The SAGE
Handbook of
Public Opinion
Research

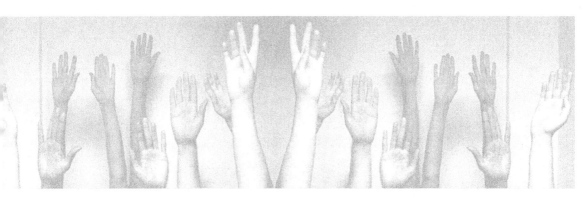

The SAGE
Handbook of
Public Opinion
Research

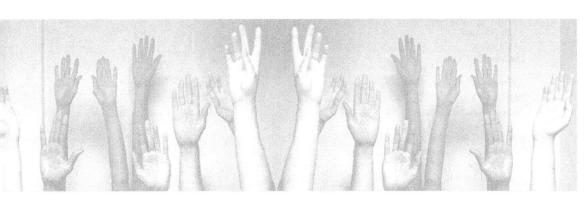

Edited by
Wolfgang Donsbach and
Michael W. Traugott

SAGE Publications
Los Angeles • London • New Delhi • Singapore

Introduction and Editorial Arrangement © Wolfgang Donsbach and
Michael W. Traugott 2008
Chapters 1–55 © SAGE Publications Ltd 2008

First published 2008

SAGE Publications Ltd
1 Oliver's Yard
55 City Road
London EC1Y 1SP

SAGE Publications Inc.
2455 Teller Road
Thousand Oaks, California 91320

SAGE Publications India Pvt Ltd
B 1/I 1 Mohan Cooperative Industrial Area
Mathura Road
New Delhi 110 044

SAGE Publications Asia-Pacific Pvt Ltd
33 Pekin Street #02-01
Far East Square
Singapore 048763

Library of Congress Control Number: 2007928091

British Library Cataloguing in Publication data

A catalogue record for this book is available from
the British Library

ISBN 978-1-4129-1177-1

Typeset by CEPHA Imaging Pvt. Ltd., Bangalore, India

Printed on paper from sustainable resources

Contents

Notes on Contributors

Danna Basson is a Survey Researcher at Mathematica Policy Research, and was previously at the University of Wisconsin Survey Center, where she managed multiple large survey projects. She is also a Ph.D. candidate in the Department of Political Science at the University of Wisconsin-Madison. Her research interests are in public opinion and survey methodology, with a focus on response latency in survey questions about political attitudes.

Adam J. Berinsky is an Associate Professor of Political Science at MIT. His research is primarily concerned with questions of representation and the communication of public sentiment to political elites, but he has also studied the continuing power of ethnic stereotypes, the effect of voting reforms, and public opinion and foreign policy. Berinsky has published articles in the *American Journal of Political Science, Journal of Politics, Public Opinion Quarterly, American Politics Research, Political Psychology*, and *Communist and Post-Communist Studies*. He is the author of *Silent Voices: Public opinion and political representation in America* (Princeton University Press, 2004).

Frank Brettschneider is Professor of Communication Studies and Communication Theory at the University of Hohenheim. His research focuses on campaign communication, public opinion, media effects, and communication performance management. He is member of the advisory board of the international institute for media analysis 'Media Tenor' and director of the Centre for Communication Performance Management.

Yun-han Chu is distinguished Research Fellow of the Institute of Political Science at Academia Sinica and Professor of political science at National Taiwan University. He serves concurrently as the President of Chiang Ching-kuo Foundation for International Scholarly Exchange. He specializes in politics of Greater China, East Asian political economy and democratization. He is the Coordinator of Asian Barometer Survey, a regional network of survey on democracy, governance and development covering more than 16 Asian countries. He currently serves on the editorial board of *International Studies Quarterly, Pacific Affairs, Journal of Contemporary China, Journal of East Asian Studies* and *Journal of Democracy*. He is the author, co-author, editor or co-editor of 11 books.

Bernhard Debatin is Associate Professor for Multimedia Policy at the E.W. Scripps School of Journalism and Director of Tutorial Studies in Journalism, Ohio University in Athens, Ohio. He received his doctorate in philosophy at Technical University Berlin (Germany), 1994, and his M.A. in Mass Communication at Free University Berlin (Germany), 1988. He is author or editor of six books and over 50 scholarly articles on media ethics, public communication, online journalism, and metaphor theory. He served as chairman of the media ethics section of the German Association of Communication Studies (DGPuK) from 2001–2005.

Don A. Dillman is Regents Professor and the Thomas S. Foley Distinguished Professor of Government and Public Policy at Washington State University. He has written extensively on data collection methods, authoring or editing more than 100 methodological publications including six books. His current research emphasizes understanding visual layout effects in Internet and mail surveys and measurement consequences for mixed-mode surveys.

Wolfgang Donsbach is a Professor of Communication at the Department of Communication at Dresden University of Technology, Germany, of which he also has been the founding director. He received his Ph.D. and his postdoctoral dissertation (Habilitation) at the University of Mainz. Prior to his current position he taught at the universities of Dortmund, Mainz and Berlin. In 1989/90 he was a fellow at the Gannett Center for Media Studies, Columbia University, New York, and in 1999 Lombard Visiting Professor at Harvard University. From 1995 to 1996 he was President of the World Association for Public Opinion Research (WAPOR) and from 2004 to 2005 President of the International Communication Association (ICA). Donsbach is managing editor of the *International Journal of Public Opinion Research* (Oxford University Press) and general editor of the ten-volume *International Encyclopedia of Communication*.

Jennifer Dykema is an Associate Scientist with the University of Wisconsin Survey Center and the Center for Demography and Ecology-Madison. Her research interests focus on questionnaire design, interaction in the interview, and cognition and survey measurement. She has published articles on these topics in the *American Sociological Review* and the *Journal of Official Statistics*.

Robert M. Eisinger (B.A., Haverford College, 1987; Ph.D., University of Chicago, 1996) is the Chair of the Political Science Department at Lewis & Clark College in Portland, Oregon. His research interests include public opinion, the history of presidential polling, and media bias. He is the author of *The Evolution of Presidential Polling* (2003: Cambridge University Press), as well as articles published in *The Harvard International Journal of Press/Politics*, *Presidential Studies Quarterly*, and *The International Journal of Public Opinion Research*.

William P. Eveland, Jr. (Ph.D., University of Wisconsin-Madison, 1997) is Associate Professor of Communication and Political Science and Director of Graduate Studies in the School of Communication at The Ohio State University. His research interests focus on the influence of political discussion and both traditional and non-traditional news media on informed participation in politics and perceptions of public opinion, with a particular interest in the mediating and/or moderating roles of motivation and information processing in these relationships.

Collin E. Fellows is a Graduate Student in Sociology at Portland State University and Program Manager of Students First Mentoring Program. His research interests focus on making higher education accessible to students who do not have a family history with higher education. He is also working on developing a practical measure of expertise and advancements in qualitative research methodology.

Kathleen A. Frankovic is Director of Surveys and Producer at CBS News, where she is responsible for the overall supervision of the CBS News opinion polls. Since 2002, she has also managed CBS News Election Night projections. She holds a Ph.D. in Political Science and speaks and writes extensively on the relationship between the news media and public opinion. She was President of WAPOR in 2003–2004.

Yang-chih Fu (Ph.D., University of Chicago) is Research Fellow and Director of the Institute of Sociology, Academia Sinica, Taiwan. He is working on how to perceive social capital with a network perspective that focuses on daily contact, on which he has published articles in *Social Networks* and *Field Methods*. He has helped initiate the East Asian Social Survey (EASS) and served in both the Methodology and Standing Committees of the International Social Survey Programme (ISSP).

Mirta Galešić is a Postdoctoral Research Fellow at the Center for Adaptive Behavior and Cognition, Max Planck Institute for Human Development in Berlin, Germany. She has a Ph.D. in Psychology from the University of Zagreb, Croatia, and a M.S. in Survey Methodology from the Joint Program in Survey Methodology, University of Maryland, USA. She is interested in cognitive aspects of survey response, communication of risks, and decision making.

Carroll J. Glynn is a Professor and Director of the School of Communication at The Ohio State University. She received her B.S. and M.S. from the University of Florida and her Ph.D. from the University of Wisconsin-Madison. Prior to her position at Ohio State, Dr. Glynn was a Professor and Chair in the Department of Communication at Cornell University where she taught and conducted research for 14 years. Her research interests focus on the understanding of public opinion formation and process and the relationship of public opinion to social norms.

Murray Goot is Professor of Politics and International Relations at Macquarie University, a Fellow of the Academy of the Social Sciences in Australia and a former President of the Australasian Political Studies Association. He has written widely on Australian public opinion. His current research is focused on competing concepts of public opinion, a critique of deliberative polling, and a history of opinion polling in Australia.

Albert C. Gunther (Ph.D., Stanford University, 1987) is Professor and Director of Graduate Studies in the Department of Life Sciences Communication at the University of Wisconsin-Madison. His research focuses on the psychology of the mass media audience, with particular emphasis on perceptions of media influence on others (the presumed influence hypothesis) and biased evaluations of message content (the hostile media effect). His theoretical work has been applied in contexts ranging from science controversies like genetically modified foods to health issues like adolescent smoking adoption. Gunther's most recent research concerns the role of media in public health issues.

Michael Häder holds the chair for Empirical Research Methods at the Institute for Sociology in Dresden (Technical University) since 2001. He studied sociology at the Humboldt-University in Berlin. Thereafter Michael Häder was scientific co-worker at the University in Leipzig, at the Academy of Sciences in Berlin and at the Centre for Survey Research and Methodology (ZUMA) in Mannheim. His current working fields are: Delphi-Method and Survey Research.

Lutz M. Hagen is a Professor of Media and Communication Studies and Director of the Institute of Media and Communication at Dresden University, Germany. He received his Ph.D. and his postdoctoral dissertation at the University of Erlangen and Nuremberg. His main research interests are in economic and political communication, especially concerning structure and effects of the news, content analysis and empirical research methods.

Jochen Hansen is a Senior Research Staff Member at the Institut für Demoskopie Allensbach, Germany. He studied economics and social sciences, receiving his degree in 1966. He has lectured at German universities and has many years of experience in conceptualizing and coordinating panel studies on market and social research issues. He is the author of numerous publications on survey research.

Sibylle Hardmeier (Dr. phil., University of Berne, Switzerland) is working as Political and Social Scientist in Berlin and Zurich. She studied at the University of Berne (history, political science, sociology), the George Washington University (Washington DC) and the Stanford University (CA) and graduated in history. After receiving her Ph.D. (1996) she worked as senior assistant and Assistant Professor at the University of Zurich, Department of Political Science; 2005–2006 she was research professor at the Social Science Research Center Berlin (WZB). Her research interest focus on opinion polling and public opinion, political behavior, election and referenda studies, as well as gender studies and democratic theory.

Uwe Hartung received his academic education at the University of Mainz, Germany, and the University of Maryland, College Park. Up to 2001 he was on the staff of the Institut für Publizistik at Mainz. He has worked in the editorial office of the *International Journal of Public Opinion Research*, first in affiliation with Mainz, then Institut für Demoskopie Allensbach, Germany, then with Technische Universität Dresden. He is also a freelancing advisor for social science methods to the Health Care Communication Lab of the Università della Svizzera Italiana in Lugano.

Ottar Hellevik is Professor of Political Science at the University of Oslo, where he has been Chairman of the Department and Dean of the Faculty of Social Sciences. He is also director of research at the market research institute Synnovate MMI. Hellevik has been member of the board of WAPOR and is currently member of the editorial board of *International Journal of Public Opinion Research*. His main research interests are values and value change, voter behavior and political recruitment, social inequality, and survey research methodology.

Anne Hildreth is an Associate Professor in the Political Science Department of Rockefeller College of Public Affairs and Policy at the University at Albany, a State University of New York. Her research focuses on public consumption of public opinion and the citizen level environment of political communication. She has published work in the *International Journal of Public Opinion Research* and the *American Journal of Political Science*.

Ursula Hoffmann-Lange is Professor of Political Science at the University of Bamberg, Germany. Her current research interests include elites, political culture, democratization and comparative politics. She is author of numerous publications on the structure of elites in developed democracies, political representation and the role of elites in democratic transitions.

Allyson Holbrook (B.A., Dickinson College; M.A., Ph.D., The Ohio State University) is an Assistant Professor of Public Administration and Psychology at the Survey Research Laboratory at the University of Illinois at Chicago. Dr. Holbrook teaches courses primarily in methodology and statistics and conducts research in two areas: (1) survey methodology, particularly the role that social and psychological processes play in the task of answering survey questions, and (2) attitudes and persuasion, and the role attitude strength plays in moderating the impact of attitudes on thoughts and behaviors. She came to UIC in 2002 after receiving her Ph.D. from The Ohio State University.

Wolfgang Jagodzinski is President of the General Social Science Infrastructure GESIS in Germany and Professor at the University of Cologne. He is involved in several international survey programs such as the European Values Survey and the International Social Survey Program. His publications focus on methodological issues, political sociology, and cultural change.

Hans Mathias Kepplinger is Professor of Communications at University of Mainz (since 1982). He earned his Ph.D. in Political Science (1970) and his postdoctoral lecturing qualification in communications (1977). He was a Heisenberg scholarship holder of the German Science Foundation (1978–1980) and served as director of the Institut für Publizistik and dean of the social science. He was a research fellow at UC Berkeley and guest lecturer at University of Tunis and Southern Illinois University. His most recent book (2005), *Abschied vom rationalen Wähler* (*Farewell to the rational voter*), looks at the effects of TV upon the images of politicians and their impact upon voting behavior. It is based upon 11 panel surveys (1998–2002) combined with content analysis of TV news.

Gašper Koren is Ph.D. student of Statistics at University of Ljubljana. His current research is focused on Web survey applications in the field of ego-centered social networks.

Jon A. Krosnick (B.A., Harvard University; Ph.D., University of Michigan) is Frederic O. Glover Professor in Humanities and Social Sciences and Professor of Communication, Political Science, and Psychology at Stanford University. Author of four books and more than 120 articles and chapters, Dr. Krosnick conducts research in three primary areas: (1) attitude formation, change, and effects, (2) the psychology of political behavior, and (3) the optimal design of questionnaires used for laboratory experiments and surveys, and survey research methodology more generally. He has taught courses on survey methodology around the world, has provided expert testimony in court, and has served as an on-air election-night television commentator and exit poll data analyst.

Michael Kunczik is Professor of Communication in the Institut für Publizistik at the Johannes Gutenberg-University of Mainz, Germany. He has researched mass media effects (violence and the mass media), theories of mass communication, international communication (images of nations and international public relations), mass media and social change as well as media economics and ethics in journalism. Recent publications include *Images of Nations and International Public Relations* (1997, second edition), *Ethics in Journalism* (1999), and the German book *Public Relations* (2002, fourth edition) which appeared also in a Romanian (2004) and a Croatian translation (2005).

Marta Lagos is founding Director of the Latinobarómetro, a yearly regional opinion barometer survey in 18 Latin American countries. Formerly the head of a Chilean think tank (CERC) that conducted opinion polls during Pinochet's regime, Lagos is founding director of her own polling company MORI (Chile), which has been associated with MORI UK since 1994. She is member of the World Values Survey team and the steering committee of the Comparative Study of Electoral Systems (CSES). Lagos is a consultant to international organizations like UNDP, World Bank, and the ILO. She is also editor of the World Opinion Section of the *International Journal of Public Opinion Research*.

Kenneth C. Land is the John Franklin Crowell Professor of Sociology and Demography at Duke University (Durham, North Carolina, USA). His research interests are in mathematical sociology/demography, statistical methods, demography, social indicators/quality-of-life measurement, and criminology. He is the co-author or co-editor of five books and author or co-author of over 150 peer-reviewed journal articles and book chapters.

Kurt Lang and **Gladys Engel Lang** are Professors emeriti of Communication, Sociology, and Political Science at the University of Washington. Their collaboration began in 1951 with a prize-winning joint paper on the 'unique perspective of television' of the rousing welcome given General MacArthur. Other publications include: *Collective Dynamics* (1961) about crowds, masses, publics, and social movements; *Politics and Television* (1968, 1984, and 2002); *The Battle for Public Opinion* (1983) about the interplay among political actors, the media, and the public during Watergate; and *Etched in Memory: The Building and Survival of Artistic Reputation* (1990 and 2001), based on near 300 men and women artists associated with the 'etching revival.' They received special awards for their lifetime achievement from American Association for Public Opinion Research and from the Political Communication Section of the American Political Science Association.

Paul J. Lavrakas, Ph.D., a research psychologist, served as Vice President and Senior Research Methodologist for The Nielsen Company since 2000–2007. He was a Professor of Journalism & Communication Studies at Northwestern University (1978–1996) and at Ohio State University (1996–2000). During his academic career he was the founding Faculty Director of the Northwestern University Survey Lab (1982–1996) and the OSU Center for Survey Research (1996–2000). Among his publications, Dr. Lavrakas has written a widely read book on telephone survey methodology. He was a co-recipient of the 2003 AAPOR Innovators Award for his work on the standardization of survey response rate calculations.

Katja Lozar Manfreda, Ph.D., is an Assistant Professor of Statistics and Social Informatics at the Faculty of Social Sciences, University of Ljubljana. Her research interests include survey methodology, new technologies in social science data collection and web surveys. She is involved in WebSM site developments from its beginnings in 1998. She is also a member of the ESRA (European Survey Research Association) committee and the secretary of RC-33 (Research Committee on Logic and Methodology) of the International Sociological Association.

Robert Mattes is Professor of Political Studies and Director of the Centre for Social Science Research at the University of Cape Town. He is also a co-founder and co-Director of the Afrobarometer, a regular survey of public opinion in 18 African countries. His research has focused on the development of democratic attitudes and practices in Africa. He is the co-author (with Michael Bratton and E. Gyimah-Boadi) of *Public Opinion, Democracy and Markets In Africa* (Cambridge University Press, 2004) and has authored or co-authored articles in journals such as *American Journal of Political Science, British Journal of Political Science, World Development*, and *Journal of Democracy*.

Debra Merskin, Associate Professor, teaches in and is Head of the Communication Studies sequence in the School of Journalism & Communication at the University of Oregon. Her research on race, gender, and media appears in journals such as *The Howard Journal of Communication, Sex Roles, Feminist Media Studies, Peace Review*, and *Mass Communication & Society*. She has contributed chapters to *Bring 'em on: Media and politics in the Iraq war, Sex in consumer culture: The erotic content of media and marketing, The girl wide web: Girls, the Internet, and the negotiation of identity*.

David L. Morgan is a University Professor at Portland State University where he also holds an adjunct appointment in Sociology. He is the author of three books and numerous articles on focus group research. In addition to his work on focus groups, Dr. Morgan's current interests center on issues in research design, with an emphasis on topics related to combining qualitative and quantitative methods.

Meinhard Moschner (Ph.D., University of Cologne, 1982) is staff member of the Central Archive for Empirical Social Research in the German Social Science Infrastructure Services (GESIS-ZA). His activity focuses on the processing and documentation of international data collections (Eurobarometer) and the related archive services.

Patricia Moy (Ph.D., University of Wisconsin-Madison) is the Christy Cressey Associate Professor of Communication at the University of Washington, where she is adjunct faculty in the Department of Political Science. Her research focuses on public opinion and political communication; she studies how communication shapes public opinion, citizens' trust in government, and civic and political engagement. Moy's work has appeared in leading refereed journals such as *Journal of Communication* and *Political Communication,* and a book, *With Malice Toward All?* (co-authored with Michael Pfau). She currently serves as Associate Editor of *Public Opinion Quarterly* and sits on the Executive Council of the World Association for Public Opinion Research.

Peter Neijens is Chair of Persuasive Communication in The Amsterdam School of Communications Research *ASCoR* (University of Amsterdam). His research interests include public opinion, referendums, public information campaigns, and media & advertising. His publications include over 100 peer-reviewed publications in national and international journals and books. Peter Neijens served as Scientific Director of The Amsterdam School of Communications Research *ASCoR* from 1998 to 2005. His research has received several awards, such as the Worcester Prize for the best article in the *International Journal of Public Opinion Research* (1997) and the Top Paper Award of the International Communication Association (in 2000 and 2006).

Anne Niedermann (M.A., Ph.D., Johannes-Gutenberg University of Mainz, 1991) is research director for legal evidence at the Allensbach Institute (Institut für Demoskopie Allensbach) in Germany. In this position she is responsible for giving expert opinions based on surveys in the areas of competition and trademark law. She also serves as a lecturer at the Faculty of Law at the University of Constance and is the chairperson of the complaints council of the Rat der Deutschen Markt- und Sozialforschung e.V., a joint disciplinary body of the German associations of market, opinion and social research. Her areas of research include the theory of public opinion, survey research as legal evidence, survey research methodology, quality criteria in survey research, brands, market research and media law.

Anthony Oberschall is emeritus Professor of Sociology at the University of North Carolina, Chapel Hill. He studied with Paul Lazarsfeld at Columbia in 1958–1962. He has written extensively on the history of social research. In the past decade he has studied and written on conflict and peace making in deeply divided societies, such as Bosnia, Northern Ireland, and Palestine.

Colm O'Muircheartaigh is Professor in the Irving B Harris Graduate School of Public Policy Studies and Senior Fellow in the National Opinion Research Center (NORC), both at the University of Chicago. His research interests are in sample design, question form and wording, modeling response and nonresponse errors, and issues of inference in surveys and social experiments.

Nicholas L. Parsons is a Ph.D. candidate in the Department of Sociology at Washington State University. His scholarly interests include quantitative methods, criminology, and the sociology of culture. He is currently conducting research on the epidemiology of methamphetamine use in the United States and media coverage of the 'Meth Epidemic.' He is also engaged in research on collective memory in sport, and the effectiveness of adult drug courts.

Thomas E. Patterson is Bradlee Professor of Government and the Press at Harvard University's John F. Kennedy School of Government. His book's include *The Vanishing Voter* (2003), which looks at the causes and consequences of declining electoral participation; *Out of Order* (1993), which received the American Political Science Association's inaugural Graber Award for best book in political communication of the last decade; and *The Unseeing Eye* (1976), which was named by the American Association for Public Opinion Research as one of the 50 most influential books on public opinion in the past half-century.

Richard M. Perloff is Professor and Director of the School of Communication at Cleveland State University. He has published widely on the third-person effect and is the author of *The Dynamics of Persuasion: Communication and Attitudes in the 21st century* (2nd ed.) and *Political Communication: Politics, Press, and Public in America*. Perloff's scholarship has focused on the confluence of communication and the psychology of perceptions of media effects. He recently edited a special issue of *American Behavioral Scientist* on communication and health care disparities.

Thomas Petersen is member of the Institute für Demoskopie Allensbach's research staff since 1993. He was lecturer at the University of Constance (1995/96), the University of Dresden (2002/2003) and the University of Mainz (since 2003). He is national representative of the World Association of Public Opinion Research (WAPOR) for Germany since 1999, since 2007 Vice President and President-Elect of WAPOR, since 2004 vice chair of the Visual Communication Division of the German Society for Communication Research (DGPuK). His research focuses survey research methodology, field experiments, international values studies, political survey research, visual communication and panel analyses on political topics and in market research.

Vincent Price is the Steven H. Chaffee Professor of Communication and Political Science at the Annenberg School for Communication and Associate Provost, University of Pennsylvania. He was formerly chair of the Department of Communication Studies at the University of Michigan and editor of *Public Opinion Quarterly*. Price has published extensively on mass communication and public opinion, social influence processes, and political communication. His most recent research, funded by grants from the National Science Foundation, the National Institutes of Health and the Pew Charitable Trusts, focuses on the role of political conversation, particularly Web-based discussion, in shaping public opinion.

Kenneth A. Rasinski, Ph.D., is Principal Research Scientist at the National Opinion Research Center and lecturer at the University of Chicago. He conducts research on psychological aspects of survey responding, and on public opinion in areas related to mental health, substance abuse and criminal justice, and on the experiences of public housing residents. His work has appeared in such journals as *Public Opinion Quarterly, the Journal of Experimental Social Psychology, Social Science Quarterly*, and *Crime and Delinquency*.

John P. Robinson is Professor of Sociology at the University of Maryland, College Park, where he directs the Americans' Use of Time Project and the Internet Scholars Program. His areas of research specialization include social science methodology, attitude and behavior measurement, social change, and the impact of information communication and other home technology. He directed the pioneering trend studies of how Americans spend time and the impact of the Internet (with main support from the National Science Foundation), as well as Americans' participation in the arts (SPPA) for the National Endowment for the Arts. Dr. Robinson was an American Statistical Association/ National Science Foundation Fellow at the Bureau of Labor Statistics, a Fulbright scholar at Moscow State University and Soviet Academy of Sciences, a Research Consultant at BBC News and acted as Research Coordinator for the US Surgeon General's Committee on Television and Society.

Patrick Roessler studied communication, political science and law, Ph.D. in communication (1987, University of Stuttgart-Hohenheim). 1989–1997 Research Assistant at the University of Stuttgart-Hohenheim, 1997–2000 Assistant Professor at the University of Munich, Department of Communication. 2000 to 2003 Full Professor of Media Sociology and Media Psychology, since 2004 Full Professor of Communication Science/Empirical Research at the University of Erfurt. Board Member of the German Communication Association (DGPuK), representative of the International Communication Association (ICA) in Germany. Editor of the book series *Internet Research* and *medien + gesundheit*, co-editor of the book series *Reihe Rezeptionsforschung* (all R. Fischer Verlag, Munich). Main fields of scholarly interest: media effects research, new media developments and online communication, audience research, health communication.

Nora Cate Schaeffer is Professor of Sociology at the University of Wisconsin-Madison, where she teaches survey research methods and conducts research on instrument design and interaction in the survey interview. She also serves as Faculty Director of the University of Wisconsin Survey Center. She recently co-edited (with Douglas W. Maynard, Johannes van der Zouwen, and Hanneke Houtkoop) *Standardization and Tacit Knowledge: Interaction and Practice in the Survey Interview*. She is a member of the Committee on National Statistics of the National Research Council and the Public Opinion Quarterly Advisory Committee of the American Association for Public Opinion Research.

Dietram A. Scheufele is a Professor of Life Sciences Communication and Journalism & Mass Communication at the University of Wisconsin, Madison. He is past President of the Midwest Association for Public Opinion Research and has served as journal review editor for the International Journal of Public Opinion Research. Scheufele has published extensively in the areas of political communication, public opinion and science communication. His most recent work, funded by the National Science Foundation, focuses on public opinion formation about emerging technologies.

Winfried Schulz is emeritus Professor of Mass Communication and Political Science at the University of Erlangen-Nuremberg (Germany). His publications and his continuing research focus on political communication, mass media audiences and effects, news analysis, media policy and media performance.

Norbert Schwarz is Professor of Psychology at the University of Michigan, Research Professor at the Institute for Social Research, and Professor of Marketing at the Ross School of Business. His research interests focus on human judgment and cognition, including the interplay of feeling and thinking, the socially situated nature of cognition, and the implications of basic cognitive and communicative processes for public opinion, consumer behavior and social science research.

Eva Johanna Schweitzer is a doctoral candidate in the Institut für Publizistik at the Johannes Gutenberg-University of Mainz, Germany. She has studied mass communication, comparative literature, and psychology. Her research interests concern political communication and online communication.

Tom W. Smith is an internationally recognized expert in survey research specializing in the study of societal change and survey methodology. Since 1980 he has been co-principal investigator of the National Data Program for the Social Sciences and director of its General Social Survey (GSS) at the National Opinion Research Center, University of Chicago. Smith was co-founder and Secretary General of the International Social Survey Program (1997–2003).

Fred Steeper is a Consultant at Market Strategies, Inc., Livonia, Michigan and one of its founders in 1989. He was a Senior Vice President of Market Opinion Research, Detroit, where he was employed, 1972–1989. He studied at the Institute for Social Research and the University of Michigan. He has designed polling, focus group and ad testing research in more than 100 U.S. Senate and gubernatorial campaigns since 1972. He served various research roles in nine Presidential elections including a principle role in three. His international experience includes campaign and issue research in Canada, the Philippines, and Moscow.

Jonathan David Tankel is Associate Professor of Communication at Indiana University—Purdue University Fort Wayne. He earned his Ph.D. at University of Wisconsin-Madison. He taught previously at the University of Maine and Ithaca (NY) College. His work has appeared in *Critical Studies in Mass Communication*, *Journal of Communication*, *Free Speech Yearbook*, and *Journal of Radio Studies,* as well as various book chapters. He served as Chair of the Popular Communication Division of the International Communication Association (2002–2004).

Humphrey Taylor is the Chairman of the Harris Poll, a service of Harris Interactive. He was educated in Britain and has lived in Asia, Africa, South America, Europe and, for the last 30 years, the United States. He has had responsibility for more than 8,000 surveys in more than 80 countries. In Britain he conducted proprietary polling for the Conservative Party and two Prime Ministers. He has published more than 1,000 columns, papers and book chapters. He has written op-ed articles for the *New York Times*, *Wall Street Journal* and (London) *The Times,* and has lectured at Oxford, Harvard, Princeton and Yale.

Roger Tourangeau is a Research Professor at the University of Michigan's Institute for Social Research and the Director of the Joint Program in Survey Methodology at the University of Maryland. He received his Ph.D. in Psychology from Yale University. Prior to coming to Institute for Social Research, he has worked for the National Opinion Research Center and the Gallup Organization. His book, with Lance Rips and Kenneth Rasinski, *The Psychology of Survey Response*, won the 2006 Book Award from the American Association of Public Opinion Research. During 2006, he served as the Chairman of the Survey Research Methods Section of the American Statistical Association.

Michael W. Traugott is Professor of Communication Studies and Political Science and Research Professor in the Center for Political Studies at the Institute for Social Research at the University of Michigan. His research focuses on public opinion, campaigns and elections, and survey methods. He is a former president of the American Association for Public Opinion Research and the current president of the World Association for Public Opinion Research.

Yariv Tsfati (Ph.D., University of Pennsylvania, 2002) is a Senior Lecturer in the Department of Communication, University of Haifa, Israel. His research focuses on audience trust in news media institutions as a factor influencing media exposure and as a moderator in media effects. His work also considers audience perceptions of media influence as a source of behavioral effects in a variety of areas, ranging from residential mobility to parental mediation of television content.

Vasja Vehovar, Ph.D. is a full Professor of Statistics at the Faculty of Social Sciences, University of Ljubljana, Slovenia. He teaches courses on Sampling, Survey methodology and Information Society. From 1996 he is the principal investigator of the national project Research on Internet in Slovenia (RIS). He is also responsible for the developments of WebSM portal devoted to web survey methodology and was the coordinator of the corresponding EU framework project. His research interests span from survey methodology to information society issues.

Penny S. Visser (B.S., Grand Valley State University, M.A., Ph.D., The Ohio State University) is an Associate Professor in the Psychology Department at the University of Chicago. Her research focuses primarily on the structure and function of attitudes, including the dynamics of attitude formation and change, the impact of attitudes on thought and behavior, the antecedents and consequences of attitude strength, and issues associated with attitude measurement and research methodology. Crosscutting Dr. Visser's specific interests in attitudes and persuasion is a more general interest in political psychology, and several strands of her research have been carried out within the political context.

David H. Weaver is the Roy W. Howard Professor in Journalism and Mass Communication Research at Indiana University's School of Journalism where he has been on the faculty since receiving his Ph.D. in mass communication research from the University of North Carolina at Chapel Hill in 1974. He has written extensively on media agenda setting, voter learning, and the characteristics and opinions of US journalists. His recent books include *The American Journalist in the 21st Century*, *Mass Communication Research and Theory*, *The Global Journalist*, and *Communication and Democracy*.

Herbert F. Weisberg (Ph.D., University of Michigan) is Professor of Political Science at The Ohio State University, where he chairs the Department and teaches in their Graduate Interdisciplinary Specialization in Survey Research. He is a specialist in American political behavior, and has written and edited several books on US voting behavior. He is the author of *The Total Survey Error Approach* (University of Chicago Press, 2005) and *An Introduction to Survey Research, Polling, and Data Analysis* (Sage, 1996). He has served as President of the Midwest Political Science Association and as editor of the *American Journal of Political Science*.

Hans L. Zetterberg has taught sociology at Columbia University in The City of New York and at Ohio State University where he was Chairman of the Sociology Department. He has also been a publisher of scholarly books (Bedminster Press), the chief executive of a big foundation in his native Sweden (The Tri-Centennial Fund of the Bank of Sweden), a long-time pollster and market researcher (Sifo AB), and the editor-in-chief of a large Stockholm newspaper (*Svenska Dagbladet*). He is a past President of The World Association of Public Opinion Research (WAPOR). He lives retired in Bromma, Sweden.

Introduction

Wolfgang Donsbach and
Michael W. Traugott

PUBLIC OPINION—A NEBULOUS CONCEPT

In 1968, W. Phillips Davison wrote the entry for 'public opinion' for the International Encyclopedia of the Social Sciences, concluding that 'there is no generally accepted definition of the term' (p. 188). Three years earlier Harwood Childs (1965) had described no less than 48 different definitions of public opinion in the relevant research literature.

Since then, the definitional situation has certainly not become any clearer; and after almost half a century of empirical research, not much has changed. But at the same time, public opinion is, as Vincent Price (1992, p. 1) wrote, 'one of the most vital and enduring concepts in the social sciences.' Public opinion continues to be one of the fuzziest terms in the social sciences— and nevertheless, it has received increasing attention from researchers in a variety of fields and disciplines.

The confusion about the term starts with both of its elements. Neither 'public' nor 'opinion' is a clearly defined concept. In his historical analysis of the public sphere, German sociologist Jürgen Habermas (1962) found no less than four meanings of the term 'public': juridical (as in the meaning of public access), political (as in the meaning of public interest), representational (as in

a public event), and communicative (as in making something public). Later, Elisabeth Noelle-Neumann (1993) within her spiral-of-silence theory added a fifth aspect to the meaning of 'public' that she claims was always part of the concept: the social psychological dimension, as in the individual's awareness of being 'in the public eye.'

In a similar vein, 'opinion' is not a terminologically clear concept. At first, opinion and *opinion* in French were used like the term 'doxa' by the ancient Greeks, to represent an uncertain and not very well based judgment. As such, it was much less than 'knowing' and had no inherent political power. Again, it was Habermas who described how the meaning of the term had evolved over time and been endowed with a certain quality and rationality—a prerequisite for opinion to be used in 'public opinion' as a political term against the existing power of the authoritarian state. Despite this evolutionary history of both essential elements in 'public opinion,' the fact that the term has been in use for centuries in philosophy, politics, literature, and the social sciences is a strong indicator of the fact that it describes an important and real phenomenon, one that cannot be described by any other term. And without claiming that we could or should strive in the field of public opinion research for a common use of the term, we can at least reflect on these variations.

This is simply a demonstration of its centrality as a legitimate and focal term in the social sciences.

PUBLIC OPINION AS AN INTERDISCIPLINARY TERM

Public opinion is also one of the most interdisciplinary concepts in social science. For *political scientists,* it is a key term applied in theories of democracy, because it denominates the relationship between the government and the people. Public opinion is also often the watershed for discussions about the representation of the public's will in political decision making by the government. As such, public opinion is a central concept that can be applied from a variety of theoretical perspectives to encompass discussions of too much (populism) and too little responsiveness of the government. And of course, public opinion is a key term for political scientists studying elections and electoral behavior.

For *historians*, public opinion is an element and a factor in understanding social change, particularly in the transition from authoritarian to democratic governments, or in the way certain major historical events—like the French Revolution or the psychological mobilization of the people for warfare—develop and evolve. In *law*, and here particularly in the philosophy and sociology of the law, scholars are interested in the question of the degree to which law-making and jurisdiction should be responsive to changes in public opinion, e.g. when behavioral norms—such as in the case of sexuality and sexual behavior—have changed. *Social psychologists* are either interested in public opinion as a force that affects the individual's behavior in the public sphere, as a reflection of our social nature and the motivation to be socially accepted, or they see public opinion as an element in our 'social perception,' as an aid to making judgments in undetermined situations (Hofstätter, 1971).

Particularly in the first half of the 20th century, many *sociologists* studied public opinion as a rather threatening phenomenon of 'mass societies,' leading the individual to irrational and often dangerous behaviors guided by the protection of the group or 'mass.' Public opinion is also an important concept within theories of social control and the enforcement of norms within a society. *Communication scholars* on the other hand study the influence of the mass media on public opinion, used as a term to describe opinions held by the people, as well as on the perception of ruling opinions as a dynamic concept explaining changes in public opinion. In this latter context, the mass media are seen as one source for our perception of what our fellow citizens think. Similarly, *economists* have found public opinion to be an important factor for predicting the economic development of a country. And of course, the techniques of *public opinion research*, especially survey research, have become useful tools for many disciplines, not just for the social sciences, where they have become the most important and the most frequently used method.

If one looks at the use of the term throughout the history of the social sciences and tries to construct a terminological genealogy, five different traditions become evident. In the *political-normative tradition*, particularly as represented in the works of Habermas, public opinion is a normative concept that describes the ideal process through which informed citizens achieve rational judgments well-grounded in knowledge and good will and for the greatest good of society. In the *functional tradition*, represented in Lippmann's (1922) and Luhmann's (1970) writings, public opinion is perceived as a social institution that helps people to cope with the complexity of their social reality. While Lippmann is more concerned with the individual citizen's problems in dealing with the news, Luhmann uses the societal perspective as a technical tool that reduces the political agenda to a manageable number of issues and policies.

In the *sociological tradition*, e.g. as seen by Edward Ross (1901), public opinion is one institution through which society exerts social control on the individual. 'Social control is concerned fundamentally with orderliness in the human world' (Landis, 1956, p. 12), and public opinion is one of the forces that creates conformity among people. The *survey research tradition* is the least complex and most straightforward concept of public opinion. Born with the advent of modern survey methodology in the 1930s, it defines public opinion as any measurement that indicates what a population thinks on an issue as measured in representative surveys. Finally, the *social psychological tradition* comes closest to the sociological one, but combines the elements of all four of the aforementioned roots. Here, public opinion is the distribution of opinions on controversial issues that is, rightly or wrongly, part of what is perceived as the dominant position in society, and as such affects the individual's readiness to talk about his or her own opinion in public situations. These are the core elements of Elisabeth Noelle-Neumann's (1993) 'spiral-of-silence theory.'

All in all, some scholars might regret the lack of a clear and common definition and use of the term 'public opinion.' On the other hand, it is obviously a concept of great relevance and a very vivid one, too. In most disciplines, the concept of public opinion either relates to key questions of the respective field, or to central norms, or to both—as is the case, for instance, with democratic theory. Nevertheless, the fact remains that researchers and social commentators can address many different topics when using the term 'public opinion.'

PUBLIC DISCOURSES ON PUBLIC OPINION POLLING

Two technologies have changed our modern political systems more than anything else: television and public opinion research. Television has popularized politics among almost all segments of society, personalized the face of politics, changed the behavior and the required skills of politicians, and, finally, led some researchers to believe that it has replaced the traditional political institutions as the center of power. Public opinion research, on the other hand, has made the most important element in democracy, the will of the people, measurable and thus available for political decision making on an almost daily basis, be it by political leaders or the electorate. This revolution has affected the very nature of the political system at its core, because it has made it possible to evaluate straightforwardly claims about acting with the consent of the majority of the people. Television, and nowadays also the Internet, as well as opinion polls, have been the target of many critical discussions about the state of democracy, particularly regarding their role in campaigns and elections. But even if no one ever talks about the possibility of banning television, many have talked about prohibiting access to or the dissemination of results from opinion polls; in some countries, this has even become law.

The possibility of measuring public opinion has been a provocation for many elites generating their political influence from such claims, particularly politicians in campaigns and journalists. The former can no longer maintain that they have the backing of the people and would be the likely winner of an upcoming election when the polls show the contrary. Journalists, on the other side, can no longer make assessments about what the majority thinks on the basis of discussions with their fellow journalists in newsrooms and bars or with party leaders and strategists—as was the case in the 1930s and 1940s (Herbst, 1990).

Thus, public opinion research, besides being a social research activity, has itself come into the focus of public discourses. There is a legal discourse as to whether it might be appropriate to ban the publication of poll data before elections, as well as a democratic theory discourse about the quality and nature of what modern polls do indeed measure. Many authors question the linking of data derived from representative samples of the population with an empirical equivalent of what theorists of democratic theory had in mind when describing the essential nature of democracies. This discourse is often combined with the question of how much 'rationality' there is in the opinions of the many as measured in these representative samples. Still another discussion thread shows how deeply the existence of opinion research relates to democratic theory: Can and should we assume that citizens must be protected from the possible influence of published poll data, as some critics hold, or must we simply start from the assumption that: (a) survey data are rather objective social data on the views of the public, and (b) that citizens are mature enough to make the best use of them?

This question of 'best use' relates, of course, also to politicians. In the literature, one can find almost a linear scale of benevolent uses of surveys, ranging from a representation of the views that governments must follow in the name of the will of the people to an elite concept where this will is seen as a result of manipulation with the help of polls. For Lijphart (1984, p. 2), 'an ideal democratic government would be one whose actions were always in perfect correspondence with the preferences of all its citizens,' and for Sudman (1982, p. 302), 'no elected official can govern wisely without knowing what the public thinks on major issues.' But for Habermas, opinion surveys are only a tool by which governments manipulate the so-called public by engineering its political decisions. However one answers the question about the degree of responsiveness or the level of independence governments should practice towards the will of the people, there is no doubt that the very existence of opinion polls has increased the likelihood that political actors can become more populist and less principled.

Finally, society discusses the accuracy of poll data and their possible effects on citizens. The increasing social mobility of citizens and the decrease in their party loyalty, combined with shrinking response rates, have made it harder for survey researchers to assess public opinion, especially political preferences, in a valid and reliable way. Almost every modern democracy has seen its Waterloo involving public pollsters in the last few years. In addition, in almost every election anywhere in the world, there is at least one politician blaming the publication of poll data prior to the election day as the reason for opinion changes in the electorate, and thus for his or her defeat.

For all of these reasons and from these various perspectives, this *Handbook of Public Opinion Research* addresses these critical discourses around public opinion research and their possible consequences.

HOW THIS *HANDBOOK* IS ORGANIZED

It is obvious that this handbook will not be able to deal with all the theoretical, terminological and disciplinary issues surrounding public opinion. However, as a handbook, it should give the reader an overview of the most important concepts included in and surrounding the term public opinion and its application in modern social research. We have assembled a set of authors who are active researchers and experts in the fields on which they were asked to write a contribution. That being said, we will neither achieve a 'canonization' of the field, nor produce a final word about the 'correct' use of the term. But our readers should become aware of these different concepts, and they will be able to use the contents to separate the chaff from the wheat in good public opinion research.

The book is organized into five different parts: *History, philosophy of public opinion and public opinion research* (Part I), *Theories of public opinion formation and change* (Part II), *Methodology* (Part III), *The social and political environment of public opinion research* (Part IV), and *Special fields of application* (Part V). Four of the five parts have two sections that further distinguish the broad topics addressed within them. Cross-references between different chapters of the Handbook are marked with an arrow (→) pointing to the title of the related chapter.

Part I is about the history and philosophy of public opinion and public opinion research, and is divided into coverage of the nature of public opinion and the development of public opinion research. The first, more theoretical section, contains seven chapters on the origin and nature of the term, on different expressions of public opinion, and on its relationship to democratic theory. The second, more methodological section turns to the development of the methods with which public opinion has been measured throughout history.

Part II is dedicated to theories of public opinion formation and change. The eight chapters present the basic empirical concepts for assessing public opinion and opinion changes in society—for instance the concepts of knowledge, opinions and attitudes, and in the second section, different theories that explain how public opinion develops and changes in societies are outlined. Among these are the third-person-effect, agenda-setting and the spiral-of-silence theory. A special chapter in this section is dedicated to the role of the news media as molders of public opinion.

Part III on methodology contains 19 chapters and is thus the longest in the handbook. This reflects the enormous research evidence that has been accumulated over the last decades, when survey research changed from the 'art of asking questions' (Payne, 1951) to the scientific paradigm for survey methodology as it is reflected, among others, in the cognitive-psychological approach to survey methodology (e.g. Tourangeau, Rips, & Rasinski, 2000). In this part, we further distinguish between two sections, 'the design of surveys' and 'the measurement of public opinion.' The former presents the different designs or modes of data collection and their potentials and risks, the latter goes more into the details of measurement such as the psychology of asking questions, the use of scales or the measurement of specific concepts like values.

Part IV focuses on the social and political environment of public opinion research and offers eight chapters on the social, political and legal status of public opinion research and on how it is perceived by the public and by journalists. The second section in this part looks into the uses and effects of public opinion research by governments and the media, as well as into the effects that the publication of poll data might have on citizens.

Finally, Part V offers a review of the role and use of surveys for selected special fields of application, ranging from their use in legal cases to the use of polls in marketing and political campaigns.

REFERENCES

Childs, H. L. (1965). *Public opinion—Nature, formation and role*. Princeton: D. Van Nostrand.

Davison, W. P. (1968). Public opinion. Introduction. In D. L. Sills (Ed.), *International Encyclopedia of the Social Sciences* (Vol. 13, pp. 188–197). New York: Macmillan & Free Press.

Habermas, J. (1962). *Strukturwandel der Öffentlichkeit. Untersuchungen zu einer Kategorie der bürgerlichen Gesellschaft* [The structural transformation of the public sphere: An inquiry into a category of bourgeois society]. Neuwied: Luchterhand.

Herbst, S. (1990). Assessing public opinion in the 1930s–1940s: Retrospective views of journalists. *Public Opinion Quarterly, 67,* 943–949.

Hofstätter, P. (1971). *Gruppendynamik. Kritik der Massenpsychologie* [Group dynamics. Criticism of crowd psychology]. Hamburg: Rowohlt.

Landis, P. H. (1956). *Social control*. Chicago: Lippincott.

Lijphart, A. (1984). *Democracies: Patterns of majoritarian and consensus government in twenty-one countries*. New Haven, London: Yale University Press.

Lippmann, W. (1922). *Public opinion*. New York: Harcourt, Brace & Comp.

Luhmann, N. (1970). Öffentliche Meinung [Public opinion]. *Politische Vierteljahresschrift, 11,* 2–28.

Noelle-Neumann, E. (1993). *The spiral of silence: Public opinion—Our social skin*. University of Chicago Press.

Payne, S. L. (1951). *The art of asking questions*. Princeton: University Press.

Price, V. (1992). *Public opinion*. Newbury Park, CA: Sage.

Ross, E. A. (1901). *Social control. A survey of the foundations of order*. New York: Macmillan Company.

Sudman, S. (1982). The presidents and the polls. *Public Opinion Quarterly, 46,* 301–310.

Tourangeau, R., Rips, L. J., & Rasinski, K. (2000). *The psychology of survey response*. Cambridge: University Press.

PART I

History, Philosophy of Public Opinion and Public Opinion Research

The Nature of Public Opinion

The Public and Public Opinion in Political Theories

Vincent Price

The origins of our modern conception of public opinion are usually traced to liberal democratic theories of the eighteenth century, with precursors reaching all the way back to ancient Greece (Palmer, 1936). And yet the connections between empirical public opinion research and political theory have been remarkably loose. Despite the encouragement of leading researchers such as Berelson (1952), Lazarsfeld (1957), and Noelle-Neumann (1979), public opinion researchers have only recently taken up the task of trying to integrate empirical and philosophical models (e.g., Herbst, 1993; Price & Neijens, 1997; Althaus, 2006).

This chapter explores some fundamental connections between public opinion research and democratic theories, with several interrelated aims: (a) illustrating briefly the historical span of democratic theories and the wide range of views they adopt with respect to citizens, publics, public opinion and governance; (b) considering some of the normative models implicit in public opinion research; and (c) exploring some of the enduring theoretical tensions, dialectics, and debates that empirical

research might conceivably help to inform, if not resolve.[1] In view of a general model of democracy as collective decision making, this chapter considers the variable sorts of expectations democratic theories harbor for political leaders, news media, publics, and citizens.

ENTWINED CONCEPTS: PUBLIC, OPINION AND DEMOCRACY

The concept of public opinion emerged during the Enlightenment, but the separate concepts of the *public* and *opinion* have much older histories, each with a range of meanings that continue to inform their use to the present day (Price, 1992). *Opinion* was used primarily in two ways. In an epistemological sense, opinion indicated a particular and to some extent inferior way of knowing, distinguishing a matter of judgment (an 'opinion') from a matter known as fact or asserted on faith. In a second sense, the term was used to indicate regard, esteem, or reputation (as in holding a high opinion of someone). Both senses relate to the notion of judgment, though in the one case the emphasis is on the uncertain truth-value of something believed, whereas in the other the emphasis is on a moral dimension of judgment, that is, approval or censure. As we shall see, political theories variously seize upon one or the other of these senses of 'opinion,' at times emphasizing cognition and knowledge and at others moral sensibility or sentiment. The term *public*, from the Latin *publicus* meaning 'the people,' similarly had several discernible meanings. In some of its earliest uses it referred to common access, with areas open to the general population deemed public (Habermas, 1962/1989). In a second usage, public referred to the common interest and common good, not in the sense of access (or belonging to) but rather in the sense of representing (that is, in the name of) the whole of the people. Thus the monarch under the theory of royal absolutism was the sole public figure, representing by divine right the entirety of the kingdom in his person (Baker, 1990).

The compound concept *public opinion* came into widespread use only in the eighteenth century and as the product of several significant historical trends, primarily the growth of literacy, expansion of the merchant classes, the Protestant Reformation, and the circulation of literature enabled by the printing press. An ascendant class of literate and well-read European merchants, congregating in new popular institutions such as *salons* and coffee houses and emboldened by new liberal philosophies arguing for basic individual freedoms, began to articulate a critique of royal absolutism and to assert their interests in political affairs (Habermas, 1962/1989). In early usage, public opinion referred to the social customs and manners of this growing class of prosperous 'men of letters' but by the close of the century it was being used in an expressly political context, often in conjunction with cousin phrases such as 'common will,' and 'public conscience.' Baker (1990) argues that with the dissolution of absolute monarchical power, both the crown and its opponents alike invoked public opinion as a new source of authority and

legitimacy, largely in rhetorical fashion and without any fixed sociological referent. Hence the term remained, in some sense intentionally, vague. It was linked quite explicitly with free and open discussion of political affairs among educated men of financial means. Yet it often acquired (as in the writings of Rousseau, 1762/1968) an abstract and almost super-human quality as an expression of the common will, divined through reasoned debate, and framed as a powerful new tribunal for checking and thus controlling, as right would have it, the actions of the state.

Despite these communitarian origins, however, the concept of public opinion came to acquire much of its contemporary meaning from its deployment in the work of later liberal thinkers, particularly 'utilitarian' philosophers such as Mill (1820/1937) and Bentham (1838/1962). While continuing to argue for full publicity of government affairs and strongly advocating freedom of expression, these analysts saw the polity less as the coming together of separate minds reasoning together toward a shared, common will than as a collection of individuals attempting to maximize their own interests and utilities. The harmonization of these conflicting interests was best achieved not through public reasoning to any consensual conclusion, but instead through rule by majority, requiring regular election and plebiscite, with the state functioning as a referee to individuals and groups vying to achieve their economic and political ends. 'A key proposition,' writes Held (1996, p. 95), 'was that the collective good could be realized only if individuals interacted in competitive exchanges pursuing their utility with minimal state interference.' Thus public opinion was wedded to the liberal idea of an unregulated 'marketplace of ideas,' with the majority view, ascertained through a free popular vote, as its operational definition.

The early development and use of the concept of public opinion, then, were part and parcel of the Enlightenment project to replace European monarchies with civil democracies. What the Enlightenment accomplished, according to Peters (1995), was to transform the classical assembly of the people—in Athenian democracy a physical, face-to-face forum—into a mass-mediated, fictive body constituted by newspapers bringing people together, not in physical space but in shared stories and conversations at a distance. 'The imagined public is not, however, *imaginary*: in acting upon symbolic representations of 'the public' the public can come to exist as a real actor' (p. 16). Implicitly, notions of the public and public opinion followed the complete arc of thinking about just what forms such 'imagined assemblies' might take, from highly communitarian formulations of the public as a fluid and amorphous group of freely associating citizens willing to think and debate in consideration of the good of the whole community, to highly individualist formulations equating it with the mass of citizens freely pursuing their personal and group interests as they wished, and by majority vote aggregating those interests to choose wise political leaders.

NOT ONE, BUT MANY, DEMOCRATIC THEORIES

Despite references to 'democratic theory' and 'classical democratic theory' that imply some sort of unified conception of democracy, writings on the subject offer myriad competing models. Indeed, while democracy is generally held to mean 'rule by the people,' there has been historically some dispute over the definition of 'the people,' and, even more so, over just what it means for them to 'rule' (Lively, 1975). Held's (1996) review identifies no fewer than a dozen variations. He describes four basic models, appearing roughly in chronological order—fifth-century *Athenian democracy*, with its sovereign assembly of the whole citizenry; *republicanism*, from its Roman and Italian Renaissance manifestations through the Enlightenment conceptions of Rousseau; eighteenth- and nineteenth-century *liberal democracy*, with its commitment to individual rights and electoral representation; and Marxist models

of *direct democracy*, predicated on complete economic and political equality.

These were then supplemented and expanded by twentieth-century models, drawing in various ways upon all four basic formulations but principally from the republican and liberal traditions (Habermas, 1966). Among these are theories Held (1996) names *competitive elitism, neo-pluralism, legal democracy* and *participatory democracy*. Each in various ways resulted from grappling with perceived problems of the public in the face of modern industrial life. These perceived ailments of the body politic included: a poorly informed and emotional mass citizenry subject to demagoguery and manipulation; widening inequalities in private economic, and hence political, power; expanding centralization of government and bureaucratic regulation; a growing and pervasive lack of citizen concern for the collective welfare; and the political withdrawal of citizens who feel inefficacious and effectively disenfranchised.

Worry over the emotionality and irrationality of ordinary citizens, and a near complete lack of confidence in their ability to discriminate intelligently among various policies, led some democratic theorists to fear that catering to a 'popular will' would prove at the least inefficient and at the worst disastrously unstable, particularly in times of cultural and political stress. Contemplating a complex industrial world that had collapsed into international confusion and warfare, and despairing any hope of wisdom in popular democracy, both Lippmann (1922) and Schumpeter (1942) argued that an independent, expert bureaucracy was needed to aid elected representatives in formulating and administering intelligent public policy, and also that public influence on policy matters should be strictly limited. In making the case for a 'leadership democracy' or '*competitive elitism*,' Schumpeter (1942, p. 269) proposed that citizens' choices should extend only to periodic selection of 'the men who are able to do the deciding.' Lippmann (1922, p. 32) argued that expert advisors with unrestricted access to information should make the 'unseen facts' intelligible to political decision makers and 'organize public opinion' for the press and the citizenry.

Such minimalist conceptions of democracy equate it with any system offering competitive elections, often placing considerable distance between the decisions of governing elites and the desires of the masses. *Pluralist* formulations, which became ascendant in American political science in the 1950s and 1960s, accept many of the minimalists' views of citizens but emphasize the role of intermediary interest groups and quasi-elite 'issue publics' in maintaining a competitive balance of power and providing a critical 'linkage' function in tying popular wishes to governmental decisions. Analysts including Almond (1950) and Key (1961) invoked the concept of 'issue publics' (or 'special publics') to explain how policy in democratic societies can, despite wide swaths of inattention and ignorance in the citizenry, nevertheless respond to public opinion in a fairly rational manner. It stands to reason that, because politics routinely gives way to more pressing matters of family, work and recreation, people should focus their attention on just a few matters of the most direct interest and importance. Nonetheless, for most issues at least a segment of the population is aroused and interested enough to learn, discuss and form opinions. Issue publics represent the small, policy-oriented segments within the mass polity that attend to particular problems, engage their political leaders and the media over these issues, and demand some degree of elite responsiveness and accountability. Elections by themselves do not ensure a stable and publicly responsive democratic state; rather, it is a multiplicity of contending minority interests, which, in pressing their claims, are able to bargain for policy accommodations. Hence modern democracies, at least those offering relatively open electoral systems and guarantees of civil liberties that protect contending minority interests, are 'polyarchies' (Dahl, 1971), where political power is effectively disaggregated and where specific policies are—unlike in the elite

model proposed by Schumpeter—anchored to popular wishes through politically active segments of the citizenry (Held, 1996).

Pluralist conceptions of disaggregated and in some sense 'fairly' distributed power in society were challenged by many. Some critics cast the model as elevating a descriptive account of contemporary Western democracies to the status of a normative theory, and in so doing enshrining the *status quo*. Others (e.g., Pateman, 1970) argued that social, financial and political resources, including knowledge and efficacy, are so maldistributed in the population that many groups in society lack the ability to mobilize. Assumptions made by liberal theory that people are 'free and equal,' argued Pateman, do not square with actual social and economic disparities, which effectively undermine any formal guarantees of equal rights. True democracy requires that such inequities be ameliorated, and that the active participation of all segments of society be fostered in democratic institutions of all kinds, which must be fully open and publicly accountable (Barber, 1984).

Participatory democratic theorists argue, drawing upon the communitarian notions of Rousseau and other 'developmental republicans,' that political autonomy arises from collective engagement in political action and discussion. As Dewey (1927, p. 208) had earlier proposed in rebutting Lippmann's (1922) withering attack on citizens, 'the essential need [is] improvement in the methods and conditions of debate, discussion, and persuasion.' The problem, many writers submit, is that the mass media transform politics into a kind of spectator sport. Opinion polls and popular referenda, despite their democratic aims, merely amplify defective opinions formed without any meaningful public debate. The result is a citizenry converted into a body that *consumes* political views disseminated by elites through the mass media, rather than an autonomous, deliberating body that *discovers* its own views through conversation. The sovereign, reasoning public is displaced by a mass audience assembled around political spectacle (Mills, 1956; Habermas, 1962/1989).

These conditions, however, are not viewed as inevitable. Were people more broadly empowered, this line of argument runs, they would become politically transformed: 'they would become more public-spirited, more knowledgeable, more attentive to the interests of others, and more probing of their own interests' (Warren, 1992, p. 8). The act of deliberating, in many treatments (e.g., Gutmann & Thompson, 1996) is thought to be especially transformative: it fosters mutual respect and trust, leads to a heightened sense of one's value as part of an active political community, and stimulates additional forays into political engagement. The presumed value of discussion in stimulating and engaging the citizenry has thus figured heavily in recent proposals for revitalizing the modern electorate. Participatory democratic theory in general and 'deliberative democracy' theories in particular have emerged in tandem with a multi-faceted critique of contemporary social and political life (e.g., Fishkin, 1991).

Participatory democratic theory is countered by another contemporary trend in political philosophy that draws its inspiration not from classical republican and communitarian notions but instead from democratic theory's liberal foundations. Much of the emphasis in liberal democratic theory has to do with delineating the rights of the citizen against the state, and balancing and distributing power to avoid its untoward concentration of power in the hands of any single actor or alignment of actors. Proponents of *legal democracy* (e.g., Hayek, 1979), who are sometimes called neo-liberals, view state efforts to ameliorate social inequities as inevitably coercive and likely to come at the expense of individual liberty. In this view, democracy is valuable primarily in its protection of individual liberty; and the more expansive the state, the larger its legislative and bureaucratic reach, the more grave the dangers to freedom. The potentially coercive powers of the state must consequently be highly circumscribed by the rule of law. The most legitimate means of collective choice and—thus the basis for any genuinely liberal society, legal democrats argue—is the free-market; and this mechanism operates best when unencumbered by government intervention and regulation (e.g., Friedman, 1962).

Twentieth-century models of democracy have thus moved beyond classical notions in grappling with ever more complex industrial and corporate societies; yet they continue to range from the highly communitarian to the highly individualistic in their conceptions of the public and public opinion, drawing freely from several centuries of philosophical inquiry. 'Democratic theory is in a state of flux,' writes Held (1996, p. 231), 'There are almost as many differences among thinkers within each of the major strands of political analysis as there are among the traditions themselves.' As Price (1992, p. 2) has noted, connecting the concepts *public* and *opinion* represented an attempt by liberal democratic philosophy to unite the 'one' and the 'many,' to devise ways of producing coordinated, collective action out of disparate and conflicting individual choices. It did so by turning to the idea of democracy, that is, collective decision making through discussion and debate among members of the citizenry, under conditions of openness and fairness. Yet the particular mechanisms of decision making proposed by democratic theorists have always varied widely.

DEMOCRACY AS COLLECTIVE DECISION MAKING

A useful matrix for conceptualizing the complex, temporally extended process of collective decision making was proposed by Price and Neijens (1997). Their matrix serves our particular purposes here by illustrating and summarizing a very wide range of possible collective decision-making processes, and myriad roles the public might play.

Price and Neijens note general similarities between traditional models of the stages through which public opinion develops (e.g., in the work of Bryce, 1888) and the phases of decision making later adopted by decision analysts and policy researchers. Five main phases of collective decision making can be distilled. First is the process of *eliciting values*, sometimes called the 'problem' stage, which involves recognizing a matter of collective worry or concern, and then articulating various goals thought to be important in addressing the issue. Next is a phase that involves *developing options* or proposals for resolving the problem, and sifting these down into a small set of potentially viable alternatives. Once these have been developed, decision makers turn to *estimating consequences* of selecting one over another option, a task that often falls to technical and policy experts. The fourth stage involves *evaluating the alternatives*, with advocates of competing options actively engaged in persuasive appeals aimed at garnering both public and elite support, and the issue typically receiving broad media attention through news coverage and opinion polling. This public debate ultimately leads to the *making of a decision*, either through bureaucratic or governmental action or in some cases by electoral choice.

The Price and Neijens decision matrix crosses each of these five stages with six different groups of actors in a democratic society who may be implicated to varying degrees at any particular phase of the process: political leaders, technical experts, interest groups, the journalistic community, attentive publics and much larger mass audiences (see Figure 1.1). Political leaders, policy experts and interest groups comprise the political 'elites,' both within and outside the sphere of formal government, who play active roles throughout all phases of decision making. Members of the press serve as critical conduits for information and opinion exchange between these elites, their followers in attentive publics, and much larger mass audiences.

Large-scale, democratic choices are especially complicated—due not only to the interactive engagements of each of these myriad groups, but also because the process does not necessarily unfold in any neatly linear fashion. It is often a rather ambiguous and politically-charged affair, far less rational than the formal stage-model would imply. While the model suggests that the discovery of problems gives rise to solutions, for example, Price and Neijens (1997) note that the entire process can be turned on its head when interest groups or political leaders adhere to ideologically favored political 'solutions' and merely lie in wait opportunistically for the right 'problems' to which they can readily be applied to appear on the scene. Despite these

	Elicitation of goals/ values	Development of options	Estimation of consequences	Evaluation of options	Decision
Political leaders					
Technical experts					
Interest groups					
Reporters and editors					
Attentive publics					
Mass audiences					

Figure 1.1 The collective decision-making process—matrix of phases and participants
Reproduced from Price and Neijens (1997, p. 342) with permission from Oxford University Press and the World Association for Public Opinion Research

complications, the matrix helps to summarize the full range of possible interactions that might potentially feed into decisions made by democratic states. It also visually reinforces two main dimensions underlying differing conceptions of democratic decision making.

Elite/mass relationships

Comparisons of activities across the vertical dimension of the matrix—from political leaders and technical policy experts at the top to mass audiences at the bottom—capture the relative degree to which the process is 'top-down' or 'bottom-up' in nature. At one end of the theoretical spectrum, elite models of democracy propose that collective decision making unfolds best when it is largely technocratic, with elected leaders and expert policy advisors deciding the relevant course of collective action and then organizing public opinion for the masses (a position embraced as noted above by Lippmann, 1922, in view of what he considered irremediable deficiencies in both the public and the press, for which he saw little hope). At the other end of the spectrum are models of direct or participatory democracy. More communitarian in spirit, as suggested earlier, they advocate a strong and engaged role for ordinary citizens across all phases of the collective decision-making process (e.g., Pateman, 1970). All seek some sort of 'linkage' from top to bottom (or bottom to top); but the degree of looseness of the linkages desired and the preferred means by which they are to be achieved is quite variable.

The nature of mass involvement

Comparisons of activities across the horizontal dimension of the matrix—from elicitation of goals and values, to developing options, estimating consequences, evaluating options, and finally deciding a course of action—capture the relative degree to which the process attempts to respond to general popular views about desirable end states, on the one hand, or aims at soliciting far more focused public evaluations of policy alternatives on the other. A number of democratic theories—while placing most of the burden for developing, debating, and evaluating policy options on elite political leaders, experts, and interest groups—nonetheless propose that ordinary citizens should play critical roles in conveying, if not highly directive views on specific policies, at least general signals of popular values and desires. 'Minimal' democratic models view periodic selection and removal of political leaders as a sufficient means of public participation. Other theories argue for the more regular and substantial involvement of ordinary citizens, for instance through referenda on specific policy actions (a primary role advocated for public opinion polls by Gallup & Rae, 1940). Different political theories, then, seize upon one or the other of the two traditional senses of opinion discussed above: Some seek citizens' knowledgeable contributions (their informed preferences for particular policies), while others seek merely to ground elite decision making in popular moral sensibilities or broad judgments related to a governing regime's overall success in meeting the citizens' basic needs. Some ask the public to think carefully about exactly what the government is doing; others are more concerned with leaders' legitimate public standing ('opinion' here equated with popular regard or reputation).

Various democratic theories, then, place a range of expectations and demands on the shoulders of citizens. They range from relatively top-down or 'weak' forms of democracy to bottom-up, 'strong' forms (Barber, 1984); and they range from models positing that ordinary citizens are best consulted by seeking diffuse judgments of satisfaction with elite performance to models that seek much more direct and detailed public input on the substance of pressing policy questions.

Polls as policy referenda

Implicit in contemporary understandings of public opinion and opinion polling, Price and Neijens (1997) and Althaus (2006) submit, is a particular decision-making model.

Mass audiences enter the process at the evaluation phase, during which time they follow elite debate over a limited number of options and are asked, via polling, to register opinions as to which they prefer. However, this informal 'policy referendum' model can be seen as problematic, even contradictory (Althaus, 2006). If members of the mass audience have no engagement in the process until they are asked their opinions at the evaluation phase, then it places quite heavy and perhaps unreasonable burdens on the press to inform their previously (perhaps habitually) unengaged audiences at this juncture. Even assuming these burdens are met, the capacity for sovereign citizen judgments may be heavily circumscribed, both because they have at their disposal little or no knowledge of alternatives that were considered and rejected (or indeed not considered) by elites, and because they are unlikely to fathom the consequences of various options (aside from whatever can be gleaned from political contestants as they attempt to recruit supporters for their side; Price & Neijens, 1997).

The decision-making matrix suggests at least two potential remedies to this problem, each consistent with a rather different normative-theoretical approach to democracy. Despairing of any expectation for intelligent mass contributions at the evaluation stage, one might shift the focus of mass engagement to the very first, problem-oriented phase of decision making. Citizens may not be competent to judge the intricacies of policy, this line of reasoning goes, but they may be fully capable of telling elite decision makers what bothers them, what needs policy attention, and what they most desire in terms of collective outputs. Such a model emphasizes public agenda setting over the monitoring of policy alternatives. Alternatively, one might propose, as do deliberative theorists, that ordinary citizens *would be* fully capable of rendering intelligent judgments, if only they enjoyed a different communication apparatus for doing so and were not hamstrung by the conventional press and

polling model as presently institutionalized. Hence the 'deliberative poll,' which seeks to unite the mass-representative capabilities of probability sampling with something very like the Athenian assembly (Fishkin, 1991), along with related notions of citizen juries, shadow assemblies, and the like.

The omnicompetent straw man

A theme running throughout our discussion deserves to be stated explicitly at this juncture. Empirical opinion research in the twentieth century—though often framed as rebutting classical democratic theory—in fact bore out the low expectations of most pre-empirical theorists, documenting the shallow diffusion of political information across the electorate, low levels of popular political knowledge, and the tendency of mass belief systems to exhibit poorly integrated or weakly 'constrained' opinions across different issues (Converse, 1964). Contrary to many claims that 'classical' democratic theory called for omnicompetent citizens, however, the majority of social-philosophical writers of the eighteenth and nineteenth centuries largely eschewed any expectation that many ordinary people would bother to spend more than a modest amount of time thinking about politics and public policy (Pateman, 1970). As Bryce (1888) and others had long suggested, most people, most of the time, are weakly if at all engaged in political issues of the day. Schudson (1998), after examining models of citizenship over the course of American history, argues that the ideal of an informed citizen is actually the product of early twentieth century progressive thought. So empirical renderings of citizen ignorance, if they indeed undercut a 'classical' theory, may actually address a relatively recent one (hypostasizing Lippmann's critique of contemporary American progressive hopes as a critique of 'democratic theory'). Althaus (2006) sums up the matter by pointing to two 'false starts' in public opinion research: the idea that opinion surveys are best used to assess government policies, and the idea that popular disinterest in politics is a grave and unanticipated problem for democratic rule.

RESEARCHING COLLECTIVE DECISION MAKING

It would be difficult at this point to conclude that empirical public opinion research has convincingly overturned any particular democratic theory. It has arguably helped, however, to refine various concepts, and has at times called certain philosophical-theoretical assumptions into question. Significant amounts of survey research have accumulated, for example, detailing the nature of mass political engagement (e.g., Verba, Schlozman, & Brady, 1995) and the diffusion of political information (e.g., Delli-Carpini & Keeter, 1996). This work highlights important inequities in both knowledge and participation, offers clues as to their origins, and considers various ramifications for democratic practice. As Held (1996, chap. 6) recounts, survey research in America and Britain proved central in early arguments supporting pluralistic democratic theory, but also, as it turned out, provided evidence of the broad socioeconomic inequalities and cultural chasms in political resources marshaled by critics of the pluralistic model.

A full, perhaps even a satisfying integration of empirical opinion research with democratic theory is beyond the scope of this chapter. Still, as a way of concluding our discussion, we can paint in broad strokes a few of the key ways empirical studies and democratic theories might profitably inform each other.

The empirical contours of 'opinion'

Price (1992) notes that while some sociologists adopted an organic, discursive model of public opinion more or less aligned with republican theory, developments in attitude measurement and survey research techniques in the 1920s and 1930s deflected public opinion research onto a much more individualistic trajectory. This trajectory has proved occasionally contentious (most notably when Blumer in 1948 attacked the field for having entirely missed the mark); however, the operational definition of public opinion as the aggregated attitudes of a population gained wide, indeed nearly universal acceptance. At any rate, in pursuing the study of individual attitudes and opinions over a half century, the field has inarguably accumulated a considerably refined understanding of both.

Many of the most profound developments have been methodological in origin. In the early days of opinion research, pollsters tended to view instabilities and inaccuracies in survey responses as mere artifacts of measurement (Sudman & Bradburn, 1974). However, a shift toward more theoretically oriented research in opinion measurement, which began in the late 1970s, led to an understanding that many variations in survey responses were far from random. Over the past few decades, research has tried to develop comprehensive models of the way people respond to survey questions, drawing heavily from theories of cognitive processing ($\rightarrow$ *Designing Reliable and Valid Questionnaires;* $\rightarrow$ *The Psychology of Survey Response*). The clear trend has been to interpret opinion responses, not as self-evidently interpretable, but in light of how respondents react to wording or context changes, how they respond to rhetorical manipulations, how they are influenced by social perceptions, and how the responses vary across groups in the population. There has also been conceptual clarification of the *range* of phenomena relevant to opinion expression, with researchers examining not only opinions (e.g., preferences related to policy matters or public officials), but also broad underlying values and attitudes, beliefs, perceptions of groups, and the complex relationships among these ($\rightarrow$ *Conceptions of Opinions and Attitudes;* $\rightarrow$ *Identifying Value Clusters in Societies*).

In any democratic decision-making process one can imagine, the public's opinions must at some point be gathered. Empirical research offers extensive guidance, far beyond anything speculation might offer, on *how to ask*. However, empirical research does not, in and of itself, offer any guidance on *what to ask*. That is properly the role of democratic theory which, in return for technical guidance, can offer the field some normative direction—in emphasizing, say, expressions of basic wants and desires, or demands for elite action on problems seen as pressing, over the usual 'approval voting' on policies of the day (Althaus, 2003).

The Internet may presage another important development for public opinion research. Despite continuous methodological improvements, survey research has generally consisted of randomly sampled, one-on-one, respondent-to-interviewer interactions aimed at extracting pre-coded answers or short verbal responses. Web-based technologies, however, may now permit randomly constituted *respondent-with-respondent group conversations* integrating general-population survey methods and focus-group techniques (Price, 2003). The conceptual fit between such conversations and the phenomenon of public opinion, itself grounded in popular discussion, renders it theoretically quite appealing (→ *The Internet as a New Platform for Expressing Opinions and as a New Public Sphere*).

The empirical contours of 'the public'

Although sublimated, the concepts of public opinion as an emergent product of widespread discussion, and of the public as a dynamic group constituted by the give-and-take of debate and deliberation, have never been entirely absent from public opinion research. Early scientific analysts, most prominently Allport (1937), found the notion of public opinion as an emergent product of discussion difficult to grasp empirically and problematic in a number of respects, and hence came to accept mass survey data as the only workable empirical rendering of public opinion. Yet the

extent to which general population surveys themselves render a valid representation of the public has been questioned by scholars of many stripes. Opinions given to pollsters and survey researchers—often unorganized, disconnected, individual responses formed without the benefit of any debate—have indeed been called 'pseudo' public opinion (Graber, 1982).

These debates echo enduring republican/liberal tensions in democratic theory, which has variously cast 'the public' as one or another of any number of sociological entities: a complex of groups pressing for political action (i.e., interest groups); people engaged in debate over some issue; people who have thought about an issue and know enough to form opinions (whether or not they have been engaged in conversation or debate); groups of people who are following some issue in the media (i.e., audiences or attention aggregates); an electorate; an agglomeration of all citizens; the general population of some geopolitical entity; or even some imagined community in the minds of citizens. These varying conceptions implicate a number of empirical phenomena—conversations, the holding of opinions, media use, knowledge, participation, the perceived climate of opinion—as criterial attributes. And each of these phenomena has been studied, some of them quite extensively, in empirical research. In one way or another, normative theories will only make contact with public opinion research if we are able to *find* the public (or publics) as conceptualized in theory.

The study of public knowledge serves as a case in point, one that drives directly at issues of rationality and equity, and indirectly at how we define the public. Suppose we dismiss general-population survey results as expressing, not true public opinion, but instead rather thoughtless, lightly rooted 'top-of-the-head' reactions to some issue. How would our reading of public opinion look if we confined 'the public' to only knowledgeable citizens? Would it render a substantially different portrait of public preferences? Perhaps surprisingly, Page and Shapiro (1992) argue 'no.' Despite the relative incoherence of many sampled opinions, when survey data are aggregated they reveal essentially rational collective preferences, since most of the thoughtless 'noise,' the flotsam and jetsam of mass pseudo opinions, ends up canceling out. Such collective rationality is reassuring to pollsters; however, it does not necessarily solve the problems arising from a large number of uninformed voters in the population (Delli-Carpini & Keeter, 1996; → *Studying Elites vs Mass Opinion*). Recently Althaus (2003) has demonstrated that, at least on some issues, systematic inequalities in knowledge distribution among groups in the population can distort even aggregate readings of public opinion. And because political knowledge is a resource (just like financial capital) that underwrites participation and facilitates mobilization, the implications of its distribution in society extend far beyond the impact on polling results. In pluralistic formulations of democratic decision making, government policies are linked to mass preferences through representative issue publics. Although they may vary in size and composition from issue to issue (Krosnick, 1990), issue publics may be drawn disproportionately from a generally well-educated, attentive and knowledgeable stratum of the population (at best one-fifth of the electorate at large, by most methods of accounting; see e.g., Delli-Carpini & Keeter, 1996). These are not just empirical lines of inquiry; they take on deep theoretical meaning when viewed through the prism of one or another model of democratic decision making. The public is a complex blending of 'active' and 'passive' segments, of 'engaged' citizens and mere 'spectators.' The size and representative composition of these segments, which surely changes across issues and over time, indexes in many ways the health of a democracy.

The empirical contours of 'the citizen'

Implicit in any model of democracy is a model of the citizen: a set of assumptions about what motivates him or her, about her cognitive capacities, about his behavioral tendencies. Here again we find significant opportunities for empirical research and democratic theory to inform one another, with the latter proposing what to look for, and the former serving to refine and correct theoretical assumptions.

Fundamental to the project of understanding citizens is some recognition that they are, in large part, products of their surrounding political culture. Consequently, understanding them requires two tasks: learning how they *are* at present, and learning how, under different conditions, they *might be*. A fitting illustration is provided by participatory democratic theory, developed as it was with the understanding that many citizens are poorly informed, politically apathetic and inefficacious, but also in the belief that these very people could be transformed through everyday democratic *praxis* into different and more productive citizens. In its deliberative variant, this theoretical model proposes that public discussion serves to broaden public perspectives, promote tolerance and understanding between groups with divergent interests, and generally encourage a public-spirited attitude.

Advocates of deliberative theory are presently legion, but its fundamental propositions are not without critics (e.g., Hibbing & Theiss-Morse, 2002), and they have been increasingly subjected to empirical scrutiny (e.g., Fishkin & Luskin, 1999; Mutz, 2006; Price, in press). Group discussion has, after all, been known to produce opinion polarization, shifts in new and risky directions, and other undesired outcomes. Disagreement may also be fundamentally uncomfortable for citizens, particularly those uncertain of their views and feeling ill-equipped to defend them. Some have argued that encouraging citizen discussion, despite its democratic intentions, will make reaching out to the disenfranchised, who tend to lack status and deliberative ability, even more difficult (Sanders, 1997). As deliberative theory is played out in actual practice and as empirical research accumulates, we should come to better understand conditions of discussion that facilitate or retard democratic aims. Comparisons of citizen behavior across different contexts—local, national, and international—should also prove highly informative.

Empirical monitoring of collective decision making

There is another, perhaps even more important way in which public opinion research and democratic theory should intersect. Some 50 years ago, Hyman (1957) pointed out that opinion research tended to pursue, using sociologist Robert Merton's phrase, 'theories of the middle range.' While this strategy stood to produce useful and valuable psychological insights, Hyman opined, it had potential liabilities as well. 'We may concentrate on the trivial rather than the important,' Hyman worried, 'We may even institutionalize the neglect of some important part of our ultimate larger theory' (p. 56). What was needed to avoid these problems, he suggested, was careful monitoring of large-scale social processes over time, with a focus on the relationship of popular thinking to governmental processes and policy outcomes.

In the terms adopted here, Hyman's call is for the monitoring over time of key cells in the decision-making matrix, as collective problems are first identified and addressed, and as decisions work their way through processes of social and political negotiation. Attention would be paid to the goals and interests of each of the participants identified by the matrix, with the aim of determining how—and indeed if—democratic mass–elite linkages occur. This is admittedly a tall order to fill. Yet here again, empirical public opinion research has been evolving in this direction, albeit not always with the explicit connections to democratic theories that it might have marshaled. Research on agenda setting, for example, though very often tethered to 'middle-range' theoretical goals, has at times turned to big-picture questions and produced interesting examinations over time of the complex interactions of public,

press, and policy agendas. Some exemplary works in this tradition include the 'agenda-building' research of Lang and Lang (1983), who examined the ways in which Watergate developed as a public issue through persistent elite efforts, constrained by political events and contemporary currents in mass opinion; or the series of detailed case studies conducted by Protess and colleagues (1991), who studied the ways investigative journalists often collaborate with public policy makers to set a 'public' reform agenda, in some instances apparently without much engagement of attentive publics or mass audiences.

Price and Neijens (1997) suggest a large number of collective 'decision-quality' concerns that might be empirically examined in opinion research. These sorts of quality criteria—for example, the extent to which the problems addressed appear responsive to popular concerns, the extensiveness of popular discussion and debate, the degree to which those who are engaged represent the affected population, the generation of differing viewpoints on the problem at hand, the degree to which the consequences of chosen policies are clearly understood by the public, or the degree to which the process is perceived as fair and legitimate—all have import for the democratic character of the public opinion and policy making process. Democratic theories construct various models of the way decision making ought to unfold, but empirical research is required to inform judgments about the way they actually unfold in practice.

This brief overview has necessarily taken a rather broad sweep at identifying some of the major lines of normative theoretical thinking that feed into modern opinion research, suggesting just a few of the ways empirical and philosophical inquiry might inform one another. Readers are encouraged, as they consider the many lines of study summarized elsewhere in this volume, to look for other useful connections to democratic theory not explored here. Finding and nurturing those connections should help an already vibrant field of research to become even more fruitful.

NOTES

1 Our review must of necessity be brief. Thorough reviews of political theory can be found, for instance, in Held (1996). For a review of the history of the concept of public opinion see Price (1992), Peters (1995), or Splichal (1999).

REFERENCES

Allport, F. H. (1937). Toward a science of public opinion. *Public Opinion Quarterly, 1,* 7–23.

Almond, G. (1950). *The American people and foreign policy.* New York: Harcourt.

Althaus, S. L. (2003). *Collective preferences in democratic politics: Opinion surveys and the will of the people.* New York: Cambridge University Press.

Althaus, S. L. (2006). False starts, dead ends, and new opportunities in public opinion research. *Critical Review, 18,* 75–104.

Baker, K. M. (1990). Public opinion as political invention. In K. M. Baker (Ed.), *Inventing the French Revolution: Essays on French political culture in the eighteenth century* (pp. 167–199). Cambridge, UK: Cambridge University Press.

Barber, B. (1984). *Strong democracy: Participatory politics for a new age.* Berkeley: University of California Press.

Bentham, J. (1962). *The works of Jeremy Bentham* (J. Browning, Ed.) (Vols. 1–11). New York: Russell & Russell (Original work published 1838–1843).

Berelson, B. (1952). Democratic theory and public opinion. *Public Opinion Quarterly, 16,* 313–330.

Blumer, H. (1948). Public opinion and public opinion polling. *American Sociological Review, 13,* 542–554.

Bryce, J. (1888). *The American commonwealth* (Vol. 3). London: Macmillan.

Converse, P. E. (1964). The nature of belief systems in mass publics. In D. E. Apter (Ed.), *Ideology and discontent* (pp. 206–261). New York: Free Press.

Dahl, R. A. (1971). *Polyarchy: Participation and opposition.* New Haven: Yale University Press.

Delli-Carpini, M. X., & Keeter, S. (1996). *What Americans know about politics and why it matters.* New Haven: Yale University Press.

Dewey, J. (1927). *The public and its problems.* New York: Holt, Rinehart & Winston.

Fishkin, J. S. (1991). *Democracy and deliberation: New directions for democratic reform.* New Haven: Yale University Press.

Fishkin, J. S., & Luskin, R. C. (1999). Bringing deliberation to the democratic dialogue. In M. McCombs & A. Reynolds (Eds.), *The poll with a human face: The national issues convention experiment in political communication.* Mahwah, NJ: Lawrence Erlbaum.

Friedman, M. (1962). *Capitalism and freedom.* Chicago: University of Chicago Press.

Gallup. G., & Rae, S. (1940). *The pulse of democracy.* New York: Simon & Schuster.

Graber, D. A. (1982). The impact of media research on public opinion studies. In D. C. Whitney, E. Wartella, & S. Windahl (Eds.), *Mass communication review yearbook* (Vol. 3, pp. 555–564). Newbury Park, CA: Sage.

Gutmann, A., & Thompson, D. (1996). *Democracy and disagreement.* Cambridge, MA: Harvard University Press.

Habermas, J. (1966). Three normative models of democracy. In S. Benhabib (Ed.), *Democracy and difference: Testing the boundaries of the political* (pp. 21–30). Princeton, NJ: Princeton University Press.

Habermas, J. (1989). *The structural transformation of the public sphere: An inquiry into a category of bourgeois society* (T. Burger, Trans.). Cambridge, MA: MIT Press (Original work published 1962).

Hayek, F. A. von (1979). *The political order of a free people.* Chicago: University of Chicago Press.

Held, D. (1996). *Models of democracy* (2nd ed.). Stanford, CA: Stanford University Press.

Herbst, S. (1993). *Numbered voices: How opinion polling has shaped American politics.* Chicago: University of Chicago Press.

Hibbing, J. R., & Theiss-Morse, E. (2002). *Stealth democracy: American's beliefs about how government should work.* Cambridge, UK: Cambridge University Press.

Hyman, H. H. (1957). Toward a theory of public opinion. *Public Opinion Quarterly, 21,* 54–60.

Key, V. O., Jr. (1961). *Public opinion and American democracy.* New York: Knopf.

Krosnick, J. A. (1990). Government policy and citizen passion: A study of issue publics in contemporary America. *Political Behavior, 12,* 59–92.

Lang, G. E., & Lang, K. (1983). *The battle for public opinion: The president, the press, and the polls during Watergate.* New York: Columbia University Press.

Lazarsfeld, P. F. (1957). Public opinion and the classical tradition. *Public Opinion Quarterly, 21,* 39–53.

Lippmann, W. (1922). *Public opinion.* New York: Harcourt Brace Jovanovich.

Lively, J. (1975). *Democracy.* Oxford, UK: Blackwell.

Mill, J. (1937). *An essay on government.* Cambridge, UK: Cambridge University Press (Original work published 1820).

Mills, C. W. (1956). *The power elite.* Oxford, UK: Oxford University Press.

Mutz, D. C. (2006). *Hearing the other side: Deliberative versus participatory democracy.* Cambridge, UK: Cambridge University Press.

Noelle-Neumann, E. (1979). Public opinion and the classical tradition. *Public Opinion Quarterly, 43,* 143–156.

Page, B. I., & Shapiro, R. Y. (1992). *The rational public: Fifty years of trends in Americans' policy preferences.* Chicago: University of Chicago Press.

Palmer, P. A. (1936). Public opinion in political theory. In C. Wittke (Ed.), *Essays in history and political theory: In honor of Charles Howard McIlwain* (pp. 230–257). Cambridge, MA: Harvard University Press.

Pateman, C. (1970). *Participation and democratic theory.* London: Cambridge University Press.

Peters, J. D. (1995). Historical tensions in the concept of public opinion. In T. L. Glasser & C. T. Salmon (Eds.), *Public opinion and the communication of consent* (pp. 3–32). New York: Guilford.

Price, V. (1992). *Public opinion.* Newbury Park, CA: Sage.

Price, V. (2003, September). *Conversations at random: New possibilities for studying public opinion online.* Invited paper presented to the Innovative Research Methodologies Symposium, New Research for New Media, Institute for New Media Studies, University of Minnesota.

Price, V. (in press). Citizens deliberating online: Theory and some evidence. In T. Davies & E. Noveck (Eds.). *Online deliberation: Design, research, and practice.* Chicago: University of Chicago Press.

Price, V., & Neijens, P. (1997). Opinion quality in public opinion research. *International Journal of Public Opinion Research, 9,* 336–360.

Protess, D. L., Doppelt, J. C., Ettema, J. S., Gordon, M. T., Cook, F. L., & Leff, D. R. (1991). *The journalism of outrage: Investigative reporting and agenda building in America.* New York: Guilford Press.

Rousseau, J. J. (1968). *The social contract* (M. Cranston, Trans.). Hamondsworth, UK: Penguin (Original work published 1762).

Sanders, L. M. (1997). Against deliberation. *Political Theory, 25,* 347–376.

Schudson, M. (1998). *The good citizen: A history of American civic life.* New York: Free Press.

Schumpeter, J. A. (1942). *Capitalism, socialism and democracy.* New York: Harper and Brothers.

Splichal, S. (1999). *Public opinion: Developments and controversies in the twentieth century.* Lanham, MD: Rowman and Littlefield.

Sudman, S., & Bradburn, N. (1974). *Response effects in surveys.* Chicago: Aldine.

Verba, S., Schlozman, K. L., & Brady, H. E. (1995). *Voice and equality: Civic voluntarism in American politics.* Cambridge, MA: Harvard University Press.

Warren, M. (1992). Democratic theory and self-transformation. *American Political Science Review, 86,* 8–23.

2

The Deliberating Public and Deliberative Polls[1]

Peter Neijens

Since the first scientific studies of public opinion were conducted, survey researchers and democratic theorists alike have pondered the central concept of public opinion and its relationship to mass survey data (Price & Neijens, 1997). Early theorists of public opinion framed it as an emergent product of broad discussion—emanating ideally from a debate open to wide popular participation, free-flowing and uncensored, and well-informed (Lasswell, 1941). However, early scientific analysts (e.g., Allport, 1937) found the concept of public opinion as an 'emergent product' of discussion difficult to grasp empirically and problematic in a number of respects, and over time they came to accept mass survey data as the only workable empirical expression of public opinion (Key, 1961; Converse, 1987; → *The Public and Public Opinion in Political Theories*).

The extent to which general population surveys provide valid measures of what was traditionally defined as public opinion—grounded in public discussion and well-informed by debate—has been questioned by scholars of many stripes (Crespi, 1989; Price & Neijens, 1998; Saris & Sniderman, 2004). Empirical evidence does seem to support the view that opinions given to pollsters and survey researchers can often be unorganized, disconnected, individual responses that have not been influenced by public debate (Bishop, Oldendick, Tuchfarber, & Bennet, 1980).

The question of the relationship of mass survey data to informed public opinion has produced a vigorous and sometimes contentious debate. As a result, public opinion scholars have developed and advanced 'deliberative polls,' 'educational polls,' polls of 'informed public opinion,' and various kinds of focus group discussions as supplements—and in some cases alternatives—to mass opinion surveys. These alternative methods attempt to provide measures of public opinion of higher quality (i.e., ones that are better informed or more deliberative) than those recorded in typical mass opinion surveys (Price & Neijens, 1998). Some researchers have attempted to gather representative samples of citizens to engage in extensive deliberation and discussion, in order to produce measures of better-informed public opinion based on meaningful public discourse (e.g., Dienel, 1978, 1989; Fishkin, 1991, 1995). Other researchers have proposed less drastic modifications of standard surveys, using 'information and choice surveys' that attempt to inform respondents about complex public issues in order to gather assessments of more thoughtful opinion (e.g., Saris, Neijens, & de Ridder, 1984; Kay, Henderson, Steeper, & Lake, 1994; Kay, Henderson, Steeper, Lake, Greenberg et al., 1994). Two of the best-developed 'deliberative polling' and 'information and choice surveys' methods will be presented later, after discussions of the concept and practice of the deliberating public, and the quality of public opinion.

DELIBERATIVE PUBLIC OPINION: THEORY AND PRACTICE

The last ten years have witnessed an increasing interest in the notion of deliberation, ranging from face-to-face and mediated deliberation processes in formal institutional settings, such as parliaments, political parties, citizens' groups, and social movement groups, to informal political talk in people's homes, workplaces, bars, etc. The growing popularity of online forums and other electronic discussions on the Internet has contributed to the interest in deliberation processes (→ *The Internet as a New Platform for Expressing Opinions and as a New of Public Sphere*).

Communication scholars and political scientists have paid attention to both normative and empirical questions regarding deliberation. The list of norms for 'full' or 'good' deliberations developed by the scientific community is almost endless: equality, diversity, reflexivity, respect, empathy, sincerity, freedom, quality, and openness are a few. Such deliberations are also characterized as free-flowing, uncensored, well-informed, directed at consensus, balanced, conscientious, substantive, comprehensive, tolerant,

autonomous, and featuring reciprocity of raising and responding to validity claims, the use of justifying reasons, the direct or indirect inclusion of all those affected, and the absence of interfering pressures with the exception of the 'forceless force of the better argument' (Habermas, 2005, p. 384), to name a few criteria (Habermas, 1962/1989; special issues of *Acta Politica*, 2005, issues 2 and 3). Price and Neijens (1997) give a descriptive review of these criteria distilled from the literature to evaluate the quality of public opinion. These criteria can be applied either to public opinion as an *outcome* or as a decision-making *process*, and to either *individual* opinions or to *collective* ones.

In addition to these normative approaches, there have been empirical studies of deliberation processes. Although some scientists argue that much is still unknown (Barabas, 2004; Rosenberg, 2005), these studies have contributed to our insight into the effects of debates on individual opinion formation and collective decision-making, and the factors that influence these effects. For systematic overviews, see Price and Cappella (2002), Mendelberg (2002), Delli Carpini, Cook and Jacobs (2004), and the special issues of *Acta Politica*, 2005, issues 2 and 3. First, deliberation may expand the range of ideas and arguments related to an issue and the individual's knowledge of the issue (Price & Cappella, 2002). Second, deliberation forces people to consider and defend their views. Third, deliberation fosters understanding of multiple points of view and enhances tolerance for opposing points of view (Gutmann & Thompson, 1996). Fourth, deliberation helps people develop the skills, motivations, and attitudes that enable deeper engagement (Finkel, 1985). Fifth, research has shown that face-to-face communication greatly increases the likelihood of cooperation (Delli Carpini et al., 2004). Sixth, 'choices have been shown to be markedly more coherent when people are exposed to competing interpretations (or frames) of an issue' (Jackman & Sniderman, 2006, p. 273).

Against these advantages, deliberation has shortcomings as well. Conversations usually take place within primary groups of family and close friends—that is, among like-minded people who largely resemble each other socially and politically (Wyatt, Katz, & Kim, 2000; Price & Cappella, 2002). Participation in group discussions and decision-making processes is usually not egalitarian, requiring cultural capital that is unequally distributed in society (Schudson, 1997). Some people may feel uncomfortable speaking up in public, especially in heterogeneous groups. Disagreement can annoy and intimidate some people and cause them to withdraw. Small groups also tend to polarize or become more extreme (Sunstein, 2000). Discussion tends to move collective opinion in the direction of the preexisting views of the majority (Dell Carpini et al., 2004). 'Group think' (Janis & Mann, 1977) may negatively influence decision-making. Group processes may lead to shifts of opinion in new and risky directions (Brown, 2000; Price & Cappella, 2002).

QUALITY OF PUBLIC OPINION

Average citizens have few opportunities to deliberate rigorously in formal institutional settings (Mansbridge, 1999; Conover & Searing, 2005). Although surveys show that talking about political issues is fairly widespread among the American public (Dell Carpini et al., 2004), studies of everyday political talk among ordinary citizens outside formal settings show that these discussions 'fall short of deliberative ideals' in many respects (Conover & Searing, 2005, p. 278). Furthermore, political debates are not equally distributed in society: People who discuss public affairs are better educated, more attentive to media messages, more knowledgeable about politics, and more politically involved (Robinson & Levy, 1986; McLeod et al., 1999). It therefore comes as no surprise that the quality of public opinion is disputed.

Lippmann (1922) long ago called it a false ideal to imagine that voters were inherently competent to manage public affairs. Later empirical studies confirmed this notion, finding that citizens' judgments are 'impulsive, oversimplified, intemperate, ill-considered, and ill-informed' (Sniderman & Theriault, 2004, p. 134). In his often quoted publication, Converse (1964, p. 245) wrote that 'large proportions of the electorate do not have meaningful beliefs, even on issues that have formed the basis of intense, political controversy among elites for substantial periods of time.' Findings in the US show that voters know little about politics (Delli Carpini & Keeter, 1996), are misinformed (Kuklinski, Quirk, Jerit, Schwieder, & Rich, 2000), and possess unstable attitudes (Barabas, 2004).

MEASURING DELIBERATIVE PUBLIC OPINION

Two important types of alternative polling techniques have been developed to measure public opinion that is of higher quality than that measured in standard mass opinion surveys: surveys of informed public opinion and deliberative polls. Surveys of informed public opinion are modifications of standard surveys that attempt to gather more informed or deliberative opinion, for example the 'Americans Talk Issues' program led by Alan Kay and associates in the United States (Kay, Henderson, Steeper, & Lake, 1994; Kay, Henderson, Steeper, Lake, Greenberg et al., 1994) or the Dutch 'Information and Choice Questionnaire' developed by Saris et al., 1984. These surveys provide respondents with written information about a specific problem before asking them for their opinions. The Information and Choice Questionnaire (Neijens, 1987; Neijens, de Ridder, & Saris, 1992) will be presented in detail in the next section.

Second, some researchers have attempted to bring together representative samples of citizens who then participate in an extensive program of deliberation and discussion, in order to produce examples of better-informed public opinion grounded in meaningful public discourse. Examples include Planning Cells (Dienel, 1978, 1989; Renn, Stegelmann, Albrecht, Kotte, & Peters, 1984), Citizens Juries (Crosby, 1995) or 'Deliberative Polls' (Fishkin, 1991, 1995; McCombs & Reynolds, 1999; Luskin, Fishkin, & Jowell, 2002). Deliberative Polls have most of the same goals as the Information and Choice Questionnaire, but add the goal of advancing discussion and debate, and creating a communicative forum that is representative of the population at large (Price & Neijens, 1997).

The Information and Choice Questionnaire (ICQ)

Designed for use in large-scale surveys, the Information and Choice Questionnaire (ICQ) provides citizens with a broad base of reasonably objective information provided by experts, summarizing a full range of viable policy options and the probable consequences of each.

The information included in the ICQ is based on criteria derived from 'decision analysis' theory (Keeney & Raiffa, 1976; Edwards, 1979). According to this theory, information about the consequences of each option, and the probabilities that each will occur, are necessary to make a responsible choice. Consequences include such things as financial and political consequences, consequences for the environment, etc. Information on the various consequences is given in the form of statements. Each statement considers one consequence, mentioning one aspect (attribute) and indicating the possible outcomes thereof, as well as the likelihood of their occurrence. If experts disagree about the outcomes, the experts' differing opinions are included in the statement. An independent, politically and scientifically balanced committee is responsible for the information provided in the ICQ.

Information processing in the ICQ is facilitated by an evaluation procedure. Respondents are asked to evaluate the attractiveness of the consequences of each option before making a choice. The rationale behind this procedure is that the respondents will absorb the information more thoroughly as a result of the various judgments they have made; they will be more actively involved with the information. It is also assumed that evaluating the consequences in the same units will help respondents compare the consequences (Slovic & MacPhillamy, 1974). The respondents' task will also be simplified if they summarize their evaluations of each option, since this 'bookkeeping system' will allow them to make their choice without having to recall all the information. The ICQ thus tries to provide respondents both with information about a problem and a procedure to process this information.

A number of studies have investigated the effects of providing information in an ICQ format. The first application of the ICQ dealt with future energy options for electricity generation (Neijens, 1987; Neijens et al., 1992). First of all, this research showed that citizens were both able and willing to fill out the questionnaire. A random sample of the Dutch population participating in a face-to-face interview was asked to fill out a booklet with the ICQ. They were given one week to do this. All the tasks were completed by 81% of the respondents. Though non-response was biased with respect to age (older people) and education (people with lower levels of education), the differences were small (these two variables explained 5% of the variance in participation). The profile of the participants taking part in the ICQ was thus only slightly different from the Dutch population as a whole.

The evaluation study showed that a majority of participants (68%) made a consistent choice, i.e., one based on the information provided. They did so by weighing positive and negative evaluations of the consequences of the options. Moreover, the ICQ had an effect on the respondents' choice-making process: 50% of the respondents made a *different* choice after reading and evaluating the information on the consequences of the policy options that was included in the ICQ. The evaluation study also investigated to what extent these choices were *better* choices, ones that took the information into account.

The majority (68%) of the respondents filling out the ICQ made energy-policy choices that were consistent with their evaluations of the consequences of each energy alternative mentioned in the information, compared with 37% in a standard survey format. That means that the choices made based on the ICQ were not only different, but also better informed (Neijens *et al.*, 1992).

Further results showed that all three aspects of the ICQ—the provision of information, the evaluation of consequences task, and the book-keeping system whereby evaluations for each option are added up—contributed to its effect on the use of information. Each aspect is important, with each contributing about 10 percentage points (Neijens *et al.*, 1992). These data also show that the results were systematically related to the various questionnaire types. This supports the interpretation that the results obtained with the ICQ can be attributed to the information provided and the information processing aid offered, instead of being merely an artifact of the research situation itself (see also van der Salm, van Knippenberg, & Daamen, 1997). It also shows that the ICQ is an instrument that not only offers people (new) information, but that also helps them to organize their own thoughts and allow them to arrive at a structured evaluation of the different issues at stake (see also Bütschi, 2004).

Further research has shown the effect of *option characteristics* (Bütschi, 2004): the ICQ is especially effective when dealing with complex or less known topics, and topics that do not touch on basic values.

Respondent characteristics also have an effect. 'Cognitive ability' and 'involvement with the issue' (variables taken from the Elaboration Likelihood Model, ELM, Petty & Cacioppo, 1981) were positively associated with elaboration of the information and the consistency and stability of the choices made with the ICQ (Neijens, 1987; van Knippenberg & Daamen, 1996). Bütschi (2004) found that the ICQ primarily influenced respondents who did not have structured beliefs about the policy alternatives in question.

Deliberative polls

According to Fishkin (1991), an ordinary poll 'models what the electorate thinks, given how little it knows. A deliberative opinion poll models what the electorate *would* think if, hypothetically, it could be immersed in intense deliberative processes' (p. 81, italics in original). The basic idea of the deliberative poll is to select a national, random sample of the voting-age population and transport them as 'delegates' to a single site for several days of debate and deliberation. After debating issues with political leaders and with each other, the delegates are then polled on their preferences. The National Issues Convention (NIC), held in Austin Texas, in January 1996, was the third Deliberative Poll (two earlier ones had been held in Britain in 1994 and 1995).

The delegates had received non-partisan briefing materials on the topics beforehand. The 'on-site' discussion of each topic began with key figures and definition of terms, and then continued with outlines of three packages of related policy proposals and their alleged advantages and disadvantages. Upon their arrival, delegates were randomly assigned to one of 30 small groups. Each group was led by a moderator, and there were about 15 people in each. They spent a total of nine hours (three on each topic) spread out over two days, discussing the issues and preparing three questions to ask presidential candidates. Then, delegates met together with issue experts and politicians. Later, they met again in their small groups to discuss candidates and issues.

Of the delegates, 54% said they had read most or all of the materials before coming to the NIC, and 14% said that they had 'only glanced' at them. It was found that just four or five delegates in each group accounted for the majority of the discussion (Smith, 1999). Smith also notes: 'On the positive side, delegates were serious and attentive. In some groups, note taking was common and many people kept the briefing materials handy…. On the negative side, most discussion was general. It was anchored in personal experience and not closely tied to public policy. When the discussion moved beyond private lives and beliefs, the quality of the information and asserted facts was mixed, with wrong assertions nearly equaling correct evidence' (p. 49f.). It was also observed that 'the discussions were often dangerously shallow. Because the NIC moderators were facilitators and not teachers, they permitted all manner of outrageous claims to be made' (Hart & Jarvis, 1999, p. 82).

Since 1994, more than 20 Deliberative Polls have been conducted, in the US, Britain, Denmark, Australia, and Bulgaria. Table 2.1 shows the most important findings based on the analyses of a number of these Deliberative Polls (see Luskin *et al.*, 2002; Fishkin & Luskin, 2005, p. 290ff.). Luskin *et al.* (2002, p. 484) conclude: 'The result, in the aggregate is a picture of a better informed and more thoughtful public opinion. We say "better" advisedly, claiming only for our results a window on the comparative, not the superlative.'

These findings raise a lot of interesting questions (Price & Neijens, 1998). A number of factors could have contributed to the increased knowledge and change of opinions. Was it the additional information, additional thought, or additional deliberation, or combinations thereof? Luskin *et al.* (2002, p. 459) conclude: 'From a scholarly perspective, the most important aspect of the Deliberative Poll is as quasi-experiment. The one grand treatment consists of everything that happens from the moment of recruitment, immediately following the pre-deliberation questionnaire, to the post-deliberation questionnaire at the end.' Further research is needed to sort out whether, and to what extent, the briefing

material, the debates with other participants and the policy experts, the attention to political news in the media, and talks about politics with friends and family long before the poll itself contributed to opinion change.

CONCLUSIONS

Each of these approaches attempts to advance a variety of specific qualities in obtained public opinions. The ICQ has limited objectives, seeking to expand the information base of survey respondents, to enable them to consider the consequences of alternative proposals or policies, and thus to gather more thoughtful and consistent individual opinions that, when aggregated, better express collective interests and collective desires. The ICQ confines itself to attempting to improve the quality of participation in the evaluation phase of collective decision making, and shares many of the objectives of conventional opinion polling.

The Deliberative Poll, on the other hand, has a broader range of objectives, aiming to create conditions that allow direct or participatory democracy to operate. This approach not only seeks to improve the same qualities of opinion formation and expression as the ICQ survey program does, but also to make the process *publicly deliberative* and *discursive*. The Deliberative Poll seeks to improve the discursive quality of mass participation in the decision-making process, albeit for short periods of time (e.g., several days to a week) and under laboratory conditions.

Table 2.1   Overview of the most important effects of deliberative polls

− The participants are representative − Opinions often change − Vote intentions often change − The participants gain information − The changes in opinions and vote intentions are information driven − The changes in opinions and vote intentions are unrelated to social position (sociodemographics)	− Policy attitudes and vote intentions tend to be more predictable after deliberation, and to hinge more on normatively desirable criteria − Preferences do not necessarily 'polarize' within groups − Preferences do not necessarily homogenize within groups

Source: Fishkin & Luskin, 2005, 290–292. *Reprinted by permission from Macmillan Publishers Ltd: Acta Politica (40, 290–292), copyright (2005) published by Palgrave Macmillan*

Studies have shown that the two methods have produced at least some of their intended effects, and that they seem viable as ways of registering more informed public opinion than those offered by typical polls or surveys. The studies have also revealed some of the mechanisms that produce these effects. Further study is needed to broaden our insight into the information and deliberation processes behind these methods. This will not only contribute to improving the methods, but also advance a meaningful interpretation of the results: the measured public opinions. Of course, like every expression of opinion—be it in a standard survey or in face-to-face exchanges between peers—the opinions expressed in the Information and Choice Questionnaire and the Deliberative Poll depend on the context. Context inevitably affects the expression (and measurement) of opinion, and the better we understand the role of the context, the better we can assess the quality of public opinion acquired in them.

NOTES

1 This chapter is partly based on Price and Neijens (1998).

REFERENCES

Allport, F. H. (1937). Toward a science of public opinion. *Public Opinion Quarterly, 1*, 7–23.

Barabas, J. (2004). How deliberation affects policy opinions. *American Political Science Review, 98*, 687–701.

Bishop, G. F., Oldendick, R. W., Tuchfarber, A. J., & Bennett, S. E. (1980). Pseudo-opinions on public affairs. *Public Opinion Quarterly, 44*, 198–209.

Brown, R. (2000). *Group processes: Dynamics within and between groups.* Oxford: Blackwell Publishers.

Bütschi, D. (2004). The influence of information on considered opinions: The example of the Choice Questionnaire. In W.E. Saris & P. Sniderman (Eds.), *Studies in public opinion: Attitudes, nonattitudes, measurement error and change* (pp. 314–334). Princeton: Princeton University Press.

Conover, P. J., & Searing, D. D. (2005). Studying 'everyday political talk' in the deliberative system. *Acta Politica, 40*, 269–283.

Converse, P. E. (1964). The nature of belief system in mass publics. In D. Apter (Ed.), *Ideology and discontent* (pp. 206–261). New York: Free Press.

Converse, P. E. (1987). Changing conceptions of public opinion in the political process. *Public Opinion Quarterly, 51*, 12–24.

Crespi, I. (1989). *Public opinion, polls, and democracy.* Boulder, CO: Westview Press.

Crosby, N. (1995). Citizens juries: One solution for difficult environmental questions. In O. Renn, T. Webler, & P. Wiedemann (Eds.), *Fairness and competence in citizen participation: Evaluating models for environmental discourse* (pp. 157–174). Dordrecht: Kluwer Publishers.

Delli Carpini, M. X., & Keeter, S. (1996). *What Americans know about politics and why it matters.* New Haven: Yale University Press.

Delli Carpini, M. X., Cook, F. L., & Jacobs, L. R. (2004). Public deliberation, discursive participation, and citizen engagement: A review of the empirical literature. *Annual Review of Political Science, 7*, 315–344.

Dienel, P. C. (1978). *Die Planungszelle: Ein Alternative zur Establishment-Demokratie. Der Bürger plant seine Umwelt* [The Planning Cell: An alternative to establishment democracy. The citizen plans its environment]. Opladen: Westdeutscher Verlag.

Dienel, P. C. (1989). Contributing to social decision methodology: Citizen reports on technological problems. In C. Vlek & G. Cvetkovich (Eds.), *Social decision making for technological problems* (pp. 133–151). Dordrecht: Kluwer Academic Publishers.

Edwards, W. (1979). Multiattribute utility measurement: Evaluating desegregation plans in a highly political context. In R. Perloff (Ed.), *Evaluator interventions: Pros and cons* (pp. 13–54). Beverly Hills, CA: Sage.

Finkel, S. E. (1985). Reciprocal effects of participation and political efficacy: A panel analysis. *American Journal of Political Science, 29*, 73–93.

Fishkin, J. S. (1991). *Democracy and deliberation: New directions for democratic reform.* New Haven: Yale University Press.

Fishkin, J. S. (1995). *The voice of the people: Public opinion and democracy.* New Haven: Yale University Press.

Fishkin, J. S., & Luskin, R. C. (2005). Experimenting with a democratic ideal: Deliberative polling and public opinion. *Acta Politica, 40*, 284–298.

Gutmann, A., & Thompson, D. (1996). *Democracy and disagreement.* Cambridge: Harvard University Press.

Habermas, J. (1989). *The structural transformation of the public sphere: An inquiry into a category of bourgeois society* (T. Burger, Trans.). Cambridge, MA: MIT Press (Original work published 1962).

Habermas, J. (2005). Concluding comments on empirical approaches to deliberative politics. *Acta Politica, 40*, 384–392.

Hart, R., & Jarvis, S. (1999). We the people: the contours of lay political discourse. In M. McCombs & A. Reynolds (Eds.), *The poll with a human face: The national issues convention experiment in political communication* (pp. 59–84). London: LEA.

Jackman, S., & Sniderman, P. M. (2006). The limits of deliberative discussions: A model of everyday political arguments. *Journal of Politics, 68*, 272–283.

Janis, I. L., & Mann, L. (1977). *Decision making: A psychological analysis of conflict, choice, and commitment.* New York: Free Press.

Kay, A. F., Henderson, H., Steeper, F., & Lake, C. (1994). *Interviews with the public guide us … On the road to consensus.* St. Augustine, Florida: Americans Talk Issues Foundation.

Kay, A. F., Henderson, H., Steeper, F., Lake, C., Greenberg, S. B., & Blunt, C. (1994). *Steps for democracy: The many versus the few.* St. Augustine, Florida: Americans Talk Issues Foundation.

Keeney, R. L., & Raiffa, H. (1976). *Decisions with multiple objectives: Preferences and value tradeoffs.* New York: Wiley.

Key, V. O., Jr. (1961). *Public opinion and American democracy.* New York: Knopf.

Knippenberg, D. van, & Daamen, D. (1996). Providing information on public opinion surveys: Motivation and ability effects in the information-and-choice questionnaire. *International Journal of Public Opinion Research, 8*, 70–82.

Kuklinski, J. H., Quirk, P. J., Jerit, J., Schwieder, D., & Rich, R. F. (2000). Misinformation and the currency of citizenship. *Journal of Politics, 62*, 790–816.

Lasswell, H. D. (1941). *Democracy through public opinion.* Menasha, WI: George Banta.

Lippmann, W. (1922). *Public opinion.* New York: Macmillan.

Luskin, R., Fishkin, J. S., & Jowell, R. (2002). Considered opinions: Deliberative polling in Britain. *British Journal of Political Science, 32*, 455–487.

Mansbridge, J. (1999). Everyday talk in the deliberative system. In S. Macedo (Ed.), *Deliberative politics: Essays on democracy and disagreement* (pp. 211–242). Oxford, UK: Oxford University Press.

McCombs, M., & Reynolds, A. (Eds.). (1999). *The poll with a human face: The national issues convention experiment in political communication.* London: LEA.

McLeod, J. M., Scheufele, D. A., Moy, P., Horowitz, E., Holberg, R., & Zhang, W. (1999). Understanding deliberation: The effects of discussion networks on participation in a public forum. *Communication Research, 26*, 743–774.

Mendelberg, T. (2002). The deliberative citizen: Theory and evidence. In M. X. Delli Carpini, L. Huddy, & R. Shapiro (Eds.), *Research in micropolitics: Political decision making, deliberation and participation* (Vol. 6, pp. 151–193). Greenwich, CT: JAI Press.

Neijens, P. (1987). *The choice questionnaire: Design and evaluation of an instrument for collecting informed opinions of a population.* Amsterdam: Free University Press.

Neijens, P. C., de Ridder, J. A., & Saris, W. E. (1992). An instrument for collecting informed opinions. *Quality & Quantity, 26*, 245–258.

Petty, R. E., & Cacioppo, J. T. (1981). *Attitudes and persuasion: Classic and contemporary approaches.* Dubuque, IA: W. C. Brown Co.

Price, V., & Cappella, J. N. (2002). Online deliberation and its influence: The electronic dialogue project in campaign 2000. *IT & Society, 1*, 303–329.

Price, V. E., & Neijens, P. C. (1997). Opinion quality in public opinion research. *International Journal of Public Opinion Research, 9*, 336–360.

Price, V. E., & Neijens, P. C. (1998). Deliberative polls: Toward improved measures of 'informed' public opinion. *International Journal of Public Opinion Research, 10*, 145–176.

Renn, O., Stegelmann, H. U., Albrecht, G., Kotte, U., & Peters, H. P. (1984). An empirical investigation of citizens' preferences among four energy alternatives. *Technological Forecasting and Social Change, 26*, 11–46.

Robinson, J., & Levy, M. R. (1986). Interpersonal communication and news comprehension. *Public Opinion Quarterly, 50*, 160–175.

Rosenberg, S. (2005). The empirical study of deliberative democracy: Setting a research agenda. *Acta Politica, 40*, 212–224.

Salm, C. A. van der, Knippenberg, D. van, & Daamen, D. D. L. (1997). A critical test of the choice questionnaire for collecting informed public opinions. *Quality & Quantity, 31*, 193–197.

Saris, W. E., & Sniderman, P. M. (Eds.). (2004). *Studies in public opinion: Attitudes, nonattitudes, measurement error and change.* Princeton: Princeton University Press.

Saris, W. E., Neijens, P. C., & de Ridder, J. A. (1984). *Kernenergie: ja of nee?* [Nuclear power: yes or no?]. Amsterdam: SSO.

Schudson, M. (1997). Why conversation is not the soul of democracy. *Critical Studies in Mass Communication, 14*, 297–309.

Slovic, P., & MacPhillamy, D. (1974). Dimensional commensurability and cue utilization in comparative judgment. *Organizational Behavior and Human Performance, 23*, 86–112.

Smith, T. W. (1999). The delegates' experience. In M. McCombs & A. Reynolds (Eds.), *The poll with a human face: The national issues convention experiment in political communication* (pp. 39–58). London: LEA.

Sniderman, P. M., & Theriault, S. M. (2004). The structure of political argument and logic of issue framing. In W. E. Saris & P. M. Sniderman (Eds.), *Studies in public opinion: Attitudes, nonattitudes,* *measurement error and change.* Princeton: Princeton University Press.

Sunstein, C. R. (2000). Deliberative trouble? Why groups go to extremes. *Yale Law Journal, 110,* 71–120.

Wyatt, R. O., Katz, E., & Kim, J. (2000). Bridging the spheres: Political and personal conversation in public and private spaces. *Journal of Communication, 50,* 71–92.

3

The News as a Reflection of Public Opinion

Thomas E. Patterson

'Public opinions must be organized for the press if they are to be sound, not by the press as is the case today.' The US journalist Walter Lippmann (1922, p. 19) thus stated what he believed was a defective tendency in the practice of democracy. Since then, the tendency has intensified. The news media are no longer asked just to keep an eye out for wrongdoing and to help keep citizens abreast of public affairs. They are expected also to take a lead role in organizing public debate—a function that traditionally has been the responsibility of political organizations and institutions.

Can the media carry this burden? Can they organize public opinion in a meaningful way? Many journalists believe they can. A study of journalists in five Western democracies found in each case that they regard 'news reports' as a more accurate expression of public opinion than 'parliamentary debates' (Patterson & Donsbach, 1992). The belief was stronger in the continental European countries of Germany, Sweden, and Italy, but it also characterized the thinking of US and British journalists.

Research has shown, however, that news content is an imperfect indicator of what citizens are thinking and doing. Contrary to what some journalists have argued (Mickelson, 1972), the news is not a 'mirror' held up to society. The news is instead a selective version of reality governed by conventions that lead journalists to provide limited and sometimes misleading portrayals of public opinion.

This chapter will discuss what content-analytic studies reveal about the relationship between news and public opinion. The chapter will also suggest how content analysis could be used to further our understanding of this relationship.[1] Although media effects and observational studies shed some light on the relationship, news content is the most precise indicator.

POLLS IN THE NEWS

How should we define public opinion when trying to determine how accurately it is reflected in the news? Should we see it narrowly, in the way measured by public opinion surveys? Is it simply an issue of how people feel about the topical issues of the day? If this is what we mean, then the answer is fairly straightforward and the content-analytic requirement is modest. We need to ask and answer three questions: Do the media make regular use of polls, their own or those of others? Are these polls presented fully and accurately? Do these polls cover a reasonable proportion of what citizens experience and care about? The respective answers to these three questions are 'yes,' 'not always,' and 'not really.'

Polls are a regular component of news coverage, particularly during election campaigns (Welch, 2002). During US presidential general elections, it is a rare day when a new poll is not released (Erikson & Wlezien, 1999). In the final two months of the 2004 election, for example, about 200 different polls were reported by one or more of the leading US news outlets (Rosenstiel, 2005). Other countries' media are not as poll-driven, but their coverage, too, has increasingly included poll results (Brettschneider, 1997; Hardmeier, 1999; Anderson, 2000; → *The News Media's Use of Opinion Polls*).

When reporting polls, journalists nowadays usually mention sampling error, which is an advance over earlier practices (Patterson, 2005). Studies indicate, however, that journalists do not always respect this parameter when interpreting polling data. In election campaigns, small differences—within the range of sampling error—between a recent poll and a previous one are often portrayed as representing real change in opinion (Erickson & Wlezien, 1999). Shaw and Roberts (2000) conclude that small shifts in poll results within a relatively short period without an identifiable triggering event are usually due to polling error rather than any underlying true change.

Journalists also tend to analyze polls for what they might say about the candidates, as opposed to what they reveal about the voters. Rhee (1996) found that, as poll references increase in news stories, references to candidates' strategies also increase. Journalists use polls transcendentally, as a basis for claims about whether the candidates' strategic maneuvers are having their intended effect. With their eyes fixed on the candidates, journalists find their explanations for poll results in what the candidates are attempting to achieve rather than in what the public is actually thinking, a tendency that derives from journalists' habit of looking for news in what leaders say and do.

Even if polls were interpreted with greater precision, they would be an imperfect indicator of public opinion. Transitory responses to poll questions are only a sliver of public opinion, which also includes people's deep-seated values and associational activities (Mutz, 2006) as well as what Lippmann called 'the pictures in our heads' of the world outside (1922, p. 3). A central issue for Lippmann was whether the media could portray the world in a way suited to the public's needs. 'To traverse the world men must have maps of the world,' Lippmann wrote. 'Their persistent difficulty is to secure maps on which their need, or someone else's need, has not sketched in the coast of Bohemia' (p. 11).

Content analytic studies indicate that the media's portrayal of reality is an inexact map at best. The problem resides in three potentially distortive orientations of the press: those to novelty, events, and leaders.

THE NEWS MEDIA'S FILTERS

Novelty

Time affects the work of every institution, but few so substantially as the news media. The news is intentionally shortsighted. *The New York Times'* James Reston described reporting as 'the exhilarating search after the Now' (Taylor, 1990, p. 25). The latest news abruptly replaces the old. In the world of news, each day is a new reality. The speed of the news cycle and the relentless search for fresh stories steer the journalist toward certain developments and away from others. In early February 2006, for example, front-page stories in the US press told of church bombings in the rural South and of unrest in the Arab world over a Danish newspaper's publication of cartoons depicting the Prophet Muhammad in terrorist garb. Suddenly, these subjects disappeared from the front pages, not because they were resolved but because they had been displaced by news that Vice President Dick Cheney had accidentally shot a hunting companion in Texas. For a week, the Cheney story was at the top of the news. Then, it, too, slipped from sight.

In the world beyond news, issues stem from societal problems and values, and are woven into the social fabric. News has shallower roots. The news is a selective account of recent developments. Issues abound, but whether they make the news depends on whether they take a form that journalists recognize as news. Breaking developments catch journalists' eye. Chronic conditions do not.

Other things being equal, larger problems get more attention than smaller ones. In the world of news, however, these 'other things' are rarely equal. Novelty and disruption trump regularity. As African Americans in the late 1940s and 1950s moved into northern US cities by the hundreds each day, seeking work and a new start, white city dwellers, pushed by racial fears and drawn by the lure of the suburbs, moved out. Within a few decades, the political, social, and economic landscape of urban America had been remade. Few developments in mid-century America had a greater impact on US society than the northward trek of southern blacks, but it was rarely mentioned in the news, much less emblazoned in the headlines.

In the late 1960s, America's urban trans-formation finally caught reporters' attention. US cities burst into flames as the pent-up frustration and anger in the black community turned violent. It was a scene and a story seen again in 1992, when Los Angeles policemen were acquitted by an all-white jury after having been caught on videotape savagely beating a defenseless black man. In each instance, the news coverage flared with the violence and receded when it died out. During the three weeks of the 1992 Los Angeles riots, urban scenes were contained in 35% of network evening newscasts. Thereafter, such scenes were nearly absent from the news (Center for Media and Public Affairs, 1992).

Although journalists' preoccupation with the moment and the distortions that result from it are amply documented, some aspects of this tendency deserve further study. The 'running story'—one that stays in the news for more than a day or two (for example, the Cheney 'shotgun' story)—is one of them. The verb tense changes when journalists pursue a running story. Most news stories are narrated in the past tense. The running story, in contrast, is told through the future tense and through a journalistic version of the 'continuous present' tense (Schudson, 1986, pp. 5–8). Running stories branch outward, covering a wider and wider area as they unfold. When and how does public opinion enter into these stories? For example, is there a predictable pattern in the way that journalists bring public opinion into the 'rally round the flag' stories that arise in the face of national crises?

Another understudied time-related subject is the 'meta-narrative'—the storyline that takes on a life of its own (Rosenstiel, 2004). It gets embedded in journalists' thinking and is imposed on subsequent coverage. Blendon and his colleagues (1997) suggest that a meta-narrative underpinned their remarkable finding in the mid-1990s that, contrary to fact, a majority of Americans believed that inflation, unemployment, crime, and the federal budget deficit had been getting worse during the previous five years. The researchers concluded that the media's relentlessly down-beat portrayal of government was a con-tributing factor. Kepplinger (1989) reached a similar conclusion about Germans' opinions on environmental pollution from a study of print coverage of the issue. Such studies raise questions about how journalists form their judgments about social conditions, and about the adequacy of feedback mechanisms that could alert them when their judgments go awry.

Events

News is mostly about events. Although there is no precise rule for determining which obtruding developments will get attention, events of the past day are the foci of news. Accordingly, issues predictably surface in the news only when they take event form. For example, Nisbet and Lewenstein (2002) found for a 30-year period that biotechnology, except for the cloning issue, was a news topic only when scientific breakthroughs were announced. Another example is terrorism coverage in the United States before the attacks of September 11, 2001. Storin (2002) found that, although the press heavily covered the first World Trade Center attack in 1993, the same-day bombings of US embassies in Kenya and Tanzania in 1998, and the Yemen-harbor bombing of the USS *Cole* in 2000, it glossed over the larger issue of terrorism. Government reports that warned of a growing terrorist threat were virtually ignored even by America's top newspapers on those earlier occasions. Nor did reporters substantially explore the possibility of any links between the three major terrorist attacks that preceded those of September 11, 2001.

Without hard events to lend them immediacy, social problems seldom get much attention in the news. Most of society's problems look the same today as they did yesterday—a monotonous sameness that reduces their news value. Conversely, any problem that routinely presents itself in the form of a hard event is likely to get substantial coverage. Crime is the preeminent example. Crimes are events—in each case, there is an act, a victim, a perpetrator, a time, and a place. Not surprisingly, crime has been a mainstay of news from the earliest days of journalism and, at times, the core of it, as in the case of the 'if it bleeds, it leads' approach that dominated US television news in the early 1990s. Responding to the steady loss of audience to cable television's entertainment programs, US broadcasters jacked up their crime coverage, hoping to hold onto marginal viewers by doing so. Between 1992 and 1993, the reporting of crime tripled. On network television, crime overshadowed all other issues, including the economy, health care, and the Bosnian crisis. The impact on public opinion was dramatic. At no time in the previous decade had even as many as 8% of Americans named crime as the nation's most important problem. In an August 1994 Gallup poll, however, an astonishing 39% labeled it the country's top issue. The facts told a different story. Justice Department statistics indicated that levels of crime, including violent crime, had been decreasing for three years (Patterson, 1999, p. 308).

Was this coverage a complete aberration? The few content analytic studies that have simultaneously tracked news coverage and policy developments suggest that news reality and social reality are often at odds. In their study of Swedish coverage of seven major policy areas, including the economy, crime, and defense, Westerstahl and Johansson (1986) found that in practically no case was there 'any correspondence between the factual and reported development' (p. 141). In a US study, Lichter and Smith (1994) reached a similar conclusion upon comparing economic coverage with economic data for the period 1982–1987. In fact, they found a negative correlation between the two measures, noting that 'as the economy improved, economic news actually grew more pessimistic, moving from a five-to-one negative ratio in the first year of the study to a seven-to-one ratio in the last' (p. 84).

Findings such as these speak to the shortsightedness that can result from looking at society through the lens of events. Events are like anecdotes; they are examples, not systematic observations. In a study of the German media, Kepplinger and Habermeier (1995) found that key events alter news selections. When a momentous event occurs, reporters tend to look for and report similar events, thus giving the impression that these episodes are increasing in frequency and magnitude even though empirical evidence would indicate otherwise. Studies like Kepplinger and Habermeier's are few in number, and more research is needed to determine the conditions under which journalists are particularly likely to misjudge reality.

Iyengar's (1991) finding that television reporters only occasionally frame event-based stories thematically—that is, as part of a larger reality—is also a promising path for additional research. Iyengar found that when journalists frame events thematically, viewers tend to think about the relationship between social conditions and public policy. However, such stories are the smaller part of event-based reporting. Journalists typically apply an episodic frame—one that focuses on a particular event without placing it in a larger context. Episodic framing leads viewers to concentrate on the individuals directly involved, to make few connections to the broader society ('the big picture'), and to deny accountability to anyone but those directly involved. Although the Iyengar study has prompted research on framing effects, it has not stimulated content-analytic studies that would reveal the situations in which reporters apply episodic frames as opposed to thematic frames.

Leaders

By tradition, news is the story of powerful people. Journalists gather where top leaders are found, and most reporting stems from what these leaders do. Official routines—press conferences, legislative debates, public speeches, and the like—are the staples of political coverage. This tendency stems from reporters' need to find and file stories on deadline and from their assumption that governing is what takes place in institutional settings. As Steele (1995) notes, reporters have an 'operational bias' in favor of top leaders. Even when journalists venture outside the realm of official circles, they usually turn to experts and former top officials—individuals who are perceived as part of the policy community and can be relied on to speak authoritatively on what is happening

inside government. Citizens, and the public opinion they represent, are at the bottom of the news hierarchy. Indeed, public opinion serves nearly as a backdrop to official action, being considered noteworthy only insofar as it empowers or constrains top leaders (Weaver, 1972, p. 69).

Bennett (1990) notes that 'news is "indexed" to the range of governmental debate and has little relationship to expressed public opinion' (p. 106). Journalists are source dependent. What their sources say—and most of them are top-ranking officials—defines the range of relevant opinions. When top officials agree on a course of action, dissenting opinion tends to be ignored by the press, even in cases where that opinion is widely held in the population. Only when the top leaders are divided in their positions are journalists inclined to open their stories to grassroots opinion. Bennett concludes that this tendency enables top-ranking officials 'to define their own publics' (p. 125).

Although indexing is one of political communication's most intriguing theories, and perhaps the one that raises the most troubling questions about the media's contribution to democracy, it has not been applied nearly as widely as framing theory or agenda-setting theory. An exception is Entman's (2003) 'cascading model,' which has roots in indexing theory and reveals its analytical power.

Research on the extent to which various publics are represented in the news is also a priority. Studies have documented the allocation of news coverage among elites—candidates, legislators, chief executives, and so on. Scholars know much less about the distribution of news coverage across society's other groups. What are the conditions under which a group becomes a news subject? What determines the way in which it is presented? Does sudden attention to an otherwise uncovered group raise journalists' awareness of countervailing interests? Are there ideological and class biases in the selection process? These are among the many lines of inquiry such research could take.

NEED FOR FUTURE RESEARCH

In Frank Baum's classic, *The Wizard of Oz*, a young Kansas girl dreams of being swept away to a land of witches and talking lions. The world as portrayed by the news media is not Oz, but it is not Kansas either. As content analytic studies have made clear, the news is a world in which novelty is prized, where obtruding events are far more visible than are the social forces propelling them into view, and where public opinion tends to become news only in the context of official action.

But if much is known about the press and public opinion, much is yet to be learned. Comparative research would be particularly useful. It cannot be assumed that all news systems handle public opinion in more or less the same way. Even within Western news systems, there are important variations (Hallin & Mancini, 2004). Continental European journalists appear to be less driven by time, events, and leaders than are US and British journalists (Donsbach & Patterson, 2004). German journalists, for example, see themselves to some extent as analysts charged with some degree of responsibility for assessing social trends (Köcher, 1986). Studies of the type that Westerstahl and Johansson conducted of the Swedish media—where they examined news coverage on a range of issues over a period of time—would seem particularly useful in identifying differences in news systems, as well as tendencies shared by all or most of them.

As is generally true of communications research, however, the greatest need is the development of concepts and frameworks that will foster inquiry that is systematic and cumulative. A great many studies have noted the news media's dependence on time, events, and leaders. Yet there has been relatively little theoretical specification or conditional identification of these dependencies. The media's tendencies are robust enough that generalization ought to be possible: the media are time bound, are event-driven, are leader-preoccupied. But existing research does not allow these generalizations to be taken to second- or third-order levels. Future research

should seek to develop that knowledge. The degree to which the news media reflect public opinion is an important issue in democratic governance, and one that scholarship can illuminate.

NOTES

1 For methodological ways on how to relate data from media content analyses to data from public opinion surveys, see → *Content Analyses and Public Opinion Research*.

REFERENCES

Anderson, R. (2000). Reporting public opinion polls: The media and the 1997 Canadian election. *International Journal of Public Opinion Research, 12*, 285–298.

Bennett, W. L. (1990). Toward a theory of press-state relations in the United States. *Journal of Communication, 40*, 103–125.

Blendon, R. J., Benson, J. M., Brodie, M., Morin, R., Altman, D. E., & Gitterman, D. (1997). Bridging the gap between the public's and economists' views of the economy. *Journal of Economic Perspectives, 11*, 105–118.

Brettschneider, F. (1997). Press and polls in Germany, 1980–1994. *International Journal of Public Opinion Research, 9*, 248–265.

Center for Media and Public Affairs. (1992, November). Clinton's the one. *Media Monitor, 9*, 1–8.

Donsbach, W., & Patterson, T. E. (2004). Political news journalists: Partisanship, professionalism, and political roles in five countries. In F. Esser & B. Pfetsch (Eds.), *Comparing political communication: Theories, cases, and challenges* (pp. 251–270). Cambridge: Cambridge University Press.

Entman, R. (2003). *Projections of power: Framing news, public opinion, and U.S. foreign policy*. Chicago: University of Chicago Press.

Erikson, R. S., & Wlezien, C. (1999). Presidential polls as a time-series. *Public Opinion Quarterly, 63*, 163–177.

Hallin, D. C., & Mancini, P. (2004). *Comparing media systems: Three models of media and politics*. New York: Cambridge University Press.

Hardmeier, S. (1999). Political poll reporting in Swiss print media. *International Journal of Public Opinion Research, 11*, 257–274.

Iyengar, S. (1991). *Is anyone responsible? How television frames political issues*. Chicago: University of Chicago Press.

Kepplinger, H. M. (1989). *Künstliche Horizonte. Folgen, Darstellung und Akzeptanz von Technik in der Bundesrepublik* [Artificial horizons. Consequences, representation and acceptance of technology in the Federal Republic of Germany]. Frankfurt & New York: Campus.

Kepplinger, H. M., & Habermeier, J. (1995). The impact of key events on the presentation of reality. *European Journal of Communication, 10,* 371–390.

Köcher, R. (1986). Bloodhounds or missionaries: Role definitions of German and British journalists. *European Journal of Communication, 1,* 43–64.

Lichter, S. R., & Smith, T. J. (1994). Bad news bears. *Forbes Media Critic, 1,* 81–87.

Lippmann, W. (1922). *Public opinion* (reissue edition 1997). New York: Free Press.

Mickelson, S. (1972). *The electric mirror: Politics in an age of network television.* New York: Dodd Mead.

Mutz, D. (2006). *Hearing the other side: Deliberative versus participatory democracy.* New York: Cambridge University Press.

Nisbet, M. C., & Lewenstein. B. V. (2002). Biotechnology and the US media: The policy process and the elite press, 1970 to 1999. *Science Communication, 23,* 359–391.

Patterson, T. E. (1999). *The American democracy* (4th ed.). New York: McGraw-Hill.

Patterson, T. E. (2005). Of polls, mountains: US journalists and their use of election surveys. *Public Opinion Quarterly, 69,* 716–724.

Patterson, T., & Donsbach, W. (1992, May). *Journalists' perceptions of public opinion: A cross-national comparison.* Paper presented at the annual meeting of the International Communication Association, Miami.

Rhee, J. W. (1996). How polls drive campaign coverage: The Gallup/*CNN*/*USA Today* Tracking Poll and *USA Today's* coverage of the 1992 presidential campaign. *Political Communication, 13,* 213–229.

Rosenstiel, T. (2004). *Character and the campaign: What are the master narratives about the candidates and how are voters reacting to them.* Project for Excellence in Journalism, Washington, D.C. Retrieved October 31, 2006, from http://www.journalism.org/node/168.

Rosenstiel, T. (2005) Political polling and the new media culture: A case of more being less. *Public Opinion Quarterly, 69,* 698–715.

Schudson, M. (1986). *What time means in a news story* (Occasional Paper No. 4). New York, NY: Columbia University, Gannett Center for Media Studies.

Shaw, D. R., & Roberts, B. E. (2000). Campaign events, the media, and prospects of victory: The 1992 and 1996 US presidential elections. *British Journal of Political Science, 30,* 259–289.

Steele, J. (1995). Experts and the operational bias of television news: The case of the Persian Gulf War. *Journalism and Mass Communication Quarterly, 72,* 799–812.

Storin, M. (2002). *While America slept: Coverage of terrorism from 1993 to September 11, 2001* (Working Paper #2002–7). Cambridge, Mass.: Harvard University, The Joan Shorenstein Center on the Press, Politics, and Public Policy.

Taylor, P. (1990). *See how they run: Electing the president in an age of mediaocracy.* New York: Alfred A. Knopf.

Weaver, P. (1972). Is television news biased? *The Public Interest, 27,* 57–74.

Welch, R. L. (2002). Polls, polls, and more polls. *Harvard International Journal of Press/Politics, 7,* 102–114.

Westerstahl, J., & Johansson, F. (1986). News ideologies as molders of domestic news. *European Journal of Communication, 1,* 126–145.

4

Advocacy: Alternative Expressions of Public Opinion

Kurt Lang and Gladys Engel Lang

Citizens have multiple ways of making themselves heard on matters of general concern, most directly when they vote and when they respond to public opinion polls. These are not their only options. They can also sign petitions, join in letter-writing campaigns, stage rallies, parade, celebrate, strike, boycott, engage in civil disobedience, even commit violence, or become otherwise involved in 'social movement' activity. Most likely to turn to such alternatives are those to whom more routinely available means for expressing their opinions appear less than fully effective. Such alternative expressions can also contradict what electoral results and polls suggest about the state of public opinion.

We refer to these forms of collective behavior as 'advocacy' rather than 'protest' or 'contentious claim-making,' terms favored in the more recent social movement literature (McAdam, Tarrow, & Tilly, 2001), because it encompasses the full range of responses— from what Hirschman calls 'exit,' when dissatisfied persons decide to opt out, to 'voice' when people seek redress for their grievances and even find ways to express approval. 'Exit' can be extended to the detachment of a group from a larger one (Hirschman, 1978, p. 93) and, we would add, to include individuals who withdraw from the public sphere and normal institutional activities without actually leaving their country.

Our more general point is that discontented people who remain silent may still be 'voting with their feet' in various ways: by emigrating, sending capital assets abroad, evading military service, not exercising their franchise, ignoring laws and regulations with which they disagree just as they may demonstrate loyalty to a regime through voluntary commitments of time, service, and money. But, unless their dissatisfaction turns into group action, none of the above manifestations would qualify as protest events; nor, for altogether different reasons, would the actions of people cheering at coronations, patriotic rallies, public hangings, ticker tape parades or similar occasions. All are nevertheless signals of what citizens are for and against, what they are likely to put up with, how willingly they assume their obligations as citizens, and the extent to which they approve or disapprove of their government and its policies. Insofar as the legitimacy of all regimes, including despotic ones, depends in the last analysis on the will of the people (Hume, 1752/1906, pp. 243ff.), governments create special festive occasions to secure their loyalty while monitoring as best they can opposition that they cannot control.

Some distinctions are in order. The first is between the collective expression of diffuse sentiment and its articulation into something more concrete. Citizens may grumble, give in to their fears, vent their frustrations, or express their enthusiasms for whatever objects present themselves without articulating just what it is that they want. A second one stems from the fact that it takes more than initial mobilization to get a serious hearing for protestations or demands. Aggrieved citizens have to have staying power, develop strategies, delegate spokespersons, all of which require some minimal organization.

A third distinction derives from another set of facts, namely that, insofar as they involve novice political actors and/or employ unconventional means, many actions in support of a claim or demand transgress what is institutionally sanctioned. They range along a continuum with no sharp line of division between 'transgressive' protests at one end and demonstrations that qualify as 'contained,' though they may sometimes get out of hand, at the other. Whether they do or do not depends not only on the exuberance or despair of participants, but also on the behavior of control agents who, instead of negotiating, might become overzealous in their enforcement of every letter of the law, thereby turning perfectly peaceful and legitimate advocacy into violent confrontation.

HOW ADVOCACIES WORK

In what follows, our emphasis is on the kind of collective advocacy that takes place in the streets and other public places sidestepping normal political channels. Participation in these actions, including those that are clearly 'contained,' rarely draws more than a minority (often a very small minority), whose views are more likely to diverge from, rather than reflect, those of the majority of citizens. If this is the case, why consider them alternative expressions of *public* opinion?

Five reasons suggest themselves. To begin with, complete unanimity of opinion may be an ideal, but is never quite reached. Contrary to impressions conveyed by organized spectacles scripted as 'conquests' to celebrate extraordinary achievement or as 'coronations' that are entirely ceremonial (cf. Dayan & Katz, 1992, pp. 25–27), the public, except when muted by strict censorship, always speaks with more than one voice. This does not keep many of us from pointing to the loudest chorus as *the* opinion of the public.

Second, active advocacy—even by small minorities—does matter. Participation by just one out of every thousand Americans in a March on Washington would generate nearly 300,000 demonstrators, a crowd too large for leaders, officials, or anyone sensitive to public opinion to ignore. An even smaller but strategically located minority—such as a massive walkout by employees in a critical industry, or an unacceptably high rate of desertions and refusals to serve in the armed forces—can carry a threat greater than the actual number involved.

Third, participants in such actions are largely self-recruited, but from that part of the public most strongly moved by whatever issue is in contention, as well as prepared to act and propagate their point of view. Given the over-representation of influentials and opinion leaders in such actions, their potential for attracting mass support is something to which anyone interested in the dynamics of public opinion should pay special attention.

Fourth, political elites are indeed sensitive to a variety of signals, including those from lobbyists, not solely because of likely campaign contributions but also because their expertise, as that of other informed citizens, can be useful in drafting laws and regulations and their cooperation crucial if these are to work as intended. They rely on such input, together with letters and phone calls, which many legislators tally (and like to cite when numbers are in their favor), to orient them to what their constituents want. For them, at least on some issues, these are the opinions that 'count' (cf. Herbst, 1998). While not always as effective as advocates may believe, especially when they run counter to what polls show, an overwhelmingly one-sided deluge has a good chance of forcing an immediate response. The large number of calls and telegrams reaching the White House after Nixon ordered the immediate dismissal of Archibald Cox, the special prosecutor investigating the Watergate break-in, was a major turning point in the controversy—one that ultimately forced the president to resign (Lang & Lang, 1983, pp. 96–105). Similarly, when official results of the 2004 presidential election in the Ukraine declared Prime Minister Yanukovich the winner over Yushchenko, his challenger, the opposition charged the ruling party with fraud and intimidation. Tens of thousands took to the streets for days. These protests, accompanied by widespread acts of civil disobedience, led the country's Supreme Court to order a new election, which Yushchenko won by a comfortable margin.

Finally, all these forms of advocacy take place in a context where people express themselves freely, i.e. not harnessed to the framework imposed by an interview schedule and certainly not restricted to the partisan choices offered only at election time. These behaviors, when properly understood, can serve as 'nonreactive' indicators of what people want (Webb, Campbell, Schwartz, Sechrest, & Grove, 1981). To ignore them is to risk missing something important. Researchers have made inferences from historical records of protests (Rudé, 1980), from petitions addressed to governments (Shapiro & Markoff, 1998), from all sorts of written accounts (Tilly, 2002a), from topics taken up in major newspapers and magazines (Hart, 1933) and even from the directions of 'the gaze' of the main subjects in paintings (Bogart, 2003). Alternative

expressions remain an indispensable source of information about public opinion in countries where polls are prohibited, as they were in the Soviet Union for a long time (Inkeles, 1950), and/or adverse results kept secret.

Even with survey data as widely available in many countries as they are today, protest events can often be more useful than polls in signaling those undercurrents of agitation within some group that have not yet surfaced as issues of general public concern. Testing the relation between survey questions on race and activities of the American civil rights movement, Lee (2002) found an 'unambiguous' relation between the number of movement-initiated events in a given year and the number of racial attitude items the year after (p. 89). Though polls often lag, monitoring such events can enhance our understanding of what moves opinion even before it has crystallized.

METHODS FOR STUDYING ADVOCACY

There are two basic approaches to the study of advocacy as alternative expressions of public opinion: event (or event-history) analysis and the case study. Analyses of protests and similar events rely heavily on records that are collected by outsiders and amenable to quantification. Case studies of one or just a few events are more diagnostic and make a fuller use of participant and observer reports. The two approaches can complement one another.

Event analysis

Beginning in the 1960s when widespread riots erupted in America's black ghettoes and student protest created confrontations in colleges and universities all over the United States, in much of Europe, and elsewhere, many of those studying collective behavior and social movements increasingly turned to this kind of analysis. Significant investments of time and effort have gone into tracking the incidence of certain events and the characteristics associated with them—their size, duration, distribution in space and over time, resolution, frequency of violence, etc. These inquiries have mainly focused on the conditions likely to generate protest and to affect its chances for success or failure (cf. Tilly & Rule, 1965; Koopmans & Rucht, 2002). Patterns of growth and decline show that typically such events are neither randomly distributed nor responses to unique circumstances. Most such events reflect a more general current of unrest that can culminate in demonstrations, boycotts, property seizures that are part of an organized campaign or, alternatively, they can give rise to the kind of crowds that stormed granaries in pre-Revolutionary France, acted as vigilantes in the rural West, were responsible for lynchings in the Southern states of America and, decades later, for rioting in its black ghettoes and, most recently, in Parisian suburbs and other parts of France. The claims that the participants in these activities seek to advance, or the grievances that motivate them, may not always be inscribed on banners; nor their demands clearly formulated in petitions. They are, nevertheless, dispensing their own kind of 'justice.' Usually the violence does not quite have the anomic character that control agents read into it. Both the locations at which these actions take place and their targets offer clues to the nature and sources of the underlying discontent.

While this line of inquiry has yielded much useful information, it has also encountered some vexing problems. One has to do with the adequacy of data sources. There is a heavy reliance on rather selective media reports. Large events, especially in metropolitan centers, get more attention than smaller events in the peripheries, especially those of purely local import. Analysts who continue to use such data do so on the partly substantiated assumptions that, given careful sampling of media outlets (supplemented with data bases under development), the patterns they find will not deviate significantly from reality and, more importantly, that the yield of events obtained in this way includes those that are politically most relevant (Earl, Martin, McCarthy, & Soule, 2004).

Official records, at least for some classes of events, may be more complete but usually lack the uniformity needed for meaningful aggregation at a national level. Data collection by each agency is guided by its own administrative and legal requirements. The most complete records tend to involve work stoppages. These extend farthest back in time, because the monitoring task was usually delegated to a government department or ministry. Yet, another set of problems surfaces here. The current of opinion that generates strikes can vary significantly. In many situations, it is employed by organized labor as a conventional bargaining tactic, especially when workers are sufficiently well off to welcome a temporary vacation and economic circumstances are favorable. Wildcat strikes or walkouts during the term of an agreement are rather rare. Many more have been set off by union leaders seeking recognition, an increase in power, or jurisdiction over additional trades. Still other strikes, especially those prone to violence, may signal an intransigent management that has driven workers to desperation, and these are more likely to be fought to the bitter end with the outcome dependent on their relative strength. Apart from clearly political strikes, such as the four massive walkouts by Belgian workers who were seeking an extension of the franchise within the 12-year period from 1891 to 1913, the opinion that drives a particular work stoppage can be hard to judge from the outside or to divine in advance. The same holds for other advocacy activities.

As to actual counts, it is essential that the analyst be explicit about the rationale behind the definition of the class of events being enumerated (Tilly, 2002b). It can be in terms of the constituency from which participants are recruited, the localities of the events, the target of the actions, the demands articulated, the tactics employed, and so forth. The choice depends on the objective pursued. What to count as a unit is another decision. Do the massive student walkouts in 1968 at several Paris universities constitute a single episode or a number of separate events? And where, when estimating size and frequency, does one draw the lines as demonstrations spread and/or continue over days? Statistics on total 'participation' also need to differentiate between committed demonstrators and accidental bystanders caught up in the action, and to avoid double-counting militants who participate in more than one action.

Case studies

Case studies help public opinion analysts understand the role of these advocacies in an elusive public discourse. To obtain something more than impressionistic accounts of activities that are often unscheduled and, if they are, may not follow a prescribed or predictable course is difficult, and can be expensive. It requires field workers taking notes, keeping a diary, conducting interviews, and/or recording electronically data that might be otherwise easily lost. Few research organizations have developed the capability for deploying adequately trained observers on short notice at pre-selected sampling points first developed for the study of such unscheduled events as disasters. There is also the risk of being mistaken for police informers or spies for one side. As a consequence, much of the richest data on advocacy as an expression of public opinion come from retrospective accounts, including those elicited in interviews with participants, rather than from observations and conversations on the scene. This is a shortcoming that inevitably plagues any effort to grasp data that by their nature are fugitive.

To see what detailed scrutiny of all relevant data can contribute let us consider the category of riots on the basis of a historical example: the 1863 New York City 'draft riots,' as they are still called. The focus of officials on maintaining order distracts attention from whatever discontent is signaled by such collective outbursts. In their view, the violence that shook the city for days was a protest against the first federal conscription bill ever passed in the United States. The selection of recruits by way of a national lottery, but with a loophole for anyone willing to shell out $300, turned out to be manifestly unfair. The first posting of names, nearly

all of them 'laborers and mechanics,' drew immediate objections and was followed by attacks against the military, which officials interpreted as an objection not just to the draft, but to the war itself—or even as sympathy for the Confederate cause, according to the following convoluted logic: 'There would have been no draft but for the war—there would have been no war but for slavery. But the slaves were black, ergo, all blacks are responsible for the war ... so they proceeded to wreak their vengeance on them' (Headley, 1873, p. 169ff.). As it turned out, the action that triggered the rioting reflected the 'hostile attitude of a large segment of Northern labor to the Negro [sic] and towards plans for emancipation ...' reflective of their latent fear of labor market competition by an influx of freed slaves (ibid.). In the prolonged rioting, workers who had heretofore expressed these concerns through strikes and agitation directed against employers of such labor now aimed them directly at those by whom they might be displaced (Lofton, 1949). This is borne out by arrest records. Almost all came from the bottom of the social pyramid, mostly Irish, with no prior involvement with the law. The high proportion below draft-age underlines the conclusion that the draft alone could not have accounted for the disorder (Cook, 1974, p. 175ff.). Still, it took nearly a century to develop a more nuanced interpretation of the so-called 'draft riots.'

In the current media environment, interpretations hinge more directly on how advocacy behavior plays on television. As a case in point, we review the public response to the drama that played out on television after the abrupt dismissal (1951) by President Harry S. Truman of General Douglas MacArthur as supreme commander in the Far East for publicly championing a policy contrary to that of the White House. Televised reports of the enthusiastic reception given this World War II hero in city after city to celebrate his return home suggested an aroused public actively demonstrating for the general and against the president. Acting on this impression, which they shared with many others, Lang and

Lang (1953) recruited 31 specially briefed observers who volunteered to mix with the crowds gathered on the streets of Chicago to greet MacArthur. What they found, contrary to expectations, was a predominantly apolitical crowd, making the most of an unexpected holiday. There is more evidence from polls that the public did not overwhelmingly rally to the general's side; nor did it demand that President Truman be sanctioned. In the Gallup poll reading of public opinion right after the firing, 56% of respondents disapproved this action by the president, with just 29% approving (Gallup Organization, 1951). Nevertheless, the climate of opinion created by the media—above all by television, then still in its infancy—illustrates a landslide effect. The media depiction of a public seemingly aroused to side with MacArthur against the incumbent president impeded rational discourse, at least for a while, until things quieted down—as they did gradually after Congressional hearings were held.

A somewhat similar methodology was employed in a study of the large march against the war in Vietnam in London in 1969 (Halloran, Elliott, & Murdock, 1970). Organized by the Campaign for Nuclear Disarmament, the march was a clearly political demonstration. Although organizers were determined to keep everything peaceful, the control points set up by police for searches of coaches and private cars, as well as the scale of visible security preparations along the designated route, testified to a widespread expectation of trouble. This expectation was not fully confirmed. Some 60,000 marchers, many of them students, moved along the designated route without serious incident. The one confrontation to mar this orderly march was provoked by a small breakaway group of flag-carrying 'anarchists.' Cordons of police held them back as they converged upon the American embassy on Grosvenor Square. Other scuffles were minor, including several attacks on homeward-bound demonstrators by youths shouting pro-American and anti-student slogans. Comparisons with reports by observers, following instructions similar to those in Chicago, revealed an undue emphasis

in the press coverage on these isolated incidents. The 'largely negative presentation was almost bound to devalue the case of the protestors and ... almost certainly created a backlash and moved doubters further away from the demonstrators' position ...' (ibid., p. 315ff.). In this instance, the coverage driven by news values had negated the message that the marchers wanted to send.

COLLECTIVE ADVOCACY AND THE PUBLIC OPINION PROCESS

Advocacy by the relatively small number of citizens who do more than just pay attention is often the driving force behind the discourse through which a constituency gains voice. Without active input from citizens, much of what is read as a mandate amounts to little more than a general acquiescence to whatever a government does in the name of its people. Turnout for national elections in the USA, as in other democracies, is below optimum; that for local elections and referenda typically much lower yet, except when citizens are aroused to impose their will on legislators by passing a binding ballot initiative. But even this practice, instituted as reform, has often provided opportunities for interest groups with money to hire professional manipulators of opinion (Broder, 2000). On more rare occasions, the voice of dissatisfied but normally acquiescent citizens can gain sufficient volume to cause a government to fall. This can happen even in a democratic polity, such as France in 1968, which enjoys freedom of expression. More recent examples are the 'velvet revolutions' that brought down communist regimes, particularly the demonstrations preceding the collapse of the German Democratic Republic in 1989, and the subsequent reunification of Germany. For months before their capitulation, leaders of the Communist Party had sought to stem a threatened mass exodus of highly dissatisfied citizens to the West, only to be overwhelmed by an increasing chorus of protest from people seeking escape, now under the leadership of active resisters, that the Wall come down and the border be reopened (Mueller, 1999). As word of this demand spread, it became the rallying cry for an entire people, though not quite 'everyone.' Essentially private escape turned into group action.

In assessing how active advocacy actions contribute to the more general discourse through which issues normally get resolved, one needs to look beyond the participants to the larger public. Its members function essentially as bystanders. Those physically present in the space where a demonstration or advocacy action takes place may not even be aware of its purpose. Yet their cheers can render it more effective, just as their jeers can diminish it. Citizens who join or organize in opposition are no longer bystanders; they become active participants. Another kind of bystander, as we define the category, includes anyone alerted—be it by word-of-mouth, via the news media, or (most recently) through the Internet—to pay at least some attention. These bystanders, even without acting as advocates, have some influence on the outcome insofar as their consent is needed. It helps the advocates' cause if a majority sympathizes with them—or better yet, shares their grievances and supports their goals—or conversely it hurts it if the majority sees itself being adversely affected, or inconvenienced should demands be met. Tactically sophisticated advocates therefore seek leverage by claiming to represent public opinion, or at least speaking for a constituency much larger than the number of active participants. Even when not actually invoked by the parties in a contentious dispute, the potential that inheres in this bystander public to play a critical third-party role always lurks in the background.

Final outcomes, particularly in polities where much of the public discourse is conducted via the mass media, hinge less on the actions of the aggrieved than on intervention by the public, or some part of it, into the dispute. '[I]t is no longer the co-present public that counts the most but the mass audience that sits at home and watches or reads the media coverage of the demonstration.' (Koopmans, 2004, p. 368; see also Lipsky, 1968). It follows that public

indifference, whether due to media inattention or to the action of censors, leaves room for both advocates and their opponents to mount the barricades or to settle their disputes as they see fit, without regard to public opinion.

There is a tendency to identify advocacies by their place of origin; that is, the storming of the Bastille, the occupation of the Winter Palace in St. Petersburg, the Montgomery bus boycott sparked by the refusal of Rosa Parks to vacate her seat, the breaching of the Berlin Wall, and so forth. By putting the event on the map, an existing but unheard current of opinion makes itself sufficiently audible to enter the public discourse and, as in the above instances, ultimately to dominate it. This happens in steps. Protests grow, often from modest beginnings, when sympathizers join the few activists who have started things rolling. In 1989, when no more than a few hundred Chinese university students started their hunger strike in Tiananmen Square, word spread quickly. Within a day, more than a 100,000 'ordinary' people, emotionally involved in what these students were doing, had converged on the square. As the strikers found themselves the center of attention, their numbers expanded, and so did their initially quite modest demands (Simmie & Nixon, 1989, p. 97; Brook, 1992, p. 37). A few months later, similar radicalization was observed during demonstrations in the East-German city of Leipzig as citizens sought the right to emigrate to the West. The slogans on the banners they carried changed even while opinions recorded in a survey of protesters, remained steady (Opp & Voß, 1993, pp. 100–107). Both in Beijing and Leipzig, nearly all the evidence pointed to massive support for the demonstrators.

Advocacies gain further strength when they generate a wave of similar activity beyond their immediate locality. Successful actions have a demonstration effect on people in essentially similar situations, and especially on activists committed to the same cause. As Conell concluded from statistics on strikes in the French coal mining industry from 1890 to 1935, workers who go out on strike 'transmit [to other workers] information about grievances, opportunities for striking, and the favorability of bargaining conditions' (Conell & Cohn, 1995, p. 367). It is not just strikes but specific strike tactics that diffuse. In 1936 during the Great Depression, the newly formed United Automobile Workers, after years of declining employment and wage cuts, called a walkout at the Flint plant of General Motors to gain recognition as the bargaining agent for employees, who knew that by walking off the job they risked being shut out of their work place by management. Aware that French workers, by taking possession of their own plants, had deprived management of an effective tactical weapon, strike leaders urged workers to 'sit down' and lock themselves in instead of walking out. Their call for an assembly at the main square in neighboring Detroit, the center of the automobile industry, attracted an overflow crowd in support of the strike (Baulch & Zacharias). Very soon workers in other locations occupied their own work places to force management into negotiation.

Diffusion of a tactic proven effective is not unique to organized labor. Campus sit-ins originating at the University of California in Berkeley in 1964, where students took over buildings to press for free speech, became within a few years the *modus operandi* for dissatisfied students everywhere (Lipset, 1971/1993). A generation later, students constructed 'shantytown' shacks from scraps of wood, tar paper, and plastics on campus lawns to get their university administrations to divest themselves of holdings in South Africa (Soule, 1997).

The purpose of all such tactics is to wrest concessions from authorities, which have some leeway in dealing with the challenge. They can concede, negotiate, engage the advocates in a public discourse, or pretend not to hear. The Nazi leaders of the Third Reich, where opposition was muted, organized huge party rallies and had them filmed by Leni Riefenstahl as part of its propaganda effort. Contrariwise, the uncertainty of the East-German communist leadership about how to cope with rising opposition led to a series of misunderstandings, with disastrous results when a lower-level official's granting of passage to a few would-be emigrants set the stage for the assault on the Berlin wall as the prelude to the collapse of the government (Keithly, 1992).

ROLE OF THE NEWS MEDIA

Just how these alternative expressions of public opinion become part of the public discourse depends very much on how they play in the news. The media are not, and nor can they be, entirely neutral transmitters of all that goes on. When it comes to reporting advocacy actions, they are similarly selective. Sensational and dramatic confrontations command more attention than typical but unremarkable events. There are, to be sure, other criteria of newsworthiness. Once an advocacy group breaks through the curtain of inattention, it can set in motion a media attention cycle. Toward the peak of such a cycle, even minor advocacies, which are otherwise unlikely to attract coverage in their own right, get space in newspapers and time on television as enhancements of one or more similar events (McCarthy, McPhail, & Smith, 1996).

The portrayal of advocates or advocacy groups by the media functions as a reference group for participants as much as for the public at large. That is why those who take their advocacy to the street do so with at least one eye on the media as the arena in which much public discourse takes place. The publicity is free, though not invariably favorable, notwithstanding efforts at impression management (Goffman, 1959). But not even positive coverage can assure that demands will be met or that grievances will receive serious consideration. While it can improve morale and stiffen resolve, it can also induce leaders to grandstand and to raise unrealistic demands with no chance of their ever being met.

The public also pays attention to media reports, but probably not nearly as much as do activists. Some may be persuaded and some repelled by what they read or hear.

Even greater significance accrues to reactions people impute to others—what has been called a third-person effect (Davison, 1983). Actions by political leaders in anticipation of a public response that may never occur can create issues and change the direction of the discourse in unexpected ways. By magnifying an external threat, leaders can set off a rally-round-the-flag effect that may justify new limitations on an area of legitimate dissent. Media attention can also favor demonstrators. The vivid pictures of police brutality against blacks participating in peaceful civil rights marches, in clear violation of accepted norms, could not have been welcomed by elites in the Southern states of America. More than the demonstrations themselves, this embarrassing publicity helped overcome hardcore resistance to court-ordered desegregation by undermining its moral basis. Segregationist opinion, though not abandoned by everyone, pretty much disappeared from the public discourse.

IMPLICATIONS FOR DEMOCRACY

More frequently public discourse is enlarged rather than constrained by advocacy action. Burstein (1979, p. 170), for one, found that '… demonstrations preceded the rise in public concern (and in media attention to civil rights), and that all these helped transform continuing changes in public opinion into support for specific legislation.' It was by capturing the attention of both the public and policy makers, according to Santoro (2002), that protests pushed civil rights legislation to the top of the policy agenda. Previously the public, while broadly supportive of the goals sought by protesters, had not cared very much about the issue. After this initial breakthrough, protests took second place to action by Congress and the administration. The same would also hold for the women's and gay rights movements, as well as the more subtle recent campaign to put teaching of the 'theory' of intelligent design on a par with evolution.

The question of the extent to which attention-catching demonstrations influence policy makers and public opinion defies simple answers. It is, however, a matter of record that, at the very time that American opinion was turning against the war in Vietnam, a majority of Americans had a negative view of anti-war protesters (Berkowitz, 1973; Schreiber, 1976). Mounting casualty figures and pessimism about prospects for an easy victory, especially after the Tet offensive, gradually turned people against the war. Still, by making their opposition so highly visible, protesters gained enough 'voice' to bypass the specialized agencies and elite forums within which discussion of such policy questions is normally confined. An analysis by McAdam and Su (2002) of anti-Vietnam War protests indicated that these actions '—especially those of a large or injurious nature—compelled public and Congressional attention,' as had been the case for civil rights, but apparently did not move lawmakers toward a peaceful solution of the conflict. Similarly limited and analogous effects, not quite as thoroughly documented, accompanied anti-nuclear protests in Europe in the 1970s and 1980s, pro-environmental actions in many parts of the world, and more recently the movement against globalization, where the protesters' presence at several conference sites of the World Trade Organization distracted public attention from the policy decisions of conferees.

Inputs from various forms of advocacy into the democratic process are largely positive, unless too many people feel threatened by the disruptive behavior and violence associated with the action. Thus, video shots of pertinacious demonstrators clashing with control agents, taken from behind police lines (as they usually are), would likely have contributed to the backlash against those demonstrating against the war in Vietnam. The reaction of the bystander public hinges on whether or not the use of force by police appears legitimate. Social distance is still another factor. That many of the protesters were young and privileged college students did not sit well with elders concerned over their own peace and security.

The lack of contact between those seeking redress and forces assigned to the maintenance of public order cannot only increase the likelihood of violence in a confrontation but may also have any number of other consequences. An incident at Sharpeville, South Africa, where an aggrieved but non-threatening crowd of protesting locals was greeted with gunfire from white police, illustrates this point. Though a total of 57 were shot dead and another 299 wounded, no convincing evidence of provocation was ever produced. The year was 1960, before the introduction of television enabled a mass audience to 'see for themselves.' An investigative commission found that the crowd surrounding the police station had gone there for various reasons: 'Some wanted to protest against the [newly enacted] pass laws, some were present because they had been coerced [by representatives of the Pan African Congress or the African National Congress], some were there out of idle curiosity, some had heard that a statement would be made about passes. ...' (Reeves, 1966, p. 2). The crowd, however noisy and excitable, was not hostile, but military personnel sent to break it up felt sufficiently threatened to open fire. Afterwards, in reaction to so great a toll, black Africans mobilized protests against apartheid. This clearly unjustified violence against law-abiding citizens, fully documented by an investigation, proved to be the turning point in the struggle by Africans for their rights. Heretofore protest had been essentially peaceful but, after Sharpeville, with the world's attention on South Africa, activists were noticeably emboldened.

From a more analytic perspective, how does one decide what kinds of action contribute to the public discourse and which are intended to circumvent it? In some cases the answer seems rather obvious. Violence against a despotic government substitutes for the absence of the discourse through which public opinion normally develops. Other less sanctioned examples of violence include 'insurgencies' by fringe groups, intent on overthrowing or forcing concessions from an established

government, and coercion against a national, ethnic, religious, or racial minority by a dominant group. Labels alone do not fully resolve the question of whether or not an action should be seen as a just demand or countered with sanctions. Who would deny, for example, that terrorists do indeed mean to enter the public discourse with the messages they send? The difference between what is and what is not legitimate is, albeit within limits, a matter of public perceptions about the action. Reactions primarily based on fear call for repressive measures. But a willingness to consider the conditions that have caused people to riot, rebel, seize property, or otherwise act out their discontent is apt to expand the public discourse. This did not happen during the violent days that have gone down in history as the draft riots. The complex motives and underlying grievances that provoked them eluded contemporary observers, or perhaps they may not have wanted to know. The old label sticks, notwithstanding everything we have learned since.

Still, labels are frequently contested—as, for example, those used by local authorities to vilify the protesting students at Kent State. It is through an ongoing political process, rather than by some objective test, that the public arrives at a collective definition of transgressive behavior. From the labeling point of view, the shooting of demonstrators at Sharpeville was as much a 'police riot' as the action of the police against protesters at the 1968 Democratic conventions, for which the investigative commission looking into these disorders coined precisely this term (Walker, 1968). It was in connection with the collective violence in black ghettoes that shook American cities during the 1960s that Turner (1969) tried to answer the more basic question: When are riots perceived (or labeled) as protest rather than criminal behavior? One condition, he hypothesized, was the right mix of threat and appeal—enough incentive to identify the unresolved issues that could have induced residents of the ghetto to battle police, set fires, and loot stores. It also helps when the disorder appears as a spontaneous response to long-standing deprivation rather than one deliberately planned. In addition to these preconditions, authorities should be ready to make some conciliatory gesture and involve third parties that appear even-handed in any negotiation.

The political consequences of protest are mediated by way of the public's response. General indifference gives authorities a free hand. What seems obvious is that a government unable to maintain public order and otherwise protect its citizens is bound eventually to lose support. For it to fall, however, there has to be a group, a party, or a coalition ready and willing to take over the reins. In May 1968, France was convulsed by rapidly spreading student demonstrations and industrial strikes that brought down de Gaulle, who resigned his presidency not long after. This result came about, first, because a large number of middle-class citizens joined the protesters and, second, because the massive unrest fed into existing partisan divisions, causing de Gaulle to lose a crucial vote in parliament. By the same token, anti-Vietnam War protests together with signs of growing opposition in and out of Congress were crucial factors in President Lyndon Johnson's decision not to stand for reelection. It is possible, though rare, for a committed group to seize power by force. Geared as they are toward influencing the public discourse, for advocacies to have effective input into policy requires something more, namely the political skill to convert demands into laws and see that they are passed (Tarrow, 1998). That requirement applies not only to advocacy groups: it applies equally to all expressions of public opinion, including those disclosed by polls.

REFERENCES

Baulch, V. M., & Patricia, Zacharias (n.d.). The Historic 1936–37 Flint Auto Plant Strikes. *The Detroit News*. Retrieved December 4, 2005, from http://info.detnews.com/history/story/index.cfm?id=115&category=business.

Berkowitz, W. R. (1973). The Impact of Anti-Vietnam Demonstrations Upon National Public Opinion. *Social Science Research, 2,* 1–14.

Bogart, L. (2003). Reconstructing Past Social Moods from Paintings: The Eye of the Beheld. *International Journal of Opinion Research, 15,* 119–32.

Broder, D. S. (2000). *Democracy Derailed: Initiative Campaigns and the Power of Money.* New York: Harcourt.

Brook, T. (1992). *Quelling the People: The Military Suppression of the Beijing Democracy Movement.* New York: Oxford University Press.

Burstein, P. (1979). Public Opinion, Demonstrations, and the Passage of Antidiscrimination Legislation. *Public Opinion Quarterly, 43,* 157–72.

Conell, C., & Cohn, S. (1995). Learning from Other People's Actions: Environmental Variation and Diffusion in French Coal Mining Strikes, 1890–1935. *American Journal of Sociology, 101,* 366–403.

Cook, A. (1974). *The Armies of the Streets: The New York City Draft Riots of 1863.* Lexington, KY: University of Kentucky Press.

Davison, W. P. (1983). The Third-Person Effect in Communication. *Public Opinion Quarterly, 47,* 1–15.

Dayan, D., & Katz, E. (1992). *Media Events.* Cambridge, MA: Harvard University Press.

Earl, J., Martin, A., McCarthy, J. D., & Soule, S. A. (2004). The Use of Newspaper Data in the Study of Collective Action. *Annual Review of Sociology, 30,* 65–80.

Gallup Organization (1951). *Gallup Poll # 1951-0475, May 19–24.* Storrs, CT: Roper Center.

Goffman, E. (1959). *The Presentation of Self in Everyday Life.* Garden City, NY: Doubleday.

Halloran, J. D., Elliott, P., & Murdock, G. (1970). *Demonstrations and Communication: A Case Study.* Harmondsworth, Middlesex: Penguin Books.

Hart, H. (1933). Changing Social Attitudes and Interest. In W. F. O. Ogburn, W. Howard, & E. E. Hunt (Eds.), *Recent Social Trends in the United States* (pp. 382–442). New York: McGraw-Hill.

Headley, J. T. (1873). *The Great Riots of New York, 1712 to 1873.* New York: E. B. Treat.

Herbst, S. (1998). *Reading Public Opinion: How Political Actors View the Democratic Process.* Chicago: University of Chicago Press.

Hirschman, A. O. (1978). Exit, Voice, and the State. *World Politics, 31,* 90–107.

Hume, D. (1752/1906). *Hume's Political Discourses.* Edited by W. B. Roberston. London: Walter Scott.

Inkeles, A. (1950). *Public Opinion in Soviet Russia: A Study in Mass Persuasion.* Cambridge, MA: Harvard University Press.

Keithly, D. M. (1992). *The Collapse of East German Communism: The Year the Wall Came Down, 1989.* Westport, CT: Praeger.

Koopmans, R. (2004). Movements and Media: Selection Processes and Evolutionary Dynamics in the Public Sphere. *Theory and Society, 33*, 367–91.

Koopmans, R., & Rucht, D. (2002). Protest Event Analysis. In B. Klandermans, & S. Staggenborg (Eds.), *Methods of Social Movement Research* (pp. 231–59). Minneapolis: University of Minnesota Press.

Lang, K., & Lang, G. E. (1953). The Unique Perspective of Television: A Pilot Study. *American Sociological Review, 18*, 3–12.

Lang, K., & Lang, G. E. (1983). *The Battle for Public Opinion: The President, the Press and the Polls During Watergate.* New York: Columbia University Press.

Lee, T. (2002). *Mobilizing Public Opinion: Black Insurgency and Racial Attitudes in the Civil Rights Era.* Chicago: University of Chicago Press.

Lipset, S. M. (1971/1993). *Rebellion in the University.* New Brunswick: Transaction.

Lipsky, M. (1968). Protest as Political Resource. *American Political Science Review, 62*, 1144–1158.

Lofton, W. (1949). Northern Labor and the Negro During the Civil War. *Journal of Negro History, 34*, 251–73.

McAdam, D., & Su, Y. (2002). The War at Home: Antiwar Protests and Congressional Voting, 1965 to 1973. *American Sociological Review, 62*, 696–721.

McAdam, D., Tarrow, S., & Tilly, C. (2001). *Dynamics of Contention.* Cambridge: Cambridge University Press.

McCarthy, J. D., McPhail, C., & Smith, J. (1996). Protest: Estimating Selection Bias in Media Coverage of Washington Demonstrations 1982 and 1991. *American Sociological Review, 61*, 478–99.

Mueller, C. (1999). Escape from the GDR, 1961–1989: Hybrid Exit Repertoires in a Disintegrating Leninist Regime. *American Journal of Sociology, 105*, 697–735.

Opp, K.-D., & Voß, P. (1993). *Die volkseigene Revolution* [The people's own revolution]. Stuttgart: Klett-Cotta.

Reeves, R. A. (1966). *The Sharpeville Massacre— a Watershed in South Africa.* Published to promote the International Day for Elimination of Racial Discrimination. New York: Unit for Apartheid, United Nations.

Rudé, G. F. E. (1980). *Ideology and Popular Protest.* New York: Pantheon.

Santoro, W. A. (2002). The Civil Rights Movement's Struggle for Fair Employment: A 'Dramatic Events-Conventional Politics Model.' *Social Forces, 81*, 177–206.

Schreiber, E. M. (1976). Anti-War Demonstrations and American Public Opinion on the War in Vietnam. *British Journal of Sociology, 27*, 225–36.

Shapiro, G., & Markoff, J. (1998). *Revolutionary Demands: A Content Analysis of the Cahiers de Doléances.* Stanford: Stanford University Press.

Simmie, S., & Nixon, B. (1989). *Tiananmen Square.* Vancouver/Toronto: Douglas & McIntyre.

Soule, S. (1997). The Student Divestment Movement in the United States and Tactical Diffusion: The Shantytown Protest. *Social Forces, 75*, 855–82.

Tarrow, S. (1998). Social Protest and Policy Reform: May 1968 and the Loi d'Orientation in France. In M. G. Giugni, D. McAdam, & C. Tilly (Eds.), *From Contention to Democracy* (pp. 31–56). Lanham, MD: Rowman & Littlefield.

Tilly, C. (2002a). Event Catalogs as Theories. *Sociological Theory, 20*, 248–54.

Tilly, C. (2002b). *Stories, Identities and Political Change.* Lanham, MD: Rowman & Littlefield.

Tilly, C., & Rule, J. (1965). *Measuring Political Upheaval.* Princeton, NJ: Center for International Studies, Woodrow Wilson School of Public and International Affairs, Princeton University.

Turner, R. H. (1969). The Public Perception of Protest. *American Sociological Review, 34*, 815–30.

Walker, D. (1968). *Rights in Conflict; Convention Week in Chicago, August, 25–29, 1968: A Report.* New York: Dutton.

Webb, E. J., Campbell, D. T., Schwartz, R. D., Sechrest, D. & Grove, J. B. (1981). *Nonreactive Measures in the Social Sciences.* Boston: Houghton Mifflin.

5

Studying Elite *vs* Mass Opinion

Ursula Hoffmann-Lange

INTRODUCTION: THE ELITE CONCEPT AND ITS IMPLICATIONS FOR THE STUDY OF PUBLIC OPINION

Power and elites are universal social phenomena. The distinction between elites and non-elites is therefore an important aspect of social analysis. The fathers of elite theory, Vilfredo Pareto and Gaetano Mosca (cf. Bottomore, 1993), conceptualized power as dichotomous and therefore assumed the existence of a clear distinction between elites and non-elites (or 'the masses'). While this crude distinction may be an acceptable simplification of social reality for studying ancient and feudal societies in which power was concentrated in the hands of a small hereditary nobility, it is certainly a gross misrepresentation of the character of modern democratic societies. These societies are not only characterized by a more or less continuous distribution of power, but also by the lack of a single center of (political) power and a high degree of horizontal differentiation.

In pluralist societies, power and influence are based on a variety of resources. The most important of these are political authority,

judicial discretion, economic power, academic or administrative expertise and, last but not least, influence on public opinion. Moreover, while intra-organizational power relations can be assumed to follow the model of a clearly defined hierarchy of power, such a model is certainly unrealistic with respect to inter-organizational interactions, which involve multilateral bargaining on a more or less equal footing. This is especially true for political decision making, which routinely involves a broad set of political institutions as well as public and private organizations (public administrations, political parties, voluntary associations, private businesses, mass media, academic institutions, etc.). It also implies the existence of a free market of ideas and associations, considerable conflict over what collective goals should be, and a pluralist elite structure (cf. Aron, 1950; Keller, 1963).

Elites are customarily defined as incumbents of leadership positions in powerful political institutions and private organizations who, by virtue of their control of intra-organizational power resources, are able to influence important (political) decisions. They belong to the small stratum of top (political) influentials who are part of a more or less inclusive elite network. In modern democracies, this network does not have any clearly demarcated outer boundaries, but instead influence levels off as we move from more central to more peripheral actors. Moreover, the composition of the network of relevant actors depends on the subject matter at stake, and it is also not invariant over time.

Because of their regular involvement in public affairs, elites are generally more knowledgeable about politics than non-elites (or the general public). This is due to their greater interest in public affairs, their regular interactions with the elites of other organizations, and their involvement in elite bargaining over public policies. It can therefore be assumed that the value orientations and political attitudes of elites differ from those of the broader public. For studying the determinants of public opinion formation, it is thus not sufficient to rely exclusively on public opinion surveys. Instead, complementary data on elites are required as well.

SURVEYING ELITES WITH STRUCTURED QUESTIONNAIRES

While general population surveys based on probability samples are well-established, a great deal of skepticism continues to prevail with respect to the possibility of surveying elites with structured questionnaires. Many scholars have claimed that elites are unwilling to reveal their true beliefs, and also resent structured questionnaires because they feel that the differentiated nature of their political views cannot be adequately captured by questions with fixed-choice options. It has therefore frequently been assumed that elite interviewing requires a different approach, thus making elite–mass comparisons inherently difficult if not impossible.

However, the sheer number of elite surveys that have been conducted in a variety of countries does not support such an assertion. Experience shows that only few elite respondents refuse to accept structured questionnaires. On the contrary: missing values due to *don't knows* or refusals are generally lower among elite respondents (cf. Wildenmann, Kaase, Hoffmann-Lange, Kutteroff, & Wolf, 1982, p. 20; Czudnowski, 1987; Sinclair & Brady, 1987). Response rates are generally somewhat lower, though; this is primarily because elites are busy people and have little spare time for lengthy interviews even if they are willing to participate in a survey. Time constraints as well as distrust in either the purpose of the research or the trustworthiness of the researcher may therefore contribute to less than satisfactory response rates. Thus, organizing the field-work for elite surveys requires more efforts in explaining the purpose of the research to potential respondents, making appointments and actually completing the interviews. Response rates also vary considerably depending on the elite sector involved. While response rates among parliamentarians come close to those of general population surveys, they tend to be much lower among business elites, military elites and religious leaders, let alone politically dissatisfied *counter-elites* (Wagstaffe & Moyser, 1987).

Compared to public opinion surveys, elite surveys have been relatively rare, and the number of studies that have included both elite and non-elite respondents is even smaller. Moreover, most of the latter surveys have been limited to comparing parliamentarians and voters in established democracies. Without denying the merits of such studies, it is obvious that more comprehensive elite surveys, including a larger set of elites from a broad spectrum of sectors, are needed to gain insight into the differentiated nature of elite beliefs. Unfortunately, such studies have been rare, and empirical evidence is therefore limited. The most favorable situation exists for Germany, where two comprehensive surveys were conducted in 1981 and 1995, involving interviews with both a broad spectrum of German top elites and a cross-section of the general population (Hoffmann-Lange, 1992; Bürklin & Rebenstorf, 1997). Additionally, a number of community studies have also included surveys of elites as well as voters (e.g. for Germany: Arzberger, 1980; for Great Britain: Parry, Moyser, & Day, 1992).

Finally, two American attitude surveys on civil libertarianism provide relevant data on elite and non-elite attitudes (McClosky & Brill, 1983; Lock, 1999).

THE ELITE THEORY OF DEMOCRACY: ELITES, NON-ELITES AND SUPPORT FOR DEMOCRATIC VALUES

The breakdown of democracy in a number of western European countries in the 1920s and 1930s, as well as public opinion research, have shattered optimistic expectations regarding the existence of high levels of support for democratic values among mass publics. Opinion surveys comparing political activists and political leaders to the electorate at large have regularly shown that elites have a much better understanding of basic democratic values and their implications for everyday life. Herbert McClosky's study, which compared the democratic value orientations of convention delegates and voters, showed for instance that while support for fundamental principles of democracy (universal suffrage, free and competitive elections, majority rule) was nearly universal among both political elites and the general public, support for some of the less obvious institutional implications of these democratic principles was much lower among the general public than among the elites (McClosky, 1964). These included the rule of law, the protection of civil liberties and minority rights, political equality, the right to organized opposition, party competition, a free market economy, etc. McClosky therefore concluded that it is the elites who should be considered as the main carriers of the *democratic creed*. Later surveys in the US and other countries have confirmed his conclusions. Based on these results, the *elite theory of democracy* concluded that the stability of democracy rests primarily on the existence of an elite consensus on democratic rules of the game.

The differences between elites and mass publics have been explained by several factors. The most important among them is the higher educational level of elites, which implies a longer exposure to civic education. Other authors have argued that elites enjoy a more secure social status and can therefore afford to be more tolerant of deviant minorities. Finally, it has been assumed that elites are inclined to support the existing political order for obvious reasons, since this order provides the basis of their superior social status, regardless of whether this order is a democratic or a non-democratic one. The latter argument especially has far-reaching theoretical ramifications, because it implies that elites in autocratic societies should be less supportive of democratic values, even if they are highly educated. A summary of these arguments can be found in McClosky and Brill (1983), as well as in Lock (1999).

Civil libertarianism

While relatively few studies have dealt directly with democratic value orientations, the available evidence from elite surveys in a variety of democratic countries confirms that elites show more support for civil libertarianism than the public at large. The two most elaborate studies on civil libertarianism were conducted in the US and surveyed a broad spectrum of elites (McClosky & Brill, 1983; Lock, 1999). In the introduction to their comprehensive volume, McClosky and Brill argued that tolerance is not an innate human trait, but rather a posture that has to be learned (McClosky & Brill, 1983, pp. 13–24).[1] This assumption was tested by not only studying elite–mass differences, but also by performing separate analyses for several specialized elite groups, among them lawyers, leaders of the American Civil Liberties Union (ACLU) and police officers. The study showed that the elite groups were generally much more supportive of civil liberties than the mass public. This held true for a broad range of attitude questions, from support for freedom of speech, freedom of assembly, freedom of religion and the guarantee of due process all the way to the right to privacy and personal lifestyle.

The authors identified four explanatory factors that accounted for these attitudinal differences between elites and the general public. The first factor is the elites' socialization into the dominant values of American democracy acquired through formal education. This explains why elites are on average more supportive of civil liberties than the general public. A second factor is the socializing effect of elites' participation in public affairs. It explains why political activists are more tolerant of deviating opinions than their non-active counterparts. Professional norms are a third factor. Defense lawyers who were professionally engaged in protecting the rights of their clients were the second most libertarian group, only surpassed by the activists of the American Civil Liberties Union (ACLU). On the other hand, police officers took a more restrictive stance and tended to attribute primacy to upholding law and order. Finally, political ideology was also related to civil libertarianism. Respondents with high scores on (economic) conservatism measures were less supportive of civil liberties than those with liberal policy preferences.

Shmuel Lock's (1999) more recent study partly supports and partly challenges the earlier results of McClosky and Brill (1983).[2] Lock found that lawyers as well as non-elite respondents with higher educational levels and higher levels of political information showed more support for civil liberties, albeit the differences he found between lawyers and ordinary citizens were not as great as might have been expected on the basis of previous studies. Moreover, it turned out that the level of political information was more important than formal education. Lock also studied the effects of an important mediating factor that had not been taken into account earlier, namely the beliefs of respondents about the root causes of crime. Those who believed that crime is caused by inequality of opportunities, and that the judicial system is biased against members of underprivileged minorities, were more supportive of civil liberties. Finally, Lock's data also show an impact of the more conservative political climate of the 1990s. Even lawyers and political knowledgeables with otherwise libertarian attitudes tended to approve of a number of recent Supreme Court decisions curtailing the rights of the accused and strengthening law enforcement.

Lock's study confirmed previous results as far as the more civil libertarian attitudes of elites are concerned. It also showed, however, that political reality is more muddled than had been assumed. Political and judicial decision-making frequently involves a conflict between civil libertarian values and the perceived necessity of upholding law and order. Lock's questionnaire asked respondents specifically how they felt about a number of issues that implied a conflict between the rights of the accused and the protection of public safety. This may explain why the differences between elites and non-elites were less pronounced in his study than in previous ones.

The conflict over *civil liberties* and *law and order* is deeply rooted in virtually all democratic party systems. It distinguishes leftist and liberal parties on one side from conservative parties on the other. As the empirical results show, the general public is much more *conservative* than the elites in this respect, even if party affiliation is being controlled for. This is probably due to the fact that elites are more inclined to accept the public expression of dissent because they are themselves regularly involved in policy disputes. They are therefore less inclined to curtail civil liberties for the sake of public order.

Competing conceptions of democracy: Representative vs plebiscitary democracy and the role of government

In the late 1960s, activists of the students' movement as well as a number of younger social scientists were the first to raise entirely new questions regarding the quality of democracy in western democratic societies. Having grown up during an extended period of political stability following World War II, they were no longer as preoccupied with the stability of democracy as the members of preceding generations, because they took it for granted. Instead, they started to dispute the narrow conception of representative democracy institutionalized in the constitutions of their countries and demanded more participation rights for ordinary citizens. Ronald Inglehart's theory of postmaterialism (1977, 1990) aptly explains the causes and the impact of these new political demands. Inglehart has argued that among the cohorts whose members have been socialized after World War II under conditions of economic affluence and political security, materialist value priorities have increasingly been replaced by postmaterialist ones. He also expects this development to be strongest among the most highly educated segments of the younger generation.

There is a wealth of data confirming Inglehart's hypothesis that age and educational level are the strongest predictors of postmaterialist value orientations in mass publics. Since most elites have completed a secondary or even tertiary degree, we should therefore expect postmaterialism to be even more prevalent among elites. The two German elite surveys of 1981 and 1995 confirm this expectation. However, due to the very high average educational level of the elites, the impact of education on postmaterialist value orientations is negligible at the elite level. At the same time, the degree of postmaterialism is more strongly related to political ideology and party preference (Hoffmann-Lange, 1992, p. 277; Bürklin & Rebenstorf, 1997, pp. 374–379). The percentage of postmaterialists is disproportionately higher among elites with leftist policy preferences. At the same time, the impact of age on postmaterialist value orientations is as strong among elites as it is among the electorate at large. A slow, but steady replacement of older, more materialistic cohorts by more postmaterialistic ones can therefore be expected in the future within both elites and the public.

One essential element of postmaterialism is support for 'more influence for citizens on governmental decision making.' It is therefore not surprising that postmaterialist value orientations and the dissatisfaction with traditional elite-dominated representative democracy are closely related. *Postmaterialists* tend to advocate the introduction of direct democratic instruments (voter initiatives, referenda, recalls, and the like) more often than *materialists*. They are also more prone to engage in *elite-challenging* modes of political participation.

Among elites, support for participatory democracy is closely related to cohort membership and party preference. Younger German elites and those supporting political parties of the left (SPD, PDS, Green Party) or the liberal FDP show greater support for direct democracy than those with a preference for the conservative Christian Democratic Party (Bürklin & Rebenstorf, 1997, pp. 391–419).

Elite–mass comparisons, however, show that overall support for participatory democracy is somewhat higher among the voters than among the elites, even if cohort membership and party preference are controlled for. This indicates the existence of a conflict of interest between elites and ordinary citizens. Elites have a natural interest in protecting their freedom of action by reducing non-elite involvement in decision making, while citizens emphasize the need for controlling elite actions.

The new central-eastern and eastern European democracies are especially pertinent cases for studying elite–mass differences in the meanings associated with the concept of democracy. Miller, Hesli, and Reisinger (1997) found that elites in Russia and the Ukraine tend to emphasize different aspects of democracy than the electorate. While elites associate democracy primarily with the rule of law, voters tend to associate it with individual freedom. The elites also favor a market economy (individual rather than government responsibility for employment, economic reforms, acceptance of socioeconomic inequality) to a much higher degree, while voters tend to emphasize governmental responsibility for the economy and for social security instead. Data for East Germany confirm that support for a strong welfare state is generally higher among the electorates of post-communist countries than among those in established liberal democracies. Longstanding experience with a paternalistic state has obviously shaped the preferences of the eastern

European mass publics. While they cherish their newly won political liberties, they still expect government to take responsibility for the economic well being of the populace.

At the same time, data from the two German elite studies conducted in the mid-1990s mentioned above show that East German elites are more skeptical regarding the benefits of an unfettered market economy than the elites in the other two post-communist countries as well as the bulk of West German elites (Welzel, 1997; Rohrschneider, 1999). However, since economic policy positions are closely related to party preference, the overall distribution of answers to these questions depends to a considerable degree on the partisan composition of the elite sample which, in turn, is determined by the electoral strengths of the different political parties. These may vary considerably from one electoral term to the next. Without sufficiently large elite samples that can be broken down by political party, it is therefore not possible to draw any definite conclusions regarding the existing spectrum of policy positions in different countries.

STUDIES OF POLITICAL REPRESENTATION: COMPARING PARLIAMENTARIANS AND VOTERS

In 1963, Warren Miller and Donald Stokes published a groundbreaking article on political representation in the US. Their analysis started out from a theoretical distinction between three different normative models of political representation: the *trustee model*, the model of the *instructed delegate*, and the *responsible party model*. The trustee model is based on Edmund Burke's notion of a free mandate and demands that deputies should follow their own judgments of what they consider to be in the best interest of the country, even if these are not in line with the actual preferences of their voters. This model implies a great deal of discretion on the part of the deputies, and of trust in the deputies' good judgment on the part of the electorate. Conversely, the model of

instructed delegate requires deputies to act in line with the policy preferences of their voters, regardless of their own preferences. The responsible party model, finally, is based on the assumption that representation is achieved through the collective efforts of political parties to aggregate the interests of their followers into coherent policy programs, which they try to implement once they come to power. In this model, political parties serve as mediators of representation, resulting in shared policy preferences of deputies and voters. Moreover, deputies are also considered to represent only the voters of their own parties rather than the electorate at large.

In order to determine which of these models governed the actual roll call behaviors of members of the House of Representatives, Miller and Stokes (1963) developed an elaborate research design, their famous diamond. Based on opinion surveys among members of the House and voters, their questionnaire included indicators for three independent variables: the policy preferences of the voters, the representatives' preferences and the representatives' perceptions of their constituents' preferences. In their analysis, the authors tried to determine how these three independent variables affected the roll call behavior of the deputies on a number of policy issues (see Figure 5.1).

Miller and Stokes (1963) found that different models of representation explained the roll call behavior, depending on the specific issue at stake. In foreign policy matters, deputies mostly followed the trustee model, i.e. they voted according to their own political preferences, regardless of their constituents' preferences. Moreover, their perceptions of constituency preferences were frequently inaccurate. In matters of social welfare, roll call behavior instead conformed to the responsible party model. The deputies' positions on these issues as well as their roll call behavior were generally in line with their party affiliations. At the same time, the deputies' own preferences mostly coincided with the preferences of the electoral majority in their constituencies. This congruence was reflected in more accurate perceptions of their

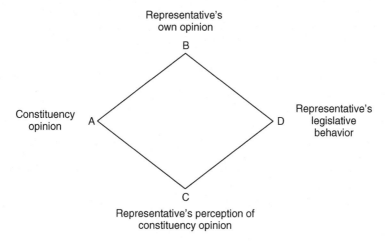

Figure 5.1   The Miller/Stokes diamond of constituency representation
Source: Adapted from Miller and Stokes (1963, p. 50). Reprinted by permission of Cambridge University Press: American Political Science Review, vol. 57, pp. 45–56

constituents' preferences. Finally, in matters of civil rights, deputies mostly followed the instructed delegate model. They voted according to the perceived policy preferences of their constituencies even if their own preferences were different.

Taking the same theoretical framework as a starting point, similar representation studies were later conducted in France (Converse & Pierce, 1986), Germany (Farah, 1980), Italy (Barnes, 1977), the Netherlands (Thomassen, 1976), and Sweden (Essaiason & Holmberg, 1996). However, the research design, which made sense in the American context of a presidential system with plurality elections in single-member districts and a strong emphasis on constituency-based representation, was not well suited to these other countries. Unlike the United States, all of them are parliamentary democracies in which parliamentary votes are characterized by a high degree of party discipline. The original design of comparing constituency voters to constituency deputies does not make much sense under these conditions. Moreover, Italy,[3] the Netherlands and Sweden use proportional electoral systems with multi-member districts. This precludes constituency-based comparisons. Finally, roll call votes are rarely taken in parliamentary democracies. Thus, the subsequent studies

also lacked the dependent variable of the American study.

The authors therefore had to change the focus of their analyses to studying the degree of congruence in policy preferences among the deputies and voters of the same party. This *dyadic correspondence* (Dalton, 1985) was then interpreted as indicator of the quality of representation for a particular political party in a particular country. For most of the issues studied, the data showed a very low degree of congruence. Systematic variations according to country, issue, and party were not very pronounced either. The single exception was a much higher congruence for the small political parties of the extreme left and right.

In a volume summarizing the results of the entire set of studies, Roy Pierce (1999) explained the low level of dyadic correspondence among deputies and voters in the European democracies by referring to the complexity of the multi-party systems of these countries. Ironically, and contrary to the theoretical expectations, attitude congruence among deputies and voters of the same party turned out to be higher in the American two-party system, even though party discipline is considerably lower in the US Congress. Pierce therefore concluded that political representation in continental European countries with multi-party systems does not conform to the responsible party model, at least as far as specific issue positions are concerned. He suspected that representation in these countries is based on ideology rather than particular policies, and that the left–right continuum is serving as a kind of 'super-issue' instead.

One interesting final result was the lack of any relationship between attitude congruence and citizen satisfaction. This indicates that other aspects of representation are obviously more relevant, thus giving elected representatives a good deal of latitude in making policy decisions.

THE POLARIZATION THESIS

Disagreement over policies is the essence of politics, and differences in the positions of political parties on policy issues provide empirical evidence of the degree of political polarization in a party system. In this vein, data on the political attitudes of elites and non-elites can also be used to study the degree of attitudinal polarization at the level of both party leaders and party supporters. Studies that have looked into such differences have frequently found that the policy positions of politicians and party activists are much more polarized than those of the party voters. This pattern was first described by McClosky, Hoffman, and O'Hara (1960), and has been confirmed by other studies in the US and West Germany (Jackson, Brown, & Bositis, 1982; Hoffmann-Lange, 1992).

McClosky et al. (1960) were also the first to point out the theoretical implications of these findings. They contradict the assumption that elites represent the policy preferences of the voters, instead suggesting that things might actually be the other way round. 'Little support was found for the belief that deep cleavages exist among the electorate but are ignored by the leaders. One might, indeed more accurately assert the contrary, to wit: that the natural cleavages between the leaders are largely ignored by the voters' (p. 426). This view is also consistent with Philip Converse's (1964) influential article on the

belief systems of mass publics, in which he demonstrated that the political knowledge and sophistication of most voters is rather low, and that their attitudes on specific policies show little ideological constraint and are not stable over time.

The prevalence of *non-attitudes* in the general population supports the conclusion that the *silent majority* is not silent because of a lack of opportunities to make itself heard, but primarily because it does not have much to say after all. Many democratic theorists have therefore assumed that it is the political elites who develop the political agendas which will then be adopted or rejected by the voters (Schumpeter, 1942).

However, the empirical evidence does not justify the assumption that the political attitudes of party elites are always more polarized than those of voters. Based on Dutch data, Galen Irwin and Jacques Thomassen (1975) demonstrated that multi-party systems may produce different empirical configurations, depending on the format of the party system and the issues at stake. While greater polarization at the elite level generally prevails for issues related to traditional party ideologies, novel issues may produce different patterns. In the early 1980s, for instance, West German voters were much more divided over the use of nuclear energy than the West Germany parties. While a significant minority of more than 10% of the voters were in favor of closing down all existing nuclear power plants and only slightly more than a third favored new constructions, the great majority of the (political) elites favored new constructions and only a tiny minority opted for closing down the existing plants. Even though there was some disagreement between the political parties over the amount of nuclear power needed for satisfying future energy demands, its continued use was not controversial among elites. This reflected a deep-seated concern among voters about the safety of nuclear reactors, while the elites took a much more sanguine stance.

Many studies have also demonstrated the existence of elite–mass displacement on important issues (Putnam, 1976, p. 118).

As reported above, support for civil liberties is much higher among elites, while support for the welfare state and direct democracy is higher among non-elites. Voters also tend to place themselves more to the right on the left–right continuum than party elites, as Russell Dalton (1985, pp. 275–277) found in his comparative analysis of candidates and voters for the European parliament.

Moreover, Holmberg's (1991) analysis of political representation in Sweden demonstrates that these patterns may change over time. Comparing data on members of the Swedish Riksdag and Swedish voters at two points in time, it turned out that issue attitudes were characterized by an elite–mass displacement in 1968/1969, but that the elites of the bourgeois parties had moved to the right by 1985, thus producing a higher level of polarization among the political elites. Holmberg's data also show a linear relationship between the degree of attitudinal polarization and the level of political activity. Of the four groups included in the analysis (namely party voters, party members, party activists, members of the Riksdag), party voters held the most centrist views and members of the Riksdag the most polarized ones (pp. 313–314). This contradicts the widespread assumption of a curvilinear relationship between political status and attitudinal polarization that expects attitudinal polarization to be highest among party activists.

Recent studies on partisan polarization in the US confirm these assumptions. In his book *Culture War? The Myth of a Polarized America*, Fiorina (2005) refutes the widespread assumption that today's American electorate is deeply polarized over values and moral issues such as abortion and homosexuality. Instead, he argues that this inaccurate picture of deep polarization between the red and the blue states reflects the fact that 'the thin stratum of elected officials, political professionals, and party and issue activists who talk to the media are indeed more distinct, more ideological, and more polarized than those of a generation ago' (p. 28). While Fiorina did not provide

empirical evidence to support this claim in his book, he later referred to a *New York Times* Poll conducted in 2004 that had revealed a 72 percentage point difference on the question of 'active government' between Democratic and Republican convention delegates, while the difference between Democrats and Republicans in the population at large was only 13 percentage points (www.vailvalleyinstitute.org/amdiv/Fiorina.html).[4] These data confirm that elite and voter attitudes vary independently of each other. It can be assumed, though, that they influence each other in complex ways that still need to be studied in more detail.

CONCLUSION

Even though most of the studies discussed in this chapter have been conducted in a rather small number of socio-economically developed democratic countries, some general conclusions can be drawn from the available empirical evidence. First, the substantial differences found between elites and non-elites indicate that elite (political) culture is an object of study in its own right. The value orientations and political attitudes of elites cannot simply be inferred from general population surveys. Instead, special elite surveys are needed to compare elite opinions to (general) public opinion. Second, all of the studies have confirmed the tremendous impact of formal education on the opinion-formation of individuals. Higher educational levels do not only foster interest and involvement in social and political affairs: a higher level of (political) information also implies that citizens have a better understanding of the way social and political institutions work, and of the interrelations that exist between specific policy issues and more abstract values and ideologies.

This is not the whole story, though, since elites are not only distinguished by their much higher average education, but also by their professional backgrounds and experiences. Lawyers are on average much more supportive of civil liberties than other elites, let alone the general public. Journalists are another professional group whose members are generally more libertarian in their outlook, because of the mass media's function of providing information on social and political developments which, in turn, is the basis for an effective public control of government actions. The 'liberal media bias' denounced by the American Media Research Center (see also Lichter, Rothman, & Lichter, 1986) can therefore not be considered a conspiracy of the media against a silent, much more conservative majority, but rather as resulting from the role of the media, which requires a critical stance of journalists vis-à-vis the established structures of social and political power.

Finally, the available evidence confirms that neither elites nor non-elites should be considered as cohesive groups. Instead, both are internally divided according to age, education, political ideology, party affiliation, and professional background. Not much is therefore to be further gained by simply comparing elites to non-elites. Instead, more differentiated analyses are needed that take into account those additional factors.

NOTES

1 McClosky and Brill's study was based on two different mail surveys, the Civil Liberties Survey (CLS) of 1978–1979 and the Opinion and Values Survey (OVS) of 1976–1977. These surveys encompassed representative population samples of 1,993 and 938 respondents respectively, as well as elite samples. The elite component of the CLS survey included 1,891 community leaders from government, colleges, the press, the clergy, the police, schools, labor unions, other voluntary organizations and the legal profession (lawyers and judges). For the OVS survey 2,987 national elite respondents were interviewed, who had been randomly drawn from the membership lists of 23 national organizations and two sub-samples from the *Who's Who*. Both surveys covered a large number of attitudinal questions.

The Opinion and Values Survey focused on political ideologies, the Civil Liberties Survey on attitudes toward civil liberties (1983, pp. 25–31). Taken together, this huge project is the most comprehensive survey of opinion-leaders conducted to date, even though it cannot be regarded as elite study in the strict sense. The focus was on opinion-leaders rather than holders of powerful positions.

2 Lock's study encompassed a telephone survey of the adult population ($n = 811$) and a mail survey of 410 lawyers.

3 Italy introduced single-member electoral districts for its lower house only in the 1990s.

4 A report on the marginals for this survey is posted on the web: www.nytimes.com/packages/html/politics/20040829_gop_poll/2004_gop_results.pdf. The full wording for the item quoted by Fiorina (2005) was: 'Which comes closer to your view: Government should do more to solve national problems; or Government is doing too many things better left to businesses and individuals?' Support for the first position was 79% among the Democratic delegates, 7% among the GOP delegates, 48% among Democratic voters and 35% among GOP voters (p. 6).

REFERENCES

Aron, R. (1950). Social structure and the ruling class. *British Journal of Sociology, 1*, 1–17 and 126–144.

Arzberger, K. (1980). *Bürger und Eliten in der Kommunalpolitik* [Citizens and elites in local politics]. Stuttgart: W. Kohlhammer.

Barnes, S. H. (1977). *Representation in Italy.* Chicago: University of Chicago Press.

Bottomore, T. (1993). *Elites and society* (2nd ed.). London: Routledge.

Bürklin, W., & Rebenstorf, H. (Eds.) (1997). *Eliten in Deutschland. Rekrutierung und Integration* [Elites in Germany. Recruitment and Integration]. Opladen: Leske + Budrich.

Converse, P. E. (1964). The nature of belief systems in mass publics. In D. E. Apter (Ed.), *Ideology and discontent* (pp. 206–261). New York: The Free Press.

Converse, P. E., & Pierce, R. (1986). *Political representation in France.* Cambridge, Mass: The Belknap Press of Harvard University Press.

Czudnowski, M. M. (1987). Interviewing political elites in Taiwan. In G. Moyser & M. Wagstaffe (Eds.), *Research methods for elite studies* (pp. 232–250). London: Allen & Unwin.

Dalton, R. J. (1985). Political parties and political representation: Party supporters and party elites in nine nations. *Comparative Political Studies, 18,* 267–299.

Essaiason, P., & Holmberg, S. (1996). *Representation from above: Members of parliament and representative democracy in Sweden.* Aldershot: Dartmouth.

Farah, B. (1980). *Political representation in West Germany.* Unpublished doctoral dissertation, University of Michigan, Ann Arbor.

Fiorina, M. P. (with Abrams, S. J., & Pope, J. C.) (2005). *Culture war? The myth of a polarized America.* New York: Pearson Longman.

Hoffmann-Lange, U. (1992). *Eliten, Macht und Konflikt in der Bundesrepublik* [Elites, power and conflict in the Federal Republic of Germany]. Opladen: Leske + Budrich.

Holmberg, S. (1991). Political representation in Sweden. In H.-D. Klingemann, R. Stöss, & B. Weßels (Eds.), *Politische Klasse und Politische Institutionen* [political class and political institution] (pp. 290–324). Opladen: Westdeutscher Verlag.

Inglehart, R. (1977). *The silent revolution.* Princeton: Princeton University Press.

Inglehart, R. (1990). *Culture shift in advanced industrial society.* Princeton: Princeton University Press.

Irwin, G. A., & Thomassen, J. (1975). Issue-consensus in a multi-party system: voters and leaders in the Netherlands. *Acta Politica, 10*, 389–420.

Jackson, J. S., III, Brown, B. L., & Bositis, D. (1982). Herbert McClosky and friends revisited. 1980 Democratic and Republican party elites compared to the mass public. *American Politics Quarterly, 10*, 158–180.

Keller, S. (1963). *Beyond the ruling class. Strategic elites in modern society.* New York: Random House.

Lichter, S. R., Rothman, S., & Lichter, L. S. (1986). *The media elite.* Bethesda: Adler and Adler.

Lock, S. (1999). *Crime, public opinion, and civil liberties.* Westport: Praeger.

McClosky, H. (1964). Consensus and ideology in American politics. *American Political Science Review, 58*, 361–382.

McClosky, H., & Brill, A. (1983). *Dimensions of tolerance.* New York: Russell Sage Foundation.

McClosky, H., Hoffman, P. J., & O'Hara, R. (1960). Issue conflict and consensus among party leaders and followers. *American Political Science Review, 54*, 406–427.

Miller, A. H., Hesli, V. L., & Reisinger, W. M. (1997). Conceptions of democracy among mass and elite in post-Soviet societies. *British Journal of Political Science, 27*, 157–190.

Miller, W. E., & Stokes, D. E. (1963). Constituency influence in congress. *American Political Science Review, 57*, 45–56.

Parry, G., Moyser, G., & Day, N. (1992). *Political participation and democracy in Britain.* Cambridge: Cambridge University Press.

Pierce, R. (1999). Mass-elite issue linkages and the responsible party model of representation. In W. E. Miller, R. Pierce, J. Thomassen, S. Holmberg, P. Esaiasson, & B. Weßels (Eds.), *Policy representation in Western democracies* (pp. 9–32). Oxford: Oxford University Press.

Putnam, R. D. (1976). *The comparative study of political elites.* Englewood Cliffs: Prentice-Hall.

Rohrschneider, R. (1999). *Learning democracy. Democratic and economic values in unified Germany.* Oxford: Oxford University Press.

Schumpeter, J. A. (1942). *Capitalism, socialism and democracy.* New York: Harper & Brothers.

Sinclair, B., & Brady, D. (1987). Studying members of the United States congress. In G. Moyser & M. Wagstaffe (Eds.), *Research methods for elite studies* (pp. 48–71). London: Allen & Unwin.

Thomassen, J. (1976). *Kiezers en gekozenen in een representatieve demokratie* [Electors and the elected in a representative democracy]. Alphen aan den Rijn: Samsom.

Wagstaffe, M., & Moyser, G. (1987). The threatened elite: studying leaders in an urban community. In G. Moyser & M. Wagstaffe (Eds.), *Research methods for elite studies* (pp. 183–201). London: Allen & Unwin.

Welzel, C. (1997). *Demokratischer Elitenwandel. Die Erneuerung der ostdeutschen Elite aus demokratiesoziologischer Sicht* [Democratic elite transformation. The renewal of the East German elite from the perspective of sociology of democracy]. Opladen: Leske + Budrich.

Wildenmann, R., Kaase, M., Hoffmann-Lange, U., Kutteroff, A., & Wolf, G. (1982). *Führungsschicht in der Bundesrepublik Deutschland 1981* [Elites in the Federal Republic of Germany 1981]. Köln: Zentralarchiv für empirische Sozialforschung (Codebook of the West German Elite Study 1981).

6

The Internet as a New Platform for Expressing Opinions and as a New Public Sphere

Bernhard Debatin

Until the advent of the World Wide Web (WWW) in the early 1990s, the Internet was an exclusive medium of communication, mostly used by scientists and computer experts. Plummeting prices for computer technology and user-friendly software have driven the WWW's rapid growth and broad, albeit uneven, diffusion throughout Western societies. This has enabled its commercialization and turned the formerly esoteric medium into a mass communication medium: anybody with Internet access can now participate in it. Relatively low production costs and equally low publication barriers today allow almost anybody with basic computer skills to create Web content. By September 2006, the Internet had more than a billion users, and nearly 70% of all North Americans and more than 50% of the European Union's population were online.[1] At least in the developed countries, the Internet has changed from an early adopter technology to one used by the vast majority of the public.

The Internet has evolved into a mass medium that allows its users to overcome their traditional role as mere recipients and to become active participants in gathering, producing, and disseminating news. It is also a valuable tool for political action and for accessing large amounts of information. At the same time, the flood of available information and the mechanisms for dealing with it have contributed to further fragmentation of issues and audiences. This chapter shows how the Internet has changed the structures and the functions of the public sphere. The Web's participatory features are revitalizing public discourse and providing a new venue for public opinion even as corporate media increasingly dominate Internet content.

EARLY ASPIRATIONS FOR THE INTERNET AS PUBLIC SPHERE

Unsurprisingly, in its early days the WWW was charged with euphoric expectations for a vibrant deliberative *cyberdemocracy*, the scope of which ranged from proposals for continual electronic plebiscites and oppositional public spheres to discourse-ethical concepts of online dialogues and Internet-based education (Ess, 1996). These expectations were frequently connected to libertarian 'last frontier' myths, such as prospect of direct democracy in the electronic agora, the anarchic self-organization of the Internet, and a perfectly free and unregulated digital economy (Rheingold, 1993). The Internet was heralded as a promising means of creating a transnational global village, which would shake off both the boundaries of nations and the ballast of social welfare institutions, culminating directly in the formation of a perfectly free cyberstate. This libertarian cyber society would secure the supply of information and goods independent of spatial, temporal, and personal limitations (Negroponte, 1995).

It quickly became clear, however, that even in the most developed countries a *digital divide* had emerged—the exclusion of poor, disadvantaged, or minority citizens from using this medium (DiMaggio, Hargittai, Celeste, & Shafer, 2004). In reality, the global village is a gated community, where the costs of admission include those pertaining to the purchase price of the technology, the acquisition of the skills necessary to use it, and access to the network infrastructure. Moreover, as non-western societies joined this community, they have demonstrated impressive resistance against assimilating Western values and ideas, thus belying the naive deterministic assumption that introducing information technology automatically leads to a democratic polity. Even optimistic approaches that presuppose the Internet's inherent 'democratizing powers' have had to tone down their euphoric assumptions in view of strict governmental control and censorship in many Arab and Southeast Asian countries (Ess, 2000).

And while the digital divide in developed countries may increasingly narrow (or rather, become indistinguishable from general social inequality and injustice),[2] the gap between rich countries of the western hemisphere and developing countries is still huge. According to *Internet World Stats*, only 15.7% of the world population has access to the Internet. Half of them are in Europe and North America, where only 17.5% of the world population lives.[3] A 'quick fix' of this global digital divide is unlikely as long as the underlying structural issues, such as unequal distribution of wealth, health, and education, are not addressed— that is, as long as the global economy of 'informational capitalism' favors 'skill-biased technological change' that widens the gap between highly-paid skilled workers and the mass of unskilled laborers (Parayil, 2005). Therefore, regarding the Internet as a new platform for the formation of a public sphere always implies a certain level of exclusiveness. This, however, is not dissimilar to the propagation of the early bourgeois public sphere among elites, as described in Habermas' (1962/1989) seminal work on the public sphere.

POTENTIALS: CREATING A NEW PUBLIC SPHERE

The parallels between the Internet and the early public sphere are striking. In its early days, the WWW held out a promise of realizing the Habermasian utopia of unconstrained *public discourse*. The role of virtual communities as agents of a new public sphere has been widely discussed and criticized (Slevin, 2000). As the Web became more commercialized, however, the euphoria of the Internet community dissipated, and it has become clear that the Internet will not solve the political and social problems of modern societies. But this does not negate the Internet's potential role in providing new channels of communication and revitalizing public discourse (for an overview see Paracharissi, 2002).

Habermas' structural *discourse criteria*—openness to all themes, unlimited access, and the 'unforced force of the better argument'—can be seen as counterfactual presuppositions shaping both the early public sphere of real communities and subsequently the public sphere of virtual communities. The correlation between these criteria and the Internet's structure might suggest that the Internet is an ideal means for *revitalizing* public discourse. However, the public sphere of the Internet may well be undergoing a structural transformation: the user friendliness and availability of the World Wide Web that made the Internet a mass medium also appear to have initiated the decline of this new virtual public sphere, in a manner similar to the transformation of the public sphere from the Enlightenment to late capitalism described by Habermas. Critics of the revitalization thesis argue that commercialization, governmental regulation, lack of attention, and a shift to mere entertainment are significantly shaping this transformation (Muhlberger, 2005). Structural limitations on discourse and engagement caused by the virtuality of the Internet and inadequate inclusiveness are seen as further hurdles for a true revitalization of the public sphere (Stegbauer, 2001).

This interpretation, however, fails to take into account that the Web has also provided a communicative space where professional and lay online journalists, as well as web-based interest groups and individuals, can broach and explore topics ignored by the mainstream media and sometimes thereby substantially influence *agenda setting* processes (Selnow, 1998, p. 187). This strongly resembles the 'outside initiative model' of agenda setting as described by Habermas (1992/1996, p. 379ff.), and shows how new media can open up room for new forms of public discourse. In part, this has to do with the specific media characteristics of the Internet. In contrast to conventional mass media, the Internet permits true nonhierarchical multidirectional communication. Its low access and publication barriers enable its users to advance from mere mass media recipients to producers of and participants in digitally

mediated mass communications. As a *hybrid medium*, the Internet combines interpersonal, group, and mass communication, and permits not only information distribution but also interaction among its users. It is thus an ideal medium for the interactive forms and needs of communication in the *lifeworld*, and can function as a sounding board for lifeworld problems—a central function of *autonomous public spheres* as described by Habermas (1992/1996, chap. 8). Such a revitalization of the public sphere by the Internet is not only feasible; it can actually be demonstrated empirically (Paracharissi, 2004). This revitalization occurs on three main levels of public communication on the Internet:[4]

Level 1: Virtual *episodic public encounters*, like those that take place in everyday life on the street or in bars, are found especially in chat rooms and other loose virtual communities where persons enjoy the protection of 'intimate anonymity.' Although these encounters do not translate automatically into political action (Jankovski & Van Selm, 2000), they provide the structural background for the emergence of an Internet-based public discourse at the second level.

Level 2: Internet-based forms of *public assembly* (Versammlungsöffentlichkeit) can be observed primarily in discussion forums, newsgroups, and mailing lists. They are instrumental in the creation and implementation of *counter-publics* (Gegenöffentlichkeiten) by protest movements, grassroots activists, and political groups (Rucht, 2004).

Level 3: Even *news media-based public communication* is undergoing a transformation due to the Internet. Conventional media are pressured to react constantly to the Internet because of its new role in agenda setting (Althaus & Tewksbury, 2002). News media also constitute a new form of mass communication by increasingly participating in the Internet with their own content, as shown by the Internet presence of nearly all print and broadcast media, as well as in the media-mix and cross-media productions of established media conglomerates in the newly converging digital environment.

All in all, the Internet has created new information channels and opened new opportunities for communication and democratic participation. A multitude of autonomous public spheres can flourish through the unforced interplay of the Internet's three main levels of public communication. For example, citizen initiatives and grassroots groups use the Internet to communicate cheaply and to coordinate their activities effectively (van de Donk, Loader, Nixon, & Rucht, 2004). Issue- and group-specific discussion forums foster the discursive formation of opinion and political will. Websites of a wide variety of organizations on every imaginable issue can be accessed, and provide a valuable and up-to-date information pool. Political activists produce their own Internet newspapers at low cost and thus contribute to the development of an alternative virtual public sphere.

Political mobilization and the coordination of transnational political action, such as demonstrations against nuclear power or globalization, are significantly simplified with the Web, and activist groups are intensively using the Internet in just this way (Pickerill, 2003). A defining event was certainly the 9/11 attacks and their aftermath, which not only generated the most traffic ever to news sites on the Internet, but also brought to researchers' attention 'the importance of the Web as a significant component of the public sphere, enabling coordination, information-sharing, assistance, expression and advocacy in a time of crisis' (Rainie, Fox, & Madden, 2002, p. 25).

RISKS: FRAGMENTATION OF ISSUES AND AUDIENCES

The flip side of the Internet as a new public sphere, with its multiplicity of voices and its potential for virtually unlimited communication, is the danger of increasing social fragmentation and polarization. While the Internet has broken up the uniformity of

the opinions published in the news media, it has at the same time created a digital obscurity due to the constant flow of huge masses of unfiltered information, which pose novel problems of selection for the user. Intelligent filtering tools, such as targeted content and personalization of news and other information, can help in coping with the digital information flood and users' limited cognitive and temporal resources of *attention*. Selnow (1998, p. 191) argues, however, that 'the Internet's capacity to ultratarget runs the risk of fragmenting the population.' And although audience fragmentation through the definition of target groups and special-interest issues is nothing new, the Internet, with its nearly infinite specialized websites, has taken this trend to a new extreme and enabled the fragmentation of issues into a myriad of narrow topics, each attracting the attention of tiny audience segments.

Users' selection of web-based information through 'push' technologies, such as portals, personalized web pages, and automated updating (RSS feed), can easily result in *tunnel vision*, as Sunstein (2001) shows. Active citizens should expose themselves to ideas and issues that they would not have chosen in advance. Instead, personalization of news and self-imposed restriction to only familiar sources create a strong consonance of opinions, which may then lead to '*cybercascades*' of identically repeated and amplified opinions that, for example, foster and enflame hate groups. Similarly, Selnow (1998) maintains that the 'information blind spot' of fragmented audiences ultimately leads to isolated, ideologically oriented groups that lack empathy and a common point of reference. This gives way to polarization and factionalism, demonization of opposing views, preference for partisan sources of information, and the acceptance of fringe ideologies and rumors (Plake, Jansen, & Schuhmacher, 2001, pp. 112–132).

Because of its low publication barrier, the Internet is indifferent to the actual content of communication and therefore acts as an amplifier for *any* sort of message. This not only further promotes the fragmentation of issues, but also systematically gives fringe groups, conspiracy theorists, fanatics, and fundamentalists a disproportionately strong presence on the Internet (Fox, Anderson, & Rainie, 2005, pp. 30ff.). The digital proliferation of 'memes'—self-replicating bits of cultural material, such as ideas, rumors, myths, and ideologies (Balkin, 2003)—takes advantage of the *self-referentiality* of the Internet, i.e. its hypertextual organization and its ubiquitous and ahistoric structure. Circular references and decontextualized information often supplant proper fact-checking and social and historical contextualization.

NEW FORMS OF JOURNALISM

Online journalism

The digital information flood and constraints on attention make it difficult to distinguish between high-quality and dubious information. The conventional media's mechanisms of quality control and issue selection cannot be seamlessly transferred to a hybrid medium characterized by interactivity, volatility, a decentralized network structure, and multidirectional communication. Yet the new multimedia obscurity presents a great opportunity for professional and lay online journalism. Plake *et al.* (2001, p. 89) maintain that the conventional news media should play a key role in filtering the Internet, because only they can provide highly selective and reliable relevance structures, such as salience and currency. These relevance structures orient the user and allow filtering of the otherwise unmanageable information flood. This filtering process is one of the most important functions of the public sphere (Habermas, 1992/1996, p. 360).

The conventional news media filter and homogenize information through the *gatekeeping function* of their journalists. This process usually results in media consonance and 'mainstreaming,' the reduction of issues to an amazingly small number of 'hot topics' on the media agenda. Long before the Internet, this reductive process drew strong criticism

and motivated the development of counterpublics, alternative press, and civic journalism (Rucht, 2004). However, the traditional role of the journalist as gatekeeper cannot be applied directly to the Internet. Some scholars see the Internet as threatening the traditional role of journalists as information providers and watchdogs (Tumber, 2001). The Internet has in fact undermined the information privilege of traditional journalism formerly secured through high production costs, scarcity of broadcast frequencies, and regulatory intervention.

Even so, traditional news media have all gone online and are among the most popular news providers on the Internet, thus retaining some of their gate-keeping function. Only one of the top six parent companies on the Internet is not a producer or provider of online news (eBay, ranked fifth). The other five are, in order of ranking, Microsoft, Yahoo!, Time Warner, Google, and News Corporation Online (Project for Excellence in Journalism, 2006). The remarkable breakthrough of Yahoo! and Google as nonjournalistic entities into the top ranking news sites relies on two new Internet technologies: intelligent, usage-driven search algorithms and RSS feed ('Really Simple Syndication'), a unidirectional content subscription service that allows tracking of regularly changing web content, such as news sites or weblogs. Google and Yahoo! use these mechanisms to provide permanently updated news summaries from a large number of news media. While some researchers and journalists worry that these automated news feeds undermine journalism, others note that these services depend crucially on journalists' filtering and editing skills (Schroeder & Kralemann, 2005).

In addition to these conventional skills, online journalists must exploit the Internet's unique properties of multimediality, interactivity and hypertextuality (Deuze, 2002, p. 133). Online stories can be told in a more complex way: instead of using the formulaic inverted pyramid, online journalists must think laterally to expand a story beyond the linear narrative and include multimedia elements. They must also layer information, i.e. dividing the story into small, well-organized hyperlinked portions that provide various degrees of background information and give the user choices about how deeply to go into the story (Stovall, 2004, chap. 4). Online journalism has become a serious competitor with conventional journalism, as shown by the emergence of professional-quality, independent online-only media (such as Salon.com in the U.S. or Netzeitung in Germany) and the dramatic growth in original online content produced by offline media. With the diffusion of broadband connections, true multimedia online journalism is possible, and broadcast media can now increasingly put their original audiovisual material online. At the same time, new ethical challenges arise due to increased time pressure (need for constant updates), the lack of accountability (understaffed online newsrooms), and the digitization of information (ease of plagiarism, fabrication, and falsification), all of which demonstrate the need for a systematic ethics of online journalism (Debatin, 2004).

Participatory journalism and the blogosphere

The Internet not only promotes professional mainstream journalism, it is also an ideal platform for participatory journalism, a bottom-up type of journalism in which citizens actively gather, prepare, disseminate, and comment on news (Bowman & Willis, 2003). Internet-based participatory journalism has dramatically changed the media landscape and also the way interest groups and grass-roots initiatives interact and report (Reynolds, 2004).

The best-known form of audience-driven journalism is blogging. *Weblogs* (blogs) range from personal journals and political punditry to fairly objective criticism, such as Romenesko's renowned media criticism blog at Poynter.org. Most serious blogs track how often they are accessed and quoted by other bloggers. This contributes to a hierarchy, where well-established blogs function as opinion leaders and other blogs

both feed on them and provide them with thematic input. As a whole, the *blogosphere* is a highly sensitive sounding board that anticipates media and public agendas, and has achieved a high level of influence on politicians and journalists as bloggers 'weave together an elaborate network with agenda-setting power' (Drezner & Farrell, 2004). Blogs have played a decisive role in first-person accounts of 9/11, in political campaigns, in watching the watchdogs (media journalism), in war reporting, in political and celebrity scandals, and in pushing neglected issues into the mainstream media.[5] Blogging can thus reverse the usual agenda setting mechanisms (Delwiche, 2005): its audience-generated agenda is reviving and fulfilling the public sphere's roles as a sensor and a sentinel for lifeworld issues (Habermas, 1992/1996, chap. 8). Reacting quickly to this, mainstream media have introduced their own blogs, functioning as new forms of op-ed columns and reader inclusion.

In addition to blogs, other Internet-based forms of communication, such as online discussion groups, e-mail-newsletters (e.g. *moveon.org*), collaborative writing and publishing (e.g. Slashdot and the Wiki platform), peer-to-peer information sharing (such as IM and SMS), and RSS feeds help make grassroots journalism a feasible alternative to mainstream journalism. The most impressive and frequently cited example of powerful citizen journalism may be the Korean online newspaper *OhmyNews*. Based almost exclusively on reader contributions, it published stories from more than 15,000 different readers within its first four years (Reynolds, 2004, pp. 93, 125–129). Although similar projects have not succeeded on this scale, there are scores of examples of successful *hyperlocal citizen media* that focus on the needs and interests of their communities (Glaser, 2004). The Internet, with its constantly emerging technologies—most recently video blogging ('vlogging') or audio and video podcasts—will continue to provide an attractive and accessible platform for audience-driven journalism.

CONCLUSION

Throughout the Internet, one finds the *critical functions* of the public sphere—watchdog, informational, and opinion formation functions—essential to a thriving democracy. This has created new relations and a new distribution of power among the public, the media, and politicians. As the Internet is increasingly integrating conventional mass media while at the same time providing a platform for participatory journalism, the way that public opinion is formed and expressed is changing considerably. More research is needed on the Internet-based interactions among conventional media, grassroots media and the audience. For instance, classic models such as the *spiral of silence* that are solely based on the distinction between conventional mass media and the audience will need to be thoroughly reevaluated.

It is safe to say that the Internet has become an important platform for expressing opinions and for revitalizing the public sphere. Although it does foster audience and issue fragmentation, it has a great potential for promoting audience-driven public discourses. It thus opens up public discourse to the periphery, instead of focusing on the central forces of the media system and the political system. As sentinels and sensors, the virtual public spheres of the Internet do not have actual problem-solving capacities, but they can strongly influence the public agenda. Thus, they can force conventional media and the political system to recognize and address socio-political problems and under-represented issues. Future research will have to focus on this new and constantly evolving mechanism of agenda setting, as well as on the development of Internet-driven audience segmentation.

The low access and publishing barriers of the Internet have turned participatory journalism from an ideal to a vivid reality, albeit one demanding substantial involvement. The primary users of the Internet for political communication are usually educated and politically sophisticated, and political communication makes up only a small portion of overall Internet traffic. At the same time, online attention is increasingly 'colonized' by large corporations, which has a marginalizing effect on critical voices (Dahlberg, 2005). Commercialization of content, the growing involvement of media conglomerates, and the increasing diffusion of broadband suggest that in the future, large portions of the Internet may be converted to a distribution mode in the hands of few major media corporations, with interactivity restricted largely to e-mail feedback. Though this is not likely to entirely roll back the participatory aspects of the Internet, it will significantly strengthen the role of the Web as a platform for conventional media content in a converging digital environment. Researchers in mass communication and public opinion will have to keep a close eye on how the Internet continues to change the media landscape—and how this changes the formation and expression of public opinion.

NOTES

1 Figures from the *Internet World Stats* website at http://www.internetworldstats.com/.

2 See DiMaggio *et al.* (2004) and the six online penetration studies of the National Telecommunications and Information Administration (NTIA) at http://www.ntia.doc.gov/.

3 Figures as of September 2006, from the *Internet World Stats* website at http://www.internet worldstats.com/.

4 These three main levels of public communication are derived from Habermas (1992/1996, chap. 8).

5 For an overview on various aspects of blogging see the special issue articles in *Nieman Reports* (2003). According to the blog tracker *technorati.com*, 48.6 million blogs existed as of July 2006.

REFERENCES

Althaus, S. L., & Tewksbury, D. (2002). Agenda setting and the 'new' news: Patterns of issue importance among readers of the paper and online versions of the *New York Times. Communication Research, 29,* 160–207.

Balkin, J. M. (2003). *Cultural software: A theory of ideology.* Yale University Press.

Bowman, S., & Willis, C. (2003). *We media. How audiences shape the future of news and information*. Reston: The Media Center at the American Press Institute. Retrieved January 12, 2006, from http://www.hypergene.net/wemedia/download/we_media.pdf.

Dahlberg, L. (2005). The corporate colonization of online attention and the marginalization of critical communication? *Journal of Communication Inquiry, 29*, 160–180.

Debatin, B. (2004). Ethik des Online-Journalismus—Medienethische Kriterien und Perspektiven [Ethics of online journalism—Criteria and perspectives of media ethics]. In K. W. Schweiger & W. Wirth (Eds.), *Gute Seiten—schlechte Seiten: Qualität in der Online-Kommunikation* (pp. 80–99). Munich: R. Fischer.

Delwiche, A. (2005). Agenda-setting, opinion leadership, and the world of web logs. *First Monday, 10* (12). Retrieved February 12, 2006, from http://www.firstmonday.org/issues/issue10_12/delwiche/index.html.

Deuze, M. (2002). *Journalists of the Netherlands*. Amsterdam: Askant Academic Publishers.

DiMaggio, P., Hargittai, E., Celeste, C., & Shafer, S. (2004). Digital inequality: From unequal access to differentiated use. In K. Neckerman (Ed.), *Social Inequality* (pp. 355–400). New York: Russell Sage Foundation. Retrieved April 12, 2006, from http://www.eszter.com/research/c05-digitalinequality.html.

Drezner, D. W., & Farrell, H. (2004). Web of influence. *Foreign Policy, November/December*. Retrieved December 18, 2005, from http://www.foreignpolicy.com/story/cms.php?story_id=2707&print=1.

Ess, C. (Ed.). (1996). *Philosophical perspectives on computer-mediated communication*. New York: SUNY Press.

Ess, C. (2000). We are the borg: The web as agent of assimilation or cultural renaissance? *e-philosopher*. Retrieved May 27, 2006, from http://ephilosopher.com/modules.php?op=modload&name=Sections&file=index&req=printpage&artid=31.

Fox, S., Anderson, J. Q., & Rainie, L. (2005). *The future of the Internet*. Washington: Pew Internet & American Life Project. Retrieved January 20, 2006, from http://www.elon.edu/e-web/predictions/expert surveys/2004_experts_survey.pdf.

Glaser, M. (2004, November 11). The new voices: Hyperlocal citizen media sites want you (to write)! *Online Journalism Review*. Retrieved June 24, 2006, from http://ojr.org/ojr/glaser/1098833871.php.

Habermas, J. (1989). *The structural transformation of the public sphere. An inquiry into a category of bourgeois society* (T. Burger with F. Lawrence, Trans.). Cambridge, MA: MIT Press. (Original work published in 1962).

Habermas, J. (1996). *Between facts and norms* (W. Rehg, Trans.). Cambridge, MA: MIT Press. (Original work published in 1992).

Jankovski, N. M., & Van Selm, M. (2000). The promise and practice of public debate in cyberspace. In K. Hacker & J. van Dijk (Eds.), *Digital democracy: Issues of theory and practice* (pp. 149–165). London: Sage.

Muhlberger, P. (2005). Human agency and the revitalization of the public sphere. *Political Communication, 22*, 163–178.

Negroponte, N. (1995). *Being digital*. New York: Random House.

Nieman Reports (2003). Journalist's trade: Weblogs and journalism. *Nieman Reports, 57* (3), 59–98.

Paracharissi, Z. (2002). The virtual sphere. The Internet as a public sphere. *New Media & Society, 4*, 9–27.

Paracharissi, Z. (2004). Democracy online: Civility, politeness, and the democratic potential of online political discussion groups. *New Media & Society, 6*, 259–283.

Parayil, G. (2005). The digital divide and increasing returns: Contradictions of informational capitalism. *The Information Society, 21*, 41–51.

Pickerill, J. (2003). *Cyberprotest. environmental activism online*. Manchester, New York: Manchester University Press.

Plake, K., Jansen, D., & Schuhmacher, B. (2001). *Öffentlichkeit und Gegenöffentlichkeit im Internet* [The public sphere and counter-publics on the Internet]. Wiesbaden: Westdeutscher Verlag.

Project for Excellence in Journalism (2006). *Online//Ownership. The State of the News Media 2006*. Retrieved June 27, 2006, from http://www.stateofthemedia.org/2006/narrative_online_ownership.asp?cat=5&media=4.

Rainie, L., Fox, S. & Madden, M. (2002). *One year later: September 11 and the Internet*. Washington, DC: Pew Internet & American Life Project. Retrieved on Jan. 26, 2006, from http://www.pewinternet.org/pdfs/PIP_9-11_Report.pdf.

Reynolds, D. (2004). *We the media. Grassroots journalism by the people, for the people*. Sebastopol: O'Reilly Media.

Rheingold, H. (1993). *The virtual community*. Cambridge: MIT Press.

Rucht, D. (2004). The quadruple 'A'. Media strategies of protest movements since the 1960s. In W. van de Donk, B. Loader, P. G. Nixon & D. Rucht (Eds.), *Cyberprotest. New media, citizens, and social movements* (pp. 29–56). London, New York: Routledge.

Schroeder, R., & Kralemann, M. (2005). Journalism ex machina—Google News Germany and its selection process. *Journalism Studies, 6*, 245–247.

Selnow, G. W. (1998). *The impact of the Internet on American politics.* Westport, London: Praeger.

Slevin, J. (2000). *The Internet and society.* Cambridge: Polity Press.

Stegbauer, C. (2001). *Grenzen virtueller Gemeinschaften—Strukturen internetbasierter Kommunikationsforen* [Boundaries of virtual communities—Structures of Internet-based communication fori]. Wiesbaden: Westdeutscher Verlag.

Stovall, J. G. (2004). *Web journalism. Practice and promise of a new medium.* Boston, New York: Pearson.

Sunstein, C. (2001). *Republic.com.* Princeton, NJ: Princeton UP.

Tumber, H. (2001). Democracy in the information age: The role of the fourth estate in cyberspace. *Information, Communication & Society, 4,* 95–112.

van de Donk, W., Loader, B., Nixon, P. G., & Rucht, D. (Eds.). (2004). *Cyberprotest. New media, citizens, and social movements.* London, New York: Routledge.

7

Popular Communication and Public Opinion

Debra Merskin and Jonathan David Tankel

The study of popular communication and culture is, by definition, an examination of public opinion. Cultural studies scholars investigate how publics (audiences) negotiate the symbolic world of mass media and express opinions (preferences) through the adoption, consumption or rejection of and resistance to popular culture. The symbolic nature of mass media content, the influence of media corporations, and the subjectivity of audiences are the key concerns of this perspective. The artifacts, practices, and experiences of popular communication are incorporated into daily life. In this way, a cultural perspective views public opinion in terms of how lived experience is expressed and interpreted by those studied. Cultural studies as a method provides public opinion research with an interpretive lens through which interpretations and preferences can be illustrated and measured.

This chapter summarizes the underlying assumptions of a popular communication perspective as it applies to the study of public opinion by examining two forms of popular culture expression: music production and fashion. These examples illustrate the complex relationship between popular communication, power, and public opinion.

BACKGROUND

The field of cultural studies, defined as 'the study of culture as politics ... ordinary life ... [and] text ...' (Hartley, 2004, p. 49), is concerned with the intersections of power, consciousness, identity, and difference in our symbolic environment. *Popular* culture, as the subject of study, simply put, is the culture of the people. Examples include cooking, mass media, entertainment, sports, literature, music, and fashion. Influenced by commercialization and industrialization, popular culture plays an ideological role in mainstreaming socialization and education, thereby ensuring conformity to social norms. The everyday interactions of people and social institutions are fertile fodder for the production of popular culture. Traditionally, what is popular (widely available) is regarded as lesser than that which is available only to a limited (wealthy) few. In his time, for example, Shakespeare's plays were popular culture, available widely, drawing upon language, interests, fantasies, and concerns of people of the day. Today, these same performances are regarded as high (elite) culture. Gans' (1974/1999) classic study of the cultural dichotomy of high and low (kitsch) culture posited that hierarchal visions of culture reinforce social distinctions and prevent democratization of production of and access to expressive arts. As forms of expression of a public's preferences, *popular* culture products are expressions of public opinion. But how do we measure the success (popularity) or failure of a particular television program, book, movie, recording artist, or fashion designer?

Typically, the public's opinions about fashion or music are measured by quantitative sales figures and responses to polls. Number of albums sold or demand for a particular dress are often used as measures of acceptance, and thus favorable expressions of public opinion. The popular communication perspective, however, examines popular culture preferences qualitatively and acknowledges the reality of underlying meaning built in by those who benefit from a positive response to 'the message.'

Hegemony and ideology play a central role in the cultural perspective. Defined as a method of social control by the ruling classes through political, religious, educational, social, and cultural ideas (ideologies), rather than by force, hegemony is unique because it requires 'winning consent' (Hartley, 2004, p. 99). Hegemony is comprised of pervasive ideologies that valorize consumerism and consumption and contribute to a blurring of the *origins* of public opinion. Merchants of popular culture work the tensions between satisfying and manufacturing public opinion, content choices, and preferences and consent. Commentators such as Lippmann (1922), Herman and Chomsky (1988), and Klaehn (2002) define the process of the *manufacture* of consent as one in which democracy is

inverted as the powerful cultivate a desire (hegemony) for their products amongst the masses, which include political acquiescence (the concern of political communication scholars) and cultural artifacts (the concern of popular communication scholars), while simultaneously justifying their actions by reference to the power of public opinion. Thus, cultural theorists approach the notion of public opinion by highlighting and interrogating the ways cultural practices and artifacts are represented and re-presented in media and in everyday life and the extent to which these are imposed by the dominant culture.

In this chapter we argue that, in addition to quantitative measures, qualitative research in general, and cultural studies in particular, offer a rich perspective on how fashion and music, as examples of popular culture, not only express what dominant culture wants seen and heard, but also how public opinion can be subverted or expressed by resisting the popular. The following section describes popular communication research and how it examines and reflects public opinion perspectives.

RESEARCH PERSPECTIVES

Novelist William Gibson demonstrates an uncanny prescience about the ways technology alters the nature of reality. In *Pattern Recognition* (2003), lead character Cayce Pollard is a 'cool hunter.' Pollard's job is to roam the postmodern image-obsessed materialist world in search of the 'next big thing.' She is keenly aware of products and consumer trends that are adapted, adopted, commodified, and standardized by the culture industries. Pollard in fact sees herself as a conduit between an authentic *culture of everyday life* and the culture *manufactured* by corporate marketers. She is surprised to learn that the *cool* she has been seeking and finding (and in effect selling) is not spontaneous, but rather is itself the product of a corporate strategy: individuals are hired and trained to circulate among friends in local venues, such as bars and parties, to create awareness of the company's products. While Gibson's tale is fiction, a year later the *New York Times Magazine* asked the question this way: 'Your friends are all buzzing about the hot new whatever. Whom are they really working for?' (Walker, 2004, cover).

Both scenarios, one imaginary and one real, illustrate not only the power of corporate 'guerilla' marketing (subversive word-of-mouth advertising that flies below most consumers' radar), but also demonstrate the ambiguous nature of what traditional public opinion researchers measure. In other words, at what point does the very concept of constructed public opinion become a marketing strategy and no longer indicative of any demonstrably authentic public opinion? What is the *real* source of a public's opinion?

Noelle-Neumann (1984, p. 115) calls people's invisible, yet fully functioning perception of what is popular, acceptable, and therefore desirable a 'statistical sense organ.' Through this ability, each individual apprehends the collective conscious, knows what is approved and disapproved, and is aware of 'shifts and changes' (p. 115), whether he or she agrees with them. Cultural studies embrace this immeasurable tension and make it the object of study. Research over the last forty years, beginning primarily with the work of the British Open University cultural studies scholars such as David Morley and Stuart Hall, regard media content as coded by the creators of the content and decoded by the receivers of it. Thus, interpretations are as diverse as is the audience. Cultural studies research can be categorized according to three general areas: consumers (audiences), content, and corporations.

Hall (1980), in his seminal essay 'Encoding/Decoding,' recognized explicitly the tensions between the construction of public messages and the ways those messages are received by the *consumers*. His work underscores many cultural studies projects by combining semiotics (the study of how meaning is made through signs and symbols) and observations of specific media production practices. Importantly, Hall notes, attention

must be paid to how individuals and groups, that is, audiences, engage with the media. The classic 'Nationwide' study of television news magazine viewing in the UK (Morley, 1980) employed this multidimensional approach and became a template for the most rigorous of cultural studies projects (see also Bird, 2003, for a contemporary look at media in everyday life). Popular communication studies that examine the *content of mass media* as sources of public opinion include a variety of topics from news to music.

The 'popular' is intimately linked with the commercial and *corporations*. Popular and commercial culture are 'allied symbol systems' (Fowles, 1996, p. xiv) because of the economic imperative underlying the production, distribution, presentation, and reception of content. Researchers using cultural theory assess the construction and maintenance of public opinion as practices of culture industries that work to transform public desire into corporate profit (Frank, 1997). Combined, these approaches offer a complex and nuanced understanding of how people make meaning of their world, an understanding of which is fundamental to discerning the dynamics of public opinion.

MUSIC AND FASHION

As creative cultural expressions and commodity products, fashion and music function ecologically as systems of meaning. To survive and thrive, both fashion and music require the constant cultivation, renewal, commodification, and reproduction of public desire, thus affording us the opportunity to examine the cyclical dynamics of public opinion as it operates in the realm of popular culture and, if rejected, the process of resistance.

Because music and fashion are 'playful,' it is easy to overlook their roles in maintaining social cohesion, marking social class and rank, and their 'disciplinary power' in pressuring people to conform (Noelle-Neumann, 1984, p. 117). Boy bands and hip hop, school uniforms and dress codes, are all used to make distinctions between youth and age, men and women, social class, occupation, attitudes, values, and beliefs. As effective social control mechanisms and means of integration, music and fashion should be taken seriously for their power to instil fear of ostracism and isolation if an individual is perceived to be 'in' or 'out' of touch with the music or fashion scenes. As expressions of dominant ideology, music and fashion are: functional (sound and clothing), forms of communication, political statements, tools of conformity, mechanisms of ideology, and weapons for resistance.

Music

In August 2005, New York Attorney General Elliot Spitzer announced a settlement with Sony BMG. The company had been accused, as had record companies since the 1950s, of paying to have their music played on the radio (payola). According to *Billboard* (Garrity, 2005, p. 5), 50 years after the payola (bribery) scandals led to scrutiny of the music industries' promotion and distribution practices, the industry still engages them. Fifty years from now public officials will probably garner similar headlines. The reason these practices continue is simple: record companies maintain that success is based on limiting production and controlling distribution and exhibition.

The commodification of music illuminates the public opinion paradox. Music has always been an integral part of social experience, from family/clan entertainment to religious worship to state ceremonies. Music has been a status symbol for the powerful and a comfort for the poor, often acting as an all-encompassing mechanism of artistic expression. The technology that made it possible to store and distribute music allowed an industry to develop that could sell music, just as the fashion industry evolved from a basic need for protection to industrialized mass production. From its origins in sheet music publishing, the music industry developed techniques to 'cultivate popularity' (see Whitcomb, 1973). Interestingly, the practices of 19th century song promoters were no different from the

Sony BMG executives mentioned earlier who settled with the Attorney General. Placing songs, whether in a vaudeville act or in nationally syndicated format radio, has always involved limiting the range of public choice in order to increase the odds of a song being 'plugged' and becoming a hit through both repetition and scarcity of competition.

The legal jeopardy and the public opprobrium that payola generates, however, muddles the issue most pertinent to the study of public opinion: how can researchers define public opinion in terms of 'authentic' popular music if the system of production and distribution distorts and manipulates the public's desires?

Music production and recording have a long history as mechanisms of social control (as in religious and governmental use) and resistance (as in songs of dissent and revolution). As the recorded music industry developed, the social utility of local, social, non-commercial music was replaced by commodified/saleable forms, for which demand (public opinion) had to be (constructed and) satisfied. Since the 19th century, the music industry has used 'authentic' popular music as raw material for its musical assembly line. By the 20th century, it became clear that creating public opinion was more efficient than relying on word-of-mouth to generate interest and acquisition. Today, music companies send out their own cool hunters, namely talent scouts, to find new and innovative musicians and composers. Once the innovation is identified (usually a modification of an already existing music genre), the music companies then work to adapt and standardize that particular innovation. In this way, the artistic expression of specific individuals and groups is categorized and labeled, as a product to be sold, whether it is Mersey Beat, Cool Jazz, or Christian Rock. As the public ardor for any particular genre cools, the industry responds by (1) maintaining an orderly presence in whatever genres they choose to continue production, and (2) searching for the next authentic expression to adapt and standardize (Hirsch, 1972/1990; Peterson & Berger, 1975/1990).

The music-as-product cycle explicitly recognizes that the expression of public opinion (as exemplified by authentic musical expression) is viewed by the recorded music industry simply as the signal to co-opt that expression for commercial gain if possible. For those who participate, the subculture serves both as respite from, and resistance to, the mainstream, just as it does in the world of fashion. Ironically, the expression itself, and its initial popularity, is a result of resistance to the hegemony exercised by the music industry, while the long-term viability of that expression is often dependent upon being absorbed into that ever-changing hegemony. Therefore, the recorded music industry serves its purposes by both *satisfying* authentic public opinion and *creating* new public opinion that can be exploited.

Fashion

One of the oldest ways people express opinions, values, preferences, rank, and role is through the ways they adorn and decorate themselves. The social action of transformation and display for self and others is a behavior true of all animals, but takes on the added dimension of status conferral or rebellion when performed by human beings. Once their ancient material function as protection against the elements is fulfilled and exceeded, clothing choices become fashion options and enter the realm of social construction, a fluid 'constituent feature of modernity ... marked by constant innovation, constant sloughing off of the old' (Barnard, 2002, p. 159). Hence, the types of clothing/fashion (which includes attire, jewelry, cosmetics, and other forms of adornment) used to constitute social class and the (re)production of appropriateness that goes with it, become naturalized as that which is right and proper for the maintenance of particular class and gender identities. Thus, the old is made new again by way of the 'recombinant' nature of fashion (Gitlin, 1985). The message is that to be fashionable, and hence desirable, one has to possess the 'latest thing' which is itself unobtainable—always

just out of reach—thus requiring participation in a continuous cycle of adopting what's hot while quickly abandoning what's not. Newness is therefore 'embedded in our psyche as the ultimate mark of prestige, status, and sophistication,' wedded to our desire for social acceptance and recognition (Catani, 1999, p. 1).

Fashion is an extension beyond the corporeal and a tool for demarcating both sameness and difference. As communicated through advertising, fashion thereby reflects not only an individual's self-image, but also anticipates how others will regard the dramatalurgical display (Goffman, 1959). As an expression of popular preferences and culture, fashion is constructed not only by the garment, but also by the desire it creates in others (Barthes, 1983).

The most prominent sociological theory of fashion disbursement comes from Blumer (1969), who described fashion as a 'class differentiation' theory, a trickle-down effect. This theory posits that fashion is launched at the top of the social and economic hierarchy and then trickles down to the lower levels, where it then becomes no longer fashionable. At that moment, the upper class has already moved on to the next thing that will eventually go the way of its predecessor.

Throughout history, people of means have used fashion to distance themselves from people without (Tseëlon, 1994). In the late 1800s, economist Thorstein Veblen (1899/1994) recognized the process of social classing through fashion. He declared fashion to be a reproductive act of the elite leisure class designed to communicate and affirm to others ('conspicuous consumption') their position in society. Beyond its functional and aesthetic aspects, fashion is 'used to construct, signal, and reproduce positions of economic class' (Barnard, 2002, p. 116). Scarce materials such as silk often mark boundaries of the social order. Fashions are transient and upper classes frequently change what they are wearing in order to stress social difference.

Today, however, in light of widespread literacy, mass production, social mobility, cultural appropriation, and access to

fashion-oriented television programs, magazines, and films, appearances in fashion can be
deceiving. Whereas the trickle-down theory
conceives of consumers as passive rather than
active selectors of fashion and strict imitators
of the elite, McCracken (1985, p. 42) suggests
an entirely new direction to describe the
redistribution of what is fashionable today
as 'trickle-across' theory (otherwise called
'affordable luxury'). This theory suggests
that the spread of fashion is a process of
'collective selection' made not as much in
response to social class differentiation, but
more so to differentiate taste cultures. Thus,
while fashion can clearly mark economic
identities, it is also used to communicate
sexuality, ethnicity, religion, and age, that is,
fashion-as-sign.

Barthes (1983) argues the public appre-
ciates fashion insofar as it marks the *new*.
A German study of attitudes toward fashion
asked respondents whether they follow a
new trend immediately or wait until the
style is established. Most wait and watch,
preferring to see if the new look takes hold
in the culture (31%), while 23% were mixed,
and 36% stated they do not follow fashion
trends. Another question asked whether these
same individuals find constantly changing
fashion styles annoying. Most did (39%), but
nearly as many (36%) like fashion's ever-
changing nature, and the rest were undecided
(Noelle-Neumann & Köcher, 2001).

Closely connected with the human desire
for recognition, newness becomes embedded
as a sign of status, prestige, and sophistication.
In some cases, it is the newness more than
the actual item that assumes the greatest
importance. This newness, or *néomanie,* has,
since the 19th century, become 'exploited and
reinforced in discourse,' and since established
itself as 'the absolute criterion for the
acquisition of garments' (Catani, 1999, p. 1).

Davis (1992) describes fashion as cyclical,
in order to explain how a particular look
moves from one phase to the next. Fashion
engages in a kind of mock reality and/or
masquerade concealing the real nature of cultural and economic (re)production behind it.
Baudrillard's (1993) groundbreaking work

describes changes in fashion as 'orders of
simulacra' (p. 50), or copies of copies
of an original idea that are so real, they
seem to be new. This way the 'continued
existence of these things is ensured' (Barnard,
2002, p. 103), and fashion attains a level
of pure and perfect simulacrum—fashion-
as-sign. Fashion-as-sign has three possible
phases: (1) *imitation,* wherein appearances
disguise reality, (2) *production,* which creates
an illusion of reality, and (3) *simulation,* the
order in which appearances invent a reality
(Baudrillard, 1993).

Choice, and the belief that it is available,
is key to understanding how fashion serves
as a distinctive aspect of the reflection of
cultural preferences. Purchases of particular
fashion items *from those made available to us,*
become an expression of a public's opinion.
Fashion's illusion of choice from among those
predetermined options, as well as its function
as a site of resistance for those who do
not adhere to society's definition of what is
fashionable, is demonstrated by the 'dressing
down' or 'casual Friday' phenomenon when,
for example, 'middle class people adopt
working class style' by wearing jeans or
khakis to the office (Polhemus, 1994, p. 24).
Hundreds of college students who want to
make anti-fashion statements shop at venues
such as vintage or second-hand clothing stores
(and these are usually individuals who can
afford *not* to shop there).

Just as fashion can naturalize inequities
in gender, status, and class, so too can
it bring attention to them. Blue jeans, for
example, reproduce the concepts of freedom,
individuality, and naturalness (Fiske, 1989).
At one time, jeans communicated lower
and working class/agricultural occupational
information. Over the past 20 years or so,
jeans, particularly when they are mechan-
ically ripped, torn, bleached, or otherwise
disfigured, communicate upper class status
(Tagliabue, 2006, C1). Jeans are global in
popularity and production, particularly in
China, Europe, and America. Brand names
such as Diesel, Replay, and Seven for all
Mankind are popular at anywhere from
$35–60 per pair, while high-end designers

such as Galliano (for Dior) have brought denim and jeans into haute couture, with prices in the high hundreds.

Fashion can also be used as a way of 'distancing oneself from ... ideologies and shared meanings' (Fiske, 1989, p. 4). Barnard (2002, p. 129) uses the terms 'refusal' and 'reversal' to describe attempts to step outside the boundaries of dominant social structure or to reverse power positions and privilege within that system. In the 1980s, the British Punk style was seen as 'a reaction against the massive commercialization of both music and fashion for the young' (Rouse, 1989, p. 297). Early US rappers and hip hoppers originally wore clothing that represented resistance to and defiance of society and the music industry in order to bring attention to the inherent conditions of racism, unemployment, inequitable legal treatment, and higher incarceration rates of young Black men.

Some of the very elements that at first distanced dominant culture from punk or Black hip-hop culture eventually found their way into the mainstream, crossing social, cultural, and economic barriers. In the 1980s, for example, middle-class fashion designers such as Isaac Mizrahi created a 'homeboy chic' and White rapper Marky Mark appeared in Calvin Klein ads. In the 1990s, one-time baggy-assed jean and chain-wearing rappers took the bounty of their winnings and created their own fashion lines.

Trickle-down, up, or side-ways? Baudrillard (1993, p. 67) argues three logics are entangled with fashion: (1) functional (use-value), (2) economic (exchange value), and (3) symbolic exchange (ambivalence). Together, whether describing fashion or music or their intersections, these logics work as sources of meaning, conveying aspects of the item's modernity.

SUMMARY AND CONCLUSION

Thought of in this way, fashion and music function symbolically to articulate social class distinctions, gender identities, and otherwise silenced or ignored political voices as a particular public's opinion. Cultural studies theories suppose and propose that audiences/consumer liking/disliking are expressed in ways that reflect not only what people value and desire, but also what producers *want* them to value and desire. Thus, music-as-sound and fashion-as-clothing can work as discursive acts of boundary confirmation or as disruptive agents of cultural distinction that can simultaneously disturb the master narrative of appropriateness. As material, commercial, and communicative phenomena, music- and fashion-as-political tools frame and liberate boundaries of personal identity. Music- and fashion-as-communication thereby work both to conceal from consumers and to create distance between consumers and corporations, which benefit from continually renewing the fashion cycle. Music- and fashion-as-industries thereby involve the fusing of economic interests of manufacturers, advertisers, critics, merchants, models, and magazines in a 'profit driven alignment of structural interdependent economic interests' (Davis, 1992, p. 12). Finally, music- and fashion-as-ideology serve a reproductive role by constructing, reinforcing, and maintaining distinctions between groups, whether it be on the basis of race, sexual preference, gender, or class.

When it comes to measuring public opinion about music and fashion, information is hard to come by. Largely proprietary, most reports rely upon sales figures released by industry insiders and made available in annual reports. What people think about the music and fashion they buy and the music and fashion they do not, is also largely unknown. Perhaps this is because both industries are, in many cases, regarded as insignificant, just appearances or entertainment, simply 'playful'. These challenges, however, present interesting opportunities for scholars wishing to examine liking/disliking, conformity/rebellion as expressions of popular opinion. Future research could examine, through multi-level analysis, the corporations, content, and audiences behind a variety of popular culture forms using the popular communication perspective to get at the richness of the multi-dimensional, polysemous dialogue about cultural, economic, political expressions of popular opinion.

REFERENCES

Barnard, M. (2002). *Fashion as communication.* London: Routledge.

Barthes, R. (1983). *The fashion system.* Berkeley: University of California Press.

Baudrillard, J. (1993). *Symbolic exchange and death.* Newbury Park, CA: Sage.

Bird, E. (2003). *The audience in everyday life: Living in a media world.* New York: Routledge.

Blumer, H. (1969). *Symbolic interactionism: Perspective and method.* Englewood Cliffs, NJ: Prentice-Hall.

Catani, D. (1999, May). Consumerism and the discourse of fashion in Mallarmé's 'La dernière mode.' *Mots Pluriels, 10.* Retrieved August 6, 2005, from http://www.arts.uwa.edu.au/MotsPluriels/MP1099dc. html#fn0.

Davis, F. (1992). *Fashion, culture, and identity.* Chicago: University of Chicago Press.

Fiske, J. (1989). *Understanding popular culture.* Boston: Unwin Hyman.

Fowles, J. (1996). *Advertising and popular culture.* Thousand Oaks, CA: Sage.

Frank, T. (1997). *The Conquest of Cool: Business culture, counterculture, and the rise of consumerism.* Chicago, IL: University of Chicago Press.

Gans, H. (1999). *Popular culture and high culture: An analysis and evaluation of taste.* New York: Basic Books (Original work published 1974).

Garrity, B. (2005). Payola probe fallout begins. *Billboard, 117*(32), 5–6.

Gibson, W. (2003). *Pattern recognition.* New York: Putnam.

Gitlin, T. (1985). *Inside prime time.* New York: Pantheon.

Goffman, E. (1959). *The presentation of self in everyday life.* New York: Penguin.

Hall, S. (1980). Encoding/decoding. In S. Hall, D. Hobson, A. Lowe, & P. Willis (Eds.), *Culture, media, language* (pp. 128–138). London: Hutchinson.

Hartley, J. (2004). *Communication, cultural, and media studies: Key concepts.* London: Routledge.

Herman, E., & Chomsky, N. (1988). *Manufacturing consent: The political economy of the mass media.* New York: Pantheon.

Hirsch, P. (1990). Processing fads and fashions: An organization-set analysis of cultural industry systems. In S. Frith & A. Goodwin (Eds.), *On record: Rock, pop, and the written word* (pp. 127–139). New York: Pantheon. (Original work published 1972)

Klaehn, J. (2002). A critical review and assessment of Herman and Chomsky's 'propaganda model.' *European Journal of Communication, 17,* 147–182.

Lippmann, W. (1922). *Public opinion.* New York: Free Press.

McCracken, G. D. (1985). The trickle-down theory rehabilitated. In M. R. Solomon (Ed.), *The psychology of fashion* (pp. 39–54). Boston: Lexington Books.

Morley, D. (1980). *The nationwide audience.* London: British Film Institute.

Noelle-Neumann, E. (1984). *Spiral of silence: Public opinion—our social skin.* Chicago: University of Chicago Press.

Noelle-Neumann, E., & Köcher, R. (Eds.). (2001). Allensbacher Jahrbuch der Demoskopie 1998–2002: Balkon des Jahrhunderts [Allensbacher yearbook of the demoscopy: Balcony of the century]. München: Verlag für Demoskopie.

Peterson, R., & Berger, D. (1990). Cycles in symbol production: The case of popular music. In S. Frith & A. Goodwin (Eds.), *On record: Rock, pop, and the written word* (pp. 140–159). New York: Pantheon. (Original work published 1975)

Polhemus, T. (1994). *Streetstyle: From sidewalk to catwalk.* London: Thames & Hudson.

Rouse, F. (1989). *Understanding fashion.* Oxford: BSP Professional Books.

Tagliabue, J. (2006, July 12). Yeah, they torture jeans. But it's all for the sake of fashion. *New York Times,* C1.

Tseëlon, E. (1994). Fashion and signification in Baudrillard. In D. Kellner (Ed.), *Baudrillard: A critical reader.* London: Blackwell.

Veblen, T. (1994). *Theory of the leisure class.* New York: Penguin Classics. (Original work published 1899)

Walker, R. (2004, December 5). The hidden (in plain sight) persuaders. *The New York Times Magazine,* 68–75.

Whitcomb, I. (1973). *After the ball.* New York: Simon & Schuster.

The Development of Public Opinion Research

8

The Historical Roots of Public Opinion Research

Anthony Oberschall

FORMATION OF PUBLICS

Public opinion has been recognized as a political force since the eighteenth century by prominent political theorists as varied as Rousseau, Tocqueville, Bentham, Lord Acton, Bryce and others, but measuring and accounting for it through quantitative social science methods started in the early twentieth century (→ *The Public and Public Opinion in Political Theories*). By the 1950s, the study and measurement of public opinion via commercial polling and scholarly research had become institutionalized.

To explain the institutionalization of an intellectual activity, one needs to explain both demand and supply. On the demand side, in the nineteenth century, governments, reformers and intellectuals wanted information on the state of mind, social problems, and political dispositions of ordinary people. As suffrage, literacy, and consumption increased, newspapers competed on predicting election outcomes and advertisers wanted to know the tastes and wants of ordinary people. This led to market, audience and public opinion research and organizations. Of great importance as well was the demand for and sponsorship of social research by the US government in the depression and in World War II for measuring unemployment and the effectiveness of relief programs, and for assessing the morale of the armed forces and domestic public opinion support for the war, for which it recruited leading social scientists. During and after the war, when they returned to universities, these social scientists created and perfected new social research methodologies (content analysis, large sample surveys, probability sampling) and research organizations (Michigan Survey Research Center, National Opinion Research Center), which institutionalized scientific public opinion surveys in academia.

On the supply side, there had to develop a clear understanding of what public opinion was, who were the public and which of their attitudes, beliefs and opinions mattered for public affairs and could be measured. Competent research staff had to be recruited and trained, methods of inquiry had to cumulate and be refined, and organizations carrying out quantitative public opinion studies had to be financed on a continuing basis. Professional and scholarly organizations, institutes, and journals publishing the results of public opinion and mass communications research had to be founded and earn acceptance in the academic world and by sponsor foundations. Such a critical mass of resources, incentives and legitimacy for public opinion research solidified for the first time in the US from the 1930s to the 1940s. In Europe, the physical and moral destruction from World War I undermined the opportunity for the same.

Among the first groups to challenge the authority of state elites on public policy were religious dissenters like the Puritans in England, who insisted on liberty in matters of conscience and worship denied by the state and the Anglican Church. There was an extraordinary outpouring of religious pamphlets that challenged orthodoxy. Religious dissenters insisted that in matters of religion, they, and not the state, had the right to create their own institutions. They wanted recognition as a public in this limited sense, and the right to practice their religion openly, unlike the Christians in the first two centuries in ancient Rome.

Much the same was true for many subsequent socio-political-religious movements in England, be it for political rights (Wilkes and liberty), wider suffrage and the reform of Parliament (the Chartists), humanitarian and reform goals (the abolition of the slave trade and of slavery): huge pamphlet literature, mass rallies, speakers filling public halls, petitions signed by tens of thousands presented to the House of Commons, huge processions and similar manifestations of public opinion. Gradually the British government and law accepted the enlargement of public opinion, a free press, the right to petition Parliament, and other political reforms that made for evolution in British political institutions.

In the continental absolutist monarchies without elected legislatures, in particular France, public opinion existed because there were people of substance outside the government with influence in public affairs, either because of resources the government needed from them (financing the state debt), or because they disseminated political beliefs and doctrines to educated circles including the elites that challenged prevailing orthodoxy (the *philosophes* in France). Thus Jacques Necker, the minister responsible for reforming the French monarchy's finances, stated that the minister of finance 'stands most in need of the good opinion of the people' for raising loans for the state, which he tried to accomplish with transparency for the state's creditors, publishing fiscal statements of state expenditures and revenues (Speier, 1950, p. 380), an innovation at the time. Public opinion was formed in salons, coffee houses, reading societies and literary clubs where the aristocracy, civil servants and state officials rubbed elbows with the bourgeoisie and intellectuals. State elites were quite conversant with the state of public opinion. The state tried to limit the dissemination of reform and opposition opinion through censorship, but failed miserably. On the eve of the French Revolution, a large part of the public had been convinced of the need for major reform in governance, and the Third Estate, joined by a segment of the nobility and the Church, proclaimed itself the National Assembly, i.e. the legitimate representative of the public speaking on behalf of the entire population.

As a consequence of the French Revolution, nation building (nationalism) by European states, the growth of literacy and newspaper readership, and the democratic revolution (the founding of political parties and the progressive extension of the franchise), the initially small public gradually became the entire citizenry of the state, eventually including even those without property, women, and religious minorities. As the public expanded, the state of public opinion became problematic, and various ways of measuring it, from social surveys to newspaper content, were perfected in addition to electoral and party politics. Rapid urbanization and the growth of an industrial working class had uprooted rural migrants from their traditional social milieu and the supervision of village parish ministers and rural notables and traditional record keeping in parish registers.

In cities, the incidence of crime, poverty, and public health problems sowed apprehension among the authorities and the bourgeoisie about what became known as the *social question* or (German) *Arbeiterfrage*. Governments and reform advocates, scientific and humanitarian associations and individuals undertook to gather information about the new 'dangerous' or 'criminal' classes. Governments instituted censuses, at first episodically and then with regular frequency, and published public records on crime, health, literacy, mortality, and material welfare. Scholars like Quetelet built a new field of *moral statistics* from these data, which purported to measure the moral as well as the material and social conditions of the population, thus creating a social barometer that measured threats to social stability. Embedded in a growing international statistical movement fueled by statistical enthusiasm, census taking, social surveys and moral statistics spread far and wide in Europe and the US.

SOCIAL SURVEYS

Civic, scientific and philanthropic organizations and individuals in the nineteenth century believed that the governments were doing much less information collecting and analysis than reform required. Consequently, such associations as the Manchester and London (later Royal) Statistical Societies in Britain, the *Académie des Sciences Morales* in Paris, and the *Verein für Sozialpolitik* in Germany undertook empirical social investigations (surveys, *enquêtes*, *Umfragen*) at their own expense. Some consisted of inquiries with knowledgeable individuals—usually priests and ministers, physicians, social workers and teachers whose profession put them in regular touch with the lower classes. Others used house-to-house inquirers armed with

questionnaires who interviewed householders themselves (Cole, 1972). These investigations were proto-social surveys, but differed from contemporary practice: they lacked clear ideas about sampling, used rudimentary questionnaire construction (e.g. no filters for those who are not in a position to answer particular items, use of biased questions, distinguishing 'don't know' as ignorance from reluctance to answer and uncertain as to choice, and the like) and simple univariate and bivariate tabular presentations of findings. As well, periods of reform did not last beyond a decade or two, and the concerns of reformers, civic organizations and intellectuals for social problems fluctuated over time. These groups assembled resources for surveys episodically, and no permanent research institutes were founded. Hence methodology and experiences with social surveys did not cumulate during the nineteenth century.

Moreover these surveys were on matters of fact, not of opinion, attitudes, hopes, and aspirations: the notion that states of mind could be measured, especially in an uneducated population, was counter to the conventional wisdom. In the preparatory prospectus for 1909–1911 *Verein für Sozialpolitik* survey of industrial workers in Germany, German sociologist Max Weber showed considerable ambivalence on this issue, whereas he had no hesitation on questioning workers about physiological variables ('after how many hours do you generally get tired?') and bread and butter issues (e.g. 'do you rent beds ... do you have boarders?'). It remained for the self-educated worker Adolf Levenstein (1912) to undertake the first large attitude-opinion survey of industrial workers on record. He sent 8,000 self-administered questionnaires to miners, steel workers, and textile workers in Germany, using a snowball procedure which started with his many worker friends and trade unionists. He achieved a remarkable 63% return. The schedule explored the workers' attitudes on important issues—their material and political hopes and wishes, their aspirations, religious beliefs, political activities, cultural and recreational pursuits, in addition to factual information on social background, wages and work. Weber convinced Levenstein to code, tabulate, and publish the results (Oberschall, 1965, chap. 6). There was no follow up, partly because Levenstein was marginal for German scholars and partly because World War I set back German social science.

Two non-survey methods were created for getting more directly at state of mind variables than moral statistical indicators. Particular individuals decided to participate in the way of life (work place, rooming house life) of ordinary working people for a period of time—participant observation—and reported on the insights they gained on the dispositions, worldviews and moral habits of their subjects through their experience (Göhre, 1891; Williams, 1920). The most comprehensive methodology was developed by Le Play (1877–1879) for his family monographs and family budgets. He used his travels as a mining engineer and consultant throughout Europe for case studies of selected working class families in many European countries.

A second method was the proto-content analysis of newspapers based on measures of the space provided for entertainment, political news, education, and so on. The assumption was that the readers were proportionately influenced by opinions reflected in the newspaper. Content itself was not analyzed in a quantitative manner: instead repeated phrases and words which the analyst thought typified a particular content were listed. Trend analyses and newspaper comparisons (e.g. capital versus provinces) were also made. These activities flourished especially in Germany, where Karl Bücher founded a journalism program at the university in Leipzig in 1915 (Bücher, 1926). Content analysis during World War I was applied to war propaganda by the principal belligerents, and it acquired a quantitative cast in the 1920s with the spread of market research and audience research in the US (Lasswell, 1927). Berelson (1952) later codified the accumulated knowledge and techniques of content analysis in a textbook.

PUBLIC OPINION POLLING

In the 1880s, mass circulation newspapers and magazines eclipsed the local daily press and cashed in on the growing advertising market sparked by national brand products on sale in the recently founded department stores. Joseph Pulitzer and William Randolph Hearts applied a new formula for muckraking journalism: love and romance for women, and sports and politics for men. Advertisements aimed at women who made consumer decisions for the household flooded the Sunday papers. Market research was financed by the corporations competing in the new US mass market, and in the 1920s got an added boost from radio audience research. Newspapers and magazines competed fiercely and boosted their circulations during election campaigns by conducting straw polls among their readers for predicting election outcomes (Park, 1923). A straw poll referred to an unofficial vote taken at some gathering or in a district for measuring public opinion. Newspapers and magazines included straw ballots in their pages that readers were asked to fill out and mail back, and the responses would be tabulated and published, and the winners thence predicted. A successful newspaper would boast of its greater accuracy compared to rivals. For instance, *The Literary Digest* embarked on a national poll in 1916 and correctly predicted Woodrow Wilson's election, which boosted its circulation.

At this time, the recently founded academic discipline of political science started taking a research interest in understanding electoral choices, the appeals of different parties, candidates and issues for the voters, and regional variations in political behavior. Utilizing census information on electoral districts, shadings on maps, simple descriptive statistics and later on multiple regression, scholars like William Ogburn (Ogburn & Goltra, 1919) and Stuart Rice (1928) in the US and André Siegfried (1913) in France created the field of political geography for understanding the formation of public opinion and electoral behavior, albeit based on ecological data and not individual votes and opinions. These techniques were also used to predict election outcomes and electoral trends.

In 1933, the young George Gallup, who earned a Ph.D. in psychology from a small mid-western university and who combined careers in academia and market research, decided to draw on both these fields to create public opinion polling. He collected and studied detailed voting records going back 100 years for the US, and sent out ballots to a small but carefully selected group of voters in each state based on his analysis of past electoral behavior. He estimated results for the 1934 congressional elections with great accuracy. He continued to experiment with these hybrid methods of choosing purposive samples of voters based on political geography, and founded the American Institute of Public Opinion (AIPO) in 1935, whose goal was 'impartially to measure and report public opinion on political and social issues of the day without regard to the rightness and wisdom of the views expressed.' AIPO conducted national public opinion surveys using Gallup's method of combining purposive sampling with quotas for relatively small numbers of respondents (compared to the tens of thousands of responses in straw polls), and distributed the results to subscribing newspapers in the form of press releases. Gallup caught national attention when he predicted Roosevelt over Landon in 1936, whereas the *Literary Digest* straw poll with over 2 million responses mistakenly predicted Landon with 54% (Roosevelt won with 62.5%). The *Digest* used its own subscribers and other lists such as automobile owners that were biased to upper income groups in an election in the midst of depression where class differences were salient.

Gallup's success found imitators and his methodology and polling organization became the norms in the rapidly growing polling industry: the Fortune survey was headed by Paul Cherrington and Elmer Roper; the Crossley poll by Archibald Crossley; later also the Louis Harris Survey, the Field poll, and many others. These polling organizations collected and released an enormous amount of data on beliefs, attitudes, preferences, expectations and behaviors on salient public issues, and did so repeatedly, which made the analysis of trends possible in addition to the demographics of public opinion. As well, Harry Field, the director of Gallup's first overseas affiliate in London, established the National Opinion Research Center (NORC), the first non-profit public opinion research organization in 1941, affiliated first with the University of Denver, and subsequently in 1946 with the University of Chicago under Clyde Hart.

The census and political geography were used to select a small number of representative districts (later called primary sampling units) where a field staff was trained and maintained, and face to face interviews were made according to quotas on age, gender, and income to match the census data in the selected districts. The results were collected by the polling organization, tabulated and rapidly released to the news media. Gallup suffered a temporary setback in the 1948 election when he predicted Dewey over Truman (the winner) by a wide margin. Gallup attributed his faulty prediction to a misunderstanding of the 'undecided' respondents' choices and to the failure to conduct a last minute poll in an election where there was a late shift in voter sentiment. In 1949, the Social Science Research Council (SSRC) investigated the methodology of polling, including the 1948 failures, and it attributed the problems to the errors inherent in quota sampling and in interviewing besides the handling of the undecided and of late voter shifts that Gallup had cited. The SSRC was founded in 1923 with the help of Rockefeller Foundation support by a group of scholars from the professional associations of the new social science disciplines interested in interdisciplinary policy research and in improving the infrastructure and training for social research. It soon became a facilitator and evaluator of academic research (it helped fund the scholars who produced 'The American Soldier'). Responding to these intellectual trends, for the 1956 election, Gallup switched to probability sampling, which eventually developed into the multistage probability samples of contemporary polling with 1,500–3,000 respondents nationwide in the US.

Gallup had academic credentials and sought to put polling on a firm scientific basis. Close ties between the academic community, opinion pollsters, and market researchers were forged early on with the founding of the American Association of Public Opinion Research (AAPOR) in 1947, which met annually and which in 1948 started publishing the *Public Opinion Quarterly* in whose pages the theory, methodology, practice and findings of public opinion polling were debated and published. There were three further critical inputs into the theory and practice of public opinion polling: on probability sampling, on survey methodology, and on mass communications.

SAMPLING

Starting with Laplace, Poisson, Gauss and followed later by the British Galton-Pearson-Yule-Fisher school of mathematical statisticians, probability theory had laid the foundations for probability sampling and quantitative multivariate analysis of data from both experimental and quasi-experimental designs; yet social scientists and pollsters were slow in applying them. Randomness in sampling was counterintuitive: the conventional wisdom held that a large entity had to be faithfully represented with a smaller scale replica, as in an architectural model for a building or a toy locomotive for a real one. Representative samples in the hands of seasoned practitioners seemed to provide accurate information when total enumeration was cumbersome. Even though Bowley and Burnett-Hurst (1915) demonstrated in a six city study of urban poverty that random sampling was as suited for assessing the incidence and demographics of poverty as Booth's laborious, time consuming and expensive methodology (Booth, 1889–1891), and Yule (1899) showed, using Booth's own data, that multiple regression techniques provided a more efficient and superior

insight into the causes of poverty than the descriptive presentation and analysis used by social reformers, the conventional wisdom on probability sampling persisted. The decisive breakthrough occurred in the US during the depression when the government, and the Department of Agriculture (USDA) in particular, hired mathematical statisticians who understood probability sampling and who demonstrated its greater accuracy and lower cost compared to purposive sampling and enumeration. Unemployment was estimated from probability samples of households, and crop yields from probability samples of farm plots. Jerzy Neyman (1934) compared the results from purposive and from probability samples and demonstrated the scientific strengths of probability theory. Rensis Likert (creator of the Likert scale) headed the USDA Division of Program Surveys, which studied farm opinion and pioneered the probability sampling of households as well as other survey techniques such as the use of open-ended questions and batteries of questions for forming scales and indices. But it was in the aftermath of World War II, when an intimate and unique collaboration was forged between academic, government and public opinion social scientists, that probability sampling became accepted. The 1948 election poll errors and the SSRC critique of polling techniques also played a part in this change.

SURVEY RESEARCH METHODOLOGY

Around 1900 in the US, social surveys of cities were conducted by social reformers, social workers and some social science scholars for the purpose of civic improvement and for raising awareness of urban poverty and social problems. Financing was provided in part by the Russell Sage Foundation, and later by the Rockefeller Foundation, which got interested in non-metropolitan towns and rural places and the quality of life there (Lynd & Lynd, 1929). Census data, the reports of social work agencies, health departments, the police and other agencies, participant observation by news reporters and social workers, and other sources were combined with data from questionnaire surveys to describe industrializing cities such as Pittsburgh and Springfield, which had been rapidly growing with the influx of immigrants from overseas and migrants from farm areas. Findings were publicized with huge public exhibits of photographs and maps, speeches, and newspaper articles in addition to books. The recently founded University of Chicago (also by Rockefeller) and Columbia University in New York created sociology departments with endowed professorships, and developed academic curricula for social workers that included field work and data analysis in collaboration with social agencies and civic organizations. The University of Chicago organized an interdisciplinary Local Community Research Committee, located all social science departments in the same building, and received Rockefeller Foundation financing for its pioneering research on the city of Chicago—Robert Ezra Park (1929) referred to the city as a social science laboratory—and on the assimilation of European migrants to American life and institutions. The linkage of survey research with the social reform enterprise, however, hindered a focus on methodological issues and advances in techniques of social inquiry (Oberschall, 1972).

The decisive change came during World War II and its aftermath, when the Information and Education Division of the US Army created a Research Branch for investigating soldier morale in the armed forces by means of self-administered questionnaire surveys distributed by field teams in war theaters across the world. For this purpose, a sterling cast of social scientists was invited to participate or serve as advisers (Rensis Likert, Frederick Mosteller, John Dollard, Louis Guttman, Hadley Cantril, Paul Lazarsfeld, Carl Hovland, to name but the most prominent) under technical director Samuel Stouffer of Harvard University. The Research Branch focused on attitudes and motivations in over 200 surveys, some of which had samples of several thousand respondents. These surveys occasioned many advances in opinion/attitude/motivation research in actual field settings (in contrast to controlled laboratory conditions), in questionnaire construction, in scaling, in causal analysis for quasi-experimental design, in data processing with Hollerith punch card counter sorters, and the organization of widely scattered field offices and research teams. These wartime activities demonstrated the usefulness of social science and enhanced the prestige of empirical research oriented academics, just as in World War I the IQ testing of two million recruits—the first large scale mental testing in history—had led to recognition of psychology as a science and to methodological advances (Madge, 1962, chap. 9).

Just as important was the secondary analysis of these massive data by the social scientists after the war that produced the four-volume 'Studies in Social Psychology in World War Two' (1949–1950) made possible by funding from the Carnegie Corporation and the Social Science Research Council, the best known of which were the first two volumes titled 'The American Soldier' (Stouffer, Suchman, Devinney, Star & Williams, 1949; Stouffer, Lumsdaine et al., 1949). Capitalizing on his Research Branch experience, Stouffer resumed his Harvard professorship and founded the Harvard Social Relations Laboratory where he trained a succession of sociologists in quantitative techniques; Carl Hovland (Hovland, Janis & Kelly, 1953) created the Yale psychology laboratory to pursue the study of attitudes and communication in controlled experiments. The Michigan Survey Research Center grew out of the work of the Division of Program Surveys in the Department of Agriculture headed by Rensis Likert, when at the war's end Likert and his young staff of experts in sampling and social surveys (George Katona, Leslie Kish, Angus Campbell, Dorwin Cartwright) managed to affiliate with the University of Michigan. These war time activities and the post-war transfer of personnel and research experience to universities provided a critical mass for the institutionalization of quantitative empirical research, including research on public opinion, in the academic social science disciplines in the US.

In Britain, at the start of World War II, large questionnaire surveys of the population using probability sampling—called the Wartime Social Survey—were organized under the Ministry of Information for measuring the morale of the civilian population and its reaction to hardships. At war's end the surveying continued as the Government Social Survey and focused on data and issues connected with the expansion of the welfare state. Unlike the US, the UK government maintained direct control of surveying rather than contracting it out to universities and non-profits (UK Office of National Statistics, 2001).

MASS COMMUNICATIONS

The remaining intellectual advance that marked public opinion research was the new field of mass communications, which provided an understanding of public opinion formation and the effects of mass communication in a natural social milieu. The key actor in this story was Paul F. Lazarsfeld. When Lazarsfeld came to the US from Vienna in 1933 on a Rockefeller fellowship, he brought with him a doctorate in applied mathematics, research experience in social psychology with Karl and Charlotte Bühler, strong methodological interests, and the successful directorship of a team of social researchers who had done a field study of a textile town, Marienthal, in the grip of depression and long term unemployment (Jahoda, Lazarsfeld & Zeisel, 1933). In the US, he carved out a leading research role in the new field of radio research. He and his associates transformed the typical market research of radio audiences that used audience demographics, content classification and program effects on small groups in laboratories into survey research of the public, listeners, readers, consumers and voters in the social milieu of everyday life such as an election campaign. He forged professional and personal links with key influentials like Frank Stanton, who headed research at the Columbia Broadcasting System (CBS) where he later rose to be President; Hadley Cantril,

a pioneer in public opinion research who headed the Office of Radio Research (ORR) at Princeton University; Samuel Stouffer of Harvard; the Rockefeller Foundation for funding; the Gallup organization for data on newspaper readers and radio audiences, and others. Upon his appointment in the sociology department at Columbia he moved his research team to the university, where they became the Bureau of Applied Social Research (BASR), the intellectual and organizational setting that further pioneered survey research in the 1940s and 1950s (Lazarsfeld, 1968).

A path breaking longitudinal BASR survey was on political attitude and opinion formation and its effects on voting in the 1940 presidential election, in Erie county, Pennsylvania, entitled 'The people's choice' (1944) and subtitled 'How the voter makes up his mind in a presidential campaign.' The study was funded by the Rockefeller Foundation, *Life* magazine, the ORR, Elmo Roper, and funds from commercial contract research at the BASR, which gives an indication of how Lazarsfeld managed to link academic scholarship with market research and public opinion polling (Morrison, 1988).

The BASR became the training organ for a generation of communications and public opinion researchers and survey analysts. The Lazarsfeld group developed panel surveys (longitudinal surveys of the same sample of respondents over a time period), the statistical analysis of survey data from quasi-experimental designs, snowball sampling, deviant case analysis, the focused interview, the logic underlying typologies and index formation, the design of complex questionnaire with batteries and filters, and contextual analysis, to mention the best known on the methodological side. In the course of their work, they discovered the selective exposure of the public to media messages, the role of opinion leaders in the social milieu of ordinary citizens, the two-step flow of communications and its dampening effect on the power of the mass media, and a theory of choice that became a paradigm for the empirical study of action, on the theoretical side. Many of these substantive and methodological results were published in *The Language of Social Research* in 1955 (Lazarsfeld & Rosenberg, 1955).

By the 1950s there was a strong and persistent demand for public opinion information. The US had the largest and most competitive mass media audience and market in the world, and a huge electorate within a highly competitive two-party system. On the supply side, it possessed a vigorous polling industry, two non-profit university affiliated survey research organizations (NORC and the Michigan SRC) with high professional standards and capable of conducting nation-wide multistage probability sample surveys on public affairs topics. As well, the social science departments of the leading universities trained students in quantitative methods and theories such as public opinion and mass communications. Last but not least, wealthy foundations and US government agencies were financial sponsors of large-scale research on social policy and public affairs. European scholars came to study public opinion research in the US and returned to start public opinion institutions. Among the best known were Jean Stoetzel, who founded the *Institut Francais d'Opinion Publique* in Paris in 1938, and Elisabeth Noelle-Neumann, who founded *Institut für Demoskopie Allensbach* in West Germany in 1947. From these beginnings, after the 1950s, opinion polling spread throughout the world.

SUMMARY

The growth of citizenship and the democratization of politics in the nineteenth century enlarged the boundaries of the public, which claimed the right to have a voice in public affairs—from elites to the population at large. As the boundaries expanded, there was a lack of information about the opinions and attitudes of new publics, in particular the public opinions and the political loyalties of the working class. Governments, professional associations, social reformers and scholars experimented with and developed a variety of techniques for obtaining such information, but it wasn't until the period 1935–1955 that modern public opinion research became institutionalized in the US with the creation of independent public opinion polling organizations, a professional association (AAPOR), and a professional journal (POQ). Successful institutionalization was due to the conjunction of four trends. In the 1930s, the depression and World War II saw the development and application of random sampling and of rigorous large sample survey methodology. Newspapers and radio broadcasters had a competitive interest in audience research and election outcome predictions. Private foundations financed empirical research for public policy. Academics created a theory of mass communications and methodologies for explaining public opinion formation and electoral choices. Together, they were responsible for routinizing the measurement of public opinion in the US, which subsequently diffused worldwide.

REFERENCES

American Institute of Public Opinion. (2002). American Institute of Public Opinion Records. Organizational History. *Truman Presidential Museum and Library website.* Retrieved January 30, 2006 from http://www.trumanlibrary.org/hstpaper/amerinst.htm

Berelson, B. (1952). *Content analysis in communication research.* New York: Free Press.

Booth, C. (1889–1891). *Life and labor of the people in London.* (Vols. 1–17). London: Macmillan.

Bowley, A., & Burnett-Hurst, A. R. (1915). *Livelihood and poverty.* London: Bell.

Bücher, K. (1926). *Gesammelte Aufsätze zur Zeitungskunde* [Collected essays on journalism]. Tübingen: Laupp.

Cole, S. (1972). Continuity and institutionalization in science: a Case Study of Failure. In A. Oberschall (Ed.), *The establishment of empirical sociology* (pp. 73–129). New York: Harper Row.

Göhre, P. (1891). *Drei Monate Fabrikarbeiter und Handwerksbursche* [Three months as a factory worker and apprentice]. Leipzig: Grunow.

Hovland, C. I., Janis, I. L., & Kelley, H. H. (1953). *Communication and persuasion.* New Haven: Yale University Press.

Jahoda, M., Lazarsfeld, P., & Zeisel, H. (1933). *Marienthal.* Leipzig: Hirzel.

Lasswell, H. (1927). *Propaganda techniques in the World War.* New York: Knopf.

Lazarsfeld, P. F. (1968). An episode in the history of social research: a memoir. In D. Fleming, & B. Bailyn (Eds.), *The intellectual migration* (pp. 270–337). Cambridge: Harvard University Press.

Lazarsfeld, P. F., & Rosenberg, M. (Eds.). (1955). *The language of social research.* New York: Free Press.

Lazarsfeld, P. F., Berelson, B., & Gaudet, H. (1944). *The people's choice.* New York: Columbia University Press.

Le Play, F. (1877–1879). *Les ouvriers europeens* [The European workers]. (Vols. 1–6). Paris: Alfred Manne et Fils.

Levenstein, A. (1912). *Die Arbeiterfrage* [The working class question]. München: Reinhardt.

Lynd, R., & Lynd, H. (1929). *Middletown.* New York: Harcourt.

Madge, J. (1962). *The origins of scientific sociology.* New York: Free Press.

Morrison, D. (1988). The transference experience and the impact of ideas: Paul Lazarsfeld and communications research. *Communication, 10,* 185–209.

Neyman, J. (1934). On the two different aspects of the representative method: The method of stratified sampling and the method of purposive selection. *Journal of the Royal Statistical Society, 97,* 558–606.

Oberschall, A. (1965). *Empirical social research in Germany 1848–1914.* Paris: Mouton.

Oberschall, A. (1972). The institutionalization of American sociology. In A. Oberschall (Ed.), *The establishment of empirical sociology* (pp. 187–251). New York: Harper Row.

Ogburn, W. F., & Goltra, I. (1919). How women vote. *Political Science Quarterly, 34,* 413–433.

Park, R. E. (1923). The natural history of the newspaper. *American Journal of Sociology, 29,* 273–289.

Park, R. E. (1929). The city as a social laboratory. In R. Turner (Ed.). (1967), *Robert Ezra Park on social control and collective behavior* (pp. 3–18). Chicago University Press.

Rice, S. (1928). *Quantitative method in politics.* New York: Knopf.

Siegfried, A. (1913). *Tableau politique de la France de l'Ouest sous la Troisieme République* [Political description of western France during the third republic]. Paris: Armand Colin.

Speier, H. (1950). Historical development of public opinion. *American Journal of Sociology, 55,* 376–88.

Stouffer, S. A., Suchman, E. A., Devinney, L. C., Star, S. A., & Williams, R. M. (Vol. Eds.) (1949). *Studies in social psychology in World War Two: Vol. 1. The American soldier: Adjustment during army life.* Princeton University Press.

Stouffer, S. A., Lumsdaine, A. A., Lumsdaine, M. H., Williams, R. M., Smith, M. B., Irving, L. J. *et al.* (Vol. Eds.) (1949). *Studies in social psychology in World War Two: Vol. 2. The American soldier: Combat and its aftermath.* Princeton University Press.

UK Office of National Statistics. (2001). *60 years of social survey 1941–2001.* London.

Williams, W. (1920). *What's on the workers mind.* New York: Scribner.

Yule, G. U. (1899). An investigation into the causes of changes pauperism in England, chiefly during the last two intercensal decades. *Journal of the Royal Statistical Society, 62,* 249–286.

9

Mass-Observation and Modern Public Opinion Research

Murray Goot

In Britain between 1937 and 1949, two under-standings of public opinion contested the intellectual, political and social terrain. One, represented by the Gallup Poll, was the child of market research and American journalism; the other, Mass-Observation (M-O), a hybrid of British anthropology, American commu-nity studies and French surrealism. One was a business, whose public face, financed by the press, focused largely on politics and public affairs; the other, an organization made up mostly of volunteers, financially dependent on benefactors, documented attitudes to politics, but also practices, utterances and beliefs of every other kind. Both ridiculed the idea of the press making pronouncements about the state of public opinion without 'real' evidence; both were concerned that governments should be properly informed about public opinion, especially during times of war; and both, though strong believers in 'the public,' wanted to see public opinion improved.

More striking, however, are the things that kept them apart. Gallup, more interested in people's opinions than in their behavior,

equated public opinion with polled opinion; M-O, more concerned with what people said in ordinary conversation, to friends as much as to strangers, thought the polls potentially misleading. And while Gallup was interested in national surveys based on systematic sampling that generated quantitative data, M-O's work focused on smaller areas and the generation of qualitative data. In short, while both were committed to a 'science' of public opinion, each understood public opinion differently, attached different weights to different aspects of it, and employed different methods to study it.

This chapter outlines M-O's diverse meth-ods, evaluates its record, and suggests the reasons for its demise. It explores the different understandings of public opinion that distinguish M-O from Gallup, argues that M-O's ideas about the relationship between 'public' and 'private' opinion anticipated Noelle-Neumann's (1974) 'spiral of silence,' and demonstrates that M-O's views of how public opinion is best ascertained came closer than Gallup's to realizing Bryce's ideal.

It concludes by noting the ways that M-O's practices are reflected in later research.

OBSERVERS AND THEIR OBSERVATIONS

The differences between M-O and Gallup were partly differences of method. Unlike Gallup, M-O did not hire interviewers; while some of its Observers were paid, especially for commissioned work, M-O depended mostly on volunteers. In addition, M-O held out the promise of giving its recruits a collective voice in public affairs, of increasing their social awareness and of modifying their social consciousness (Jennings & Madge, 1937/1987, p. iv; Madge & Harrisson, 1937, p. 30). In the first months of 1937, through advertisements in newspapers and magazines, it recruited some 500 Observers (Jeffery, 1999, p. 28). By the end of the war nearly 3,000 volunteers had taken some part in its work, though only about 1,000 involved themselves more than once (N. Stanley, 1981, pp. 155ff.).

Observers were disproportionately drawn from South East England, and were middle class or lower middle class, male, and young (especially the men), though that changed with the war (N. Stanley, 1981, p. 154ff.). Some of the men were manual workers, but the largest group was made up of clerks or schoolteachers; the same was true of the women who had paid jobs. Though often widely read, few had gone to University; their urge to expand their education, particularly their understanding of current affairs, was one reason for joining; in that sense, M-O was a social movement (Summerfield, 1985).

What did Mass-Observers do? Between 1937 and 1940, a relatively small group, including a number of artistic and literary types, worked under Tom Harrisson's direction, initially, in Bolton (Worktown) and Blackpool (Holiday Town or Seatown), where Worktowners took their holidays (Cross, 1990). Others, initially under Charles Madge, formed a National Panel. On the 12th of each month, commencing February 12th, 1937,

until February 12th, 1938, 'they set down plainly all that happened to them that day' (Madge & Harrisson, 1938, p. 7). In the beginning, Madge wanted accounts of people's dreams so that he could search for coincidence, mass fantasies, and dominant images and uncover the 'collective unconscious' (Jeffery, 1999, p. 23). The diaries for the 12th May, the coronation of George VI, form the centerpiece for M-O's first book, 'May the twelfth' (Jennings & Madge, 1937/1987).

Panelists also answered Directives, a series of questions about their own attitudes, personal histories or current behavior in relation to particular topics. The first, in July 1937, was on smoking; among other things it invited respondents to suggest other questions and criticize the questions they had been asked (Author's collection). During the war, over 2,000 Observers answered at least one Directive, while for some time about 500 kept daily diaries (Jeffery, 1999, p. 42; see Garfield, 2004, for five of the diaries). A disparate array of other material relating to 'Housing,' 'Pacifism,' 'Wall Chalkings,' 'Dreams,' and so on was also collected (Calder, 1985, p. 124; Jeffery, 1978, pp. 50ff., for a list of Worktown and Holiday Town projects).

In addition to describing their own conduct and opinions, Observers—'whole-time,' 'half-time,' but mostly 'part-time'—were asked to describe other people's behavior, including their 'verbal behavior.' Nonobtrusive measures included: 'counts' of particular kinds of behavior; 'observations' of exactly who did what and how; and 'overheards' of conversations in cinemas, buses and the like. These activities sometimes involved following people around or 'follows' (L. Stanley, 2001, pp. 97ff.). Observers were also asked to elicit other people's opinions by indirect interview, by informal interview, or (at least post-1940) by formal interview (N. Stanley, 1981, pp. 230ff.). Only in the case of formal interviewing did M-O's methods resemble Gallup's.

Most of M-O's reports drew on more than one of these approaches. This may have reflected the way M-O 'changed over time,' its 'loose structure,' or its 'fractures' (L. Stanley, 2001, p. 95). Most of the studies brought together in *Britain* incorporate data from informal and (possibly) formal interviews. The series of studies for advertising agencies, through the Advertising Services Guild (for example, Mass-Observation, 1944, 1949), include data from formal interviews. But *The Pub and the People* (Mass-Observation, 1943/1987) draws on some of the 15,000 conversations—indirect interviews—M-O conducted in Bolton (Harrisson & Madge, 1939/1986, p. 42).

PUBLIC OPINION AND HOW TO ASCERTAIN IT

Along with differences in methods were differences in the weights M-O and Gallup attached to private opinion, and the ways in which M-O's approach effectively challenged Gallup's claim to have inherited the mantle of Bryce.

The concept of public opinion

In *The Pulse of Democracy*, Gallup acknowledged 'the distinction between the "public" opinion which an individual expresses and the "private" opinion which he keeps to himself' (quotes in this paragraph are from Gallup & Rae, 1940, pp. 228ff.). But thinking through its implications defeated him. On the one hand he insisted that polls, like 'any other method of assessing public opinion,' could only measure 'overt indications' of 'basic attitudes' and that the question 'Do opinions represent basic convictions?' was 'unanswerable.' On the other, he argued that 'once people become familiar with [the polls'] objectives,' polls were in a 'strong position' to get at their 'true convictions.' Far from being beyond the reach of the polls, what people actually thought was precisely what polls uncovered: 'the anonymity of surveys, their fact-finding objectives, and the natural though often shy curiosity which most people feel in their own and in their neighbor's opinions' disposed 'the public to co-operate with the surveys.'

There seemed to be few, if any, attitudes 'too personal for the polls to reach.' At the end of an interview 'most people' asked: 'How do my opinions stack up against the other people's answers?' But nothing in Gallup's account suggests that respondents showed any anxiety about *how* their answers might 'stack up.'

M-O subscribed to another view. Puzzled by an apparent decline, during 1938, in the proportion who told M-O that there would be no war, Harrisson and Madge (1939/1986, p. 53) cautioned that if this is 'what people *say* they think' it could not be assumed that this is 'what they actually think.' In 1940, the year in which *The Pulse of Democracy* was published, Harrisson set out a six-point scale with 'public opinion' at one end and 'private opinion' at the other. Public opinion was 'What a person says to a stranger,' what someone 'would *say out loud to anyone*.' Private opinion was 'What a person says in his sleep.' In between came 'What a person would say to an acquaintance,' or perhaps 'What a person would say to a friend' (weaker forms of public opinion); and 'What a person would say to himself,' or perhaps 'What a person would say to his wife' (weaker forms of private opinion). 'Logically,' he reminded readers, 'a person's "real opinion" is the opinion he holds privately.' A person's willingness to express private views in public depended on a number of things—above all, on how far it was respectable, 'the done thing,' to voice such opinions at that time and in that place (1940, pp. 369ff.; also Mass-Observation, 1943, p. 7).

Unless one grasped the fact that what a person said to a stranger—a journalist, an MP, an interviewer—was not necessarily what that person would say to themselves, one would not be able to anticipate how quickly public opinion might change. The point was easily illustrated by reference to Appeasement. According to the British Institute of Public Opinion (BIPO), Britain's Gallup Poll, from October 1938 until his resignation in May 1940, the public approved Neville Chamberlain's performance as Prime Minister (Gallup, 1976, pp. 9ff.). And with most

MPs and newspapers saying the country was united behind Chamberlain, Harrisson (1940, p. 372) thought support in the polls hardly surprising. However, M-O data showed something quite different. In the darkness of British cinemas, where people could express their private views, 'applause for Mr. Chamberlain, when he appeared on newsreels' fell steadily from September 1939 until the point where, he resigned eight months later. The number of unfavorable comments made in diaries, kept by members of the Panel, showed the same thing (Harrisson, 1940, p. 371). But private opinion could not surface as public opinion because the press had 'made people feel that being anti-Chamberlain was old, anti-social or Socialist.' Moreover, while people felt 'increasingly bewildered, fearful and ashamed' they did not realize that that was how other people also felt (Harrisson & Madge, 1939/1986, pp. 105ff.).

Heirs to Bryce

Shortly before the emergence of opinion polling, Bryce (1923, pp. 262ff.) noted that a new 'stage of democracy would be reached if the will of the majority of the citizens were to be ascertainable at all times,' although he predicted that 'the machinery for weighing or measuring the popular will' was 'not likely to be invented.' But were the machinery to be invented, how did he envisage it operating? 'The best way,' he argued, 'in which the tendencies which are at work in any community may be discovered is by moving freely about among all sorts and conditions of men and noting how they are affected by the news or arguments brought from day to day to their knowledge.' And 'Talk is the best way of reaching the truth, because in talk, one gets directly at the facts' (1921, pp. 175ff.).

Gallup embraced Bryce as a legitimating icon. He accepted Bryce's view about the importance of linking public opinion to democratic government, endorsed his method by which 'the tendencies' might be 'discovered,' and argued that polls embodied the method (Gallup & Rae, 1940, chaps. 2

and 9). But Gallup's claim to Bryce's mantle is not a strong one. Interviewers for Gallup do not know their respondents. They do not know how their fellow citizens 'are affected by the news or arguments brought from day to day to their knowledge' because they hardly ever find out what news or arguments have been brought to their knowledge. And if it lies outside the terms in which a question is asked, what a respondent wishes to convey cannot be recorded (*pace* Gallup, 1944, p. 45); it is either forced into a procrustean bed or discarded.

M-O's entitlement to Bryce's mantle is stronger. Observers were better than interviewers at noting how 'all sorts and conditions of men' were affected by the news or arguments brought from day to day to their knowledge, partly because in many cases they knew something about the people on whom they were reporting (for example, when they were asked to interview family and friends); partly because they could report their findings in the language people actually used via remarks overheard, indirect interviewing or informal interviewing; and partly because they sought to distinguish 'private' opinion from 'public' opinion, and what people did from what they said. If there was something as clear as a majority 'will,' M-O had a better chance than Gallup of detecting it.

EVALUATION

If Harrisson and Madge sought to 'annoy' academic sociologists whom they regarded as 'timid, bookish and unproductive' (Harrisson, 1961, p. 278), and too little focused on how people actually behaved (Madge, 1976), they largely succeeded.

Beyond that, how successful was M-O? To say that its performance was not 'quite commensurate' with its 'early ambitions' (Madge in Harrisson, 1961, p. 280) is an understatement. It didn't get 'the unwritten laws of social behavior' written down, generate 'a new philosophical synthesis,' or fulfill Huxley's dream of a society under 'scientific control' (Madge & Harrison, 1937, p. 6). It didn't succeed in separating the reporting of facts from the attribution of values. Nor did its own practices succeed in subverting hierarchically organized research for research based on democratic control. But, in the context of its time, when 'little serious research was being done in (the then very small) academic circles' (Platt, 1986, pp. 104ff.), what it produced—which included a large number of books, pamphlets and reports (see Harrisson, 1976, pp. 346ff., for one list)—was better, as Calder (1985, pp. 133ff.; 1969/1971, p. 13) and Summerfield (1985, p. 449) observe, and more important, than many of its critics allow.

Sampling and representativeness

A common criticism of M-O is that its data were not necessarily representative of the opinions or practices it was attempting to document or explain (Robinson, 1948, pp. 372ff.; Albig, 1956, p. 128). Observers were not a microcosm of the British public and even if they had been representative in demographic terms, they would not have been representative—as Madge and Harrisson (1938, p. 66) knew—of 'the mass of people who are unobservant and inarticulate.' Samples were often small and their geographical spread limited; generalizations from a single London borough, Metrop, were not unusual (Madge & Harrisson, 1938, p. 52; Harrisson & Madge, 1939/1986; Firth, 1939, pp. 183ff.; Abrams, 1951, p. 107). Gallup's quota sampling, though far from ideal, was a good deal better; so, too, were its sample sizes and their spread.

Nonetheless, M-O's reports were not necessarily misleading. As Calder (1969/1971, p. 13) suggests, while M-O's wartime statistics 'aren't definitive'—'which statistics of that time are?'—'they generally conform, where comparison is possible, with Gallup Polls,' so that 'even if the absolute percentages are too high or too low, the trends and variations must surely be real.' In addition, Summerfield (1985, p. 449) found 'a strong consistency' between M-O's findings and the 'sample–based questionnaire research' undertaken by the Wartime Social Survey.

Nor should we forget that M-O did not always *want* to generalize. Bolton was chosen not because it was 'typical' or 'special,' Harrisson insisted, but 'because it is just a town that exists and persists on the basis of industrial work … where most of our people now earn and spend.' He did not assume 'that Worktown pubs are "typical," any more than Professor Malinowski considers the Trobriand Islands typical' (Mass-Observation, 1943/1987, p. xiv ff.). For much of M-O's work, Sheridan (1996, pp. 2ff.) argues the relevant paradigm may not be the sample survey but the life history.

Quantitative versus qualitative

If sampling was a weakness, the qualitative data M-O generated were a strength. Within its first two years, M-O had 'millions of words' on file (Harrisson & Madge, 1939/1986, p. 217). Ultimately, it accumulated 'more than 1,000 boxes of raw material' (Calder, 1985, p. 124), the diaries alone running to 'about one million pages' (Garfield, 2004, p. 2). Without M-O, important contributions to the social history of the period—including '*Living through the Blitz*' (Harrisson, 1976), 'one of the finest pieces of social research of the period' (Marsh, 1982, p. 33)—would never have been gathered. The 'extremely gripping' account of the Munich crisis, says Calder in *Britain* (1986, p. xi), 'surely provides the first comprehensive and sophisticated account of British public opinion in rapid flux'—an assessment based not on M-O's quantitative, primarily, but on its qualitative work.

Many of the Observers may have been 'untrained,' as sociologists and other critics complained (for example, Abrams, 1951, p. 110), but the 'details' conveyed 'a sense of depth never, surely, attained by any social scientist or reporter before' (Calder, 1986, p. xii). Part of M-O's success lay in its idea of Observers as 'subjective cameras,' with the 'how' of the observation varying between Observers as well as the 'what' (L. Stanley, 2001, p. 95); in that sense, the lack of training may not have been a hindrance but a help.

Though M-O set great store by its qualitative approach it was not 'religiously qualitative' (*pace* Jeffery, 1978, p. 5). Not only did Observers count things, they could be obsessive about it. In Bolton, they counted the number of customers in each pub, each hour of each day, noting the hours in which drinking was heaviest and the rate at which customers drank, and so on (Mass-Observation, 1943/1987). An interest in numbers is also evident in M-O's attempts to report the distribution of opinion in quantitative terms. '[I]nterviewing' may have been 'the least intelligent process in social science' (Harrisson, 1947b), but it didn't stop M-O from using it.

What Harrisson stressed was that science could not be equated with quantitative work or 'the statistical obsession' peculiar to Britain (but see Wootton, 1950, pp. 45ff.); that, as anthropologists knew, scientific work could be replicable even if it was qualitative or used non-standardized instruments (*pace* Bogart, 1972, p. 60); and that qualitative work, as American sociology had shown, allowed 'vertical exploration' of the 'stuff of ordinary living,' not just 'horizontal fieldwork' (Harrisson, 1947a). In this sense M-O did not (*pace* Bulmer, 1985, p. 11) focus on 'externals without an attempt to elicit the meanings attached to action.' Harrisson was a methodological pluralist. A synthesis of both approaches, he argued, was 'long overdue' (Mass-Observation, 1943, pp. 7ff.).

What, then, was his view of Gallup? When Henry Durant, founder of the BIPO, argued that ultimately 'everything' is quantitative, Harrisson responded by saying that while quantitative methods were 'essential,' the 'primary and vital acts of empirical social study must always be qualitative' (Harrison & Durant, 1942, pp. 516ff.). Polls owed their 'increased acceptance' to 'their accuracy in predicting election results.' But voting, he pointed out, was unlike most things the polls sought to measure because most people already knew how they were going to vote. Too often for other questions polls elicited 'respectable' rather than honest answers, or answers that respondents had not really thought about. Some questions, too, were poorly formed—a criticism also leveled at M-O (Firth, 1939, p. 191; Calder, 1985, pp. 133ff.)—or the answers an artifact of how the questions were asked. Moreover, the press was prone to over-interpret the results (Harrisson, 1947d).

Validity

Defending M-O from its competitors in market research after the war, Bob Willcock (1947) argued that if the 'verbal statements' of 'a sample which is a perfect microcosm of the population … consist largely of truisms and the repetition of socially respectable opinions and attitudes,' it 'reflects only the topmost level of social talk. An imperfect sample which tells the "truth" provides data of far greater objective value than a perfect sample which skims the surface of safe conversation.'

One of M-O's most important claims was to be able to distinguish between 'private' opinion and 'public' opinion. But both the distinction and the way the relationship is supposed to work are problematic. First, the distinction between private and public is tangled up with the distinction between sincere, partly sincere and insincere. There might well be private views that people are prepared to confide to an interviewer in part or in whole (public and sincere) that they are not prepared to confide to their friends, or if prepared to confide to their friends then not prepared to confide to their partners; indeed, they may even dissemble about them (private and insincere). Part of the way around this would be to deny that responding to a poll-taker is a public rather than a private act; certainly, it seems odd to equate it, as Harrisson (1940, pp. 374ff.) does, with talking anonymously to an interviewer with '*what you will say out loud to anyone.*' But of course this way around the problem would undermine one of Harrisson's key points.

Second, the conditions under which 'private' opinions go 'public' are not always clear. For example, when Harrisson, in 1944, used the reaction of cinema audiences to Stanley Baldwin to predict that Churchill would lose in 1945, he did not explain what change at the public level would allow this 'private' opinion to come to the fore. (Nor, even more basically, did he say what is 'public' about a secret ballot.)

Third, the rules for establishing the effect of 'social expectations' (assumed to be uniform) on public opinion are never made clear. While it is relatively easy to check, say, men's claims about shaving with a new blade every day against sales for blades (Willcock, 1947)—that is, the difference between how people describe their behavior to an interviewer and how they actually behave—and to see whether any over-reporting is consistent with some of their number conforming to the 'socially acceptable,' it is usually very difficult to see whether people's stated beliefs are the same as their actual beliefs. In what he supposes is a straightforward illustration of the difference, Harrisson (1940, p. 373) notes that the day before conscription was introduced in 1939, Gallup reported 39% in favor of it and 53% against; a week later the figures were reversed, 58:38. The turnaround, he insists, demonstrates the force of the 'socially done thing.' But does it? What of the possibility of a turnaround not because private opinion, suddenly legitimized, went public but because private opinion shifted in response to a change in public policy? Even if respondents saw support for conscription as 'the socially done thing,' no evidence for it is offered.

DEMISE

Why did M-O fade while Gallup went on to flourish? One reason is that M-O, built around an 'underlying contradiction' between the approach favored by Harrisson and that favored by Madge, gradually lost its key personnel. How to characterize this 'contradiction' is itself a matter of dispute. Towards the end of his life Harrisson described it as a conflict between his commitment to science and objectivity and Madge's commitment to poetry and subjectivity (Harrisson, 1976, p. 11f.). Madge, looking back, described

it in terms of his own fealty to science versus Harrisson's flirtation with politics and personal power (Madge, 1987, p. 71, 115).

Another reason for the effective demise of M-O was the changes rung by the war. As Harrisson noted in *Living through the Blitz* (1976, p. 11), M-O had originated 'as a several-pronged reaction to the disturbed condition of Western Europe under the growing threat of fascism'; the defeat of Germany brought this to an end. M-O was also a reaction to a sense that working people were being ignored; the election of a Labour Government in 1945 may have changed that, too (Summerfield, 1985, p. 450). Before the war, M-O had depended on a few benefactors, generous advances from Victor Gollancz for four books on Bolton and Blackpool—on the pub, religion, politics and the non-voter, and leisure (N. Stanley, 1981, p. 9)—only one of which was ultimately published, and subscriptions to its newsletter. At the beginning of the war, contracts with the Ministry of Defence were a considerable boon; contracts with the NIESR and with the Advertising Services Guild also helped. After the war, only the connection with the ASG survived. Under these circumstances, it became increasingly difficult to resist the pressures and temptations of orthodox market research.

The Gallup poll, by contrast, had always been geared to the needs of the press. What Gallup and similar organizations had to offer, and what the press was prepared to finance, were answers to questions on topical issues, presented in the form of news: answers to questions asked in simple, even simplistic, ways—typically in binary form, modeled on referenda, about things on which respondents may or may not have had views; answers to questions in the news—often on issues the press had helped turn into news; and answers to questions whose exact form, if not determined by the press was heavily influenced by it (Gallup, 1944, p. 39). When Gallup (1947) proposed a 'new system' of polling—the 'quintamensional' method, two 'open' and three 'closed' questions on every issue—Mass-Observation (1948) welcomed it. But there was never any prospect of the press underwriting the method, because the cost of asking questions that way and the space it would take to report the results made it impractical. As polls and public opinion became synonymous, M-O's fate as originally conceived was finally sealed.

CONCLUSION

M-O's 'heroic' period ran from January 1937 to June 1940; after Madge's departure, 'the pretensions of M-O to maintain a pioneering experiment cannot be sustained' (N. Stanley, 1981, p. 15, p. 24; but cf. Harrisson, 1976, p. 12). Its second period, when it worked for government and commercial interests and increasingly responded to criticisms 'in the terms set by their critics' (Finch, 1986, p. 100), ended in 1949. Yet even as he boasted that some of its major work now contained 'little else but the results of questionnaires,' M-O's last Managing Director insisted there had been 'no change of basic policy' and that it stood 'unreservedly by its original principles' (England, 1949, p. 592). Nonetheless, from 1949, when it became Mass-Observation Ltd, it was largely indistinguishable from other firms doing market research. Len England (1949–1950), now director of the newly incorporated body, even concurred with Gallup that, interviewed by strangers, respondents were prepared to be remarkably open about their attitudes to sex.

In Britain, M-O's 'greatest significance in the history of social science,' Calder (1985, p. 122) concludes, was 'that its reputation accustomed people to the idea that ... surveys should be taken seriously.' M-O contributed 'powerfully,' if ironically, 'to growing public acceptance of the usefulness of sample polls' (Calder 1986, p. x). The irony is not that M-O had no use for opinion; the view that M-O focused on 'behaviors' not on 'opinions or thoughts' and that Harrison in particular focused on public behavior not private opinion (L. Stanley, 2001, pp. 95ff.) is mistaken. Rather, the irony is that a critic of the polls should be

thought of as someone who helped secure their future.

What was distinctive about M-O was not its ability to predict but its ability to explain— 'to get at beliefs, opinions and motives for action' (N. Stanley, 1981, p. 234): in the case of Churchill's defeat, its ability to explain why people wanted a change (Harrisson, 1944); in relation to the Wartime Social Survey, its ability to explain why women were or were not willing to undertake wartime work (Summerfield, 1985, p. 450). With 'an ear for the fluid, ambiguous, contradictory character of popular attitudes' (Hinton, 1997, p. 269), M-O distinguished differences of meaning among respondents in the polls who said 'don't know' or 'don't care' (Mass-Observation, 1948), and differences in tone or certainty among those voicing their 'approval' or 'disapproval' (Harrisson, 1947c).

Indirectly its contribution went a good deal further. Its 'assertion that you did not need to be an expert in order to take part in the study of society, or in writing your own history, prefigured the claims of the ... radical social movements of the late 1960s and 1970s, including black activism and feminism' (Sheridan, 1996, p. 9). Its monthly bulletins (Madge & Harrisson, 1937, p. 41) can be seen as an early form of what Rosen (1999) calls 'public journalism.' And M-O anticipated 'by some two decades, the first large stirrings of "serious" interest in popular culture' (Calder, 1986, p. xii; see also, Johnson, 1979, p. 43), partly through its ploughing into areas 'rarely touched by earlier academic students of society' (Abrams, 1951, p. 106), and partly through its use of 'oral history' that was 'little practiced then,' but 'commonplace now' (Calder, 1986, p. xii).

More broadly, M-O's legacy ranged from pioneering work on the 'economics of everyday life' to the development of a 'surrealist ethnography' (L. Stanley, 2001). It was an 'important precursor' (Marsh, 1982, p. 33) to the systematic social observation method pioneered by Reiss (1968, 1971). Its shadow lies across the development of social research based on 'unobtrusive measures'

(Webb, Campbell, Schwartz, & Sechrest, 1966, chap. 5). Recent work on 'observational research,' where manufacturers go out and talk with customers while observing their behavior, is consistent with M-O's approach, though Becker's (1967/1971) rediscovery of 'immersion research' was more profound. And the development of discussion groups, where opinions about issues are discussed *not* among strangers—as they are in most focus groups—but among people who know one another and are asked to discuss a topic rather than answer a set of questions, and where the researcher sits in the background (Mackay, 1983), is redolent of M-O as well. In sum, the 'combination of quantification and interpretative analysis of qualitative material,' said by Lazarsfeld in 1971 to be at 'the forefront of the research fraternity's interest' (Jahoda, Lazarsfeld, & Zeisel, 1933/1971, p. xii), had been pioneered in Britain by M-O long before.

Like Gallup, M-O thought 'the people' ought to be heard, even if neither Gallup nor M-O was entirely clear about how they spoke, the extent to which they should be heeded, or particularly mindful of the distinction between public opinion as a means of popular empowerment and public opinion as a means of strengthening elite control. But if Gallup and M-O were both populists, they were populists of very different stripes. Gallup distrusted all inferences about public opinion based on electoral outcomes, sought to challenge the claims about public opinion advanced by 'strident minorities,' and in particular established a pattern of polling weighted against organized labor (Gallup & Rae, 1940, pp. 149ff.; Kornhauser, 1946). By contrast, M-O (like Bryce) sometimes maintained that an election was the way of determining public opinion (Harrisson & Madge, 1939/1986, p. 44 but cf. p. 107); and though 'politically ill-defined' (Jeffery, 1999, p. vii), practised a kind of radicalism that placed it to the left of Gallup. Above all, while Gallup and M-O wanted 'the people' to be heard they had very different views of what one had to do to hear them.

ACKNOWLEDGMENTS

Research costs and writing time were funded by grants from the Australian Research Council, DP0559334, and the Macquarie University Research Development Grant Scheme. I am also grateful to Kylie Brass, Mick Counihan, Uwe Hartung, Marion Orchison, Vicky Paine and the staff of the Mass-Observation Archive at the University of Sussex for assistance with the research, and to Mike Traugott for helping to compress what was originally a more extensive account.

REFERENCES

Abrams, M. (1951). *Social surveys and social action.* London: William Heinemann.

Albig, W. (1956). *Modern public opinion.* New York: McGraw-Hill.

Becker, H. S. (1971). Whose side are we on? In H. S. Becker (Ed.), *Sociological work: Method and substance* (pp. 123–134). New Brunswick, N.J.: Transaction Books. (Original work published 1967)

Bogart, L. (1972). *Silent politics: Polls and the awareness of public opinion.* New York: Wiley-Interscience.

Bryce, J. (1921). *The American commonwealth.* (Vol. 1). New York: Macmillan.

Bryce, J. (1923). *The American commonwealth* (new ed., Vol. 2). New York: Macmillan.

Bulmer, M. (1985). The development of sociology and of empirical social research in Britain. In M. Bulmer (Ed.), *Essays on the history of British sociological thought* (pp. 3–36). Cambridge: Cambridge University Press.

Calder, A. (1971). *The people's war: Britain 1939–45* (2nd ed.). London: Panther. (Original work published 1969)

Calder, A. (1985). Mass-observation 1937–1949. In M. Bulmer (Ed.), *Essays on the history of British sociological thought* (pp. 121–136). Cambridge: Cambridge University Press.

Calder, A. (1986). Introduction to the Cresset Library edition. In T. Harrisson & C. Madge (Eds.) (1939/1986), *Britain by mass-observation.* London: The Cresset Library.

Cross, G. (Ed.). (1990). *Worktowners at Blackpool: Mass-observation and popular leisure in the 1930s.* London: Routledge.

England, L. R. (1949). Progress in mass-observation: An internal view. *International Journal of Opinion and Attitude Research, 3,* 591–595.

England, L. R. (1949–1950). Little Kinsey: An outline of sex attitudes in Britain. *Public Opinion Quarterly, 13,* 587–600.

Finch, J. (1986). *Research and policy: The uses of qualitative methods in social and educational research.* Lewes, East Sussex: The Falmer Press.

Firth, R. (1939). An anthropologist's view of mass observation. *Sociological Review, XXXI*(2), 166–193.

Gallup, G. (1944). *A guide to public opinion polls.* Princeton: Princeton University Press.

Gallup, G. (1947). The quintamensional plan of question design. *Public Opinion Quarterly, 11,* 385–393.

Gallup, G.H. (Ed.). (1976). *The Gallup international public opinion polls: Great Britain, 1937–1975* (Vol. 1, 1937–1964). New York: Random House.

Gallup, G., & Rae, S. F. (1940). *The pulse of democracy: The public-opinion poll and how it works.* New York: Simon and Schuster.

Garfield, S. (2004). *Our hidden lives: The everyday diaries of a forgotten Britain 1945–1948.* London: Ebury Press.

Harrisson, T. (1940). What is public opinion? *Political Quarterly, XI,* 368–383.

Harrisson, T. (1944). Who'll win? *Political Quarterly, 15,* 210–219.

Harrisson, T. (1947a). The future of British sociology. *International Journal of Opinion and Attitude Research, 1,* 47–62 (reprinted from *Pilot Papers, 2*(1), 10–25).

Harrisson, T. (1947b). A British view of 'cheating.' *Public Opinion Quarterly, 11,* 172–173.

Harrisson, T. (1947c). British opinion moves toward a new synthesis. *Public Opinion Quarterly, 11,* 327–341.

Harrisson, T. (1947d). Galluping consumption. *Fabian Quarterly, March,* 1–4.

Harrisson, T. (1961) *Britain revisited.* London: Victor Gollancz.

Harrisson, T. (1976) *Living through the blitz.* London: Collins.

Harrisson, T., & Durant, H. (1942, May 9). Quantitative and qualitative method in sociological research. *Nature, No. 3784,* 516–518.

Harrisson, T., & Madge, C. (1986). *Britain by mass-observation.* London: The Cresset Library. (Original work published 1939)

Hinton, J. (1997). 1945 and the Apathy school. *History Workshop Journal, 43,* 266–273.

Jahoda, M., Lazarsfeld, P. F., & Zeisel, H. (1971). *Marienthal: The sociography of an unemployed community.* Chicago: Aldine-Atherton. (Original work published 1933)

Jeffery, T. (1978). *Mass observation–A short history.* (Stencilled Occasional Paper No. 55). Birmingham: Centre for Contemporary Cultural Studies.

Jeffery, T. (1999). *Mass observation: A short history* (new ed., Occasional Paper No. 10). Mass-Observation Archive: University of Sussex.

Jennings, H., & Madge, C. (Eds.). (1987). *May the twelfth: Mass-observation day-surveys 1937.* London: Faber & Faber. (Original work published 1937)

Johnson, R. (1979). Culture and the historians. In J. Clarke, C. Critcher & R. Johnson, (Eds.), *Working class culture: Studies in history and theory* (pp. 41–71). London: Hutchinson in association with the Centre for Contemporary Cultural Studies.

Kornhauser, A. (1946). Are public opinion polls fair to organised labor? *Public Opinion Quarterly, 10,* 484–500.

Mackay, H. (1983). *Reinventing Australia.* Pymble, NSW: Angus & Robertson.

Madge, C. (1976, November 5). The birth of mass-observation. *Times Literary Supplement,* p. 1395.

Madge, C. (1987). Ts draft of CM's autobiography sent to and returned by the literary agent John Farquharson. ff.278. Special Collections. The Library, University of Sussex.

Madge, C., & Harrisson, T. (1937). *Mass-observation.* London: Frederick Muller.

Madge, C., & Harrisson, T. (Eds.). (1938). *First year's work 1937–1938 by mass-observation.* London: Lindsay Drummond.

Marsh, C. (1982). *The survey method: The contribution of surveys to sociological explanation.* London: George Allen & Unwin.

Mass-Observation (1987). *The pub and the people.* Introduction by Tom Harrisson. London: The Cresset Library. (Original work published 1943)

Mass-Observation (1943). *War factory: A report.* London: Victor Gollancz.

Mass-Observation (1944). *The journey home: A report prepared by Mass-Observation for the Advertising Services Guild.* London: John Murray.

Mass-Observation (1948). Don't know, don't care. In A. G. Wiedenfeld (Ed.), *The adventure ahead.* London: Contact Publications.

Mass-Observation (1949). *The press and its readers: A report prepared by Mass-Observation for the advertising service guild.* London: Art & Technics.

Noelle-Neumann, E. (1974). The spiral of silence: A theory of public opinion. *Journal of Communication, 24,* 43–51.

Platt, J. (1986). Qualitative research for the state. *Quarterly Journal of Social Affairs, 2*(2), 87–108.

Reiss, A. J. (1968). Stuff and nonsense about social surveys and observation. In H. S. Becker, B. Geer, D. Riesman, & R. S. Weiss (Eds.), *Institutions and the person* (pp. 351–367). Chicago: Aldine.

Reiss, A. J. (1971). Systematic observation of natural social phenomena. In H. Costner (Ed.), *Sociological methodology* (pp. 1–33). San Francisco: Jossey Bass.

Robinson, R. (1948). Progress in mass-observation. *International Journal of Opinion and Attitude Research, 2*, 371–378.

Rosen, J. (1999). *What are journalists for?* New Haven: Yale University Press.

Sheridan, D. (1996). *Damned anecdotes and dangerous confabulations: Mass-observation as life history.* Occasional Paper No. 7, Mass-Observation Archive, University of Sussex Library.

Stanley, L. (2001). Mass-observation's fieldwork methods. In P. Atkinson, A. Coffey, S. Delamont, & J. Lofland (Eds.), *Handbook of ethnology* (pp. 92–108). London: Sage.

Stanley, N. S. (1981). The extra dimension: A study and assessment of the methods employed by Mass-Observation in its first period 1937–1940. Doctoral dissertation. Department of Sociology and Applied Social Studies, Birmingham Polytechnic.

Summerfield, P. (1985). Mass-Observation: Social research or social movement? *Journal of Contemporary History, XX*, 429–452.

Webb, E. J., Campbell, D. T., Schwartz, R. D., & Sechrest, L. (1966). *Unobtrusive measures: Nonreactive research in the social sciences.* Chicago: Rand McNally.

Willcock, H. D. (1947). Mass-Observation. Draft for handout, 30.1.47. In Polls apart. Unpublished Manuscript. Mass-Observation Archive, University of Sussex.

Wootton, B. (1950). *Testament for social science.* London: George Allen & Unwin.

10

The Start of Modern Public Opinion Research

Hans L. Zetterberg

For centuries, elite opinions have been gauged by messengers or spies, or by searching letters, diaries, or pamphlets. Opinions of illiterate masses, to the extent they were not totally ignored, had been gauged by thumbs ups or thumbs downs in local stadiums and rinks. Countrywide public opinion polling of the general population by statistical methods has a shorter history. It is a child of the American newspaper world, born in the 1930s. In this chapter, we meet the launching actors, their ideas about the nature and use of opinion reporting, and their methods of researching opinions. We sketch the expansion of opinion research into the universities, and its worldwide expansion after World War II.

OPINION POLLS: A NEW FEATURE IN JOURNALISM

The founding fathers: George Gallup and Elmo Roper

The previous half century before the launch of opinion polls in the 1930s had seen a tremendous increase in the number of newspapers and their circulation and advertising revenues. The journalistic contents of the papers had changed from dealing exclusively with news to an increasing involvement with features. Features in American newspapers had begun as comic strips, special pages for sports and entertainment, fashion, holiday travel, religious sermons, serialized novels, and the like. European newspapermen had long thought that such features degraded journalism and diverted it from the task of delivering the news. But the readers wanted features; circulations increased, advertising space and revenue increased, and increased income allowed the papers to do a more far-reaching and cavernous journalistic job.

In this positive spiral, opinion polls became a late addition to the line of features in the media. Independently of one another, two Midwesterners of the United States, Elmo Roper (1900–1971) and George H. ('Ted') Gallup (1902–1984), who had both come to the New York area to do market research, became the pioneers of featuring opinion polls in mass media.

In 1933, Elmo Roper co-founded one of the first market research firms, Cherington, Wood, and Roper. He started Fortune Surveys in 1935 and remained its director until 1950. He polled for one single publication, the business magazine *Fortune*. He had journalistic talents and civic concerns. He became an editor-at-large for the *Saturday Review,* a magazine for culture, science and politics, which also carried polls and commentaries based on polls. Roper was promoter of many causes: among them the Urban League, Fund for the Republic, and Planned Parenthood. A lasting contribution is his social science data archive, the Roper Center for Public Opinion Research at Williams College, founded in 1946. It started as a depository for his surveys and those of Gallup. Later located at the University of Connecticut, the Roper Center is the world's largest repository of polling data, with collections from numerous organizations and many countries beginning in the 1930s to the present.

George H. Gallup got his Ph.D. in psychology with the thesis 'An objective method for determining reader interest in the content of a newspaper.' He found that more readers preferred comics to the front page, and feature stories to news. Gallup became head of the journalism department at Drake University (1929–1931), professor of journalism and advertising at Northwestern University outside Chicago (1931–1932), and visiting professor at the Pulitzer School of Journalism, Columbia University in the City of New York (1935–1937). A research piece at Northwestern that showed how men and women differently rated appeals in advertisements in terms of economy, efficiency, sex, vanity, and quality changed Gallup's career. It caught the attention of Ray Rubicam, the rising advertising star, who asked Gallup to establish a research department, the first of its kind, in his advertising agency Young & Rubicam in New York. This private research house became a more congenial and supportive structure to Gallup's interests than the research opportunities in the university world, where departments of social science still generally lacked research facilities. He remained affiliated with Young & Rubicam as vice president while also pursuing his university teaching and starting small businesses of his own. In 1935, he created The American Institute of Public Opinion. He did not deliver his write-ups of polling results directly to any paper. He had a partner in Chicago, Harold Anderson, who ran Publisher-Hall Syndicate, a business providing papers with editorial material. Gallup furnished Anderson with a new and unique product that no one else in his line of business had. Anderson loved the Gallup material and marketed it with enthusiasm. He offered it in the first place to the biggest paper in each city. At best over 200 papers subscribed to the Gallup releases.

These pioneering pollsters developed two different research products for the media: issue polls and electoral polls.

Issue polls as a social innovation

Issue polls deal with the public's concerns, political or non-political. Of course, the early pollsters did not think that politicians were constitutionally bound to follow public opinion as revealed in polls, but they felt that they were morally obliged to pay attention. They believed in the populist rhetoric of the American Revolution. In a democracy, the people constitute the ruling class. In a democracy, politicians are the servants of the people, not their lords. The source and legitimacy of political actions and programs were found in the general public. Gallup, in particular, believed that the public's views were loaded with political wisdom, and that a poll was the key to unlock it (Gallup & Rae, 1940).

Elmo Roper's first national poll was published in July 1935. The country and the rest of the world were then in the middle of the Great Depression. His interview question was one of considerable interest to anyone who wanted to prepare for an end of the depression: 'If you get more money this year, what will you spend it for first?' The answers showed a concern to restore personal finances: 13.7% wanted to save the money; their savings had obviously been drained during the Depression. An almost equal number wanted to use the money to repay debts. But the relatively highest number of the respondents (14.4%) wanted to buy clothes. This priority, heavily loaded with a need to improve the presentation of self to others, beat the more material concerns such as house repairs, furniture, automobiles, and also travel. It overwhelmed the need to spend the extra money on food, a need which had figured prominently in the comments on the state of the nation during the Great Depression. All this was more than a human-interest story; it helped commercial planning in the business community, the readers of *Fortune*.

George Gallup produced fortnightly nation-wide opinion polls, which were reported in newspaper columns with the bold logo 'America Speaks.' The first one appeared on October 20, 1935, three months after Roper's first release. It dealt with the spending of Roosevelt's New Deal program to cope with the Depression. The question asked was: 'Do you think expenditures by the government for relief and recovery are too little, too great, or about right?' The answers: 60% said 'too great,' 31% said 'about right,' and 9% said 'too little.' Dr. Gallup signed his press releases with his name, a fact that made most people talk about the 'Gallup Poll' rather than 'The American Institute of Public Opinion,' or, 'America Speaks.'

The issues of the first Roper and Gallup polls grew out of the Great Depression. A critical task in all public opinion polling on issues is the choice of topics for the questionnaire. It is important to ask questions revealing the public's concerns, and not only questions that interest the pollsters or their editors or sponsors. Gallup solved this problem in the late 1930s by regularly asking: 'What is the most important problem facing the country today?' He did not want to define all issues by himself, or to have his editors take all the initiatives. In the ideal issue poll, his respondents, the general public, should have the main say in defining the issues! Their

views on the issues should be known to the public and to the leaders of the public through the media without any filters or restrictions. The full measure of Gallup's contribution is not only a scientific application of sampling, interviewing, and calculation of percentages of responses, but a *social innovation*, that is, polling *of* the public, on the issues defined *by* the public, *for* the benefit of the public (Gallup & Rae, 1940).

Gallup did not want to poll for interest groups. In fact he regarded his poll as an anti-dote to the influence of organized interests in his country's politics. His collaborator Claude Robinson thought it would be good business to sell opinion research to interest groups. The conflict was resolved by launching a separate company, Opinion Research Corporation, to serve pressure groups but not the mass media. Shortly after it got underway, Gallup left it to Robinson. It is to the credit of Gallup's sons and heirs, Alec and George Jr., that during their ownership of the family poll they continued this rather unique policy of polling integrity.

As issue polls by pollsters grew in numbers, they changed the meaning of 'public opinion.' Prior to the work of Roper and Gallup, public opinion on an issue was an informed summary formulated in ordinary language about the views of some of those who had made their opinions heard. In the view of MacKinnon (1828/1971), who published the first book in English with the title *Public Opinion*, it was the opinions of the best informed and honorable. Or, in the view of Lowell (1913), a political scientist who became president of Harvard University and who also influenced the scholars of the Chicago School of Sociology, it was opinions emerging in lasting and functioning 'publics' that had such a density that the participants could talk and argue about a common issue so that everyone's view became known and influenced by everyone else's view. Or, in the view of Lippmann (1922) and others, public opinion was the degree of consensus that could be distilled from public speeches, editorial comments, pamphlets, and publications ($\rightarrow$ *The Public and Public*

Opinion in Political Theories, → *Advocacy: Alternative Expressions of Public Opinion*). After the advent and spread of issue polling, public opinion was a mathematical expression of frequencies of views of representatives of all in a population and their demographic subgroups, both those who had expressed their opinion in public and those who had not.

The volume of opinion research grew. The Rockefeller Foundation provided Princeton University with the funds for a first volume about all opinion findings between 1935 and 1946 from the United States and from other countries with established polls (Cantril & Strunk, 1951). The polled topics were cat-alogued by the system used by the Library of Congress. The large number of categories invoked in the issue polls demonstrated that public opinion research fits the study of popular art, science and education, religion and morality, family life and household living, health and sports—all this in addition to the many issues that had to do with policy making and legislation. From the start it thus became clear that opinion research was much more than a branch of political science. The work on this catalog was carried out by Mildred Strunk. It got 'greater proportions than we originally envisaged,' said Professor Hadley Cantril—the project was his initiative—in his preface to the volume of 1191 over-sized, densely printed pages (ibid.). By 1946, the world thus had seen about 17,500 polls. No one has made a detailed tabulation of all the topics. A sample tabulation shows that about 11,000 were issue polls conducted in the United States between 1935 and 1946. In the following years, polling activities expanded so much that it became inconceivable to continue the project to reprint and classify all findings.

Electoral polls

Regular polls between elections show the level of support for a government and opposition and/or the public's confidence in elected leaders. Here we deal, of course, with polling in the realm of political science.

In 1936 Gallup had 20 newspapers sub-scribing to his column. He promised he would refund their money if he did not predict the results of the 1936 election more accurately than the then well-established magazine *Literary Digest*, which used to tell its readers how elections were going by mailing millions of questionnaires to people whose names and addresses were obtained from the phone book and automobile registry. In the 1936 election, *The Digest* had reported that Roosevelt would lose, 56% to 44%. Many pundits agreed: Roosevelt seemed helpless to stop the Great Depression, too free-spending (as Gallup himself had shown), too controversial not only in the business community, but in the broad middle classes. Gallup's quota sample included 3,000 people who answered his mail ballot. It was better designed than that of the *Digest*, whose questionnaire—despite its huge numbers—was far from being representative due to the correlations between the socio-economic status of the population, since it was based on car and telephone owners and party preferences (Squire, 1988). Gallup also had an advantage in that he used information from a question in his questionnaire on how his respondents had voted in the previous presidential election 1932. With this information, he could balance his piles of questionnaires from the field by comparing his counts with the official statistics of Republican and Democrat votes four years earlier.

On Election Day, Roosevelt's Republican opponent, Al Landon, won a total of two states. Roosevelt swept the rest of the nation, the greatest landslide to that date in American presidential history. Electoral polls thus became established in the United States with a bang. They have no constitutional consequences, but they have nevertheless become an integral part of the electoral process. They are particularly relevant to politicians toward the end of their terms in office when they face re-election. Polls on electoral standing are a helpful part of the mental and practical preparation for the peaceful transition from one government to another that is a *sine qua non* in democracy.

Many governing politicians feel that they deserve to continue in office until they reach the limit set by a constitution, incapacity, or death. Without the early warning of electoral polls, the transition from one government to another would be less orderly and more susceptible to chaotic and emotional episodes.

THE METHODS OF THE EARLY POLLSTERS

The first polls in the United States in the 1930s—including the 1936 election studies—used mail ballots. Face-to-face and in-home interviewing became the rule when polling began in earnest after the 1936 success.

The pioneers had to create a new occupation, that of the survey interviewer. It took more than a decade and much publicity to accustom the American public to survey interviewers. He, or more often she, is a stranger who assumes and normally is given the right to ask and record other people's views. The stranger is a well-known sociological type, first analyzed by Georg Simmel (1923, pp. 509–512), who showed that often you can tell a stranger something that you do not readily tell a neighbor. The first cadres of interviewers were strangers to their employer as well. They were recruited by mail and trained by a one-shot correspondence course.

Gallup's organization in Princeton, New Jersey was a small business, but it became as important as an ancient Greek temple, consulted by the lords of the day. It had four supporting pillars. Three were the outside pillars, in charge of communication with the outside world. The center outside pillar was the tall broad-shouldered George H. Gallup. He was eventually flanked by his sons Alec and George, Jr., who grew to be active promoters of the family name and business. The solid inside pillar was Paul K. Perry, head of the temple servants in charge of the rites of opinion research. They transformed Dr. Gallup's questions, first into finished and pre-tested questionnaires sent

to the interviewers, and then returned them completed. In the office, they were then converted into statistical tables of opinions. In the last step, Gallup himself wrote and signed the press releases. Here then was the twentieth century Delphi oracle, which also in its days had had a network of informants from all over the known world, whose messages were used to cook advice for the rulers of those days.

Paul Perry was one of Gallup's six original employees. An economist by training, he learned additional statistics from friends at Princeton University and became chief statistician and later president of the Gallup Organization. He and his colleagues counted questionnaires by hand for over a year until an IBM counter-sorter was installed. He organized the switch from mail questionnaires to face-to-face interviews used in the 1940 election. He took part in setting up a field team and an interview recruitment and training program. The instructions he wrote were copied by several of the emerging pollsters in Europe and Australia. After the 1948 election, Perry aided Gallup, as the first commercial survey organization, to adopt nationwide probability sampling. In the 1950s, he devised two standard ingredients for all election research: a scale to identify likely voters, and a method to allocate undecided voters to candidates. He also tested the use of secret ballots in election research so that the respondents would not openly have to reveal their political preference to the interviewer. All this was done with the support and inspiration of Dr. Gallup, who rightly let Perry publish the work in professional journals in his own name, for example, his description of the Gallup methodology of the late 1950s (Perry, 1960).

SURVEY METHODOLOGY SPREADS

Entering the universities

During and after World War II, several American colleges and universities began to give courses in public opinion.

Advanced analysis of surveys originated in facilities at several universities, the most well known being The Bureau of Applied Social Research at Columbia University. Only two universities—Chicago and Michigan—also developed fieldwork services with national interviewing staffs.

These academic centers conducted mission-oriented social research on a contractual basis. Their main clients were government agencies and foundations. They served the ideals of science, not the ideals of journalism. Thus they published primarily to establish priority of discovery within the scholarly community. They have shown less interest in Gallup's social innovation to poll the public, on the issues defined by the public, for the benefit of the public.

Harry H. Field, a British-born salesman, introduced to surveys by George Gallup at Young and Rubicam's research department, established the National Opinion Research Center (NORC) at the University of Denver. He hired his sampling statistician and field supervisor from Gallup in Princeton. The latter was instructed to see to it that all interviewers were personally contacted and evaluated, a mark of improved research quality. NORC soon moved to the University of Chicago. During World War II, NORC was contracted to serve as the operational arm of the survey division of the Office of War Information (OWI), which regularly reported on civilian morale and public attitudes to war-related issues, such as regulations and shortages. The survey division of OWI was headed by Elmo C. ('Bud') Wilson, another Midwestern journalist who had been a senior researcher at *Time Magazine* and was trained in survey work by Elmo Roper.

NORC did social research on health, education, housing, labor relations, and other areas of public policy interest. It conducted the first major study of public attitudes toward mental illness. In 1972, it started its regular General Social Survey (GSS), which follows indicators in many aspects of American society. The GSS has continued into the twenty-first century.

In 1946, the University of Michigan established *The Survey Research Center (SRC)* as part of its existing Institute of Social Research (ISR). Its founder, Rensis Likert, like most of the other pioneers in opinion research, was a Midwesterner. But unlike them, he had no involvement with journalism. His Ph.D. thesis in psychology from Columbia University dealt with a simplification of the then prevailing method to measure attitudes developed by L. L. Thurstone. Likert's five-point scale eventually replaced Thurstone's more cumbersome method of paired comparisons in academic attitude research.

In the first half of the 1940s, Likert worked for the US Department of Agriculture as head of the Division of Program Surveys. It used interview surveys among farmers to evaluate many of the department's programs. During the war, this organization was called upon to broaden its activities beyond agriculture; among other things it studied the public's willingness to buy war bonds. Likert gathered in his division a creative team of young social scientists, including Angus Campbell, Charles Cannell, George Katona, and Leslie Kish. Together, they began developing their own routines for interviewing, for coding questionnaires with open-ended questions, and new applications of scaling responses, for example, on consumer confidence.

Likert and his staff also developed a routine to sample households in a country without a national register of inhabitants or dwellings by dividing the country into small geographical areas. These maps were stratified and sampled and the households in each selected area were enumerated. Interviewers were randomly assigned households to visit and interview. The procedure became known as 'area probability sampling' ($\rightarrow$ *Sampling*). Leslie Kish was the master sampler on Likert's staff.

SRC was successful in attracting grants to study numerous emerging issues such as drug abuse, pollution, and poverty, as well as major grants for election research. Its monthly opinion poll on consumer confidence—developed by Georg Katona—became one of the leading business cycle indicators of the

US Department of Commerce. It developed the nation's largest program offering a Ph.D. in survey methodology. It has a summer training program in survey research and analysis with students from all over the world. By the turn of the century, SRC had become the home of the widely cited World Values Surveys, coordinated by Ronald Inglehart.

NORC and SRC differed originally from one another in that NORC had a founder and key staff members with roots in the Gallup/Roper tradition of polling for journalism. SRC, with its roots in the Washington bureaucracy, remained divorced from this tradition. One might say that SRC successfully created its own world of opinion research. It got its counterpart to the Roper Center in a data archive of its own, the Inter-University Consortium for Political and Social Research. Since the middle of the 1950s, SRC has also initiated and participated in many international surveys. It was consulted about the establishment of survey research centers in Europe, Latin America, India, South Africa, and China.

Entering other continents

After World War II, more polls surfaced among the victorious and neutral powers. The defeated countries, Germany and Japan, also got hands-on demonstrations of the methodology of American survey practice in the 'bombing surveys' conducted by the occupation powers to assess the effects their mass bombing had had on their civilian life and morale.

The men and women who took national opinion polling from the United States to their native countries deserve a book of their own. They were great personalities who combined entrepreneurial, writing, media, social and scientific skills. Many also became public personalities in their home countries, just as Roper and Gallup had become in the United States. Some like Elisabeth Noelle-Neumann in Germany and Sten Hultgren in Sweden were journalists when they started polling. One was already

a professor when he discovered polling: Italy's Pierpaolo Luzzato-Fegiz. Several became professors after they had started polling, as did Jean Stoetzel at the Sorbonne and Elisabeth Noelle-Neumann at the University of Mainz. Henry Durant, the father figure of public opinion polling in Great Britain, came right out of the London School of Economics. So did Björn Balstad of Norway, inventor of the omnibus survey that saved the financing of private polling when the newspaper market changed to one-city-one-paper. Two or three of the early pollsters of the world came from the overseas marketing departments of large US corporations, as did Arturi Raula in Finland. Many others had their backgrounds in market research, public relations and advertising agencies.

In addition, outside the United States it was common that commercial polling of opinions became established before academic institutions and government agencies became regular practitioners of opinion research. An exception is Israel, where academic polling got a superior start through Louis Guttman, an American immigrant who had been at Cornell University and took a new position at the Hebrew University in Jerusalem. In 1947, he started the Israel Institute of Applied Social Research, where he continued his research into the sophisticated scaling of opinions originally published in *The American Soldier*, the summary of social research conducted on the armed forces of the United States in World War II.

In 1947, Dr. Gallup and his French and English colleagues, Jean Stoetzel and Henry Durant, called an international conference of 14 polling organizations. They met in Loxwood Hall in Sussex, England. From the compilation of Cantril and Strunk (1951), we can calculate that at that time two-thirds (64%) of nationwide public opinion polls had been carried out in the United States and one-third (36%) in the 15 other nations in the world that had established polls. The market shares of the Loxwood participants can also be ascertained: 66% in the United States and a whopping 91% of polls outside the US.

At Loxwood the participants worked on questionnaires for international polls to be sold to newspapers. They formed a voluntary association, The International Association of Public Opinion Institutes (IAPOI), an organization for cooperation in survey research that eventually became known as the *Gallup International Association*. They admitted one survey organization in each country that was led by competent and solvent nationals, not foreigners. Membership in this association grew from 14 in the 1940s to 62 in 2004. Table 10.1 shows how membership spread to new countries and continents. It may be read as an index of how public opinion polling conquered the globe; we have no other statistic. No one has figured out which country conducted the most national polls in the last half of the twentieth century. Probably it is France (Blondiaux, 1998). For shorter reviews

of political polling in important countries see Worcester (1983).

Norman Webb, a British mathematician who became Secretary General of the Gallup International Association, used legislative restrictions placed on survey interviewing across countries to arrive at an important classification. He placed opinion polls in the context of the success story of the market economy and democracy. He distinguished between: (1) countries where neither market nor political research were permitted, (2) countries that permitted market interviewing but not interviewing on political issues, and (3) countries that permitted both. The latter were in ascendancy in the second half of the twentieth century.

In time, the initial high market share of the Gallup International Association became

Table 10.1 Accumulation of member countries in the Gallup International Association, 1947–2004

	1940s	1950s	1960s	1970s	1980s	1990s	2000s
North America	Canada# USA#						
Latin America	Brazil*		Argentina Uruguay#	Colombia# Mexico# Puerto Rico* Venezuela#	Ecuador# Peru# Costa Rica*	Bolivia Chile*	Dominican Rep.
Europe	Austria Czechoslovakia Denmark Finland France# Italy Netherlands Norway Sweden UK*	Germany Switzerland	Spain# Belgium Luxembourg	Ireland Portugal#	Belgium Greece Hungary Iceland	Bosnia Bulgaria Croatia Czech Rep Estonia Latvia Poland Rumania Russia Ukraine	Georgia Macedonia Serbia & Montenegro
Asia		India#	Japan Lebanon*	Israel# Korea UAE	Hong Kong# Pakistan Taiwan# Turkey	Singapore Thailand	Vietnam
Australia/ Oceania	Australia			Philippines	New Zealand	Malaysia	Indonesia
Africa			Ivory Coast* South Africa		Egypt Nigeria	Zimbabwe	Cameron Kenya
Countries added	14	3	9	10	13	16	8

Membership 2004 64

Note: *Not member 2004; #Original member firm has changed
Source: '*Gallup goes international*' (*forthcoming*), preliminary data

more modest. In the immediate postwar years, the State Department in Washington commissioned several international surveys to test the effect of US policies and collect information useful to the execution of foreign policy. They were designed by a staff member, Eric Stern, who should be counted as one of the pioneers in international opinion research. When USIA, the United States Information Agency, was created in 1953 it got a full-fledged division for survey analysis. The agency could not normally own research facilities in the countries it studied, but it could supply its questionnaires to foreign market research firms with national fieldwork capacities.

To serve the needs of the State Department and of the USIA for international opinion research, Elmo 'Bud' Wilson created INRA, the *International Research Associates*. INRA had a central office in New York to coordinate overseas research with a competent staff, including Helen Dinerman, among others. They investigated, educated, and selected independent research firms around the world that provided the basic services. It became a chain of size approximately equal to the Gallup International Association. With its tight contract of cooperation, INRA also became very fit to do market research for the American corporations that were conquering the world market at that time: Coca-Cola, Reader's Digest, Procter and Gamble, and the like.

The spread of public opinion research can be seen as a part of the Americanization of the world. The Gallup International Association stands out as an unusual part of this process. It was not promoted by the US government and not organized as a US multinational corporation. It was a voluntary association of one American and many non-American institutions. It represents Americanization with a human face. In fact, it is another great social innovation of George H. Gallup. It suited his personality to create an international organization based on friendship and mutual aid in pursuit of the enormous task of giving a voice to the common man around the world.

REFERENCES

Blondiaux, L. (1998) *La fabrique de l'opinion: une histoire sociale des sondages* [The manufacturing of opinion: a social history of opinion surveys]. Paris: Broché.

Cantril, H., & Strunk, M. (1951). *Public opinion, 1935–1946*. Princeton: Princeton University Press.

Gallup, G. H., & Rae, S. F. (1940). *The pulse of democracy; the public-opinion poll and how it works*. New York: Simon & Schuster.

Lippmann, W. (1922). *Public opinion*. New York: Harcourt, Brace.

Lowell, L. A. (1913). *Public opinion and popular government*. New York: Longmans Green.

MacKinnon, W. A. (1971). *On the rise, progress, and present state of public opinion in Great Britain, and other parts of the world* (reissued). Shannon: Irish University Press. (Original work published in 1828)

Perry, P. K. (1960). Election survey procedures of the Gallup poll. *Public Opinion Quarterly, 24*, 531–542.

Simmel, G. (1923). *Soziologie. Untersuchungen über die Formen der Vergesellschaftung* [Sociology. Forms of associating] (3rd ed.). Berlin: Dunker & Humblot.

Squire, P. (1988). Why the 1936 Literary Digest poll failed. *Public Opinion Quarterly, 52*, 125–133.

Worcester, R. M. (Ed.). (1983). *Political opinion polling: An international review*. London: Macmillan.

11

Public Opinion Research in Emerging Democracies

Robert Mattes

As late as the 1878 Berlin Conference, Western geographers knew more about the topography of the moon than the interior of Africa (Pakenham, 1991). Yet as late as the 1989 fall of the Berlin Wall, much the same thing could be said about social scientists' knowledge of ordinary Africans. As scholars of political behavior scrutinized virtually every aspect of the opinions and behaviors of American and European voters, we knew virtually nothing about the values, preferences or knowledge of the mass of humanity living in Africa—and indeed throughout the developing post colonial world—even though much of this world stood on the precipice of breaking its authoritarian chains and embarking on a wide range of democratic experiments.

One would not have necessarily predicted such a continuing dearth of knowledge just 30 years earlier. In the middle of the 1960s, there were reasons to hope that this deficit would be cut rapidly through pioneering surveys in Latin America, Asia and Africa conducted by scholars like Gabriel Almond,

Sydney Verba, Norman Nie, Jae-On Kim, Lucian Pye, Alex Inkeles, Daniel Lerner and Joel Barkan. But a second generation of empirical scholars never emerged to build on this formative work as evolving trends in both politics and social science fashion set back the exploration, mapping and explanation of public opinion in the developing world for another three decades (Almond, 1990).

Fortunately, the widespread collapse of authoritarian and totalitarian political systems that followed the fall of the Berlin Wall eclipsed both those social systems as well as the social science paradigms that had prevented the widespread application of survey research, and the comparative cross-national exploration of public opinion in the developing world finally took off. Dozens of transitions away from authoritarian rule toward open, competitive, multi-party politics led scholars either to dust off unfashionable theories of political legitimacy and civic culture, or develop new applications of theories from other fields—like social capital—to the study of democratization. At the same time, the rapidly changing priorities of scientific funders, international agencies and bilateral aid agencies with newfound missions in democratic strengthening led to a unique fusion of analytical interest, normative commitment, and political need that supported an unprecedented proliferation of comparative survey research.

This proliferation represents more than the simple spread of Western social science paradigms and technologies to new areas and the accumulation of new knowledge about heretofore understudied subjects. Rather, the extension of survey research to the developing, democratizing world portends important shifts in the way we study public opinion, democracy, and comparative politics. While the actual *tool* of the survey appears the same in form, social conditions often mean that its *application* differs from the Western standard in important ways, and may produce some important alternatives to the normal Western textbook methods. Moreover, the political and social context of transition means that the *content* of questionnaires as well as the *purpose* of systematic public opinion research also differs quite substantially from the standard academic survey research paradigm in Western democracies, producing as many political impacts as scientific ones.

COMMON CHALLENGES

In order to understand how the new comparative survey research in emerging democracies differs from its older sister in the West, one must begin from the basic fact that this work is conducted largely in poor, post-colonial states. This entails a range of important consequences. First, a large proportion of these societies were created by colonial mapmakers who often divided groups of people with common ethnic backgrounds (in terms of language, religion, tribe, clan), forced dissimilar groups together within the same borders, or left behind significant proportions of settlers. Thus, compared to the Western societies in which public opinion research originally developed, the relative social heterogeneity of

these societies creates a range of challenges to drawing representative samples. Second, without resorting to either imperialist or underdevelopment theories of colonialism, it is clear that these societies are characterized by relatively high levels of poverty and inequality, and that this is connected in some way to the legacies of their colonial experiences. Economic inequality not only creates yet another social cleavage that must be factored into sampling designs and data analysis, but low levels of infrastructural development and high levels of poverty mean that these societies often have limited bases of social data that can be used as a sampling frame. Third, the ideologies of anti-colonial movements and ensuing post independent governments of both the left and the right have left a range of bitter political legacies that to this day question the role of, and shrink the space for, independent and open intellectual inquiry, whether conducted by universities or civil society organizations. Fourth, these same ideologies have bequeathed a great deal of skepticism and suspicion toward the positivist systematic empirical methodology of behavioral social science. Yogendra Yadav (2005, p. 1), co-director of the Asia Barometer, recalls that as a graduate student at Jawaharlal Nehru University:

> The worst thing you could say about any political scientist was that he or she 'did survey research.' The label 'survey research' stood for what was considered to be most inappropriate in the third world imitations of the American science of politics: it was methodologically naïve, politically conservative and culturally inauthentic.

The combination of political hostility to independent inquiry and anti-positivist hostility to empirical research has had important impacts on both the demand and supply of survey research in the developing world. On the supply side, it has severely reduced the stock of scholars trained in systematic empirical research and quantitative methods in general, let alone survey research. On the demand side, it has produced a relatively innumerate and skeptical political class of elected leaders, policy makers, civil society leaders and news journalists.

A final important factor is the considerable interest that international organizations and Western governments now take in comparative multi-country studies and the substantial funds they invest in them. While certainly welcome, one clear consequence is that comparative cross-national survey research cannot now, if it ever could, be seen as a purely social scientific enterprise. The rest of this chapter will trace the implications of these factors for the purpose, design and execution of both national and cross-national survey research in the democratizing world.[1]

METHODOLOGICAL IMPLICATIONS

These factors entail a wide range of potential methodological dilemmas for comparative public opinion researchers, ranging from relatively simpler issues like collaboration with local partners to more complex issues such as fieldwork, sampling and questionnaire design. Many of these dilemmas involve trade-offs between a strict adherence to standard survey methodologies and the incurring of greatly increased project costs.

Local collaboration

Given the sheer scope of conducting fieldwork in and across these societies, comparative surveys are almost always collaborative, involving varying forms of partnerships between international (usually European or North American based) and national researchers with survey expertise in the countries of interest. Collaborative partnerships are also a realistic way to establish the local legitimacy of the project. Local legitimacy is important not only where the formal approval of cabinet ministers or security officials, or the informal consent of local leaders, is necessary to conduct fieldwork, but also where the intended political impact of the project is premised on national leaders' acceptance of the survey results.

But legitimacy usually requires local researchers to do more than simply contribute their knowledge to sampling, fieldwork and questionnaire design. They must also be involved in the analysis and dissemination of survey data, avoiding the simple replication of colonial patterns whereby local researchers 'mine' raw data but 'export' it to European and North American researchers who 'refine' it and receive the scholarly credit and recognition. Yet in this pursuit, opinion researchers soon confront the paucity of local social science quantitative research capacity. On one hand, those local survey researchers with the requisite skills to draw samples and conduct systematic fieldwork usually draw their experience from demographic and econometric household surveys, but are often unfamiliar with the substantive political science or sociological literatures that underpin the questionnaire. On the other hand, local sociologists and political scientists who might be conversant with key concepts and literatures often have little or no training in research design, survey research, or data analysis. Thus, comparative researchers interested in more than simple data mining should be prepared to devote significant time to building basic capacity in survey research and data analysis. As Seligson (2005, p. 55) has observed, 'without local collaboration, the standards established might be rejected as "gringo imposed." '

Fieldwork

Social heterogeneity and low levels of development pose a range of challenges to contacting and interviewing representative samples of respondents. Because all respondents should be able to hear the survey in the language of their choice, researchers must select fieldworkers, or firms whose fieldworkers are fluent in all languages likely to be needed to interview any particular sample as well as conversant with local norms of interaction and dress. Questionnaires must also be translated into all relevant languages to avoid forcing interviewers to produce on the spot translations. This in turn necessitates identifying and hiring the services of trained linguists for each of as many as a dozen different languages in places like Nigeria,

Kenya or South Africa. This is just the first of many factors that drive up survey costs in developing societies.

Outside of a handful of countries, low and/or extremely uneven rates of telephone ownership (let alone access to telephone service) mean that telephone interviews are simply not an option.[2] Yet the combination of heterogeneous, relatively rural and dispersed populations with poor road networks means that contacting and conducting personal interviews with a random, nationally representative sample of 1, 200 or 2, 400 respondents can be an extremely demanding and expensive proposition (though Latin America, which is relatively urbanized, seems to be an exception: see Seligson, 2005, p. 51).

In some places, fieldwork teams have absolutely no roads to use to reach selected sampling areas. In mountainous Lesotho, for example, Afrobarometer researchers ride on horseback to conduct interviews in selected villages. In many cases, fieldwork teams have to traverse tortuous dirt or gravel roads which require renting expensive four wheel drive vehicles. In Mozambique, most good roads run from mining towns to the closest coastal port, and few if any connect these towns with each other, posing significant challenges to devising cost effective ways to move fieldwork teams around the country.

Low levels of infrastructural development pose other significant burdens. There may be no appropriate sources of lodging or even food near selected interview areas. And vague maps and poor signposting make it difficult for interview teams to determine when they have entered (or exited) a selected sampling area, and may necessitate the use of GPS instruments. In sum, a week of interviews in rural areas often turns into an exotic and challenging camping expedition.

At the same time, one advantage of doing opinion research in new democracies is that respondents are far more willing to allow themselves to be interviewed and to give interviewers a significant amount of their time. Virtually all researchers I have spoken to working in the developing world agree that it is possible to conduct surveys lasting an average of at least 45 minutes. Some questionnaires, such as the World Values Survey, take far more time, though the impact of this on response quality is a real question. In general, respondents are engaged and genuinely interested, which is fortunate since prevailing customs or overcoming initial suspicions may require interviewers to engage in extended cordialities with the head of household or respondent, adding additional time over and above that required for the actual interview. Indeed, fieldworkers often report difficulties ending interviews because respondents want to carry on their discussion.

But while most respondents are quite willing to be interviewed, the lack of familiarity with the entire idea of surveys as well as the general innumeracy of the respondents present a range of problems for simply applying the standard methods contained in Western textbooks. First of all, typical methods of random selection within a household, whether it be pre-selection from a register of citizens or voters, or other random devices like the Kish or Politz Grids or even a birthday rule, are not transparent and may confuse respondents and create unnecessary suspicion. This is especially true in patriarchal societies where male heads of households may be open to the idea of being interviewed, but object to being told that the interview has to be done with their wife or daughter. Such situations, however, present wonderful laboratories where we can use local knowledge to advance survey methodology. For example, dealing playing cards to either all eligible males, or all eligible females in the household, and then allowing the patriarch to pull the card of the sampled person, simultaneously respects local traditions while yet retaining randomness, and allows researchers to introduce a gender stratification.

Sampling

Drawing samples of respondents that are representative of the typical developing society presents comparative survey researchers with a wide range of obstacles and trade-offs.

To begin with, relatively high levels of social heterogeneity (featuring politically important cleavages along linguistic, religious, racial or class lines) means that researchers need to consider drawing relatively larger samples (compared to the typical $n = 1,200$ survey sample in the West) to ensure that they represent socially and politically significant sub national groups or regions, and are thus able to test adequately for statistically significant differences across these cleavages. But besides the costs of the additional interviews, mapping these cleavages requires high quality demographic data, something which developing societies with weak census bureaus may not be able to provide. In a small number of countries, especially those marred by recent histories of civil war, available census data (if any) is simply too old to be of any use. In other countries, the census may have once been reliable, but the information used to update it is often suspect.

Matters are even more difficult when it comes to the nature of the sampling frame. A large number of countries have no reliable lists of citizens, households or even registered voters. Census department maps often feature only the boundaries of enumerator areas and contain no information about the locations or densities of households. And even where such lists or household maps exist, high levels of mobility mean that they quickly go out of date and research teams find that they bear little resemblance to the reality they confront in the field, especially in informal housing areas.

Thus, census enumerator areas are typically the smallest bit of reliable information that survey researchers have to create a sampling frame. If researchers want to calculate selection probabilities at second or third stages of household and respondent selection, they must map and enumerate the selected area themselves, which significantly increases the amount of time interview teams need to be present in selected areas and drastically increases fieldwork costs. The lack of good data at this level also raises the issue of substitution. Standard survey texts warn against substitution (generally because of the belief that it grants too much discretion to interviewers and precludes the possibility of calculating contact, refusal and response rates). Instead, they recommend that researchers draw larger than required samples that anticipate refusals, or draw additional, smaller sample 'packages' that are only opened and contacted in their entirety if the realized sample falls short.

However, accurately anticipating refusal rates presumes that survey researchers have a firm idea of what that rate is likely to be across their country and within specific regions based on the track record of previous surveys. But such a reliable track record does not exist where survey research is in its infancy. And drawing packages of over-samples to be interviewed after the original sample requires interviewers to move back into the countryside, greatly increasing survey costs.

These costs also have to be set against other considerations. For example, clustering interviews within primary sampling units, and primary sampling units within secondary sampling units, might reduce travel costs significantly. But where a project's goal is not only to produce scientific data but also to have local policy impact, an overly-clustered sample may be counter-productive. Policy makers unfamiliar with the logic of sampling may be far less convinced of the representativeness of a sample of even 2,400 interviews if that sample was clustered into 200 primary sampling units located within just 20 districts, compared to one dispersed across PSU's in 600 different districts across the width and breadth of the country (but which would mean far higher fieldwork costs).

It is true that few, if any, single surveys in the developing world are anywhere as expensive as something like the US National Election Study (Seligson, 2005, p. 51). But a more appropriate comparison should take into consideration the fact that the most important projects in the democratizing world are multi-country, and multi-wave, and have no institutional base of predictable financial support like the US National Science Foundation. Thus, while the cost considerations of any single factor mentioned above or below might be sustainable in a one-off, single country study, they become extremely important considerations when scholars want to generate donor support for a dozen or so such surveys and repeat the exercise in two or three years time.

Thus, comparative survey research in the democratizing world is unlikely to meet the 'gold standard' of international survey research, if by that we mean full probability based samples with no substitution (Heath, Fisher, & Smith, 2005, p. 319). However, there are reasonable alternative methodologies which, if strictly enforced and monitored, might constitute a 'silver standard' of research in developing contexts. Reliable population lists of census enumerator areas can be stratified into socially and politically relevant sub-lists, along provincial, regional, or urban and rural lines, enabling researchers to draw a scientific, representative area probability sample with probability proportionate to size. Within the primary sampling unit, researchers can devise systematic, random methods of start points and walk patterns of household and respondent selection, with rules for household substitution that are strictly enforced by field supervisors to ensure that fieldworkers have no discretion over whom to interview. All household visits need to be rigorously documented to enable the calculation of contact, refusal and response rates. Fieldwork should also be done at times when respondents are most likely to be available and when fieldworkers are able to make multiple callbacks, minimizing the need for household substitution. The image of a 'silver standard' might imply to some a 'second-best method' yielding necessarily inferior, biased data. But this is ultimately an open question that needs to be tested through a systematic comparison of the results generated by alternative methods used on the same populations.[3]

Questionnaire design

Low levels of formal education of potential respondents pose special challenges for questionnaire design. Innumeracy and/or a lack of familiarity with linear logic means that the numeric scales widely used in the West (like feeling thermometers running from 0 to 100) are often inappropriate. And attempting to convey the idea of a linear or symmetric response scale visually through show cards is often not an option because of high rates of illiteracy. In response, local investigators have developed some ingenious responses such as building a wire anchored on two ends and asking respondents to slide a bead back and forth along the wire to indicate where their opinions lie between the two designated endpoints. In other places, researchers have laid out mats with cards representing differing groups, and then asked respondents to pick or rank liked and disliked groups, both in overall terms or in paired comparisons (Miles & Rochefort, 1991).

Many scholars who design questionnaires for use in developing societies also worry that typical Likert scales induce an acquiescence bias, especially where people have newly formed, or weakly held attitudes toward subjects such as democracy. Not only do such measures overestimate the apparent support for democracy or agreement with items measuring democratic values, they may also overestimate the validity and reliability of scales based on several such items. Scholars usually respond by reversing the valence of several scale items to keep respondents alert and avoid rote responses. Yet reversing item valence may serve only to confuse respondents by removing their ability to anchor their responses against some fixed referent (see Robinson, Shaver, & Wrightsman, 1999). Thus, it is often necessary to resort to ordinal items that force respondents to choose from a balanced or unbalanced set of statements.

A final challenge to questionnaire design in the democratizing world comes from social heterogeneity. Linguistic diversity not only drives up survey costs through the necessity of translating questionnaires into several local languages, but also raises serious issues of validity and reliability. Investigators need to ensure not only that respondents understand concepts like 'trust,' 'tolerance' or the 'rule of law' in the intended way, but also that respondents across different language groups and countries understand it in the same way. This is usually accomplished through the process of 'double-blind' translation, which adds significant costs in terms of both time and finances (but see Heath *et al.*, 2005, p. 320, who recount several doubts as to what the double-blind method actually accomplishes). But perhaps the best way to accomplish this is by writing short, simply structured questions that use broadly accessible language.

THE PURPOSE OF OPINION SURVEYS IN THE DEMOCRATIZING WORLD

Another factor that distinguishes social scientific surveys in new democracies from standard large-scale academic surveys in the West is their political purpose. Put simply, surveys of transitional societies are not purely social scientific instruments. While surveys like the American National Election Study or General Social Survey may produce conclusions that ultimately have important policy consequences, they are organized and funded primarily as scientific vehicles. But while political scientists and sociologists might initiate public opinion surveys in transitional societies as vehicles for scientific inquiry, the vast majority of cross-national research is supported by international foundations and bilateral aid agencies precisely because of their potential political and developmental impacts.

First, these surveys inform the larger process of institutional reform by offering a *feedback mechanism to decision makers*. Second, they enhance political accountability by *letting everyone else know what the government knows*.[4] The first function can be accomplished by communicating results directly to government officials in personal briefings and written reports. Yet survey researchers working in the developing world often express surprise at how little interest most government officials express in their data. Part of this is a product of official inexperience with the necessity of learning about voter opinions. Yet a major part of this

also has to do with the innumeracy and/or skepticism toward survey research discussed above.

The second function can be achieved through the dissemination of results directly to key political actors like legislators and opposition party officials, but also more widely to the public in general through the news media. Elected officials can be persuaded to take more interest in survey results if they know that their political opponents have the same information—information that might be politically embarrassing or damaging. Yet in many places in the developing world, innumeracy means that the news media are surprisingly hesitant to engage with survey results. And where newspapers and television channels commonly join to commission and report surveys, such as Latin America, media organizations are not independent from the government or from specific political parties. On other occasions, the media report uncritically the results of pre-cooked, partisan surveys as if they were fact (Seligson, 2005, p. 54). In both cases, the image of survey research may be undermined rather than strengthened.

Survey researchers in transitional societies are also political actors, because public opinion data can constitute real political threats to the leaders of the often hybrid regimes that comprise the 'new democracies.' Survey results may threaten the claims of elected leaders to be the sole, authentic representatives of their societies and challenge their attempts to overload the meaning of their electoral 'mandates.' But while survey researchers may locate receptive allies in smaller civil society organizations devoted to policy research and democracy advocacy, they find no automatic alliance with civil society in general. As Ginsberg (1986) has pointed out, survey research transforms our very concept of public opinion from a behavioral assertion and a property of interest groups who control the timing, framing and method of expression, to an attitudinal response that is constrained by researchers' decisions about when to conduct surveys, which questions to ask, and how to frame and word questions and responses.

Thus, survey research may pose a threat to the political power of mass organizations like trade unions, citizen movements, policy advocacy groups or political parties—groups that are often already suspicious of surveys because of ideology or innumeracy.

Finally, the international financial support that underpins public opinion research in the democratizing world can be a double-edged sword. While it provides the resources that otherwise could not be found in the typical transitional society, foreign sponsorship may undercut the legitimacy of a survey and limit its local political impact. On rarer occasions, funders may even decline to release results that could be seen to show anti-democratic actors or processes in a favorable light and damage the local democratization process. In one innovative response, Indian survey researchers have created 'national local funders,' who provide small amounts of financial support but then publicize, use and defend the survey results (Yadav, 2005).

THE CONTENT OF PUBLIC OPINION SURVEYS IN DEMOCRATIZING COUNTRIES

Finally, the larger social, economic and political context of transition has profound implications for the content of public opinion surveys in democratizing societies. Until the fall of the Berlin Wall, the dominant paradigm of the relevance of public attitudes to democracy (based on Almond & Verba's, 1963, classic 'The Civic Culture') assumed that democratic stability was predicated on the existence of a series of deeply held cultural values such as pragmatism, moderation, efficacy, tolerance, and a high degree of interpersonal trust, balanced with a healthy skepticism of political leaders. A more recent variant has focused on a syndrome of 'self-expression' values (Inglehart & Welzel, 2005). Rose, Mishler, and Haerpfer (1998, p. 84) have described surveys based in this paradigm as 'destination studies' because they measure 'how near or far countries are to a Western-style ideal' and

whether they are becoming 'just like us' or 'enough like us.'

But with the spread of cross national opinion research in the democratizing world, a second, quite different approach to surveying transitional societies emerged. Based on Linz and Stepan's (1996) argument that democracy can only be consolidated once it has been 'legitimated,' that is seen by all significant political actors and an overwhelming majority of citizens as 'the only game in town,' this new approach assumes that in new democracies, whether or not citizens hold norms, values or personality traits conducive to democracy is much less important than whether they see democracy as better than and prefer it to alternative political regimes. Rose et al. (1998) call this the 'Churchill Hypothesis,' stemming from Winston Churchill's famous dictum that 'Democracy is the worst form of government, except for all the others that have been tried from time to time.' Questionnaires anchored in this approach tap not how close societies are to an ideal, Western set of norms and values, but the direction in which they are going and why; Rose et al. (1998, p. 85) call this type of survey a 'transformation model.'

The transformation model informs the measurement strategy of the various Global Barometer surveys in Africa, Asia, Latin America and Eastern Europe (see Uno, 2005). While accepting that norms and values are undoubtedly important, they ultimately prefer to devote scarce questionnaire space to measuring how citizens of democratizing societies experience change, how they understand democracy, whether they are willing to choose democracy against its alternatives, and how they evaluate the performance of their new, reforming regimes and institutions compared to the old.

To be sure, both traditions are based on the *legitimation theory of democratic consolidation*: that is, regardless of how well-designed a country's political institutions and processes, a sustainable democracy requires people who are willing to support, defend and sustain democratic practices. At the same time, the transformation model questionnaire offers the additional advantage that the data it produces is simultaneously suitable to test *institutional explanations of consolidation*. Institutional theories argue that democratic citizens are the result of, rather than the necessary condition for, effectively functioning democratic institutions (e.g. DiPalma, 1990; Norris, 2004). In this case, the resulting data can be used to test the effectiveness of new political institutions as well as the extent to which institutions actually do (re)shape public attitudes towards democracy and politics. The results of value-based surveys, by contrast, cannot provide such a test because values— according to the theory's proponents—are deeply held and only evolve slowly, over generations rather than within a few years in response to specific institutional reforms. Thus, the discipline is well served by the existence of both the World Values Survey (which measures broad change across an impressive range of societies at five to seven year intervals) and the Global Barometers (which tap more immediate changes in regime preferences and institutional evaluations on a more regular basis).

In addition to measuring the extent of public support for democracy, researchers studying democratizing societies face the challenge of ascertaining precisely *what* citizens of new democracies understand democracy to be. This usually requires open-ended questions to get at least at surface understandings (see Bratton & Mattes, 2001; Chu, Diamond, & Shin, 2001; Lagos, 2001), or specially designed closed-ended probes that ask whether specific procedures or substantive outcomes are essential to democracy (McIntosh, McIver, & Abele, 1994; Bratton, Mattes, & Gyimah-Boadi, 2005).

An equally important issue for new democracies is *how much* people know about democracy and politics. Besides asking people to recall or recognize specific information about institutions, policies or incumbents, political knowledge can be effectively assessed by attaching to questions such as 'How well or badly would you say the government is combating HIV/AIDS?' a filter which adds 'or haven't you had a chance to find out about this yet?' (Bishop, Odendick, & Turfbacher, 1983). Because people who really don't have an opinion are given the space and encouragement to say so, this significantly increases the level of 'don't know' responses. However, while such filters provide civil society, the news media, policy makers and donors with crucial details about the contours and limits of public engagement, they also present data analysts with thorny question of whether to treat 'don't know' responses as missing data or as meaningful responses that should be re-assigned to a defensible place on the response scale.

CONCLUSIONS

While Western political scientists and sociologists have exported the tool of public opinion research to new settings, the different economic, social and political contexts of those settings often mean that social scientific surveys of public opinion are designed, executed, and received in very different ways than in the West. But rather than simply seeing these differences as blemishes that need to be gradually ameliorated, we may have much more to learn from the globalization of public opinion research than the simple accumulation of more data from exotic settings. As Heath *et al.* (2005) have recently observed: 'Rather than a simple export of Western methods, assumptions and intellectual frameworks to non-Western societies, public opinion research might benefit from imports in the reverse direction' (p. 330).

NOTES

1 While I refer to the democratizing world in general, my remarks apply more directly to survey research in Africa and Asia, and to a lesser extent Latin America. I illustrate this argument primarily with examples from Africa, the region most widely thought to be inhospitable to systematic survey research, though I tap examples from Asia and Latin America wherever possible.

2 On the other hand, this could be an advantage given the rising levels of non-response in developed

countries created by refusals, answering machines and call-blocking, let alone the problems created by mobile phones.

3 Heath *et al.* (2005, p. 328) conclude: 'We consider it a priority … for methodologists to establish empirically whether findings from random-route samples, for example, show different patterns from those obtained by strict probability samples with high response rates.'

4 Bilateral aid agencies also support these surveys, because they simultaneously provide a needs assessment, as well as program monitoring and evaluation.

REFERENCES

Almond, G. (1990). *A discipline divided: Schools and sects in political science.* Newbury Park, CA: Sage.

Almond, G., & Verba, S. (1963). *The civic culture: Political attitudes and democracy in five countries.* Princeton: Princeton University Press.

Bishop, G., Odendick, R., & Turfbacher, A. (1983). The effects of filter questions in public opinion surveys. *Public Opinion Quarterly, 47,* 528–546.

Bratton, M., & Mattes, R. (2001). Africans' surprising universalism. *Journal of Democracy, 12*(1), 107–121.

Bratton, M., Mattes, R., & Gyimah-Boadi, E. (2005). *Public opinion, democracy and market reform in Africa.* London: Cambridge University Press.

Chu, Y., Diamond, L., & Shin, D. C. (2001). Halting progress in Korea and Taiwan. *Journal of Democracy, 12*(1), 122–136.

DiPalma, G. (1990). *To craft democracies: An essay on democratic transition.* Berkeley: University of California Press.

Heath, A., Fisher, S., & Smith, S. (2005). The globalization of public opinion research. *Annual Review of Political Science, 8,* 297–333.

Ginsberg, B. (1986). *The captive public: How mass opinion promotes state power.* New York: Basic Books.

Inglehart, R., & Welzel, C. (2005). *Modernization, cultural change and democracy.* New York: Cambridge University Press.

Lagos, M. (2001). Between stability and crisis in Latin America. *Journal of Democracy, 12*(1), 137–145.

Linz, J., & Stepan, A. (1996). *Problems of democratic transition and consolidation: Southern Europe, South America and post communist Europe.* Baltimore: Johns Hopkins University Press.

McIntosh, M., McIver, M., & Abele, D. (1994). Publics meet market democracy in Central and Eastern Europe. *Slavic Review, 53,* 483–512.

Miles, W., & Rochefort, D. (1991). Nationalism versus ethnic identity in sub-Saharan Africa. *American Political Science Review, 85,* 393–403.

Norris, P. (2004). *Electoral engineering.* New York: Cambridge University Press.

Pakenham, T. (1991). *The scramble for Africa.* Johannesburg: Jonathan Ball Publishers.

Robinson, J., Shaver, P., & Wrightsman, L. (Eds.). (1999). *Measures of public attitudes.* San Diego: Academic Press.

Rose, R., Mishler, W., & Haerpfer, C. (1998). *Democracy and its alternatives: Understanding post communist societies.* Baltimore: Johns Hopkins University Press.

Seligson, M. (2005). Improving the quality of survey research in democratizing countries. *Political Science & Politics, 38,* 51–56.

Uno, S. (2005). Comparing the global barometers. *APSA Comparative Politics Newsletter, 16*(2), 30–32.

Yadav, Y. (2005, February). *Setting standards for international survey research.* Paper presented to the Afrobarometer round 3 planning workshop, Accra, Ghana.

PART II

Theories of Public Opinion Formation and Change

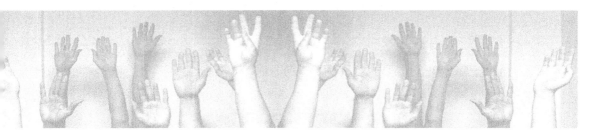

Formation of Opinion

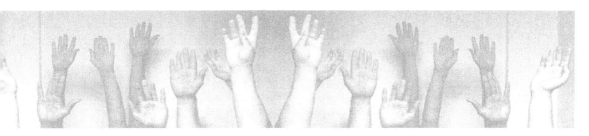

12

Knowledge and Attitudes

Penny S. Visser, Allyson Holbrook and
Jon A. Krosnick

The simple notion that citizens elect representatives who implement policies with which they agree is central to democratic theory. In this way, all citizens can pursue their own interests as well as the interests of the common good in an orderly and efficient way. According to many political theorists, this simple process enables democratic governments to maintain stability and legitimacy.

On close inspection, however, this process is far from simple. It depends critically on a number of fairly demanding steps. It first requires that at least a substantial majority of citizens carefully attend to political events on the local, state, and national stages. Further, citizens must consolidate the constant stream of political information provided by the news media, advocacy groups, and other individuals within the social environment, and they must store this information in memory for later use. From this elaborate and diverse set of stored information, citizens must derive attitudes on salient issues of the day that reflect their interests and other core predispositions. Citizens must then discriminate among various candidates for political office, identifying

those who hold issue positions closest to their own, and they must cast ballots in support of those candidates during elections. This can be difficult, because candidates often do not clearly and consistently state their positions on issues (Page, 1978), and the media do not make special efforts to communicate candidates' positions to the public (Patterson & McClure, 1976; Graber, 1980; Patterson, 1980). Finally, citizens must monitor the actions of their elected officials, holding them accountable for pursuing the appropriate policies and in other ways serving the citizens' goals and interests.

All of this suggests that the functioning of a healthy democracy requires an engaged and informed citizenry whose attitudes and preferences reflect careful consideration of a broad set of political information. In this chapter, we consider the extent to which ordinary citizens live up to this ideal. We also consider the antecedents of and barriers to the acquisition of political knowledge and trace the various consequences of knowledge for political attitudes, judgments, and behavior.

HOW KNOWLEDGEABLE?

So how much do ordinary citizens know about political matters? Several decades of research provide a resounding answer: not much at all. Looking first at young adults, research on civic education within the US suggests that most young people enter adulthood with a rather tenuous grasp of the basic features of the political system. In fact, a recent survey administered by the US Department of Education (Lutkus, Weiss, Campbell, Mazzeo, & Lazer, 1999) revealed that by the time they reach twelfth grade, only about a quarter of US students performed at or above the level of expected proficiency in civic knowledge. And fully 35% of high school seniors tested below the most basic level, reflecting virtually no knowledge about the political system.

Research with representative samples of US adults suggests that these early deficits often persist. In one especially comprehensive investigation, Delli Carpini and Keeter (1996) analyzed over 2000 political knowledge questions posed to representative samples of American adults, covering basic features of political institutions and processes, salient policy domains, and prominent political leaders. They found that most Americans were at best moderately informed about political matters, and many were exceedingly uninformed. For example, only 44% of Americans could name one of the three branches of government. When presented with the three branches, less than 60% could say which one determines the constitutionality of a law. Just over 30% of American adults could provide even the most rudimentary definition of affirmative action, and less than 60% knew that Roe v. Wade involved the issue of abortion rights. Overall, Delli Carpini and Keeter (1996) found that only 41% of Americans knew the answers to 50% or more of the political knowledge questions, and only 13% were able to answer 75% of the questions. Findings like these have led to much hand-wringing across the social sciences, as political scientists and others lament 'the breadth and depth of citizen ignorance' (Lupia & McCubbins, 1998, p. 1). These alarmingly low levels of political

knowledge have typically been viewed as a serious threat to the functioning of democracy.

Interpreting these findings

Recently, however, scholars have begun to question the degree to which these observed low levels of political knowledge do in fact repudiate the competence of ordinary citizens to participate in the democratic process. Some scholars have pointed out, for example, that it is not clear precisely what knowledge is necessary for people to be effective democratic citizens, or if the questions posed to survey respondents measure that knowledge (Krosnick, 1998; Kuklinski & Quirk, 2001; Lupia, in press). No effort has been made to define the universe of necessary knowledge or to sample from such a universe in any systematic way (Krosnick, 1998). In fact, only recently have scholars begun to articulate the conceptual foundations of citizen competence, explicitly delineating the specific tasks that confront citizens, the criteria by which their performance of these tasks should be evaluated, the observable indicators of the criteria, and the standards against which the indicators should be evaluated (Kuklinski & Quirk, 2001). Because such systematic analysis has been absent, it is difficult to know what to conclude from responses to the apparently arbitrary set of knowledge questions that have been posed to survey respondents over the years.

Others have challenged the way that political knowledge is assessed, suggesting that the 'pop quiz' format of the typical telephone survey is misleading regarding the process by which citizens wield political information in consequential judgments and decisions (Prior & Lupia, 2005). They suggest that, as in most domains in life, the critical element is not the number of discrete bits of information stored in memory and available for instantaneous retrieval, but rather the ability and motivation to access and utilize relevant pieces of information when the task at hand calls for it. Thus, the fact that most people do not have an encyclopedic set of political facts at their fingertips does not mean that the political judgments and decisions they make are groundless. When faced with a consequential judgment or decision, people may well seek out and then make use of relevant information. Telephone surveys that pose unexpected knowledge questions provide respondents with neither the motivation nor the opportunity to do so, and thus may offer a distorted portrait of the role of political information in citizens' judgments, decisions, and behaviors. Indeed, when provided with both opportunity and motivation, ordinary citizens prove to be quite capable of acquiring and utilizing political information (Prior & Lupia, 2005).

Some have suggested that the volume of political information retained in memory (and therefore available for retrieval during an interview) may vastly underestimate the amount and diversity of information upon which people's political opinions are based (Lodge, Steenbergen, & Brau, 1995). Rather than meticulously cataloging and storing the vast array of political information to which they are exposed, people may simply adjust their attitudes on-line, modifying their views in light of new information. Having incorporated the information into their relevant opinions, people may choose not to expend the additional effort to retain the information in memory. It may be misleading, therefore, to use tests of political knowledge to draw inferences about the degree to which ordinary citizens hold informed opinions.

As this discussion illustrates, the interpretation of political knowledge levels among the mass public is somewhat controversial. Regardless of one's interpretation, however, the fact remains that most citizens do not know very much about the people, policies, and institutions that comprise their political system.

WHY SUCH LOW LEVELS OF POLITICAL KNOWLEDGE?

To begin to understand these low levels of political knowledge, we must consider the general processes by which people become knowledgeable about various topics. People gain knowledge in two primary ways: (1) through direct experiences with an attitude object (Fazio & Zanna, 1981; Wood, Rhodes, & Biek, 1995); and (2) through exposure and attention to information about the object from other people, transmitted during informal conversations (Robinson & Levy, 1986), formal schooling (Nie, Junn & Stehlik-Barry, 1996), or through the mass media (Roberts & Maccoby, 1985; McGuire, 1986). They acquire knowledge about social and political issues primarily through exposure and attention to information provided by other people, especially by the news media (Clarke & Kline, 1974; Clarke & Fredin, 1978; Perse, 1990).

Exposure, however, is just the first of several steps in the process of knowledge acquisition. After individuals are exposed to new information, they must devote perceptual attention to it, bringing it into short-term or working memory (Baddeley & Hitch, 1974). Of course, it is impossible for individuals to attend to all of the stimuli that bombard their senses at any given moment, so people selectively attend to some things and filter out the vast majority of others. Some of the information that is brought into short term or working memory undergoes elaboration, during which an individual actively thinks about the new information and relates it to information already stored in memory. Through this process, associative links are built, connecting new information to previously acquired information (Craik & Lockhart, 1972). The more extensively an individual processes new information, the stronger the neural trace and the more likely it will be available for later retrieval (e.g., Craik, 1977; Tyler, Hertel, MacCallum, & Ellis, 1979). Thus, the process of acquiring knowledge about the political world is costly, imposing tremendous cognitive demands (Downs, 1957).

These demands are especially high for people who have little political knowledge to begin with. Prior knowledge on a particular topic improves people's ability to comprehend new information, enabling them to extract the central elements of a message and draw appropriate inferences efficiently (Recht & Leslie, 1988; Eckhardt, Wood, & Jacobvitz, 1991). Prior knowledge also enhances people's ability to store new information on that topic and retrieve the information later (e.g., Recht & Leslie, 1988; Fiske, Lau, & Smith, 1990; McGraw & Pinney, 1990; Cooke, Atlas, Lane, & Berger, 1993; Schneider, Gruber, Gold, & Opwis, 1993; Hambrick, 2003). So the less political information individuals have stored in memory, the more difficult it is for them to acquire new information.

In addition to the substantial cognitive burdens it imposes, the acquisition of political knowledge involves other costs as well. In particular, it reduces the resources available for acquiring information about other topics. The more a person is exposed to information about political issues and objects, and the more resources he or she devotes to attending to and elaborating this information, the less likely it is that other available information will be stored in his or her long-term memory and available for later retrieval (e.g., Kahneman, 1973). Thus, becoming more knowledgeable about political matters often comes at the cost of gaining knowledge about other topics.

DETERMINANTS OF POLITICAL KNOWLEDGE

Under what circumstances are people willing to bear the cognitive burdens and opportunity costs of becoming politically knowledgeable? And how do people select among the myriad of political issues and objects that vie for their attention?

Incidental media exposure

People sometimes learn about the political world through incidental exposure to news media coverage of politics (Krugman & Hartley, 1970; Zukin & Snyder, 1984; Tewksbury, Weaver, & Maddex, 2001). For example, a person with no particular interest in politics may nonetheless become politically knowledgeable because he or she routinely watches the evening news, either out of

habit or because another household member regularly tunes in. Such passive learning may be especially likely from televised news broadcasts, which often contain vivid graphics and visual images that require fewer cognitive resources to decode and retain in memory (Graber, 1990).

Non-selective media exposure

People also intentionally expose themselves to information about the political world. Many people tune in to general television or radio news programs or regularly visit pages on the Internet that cover a range of political topics, for example, leading to increases in political knowledge (e.g., Roberts & Maccoby, 1985; Delli Carpini & Keeter, 1997). The flowing nature of television and radio news programs does not easily afford news consumers opportunities to expose themselves to some stories and not others. Therefore, choosing to watch or hear such programs typically produces nonselective exposure to information on many topics.

The decision to tune in to television or radio news broadcasts is, of course, influenced by interest in politics: those who find politics intrinsically interesting are much more likely to expose themselves to news programming intentionally than those who are disinterested in politics (e.g., Luskin, 1990; Delli Carpini & Keeter, 1997). News media consumption is also influenced by more general surveillance motives: those who are more intrinsically motivated to monitor their environment pay more attention and give more thought to news broadcasts than those with lower motivation (e.g., Eveland, Shah, & Kwak, 2003).

Issue-specific selective attention

People are selective not only in terms of the overall amount of attention they pay to the news media, but also regarding the amount of attention they pay to coverage of specific issues. Indeed, people sometimes actively seek out information about some issues but make no special effort to gain information about others, rendering them deeply knowledgeable about the former and less informed about the latter.

How do people decide which issues to attend to? One answer is suggested by the positive correlation between the volume of knowledge a person has stored in memory about an object and the importance people attach to their attitude toward the object. People consider themselves more knowledgeable about an object when their attitudes toward it are important to them (e.g., Krosnick, Boninger, Chuang, Berent, & Carnot, 1993; Bassili, 1996; Prislin, 1996; Visser, 1998), and they can retrieve more information about the attitude object from memory (Wood, 1982; Krosnick *et al.*, 1993; Berent & Krosnick, 1995). The knowledge accompanying more important attitudes is also more likely to be accurate (Krosnick, 1990). These associations suggest that attitude importance may provide the impetus for knowledge acquisition, motivating people to gather and retain information about some attitude objects at the expense of learning about others. Attitude importance is a person's subjective sense of how much significance to attach to an attitude—how much to care and be concerned about it (see Boninger, Krosnick, Berent, & Fabrigar, 1995). Attaching importance is highly consequential—it leads people to use the attitude in processing information, making decisions, and selecting a course of action (for a review, see Boninger, Krosnick, Berent, & Fabrigar, 1995). And having substantial knowledge about the attitude object seems likely to be quite useful to facilitating effective attitude use. As a result, attitude importance may motivate the acquisition of relevant knowledge in long-term memory.

This may occur because attitude importance guides people's choices when they are deciding to which information they will attend. They may selectively attend to information relevant to their more important attitudes, particularly when available information is abundant and time or cognitive resources are limited. After they have been exposed to information, people may process it more deeply if it is relevant to important attitudes, because such processing is likely to serve

strategic purposes later. As a result, this new information is more likely to be stored in long-term memory and available for later retrieval.

In a program of research employing both naturalistic and laboratory investigations, Holbrook, Berent, Krosnick, Visser, & Boninger (2005) recently documented precisely these causal processes. They found, for example, that after watching a televised presidential debate under naturalistic conditions, viewers were better able to remember the candidates' statements about policy issues on which they had more personally important attitudes. And they found that attitude importance regulated knowledge acquisition by inspiring selective exposure and selective elaboration: when given the opportunity to choose, people sought information about policies toward which they had more personally important attitudes, and chose to think more about these policies as well. Further, they demonstrated that when the opportunity for selective exposure and selective elaboration was eliminated, the relation between importance and knowledge also disappeared. Taken together, these findings suggest that attaching personal importance to an attitude motivates people to expose themselves selectively to attitude-relevant information and elaborate that information, leading to the acquisition and maintenance of information in long-term memory.

But why do people attach importance to some issues and objects and not others? Three primary antecedents of attitude importance have been identified (see Boninger, Krosnick, & Berent, 1995). People attach importance to some attitudes because they perceive that the attitude object impinges on their material self-interests. For example, senior citizens who rely on Medicare would be especially likely to attach importance to their attitudes toward new Medicare policies.

People attach importance to other attitudes because they perceive a link between the attitude object and their core values. Values refer to a person's fundamental beliefs about how people ought to behave, or about what end-states are desirable (Rokeach, 1968). Attitudes that are tightly linked to one or more of a person's core values are deemed more important than attitudes that are loosely associated with his or her values. For example, an individual who cherishes the end-state of a world at peace may see a connection between this core value and his or her attitude toward the Iraq war. This connection would lead him or her to attach personal importance to this attitude.

Finally, people attach importance to some attitudes because the groups or individuals with whom they identify are materially affected by the object or consider their attitudes toward the object to be important. For example, even if she never expects to be personally affected by changes in abortion laws, a woman may attach importance to her attitude toward legalized abortion because she identifies with women everywhere, some of whom would be affected by changes in abortion laws.

Links to self interest, core values, or social identities often lead people to attach personal importance to particular political issues such as Medicare reform or legalized abortion. But these antecedents can also lead people to attach importance to the domain of politics more generally, increasing their motivation to acquire knowledge about a wide range of political topics and issues. Thus, importance can inspire selective expertise on political topics of particular significance to an individual, or it can inspire more general information gains across a broad spectrum of currently salient political topics.

An illustration: Attitudes toward legalized abortion

One recent investigation illustrates several of these processes. Visser, Krosnick, and Norris (2004) explored the determinants of knowledge about legalized abortion. Replicating past research, they found that self-interest, the importance of the issue to reference groups and individuals, and value-relevance each predicted unique variance in the personal importance that people attached to their attitudes on this issue. And attitude importance was a strong predictor of the volume of information people sought and possessed about legalized abortion. This suggests that people who cared deeply about the issue of abortion sought out information about the issue, thought deeply about it, and retained the information in memory. Exposure to news media, on the other hand, was unrelated to the importance people attached to this issue, but it was a strong predictor of knowledge about legalized abortion (see Figure 12.1). Thus, both selective and nonselective media exposure appear to have contributed to levels of knowledge about abortion.

CONSEQUENCES OF KNOWLEDGE

We began this chapter by noting that democratic theory rests on the assumption that citizens are both informed and engaged,

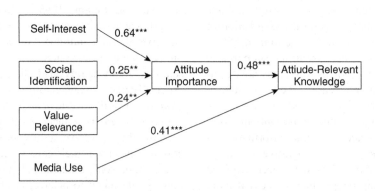

Figure 12.1   Determinants of knowledge as documented by Visser, Krosnick, and Norris (2004)
Note: **$p < 0.01$; ***$p < 0.001$

capable of selecting political leaders who represent their goals and interests, and of holding those leaders accountable once in office. As we have seen, however, an overwhelming body of evidence calls into question ordinary citizens' ability to perform these duties. Just how concerned should we be about the dearth of political knowledge within the general public? In other words, what are the consequences of possessing or failing to possess political knowledge?

Generally speaking, possessing a large store of information confers a host of cognitive abilities, with clear implications for attitudes and behavior. In addition to aiding comprehension and retention of new information, knowledge increases the speed of relevant judgments (e.g., Fiske *et al.*, 1990; Paull & Glencross, 1997) and improves people's ability to utilize cues in decision tasks (Paull & Glencross, 1997). This suggests that people with more political knowledge are better able to integrate various aspects of political issues efficiently and effectively, weigh the advantages and disadvantages of specific political policies, and synthesize the diverse attributes of political candidates. Thus, their political attitudes are likely to reflect a more thorough and sophisticated combination of the positive and negative aspects of the objects, issues, and people they encounter in the political realm.

Consistent with this notion, a good deal of evidence suggests that people who possess a large store of political knowledge are better able to recognize links between particular political policies and their own material interests or other core predispositions, and they are better able to identify political candidates who are likely to share their views and work to enact laws that they support (Zaller, 1992; Delli Carpini & Keeter, 1996). The politically knowledgeable are also better able to recognize the ideological underpinnings of various policy positions, and are more likely to adopt ideologically coherent attitudes across a range of issues (Delli Carpini & Keeter, 1996). Thus, knowledge enables people to utilize incoming political information efficiently and effectively.

Knowledge also improves people's ability to evaluate critically the cogency of persuasive messages (Wood, Kallgren, & Preisler, 1985; Ratneshwar & Chaiken, 1991) and to generate effective counter-arguments to a persuasive appeal, rendering these people resistant to attitude change (Wood, 1982; Wood *et al.*, 1995; Muthukrishnan, Pham, & Mungale, 1999). This suggests that the politically knowledgeable are less likely to be buffeted about by the constantly shifting winds of political rhetoric. Instead, they scrutinize counter-attitudinal information and defend their views against all but the most compelling challenges to their attitudes. Indeed, people with more political knowledge exhibit greater attitude stability over time than people who possess less knowledge (Delli Carpini & Keeter, 1996).

Knowledge also equips people with the information they need to plan and execute effective behavioral strategies, enabling them to engage in attitude-expressive behaviors efficiently. For example, knowledge about environmental conservation has been shown to enable people with pro-environmental attitudes to express their views behaviorally (e.g., Kallgren & Wood, 1986; Meinhold & Malkus, 2005). And knowledge about the political world is a highly significant predictor of voting behavior: people who possess a large store of political knowledge are far more likely to turn out on election day than those who are less knowledgeable (Delli Carpini & Keeter, 1996; Popkin & Dimock, 1999).

THE LIMITED IMPACT OF KNOWLEDGE

As the preceding review illustrates, there is a wealth of evidence suggesting that knowledge confers a host of cognitive abilities, all of which would seem to facilitate effective navigation of the political terrain, suggesting that interventions that raise the public's level of political knowledge will have positive consequences for the functioning of democracy. This conclusion may be premature, however. In other domains, the acquisition of knowledge has very limited consequences.

In the realm of public health, for example, practitioners have often sought to raise knowledge levels in hopes of improving health decisions and modifying behavioral choices. But interventions that have successfully increased the public's level of knowledge have often failed to produce the anticipated consequences of this newfound knowledge.

This was certainly the case in the initial efforts to combat AIDS in the United States. Public health officials assumed that if they could increase people's knowledge about the disease, people would make the appropriate modifications to their behaviors (Helweg-Larsen & Collins, 1997). A massive public education campaign was developed to educate people about the disease (for a review, see Fisher & Fisher, 1992). In terms of its primary goal, this campaign was a resounding success. By the early 1990s, virtually all US adults knew what AIDS was, had some sense of how the disease is transmitted, and knew what steps could be taken to avoid exposure (DiClemente, Forrest, Mickler, & Principal Site Investigators, 1990; Rogers, Singer, & Imperio, 1993). But in terms of its broader aims, this public education campaign was largely a failure, yielding virtually no reliable effects on people's actual behaviors (e.g., Mann, Tarantola, & Netter, 1992). Knowledge, in and of itself, was insufficient for changing judgments and behaviors.

Similar efforts have been initiated in recent years to increase the public's knowledge about the health consequences of obesity. As a part of this effort, the US Department of Health and Human Services hosts a webpage designed to provide health information based on the premise that 'accurate scientific information on nutrition and dietary guidance is critical to the public's ability to make the right choices in the effort to curb obesity and other food related diseases' (www.healthierus.gov). So far, though, these kinds of information campaigns seem not to have had their intended effect: the proportion of US adults who are overweight or obese has risen steadily over the last decade, reaching a startling 66% in one recent national study (Hedley, Ogden, Johnson, Carroll, & Curtin, 2004).

And the same sorts of findings have emerged in the political domain. For example, results from 'deliberative polls' suggest that even substantial increases in political knowledge often exert little impact on political views (Fishkin, 1991, 1995). According to its proponents, deliberative polling provides insight into the issue positions that ordinary citizens would hold 'were they better informed on the issues and had the opportunity and motivation to examine those issues seriously' (Fishkin, 1995, p. 162). But the results of these intensive interventions have often been quite modest.

The first and most widely publicized deliberative poll, held in early 1996, provides a dramatic illustration (Merkel, 1996). Nearly 500 US citizens were assembled in Austin, Texas, for an intense weekend of education and deliberation. Leading up to the weekend, participants were provided with briefing reports on several of the most salient issues of the day, and during the weekend, experts in various policy domains provided further information and answered questions about the issues. In small groups, participants engaged in face-to-face discussions with other citizens, further expanding the range of perspectives and information to which participants were exposed.

Despite the intensity of this experience and the volume of information that participants were exposed to, substantive shifts in political views were the exception rather than the rule (Kohut, 1996; Mitofsky, 1996). In fact, of the 81 political opinions that were assessed before and immediately after the event, only 20 registered statistically significant change at the aggregate level; the remaining 60 political opinions were impervious to the intense barrage of political information (Kohut, 1996). And very few of these involved changes from one side of an issue to another. These findings suggest that even dramatic increases in political knowledge have modest effects on political opinions.

More tightly controlled experimental investigations have yielded similar evidence. In one recent demonstration, Tichy and Krosnick (2001) examined knowledge among the general public about US energy policies. Specifically, they assessed how much ordinary citizens knew about the costs and benefits of various modes of electricity generation, and they explored the implications of this knowledge for people's preferences about how electricity should be generated in the future. They found remarkably low knowledge levels: only about 30% of participants recognized that coal was the most prevalent source of electricity in the US. And the vast majority mistakenly believed that the production of solar energy is inexpensive (63%) or only moderately expensive (26%) when in fact it is very expensive to produce. Overall, few people correctly understood how electricity was being generated, or the advantages and disadvantages of various methods of electricity generation.

Tichy and Krosnick (2001) then explored the consequences of increasing the amount of knowledge people possessed about electricity generation. They presented a randomly selected subset of their participants with accurate information about electricity generation, specifically, about the percentage of America's electricity that is currently produced by various methods, the cost, type(s) and quantity of pollution each produces, and other notable advantages or drawbacks characteristic of each method. Subsequently, participants were asked about their preferences regarding specific energy policies. Other participants were asked the same set of questions about their energy policy preferences without being given the background information.

Tichy and Krosnick (2001) found that providing participants with accurate information induced very modest opinion shifts. For example, increasing people's knowledge about electricity generation led to a modest increase in the proportion of people who supported the use of coal (21% *vs.* 11%), presumably because few people had realized that coal is as inexpensive as it is. Educating participants also led to a decrease in support for solar power generation (19% *vs.* 13%), probably because few people had realized that wind is considerably less expensive

than solar power. Although statistically significant, the magnitudes of these changes suggest that information did little to alter people's preferences regarding electricity generation.

This pattern of findings has been corroborated in the domain of welfare policy (Kuklinski, Quirk, Jerit, Schwieder, & Rich, 2000). Most Americans are dramatically misinformed about basic facts relevant to the current welfare policy debate. In one recent survey, containing six factual questions about welfare, none of the questions was answered correctly by more than half of the participants, and only 3% of participants got more than half of the questions correct. Remarkably, however, providing people with accurate information about welfare had no impact on people's welfare policy preferences; they were no different for people who had and had not received the information (Kuklinski *et al.*, 2000). Here too, people's attitudes seem not to be tightly bound to the knowledge they possessed about the attitude object.

WHY SUCH MODEST EFFECTS?

Taken together, a diverse set of evidence suggests that even fairly drastic increases in the amount of political information people have about an object don't always lead to discernible changes in relevant attitudes or behaviors. This may seem at odds with the litany of powerful consequences of knowledge that we reviewed earlier, but one resolution lies in a clearer understanding of how knowledge operates.

Knowledge is a powerful enabler. It confers particular cognitive and behavioral abilities, facilitating a great number of tasks. But virtually all deliberate judgments or behaviors require more than ability alone—they also require sufficient levels of motivation. Motives exert an energizing influence, instigating, directing, and sustaining actions aimed at achieving currently salient goals. Without adequate motivation, even dramatic increases in ability will have little impact on judgments or behavior. Unless people are already motivated to engage in the political process, interventions that increase knowledge alone are likely to have modest effects on political judgments and behavior.

Disentangling the impact of motivation and ability

All of this suggests that when an outcome (e.g., a particular judgment, the formation of an opinion, the enactment of a behavior) requires specific information and does not require the energizing and directive force of motivation, levels of political knowledge regulate the outcome. When an outcome requires motivation but does not require specific information, political knowledge will not regulate the outcome (though motivating factors will). And when an outcome requires the copresence of information and motivation, political knowledge will regulate the outcome in conjunction with motivating forces.

Recent evidence supports each of these contentions (Visser *et al.*, 2004). For example, when people evaluate the fairness of media coverage of an issue, they often exhibit a 'hostile media' bias, or the tendency to perceive that a balanced presentation of information on a controversial issue is biased against one's own side of the issue (Vallone, Ross, & Lepper, 1985).

This bias is driven at least partly by the fact that people spontaneously compare their own store of information about an issue to the information presented by the media. Because people tend to possess more attitude-congruent than attitude-incongruent information, even a balanced media presentation appears to have omitted more of the former than of the latter, producing the perception of a bias against one's own side of the issue. This suggests that possessing information, regardless of one's level of motivation, should regulate the hostile media bias. And indeed, people who are very knowledgeable about an issue perceive a much stronger hostile media bias than do people who are less

knowledgeable about the issue (Visser *et al.*, 2004). The amount of importance people attach to the issue, on the other hand, does not regulate the magnitude of the hostile media bias.

A different outcome produced the opposite pattern of results. When told that they would be evaluating a series of political candidates and given an opportunity to selectively expose themselves to information about each candidate, attitude importance (and not attitude-relevant knowledge) regulated the type of information people chose. For example, people who attached importance to the issue of capital punishment requested candidates' positions on that issue significantly more often than those who attached little importance to the issue. The volume of issue-relevant information stored in memory had no impact on selective exposure. Thus, attaching importance to the issue motivated participants to seek information that enabled them to use their attitudes when evaluating candidates, but possessing knowledge did not.

A third outcome revealed yet another pattern of results. Performing an attitude-expressive behavior requires sufficient motivation to do so, as well as sufficient knowledge to plan and execute appropriate behavioral strategies. And indeed, across two studies, higher attitude importance and attitude-relevant knowledge both predicted subsequent increases in attitude-expressive behavior, but the combination of high importance and high knowledge predicted a particularly pronounced surge in attitude-expressive behavior (Visser *et al.*, 2004).

The consequences of knowledge, therefore, depend on the nature of the outcome. Knowledge confers a host of important cognitive and behavioral abilities, and for outcomes that depend solely on these abilities, knowledge has powerful consequences. Ability alone, however, is insufficient for many outcomes. For outcomes that are primarily driven by motivational forces, knowledge is quite inconsequential. And for outcomes that demand both ability and motivation, knowledge is a necessary but not a sufficient antecedent.

CORRELATION AND CAUSATION

Taken together, these findings raise an important caveat about interpreting past findings regarding the consequences of political knowledge. With exceedingly few exceptions, inferences about the implications of political knowledge for political opinions and behaviors have been based on observed correlations between levels of political knowledge and other variables. Political knowledge has been shown to correlate with factors such as political participation, tolerance, and ideological constraint, among other things (for a review, see Delli Carpini & Keeter, 1996).

The preferred explanation for these findings is that political knowledge causes a wide range of desirable outcomes, and such causal claims are ubiquitous in the literature. For example, Delli Carpini and Keeter (1996) concluded that political knowledge 'boosts participation' (p. 224), 'promotes a number of civic attitudes such as political interest and efficacy' (p. 224), 'leads citizens to develop more numerous, stable, and internally consistent attitudes' (p. 228), among other things.

The broad acceptance of these causal claims about the profound impact of political knowledge on the basis of correlational evidence is remarkable, particularly in light of the fact that other causal processes provide equally plausible accounts for the observed relations between political knowledge and other variables. Rather than knowledge 'promoting' political interest or efficacy, for example, it is equally reasonable to suppose that being interested in politics or feeling politically efficacious motivates people to acquire political knowledge, reflecting the reverse causal mechanism. And rather than knowledge 'boosting' political participation, it is entirely plausible that some third factor may produce both outcomes. We know, for example, that the importance people attach to politics is likely to inspire both knowledge acquisition and political participation. Thus, the relation between knowledge and participation could be entirely spurious, driven by their mutual relation to importance.

FUTURE DIRECTIONS

This discussion makes clear that a number of issues remain unresolved, and provides guidance for future research. Perhaps most fundamental is the need for greater clarity about precisely what kind of information is necessary for the successful execution of citizen duties (Krosnick, 1998; Kuklinski & Quirk, 2001; Lupia, in press). This poses a significant challenge, but it is one that the field must confront before real progress can be made toward understanding the antecedents of political knowledge as well as its consequences for the attitudes, beliefs, and behaviors of individuals.

Another high priority is the accumulation of more experimental evidence regarding the causal effects of political knowledge. Continuing to assess the correlations between measures of political knowledge and other variables is unlikely to yield important new insights regarding the consequences of knowledge. But directly manipulating political knowledge and tracing the implications for other outcomes and processes may well do so. Such investigations should also explore potential moderators of the impact of political knowledge. Its consequences are likely to vary depending on a host of other factors.

In particular, additional research is necessary to explore more fully when and how knowledge interacts with various motivational factors to influence behavior. Contributions of this sort would provide much more precise leverage for identifying the necessary and sufficient conditions under which political knowledge exerts its impact.

CONCLUSION

A wealth of evidence from decades of survey research suggests that most citizens know remarkably little about the political world, raising deep concerns among social scientists about the degree to which citizens' attitudes and beliefs reflect careful consideration of relevant political information. Indeed, evidence from the psychological literature indicates that knowledge confers important cognitive abilities, many of which would seem to be important for meeting the obligations of democratic citizenship. Inferences about current levels of political knowledge among the general public and the impact of these knowledge levels on citizens' attitudes, beliefs, and behavior must be drawn with caution, however. A number of important conceptual and methodological limitations must be addressed before strong conclusions can be drawn about the antecedents and consequences of political knowledge.

REFERENCES

Baddeley, A. D., & Hitch, G. J. (1974). Working memory. In G. Bower (Ed.), *The psychology of learning and motivation: Advances in research and theory* (pp. 47–90). New York: Academic Press.

Bassili, J. N. (1996). Meta-judgmental versus operative indexes of psychological features: The case of measures of attitude strength. *Journal of Personality and Social Psychology, 71*, 637–653.

Berent, M. K., & Krosnick, J. A. (1995). The relation between political attitude importance and knowledge structure. In M. Lodge & K. McGraw (Eds.), *Political judgment: Structure and process* (pp. 91–110). Ann Arbor, MI: University of Michigan Press.

Boninger, D. S., Krosnick, J. A., & Berent, M. K. (1995). Origins of attitude importance: Self-interest, social identification, and value relevance. *Journal of Personality & Social Psychology, 68*, 61–80.

Boninger, D. S., Krosnick, J. A., Berent, M. K., & Fabrigar, L. R. (1995). The causes and consequences of attitude importance. In R. E. Petty & J. A. Krosnick (Eds.), *Attitude strength: Antecedents and consequences* (pp. 159–189). Mahwah, NJ: Erlbaum.

Clarke, P., & Fredin, E. (1978). Newspapers, television and political reasoning. *Public Opinion Quarterly, 42*, 143–160.

Clarke, P., & Kline, F. G. (1974). Media effects reconsidered: Some new strategies for communication research. *Communication Research, 1*, 224–240.

Cooke, N. J., Atlas, R. S., Lane, D. M., & Berger, R. C. (1993). Role of high-level knowledge in memory for chess positions. *American Journal of Psychology, 106*, 321–351.

Craik, F. I. M. (1977). Depth of processing in recall and recognition. In S. Dornic (Ed.), *Attention and performance VI* (pp. 679–697). Hillsdale, NJ: Erlbaum.

Craik, F., & Lockhart, R. (1972). Levels of processing: A framework for memory research. *Journal of Verbal Learning and Verbal Behavior, 11*, 671–684.

Delli Carpini, M., & Keeter, S. (1996). *What Americans know about politics and why it matters.* New Haven: Yale University Press.

DiClemente, R. J., Forrest, K. A., Mickler, S., & Principal Site Investigators. (1990). College students' knowledge about AIDS and changes in HIV-preventative behaviors. *AIDS Education and Prevention, 2*, 201–212.

Downs, A. (1957). *An economic theory of democracy.* New York: Addison Wesley.

Eckhardt, B. B., Wood, M. R., & Jacobvitz, R. S. (1991). Verbal ability and prior knowledge: Contributions to adults' comprehension of television. *Communication Research, 18*, 636–649.

Eveland, W. P., Shah, D. V., & Kwak, N. (2003). Assessing causality in the cognitive mediation model: A panel study of motivations, information processing, and learning during campaign 2000. *Communication Research, 30*, 359–386.

Fazio, R. H., & Zanna, M. P. (1981). Direct experience and attitude-behavior consistency. In L. Berkowitz (Ed.), *Advances in experimental social psychology* (Vol. 14, pp. 161–202). San Diego, CA: Academic Press.

Fisher, J. D., & Fisher, W. A. (1992). Changing AIDS-risk behavior. *Psychological Bulletin, 11*, 455–474.

Fishkin, J. S. (1991). *Democracy and deliberation: New directions for democratic reform.* New Haven, CT: Yale University Press.

Fishkin, J. S. (1995). *The voice of the people: Public opinion and democracy.* New Haven: Yale University Press.

Fiske, S. T., Lau, R. R., & Smith, R. A. (1990). On the varieties and utilities of political expertise. *Social Cognition, 8*, 31–48.

Graber, D. A. (1980). *Mass media and American politics.* Washington, DC: Congressional Quarterly Press.

Graber, D. A. (1990). Seeing is remembering: How visuals contribute to learning from television news. *Journal of Communication, 40*, 134–155.

Hambrick, D. Z. (2003). Why are some people more knowledgeable than others? A longitudinal study of knowledge acquisition. *Memory and Cognition, 31*, 902–917.

Hedley, A. A., Ogden, C. L., Johnson, C. L., Carroll, M. D., & Curtin, L. R. (2004). Overweight and obesity among US children, adolescents and adults, 1999–2002. *Journal of the American Medical Association, 291*, 2847–2850.

Helweg-Larsen, M., & Collins, B. E. (1997). A social psychological perspective on the role of knowledge about AIDS in AIDS prevention. *Current Directions in Psychological Science, 6*, 23–26.

Holbrook, A. L., Berent, M. K., Krosnick, J. A., Visser, P. S., & Boninger, D. (2005). Attitude importance and the accumulation of attitude-relevant knowledge in memory. *Journal of Personality and Social Psychology, 88*, 749–769.

Kahneman, D. (1973). *Attention and effort*. Englewood Cliffs, NJ: Prentice-Hall.

Kallgren, C. A., & Wood, W. (1986). Access to attitude-relevant information in memory as a determinant of attitude-behavior consistency. *Journal of Experimental Social Psychology, 22*, 328–338.

Kohut, A. (1996). The big poll that didn't. *Poll Watch, 4*, 2–3.

Krosnick, J. A. (1990). American's perceptions of presidential candidates: A test of the projection hypothesis. *Journal of Social Issues, 46*, 159–182.

Krosnick, J. A. (1998). Review of 'What Americans know about politics and why it matters' by M. X. Delli Carpini and S. Keeter. *Annals of the American Academy of Political and Social Science, 559*, 189–191.

Krosnick, J. A., Boninger, D. S., Chuang, Y. C., Berent, M. K., & Carnot, C. G. (1993). Attitude strength: One construct or many related constructs? *Journal of Personality and Social Psychology, 65*, 1132–1149.

Krugman, H. E., & Hartley, E. L. (1970). Passive learning through television. *Public Opinion Quarterly, 34*, 184–190.

Kuklinski, J. H., & Quirk, P. J. (2001). Conceptual foundations of citizen competence. *Political Behavior, 23*, 285–311.

Kuklinski, J. H., Quirk, P. J., Jerit, J., Schwieder, D., & Rich, R. F. (2000). Misinformation and the currency of democratic citizenship. *Journal of Politics, 62*, 790–816.

Lodge, M., Steenbergen, M., & Brau, S. (1995). The responsive voter: Campaign information and the dynamics of candidate evaluation. *American Political Science Review, 89*, 309–326.

Lupia, A. (in press). How elitism undermines the study of voter competence. *Critical Review*.

Lupia, A., & McCubbins, M. (1998). *The democratic dilemma: Can citizens learn what they need to know?* New York: Cambridge University Press.

Luskin, R. C. (1990). Explaining political sophistication. *Political Behavior, 12*, 331–361.

Lutkus, A. D., Weiss, A. R., Campbell, J. R., Mazzeo, J. & Lazer, S. (1999). *The NAEP 1998 Civics Report Card for the Nation* (NCES 2000-457). Washington, DC: US Department of Education.

Mann, J. M., Tarantola, D. J. M., & Netter, T. W. (1992). *AIDS in the World*. Cambridge, MA: Harvard University Press.

McGraw, K. M., & Pinney, N. (1990). The effects of general and domain-specific expertise on political memory and judgment. *Social Cognition, 8*, 9–30.

McGuire, W. J. (1986). The myth of massive media impact: Savagings and salvagings. In G. Comstock (Ed.), *Public communication and behavior* (Vol. 1, pp. 173–257). San Diego, CA: Academic Press.

Meinhold, J. L., & Malkus, A. J. (2005). Adolescent environmental behaviors: Can knowledge, attitudes, and self-efficacy make a difference? *Environment and Behavior, 37*, 511–532.

Merkel, D. (1996). The polls—Review. The National Issues Convention Deliberative Poll. *Public Opinion Quarterly, 60*, 588–619.

Mitofsky, W. J. (1996). The emperor has no clothes. *The Public Perspective, 7*, 17–19.

Muthukrishnan, A.V., Pham, M. T., & Mungale, A. (1999). Comparison opportunity and judgment revision. *Organizational Behavior and Human Decision Processes, 80*, 228–251.

Nie, N., Junn, J., & Stehlik-Barry, K. (1996). *Education and democratic citizenship in America*. Chicago: University of Chicago Press.

Page, B. I. (1978). *Choices and echoes in presidential elections*. Chicago: University of Chicago Press.

Patterson, T. E. (1980). *The mass media election*. New York: Praeger.

Patterson, T. E., & McClure, R. D. (1976). *The unseeing eye: The myth of television power in national elections*. New York: Putnam.

Paull, G., & Glencross, D. (1997). Expert perception and decision making in baseball. *International Journal of Sport Psychology, 28*, 35–56.

Perse, E. M. (1990). Media involvement and local news effects. *Journal of Broadcasting and Electronic Media, 34*, 17–36.

Popkin, S. L., & Dimock, M. A. (1999). Political knowledge and citizen competence. In S. L. Elkin and K. E. Soltan (Eds.), *Citizen competence and democratic institutions* (pp. 117–146). University Park, PA: Pennsylvania State University Press.

Prior, M., & Lupia, A. (2005, August/September). *What citizens know depends on how you ask them: Experiments on political knowledge under respondent-friendly conditions*. Paper presented at the 101st annual meeting of the American Political Science Association, Washington, DC.

Prislin, R. (1996). Attitude stability and attitude strength: One is enough to make it stable. *European Journal of Social Psychology, 26*, 447–477.

Ratneshwar, S., & Chaiken, S. (1991). Comprehension's role in persuasion: The case of its moderating effect on the persuasive impact of source cues. *Journal of Consumer Research, 18*, 52–62.

Recht, D. R., & Leslie, L. (1988). Effect of prior knowledge on good and poor readers. *Journal of Educational Psychology, 80*, 16–20.

Roberts, D. F., & Maccoby, N. (1985). Effects of mass communication. In G. Lindzey & E. Aronson (Eds.), *Handbook of social psychology* (3rd ed., Vol. 2, pp. 539–598). New York: Random House.

Robinson, J. P., & Levy, M. R. (1986). *The main source: Learning from television news.* Beverly Hills, CA: Sage.

Rogers, T. F., Singer, E., & Imperio, J. (1993). AIDS—An update. *Public Opinion Quarterly, 57*, 92–114.

Rokeach, M. (1968). *Beliefs, attitudes and values.* San Francisco: Jossey-Bass Inc.

Schneider, W., Gruber, H., Gold, A., & Opwis, K. (1993). Chess expertise and memory for chess positions in children and adults. *Journal of Experimental Child Psychology, 56*, 328–349.

Tewksbury, D., Weaver, A., & Maddex, B. (2001). Accidentally informed: Incidental news exposure on the World Wide Web. *Journalism & Mass Communication Quarterly, 78*, 533–554.

Tichy, M. P., & Krosnick, J. A. (2001). *Public perceptions of electricity generation: An exploratory study.* Unpublished manuscript, Ohio State University, Columbus, OH.

Tyler, S. W., Hertel, P. T., McCallum, M. C., & Ellis, H. C. (1979). Cognitive effort and memory. *Journal of Experimental Psychology: Human Learning and Memory, 5*, 607–617.

Vallone, R. P., Ross, L., & Lepper, M. R. (1985). The hostile media phenomenon: Biased perception and perceptions of media bias in coverage of the Beirut massacre. *Journal of Personality and Social Psychology, 49*, 577–585.

Visser, P. S. (1998). *Assessing the structure and function of attitude strength: Insights from a new approach.* Unpublished doctoral dissertation, Ohio State University.

Visser, P. S., Krosnick, J. A., & Norris, C. M. (2004). *Challenging the common-factor model of strength-related attitude attributes: Contrasting the antecedents and consequences of attitude importance and attitude-relevant knowledge.* Unpublished manuscript, University of Chicago, Chicago, IL.

Wood, W. (1982). Retrieval of attitude-relevant information from memory: Effects on susceptibility to persuasion and on intrinsic motivation. *Journal of Personality & Social Psychology, 42*, 798–810.

Wood, W., Kallgren, C. A., & Preisler, R. M. (1985). Access to attitude-relevant information in memory as a determinant of persuasion: The role of message features. *Journal of Experimental Social Psychology, 21*, 73–85.

Wood, W., Rhodes, N., & Biek, M. (1995). Working knowledge and attitude strength: An information-processing analysis. In R. E. Petty & J. A. Krosnick (Eds.), *Attitude strength: Antecedents and consequences* (pp. 283–313). Mahwah, NJ: Lawrence Erlbaum Associates.

Zaller, J. (1992). *The nature and origins of mass opinion.* Cambridge University Press.

Zukin, C., & Snyder, R. (1984). Passive learning: When the media environment is the message. *Public Opinion Quarterly, 48*, 629–638.

13

Conceptions of Attitudes and Opinions

Roger Tourangeau and Mirta Galešić

It is hard to think of a concept that is more central to social psychology than the concept of attitudes. Social psychology began as the study of attitudes (Thomas & Znaniecki, 1918), and attitudes have remained a major preoccupation of social psychologists ever since. This interest in attitudes and such closely related notions as public opinion is hardly restricted to social psychologists: these are key concepts for pollsters, sociologists, political scientists, and policy makers as well. Like most concepts in the social sciences, the concept of attitudes has evolved considerably over the years in response both to empirical findings and theoretical developments. As a result, there have been multiple definitions for the concept of attitudes, and the concept is embedded in several rival theoretical frameworks. In addition, researchers have attempted over the years either to distinguish attitudes from such related concepts as beliefs, opinions, and stereotypes or to collapse such distinctions. Still, as we shall see, it is

probably fair to say that the concept of attitudes has shrunk somewhat over the years, and researchers have converged on a rather narrow core definition; attitudes are typically defined as evaluations, as likes and dislikes (see, e.g., Eagly & Chaiken, 1993).

THE EVOLUTION OF THE TRADITIONAL VIEW

Gordon Allport's (1935, p. 310) famous definition of attitudes ('a mental and neural state of readiness, organized through experience, exerting a directive and dynamic influence upon the individual's response to all objects and situations to which it is related') illustrates the early view of attitudes as broad and enduring structures that are closely tied to behaviors. Virtually every aspect of Allport's definition has come under attack at one time or another. For example, Tesser (1993) has argued that some attitudes are the product of heredity rather than experience. Others have questioned the link between attitudes and behaviors. Still others have expressed doubt about how enduring attitudes are (e.g., Converse, 1964).

Despite these challenges, the notion that attitudes involve a predisposition to respond in a specific way—positively or negatively—toward some object or class of objects continues to play a central role in contemporary discussions of attitudes (see, e.g., Eagly & Chaiken, 1993). Almost any concept at any level of abstraction can be the object of an attitude. We can like or dislike fish, eating fish, eating anchovies, eating anchovies on pizza, or the government's policies on commercial fisheries involving anchovies.

Attitudes vs. opinions

Traditional views of attitudes distinguish attitudes from several related concepts. Attitudes are, as we noted, linked to behaviors, but are distinct from them. Behaviors toward an attitude object are generally seen as manifesting the underlying attitudes. In addition, attitudes are also traditionally linked to emotions or feelings about the object and to beliefs about it. Beliefs are the cognitions or thoughts that are associated with the attitude object, not all of which are necessarily evaluative in character. Another term related to attitudes is *opinions*; this term is used in several different ways in the literature, prompting McGuire (1969) to note, 'Perhaps more effort has been expended to distinguish attitudes from opinions than any other construct' (p. 152). Some authors use 'opinion' as a near-synonym of belief. As we drain the evaluation from an attitude, it becomes an opinion, a belief, or, at the extreme, a bit of factual knowledge. Others, however, regard opinions as more specific manifestations of broader underlying attitudes. Under this conception, one would have an attitude about affirmative action, say, but an opinion about the affirmative action policies at a specific university. To complicate matters further, *public opinion* is sometimes used as a synonym for mass political attitudes (e.g., Zaller & Feldman, 1992). McGuire

(1969, p. 152) may have had a point when he noted that the 'situation involv[es] names in search of a distinction.'

Internal attitude structure

Traditionally, attitude researchers have adopted one of two approaches for describing the internal structure of attitudes. One approach (Breckler, 1984) treats attitudes as consisting of beliefs (the *cognitive* component), feelings (the *affective* component), and intentions (the *behavioral* component). All three components have evaluative aspects (for example, one's belief that Mozart is a great composer, one's enjoyment in hearing *The Magic Flute*, and one's intention to attend a Mozart concert next week all suggest a positive evaluation of Mozart). Although the three components tend to coalesce around a single evaluation, they need not converge in this way; when they don't, inconsistent attitudes are the result. It is easy to think of situations when the head conflicts with the heart ('I know broccoli is good for me, but I hate to eat it!') or behavioral intentions don't reflect our feelings ('It's not that I want to miss Mozart but I have to be out of town'). In addition, it is possible for attitudes to lack one or more of the three components. Zajonc's work has been particularly influential in showing that there can be affective evaluations without much in the way of supporting cognitions (Zajonc, 1980); these cognition-free attitudes can arise through several processes, such as classical conditioning or repeated exposure to subliminal stimuli.

The work of Millar and Tesser (e.g., 1989) supports a variation on this traditional three-component conception of attitude structure. Their studies suggest that some attitudes (*consummatory* attitudes) are based mainly on affect whereas others (*instrumental* attitudes) are based mainly on cognitions. They note that this distinction may explain some of the findings reported by Wilson and his colleagues on the disruptive effects of thinking about an attitude object (e.g., Wilson & Dunn, 1986). If the underlying attitude is based primarily on affect, but the measurement procedure emphasizes cognition (for example, by asking the respondent to explain the reasons for his or her attitude), then the resulting attitude report may be a poorer predictor of behavior or indicator of the person's actual evaluation of the object in question than a measurement procedure (such as a simple rating scale) that doesn't bring cognition to the fore.

The second major approach to the internal structure of attitudes is based on the idea that evaluations of an object or course of action are based on the perceived utility of the object or action (e.g., Fishbein, 1967). For example, one's attitude toward voting would depend on one's beliefs about the likely consequences of voting and one's evaluation of each of those consequences. Similarly, one's evaluation of a specific group of people (say, bankers) depends on what attributes one believes bankers to have (conservative, wealthy) and one's evaluation of those attributes:

$$A_O = \sum_{}^{n} b_i e_i \qquad (1)$$

where A_O is the attitude toward the course of action or object in question, b_i is the subjective probability that the course of action leads to consequence i (or that the object has attribute i), e_i is the evaluation of that consequence or attribute, and n is the number of relevant consequences or attributes. This view of attitude structure has obvious links to the notion of subjective expected utility (SEU). Essentially, the attitude toward an object *is* its SEU, and we like things with attractive attributes or high expected payoffs.

Contemporary versions of the traditional view

Perhaps the most influential contemporary advocate of the traditional view of attitudes as pre-existing and relatively enduring evaluations has been Russell Fazio. Like other contemporary attitude theorists, Fazio sees attitudes as structures in long-term memory (LTM), with the same properties as other structures in LTM. One widely accepted model (Anderson, 1983) depicts memory as an associative network, in which concepts are the nodes in the network and the relations between concepts are the links; the links between two concepts become stronger when the concepts are activated together. According to Fazio (e.g., Fazio, 1990), an attitude is a structure consisting of an attitude object, an evaluation, and the link between them. A key property of an attitude is the strength of the object-evaluation link, which determines the accessibility of the attitude: the stronger the link, the more likely that the evaluation will be activated (that is, will come to mind) when the object of the attitude is encountered. With highly accessible attitudes, the evaluation will come to mind automatically whenever the object of the attitude is encountered or mentioned. At the other end of the spectrum, some people will have weak links (or no link at all) between the object and an evaluation. In such cases, an evaluation 'may be constructed on the spot on the basis of whatever information and features of the object happen to be salient at that moment' (Dovidio & Fazio, 1992, p. 206).

To summarize, then, contemporary versions of the traditional view of attitudes retain several key components of the conception of attitudes embodied in Allport's (1935) famous definition. Attitudes (or at least accessible or strong ones) are enduring structures in long-term memory that link an attitude object with an evaluation of it and that guide both perceptions of the object and behaviors toward it (see also Krosnick & Petty, 1995).

CHALLENGES TO THE TRADITIONAL VIEW

Since the 1990s, various features of this view of attitudes have come under fire. One basic line of argument is that people just don't have attitudes as they have been traditionally defined, or if they do have such attitudes, they are not relevant to the kinds of questions that appear in polls and attitude surveys. For example, Zaller and Feldman (1992, p. 79) argue that 'most citizens ... simply do not possess preformed attitudes at the level of specificity demanded in surveys.' Similarly, Tourangeau and Rasinski (1988) argue that attitude questions in surveys typically bring to mind a sample of considerations (relevant beliefs, values, or impressions) from which respondents cobble together a judgment about the issue. By contrast, the traditional view of attitudes assumes that people have stable, pre-existing views about an issue and that they simply recall and report those views when asked to do so. Wilson and Hodges (1992) dub this account the 'file drawer' model, suggesting that respondents search their memories for an attitude and simply read out the result they find (p. 38):

> When people are asked how they feel about something, such as legalized abortion, their uncle Harry, or anchovies on a pizza, presumably they consult a mental file containing their evaluation. They look for the file marked *abortion*, *Uncle Harry*, or *anchovies*, and report the evaluation it contains.

A number of findings have been cited as demonstrating the inadequacy of the file drawer model.

Nonattitudes

One type of evidence against the traditional view is that attitudes just don't appear to be very stable. Data from surveys about various topics show significant inconsistencies in the answers given to the same questions at different time points. Tourangeau, Rips, and Rasinski (2000) describe a study documenting substantial shifts in responses to survey items on abortion and welfare over the space of three weeks. In an another example, Schuman and Presser (1981, p. 255) report a study in which approximately 28% of respondents changed their answers to a question about who is more to blame for crime and lawlessness in the country (individuals or social conditions) within several months. These shifts at the individual level appear essentially random;

there was no overall movement in one direction or the other over the same time frame.

Perhaps the most famous study documenting the apparent fickleness of public attitudes was conducted by Converse (1964). Based on data collected in the SRC NES panels in the years 1956, 1958 and 1960, Converse concluded that 'large portions of an electorate do not have meaningful beliefs' even on widely discussed public issues (p. 245). He found very low correlations between attitudes across waves of the panel, and only weak associations between ideological labels, such as liberal or conservative, and relevant policy positions. For example, one respondent declared himself as 'socialist,' although he thought that services like gas and electricity should be privately owned. Other respondents supported expansion of government services and reducing taxes at the same time (a rather familiar problem to students of American politics). Converse concluded that most of the respondents did not have any real attitudes, but gave answers simply to hide their ignorance or to please the interviewers. Although researchers have noted other possible explanations for the apparent inconsistency of answers to attitude questions, including the unreliability of the questions and true change of attitudes (e.g., see Judd & Krosnick, 1982), the sheer level of inconsistency noted in the studies by Converse, Zaller and Feldman, and others does not sit well with the assumption that people have underlying 'true attitudes' and that these are relatively enduring structures.

Converse (1964) dubbed the highly unstable answers to attitude questions that he observed in the NES panelists 'nonattitudes.' Later experiments have confirmed his contention that respondents often generate answers to attitude questions on the spot without any real grounding in a pre-existing judgment (see Smith, 1984, for a review). One line of research on the use of 'don't know' filters (e.g., Schuman & Presser, 1981) shows that many respondents are willing to offer opinions about issues that are either very obscure or completely fictitious when the question does not explicitly mention 'don't know' or 'no opinion' among the possible responses. An additional 20 to 25% of respondents admit their ignorance about such issues when the question offers an explicit 'don't know' option compared to questions that force respondents to volunteer these responses. How respondents select their answers in such situations—whether they answer completely at random (based on what Converse called a 'mental coin flip') or are biased by acquiescence, social desirability, or in some other way—depends on characteristics of the items, the context, and other variables (Smith, 1984).

Another line of research also seems to reveal the haphazard nature of people's political preferences. These are the studies by Achen and Bartels (2004) that suggest that voters' support for the incumbent party results not from their ideological agreement with that party or even from their overall evaluation of its performance in office, but from highly visible natural events (droughts, shark attacks, and similar catastrophes) that occurred during the incumbent's term in office and that were seen—accurately or not—as being under the incumbent party's control. For example, they show that the highly publicized shark attacks on the New Jersey shore in 1916 resulted in significantly lower support for the incumbent president (Wilson) in the beach counties of New Jersey, although Wilson could hardly have had any influence over these events. Similarly, they argue that bad weather—whether it involves droughts or floods—systematically works against incumbent presidents, because voters blame them for the resulting losses. In the US Presidential elections of 2000, Achen and Bartels estimated that droughts in some parts of the country might have cost Democrat Al Gore 2 to 3% of the votes, as well as up to seven tightly contested states that were hit by bad weather that year. They concluded that most voters simply cannot grasp all the connections between politicians' actions and their own (mis)fortunes.

Context effects

Not only do attitudes seem to vary markedly over time and in response to transient conditions like droughts and shark attacks, they seem to shift even within a questionnaire as a result of seemingly minor changes in question wording or question order. Many studies have shown that attitude judgments are highly context-dependent (see Tourangeau et al., 2000, chap. 7, for a review). Respondents' answers to attitude questions may depend on the general survey context, including the preceding questions, the name of the survey, its sponsor, or even broader circumstances unrelated to the survey topic, such as the weather. Schwarz and Clore (1983) showed that people reported higher overall life satisfaction when they were interviewed on sunny days than on rainy days, presumably because their current mood affected their answers.

Most studies on context effects deal with the effects of one or more prior questions, the *context* items, on responses to a target attitude question that follows them. Two basic types of context effects can occur—assimilation or contrast effects. Assimilation occurs when answers to the target question move in the direction of answers to the context item or when the correlation between the target and context items increases. Contrast effects produce the opposite results—the responses to the target question move away from the answers to the context items or the correlation between the target and context items drops. Most theoretical explanations of context effects share the assumption that attitudes are often ad hoc constructions, created using whatever information is available at the moment the question is asked and using whatever standard of comparison is highlighted by a given context.

According to Tourangeau and colleagues (2000; for a similar model, see Schwarz & Bless, 1992), context effects can originate as respondents carry out the various components of the process of formulating an answer. For example, in trying to understand a question, respondents may use the information from the previous questions as an interpretive framework. Or while trying to recall information to formulate their answers, respondents can be affected by what they have already retrieved in answering earlier items; it is easier for respondents to recall material that they have already retrieved in answering earlier questions. For example, respondents who first answered several questions on society's obligations to the poor showed greater support for welfare spending than respondents who had answered prior questions about economic individualism.

Context can affect not only how respondents construe an issue, but how they arrive at their judgments about it as well. In a famous example originally reported by Hyman and Sheatsley (1950) and later replicated by Schuman and Presser (1981), respondents were much more likely to support Communist journalists reporting news in the United States if they were first asked about US journalists reporting from Russia. When the item on the US journalists came first, respondents' answers to the item about communist reporters reflected the norm of evenhandedness, which mandates similar treatment of journalists from both countries. By contrast, when the communist reporter item came first, answers reflected the prevailing anti-communist sentiments in the US. Schuman and Ludwig (1983) report several conceptual replications of this question order effect (e.g., one pair of items concerned restrictions on imports to the US from Japan and restrictions on exports from the US to Japan), and again found large context effects.

Not all context effects pose problems for the view that attitudes are pre-existing judgments which are read out in response to survey questions. For example, if context alters what issue(s) or attitude object(s) the respondents see as relevant to the question, it may merely affect which file folder they consult. But a large number of context effects appear to involve changes in how respondents think about or evaluate an issue rather than which issue they think about, and such effects clearly present problems for the traditional view.

Framing effects

Another line of research that supports the notion that people's expressed preferences are often constructed on the spot is the work of Kahneman and Tversky (e.g., 1984) and the many papers that elaborate and extend their ideas. In opposition to classical economic theory, which assumes the existence of stable preferences, Kahneman and Tversky propose that people's preferences are constructed on the spot, depending on the context or framing of a particular situation. Their prospect theory explains some of the mechanisms underlying the apparent discrepancies between the preferences predicted by classical economic theory and those actually observed in areas such as consumer behavior, political choice, and risk-taking.

CONSTRUCTIVE ACCOUNTS

If respondents don't have pre-existing views and preferences, then how do they respond to attitude questions about an object or issue? According to Tourangeau *et al.* (2000), formulating a response to any survey question, including factual questions, typically involves four component processes—interpreting the question, retrieving relevant information from memory, integrating that information into a judgment, and reporting the result. What distinguishes attitude questions from factual questions is the type of material that respondents retrieve in formulating their answers and the strategies they use in coming up with an overall judgment.

Retrieval processes and the content of attitudes

Schwarz and his colleagues have argued that 'to arrive at a feature-based evaluation of the attitude object, respondents need to recall relevant information from memory to form a mental representation of the object and of a standard against which it can be evaluated' (Schwarz & Bohner, 2001, p. 439). What particular information a respondent calls to mind will depend largely on the accessibility of the information in memory.

Some information may be temporarily accessible because it was activated while respondents were formulating answers to earlier questions; as we noted in our discussion of context effects, these temporary increases in activation may lead respondents to incorporate information in their representation of the target that they would otherwise have left out. For example, Schwarz and Bless (1992) showed that German respondents evaluated the Christian Democrats more favorably just after they had answered a question that linked a popular politician (Richard von Weizsäcker, then the President of the Federal Republic of Germany) to that party. Apparently, respondents were more likely to include von Weizsäcker in their representation of the Christian Democratic Union (CDU), having just answered a question about him. Of course, other information is chronically accessible and is likely to be retrieved and included in the representation of the target across contexts and occasions. Tourangeau *et al.* (2000, chap. 6) argue that this overlapping material that is retrieved each time the respondent thinks about an issue or object is an important source of consistency in attitude reports.

Apart from exemplars of a category (like von Weizsäcker), respondents may incorporate a wide range of material in constructing a representation of an attitude object or category. Specific experiences, the respondent's mood, impressions, beliefs, and values may all be retrieved and incorporated directly or indirectly into the representation the respondents put together. As Wilson and Hodges (1992, p. 39) put it, 'When people construct their attitudes they have a large data base to draw from, including their behavior, their moods, and a multitude of (often contradictory) beliefs about the attitude object.' Tourangeau *et al.* (2000) refer to the material retrieved in answering attitude questions simply as *considerations*.

Still, what gets retrieved is clearly not the whole story in determining how respondents represent the attitude issue or object.

Respondents often actively exclude material from their representation of the target. The material that they disregard may be seen as irrelevant to the judgment at hand or tainted in some way; or the respondents may infer that the current question calls for them to make a judgment based on new considerations to avoid redundancy with their earlier answers. For example, in the Schwarz and Bless (1992) study, ratings of the Christian Democrats were systematically *lower* when the prior item on von Weizsäcker noted the apolitical character of his office, leading respondents to exclude him from the representation of the CDU. In another example of the deliberate exclusion of accessible material, Schwarz, Strack, and Mai (1991) showed that asking respondents how happy their marriage or romantic lives were just before asking them how happy they were in general ('Taking things all together, would you say that you are very happy, somewhat happy, or not too happy?') reduced the correlation between the two judgments. The study by Schwarz and his colleagues strongly suggested that, when the item on marital happiness came first, respondents reinterpreted the item on overall happiness to mean 'Apart from your marriage, would you say . . . .'

Belief-sampling and the role of mixed beliefs

A key assumption of the attitudes-as-constructions approach is that although any particular person might draw on a very large number of potentially relevant considerations in formulating an answer to an attitude question, most respondents retrieve only a small portion of them. For example, Tourangeau and Rasinski (1988, p. 300) argue that 'because respondents are unlikely to retrieve all their beliefs about an issue, the retrieval stage can be seen as kind of sampling process that overrepresents the most accessible beliefs or situational cues.' Zaller and Feldman (1992, p. 580) make the same point: 'When questioned, [respondents] call to mind a sample of these ideas, including an oversample of ideas made salient by the questionnaire and other recent events.'

One implication of this viewpoint is that variability in the answers respondents give over time and across question contexts partly reflects variability in what they consider as they generate their answers. The problem is not that people know too little about these issues to give stable answers; the problem is that they know too much and base their answers on different considerations every time. Context and other response effects in attitude surveys are often thought to reflect weak or nonexistent attitudes. Tourangeau and his colleagues (2000) argue for the opposite conclusion. To be affected by context, respondents' attitudes must be sufficiently developed for respondents to see the implications of the accessible considerations for the question at hand. For example, respondents' judgments about welfare spending won't be affected by prior items about society's obligations to the poor unless the respondents know enough to make the connection between the two.

A second implication of the idea that inconsistent answers reflect variation in what people retrieve is that many people must have mixed beliefs about many issues. Changing what respondents consider as they formulate their answers will only change their answers if the different considerations point to different judgments. When all the potentially relevant considerations support the same judgment, then sampling variability won't matter. Thus, a key assumption of Zaller and Feldman (1992, p. 585) is that 'most people possess opposing considerations on most issues, that is, considerations that might lead them to decide the issue either way.' Zaller and Feldman present evidence of the impact of mixed considerations on response consistency over time: when the underlying pool of considerations from which respondents sample support different judgments, answers to attitude questions are much more likely to vary over time (see also Tourangeau *et al.*, 2000, p. 189, for related findings).

The findings by Schwarz and his colleagues (Schwarz & Clore, 1983; Schwarz *et al.*, 1991) on the impact of context on judgments of life satisfaction illustrate these broader points about the variability in attitudinal responses over time and across contexts. Instability results when a large base of information that includes a mix of considerations (what do we know more about than our own joys and sorrows, and whose life doesn't include its allotment of both?) is represented by a small, hastily assembled sample from which an overall judgment is derived.

There may be systematic sources of variability within a single attitude structure as well. For example, attitudes may be predominantly cognitive or predominantly affective in character, and respondents may be misdirected by the question to consider mainly their beliefs about the topic or mainly their feelings. This will lead to unstable judgments if the considerations used to construct an answer don't match those that ordinarily guide the judgment of the object (see Wilson & Hodges, 1992, for a summary of research along these lines). Wilson and his colleagues have also argued that respondents may maintain multiple evaluations of the same object, often involving a relatively conscious (or *explicit*) evaluation of the object and a relatively unconscious (or *implicit*) evaluation of it (Wilson, Lindsey, & Schooler, 2000).

Dual and multi-track models

Of course, it is possible that the traditional model applies perfectly well to some people and some attitudes, but that the constructive account applies to others. Fazio clearly intended for his model of the automatic activation of accessible attitudes to apply only to some attitudes—those with strong object-evaluation links. Strack and Martin (1987) also explicitly propose that there are two main routes through which respondents generate answers to attitude questions. In one, respondents retrieve and report an existing evaluation (as in the file drawer model); in the other, they retrieve more specific considerations and integrate them into a judgment (as in the constructive accounts). Tourangeau *et al.* (2000) argue that across a range of survey questions, respondents generally follow one of four main routes to arrive at an answer: Respondents may retrieve an existing answer; they may derive their answers from the top down, inferring an answer based on some more general principle; they may build their judgments from the bottom up, retrieving detailed considerations about the object or issue and integrating these; or, finally, they may base their judgment on an impression, a kind of broad or vague existing judgment. For example, survey respondents asked about their support for the US invasion of Iraq might have an existing judgment about this policy and base their answers on that evaluation. Or they may oppose such interventions on principle or favor them on principle as part of the war on terror, and infer their position on the war from those broader principles. Or they may generate a judgment after considering such specifics as US and Iraqi casualties, the prospects for peace or democracy in the Middle East, the burden of the war on the US Treasury, and so on. Finally, they may simply respond based on their impressions of Bush, Saddam Hussein, or the Middle East. Analogous strategies are used when respondents answer other types of survey questions, such as those asking for frequency estimates.

OTHER APPROACHES

The last few decades have seen a tremendous increase in research on the physiological underpinnings of attitudes. The emerging social neuroscience approach, which examines how nervous, endocrine, and immune systems affect social processes, is being increasingly applied in studies of attitudes and related phenomena (Cacioppo & Berntson, 1992). Bodily responses have been used as a means of capturing 'real' attitudes about sensitive topics, such as those related to racial prejudice or interpersonal attraction. The key idea underlying this research is when respondents have extremely positive or extremely negative attitudes toward an object, that object will provoke greater physiological arousal than when respondents have less

extreme attitudes. This increased arousal can then be detected via physiological measures, such as sweating, heart rate, blood pressure, or respiration. More recently, attitude researchers have applied more sophisticated measurement techniques, such as recording event-related brain potentials (e.g., Cacioppo, Crites, Berntson, & Coles, 1993) or using fMRI to record amygdala activation (e.g., Cunningham, Johnson, Gatenby, Gore, & Banaji, 2003) during exposure to various attitude objects.

One of the most active research areas of social neuroscience deals with the underlying nature of evaluative categorizations. Are positive and negative evaluations reciprocal, that is, negatively correlated? Or can an object be evaluated both positively and negatively? Most measures of attitudes are based on the first assumption and use bipolar scales with both positive and negative ends. Yet some studies have shown that the same attitude object can activate both positive and negative evaluations, only positive, or only negative evaluations. For example, White participants in racial studies sometimes report both strong positive and strong negative attitudes toward Blacks (Hass, Katz, Rizzo, Bailey, & Eisenstadt, 1991). A study by Ito, Cacioppo, and Lang (1998) showed that some attitude objects (such as pictures of a mutilated body or of rabbits with flowers) provoke only one kind of activation, without a reciprocal decrease in the other kind.

Moreover, research in various domains shows that positive and negative information has differential effects on people's evaluations. Negative information affects evaluations more strongly than comparably extreme positive information. This *negativity bias* has been observed in studies of attitudes toward blood and organ donations (Cacioppo & Gardner, 1993), evaluation of political candidates (Holbrook, Krosnick, Visser, Gardner, & Cacioppo, 2001), and risk-taking behaviors (Kahneman & Tversky, 1984). On the other hand, people seem to have slightly positive attitudes when faced with relatively neutral or unknown objects. Such a *positivity offset* is well known in the impression formation literature, where it is often found that previously unknown others are evaluated positively. Both phenomena could have evolutionary benefits: positivity offset motivates organisms to approach novel objects and explore their environment, while negativity bias prevents potentially irreversible harm from hostile situations.

The evidence for nonreciprocal evaluative activations and the existence of both positivity offset and negativity bias suggest that different biological mechanisms may underlie positive and negative activation. In a widely cited paper, Cacioppo and Berntson (1994) proposed a model of the evaluative space in which an object may simultaneously evoke both positive and negative evaluative activation. A number of neuroscience findings support this model. Different areas of the brain have reinforcing and punishing effects when stimulated (Delgado, Roberts, & Miller, 1954); recent research shows that different brain systems may be important to the experience of reward and punishment. The existence of separate systems for positive and negative evaluation presumably allows for more efficient, simultaneous processing of positive and negative information from the environment.

Besides providing insight into neurobiological mechanisms underlying attitudes, the neuroscientific approach to the study of attitudes has inspired new ways of measuring attitudes. For example, Phelps and colleagues (2000) recorded amygdala activity in White respondents while they were evaluating Black and White faces. The respondents who showed negative reactions to Black faces in implicit attitude tests (by classifying negative words as negative more quickly when they followed a photograph of a Black face than one of a White face) had significantly higher amygdala activity than respondents who did not have such negative reactions. There was no correlation between amygdala activity and direct measures of racial attitudes (such as the Modern Racism Scale) on which the respondents presumably could adjust their answers in a more socially desirable direction. These results

are in line with other studies showing that some basic evaluative mechanisms operate automatically outside of conscious awareness (Bargh, 1994).

Another approach to studying the physiological foundations of attitudes is investigating the extent to which certain attitudes are heritable. The idea that attitudes can be inherited does not imply that there is a gene for any particular attitude, but rather that certain heritable physical differences affect the way a person perceives and reasons about the environment (Tesser, 1993). For example, one's sensory structures (taste, hearing, touch), hormonal levels, intelligence, or activity levels may all affect the formation of one's attitudes. Indeed, different studies have shown a heritable component in various attitudes, ranging from broad social attitudes such as aggression and altruism, to more specific vocational and religious attitudes, and even to conservatism (cf. Tesser, 1993).

STEREOTYPES

The concept of stereotypes, first introduced by Lippmann (1922), who called them 'pictures in our heads,' are closely related to attitudes, and stereotypes have been the subject of considerable research and theoretical development over the last 20 years. Stereotypes are usually described as beliefs about the traits, behaviors, and other characteristics of members of a particular group (Schneider, 2004). When stereotypes toward a group are coupled with negative affective reactions or attitudes toward that group, prejudice occurs. In an important study, Devine (1989) showed that mere knowledge of a stereotype might not lead to prejudice if the stereotype is incongruent with one's personal beliefs. It is difficult to imagine a White American who isn't familiar with the stereotype of Black Americans; however, knowing a stereotype isn't the same as subscribing to it. Still, since the stereotypes are typically learned earlier than the opposing personal beliefs, they can be automatically activated in the presence of members of stereotyped groups and can be detected through implicit measures of attitudes.

Implicit measures of attitudes represent an attempt to measure the automatic components of attitudes; these are evaluative reactions that take place outside of our awareness, that don't require any intention to initiate (and cannot be consciously terminated or controlled), and that create minimal interference with other ongoing cognitive processes (see, for example, Bargh, 1994). In contrast with the traditional direct measures of attitudes (such as rating scales), implicit attitude measures are thought to be useful for predicting behaviors that are performed without much thought or behaviors on sensitive issues, where direct attitude measures might be prone to social desirability biases (Dovidio & Fazio, 1992). The most popular implicit tests involve 'priming' procedures, in which the presentation of a stimulus facilitates some judgment, presumably by triggering an automatic evaluative response. For example, Fazio, Jackson, Dunton, and Williams (1995) used affective priming to measure prejudice indirectly. Their respondents were first briefly presented with a Black or a White face and were then asked to indicate whether an adjective was negative or positive. For White participants, Black faces facilitated responding to negative adjectives and interfered with responding to positive adjectives; these effects were reflected in shorter response times for the negative adjectives and longer for the positive ones. The same pattern occurred for Black participants with White faces.

Greenwald, McGhee, and Schwartz (1998) developed an alternative technique for measuring implicit attitudes—the Implicit Association Test (IAT). In this test, respondents first learn the desired responses to two pairs of stimuli, for example 'white' and 'black' and 'good' and 'bad.' They learn to respond differently to each stimulus in the pair; for example, they learn to press the left key when they see a word whose meaning is related to 'good' and to press the right key when they see a word whose meaning is related to 'bad.' The two pairs are then

combined in such a way that the response mapping for one of the pairs is switched. For example, the respondents now have to press the left key when they see a word related to 'white' or 'bad,' and the right key when they see a word related to 'black' or 'good.' Response times are recorded. The basic assumption is that the response times will be longer for incongruent mappings. For example, a person who holds negative stereotypes toward Blacks will have more trouble in using the same key for both 'black' and 'good,' compared to a person who holds positive stereotypes toward Blacks. This incongruency effect was found not only in studies of racial attitudes (Greenwald *et al.*, 1998), but also with attitudes toward other groups, such as older people and women.

What remains unclear in the literature on implicit attitudes is what exactly is triggered by the presentation of stimuli like these. For example, what the 'attitude' object in these studies (a picture of a Black face; the word 'Black') may trigger could be a connotation that is more semantic in character than it is attitudinal. Or the stimulus could automatically activate a stereotype that the respondent doesn't subscribe to or in fact rejects. The spread of activation from one concept to another is an automatic process, but the fact that two concepts are linked in memory doesn't mean that the one represents the evaluation of the other; sometimes an associative link is just a link, not a belief or an evaluation. There are different levels and types of evaluative reaction, ranging from connotative meanings to cognitive associations to visceral reactions. It is not clear that the presence of *any* type of evaluative association really indicates the existence of an attitude, at least not an attitude that traditional attitude theorists would recognize.

CONCLUSION

The last few decades have seen considerable refinement in the traditional view of attitudes. People clearly make evaluative judgments, and, though many of these judgments are generated on the spot (rather than retrieved from memory) and are context-dependent (rather than stable across contexts and occasions), they nonetheless reflect what people know and feel about different topics. The evolution in the concept of attitudes over the last 20 years or so has been strongly influenced by developments within cognitive psychology. Attitude researchers have borrowed such key notions from cognitive psychology as the conception of long term memory as an associative network, the spread of activation from one concept to related concepts, and the distinction between automatic and controlled processes, and they have proposed analyses of the processes involved in answering attitude questions modeled on those for other cognitive tasks. As cognitive psychology itself continues to be affected by the neuroscience revolution and becomes 'warmer' (Schwarz, 1998)— that is, more attuned to 'the interplay of thinking and feeling' in Schwarz's phrase— the next wave of development in our conception of attitudes is likely to be based on advances in our understanding of their neurophysiological and emotional bases.

REFERENCES

Achen, C. H., & Bartels, L.M. (2004). Musical Chairs: Pocketbook voting and the limits of democratic accountability. Paper presented at the Annual Meeting of the American Political Science Association, Chicago.

Allport, G. W. (1935). Attitudes. In C. Murchison (Ed.), *A handbook of social psychology* (pp. 798–844). Worcester, MA: Clark University Press.

Anderson, J. R. (1983). *The architecture of cognition.* Cambridge: Harvard University Press.

Bargh, J. A. (1994). The four horsemen of automaticity: Awareness, efficiency, intention, and control in social cognition. In R. S. Wyer, Jr. & T. K. Srull (Eds.), *Handbook of social cognition* (2nd ed., pp. 1–40). Hillsdale, NJ: Erlbaum.

Breckler, S. J. (1984). Empirical validation of affect, behavior, and cognition as distinct components of attitude. *Journal of Personality and Social Psychology, 47,* 1191–1205.

Cacioppo, J. T., & Berntson, G. G. (1992). Social psychological contributions to the decade of the brain: Doctrine of multilevel analysis. *American Psychologist, 47,* 1019–1028.

Cacioppo, J. T., & Berntson, G. G. (1994). Relationship between attitudes and evaluative space: A critical review, with emphasis on the separability of positive and negative substrates. *Psychological Bulletin, 115,* 401–423.

Cacioppo, J. T., & Gardner, W. L. (1993). What underlies medical donor attitudes and behavior? *Health Psychology, 12,* 269–271.

Cacioppo, J. T., Crites, S. L., Jr., Berntson, G. G., & Coles, M. G. H. (1993). If attitudes affect how stimuli are processed, should they not affect the event-related brain potential? *Psychological Science, 4*(2), 108–112.

Converse, P. (1964). The nature of belief systems in mass publics. In D. Apter (Ed.), *Ideology and discontent* (pp. 206–261). New York: Free Press.

Cunningham, W. A., Johnson, M. K., Gatenby, J. C., Gore, J. C., & Banaji, M. R. (2003). Neural components of social evaluation. *Journal of Personality and Social Psychology, 85,* 639–649.

Delgado, J. M. R., Roberts, W. W., & Miller, N. E. (1954). Learning motivated by electrical stimulation of the brain. *American Journal of Physiology. 179,* 587–593.

Devine, P. G. (1989). Stereotypes and prejudice: Their automatic and controlled components. *Journal of Personality & Social Psychology, 56,* 5–18.

Dovidio, J. F., & Fazio, R. H. (1992). New technologies for the direct and indirect assessment of attitudes. In J. M. Tanur (Ed.), *Questions about questions: Inquiries into the cognitive bases of surveys* (pp. 204–237). New York: Russell Sage Foundation.

Eagly, A. H., & Chaiken, S. (1993). *The psychology of attitudes.* Ft. Worth, TX: Harcourt Brace Jovanovich.

Fazio, R. H. (1990). Multiple processes by which attitudes guide behavior: The MODE model as an integrative framework. In M. P. Zanna (Ed.), *Advances in experimental social psychology* (Vol. 23, pp. 75–109). New York: Academic Press.

Fazio, R. H., Jackson, J. R., Dunton, B. C., & Williams, C. J. (1995). Variability in automatic activation as an unobtrusive measure of racial attitudes: A bona fide pipeline? *Journal of Personality and Social Psychology, 69,* 1013–1027.

Fishbein, M. (1967). A behavior theory approach to the relations between beliefs about an object and the attitude toward the object. In M. Fishbein (Ed.), *Readings in attitude theory and measurement* (pp. 389–400). New York: John Wiley.

Greenwald, A. G, McGhee, D. E., & Schwartz, J. L. K. (1998). Measuring individual differences in implicit cognition: The Implicit Association Test. *Journal of Personality and Social Psychology, 74*, 1464–1480.

Hass, R. G., Katz, I., Rizzo, N., Bailey, J., & Eisenstadt, D. (1991). Cross-racial appraisal as related to attitude ambivalence and cognitive complexity. *Personality and Social Psychology Bulletin, 17*, 83–92.

Holbrook, A. L., Krosnick, J. A., Visser, P. S., Gardner, W. L., & Cacioppo, J. T. (2001). Attitudes toward presidential candidates and political parties: Initial optimism, inertial first impressions, and a focus on flaws. *American Journal of Political Science, 45*, 930–950.

Hyman, H. H., & Sheatsley, P. B. (1950). The current status of American public opinion. In J. C. Payne (Ed.), *The teaching of contemporary affairs: Twenty-first yearbook of the National Council for the Social Studies* (pp. 11–34). New York: National Education Association.

Ito, T. A., Cacioppo, J. T., & Lang, P. J. (1998). Eliciting affect using the international affective picture system: Trajectories through evaluative space. *Personality and Social Psychology Bulletin, 24*, 855–879.

Judd, C. M., & Krosnick, J. A. (1982). Attitude centrality, organization, and measurement. *Journal of Personality and Social Psychology, 42*, 436–447.

Kahneman, D., & Tversky, A. (1984). Choices, values, and frames. *American Psychologist, 39*, 341–350.

Krosnick, J. A., & Petty, R. E. (1995). Attitude strength: An overview. In R. E. Petty and J. A. Krosnick (Eds.), *Attitude strength: Antecedents and consequences* (pp. 247–282). Hillsdale, NJ: Erlbaum.

Lippmann, W. (1922). *Public opinion*. New York: Free Press.

McGuire, W. J. (1969). The nature of attitudes and attitude change. In G. Lindzey & E. Aronson (Eds.), *The handbook of social psychology* (2nd ed., Vol. 3, pp. 136–314). Reading, MA: Addison-Wesley.

Millar, M. G., & Tesser, A. (1989). The effects of affective-cognitive consistency and thought on the attitude-behavior relation. *Journal of Experimental Social Psychology, 25*, 189–202.

Phelps, E. A., O'Connor, K. J., Cunningham, W. A., Funayama, E. S., Gatenby, J. C., Gore, J. C. *et al.* (2000). Performance on indirect measures of race evaluation predicts amygdala activation. *Journal of Cognitive Neuroscience, 12*, 729–738.

Schneider, D. J. (2004). *The psychology of stereotyping*. New York: The Guilford Press.

Schuman, H., & Ludwig, J. (1983). The norm of evenhandedness in surveys as in life. *American Sociological Review, 48*, 112–120.

Schuman, H., & Presser, S. (1981). *Questions and answers in attitude surveys*. New York: Academic Press.

Schwarz, N. (1998). Warmer and more social: Recent developments in cognitive social psychology. *Annual Review of Sociology, 24*, 239–264.

Schwarz, N., & Bless, H. (1992). Scandals and public trust in politicians: Assimilation and contrast effects. *Personality and Social Psychology Bulletin, 18*, 574–579.

Schwarz, N., & Bohner, G. (2001). The construction of attitudes. In A. Tesser & N. Schwarz (Eds.), *Blackwell handbook of social psychology: Intraindividual processes* (Vol.1, pp. 436–457). Oxford, UK: Blackwell.

Schwarz, N., & Clore, G. L. (1983). Mood, misattribution, and judgments of well-being, Informative and directive functions of affective states. *Journal of Personality and Social Psychology, 45*, 513–523.

Schwarz, N., Strack, F., & Mai, H. (1991). Assimilation and contrast effects in part-whole question sequences: A conversational logic analysis. *Public Opinion Quarterly, 55*, 3–23.

Smith, T. W. (1984). Non-attitudes: A review and evaluation. In C. F. Turner & E. Martin (Eds.), *Surveying subjective phenomena* (Vol. 2, pp. 215–255). New York: Russell Sage Foundation.

Strack, F., & Martin, L. (1987). Thinking, judging, and communicating: A process account of context effects in attitude surveys. In H. Hippler, N. Schwarz, & S. Sudman (Eds.), *Social information processing and survey methodology* (pp. 123–148). New York: Springer-Verlag.

Tesser, A. (1993). On the importance of heritability in psychological research: The case of attitudes. *Psychological Review, 100*, 129–142.

Thomas, W. I., & Znaniecki, F. (1918). *The Polish peasant in Europe and America*. Vol. 1. Boston, MA: Badger.

Tourangeau, R., & Rasinski, K. (1988). Cognitive processes underlying context effects in attitude measurement. *Psychological Bulletin, 103*, 299–314.

Tourangeau, R., Rips, L. J., & Rasinski, K. (2000). *The psychology of survey response*. New York: Cambridge University Press.

Wilson, T. D., & Dunn, D. (1986). Effects of introspection on attitude-behavior consistency: Analyzing reasons versus focusing on feelings. *Journal of Experimental Social Psychology, 22*, 249–263.

Wilson, T. D., & Hodges, S. (1992). Attitudes as tempo-
rary constructions. In L. Martin & A. Tesser (Eds.),
The construction of social judgments (pp. 37–66).
New York: Springer-Verlag.

Wilson, T. D., Lindsey, S., & Schooler, T. Y. (2000).
A model of dual attitudes. *Psychological Review, 107*,
101–126.

Zajonc, R. B. (1980). Feeling and thinking: Preferences
need no inferences. *American Psychologist, 35*,
151–175.

Zaller, J., & Feldman, S. (1992). A simple theory of
the survey response: Answering questions versus
revealing preferences. *American Journal of Political
Science, 36*, 579–616.

14

Theories on the Perception of Social Reality

William P. Eveland, Jr. and Carroll J. Glynn

Work on the concept of social reality perception is at the foundation of 20th century social scientific research, and there is no indication of a decline in academic interest in this topic in the 21st century. Importantly, this topic has drawn together researchers from across the core social sciences, including psychology, sociology, communication, and political science. The broad range of scholars working in this area has led to some confusion regarding terminology, which we attempt to clarify in this chapter. We also review the major themes of social reality perception theory and research as an introduction to other chapters later in this volume.

DEFINING SOCIAL REALITY

The understanding of social reality has its roots in the late 19th and early 20th centuries, when scholars argued against the prevailing notion that instinct, heredity and social evolution were the 'deterministic mechanisms that caused humans to tick'

(Glynn, Ostman, & McDonald, 1995, p. 250). Scholars in the 20th century increasingly found that external factors such as culture and the social environment (Irion, 1950) had an impact on human behavior and attitudes.

Cooley (1902/1983) and others argued that humans were different from other animals for a number of important reasons, including their greater inherent potential. He felt that a critical difference between humans and other animals was that humans had social and moral realities ('ideas') that existed in their minds and imaginations. Cooley believed that these ideas would stimulate motives, and that from these motives the reflective observer could gauge behaviors and thence others' 'social reality.' Cooley argued that an understanding of humans required knowledge of both a stream and a path running parallel to the stream along its banks. The stream in this analogy was heredity; the path was communication.

Cooley also felt that self and other do not exist as mutually exclusive social entities. He wrote that 'I' was a term with meaning only insofar as the 'I' thought of him- or herself in reference to an 'Other.' The 'I' required an association with the 'Other,' which in turn made communication both fundamental and critical. In order to communicate, Cooley claimed, the 'I' had to enter into and share the mind of an Other or Others. This capacity was called sympathy—the sharing of mental states that can be communicated. Cooley labeled the symbiosis between the I and the Other the 'looking glass self.' He reasoned that a 'self-idea' has three principal elements: the imagination of what we are to another person, the imagination of that person's judgment of us and 'some sort of self-feeling, such as pride or mortification' (Cooley, 1902/1983, p. 184). He also noted that communication is 'truly the outside or visible structure of thought, as much cause as effect of the inside or conscious life of men' (1909/1962, p. 64).

However, the understanding of the relationship of communication with perceptions of social reality was not a focus for communication scholars until McLeod and Chaffee's (1972) classic work concerning the construction of social reality. They attempted to incorporate the understanding of social reality into the mainstream of communication research. McLeod and Chaffee argued that it is important to understand communication in relation to social influence processes because 'much of the information obtained from others is given the status of *reality*, as if it were no less valid than if it had been a direct observation of physical reality' (p. 50). We perceive that others share the same ideas and information we do and agree that people 'ought' to share our perceptions. Social reality is often considered to be this 'normative sharing of "oughtness"' (p. 51). Because we often do not directly experience events but rather must rely on communicating with others about those events, the communication experience actually describes our social reality. And, because individuals differ in terms of their communication experiences, their 'maps' of social reality will differ as well.

In order to examine social reality in a communication context, McLeod and Chaffee explored the term as *social* reality and social

reality, two very different levels of abstraction. When focusing on *social* reality, the cognitive system of the individual is the unit of analysis, referring to an individual's frame of reference in a social situation (Cooley, 1909/1962; McLeod & Chaffee, 1972). Social *reality* on the other hand is a social system level concept and can be thought of as the degree of agreement or consensus among the members of that system (Katz & Lazarsfeld, 1955; McLeod & Chaffee, 1972). In essence, *social* reality is the view of the world held cognitively by individuals, whereas social *reality* is a system level concept that implies a perception of the world commonly shared in society.

SOCIAL REALITY PERCEPTION RESEARCH

The domain of empirical study under the label of social reality perception research is vast, as implied by the definitions of social reality described above. Our focus is on a subset that is particularly relevant to the study of public opinion, and addresses both of McLeod and Chaffee's (1972) definitions (*social* reality and social *reality*). Below we organize relevant research that provides insight into: (a) whether or not individuals are capable of accurately perceiving reality; (b) the cognitive and social processes through which social reality perceptions are generated; and (c) the social implications—in particular for public opinion and public behavior—of social reality perceptions.

Accuracy in social reality perception

One of the most common findings in the study of social reality perceptions is that these perceptions are often erroneous. Work on errors in social reality perception can be found under labels such as social projection (Robbins & Krueger, 2005), false consensus effect (Ross, Greene, & House, 1977), false uniqueness (Bosveld, Koomen, van der Pligt, & Plaisier, 1995), third-person perceptions (Perloff, 1999), and cultivation

(Gerbner & Gross, 1976), among others. Early work by Allport and his students (Katz & Allport, 1931; Schank, 1932) coined the term 'pluralistic ignorance' to describe the situation in which an individual perceives him- or herself to be in the minority when in fact that individual is in the majority. Later, the definition of pluralistic ignorance was expanded by Merton (1968, p. 431): 'There are two patterns of pluralistic ignorance— the unfounded assumption that one's own attitudes and expectations are unshared and the unfounded assumption that they are uniformly shared.'

An even more inclusive definition, and one that we will follow here, was provided by O'Gorman (1986, p. 333): 'Pluralistic ignorance refers to erroneous cognitive beliefs shared by two or more individuals about the ideas, feelings, and actions of others.' It seems that pluralistic ignorance has come to refer to a shared error in social reality perception that is not specific with regard to direction. The concept thus serves as an inclusive general term for what O'Gorman (1988, p. 145) calls 'false social knowledge of other people,' and it can subsume all of the terms mentioned in the previous paragraph.[1]

A *false consensus* effect occurs when individuals 'see their own behavioral choices and judgments as relatively common and appropriate to existing circumstances while viewing alternative responses as uncommon, deviant, or inappropriate' (Ross *et al.*, 1977, p. 280). It is important to emphasize that the concept of false consensus is *relative* (Gilovich, 1990); that is, research on the false consensus tends to ignore the notion of accuracy that is necessary for defining a consensus as actually false. Instead, researchers generally operationalize the false consensus as an association between one's own response and the perceived responses of others. The false consensus describes the opposite outcome of the original notion of pluralistic ignorance; false consensus suggests that individuals tend to see others as similar to themselves.

Current research on perceptions of uniqueness compared to others can be found under the labels of *pluralistic ignorance* (using the more restrictive definition, e.g., Miller & Prentice, 1994), *false uniqueness* (Bosveld *et al.*, 1995), and *false idiosyncrasy* (Sherman, Presson, & Chassin, 1984).[2] The false consensus effect and the false uniqueness effect are mutually exclusive outcomes, and some work has been done to understand when one or the other will occur (Biernat, Manis, & Kobrynowicz, 1997).

The concepts of projection, false consensus, false uniqueness, and pluralistic ignorance tend to be addressed primarily in sociology, psychology, and social psychology. The *third-person perception*—the belief that others are more susceptible to the negative impact of persuasive mass media messages than the self (Davison, 1983)—might be considered similar to a false uniqueness effect. That is, by reporting that they are not as susceptible as others to media influence, individuals are demonstrating an error of false uniqueness (→ *Public Opinion and the Third-Person Effect*). The related concept of a 'first-person' (or reverse third-person) perception, in which individuals see themselves as more likely to be influenced by positive mass media messages (Atwood, 1994), would also be consistent with a false uniqueness effect.

Processes in social reality perception

Although it is obviously very useful to understand tendencies in social reality perceptions—or what Glynn *et al.* (1995) call product models of social reality perception— what is at least as important is explaining how these products come to be. Glynn *et al.* (1995) refer to these explanations as 'process models.' The section above described two key products of social reality perceptions that at least *implied* errors in perception. One product is some form of shared perception of similarity (i.e., false consensus) and the other is some form of shared feeling of uniqueness (i.e., false uniqueness). We also know from considerable research that both of these shared misperceptions can be reliably identified empirically. The question then becomes: what intrapersonal, interpersonal, and/or mass mediated processes produce one or the other misperception—or accurate perceptions?

Prentice and Miller (1993) suggest that *impression management* may explain false uniqueness effects, and we believe that it could just as easily explain false consensus effects. The impression management explanation states that in order to appear somehow different from others, respondents intentionally misrepresent their own characteristics (or their perceptions of others) to achieve this distinctiveness. In short, impression management explains pluralistic ignorance as the product of some intentional misreporting in order to appear more socially desirable.

Another, more cognitive explanation for the false consensus is *social projection*. That is, we observe a false consensus because individuals use information about themselves to infer information about specific or generalized others about whom little direct information is available. Nickerson (1999), for instance, offers a model of how perceptions of oneself serve as a starting point for making estimates of the characteristics of others. This use of the self as a baseline may be a conscious technique, but it may also reflect a process in which individuals generate their estimates of the characteristics of others using various exemplars. The availability of the self as just one—but one very accessible—exemplar thus leads to projection. Although much of the work on the process of projection starts with the assumption that projection will produce errors in social reality perception, a number of scholars have demonstrated that sometimes, or even often, projection can lead to increased accuracy in perceptions (Hoch, 1987).

A related explanation of false consensus considers how *selective exposure to exemplars* similar to the self can bias perceptions of others (Marks & Miller, 1987). Since individuals often have relatively homogeneous interpersonal contacts, both by choice and based on social structural factors, a quick mental search for exemplars to draw conclusions about others will produce exemplars biased toward individuals similar to the self. Thus, the projection may not be directly from the

self, but instead based on the use of exemplars that are similar to the self (Christen & Gunther, 2003).

Errors in social reality perception may also stem from a *mismatch between the behaviors and the attitudes of others*, or in how the behaviors of others are interpreted by the self. For instance, Prentice and Miller (1993) suggest that public behavior and statements tend to be biased in favor of the existing perceived norm. When personal opinions (and private behaviors) change, norms may be slow to follow. Even based on an accurate sampling of public behaviors and social contacts, private attitudes may be misperceived if the public statements and behavior of others are inconsistent with their private opinions and beliefs.

This explanation, which assumes that some opinions are expressed in public at a different rate than others based on their consistency with perceived norms, has much in common with Noelle-Neumann's (1993) account of the social reality perception process she calls the 'spiral of silence.' The general principle of the theory is that individuals continually scan their social environments for clues related to majority and minority opinions on issues to determine whether or not to speak up or remain silent. The theory states that people have a 'quasi-statistical sense' that they employ in developing estimates of opinions that appear to be gaining or losing ground. The theory also has been examined in terms of normative influences (cf., Glynn & McLeod, 1984, → *Spiral of Silence Theory*).

The *differential interpretation hypothesis* suggests that false uniqueness can be produced when individuals consciously misrepresent their private behaviors to conform to the public norm, but do not realize that others also engage in the same behavior. The *differential encoding hypothesis* suggests that individuals are not aware of how they unintentionally misrepresent their private beliefs, and do not realize that others also unintentionally do the same. For instance, when the self remains silent and does not offer an opinion in a social setting where others are expressing opinions, those others might infer this to imply acquiescence by the self. However, the self might believe that others interpret the self's silence accurately as contempt for the views expressed by others. But, by the same token, the self infers that some other's silence implies acquiescence.

Media influence on reality perception

In addition to these intrapersonal and interpersonal processes offered as explanations for false consensus and false uniqueness effects, communication researchers have worked for decades to identify mass media explanations for pluralistic ignorance, as in Noelle-Neumann's (1993) spiral of silence theory. Another strain of research indicates that different journalistic approaches to presenting information about social reality may produce different effects. Distinguishing between 'base rate' information presented in news coverage (e.g., public opinion polls, government statistics) and *exemplification* in the form of personal examples of cases from statistical categories, researchers have found that audiences infer social reality perceptions more strongly from exemplification than from base rates (Daschmann, 2000). Inferring social reality from exemplification could produce errors in perception because base rate information is typically the more accurate information, and exemplars are not necessarily distributed in a news story in strict accordance with base rates.

Gunther (1998) discusses what he calls the *persuasive press inference* as one explanation for media effects on social reality perceptions. In the context in which media appear to be slanted in favor of one position or another (whether due to partisan media bias or simply because facts favor one position over another), viewers make two related assumptions. First, they assume others are exposed to this same information; second, they assume that this information influences the opinions of others in the direction of the slant. Together, this produces a perception of change in either current or future opinion in the direction of the news slant. But in reality, no change may

take place, or the slant in the news media may be misperceived due to factors including, but not limited to the hostile media phenomenon (see Eveland & Shah, 2003).

Finally, the *cultivation effect* describes a process by which individuals use mass mediated information to infer social reality. Originally, the theory was proposed only to address the influence of entertainment television as a medium because of assumptions about standardized themes across genres and a lack of selectivity in viewing (see Gerbner & Gross, 1976). As such, it focused on the influence of viewing television on broad social themes such as the prevalence of violence and the relative prominence of various social groups. Early modifications to the theory took into account differences in the content conveyed across various genres of television (Hawkins & Pingree, 1981). The original cultivation model implied that a long-term learning process accounted for television effects on social reality perceptions (see Hawkins & Pingree, 1990), although other models have been offered (e.g., Shapiro, 1991). Recent work suggests that these effects are most closely related to the use of heuristics (see Shrum & O'Guinn, 1993), and thus theoretically they tie in nicely with other explanations of pluralistic ignorance.

IMPLICATIONS OF SOCIAL REALITY PERCEPTIONS

Do perceptions of social reality matter, in that they ultimately impact attitudinal or behavioral outcomes? Mutz (1998) calls the influence of perceptions of generalized others on the self 'impersonal influence.' Aside from this general label, there are numerous theories and domains of research that predict or have demonstrated an influence of perceptions of social reality on public attitudes or behaviors. In fact, many of the most prominent theories of persuasion consider perceptions of the beliefs, opinions, or behaviors of others as central determinants of human behavior (see Eveland, 2002, for a review).

Noelle-Neumann's (1993) spiral of silence theory is possibly the most prominent among the public opinion theories that imply an important role for social reality perceptions in determining public behavior. It suggests individuals who generally fear social isolation and perceive themselves to be in the minority on 'moral' issues will be less likely to express their opinions in public. This alters the climate of opinion, which then further influences opinion expression, leading to the spiral (→ *Spiral of Silence Theory*).

There is also a 'behavioral component' in the third-person-effect hypothesis. As Davison (1983) initially noted, based on their perceptions of the impact of a persuasive message, individuals will then take some action in response to the perceived effects. Most research on the third person effect has examined support for censorship as a logical outcome of the (aggregate) misperception of media effects. Although the findings still have some degree of ambiguity, a number of studies have now demonstrated greater support for censorship among those perceiving high levels of media influence on others *or* a large differential between perceived impact on self and other (see Perloff, 1999). Considerable work has been done that examines other attitudinal and behavioral outcomes, including work on public opinion, stereotypes and intergroup behavior, and attitudes toward and engaging in risky behavior. We briefly address each of these areas below.

A number of studies of pluralistic ignorance have sought to understand the possible social implications of social reality misperceptions. A common theme in this work is the impact of misperceived norms for engaging in risky behavior among adolescents. Numerous studies have demonstrated that misperceptions of heavy alcohol use on campus as normative are positively associated with drinking behavior (Perkins & Wechsler, 1996), and longitudinal studies indicate that this relationship appears to be causal in the direction of perception influencing behavior (Prentice & Miller, 1993). Attempts to correct the misperceptions or make them less influential for later behavior

have been somewhat successful (Schroeder & Prentice, 1998). In addition to social reality perceptions on alcohol use, adolescent participation in other risky behaviors, including tobacco (Botvin, Botvin, Baker, Dusenbury, & Goldberg, 1992) and marijuana (Bauman & Geher, 2002–2003) use, have also been shown to be related to misperceptions about the prevalence of these behaviors.

The process of projection, when differentially applied to ingroups and outgroups, can also have important implications for intragroup and intergroup attitudes and behavior. Robbins and Krueger (2005, p. 44), for instance, argue that 'differential projection is sufficient to produce attribute-based ingroup-favoritism and perceptions of group homogeneity. Cooperative behavior with other individuals within one's own group can be understood as a behavioral extension [of] projection-based ingroup-favoritism.' A considerable body of literature on the formation of stereotypes and other perceptions related to ingroups and outgroups may be closely linked to pluralistic ignorance.

Another common framework for understanding the influence of perceived public opinion on public opinion falls under the term 'bandwagon effects' (Fleitas, 1971, → *The Effects of Published Polls on Citizens*). Similarly, Kerr, MacCoun, Hansen and Hymes (1987) investigated what they labeled a 'momentum effect,' the idea that if some members of a group move toward a particular opinion, others will follow. Here, the individuals seek to bask in the reflected glory of the winning side on some issue (or candidate), and so they publicly express opinions (or even privately change their opinions) that conform to the majority. It appears that perceptions of opinion climates are not only related to opinions and opinion expression, but also to willingness to engage in various forms of political participation that imply support for a candidate (Scheufele & Eveland, 2001). Unfortunately, without longitudinal data it is difficult to demonstrate the difference between projection and bandwagon effects (Nadeau, Niemi, & Amato, 1994), because both models employ the same variables, but work in the opposite causal order (bandwagon from perception to own opinion, and projection from own opinion to perception). Although there is empirical evidence for bandwagon effects based on both survey and experimental data, there is also some evidence for the reverse, an 'underdog effect,' in which supporters rally to the losing candidate or side of an issue (Mutz, 1998; Scheufele & Eveland, 2001). But more generally, it seems that bandwagon effects would be more likely in low involvement issues or elections than for issues or elections about which opinions were already strong (Fleitas, 1971). Clearly, more work is needed to better understand the contextual factors or personality types that lead to bandwagon versus underdog effects.

CONCLUDING COMMENTS

Interest in social reality perceptions has a long history in the theoretical and empirical literatures of social science. A number of common findings—often centered on errors in social reality perception—have emerged from this literature. This literature on pluralistic ignorance has produced two key regularities. First, in some instances people perceive their behavior or attitudes to be relatively more common; second, in other instances, people perceived their behavior or attitudes to be relatively unique. Numerous explanations, based on either motivational or cognitive processes at the intraindividual, interpersonal, or mass mediated levels have been offered as explanations for these social reality perceptions. Although there is empirical support for most of these explanations, researchers are still working to understand the relative weights of each explanation in predicting social reality perceptions. They are also attempting to identify important moderating factors that lead to different explanations in different contexts.

There is also considerable evidence that these social reality perceptions can influence other attitudes and behaviors. This is particularly relevant when the social reality perceptions are, in an objective sense, in error. When errors exist in social reality perception—that is, a state of pluralistic ignorance holds—then attitudes and behaviors of the public may be at odds with the best interests, or at least the intentions, of the public. It is no surprise, then, that the study of social reality perceptions has been, and likely will continue to be, a central component of the study of public opinion.

NOTES

1 For a narrower definition see e.g., Miller & McFarland, 1987.

2 For definitional consistency, we will use the term false uniqueness for this phenomenon and reserve the term pluralistic ignorance for the more general perceptual error, even if the original authors employ a different term.

REFERENCES

Atwood, L. E. (1994). Illusions of media power: The third-person effect. *Journalism Quarterly, 71*, 269–281.

Bauman, K. P., & Geher, G. (2002–2003). We think you agree: The detrimental impact of the false consensus effect on behavior. *Current Psychology: Developmental, Learning, Personality, Social, 21*(4), 293–318.

Biernat, M., Manis, M., & Kobrynowicz, D. (1997). Simultaneous assimilation and contrast effects in judgments of self and others. *Journal of Personality and Social Psychology, 73*, 254–269.

Bosveld, W., Koomen, W., van der Pligt, J., & Plaisier, J. W. (1995). Differential construal as an explanation for false consensus and false uniqueness effects. *Journal of Experimental Social Psychology, 31*, 518–532.

Botvin, G. J., Botvin, E. M., Baker, E., Dusenbury, L., & Goldberg, C. J. (1992). The false consensus effect: Predicting adolescents' tobacco use from normative expectations. *Psychological Reports, 70*, 171–178.

Christen, C. T., & Gunther, A. C. (2003). The influence of mass media and other culprits on the projection of personal opinion. *Communication Research, 30*, 414–431.

Cooley, C.H. (1962). *Social organization: A study of the larger mind.* New York: Schocken Books (Original work published in 1909).

Cooley, C. H. (1983). *Human nature and the social order*. New Brunswick, NJ: Transaction Books (Original work published in 1902).

Daschmann, G. (2000). Vox pop & polls: The impact of poll results and voter statements in the media on the perception of a climate of opinion. *International Journal of Public Opinion Research, 12*, 160–179.

Davison, W. P. (1983). The third-person effect in communication. *Public Opinion Quarterly, 47*, 1–15.

Eveland, W. P., Jr. (2002). The impact of news and entertainment media on perceptions of social reality. In J. P. Dillard & M. Pfau (Eds.), *The persuasion handbook: Developments in theory and practice* (pp. 691–727). Thousand Oaks, CA: Sage.

Eveland, W. P., Jr., & Shah, D. V. (2003). The impact of individual and interpersonal factors on perceived news media bias. *Political Psychology, 24*, 101–117.

Fleitas, D. W. (1971). Bandwagon and underdog effects in minimal-information elections. *American Political Science Review, 65*, 434–438.

Gerbner, G., & Gross, L. (1976). Living with television: The violence profile. *Journal of Communication, 26*(2), 173–199.

Gilovich, T. (1990). Differential construal and the false consensus effect. *Journal of Personality and Social Psychology, 59*, 623–634.

Glynn, C. J., & McLeod, J. M. (1984). Public opinion du jour: An examination of the spiral of silence. *Public Opinion Quarterly, 48*, 731–740.

Glynn, C. J., Ostman, R. E., & McDonald, D. G. (1995). Opinions, perception, and social reality. In T. L. Glasser & C. T. Salmon (Eds.), *Public opinion and the communication of consent* (pp. 249–277). New York: Guilford Press.

Gunther, A. C. (1998). The persuasive press inference: Effects of mass media on perceived public opinion. *Communication Research, 25*, 486–504.

Hawkins, R. P., & Pingree, S. (1981). Uniform messages and habitual viewing: Unnecessary assumptions in social reality effects. *Human Communication Research, 7*, 291–301.

Hawkins, R. P., & Pingree, S. (1990). Divergent psychological processes in constructing social reality from mass media content. In N. Signorielli & M. Morgan (Eds.), *Cultivation analysis: New directions in media effects research* (pp. 35–50). Newbury Park, CA: Sage.

Hoch, S. J. (1987). Perceived consensus and predictive accuracy: The pros and cons of projection. *Journal of Personality and Social Psychology, 53*, 221–234.

Irion, F. C. (1950). *Public opinion and propaganda*. New York: Thomas Y. Crowell Co.

Katz, D., & Allport, F. H. (1931). *Student attitudes*. Syracuse, NY: Craftsman Press.

Katz, E., & Lazarsfeld, P. F. (1955). *Personal influence: The part played by people in the flow of mass communications*. Glencoe, IL: Free Press.

Kerr, N. L., MacCoun, R. J., Hansen, C. H., & Hymes, J. A. (1987). Gaining and losing social support: Momentum in decision-making groups. *Journal of Experimental Social Psychology, 23*, 119–145.

Marks, G., & Miller, N. (1987). Ten years of research on the false-consensus effects: An empirical and theoretical review. *Psychological Bulletin, 102*, 72–90.

McLeod, J. M., & Chaffee, S. H. (1972). The construction of social reality. In J. T. Tedeschi (Ed.), *The social influence processes* (pp. 50–99). Chicago: Aldine.

Merton, R. K. (1968). *Social theory and social structure* (enlarged edition). New York: Free Press.

Miller, D. T., & McFarland, C. (1987). Pluralistic ignorance: When similarity is interpreted as dissimilarity. *Journal of Personality and Social Psychology, 53*, 298–305.

Miller, D. T., & Prentice, D. A. (1994). Collective errors and errors about the collective. *Personality and Social Psychology Bulletin, 20*, 541–550.

Mutz, D. C. (1998). *Impersonal influence: How perceptions of mass collectives affect political attitudes*. New York: Cambridge University Press.

Nadeau, R., Niemi, R. G., & Amato, T. (1994). Expectations and preferences in British general elections. *American Political Science Review, 88*, 371–383.

Nickerson, R. S. (1999). How we know—and sometimes misjudge—what others know: Imputing one's own knowledge to others. *Psychological Bulletin, 125*, 737–759.

Noelle-Neumann, E. (1993). *The spiral of silence: Public opinion—our social skin* (2nd ed.). Chicago: University of Chicago Press.

O'Gorman, H. J. (1986). The discovery of pluralistic ignorance: An ironic lesson. *Journal of the History of the Behavioral Sciences, 22*, 333–347.

O'Gorman, H. J. (1988). Pluralistic ignorance and reference groups: The case of ingroup ignorance. In H. J. O'Gorman (Ed.), *Surveying social life: Papers in honor of Herbert H. Hyman* (pp. 145–173). Middletown, Connecticut: Wesleyan University Press.

Perkins, H. W., & Wechsler, H. (1996). Variation in perceived college drinking norms and its impact on alcohol abuse: A nationwide study. *Journal of Drug Issues, 26*, 961–974.

Perloff, R. M. (1999). The third-person effect: A critical review and synthesis. *Media Psychology, 1*, 353–378.

Prentice, D. A., & Miller, D. T. (1993). Pluralistic ignorance and alcohol use on campus: Some consequences of misperceiving the social norm. *Journal of Personality and Social Psychology, 64,* 243–256.

Robbins, J. M., & Krueger, J. I. (2005). Social projection to ingroups and outgroups: A review and meta-analysis. *Personality and Social Psychology Review, 9,* 32–47.

Ross, L., Greene, D., & House, P. (1977). The 'false consensus effect': An egocentric bias in social perception and attribution processes. *Journal of Experimental Social Psychology, 13,* 279–301.

Schank, R. L. (1932). A study of a community and its groups and institutions conceived of as behaviors of individuals. *Psychological Monographs, 43*(2, Serial No. 195).

Scheufele, D. A., & Eveland, W. P., Jr. (2001). Perceptions of 'public opinion' and 'public' opinion expression. *International Journal of Public Opinion Research, 13,* 25–44.

Schroeder, C. M., & Prentice, D. A. (1998). Exposing pluralistic ignorance to reduce alcohol use among college students. *Journal of Applied Social Psychology, 28,* 2150–2180.

Shapiro, M. A. (1991). Memory and decision processes in the construction of social reality. *Communication Research, 18,* 3–24.

Sherman, S. J., Presson, C. C., & Chassin, L. (1984). Mechanisms underlying the false consensus effect: The special role of threats to the self. *Personality and Social Psychology Bulletin, 10,* 127–138.

Shrum, L. J., & O'Guinn, T. C. (1993). Processes and effects in the construction of social reality. *Communication Research, 20,* 436–471.

15

Pluralistic Ignorance and Nonattitudes

Patricia Moy

A decades-old concept, 'pluralistic ignorance' is a term used broadly to refer to perceptual inaccuracies of the collective, by the collective. Drawing from research in communication, psychology, sociology, and related fields, this chapter examines various aspects of pluralistic ignorance. First, it highlights various definitions of the concept and the contexts in which pluralistic ignorance has been studied, and puts forth the theoretical assumptions on which this concept is grounded. Second, the chapter summarizes commonly offered explanations for and implications of this phenomenon.

The chapter ends by addressing some methodological aspects of pluralistic ignorance, presenting a section on the significance of nonattitudes. The problem of nonattitudes—or the tendency of respondents to answer survey questions regarding issues that they know nothing about or issues about which they hold no opinion—has become increasingly crucial for public opinion researchers. This last section focuses

on the nature of this problem and its implications for the study of public opinion.

PLURALISTIC IGNORANCE

Intellectual evolution

Social scientists long have shown that perceptions of the collective can influence individual attitudes and behaviors. However, one's ability to accurately perceive how the collective thinks or feels is flawed. Misperceptions of the collective—in particular, public opinion—abound (for reviews, see Glynn, Ostman, & McDonald, 1995; → *Theories on the Perception of Social Reality*); this chapter focuses on a particular perceptual inaccuracy—pluralistic ignorance.

Often credited as the individual responsible for bringing pluralistic ignorance to the fore, psychologist Floyd Allport (1924) believed that individuals defined 'the public' as 'an imagined crowd in which ... certain opinions, feelings, and overt reactions are universal' (p. 308). According to others, however, pluralistic ignorance is more than simply the phenomenon of members of a system falling prey to the 'illusion of universality' (p. 309). Merton (1949) posited that pluralistic ignorance comprises not only 'the unfounded assumption that one's own attitudes and expectations are unshared,' but also 'the unfounded assumption that they are uniformly shared' (p. 377).

In general, explications of pluralistic ignorance have generated some degree of conceptual variance, particularly regarding the direction of misperception. Whereas early formulations of pluralistic ignorance (Allport, 1924; Schanck, 1932) emphasized the individual's misperceiving himself or herself to hold the minority view (when in fact, he or she holds the majority view), current conceptualizations focus on the presence, not direction, of the misperception. That is, pluralistic ignorance no longer refers to the underestimation of majority opinion, but the overestimation or underestimation of opinion (O'Gorman, 1976; Taylor, 1982). The concept now includes situations in which individuals perceive minority opinion to be the majority, and majority opinion to be the minority (Glynn *et al.*, 1995).

Pervasiveness of pluralistic ignorance

A classic example of pluralistic ignorance, Hans Christian Andersen's *'The Emperor's New Clothes'* tells the story of some swindlers who sell the emperor an invisible robe, proclaiming that only unfit or stupid individuals cannot see the robe. The emperor obviously cannot see the robe, nor can anyone else. However, no one will admit to not being able to see the robe as everyone fears being exposed as unfit. Centola, Willer, and Macy (2005) describe how continued admiration for the new clothes generates widespread support for the norm, with the 'spell' breaking only when a child, innocent of the norm, laughs at the emperor.

Pluralistic ignorance may be an academic term relegated to academic journals, but its manifestations are clear. The phenomenon emerges, for instance, in the classroom setting, when students unclear about course content may not ask a question because they assume from the lack of questions that others understand the material (Miller & McFarland, 1987). That is, each student assumes he or she is the only one to not understand the course content when in fact virtually every student feels the same way.

Similar to the classroom situation, pluralistic ignorance arose when the Kinsey Reports on Americans' sexual behavior were published. Many readers expressed great surprise at the findings, leading Udry (1993) to cite this as a prime example of the phenomenon: many individuals were shocked to read about the pervasiveness of certain sexual behaviors—'things that readers never dreamed of doing themselves, or that they did, but thought in their private shame that hardly anyone else did' (p. 105).

Theoretical assumptions

If pluralistic ignorance represents a particular case of misperceived (over- or underestimated) public opinion, its being rests on several theoretical pillars. First, and most broadly, pluralistic ignorance is grounded in social-psychological phenomena. According to Price and Oshagan (1995), 'ideas and opinions are shaped and altered through interaction among people and the social groups they constitute' (p. 178). The authors cite research showing how attitudinal and behavioral change can stem from informational social influence—when a group member receives information that he or she perceives to be reality—or normative social influence, when change occurs so that the group member can secure social approval from other members. Indeed, the influence of the group (or society) underlies long-standing public opinion theories such as the spiral of silence (Noelle-Neumann, 1993; → *Spiral of Silence Theory*).

Second, because pluralistic ignorance concerns a group member's misperception of that group's distribution of opinion, the concept invokes not only the power of the group, but also the difference between private thoughts and public behaviors. The two need not be congruent, and in the case of pluralistic ignorance, they most likely are not. After all, pluralistic ignorance appears to be grounded in a discrepancy between personal attitudes and public behaviors—specifically, one in which public behaviors misrepresent unexpressed, private views (Miller & Prentice, 1994). That is, group members behave publicly in a manner that reflects pervasive conformity to a social norm—a norm sufficiently powerful so as to produce level behavior that is incongruent with individuals' attitudes (Prentice & Miller, 1996). Individuals recognize their own attitude-behavior discrepancy, but assume no such discrepancy among others.

A third assumption undergirding pluralistic ignorance concerns individuals' ability to assess the distribution of opinion. In her spiral of silence theory, Noelle-Neumann (1993) referred to this ability as individuals' quasi-statistical sense, which allows them to gauge the climate of opinion. Naturally, the premise behind pluralistic ignorance is strongly interwoven with this third assumption: individuals are unable to correctly assess the distribution of opinion.

Antecedents: Why does pluralistic ignorance occur?

The above theoretical assumptions situate pluralistic ignorance, but do not offer much in terms of explaining why it occurs, and with what effects. Because pluralistic ignorance is, at its heart, a discrepancy between perceptions of oneself and perceptions of others, researchers have examined a host of explanations. These explanations can be categorized as those implicating individual-level factors as well as the information environment.

Some researchers (Allport, 1924; O'Gorman, 1986) argue that as a shared cognitive error, pluralistic ignorance can be explained in part by the individual processes involved in social comparison. After all, individuals tend to make more extreme judgments when they are alone as compared with when they are with others.

Others, who focus on pluralistic ignorance as the discrepancy between personal attitudes and public behaviors, have examined why people attribute the same actions of oneself and others differently, looking specifically at fear of embarrassment. Individuals are indeed likely to believe they are more socially inhibited relative to others, and they avoid things and situations that would cause embarrassment (Miller & McFarland, 1987). According to this line of reasoning, because fear of embarrassment is largely internal, individuals would be more aware of their own fear compared to that of others. By believing themselves to be more fearful of embarrassment, individuals err in other judgments of the collective, and as a group, manifest pluralistic ignorance (→ *Public Opinion and the Third-Person Effect*).

Similarly, it is likely that individuals underestimate the impact of social motives on behavior. In inferring their own motivations for behaving in a particular way, individuals tend to believe they are striving to maintain their social identity and social standing. However, in inferring others' motives, the desire to maintain one's social identity and social standing gets downplayed. Rather, others' behaviors get attributed to their personal beliefs and attitudes. As a result, when asked about perceived social norms, individuals erroneously report a majority opinion that is reflected by others' behaviors.

Prentice and Miller (1993) offer two individual-level interpretations of pluralistic ignorance. The first, the two-pronged differential interpretation hypothesis, posits that individuals not only report being more in line with perceived group norms (to make themselves appear more socially desirable and less deviant), but also are unaware that others, like them, are misrepresenting their true attitudes. The second interpretation involves differential encoding, in which individuals assume true attitudes are reflected in public behaviors (when in fact they are misrepresented). In other words, when individuals believe that there is an attitude–behavior correspondence that does not exist, they believe that others truly adhere to the social norm and that they are alone in holding the minority opinion.

For other scholars, pluralistic ignorance arises from a misleading information environment. In other words, the media and interpersonal channels can provide information about climates of opinion that may or may not mesh with reality. This can happen if, as Lippmann (1922) noted, the media highlight certain aspects of the unseen environment for audience members—and given the time and space constraints of most media outlets, it is only reasonable to expect that not all information is conveyed. The salience of any particular issue in the news media, similar to what Shamir and Shamir (1997) call the issue's overall 'visibility,' can mean that more polls and other information suggestive of public opinion distributions are printed or broadcast.

Unfortunately, there is not always perfect correspondence between the number of media polls and the range of voices reflected in the polls (Lewis, 2001). Absent specific polls, the news media can reference public opinion by including interviews with individuals who are quoted and provide a personal description. News media consumers exposed to such non-representative exemplars tend to estimate minority and majority opinion in a way that closely reflects the distribution of exemplars in a given story (Brosius & Bathelt, 1994). News media consumers exposed to official sources, on the other hand, will see that journalists turn to and cite these elite in proportion to their relative power (Bennett, 1996). Thus, regardless of whether manifestations of public opinion in the media appear as polls, exemplars, or elite sources, there is evidence that people who consume such content believe this information to reflect opinions at large (→ *The News as a Reflection of Public Opinion*).

However, the issues covered by the media can be portrayed less than fully accurately.

Factors both internal and external to media organizations can influence what issues warrant coverage, and the nature of that coverage. Such factors include the issues or events themselves that, coupled with journalists' ideology, attitudes, and professional values, as well as organizational routines and news values (for an overview, see Shoemaker & Reese, 1996), can generate incomplete or skewed coverage. As with all studies of content, such influences need be considered in light of the pluralism and diversity reflected in a given media system.

If individuals look to the media to assess the state of public opinion, they turn to others as well. And just as the diversity of media content can influence us, so can the nature of our interpersonal networks, and the issue-based discussion that takes place within those networks. Heterogeneous networks typically comprise individuals who are more accustomed to encountering opposing points of view, and therefore may be more likely to share minority opinions (Krassa, 1990). However, such exposure to 'cross-cutting' views is not as common as once believed, with citizens increasingly living in areas segregated by particular demographics (Mutz, 2006). Although one might argue that an increase in such similarities might reduce pluralistic ignorance (as people can more accurately perceive how those similar to themselves feel about an issue), the discrepancy between private attitudes and public behaviors remains.

Looking to the information environment as a cause of pluralistic ignorance then shifts culpability from individual-level processing of data to a skewed distribution of the expression of opinion, whether in the media or by those who are more willing to express dissonant views. Prentice and Miller (1993) consider this a 'biased sample' interpretation of the pluralistic ignorance.

Consequences of pluralistic ignorance

What implications does pluralistic ignorance have for the individual, the group, and public opinion at large? Given the social nature of human beings, pluralistic ignorance can significantly impact the individual. On a psychological level, it can generate considerable stress as people believe they are the only ones deviating from a socially held norm (Miller & McFarland, 1987). As a result, individuals begin to distance themselves socially from, and reduce communication with, the group. Another outcome could involve just the opposite: individual members may change their behaviors to conform to what they perceive to be the group norm (Miller & Prentice, 1994). For those situations involving health risk behaviors (e.g., unsafe sex or substance abuse), pluralistic ignorance may increase the frequency of such behaviors. Whether the individual member alienates himself or herself, or internalizes the perceived social norm, appears to depend partly on gender, at least in the case of college drinking (Prentice & Miller, 1996). Understanding the nuances of such consequences better would therefore aid in the development of social change programs.

The aforementioned individual-level outcomes point to the power of the group, but the collective also is affected by pluralistic ignorance. In particular, misperceptions can lead a group to act inconsistently with the attitudes of its individual members. In Janis' (1982) seminal work on groupthink, decisions endorsed collectively by group had been misperceived by many members to be the majority view. In situations that implicate polls and policy, reported perceptions of support can lead to the implementation of policy that really goes against the wishes of the public. Shamir and Shikaki (2005), for example, illustrate how a majority of Palestinians and Israelis support mutual recognition of national identity; yet each group misperceives the other group's level of support for such recognition.

Finally, the relationship between pluralistic ignorance and public opinion at large needs to be addressed. If individuals erroneously report their perceptions of public opinion, these misperceptions coupled with changes in behavior, might influence the policy-making process. That is, what politicians and elected officials believe to be the will of the people might not reflect citizens' true attitudes. Depending on how public opinion gets reported, those in a position to effect policy may very well be reacting to misperceptions of public opinion rather than true opinions.

NONATTITUDES

Methodological issues of pluralistic ignorance

The body of research on pluralistic ignorance reviewed thus far indicates that it is a robust phenomenon, existing across a vast number of contexts and emerging in empirical studies that employ different methodologies. Can anything be done to reduce the occurrence of pluralistic ignorance? Apparently, greater visibility of an issue in the information environment—as reflected in elections and media coverage—can help (Shamir & Shamir, 1997). Shamir (1998) examined whether respondents who were motivated (i.e., they were promised a present) were also more likely to generate accurate estimates of opinion distributions. They found that although the respondents tried harder, they were no more likely to be accurate in their perceptions.

From a methodological standpoint, researchers have questioned whether misperceptions of opinion reflect a response bias—for example, respondents being reluctant to admit their preference for a particular way of thinking or behavior (O'Gorman, 1975)—or question wording. For instance, Whitehead, Blankenship, and Wright (1999) found spurious support for the death penalty, and varying reports of attitudes depending on the question asked. The researchers thus concluded that legislators can interpret data based on single-item measures of attitudes toward the death penalty very differently from data based on multiple items. Such a discussion on the utility of public opinion surveys raises an issue that perennially plagues public opinion researchers—that of nonattitudes.

In democratic systems, citizens elect the officials they believe are in a position to enact policies that reflect their constituents' interests. Citizens also communicate such interests and attitudes in a number of ways, including voting, writing letters to the editor, protesting, signing petitions, and expressing their opinions in public opinion surveys. Despite such expressions of opinion, one cannot necessarily assume that all poll data accurately reflect public opinion as it truly exists. After all, some respondents answer survey questions regarding issues that they know nothing about, or regarding issues about which they hold no opinion. As a result, analyses and interpretations of the data can mislead consumers of such data—including policy makers—into believing that public opinion falls a certain way on a given issue. This section deals with the nature of this problem and its implications for the study of public opinion.

The nature of nonattitudes

Converse (1964, 1970) coined the term 'nonattitudes' after seeing how many panel participants offered unstable or inconsistent responses to the same questions asked over time. His 'black and white' model assumed that 'a mass public contains significant proportions of people who, for lack of information about a particular dimension of controversy, offer meaningless opinions that vary randomly in direction during repeated trials over time' (1964, p. 243).

Robust evidence of nonattitudes has emerged across numerous studies, with respondents reporting attitudes about members of nonexistent nationalities (Hartley, 1946), fictitious acts, and real but highly obscure issues (see Bishop, 2005 for an overview). Scholars generally agree that there is a fine line between attitudes and nonattitudes, and that questions about nonobjects can elicit real attitudes.

Converse's (1964, 1970) condemnation of the mass public, in conjunction with studies documenting the existence of nonattitudes, generated a stream of research that sought to redeem the public and show that its attitudes were in fact quite stable. Scholars in this camp (e.g., Achen, 1975) attribute such attitude instability to measurement error stemming from methodologically faulty survey items. Taking a middle ground, one that reflects contemporary thought in this area, Zaller and Feldman (1992) illustrate how response stability is a function of both the respondent and the survey instrument. They write: 'Survey questions do not *simply* measure public opinion. They also shape and channel it by the manner in which they frame issues, order the alternatives, and otherwise set the context of the question' (p. 582). Tourangeau, Rips, and Rasinski (2000) acknowledge that absent a well-articulated attitude (when the respondent has a preformed opinion that can be offered easily to the interviewer), reported attitudes derive in part from top-of-mind considerations, pre-existing stereotypes and schemas, and question wording or order.

What scholars choose to pinpoint as the source of nonattitudes has implications for measures taken to reduce the occurrence of these pseudo-opinions. For example, if a desire to appear knowledgeable generates nonattitudes (Converse, 1970), then including a filter question (e.g., 'Do you have an opinion on Issue X?') before the actual attitude item can reduce the likelihood of nonattitudes emerging (Bishop, Oldendick, & Tuchfarber, 1980). After all, respondents generally are reluctant to volunteer that they do not have an opinion unless presented with an opportunity to do so (Bishop, 2005).

Others believe that nonattitudes reflect respondents' attempts to impute meaning to the survey question. Because the interview situation simulates a conversation, respondents have no reason to believe that an interviewer would ask them questions about issues that did not exist (Schwarz, 1995, cited in Bishop, 2005). Consequently, in providing an answer to an attitude item, the respondent will use the context of the question to help themselves define the question. Because the interview situation presupposes various 'sincerity conditions' (Tourangeau *et al.*, 2000, p. 247)—that questions concern real issues, and that the response for closed-ended questions is present among the options provided—what some interpret as nonattitudes might really be respondents' attitudes based on meanings imputed from the question context. According to this line of reasoning, adding a 'no opinion' option can reduce the level of nonattitudes expressed in a survey (Bishop, Oldendick, & Tuchfarber, 1986).

Coping with nonattitudes

Because Converse's (1964, 1970) original formulation of nonattitudes implicated the stability of attitudes over time, scholars have turned to old and new methodological developments to examine the volatility of respondents' attitudes. Gallup (1947) advanced a series of survey questions that would assess various dimensions of one's opinion. His 'quintamensional plan' entailed: (1) a filter question measuring respondents' level of information about an issue; (2) an open-ended question getting at respondents' general attitudes about that issue; (3) closed-ended questions about specific aspects of the issue; (4) open-ended questions assessing why the respondent held a particular attitude; and (5) a closed-ended question concerning the respondent's intensity of feeling. In a similar vein, Yankelovich, Skelly, and White's 'mushiness index' attempts to identify respondents who hold nonattitudes (Keene & Sackett, 1981). This four-item index comprised questions measuring: respondents' perception of how much the issue affected them personally; their perception of how well-informed they believed they were on the issue; respondents' level of engagement with the issue, as reflected in their level of interpersonal discussion; and their conviction or how much they believed their opinions on the issue would change (Asher, 1992). Although Gallup's quintamensional plan and the mushiness index may identify which respondents hold 'true' or more stable attitudes, the number of questions required and the cost of asking so many additional questions per item discourage practitioners from using them often.

To date, methodological studies involving questionnaire design, interviewing, and related areas collectively suggest effective ways to measure public opinion accurately. There is no consensus as to what constitutes the single best practice. It is only through the interplay of the issue under study, existing information that individuals have, the interview situation, and cognitive and social processes that researchers can better understand how to assess opinions expressed.

REFERENCES

Achen, C. (1975). Mass political attitudes and the survey response. *American Political Science Review, 69,* 1218–1231.

Allport, F. H. (1924). *Social psychology.* Boston: Houghton Mifflin.

Asher, H. (1992). *Polling and the public: What every citizen should know* (2nd ed.). Washington, DC: CQ Press.

Bennett, W. L. (1996). An introduction to journalism norms and representations of politics. *Political Communication, 13,* 373–384.

Bishop, G. F. (2005). *The illusion of public opinion: Fact and artifact in American public opinion polls.* Lanham, MD: Rowman & Littlefield.

Bishop, G. F., Oldendick, R. W., & Tuchfarber, A. J. (1980). Pseudo-opinions on public affairs. *Public Opinion Quarterly, 44,* 198–209.

Bishop, G. F., Oldendick, R. W., & Tuchfarber, A. J. (1986). Opinions on fictitious issues: The pressure to answer survey questions. *Public Opinion Quarterly, 50,* 240–250.

Brosius, H. -B., & Bathelt, A. (1994). The utility of exemplars in persuasive communications. *Communication Research, 21,* 48–78.

Centola, D., Willer, R., & Macy, M. (2005). The emperor's dilemma: A computational model of self-enforcing norms. *American Journal of Sociology, 110,* 1009–1040.

Converse, P. E. (1964). The nature of belief systems in mass publics. In D. E. Apter (Ed.), *Ideology and discontent* (pp. 206–261). New York: Free Press.

Converse, P. E. (1970). Attitudes and nonattitudes: Continuation of a dialogue. In E. R. Tufte (Ed.), *The quantitative analysis of social problems* (pp. 168–189). Reading, MA: Addison-Wesley.

Gallup, G. (1947). The quintamensional plan of question design. *Public Opinion Quarterly, 11,* 385–393.

Glynn, C. J., Ostman, R. E., & McDonald, D. G. (1995). Opinions, perception, and social reality. In T. L. Glasser & C. T. Salmon (Eds.), *Public opinion and the communication of consent* (pp. 249–277). New York: Guilford.

Hartley, E. (1946). *Problems in prejudice*. New York: Kings Crown Press.

Janis, I. L. (1982). *Victims of group think: A psychological study of foreign-policy decisions and fiascos* (Rev. ed.). Boston: Houghton Mifflin.

Keene, K. H., & Sackett, V. A. (1981). An editor's report on the Yankelovich, Skelly and White 'mushiness index,' *Public Opinion, 4*(2), 50–51.

Krassa, M. (1990). The structure of interaction and the transmission of political influence and information. In J. A. Ferejohn & J. H. Kuklinski (Eds.), *Information and democratic processes* (pp. 100–113). Urbana, IL: University of Illinois Press.

Lewis, J. (2001). *Constructing public opinion: How politics elites do what they like and why we seem to go along with it.* New York: Columbia University Press.

Lippmann, W. (1922). *Public opinion.* New York: Macmillan.

Merton, R. K. (1949). *Social theory and social structure.* Glencoe, IL: Free Press.

Miller, D. T., & McFarland, C. (1987). Pluralistic ignorance: When similarity is interpreted as dissimilarity. *Journal of Personality and Social Psychology, 53,* 298–305.

Miller, D. T., & Prentice, D. A. (1994). Collective errors and errors about the collective. *Personality and Social Psychology Bulletin, 20,* 541–550.

Mutz, D. C. (2006). *Hearing the other side: Deliberative versus participatory democracy.* New York: Cambridge University Press.

Noelle-Neumann, E. (1993). *The spiral of silence: Public opinion—our social skin.* Chicago: University of Chicago Press.

O'Gorman, H. J. (1975). Pluralistic ignorance and white estimates of white support for racial segregation. *Public Opinion Quarterly, 39,* 313–330.

O'Gorman, H. J. (with Garry, S. L.). (1976). Pluralistic ignorance—A replication and extension. *Public Opinion Quarterly, 40,* 449–458.

O'Gorman, H. J. (1986). The discovery of pluralistic ignorance: An ironic lesson. *Journal of the History of the Behavioral Sciences, 22,* 333–347.

Prentice, D. A., & Miller, D. T. (1993). Pluralistic ignorance and alcohol use on campus: Some consequences of misperceiving the social norm. *Journal of Personality and Social Psychology, 64,* 243–256.

Prentice, D. A., & Miller, D. T. (1996). Pluralistic ignorance and the perpetuation of social norms by unwitting actors. In M. P. Zanna (Ed.), *Advances in experimental social psychology: Vol. 28* (pp. 161–209). San Diego: Academic Press.

Price, V., & Oshagan, H. (1995). Social-psychological perspectives on public opinion. In T. L. Glasser & C. T. Salmon (Eds.), *Public opinion and the communication of consent* (pp. 177–216). New York: Guilford.

Schanck, R. L. (1932). A study of a community and its groups and institutions conceived of as behaviors of individuals. *Psychological Monographs, 43*(2), No. 195.

Shamir, J. (1998). Motivation and accuracy in estimating opinion distributions: A survey experiment. *International Journal of Public Opinion Research, 10,* 91–108.

Shamir, J., & Shamir, M. (1997) Pluralistic ignorance over issues and over time: Information cues and biases. *Public Opinion Quarterly, 61,* 227–260.

Shamir, J., & Shikaki, K. (2005). Public opinion in the Israeli-Palestinian two-level game. *Journal of Peace Research, 42,* 311–328.

Shoemaker, P. J., & Reese, S. D. (1996). *Mediating the message* (2nd ed.). White Plains, NY: Longman.

Taylor, D. G. (1982). Pluralistic ignorance and the spiral of silence: A formal analysis. *Public Opinion Quarterly, 46,* 311–335.

Tourangeau, R., Rips, L. J., & Rasinski, K. (2000). *The psychology of survey response.* New York: Cambridge University Press.

Udry, J. R. (1993). The politics of sex research. *The Journal of Sex Research, 30,* 103–110.

Whitehead, J. T., Blankenship, M. B., & Wright, J. P. (1999). Elite versus citizen attitudes on capital punishment: Incongruity between the public and policymakers. *Journal of Criminal Justice, 27,* 249–258.

Zaller, J., & Feldman, S. (1992). A simple theory of the survey response: Answering questions versus revealing preferences. *American Journal of Political Science, 36,* 579–616.

Dynamics of Public Opinion

16

Spiral of Silence Theory

Dietram A. Scheufele

Formulated by Noelle-Neumann in the early 1970s, the spiral of silence theory is one of the most prominent theoretical models of opinion formation and consensus building in modern societies. Since its initial formulation, there have been more than three decades of research testing the key hypotheses of the theory and also its implicit assumptions. This chapter provides an overview of Noelle-Neumann's original work and critically discusses challenges to the theory and related follow-up research. It also highlights the continued importance of the spiral of silence model in public opinion research.

The spiral of silence model assumes that people are constantly aware of the opinions of people around them and adjust their behaviors (and potentially their opinions) to majority trends under the fear of being on the losing side of a public debate. In particular, Noelle-Neumann based her theorizing on the premise that individuals have a 'quasi-statistical sense' that allows them to gauge the opinion climate in a society, i.e., the proportions of people who favor or oppose a given issue. This quasi-statistical sense may be accurate, but very often it is not, i.e., people are wrong in their assessments of what

everyone else thinks. This point is largely irrelevant for the spiral of silence theory, however, since it is the *perception* of opinion distributions rather than the *real* opinion climate that shapes people's willingness to express their opinions in public (Scheufele & Moy, 2000).

In addition to the quasi-statistical sense, Noelle-Neumann's theory introduces a second key concept: fear of isolation. This concept is based on the assumption that social collectives threaten individuals who deviate from social norms and majority views with isolation or even ostracism. As a result, individuals are constantly fearful of isolating themselves with unpopular views or behavior that violates social norms.

Based on these assumptions, the spiral of silence predicts that groups who see themselves in a minority or as losing ground are less vocal and less willing to express their opinions in public. This, in turn, will influence the visibility of majority and minority groups, and the minority group will appear weaker and weaker over time, simply because its members will be more and more reluctant to express their opinions in public. Ultimately, the reluctance of members of the

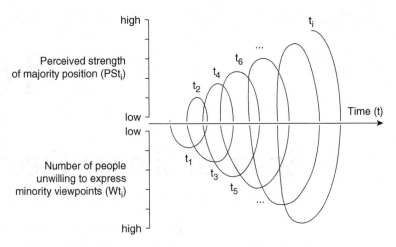

Figure 16.1   The spiral of silence as a dynamic, macrosocial process
Note: Based on ideas first outlined in Scheufele & Moy (2000)

perceived minority to express their opinions will establish the majority opinion as the predominant view, or even as a social norm.

Noelle-Neumann's (1984) theorizing comes out of two broad theoretical traditions. The first theoretical tradition that the spiral of silence theory evolved from are the works of philosophers, such as Locke or Montaigne, whose writings had dealt extensively with the effects of public opinion and public ostracism. The second theoretical foundation of the spiral of silence theory is social-psychological, particularly theories about conformity to majority pressures (Asch, 1955, 1965) and the influence of group norms on judgments and attitudes (Sherif, 1967).

THE SPIRAL OF SILENCE AS A DYNAMIC PROCESS

The most critical component of the spiral of silence is also the one that has been overlooked most in previous research on the theory: its dynamic character. The spiral of silence is a process that works over time. As people who perceive themselves to be in the minority fall silent, perceptions of opinion climates shift over time, and ultimately the majority opinion is established as the predominant one or even as a social norm.

Figure 16.1 illustrates this spiraling process over time. People's willingness to publicly express their views depends heavily on their perceptions of which viewpoints are represented by a majority of citizens or which viewpoints are gaining ground. As people with minority viewpoints fall silent over time, perceptions of the majority opinion gaining ground increase. This creates a mutually reinforcing spiral where the reluctance of the minority group to speak out leads to perceptual biases in favor of the majority group, which, in turn, further discourages the minority group from speaking out.

There are two contingent conditions for this spiraling process to take place. The first one is the nature of the issue that is being discussed. Previous research suggests that the spiral of silence only works for issues with a moral component, or value-laden issues 'by which the individual isolates or may isolate himself in public' (Noelle-Neumann, 1993, p. 231). The recent debate about embryonic stem-cell research in many countries is a good example of an issue where religious and moral concerns are intertwined with more rational, scientific arguments in public discourse. Public debate around this issue is therefore morally charged, and it is impossible to 'objectively' answer the question if a given country should proceed with this new technology and provide federal funds to do so. As a result, opinion climates provide critical cues for citizens about when they have to decide if they want to express their own views in public or not.

The second factor that can play an important role in the process of the spiral of silence are the news media. Based on Noelle-Neumann's early theorizing (Noelle-Neumann, 1977, 1984), the quasi-statistical sense that people use to gauge opinion climates depends at least to some degree on media portrayals of the issue. In particular, people rely on two sources when making assessments of what everyone else around them thinks. The first source is their immediate social environment. In fact, more recent research suggests that people project from recent discussions in their immediate social circles when making assessment about the larger opinion climates surrounding them (Scheufele, Shanahan, & Lee, 2001). The second source is the news media. Especially for issues that citizens have little direct experience with, or where they may have a hard time gauging opinion climates, the news media provide an important heuristic.

Other chapters in this book will talk about phenomena, such as pluralistic ignorance and other collective perceptual errors. One specific error is especially noteworthy when discussing the role of media in the process of the spiral of silence. It is usually referred to as a 'dual climate of opinion.' A dual climate of opinion exists when the majority of the population has a specific stance on an issue, but perceptions of which group is winning or losing the debate are just the opposite.

This could happen in an election, for example, when a majority of the population supports candidate X. A dual climate of opinion exists if there is also prevalent perception among the electorate that there is a majority who supports candidate Y. Why would that happen? One possible explanation is the content of the news media. If media portray the race in a way that suggests that the majority of the electorate supports candidate Y, we have a dual climate of opinion where collective perceptions deviate from collective preferences. The implications for

the spiral of silence are obvious. As a result of a dual climate of opinion, we may see a spiral of silence against the real opinion distribution, i.e., against candidate X and in favor of candidate Y, simply because the media inaccurately portray the opinion climate, which, in turn, influences people's willingness to express their opinions and accelerates a spiraling process of the opinion climate and opinion expression against candidate X.

In order to fully understand the idea of dual climates of opinion, it is necessary to briefly examine Noelle-Neumann's understanding of how media can shape public opinion. According to Noelle-Neumann, dual climates of opinion can develop because media coverage of controversial issues tends to be consonant and cumulative (Noelle-Neumann, 1973). Consonance refers to the tendency of different media outlets to portray controversial issues in a homogeneous fashion. The idea of consonance is consistent with other concepts, such as inter-media agenda setting (McCombs, 2004) or news waves (Fishman, 1978), which both suggest that journalists' choices about what to cover and how to spin a story are often influenced by peer or elite media, and such as group dynamic processes among journalists to resolve undetermined situations (Donsbach, 2004). According to Noelle-Neumann, consonant coverage of an issue therefore likely strengthens media effects, since it undermines the ability of audience members to selectively expose themselves only to media messages that are consistent with their own views. More importantly, however, Noelle-Neumann assumes that media effects are cumulative, i.e., they work *over time*. As a result, dual climates of opinion can develop when a cumulative stream of consonant media messages creates public perceptions of the opinion climate that deviate from the real opinion distribution in the population.

THE SPIRAL OF SILENCE AS A MACRO-THEORY

The example of the dual climate of opinion highlights how the spiral of silence theory bridges individual and aggregate levels of analysis. In this sense, the theory is one of the few truly macro-social theories of public opinion, i.e., it links macro-, meso-, and micro-levels of analysis.

As a micro-theory, the spiral of silence examines opinion expression, controlling for people's predispositions, such as fear of isolation, and also demographic variables that have been shown to influence people's willingness to publicly express controversial opinions. In particular, previous research showed that younger respondents and male respondents were more likely to express their views in public, regardless of fear of isolation or perceptions of the dominant climate of opinion (for an overview, see Scheufele & Moy, 2000).

Figure 16.2 lists some of these individual-level controls. It also shows the interplay between a person's own opinions and his or her perceptions of the opinion climate. If the two are incongruent, the person is less likely to express his or her views. This public expression of opinion is what

moves the spiral of silence to a more macroscopic level of analysis. If more and more members of the perceived minority fall silent, as outlined earlier, public perceptions of the opinion climate and the societal level begin to shift. In other words, a person's individual reluctance to express his or her opinion, simply based on perceptions of what everyone else thinks, has important implications at the social level. These social, macro-level perceptions, of course, in turn influence individual perceptions and people's willingness to express opinions.

In addition to linking macro- and micro-levels of analysis, the spiral of silence theory also incorporates evidence from meso-levels of analysis. In particular, Noelle-Neumann's original theorizing relied heavily on con-formity experiments conducted by Solomon Asch (Asch, 1955, 1965) that showed that individuals, when faced with overwhelming social opposition in a group setting, were unwilling to speak out against the group, even when they knew that the group's judgment was wrong.

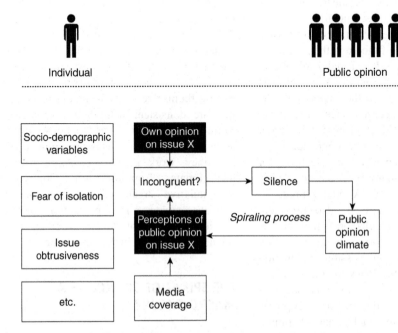

Figure 16.2   The spiral of silence: linking individual and mass opinion
Note: Based on ideas first outlined in Donsbach (1987)

Beyond laying the theoretical foundation of much of Noelle-Neumann's work, social groups are also directly relevant as explanatory mechanisms for two phenomena related to the spiral of silence. First, more recent research has shown that reference groups can provide important social cues when people try to gauge the social climate of opinion. The second role that reference groups can play in the process of the spiral of silence is to provide a protective environment for people who resist or choose to counter hostile opinion climates. Noelle-Neumann (1984) refers to these groups as 'avantgardes' and 'hard cores.' Hard cores are groups who stick with a minority position even as the spiral of silence grows stronger and stronger against their own position. Avantgardes may base their resistance to hostile opinion climates on strong ideological belief systems, on a strong concern about the issue being discussed, or— most important for our discussion here—on reference groups that reinforce their existing beliefs. While hard cores hold on to existing issue stances, even as the opinion climate turns against them, avantgardes promote *new*, unpopular viewpoints that go against existing social norms of predominant opinion climates. As a result, reference groups are likely to play an important role for avantgardes—as for hard cores—by creating a protective social environment that provides the necessary social support for members of the avantgarde who speak out against an existing majority opinion.

The notion of avantgardes and hard cores is consistent with findings from Asch's (Asch, 1955, 1965) conformity experiments. In his studies, the proportion of respondents who were willing to speak out against a group majority increased dramatically if at least one person in the room sided with the respondent. Most recently, McDonald and his colleagues (McDonald, Glynn, Kim, & Ostman, 2001) examined hard cores in their secondary analysis of Lazarsfeld *et al.*'s 1948 Elmira study (Lazarsfeld, Berelson, & Gaudet, 1948). McDonald *et al.*'s analysis showed that hard cores were in fact less susceptible to opinion trends than other respondents in the sample,

providing at least tentative support for Noelle-Neumann's initial theorizing.

NEW AND CRITICAL APPROACHES TO THE SPIRAL OF SILENCE

The spiral of silence theory has drawn criticism from a number of scholars since its first formulation in the mid-1970s, both on methodological and theoretical grounds (for a recent overview, see Scheufele & Moy, 2000). The areas in which the spiral of silence was initially critiqued have also been the most fruitful areas for new research on the spiral of silence, more specifically, and public opinion, more generally. First, some researchers have questioned whether fear of isolation adequately and sufficiently explains the willingness to speak out in both experimental and survey designs (Glynn & McLeod, 1984). Most importantly, fear of isolation was an assumption underlying most of the initial research on the spiral of silence in the 1970s and 1980s, and only in the 1990s did researchers begin to operationalize the construct (Neuwirth, 1995; Scheufele, 1999).

Most recently, Hayes, Glynn and Shanahan (2005) suggested that a construct called 'willingness to self-censor' may be more appropriate to tap individuals' tendency to withhold their true opinions from an audience perceived to disagree with that opinion. They also provide evidence that willingness to engage in self-censorship can be measured reliably and validly, and that it is distinguishable from conceptually related individual differences.

Second, and somewhat relatedly, Noelle-Neumann's original research on the spiral of silence was criticized for focusing too narrowly on fear of isolation as the *only* explanatory mechanism for willingness to speak out at the individual level. Since then, a number of researchers—including Noelle-Neumann herself—have examined various contingent conditions other than fear of isolation under which individuals are in fact willing to express their opinions in public (Lasorsa, 1991; Noelle-Neumann, 1993; Neuwirth, 1995).

Most of these studies suggest that younger respondents, male respondents, and respondents who care more strongly about the issue being discussed, are also more likely to express their opinions, regardless of fear of isolation or opinion climates (for an overview, see Scheufele & Moy, 2000).

Third, previous research raised criticism of the notion of reference groups impacting respondents' willingness to express their opinion. Most importantly, some researchers suggested that reference groups can serve as proxies for the climate of opinion. In other words, do people make inferences from their reference groups to the general climate of opinion? And are the opinion distributions within reference groups therefore a better predictor of the willingness to speak out than the national climate of opinion?

Two recent studies suggest that this may indeed be the case. Scheufele and his colleagues examined the role of reference groups in shaping people's perceptions of the opinion climates surrounding them (Scheufele *et al.*, 2001). Their findings suggest that individuals may project from their experiences in reference groups to the world around them when asked to assess the broader climate of opinion. More importantly, however, Moy and colleagues (Moy, Domke, & Stamm, 2001) argue that opinion climates within reference groups matter above and beyond projection errors. Rather, the opinion climate within a person's reference group may in fact matter more than the national climate of opinion, given that the reference group is the environment in which the individual is experiencing the most immediate threat of being isolated.

Moy *et al.* (2001) used the public opinion dynamics surrounding a referendum on affirmative action to test the spiral of silence theory and found strong support for its hypotheses. That is, the congruity between a person's own opinion and his or her perceptions of the predominant opinion climate in the reference group was also related to his or her willingness to publicly express an opinion on affirmative action. In other words, the climate of opinion in a person's reference group was a significant predictor of opinion expression, even after controlling for fear of isolation and other individual-level controls.

The fourth area of new research has focused on Noelle-Neumann's initial operationalization of outspokenness. Some researchers have argued that Noelle-Neumann's use of what she called the 'train test' was not only too narrow, but also too culturally specific. In order to simulate a public situation and test mothers' willingness to speak out about their views on spanking their children, for example, Noelle-Neumann asked a representative sample of mothers the following question: 'Suppose you are faced with a five-hour train ride, and there is a woman sitting in your compartment who thinks ... that spanking is part of bringing up children/that spanking is basically wrong. Would you like to talk to this woman so as to get to know her point of view better, or wouldn't you think that worth your while?' (Noelle-Neumann, 1993, pp. 17–18). The questionnaire was based on a split-ballot design, and women who opposed spanking were asked to have a discussion with a proponent of spanking and vice versa.

This train test has been criticized for being potentially culturally biased, given that long train rides and conversations with strangers in train compartments may not be realistic enough to be used in surveys in the US or other countries. Noelle-Neumann, however, suggested a whole range of other, more indirect measures. These include displaying campaign buttons and bumper stickers, participating in public meetings, or other forms of public participation (Noelle-Neumann, 1993).

Subsequent studies often used measures of people's willingness to speak out that were less culturally specific. In their study of the spiral of silence in the context of agricultural biotechnology, Scheufele *et al.* (2001) suggested a wording that takes the public element of discussion into account and also addresses the issue of speaking out in the face of a hostile environment: 'Imagine you're at a party where you don't know most people. You're talking to a group of people when somebody brings up the issue of genetic engineering. From the discussion you can tell that most people in the group do not support your point of view. In this kind of situation, some people would express their opinions and some would not ... How likely is it that you would express your own opinion in a situation like this?' (Scheufele et al., 2001, pp. 321–322).

Of course, all of these measures (for an overview of different survey-based measures of speaking out, see Glynn, Hayes, & Shanahan, 1997) share one potential shortcoming. They are based on hypothetical situations that may not emphasize the potential threat of isolation enough. This element of social pressure, of course, is critical for the spiral of silence to work. Scheufele et al. (2001) therefore compared a hypothetical operationalization of speaking out to a measure that tapped people's willingness to participate in a real discussion. Specifically, their split-ballot design asked college students about their willingness to speak out in one of two scenarios: the hypothetical conversational situation outlined earlier, and a fictional follow-up study where respondents were told that they would be assigned to focus groups. The exact wording for the focus group condition was: 'As we explained earlier, we will conduct focus groups with participants from this study who hold different viewpoints on this issue. In order to select subjects for our focus groups, we would like to know how willing you would be to participate in this second stage of our study' (Scheufele et al., 2001, p. 322). Scheufele et al.'s findings provided overall support for the spiral of silence model. They also showed, however, that the model worked consistently better for the 'real' measure of speaking out than for the hypothetical one.

The most fruitful areas of new research on the spiral of silence, finally, are cross-cultural differences. In 2000, Scheufele and Moy (2000) had suggested that many of the inconsistencies among different studies of the spiral of silence could be explained by taking into account intercultural differences, such as differences with respect to conflict styles and norms of opinion expression. Most recently, two studies directly addressed this issue.

Willnat and his colleagues examined the spiral of silence model in Singapore, using two morally charged issues: interracial marriage and equal rights for homosexuals (Willnat, Lee, & Detenber, 2002). In addition to the opinion climate and fear of isolation, they also tested a host of variables that might help explain culture-specific variations of people's willingness to speak out. These variables included communication apprehension, fear of authority, and social interdependence. Interdependence is especially interesting as a potential attenuating force on people's willingness to speak out. As Willnat et al. (2002) point out, 'people with an interdependent self-concept ... value fitting in, and regard speaking out in such circumstances as a threat to group harmony and hence inappropriate' (p. 394). Willnat and his colleagues found some support for the traditional spiral of silence model. Variations in people's interdependent self-concept, however, were not found to be related to their willingness to express their opinions on interracial marriage and equal rights for homosexuals.

One potential explanation for the lack of a significant influence of interdependence, of course, is the fact that Willnat and his colleagues only tested their model in Singapore. If it is really cross-cultural *variations* that explain differences in people's willingness to speak out, we should explore these variations across cultures. A recent study did just that (Huang, 2005). Huang assumes that cultures differ with respect to their degree of collectivism or individualism. Similarly to Willnat and his colleagues, she expects collectivistic cultures to be more concerned with harmony and social cohesion, whereas individualistic cultures are more concerned with self-fulfillment and an emphasis on individual goals. Huang compares Taiwan and the US as exemplars of collectivistic and individualistic societies, respectively. As expected, she found support for her tests of the spiral of silence model in Taiwan, but not in the US.

In spite of these cross-cultural differences, however, most research suggests that social pressure and opinion climates are powerful forces in all cultures, including highly individualistic ones, such as the US (e.g., Katz & Baldassare, 1994), and very collectivistic ones, such as Japan (e.g., Ikeda, 1989).

THE SPIRAL OF SILENCE: TESTING MACRO-MODELS OF PUBLIC OPINION

As this chapter shows, research on the spiral of silence has branched out in different directions and has helped refine the theory over the course of the last 30 years. It has examined individual-level predictors of the basic mechanism underlying the model, and it has examined cross-cultural aggregate-level differences in how these mechanisms work. It has focused on conceptual questions with respect to important assumptions underlying the spiral of silence model, and it has tackled operational issues linked to willingness to speak out and its antecedents.

As outlined earlier, however, the spiral of silence is one of the true macroscopic theories in our field. It assumes that social settings and individual predispositions interact, and that this interaction over time is what drives public opinion and helps build public consensus. Unfortunately, many of the tests of the spiral of silence continue to pay less attention to the interplay between these different levels of analysis as they should. The critical question is not: Which factors help explain people's willingness or unwillingness to express an opinion? Rather, the question we need to ask is: Under which circumstances does the spiral of silence process work better, and what are the variables that can attenuate the relationships between fear of isolation, perceptions of the opinion climate, and willingness to speak out?

Future tests of the spiral of silence therefore need to include both aggregate-level variables, such as cross-cultural comparisons, and individual-level predictors, such as willingness to self-censor or fear of isolation. Most importantly, however, future studies will have to examine the *interactions* between these aggregate-level differences and

individual-level predictors of outspokenness. Does willingness to self-censor, for example, influence outspokenness the same way in collectivist cultures as it does in individualistic cultures? Only if we answer some of these questions more systematically, will we be able to fully explore the potential of the spiral of silence as one of the few truly macroscopic theories of opinion formation in modern societies.

REFERENCES

Asch, S. E. (1955). Opinions and social pressure. *Scientific American, 193*(5), 31–35.

Asch, S. E. (1965). Effects of group pressure upon the modification and distortion of judgements. In J. H. Campbell & H. W. Hepler (Eds.), *Dimensions in communication: Readings* (pp. 125–137). Belmont, CA: Wadsworth.

Donsbach, W. (1987). Die Theorie der Schweigespirale [The theory of the spiral of silence]. In M. Schenk (Ed.), *Medienwirkungsforschung* (pp. 324–343). Tübingen: Mohr.

Donsbach, W. (2004). Psychology of news decisions. Factors behind journalists' professional behavior. *Journalism, 5*, 131–157.

Fishman, M. (1978). Crime waves as ideology. *Social Problems, 25*, 531–543.

Glynn, C. J., & McLeod, J. M. (1984). Public opinion du jour: An examination of the spiral of silence. *Public Opinion Quarterly, 48*, 731–740.

Glynn, C. J., Hayes, A. F., & Shanahan, J. (1997). Perceived support for one's opinions and willingness to speak out: A meta-analysis of survey studies on the 'spiral of silence.' *Public Opinion Quarterly, 61*, 452–463.

Hayes, A. F., Glynn, C. J., & Shanahan, J. (2005). Willingness to self-censor: A construct and measurement tool for public opinion research. *International Journal of Public Opinion Research, 17*, 298–323.

Huang, H. P. (2005). A cross-cultural test of the spiral of silence. *International Journal of Public Opinion Research, 17*, 324–345.

Ikeda, K. (1989). 'Spiral of silence' hypothesis and voting intention: A test in the 1986 Japanese national election. *Keio Communication Review, 10*, 51–62.

Katz, C., & Baldassare, M. (1994). Popularity in a freefall—Measuring a spiral of silence at the end of the Bush presidency. *International Journal of Public Opinion Research, 6*, 1–12.

Lasorsa, D. L. (1991). Political outspokenness—Factors working against the spiral of silence. *Journalism Quarterly, 68*, 131–140.

Lazarsfeld, P. M., Berelson, B. R., & Gaudet, H. (1948). *The people's choice: How the voter makes up his mind in a presidential campaign.* New York: Duell, Sloan & Pearce.

McCombs, M. E. (2004). *Setting the agenda: The mass media and public opinion.* Malden, MA: Blackwell.

McDonald, D. G., Glynn, C. J., Kim, S. H., & Ostman, R. E. (2001). The spiral of silence in the 1948 presidential election. *Communication Research, 28*, 139–155.

Moy, P., Domke, D., & Stamm, K. (2001). The spiral of silence and public opinion on affirmative action. *Journalism & Mass Communication Quarterly, 78*, 7–25.

Neuwirth, K. J. (1995). *Testing the 'spiral of silence' model: The case of Mexico.* Unpublished doctoral dissertation, University of Wisconsin-Madison, Madison, WI.

Noelle-Neumann, E. (1973). Return to the concept of powerful mass media. *Studies in Broadcasting, 9*, 67–112.

Noelle-Neumann, E. (1977). Turbulences in the climate of opinion: Methodological applications of spiral of silence theory. *Public Opinion Quarterly, 41*, 143–158.

Noelle-Neumann, E. (1984). *The spiral of silence: Public opinion, our social skin.* Chicago: University of Chicago Press.

Noelle-Neumann, E. (1993). *The spiral of silence: Public opinion, our social skin* (2nd ed.). Chicago: University of Chicago Press.

Scheufele, D. A. (1999). Deliberation or dispute? An exploratory study examining dimensions of public opinion expression. *International Journal of Public Opinion Research, 11*, 25–58.

Scheufele, D. A., & Moy, P. (2000). Twenty-five years of the spiral of silence: A conceptual review and empirical outlook. *International Journal of Public Opinion Research, 12*, 3–28.

Scheufele, D. A., Shanahan, J., & Lee, E. (2001). Real talk: Manipulating the dependent variable in spiral of silence research. *Communication Research, 28*, 304–324.

Sherif, M. (1967). *Social interaction: Processes and products.* Chicago, IL: Aldine Publishing Company.

Willnat, L., Lee, W. P., & Detenber, B. H. (2002). Individual-level predictors of public outspokenness: A test of the spiral of silence theory in Singapore. *International Journal of Public Opinion Research, 14*, 391–412.

17

Public Opinion and the Third-Person Effect

Albert C. Gunther, Richard M. Perloff and Yariv Tsfati

Much contemporary theoretical research on public opinion is concerned not with actual but rather with perceived public opinion—that subjective form embodied in individuals' perceptions of the attitudes and beliefs of others. In many ways, perceived public opinion is the form that matters most. It is important because people will do many things—decide to vote, buy a new blouse, stop smoking, argue about politics, trade in that SUV, sell stock, cut down on pasta—at least partially in response to their perceptions of the opinions of others.

But where do perceptions about the opinions of others arise? How and why do people form these perceptions? Among the many possible answers to these questions is a communication phenomenon, first named and described by Princeton Sociologist W. Phillips Davison in the 1983 issue of *Public Opinion Quarterly*, known as the third-person effect.

Davison's conception of the third-person effect focused primarily on mass communication messages and the notion that people might not feel that such messages influence themselves personally, but that the same messages will have a substantial influence on others. Davison's model does not stop there, however; he also proposed that people will react in some way to their perception of influence on others. These two steps are now often respectively referred to as the perceptual and behavioral components of the third-person effect. His original article was thin on empirical evidence, being based primarily on engaging examples and exploratory data from classroom experiments. But it was rich in thoughtful speculation and, though well over a 100 third-person effect articles have since been published (at this writing, Davison's article alone has been cited 138 times according to the social science citation index), the original still makes provocative reading.

At several stages over the past 20 years, a social scientist interested in this area is likely to have heard eulogies muttered over the body of third-person effect research. Scholars may have paused to wonder if this was a dead, or dead-end, avenue of inquiry. But if there have been moribund periods, there have also been vigorous revivals. At the time of this writing, the third-person effect is one of the most-researched topics in the field of mass communication and public opinion. It was recently ranked fifth on a list of 'most popular theories' in 21st century communication research, and first in the three newest, 'cutting-edge' journals (*Communication Research, Mass Communication and Society* and *Media Psychology*) included in the sample (Bryant & Miron, 2004).

What explains premature reports of the demise of third-person effect research? Perhaps this is due in part to the failure of much early research to take a theoretical approach. On its face, the third-person effect describes a phenomenon, not an explanatory theory. Its early literature saw many replications of the tendency for people to estimate a greater influence of communication on others than on themselves, but not much attention to why.

And what explains the apparent ongoing vitality of third-person effect research? Again, the answer lies in theory, and much of this theory is intimately related to public opinion research. First, the third-person effect is an arena that links self and others and thus places individuals in a larger social sphere—a crucial setting for many of the most engaging ideas in the field of public opinion. Second, third-person effect models involve multiple stages (and, it should be noted, perceived public opinion lies precisely at the center of these models), and thus several theoretical constructs can come into play. And finally, many of the most interesting theoretical questions about the third-person effect, while receiving increasing attention, have not been resolved. Hence, the third-person effect meets Popper's

standard for a robust area of theoretical inquiry.

FIRST COMPONENT: THE THIRD-PERSON PERCEPTION

Is the third-person perception, the sense that communication will influence others more than the self, a new phenomenon that originated with the broadcast media, or does it date back to the dawn of civilization? Plato feared that the 'ascendancy of the written word over the spoken word' (Starker, 1989, p. 7) would cause great harm. Nineteenth century critics worried that reading novels would lead to 'the entire destruction of the powers of the mind' (Starker, p. 8). It seems likely that fears of media effects and accompanying third-person perceptions have greeted the initiation of all new media (Wartella & Reeves, 1985; Perloff, 2002). Yet our current era seems to be particularly susceptible to the perception of powerful media effects. The vividness and reach of television invites attributions of strong effects. As a result of formal features or content that gives rise to hostile media perceptions, 'media direct attention outward, to the mass media audience and the undesirable influence that audience may experience' (Gunther & Schmitt, 2004, p. 69). Due to media's formal properties and widely-publicized discussions of media effects, mass media direct the gaze of observers onto the audience, leading them to consider how the audience is influenced by media content. This is itself a media effect.

Contemporary media genres—television entertainment, MTV, video games and the Internet—are particularly likely to invite perceptions of media impact. For example, a preeminent meaning of video games in today's culture involves descriptions of new generations of video games, widespread use by young people, and adult concern that games are harming adolescents (Perloff, 2005). Third-person perceptions are built into the fabric of media and are part of the public discourse in a way they have never been before.

The third-person perception is one of a family of social scientific concepts that focuses on perceptions of others or collectives outside an individual's personal life space (Mutz, 1998). It is unique in several respects. First, it focuses on the intriguing bifurcation between perceptions of message effects on others and the self. In this way, it flows from the time-honored duality of Western thought (i.e., the subject–object dichotomy), in which we experience ourselves as different from the objects of our perception. Second, it is most commonly operationalized as a relational concept. The focus is not perceived media effects on others or perceived effects on the self, but the discrepancy between these beliefs. The key element is the 'disconnect' between perceptions of others and the self. In addition, the third-person effect is a perceptual distortion arising from the logical inconsistency implicit in the notion that media influence others more than oneself (Tiedge, Silverblatt, Havice, & Rosenfeld, 1991).

There have been two authenticity-based concerns—one methodological, the other psychological. Some researchers have speculated that the effect is an artifact of question order or measurement issues. Yet the third-person effect has survived many methodological controls designed to evaluate these alternative explanations (e.g., Gunther, 1995; Brosius & Engel, 1996; Price & Tewksbury, 1996; Salwen & Driscoll, 1997). In a rigorous series of tests, David, Liu, and Myser (2004) reported the third-person effect persisted despite such controls as counterbalancing order of evaluation of others and self, use of a bipolar scale with 'no effect' of media as the midpoint, and shift from a within-subjects to a between-subjects comparison.

The second threat to third-person effect authenticity concerns the disowning projection (Fields & Schuman, 1976). From the very beginning, skeptics argued that the third-person effect is nothing more than the desire to project one's own socially undesirable perceptions onto others. It is difficult to unequivocally rule out a disowning projection. However, this scenario is weakened by the absence of supportive data, predominance of other explanations, and its counterintuitive quality. It strains credulity to believe that individuals are so threatened by media content that they unconsciously project their own vulnerability to media influence onto others.

Whether people overestimate the effects of messages on others, underestimate their effects on the self or engage in some combination of both is difficult to determine, but a few early experiments tackled this problem. By using control groups to establish baseline opinion in a sample and then measuring actual opinions along with perceived opinion changes for self and others in treatment groups, researchers were able to assess the apparent accuracy of perceived message influence (e.g., Gunther, 1991). In general, results favored overestimation of influence on others, but at least one study (Douglas & Sutton, 2004) has revealed underestimated influence on the self. In any event, such studies are too few to justify any generalizations; this important question deserves more attention.

It is, however, safe to say that the third-person perception is no mere artifact, and is in fact empirically robust. In their meta-analytic study, Paul, Salwen, and Dupagne (2000) found that the effect size (magnitude of difference between estimated media effects on self and others) was substantial, with an r of 0.50. This is larger than that reported for the impact of TV violence on antisocial behavior ($r = 0.31$), and pornography on aggression ($r = 0.13$; cf. Paul *et al.*, 2000).

But robust correlations do not answer the question of why. What explains the pervasive evidence of third-person perceptions? The prevailing explanation is ego-maintenance. Admitting one has been influenced by media messages, particularly undesirable messages, is tantamount to acknowledging gullibility or vulnerability. By assuming that the self is invulnerable to media effects, while perceiving others as susceptible, the individual preserves a positive sense of self (Perloff, 2002). In support of this view, messages associated with undesirable outcomes are perceived to have stronger effects on others than the self (e.g., Gunther & Mundy, 1993; Duck & Mullin, 1995). By contrast, content that is seen as socially desirable or good for the self has in some cases yielded first-person effects, or perception of greater impact on the self than others (Henriksen & Flora, 1999).

The ego-maintenance view argues that third-person perceptions have their roots in motivational processes. A second interpretation argues that when assessing media effects on others, individuals invoke a simple 'exposure equals influence' heuristic (McLeod, Detenber, & Eveland, 2001, p. 692). However, when considering media effects on the self, individuals employ a more complex, conditional-effects perspective that takes into account one's own ability to discount or reject harmful messages. McLeod and his colleagues speculate that the self–other disparity can be viewed as a subset of the fundamental attribution error. When estimating media effects on themselves, individuals take into account the impact of situational factors like persuasive intent (Gunther, 1991), but when examining message effects on third persons, they assume others' shortcomings render them incapable of appreciating the impact of factors that they, of course, see through.

Explanations for the third-person effect are by no means resolved. Self-enhancement processes seem clearly implicated, but do not explain all findings, and first-person effects that presumably reflect self-enhancement are not universally obtained (Salwen & Dupagne, 2003; David et al., 2004). Researchers have proposed a host of additional explanatory mechanisms, including self-categorization (Reid & Hogg, 2005), anxiety (Tewksbury, Moy, & Weis, 2004), perceptions of message severity (Shah, Faber, & Youn, 1999) and central/peripheral processing (White, 1997). Clearly, research on the first component of the third-person effect will benefit from continued, theoretically grounded studies on mediating mechanisms.

Although infrequently discussed, the normative implications of the third-person perception deserve consideration. The actual (and perceived) increase in polarized voices in the media, exemplified on any issue from social security to the right-to-die debate, has a way of encouraging people to think in bipolar terms. When people hear of Democrats waging war against Republicans, those who do not turn off the media entirely are encouraged to pick sides. When they do so, they may fall prey to a situationally based hostile media perception, in which they do not assimilate many of the viewpoints they hear. Instead, they assume that media views are discrepant from their perspective, and are bound to persuade the public to the opposing viewpoint (Gunther, Christen, Liebhart, & Chia, 2001). Viewing media in this way, they conclude that the public is becoming more hostile toward their attitudes, which may polarize their attitudes even further. Thus, strident media content (amplified on the web), along with increased public perceptions of news bias (Healy, 2005) and the hostile media effect, may produce a more polarized, less open-minded electorate. To the extent that contemporary media encourage a bifurcation of self and other and cultivate perceptions that polarize public opinion, they may be unwittingly contributing to an increasingly fragmented, disconnected public.

SECOND COMPONENT: THE THIRD-PERSON EFFECT

Although a majority of studies on this phenomenon have addressed the perceptual hypothesis, scholarly interest is increasingly turning to its real-world 'behavioral' implications (see Perloff, 2002). The second component of the third-person effect suggests that people's expectations regarding media impact produce a reaction. These reactions, although often described under the umbrella of the so-called behavioral component, can involve cognitive, perceptual, attitudinal and other responses. While research on this component of the hypothesis has received less attention, more and more evidence has appeared in recent years suggesting that third person perceptions have important consequences. As Elihu Katz (2005) maintains, 'the *myth* of media impact is influential, too.'

The consequences of perceiving large media influences on others (though little influence on the self), fall into two general classes: prevention and accommodation (Gunther, Bolt, Borzekowski, Liebhart, & Dillard, 2006). Prevention refers to the impulse to thwart an apparently harmful message, and this reaction received the earliest research attention. Support for message restrictions has been documented in various contexts, including pornography (Gunther, 1995), violence (Rojas, Shah, & Faber, 1996), and misogynic rap music (McLeod, Eveland, & Nathanson, 1997). Prevention reactions suggest that people will support censorship based on a false perception of harmful influences on others, an outcome with important implications for the freedom of speech.

Accommodation reactions, which are more complex and more recently documented, appear to fall into at least four conceptually different categories: 'comply,' 'defy,' 'withdraw' and 'oblige' (drawing on Katz, 2005). In the first condition, perceiving that media promote the adoption of a social norm may cause individuals to *comply* with that norm. For example, adolescents perceiving that pro-smoking messages make their peers more favorably inclined toward smoking are significantly more likely to start smoking themselves, presumably to comply with the perceived social norm (Gunther et al., 2006). Studies of body image suggest that young people may change eating behaviors because of their perceptions of media influence on normative attitudes toward the ideal body type (Milkie, 1999).

In contrast, the second category describes situations where individuals who believe that media influence the opinions and behaviors of others will react in *defiance* of those perceived trends. For example, right-wing Jewish settlers in the Gaza Strip, feeling that Israeli public opinion toward the settlements was heavily influenced by unfavorably biased media coverage, were more likely to say they would forcefully resist evacuation from their homes (Tsfati & Cohen, 2005).

In the third scenario, believing that media foster a social norm causes people to *withdraw*, to stop doing something, or *not* to do something they would have done otherwise, because they think other people would not like it. Noelle Neumann's (e.g., 1993) classic spiral-of-silence model falls into this category. Her theory describes people not speaking their minds because they feel that media influence other people to hold contrary opinions. A withdrawal reaction was also described in a study of residents of peripheral towns in Israel (Tsfati & Cohen, 2003). If residents, even those who liked where they lived, perceived that negative media portrayals of their towns would generate unfavorable public opinion about their towns, they were more likely to consider moving away.

The fourth type of consequence of perceived media influence takes place when people feel *obliged* to react to the fact that others are affected, regardless of their personal compliance with the norm. This may be true especially when people are serving dependent others. For example, grocers place well-advertised goods (rather than poorly advertised products) on prominent shelves, because they assume advertising influences customers and they feel obliged to accommodate that effect. As Schudson (1986, p. xv) maintains, the result is that 'widely advertised brands become the brands most widely available.' Schudson concludes that in this way 'it is entirely plausible ... that advertising helps sell goods even if it never persuades a consumer of anything' (p. xv).

Other 'oblige' reactions can be found in studies of so-called unintended audiences. Doctors, for example, who perceived that direct-to-consumer (DTC) prescription drug advertising had negative effects on their clients were more likely to refuse to prescribe these DTC drugs (Huh & Langteau, 2005). Patients' beliefs on the influence of a Nepalese radio drama containing health-delivery messages, messages targeted at doctors and nurses, were found related to patients' beliefs about, and interactions with, health care providers (Gunther & Storey, 2003).

Parents believing that controversial or violent media content impacts other children (more than their own) were more likely to provide parental mediation to their children and more likely to monitor their own kids' social activities as well as their media consumption (Tsfati, Ribak, & Cohen, 2005). Parents apparently worry about the indirect effects of such programs on their own children because they perceive negative influences on their children's friends and playmates.

Exploring the third-person effect in a book on public opinion is particularly appropriate because the subjective or perceived public opinion discussed throughout this chapter is a fulcrum in the third-person effect model. Not only is it the critical mediating variable, it is also—conceptually and theoretically— the most fertile area for future research. Though traditionally defined as a self–other difference, for example, the third-person perception has recently been cast in arguably broader terms—as simply perceived influence on others (Gunther & Storey, 2003).[1]

This view begs the question of what we mean by influence. When we ask that question, aren't we really just as interested in the immediate consequences of such influence— changes in attitudes, opinions, beliefs (or even behaviors) of others (see Jensen & Hurley, 2005)? If we simply consider question wording, much third-person effect research seems to elicit the former—perceptions of influence. But other studies take this a bit further, asking about perceived peer norms, public attitudes, or even perceived behaviors of others as the mediating variables. These are in large part public opinion variables, and their consequences are what ultimately make third-person effect research important to pursue.

Crucial theoretical issues lurk here. Is it influence, or the thing we assume to be influenced (beliefs, norms, even behaviors), that give rise to prevention or accommodation outcomes? And is it a disconnect between self and others, or simply (overestimated) influence on others that predicts these 'behavioral' reactions? The answer, of course, may turn out to be all of these—and for

a variety of interesting, practical and useful reasons. Our task is to find out what these reasons are.

NOTES

1 Methodologically, a case could be made for investigating the 'me' and 'them' items separately in models examining the consequences of the third-person effect. Using a difference score may conceal the effects of the separate presumed influence items (see Tsfati, Ribak, & Cohen, 2005). This happens when both presumed influence items are positively or negatively correlated with the dependent variable, and thus the effect of the difference score may be null.

REFERENCES

Brosius, H.-B., & Engel, D. (1996). The causes of third-person effects: Unrealistic optimism, impersonal impact, or generalized negative attitudes towards media influence? *International Journal of Public Opinion Research, 8*, 142–162.

Bryant, J., & Miron, D. (2004). Theory and research in mass communication. *Journal of Communication, 54*, 662–704.

David, P., Liu, K., & Myser, M. (2004). Methodological artifact or persistent bias? Testing the robustness of the third person and reverse third-person effects for alcohol messages. *Communication Research, 31*(2), 206–233.

Davison, W. P. (1983). The third-person effect in communication. *Public Opinion Quarterly, 47*, 1–15.

Douglas, K. M., & Sutton, R. M. (2004). Right about others, wrong about ourselves? Actual and perceived self-other differences in resistance to persuasion. *British Journal of Social Psychology, 43*, 585–603.

Duck, J. M., & Mullin, B. (1995). The perceived impact of the mass media: Reconsidering the third person effect. *European Journal of Social Psychology, 25*, 77–93.

Fields, J. M., & Schuman, H. (1976). Public beliefs about the beliefs of the public. *Public Opinion Quarterly, 40*, 427–448.

Gunther, A. C. (1991). What we think others think: Cause and consequence in the third-person effect. *Communication Research, 18*, 355–372.

Gunther, A. C. (1995). Overrating the X-rating: The third-person perception and support for censorship of pornography. *Journal of Communication, 45*(1), 27–38.

Gunther, A. C., & Mundy, P. (1993). Biased optimism and the third-person effect. *Journalism Quarterly, 70*, 58–67.

Gunther, A. C., & Storey, J. D. (2003). The influence of presumed influence. *Journal of Communication, 53*, 199–215.

Gunther, A. C., & Schmitt, K. (2004). Mapping boundaries of the hostile media effect. *Journal of Communication, 54*(1), 55–75.

Gunther, A. C., Christen, C. T., Liebhart, J. L., & Chia, S. C. (2001). Congenial public, contrary press, and biased estimates of the climate of opinion. *Public Opinion Quarterly, 65*, 295–320.

Gunther, A. C., Bolt, D., Borzekowski, D. L. B., Liebhart, J. L., & Dillard, J. P. (2006). Presumed influence on peer norms: How mass media indirectly affect adolescent smoking. *Journal of Communication, 56*, 52–68.

Healy, P. D. (2005, May 22). Believe it: The media's credibility headache gets worse. *The New York Times*, Week in Review, p. 4.

Henriksen, L., & Flora, J.A. (1999). Third-person perception and children: Perceived impact of pro- and anti-smoking ads. *Communication Research, 26*, 643–665.

Huh, J., & Langteau, R. (2005, August). *Perceived influence of DTC prescription drug advertising: Do the general public and the expert think differently?* Paper presented at the 2005 Annual Conference of the Association for Education in Journalism and Mass Communication, Austin, TX.

Jensen, J. D., & Hurley, R. J. (2005). Third-person effects and the environment: Social distance, social desirability and presumed behavior. *Journal of Communication, 55*, 242–256.

Katz, E. (2005, June). *The myth of media impact is influential, too.* Keynote address delivered at 'The Influence of Presumed Media Influence' research workshop, Haifa, Israel.

McLeod, D. M., Eveland, W. P., Jr., & Nathanson, A. I. (1997). Support for censorship of violent and misogynic rap lyrics: An analysis of the third-person effect. *Communication Research, 24*, 153–174.

McLeod, D. M., Detenber, B. H., & Eveland, W. P., Jr. (2001). Behind the third-person effect: Differentiating perceptual processes for self and other. *Journal of Communication, 51*(4), 678–695.

Milkie, M. A. (1999). Social comparisons, reflected appraisals, and mass media: The impact of pervasive beauty images on black and white girls' self-concepts. *Social Psychology Quarterly, 62*, 190–210.

Mutz, D. C. (1998). *Impersonal influence: How perceptions of mass collectives affect political attitudes.* Cambridge, England: Cambridge University Press.

Noelle-Neumann, E. (1993). *The Spiral of Silence: Public opinion—our social skin* (2nd ed.). Chicago: University of Chicago Press.

Paul, B., Salwen, M. B., & Dupagne, M. (2000). The third-person effect: A meta-analysis of the perceptual hypothesis. *Mass Communication & Society, 3*, 57–85.

Perloff, R. M. (2002). The third-person effect. In J. Bryant & D. Zillmann (Eds.), *Media effects: Advances in theory and research* (2nd ed., pp. 489–506). Mahwah, NJ: Lawrence Erlbaum Associates.

Perloff, R. M. (2005, June 10). Video games' benefits. (Letter to the Editor). *USA Today*, 22A.

Price, V., & Tewksbury, D. (1996). Measuring the third-person effect of news: The impact of question order, contrast and knowledge. *International Journal of Public Opinion Research, 8*, 120–141.

Reid, S. A., & Hogg, M. A. (2005). A self-categorization explanation for the third-person effect. *Human Communication Research, 31*, 129–161.

Rojas, H., Shah, D. V., & Faber, R. J. (1996). For the good of others: Censorship and the third-person effect. *International Journal of Public Opinion Research, 8*, 163–186.

Salwen, M. B., & Driscoll, P. D. (1997). Consequences of third-person perception in support of press restrictions in the O. J. Simpson trial. *Journal of Communication, 47*(2), 60–75.

Salwen, M. B., & Dupagne, M. (2003). News of Y2K and experiencing Y2K: Exploring the relationship between the third-person effect and optimistic bias. *Media Psychology, 5*, 57–82.

Schudson, M. (1986). *Advertising, the uneasy persuasion.* New York: BasicBooks.

Shah, D. V., Faber, R. J., & Youn, S. (1999). Susceptibility and severity: Perceptual dimensions underlying the third-person effect. *Communication Research, 26*, 240–267.

Starker, S. (1989). *Evil influences: Crusades against the mass media.* New Brunswick, NJ: Transaction.

Tewksbury, D., Moy, P., & Weis, D. S. (2004). Preparations for Y2K: Revisiting the behavioral component of the third-person effect. *Journal of Communication, 54*(1), 138–155.

Tiedge, J. T., Silverblatt, A., Havice, M. J., & Rosenfeld, R. (1991). Discrepancy between perceived first-person and perceived third-person mass media effects. *Journalism Quarterly, 68*, 141–154.

Tsfati, Y., & Cohen, J. (2003). On the effect of the 'third-person effect': Perceived influence of media coverage and residential mobility intentions. *Journal of Communication, 53*(4), 711–727.

Tsfati, Y., & Cohen, J. (2005). The influence of presumed media influence on democratic legitimacy: The case of Gaza settlers. *Communication Research 32*, 794–821.

Tsfati, Y., Ribak, R., & Cohen, J. (2005). Rebelde Way in Israel: Parental perceptions of television influence and monitoring of children's social and media activities. *Mass Communication & Society, 8*(1), 3–22.

Wartella, E., & Reeves, B. (1985). Historical trends in research on children and the media: 1900–1960. *Journal of Communication, 35*, 118–133.

White, H. A. (1997). Considering interacting factors in the third-person effect: Argument strength and social distance. *Journalism & Mass Communication Quarterly, 74*, 557–564.

18

Effects of the News Media on Public Opinion

Hans Mathias Kepplinger

The term *opinion* is used to express at least two different meanings. On the one hand, it denotes an appraising comment about a person, an animal or a thing. An example for this is the statement 'I have a good opinion of ….' On the other hand, it denotes an uncertain assertion of a fact. An example for this is the statement 'In my opinion, it is going to rain.' In the following overview, both meanings are used. Because *opinion* here also indicates the uncertain assertions of facts, the term is sometimes replaced by terms like *cognition* or *knowledge* used in the literature cited. The term *public opinion* therefore describes appraising judgments concerning reality and/or uncertain ideas about reality.

In order to analyze the impact of media coverage on public opinion, three different concepts of public opinion have to be distinguished. In the *quantitative concept*, public opinion is regarded as distribution of individual opinions within a population. While some authors include opinions on all issues and others restrict it to political issues, they agree that public opinions are measured by representative opinion polls (Glynn, Herbst, Garrett, O'Keefe, & Shapiro, 1999; Bardes & Oldendick, 2003; Saris & Sniderman, 2004). Although most theorists stress the distribution of opinions, most empirical researchers use the term to identify the majority opinion on issues. The origin of the quantitative concept can be found in Rousseau's 'volonté de tous,' the countable will of the majority.

In the *qualitative concept,* public opinion is regarded as the opinion of interested and well-informed citizens on political issues. It is assumed that they pursue collective goods, besides individual goals, derive their opinions from general values and detailed information about current affairs, and take a stand for their opinion in public (Hennis, 1957). In this view, public opinion is composed of the opinions of elites, among which editorial writers and other top journalists play an important role. Therefore, this public opinion cannot be measured by opinion polls but has to be deduced from public statements (Herbst, 1998). As even the elites mentioned might not be able to recognize a reality independent of their individual preferences (Lippmann, 1922), one might question if they really represent what Rousseau called 'volonté générale.'

In the *functional concept*, public opinion can be regarded as a mechanism that reduces the unlimited number of possible topics to a limited number of issues that can be discussed in public. It is driven by attention rules (news factors and news values), which have to be distinguished from decision rules that guide the process of decision making in politics, business and other institutions. If a topic has become an element of public opinion, it might fit decision rules and thus have lasting consequences, or it might not fit decision rules (for example, because shortly before an election the government is not able to react) and fade away without leaving an effect (Luhmann, 1970). It also can be regarded as a mechanism that establishes and stabilizes dominant opinions concerning controversial issues by discouraging public statements by people holding divergent views (the *spiral of silence*). Here, the impact of public opinion is restricted to morally loaded issues but can affect opinion formation about political and non-political issues. Public opinion, the opinion 'that one can express in public without isolating oneself' (Noelle-Neumann, 1993, p. 62), can be identified with opinion polls, but is not necessarily identical with the majority opinion. The functional concept can be traced back to ancient texts, the origin of its modern version being John Locke's 'law of opinion' (→ *The Public and Public Opinion in Political Theories*).

Theories about the influence of media on public opinion depend on the particular concept of public opinion used. According to the qualitative concept, the coverage of the (leading) news media and public opinion are more or less identical. Therefore, the news media do not exert a remarkable influence upon public opinion. Instead, public opinion has to be concluded from media coverage and from personal contacts with reporters and editorial writers. According to the quantitative concept, the focus of research will be on

the relationship between the tenor of media coverage and the opinion of the majority. Here, media coverage can be regarded as an independent variable, and majority opinion as a dependent variable (→ *Agenda-Setting, Framing and Priming*). According to the functional concept, public opinion is regarded as an intervening variable, influencing individuals to take a stand in public, which in turn influences public opinion—the opinion perceived by individuals as the dominant opinion. In so far as this process stimulates individual opinion changes, it is related to the quantitative concept of public opinion. Other than in the quantitative concept, the opinion of the majority is not necessarily regarded as a direct effect of media coverage but as a consequence of a complex process in which media coverage plays an important role (see Figure 18.1).

EXPOSURE AND EFFECTS

According to an unspoken axiom of media effects research, there is 'no effect without contact.' Media coverage is used and processed selectively. Therefore, selective use of mass media is often said to minimize or even prevent media effects on public opinion. With respect to selectivity, three stages can be identified—the selective attentiveness to offers of the media (pre-communicative phase), the selective reception of the offers taken up (communicative phase) as well as the selective remembering of the offers received (post-communicative phase). Reasons for the selection are the availability of media coverage, clear-cut editorial policy of various media outlets, individual usefulness of media coverage as well as the values of recipients. Selective use and processing of media coverage has been empirically well anchored by numerous investigations and can be explained by the theory of cognitive dissonance and related approaches. It is often put forward as proof of the validity of the *amplifier thesis,* according to which the media do not change attitudes and opinions, but only reinforce them. This is a matter of

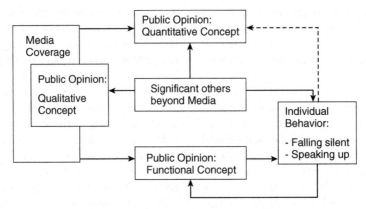

Figure 18.1   Three concepts of public opinion and their respective relations to media coverage

an unreliable generalization. The recipients' system of values has a moderate influence on the use of national daily newspapers, the tabloids, weekly papers and political TV magazines, and a weak influence on the use of regional daily newspapers and radio and TV news (Kepplinger, Brosius, & Staab, 1991). It has a moderate influence on the reading of articles in regularly used newspapers. The slight tendency of readers to read selectively in their newspapers can, moreover, be overcome by journalistic page design. The general tendency to select in no way presents an impermeable barrier for dissonant or inconsistent information. It reduces the effect of the media, but does not, however, prevent it (Donsbach, 1991).

Most people receive some of the information and opinions circulated by the media indirectly, i.e. from people who got their information from the media (*two step flow → Studying Elite vs Mass Opinion*). The conveyers of this information have been named 'opinion leaders' (Lazarsfeld, Berelson, & Gaudet, 1968). They are found in all segments of society, have specific personality traits and hold key positions in their social networks (Weimann, 1991). The influence of opinion leaders on other persons is—corresponding to the unspoken axiom of media effects research 'no effect without contact'—usually not considered as an effect of the media reports they use. This assumption is only correct if at least one of two conditions

is fulfilled: (1) opinion leaders only pass on the information and opinions of the media that correspond to their own convictions. In this case they act as filters, which minimize the effect of the media reports. (2) Opinion leaders change the input from the media by adding information and opinions. In this case they act as independent sources that were activated by the media reports. A systematic test of these assumptions has never been carried out. As a consequence, the most important question is still open: must opinion leaders be regarded as filters who minimize media effects or as amplifiers of media effects who exert their impact upon those who had no contact with their coverage?

DIRECT INFLUENCE OF THE MEDIA ON PUBLIC OPINION (QUANTITATIVE CONCEPT)

Learning theory approaches

According to the learning theory, learning is based on the association (*conditioning*) of stimulus and reactions (*stimulus-response associations*). In the present context, *operant conditioning* is especially significant. According to this formulation, rewarding a specific behavior establishes a link to a stimulus (*amplification*). In the area of media effects, the reward consists, for example, in social recognition for knowledge about political issues. In the case of the learning theory approaches, opinion is a matter of the correct learning of information. Divergences between opinions and media coverage thus count as learning deficits, which are interpreted as a lack of media effects. For learning, *attentiveness* to certain stimuli is necessary, as also the *storing* (cognitive representation) of the information as well as the *motivation* to use it. Attentiveness depends on individual interests. A flaw in most of the effects studies oriented to learning theory is that the different variables—objective contents and subjective understanding, attentiveness and effect—are not distinguished and recorded separately, because measuring them in primary studies would take too much time and effort and the data necessary for secondary analyses are usually not available.

Influence on relevance of issues (*agenda-setting function*). The current news coverage by the media has a relatively great influence on the population's assessment of the significance of social problems, especially on the urgency for solving them. However, it has only a very weak influence on the significance of the same facts for the individual's own life. In agenda-setting research, two research directions have been established: (1) Comparisons of the media's agenda with the population's agenda at a few points in time within a short period of time. Of particular significance here are panel studies that reveal the changes of opinions of single persons. (2) Comparisons of the development of the tenor of the media and beliefs of the population on the basis of one topic at many points in time, over a long period of time (McCombs & Shaw, 1993; Rogers & Dearing, 1993). The media agenda, and the tenor of the media, depend on the *current events situation*—for example, the frequency of crimes. The population knows about some of these events from their own experiences. Therefore, changes in opinions might be caused by personal contact and/or media coverage. Even if people get first-hand information, media coverage exerts an influence on public opinion on many

topics (Combs & Slovic, 1979; Behr & Iyengar, 1985, → *Agenda-Setting, Framing and Priming*).

Most studies about the effects of the mass media on public opinion contain the unspoken assumption that a linear relationship exists between the quantity of media reports and the opinions of the population (cumulative model). Starting with this assumption, the opinions of the population follow the ups and downs of the emphases given to the topics in the media. However, this assumption is not true in many cases. Thus, for example, the population still remains worried about disasters following extensive reports concerning serious disasters, even after news coverage has already subsided (echo model). In such cases there is obviously no linear relationship between media coverage and opinions of the population. If one calculates the connections with methods that presume a linear relationship, the results paradoxically demonstrate a weak effect, because the effect was so strong that worries continued to exist after the news coverage had abated. As a consequence, a variety of non-linear models have been proposed and tested (Potter, 1991; Brosius & Kepplinger, 1992). Figure 18.2 shows, on the left, a representation of a linear connection between the news coverage of several topics and the beliefs at a certain point in time (cumulative model), and on the right, the development of the news coverage concerning one topic and related opinions during a longer period of time.

Influence on assessments of risks (*risk perception*). People have a rather good judgment concerning the relative frequency of causes of death: they naturally know which occur often and which are rarer. They typically make two mistakes, however: they overestimate the occurrence of the rare causes and underestimate the occurrence of more frequent causes of death. One reason for this is found in the media's news coverage: they report very intensively about rare causes of death (tornados, death by poisoning, lightning, and the like), because these have a great news value due to their rareness. In contrast, they rarely report about frequent causes of death

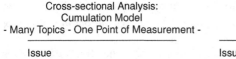

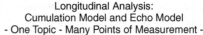

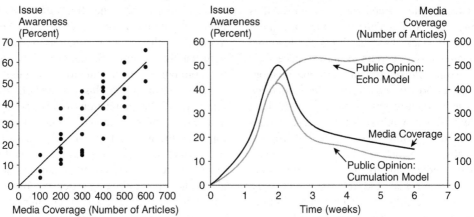

Figure 18.2   Cumulative model of media effects in cross-sectional and longitudinal analysis compared to echo model

(heart attacks, lung cancer, diabetes, and the like), which for the same reasons do not have a great news value. The population's beliefs about the frequency of various causes of death follow the media's focusing on the causes of death rather than their actual frequency (Combs & Slovic, 1979). Thus, opinions about the risks of technologies rather follow the representation of damage and risks than the damage actually documented (Kepplinger, 1992; Ader, 1995). The effect of the representation of the dangers depends not only on the magnitude of the risk represented, but also on the way it is covered. Using photographs or descriptions, the media often give the impression that the damage is greater than it actually is. The more extreme the photographs and descriptions are, the more typical the crimes appear to the audience, and thus the audience is more likely to regard them as a national problem. These misinterpretations do not become smaller over the course of time, but actually increase (Gibson & Zillmann, 1994). It follows that the population at times is not afraid of what really is threatening them, but of what they mistakenly consider especially threatening, on the basis of media reports.

According to Gerbner and his co-authors, the representation of death and distress,

especially on TV, shapes the opinions of the population about the risk of becoming the victim of a crime: the more TV people watch, the more their ideas are influenced by TV's presentation of reality. *Frequent viewers* thus are more likely to overestimate the tenor of the television offerings according to the frequency of violence than *infrequent viewers* (Gerbner, Gross, Signorielli, Morgan, & Jackson-Beeck, 1979; Morgan, 1983). The studies by Gerbner and his colleagues were criticized due to shortcomings in method (Hirsch, 1980, 1981). More recent studies show no uniform findings, but argue, however, rather more for than against an influence of television on fear about crime and opinions on what should be done against it (Gross & Aday, 2003; Kepplinger, 2003; Lowry, Nio, & Leitner, 2003; Romer, Jamieson, & Aday, 2003; → *Theories on the Perception of Social Reality*).

Influence on suppositions about effect. Most people attribute stronger effects of media messages on others compared to themselves (*third-person effect* → *Public Opinion and the Third-Person Effect*). For example, they tend to deny the effects of violent movies upon themselves, but believe they have strong effects upon most other people. Third-person effects occur especially when the media or the effects are regarded as negative or undesirable (Davison, 1996). People who are highly involved in an issue tend to overestimate the effect of news reports more strongly than neutral people (Perloff, 1999). The more distant and different third persons are, and the larger the category of third persons is, the more protagonists will attribute strong effects to them (Gunther, 1991; Tewksbury, 2002). 'Although perceived public opinion has not been incorporated in the third-person effect hypothesis, it is a logical extension of the model to expect that when people perceive substantial media influences on others, they should also perceive consonant influences on aggregated public opinion' (Gunther, 1998, p. 487). There is some evidence that when the public perceives any potentially immoral or harmful effects of media news coverage (for example television violence) or other information dissemination (advertising for controversial products), they will increase their support for censorship or other restrictions on the general population (Driscoll & Salwen, 1997; Eveland & McLeod, 1999; Salwen & Dupagne, 1999). In turn, these opinions—as measured by opinion polls or deduced from media coverage—might have an impact on policy makers.

Cognitive theory approaches

Cognitive theories pose the general question concerning how people perceive their environment and themselves, how they interpret these purposefully, and how they experience them emotionally. At its center is human information processing and the triggering of these processes by media coverage. The theories go back primarily to assumptions of Fritz Heider: (1) People do not take the reality surrounding them as single elements, but as pre-structured units and derive their judgments about the elements from them. This assumption became the foundation of the *consistence and dissonance theories*. (2) People are compulsive cause-seekers. Following specific rules, they attribute causes to occurrences (Heider, 1958). This assumption became the

foundation of the *attribution theory*. It is a common denominator of these theories that the opinions of the readers, listeners and viewers cannot be regarded as copies of media representations of reality. They go, in fact, clearly beyond the representation, but are based on the representation. Differences between the representation and opinions of the population are regarded as predictable results of their processing of information provided by—among other sources—media coverage.

Processing of Media Information. Schema theory and closely related *framing theory* are based on the assumption that recipients of media coverage do not take up the individual pieces of information in the news independent of one another, but interpret them coherently according to a predetermined schema or frame (→ *Agenda-Setting, Framing and Priming*). In the case of the schemata/frames it is a matter of perspectives that are often established at the beginning of the report and control the reception of further information (Graber, 1984; Brosius, 1995). Both theories can be integrated in a 'process model of media framing.' Here 'frame building' is established by social actors, 'frame setting' by the media and the 'frame effects' by readers, listeners and viewers (Scheufele, 1999). Close relationships also exist between framing and priming theory (Price & Tewksbury, 1997). It has been demonstrated that readers primarily remember information and erroneously believe they have read information conforming to the frame in which it is presented (Brosius, 1995, pp. 214–238). They interpret the information in the context (frame) established by media reports (Price, Tewksbury, & Powers, 1997; Domke, Shah, & Wackman, 1998); and make conclusions in line with the frame given (Nelson, Clawson, & Oxley, 1997; McLeod & Detenber, 1999). The influence of frames or schemata in news coverage must be distinguished from the influence of opinions, which are simply taken over by the recipients according to the valence model of media effects and thus can be better explained with the help of learning theories (Fan, 1988; Zaller, 1992).

Priming theory is based on the assumption that one can regard certain feelings, thoughts and memories as knots in a network, which are more or less closely related to other parts of this network. Information activates such knots as well as the parts of the network connected to them and sensitizes them to acquire similar information, which as a consequence is taken up more attentively and processed more intensively (Price & Tewksbury, 1997). The basic assumptions of the theory can be specified as follows: (1) Opinions about politicians (and parties) as well as the voting intentions resulting from this are based, among other things, on the public's beliefs about the skills of the politicians, i.e. about their capabilities of solving certain problems. (2) Repeated coverage concerning individual problems—for example internal security or unemployment—sensitizes the recipients to these topics and so improves the taking up and remembering of information. (3) Concentration of attention on individual problems makes the solution of these problems seem particularly urgent. (4) Thus the presumed ability of the politicians to solve these problems becomes more significant for their overall assessment, which, according to how their capability is rated, has a positive or negative effect on general overall opinions about politicians. General opinions about politicians and voting intentions can thus change, although the judgments of the politicians' individual abilities remain constant. If one considers the beliefs about the skills of the recipients to be attitudes, then it may be said that the attitudes will not be changed, but will become more or less relevant (Iyengar & Kinder, 1986; Iyengar, 1991; Domke, Shah, & Wackman, 1998).

Interaction of cognitions and emotions. Appraisal theory posits a connection between the cognitions/opinions based on the information available (*appraisal*) and the type of emotions felt. It is not clear whether the assessments are the causes of the emotions (Smith & Ellsworth, 1985) or whether people assess the situations in a special way due to the emotions felt (Frijda, 1993). The theory is based on the following assumptions:

(1) Reports about extensive damage trigger great attention. (2) They convey opinions about the reasons for the damage. (3) If the damage is portrayed as the result of circumstances that nobody could change, sadness is felt. If it is portrayed as the result of the action of someone who could have acted differently, anger is felt. (4) Emotions are not only a consequence of cognitions/opinions, but also the cause of coherent cognitions/opinions. For example, if an article causes anger about a person depicted in it, readers tend to deny higher objectives, even if nothing was said about this in the reports. Thus there are interactions between cognitions/opinions and emotions that tend to a consistent condition. Strong emotions arouse behavior intentions—the tendency to boycott based on anger, and the tendency to help based on sadness. This theory has been confirmed by laboratory experiments (Nerb & Spada, 2001).

The *theory of instrumental actualization* regards public controversies as disputes between contending groups, in which the media function as more or less independent actors. It is based on the following assumptions: (1) In all conflicts, there are many information occurrences that argue for one or the other side. In this sense they are 'instrumental.' (2) Contenders and the media supporting them concentrate on information that speaks for their own side and against the opponent's side (*instrumental actualization*). (3) Legitimization of the one side is based mainly on discrediting the opposing side. (4) Reception and knowledge of information, which speaks for the one respectively against the other side, is reflected in positive (or negative) opinions about the opponents. The theory has been confirmed by a field study, in which the type and quantity of the media information used was determined, and its influence on the knowledge and opinions of the individual readers, listeners and viewers was established (Kepplinger, Brosius, & Staab, 1991).

De facto effects

In experimental studies, researchers use isolated representations of media content and measure its processing by the recipients. This procedure represents a great reduction of the complexity of the typical news coverage. In social life, media content is not found to be isolated, but part of a recurring diversity of interests made up of correct and false assertions of facts, presumptions, opinions and the like. Thus it is hardly possible to distinguish whether it is a matter of a statement concerning an assertion of a fact or concerning an evaluation. Media coverage can influence the opinions of the recipients in two ways. The recipients can learn opinions by taking over statements of opinions from journalists and others (Gunther & Christen, 1999). This is increasingly the case the more often they read or hear those sorts of statements. They can also derive their opinions, however, from the neutral account of successes or failures or of chances and risks. Here their conclusions can reach distinctly beyond the explicit information presented in the media. The recipients' opinions have various sources, which cannot be isolated ex post facto. These sorts of effects are called *de facto effects*. De facto effects may always be assumed if the formation of opinion follows the tenor of the media, and other sources can, with great probability, be excluded. They have been documented for numerous topics—concerning opinions on politicians such as Chancellor Helmut Kohl (Kepplinger, Donsbach, Brosius, & Staab, 1989), President George Bush (Lichter & Lichter, 1992), George Bush and Michael Dukakis (Fan & Tims, 1989); concerning opinions on special topics such as general economic developments (Hagen, 2005), as well as opinions on the state of the parties (Moy & Pfau, 2000; Maurer, 2003).

INDIRECT INFLUENCE OF THE MEDIA ON PUBLIC OPINION (FUNCTIONAL CONCEPT)

Influence on the belief about majorities. Almost all people form opinions about the opinions of the majority in the relevant population (town, country, state). Here various mistaken judgments can occur. 'False consensus' is the tendency of people 'to see their own behavioral choices and judgments as relatively common and appropriate to existing circumstances while viewing alternative responses as uncommon, deviant and inappropriate' (Ross, Greene, & House, 1977). 'Looking glass perception' is the conviction that most other people, including most people one considers important, have the same opinion as oneself (Fields & Schuman, 1976). 'Pluralistic ignorance' is the mistaken conviction that the opinion of the majority is the opinion of a minority (O'Gorman & Garry, 1976) (→ *Theories on the Perception of Social Reality,* → *Pluralistic Ignorance and Nonattitudes*).

Opinions about the opinion of the majority theoretically have two sources—direct observation, mainly through conversations with other people, and indirect observation through the news coverage of the media concerning the opinion of the population. In the second case, we can distinguish between two types of representation: reports with quantitative information ('the majority believes …' or '55% think …') and interviews with individual persons or 'exemplars,' who represent different perspectives (case reports, witnesses' statements, or 'man in the street' interviews). The selection of persons interviewed can correspond to the actual distribution of opinion or can depart from it. Reports about the opinions of a few persons, the majority of whom represent one view, influence the estimates of the recipients of the distribution of opinions more strongly than reports with quantitative statements concerning the opinion of the majority (Zillmann & Brosius, 2000; Daschmann, 2001). The comparatively strong effect of the exemplars is probably based on the fact that the generalization of individual cases belongs to the traditional and accordingly deeply anchored mechanisms, using which we form general beliefs, whereas statistical details have only been available for a few generations (and in many cases are understood only with difficulty).

Influence on the readiness to make public statements on controversial issues. According to the spiral of silence theory, the perception of what is majority and what minority opinion has an impact on the voicing of one's own opinion in public (→ *Spiral of Silence Theory*). For example, as the balance of negative and positive information about nuclear energy in the German press had become increasingly unfavorable, a growing percentage of the population believed the majority would oppose nuclear energy plants. As a consequence, a shrinking portion of supporters of nuclear energy was willing to express in public his/her own view to someone who started talking very unfavorably about nuclear energy (Noelle-Neumann, 1991).

ROLE OF THE MEDIA IN DEMOCRACY

The role of the media in a democracy must be evaluated against the background of theories of democracy (→ *The Public and Public Opinion in Political Theories*). A basis for this is provided by the distinction between the theory of the direct or plebiscitary democracy, in which all citizens should decide about everything themselves, and the theory of indirect or representative democracy, in which elected bodies make most of the decisions.

The prerequisite of the *theory of plebiscitary democracy*, which largely goes back to Jean-Jacques Rousseau and Karl Marx, is that the majority of the citizens behave rationally and according to rules if no one deters them from doing so. According to the theory of plebiscitary democracy, public opinion, in the sense of the quantitative concept, forms an important basis, if not the most important one, for political decisions. In contrast, public opinion in the sense of qualitative and functional concepts represents troublesome foreign bodies that prevent the mass of the population from forming their own opinions without being influenced. To enable citizens to take part in political life, several prerequisites must be fulfilled: (1) The mass media have to report current events intensively and in detail. (2) Journalists have

to be unprejudiced conveyors of information. (3) The media have to portray current events in a neutral way. (4) The citizens have to be interested in current events and make use of media reports about these events. (5) Citizens have to be able to process the media's information adequately and thus improve their knowledge and form their own opinions.

The prerequisites for the *theory of representative democracy*, which largely goes back to Alexander Hamilton, James Madison and John Jay and was elaborated by John Stewart Mill, are that the majority of citizens by nature do not have a great interest in politics, that they do not possess sufficient knowledge, and that their opinions depend on moods and are easily manipulated. Although the majority should take part in political decision-making, political decisions must be made by minorities in representative bodies who are relatively independent of the momentary moods of the majority. This is possible in society if a consensus exists concerning fundamental questions. Because such a consensus does not come into being on its own on the basis of rational discussions, it must be brought about. Here we find the essential task of the mass media. According to the theory of representative democracy, public opinion in the sense of the qualitative concept forms an important basis, if not the most important one, for political decisions. By contrast, public opinion in the sense of the quantitative concept may represent a troublesome foreign body in emotional public disputes that hinders the government from taking factually necessary decisions that are in everybody's interest. The judgment about the influence of the media on public opinion depends on whether the news coverage makes short-term sound opinions and a consensus in the long term possible (Graber, 1993; Hart, 1993; Jamieson, 1993; McLeod, 1993; Patterson, 1993).

The assumptions, upon which the theory of direct democracy is based, have been questioned in past decades by empirical investigations: the media, which reach the majority of the citizens, do not report extensively and in enough detail about current events (Robinson, 1976). Journalists of the influential media are not always neutral transmitters, but often portray the events from the viewpoint of the urban middle class (Lichter, Rothman, & Lichter, 1986). Journalists increasingly tend to put their own point of view in the foreground. Their reports thereby reduce the chances of social actors presenting their points of view (Patterson, 1994). Most citizens are not interested in extensive and detailed reports about current events. Their knowledge of current events does not increase (Neuman, 1986), their opinions do not become sounder, their confidence in politics dwindles (Lipset & Schneider, 1987), and their political participation decreases (Patterson, 2003). Thus the mass media do not possess the influence on public opinion that they could and should have. Moreover, public opinion does not have the quality that can be regarded as the prerequisite for decision making in a democracy.

Some authors regard the deficits and mistakes of the media and citizens as the consequence of their manipulation by the economic and political elites, who thereby defend their privileges (Chomsky & Herman, 2002). Accordingly they support a fundamental reform of the media and political institutions. Here the question remains unresolved as to whether the mass of the people bring with them the prerequisites that are implicitly attributed to them. Most authors attribute the deficits and mistakes of the mass media and the citizens to more or less unavoidable shortcomings of individuals and the institutions in which they work (Lippmann, 1925). Accordingly they implicitly or explicitly advocate a reduction of the deficits and mistakes, as well as an adaptation of the idealistic assumptions of the theory of plebiscite democracy to social reality. This includes the differentiation between the very small section of politically active people, the large mass of politically passive people, and the small section of politically alienated people, as well as the insight that the institutions of a democracy function relatively well, although the majority only occasionally becomes politically involved (Neuman,

1986, pp. 167–189; Page & Shapiro, 1992, pp. 383–398).

REFERENCES

Ader, C. R. (1995). A longitudinal study of agenda setting for the issue of environmental pollution. *Journalism & Mass Communication Quarterly, 72*, 300–311.

Bardes, B. A., & Oldendick, R. W. (2003). *Public opinion. Measuring the American mind* (2nd ed.). Belmont, CA: Wadsworth.

Behr, R. L., & Iyengar, S. (1985). Television news, real-world cues, and changes in the public agenda. *Public Opinion Quarterly, 49*, 38–57.

Brosius, H.-B. (1995). *Alltagsrationalität in der Nachrichtenrezeption. Ein Modell zur Wahrnehmung und Verarbeitung von Nachrichteninhalten* [A model of perception and processing of news]. Opladen: Westdeutscher Verlag.

Brosius, H.-B., & Kepplinger, H. M. (1992). Linear and nonlinear models of agenda-setting in television. *Journal of Broadcasting & Electronic Media, 36*, 5–23.

Chomsky, N., & Herman, E. S. (2002). *Manufacturing consent. The political economy of the mass media* (2nd ed.). New York: Pantheon.

Combs, B., & Slovic, P. (1979). Newspaper coverage of causes of death. *Journalism Quarterly, 56*, 837–843, 849.

Daschmann, G. (2001). *Der Einfluss von Fallbeispielen auf Leserurteile. Experimentelle Untersuchungen zur Medienwirkung* [Impact of case reports on readers' judgments]. Konstanz: UVK.

Davison, W. P. (1996). The third-person effect revisited. *International Journal of Public Opinion Research, 8*, 113–119.

Domke, D., Shah, D. V., & Wackman, D. B. (1998). Media priming effects: Accessibility, association, and activation. *International Journal of Public Opinion Research, 10*, 51–74.

Donsbach, W. (1991). Exposure to political content in newspapers: The impact of cognitive dissonance on readers' selectivity. *European Journal of Communication, 6*, 155–186.

Driscoll, P. D., & Salwen, M. B. (1997). Self-perceived knowledge of the O. J. Simpson trial: Third-person perception and perceptions of guilt. *Journalism & Mass Communication Quarterly, 74*, 541–556.

Eveland, W. P., Jr., & McLeod, D. M. (1999). The effect of social desirability on perceived media impact: Implications for third-person perceptions. *International Journal of Public Opinion Research, 11*, 315–333.

Fan, D. P. (1988). *Predictions of public opinion from the mass media.* New York: Greenwood Press.

Fan, D. P., & Tims, A. R. (1989). The impact of the news media on public opinion: American presidential election 1987–1988. *International Journal of Public Opinion Research, 1,* 151–163.

Fields, J. M., & Schuman, H. (1976). Public beliefs about the beliefs of the public. *Public Opinion Quarterly, 40,* 427–448.

Frijda, N. H. (1993). The place of appraisal in emotion. *Cognition and Emotion, 7,* 357–387.

Gerbner, G., Gross, L., Signorielli, N., Morgan, M., & Jackson-Beeck, M. (1979). Growing up with television. The demonstration of power: Violence profile no. 10. *Journal of Communication, 29*(3), 177–196.

Gibson, R., & Zillmann, D. (1994). Exaggerated versus representative exemplification in news reports. Perception of issues and personal consequences. *Communication Research, 21,* 603–624.

Glynn, C. J., Herbst, S., Garrett, J., O'Keefe, G., & Shapiro, R. Y. (1999). *Public opinion.* Boulder, CO: Westview Press.

Graber, D. A. (1984). *Processing the news. How people tame the information tide.* New York: Longman.

Graber, D. A. (1993). Two hundred years of press freedom: Has the promise been fulfilled? Editor's foreword to the debate. *Political Communication, 10,* 1.

Gross, K., & Aday, S. (2003). The scary world in your living room and neighborhood: Using local broadcast news, neighborhood crime rates, and personal experience to test agenda setting and cultivation. *Journal of Communication, 53,* 411–426.

Gunther, A. C. (1991). What we think others think. The role of cause and consequence in the third-person effect. *Communication Research, 18,* 355–372.

Gunther, A. C. (1998). The persuasive press inference. Effects of mass media on perceived public opinion. *Communication Research, 25,* 486–504.

Gunther, A. C., & Christen, C. T. (1999). Effects of news slant and base rate information on perceived public opinion. *Journalism & Mass Communication Quarterly, 76,* 277–292.

Hagen, L. (2005). *Konjunkturnachrichten, Konjunkturklima und Konjunktur: Wirkungen und Ursachen der Medienberichterstattung im transaktionalen Wirkungsgeflecht* [Coverage about Economic Cycle, Public Opinion about Economic Cycle and Actual Economic Cycle]. Köln: Halem.

Hart, R. P. (1993). Politics and the media two centuries later. *Political Communication, 10,* 23–27.

Heider, F. (1958). *The psychology of interpersonal relations.* New York: Wiley.

Hennis, W. (1957). *Meinungsforschung und repräsentative Demokratie* [Opinion polls and representative democracy]. Tübingen: Mohr.

Herbst, S. (1998). *Reading public opinion: how political actors view the democratic process.* Chicago: University of Chicago Press.

Hirsch, P. (1980). The 'scary world' of the nonviewer and other anomalies. A reanalysis of Gerbner et al.'s findings on cultivation analysis. Part I. *Communication Research, 7,* 403–456.

Hirsch, P. (1981). On not learning from one's own mistakes. A reanalysis of Gerbner et al.'s findings on cultivation analysis. Part II. *Communication Research, 8,* 3–37.

Iyengar, S. (1991). *Is anyone responsible? How television frames political issues.* Chicago: University of Chicago Press.

Iyengar, S., & Kinder, D. R. (1986). More than meets the eye: TV news, priming, and public evaluations of the president. In G. A. Comstock (Ed.), *Public communication and behavior 1* (pp. 135–171). Orlando: Academic Press.

Jamieson, K. H. (1993): The first amendment is alive and well. *Political Communication, 10,* 3–8.

Kepplinger, H. M. (1992). Artificial horizons: How the press presented and how the population received technology in Germany from 1965–1986. In S. Rothman (Ed.), *The mass media in liberal democratic societies* (pp. 147–176). New York: Paragon House.

Kepplinger, H. M. (2003). Public opinion and violence. In W. Heitmeyer & J. Hagan (Eds.), *International Handbook of Violence Research* (pp. 1151–1166). Dordrecht: Kluwer Academic Publishers.

Kepplinger, H. M., Donsbach, W., Brosius, H.-B., & Staab, J. F. (1989). Media tone and public opinion: A longitudinal study of media coverage and public opinion on chancellor Kohl. *International Journal of Public Opinion Research, 1,* 326–342.

Kepplinger, H. M., Brosius, H.-B., & Staab, J. F. (1991). Opinion formation in mediated conflicts and crises: A theory of cognitive-affective media effects. *International Journal of Public Opinion Research, 3,* 132–156.

Lazarsfeld, P. F., Berelson, B., & Gaudet, H. (1968). *The people's choice. How the voter makes up his mind in a presidential campaign* (3rd ed.). New York: Columbia University Press.

Lichter, S. R., Rothman, S., & Lichter, L. S. (1986). *The media elite.* Bethesda: Adler & Adler.

Lichter, S. R., & Lichter, L. S. (Eds.). (1992). *Abortion rights and wrongs: Media coverage of the abortion debate 1991–1992* (Media Monitor, 6(6)). Washington, DC: Center for Media and Public Affairs.

Lippmann, W. (1922). *Public opinion*. New York: The Macmillan Company.

Lippmann, W. (1925). *The phantom public*. New York: Macmillan.

Lipset, S. M., & Schneider, W. (1987). *The confidence gap: Business, labor, and government in the public mind* (expanded ed.). Baltimore: The Johns Hopkins University Press.

Lowry, D. T., Nio, T. C. J., & Leitner, D. W. (2003). Setting the public fear agenda: A longitudinal analysis of network TV crime reporting, public perceptions of crime, and FBI crime statistics. *Journal of Communication, 53*, 61–73.

Luhmann, N. (1970). Öffentliche Meinung [Public opinion]. *Politische Vierteljahresschrift, 11*, 2–28.

Maurer, M. (2003). *Politikverdrossenheit durch Medienberichte. Eine Panelanalyse* [Political alienation caused by media coverage. A Panel Study]. Konstanz: UVK.

McCombs, M. E., & Shaw, D. L. (1993). The evolution of agenda-setting research: Twenty-five years in the marketplace of ideas. *Journal of Communication, 43*(2), 58–66.

McLeod, D. M., & Detenber, B. H. (1999). Framing effects of television news coverage of social protest. *Journal of Communication, 49*(3), 3–21.

McLeod, J. M. (1993). On evaluating news media performance. *Political Communication, 10*, 16–22.

Morgan, M. (1983). Symbolic victimization and real-world fear. *Human Communication Research, 9*, 146–157.

Moy, P., & Pfau, M. (2000). *With malice toward all? The media and public confidence in democratic institutions*. Westport, Con. Praeger.

Nelson, T. E., Clawson, R. A., & Oxley, Z. M. (1997). Media framing of a civil liberties conflict and its effect on tolerance. *American Political Science Review, 91*, 567–583.

Nerb, J., & Spada, H. (2001). Evaluation of environmental problems: A coherence model of cognition and emotion. *Cognition & Emotion, 15*, 521–551.

Neuman, R. W. (1986). *The paradox of mass politics. Knowledge and opinion in the American electorate*. Cambridge, MA: Harvard University Press.

Noelle-Neumann, E. (1991). The theory of public opinion: The concept of the spiral of silence. In J. A. Anderson (Ed.), *Communication Yearbook 14* (pp. 256–287). Newbury Park: Sage.

Noelle-Neumann, E. (1993). *The spiral of silence. Public opinion—our social skin* (2nd ed.). Chicago: University of Chicago Press.

O'Gorman, H. J., & Garry, S. L. (1976). Pluralistic ignorance—A replication and extension. *Public Opinion Quarterly, 40*, 449–458.

Page, B. I., & Shapiro, R. Y. (1992). *The rational public. Fifty years of trends in Americans' policy preferences*. Chicago: The University of Chicago Press.

Patterson, T. E. (1993). Fourth branch or fourth rate? The press's failure to live up to the founders' expectations. *Political Communication, 10*, 8–16.

Patterson, T. E. (1994). *Out of Order* (2nd ed.). New York: Vintage Books.

Patterson, T. E. (2003). *The vanishing voter: Public involvement in an age of uncertainty*. New York: Vintage Books.

Perloff, R. M. (1999). The third-person effect: A critical review and synthesis. *Media Psychology, 1*, 353–378.

Potter, W. J. (1991). The linearity assumption in cultivation research. *Human Communication Research, 17*, 562–583.

Price, V., & Tewksbury, D. (1997). New values and public opinion: A theoretical account of media priming and framing. In G. A. Barnett & F. J. Boster (Eds.), *Progress in communication sciences: Advances in persuasion 13* (pp. 173–212). Greenwich, Conn.: Ablex.

Price, V., Tewksbury, D., & Powers, E. (1997). Switch trains of thought. The impact of news frames on readers' cognitive responses. *Communication Research, 24*, 481–506.

Robinson, M. J. (1976). Public affairs in television and the growth of political malaise: The case of 'The selling of the Pentagon.' *American Political Science Review, 70*, 409–432.

Rogers, E. M., & Dearing, J. W. (1993). The anatomy of agenda-setting research. *Journal of Communication, 43*(2), 68–84.

Romer, D., Jamieson, K. H., & Aday, S. (2003). Television news and the cultivation of fear of crime. *Journal of Communication, 53*, 88–104.

Ross, L., Greene, D., & House, P (1977). The 'False Consensus Effect.' An egocentric bias in social perception and attribution process. *Journal of Experimental Social Psychology, 13*, 279–301.

Salwen, M. B., & Dupagne, M. (1999). The third-person effect. Perceptions of the media's influence and immoral consequences. *Communication Research, 26*, 523–549.

Saris, W. E., & Sniderman, P. M. (Eds.). (2004). *Studies in public opinion: Attitudes, nonattitudes, measurement error, and change*. Princeton: Princeton University Press.

Scheufele, D. A. (1999). Framing as a theory of media effects. *Journal of Communication, 49*(1), 103–122.

Smith, C. A., & Ellsworth, P. C. (1985). Patterns of cognitive appraisal in emotion. *Journal of Personality & Social Psychology, 48*, 813–838.

Tewksbury, D. (2002). The role of comparison group size in the third-person effect. *International Journal of Public Opinion Research, 14*, 247–263.

Weimann, G. (1991). The influentials: Back to the concept of opinion leaders? *Public Opinion Quarterly, 55*, 267–279.

Zaller, J. (1992). *The nature and origins of mass opinion.* Cambridge: Cambridge University Press.

Zillmann, D., & Brosius, H.-B. (2000). *Exemplification in communication. The influence of case reports on the perception of issues.* Mahwah, NJ: Erlbaum.

19

Agenda-Setting, Framing and Priming

Patrick Roessler

Issues help to structure our perception of reality. They provide typical categories which organize our knowledge and our experiences in a larger semantic framework relevant for communication in society (Luhmann, 1970). This is true for the depiction of current events in the news media, where headlines and keywords clearly indicate the issues the respective coverage refers to. And it corresponds with the audience members' processing of news, which needs a principle to store and retrieve this information. Cognitive schemata emerge as a result of these mental networks, and very often they relate to the schemata applied by the news media and reproduced in media coverage (Brosius, 1991; Roessler, 1999).

This chapter focuses on three relevant concepts in the field of cognitive media effects: *Agenda-setting*, which describes the process of mutual influence between media and audience perceptions of what the important issues in public life are; *framing*, which refers to the patterns of interpretation which are prevalent in media coverage and in people's minds and emphasize certain aspects of reality while ignoring others; and *priming* as the process in which dominant aspects of media coverage serve as criteria for individual decision making.

It is noteworthy that this line of research started as a counter-concept to the traditional media effects paradigm of persuasion, which looks for influences on attitude formation and public opinion: 'News media may not be successful in telling people what to think, but they are stunningly successful in telling them what to think about' (Cohen, 1963). People's perceptions of reality were assumed to be the main target of media impact, but more recently this cognitive perspective (agenda-setting) was complemented by additional approaches (framing and priming) which integrate aspects of opinion-formation.

AGENDA-SETTING

The agenda metaphor: Historical development and meaning

With its growing accumulation of empirical evidence—recent reviews have counted several hundred corresponding studies (McCombs & Reynolds, 2002)—the agenda-setting approach represents one of the dominant paradigms in political media research. The term 'agenda' refers to the rank-ordered set of issues perceived to be most important at a given point in time. On the media side, coverage without an agenda is impossible: the front-page story is assumed to be the most important one in the newspaper that day, and television news shows carefully choose the order of their reports. Nevertheless, the idea of an overall 'media agenda' as a spin-off from regular media coverage is a mere analytical construct based on the (questionable) assumption that adding up the number and size of media reports related to a certain issue leads to 'the' *media agenda*.

The term 'setting,' on the other hand, indicates a process in which this media agenda exerts a substantial influence on audience perceptions of the issues relevant for society. Accordingly, the basic notion of *agenda-setting* goes back to the expectation that people will retrieve some assessment of how important the respective issue is considered to be by the journalists from the amount of news coverage that the issue receives. As a consequence, cumulative use of news media by audience members is supposed to convey an impression of the media agenda, which in turn should be reflected by the so-called *audience agenda*. This analytical construct empirically results from the answers to the common survey question on the 'most important problem society is facing these days' (the so-called MIP question)—or, in other terms, from summing up individual agendas across a larger population of an opinion poll.

Although rarely acknowledged, both the agenda-setting idea and its metaphorical terminology were already established by a British research team in 1938 ('The importance of the agenda-making function of the press'; PEP, 1938, p. 263): 'Perhaps the influence of the press may best be estimated by considering it as the principal agenda-making body for the everyday conversation of the ordinary man and woman, and, therefore, for that elusive element called public opinion. Newspapers in a democracy form the daily agenda of public affairs.' But it took more than 30 years until a small campaign study conducted by a research team from Chapel Hill, North Carolina (McCombs & Shaw, 1972) caused the breakthrough of the agenda-setting approach in communication research. Usually cited as the first agenda-setting study, the authors suggested that the media agenda exerted a strong influence on the public agenda of those 100 undecided voters surveyed.

The basic empirical strategy of agenda setting research—comparing the issues determined in a media content analysis with the data gathered by a voter survey—was originally developed in another British study dealing with the effects of television coverage on the electorate. Without paying further notice to their striking results, Trenaman and McQuail (1961) compiled a table showing on the one hand the importance of 15 issues as stated by the electorate and on the other hand the respective TV time and press space devoted to these issues. Nevertheless, Maxwell McCombs and Donald Shaw can be credited with melding both the agenda metaphor and the empirical test into a single media effects hypothesis labeled 'agenda-setting.' Subsequently, they moved the agenda-setting approach to the top of the research agenda in communication science of the last decades.

The comparison of the media and audience agendas is often based on a *rank-order correlation*, and results widely confirm the hypothesis of an agenda-setting function of news media: the seminal study of McCombs and Shaw (1972) already yielded an almost perfect correlation of 0.97 for the ranking of six issues on the media and the audience agenda. So far, most follow-up studies have reproduced this strong association between audience perceptions and the preceding media coverage (for an overview, see Roessler, 1997). It should be emphasized, that—in addition to the agenda of a media outlet being an inevitable by-product of fulfilling its function in public life—the agenda-setting role is more than just manipulation. By indicating the relevance of an issue, media give their audiences orientation, they suggest topics for interpersonal discussion and provide a cognitive map for the 'pictures in our heads' evoked by an increasingly confusing social environment.

This close relationship of the agenda-setting approach to social and political life was reflected by the introduction of additional agendas, e.g. the political agenda ('Agenda-building,' Dearing & Rogers, 1996) or real-world data on the emergence of social phenomena (Erbring, Goldenberg, & Miller, 1980). While the latter was introduced into agenda-setting research by Funkhouser (1973) in a pioneering time-series analysis which traced back the 'issues of the sixties' in news media, public opinion and the 'real world,' particularly the question of who sets the media agenda is crucial for the interpretation of effects. So-called opinion-leader media (such as the *New York Times* in the USA, *Asahi Shinbun* in Japan, *Le Monde* in France, or the *Frankfurter Allgemeine Zeitung* in Germany) often determine the coverage of other outlets (*intermedia agenda-setting*; Danielian & Reese, 1989), and some studies also found a *reversed effect* of the audience agenda on media agendas (Weimann & Brosius, 1994). Although all this broadens our understanding of the dynamics within issue diffusion substantially, space restrictions limit this chapter to exploring the research on the core process of agenda-setting, with public perception of issues as the dependent variable affected by media depiction of issues.

Perspectives on agenda-setting: The Acapulco typology

While the starting point of agenda-setting research relied on aggregate-level comparisons of media and audience agendas as described above, the epistemological and methodological limitations of this research strategy are obvious: evidence is mostly based on a comparison of the relationship between the share of a given population attributing importance to several issues (measured as a percentage in an opinion survey) and the amount of media space devoted to the same issues (measured in seconds, square inches or just the number of news items in the media). Even if we accept these indicators and their relationship as a valid operationalization of the agenda-setting notion, this aggregate-level analysis is an appropriate research strategy only if the unit of analysis is in fact a group itself—and not the individuals forming that group.

In fact, there are good reasons to consider agenda-setting as an effect on public opinion and the society as a whole. In the first large-scale panel study of agenda-setting, Shaw and McCombs (1977, p. 152) pointed out that 'the idea of an agenda-setting function of the press is a macro-notion of mass communication influence.' Issues presented in the news media serve as a common framework for social interaction and political participation; they provide a background for meaningful communication—'as a general functional requirement of society, agenda-setting is practically indispensable' (McCombs, 1981, p. 136).

The explanation for the occurrence of agenda-setting effects, however, is theoretically based on a modified learning theory. Audience members are supposed to learn how much importance to attach to an issue or topic from the emphasis placed on it by the media (Kraus & Davis, 1976). Consequently, the manifestation of agenda-setting lies within the information processing of every single individual, and authors have claimed that—for validity reasons—the empirical test of the hypothesis should reflect the personalized nature of the supposed effect (Becker, 1982, p. 527). Using two highly aggregated data sets instead involves the danger of an 'ecological fallacy' (see Zhu, 1992, p. 836;

Roessler, 2001). This phenomenon, observed in many sociological studies, claims that statistical associations calculated on the basis of group means are not suitable estimations for the associations within the individual members of the groups.

Obviously, the level of aggregation is crucial for our understanding of agenda-setting regarding methodology as well as the meaning of the results. In order to set a framework for further empirical research, McCombs (1981, p. 124) proposed a distinction between different levels of data aggregation. He distinguished between the level of agenda measurement (individual or aggregate) and the range of issues under study (a single issue or a set of issues). This distinction results in a four-cell matrix which is referred to as the *Acapulco typology* of agenda-setting research (McCombs & Reynolds, 2002, p. 6), named after the place where it was presented for the first time on the occasion of an international conference. Following McCombs, Danielian, and Wanta (1995), the four cells representing different perspectives of agenda-setting can be labeled as mass persuasion effects (I) or automaton effects (II) for *complete agendas* on the aggregate and the individual levels respectively, and natural history effects (III) or cognitive portrait effects (IV) for *single issues* on the aggregate and individual levels respectively. We will use this typology (see Figure 19.1) in the following section to review the main results of agenda-setting research.

Empirical evidence for the agenda-setting effect

Comprehensive reviews covering the abundance of agenda-setting studies and their differentiated (and sometimes conflicting) results can easily be found elsewhere (Rogers & Dearing, 1988; Protess & McCombs, 1991; Dearing & Rogers, 1996; Roessler, 1997; Wanta, 1997; Wanta & Ghanem, 2006). They all share the insight that empirical evidence for agenda-setting differs considerably if we analyze the supposed media effect on an aggregate level (where overall media content and issue perceptions within a whole society are compared) as compared to an individual level (where individual media use patterns and individual issue assessments are compared).

So far, most agenda-setting research has perpetuated the original idea of comparing aggregate agendas in a competition perspective (McCombs & Reynolds, 2002, p. 7), where an array of issues struggle for leadership on the agendas of the media and the audience (*Type I*). These studies are often based on a secondary analysis that takes advantage of the easily accessible and almost inexhaustible routine data collections offered by opinion polls (of which many regularly include a question on the currently most important problem) and data bases on news content such as the Vanderbilt Archive in the US. According to a recent meta-analysis of 90 studies, a mean correlation of 0.53 illustrates the close relationship between

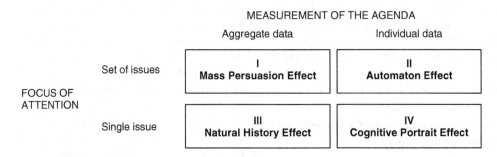

Figure 19.1   The 'Acapulco' typology of agenda-setting
Source: McCombs *et al.*, 1995, p. 285. *Reprinted by permission of Guilford Publications Inc*

media and audience agendas (Wanta & Ghanem, 2006). Altogether, Type I studies provide the most convincing evidence for agenda-setting effects, although they do not show an influence on the agenda of a single individual, but instead the influence on the distribution of the top one or two issues among some population.

This strong confirmation of the agenda-setting notion remains stable even when controlling for audience characteristics. Splitting the public into different subgroups with regard to reference groups in society, Shaw and Martin (1992) took a closer look at the agendas of men and women, non-whites and whites, young and old, higher- and lower-formally educated and rich and poor. Their results indicate that issue agendas provided by news media can serve to overcome traditional social gaps and thus enhance group consensus in society—a result that could also be interpreted more pessimistically in terms of the suppression of minority issues. Other variables involved in aggregate subgroup analysis include the interpersonal communication of respondents (Wanta & Wu, 1992; Zhu, Watt, Snyder, Yan, & Jiang, 1993), their political involvement (Tardy, Gaughan, Hemphill, & Crocket, 1981), or opinion leadership (Weimann & Brosius, 1994). Another distinctions referred to different types of media such as the 'spotlighting' effect of TV news (McCombs, 1978).

Analyzing single issues with aggregate data (*Type III*) often traces the history of one or more issues over time. In some studies, sophisticated time series models conclusively examine agenda-setting effects with high statistical validity (e.g. Neuman, 1990; Yan, Jiang, Watt, Zhu, & Snyder, 1992; Gonzenbach & McGavin, 1997). The dynamics of mutual influence between the media agenda and the public agenda follow different models, considering threshold and ceiling effects as well as different modes of acceleration (Brosius & Kepplinger, 1990, 1992). All attempts to determine the ideal time-lag for agenda-setting effects to occur yielded somewhat arbitrary results as the idiosyncrasies of the issues led to a range from

immediate responses within a single day to merely statistical top-correlations after more than two years (MacKuen, 1981; Wanta & Hu, 1994). A time-lag of approximately four weeks between the measurement of the media and audience agendas often produced the highest correlations. Nevertheless, an impressive time-series analysis of a German data set on daily basis revealed a strong agenda-setting effect of TV on the next day's audience agenda, including indirect effects on non-viewers three days later (Krause & Gehrau, 2007).

The *obtrusiveness* of issues (Winter & Eyal, 1981) and people's *need for orientation* (Weaver, 1980) have proven to be important factors that moderate agenda-setting effects. As a concept, the need for orientation is defined by two components: the personal relevance of the issues under study, and the uncertainty with regard to the extent to which the audience perceives itself to be informed about the issue. The need for information should be highest for people who assess an issue to be highly relevant for them personally while they hold little or no information. While a high need for an orientation condition (like a political campaign) enhances agenda-setting effects, the effects decrease for obtrusive issues where people display a high degree of personal involvement (McCombs & Reynolds, 2002).

Nevertheless, individual-level evidence of agenda-setting effects is scarce compared to the overwhelming body of aggregate-level research, and the results are mixed. Obviously, the automaton perspective (*Type II*) makes the greatest demands on the agenda-setting effect, as it requires a correspondence of the individual's hierarchy of personally relevant issues with the issues they were confronted with in their own media use. This is rather close to a hypodermic-needle idea of media effects, and thus a very unlikely expectation (McCombs & Reynolds, 2002, p. 7). According to the few studies available, the agenda of an individual seems only loosely related to the importance that was attributed to different issues by the coverage of the media he or she had actually perceived

(McLeod, Becker, & Byrnes, 1974; Weaver, Stehle, Auh, & Wilhoit, 1975; Stevenson & Ahern, 1979). In a more recent German study, individual correlations on a high level in the assumed direction were true for not more than 20% of the sample. For these respondents, the agenda of their received media content correlated with their personal agenda of issue importance (Roessler, 1999).

Most individual-level agenda-setting research concentrated on single issues (*Type IV*), with the pioneering study of Erbring *et al.* (1980) being one of the first to succeed in matching the individual media use of respondents with their perception of important political problems. Multiple regression analyses revealed only slight relationships between the frequency of issues in one's own newspaper and the perceived individual salience of the issue. Other variables displaced the media influence, especially the amount of interpersonal communication on politics. From the same research perspective, two German studies based on elaborated path analysis models replicated the earlier results with individual factors exerting a decisive influence (see Roessler & Eichhorn, 1999). Interpersonal communication and the closeness of the respective issue to one's own life produced the highest coefficients, while the influence of both media content and media use variables was considerably smaller (Huegel, Degenhardt, & Weiss, 1989; Roessler, 1999).

On the other hand, experimental agenda-setting studies lend strong support to the individual-level notion of agenda-setting: in a series of laboratory experiments, Iyengar and Kinder (1987) graded the importance of issues in different versions of a news program. Their comparison of pre-test and post-test scores found a strong support for short-term agenda-setting effects of television news on individual issue assessment. But as the experimental situation controlled most intervening variables, the results must be interpreted considering the limited external validity of the method. To overcome these limitations, field experiments in the US (for a summary see Protess *et al.* (1991) and in

Germany (Wolling, Wünsch, & Gehrau, 1998) were able to manipulate media coverage of outlets available to the target population. Their studies could prove substantial agenda-setting effects on the individual level in a non-laboratory setting. The strong divergence between support of individual agenda-setting in experimental designs and a lack of similar results in survey research can perhaps be explained with pre-existing knowledge.

Methodology and validity of empirical research

While the agenda-setting approach developed a large appeal for media effects scholars, its empirical pitfalls are substantial and have led to a whole variety of methodological criticism which can only be summarized here (see Roessler, 2005 in detail):

Definition of issues. The results of an agenda-setting study depend on how the empirical construct 'issue' is defined. A long-term analysis often requires broad issue categories (such as 'foreign policy' etc.), while the focus of topics represented in media coverage is usually more narrow and follows the current events closely (e.g. 'US President visits Israel'). Survey respondents, on the other hand, differentiate their answers on the MIP question rather in any way they like; in most cases, their answers are recoded according to some categories derived from media coverage, making 'the issue (...) an artifact of the study content analysis' (Shaw, McCombs, Weaver, & Hamm, 1999, p. 6).

Media agenda. Two main problems emerge in determining the media agenda: First of all, which media should be included in our sample of outlets? On the one hand, this sample should ideally reflect the media used by the survey population, cover a wide range of media types from newspapers to radio, TV and the Internet, and be weighted according to ratings or circulation. In reality, because of the cost of assembling and analyzing the content from a geographically diverse sample, most studies rely on a small sample of presumably influential national outlets (e.g. the *New York Times*); TV is included occasionally, magazines and radio almost never; and the use of the selected media by the survey population is rarely controlled.

The second problem refers to the measurement of 'importance'—is it the mere frequency of reports, or furthermore their size, placement, and additional features?

Audience agenda. Beyond the open-ended MIP question, which is difficult to handle (recoding) and produces only data on a nominal level, scholars have applied a wide range of survey stimuli. Early agenda-setting research already pointed out the difference between the individual issue salience, the perceived issue salience with regard to a general public, and the salience of an issue for interpersonal discussions (McLeod *et al.*, 1974). Furthermore, empirical tests could prove substantial differences between the results produced by an open-ended question and the rating of a closed-ended set of issue categories (Roessler, 1997).

Further limitations of agenda-setting research refer to the situational context of the empirical studies: in many cases, results were obtained during a campaign, among which the Presidential elections in the US are most popular. This can be explained by the nature of a campaign, which is restricted unequivocally to a reasonable time-frame, where issues are clearly identified and communicated by staged events, and when a lot of empirical research suitable for a secondary analysis or for complementary efforts is done anyway. Although agenda-setting research was conducted in a variety of countries so far, most of the evidence was collected in the US and cannot easily be transferred to other nations and societies with different traditions in public life, due to some unique characteristics of its political and its media system.

FRAMING AND SECOND-LEVEL AGENDA-SETTING

More recently, the original idea of agenda-setting related to the depiction and perception of issues was expanded to mechanisms on a second level, the agenda of attributes: 'Beyond the agenda of objects, there is another level of agenda-setting. Each of the objects on an agenda has numerous attributes–characteristics and properties. Just as objects vary in salience, so do their attributes. Both the selection of objects for attention and the selection of attributes for picturing these objects are powerful agenda-setting roles' (McCombs & Reynolds, 2002, p. 10). Extending Cohen's (1963) famous statement, media not only tell us what to think about, but they can also tell us *how* to think about certain issues, and even what to do about it (see also Ghanem, 1997; McCombs & Estrada, 1997).

Research on the second level of agenda-setting focused on campaign settings, with several studies about the 1996 Spanish general election. McCombs, Lopez-Escobar, and Llamas (2000) found a median correlation of 0.72 when they compared the media coverage and voters' descriptions of political candidates for substantive attributes (e.g. issue positions, integrity, personality), and for their affective dimension (positive, negative, and neutral). These survey results were later supported in an experimental design where the image attributes of candidates were manipulated and participants' criteria for judgment were influenced by the media stimulus presented (Kiousis, Bantimaroudis, & Ban, 1999).

The introduction of second-level agenda-setting did not remain undisputed, and one main reason for this criticism becomes clear when looking at the empirical study of Kiousis and McCombs (2004), who tested the relationship between media coverage and the audience's attitude strength toward candidates. But this convergence of agenda-setting and attitude change blurs the line between cognitive and persuasive media effects that originally served as a starting point for the agenda-setting hypothesis. 'The tendency of media coverage—respectively the attitudes of recipients—is now labeled as affective attributes which simply means introducing an artificial new term' (Scheufele, B., 2004, p. 406). Other comments in this critique emphasize the poor conceptualization of agenda-setting's second level, particularly with regard to related constructs such as schemata and frames.

Especially the framing approach enjoyed high popularity among media scholars during the past years (see e.g. the contributions in Reese, Gandy, & Grant, 2001). In general terms, frames can be defined as patterns of interpretation through which information is classified in order to handle it efficiently, based on (but not identical with) cognitive schemata. 'To frame is to select some aspects of a perceived reality and make them more salient in a communication context, in such a way as to promote a particular problem definition, causal interpretation, moral evaluation, and/or treatment recommendation for the item described' (Entman, 1993, p. 52).

Framing research can be organized according to three distinct types (Scheufele, B., 2004):

1   The *communicator approach* analyzes journalist's cognitions as criteria of news production or, more frequently, the structure of coverage related to one or more issues.
2   The *public discourse approach* investigates the efforts of political actors to launch their interpretation of reality in the mass media, and thus relates to the notion of agenda-building mentioned above.
3   The *media effects approach* examines how media frames translate into media users' perceptions of reality, in our case representing the most relevant expression of media framing.

The mutual relationships between different occurrences of framing in the media and the audience leads to a process model of framing research (Scheufele, D., 1999, p.115).

Comprehensive reviews of framing research (see e.g. Scheufele, B., 2004, pp. 412ff.) suggest that there is some evidence supporting the effects dimension, although the results in detail are inconclusive. Experimental studies distinguishing between episodic framing (singular cases, prototypes) and thematic framing (abstract discussion, societal responsibility) of an issue yielded support for the assumption that media framing influences attributions by the participants (Iyengar, 1991). In an elaborate study design which included the observation of individual frames with an open-ended question on

'thoughts and feelings' evoked by their stimulus, Price, Tewksbury, and Powers (1997) confirmed the impact of media frames on the respondents' cognitive responses.

Collecting evidence for framing effects from poll data is a rather difficult task, as survey data only exceptionally provides enough information on issues to reconstruct audience's frames. Accordingly, Shah, Watts, Domke, and Fan (2002) conducted a long-term content analysis, including coverage of US President Clinton's sex scandal. Three distinct frames (Clinton behavior frame, Conservative attack frame, Liberal response frame) were put against the time-trend of opinion polls on the President's job approval, indicating that the strategic framing of the scandal by political opponents extended, rather than weakened, the public support for Clinton. But it should be noted that the existence of the actual frames in respondents' heads could not be tested and observed with the data set available.

Consequently, a large-scale German study refrained from determining audience frames and concentrated upon the communicator approach instead (Scheufele, B., 2003). Results imply that journalists are involved in a process of schema-fitting with their individual frames serving as consistent frameworks of expectation to interpret events in routine coverage.

PRIMING EFFECTS OF MEDIA COVERAGE

Another approach which was aimed at expanding the cognitive perspective of the original agenda-setting approach was developed under the label of *media priming*. Derived from psychological theories, priming is the process in which news media call attention to some issues while ignoring others (agenda-setting component), and thereby influence the standard by which the public judges political figures and issues. In their landmark priming study, Iyengar and Kinder (1987) accordingly checked for agenda-setting effects as the first step: after exposing their subjects to the experimental stimulus, their individual issue agenda followed closely the media content presented (see above). In a second step, people subsequently applied these issues as criteria for rating the performance of the US President.

This argument follows the psychological concept of availability heuristics, which states that individuals do not consider all relevant information for judgment, but merely those accessible at that very moment. If an issue is covered extensively by mass media, it may serve as a prime, remains accessible and can be activated again for judgment. Although the transfer of a psychological concept based on the micro-level of mental processing (original research used single words and simple traits) did not remain undisputed as media content is much more complex and involves other factors as well (see e.g. Scheufele, B., 2004, p. 407), experimental evidence from several empirical studies proved this strong link between cognitive agenda-setting effects and attitude formation.

Further developing the media priming approach, Price and Tewksbury (1997) distinguished between *availability*, *accessibility*, and *applicability*: Available schemata exist in an individual's long-term memory and become accessible in one's working memory when it can be applied to repeated coverage. They consider *activation* to be the crucial link between agenda-setting, framing, and priming—media emphasis placed on certain issues activates those schemata which fit best with the characteristics (frames) of these issues (applicability). Over time, part of this basic activation (framing effect) is retained, and the remaining residual activation can be activated again later on if a task requires a judgment related to the schema (priming effect).

In his thorough review of priming research, Peter (2002) emphasized the prevalence of the two-step process—with media reports priming certain schemata, making them more accessible and easier to activate. In a second step, these schemata are then applied when individuals are required to interpret or judge a new stimulus or situation. The most important

contingent conditions which enhance an impact of the media prime are: (1) if the prime was encountered only recently; (2) it is encountered more frequently; and (3) if it possibly fits a large number of upcoming real-world events. The overwhelming number of studies support the notion of a priming effect triggered by media coverage (ibid., p. 34), but it is not a universal phenomenon: The predicted effect often emerges only for certain types of respondents or under certain issue-related conditions (see e.g. Miller & Krosnick, 2000).

IMPLICATIONS FOR FUTURE RESEARCH

The cognitive origin of the agenda-setting approach was meant to be an alternative to the traditional view of media effects as persuasion and attitude change. Due to its intellectual appeal, face-value in real life, compatibility with routine data collections, reference to recurring events (such as political campaigns) and a consistently changing historical background of current events, it is safe to assume that the good reasons to apply the classical agenda-setting concept will continue to exist as long as media coverage finds its audience. Agenda-setting has achieved the status of a dominant paradigm in the field of media effects, and thus forms a basis for more probing concepts such as framing and priming. In recent years, observers noted that framing was often used as a key word for labeling the results of any media content analysis, thus giving the impression of a theoretical framework. Actually, many of these studies do not even reflect the communicator approach of framing, but rather merely enumerate characteristics of media coverage with respect to some issue. Priming research, on the other hand, requires substantial empirical effort but, embracing both agenda-setting and framing effects, represents the most elaborate merger of cognitive media impact and explanations for opinion formation.

Agenda-setting

During the past decade, variations of the original metaphor such as agenda melding (Shaw et al., 1999), agenda-designing (Roessler, 1999) and second-level agenda-setting indicate that scholars have gone beyond the simple basic notion of the agenda-setting hypothesis. But future work needs to solve the theoretical, conceptual and empirical gap between agenda-setting effects on the aggregate and the individual level while avoiding the ecological fallacy trap (Roessler, 2001). Furthermore, strong evidence suggesting an influence of issue representation in the news media on audience perceptions has led to a new emphasis on the question of how the media agenda emerges.

Framing

Forthcoming research efforts need to move away from bare descriptions of issue frames in media coverage to the effects dimension, linking media depictions to audience perceptions of media frames. More importantly, further clarification of the relationship between second-level agenda-setting and framing effects is needed in this realm. Some confusion still exists when it comes to the empirical measurement of frames—due to their complexity, the procedures usually applied in quantitative research need considerable refinement. In the case of media frames, typological procedures based on principles specified by Grounded Theory (Scheufele, B., 2003) or on cluster analysis (Matthes & Kohring, 2004) have been applied successfully. To determine audience frames, methods from instructional psychology such as the Repertory grid technique (for an overview see Jonassen, Tessmer, & Hannum, 1999) could improve construct validity, but are less suitable for use in opinion polls.

Priming

In theoretical terms, the application of the priming theory still lacks convincing arguments for why a micro-level phenomenon of information-processing can be transferred to the complex and cumulative process of media news perception and retention. Additionally, current concepts have difficulties in explaining the changes of existing schemata and the establishment of new ones that are subsequently activated by media coverage; in other words, they have difficulties in explaining the feedback loop from priming effects to schema-building in the long-term memory of an individual.

REFERENCES

Becker, L. B. (1982). The mass media and citizen assessment of issue importance. A reflection on agenda-setting research. In D. Whitney, & E. Wartella (Eds.), *Mass Communication Yearbook Vol. 3* (pp. 521–536). Beverly Hills, London: Sage.

Brosius, H.-B. (1991). Schema-Theorie—ein brauchbarer Ansatz in der Wirkungsforschung? [Schema theory—A useful approach for media effects research?] *Publizistik, 36*(3), 285–297.

Brosius, H.-B., & Kepplinger, H. M. (1990). The Agenda-setting function of television news. Static and dynamic views. *Communication Research, 17*(2), 182–211.

Brosius, H.-B., & Kepplinger, H. M. (1992). Linear and nonlinear models of agenda-setting in television. *Journal of Broadcasting & Electronic Media, 36*(1), 5–23.

Cohen, B. C. (1963). *The press and foreign policy.* Princeton: Princeton University Press.

Danielian, L. H., & Reese, S. D. (1989). A closer look at intermedia influences on agenda setting: The cocaine issue of 1986. In P. Shoemaker (Ed.), *Communication campaigns about drugs* (pp. 47–66). Hillsdale, NJ: Lawrence Erlbaum.

Dearing, J. W., & Rogers, E. M. (1996). *Agenda-setting.* Thousand Oaks, London, New Delhi: Sage.

Entman, R. M. (1993). Framing: toward clarification of a fractured paradigm. *Journal of Communication, 43*(4), 51–58.

Erbring, L., Goldenberg, E.N., & Miller, A. H. (1980). Front-page news and real-world cues: A new look at agenda-setting by the media. *American Journal of Political Science, 24*(1), 16–49.

Funkhouser, G. R. (1973). The issues of the sixties: An explanatory study of the dynamics of public opinion. *Public Opinion Quarterly, 37*(1), 62–75.

Ghanem, S. (1997). Filling in the tapestry: The second level of agenda-setting. In M. E. McCombs, D. Shaw, & D. Weaver (Eds.), *Communication and democracy. Exploring the intellectual frontiers in agenda-setting theory* (pp. 3–14). Mahwah, London: Lawrence Erlbaum.

Gonzenbach, W. J., & McGavin, L. (1997). A brief history of time: A methodological analysis of agenda-setting. In M. McCombs, D. Shaw, & Weaver, D. (Eds.), *Communication and democracy. Exploring the intellectual frontiers in agenda-setting theory* (pp. 115–136). Mahwah / London: Lawrence Erlbaum.

Huegel, R., Degenhardt, W., & Weiss, H.-J. (1989). Structural equation models for the analysis of the agenda-setting process. *European Journal of Communication, 4*(2), 191–210.

Iyengar, S. (1991). *Is anyone responsible? How television frames political issues.* Chicago, London: University of Chicago Press.

Iyengar, S., & Kinder, D. R. (1987). *News that matters. Television and American opinion.* Chicago, London: University of Chicago Press.

Jonassen, D. H., Tessmer, M., & Hannum, W. H. (1999). *Task analysis methods for instructional design.* Mahwah, London: Lawrence Erlbaum.

Kiousis, S., Bantimaroudis, P., & Ban, H. (1999). Candidate image attributes: Experiments on the substantive dimension of second-level agenda setting. *Communication Research, 26,* 414–428.

Kiousis, S., & McCombs, M. E. (2004). Agenda-setting effects and attitude strength: Political figures during the 1996 presidential election. *Communication Research, 31,* 36–57.

Kraus, S., & Davis, D. (1976). *The effects of mass communication on political behavior.* University Park, London: The Pennsylvania State University Press.

Krause, B., & Gehrau, V. (2007). Das Paradox der Medienwirkung auf Nichtnutzer. Eine Zeitreihenanalyse auf Tagesbasis zu den kurzfristigen Agenda-Setting-Effekton von Fernsehnachrichten [The paradox of media effects on non-users. A time series analysis of short-term agenda-setting effects]. *Publizistik, 52*(2), 191–209.

Luhmann, N. (1970). Öffentliche Meinung [Public opinion]. *Politische Vierteljahresschrift, 11*(1), 2–28.

MacKuen, M. B. (1981). Social communication and the mass policy agenda. In M. MacKuen, & S. Coombs (Eds.), *More than news. Media power in public affairs* (pp. 19–144). Beverly Hills, London: Sage.

Matthes, J., & Kohring, M. (2004). Die empirische Erfassung von Medien-Frames [The empirical measuring of media frames]. *Medien- und Kommunikationswissenschaft, 52*(1), 56–75.

McCombs, M. E. (1978). Public response to the daily news. In L. Epstein (Ed.), *Women and the news* (pp. 1–14). New York: Hastings House.

McCombs, M. E. (1981). The agenda-setting approach. In D. Nimmo, & K. Sanders (Eds.), *Handbook of political communication* (pp. 121–140). Beverly Hills, London: Sage.

McCombs, M. E., & Shaw, D. L. (1972). The agenda-setting function of mass media. *Public Opinion Quarterly, 36,* 176–187.

McCombs, M. E., Danielian, L., & Wanta, W. (1995). Issues in the news and the public agenda: The agenda-setting tradition. In T. Glasser, & C. Salmon (Eds.), *Public opinion and the communication of consent* (pp. 281–300). New York, London: The Guilford Press.

McCombs, M. E., & Estrada, G. (1997). The news media and the pictures in our heads. In S. Iyengar & R. Reeves (Eds.), *Do the media govern?* (pp. 237–247). London: Sage.

McCombs, M. E., Lopez-Escobar, E., & Llamas, J. P. (2000). Setting the agenda of attributes in the 1996 Spanish general election. *Journal of Communication, 50*(2), 77–92.

McCombs, M. E., & Reynolds, A. (2002). News influence on our pictures of the world. In J. Bryant & D. Zillmann (Eds.), *Media effects. Advances in theory and research* (2nd ed., pp. 1–18). Mahwah, NJ: Lawrence Erlbaum.

McLeod, J. M., Becker, L. B., & Byrnes, J. E. (1974). Another look at the agenda-setting function of the press. *Communication Research 1,* 131–165.

Miller, J. M., & Krosnick, J. A. (2000). News media impact in the ingredients of presidential evaluations: Politically knowledgeable citizens are guided by a trusted source. *American Journal of Political Science, 44,* 301–315.

Neuman, W. R. (1990). The threshold of public attention. *Public Opinion Quarterly, 54,* 159–176.

Peter, J. (2002). Medien-Priming—Grundlagen, Befunde und Forschungstendenzen [Media priming—Basics, findings and research trends]. *Publizistik, 47*(1), 21–44.

Political and Economic Planning (PEP). (1938). *Report on the British Press. A survey of its current operations and problems with special reference to national newspapers and their part in public affairs.* London: PEP.

Price, V., & Tewksbury, D. (1997). News values and public opinion: A theoretical account of media priming and framing. In G. Barnett, & F. J. Boster (Eds.), *Progress in the communication sciences* (pp. 173–212). Greenwich, CT: Ablex.

Price, V., Tewksbury, D., & Powers, E. (1997). Switching trains of thought: The impact of news frames on reader's cognitive responses. *Communication Research, 24,* 481–506.

Protess, D. L., Cook, F. L., Doppelt, J. C., Ettema, J. S., Gordon, M. T., Leff, D. R., & Miller, P. (1991). *The Journalism of Outrage.* New York, London: Guilford Publ.

Protess, D. L., & McCombs, M. E. (Eds.). (1991). *Agenda setting. Readings on media, public opinion, and policymaking.* Hillsdale: Lawrence Erlbaum.

Reese, S. D., Gandy, O., & Grant, A. E. (Eds.). (2001). *Framing public life. Perspectives on media and our understanding of the social world.* Mahwah, NJ: Lawrence Erlbaum.

Roessler, P. (1997). *Agenda-setting. Theoretische Annahmen und empirische Evidenzen einer Medienwirkungshypothese* [Agenda-setting. Theoretical assumptions and empirical findings of a media effects hypothesis]. Opladen: Westdeutscher Verlag.

Roessler, P. (1999). The individual agenda-designing process. How interpersonal communication, egocentric networks and mass media shape the perception of political issues by individuals. *Communication Research, 26,* 666–700.

Roessler, P. (2001). Caught in the ecological fallacy trap? Matching media content and audience data: The level of aggregation problem. Paper presented to the WAPOR Thematic Seminar: Survey Research and Media Content Analysis, Hamburg, Germany.

Roessler. P. (2005). Zur Logik der Agenda-Setting-Forschung [On the logic of agenda-setting research]. In: W. Wirth, E. Lauf, & A. Fahr (Eds.), Forschungslogik und -design in der Kommunikationswissenschaft, Vol. 2 (pp. 139–167). Köln: Herbert von Halem.

Roessler, P., & Eichhorn, W. (1999). Agenda-setting. In H.-B. Brosius, & C. Holtz-Bacha (Eds.), *German Communication Yearbook, Vol. 1* (pp. 277–304). Creskill: Hampton Press.

Rogers, E. M., & Dearing, J. W. (1988). Agenda-setting research: Where has it been, where is it going? In J. Anderson (Ed.), *Communication Yearbook Vol. 11* (pp. 555–594). London: Sage.

Scheufele, B. (2003). *Frames—Framing—Framing-Effekte. Theorethische und methodische Grundlegung des Framing-Ansatzes sowie empirische Befunde zur Nachrichtenproduktion* [Frames—framing—framing effects. Theoretical and methodological foundation of the framing approach and empirical findings on news production]. Wiesbaden: Westdeutscher Verlag.

Scheufele, B. (2004). Framing-Effekte auf dem Prüfstand [Framing effects put to test]. *Medien- und Kommunikationswissenschaft, 52*(1), 30–55.

Scheufele, D. (1999). Framing as a theory of media effects. *Journal of Communication, 49,* 103–122.

Shah, D. V., Watts, M. D., Domke, D., & Fan, D. P. (2002). News framing and cueing of issue regimes: Explaining Clinton's public approval in spite of scandal. *Public Opinion Quarterly, 66,* 339–370.

Shaw, D. L., & McCombs, M. E. (1977). *The emergence of American political issues: The agenda-setting function of the press.* New York: West Publishing Co.

Shaw, D. L., & Martin, S. E. (1992). The function of mass media agenda-setting. *Journalism Quarterly, 69,* 902–920.

Shaw, D., McCombs, M. E., Weaver, D., & Hamm, B. (1999). Individuals, groups, and agenda melding: A theory of social dissonance. *International Journal of Public Opinion Research, 11,* 2–24.

Stevenson, R. L., & Ahern, T. J. (1979). *Individual effects of agenda-setting.* Paper presented to the AEJMC conference, Houston, USA.

Tardy, C. H., Gaughan, B. J., Hemphill, M. R., & Crockett, N. (1981). Media agendas and political participation. *Journalism Quarterly, 58,* 624–627.

Trenaman, J., & McQuail, D. (1961). *Television and the political image.* London: Methuen.

Wanta, W. (1997). *The public and the national agenda. How people learn about important issues.* Mahwah, London: Lawrence Erlbaum.

Wanta, W., & Wu, Y.-C. (1992). Interpersonal communication and the agenda-setting process. *Journalism Quarterly, 69,* 847–855.

Wanta, W., & Hu, Y.-W. (1994). The effects of credibility, reliance, and exposure on media agenda-setting: A path analysis model. *Journalism Quarterly, 71,* 90–98.

Wanta, W., & Ghanem, S. I. (2006). Effects of agenda-setting. In R. Preiss, B. M. Gayle, N. Burrell, M. Allen, & J. Bryant (Eds.), *Mass media theories and processes: Advances through meta-analysis* (pp. 37–52). Mahwah, NJ: Lawrence Erlbaum.

Weaver, D. H. (1980). Audience need for orientation and media effects. *Communication Research, 7,* 361–376.

Weaver, D. H., Stehle, T. E., Auh, T. S., & Wilhoit, C. G. (1975). *A path analysis of individual agenda-setting during the 1974 Indiana senatorial campaign.* Paper presented at the AEJMC conference, Ottawa, Canada.

Weimann, G., & Brosius, H.-B. (1994). Is there a two-step-flow of agenda-setting? *International Journal of Public Opinion Research, 6,* 323–341.

Winter, J. P., & Eyal, C. H. (1981). Agenda setting for the civil rights issue. *Public Opinion Quarterly, 45,* 376–383.

Wolling, J., Wünsch, C., & Gehrau, V. (1998). Was ich nicht weiß, macht mich nicht heiß? Eine Agenda-Setting-Untersuchung aus schematheoretischer Perspektive [What you don't know, won't hurt you? An agenda-setting-study from the perspective of schema theory]. *Rundfunk und Fernsehen, 46*, 447–462.

Yan, J., Jiang, Y., Watt, J. H., Zhu, J.-H., & Snyder, L. (1992). *A comparison of four agenda-setting models.* University of Connecticut (Mimeo).

Zhu, J.-H. (1992). Issue competition and attention distraction: A zero-sum theory of agenda-setting. *Journalism Quarterly, 69*, 825–836.

Zhu, J.-H., Watt, J. H., Snyder, L. B., Yan, J., & Jiang, Y. (1993). Public issue priority formation: Media agenda-setting and social interaction. *Journal of Communication, 43*, 8–29.

Methodology

The Design of Surveys

20

The Methodological Strengths and Weaknesses of Survey Research

Herbert F. Weisberg

Survey research is a technique that is well designed for assessing the prevalence and distribution of attitudes, as well as factual material about respondents. It has both strengths and weaknesses in comparison to other techniques for measuring public opinion.

Surveys measure the attitudes of a population of interest. In particular, scientific sample surveys ask questions of a sample of members of that population, taking enough interviews to be able to generalize to that larger population and trying to minimize nonresponse by people included in the sample, while using tested methods to measure the attitudes of respondents. Each part of this definition calls attention to a different challenge for surveys: the choice of respondents, the minimizing of nonresponse, and the measurement of attitudes. The quality of a survey depends on how well it handles each of these challenges.

Surveys can be used to measures attitudes, beliefs, and/or facts. As discussed in previous chapters, attitudes measure how positively or negatively people feel toward objects, such as broccoli or the president. Surveys sometimes also ask about respondents' preferences—comparisons of attitudes toward different objects, such as different foods or political candidates. By contrast, a belief is an opinion about the state of the world, such as whether the person believes that a particular food is healthy or that a political candidate is honest. Surveys can also obtain predictions from respondents—their beliefs about the future, such as whether gas prices are likely to rise in the coming month or whether a particular candidate will win the next presidential election. Finally, people are often asked about facts, including their past behavioral experiences.

Surveys are used to assess the prevalence of attitudes, beliefs, and behaviors. Surveys are also often used to look for changes over time in the rates of occurrence of those attitudes, beliefs, and behaviors. Additionally, surveys are used to examine differences between groups. That provides an important reason why factual questions are usually asked in public opinion surveys—so that attitudes of different types of respondents can be compared, such as seeing whether older people are more likely to have a particular attitude or to like a political candidate.

Surveys are generally weak in assessing causation. Finding that a difference between respondents is associated with a difference in their opinions does not determine the real cause of the opinion difference. This is particularly problematic with cross-section surveys that measure everything at once, making it impossible to tell, for example, whether people have different attitudes toward the president because of their stands on policy issues, or whether their different attitudes toward the president are causing them to have different issue positions. Longitudinal surveys can help disentangle causal directions, but they are not necessarily a panacea. Experiments are better suited to determining causation, since the experimenter can manipulate the presumed cause to look for effects, but experiments are generally not as realistic as surveys in examining attitudes under real world conditions. Experiments are considered to have better 'internal validity' because the well-designed experiment can eliminate possible extraneous causes, but surveys have better 'external validity' because they can generalize better to the full population under real world conditions.

Another limitation of surveys is that they measure individual opinions, whereas opinions are often generated as part of group processes. Focus groups and 'deliberative polls' may be better suited than regular surveys for measuring opinions within a group context.

The 'Total Survey Error Approach' has been developed in recent years to serve as a paradigm for the survey research field generally and for evaluating the sources of error in particular surveys. The first general presentation of this approach was in the 1989 book, *Survey Errors and Survey Costs*, in which Robert Groves provided a systematic treatment of the several types of survey errors, along with relevant cost considerations. The total survey error approach has since been used in several survey research texts (Lavrakas, 1993; Fowler, 2002), and it is the basis of the Groves *et al.* (2004) and Weisberg (2005) books on survey research.

Weisberg (2005) generalizes the total survey error paradigm by describing it as having three components: (1) a classification of survey errors, slightly extending those discussed in Groves' (1989) book; (2) a three-fold categorization of 'survey constraints' that goes beyond just survey costs; and (3) a large number of 'survey-related effects.' The following three sections of the chapter consider, in turn, each of these three components.

SURVEY ERRORS

Early work on survey accuracy emphasized mainly the sampling error in surveys, probably because the precision of the formulas for calculating sampling error for some types of samples allowed that error to be decreased by simply increasing the sample size. It was sometimes admitted that non-sampling error also exists, but the other sources of error could not be computed and minimized.

The total survey error approach recognizes that the simple distinction between sampling and non-sampling error is too primitive. Instead, it distinguishes between several types of error: sampling error, coverage error, non-response error at the unit level, nonresponse error at the item level, measurement error due to respondents, and measurement error due to interviewers. 'Postsurvey error' is sometimes added as a seventh type, because it affects the reporting of survey results, even though, by definition, it does not occur as part of the actual survey.

One way to visualize these sources of error is to regard sampling error as the tip of the iceberg and then fill in the rest of that iceberg. Figure 20.1 does so, breaking the iceberg into three tiers. Sampling error is shown as the tip, but with two other respondent selection issues also near

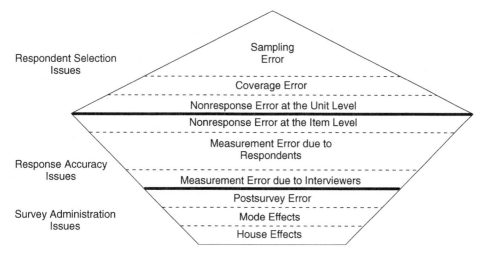

Figure 20.1   Types of survey error
Reprinted by permission of Chicago University Press: Weisberg (2005). The total survey error approach: A guide to the new science of survey research

the top: coverage error, and nonresponse at the unit level. The next tier involves response accuracy issues: nonresponse at the item level and measurement error. Several survey administration issues are depicted in the bottom tier, detachable from the rest: postsurvey error and two matters that will be discussed later in this chapter when discussing survey effects, namely mode effects and house effects. The relative sizes of the different areas in Figure 20.1 should not be taken literally, though it is the case that two of the larger areas—those for sampling error and for measurement error due to respondents—both represent major topics.

It should be emphasized that these are really 'potential sources of error' because they are not necessarily errors. For example, survey results are not necessarily biased when some people do not answer a question; bias occurs only if people who do answer are different from those who do not. However, we cannot tell how similar these groups are, since we generally lack data on those who do not answer the question, so nonresponse is a potential source of error. Yet error is inevitable in surveys, as there is never a perfect wording for questions, never a perfect sample, and so on.

Systematic bias must be distinguished from random error, because its effects are more serious. Systematic error directly distorts the mean of a variable, as when some people understate their age so that the calculation of average ages is wrong. Random error has a mean of zero, so it does not deflect the variable's mean, but random error increases the variance of a variable, and variables measured with large amounts of random error would be termed unreliable. Because of the increased variance, random error directly affects correlations with other variables, reducing the magnitude of the correlations (an effect known as 'attenuation'). Regression coefficients are similarly attenuated by random error in the independent variable, and hypothesis tests have less 'statistical power' (making it harder to obtain significant results) than if measures were perfectly reliable.

Another important distinction is between uncorrelated and correlated errors. Uncorrelated errors occur when the errors for different respondents are unrelated, as when an interviewer happens to ask a question differently from one interview to another. Correlated error occurs when errors for different respondents are related, as when an interviewer systematically asks questions in a particular wrong way. Correlated errors can occur when interviewers take multiple interviews, when coders code open-ended questions in multiple interviews, and when cluster sampling is used. Uncorrelated errors diminish the reliability of the data, but correlated errors are more serious, in that they multiply the standard errors of variables so that it is much harder to achieve results that are statistically significant.

Respondent selection issues

The first respondent selection problem is *sampling error*—the error that arises when only a subset of the population is included in a survey. The sampled units inevitably differ from the full population, and researchers want to be able to generalize from the sample to that larger population. There are mathematical formulas for calculating the sampling error for probability samples, with larger samples having smaller sampling errors. However, sampling error cannot be estimated for nonprobability samples, and there are often biases with availability samples (especially the use of volunteers), purposive samples, and quota samples ($\rightarrow$ *Sampling*). The appropriate sample size depends on the degree of precision desired, both overall and for subgroups of interest. Additionally, in taking a sample, it is necessary to consider the incidence rate (such as when trying to sample Catholics), the expected completion rate, and the expected hit rate (such as the proportion of phone numbers that are working residential numbers). Some studies suggest that sample size does not affect poll accuracy (Lau, 1994), but there would be credibility problems if sample sizes were too small.

A related respondent selection problem is *coverage error*—the error that occurs when the set of units from which the actual sample is taken (the 'sampling frame') omits some elements in the target population. Coverage error produces bias when a large part of the target population is omitted from the sampling frame, and when the mean of the sampling

frame thus differs from that for those omitted from it. Concern that many households did not have a telephone led to avoidance of telephone surveys until the 1970s when the coverage rate for telephones in the US finally went above the 90% level. Internet surveys still suffer from serious coverage problems, though Knowledge Networks attempts to avoid these problems by offering chosen respondents (obtained through telephone interviewing) free WebTVs and Internet access for their participation.

The final respondent selection problem is *nonresponse error at the unit level*, which occurs when some designated respondents are not interviewed. This is a problem to the extent that non-participation is related to variables of interest in the survey. Unit nonresponse can be due either to noncontact or to noncooperation. The traditional methods of decreasing unit nonresponse are repeated callbacks to improve contact rates as well as monetary incentives and refusal conversion to increase cooperation rates, though several studies suggest that such extra effort may not significantly change survey results (Visser, Krosnick, Marquette, & Curtin, 1996; Curtin, Presser, & Singer, 2000; Keeter, Miller, Kohut, Groves, & Presser, 2000). Research also suggests the value of tailoring the request to participate so as to maximize the chances that the person will agree to give the interview. Nonresponse can be dealt with in data analysis through weighting or through modeling nonresponse, as in Brehm's (1993) use of Heckman-selection models to analyze simultaneously willingness to be interviewed and survey responses.

Response accuracy issues

Another type of nonresponse problem is when respondents do not answer particular questions, known as *nonresponse at the item level*. This includes the problem of refusals to answer a particular question (which occur mainly on the income question) and 'not ascertained' situations (when a question is skipped, either inadvertently or intentionally), but the major item nonresponse problem is the 'don't know' answer. Don't knows can be minimized by first asking a filter question to ascertain whether the person has an opinion on the topic, though some researchers feel filters eliminate some people with valid attitudes. Similarly, there is a debate about offering 'no opinion' options; Krosnick *et al.* (2002) strongly argue that 'no opinion' options prevent the measurement of meaningful opinions. Statistically, how serious missing data are depends on whether there are systematic reasons as to why some data are missing. There is serious bias when the likelihood that a value is missing is related to the (unobserved) missing value—as would be the case if higher income people were more likely not to respond to the income question in a survey. The usual approach of analyzing only cases with full data on the variables of interest is problematic unless the data are 'missing completely at random.' Instead, there are statistical strategies for dealing with missing data, such as substituting values for the missing data (known as 'missing data imputation') on the basis of other information about or from the respondent.

Measurement error is the error that occurs when the researcher does not obtain accurate measures of the phenomena of interest. *Measurement error due to respondents* occurs to the extent that respondents are not providing the answers they should. This usually is due to questionnaire construction and, especially, question wording. Two theories have become important in understanding how respondents relate to survey questions. Tourangeau's (1984; see Tourangeau, Rips, & Rasinski, 2000) four-stage theory of replying to survey questions suggests that good question writing involves understanding how respondents: (1) comprehend the questions, (2) retrieve relevant information from their memory, (3) judge the appropriate answer, and (4) select an answer. The other important theory is Krosnick and Alwin's (1987) two-track theory: some people work through the four steps above to obtain the best answer to a question, while others 'satisfice' by doing just enough work to give a plausible answer, such as by just choosing the middle answer on

scales. Satisficing poses serious challenges to surveys, since these are not the respondents' best answers (→ *Designing Reliable and Valid Questionnaires*).

Measurement error due to interviewers occurs to the extent that interviewers affect responses. Many survey shops use standardized interviewing (Fowler & Mangione, 1990) as a means of minimizing interviewer-related error, though some researchers prefer a conversational approach in which the interviewer works with the respondent to establish the researcher's intended meaning of the question (Conrad & Schober, 2000). Interviewer error is often due to not reading the question as written—and studies show that it is common for interviewers to depart from the exact wording of questions even in standardized interviewing shops. Interviewer effects can be eliminated by switching to self-administered surveys, though many researchers would contend that well-trained interviewers who develop a good rapport with the respondent can obtain higher quality data than obtained via other modes. Interviewer training, combined with supervision and incentives for interviewers, is seen as essential for minimizing interviewer-related error.

Survey administration issues

In addition to respondent selection and response accuracy issues, there are a series of potential problems related to survey administration that directly affect the precision of survey results. One survey administration issue is the *mode* of the survey: whether it is self-administered, face-to-face interview, telephone interview, Internet, interactive voice response (IVR), or some other mode. These different modes by necessity often use different sampling approaches and confront different coverage problems, so that the types of respondents may differ depending on the mode. Mixed mode research is sometimes employed, partly because each mode can overcome some of the sampling, coverage, and nonresponse problems that the other mode encounters.

Postsurvey error is the error that occurs after the actual interviewing. Coding open-ended materials into numeric codes and entering data from paper-and-pencil questionnaires into the computer are two examples of important operations that occur after some surveys, both of which can lead to error. Postsurvey error can also occur during data file management, statistical analysis, and reporting of the survey results. The postsurvey process can also be used to look for and correct data errors (known as 'data editing'); some public-use datasets are put through so much data editing that concern has been expressed in the literature about overediting (Granquist, 1995).

SURVEY CONSTRAINTS

While the focus so far has been on survey errors, the second part of the total survey error equation involves constraints that make it impossible to eliminate errors in surveys. Groves' (1989) *Survey Errors and Survey Costs* book focused attention on one critical constraint: cost. Surveys can be very expensive (a national face-to-face survey can cost as much as $1,000 a respondent), or can be done very inexpensively (as when just mailing a questionnaire to people without follow-ups to encourage response). Minimizing survey error involves tradeoffs with costs. This is obvious with respect to sampling error: sampling error is reduced by taking more interviews, which increases costs. Coverage error can be reduced by preparing better sampling frames. Unit nonresponse can be reduced with callbacks, refusal conversion, and monetary incentives. Better interviewer training can reduce item nonresponse. More pretesting before going into the field can reduce measurement error due to respondents. Hiring more interviewers can reduce correlated measurement error due to interviewers, since each interviewer would conduct fewer interviews. Hiring higher-power computer programmers and statisticians, can minimize post-survey error. However, each of these steps adds to the cost. Note, by the way, that

personnel needs are typically included in the cost term, since hiring more and better staff increases the costs.

While cost is obviously an important constraint on surveys, so is time. Survey sponsors vary in their relevant time frames. Commercial clients sometimes require daily tracking information, while academic researchers may be content to wait a half-year to obtain their data. These time needs affect the choice of survey mode, since daily tracking requires use of computerized surveys, whereas face-to-face interviews can only be used when survey results are not needed immediately. Further, the time constraint affects the ability to minimize the different sources of error. Improving sampling frames, callbacks, refusal conversions, more pretesting, and better interviewer training all take time. Thus, minimizing error is possible only to the extent that the sponsor's time perspective permits.

The third important constraint involves ethics. Treatments of survey research often put aside the role of ethics, but ethics constitute an essential constraint. This is particularly the case for research that has to go through Institutional Review Boards that have to give preclearance for human subjects research, but it also holds for survey organizations that respect the ethical codes of the American Association for Public Opinion Research. Survey research of adults is generally exempt from IRB procedures, so long as there is no deception involved and the survey does not pose serious risks to respondents, but even getting exemption from IRB proceedings adds to the time involved in going into the field for surveys. Other ethical problems can increase costs, such as giving interviewers good enough pay that they will be less likely to fake interviews.

SURVEY-RELATED EFFECTS

The third leg of the survey research triangle involves a series of survey-related effects (Figure 20.2). These effects limit the precision of the conclusions that can be drawn from

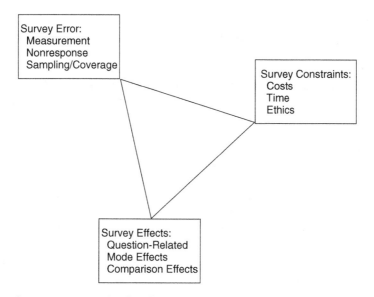

Figure 20.2   The survey research triangle
Reprinted by permission of Chicago University Press: Weisberg (2005). The total survey error approach: A guide to the new science of survey research

survey evidence, but they do not represent errors. Instead they point to the limits of possible inference.

One set of survey-related effects is question-related. No single question wording is 'correct,' but different question wordings can yield somewhat different results. The choice between open- and closed-ended questions can affect answers, as can how a question is 'framed' in the survey. What distinguishes these various effects is that there is no way to eliminate them. Different ways to structure the question yield somewhat different results, but there is rarely a perfect wording. Response-option order can affect answers to closed-ended questions, such as the recency effect that occurs when respondents in phone surveys tend to choose the last response that is read to them. Question order can affect results. One way to think about this is that attitudes are always context-dependent, so it would be chimerical to try to eliminate context. It might be best for us to conceptualize true answers as a range and then view alternative question wordings (including question orders and response-option orderings) as permitting researchers to

examine that range. Indeed, it may be better to experiment with multiple question wordings than to seek a single optimal wording.

In addition there are mode effects associated with how the survey is administered. There are several relevant distinctions, including whether the survey is self-administered or whether an interviewer is employed, whether or not the survey is computerized (in an interactive manner), and whether it is primarily aural or visual. All of these decisions can affect the results. Furthermore, these modes differ in their susceptibility to nonresponse and to satisficing behavior. The largest concern is whether particular modes are more effective for sensitive topics. Social desirability effects are particularly problematic for modes in which the respondents may worry about their answers being identifiable, so self-administered modes are generally considered best for sensitive matters.

Another set of survey-related effects involves comparisons between surveys. Comparisons of results obtained from different surveys are inherently risky. Three types of comparison effects can be distinguished. House effects are relevant when comparing results obtained by different survey organizations. House effects can occur when survey organizations bias question wording to yield results their clients desire, but these effects are often just random, due to the inevitably many differences in how organizations conduct surveys—such as differences in sampling schemes, numbers of callbacks, and interviewer training procedures. Longitudinal effects occur when comparing results of surveys taken at different points in time. Changes between polls—even differences that are larger than sampling error—can just be due to differences in survey administration or to changes in the meaning of a question over time. Cross-cultural effects occur when comparing survey results obtained from different cultures. There can be problems involving the equivalence of concepts across societies, the equivalence of question wording across languages, and the equivalence of surveys taken by different organizations in different nations.

There are several additional survey-related effects. For example, it is common to speak of interviewer effects, including probing style effects and gender-of-interviewer effects. There can be day-of-the-week effects, third-party presence effects, conditioning effects in panel studies, display effects in Internet surveys, and many others. The research literature attempts to measure these various effects through careful experiments and meta-analysis of published studies, in order to understand survey results better, even if they are not errors that can be eliminated.

THE TOTAL SURVEY ERROR APPROACH

The total survey error approach can be useful in emphasizing the tradeoffs involved in conducting surveys. Survey errors can be minimized, but that must happen within the constraints of cost, time, and ethics. Obtaining high quality data requires thinking through how best to spend resources in minimizing different types of survey error. For example, higher quality data may be obtained by spending more money on pretests and interviewer training rather than cutting sampling error by taking a few more interviews.

This tradeoff is most controversial as regards to response rate. Some survey organizations interpret the total survey design approach as implying that response rate is not all that important since there always are other sources of error. However, that argument should not be allowed to become a convenient excuse for not being able to attain a high response rate. Survey clients should understand that resources can be spent on other ways to reduce survey error, rather than just concentrating on response rate, especially since several studies suggest that a higher response rate does not necessarily translate to better data quality. Yet, survey results will always receive more credence with a higher response rate, so it is important not to go overboard with this tradeoff.

The total survey error paradigm can be useful in some additional respects. It can help survey clients understand the need for high quality in all aspects of the survey design. Some survey organizations use it when training interviewers, to help them recognize their contribution to obtaining high quality data.

The total survey error approach draws together all the elements of the survey process in a unified framework. This approach considers survey costs and other constraints as balancing the need to minimize errors, while taking into account several effects that inevitably affect surveys. Survey research will, of course, have to continue to adapt to the inevitable changes in personal communication technology, but it should do so with recognition of the need to deal with the implications of those changes for the different types of survey error.

REFERENCES

Brehm, J. (1993). *The phantom respondents.* Ann Arbor: University of Michigan Press.

Conrad, F., & Schober, M. (2000). Clarifying question meaning in a household telephone survey. *Public Opinion Quarterly, 64,* 1–28.

Curtin, R., Presser, S., & Singer, E. (2000). The effects of response rate changes on the index of consumer sentiment. *Public Opinion Quarterly, 64,* 413–28.

Fowler, F. J., Jr. (2002). *Survey research methods* (3rd ed.). Thousand Oaks, CA: Sage.

Fowler, F. J., Jr. & Mangione, T. W. (1990). *Standardized survey interviewing: Minimizing interviewer-related error.* Newbury Park, CA: Sage.

Granquist, L. (1995). Improving the traditional editing process. In B. G. Cox, D. Binder, B. N. Chinnappa, A. Christianson, M. J. Colledge & P. S. Kott (Eds.), *Business survey methods* (pp. 385–401). New York: Wiley.

Groves, R. M. (1989). *Survey errors and survey costs.* New York: Wiley.

Groves, R. M., Fowler, F. J., Couper, M. P., Lepkowski, J. M., Singer, E., & Tourangeau, R. (2004). *Survey methodology.* New York: Wiley.

Keeter, S., Miller, C., Kohut, A., Groves, R. M., & Presser, S. (2000). Consequences of reducing nonresponse in a national telephone survey. *Public Opinion Quarterly, 64,* 125–48.

Krosnick, J. A., & Alwin, D. F. (1987). An evaluation of a cognitive theory of response-order effects in survey measurement. *Public Opinion Quarterly, 51,* 201–219.

Krosnick, J. A., Holbrook, A. L., Berent, M. K., Carson, R. T., Hanemann, W. M., Kopp, R. J. *et al.* (2002). The impact of 'no opinion' response options on data quality: Non-attitude reduction or an invitation to satisfice? *Public Opinion Quarterly, 66,* 371–403.

Lau, R. R. (1994). An analysis of the accuracy of 'trial heat' polls during the 1992 presidential election. *Public Opinion Quarterly, 58,* 2–20.

Lavrakas, P. J. (1993). *Telephone survey methods: Sampling, selection and supervision* (2nd ed.). Newbury Park, CA: Sage.

Tourangeau, R. (1984). Cognitive science and survey methods. In T. Jabine, M. Straf, J. Tanur & R. Tourangeau (Eds.), *Cognitive aspects of survey methodology: Building a bridge between disciplines* (pp. 73–100). Washington, DC: National Academy Press.

Tourangeau, R., Rips, L., & Rasinski, K. A. (2000). *The psychology of survey response.* Cambridge: Cambridge University Press.

Visser, P. S., Krosnick, J. A., Marquette, J., & Curtin, M. (1996). Mail surveys for election forecasting? An evaluation of the Columbus Dispatch Poll. *Public Opinion Quarterly, 60,* 181–227.

Weisberg, H. F. (2005). *The total survey error approach: A guide to the new science of survey research.* Chicago: University of Chicago Press.

21

The Uses and Misuses of Polls

Michael W. Traugott

No matter what the issue is or the method for collecting attitudes about it, the mass media have a critical role to play in conveying information about the nature of public opinion to the majority of the population. This has historically been the case because of the media's central location in the process of exchanging and communicating social and political values as well as information. But the influence of news organizations grew and became more important as they became producers as well as disseminators of public opinion data. On the one hand, public opinion data are a means by which the mass media can establish and maintain contact with their audience members, by providing a conduit for the exchange of different perspectives and points of view as well as an indication of how prevalent they are in society. News organizations always provided these kinds of links through standard reportorial techniques such as the use of quotations from sources or 'man in the street' interviews, as well as through letters to the editor. But the advent of public polling organizations and the dissemination of their findings through the media—and eventually the establishment of independent media polling operations—provided a more scientific and systematic way to collect and present such information (Herbst, 1993; → *The News Media's Use of Opinion Polls*).

The role of journalists as intermediaries in transmitting public opinion information to a mass audience is critical, because the general public operates essentially on faith that the information that they read or view or hear is accurate and reliable. At the same time that people have a strong interest in what their fellow citizens think about important issues of the day—or even about minor elements of current events—they are by and large completely ignorant of the details of polling methodology. When they are told what 'the public thinks' about a certain issue, they generally accept this statement as fact. The vast majority of citizens do not have the skills to dissect and evaluate such information and no way to form an independent judgment about its reliability and validity, as there are few places to turn for such guidance (Traugott & Lavrakas, 2004).

THE IMPACT OF METHODOLOGY

The foundation of good reporting on public opinion is good data. The key issue is that accurate poll data rest upon: (1) probability samples that permit inferences back to the underlying population; (2) well-written questionnaires that produce unbiased measures of attitudes and behavior; (3) appropriate analysis; and (4) interpretations that do not exceed the limitations of all of the forgoing elements.

The range of inadequate data collection techniques is quite wide (→ *Sampling*). Most commonly, it includes both data collected from biased or unrepresentative samples as well as deliberate attempts to sway opinions through the use of biased question wordings or orders. As examples of the former category, there are various forms of biased, non-probability samples known as SLOP, or 'self-selected listener opinion polls,' and CRAP, 'computerized-response audience polls.' In a probability sample, every element in the population has a known, non-zero chance of being selected. Good practice excludes the use of questionnaires inserted in newspapers or made available on Web sites, for example, that permit anyone to answer (often as many times as they like). Another bad practice is the representation of the views of participants in small focus groups as the attitudes of the general public.

Under some circumstances there are also structural problems with the collection of opinions, deriving from other time-saving necessities and conventions of public pollsters. Most public polling data are collected through the use of forced choice (close-ended) questions in which the respondent is offered only two alternatives, not counting a possible option to express 'no opinion.' Using close-ended questions is generally preferable to using open-ended questions where the responses have to be coded for analysis. But this dual close end response option also conforms to the media's tendency to report news in a dichotomous fashion (on the one hand, on the other hand) that often oversimplifies the world. While adequate pretesting of questionnaires (including open end questions) goes a long way toward ensuring that such questions are balanced and cast in terms of the views that most respondents hold, the dual close end response option nevertheless constrains the ways that some respondents can offer their opinions. One difficulty with this technique is that the respondent must answer in the frame that the polling organization offers. These forced choices may reflect the division of preferences among elites, for example, in terms of their assessments of feasible policy alternatives, but they also may constrain the public's ability to express their true range of preferences.

This raises additional questions about the impact of the reporting of public opinion on the audience. The dissemination of public opinion data clearly has an impact on subsequent opinion and behavior. While many public pollsters are reluctant to acknowledge this fact, there is growing evidence from a range of academic studies that knowledge of what others think or believe—or how those opinions are changing—has an effect on an individual's opinions and behavior (→ *The Effects of Published Polls on Citizens*). These impacts are not necessarily negative, as there is usually a positive version of each of the phenomenon that many critics see as negative; but the effects are there nevertheless.

PROBLEMS OF REPORTING ON PUBLIC OPINION

Journalists face a number of problems when reporting on public opinion. Some come from difficulties they have with statistical concepts; others come from a lack of training in survey methods. An understanding of both issues is critical for deciding how to write about anyone's data, even if they were collected by the news organization where the journalist works. Many reporters are offered survey data by individuals or organizations who believe that current measures of public opinion will increase the likelihood that their point of view becomes newsworthy. In this case, reporters may face a special problem: that of trying to validate the information in the same way that they would check their facts in a more traditional story. In each instance, there are ways that journalists can be encouraged to 'get it right.'

Interest groups that want to press a point

Many interest groups believe that poll data that support their position will increase the likelihood that news organizations will produce stories that cover their interests, thus getting them on the policy agenda for elites. This is especially problematical when a press release or research report describes an issue in conceptual terms, but the underlying or supporting data present problems of operationalization that come from biased question wording or question order effects. If journalists cannot distinguish between the conceptual and operational issues, they may inadvertently present poll data as facts when their provenance is questionable.

The organization Mothers Against Drunk Driving (MADD) has advocated laws to reduce traffic accidents related to alcohol consumption in the United States. One of their major thrusts has been to have federal and state laws passed to reduce the amount of blood alcohol concentration (BAC) that is permissible when driving a car. In 1997, they reported results from a survey that indicated that seven in ten Americans supported a reduction in the allowable BAC from 0.10% to 0.08%, including this claim in testimony before Congress. That result was based upon the following question, which is clearly leading:

> Today, most states define intoxicated driving at 0.10% blood alcohol content, yet scientific studies show that virtually all safe driving skills are impaired at 0.08. Would you be in favor of lowering the legal blood alcohol limit for drivers to 0.08?

The reference to 'scientific studies' clearly gives the impression that 0.08 would be a safer alternative. Using this as part of an effort to adopt the lower limit, MADD was successful in their support of a federal law passed by

Congress in 2000 that required states to adopt the lower limit by 2004 in order to continue to receive federal highway funds.

After the law took effect, a second survey they commissioned trumpeted the fact that 88% of licensed drivers said they supported the new federal law. However, the question that was asked in this survey was:

> According to the National Highway Traffic Safety Administration, 0.08% blood alcohol concentration is the illegal drunk driving limit in all 50 states and the District of Columbia. Please tell me if you strongly support the law, support the law, oppose the law, or strongly oppose the law.

The question wording does not refer to a federal law or its requirements. From the response categories, it is unclear whether the respondents support the federal law or the law in their state. The previous question in the survey asked the respondents if they knew what the allowable legal BAC was in their state, but it did not tell them what it was. In order for journalists to be able to decode these claims against the underlying data, they have to know something about surveys and questionnaire design and how to distinguish between the concept of 'support for lowering the limit' and the specific ways that the concept was operationalized in a survey question.

Distinguishing a difference

Almost all media reporting of poll data is based upon the results from a single cross-sectional survey using one question at a time, often called 'reporting the marginals.' For example, when a survey measures whether or not Americans approve or disapprove of the job George W. Bush is doing as president, the resulting press release or news story begins with an indication that 37% of those surveyed approve of the way he is handling his job. A single proportion or percentage like that has a margin of error associated with it due to sampling alone that is based upon the sample size. In a typical media poll with a sample of 1,000 respondents, the statement is made that the 'margin of error due to sampling is plus or minus three percentage points.' This means that we would expect that 95 times out of 100, the population value for presidential approval lies between 34% and 40% (37% ± 3%).

This has two important analytical consequences for a data analyst or journalist. The first is the ability to state with confidence that more people disapprove of Bush's handling of his job than approve, i.e. that 37% is statistically significantly different from 63%. A second issue that preoccupies many analysts is the ability to make a statement that a 'majority of Americans' disapprove of the president's handling of his job, in effect a statement that 37% is statistically significantly different from 50%. This concern about majorities comes from living in a democratic society where a commonly shared assumption is that 'the majority rules.'

While these issues seem quite straightforward, they may get complicated when either the size of a sample or the differences in the proportions gets relatively small. When the public is evenly divided on an issue, it will take quite a large sample to distinguish with confidence a difference between 53% and 47%. And as the sample size decreases, the margin of error increases; so relatively small differences that are statistically significant in a sample of size 1,000 will not be in a sample of size 500. While journalists may not frequently encounter samples sizes as small as 500, the size of *subsamples* for men and women in a national sample of size 1,000 would normally approximate that. So the confidence intervals around estimates in subsamples are larger than the confidence intervals around estimates from the full sample. In general, it is a good idea for journalists not to report on differences that are less than 5 percentage points when sample sizes are in the range of 750 to 1,000 respondents; and the differences must be greater for smaller subsample sizes.

The problem of reporting on change

The extension of distinguishing a simple difference in a single survey is trying to distinguish whether a proportion or percentage is different when the same question is asked in two different surveys. Journalists frequently have a problem interpreting survey results when they involve such a description of change. One reason is they cannot distinguish between different types and causes of 'change.' Some are methodological artifacts of measurement or differences in the conceptualization of change. Others come from aggregation effects that make opinions appear to be more stable than they really are, because of counterbalancing trends. Some reports suggest that everyone has changed a little, when in fact the change has been localized in specific subgroups in the population. And sometimes the apparent lack of change in the entire sample masks significant but compensating changes in subgroups. For example, the distribution of party identification in the United States has remained virtually unchanged since 1952. But this apparent stability was the result of a growing Democratic allegiance among Blacks, offset by a movement toward the Republican Party among southern whites, as well as a movement of men toward the Republican Party and women toward the Democrats.

A common source of error in describing opinion change comes from the 'cross sectional fallacy,' in which comparisons are made in the distribution of opinions derived from asking the same question of independent samples drawn from the same population at two different points in time. The aggregate differences are assumed to represent all of the change that has taken place among the individuals in the population being sampled. If 40% of the sample supported Policy A in the first survey and 60% supported the policy in the second survey, journalists often describe a 20-percentage point shift as having taken place. But this almost certainly underestimates the total amount of shifting opinion. Some people who supported the policy in the first survey may subsequently have opposed it or become undecided; and there may have been offsetting shifts among those who initially opposed the policy. The true assessment of changes in opinion can only be made through the use of panel designs, in which the same respondents are asked the same questions at two or more points in time (→ *Panel Surveys*).

It is also important that comparisons are made between the same operational definition of a concept at multiple points in time. Sometimes analysts write in the language of concepts, ignoring the fact that different operational definitions were used at different points in time. It is no wonder, then, that journalists confuse methodological artifact for change. For example, Smith (1987) reviewed the analysis of social and behavioral science research reported by the Attorney General's Commission on Pornography (1986) and found it seriously lacking. Public attitudes were a relevant and important topic for consideration by the Commission because recent court cases suggested the application of 'contemporary community standards' as an appropriate criterion for assessing whether something is pornographic or not. And survey research seems the obvious scientific method for measuring contemporary community standards in a valid manner.

Among the many examples he cites from the report, Smith discusses a conclusion that exposure to printed pornographic material had increased between 1970 and 1985. This was based upon analysis of the responses to these two questions:

1970: 'During the past year, have you seen or read a magazine which you regarded as pornographic?'

1985: 'Have you *ever* read *Playboy* magazine or *Penthouse* magazine?'

The Commission concluded that exposure to sexually explicit magazines increased substantially across this fifteen-year period because 20% reported seeing or reading a pornographic magazine in 1970 while '(i)n contrast, two-thirds of the 1985 respondents had read *Playboy* or *Penthouse* at some time' (p. 913). Even though the report hedges on the interpretation of this difference, the point is that this interpretation should never have been made at all.

A common problem in designing questions is that of setting the time frame as a reference for a respondent, and differences in phraseology often lead to different levels of reported behavior. The earlier question asked for a report of a behavior that might have occurred 'during the past year,' while the time reference for the 1985 question was 'ever.' More importantly, the first question left the interpretation of what constitutes 'pornographic' up to the respondent; and there certainly would be a wide variation in associated meanings, including whether the respondents had either *Playboy* or *Penthouse* in mind when they answered. In the second question, the concept of 'pornography' was operationalized by referring to two specific magazines. As a result of these problems, it is impossible to know if there is any reasonable interpretation of observed differences over time at all.

One of the most frequent issues in reporting change has to do with tracking polls, those daily measures of candidate standing that are taken near the end of a campaign. In the last days of a campaign, reporters are often looking for any signs of tightening in a contest, so the reporting usually focuses on change. However, there are methodological issues associated with tracking polls that make reporting on change problematical. In the first place, most tracking polls involve rolling cross-sections in which a small number of interviews, typically ranging from 100 to 150, are taken every day; and the results are combined across three days. As a consequence, the reported results are based upon small samples ranging from 300 to 450 interviews.

A second conceptual issue is that the change from one 'day's' results to the next involves counting some of the same respondents twice. That is, the data reported on Monday will usually include combined responses from people interviewed on Friday, Saturday, and Sunday. The results reported on Tuesday will include combined responses from people interviewed on Saturday, Sunday, and Monday. So two-thirds of the data are the same, while all of the difference is essentially due to the exclusion of the Friday respondents and the addition of the Monday respondents. The one-day sample sizes are even smaller than the combined total, with even larger margins of error to account for. Almost any difference that appears will be statistically insignificant.

Conflicting reports of public opinion

On many issues, the public begins with no strongly held view or preconceived notion of what appropriate public policy might be. While forming their own views, many citizens scan the opinion horizon to see what others think as a reference. This is one of the important ways that dissemination of poll results educates the public, and they in turn rely upon accurate reporting. But evaluating the quality of data obtained in polls and surveys presents a special problem for journalists, since their formal training in interpreting poll results is generally weak and inadequate. There are even inadvertent instances where media polls have reported diametrically opposed 'findings'—sometimes even from separate polls released at about the same time. Most commonly this occurs as an artifact of question wording. It can create complicated interpretive problems for readers and viewers who might want to assess their fellow citizens' opinions by comparing poll results on the same topic.

For example, CBS News and the *New York Times*, based on their own poll, reported on public evaluations of the impact of the Enron scandal quite differently than CNN did using a specially commissioned Gallup poll. CBS produced a story on January 27, 2002 under the headline 'Poll finds Enron's taint clings more to G.O.P. than Democrats.' CNN/*USA Today* reported on January 27, 2002 the results from a Gallup Poll they commissioned under the headline 'Bush gets benefit of doubt from public in latest poll.' So was Enron hurting the Democrats or Republicans more? The answer lies in a comparison of the specific questions asked.

The CBS News/*New York Times* question and marginals were:

From what you know so far, do you think executives of the Enron Corporation had closer ties to the Republican Party or closer ties to the Democratic Party?

Republican Party	45%
Democratic Party	10%
Both equally (volunteered)	10%
Don't know	34%

From this single question, the suggestion is that Americans thought the Enron executives were closer to the Republicans than the Democrats.

When the CNN/*USA Today* released their results, they reported that Americans felt that the Enron Corporation was involved with both the Republicans and Democrats in Congress, according to the following three questions, but did not link Enron to members of the Bush administration any more than the Democrats in Congress:

Which of the following statements best describes your view of the Republicans' in Congress/Democrats' in Congress/members of the Bush administration's involvement with the Enron corporation?

	Republicans in Congress	Democrats in Congress	Members of Bush Administration
Did something illegal	33%	16%	15%
Did something unethical but nothing illegal	41%	35%	32%
Did not do anything seriously wrong	30%	18%	28%
Don't know/ No opinion	16%	31%	25%

Americans generally do not pay a great deal of attention to corporate scandals; only 23% in the Gallup sample were following the story 'very closely' for example. So this would be an instance of an issue rising rapidly to public visibility when citizens are unlikely to have strongly held prior views. But what were readers and viewers of these poll results to believe—did Americans hold the Republicans more liable than the Democrats?

Partisanship and the Republican revolution

Party identification is one of the most fundamental concepts underlying the analysis of political phenomena in the United States and elsewhere. Developed originally by political psychologists as a measure of the voter's 'affective orientation to an important group-object in his environment' (Campbell, Converse, Miller, & Stokes, 1960, p. 121), from the early 1950s it has been viewed as the most important predictor of candidate preference and voter choice among individual voters. At the same time, distinctions are made between this attitudinal predisposition to identify with a party, which can only be measured through personal interviews, and various behavioral measures of partisanship such as voting, which can be measured with election returns as well as surveys. The distributions of partisans and party-based voting behavior in any political system are two of its most important properties.

During the 'Reagan revolution,' political scientists and historians, as well as political activists and strategists, seriously debated whether the United States was undergoing another partisan realignment, that is a fundamental and durable shift in the relative distribution of people who identify themselves as Democrats and Republicans. This is a biennial debate that occurs most frequently around national elections, and it has political consequences for how the policy initiatives of the president and Congress are framed in terms of their public support.

The basic data source that fuels the controversy is a time series of survey-based estimates of party identification. In the United States, differences in partisanship have long been observed between samples of successively more restricted populations of adults: those who are registered to vote, those who indicate they are likely to vote in a given election, and those who actually go to the polls become increasingly more Republican. Borrelli, Lockerbie, and Niemi (1987) analyzed 51 poll results between 1980 and 1984 in evaluating three possible causes of these variations: (1) the relative effects of the timing of the polls in relation to Election Day, (2) differences in the population sampled, and (3) the wording of the partisanship question. Interviewing close to Election Day was strongly related to the size of the relationship between voting behavior and identification, either because respondents bring their identifications into consonance with their expected votes or because they misinterpret the question as inquiring about their intended votes. The main question wording difference involved references to partisanship 'as of today,' 'generally speaking' or 'usually,' or 'regardless of how you may vote.'

The results showed that all of these predictors were statistically significant and operated in the expected direction; and they explained a large proportion of the variance (78%) in the difference in the proportion of identifiers with the two major parties. The purpose of the analysis was not to corroborate whether or not a realignment was taking place in this period, as measured by changes in basic attitudes toward the political parties. Rather it was to alert analysts interested in this question (including journalists) to the potential effect of methodological issues on substantive interpretations. The distribution of partisanship is a function of who gets interviewed and when, and what questions they are asked. It turns out that debates about realignment that take place around election results reflect a peculiarity of the measurement of the very phenomenon itself in conjunction with impending voting behavior. And post-election surveys showed that no durable realignment occurred.

EVALUATING DATA QUALITY

Most of the poll-based reporting about politics, in the United States and elsewhere, consists of stories organized around surveys that news organizations commission or conduct. However, some stories are offered to news organizations by interest groups or individuals because they believe that public consumption of the information they want disseminated will be enhanced by the credibility of a source like a newspaper or network evening news show. When such stories are 'shopped around' to news organizations, the availability of polling data related to the content increases the likelihood that journalists will see the information as newsworthy and run the story.

An interesting example of such a strategy occurred with the Republican Party's development of the 'Contract with America,' an organizing device for their 1994 congressional campaign (Traugott & Powers, 2000). Republican officials and strategists designed the Contract as a unifying theme for the fall campaign in an attempt to nationalize their effort to gain control of the US House of Representatives. At the rollout of the Contract, they promoted it to journalists with the claim that each of its 10 'reforms' was supported by at least 60% of the American public. Although this claim was widely reported in the media across the entire campaign period, it was not true. This episode provides an interesting case study of how political strategists can take advantage of unwary and untrained journalists in order to frame a campaign by invoking public support for their agenda through (alleged or implied) polling data (→ *The Use of Surveys by Governments and Politicians;* → *The Use of Voter Research in Campaigns*).

Although many journalists may be familiar with sources of information about polls, almost none are familiar with sources of other information they can use to corroborate data from a poll they are evaluating. This information is available from data archives that contain substantial holdings of public opinion data in various forms, as well as some holdings on public opinion in many other countries (→ *Archiving Poll Data*). They provide critical information that permits journalists to make independent assessments of the reliability and validity of public opinion data collected or reported by others. Some of these archives specialize in polls conducted by and for media organizations, while others contain long-term trend data collections from academic survey organizations. This information can come in any one of three different formats: data summaries in the form of tables and charts from individual or similar polls or surveys; question databases that provide aggregate results (frequency distributions) from topical questions used by a variety of polling sources; and the

actual computerized data files that allow users to perform their own statistical manipulations. Access to most of these sources is available on-line through the World Wide Web and the Internet, and through subscriptions to services like Lexis-Nexis to which virtually every political reporter has access.

CONCLUSIONS

Consumers of poll results rely upon journalists to select and report poll results and public opinion data in a way that provides accurate information and a context for interpretation. Accurate information comes from good data that are appropriately analyzed and interpreted. Context provides a basis for understanding that often involves a comparison with other questions recently asked on the same topic, previous administrations of the same question, or analysis of relevant subgroups in the sample. Beyond the preparation of stories based upon the poll results, packages of stories can be produced that relate the poll findings to interviews with or stories about 'real people' who hold the same views or behave in the same way.

REFERENCES

Attorney General's Commission on Pornography (1986). *Final report.* Washington, D.C.: Government Printing Office.

Borrelli, S., Lockerbie, B., & Niemi, R. G. (1987). Why the Democrat-Republican partisanship gap varies from poll to poll. *Public Opinion Quarterly, 51,* 115–119.

Campbell, A., Converse, P. E., Miller, W. E., & Stokes, D. E. (1960). *The American voter.* New York: John Wiley & Sons.

Herbst, S. (1993). *Numbered voices: How opinion polling has shaped American politics.* Chicago: University of Chicago Press.

Smith, T. W. (1987). The use of public opinion data by the Attorney General's Commission on Pornography. *Public Opinion Quarterly, 51,* 249–267.

Traugott, M. W., & Lavrakas, P. J. (2004). *The voter's guide to election polls* (3rd ed.). Lanham MD: Rowman and Littlefield.

Traugott, M. W., & Powers, E. (2000). Did public opinion support the contract with America? In P. J. Lavrakas & M. W. Traugott (Eds.), *Election polls, the news media, and democracy* (pp. 93–110). New York: Seven Bridges Press.

22

Face-to-Face Surveys

Jennifer Dykema, Danna Basson and
Nora Cate Schaeffer

Face-to-face interviews are the oldest method of survey data collection and still have an important role in many studies. In their purest form, face-to-face surveys use interviewers to both contact and collect information from respondents (de Leeuw & Collins, 1997). Face-to-face surveys, along with telephone surveys, self-administered questionnaires (such as mail surveys), and e-mail and Internet surveys, comprise the four different modes of data collection discussed in this Handbook. Face-to-face surveys can be used alone, but often are used in combination with these other modes.

Decisions about whether to conduct a face-to-face survey are influenced by concerns about costs and data quality, sampling issues, design features of the instrument, and the desired length of the field period. Modes of data collection used in sample surveys differ along important dimensions related to these concerns (Tourangeau & Smith, 1996; Biemer & Lyberg, 2003). The first concerns how the sampled individual is contacted and

asked to participate (e.g., in person, over the telephone, or through surface or e-mail). The second dimension involves how questions are presented to the respondent (e.g., by an interviewer, read and answered by the respondent on their own, or presented using a recorded voice). Finally, modes vary in how they incorporate computers. In general, face-to-face surveys are used when funds are large and a high response rate is needed, when area probability sampling methods are required to improve population coverage, or when measurement is complex and includes observations or a long questionnaire.

This chapter provides an overview of face-to-face surveys. It highlights the important design and implementation steps in conducting face-to-face interviews including sampling issues, such as coverage and nonresponse; measurement issues including the influence of interviewers; and other issues related to data quality and costs. The chapter concludes with a discussion of computer-assisted personal interviewing.

SAMPLING: COVERAGE

Compared to other modes, face-to-face survey designs that use multistage area probability sampling methods have better coverage of many populations, particularly the general population, for which a list of all members is not available in the United States (Kalton, 1983). If the study requires choosing respondents using random selection methods or special screening techniques, interviewers are usually required. Face-to-face contact allows for more complicated selection methods and yields higher rates of cooperation than contact made over the telephone.

For samples of the general population, telephone sampling frames have several weaknesses in comparison to area probability frames (Biemer & Lyberg, 2003). Telephone frames necessarily omit approximately 6% of households without telephones in the United States, and they include households with more than one telephone number multiple times. Telephone frames may also omit households that rely exclusively on cell phones for phone service; this proportion is low, but increasing (Tucker, Brick, & Meekins, 2004).

Nevertheless, sampling frames for face-to-face interviews of the general population have coverage problems for some groups. The frames typically omit individuals living in institutions, group quarters, outside of the contiguous United States, and in areas that are remote or sparsely populated. Other groups that have a higher likelihood of being omitted include those residing in small buildings with multiple units (sometimes overlooked during enumeration), and demographic groups that are also under-enumerated in the US decennial census, such as African-Americans and men.

SAMPLING: RESPONSE RATES

While the preponderance of evidence indicates that response rates are declining across all modes, face-to-face surveys have had (Hox & de Leeuw, 1994) and continue to produce higher response rates than any other mode. Groves and Couper (1998) review trends for six prominent surveys that are conducted face-to-face or use a mixed-mode design (in-person for the initial interview, followed by the telephone for subsequent contacts). Results from the 1970s to 1990s show increasing nonresponse for three of the six surveys, with the refusal rate increasing for four surveys.[1] Overall, however, response rates remained high—at or above 75%—for all of the surveys. Atrostic, Bates, Burt, and Silberstein (2001) extend the comparison by presenting trends for six surveys throughout the 1990s and limiting comparisons to response rates made during the initial contact with the household. Results continue to show increasing nonresponse rates (both increasing refusal and noncontact rates) but still remarkably high response rates overall—over 70% for all six surveys and at or above 85% for four surveys.

However, nonresponse rates for face-to-face surveys are likely to continue to rise as the number of refusals increases and efforts to locate and contact respondents plateau or decline. For example, recent data from the General Social Survey indicate a decline in the overall rate to 70%, a change attributed to increases in refusals (Curtin, Presser, & Singer, 2005).

Even though they have declined, response rates for face-to-face surveys remain substantially higher than those for other modes. The response rate for the Survey of Consumer Attitudes, an academically based, national RDD survey, dropped from 72% in 1979 to 48% in 2003 (Curtin *et al.*, 2005). Evidence suggests that rates for other RDD surveys are probably lower (Steeh, Kirgis, Cannon, & DeWitt, 2001). Response rates for self-administered surveys such as mail surveys (Chapter 24) and Internet surveys (Chapter 25) are typically lower than for interviewer-administered surveys.

There are several reasons why surveys using face-to-face interviewers yield the highest response rates. Unlike self-administered modes in which an interviewer is not present, or a telephone survey where the respondent can only hear the interviewer, interviewers in face-to-face surveys can have a more direct impact on contacting respondents and getting them to participate. Because field interviewers can see respondents' neighborhoods, homes, and faces, they have considerable information to use in tailoring appeals to participate. While households may be more difficult to contact because of characteristics such as urbanicity, household size and composition (e.g., elderly respondents), fielding decisions and interviewer actions can affect contact rates within these constraints (Groves & Couper, 1998). For example, interviewers can note information about neighborhoods and housing units during the listing phase or during initial visits. Using this information, interviewers can customize their approaches, for instance by approaching single-person households in the evening or households with elderly respondents during the day. Also in face-to-face surveys, respondents have the opportunity to see that interviewers are who they claim to be and to view their credentials.

Despite the importance of gaining cooperation, it is difficult to conduct research on interviewer-level correlates of contactability and cooperation (Groves & Couper, 1998). While interviewers' characteristics are probably less important in determining cooperation than the techniques they use and when they use them, attributes including tenure on the job, self-confidence, and belief in the legitimacy of their work are related to success (Hox & de Leeuw, 2002).

Indicators of the interaction between the interviewer and respondent are related to survey cooperation. Because the initial interaction requires a quick response to the householder's concerns, the most successful interviewers are able to preempt objections and tailor effective responses. Research finds that interviewers with five or more years of experience are better able to anticipate and overcome such barriers as negative attitudes toward surveys and interview-delaying tactics (e.g., 'I'm too busy') (Groves & Couper, 1998). Evidence suggests that interviewer training aimed at satisfactorily addressing respondents' concerns with a rapid, natural

delivery increases cooperation (Groves & McGonagle, 2001). Finally, an appeal for participation made face-to-face is probably more difficult to reject than one from a faceless telephone interviewer.

MEASUREMENT: CHARACTERISTICS OF INTERVIEWERS

In addition to the impact they have on nonresponse, interviewers influence survey reports in several ways, including their characteristics, such as their physical appearance and expectations; their conduct during the interview, including the extent to which they deviate from standardization; and by their mere presence (Groves, Fowler, Couper, Lepkowski, Singer, & Tourangeau, 2004). Overall, response effects attributed to interviewers' characteristics are small. Interviewers' gender and race sometimes influence answers, but the effects are most likely to occur when the visible characteristic of the interviewer is related to the topic of study, and these effects are primarily confined to attitudinal questions. Similarly interviewers' expectations, such as concerns about a study's difficulty, only have a small impact on data quality.

MEASUREMENT: BEHAVIOR OF INTERVIEWERS

Interviewers' conduct, particularly with regard to departures from standardized procedures, also affects data quality. Unlike self-administered modes where the presentation of the survey question is held constant across respondents, in face-to-face and telephone surveys, interviewers and interviewer–respondent interactions are sources of measurement error. Systematic effects of interviewers may bias answers, and interviewers may decrease the reliability of answers by adding a component of interviewer variance (Mangione, Fowler, & Louis, 1992). Variance estimates may be smaller for face-to-face than telephone interviews, because they vary as a function of interviewers' workloads, which are typically smaller in face-to-face surveys (Biemer & Lyberg, 2003).

In order to control sources of error, interviewers' behaviors are constrained by the rules of standardization (Fowler & Mangione, 1990). Interviewers are taught to: read questions exactly as worded, use neutral probes, maintain neutrality, use feedback to reward appropriate behaviors, and avoid providing cues about how respondents should answer. However, interviewers consistently make major departures from standardization even when monitored. A large proportion of unstandardized behaviors at a given question may indicate that answers to the question will be of lower quality.

Both changes to the survey question and probing usually occur because something is problematic about the survey question (e.g., it contains terms that are hard to comprehend), and interviewers frequently behave the way they do to help the respondent to answer. Researchers attribute interviewers' and respondents' unstandardized behaviors to several causes, the most important being poorly worded and cognitively difficult survey questions (Oksenberg, Cannell, & Kalton, 1991) and the pull of conversational practices (Maynard, Houtkoop-Steenstra, Schaeffer, & van der Zouwen, 2002).

The role and importance of standardization continue to be debated. Some researchers argue that standardization undermines validity (Schober & Conrad, 1997) and that to benefit from conversational practices that promote comprehension, interviewers should be flexible. However, it is important to balance gains in accuracy against increased interviewer variability.

MEASUREMENT: MERE PRESENCE OF INTERVIEWERS AND THREATENING QUESTIONS

Interviewers also influence survey respondents by their mere presence. Social desirability bias occurs when respondents over-report desirable and under-report undesirable behaviors in order to present themselves positively (Schaeffer, 2000). Research suggests that the key to improving responses to threatening questions is to minimize aspects of answering that are threatening to respondents while making more salient features that change respondents' comfort for revealing sensitive information. Thus researchers should increase privacy and anonymity, respondents' trust in the confidentiality of their answers and the legitimacy of the survey organization, and respondents' perception of the importance of the information. No mode appears superior in all of these ways.

Many studies have varied the mode in which the data are collected for threatening questions (Tourangeau & Smith, 1996). In comparison to self-administered interviews, face-to-face interviewers are more likely to obtain lower reports of these behaviors (Turner, Lessler, & Devore, 1992). In contrast, several studies show reduced social desirability bias in face-to-face versus telephone interviews (e.g., de Leeuw & van der Zouwen, 1988; Holbrook, Green, & Krosnick, 2003) although sometimes the effect is not there or is reversed. For interviewer-administered surveys, face-to-face interviewers can manipulate the setting by conducting interviews privately and away from family members, or even outside the home (Tourangeau, Rasinski, Jobe, Smith, & Pratt, 1997). In person, interviewers may be more likely to demonstrate their legitimacy and gain respondents' trust and mitigate the effect of their presence by giving respondents a self-administered instrument.

MEASUREMENT: OTHER ISSUES

Other features of in-person interviews seem likely to improve measurement, although mode comparisons assessing them are not always available. In face-to-face interviews, visual information can be shared and visual aids such as show cards, calendars, and timelines can be used more easily and effectively than over the phone (Groves et al., 2004). Using aids in telephone surveys requires advance contact and mailing and reliance on the respondent to retain and use materials correctly. In-person interviewers can gather data impossible to collect over the phone or difficult to collect through the mail, including: visual observations about respondents and their surroundings, physical measurements (e.g., height), and biological samples (e.g., saliva).

Several different kinds of response effects have been shown to vary by mode (Tourangeau, Rips, & Rasinski, 2000; Biemer & Lyberg, 2003; Groves et al., 2004). Primacy effects, the tendency to select options at the beginning of a scale, are found in face-to-face interviews, which often present response categories visually on show cards. Recency effects, the tendency to select options at the end of the scale, occur in telephone interviews, which present responses orally. Other response effects appear to be more common over the phone than in person, including acquiescence (the tendency to agree with a question regardless of its content) and extreme responses (the tendency to choose the end-points of the scales or the first or last response categories). In order to maintain the interaction with the respondent, a telephone interviewer's pace might be faster than face-to-face. A quicker pace implies that respondents must also rush, and they may be more likely to provide 'don't know' or no opinion responses and shorter responses to open-ended questions. Holbrook et al. (2003) also find that in comparison to telephone surveys, in-person interviews result in less non-differentiation, less dissatisfaction with interview length, and more interest in the survey. Respondents were also rated as more cooperative by interviewers.

There may be other intangible advantages to face-to-face interviews (Biemer & Lyberg, 2003). In-person interviewers can adapt to potential distractions, such as the presence of others. Face-to-face interviewers can also explicitly persuade respondents to do their best and encourage them to check records or make calculations. Respondents are probably less likely to engage in other tasks in the interviewer's presence than they might be over the telephone. The interviewer may also be better able to monitor the respondent for signs of misunderstanding or fatigue. Thus, particularly for interviews lasting over an hour, face-to-face interviews may provide data of higher quality than telephone surveys (Holbrook et al., 2003).

IMPLEMENTATION: INTERVIEWERS AND ASSOCIATED COSTS

Because the interviewer must be delivered to the respondent, surveys conducted in-person are more expensive than any other mode. Higher costs for hiring, training, equipping, supervising, and monitoring interviewers are compounded by the additional cost associated with interviewers' travel. Fixed costs or design features that are typically not affected by sample size, such as developing and programming a questionnaire, tend to be comparable for face-to-face and telephone surveys. In contrast, variable costs associated with contacting and interviewing respondents can vary greatly between face-to-face and comparable telephone surveys, with the former usually being considerably more expensive than the latter (Groves, 1989). Field periods are likely to be longer for face-to-face than telephone surveys of comparable size.

Because face-to-face surveys allow for more complex survey designs (such as self-administered audio portions or show cards) and because they work without a supervisor close at hand, field interviewers require more training than telephone interviewers (Groves et al., 2004). Monitoring field interviewers requires special procedures, such as checking instrument timings, looking for indications of falsified data, and calling respondents to confirm that interviews occurred and that interviewers acted professionally. In contrast, telephone interviewers are monitored frequently and at a lower cost in centralized telephone facilities.

A key component of cost is travel time and expenses for interviewers and their supervisors. Travel increases the cost of training and of contacting respondents. The marginal cost of an additional contact is very low in a telephone facility, where any available interviewer can attempt any available case. Missed appointments by respondents are costlier for in-person interviews in terms of both time and money. Respondents in area probability samples are selected in clusters to minimize travel time. For list samples of populations that are especially mobile or do not have stable residences, such as youths in foster care, tracking and locating respondents can require multiple contacts. Face-to-face surveys of special populations may further increase costs by requiring interviewers who are bilingual and sensitive to the group's norms (de Leeuw & Collins, 1997).

Equipment costs also tend to be higher in face-to-face than telephone surveys. Each field interviewer requires a laptop, and each field computer is used in fewer interviews than those in centralized telephone facilities. Additional tools supplied to field interviewers can include global positioning system (GPS) equipment, software to enable data exchange, and cell-phones.

COMPUTER-ASSISTED PERSONAL INTERVIEWING (CAPI)

CAPI is one of several forms of computer-assisted interviewing that have transformed interviewing in the last three decades (Couper et al., 1998). CAPI questionnaires are pre-programmed onto laptop computers that interviewers bring to respondents and responses are recorded directly into the computers, thereby eliminating the need for data entry and editing.

CAPI offers several advantages over paper and pencil interviews (PAPI). A computerized instrument can accommodate complicated skip patterns; information on sample characteristics (e.g., respondents' names) can be pre-loaded and invoked as needed; data

provided at earlier questions can be incorporated into subsequent questions; and complicated calculations (e.g., for income) can be automated to be faster and more accurate. For longitudinal surveys, information gathered at earlier times can be preprogrammed to check inconsistencies in reports between waves or to remind respondents about previous answers. Computerization can be used in innovative ways by allowing interviewers and respondents access to survey definitions (e.g., Conrad & Schober, 1999).

With regard to disadvantages, CAPI appears to cost more than PAPI, probably because of the cost of computers, more complicated instruments, and programming time. Current CAPI programs constrain how questions can be presented, which can be particularly difficult for questions presented in a matrix format, such as household rosters (Moore & Moyer, 1998). It may also be difficult for interviewers to learn the overall structure of a CAPI instrument, a phenomenon that has been called a segmentation effect (House & Nicholls, 1988). Researchers are actively exploring instrument and screen designs, and usability issues (Fuchs, Couper, & Hansen, 2000).

A few studies make direct comparisons between PAPI and CAPI for the purposes of evaluating data quality. Evidence suggests that unit response rates are relatively unaffected by computerization, but that missing data and interviewer variance are reduced in CAPI (e.g., Tourangeau et al., 1997). Some research indicates that CAPI produces higher reports of sensitive behaviors than PAPI (Baker, Bradburn, & Johnson, 1995). In addition, CAPI interviewers can have respondents complete questions by themselves, referred to as computer-assisted self-interviewing (CASI) when the respondent reads the questions, or audio-CASI (ACASI) when the questions are prerecorded. ACASI offers the additional benefit of not requiring that respondents be able to read. Research indicates that in comparison to CAPI or CASI, ACASI yields higher reports of sensitive behaviors including abortions (Lessler, Weeks, & O'Reilly, 1994) and sex partners (Tourangeau & Smith, 1996). Thus, for the collection of sensitive behaviors, there appear to be advantages to ACASI (Tourangeau & Smith, 1998; Turner et al., 1998), but overall it is likely that the effect of computerization in personal interviews is small (Tourangeau et al., 1997).

CONCLUSIONS

The first, and for many years a widely used method of survey data collection, face-to-face interviewing is deployed much less often today. High costs and long timelines usually make it an impractical choice. Telephone, e-mail, and Internet modes are faster to implement, less expensive, and can achieve levels of response and data quality acceptable for many purposes. That said, face-to-face surveys survive and remain a viable, sometimes even preferred, mode in certain contexts. They are most useful when a high response rate is essential or when the measurement tasks are cognitively demanding or require a long questionnaire.

Face-to-face interviewing produces response rates substantially higher than those obtained via any other mode. It provides the best coverage of many populations. It facilitates initial cooperation and aids refusal conversion. The nationally representative panel study on labor force participation, the Current Population Survey (CPS), is one example of how researchers often leverage the advantages of face-to-face interviewing as part of a mixed-mode design. Interviewers are required to conduct the first interview in person, but then are allowed to do subsequent interviews by telephone to reduce costs and save time. If time and resources permit, face-to-face is recommended for launching a panel study or producing general population estimates.

Paradoxically, face-to-face surveys give researchers both less and more control over data collection. Interviewer performance is relatively uncontrolled. But in contrast to other modes, face-to-face interviewing

enables researchers to implement a full range of audio, visual, personal, and other tools to enhance communication, comprehension, and data recording. By their mere presence, interviewers can positively influence respondent motivation, attentiveness, and interview completion. Even aspects of in-person surveys previously identified as weaknesses, such as underreporting of sensitive behaviors and an inability to administer contingent wording and complex branching, have been mitigated by advances in interview technology and the use of self-administered instruments presented by interviewers in person. Possessing advantages that newer data collection modes cannot challenge and now invigorated by this technology, the future of face-to-face surveys appears secure.

NOTES

1 Trends in declining response rates are not limited to the United States (de Leeuw & de Heer, 2002).

REFERENCES

Atrostic, B.K., Bates, N., Burt, G., & Silberstein, A. (2001). Nonresponse in U.S. government household surveys: Consistent measures, recent trends, and new insights. *Journal of Official Statistics, 17*, 209–226.

Baker, R. P., Bradburn, N. M., & Johnson, R. A. (1995). Computer-assisted personal interviewing: An experimental evaluation of data quality and cost. *Journal of Official Statistics, 11*, 413–431.

Biemer, P. P., & Lyberg, L. E. (2003). *Introduction to Survey Quality.* New Jersey: John Wiley & Sons, Inc.

Conrad, F. G., & Schober, M. F. (1999). A conversational approach to text-based computer administered questionnaires. In Association for Survey Computing (Eds.), *Proceedings of the Third International ASC conference* (pp. 91–101). Chichester, UK: Association for Survey Computing.

Couper, M. P., Baker, R. P., Bethlehem, J., Clark, C. Z. F., Martin, J., Nicholls, W. L. II, & O'Reilly, J. M. (1998). *Computer Assisted Survey Information Collection.* New York: John Wiley & Sons, Inc.

Curtin, R., Presser, S., & Singer, E. (2005). Changes in telephone survey nonresponse over the past quarter century. *Public Opinion Quarterly, 69,* 87–98.

de Leeuw, E., & Collins, M. (1997). Data collection methods and survey quality: An overview. In L. Lyberg, P. Biemer, M. Collins, E. de Leeuw, C. Dippo, N. Schwarz & D. Trewin (Eds.), *Survey Measurement and Process Quality* (pp. 199–220). New York: John Wiley & Sons, Inc.

de Leeuw, E., & de Heer, W. (2002). Trends in household survey nonresponse: A longitudinal and international comparison. In R. M. Groves, D. A. Dillment, J. L. Eltinge & R. J. A. Little (Eds.), *Survey Nonresponse* (pp. 41–54). New York: John Wiley & Sons, Inc.

de Leeuw, E., & van der Zouwen, J. (1988). Data quality in telephone and face-to-face surveys: A comparative meta-analysis. In R. M Groves, P. P. Biemer, L. E. Lyberg, J. T. Massey, W. L. Nicholls, II & J. Waksberg (Eds.), *Telephone Survey Methodology* (pp. 283–299). New York: Wiley.

Fowler, F. J. Jr., & Mangione, T. W. (1990). *Standardized Survey Interviewing: Minimizing Interviewer-Related Error.* Newbury Park: Sage.

Fuchs, M., Couper, M. P., & Hansen, S. E. (2000). Technology effects: Do CAPI or PAPI interviews take longer? *Journal of Official Statistics, 16*, 273–286.

Groves, R. M. (1989). *Survey Errors and Survey Costs.* New York: Wiley.

Groves, R. M., & Couper, M. P. (1998). *Nonresponse in Household Interview Surveys.* New York: John Wiley & Sons, Inc.

Groves, R. M., Fowler, F. J. Jr., Couper, M. P., Lepkowski, J. M., Singer, E., & Tourangeau, R. (2004). *Survey Methodology.* New York: John Wiley & Sons, Inc.

Groves, R. M., & McGonagle, K. A. (2001). A theory-guided interviewer training protocol regarding survey participation. *Journal of Official Statistics, 17*, 249–265.

Holbrook, A. L., Green, M. C., & Krosnick, J. A. (2003). Telephone versus face-to-face interviewing of national probability samples with long questionnaires: Comparisons of respondent satisficing and social desirability response bias. *Public Opinion Quarterly, 67*, 79–125.

House, C. C., & Nicholls III, W. L. (1988). Questionnaire design for CATI: Design objectives and methods. In R. M Groves, P. P. Biemer, L. E. Lyberg, J. T. Massey, W. L. Nicholls, II & J. Waksberg (Eds.), *Telephone Survey Methodology* (pp. 421–436). New York: Wiley.

Hox, J., & de Leeuw, E. (1994). A comparison of nonresponse in mail, telephone, and face to face surveys. *Quality and Quantity, 28*, 329–344.

Hox, J., & de Leeuw, E. (2002). The influence of interviewers' attitude and behavior on household survey nonresponse: An international comparison. In R.M. Groves, D. A. Dillman, J. L. Eltinge, & R. J. A. Little (Eds.), *Survey Nonresponse* (pp. 103–120). New York: John Wiley & Sons, Inc.

Kalton, G. (1983). Introduction to Survey Sampling. *Quantitative Applications in the Social Sciences Series, 35*, Newbury Park, CA: Sage.

Lessler, J. T., Weeks, M. F., & O'Reilly, J. M. (1994). Results from the National Survey of Family Growth Cycle V Pretest. *American Statistical Association: Proceedings of the Section on Survey Research Methods, Vol. 1*, 64–70.

Mangione, T. W., Fowler, F. J., & Louis, T. A. (1992). Question characteristics and interviewer effects. *Journal of Official Statistics, 8*, 293–307.

Maynard, D. W., Houtkoop-Steenstra, H., Schaeffer, N. C., & van der Zouwen, J. (2002). *Standardization and Tacit Knowledge: Interaction and Practice in the Survey Interview.* New York: John Wiley & Sons, Inc.

Moore, J. C., & Moyer, L. (1998). Questionnaire design effects on interview outcomes. *American Statistical Association: Proceedings of the Section on Survey Research, Vol. 2*, 851–856.

Oksenberg, L., Cannell, C., & Kalton, G. (1991). New strategies for pretesting survey questions. *Journal of Official Statistics, 7*, 349–365.

Schaeffer, N. C. (2000). Asking questions about threatening topics: A selective overview. In A. A. Stone, J. S. Turkkan, C. A. Bachrach, J. B. Jobe, H. S. Kurtzman & V. S. Cain (Eds.), *The Science of Self-Report: Implications for Research and Practice* (pp. 105–121). New Jersey: Lawrence Erlbaum Associates.

Schober, M. F., & Conrad, F. G. (1997). Does conversational interviewing reduce survey measurement error? *Public Opinion Quarterly, 61*, 576–602.

Steeh, C., Kirgis, N., Cannon, B., & DeWitt, J. (2001). Are they really as bad as they seem? Nonresponse rates at the end of the twentieth century. *Journal of Official Statistics, 17*, 227–247.

Tourangeau, R., & Smith T. W. (1996). Asking sensitive questions: The impact of data collection mode, question format, and question context. *Public Opinion Quarterly, 60*, 275–304.

Tourangeau, R., Rasinski, K., Jobe, J. B., Smith, T. W., & Pratt, W. F. (1997). Sources of error in a survey on sexual behavior. *Journal of Official Statistics, 13*, 341–365.

Tourangeau, R., Rips, L. J., & Rasinski, K. (2000). *The Psychology of Survey Response.* Cambridge: Cambridge University Press.

Tucker, C., Brick, M., & Meekins, B. (2004). *Telephone service in U.S. households in 2004. Paper presented at the Annual Meeting of the American Association for Public Opinion Research*, Phoenix, Arizona.

Turner, C., Lessler, J., & Devore, J. (1992). Effects of mode of administration and wording on reporting of drug use. In C. Turner, J. Lessler, & J. Gfroerer (Eds.), *Survey Measurement and Drug Use: Methodological Studies* (pp. 177–220). Rockville, MD: National Institute on Drug Abuse.

Turner, C. F., Forsyth, B. H., O'Reilly, J. M., Cooley, P. C., Smith, T. K., Rogers, S. M., & Miller, H. G. (1998). Automated self-interviewing and the survey measurement of sensitive behaviors. In M. P. Cooper, R. P. Baker, J. Bethlehem, C. Z. F. Clark, J. Martin, W.L. Nicholls, & J.M. O'Reilly (Eds.), *Computer Assisted Survey Information Collection* (pp. 455–473). New York: John Wiley & Sons, Inc.

23

Surveys by Telephone

Paul J. Lavrakas

Telephone survey methods have undergone serious methodological development only in the past 40 years. Prior to that time, the penetration (coverage) of households with telephones in the United States, Europe, and elsewhere was too low to justify use of the telephone as a representative survey sampling mode. However, by the mid-1980s household telephone coverage in the United State exceeded 90%, and telephone surveying was becoming commonplace. Even by 2005, though, there remained geographic areas—both inner city and rural—in which telephone coverage in the US was below 90%. In Europe, telephone coverage increased to 97% of all households, with two-thirds having both a wired (fixed) line and mobile service (IPSOS-INRA, 2004).

By the late 1980s, the telephone became the sampling and data collection mode of preference for public opinion surveys in the US. This was due primarily to two reasons: (1) the data gathered via well-conceived and well-executed telephone surveys was shown to be reliable and valid (cf. de Leeuw & van der Zouwen, 1988; Groves, 1989);

and (2) telephone survey data could be gathered much more quickly than via in-person or mail surveys. Timeliness was a highly salient factor in measuring newsworthy public opinion topics. However, a series of telecommunication-related behavioral trends and government policies in the US since the mid-1990s have begun to call into question whether telephone surveys of the American public will remain representative in the coming decades. These factors are not likely to be of concern in Europe and other countries, raising the future prospect of distinct national differences in how the telephone can be used for representative sampling of the public.

THE ADVANTAGES AND DISADVANTAGES OF THE TELEPHONE SURVEY MODE

Why did telephone surveying gain prominence as a means of providing accurate and timely measures of public opinion? Simply stated, in most cases its advantages far outweighed its disadvantages.

Advantages

Although many fail to recognize or acknowledge it, a very important advantage of telephone surveying is the opportunity it provides for quality control over the entire data collection process. This includes sampling, respondent selection, administering a questionnaire, and data entry. It is this *quality control advantage* that recommends the telephone as the preferred mode for public opinion surveying, providing there are no overriding concerns that rule against it.

A second major advantage is its cost-efficiency. Telephone surveys can collect data far more efficiently than in-person interviewing. For example, in addition to the absence of travel expenses which in-person surveying requires, Groves (1989) estimated that individual questionnaire items administered via telephone take 10% to 20% less time than the same items administered in person. And, although telephone surveys are typically more expensive than mail and web surveys, their potential advantages for addressing total survey error often outweigh this cost disadvantage.

A third major advantage is the speed with which data can be gathered and processed. In less than a week, a group of skilled interviewers can gather high quality opinion data via telephone that might take a month or more using in-person interviews. An even longer period often would be needed to conduct a high quality mail survey on the same topic with the same sample size, given the necessity of follow-up mailings to increase typically low response rates to the first mailing. For example, with as few as 10 experienced telephone interviewers, working four-hour shifts per day, upward of 400 to 500 20-item questionnaires could be completed within five days (including allowance for several callbacks) with a response rate of greater than 50%. If a newspaper editor asked on Monday for some opinion poll data by the end of the week to aid him/her in writing an important Sunday editorial about satisfaction/dissatisfaction with the current city administration, a good survey unit could complete a high-quality telephone survey of adult residents in the city and provide results to the editor on deadline. High-quality opinion data could not be gathered via mail or in-person surveys within this time frame for the same costs as the telephone survey, and the editor could not be confident about data accuracy gathered via a web survey because the web—unlike the telephone—at present cannot reach a fully representative sample of the citizenry.

Disadvantages

A major disadvantage of telephone surveys—even when well executed—is the limitations they place on the complexity and length of the interview. Unlike the dynamics of face-to-face interviewing, the average respondent often finds it tiresome to be kept on the telephone for longer than 20 minutes, especially when the topic does not interest her/him. In contrast, personal interviewers do not seem to notice as much respondent fatigue even with interviews that last 30 minutes or longer. Mail and web surveys also do not suffer from this disadvantage, as the questionnaires can be completed at a respondent's leisure over multiple sessions. Similarly, complicated questions, especially those that require the respondent to see or read something, heretofore have been impossible to display via the telephone. With the advent of video telecommunications technology on the web and telephones, this limitation should diminish. However, these limitations often do not hamper opinion polls due to their typical use of relatively straightforward questionnaires of modest length.

Other traditional concerns about telephone surveys include potential coverage error that may occur. For example, not everyone in the US lives in a household with a telephone, and among those who do, not every demographic group is equally willing or can be accounted for and/or interviewed via telephone. According to Federal Communications Commission statistics, in 2004 approximately 6% of the US public lived in a home without any telephone—with

Arizona (8%), Arkansas (11%), the District of Columbia (8%), Georgia (9%), Illinois (10%), Indiana (8%), Kentucky (9%), Louisiana (9%), Mississippi (10%), New Mexico (9%), Oklahoma (9%), and Texas (8%) having the highest rates of non-coverage. In contrast, regional coverage in European Union countries is not as problematic, with only Portugal at 90% coverage and Belgium at 94% coverage, having more than five in 100 households without a telephone line (IPSOS-INRA, 2004).

Furthermore, currently there are no scientifically accepted ways to incorporate cell phone and Voice-Over-Internet (VoIP) telephone numbers into the traditional methods used to sample the US public via telephone (cf. Brick, Brick, Dipko, Presser, Tucker, & Yuan, 2007). In 2005, an estimated 7% of households had only cell phone coverage (Blumberg, Luke, & Cynamon, 2006; Tucker, Brick, & Meekins, 2007). Thus telephone surveys can be at a disadvantage in reaching certain segments of the general population, such as renters (12% cell phone only in 2005) and adults younger than 24 years of age (15% cell phone only in 2005). For other countries this is not the same problem, as the business model used to charge customers in other countries does not appear to hamper respondents' willingness to be interviewed on their wireless phone as it often does in the US, nor are there federal telecommunications policies that hamper many survey researchers in the US.

In addition, since the advent of 'number portability'[1] in the United States in 2004, an opinion researcher can no longer be certain 'where' (in a geographical sense) a respondent has been reached when contacted on a telephone. Depending on how quickly the public exercises their right to *port* their telephone number(s)—and in 2007 more than two million already had done so (Steeh & Piekarski, in press)—telephone surveys may suffer the burden of having to conduct explicit geographic screening of respondents to determine whether the respondent lives within the geopolitical area being surveyed (cf. Lavrakas, 2004). If this were not done, then serious errors of commission (false positives)

would result from interviewing respondents who are geographically ineligible for the opinion poll. Such geographic screening would lead to increases in nonresponse. These coverage problems do not exist for opinion researchers outside the US.

TOTAL SURVEY ERROR (TSE) PERSPECTIVE

As detailed by Groves (1989), in addition to considerations of sampling error, a careful public opinion researcher must attend to the potential effects of coverage error, nonresponse error, and measurement error. Together, all these potential sources of variance and bias constitute *total survey error* (see Fowler, 1993; Lavrakas, 1996). Thus, public opinion researchers should consider each element of TSE separately when planning, implementing, and interpreting a telephone survey.

Prudent concern about a survey's total error will lead the researcher to deploy methods to: (a) reduce the likely sources of error; and/or (b) measure the nature and size of potential errors. Ultimately, it remains the researcher's responsibility to allocate the resources available to conduct the survey so as to achieve the best-quality data possible within the finite budget. However, this often will require many difficult cost–benefit trade-offs, such as whether to use more resources to hire and train high-quality interviewers or, instead, to make additional callbacks to hard-to-reach respondents, or to deploy a 'refusal conversion' process, since a researcher never will have enough resources to address all potential sources of survey error.

Noncoverage

As it applies to telephone surveys, noncoverage is the 'gap' that often exists between the sampling frame (the list of telephone numbers from which a sample is drawn) and the larger population the survey is meant to represent. To the extent the group 'covered' by the sampling frame differs from the group missed by the sampling frame, the survey will have coverage bias. For example, all household telephone surveys, including those using random-digit dialing (RDD), use sampling frames that miss households and persons without telephones and those only with cell phone numbers. Thus, they have the potential for coverage error if researchers attribute any findings to the US general public about issues for which opinions are correlated with whether or not someone can be surveyed via a wired telephone. Worldwide, not having a telephone is related to very low income, low education, rural residency, younger ages of household heads, and minority racial status. In the US, having only wireless phone service is related to many of these same demographic factors and also to being a renter. Thus there will be some level of non-negligible coverage bias in many telephone surveys that sample only households with wired telephone service.

Another source of potential coverage error is multiple-line households. Approximately one in six households with wired lines in the United States as of 2005 had more than one line, whereas more than half of households in many European countries have multiple lines, when considering both wired lines and mobile lines. Whenever an RDD or a list-based frame of household telephone numbers is used, residences with more than one telephone number have a greater probability of being sampled than those with only one number. Thus, whenever one is conducting an opinion survey via telephone—e.g., measuring the proportion of adults who hold favorable views towards a particular candidate—one should include a question about the number of different telephone numbers in the household and then take this into account when conducting post hoc statistical weighting adjustments.

Nonresponse

Nonresponse error in a telephone survey occurs when people who are sampled but not interviewed differ as a group in some non-negligible way from those who are interviewed. Nonresponse in telephone surveys is due primarily to: (a) failure to contact sampled respondents; (b) sampled respondents who refuse to participate; and (c) sampled respondents who have language or health problems. Since the early 1990s, response rates for telephone surveys of the US and European publics have noticeably and continuously declined each year, albeit slowly (cf. de Heer, 1999; Curtin, Presser, & Singer, 2005). This is due to a combination of the public's increasing unwillingness to participate in telephone surveys because of busy life styles and the increase in telecommunications system challenges to reaching a sampled respondent within a fixed length field period, especially within the United States.

In the US, the growing tendency of respondents to refuse to participate in surveys also is related to the proliferation of telemarketing in the 1990s and the nuisance many citizens experience with such telephone calls. The implementation of the Do Not Call List (DNCL) in October 2003 appears to have largely stemmed the telemarketing nuisance call problem, but it is too soon to know for certain what long run effect this will have on response rates in legitimate telephone surveys. Some evidence to date is promising in that those listed on the DNCL are more likely to participate when subsequently sampled for a telephone survey than those who are not (Lavrakas, 2004). But other findings are troubling, in that a large minority of the US public would like to have the DNCL restrictions extended to opinion and other types of research surveys (CASRO, 2003).

One of the most effective ways to raise response rates in a telephone survey is to make an advance contact via mail with each sampled household before contacting them via telephone (cf. Camburn, Lavrakas, Battaglia, Massey, & Wright, 1995; Dillman, 2000; de Leeuw, Joop, Korendijk, Mulders, & Callegaro, 2005). The most effective type of advance mailed contact is a polite, informative, and persuasive letter that is accompanied by a token cash incentive. Lavrakas and Shuttles (2004) reported experimental findings in a very large national survey of gains in RDD response rates of 10 percentage points with as little as $2 mailed in advance. Of course this advance mail treatment requires the ability to match sampled telephone numbers with accurate mailing addresses, which is possible approximately 50%–60% of the time for many RDD samples in the US.

'Refusal Avoidance' training for interviewers (cf. Lavrakas, 1993) is a different approach to reducing the problem of refusals in telephone surveys. Groves and colleagues (e.g., Groves & McGonagle, 2001), O'Brien and colleagues (e.g., Mayer & O'Brien, 2001), Cantor and colleagues (e.g., Cantor, Allen, Schneider, Hagerty-Heller, & Yuan, 2004), and Shuttles and colleagues (e.g., Shuttles, Welch, Hoover, & Lavrakas, 2002) have led recent advances in devising strategies for this training. These researchers have deployed carefully controlled experiments to test a theory-based training curriculum that includes:

1 focus groups with top interviewers that identify the actual verbiage they hear from refusers and then map the persuasive replies these interviewers use to try to convert reluctant respondents to each reason for refusing;
2 communication discourse techniques for extending the time that reluctant respondents stay on the phone before hanging up on the interviewer, e.g., posing a conversational question back to the respondent to engage her/him in a two-way dialogue; and
3 correctly and rapidly identifying the reason(s) why the respondent is refusing and delivering the correct persuasive verbiage to counter those reason(s).

The results of these experiments have been mixed, with some studies showing upwards of a 10 percentage-point gain in cooperation by those interviewers receiving this training and other studies showing no effects whatsoever. Hoover and Shuttles (2005) reported on 'Advanced Response Techniques' (ART) that can be used by telephone interviewers that

focus on the critical importance the first six to eight seconds of contact with respondents in RDD surveys to avoid immediate hang-ups. These techniques include the importance of the interviewer knowing in advance where the household is located geographically, and then using this information to conversationally build a quick rapport with the adult who answers the telephone. They also involve the use of introductory scripts that are based on 'progressive engagement,' in which the opening wording creates an interpersonal expectation of the respondent to speak back to the interviewer (cf. Burks, Lavrakas, Camayd, & Bennett, 2007).

In terms of reducing nonresponse associated with noncontacts in telephone surveys, the basic technique is to make many callbacks, scheduled at various times of the day and various days of the week over as long a field period as possible. That is, the more callbacks made and the longer the field period, the higher the contact rate in RDD surveys, all other factors being equal. This is problematical for many opinion surveys, especially those conducted by the media for news purposes, because newsworthiness often exists only for a brief moment in time. In these instances, the only choices a researcher faces is to exercise care in considering the effect of noncontact-related nonresponse and to weight the data by gathering information in the survey about the propensity of the respondent to be at home over a longer field period (e.g., the past week), with those least likely to be reachable over the longer field period being assigned weights greater than 1.0 and those most likely to be at home being assigned weights less than 1.0.

In considering how to handle callbacks during any finite field period, not all RDD telephone numbers merit equal calling effort, since many of them are non-working or otherwise non-residential and yet are not reliably detected as such by autodialers or live-interviewers. In the US, this is due in part to the inconsistent manner in which local telephone companies handle such non-residential numbers. Using data from several extremely large national RDD surveys, Stec, Lavrakas, and Shuttles (2005) reported that telephone numbers in the US that have a repeated Busy-Signal outcome (> 5) or a repeated Ring-No-Answer outcome (> 10) are very unlikely to ever produce an interview, even with as many as 30 call attempts. On the other hand, when encountering a residential answering machine, persistence often appears to pay off, regardless of how many times such an outcome results (Piazza, 1993). Leaving messages on answering machines is generally thought to be a good practice to increase subsequent contact rates, but the literature is inconclusive on the issues of what should be said in the message and when, and how often, such messages should be left (cf. Shuttles & Lavrakas, 2005). Leaving too many messages is assumed to be more harmful than helpful in eventually gaining cooperation from a household, but exactly how many is 'too many' remains uncertain.

With the growth of the Caller ID technology in the United States, it is becoming harder to get people to pick up their telephone when they receive a call from an unknown source. Tuckel and O'Neill (2002) and the Pew Research Center (2004) reported that more than half of US households have Caller ID capability. Leverage-Salience theory (Groves, Singer, & Corning, 2000) would suggest that depending on what is displayed on Caller ID at the household-level, the response propensity to answer the incoming call will be affected either positively or negatively. Trussell and Lavrakas (2005) reported the results of two very large national experiments with RDD samples in which displaying the name 'Nielsen Ratings' (a generally well-known and positively valued brand in the US) raised telephone survey response rates by more than two percentage points, although these gains were not due solely to increasing the contact rate. But other results in these experiments suggested that caution should be exercised in displaying something on Caller ID too many times if a telephone survey is using a large number of callbacks (e.g., > 10). Callegaro, McCutcheon, and Ludwig (2006) found mixed results with Caller ID. Depending on the target population,

sometimes the use of a Caller ID display lowered the response rate. On the other hand, with an RDD of the general population, Caller ID increased the response rate by three percentage points.

Measurement

Not all data that interviewers record during an interview are accurate measures of the attitudes, behaviors, and demographics of interest. These inaccuracies, in the forms of both bias and variance, may be due to errors associated with: (a) the questionnaire, and/or (b) the interviewers, and/or (c) the respondents (see Biemer, Groves, Lyberg, Mathiowetz, & Sudman, 1991). In thinking about these potential sources of measurement error, the prudent opinion researcher will consider ways by which the nature and size of such errors might be measured, so that the researcher can consider post hoc adjustments to the 'raw data' gathered from respondents by interviewers. The best way to base such adjustments on sound empirical evidence is to build experiments into the telephone questionnaire. This is especially important whenever a researcher is using questions that have not been used in previous surveys, and thus their wording is not validated by solid experience. In this case, a researcher should use an experimental design to test different wordings, even if only a small part of the sample is exposed to alternative wordings. Researchers should remain flexible in thinking about how many versions of the question wording should be tested and whether there is any valid statistical need to assign equal-sized subsamples of respondents to each version randomly.

STEPS AND CONSIDERATIONS IN CONDUCTING A TELEPHONE SURVEY

Anyone planning a telephone survey should develop a detailed administrative plan that lays out all the tasks that must be accomplished and identifies the personnel to be involved in each task (see Lyberg, 1988;

Frey, 1989; Hansen, in press; Kelly, Link, Petty, Hobson, & Stork, in press; Steve, Burks, Lavrakas, Hoover, & Brown, in press; Tarnai & Moore, in press). The following are the steps an opinion researcher typically needs to perform in order to conduct a high-quality telephone survey:

1 Decide upon a sampling design, including identification of the sampling frame from which sampled units will be selected, and the method of respondent selection within a sampling unit if the sampling unit is not also the sampling element. In many telephone surveys, it will be best to use some variation of RDD sampling and some variation of the 'last birthday' within-unit respondent selection method (cf. Lavrakas, 1993; Lavrakas, Harpuder, & Stasny, 2000; Gaziano, 2005).

2 Choose a method to generate or select the set of telephone numbers that will be used in sampling (hereafter called the *sampling pool;* cf. Lavrakas, 1993) from the sampling frame (see subsequent section below). Create the sampling pool and divide it randomly into replicates to help control the allocation of the numbers that will be dialed during the field period.

3 Decide upon the length, in days, of the field period, and the calling rules that will be used to reach a 'proper' final disposition for all telephone numbers in the sampling pool that are dialed within the field period. Also, decide at what hours of each day and on which days of the week calling will occur. For the calling rules, decide upon the maximum number of call attempts per telephone number, how much time should be allowed to elapse before re-calling a busy number, and whether or not refusal conversions will be tried. In terms of refusal conversions, decide how much time should elapse before redialing the number, while recognizing that 'best practice' is to allow as many days as possible to pass, within the finite constraints of the field period, before redialing the refusing number.

4 Produce a call-record for each telephone number that will be used to track and control its call history during the field period. Most CATI systems used to control the processing of a sample have such a feature built in. The information in these call-records—sometimes referred to as 'paradata'—is very important for interviewers to review before making each callback. This helps prepare the interviewer for the recontact.

The more detailed the information recorded by the previous interviewers who contacted the household, the more prepared an interviewer will be for any subsequent contacts.

5 As the sampling design is being selected, develop and format a draft questionnaire, keeping in mind how long the questionnaire can be, given the available resources and the purposes and needs of the survey project.

6 Develop a draft introduction and respondent selection sequence, and draft 'fallback statements' (persuaders) for use by interviewers to tailor their introduction and help gain cooperation from sampled respondents.

7 Decide whether advance contact will be made with sampled respondents, such as an advance letter, and if so, whether an incentive will be included.

8 Pilot test and revise survey procedures and instruments.

9 Program the script (introduction, respondent selection method, and questionnaire) into CATI.

10 Hire interviewers and supervisors, and schedule interviewer training and the data collection sessions. When doing a survey in more than one language, it is best, from a data accuracy standpoint and response rate standpoint, to have individual interviewers interview in only one language. It is best to utilize native speakers of a language rather than using bilingual speakers whose primary language is not the one in which they will interview exclusively. The value of this approach is that native speakers also will share cultural similarities with those respondents who speak that language, and thus will be able to gain cooperation more readily and probe unclear answers more effectively.

11 Train interviewers and supervisors. When doing a survey in more than one language, each group of interviewers should have supervisory personnel whose primary language matches the language their group will use to conduct interviews.

12 Conduct fully supervised interviews. Decide what portion, if any, of the interviewing will be monitored (cf. Steve *et al.,* in press) and whether any respondents will be called back to validate the completed interviews (cf. Lavrakas, 1993).

13 Edit/code completed questionnaires. If coding open-end verbatims, devise coding categories, train coders, and monitor their reliability.

14 Assign weights (if any) to correct for unequal probability of selection (e.g., for multiple telephone line households, the number of adults in a household, the proportion of time in the past year the household did not have telephone service) and for deviations in sample demographic statistics (e.g., gender, age, race, education, etc.) from known population parameters. In the latter case, adjustments for education are likely to be the most important to make, because opinion surveys almost always oversample those with high educational attainment and undersample those with low educational attainment, and opinions on many issues are often highly correlated with educational attainment.
15 Perform data analyses and report preparation.

An additional design consideration in any telephone survey should be an explicit decision about whether experiments will be built into the study. When planning their opinion surveys, far too few researchers take advantage of the power of true experiments to address causal relationships in the data being gathered—which often can be done at essentially no additional cost. The common ways that experiments can be used in telephone surveys is to test: (a) various question wording or ordering sequences, (b) different introductory scripts and/or respondent selection methods, and (c) incentives and other treatments to raise response propensities.

SAMPLING FRAMES IN TELEPHONE SURVEYS

Prior to choosing a sampling frame, the researcher must choose between the use of a probability sample and the use of a nonprobability sample. As Henry (1990, p. 32) notes, the great advantage of probability samples is that 'the bias and likely error stemming from [their use] can be rigorously examined and estimated; [but this is not the case] for nonprobability samples.' As such, only probability samples permit the portion of total survey error that is due to sampling variance to be rigorously quantified, as only a probability sample provides every element in

the sampling frame a known nonzero chance of selection.

Once these decisions are made, the researcher must make a number of other sampling design decisions. These include explicit identification of the following:

1 *The population of inference* (i.e., the group, setting, and time to which the findings can generalize). For many public opinion surveys, this will be the entire adult population within a specific geopolitical area. For example, in the US this might be the entire nation; the 48 contiguous states; some region of the nation (e.g., the South); a state or several states; a large metropolitan area, a county or a combination of counties; a city, town, or even a neighborhood area.
   Another key consideration in choosing the population of inference is the implications such a decision has on the language(s) in which the survey will be conducted. If, for example, a researcher purports to be measuring all adults in an area populated with many Latino residents, then the researcher must include Spanish-language interviewing, as the opinions of Spanish-Dominant Hispanics are likely to be quite different from the opinions of English-Dominant Hispanics.
2 *The target population* (i.e., the finite population that is purportedly surveyed).
3 *The sampling frame*, often in list form, that will operationalize the target population.

In the United States, in most instances in which the general public within a geopolitical area is being surveyed, this means a Random-Digit Dialing (RDD) frame. On the other hand, when sampling the opinions of elites via a telephone survey, RDD is almost never the preferred frame because it is inefficient in reaching elites; instead, a list frame (e.g., members of a professional organization) needs to be acquired or built that covers the target population of elites well. In contrast, in many European countries, RDD sampling is not always necessary to reach a representative sample of the public, as unlike in the US, nearly all residences in Europe have listed telephone numbers (cf. Nicolaas & Lynn, 2002; Kuusela, 2003; Taylor, 2003). In these instances, a directory may exist that can be used as the sampling frame.

When the RDD frame was first pursued, the Mitofsky–Waksberg approach became the standard methodology, but this proved to be difficult to implement accurately and was rather inefficient. Subsequently, many approaches to list-assisted RDD sampling were devised that were more easily administered and much more efficient in reaching sampled respondents (cf. Lavrakas, 1987; Tucker, Casady, & Lepkowski, 1992; Brick, Waksberg, Kulp, & Starer, 1995; Gabler & Häder, 2001; Tucker, Lepkowski, & Piekarski, 2002). Nowadays, there are several reputable commercial organizations (Marketing Systems Group, Survey Sampling Inc., etc.) that supply accurate, efficient and reasonably priced list-assisted sampling pools for opinion researchers to survey the public in just about any geographical area in the US and in many other countries as well. Thus, it is unusual for an opinion researcher to engage in the manual approach to generate an RDD sampling pool for the target population (cf. Lavrakas, 1987, 1993). For those conducting cross-national opinion surveys, the work of Kish (1994) and Gabler and Häder (2001) is recommended for guidance in building sampling frames and probability sampling designs that best represent the respective target population in each country.

When surveying the general US public for their opinions, it is very important to make an explicit decision about whether or not known cell phone telephone exchanges will be included in the sampling frame. This is an extremely thorny issue for which Best Practices have not as yet been identified by the survey industry, but issues that must be balanced are:

1   the extent to which those who can be reached only by cell phone hold different opinions from those who can be reached via a traditional landline (cf. Callegaro & Poggio, 2004; Vehovar, Belak, Batagelj, & Cikic, 2004; Keeter, 2006);
2   how wireless phone and wired phone exchanges will be mixed in the sampling pool and how respondents reached via a wired line vs. those

reached via a wireless phone respectively will be weighted at the analysis stage;
3   how long a questionnaire is reasonable to use with someone reached on their cell phone; and
4   how respondents reached on a cell phone will be incented, have their safety protected, and how the accuracy of the responses they provide will be maximized (cf. Lavrakas & Shuttles, 2005; Nielsen, 2005);
5   the size of the final sample with whom interviews must be completed (see Kish, 1965; Groves, 1989, pp. 81ff.; Henry, 1990; Lavrakas, 1993).

A general rule is that the shorter the field period for a telephone survey, the larger the sampling pool of telephone numbers needs to be. Shorter field periods lead to lower response rates, all other things being equal. Thus, for example, opinion surveys that strive to complete 1,000 interviews over a Friday–Sunday weekend will need a much larger sampling pool than surveys striving to complete the same number of interviews during a field period of a week or two or longer.

RESPONSE RATES

A traditional indicator of a telephone survey's likely quality has been its response rate(s): Of all the telephone numbers dialed and households/persons sampled, at how many was a completed interview actually achieved? Currently, most survey professionals agree that response rates are best considered as a range rather than a single value, as there are many different ways that response rates can be calculated. Readers who need a detailed explanation of telephone survey response rates in the US should refer to AAPOR's (2006) guidelines, also adopted by WAPOR (for discussion of response rates in the United Kingdom see Lynn, Beerten, Laiho, & Martin, 2001).

In general, telephone survey response rates are affected by the survey topic, reputation of the organization sponsoring and/or conducting the survey, length of the questionnaire, caliber of the interviewing staff conducting the survey, length of the field period, rules for callbacks and refusal conversions, use of noncontingent and contingent incentives, and other factors. Furthermore, Groves (1989, p. 133) correctly warns that survey response rates, in themselves, are not a direct measure of nonresponse error, the latter being a function of: (a) the size of the nonresponse, and (b) whatever differences may exist on the survey variables between those who responded and those who did not. Response rates have not been shown to be consistently related to the presence of nonresponse bias, but that issue is far from settled (cf. Groves, 2006), and opinion researchers must consider carefully the response rates to their surveys and the likelihood of nonresponse error when interpreting results.

CONCLUSION: SURVEY QUALITY AND BASIC COST CONSIDERATIONS

Every telephone survey has a finite budget, and the key challenge the researcher faces is to get the most accurate data from these finite resources. This is best done by explicitly considering all sources of survey error and making careful *a priori* trade-off decisions about how best to allocate fixed resources. As Groves (1989) explains, efforts to reduce and/or measure the potential effects of the various types of survey error have real cost implications. Researchers should attend to the basic distinction between approaches intended to *reduce* potential errors and approaches intended to *measure* potential errors. That is, whereas it may be too expensive for an opinion researcher to implement procedures that may eliminate (or substantially reduce) a potential source of error, the researcher may be able to implement procedures to measure its approximate size, and thus take it into account when interpreting the survey's findings.

For novice opinion researchers, these considerations can seem forbidding or even overwhelming. When faced with all the potential threats to a survey's validity, some may question the value of the entire survey enterprise. However, this fails to acknowledge that highly accurate opinion surveys are routinely conducted by experienced pollsters and other researchers who exercise the necessary care. This chapter is meant to serve as an introduction to many of these considerations as they apply to telephone opinion surveys. And this discussion is meant to alert readers to the many challenges an opinion researcher faces in conducting a telephone survey that will be 'accurate enough' for the purposes for which it is meant. The message should be clear: planning, implementing, and interpreting a telephone survey that is likely to be accurate is a methodical, time-consuming process, but one well worth the effort.

NOTES

1 *Number portability* refers to an option that went into effect in November 2004 in the US allowing people to transfer (port) their 10-digit telephone number to another geographic area when they moved, and/or allowing them to keep the same number when they changed their telephone service from a landline to a cell phone or vice versa.

REFERENCES

AAPOR (American Association for Public Opinion Research). (2006). *Standard definitions. Final dispositions of case codes and outcome rates for surveys* (4th ed.). Lenexa, Kansas: AAPOR. Retrieved August 20, 2006, from http://www.aapor.org/pdfs/standarddefs_4.pdf.

Biemer, P. N., Groves, R. M., Lyberg, L. E., Mathiowetz, N. A., & Sudman, S. (Eds.). (1991). *Measurement errors in surveys.* New York: John Wiley.

Blumberg, S., Luke, J., & Cynamon, M. (2006). Telephone coverage and health survey estimates: Evaluating the need for concern about wireless substitution. *American Journal of Public Health, 96*, 926–931.

Brick, J. M., Brick, P. D., Dipko, S., Presser, S., Tucker, C., & Yuan, A. (2007). Cell phone survey feasibility in the U.S.: Sampling and calling cell numbers versus landline numbers. *Public Opinion Quarterly, 71*, 23–39.

Brick, J. M., Waksberg, J., Kulp, D., & Starer, A. (1995). Bias in list-assisted telephone samples. *Public Opinion Quarterly, 59*, 218–235.

Burks, A. T., Lavrakas, P. J., Camayd, E., & Bennett, M. A. (2007). *The use of progressive involvement techniques in a telephone survey introduction.* Presented at the annual conference of the American Association for Public Opinion Research, Anahiem, CA.

Cantor, D., Allen, B., Schneider, S. J., Hagerty-Heller, T., & Yuan, A. (2004). *Testing an automated refusal avoidance training methodology.* Paper presented at the annual meeting of the American Association for Public Opinion Research, Phoenix, AZ.

Callegaro, M., & Poggio, T. (2004). Espansione della telefonia mobile ed errore di copertura nelle inchieste telefoniche [Mobile telephone growth and coverage error in telephone surveys]. *Polis, 18*, 477–506. English version retrieved August, 20, 2006, from http://eprints.biblio.unitn.it/archive/00000680.

Callegaro, M., McCutcheon, A., & Ludwig, J. (2006, January). *Who's calling? The impact of caller-ID on telephone survey response.* Paper presented at the second International Conference on Telephone Survey Methodology, Miami, FL.

Camburn, D., Lavrakas, P. J., Battaglia, M. P., Massey, J. T., & Wright, R. A. (1995). Using advance respondent letters in random-digit-dialing telephone surveys. *American Statistical Association 1995 Proceedings: Section on Survey Research Methods, 1996*, 969–974.

CASRO (Council of American Survey Research Organizations) (2003). *28th Annual CASRO Conference*, Las Vegas.

Curtin, R., Presser, S., & Singer, E. (2005). Changes in telephone survey nonresponse over the past quarter century. *Public Opinion Quarterly, 69*, 87–98.

de Heer, W. (1999). International response trends: Results of an international survey, *Journal of Official Statistics, 15*, 129–142.

de Leeuw, E. D., & van der Zouwen, J. (1988). Data quality in telephone and face to face surveys: A comparative meta-analysis. In R. M. Groves, P. N. Biemer, L. E. Lyberg, J. T. Massey, W. L. Nicholls, & J. Waksberg (Eds.), *Telephone survey methodology* (pp. 283–300). New York: John Wiley.

de Leeuw, E., Joop, H., Korendijk, E., Mulders, G.-L., & Callegaro, M. (2005). The influence of advance letters on response in telephone surveys: A meta-analysis. In C. van Dijkum, J. Blasius & C. Durand (Eds.), *Recent developments and applications in social research methodology. Proceedings of the RC 33 Sixth International Conference on Social Science Methodology, Amsterdam 2004 [CD-ROM].* Leverkusen-Opladen, Germany: Barbara Budrich.

Dillman, D. A. (2000). *Mail and internet surveys: The tailored design method* (2d ed.). New York: Wiley.

Fowler, F. J., Jr. (1993). *Survey research methods* (2nd ed.). Newbury Park, CA: Sage.

Frey, J. H. (1989). *Survey research by telephone* (2nd ed.). Newbury Park, CA: Sage.

Gabler, S. and Häder, S. (2001). Idiosyncrasies in telephone sampling—the case of Germany. *International Journal of Public Opinion Research, 14*, 339–345.

Gaziano, C. (2005). Comparative analysis of within-household respondent selection techniques. *Public Opinion Quarterly, 69*, 124–157.

Groves, R. M. (1989). *Survey errors and survey costs.* New York: John Wiley.

Groves, R. M. (2006). *Nonresponse rates and non-response bias in household surveys. Public Opinion Quarterly, 70*, 646–675.

Groves, R. M., & McGonagle, K. A. (2001). A theory-guided interviewer training protocol regarding survey participation. *Journal of Official Statistics, 17*, 249–265.

Groves, R. M., Singer, E., & Corning, A. (2000). Leverage-saliency theory of survey participation: Description and an illustration. *Public Opinion Quarterly, 64*, 299–308.

Hansen, S. E. (in press). Cati sample management systems. In J. Lepkowski, C. Tucker, M. Brick, E. de Leeuw, L. Japec, P. Lavrakas *et al.* (Eds.), *Telephone surveys: Innovations and methodologies.* New York: Wiley.

Henry, G. T. (1990). *Practical sampling.* Newbury Park, CA: Sage.

Hoover, J. B., & Shuttles, C. D. (2005). *The evolution and expansion of advanced response techniques (ART) training.* Presented at the Council for Marketing and Opinion Research's Improving Respondent Cooperation Workshop, Washington DC.

ISPSOS-INRA (2004). *EU Telecomm Service Indicators.* Retrieved August 20, 2006 from http://europa.eu.int/information_society/policy/ecomm/doc/info_centre/studies_ext_consult/inra_year2004/report_telecom_2004_final_reduced.pdf.

Keeter, S. (2006). The impact of cell phone non-coverage bias on polling in the 2004 presidential election. *Public Opinion Quarterly, 70*, 88–98.

Kelly, J., Link, M., Petty, J., Hobson, K., & Stork, P. (in press). Establishing a new survey research call center. In J. Lepkowski, C. Tucker, M. Brick, E. De Leeuw, L. Japec, P. J. Lavrakas *et al.* (Eds.), *Advances in telephone survey methodology.* New York: John Wiley & Sons.

Kish, L. (1965). *Survey sampling.* New York: John Wiley.

Kish, L. (1994). Multi-population survey designs: Five types with seven shared aspects. *International Statistical Review, 62*, 167–186.

Kuusela, V. (2003). Mobile phones and telephone survey methods. In R. Banks, J. Currall, J. Francis, L. Gerrard, R. Kahn, T. Macer *et al.* (Eds.), *ASC 2003—The impact of new technology on the survey process. Proceedings of the 4th ASC international conference* (pp. 317–327). Chesham Bucks, UK: Association for Survey Computing (ASC).

Lavrakas, P. J. (1987). *Telephone survey methods: Sampling, selection, and supervision.* Newbury Park, CA: Sage.

Lavrakas, P. J. (1993). *Telephone survey methods: Sampling, selection, and supervision* (2nd ed.). Newbury Park, CA: Sage.

Lavrakas, P. J. (1996). To err is human. *Marketing Research, 8*(1), 30–36.

Lavrakas, P. J. (2004). *Will a perfect storm of cellular forces sink RDD sampling?* Paper presented at the Annual Conference of the American Association for Public Opinion Conference, Phoenix.

Lavrakas, P. J., & Shuttles, C. (2004). *Two advance letter experiments to raise survey responses rates in a two-stage mixed mode survey.* Paper presented at the 2004 Joint Statistical Meetings, Toronto.

Lavrakas, P. J., & Shuttles, C. W. (2005). Cell phone sampling, rdd surveys, and marketing research implications. *Alert!, 43*(6), 4–5.

Lavrakas, P. J., Harpuder, B., & Stasny, E. A. (2000). *A further investigation of the last-birthday respondent selection method.* Paper presented to the annual conference of the American Association for Public Opinion Research, Portland OR.

Lyberg, L. E. (1988). The administration of telephone surveys. In R. M. Groves, P. N. Biemer, L. E. Lyberg, J. T. Massey, W. L. Nicholls, & J. Waksberg (Eds.), *Telephone survey methodology* (pp. 453–456). New York: John Wiley.

Lynn, P., Beerten, R., Laiho, J., and Martin, J. (2001). *Recommended standard final outcome categories and standard definitions of response rate for social surveys* (Working paper No. 2001–23). Colchester: University of Essex, Institute for Social and Economic Research.

Mayer, T. S., & O'Brien, E. (2001). *Interviewer refusal aversion training to increase survey participation.* Paper presented at the 2001 Joint Statistical Meetings, Atlanta.

Nicolaas, G., & Lynn, P. (2002). Random-digit dialing in the UK: Viability revisited. *Journal of the Royal Statistical Society: Series A, 165*, 297–316.

Nielsen (2005). *Cell phone sampling summit II.* Retrieved August 20, 2006, from http://www.nielsenmedia.com/cellphonesummit/cellphone.html.

Pew Research Center (2004). *Polls face growing resistance, but still representative.* News release. Retrieved February 5, 2007, from http://www.people-press.org.

Piazza, T. (1993). Meeting the challenge of answering machines. *Public Opinion Quarterly, 57*, 219–231.

Shuttles, C., & Lavrakas, P. J. (2005). *An experimental test of answering machine message content to improve response rates.* Paper presented to the annual conference of the American Association for Public Opinion Research, Miami Beach, FL.

Shuttles, C., Welch, J., Hoover, B. & Lavrakas, P. J. (2002). *The development and experimental testing of an innovative approach to training telephone interviewers to avoid refusals.* Paper presented at the annual conference of the American Association for Public Opinion Conference, St. Petersburg.

Stec, J., Lavrakas, P. J., & Shuttles, C. (2005). *Gaining efficiencies in scheduling callbacks in large RDD national surveys.* Paper presented to the annual conference of the American Association for Public Opinion, Miami Beach, FL.

Steeh, C., & Piekarski, L. (in press). Accommodating new technologies: Mobile and VoIP communication. In J. Lepkowski, C. Tucker, M. Brick, E. de Leeuw, L. Japec, P. Lavrakas *et al.* (Eds.), *Telephone surveys: Innovations and methodologies.* New York: Wiley.

Steve, K., Burks, A. T., Lavrakas, P. J., Hoover, B., & Brown, K. (in press). The development of a comprehensive behavioral-based system to monitor telephone interviewer performance. In J. Lepkowski, C. Tucker, M. Brick, E. de Leeuw, L. Japec, P. Lavrakas *et al.* (Eds.), *Telephone surveys: Innovations and methodologies.* New York: Wiley.

Tarnai, J., & Moore, D. (in press). Measuring and improving telephone interviewer performance and productivity. In J. Lepkowski, C. Tucker, M. Brick, E. de Leeuw, L. Japec, P. Lavrakas *et al.* (Eds.), *Telephone surveys: Innovations and methodologies.* New York: Wiley.

Taylor, S. (2003). Telephone surveying for household social surveys: The good, the bad, and the ugly. *Social Survey Methodology Bulletin, 52*, 10–21.

Trussell, N., & Lavrakas, P. J. (2005). *Testing the impact of caller ID technology on response rates in a mixed mode survey.* Paper presented at the annual conference of the American Association for Public Opinion Research, Miami Beach, FL.

Tuckel, P., & O'Neill, H. (2002). The vanishing respondent in telephone surveys. *Journal of Advertising Research, 42*, 26–48.

Tucker, C., Casady, R. J., & Lepkowski, J. (1992). Sample allocation for stratified sample designs. *1992 Proceedings of the Survey Research Methods Section, American Statistical Association*, 291–296.

Tucker, C., Lepkowski, J., & Piekarski, L. (2002). The current efficiency of list-assisted telephone sampling designs. *Public Opinion Quarterly, 66*, 321–338.

Tucker, C., Brick, J. M., & Meekins, B. (2007). Household telephone service and usage patterns in the United States in 2004: Implications for telephone samples. *Public Opinion Quarterly, 71*, 1–20.

Vehovar, V., Belak, E., Batagelj, Z., & Cikic, S. (2004). Mobile phone surveys: The Slovenian case study. *Metodološki zvezki, 1*(1), 1–19.

24

Self-Administered
Paper Questionnaires

Don A. Dillman and Nicholas L. Parsons

INTRODUCTION

The mail survey may be the oldest of systematic survey methods. The earliest known such survey was conducted in 1577 by King Phillip II of Spain, who posed 38 written questions sent by official courier to leaders of his New World colonies (Erdos, 1970). Despite modern innovations in survey research methodology, including telephone and web data collection, the practice of asking people to write their answers to questions and either hand them to the surveyor or return them by mail remains a viable and much used data collection procedure to measure opinions.

An example of the current effectiveness of mail data collection methods is a general public survey of community satisfaction and involvement administered in 2005 to residents of a small urban region in the Western United States. A 12-page, 39-question survey mailed to households randomly selected from telephone listings elicited a response rate of 69%. Since many questions had sub-parts

to them, the maximum number of queries respondents could have answered was 156 (Stern & Dillman, 2005). This response rate, obtained by three contacts and a $2 token incentive sent with the first mailing, was much higher than could have been obtained by telephone, and more representative of the general public than if the survey had been limited to households with Internet access.

Although the mail survey faces numerous coverage problems as described in this chapter, it remains an effective data collection method for many populations and survey situations. In fact, its use for some types of surveys is increasing as surveyors attempt to compensate for the poor coverage of web surveys and declining response rates to telephone interviews. If implemented properly, mail data collection, and the related procedure of group administration of paper surveys, can be effective for assessing public opinion (Dillman, 2000). In this chapter, we discuss the general strengths and limitations of mail and group administered surveys, as well as the selection and design of implementation procedures that will improve the quantity and quality of results.

ADVANTAGES

Many of the advantages of self-administered questionnaires derive from the absence of an interviewer. Presumably because of their higher degree of perceived anonymity, private modes of survey administration have generally been found to elicit more accurate measures of respondent opinions and behaviors than interview modes (O'Reilly, Hubbard, Lessler, Biemer, & Turner, 1994). For example, research has found respondents to mail surveys exhibit less of a tendency than in telephone or face-to-face interviews to provide socially desirable answers, i.e., responses that make them appear more favorable in the eyes of interviewers and the more general culture (e.g., DeLeeuw, 1992). A second advantage of self-administered questionnaires is that respondents are able to complete them at their own pace. Although this option does not guarantee respondents will always take enough time to carefully read and formulate a response for each question, the self-administered mode contrasts significantly with interview surveys, which sometimes encourage less thoughtful, 'top-of-the-head' answers (Hippler & Schwarz, 1987). Another potential advantage of self-administered questionnaires is that fully labeled five or seven point answer scales can easily be provided for attitudinal questions. This contrasts with telephone surveys, where interviewers often offer polar-point labeled scales to reduce the communication effort required to convey information to respondents (Dillman & Christian, 2005).

A final advantage of self-administered paper questionnaires is that individuals and organizations with word processing equipment can construct and implement their own surveys, rather than having to depend on professional survey organizations, as is usually required for telephone, face-to-face and web surveys.

DISADVANTAGES

The absence of an interviewer that affords so many advantages of the self-administered paper questionnaire also explains some of its disadvantages. Since an interviewer is not present, instructions and question meanings cannot be clarified. Also, the researcher is unable to ensure that the respondent reads and completes each question. A related disadvantage of self-administered questionnaires is that it is difficult to motivate respondents to provide quality answers to open-ended questions that are as complete as answers obtained from interview surveys. A third disadvantage of self-administered questionnaires is the use of branching questions. Methodologists are sometimes reluctant to include many branching instructions on paper questionnaires, because they often lead to confusion and item nonresponse and add to questionnaire length (Redline, Dillman, Dajani, & Scaggs, 2003; Dillman & Christian, 2005). A final difficulty in self-administered questionnaires due to interviewer absence is the respondent's literacy level. Persons with limited literacy will have a difficult time reading and responding to the questionnaire. Also, potential respondents vary in the degree to which they possess 'forms literacy,' the ability to comprehend form structures, goals, and semantics (Lessler & Holt, 1987).

The financial costs of constructing and implementing a paper questionnaire used to be one of its largest advantages. While it is still much cheaper to administer than face-to-face interviews, particularly across large, heterogeneous populations, the cost for conducting mail surveys now approaches, and may exceed, that for telephone surveys and is significantly higher than expenditures for web survey implementation. However, it is important to note that costs associated with any mode of survey implementation partly depend on the surveyor's access to research facilities. Also, it takes much longer to conduct a mail survey than is generally required for either telephone or web surveys. A related disadvantage is the extra time required to code and compile responses to completed questionnaires. In telephone interviewing and web surveys, much of this process is carried out immediately by the telephone interviewer or web respondent. Optical mark recognition (OMR) technology makes the data compilation process for self-administered questionnaires much more efficient. However, forms utilizing OMR may yield lower response rates, particularly when they resemble standardized test forms and appear too formal and impersonal (Dillman, 2000, p. 416).

COVERAGE ERROR CONCERNS AND THE INCREASED USE OF MIXED-MODE SURVEYS

Perhaps the most significant concern facing the mail survey researcher is obtaining a random sample of respondents from the population of interest. In the United States, there is no comprehensive database of names and addresses for sampling the general public. Thus, self-administered questionnaires are difficult to administer to large, heterogeneous populations without accruing some degree of systematic coverage error. Researchers in countries where complete lists of residences and their occupants are available are less likely to encounter this coverage problem.

Coverage error, at the sampling stage, can be avoided for special groups of individuals for whom a complete sampling frame exists. For example, Visser, Krosnick, Marquette, and Curtin (1996) report that the *Columbus Dispatch* political survey consistently outperformed telephone surveys in predicting the winners of Ohio elections since 1980, precisely because the poll utilizes a list of Ohio voters for its sampling frame, which affords minimal coverage bias. Although the 2005 *Dispatch* survey failed to accurately predict election outcomes for that year, it has been speculated that contextual factors (e.g., timing) and measurement error (e.g., offering an 'undecided' option),

not coverage error, were to blame (see Blumenthal, 2005). Comprehensive lists of people from which systematic random samples may be drawn also include university faculty, members of professional organizations, licensed drivers, magazine subscribers, and others.

One of the difficult coverage issues now facing many mail survey researchers is the deterioration of postal address lists. This situation sometimes results when members of a survey population are allowed to choose what contact information they wish to make publicly available. A recent survey we conducted of Washington State University undergraduates serves to illustrate this problem. Several years ago, it was possible to obtain a nearly complete sampling frame with enrolled students' postal addresses and telephone numbers, since a University employee was actively responsible for keeping this information up-to-date. Thus, it was possible for us to survey almost every student through either mail or telephone. However, now it is the students' responsibility to keep their contact information current. This presents a coverage problem for University researchers, as many students do not update their addresses as they change. Additionally, students who choose to update their contact information are allowed to leave important data fields blank (e.g., phone numbers, e-mail addresses).

At the start of a recent survey, we learned that e-mail addresses were available to us for 64% of students (although every student is given a University e-mail address when they enroll). Eighty percent of students provided telephone numbers, but many of these were for their prior residences. Although all students provided postal addresses, 24% were for locations outside of commuting distance to the university. Instead of relying on either mail or telephone for contacting a representative sample of undergraduates, a more sensible alternative that helped us reduce coverage error was to devise a mixed-mode approach.

Our dependence upon mail survey methods exists in a paradoxical environment. While the mail mode faces coverage problems that render it less adequate as a stand-alone survey mode, its increased use is simultaneously being encouraged as a means of overcoming the coverage and nonresponse problems that now plague other survey modes (DeLeeuw, 2005). Research has demonstrated that attempting to survey people by one mode and then switching to an alternative mode can significantly improve response rates. In one study, three contacts by mail produced a response rate of 75%, which increased to 83% when nonrespondents were followed-up by telephone. In the same study, 44% of those first contacted by telephone were interviewed. This response rate increased to 80% using a mail follow-up strategy (Dillman *et al.*, 2001). Shettle and Mooney (1996) describe a survey of US college graduates in which mail, telephone and face-to-face interviews were used successively. The response rate for mailed questionnaires was 63%, increased to 74% when telephone interviews were added, and reached 86% when nonrespondents were followed-up with a face-to-face interview. While these examples show that mixing modes leads to the completion of more questionnaires, simply giving people a choice of which mode to respond to does not appear to improve response rates (Dillman, Clark, & West, 1994).

The advent of the Information Age has introduced telephone and web procedures as alternatives to mail, and it has also led to technological advancements favorable to the use of mail in a mixed-mode context. For example, it is now possible to move text document files easily from one piece of software to another. Also, the cost of mixing modes for a single survey is far less and much faster to accomplish than in the past. Thus, it is not surprising that use of mixed-mode surveys with a mail component is occurring throughout the world. However, the increased use of multiple survey modes presents another set of methodological considerations, one of which concerns measurement variations across different modes of communication.

THE MEASUREMENT CHALLENGE

The challenge of measuring people's opinions in mail surveys is formidable. First and foremost, one must communicate in writing rather than through verbal dialogue. This fundamental difference in implementation between self-administered questionnaires and interview surveys leads researchers to construct questions in different formats. For example, in interviews, researchers often choose to eliminate response options from the query, whereas researchers conducting mail surveys may list them in the questionnaire as separate categories to be checked. This is one of many typical changes made when converting from interview to paper surveys (Dillman & Christian, 2005). In addition, since an interviewer is not present and able to respond to any questions the respondent might have, additional written instructions are usually provided to clarify the researcher's intent. Should the researcher decide to limit written instructions in self-administered questionnaires, respondents may interpret questions differently than interview respondents, resulting in measurement variability across modes.

Public opinion questions seem particularly prone to certain mode effects, in part because respondents may not have formulated precise opinions, in the same way they hold knowledge of education achieved, the name of the city in which they live, or their age (Dillman & Christian, 2005). Most opinion questions ask for psychological states using vague quantifiers (e.g., somewhat, mostly, or completely satisfied) that lack the precise separations associated with age and educational achievement categories. Researchers should also think critically about what to do with 'hidden' answer categories, (e.g., neutral, don't know, no opinion) when considering mixing modes. These categories are termed 'hidden' because in face-to-face interviews and telephone surveys, researchers often omit them in an effort to encourage respondents to choose substantive answers. If non-substantive response options are provided in self-administered questionnaires, but not made available to respondents in interview surveys, measurement differences become problematic.

In addition to concerns regarding how different survey modes produce different measures, recent research on measurement differences within paper surveys has found that varying the visual layout of questions and response options can significantly affect the answers respondents provide. For example, Christian and Dillman (2004) have found:

- Larger answer spaces for open-ended questions encourage respondents to provide more words and themes.
- Greater spacing between answer categories influences answers to nominally scaled questions.
- The addition of an 'arrow' symbol increases the likelihood that respondents answer a subordinate question.
- Breaking a five-point vertically presented scalar display into three columns significantly changes the mean scale value.

Requiring respondents to write answers in a number box instead of asking them to check a number on a scale results in confusion over the meaning of the scale.

Earlier research has also shown that numerous aspects of visual layout can affect the way people navigate through a questionnaire. For example, Redline *et al.* (2003) have shown respondents make fewer branching errors when arrows, font size and boldness, and the distance of branching instructions from answer boxes are manipulated in various ways. These studies clearly demonstrate that respondents derive meaning from more than simply the words used to ask questions. Specifically, respondents assign meaning to paralanguages of symbols (e.g., arrows), numbers, and graphics (e.g., font size, brightness, contrast) associated with those words, based upon cultural learning and principles of perception identified by Gestalt psychologists and others (e.g., Jenkins & Dillman, 1997; Redline & Dillman, 2002).

OBTAINING A RESPONSE

The essential response goal of mail survey implementation, as well as other modes of implementation, is to avoid nonresponse error, i.e., differences in measured characteristics (e.g., opinions) relevant to the study between sample respondents and nonrespondents. Although the elimination of non-response error is not assured by obtaining a high response rate, doing so tends to increase our confidence that those who respond are representative of the population from which the sample is drawn.

The survey literature is consistent across many decades of research in demonstrating that two elements are particularly powerful for improving response rates: the number of contacts made (Dillman, 2000) and the inclusion of token cash incentives (Church, 1993). No other technique for improving response approaches the effectiveness of these two elements, particularly when they are used in combination with each other.

An example of an effective contact strategy in mail survey implementation is to send a pre-notice letter, the questionnaire one week later, a thank-you/reminder postcard one week later, a replacement questionnaire 2 to 3 weeks later, and yet another replacement questionnaire as a final contact in a few more weeks. This strategy, along with examples of cover letters is described by Dillman (2000).

An example of the effectiveness of token cash incentives is an analysis of eight recent studies in which enclosing an incentive of $2 to $5 with the first questionnaire mailing improved response rates an average of 18.9 percentage points, from a mean of 42.2% to 61.1% (Lesser *et al.*, 2001). Other researchers have frequently investigated whether sending material incentives (e.g., ballpoint pens, phonecards), rewarding one of a few respondents with a sweepstakes prize, or promising to pay respondents who complete and return the questionnaire increase response rates. Most of these studies have found such incentives generally have a very small effect on improving response, if any (Church, 1993). For example, James and Bolstein (1992) reported that promising respondents a $50 check after they mailed back the questionnaire improved response rates only slightly, from 52 (with no incentive) to 57%. However, sending a one-dollar token cash incentive with the questionnaire to potential respondents produced a response rate of 64%.

It is not clear exactly why the combination of multiple contacts and token incentives given in advance is such an effective means of improving response rates. However, it has been argued that social exchange processes underlie the act of deciding whether to respond to survey requests (Dillman, 1978, 2000). This argument contends that voluntarily completing a questionnaire is more social than economic in nature. The potential respondent contemplates a variety of small social costs (e.g., answering will be boring, future questionnaires might be sent if the current one is mailed back, not understanding the questions could be embarrassing) and rewards (e.g., participating will be interesting, the results could benefit society). People agree to participate when they trust the rewards of responding will outweigh the costs. Multiple contacts carried out in a manner that seems reasonable to the respondent (e.g., cordial, non-threatening) and sending the token incentive before any response instills trust necessary for encouraging participation. Put simply, if people receive trust and respect from others, they will often be motivated to reciprocate.

The social nature of multiple contacts and token cash incentives underscored by the social exchange framework suggests that the verbal content of later contacts need to differ from previous contacts. It also partly explains why self-administered questionnaires by mail that promise relatively large monetary gifts generally obtain lower response rates than surveys enclosed with a two or five dollar bill. The monetary value of the cash incentive itself is less important than the way it is given. The social exchange framework not only emphasizes these multiple aspects of the implementation process, but also suggests

that each part needs to connect with all others.

The research literature is fairly consistent in showing that five other aspects of mail survey implementation have significant positive effects on response rates. One such factor is the use of special delivery methods, such as priority postal mail service or a courier service like Federal Express. A second factor is personalizing correspondence by avoiding such terms as 'householder' or 'resident' and using the sampled person's name on the envelope and in the individually processed cover letters. Research also suggests that a small increment of response can be achieved through affixing an actual stamp to the return envelope (Armstrong & Luske, 1987). A fourth factor influencing response, though more difficult for the researcher to control, is the nature of the organization sponsoring the survey. In a meta-analysis of 214 mail surveys, Heberlein and Baumgartner (1978) found that surveys conducted by governmental agencies tend to obtain higher response rates than those conducted by businesses or market research organizations. Additionally, switching modes (e.g., from mail to telephone) after one has made a number of contacts by the first mode increases the response rate significantly (Dillman, 2000).

More recent research has found that various aspects of questionnaire design can influence response. Analyzing rates of return from 39 mail surveys implemented from 1977 to 1987, Connelly, Brown, and Decker (2003) found an inverse relationship between response rates and questionnaire length, as measured by number of pages. To combat the fear that lengthy questionnaires will lead to low response, a frequent but unfortunate tendency exhibited by surveyors has been to squeeze more questions into fewer pages. However, this often has the unintended consequence of making the questionnaire more difficult to complete, due to smaller font size, less white space, and the increase in visual clutter. There is strong evidence that reducing the number of questions will increase item response, but we know of no research that shows placing the same number of questions into fewer pages will increase item response. However, research has found questionnaires with convoluted navigational paths, created when more questions are forced into available space, leads respondents to miss important information (Jenkins & Dillman, 1997; Dillman, 2000).

In addition to length, the shape and manner in which the questionnaire is assembled are other factors associated with questionnaire design that influence response. Oddly shaped and assembled questionnaires often frustrate respondents, thus discouraging participation. Considerable research from the US Census Bureau, summarized by Dillman (2000) shows that unusual (double or accordion-like) folds caused respondents to miss answers, and also created mail-back problems. Cultural convention serves as a good guide. Constructing questionnaires as booklets emulates the familiar reading format of books.

Two final factors of questionnaire design that can affect response relate to the mail recipient's initial, visceral reaction upon receiving the questionnaire. Research has found that manipulating the design of a questionnaire's cover can affect response (Gendall, 2005). Also, presenting interesting, substantive questions first will likely pique the reader's curiosity and consequently, encourage participation (Dillman, 2000). For example, the questionnaire introduced at the beginning of this chapter was designed to measure the respondent's Internet use and participation in social networks (Stern & Dillman, 2005). Questions relating to these topics were deliberately relegated to later pages, while questions eliciting peoples' opinions about their local community, a topic introduced by a vibrant and salient cover page, were placed early in the questionnaire.

Are mail response rates declining?

Our general impression is that response rates to mail surveys have gone down only slightly in recent decades. However, attempts to summarize these effects across multiple surveys show mixed results. In the early 1990s, Hox and DeLeeuw (1994) found that while response rates to face-to-face and telephone interviews were clearly declining, mail response rates appeared to be rising. Data reported more recently indicate mail surveys are experiencing a slight decrease in rates of return, such as Connelly et al.'s (2003) analysis of natural resource surveys conducted between 1971 and 2000. Dillman and Carley-Baxter's (2001) analysis of 98 surveys of National Park visitors conducted between 1988 and 1999 also reported slight declines in response rates over time. However, they also found that the number of survey questions had more than doubled, while the number of pages remained the same. At the same time, the number of replacement questionnaires had increased from one to two. Thus, while response rates to National Park surveys in the late 1990s dropped only slightly since the late 1980s, more information was being collected and more intensive follow-up procedures were being used. Our conclusion is that mail response rates are not undergoing the substantial decline we have observed in telephone surveys in the United States, but increased efforts to obtain acceptable response rates may be part of the reason.

CONCLUSION

It is striking that paper and pencil surveys, first used more than 400 years ago, remain an important means of collecting data in today's electronic age. Their current use as a stand-alone survey method or in combination with other modes in mixed-mode designs reflects, on the one hand, the modern difficulties in coverage and response encountered by many telephone and Internet survey methodologists. On the other hand, the current use of self-administered paper questionnaires reflects their ability to obtain quality answers and respectable response rates.

Adequate coverage, the primary challenge faced by mail survey researchers, persists as a problem inherent to self-administered questionnaires implemented in the general public or any other population for which a complete sampling frame is difficult to obtain. But, new challenges are also emerging, such as the deterioration of mailing lists for populations that previously were adequately covered. As postal communication becomes a less common way for people to contact each other, updating one's postal mail address may be perceived as less important today. Consequently, mailing lists become inadequate, and researchers must seek to contact potential respondents via other survey methods by mixing modes. In addition, new research is showing that the visual layout and design of questionnaires, a factor seldom considered prior to the 1990s, is interfering with surveyors' attempts to consistently measure respondent characteristics and opinions across survey modes.

In cases where address availability allows the use of mail, successful survey implementation by this mode now depends upon using more intensive data collection strategies than before. Whereas mail surveyors of decades past might have been able to use fewer contacts, or forego token cash incentives and other response-inducing strategies, this seems less likely to produce quality data in today's survey research environment.

REFERENCES

Armstrong, J. S., & Luske, E. J. (1987). Return postage in mail surveys: A meta-analysis. *Public Opinion Quarterly, 51*, 233–248.

Blumenthal, M. (2005, November 18). *Columbus dispatch poll: Past performance no guarantee of future results*. Retrieved June 30, 2006, from http://www.mysterypollster.com/main/2005/week46/index.html.

Christian, L., & Dillman, D. A. (2004). The influence of symbolic and graphical language manipulations on answers to paper self-administered questionnaires. *Public Opinion Quarterly, 68*, 57–80.

Church, A. H. (1993). Estimating the effect of incentives on mail survey response rates: A meta-analysis. *Public Opinion Quarterly, 57*, 62–79.

Connelly, N. A., Brown, T. L., & Decker, D. J. (2003). Factors affecting response rates to natural resource—Focused mail surveys: Empirical evidence of declining rates over time. *Society and Natural Resources, 16*, 541–549.

DeLeeuw, E. D. (1992). *Data quality in mail, telephone, and face-to-face surveys*. Amsterdam: TT Publications.

DeLeeuw, E. D. (2005). To mix or not to mix data collection modes in surveys. *Journal of Official Statistics, 21*(2), 233–256.

Dillman, D. A. (1978). *Mail and telephone surveys: The total design method*. New York: Wiley-Interscience.

Dillman, D. A. (2000). *Mail and internet surveys: The tailored design method*. New York: John Wiley.

Dillman, D. A., & Carley-Baxter, L. R. (2001). Structural determinants of mail survey response rates over a 12-year period, 1988–1999. *2000 Proceedings of American statistical association survey methods section* (pp. 394–399). Alexandria, VA.

Dillman, D. A., & Christian, L. M. (2005). Survey mode as a source of instability across surveys. *Field Methods, 17*(1), 30–52.

Dillman, D. A., Clark, J. R., & West, K. K. (1994). Influence of an invitation to answer by telephone on response to census questionnaires. *Public Opinion Quarterly, 58*, 557–568.

Dillman, D. A., Phelps, G., Tortora, R., Swift, K., Kohrell, J., & Berck, J. (2001, May). *Response rate and measurement differences in mixed mode surveys using mail, telephone, interactive voice response and the Internet*. Paper presented at the 56th Annual Meeting of the American Association for Public Opinion Research, Montreal.

Erdos, P. (1970). *Professional mail surveys*. New York: McGraw-Hill.

Gendall, P. (2005). Can you judge a questionnaire by its cover? The effect of questionnaire cover design on mail survey response. *International Journal of Public Opinion Research, 17*, 346–370.

Heberlein, T. A., & Baumgartner, R. (1978). Factors affecting response rates to mailed questionnaires: A quantitative analysis of the published literature. *American Sociological Review, 43*, 447–462.

Hippler, H. J., & Schwarz, N. (1987). Response effects in surveys. In C. F. Turner & E. Martin (Eds.), *Social information processing and survey methodology* (pp. 102–122). New York: Springer-Verlag.

Hox, J., & DeLeeuw, E. (1994). A comparison of nonresponse in mail, telephone, and face-to-face surveys. Applying multilevel modeling to meta-analyses. *Quality and Quantity, 28*, 329–344.

James, J. M., & Bolstein, R. (1992). Large monetary incentives and their effect on mail survey response rates. *Public Opinion Quarterly, 56,* 442–453.

Jenkins, C. R., & Dillman, D. A. (1997). Towards a theory of self-administered questionnaire design. In L. Lyberg, P. Biemer, M. Collins, L. Decker, E. de Leeuw, C. Dippo, N. Schwarz, & D. Trewin (Eds.), *Survey measurement and process quality* (pp. 165–196). New York: Wiley-Interscience.

Lessler, J. T., & Holt, M. (1987). Using response protocols to identify problems in the U.S. census long form. *Proceedings of American Statistical Association Survey Methods Section* (pp. 262–266). Alexandria, VA.

Lesser, V. A., Dillman, D. A., Carlson, J., Lorenz, F., Mason, R., & Willits, F. (2001). Quantifying the influence of incentives on mail survey response rates and nonresponse bias. *Proceedings of American Statistical Association Survey Methods Section.* Alexandria, VA.

O'Reilly, J. M., Hubbard, M., Lessler, J. Biemer, P. P., & Turner, C. F. (1994). Audio and video computer assisted self-interviewing: Preliminary tests of new technologies for data collection. *Journal of Official Statistics, 10,* 197–214.

Redline, C. D., & Dillman, D. A. (2002). The influence of alternative visual designs on respondents' performance with branching instructions in self-administered questionnaires. In R. Groves, D. Dillman, J. Eltinge, & R. Little (Eds.), *Survey nonresponse* (pp. 179–193). New York: John Wiley.

Redline, C. D., Dillman, D. A., Dajani, A., & Scaggs, M. A. (2003). Improving navigational performance in U.S. census 2000 by altering the visual languages of branching instructions. *Journal of Official Statistics, 19,* 403–420.

Shettle, C., & Mooney, G. (1996). *Evaluation of using monetary incentives in a government survey.* Paper presented to the meeting of the American Statistical Association, Chicago, IL.

Stern, M. J., & Dillman, D. A. (2005). Does the Internet strengthen or weaken community ties? *Proceedings of the 68th Rural Sociological Society Meeting.*

Visser, P. S., Krosnick, J. A., Marquette, J., & Curtin, M. (1996). Mail surveys for election forecasting? An evaluation of the Columbus dispatch poll. *Public Opinion Quarterly, 60,* 181–227.

25

Internet Surveys

Vasja Vehovar, Katja Lozar Manfreda
and Gašper Koren

INTRODUCTION

Internet surveys are typically based on computerized self-administered questionnaires on the web, where respondents read questions from the screen of a personal computer (PC) and manually record responses. However, the scope of self-administered surveys supported with modern information-communication technology is broader, including other devices than the PC and other networks than the Internet, relying on audio/video communication, and, in particular, combining multiple survey modes.

Computer assisted data collection (CADAC) has changed many aspects of contemporary businesses, from customer payment systems, media audience measurements, retail price auditing, to survey data collection. For the latter, the corresponding applications are labeled *computer assisted survey information collection* (CASIC). Starting as *computer assisted telephone interviewing* (CATI) in the 1970s, computers have further penetrated into the survey process as *computer*

assisted personal interviewing (CAPI) and *self-interviewing* (CASI), *computerized self-administered questionnaires* (CSAQ), *touch-tone data entry* (TDE) and *interactive voice response* (IVR).

In the 1990s the Internet enabled e-mail and web types of CSAQ. Because of growing broadband access and hardware/software improvements, Internet related surveys are now continuously expanding. Technology is permanently changing two important aspects of these surveys. First, more multimedia components are introduced to survey questionnaires (e.g. pictures, sounds, video clips, and animations); secondly, more interactivity is provided (e.g. personalization, controls, feedback, virtual interviewers, and personalized help). Internet survey questionnaires are thus dramatically broadening their potential, but they are also becoming more and more complicated. Researchers now have a sophisticated spectrum of tools, while respondents may be unpredictably sensitive to specific applications and their variations. Furthermore, the growing number of potential interface devices (e.g. PCs, TVs, mobile phones, and PDAs) creates another complexity that increasingly requires highly skilled professionals to implement. On the other hand, easy-to-use software packages also allow survey implementation to non-professionals.

The impact of information and communication technology (ICT) extends beyond questionnaires; it is also changing the process of transmitting survey data to central locations. Here, we can use the notion of telesurveys (Nathan, 2001) to denote telecommunication technology used for immediate transmission of responses to the survey organization when a respondent is remote from the interviewer (e.g. CATI) or there is no interviewer (i.e. CSAQ).

Equally important, although less visible, is the revolutionary role of ICT—particularly the Internet—in the administration of the survey process. Contemporary surveys often involve hundreds of interviewers and thousands of questionnaires, so effective monitoring of this process is unthinkable without corresponding ICT support, which is now increasingly moving to the Internet (Cowling, 2005).

All these Internet related changes stimulate the perception of survey data collection as a business process. Survey organizations regularly face standard managerial issues such as returns on ICT investment, and they permanently deal with monitoring of the processes with cost optimizations and complex schemes for assuring quality standards (Biemer & Lyberg, 2003). Therefore, survey organizations increasingly apply project management tools and benchmarking approaches. The modern survey data collection process is thus shaped not only by methodological issues but also by business principles. They are becoming increasingly intertwined, because they are both so closely related to the growing role of ICT.

METHODOLOGICAL ISSUES

Sometimes, survey methodologists have difficulty accepting new modes of data collection. They were suspicious when telephone surveys emerged as a replacement technology for face-to-face surveys in the 1960s and 1970s. The resistance was not easily overcome even after studies demonstrated that the telephone surveys worked well (Groves & Kahn, 1979). There were also certain problems with the introduction of computers, but they were handled relatively easily (Saris, 1991). In addition, newly tailored approaches for new modes of data collection were developed (e.g. Dillman, 2000). With the introduction of CASIC, the basic methodological principles of survey research have thus remained more or less unchanged, while adding many new horizons in contemporary survey data collection.

However, in the mid-1990s, serious doubts appeared with the advent of Internet surveys. The main problem was not so much with the data collection specifics, but rather with the radical enthusiasm of the advocates of this mode, who exaggerated its immediate potentials. Especially in the marketing research industry, they instantly recognized the Internet as a replacement technology for the telephone, just as telephone data collection had replaced the face-to-face interviews as a dominant survey mode few decades ago. However, there are several methodological problems that need to be overcome for Internet surveys to become a valid and reliable data collection mode.

Internet surveys as CASIC mode

Today, the definition of an *Internet survey* is relatively problematic due to the number of contexts used as well as fast and continuous technological changes. To clarify and define this term, we will first sketch a broader notion of CASIC modes.

A general cost-reduction pressure—manifested in trends of replacing expensive human labor with cheap and intelligent machines—is an integral part of the transformation of contemporary work processes. Human beings are not only expensive but also unreliable and prone to errors, so automatic interactive services are increasingly removing human interactions. Historically, this trend started decades ago with self-service supermarkets and restaurants, followed by ATM banking, self-service gas stations, and call centers with automated voice instructions. Within this general trend, we can also observe the gradual tendency to eliminate interviewers from the survey data collection process and replace them with machines—in the form of computerized self-administered questionnaires (CSAQ).

The introduction of CASIC transformed the initial 'classic' form of survey data collection, based on interviewers recording responses in face-to-face paper and pencil interviews (PAPI), to modern survey data collection processes with no paper and no interviewers (CSAQ). In *paper-less* and *interviewer-less* survey data collection (Figure 25.1) a remote respondent typically answers a computerized self-administered questionnaire visually on a screen of some device (visual CSAQ). This is different from *computer assisted-interviewing* (CAI) where a 'live' interviewer is involved (CATI and CAPI) who also records the answers on the PC, or from *computer assisted self-interviewing* (CASI) where the interviewer hands the PC to a respondent for a certain part of the questionnaire. We thus avoid here the word 'interviewing'

for survey modes where there is actually no interviewer involved, so we will not use the notion of 'web CASI' (sometimes referred also as CAWI—*computer assisted web interviewing*), because it is ambiguous about the levels of interviewer presence and involvement. Instead, we will use the term CSAQ (or web CSAQ when the questionnaire runs on the web) to denote Internet surveys without any involvement of the interviewer.

In a broader sense, in this chapter we discuss the *CSAQ telesurveys* (lower right cell in Figure 25.1), which can be characterized as follows:

- *self-administration:* no interaction with the interviewer/researcher during data collection; exceptions may be certain help interventions (via e-mail, telephone or video) of the supporting staff;
- *computerization:* survey questionnaire interacts and evolves through some electronic device (PC, digital TV, PDA, mobile phone device, audio/video recording device, or the like), while responses are self-administered—either manually (keyboard, mouse, touch-screen) or with automatic voice recognition (AVR);
- *electronic networks:* responses are instantly transferred to the (remote) survey organization, typically over the Internet but also by some others such as mobile phone networks.

Interviewer involvement	Survey Mode	
	Paper and pencil	CASIC
Interviewer presence	Paper and pencil (face-to-face) interviewing (PAPI)	CAPI, CASI, Audio/Video CASI
Remote interviewer	Paper assisted telephone interviewing (PATI)	CATI, CAVI (computer assisted video interviewing)
No interviewer	Self-administered paper questionnaires (mail questionnaires)	CSAQ telesurveys (web CSAQ, TDE, IVR, Virtual interviewer)

Figure 25.1   Interviewer involvement and survey mode: the evolution of the survey data collection

We should also further clarify another important distinction within self-administered CASIC modes—the input/output technology of the respondent. Here, one specific technology can be used to convey the input (questions) to a respondent, while another can allow the respondent to express his/her output (answers). In either case, we can use visual (letters/signs) or audio (voice/sound) interfaces (Figure 25.2). When the presentation of survey questions is visual, we speak about *visual CSAQ*. Most typically this is on a PC, but mobile phones, digital TV, or PDAs can also be used. Another input alternative is the delivery of questions to respondents with some automated audio devices—*audio CSAQ*. Here, the self-administered questionnaire is still computerized, even if it is not visualized on the screen; it uses computer controlled sequences of pre-recorded spoken questions.

Similarly, there are two options when recording a respondent's output. The first is manual self-administration (keyboard, touch-screen, or mouse), most typically associated with visual CSAQ. However, in *touch-tone data entry* (TDE) procedures, respondents often listen to the pre-recorded questions and then type the responses on the keyboard of the telephone (audio CSAQ). The second recording option is self-administration via audio output, where an *automated voice recognition* (AVR) system records the answers, as in *interactive voice response* (IVR) surveys, a special CSAQ option where both components (input/output) are related to voice/audio. The AVR output component, using a PC equipped with microphones or cameras, may also be used in combination with visual CSAQ

as the input option. However, for various cultural and technical reasons, together with usability problems and cost issues, such combinations have not become very popular, partly because PCs are not yet routinely equipped with cameras and/or microphones.

Further sub-classification may follow if we observe the use of artificial voice, such as machine generated audio questions (TTS—text to speech), and/or the introduction of a virtual interviewer. This, however, should be strictly separated from audio or video IVR types of communication, where the respondent listens to or watches only the prerecorded 'true' interviewer voice or appearance.

When talking about pure types of input/output combinations, we thus have three distinguishable options:

1 *classic option*: interviewer and respondents communicate orally; interviewer records answers manually (e.g. PAPI, PATI);
2 *audio option*: questions are audio pre-recorded (including TTS), and oral responses from the interviewer are recorded (AVR) and processed automatically (IVR);
3 *visual option*: written questions appear on the screen of a device, and the respondent answers questions manually by keyboard, mouse or touch-screen.

In practice, of course, numerous combinations of input/output options are possible at each step of the data collection. We should make clear that the latter option (3) includes the *web CSAQ*, which is currently the dominant type of CSAQ telesurvey, and it also corresponds to the

Asking questions (INPUT)	Recording of responses (OUTPUT)	
	Manual recording	Automatic voice recognition
Written questions	Standard CSAQ (PC with/without Internet, TV, PDA, Mobile)	Visual CSAQ with AVR
Audio questions	Video CSAQ, Audio CSAQ, TDE	IVR, Video IVR, TTS with AVR, Virtual interview

Figure 25.2   CSAQ telesurveys according to input and output technologies used with of respondents

notion of an Internet survey in its narrow meaning.

From the perspective of its technical aspects, the standard web CSAQ is typically conducted through continuous interaction with a server at the survey organization that records each page that the respondent has completed, while it also selects and sends to the respondent's device (i.e. client) the next page of questions. The entire application is thus governed by the server.

However, the CSAQ can also be performed independently from client-server interaction and also independently from web browsers. In such a case, for example, respondents first access a stand-alone CSAQ application, which installs itself on their device, evolves the questions, records the answers and sends responses to the survey organization. Further, some non-Internet networks (e.g. mobile phone networks) can be used for the tele-transferring. Such a client-based approach—which can be run completely outside the Internet—enables much more flexibility compared to the server-based option, because researchers are free from any restrictions arising from web browsers and from network connection problems. Nevertheless, server-based web CSAQs still dominate, although client-based options have existed from the mid 1990s and were thought to have a very promising future. However, various technical limitations, broadband restrictions and security concerns on one side, as well as browser improvements accompanied by capable web software extensions (e.g. XML, JavaScript, Ajax, Flash) on the other, have preserved the initial client–server philosophy of the web CSAQ as the prevailing approach.

Sampling

The initial fascination with Internet surveys arose from their ease of implementation, low costs and simple recruiting of respondents (Pitkow & Recker, 1994). However, survey practice showed that especially sampling and recruiting for this new mode are in fact at least as complicated as with other survey modes.

In addition, thousands of popular web sites that published results from self-selected web surveys created the impression that Internet surveys are inherently associated with non-probability sampling and, consequently, also with lower quality. We must thus sharply separate non-probability from probability Internet surveys, as it is only with the latter that statistical inferences to the target population can be made.

First we have to expose the distinction between the survey mode and sampling issues, which are sometimes mistakenly interwoven. Especially in market research, we often encounter the replacement of probability samples typical in telephone or face-to-face surveys with non-probability ones in Internet surveys. However, this includes two components: shift of mode and shift of sampling design, so this replacement process should never be treated as one package. Each component—the mode and the sampling—must be observed separately. It is true that samples for telephone surveys are usually generated with some probability mechanism from lists, or, with random digit dialing (RDD), while a majority of Internet surveys rely on non-probability samples with respondents self-selecting themselves to a specific survey or panel. However, despite this apparent association, the mode and sampling mechanism are not necessarily related. There are telephone surveys based on non-probability samples (e.g. self-selected telephone surveys with call-in 800 numbers), and the same is true for mail or magazine surveys or for face-to-face surveys (e.g. convenience sampling or quota sampling). On the other hand, of course, Internet surveys can be based on probability samples using the e-mail list of the target population, such as students, employees, members, or customers.

The increased role of ICT affects only the mode of survey data collection, solicitation procedures and survey management, while there are no direct effects on principles of sampling or on statistical inference. The issues related to probability vs. non-probability samples are independent from the survey mode used, and hence from the trends toward

CSAQ and also from the concept of survey data collection as a business process. The spurious link between the Internet survey mode and non-probability samples arises only from dramatic cost savings in non-probability Internet surveys, which seduces the practitioners to omit expensive and time-consuming steps needed for assuring probability sampling principles.

The inferential potentials of non-probability samples are thus a purely statistical issue (Lynn, 2005), independent from the survey mode and from the business aspects of the survey process. They are equally relevant for quota samples, convenience samples and various opt-in self-selected surveys, which may use a mail, telephone or face-to-face survey mode.

There exist some promising attempts to approach the inferential problems of non-probability samples. Advanced calibration methods and propensity score weighting (Lynn, 2005) of non-probability samples seem to improve the adjustment procedures. When studying causal relations, the research shows much potential also when using multiple imputations, data fusion and a proper philosophy of causality (Rubin, 2005). Other than that, not many scientific solutions exist to improve the inference based on non-probability samples. Nevertheless, various practitioners have developed a few, such as the art of sample selection, modeling and post-survey adjustment procedures, and what may work relatively well for their specific purposes. Of course, the risk of being wrong cannot be quantified here. The AAPOR (2006) recommendations thus declare that the giving of confidence interval calculations for non-probability samples is a clearly misleading practice.

Internet surveys with probability samples

If we concentrate only on Internet surveys based on scientific (i.e. probability) samples—where we know the (positive) probability of inclusion into the sample for each unit in the target population—we can say that they basically suffer from two specific issues: coverage and frame problems. With regard to coverage, not all of the general population actually uses the Internet. In developed countries, we are perhaps at the stage where telephone surveys were in the 1960s. The majority of adults do already use the Internet; however, the percentages are typically below (or around) 70%, at least in the EU (Eurostat, 2006), and 73% in the United States (Pew Internet, 2006). As a comparison, there was a claim in the 1980s (Groves, 1988) that unless we had 80% telephone coverage, we needed some dual frame solutions for telephone surveys. There are no reasons for not applying this benchmark to Internet surveys as well, because Internet non-users are very much different from users.

The sampling frame problems for Internet surveys have some additional difficulties. If e-mails are used for invitations, there is no e-mail directory for the general population. Even worse, we cannot construct any surrogates, as with RDD for telephone surveys or area samples for face-to-face surveys. Of course, e-mail lists may exist for some target populations, such as students, members of organizations, customers or employees, and there we can apply standard sampling techniques relatively straightforwardly. On the other hand, for general population surveys the only option for a probability sample is to perform the initial solicitation stage using some other communication mode. In particular, telephone recruiting is often used for Internet surveys (e.g. Pratesi, Lozar Manfreda, Biffignandi, & Vehovar, 2004), and is popular also among marketing researchers (e.g. Schouten, 2005), although it provides low final response rates (around 10% or less). Of course, high non-response—together with low coverage—may easily transform a proper probability sample survey into an entirely non-probability one. We should add that a very special case of probability Internet surveys are intercept samples, where we actually select the user's session (i.e. the visit) on a certain web site or group of web sites.

Solicitation, participation, nonresponse

We should separate sampling also from the solicitation aspects of Internet surveys. We have two dimensions, each with two options—probability or non-probability samples, and personal or general types of invitation (Batagelj & Vehovar, 1998). This gives us four rough types (for a more detailed classification see Couper, 2000) of Internet surveys: probability surveys with personalized or general invitations (e.g. pop-up surveys), and non-probability surveys with personal (e.g. Internet access panels) or general (e.g. self-selected web surveys with ads on web sites) invitations. Each category has its specifics in terms of inferential approach and solicitation strategy.

Another characteristic of Internet surveys is the complexity of the survey response process. Even after the e-mail invitation is sent to the respondent, the researcher does not know whether it was actually delivered to the respondent, due to typing errors, spam filters, or simply to recipients overlooking the e-mail message (Vehovar, Batagelj, Lozar Manfreda, & Zaletel, 2002). In addition, respondents can very easily quit at any time during the process (i.e. partial respondents) or only be lurking (Bosnjak, Tuten, & Bandilla 2001). In addition, item non-response can also significantly increase during the response process, especially if forced reminders for each unanswered item are used, which may generate low satisfaction and increased partial nonresponse.

Response rates in Internet surveys are typically 6% to 15% lower compared to other survey modes, as observed in a meta-analysis of split-sample experiments (Lozar Manfreda, Bosnjak, Berzelak, Haas, & Vehovar, in press). Nevertheless, another meta-analysis of response rates in web surveys (Lozar Manfreda & Vehovar, 2002) showed that those with personal invitations have an average response rate around 35% (or 42% if partial respondents are taken into account)—still a relatively high value that is perhaps related to the specific context of these studies.

All in all, the response process in Internet surveys depends on four main components (Vehovar *et al.*, 2002): respondents' characteristics (socio-demography, survey experience, interest in the survey topic, and attitudes), social environment (general survey climate—survey tradition, perceptions of direct marketing and the legitimacy of surveys), technological environment (Internet penetration, broadband use, alternative devices, ICT literacy), and survey design (invitation, follow-ups, incentives, length of the questionnaire, questionnaire design). From those, only survey design is under the (partial) control of the researcher. Therefore, design is extremely important for any Internet survey.

Low response rates in Internet surveys also increase the importance of incentives, which were already well elaborated in other survey modes (see Singer, 2002). With Internet surveys, however, some specifics appear, particularly with regard to the nature of incentives—which may range from access to additional on-line information to lottery tickets and monetary incentives in various virtual currencies. General principles still hold: the incentive must be given in advance and it should not stimulate false responding (Göritz, 2004). The decision about the type of incentive and mode of delivery depends on the target population and survey specifics. Some standards have been established in practice: A typical incentive for a survey of up to 20 minutes using web CSAQ is roughly €5–10, $5–10, or 1000–2000 Yen.

Measurement error

Measurement error is usually understood to be the difference between the values (survey answers) reported by the respondents and true values of the variables due to the measurement process. In self-administered survey modes, we can observe two main sources of measurement error: the *measurement instrument* (questionnaire design, question wording or various technical problems), which is also closely linked to the issues of reliability, validity and sensitivity; and the *respondent himself/herself* and his/her motivation, comprehension, skills, and privacy concerns. In general, studies show that these types of errors are manageable, and in this aspect the Internet surveys typically outperform the telephone ones (Chang & Krosnick, 2002).

Respondent error in web surveys might be decreased because of the convenience of self-administration, allowing respondents to choose the most appropriate time and place for questionnaire completion. On the other hand, respondents may answer survey questions less carefully because of a less controlled survey situation—they might be doing other things while answering the questions or not reading the survey text carefully. In addition, specific problems might occur because of a potential lack of experience with computer and Internet use among specific groups of respondents.

In a typical web survey, the visual elements of the questionnaire take control over the interviewer's role (welcome, start, end, skips, answers' controls, and reminders), and are thus the most important communication channel between researcher and respondents. A very similar situation exists with self-administered paper-and-pencil questionnaires, but the Internet brings broader potential and much more complexity. First, respondents have different levels of familiarity with ICT usage and may also use different hardware/software. Second, there are issues about how people read web content: According to human–computer interaction research, individuals are not really reading but more 'scanning' the pages, and tend to answer quickly without paying enough attention to the text, while being focused on graphical elements (Spool, Scanlon, Schroeder, Snyder, & DeAngelo 1999). Inappropriate design features can therefore distract respondents and even interfere with the question answering process. The use of graphics and multimedia (sound and video) extends the power of a survey question because it provides extra stimuli; but it can also have negative effects if used inappropriately. Different layouts can significantly influence responses (see Dillman, Tortora, Conrad, & Bowker, 1998; Lozar Manfreda,

Batagelj, & Vehovar, 2002), and since the effect of graphics and multimedia is never completely clear and predictable, they should be used with caution.

In addition, when using certain graphical and multimedia elements, extra attention should be paid to the following two problems. First—unlike the standard graphics supported by all graphical web browsers—we usually need special plug-ins; and second, the size of multimedia files is much larger than the size of standard graphical elements and may cause problems in download time. Some experiments have already shown that the use of multimedia and rich graphics does not help to motivate respondents (Couper, Tourangeau, & Kenyon, 2004), so that plain designs usually outperform the fancy ones in almost all aspects of data quality (Dillman *et al.*, 1998; Coates, 2004). To stay on the safe side, it is thus wise to keep the questionnaire layout as simple as possible. Experiments with unusual elements like slider bars showed that they tend to produce higher dropout rates, higher item missing data and longer completion times than other question format types (Couper, Tourangeau, Conrad, & Singer, 2006).

The web presentation of the questionnaire is also important. While the print on paper is always an exact copy of the original, in Internet surveys we do not have full control over the presentation of the questionnaire to the respondent. Due to lack of standards in web design, the same web questionnaire can look different if we see it in different browsers, and even on different screens with different display resolutions. Experiments with PDF layouts, which could ensure an identical layout on every computer, seem not to be very fruitful. Therefore, it is crucial to test the questionnaire extensively within as many computer environments as possible, using different software and hardware.

Another important and well-elaborated component of the questionnaire layout is the so-called *progress indicator*. This is a graphical or text add-on showing how far the respondents are in the questionnaire. The idea is to present information about the duration of a task of unknown length and to encourage the respondents not to break off prematurely. Initial experiments with progress indicators showed that they have no particular role in motivating respondents or reducing the break offs (see Couper, Traugott, & Lamias, 2001). Conrad, Couper, Tourangeau, and Peytchev (2004) indicated that progress indicators may even increase dropout rates in long questionnaires. On the other hand, having no indicator usually results in much lower satisfaction with a survey (Lozar Manfreda et al., 2002). Nevertheless, the inclusion of progress indicators is recommended by professional standards and guidelines (e.g. ESOMAR, 2005).

A question of whether to use single-page web questionnaire layouts or have more pages was one of the first methodological dilemmas in web surveys. Vehovar and Batagelj (1996) found that dropout rates did not differ significantly, while completion times were slightly longer for the page-by-page option, as did subsequent studies (Tourangeau, Couper, Galesic, & Givens, 2004). Nevertheless, with long and complex questionnaires, one scrollable page is still an inappropriate choice. On the other hand, when we have a short questionnaire and (almost) all questions are relevant for all respondents, we may still consider the single-page design.

When designing online questionnaires, we have a wide range of options for presenting questions and answers through HTML forms. Classic HTML entry forms (such as radio buttons, checkboxes, drop down menus, and text boxes) have been extensively tested, and we now know which forms are more or less appropriate for certain survey tasks. Heerwegh (2005) claims that radio buttons are easier to complete than drop-down menus and can lead to lower item non-response rates. Couper, Tourangeau, and Conrad (2004) showed that some formats (e.g. a drop box with five visible and five hidden options) tend to be more prone to primacy effects; items that are visible in the box are more likely to be chosen than when presented with radio buttons or normal drop-down menus.

Another important finding is that the response format used has no significant influence on the time to complete the question. A solution to primacy effects is thus to randomize response categories within certain questions. When we have a small number of items that can be displayed normally on one screen, we should thus use radio buttons; drop down menus are used only when we have too many items for one non-scrollable screen (e.g. selection of a country or certain year input). With some more complicated technical solutions and client-side scripting, we can also use a simple input box with helper tooltips to suggest auto completion and the validation of the entry in real time.

Unfortunately, the decision about the exact types of input fields is often arbitrary, and selection of an 'appropriate' form is driven by the researcher's intuition, available tools in the survey design software, or the programmer's skills. Very often they are more likely to be influenced by web design principles than questionnaire design ones (Couper, Tourangeau, & Conrad, 2004). The problem of questionnaire layout is, however, not new or specific to web surveys. Questionnaire design is particularly important in all self-administered surveys (Dillman, 2000), but it also influences interviewer-administered surveys.

Nevertheless, even though simple designs seem to perform better, we believe that the introduction of multimedia and other dynamic elements can make web questionnaires more interesting and less boring for respondents. For example, Bälter (2005) presented an interesting approach to interactive web surveys using computer game design and human–computer interaction theory to improve response rates.

Codes and standards

Development of ethical codes and guidelines with best practices are important signs of maturity of the field. The majority of general standards for survey data collection can also be applied to Internet surveys; however, there are some specifics, so special codes and guidelines were established, or, at least added to existing ones in order to cover Internet surveys. An exhaustive list of codes and standards can be found on WebSM (2006).

Ethical and design standards are particularly important for Internet surveys. First, since Internet surveys are often conducted by non-professionals, implementation according to high ethical and design standards by professional research organizations can provide increased legitimacy to the Internet survey industry. In addition, the privacy concerns of participants in Internet surveys are more serious than in more conventional survey settings. Therefore, implementing high professional standards can help to promote participation in Internet surveys among skeptical individuals.

In addition to standards that directly relate to Internet-based research, particularly those produced by AAPOR (2006) and ESOMAR (2005), other general standards regarding the Internet may have an important value. An example is the guidelines produced by the Interactive Advertising Bureau on e-mail, pop-ups usage, privacy and other issues (IAB, 2006).

COSTS, ERRORS AND MANAGEMENT

As the survey process becomes more of a business process, it must conform to corresponding managerial principles, particularly those related to survey quality and cost optimization. The increasing role of ICT in survey data collection is thus accompanied by the growing adoption of well-established concepts of quality management, e.g. total quality management (TQM). Today, we can observe numerous applications of formal management and quality standards to the survey process, particularly in the commercial sector: the Market Research Quality Standards Association (MRQSA), the Interviewer Quality Control Scheme (IQCS), the ISO 9000 standard for Survey Quality (Biemer & Lyberg, 2003). Similarly, in official statistics, various national and international

bodies (e.g. Eurostat, United Nations, and National Statistical Offices) undertake numerous activities for developing modern quality standards for survey data collection (→ *Codes of Ethics and Standards in Survey Research*).

The cost aspects of Internet data collection are one of its key advantages; however proper cost comparisons show that web surveys are not always that much cheaper. For example, costs are relatively high for web surveys based on probability panels of the general population due to high panel maintenance costs or when incentives are used. However, simultaneous studies of costs and errors for Internet surveys are surprisingly rare. In part, this is understandable, because costs are difficult to allocate (particularly the indirect ones), and the quality of survey data is also very complex to measure. In addition, it is very complicated to establish the proper experimental environment. Very often, the survey quality aspect is reduced to mean squared error (MSE), which typically has only two components: sampling error and nonresponse bias. One of the rare studies of this kind was performed by Vehovar, Lozar Manfreda, and Batagelj (2001), who minimized the MSE at fixed costs. They found that, in the case of short questionnaires, a telephone survey with a smaller sample size but lower nonresponse bias was more cost-effective than a web questionnaire with mail invitations and larger sample size that had substantial nonresponse bias. However, with longer questionnaires, the situation was just the opposite.

The selection of a software package to conduct a web survey is one of the crucial steps in the process of on-line data collection. On the one hand, it is difficult for a non-technician to choose among a wide range of commercial software packages with different capabilities. On the other hand, the choice of appropriate software is often a long-term decision connected with considerable costs, technical problems and managerial solutions. When selecting the software package, we should first determine our needs. The most important questions are: Do we plan a simple, one-time data collection, or are we going to use online data collection as our frequent future data collection method? What kind of questionnaires do we want to implement?

In 2006, there were more than 300 software packages for implementing web surveys on the market in the English language alone (WebSM, 2006). Commercial software packages often provide integrated solutions for data analysis, database manipulation, data mining and/or decision support, while open source solutions, on the other side, are somehow limited to core aspect of Internet questionnaire design.

CONCLUSION

Modern technology, especially the ICT, is rapidly changing the survey research industry and is pushing the survey process toward paper-less and interviewer-less data collection. We observe this transformation also through growing business pressures, which have accelerated with ICT developments. These all move survey procedures toward optimizing the entire survey process, balancing the input costs with data quality outputs, ensuring the timeliness of the results, and integrating the survey procedures with the administrative and business environment. Methodological issues are thus only one piece, which needs to be optimally integrated into the entire data production processes.

When Internet surveys first appeared, there was an expectation they would become a true replacement technology, solving many problems in the survey industry (Baker, 1998), particularly the increased costs and declining response rates. There were also some brave predictions that Internet surveys would additionally be combined with, or even replaced by, various techniques of data mining and decision support systems using existing data such as consumer databases, administrative records, site visitation tracking, and Internet survey paradata (ibid.). Such optimism was not surprising. Web surveys truly offer a number of advantages: minimizing human errors, lower costs, convenient implementation and great potential for integration with other

survey modes, as well as with other business processes. Today, we can observe that those predictions are becoming a reality, although at a much slower pace and sometimes in a slightly different form than anticipated. In any case, in developed countries Internet questionnaires already dominate with respect to the number of questionnaires completed when compared with other survey modes; and they are also approaching the position of the leading survey mode in the sense of financial resources allocated.

However, there are still several unresolved methodological and technical issues. While Internet access is widespread, several population segments are significantly underrepresented, which is true even for the most developed countries (Eurostat, 2006; Pew Internet, 2006). In addition, the sampling frame problem restricts the use of probability sampling, while probability surveys of the general population suffer from high costs of recruiting and/or from low response rates. As a result, Internet surveys of the general population are usually based on panels, either in the form of some general household panels, or in the form of specific non-probability Internet panels (i.e. access panels). As of now, however, except for some successful examples and for some rare attempts from statistical science (e.g. propensity weighting, causal inference using data fusion), we still lack comprehensive approaches to this central problem of Internet surveys.

In the future, we can expect that Internet surveys will continuously create an increased fragmentation of the survey process. On the other hand, the survey process will become increasingly integrated and coordinated by centralized management. Another important direction is the development of integrated software support for interactivity between the respondent and the questionnaire, such as instant feedback information for the respondent, interactive help and guidance, animation inserts, and heavy multimedia usage. We can also expect further invasion of the technology by increasing virtualization of the survey process (e.g. virtual interviewer). According to this, the audio components will gain importance, particularly with elaborated TTS technologies, speech recognition techniques and interactive translation technologies.

Further technological developments will also raise new methodological problems, so there will be an increased need for research, especially in the following three areas: cost-error optimization problems, issues of inference from non-probability samples, and the question of mixing survey modes.

REFERENCES

AAPOR (2006). *American Association of Public Opinion Research*. Retrieved November 30, 2006, from http://www.aapor.org.

Baker, R. P. (1998). The CASIC Future. In R. P. Baker, M. P. Couper, J. Bethlehem, C. Z. F. Clark, J. Martin, W. L. Nicholls, & J. M. O'Reilly (Eds.), *Computer Assisted Survey Information Collection* (pp. 583–604). New York: Wiley.

Bälter, O. (2005). *Using computer games design to increase response rates*. Paper presented at the ESF Workshop on Internet survey methodology, Dubrovnik.

Batagelj, Z., & Vehovar, V. (1998). WWW Surveys. *Advances in Methodology and Statistics (Metodoloski zvezki), 14*, 209–224.

Biemer, P. P., & Lyberg, E. L. (2003). *Introduction to survey quality*. Hoboken: Wiley.

Bosnjak, M., Tuten, L. T., & Bandilla W. (2001). Participation in web surveys: A Typology. *ZUMA-Nachrichten, 48*, 7–17.

Chang, L. C., & Krosnick, J. A. (2002). *Comparing self-administered computer surveys and auditory interviews: An experiment*. Paper presented at the 57th Annual Conference of the American Association for Public Opinion Research (AAPOR), St. Pete Beach.

Coates, D. (2004). *Online surveys—Does one size fit all?* Paper presented at the RC33 6th International conference on social science methodology: Recent developments and applications in social research methodology, Amsterdam.

Conrad, F. G., Couper, M. P., Tourangeau, R., & Peytchev, A. (2004). *Effectiveness of progress indicators in web surveys*. Paper presented at the RC33 6th International conference on social science methodology: Recent developments and applications in social research methodology, Amsterdam.

Couper, M. P. (2000). Web surveys: A review of issues and approaches. *Public Opinion Quarterly, 64*, 464–494.

Couper, M. P., Traugott, M. W., & Lamias, M. J. (2001). Web survey design and administration. *Public Opinion Quarterly, 65*, 230–253.

Couper, M. P., Tourangeau, R., & Kenyon, K. (2004). Picture this! Exploring visual effects in web surveys. *Public Opinion Quarterly, 68*, 255–266.

Couper, M. P., Tourangeau, R., & Conrad, F. G. (2004). What they see is what we get—Response options for web surveys. *Social Science Computer Review, 11*, 111–127.

Couper, M. P., Tourangeau, R., Conrad, F. G., & Singer, E. (2006). Evaluating the effectiveness of visual analog scales: A web experiment. *Social Science Computer Review, 24*, 227–245.

Cowling, T. (2005). *Market for multi-country surveys. New tools and business solutions*. Paper presented at the joint WAPOR/ISSC conference on international social survey, Ljubljana.

Dillman, D. A. (2000). *Mail and internet surveys: The tailored design method*. New York: John Wiley & Sons.

Dillman, D. A., Tortora, R. D., Conrad, J., & Bowker, D. (1998). *Influence of plain vs. fancy design on response rates for web surveys*. Paper presented at the joint statistical meeting of the American Statistical Association, Dallas.

ESOMAR (2005). *ESOMAR Guideline on conducting market and opinion research using the internet*. Retrieved May 2, 2006, from http://www.esomar.org/web/show/id=49859.

Eurostat (2006, April). Internet usage in the EU-25 in 2005. *Eurostat news release, 45*. Retrieved April 10, 2006 from http://epp.eurostat.ec.europa.eu/pls/portal/docs/page/pgp_prd_cat_prerel/pge_cat_prerel_year_2006/pge_cat_prerel_year_2006_month_04/4-06042006-en-ap.pdf.

Göritz, A.S. (2004). The impact of material incentives on response quantity, response quality, sample composition, survey outcome, and cost in online access panels. *International Journal of Market Research, 46*, 327–345.

Groves, R. M. (Ed.). (1988). *Telephone survey methodology*. New York: John Wiley & Sons.

Groves, R. M., & Kahn, R. L. (1979). *Surveys by telephone: A national comparison with personal interviews*. New York: Academic Press.

Heerwegh, D. (2005). *Web surveys: Explaining and reducing unit nonresponse, item nonresponse and partial nonresponse*. Unpublished doctoral dissertation, Katholieke Universiteit Leuven, Leuven.

IAB (Interactive Advertising Bureau) (2006). *IAB Standards and Guidelines*. Retrieved June 10, 2006, from http://www.iab.net/standards/index.asp.

Lozar Manfreda, K. & Vehovar, V. (2002). *Survey design features influencing response rates in web surveys*.

Paper presented at the international conference on improving surveys, Copenhagen.

Lozar Manfreda, K., Batagelj, Z., & Vehovar, V. (2002). Design of web survey questionnaires: Three basic experiments. *Journal of Computer Mediated Communication, 7*(3).

Lozar Manfreda, K., Bosnjak, M., Berzelak, J., Haas, I., & Vehovar, V. (in press). Web surveys versus other survey modes—A meta-analysis comparing response rates. *International Journal of Market Research.*

Lynn, P. (2005). *Inferential potential of non-probability samples.* Paper presented at the 55th ISI Session, Sydney.

Nathan, G. (2001). Telesurvey methodologies for household surveys—A review and some thoughts for the future? *Survey Methodolgy, 27,* 7–31.

Pew Internet (2006). *Internet penetration and impact.* Retrieved July 12, 2006, from http://www.pewinternet.org/PPF/r/182/report_display.asp.

Pitkow, J. E., & Recker, M. M. (1994). Results from the first world-wide web user survey. *Journal of Computer Networks and ISDN Systems, 27,* 243–254.

Pratesi, M., Lozar Manfreda, K., Biffignandi, S., & Vehovar, V. (2004). List-based web surveys: Quality, timeliness, and nonresponse in the steps of the participation flow. *Journal of Official Statistics, 20,* 451–465.

Rubin, D. B. (2005). *The use of multiple imputation to create a null data set from nonrandomized job training data.* Paper presented at the 55th ISI Session, Sydney.

Saris, W. E. (1991). *Computer-assisted interviewing.* Newbury Park: Sage.

Schouten, B. (2005). *How to correct for survey nonresponse in a single step?* Paper presented at the First EASR Conference, Barcelona.

Singer, E. (2002). The use of incentives to reduce nonresponse in household surveys. In R. M. Groves, D. A. Dillman, J. L. Eltinge, & R. J. A. Little (Eds.), *Survey nonresponse* (pp. 163–178). New York: John Wiley.

Spool, J. M, Scanlon T., Schroeder W., Snyder C., & DeAngelo T. (1999). *Web site usability: A designer's guide.* San Diego: Academic Press.

Tourangeau, R., Couper, M. P., Galesic, M., & Givens, J. (2004). *A comparison of two web-based surveys: Static versus dynamic versions of the NAMCS questionnaire.* Paper presented at the RC33 6th International conference on social science methodology: Recent developments and applications in social research methodology, Amsterdam.

Vehovar, V., & Batagelj, Z. (1996). *The methodological issues in WWW surveys.* Paper presented at the international conference on computer-assisted survey information collection, San Antonio.

Vehovar, V., Lozar Manfreda, K., & Batagelj, Z. (2001). Sensitivity of e-commerce measurement to the survey instrument. *International Journal of Electronic Commerce, 6,* 31–52.

Vehovar, V., Batagelj, Z., Lozar Manfreda, K., & Zaletel, M. (2002). Nonresponse in web surveys. In R. M. Groves, D. A. Dillman, J. L. Eltinge, & R. J. A. Little (Eds.), *Survey Nonresponse* (pp. 229–242). New York: John Wiley.

WebSM (2006). *Web survey methodology.* Retrieved November 30, 2006, 9 from http://websm.org.

26

Different Survey Modes and International Comparisons

Yang-chih Fu and Yun-han Chu

As more research projects rely on cross-national surveys to collect comparative data, researchers must be innovative and flexible when choosing the appropriate survey modes to fit local conditions. This complicates research designs and requires thoughtful plans and strategies. This chapter discusses how researchers might accommodate specific social and cultural settings when designing sampling schemes, constructing proper questionnaires, and selecting modes of data collection. Due consideration of differences in cultural and social context helps researchers to stay clear of many common pitfalls in cross-national surveys and buttresses the internal validity of their research designs. When differences in cross-cultural comparisons are found, they can be confident that these findings result from actual differences rather than methodological flaws. When similar empirical patterns are identified cross-nationally, they can assure themselves that these patterns emerge out of shared characteristics of human societies rather than as self-imposed methodological artifacts.

In most cases, cross-national settings are so complicated that few scholars are culturally and linguistically equipped to conduct credible comparative surveys by themselves. It always pays off to work with local scholars or survey practitioners from each participating country. Not only can such international teams help conduct efficient and comparable surveys, but they also can help interpret the survey results correctly. On the other hand, by adhering to some well-established procedural checks and some necessary step-by-step process of validation, researchers can counteract the common tendency of re-inventing the methodological wheel, or even worse, repeating the same mistakes of others. We believe that many of the best practices and rules of thumb that we describe below can reduce this twin possibility to an acceptable minimum.

SAMPLING

Whenever possible, researchers should base their sampling designs on census data. There are two obvious advantages to doing this: First, a census helps generate macro-level demographic statistics. Second, it makes it possible to compile a list of individuals in the population. In countries where census data are reliable and readily available, researchers can use demographic statistics as a baseline against which they can evaluate the results of their own surveys in these terms. Also, in some countries, the list of individuals from the census is probably the only legitimate and trustworthy source from which one can draw representative samples.

However, the use of census data in sampling designs may be limited. On the one hand, census data become obsolete quickly, particularly in countries with rapidly changing populations. Even though some researchers can make reasonable estimates by modeling the population growth and the changes that occur between censuses, it may be necessary to add other sources to justify the estimation. Sometimes it is preferable to rely on other demographic statistics for sampling designs. On the other hand, census data are not normally available at the individual level, due to concerns about the right to privacy, which may be protected by law. As a result, survey researchers often need to look to other sources as guidelines for producing sampling designs.

Among the alternative sources, resident registers and voter registers are both official and may be available for conducting academic surveys. In addition, they are supposed to be current and up-to-date, another feature that can help researchers locate potential respondents. In countries where resident registration is compulsory, researchers may be able to obtain a complete list of the registered residents who are members of the population of interest. Otherwise, researchers may need to rely on voter registers, even though they only include those who voluntarily register to vote. In some countries, the percentages of registered voters within voting age populations (VAP) are high enough to provide a comprehensive population for sampling, such as 86.1% in Mongolia (in 2000) and 85.9% in Australia (in 1998, IDEA, 2006), where voting is 'compulsory' (ZA, 2005, p. 20). Despite missing a certain proportion of residents who still did not register, such voter registers remain a highly valuable source in countries that do not maintain resident registers. Particularly when the response rate of a survey reaches as high as 95.8%, as it did in the 2002 East Asia Barometer Survey in Mongolia (PEA, 2003), voter registers have helped accomplish an otherwise very difficult task of sampling in nomadic societies.

Resident registers provide another reliable source. For example, the Taiwan Social Change Survey (TSCS), the series of surveys since 1984 that has conducted the most interviews in any GSS-model national survey series in the world as of 2005 (Smith, Kim, Koch, & Park, 2005, p. 74), has relied on the Household and Population Register as its exclusive source for sampling individuals from the adult population. This procedure is also used in Japan with its Basic Resident Registers and Slovenia with its Central Register of the Population for its ISSP (International Social Survey Programme) surveys (ZA, 2006a). Each year, the TSCS samples 22 of 358 towns and cities, selects 4 villages or precincts in each, and then randomly picks 80 to 100 residents in each village/precinct. After identifying 88 villages/precincts, the Center for Survey Research, a government-funded academic institution that conducts the surveys, asks the Department of the Interior for an electronic file that contains all registered individuals over age 18 in these 88 villages/precincts. With a program that randomly selects individuals, the file helps generate a sample that lists the name, date of birth, gender, and official address for each target respondent. Such a list of specific individuals is thus an important resource available for conducting general social surveys.

In highly mobile societies, voter registers may become obsolete quickly, a problem of smaller concern when using resident registers as the source for sampling. Although resident registration is usually mandatory by law, the penalty for not complying is not always compelling or rigorously enforced. As a result, a small proportion of residents move without bothering to change their registration, and thus the registration data may provide outdated information about the sample. For the TSCS, in most cases, about 10% of the selected individuals in the sample did not live at the official addresses where they were registered (Chang & Fu, 2002, pp.17f.). In some villages or precincts, as many as one-third of the registered residents had already moved. Most of these movers became part of the floating populations that have emerged in countries facing rapid changes.

Under most circumstances, it is impossible to avoid sampling targets in the floating population, who may be very difficult to locate. Once a sample list is drawn, the interviews should include everyone on the list. Otherwise, the higher the proportion of the floating population, the more seriously the completed sample will be biased (as the floating population usually shares certain demographic characteristics, such as being young, single, and members of minority ethnic groups).

The ideal way to deal with the floating population is to follow up those who are dislocated from their registered addresses. But the success of following up varies. For example, it is easier to locate college students and young workers who live away from their parents' homes (where they are registered). Interviewers usually are able to update their addresses and forward that information to the survey administrators, who dispatch the updated lists to other interviewers, who can track these dislocated targets accordingly. In contrast, those who move out of their registered residences with their family are more difficult to track, especially in urban areas, where family and relatives do not usually live close by and neighbors rarely know one another.

In some countries, researchers conduct surveys around the most important holiday of the year, when a large portion of the floating population returns home. For instance, a large number of Filipino migrant workers travel back to their home country around the Christmas holidays, and a great majority of the rural migrant workers in China return to the countryside during the Chinese lunar New Year.

QUESTIONNAIRE DESIGN

In countries with a long history of social surveys, designing questionnaires has been relatively straightforward. Researchers often adopt conventional and well-established formats, measures, and contents that best fit the research topics of interest. When applied to cross-national surveys, however, some of these designs need to be modified, taking into account various circumstances in countries that differ markedly in political, economic, social, and cultural settings. All of these heterogeneous conditions make designing the questionnaire a complicated task, requiring the research team to reconsider some of the practices that it previously had taken for granted. In short, researchers who make comparisons across societies and cultures need to avoid potential confusions or inconsistencies when applying ordinary terms or concepts, common measurements, and familiar formats of answer categories.

Terms and concepts

Linguistic idiosyncrasies are among the most arduous barriers to optimal comparability across fieldwork undertaken in different countries. Translating questionnaires for cross-cultural research is fraught with methodological pitfalls that threaten research validity. Literal translations are more likely than not to be counterproductive when trying to achieve equivalence meanings in a questionnaire. Experienced researchers employ both qualitative and quantitative methods to establish equivalence of meaning and measurement between different country versions (Sperber, Devellis, & Boehlecke, 1994). There are two minimum requirements for a systematic method of translation. The first is detailed annotation of the source questionnaire, especially for new, potentially difficult concepts. The second is iterative back-translation, where the source questionnaire is first translated into the required languages, and then translated back to the source language to see if and in what way the original question could have been corrupted.

Back translation, however, is designed to achieve linguistic equivalence without due consideration for context and milieu. Ideally, a systematic approach to translating the source questionnaire into other languages entails multi-stage pre-testing and a piloting process to ensure functional equivalence at both the linguistic and the conceptual level (Jowell, Roberts, Fitzgerald, & Eva, 2007). Conceptual equivalence (also known as 'interpretive equivalence' in some of the literature) requires concordance of meaning across different cultural and social contexts, which is sometimes difficult to achieve in cross-national survey. One should always be mindful of the 'etic-emic' conceptual model from anthropology and psychology for assessing the degree as well as the possibility of cross-cultural equivalence (Johnson, 1998). According to this framework, concepts, ideas and behaviors represented by survey questions can be classified as universal or 'etic' to the degree that they are understood in a consistent manner across cultural and national boundaries. In contrast, some ideas and concepts are considered 'emic' if they have meaning only to a few cultural groups. It is difficult if not impossible to establish interpretive equivalence for 'emic' terms or concepts. Some advanced statistical methods such as item response theory (Van der Linden & Hambleton, 1997) can be used to evaluate interpretive equivalence. However, statistical methodology can hardly replace expert judgment when it comes to making the distinction between 'etic' and 'emic' phenomena.

For instance, some terms and concepts may be clear-cut in Western or modern capitalist societies, but they become obscure and have different connotations in other societies and cultures. Even very simple terms or concepts that people use in everyday life may have different meanings from society to society. Whenever one uses these terms or concepts in a cross-national survey, it is always wise to be cautious during questionnaire design and when interpreting the results. For example, family, household, income, monthly income, paid job, and transportation may all sound straightforward and be commonly recognized across some countries. However, when an international survey covers more diverse regions and countries, it usually becomes clear that not all countries enjoy the same modern infrastructures and not all respondents share the same life experiences and frames of reference.

In Western societies, where social surveys have been developed and most used, families and households may be relatively easy to delineate. A family usually refers to the most basic social organization that includes one's parents, spouse, and children. In most cases, the household is the unit in which these family members reside. In many societies where nuclear families predominate, it is easy to identify the boundaries of families and households accordingly. In other societies where extended families are more common, however, it may become a more complicated task to determine exactly who counts as one's 'family member.'

For example, during the discussion in the 2006 Family module of the East Asian Social Survey (EASS), the Korean team suggested that the interviewers pursue the following guidelines to identify and include a family member in the questionnaire. First, for those living with the respondent, include everybody, no matter how far they might be removed in terms of blood relationships. Second, for those living away from home (including the respondent), include only those who are right above or below their own generation—which means excluding two generations (or more) above or below (e.g., grandparents, grandchildren) and siblings who live elsewhere. Third, include any members who live with the respondent's parents.[1] Although some may argue that such an operational definition may be too far-reaching, the guidelines are a good example of wide-ranging family boundaries that may differ from what prevails in many Western societies.

Furthermore, when several related nuclear families reside in the same lodging unit (for example, all live in a multi-story building with one nuclear family residing on each floor) and share their bare necessities (cooking, eating meals, using housing facilities, and the like), it would be even more difficult to draw a boundary around the family. Even within an independent housing unit, it is not uncommon to find more than two generations living together. While some restrict the meaning of the family to one's nuclear family, others might include married siblings. Under such circumstances, respondents may use different definitions when they identify how they share 'family chores,' how much their family income (or household income) is, and so on. When the boundary extends beyond one's spouse and children, it is also difficult to add up how much income all 'household members' earn.

In addition, the concept of 'income' breakdown is hard to measure in societies dominated by subsistence farming or other non-industrial means of production. Many peasants and farmers cannot grasp the concept of 'monthly income' because they sell their crops only once or twice a year. When searching for alternative measures of family wealth or economic conditions, therefore, one should take into account the major modes of subsistence in the countries participating in cross-national surveys. For example, in the East Asia Barometer, the Mongolian questionnaire used the number of cattle or horses as an index of family property or wealth. Similarly, questions about transportation need to incorporate horse or camel rides in countries like Mongolia or boat rides in countries such as Cambodia.

Like 'monthly income,' the term 'paid job' has been helpful for referring to 'work' in many societies. However, in some societies, it may be common for individuals to work and generate income for themselves or to help their families make money without getting paid by anyone. When families or other self-employed small businesses account for a large proportion of the labor force, in particular, the general term 'paid job' may not cover all the work in the labor force, and thus it might be obscure to many respondents.

In other words, in countries where over 30% or 40% of the working population is self-employed, the concept of 'paid job' as well as 'employer' may be irrelevant to that segment of the labor force, because they are not 'employed' or 'getting paid' in the conventional sense. Under certain circumstances, therefore, a more encompassing term like 'job with income' may serve as an alternative.

Measurement and response categories

The validity and reliability of any measure is always context-specific. This nuance is especially important in international surveys. In addition to concepts and terms, other key parts of questionnaire design (such as measurement scales and response categories) also deserve careful planning. For example, as straightforward as a 0 to 10 scale may be, it is neither self-explanatory nor self-evident. Especially to some less-educated or less-informed respondents, making judgments or expressing one's feelings about daily life or social issues in terms of a point system may be unfamiliar and foreign. Thus as a rule, researchers should pretest numerical scales.

Another issue with the point scaling system is associated with the cultural values and social norms that differ from society to society. In a comparative study of American and Chinese college students, Schwarz (2003) found that different scales that ask about the frequency of behavior worked equally well for Americans. For the Chinese students, however, the responses to such scales seemed to follow cultural values. Whatever the actual numbers that were used to measure the frequencies (e.g., about how often the student visited the campus library), the responses from the Chinese sample tended to fall at the center of the scale. In other words, by picking the middle categories that seemingly reflected their peers' most frequent patterns, the Chinese appear to have conformed to social norms.

Likewise, the Japanese respondents who picked the mid-points in attitudinal scales accounted for an unusually large percentage in recent ISSP surveys. Such 'middle-category' response patterns in both China and Japan may indicate strong social conformity in East Asian countries, or reflect cultural norms that discourage people from expressing strong opinions in their daily lives. More importantly, the apparently different response patterns among countries and regions call for the thoughtful design, practice, and interpretation of cross-national surveys.

Such cross-national variations also may relate to another popular format for questionnaire response categories, one that uses the 'agree-disagree' routine. As witnessed in many large-scale national and international surveys, some questions require respondents to judge how strongly they agree or disagree with certain statements. If these statements are opinions, one might expect people to respond to whether they agree or disagree with such opinions, or more precisely, whether they also think so. Nonetheless, when these statements read like facts—as well as opinions—they may be ambiguous and cause confusion during interviews.

Take the following question that uses a positive statement: *Please tick one box on each line to show how much you agree or disagree with each of the following statements. People we elect as members of the Parliament (MPs) try to keep the promises they have made during the election* (ISSP, 2006 Role of Government). For the designers, this statement is clearly an opinion,

a 'someone says that' sentence. To some respondents, particularly the less-educated or less-sophisticated ones, the same sentence might sound like a 'fact': a statement that these MPs do 'try to keep the promises.' When a respondent says, 'agree' does that mean s/he believes that 'they will try' or that 'such an act of trying to keep the promises is such a good a thing that there is no way to disagree with it?'

Take another question that adopts a negative tone: *To what extent do you agree or disagree with the following statements. If you are not careful, other people will take advantage of you* (ISSP, 2006 Role of Government). Again, do all respondents understand that this statement is an opinion, not a social phenomenon? Can we be sure that no one would mistake the conditional statement for a precaution that is urging respondents to be careful so that other people will have no chance to take advantage of them? Does a 'disagree' response really mean that the respondent 'does not believe that other people will take advantage of them if they are not careful?' Or does it simply reflect one's disagreement with 'such a horrible social condition,' in which people will take advantage of them when they are not careful? The former answer represents the response pattern that researchers have in mind, while the latter scenario gives an answer that measures something else instead.

While some respondents in any country may experience such confusions, these interpretive problems are more likely to cause a significant distortion to survey results in countries where people do not often express their opinions freely, particularly when they face the interviewer, a stranger. Although such an 'agree/disagree' format has been widely used in countries with a long history of social surveys, it always helps to experiment with different formats through cognitive interviews in all the countries involved. While keeping this format may be appropriate for purely attitudinal questions, it is wise to avoid it when there is any possibility that it may confuse some respondents. For questions similar to the two examples in this section, one may want to skip the leading questions in each instance and ask them directly. Rather than using 'strongly agree, somewhat agree, somewhat disagree, strongly disagree' as the response categories, one may want to use clearer categories, such as, 'definitely will, probably will, probably will not, definitely will not,' which would enable respondents to think and reply in a direct, unambiguous, and undemanding manner. At least, an 'agree' response should be translated into a phrase that means, 'I think so,' which was exactly what the Japanese General Social Survey (JGSS) did in its annual surveys.[2]

MODES OF DATA COLLECTION

The appropriate modes of data collection may differ depending on the questionnaires' length and content. How effectively a specific mode functions also differs from country to country. For serious and complex academic surveys, the face-to-face, in-person interview with trained interviewers has been the mainstream mode of interviewing. Particularly in countries where a large proportion of residents is illiterate, where telecommunications are difficult, or when the questionnaire format is complicated and difficult to follow, face-to-face interviews are the most appropriate mode.

As technology advances and face-to-face interviews become more difficult and expensive to conduct, many surveys have relied on other means, especially postal mail, telephone, and the Internet. In addition to the questionnaires' length and content, the cost of conducting interviews plays another important role in selecting appropriate modes of research. Sometimes cost is a major reason why countries abandon face-to-face interviews, but in most of these countries, socio-economic conditions allow them to conduct reliable and valid surveys using less supervised modes to collect data, particularly when the vast majority of target respondents is well educated and residents usually trust the survey institutions. For international surveys

across different continents or regions of the world, there often is such variation in modes of data collection (Skjak & Harkness, 2003).

For example, nearly two-thirds of the International Social Survey Programme (ISSP) members used face-to-face interviews to collect data for their 2003 and 2004 ISSP modules, and about one-third used postal mail surveys. Not coincidentally, the countries that used postal surveys, mostly Scandinavian and West European countries, normally had higher labor costs for in-person interviews and a higher proportion of well-educated residents who could complete the questionnaires by themselves. In other cases, such as in Canada and Australia, the cost of tracking sparse target respondents would have grown so enormously that face-to-face interviews could not be justified (ZA, 2005, 2006a, 2006b).

Some survey designs mix different modes in the same study, thus modifying the practice of face-to-face interviews. They also make the common modes of interviewing insufficient. While conventional face-to-face interviews employ interviewers to administer questionnaires, and postal mail interviews rely on the respondents' self-completion, the line between such modes of interviewing is no longer clear-cut in emerging international survey programs. For example, respondents in both Japan and Great Britain were asked to complete (at least part of) the questionnaires by themselves, just as those completing the postal (and web) surveys did. However, the trained interviewers actually visited the respondents, left the questionnaire, and later picked it up. In so doing, the interviewers could answer any questions face-to-face and make sure that the respondents had understood and completed all parts of the questionnaires. Similarly, trained interviewers in Flanders used Computer Assisted Personal Interviewing (CAPI) to ask about aspects of respondents' personal backgrounds, such as socioeconomic characteristics, face-to-face, and then left the ISSP module for the respondents, who completed and mailed the questionnaires back to the survey agency

(ZA, 2006b). In addition, it is not uncommon for interviewers and supervisors to follow-up with respondents by telephone.

Although telephone interviews have been popular and efficient in many countries, they seldom are used for making comparisons among countries that differ greatly in teledensity (measured by main telephone lines per 100 inhabitants, ITU, 2004) or the percentage of households with at least one telephone. Of the large-scale, cross-national survey programs, telephone surveys have been used only in part of the Comparative Study of Electoral Systems (CSES), the Gallup International Voices of the People Survey, and the Pew Global Attitudes Survey (Heath, Fisher, & Smith, 2005, pp. 312f.). Indeed, telephone interviews are clearly not an option in many African countries where the teledensity is under 10. In contrast, in countries where fixed-line telephones cover the population well, researchers have been able to obtain representative samples by interviewing respondents over the phone, especially with the help of Computer Assisted Telephone Interviewing (CATI) systems.

However, even in these countries, it has become unrealistic to claim that there is an equal chance of reaching every resident by fixed-line phones. Within the younger generation, in particular, a new pattern of telecommunication has taken shape with mobile phones and wireless text messages. As more residents become less accessible by fixed-line telephones, the conventional mode of telephone interviews is missing them. More importantly, actual samples may be highly biased against younger residents and thus need to be adjusted by weights on age. To cover all populations, telephone interviews would also have to target those who are accessible only or mainly by mobile phones.

Conducting interviews over mobile phones enables researchers to contact respondents who are otherwise less reachable. Yet this type of interview poses a new challenge, because interviewers are more likely to catch respondents on the move, a situation disadvantageous to the already short-lasting conversations on mobile phones. Although most telephone interviews using fixed lines have been limited to relatively short and straightforward questionnaires, some interviews can last as long as 45 minutes, enough time to tackle such complicated questions, as in a U.S. Social Capital survey in early 2005 ($n = 3,000$).[3] Conducting such extended interviews would seem impossible over mobile phones.

The newest mode of interviewing takes advantage of the Internet, mainly using web surveys. Web surveys initially were designed for non-scientific purposes, with a few commercial and non-academic agencies using them to explore a limited number of Internet users. As Internet usage expands rapidly, it is becoming more feasible to interview a wide range of social groups in countries where the Internet penetration rate (the percentage of the population using the Internet) reaches as high as 50% to 80% (IWS, 2006). As is the case with teledensity, however, Internet usage remains very sparse and limited in many other countries, where face-to-face interviewing remains the only option.

However, the problems with using web surveys for international comparisons lie beyond the digital divide. Due to the nature of using the Internet, it is extremely difficult to make reliable checks on respondents' identities. More importantly, respondents and non-respondents on web surveys may differ not only in terms of their demographic backgrounds and socioeconomic characteristics, but also in their attitudes and values toward the use of online communication. For example, a study in Taiwan suggested that, compared to other Internet users, active respondents in online surveys felt e-mail messages were important. For these respondents, however, online interactions seemed so transient and fleeting that most messages were not worth preserving (Fu, 2001). Thus, while online surveys challenge traditional modes of interviewing, interviewing over the Internet faces fundamental difficulties that go beyond non-probability sampling and low response rates.

CONCLUSION

As cross-national surveys involve more regions, cultures, political systems, and economic conditions, various problems may arise in sampling, questionnaire design, and data collection. It is extremely difficult, if not impossible, to conduct cross-national surveys using identical sampling schemes, question wordings and orderings, measurement scales, and modes of data collection. In fact, there is no ideal or 'universal' approach. Because the sources of macro-level data differ greatly from country to country, researchers should allow for variable sampling strategies while insisting on probability sampling at critical stages (e.g., within the primary sampling units). To design standardized instruments, common terms and concepts must be unequivocal, and measurement scales and response categories must be appropriate for cross-cultural settings.

Although cross-national surveys have relied on different modes of data collection, face-to-face interviewing remains a reliable mode that reaches out to a vast majority of the population and facilitates the most sophisticated questionnaire designs. For face-to-face interviews, it is important to recruit heterogeneous interviewers in terms of gender, age, ethnic group, and linguistic capability. Gender and ethnicity may be the most sensitive characteristics during face-to-face interviews. In many societies, it is inappropriate to send a male interviewer to interview a female respondent in a private setting (that is, without the presence of the male head of household). Furthermore, in most Muslim countries, it is impossible to send a female worker to interview a male respondent. Sometimes it is necessary to have several male–female teams among the interviewers to accommodate various circumstances. While national surveys incorporate such considerations, social and cultural differences among nations further point to the necessity of taking macro-level variations into account when exploring how social phenomena differ across national borders.

NOTES

1 Used with permission from the instructions drafted by Sang-wook Kim, the principal investigator of the Korean General Social Survey (KGSS).

2 This is a point well taken by one of the JGSS's Principal Investigators, Noriko Iwai.

3 The project was sponsored by Academia Sinica, Taiwan. The principal investigator was Nan Lin.

REFERENCES

Chang, Y., & Fu, Y. (2002). *Taiwan Shehui Beichien Jihben Diaochia Baogao 2002* [Report on Taiwan Social Change Surveys, 2002]. Taipei: Institute of Sociology, Academia Sinica.

Fu, Y. (2001). *Wanglu Ruiko de Yangban Terxin.* [Sample characteristics of the Internet population: Web survey follow-up and personal network sampling compared.] *Survey Research, 9,* 35–72.

Heath, A., Fisher, S., & Smith S. (2005). The globalization of public opinion research. *Annual Review of Political Science, 8,* 297–333.

IDEA. (2006). *Voter turnout webpage.* Stockholm, Sweden: International Institute for Democracy and Electoral Assistance. Retrieved January 6, 2007, from http://www.idea.int/vt/.

ITU. (2004). *Teledensity of countries/territories.* International Telecommunication Union. Retrieved January 6, 2007, from http://www.itu.int/itudoc/itu-t/com3/focus/72404.html.

IWS. (2006). *Internet usage statistics—The big picture. World Internet users and population stats.* Retrieved January 6, 2007, from http://www.internetworldstats.com/stats.htm.

Johnson T. P. (1998). Approaches to equivalence in cross-cultural and cross-national survey research. In J. Harkness (Ed.), *Cross-cultural survey equivalence* (pp. 1–40). Mannheim: ZUMA.

Jowell, R., Roberts, C., Fitzgerald, R., & Eva, G., (Eds.). (2007). *Measuring attitudes cross-nationally: Lessons from the European Social Survey.* London: Sage Publication.

PEA. (2003). *Country survey report: Mongolia. East Asia Barometer Survey.* Mongolia: Political Education Academy.

Schwarz, N. (2003). Culture-sensitive context effects: A challenge for cross-cultural surveys. In J. A. Harkness, F. J. R. Van de Vijver, & P. Ph. Mohler (Eds.), *Cross-cultural survey methods* (pp. 93–100). New York: John Wiley & Sons.

Skjak, K.K., & Harkness, J. (2003). Data collection methods. In J. A. Harkness, F. J. R. Van de Vijver, &

P. Ph. Mohler (Eds.), *Cross-cultural survey methods* (pp. 179–193). New York: John Wiley & Sons.

Smith, T. W., Kim, J., Koch, A., & Park, A. (2005). Social-science research and the general social surveys. *ZUMA-Nachrichten, 56,* 68–77.

Sperber, A., Devellis, R., & Boehlecke, B. (1994). Cross-cultural translation—methodology and validation. *Journal of Cross-Cultural Psychology, 25,* 501–524.

Van der Linden, W. J., & Hambleton, R. K. (Eds.). (1997). *Handbook of modern item response theory.* New York: Springer.

ZA. (2005). *ISSP 2002 Module—Family and changing gender roles* (Document #ZA3880). Cologne, Germany: Central Archive for Empirical Social Research.

ZA. (2006a). *ISSP 2003 Module—National identity II final data CD* (Document #ZA3910). Cologne, Germany: Central Archive for Empirical Social Research.

ZA. (2006b). *ISSP 2004 Module—Citizenship (preliminary data from 35 member countries).* Cologne, Germany: Central Archive for Empirical Social Research.

27

Sampling

Colm O'Muircheartaigh

It seems implausible that a good measure of what is happening in a whole population can be obtained by examining only a tiny fraction of that population. The theory and practice of sampling underpin this claim. Sampling is the process of selecting a subset of a population; inference consists of using the measurements on that subset to make statements about the population as a whole. This chapter presents the rationale behind sampling and inference from samples, briefly traces its history, and describes the main procedures for sampling for face-to-face surveys and telephone surveys today.

This chapter consists of four sections. The first section presents my seven maxims of sampling, which serve as a foundation for the principles involved. The following two sections cover sampling for face-to-face surveys and for telephone surveys. The fourth section discusses briefly issues in pre-election polling and Internet surveys. There are some brief concluding remarks at the end of the chapter.

THE SEVEN MAXIMS OF SAMPLING

Maxim #1: Survey sampling is an applied discipline and is not a branch of mathematical statistics

Survey sampling as we know it today originated in a proposal presented in Berne in 1895 to a meeting of the International Statistical Institute (ISI) by the director of the Norwegian Central Bureau of Statistics, Anders Kiaer.[1] His audience was composed primarily of senior government statisticians, whose preference and inclination was for complete enumerations of populations, either through Censuses or from administrative records.

The objective of sampling was to identify a *miniature of the population* that mirrored important aspects of the population, but on a smaller scale. The prerequisites for selecting a sample were knowledge of the population and its important parameters. There is no reference in Kiaer's presentation or in the discussion of it to any statistical or mathematical theory, apart from the pejorative comment of von Mayr who disparaged the whole enterprise by declaring 'pas de calcul là où l'observation peut être faite' (Kiaer, 1897, p. 52). This notion that sampling and estimation is a form of guesswork legitimated by mathematical sleight of hand is still prevalent today, as we can see from the controversy that still surrounds the use of sampling in the decennial Population Census.

As a mental exercise, think about choosing a real population about which there is substantial information. Next, consider how to design a sample to use to collect data from this population. The population might be all residents of a country who are aged 18 and over, voters in an election, adults in a city, consumers of a company's products, households in a legislative district, or readers of a newspaper.

As an example I will suggest possible reasoning for a national sample in the US measuring attitudes to the war in Iraq.

Every real population has diversity, and almost certainly a researcher would want to represent that diversity in a sample. This means that the (ideal) sample should contain elements (people) that represent that diversity. For the national attitude survey, that means (at the very least) that it should represent proponents and opponents of the war, and the ambivalent. On the issue of the Iraq war there has been strong disagreement between the Democrat and Republican political parties. Thus, this might be built into the sample design by classifying the population into blue (Republican) states and red (Democrat) states and ensuring that the sample is drawn from each in proportion to their population. [These segments are called *strata* in the sampling literature.] The more the researcher knows about the population and about factors that might be related to the target variable, the more it will be possible to structure the sample to represent these dimensions of the population.

Practicality should also enter into the design. Populations are typically widely dispersed, and for face-to-face surveys of the general population, it is impractical to think of selecting individuals as the sampling units. Thus, a sample is first selected of aggregations of individuals (such as states, counties, towns, blocks, etc.), and the final sample is restricted to these selected sampling units, referred to as *clusters* in the sampling literature. The absence of lists of individuals is another reason why it is often simply impractical to contemplate a design where individuals are selected directly into the sample.

The sample design reported by Kiaer in his 1895 presentation contains just these elements. His design first categorized Norway by region, and an appropriate portion of the sample was selected from each region. Within each region, he selected a sample of districts and, in advance of the selection of districts, determined a detailed plan to select the sample within selected districts. From each district he selected households ('houses and their inhabitants') through a systematic procedure.

Thus the basic design that one might develop for this general problem would be a stratified clustered sample of households, with some method for selecting individual respondents within the selected households. The specifics of the stratification and the clustering are driven by subject matter knowledge, not statistical expertise.

The key message here is that the reasoning underlying sample design, though often couched in mathematical form, does not require any mathematics to appreciate its import.

Maxim #2: Freedom from selection bias is the most important reason for probability sampling

The conflict between the proponents of probability sampling and the supporters of other (non-probability) approaches to sampling is relatively recent. Kiaer's original proposals suggested two desirable characteristics for samples: first, they should mirror the important characteristics of the population (they should in some sense be *representative*), and second, they should be selected *objectively*, that is, not *subjectively*—the selector should not prejudice the selection by the introduction of any personal or other biases.

Over the following 40 years or so, sampling developed in two quite different ways. One branch concentrated on the principle of representativeness: purposive samples in which the units were chosen, using the judgment of the investigator, to represent important aspects of the population; this came to be known as the *Method of Purposive Selection*. The other branch favored mechanical neutrality over judgment: The units in the sample were chosen using a probability mechanism, such as random numbers; this was known as the *Method of Random Selection*.

Purposive selection generated a large number of different procedures and names. In government work, the term *balanced sampling* was often used; in commercial and market research, the term *quota sampling* eventually became the general term to describe the methods. This was because each interviewer was allocated a set of cases to complete; this set was defined not in terms of the selection process, but in terms of meeting targets for the number of cases with pre-specified characteristics—the interviewer's quota.

The method of random selection was favored by statisticians, of course, and was generally more common in official statistics. The difficulty was that only the simplest form of the method—simple random sampling— had support from mathematical statistical theory, and practitioners felt that this restricted too much their flexibility in using their knowledge of the population.

Maxim #3: We judge a sample design not by the samples it produces, but by the samples it might have produced (the Sampling Distribution)

Jerzy Neyman, a Polish mathematician, produced the breakthrough in reasoning that made it possible to compare these two competing approaches. He argued that in evaluating a sample design, the appropriate criterion was the *likelihood* that the design would produce a sample that was adequate for its purpose. Essentially, the argument boils down to saying that one can't judge a design by a single outcome; it should be judged on a consideration of all the possible outcomes of the design and how acceptable this set of possible outcomes is for a study's purpose.

This set of all possible outcomes of a sample design is called the *Sampling Distribution*. In a paper presented to the Royal Statistical Society in 1934, Neyman compared purposive selection and random selection in terms of the sampling distributions they generated. The two key characteristics of the sampling distribution are its *mean*, which is the average value of the estimates it contains, and its *standard error*, which is a measure of the dispersion of the sampling distribution (how different from each other the various estimates in the sampling distribution can be).[2]

Maxim # 4: Never use simple random sampling!

Simple Random Sampling

A sample design that gives every element in the population the same chance of selection *and also gives every combination of n elements the same chance of selection.*

Sampling textbooks often devote a great deal of time and space to simple random sampling (SRS). This can lead the unwary to believe that SRS is an appropriate sample design to use. This is not so.

In thinking about this issue, it is important to distinguish between the probabilities of selection of elements and the probabilities of selection of combinations of elements. The core characteristic of a probability sample is that every *element* in the population has a known non-zero probability of selection. Under SRS any and every *combination of elements* in the population could constitute the sample. Using SRS therefore implies that one is indifferent among combinations of elements. For a national design, it would obviously be undesirable to have the whole national sample from the same street, or the same neighborhood, or even from a single town. Similarly, in designing a sample of voters in an exit poll, even if one had in advance a list of all those who would actually vote, one would not design a sample that permitted the whole sample to be of voters in a single precinct, or from a single hour of the day.

SRS is essentially the most unrestricted form of sampling (every combination of elements is a possible sample, and every combination of elements has the same probability as every other combination of elements). As every other design can be seen as a set of restrictions on this design, SRS provides a natural benchmark for all other sample designs. Finally, SRS is the closest survey sampling comes to the crucial assumption of i.i.d. (independent identically distributed) observations in mathematical statistics. This makes it a sample design that is a natural fit for other branches of statistics.

Maxim #5: Sample design consists of manipulating the probabilities of different sample outcomes

The key to understanding sample design is to understand the sampling distribution; the key to understanding a particular sample design is to understand the particular sampling distribution it produces. Using as a reference point the sampling distribution produced by SRS, in which every possible combination of elements from the population has the same chance of occurring, one can consider all other sample designs as manipulating the probabilities of some or all of these combinations of elements.

This means that it is possible to change the sampling distribution by increasing the probabilities of some samples (combinations of elements) and decreasing the probabilities

of other samples. And this can be done without necessarily changing the probabilities of the individual elements that make up the combinations!

If one can manage to increase the probabilities of selection of samples that give estimates close to the true value (samples that are more representative of the population), then one can increase the precision of the estimate; the spread of the sampling distribution will be less, the standard error of the estimate will be smaller. Typically this happens when a stratified sample is selected; generally stratification gives more precise estimates, and typically does not cost more than not stratifying.

If a researcher wants to select a sample of 500 residents from a population of 60,000 that consists of two towns, each of population 30,000 but with different socio-demographic characteristics, this can be achieved with a selection probability of 1 in 120 for each resident (element) either by selecting an SRS of 500 residents from the whole population (thereby allowing any combination of residents to constitute the sample), or by selecting an SRS of 250 residents from within each town independently (thus allowing only samples of 500 that combine 250 from each of the two towns).

If the samples that are made more likely are less representative of the population, the spread of the sampling distribution will be greater; the precision of the estimate will decrease, the standard error of the estimate will be larger. Typically this happens when cluster or multistage samples are selected; generally clustering gives less precise samples but saves costs.

If 2,000 voters were arranged in 8 precincts of 250 voters each, for example, we can give every voter (element) a 1 in 8 chance of selection either by selecting a simple random sample of 250 voters (thereby allowing any possible combination of 250 voters to constitute the sample), or by selecting one of the 8 precincts at random (thereby allowing only 8 possible combinations of voters to constitute the sample). Because precincts will typically be relatively homogeneous, such cluster samples will on average be less representative than samples that contain voters from a variety of precincts.

There are two concepts that we use to help us understand the impact of sample design on outcome—the design effect (*deff*) and the effective sample size n_{eff}; both relate the particular design to an SRS benchmark.

Design Effect

The design effect (*deff* or d^2) is the ratio of the variance for the design to the variance for a simple random sample of the same size.

For clustered samples, the design effect is typically greater than 1; for stratified samples the design effect is typically less than 1.

Effective Sample Size n_{eff}

The effective sample size is the size of simple random sample that would give the same precision as the sample actually used. Effective sample size can be calculated as $n_{eff} = n/deff$.

Maxim #6: Optimal design does not minimize cost per case completed; it maximizes information per dollar spent

In looking at reports of a survey, we tend to look at the sample size as our first indicator of credibility or plausibility. This is appropriate as a first approximation, as precision is directly related to sample size for simple random sampling, because the variance of the estimate is inversely related to sample size (standard error is inversely related to the square root of sample size).

However, as almost no samples are simple random samples, this first approximation may be misleading. For samples with different designs, it is the effective sample size and not the absolute sample size that is important; the effective sample size measures the information content of the sample.

There are two circumstances in which this becomes relevant. The first is at the stage of designing or commissioning a study when the researcher needs to balance the cost of the survey against the information being collected. A sample of 100 clusters with 20 individuals interviewed in each may well be considerably more precise than a sample of 20 clusters with 150 individuals interviewed in each, even though the sample size in one case is $100 \times 20 = 2000$ and in the other $20 \times 150 = 3000$. The second is when a researcher is faced with analyzing data from a survey already completed. There is a tendency to analyze data using standard statistical software that treats all data as SRS. Failure to take into account the sample design, including any appropriate weights to account for it, can lead to seriously misleading results.

In general, preferred sample designs are *epsem* (equal probability of selection method) designs. Departures from epsem should really only be introduced: (i) of necessity, or (ii) when the particular objectives of a survey make a non-epsem design particularly advantageous. Epsem designs have the major advantage of simplicity in the analysis, and are generally appropriate for surveys with many objectives. In an epsem sample, each part of the population is represented by a sample whose size is proportional to the size of the part of the population it represents; this is proportional sampling.

When the primary purpose of a study is to compare two (sub-)populations, however, then the best design is one in which the sample size from each of the parts of the population is equal. This will lead to a design with relatively low precision for the parameters of the overall population, but it will compensate for this by giving much better precision for relevant comparisons within the population.

Maxim #7: Good sample design is based on knowing your population, your frame, and your objectives

There is a tendency among sampling statisticians to think about sample design generically as a technical problem and not to consult in any detail with the researcher, the client. Though one may not (wish to or be able to) appreciate the technical detail, it is important to remember that sample design is the servant of the subject matter, not the other way round. All major decisions about the design are relevant to the user, who, if willing to listen, is entitled to understand and approve them.

In the following sections, we will describe sample design for the two major modes of data collection—face-to-face interviewing and telephone interviewing, followed by a short discussion of pre-election polls, exit polls, and Internet surveys.

SAMPLING FOR FACE-TO-FACE SURVEYS

Survey sampling as we know it today has its origins in the work of government statisticians at the end of the 19th century. Early work using survey sampling was carried out by Kiaer in Norway, Bowley in England, Mahalanobis in India, and Gini in Italy. Some rudimentary work on sampling was directed for the Federal government in the US by Carroll D. Wright and Cressy L. Wilbur. In the area of opinion polling, early leaders in survey research were Archibald Crossley, George Gallup and Elmo Roper, who are credited with developing the dominant form of sample design in opinion research—*quota sampling* (Stephan & McCarthy, 1974, pp. 27ff.). It is worth noting that the primary difference between quota samples and balanced purposive selection was that the latter mostly adopted purposive selection at the early stages of sampling, while the former introduced purposiveness primarily at the stage of selection of individual respondents.

Apart from market research, probability sampling has replaced quota sampling for most purposes. National attitude surveys such as the General Social Survey (GSS) and the National Election Survey (NES) in the US and the British Social Attitude Survey (BSA) in the UK are based on multistage probability samples. The new European flagship attitude survey, the European Social Survey (ESS), also stipulates probability sampling for all participating countries.

Considerations of cost and feasibility have determined that essentially all national sample designs worldwide are multi-stage samples with administrative/political areas as the primary sampling units (PSUs). The skewedness[3] of the distribution of the sizes of administrative area units typically leads to the inclusion of the largest of these area units in the sample with certainty. These selections are sometimes called self-representing PSUs. The design also traditionally includes stratification of the area units at the various stages of selection, incorporating prior knowledge of the population structure.

Though the PSUs in almost all national demographic surveys are areas, the sampling methods for subsequent stages vary considerably. It is at the penultimate stage of selection—typically the selection of housing units—that the divergence is most important, distinguishing between those areas in which a pre-existing list frame is used and situations where there are further area selections within *ad hoc* listings for a particular survey or master sample.

In Scandinavia and the Netherlands, the state maintains up-to-date and comprehensive population registers; typically these registers are used as sampling frames for demographic surveys. In China until the mid- to late-1980s, samples were also register-based, though with the changes in the economic and political system the quality of the registers deteriorated and samples began to be designed as area samples. In Ireland, the UK, and a number of other countries, the Registers of Electors (an administrative list of those qualified to vote) were considered comprehensive enough (perhaps 90 to 98% of the adult population) that they were used as a frame. However, in the mid-1980s in the UK, the quality of the Electoral Register as a frame for the adult population deteriorated to the extent that survey designers switched to the Postcode Address File (PAF), a centrally available list of delivery points used by the postal service as a frame for mail delivery because its high coverage, frequent updating, and ease of access made it the frame of choice for household surveys. Where such lists were typically not available, sample designs tend to involve multiple area stages with *ad hoc* listing of the ultimate area units (UAUs) to provide a frame of households. In the US, the absence of any satisfactory population register had led *ab initio* to the use of area sampling with listing of addresses/housing units in the selected UAUs.

The absence of any list of acceptable quality had another major implication for sample design in the US. In register-based systems, annual or continuous updates make it feasible to select a fresh sample for each survey; the measures of size for the area units at the higher stages can be modified with changes in the population, leading to efficiencies in the overall design. In the US, however, the only measures of size for the area units were those generated by the decennial census. This implied that the selection of PSUs could be carried out once each decade, and that no new information to modify that selection would be available for a further 10 years. Consequently, until quite recently, national probability samples for face-to-face surveys in the US were based on master samples of areas selected decennially by the major survey organizations; annual or biennial changes were at the level of sampling within the selected areas.

Although there are some alternative frames, the United States Postal Service-based frame seems to have the best coverage. Interestingly, the results of direct comparisons between the new list-based frames and the earlier listings provided by field listers from survey organizations suggest that the list frames may, in some circumstances, be superior to those produced by the previous methodology (O'Muircheartaigh, Eckman, & Weiss, 2002; O'Muircheartaigh, Eckman, & English, 2004).

The overall implication of these developments is that we can move now from the straitjacket of the decennial master sample to a *tailored sample* approach, where sample designs can be modified to fit more accurately the objectives of the studies in which they are being used. The availability of these lists relaxes the constraints on sample design for face-to-face field surveys.

SAMPLING FOR TELEPHONE SURVEYS[4]

Because costs of telephone frames and telephone sampling are very low relative to the cost of samples for face-to-face surveys, there has not been the same clash between probability and non-probability sampling in telephone surveys that has existed for face-to-face surveys. To the extent that there has been a divergence, it has been between using a list frame (listed telephones only) and random digit dialing of all possible telephone numbers.

Surveys by telephone probably began in the 1920s and 1930s as soon as telephone directories were published. As early as 1952, O. N. Larson published a paper on 'The comparative validity of telephone and face-to-face interviews in the measurement of message diffusion from leaflets' (Larson, 1952). However, early surveys were local in scope, and the sampling frame was typically the local telephone directory. The principal shortcoming of the telephone directory as a frame is the absence of unlisted numbers. The extent of this noncoverage has increased over time, and current estimates for the USA range from 30% to 60% of all telephone numbers, depending on region and various demographic characteristics.

The feasibility of large-scale telephone surveys depends on the coverage and the structure of the telecommunications system. The availability of electronic frames of telephone numbers, privacy laws, and the pricing structure for telephone calls all play a part in facilitating or inhibiting telephone surveys. All countries in which probability samples of telephone numbers became widespread had highly structured systems for assigning telephone numbers that facilitated this process. Where this was not the case, as in the United Kingdom, the growth of national telephone surveys was seriously delayed. The US example is given as an illustration of the principles and requirements of a computer-driven telephone sampling system. Consequently, this section deals primarily with telephone sampling in the US; the general principles and constraints apply more broadly.

The standardized US telephone number system (NANP, the North American Numbering Plan, 3-digit area code (AC) plus a 7-digit number) was established in 1947, but it was not until the 1960s that the telephone system supported full direct distance dialing (national dialing without operator assistance). This development made the ideal of selecting a random sample of all telephone numbers, and surveying them, a practical possibility. In 1972 random-digit dialing (RDD) was proposed as a method of telephone sampling by Glasser and Metzger in *the Journal of Marketing Research*. In 1977, Thomas Danbury set up Survey Sampling Inc. (now SSI), the first major vendor of probability samples of telephone numbers.

Sample selection for RDD consists of selecting telephone numbers randomly from a frame of possible telephone numbers. The first frame of such numbers had to be constructed by amalgamating data on all area codes (ACs) and central office codes (later known as prefixes) that were in use. If all possible telephone numbers within known AC/prefix combinations are considered to be in the frame, there are about 770,000,000 possible numbers. About 13% to 17% of these are currently in service.

The first RDD studies selected numbers at random, usually as a systematic random sample from the universe of possible numbers defined by the AC/prefix combinations. However, in the 1970s the hit rate (i.e., the proportion of such numbers that were working household numbers) for this process was only 20%, leading to high costs for survey organizations in calling and screening non-working numbers.

The first breakthrough came with the development (by Joseph Waksberg and Warren Mitofsky) of a method that increased the hit rate from 20% to about 50% through a two-phase sampling method now known as the Mitofsky-Waksberg method. A random sample of telephone numbers from the universe determined by working AC/prefixes would first be selected; these numbers defined a set of 100-block, eight-digit numbers (AC/prefix combinations followed by two random digits). If the selected number was a working household number, then numbers within that 100 block would be called until k (usually a number between 4 and 8) working household numbers were selected from that block. If the number was not a working household number, another 100 block would be selected. Through a clever application of probability proportional to size sampling, this procedure generates an equal probability sample of working household numbers from the universe, but with a much higher hit rate. However, the method had a number of practical difficulties related to problems with sparsely populated 100 blocks and lack of predictability of the required number of telephone numbers to be called.

The practical problems of the Mitofsky-Waksberg method led to the exploration and introduction of a new RDD methodology in the 1980s known as *list-assisted RDD*. There are two basic differences between list-assisted and M-W sampling. First, in list-assisted sampling, the universe of (potentially) eligible numbers is defined through detailed analysis of the universe of listed numbers. Second, list-assisted sampling is a one-phase rather than a two-phase sampling method, and control of the initial sample size is considerably greater. The objective is still to be able to select an equal probability sample of working telephone numbers in the US. List-assisted sampling is now the dominant procedure for selecting RDD samples.

Mechanism and specifications

Today, there are estimated to be over 100 million telephone households in the

United States. The ability to represent all households in a telephone sample is complicated by two main factors: some households are unlisted by choice, and others are unlisted by circumstance, particularly because of mobility. Approximately 30% of telephone households in the US have unlisted numbers, and these are disproportionately distributed across the country. Statewide unlisted rates range anywhere from 11% to 46%, and rates are even higher in some urban areas. In addition, each year, about 20% of American households move, so that 12% to 15% of the residential numbers in a typical directory are disconnected. Samples drawn entirely from directories and 'plus-one' techniques, in which a directory-listed number is incremented by one in an attempt to incorporate some unlisted numbers, often significantly under-represent unlisted households.

Creation of a frame for random digit selection

Most RDD samples are generated using a database of 'working blocks.' A *block* (also known as a *100-bank* or a *bank*) is a set of 100 contiguous numbers identified by the first eight digits of a telephone number. For example, in the telephone number 312-749-5512, '31274955' is the block containing that phone number, and includes the set of all numbers between 312-759-5500 and 312-759-5599. Blocks are merged with the database of all directory-listed households in the country, and are determined to be *working* if at least one listed telephone number is found in that block. Once the working blocks are identified, the RDD frame is stratified, say by county. The number of working blocks in an exchange is multiplied by 100 (the number of possible 10-digit telephone numbers in a block) to calculate the total number of possible phone numbers.

Sample selection

Samples are typically drawn systematically from the frame. EPSEM (equal probability of selection method) samples are single stage, equal probability samples of all possible 10-digit telephone numbers in blocks with one or more listed telephone number. The Working Residential Number rate (WRN)[5] for an epsem list-assisted RDD sample is on average about 50%.

Selection options

Geographic Selection Options: Samples can be ordered from geographic areas as large as the entire US and as small as census tracts or exchanges. The exact geography from which the sample should be selected must be specified to the vendor. Some common geographic selections include states, counties, zip codes, area code/exchange combinations, and groups of census tracts.

Demographic Selection Options: Several demographic selection options are available for RDD and listed samples. Samples can be ordered to target racial or ethnic groups, particular income brackets, urban, suburban, or rural areas, and age groups. The information used to target these groups is based on census data. For example, racial groups are targeted based on their density in the population using census data, which are typically available down to tract level. RDD samples have the option of being targeted based on race, income, and urban status. Listed samples can also be targeted based on ethnicity and age group.

Sample screening

Often, there are particular types of numbers that researchers would like to exclude from a sample. For example, in a survey targeting households, it is useful to remove known businesses from the sample before beginning data collection to reduce the number of calls made to ineligible lines. In most surveys, known disconnected lines are also removed before data collection. This process of *screening* for particular types of phone numbers usually involves creating a *flag* that can later be used to remove unwanted numbers, such as disconnects, from the sample. Screening can be accomplished using various methods, including automated tone detection, database matching, and manual identification.

Automated tone detection is a method by which sampled telephone numbers are called by a machine that identifies special tones the instant a connection is made (usually before the phone even rings on the receiving end). Some tones signify non-working (disconnected) numbers, others fax or modem lines. Database matching involves comparing sampled numbers to a database in order to identify particular numbers for possible removal from (or inclusion in) the sample. One common instance of this involves matching sampled numbers to a database of known businesses. Finally, manual identification involves a human being calling each sampled number to determine whether it is a non-working (disconnected), business, fax, modem, or household line.

Coverage and hit rate

If a target population is defined by a geographic area, the coverage and hit rate become additional factors important in the design and selection of an RDD sample. Because telephone geographies do not coincide with physical geographies, it is necessary to find an appropriate balance between how well the targeted geography will be covered by a telephone sample, and how efficient the telephone sample will be in terms of incidence. Coverage refers to the proportion of numbers in the targeted geographic area that are included among the frame of telephone numbers from which the sample is selected. Incidence, or *hit rate*, refers to the proportion of numbers in the frame that are actually in the targeted geographic area. Generally there are tradeoffs between the two, and both must be considered when specifying the sample. For all RDD samples, telephone sampling vendors translate the targeted geography into a set of telephone exchanges before selecting the sample. They can then provide an analysis of how well these exchanges line up with the specified geographic boundaries. Based on this analysis, one can select the set of exchanges that represent the coverage level and geographic incidence most appropriate for the study.

Mobile phones/cell phones

Of particular concern with respect to RDD coverage and sampling is cell phone usage. The FCC indicates that over 60% of US households have at least one mobile phone. Annual supplements to the National Health Interview Survey (NHIS) have tracked the increase in cell-phone only households. The 2006 supplement indicates that more than 10% of US households now have only cell-phone service, and this percentage has increased rapidly in recent years (Blumberg, Luke, & Cynamon, 2006). Cell-only users tend to be different from others in two principal ways: first, as younger, urban, single, better-off renters, in one-person households; and second, as poorer households who previously may have had only intermittent land-line coverage. Non-coverage of cell-only users in RDD surveys could severely under-represent particular subgroups in the population.

The pricing structure in the US is such that mobile phone owners pay for all outgoing *and* incoming calls. As a result, legal restrictions for calling mobile phones have been imposed, and cell phone sampling frames are not publicly available. Another issue that complicates the sampling of cell phones relates to the idea of the sampling unit. In most RDD surveys, the household is the primary sampling unit from which household members may be selected. However, with mobile phones, which are more likely for personal or business use rather than for an entire household, the mobile phone user is the primary and final sampling unit.

Because of the increasing usage of mobile phones, it will be necessary to overcome the barriers to sampling mobile phone users. If the pricing structure were changed such that incoming calls were not charged to the mobile phone owner, the ethical difficulties and legal restrictions would likely be eased. In the meantime, free anytime minutes or other monetary incentives could be offered to offset the cost of the call, or a toll-free number to be used as a mobile phone equivalent to an 800 number could be created.

In many European countries, charges for calling a cell phone are borne by the caller;

cell phone numbers are identifiable by their prefixes, and callers are aware that they are calling a cell phone. Cell phone penetration is also much higher in many countries, as is the percentage of cell-only users. This has led to a different attitude to the inclusion of cell numbers in telephone samples. For political opinion research, a frame of phone numbers tied to individuals rather than households may in any case be preferable.

Response rates

The culture of telephone use in the United States was initially favorable to telephone surveys; respondents were comfortable being interviewed on the telephone. Though response rates were not as high as those achieved with face-to-face interviewing, it was not unusual for academic and social research organizations to achieve response rates around 70%, while market researchers could achieve response rates of 30% to 50%. There has, however, been a steady decrease in response rates over the years. With few exceptions, response rates are now rarely above 50%, except for high-cost telephone surveys with many call-backs and highly experienced interviewers. Even the better social research organizations now have difficulty achieving response rates as high as 50%; response rates of 30% to 40% are more common. Market researchers now find response rates of 15% to 20% acceptable.

The dramatic increase in privacy protection systems (the successors to the rudimentary answering machine) present telephone surveyors with an increasingly difficult task. The spread of mobile phones, and the introductions of what are essentially individually owned telephone numbers, will continue to increase the challenges. RDD telephone surveys may become an endangered species in the next ten years.

SUMMARY

Sampling is a key component of public opinion research involving surveys, as it is usually only cost effective to collect data from a subset of the relevant population. However, the selection of the subset has to be designed in such a way that the researcher can be confident that it is relevant to the population to which the researcher wants to generalize or make an inference. This requires that a probability method of selection is used to make the selection, but the researcher must work closely with the sampler, providing important information and insights into the relevant population, in order to help the sampler design and implement an efficient sampling strategy.

While simple random samples, especially those employing epsem methods, have a great deal of intuitive appeal, current sampling strategies employ a variety of techniques, such as stratification and clustering, to produce more efficient designs. While there are general principles that apply equally to both face-to-face and telephone surveys, the details of the sampling strategies differ to the extent that different frames are used and the selection of individuals within households may proceed along different lines as well.

PRE-ELECTION POLLS, EXIT POLLS, AND INTERNET SURVEYS

Pre-election polls

Practice varies across countries in the methodology applied to pre-election polls. There has been a gradual shift from face-to-face interviewing to telephone interviewing in European countries, with Internet polling (discussed in the next section) becoming increasingly common. Moon (1999) provides a nice description of the history and methods of political polling in the United Kingdom and analyzes in some detail the pre-election polls from the 1992 election in the UK.

The 2005 special issue of *Public Opinion Quarterly* provides the best overview of pre-election polling in the US; it is notable, however, how little of the issue is devoted to the methodology of the polls, and in particular the sampling designs for the polls (see Traugott, 2005). The criticisms of pre-election polls do not center on the sample designs, which in general are standard RDD probability designs, but on two other factors—response rates, which tend to be very low and are generally not reported, and the likely voter models used to determine which respondents should be included in the estimates of vote.

A constant challenge in pre-election studies is to identify the appropriate population from which to sample. It is not possible to identify in advance of an election which people eligible to vote will actually vote. Thus, in comparing probability samples of households with volunteer samples, two contrasts/issues are being confounded—identification of eligible individuals and responses from these individuals. In some situations, volunteer samples may perform better even though the selection is biased, if the characteristics of people that make them more likely to volunteer are similar to the characteristics that make them likely to turn out and vote.

The frames that are generally available for selection do not identify either those registered to vote or those who will actually vote. Unusually therefore, in contrast to most general population surveys, an important component of coverage error in pre-election polls is that of over-coverage, due to the inclusion in the sampling frame of non-voters (unregistered individuals and registered individuals who will not vote). This problem can be mitigated at the sampling stage if the survey can be confined to individuals for whom a complete sampling frame exists. For example, Visser, Krosnick, Marquette, and Curtin (1996) report that the *Columbus Dispatch* political survey consistently outperformed telephone surveys in predicting the winners of Ohio elections since 1980, precisely because the poll utilizes a list of Ohio voters for its sampling frame, which affords minimal coverage bias. Perhaps more importantly, the propensity to respond to the mail survey may have correlated strongly with the propensity to vote.

In the US, there has been a dramatic increase in 'early voting' (by mail, absentee ballot, in malls, etc.). This complicates the pre-election polling situation by changing the status of potential respondents; some may already be actual voters before the election date. Much more work needs to be done on how to identify early voters; formulating neutral filter questions may be a challenge.

Exit polls

Exit polls are seen as providing two different types of information: (i) an early assessment of trends in voting; and (ii) data that permits the analysis of reasons why different categories of voter voted the way they did. Exit polls are criticized bitterly when they fail to provide an accurate prediction of the vote; exit pollsters often contend that their primary purpose is to collect data that permits analysis of the relative reasons for voting of different subsets of the population, and that they are not designed for the prediction of results.

In the US, exit polls use a two-stage probability sampling design. In the first stage, a stratified systematic sample of precincts is selected in each state, proportional to the number of votes cast in the previous election. In the second stage, interviewers systematically select voters exiting polling places on Election Day, using a sampling interval based on the expected turnout in that precinct. The interval is computed (in advance) so that approximately 100 interviews are completed in each precinct.

One interviewer is assigned to each precinct in the sample. As voters exit the polling place, the interviewer approaches the sampled voter, shows the questionnaire and asks him/her to fill it out. After the voter fills out the questionnaire, he/she places it in a 'ballot box.' Interviewers also keep track of nonrespondents throughout the day. The response rates vary considerably by precinct, ranging from as low as 10% to as high as 95%; a primary reason is the proximity of the interviewing position to the polling place.

Merkle and Edelman (2002) found that there was no systematic relationship between the response rate at the precinct level and the accuracy of the responses in the precinct. This does not mean, of course, that there is not a systematic bias in exit polls; indeed, there is evidence from the 2004 exit polls that certain groups (in particular Republicans and older people) were systematically underrepresented. Such underrepresentation does not necessarily invalidate the cross-group analyses carried out using the data.

A further complication for exit polls is the 'Early voting' referred to above. In response to the rapid growth in this phenomenon, in states where such early voting is a significant proportion of the total vote, exit poll designs are increasingly mixed mode (usually dual mode) designs combining RDD telephone samples with the traditional precinct-based face-to-face design. Considerable challenges remain in optimizing these designs and devising appropriate composite estimators from the data.

Internet surveys (e-panels)

There has been a substantial increase in the use of the Internet for surveys in general in recent years. The increase has been greatest in market research, in particular in the areas of consumer, client, and employee research. The Internet has considerable advantages over telephone and self-administered paper and pencil surveys, previously the primary modes for these surveys. The Internet shares the advantage of other self-completion modes that no interviewer is required; it dominates all other data collection modes in its potential to present audio-visual material to respondents; the cost of transmission of information is very low; the speed of transmission of data is very high; and the data are immediately available to the analyst.

The principal concern with Internet surveys is representation. Where there is an available Internet sampling frame for the population, this concern does not apply. This is why surveys of clients, employees, and consumers comprise the bulk of Internet survey practice; the distinguishing feature of these contexts is that there is an available (population) frame from which to select the sample. Without a sampling frame, there is no scientific basis for making an inference from the sample results to the population.

The most common vehicle for Internet surveys is the volunteer panel of respondents recruited through the Internet (an *e-panel*). The *International Journal of Market Research* published two papers in 2004 presenting the competing arguments of traditional pollsters and Internet pollsters in the UK (Sparrow & Curtice, 2004; Kellner, 2005). The papers contrast the two methodologies and compare the results they obtain for a variety of political opinion measures. The evidence is mixed: sometimes the results of the e-panels correspond to those of the traditional polls, and sometimes they do not. There is however general agreement that one of the UK Internet panels (YouGov) has performed consistently well for election prediction in the UK. Of course, the election predictions are the result not just of selection, but also of weighting, and of other (sometimes undisclosed) modeling of the data.

There have been a small number of attempts over the years to recruit a panel through other modes (face-to-face or telephone), supply the panel members with computers and an Internet connection, and conduct surveys with the panel. Some French researchers used the mini-computers given by the French telecom agency to all households in France in the 1980s as the basis for Internet market research surveys. Willem Saris (1989) recruited such a panel in the Netherlands, donating a computer to each household in the panel.

Knowledge Networks (KN, then called InterSurvey) recruited a panel by telephone in 2000 as a basis for ongoing market and social research by Internet and provided all needed equipment to households. A major problem for KN has been a failure to obtain sufficiently high response rates at the recruitment stage to allay concerns about lack of representativeness.

The National Science Foundation sponsored a study in 2006–7 to investigate the feasibility of recruiting a panel through face-to-face visits (O'Muircheartaigh, Krosnick, & Dennis, 2007). Following this, the National Election Study (NES) may institute an Internet panel for the 2008 elections.

Where recruitment has been by Internet, the panels are, and should be regarded as, volunteer samples; a number of these are used in pre-election prediction (Harris Interactive and Polimetrix, for instance). The fundamental problem with such samples is that there is no rigorous way to relate the elements (people) in the sample with the population from which they were drawn. Weighting by known population characteristics can restore the appearance of representation to these samples, but this does not address the underlying weakness.

Volunteer samples suffer from all the shortcomings of non-probability sampling (see Maxim #2 and Maxim #3 above). Though such surveys can, in the right circumstances, give accurate results, their warrant depends on two assumptions: (i) that there is no systematic difference between the population of volunteers (the sampling frame for these surveys) and the population of interest (perhaps all adults, or all voters); and (ii) that within the frame, there is no additional systematic differential in dropout or nonresponse rates that biases the estimates (the issue of differential nonresponse is relevant to all frames, of course, but there may be more anxiety about differential dropout from volunteer panels; the observed response rates for such panels is also known to be extremely low).

All in all, it would be unwise to rely on Internet surveys of the general population for any social or political research that aims to make statements about the population as a whole. Whatever temporary success they might have could end in a replication of the *Literary Digest* débâcle of 1936 unless the representation issues inherent in volunteer participation are addressed.

CONCLUDING REMARKS

This chapter deals primarily with sampling, and the theoretical foundations of scientific sampling from real populations are clear and unambiguous. The seven maxims in the first part of the chapter set out the reasoning underlying the practice of probability sampling. It is only with probability samples that we have a scientific basis for making an inference from the sample to the population. But it is critical that the researcher work closely with the sampler, providing important information and insights into the structure of the relevant population, to ensure a sampling strategy that is appropriate and efficient for the specific purpose.

In practical survey work, the decisions about sampling interact with many other decisions about methodology. The choice of mode of data collection (face-to-face, telephone, mail, Internet) is contingent on having a sampling frame from which to select the sample. The probability samples of households that we use for face-to-face survey work are considered by many to be the gold standard for survey work. However, such surveys are extremely expensive and also require an extended period in the field to achieve the high response rates for which they are rightly respected. Probability sampling methods for telephone sampling have been available for 30 years or so. Initially speed, cheapness, and the efficiencies of computer-assisted interviewing propelled telephone sampling to a dominant position; now, however, plummeting response rates are bringing about a re-consideration. Internet surveys of the general population suffer from the crippling shortcoming that there is no available sampling frame with even reasonable coverage properties; until this deficiency is addressed Internet *samples* must be viewed with considerable skepticism (this does not rule out the use of the Internet as a mode of data collection for samples obtained otherwise).

The future probably lies with multi-mode/ mixed mode approaches to data collection;

the challenge for the sampler will be to provide compatible frames and methods of producing efficient composite designs and estimators.

NOTES

1 The *Proceedings* of the ISI conference contain only a brief description. A more comprehensive version of Kiaer's proposal was published in the *Papers of the Norwegian Academy of Arts and Letters* (Kiaer, 1897).

2 The standard error is the standard deviation of the sampling distribution of the estimator. It is the most widely used measure of dispersion in mathematical statistics, and is used in most standard statistical tests and estimation procedures.

3 *Skewness* to statisticians.

4 This section is an edited and updated version of Murphy and O'Muircheartaigh (2005).

5 The WRN is the percentage of telephone numbers expected to be working household lines.

REFERENCES

Blumberg, S. J., Luke, J. V., & Cynamon, M. L. (2006). Telephone coverage and health survey estimates: Evaluating the need for concern about wireless substitution. *American Journal of Public Health, 96*, 926–931.

Glasser, G. J., & Metzger, G. D. (1972). Random-digit dialing as a method of telephone sampling. *Journal of Marketing Research, 9* (February), 59–64.

Kellner, P. (2005). Clearing the fog: What really happened in the 2005 election campaign. *The Political Quarterly, 76*, 323–332.

Kiaer, A N. (1897). Den Representative Undersogelsesmethode. Oslo: *Videnskapsselskapets Skrifter* (Papers from the Norwegian Academy of Science and Letters). Reprinted with a translation into English as 'The representative method of statistical surveys' by the Norwegian Central Bureau of Statistics (Oslo, 1976).

Larson, O. N. (1952). The comparative validity of telephone and face-to-face interviews in the measurement of message diffusion from leaflets. *American Sociological Review, 17*, 471–476.

Merkle, D. M., & Edelman, M. (2002). A review of the 1996 voter news service exit polls from a total survey error perspective. In P. J. Lavrakas & M. W. Traugott (Eds.), Elections, the news media, and democracy (pp. 68–72). New York: Chatham House.

Moon, N. (1999). *Opinion polls: History, theory and practice.* Manchester: Manchester University Press.

Neyman, J. (1934). On the two different aspects of the representative method. *Journal of the Royal Statistical Society, 97*, 558–625.

O'Muircheartaigh, C., Eckman, S., & Weiss, C. (2002). Traditional and enhanced field listing for probability sampling. *2002 Proceedings of the Section on Survey Research Methods of the American Statistical Association.*

O'Muircheartaigh, C., Eckman, S., & English, N. (2004). Survey sampling in the inner city with GIS lists: Quality, coverage, practicality, and data implications. *Proceedings of City Futures: an international conference on globalism and urban change, University of Illinois at Chicago, July 2004.*

O'Muircheartaigh, C., Krosnick, J. A., & Dennis, M. (2007). Face-to-face recruitment of an Internet survey panel: Lessons from an NSF-funded demonstration project. *2007 Proceedings of the Section on Survey Research Methods of the American Statistical Association.*

Saris, W. E. (1989). Technological revolution in data collection. *Quality and Quantity, 23*, 333–349.

Sparrow, N., & Curtice, J. (2004). Measuring the attitudes of the general public via Internet polls: An evaluation. *International Journal of Market Research, 46*(1), 23–44.

Stephan, F. F., & McCarthy, P. J. (1974). Sampling opinions; an analysis of survey procedure. Westport, Conn.: Greenwood Press.

Traugott, M. W. (2005). The accuracy of the national preelection polls in the 2004 presidential election. *Public Opinion, 69*, 642–654.

Visser, P. S., Krosnick, J. A., Marquette, J., & Curtin, M. (1996). Mail surveys for election forecasting? An evaluation of the Columbus dispatch poll. *Public Opinion Quarterly, 60*(2), 181–228.

28

Survey Non-Response

Adam J. Berinsky

Sometimes, the information we do not collect on surveys is as important as the information we do collect. In recent years, social scientists and professional pollsters have paid increasing attention to survey non-response. In this chapter, I review current literature on this phenomenon and point to some areas of future inquiry.

When we speak of survey non-response, we are in fact, speaking of two distinct but related phenomena: *unit* non-response and *item* non-response. Unit non-response occurs when an entire observation unit is missing from our sample (Lohr, 1999). In the context of survey research, unit non-response occurs when we have no information about a respondent selected to be in our sample. Item non-response, on the other hand, occurs when some measurements are present for an observational unit, but at least one measure of interest is missing (Lohr, 1999). In survey research, item non-response occurs when we have some information about the respondent, but we are missing data for a given variable or variables of interest. For instance, we may know a respondent's education level and partisanship, but not her income.

These two forms of survey non-response both involve missing information, but have been dealt with separately in the literature. In this chapter, I will follow convention and take up each topic in turn. However, as my review of the literature will demonstrate, both types of non-response arise from similar causes and create related concerns for survey researchers, thereby implying that similar solutions may be in order. Future work should therefore take more seriously the theoretical and empirical links between unit non-response and item non-response.

UNIT NON-RESPONSE

Unit non-response has become an increasingly serious problem over the last 40 years. Studies in the 1990s demonstrated that face-to-face surveys by academic organizations, such as the National Election Study (NES) and the General Social Survey (GSS), have non-response rates between 25 and 30%, up from 15 to 20% in the 1950s (Brehm, 1993; Luevano, 1994; Groves & Couper, 1998). Telephone surveys conducted by commercial polling houses, which produce the majority of polling information in circulation in the political world, are often even higher. For instance, in a study of polls conducted by the news media and government contractors, Krosnick, Holbrook, and Pfent (2005) found that the mean response rate for these surveys was 36%.[1] Furthermore, indications are that unit non-response has become an even more serious problem since 2000. Since 1994, the response rate to the NES has fallen below 70%, dropping to 56% in 2002 before rebounding to 66% in 2004.[2]

These non-response rates are, in fact, the product of two distinct processes: (1) some respondents cannot be found by the poll's sponsors; and (2) other respondents decline to participate in the poll. In both cases potential data is lost. Unit non-response is therefore a function of both respondent contact and respondent cooperation (Groves & Couper, 1998).

Conventional wisdom holds that survey response rates are falling because potential respondents are harder to contact. In face-to-face surveys, physical impediments, such as locked apartment buildings have made it more difficult to access households in the sample (Groves & Couper, 1998). Likewise, researchers employing telephone surveys seem to have a more difficult time reaching respondents in recent years because of the rise of caller ID, answering machines, and other technological innovations. However, academic studies have shown that the rise in unit non-response is as attributable to increasing refusal rates as it is to decreasing contact rates. Take, for instance, the NES. In 1952, 6% of potential respondents refused to be interviewed by NES. By 1986, this number had risen to 26%. Though refusal rates have fluctuated somewhat in recent years—the 2004 refusal rate for the NES was 23%—they have remained high in the modern era (Luevano, 1994). Similar patterns of response have been found in other face-to-face surveys. Curtin, Presser and Singer (2005) study the response rates to the University of Michigan's Survey of Consumer Attitudes

and find that the response rate dropped from 1979 to 2003, with the steepest decline occurring in the 1997 to 2003 period. While non-contacts increased over this time, that increase has slowed in recent years. The majority of the decline in response rate was due to an increase in the refusal rate by nearly 1% per year from 1997 to 2003, leading to a refusal rate of almost 30% in 2003.

The primacy of refusals as an explanation for increased rates of survey non-response extends from face-to-face academic surveys to commercial telephone surveys. The Pew Center for the Study of the People & the Press carried out surveys in 1997 and 2003 over a five-day period using polling techniques typical of professional survey houses. They found that these surveys conducted in identical manners had very different rates of response in the two time periods.[3] Somewhat surprisingly, the contact rate stayed roughly the same—increasing only one percentage point to 70%—over the six years. However, over that same time period, the refusal rate increased 20 points, from 42% to 62%.[4] Thus, while the response rate was 36% in 1997, by 2003, it had dropped to 27%. Commercial polls are plagued by similar problems. A 2001 survey by the Council for Marketing and Opinion Research found that refusal rates increased from 19% in 1980 to 36% in 1990, and again rose to nearly 50% in 2000 (Weisberg, 2005). These findings are not limited to the American case. de Leeuw and de Heer (2002) examined trends in response rates across 16 countries from 1980 to 1998 and found that refusal rates increased faster than non-contact rates.

Causes of unit non-response

The increasing rates of unit non-response in surveys over the last 20 years are not an inevitable development. However, there are certain predictable determinants of unit non-response. As Groves and Couper (1998) argue, the decision to respond to a survey is a stochastic process, and they present a unified framework representing the decision to participate in survey, considering separately the impact of survey design, interviewer factors, and respondent characteristics on the processes of securing respondent contact and respondent cooperation. They find that contact rates are a function of the physical barriers to accessing a household (in face-to-face surveys), the patterns of times of the day when members of a household are present, and the timing and the number of attempted interviewer contacts. Refusal patterns also follow specific tendencies. Younger respondents and older respondents are more likely to cooperate with an interviewer than middle-aged respondents; respondents with low socio-economic status are more likely to agree to be surveyed than high status individuals. Furthermore, the socio-economic environment of a household influences co-operation rates. They find low cooperation rates among households in high-density areas (over and above specific household characteristics). The structure of the survey and interviewer practices can also influence patterns of survey refusal. For instance, Groves and Couper find that more experienced interviewers and those who are able to establish a rapport with the respondents at first contact are more likely to secure interviews. Finally, the survey design itself can influence cooperation rates. Providing advance warning of the survey request and monetary incentives (or other objects of value) increase the likelihood that a respondent will agree to be interviewed.

For survey practitioners, the message of this work is clear. Though some aspects of non-response are related to characteristics of the surveyed household and are beyond the control of survey researchers, response rates can be increased through the use of advance warning letters, respondent incentives, and highly trained interviewers who make multiple attempts to secure an interview. With some effort, rates of unit non-response can be held down, even in the era of increasing refusal rates and declining cooperation rates.

Implications of non-response

High response rates, however, often come with a high monetary cost. All of the methods of reducing unit non-response described above—using experienced interviewers, varying patterns of attempted contact, and employing respondent incentives—are expensive. Although no practitioner would disagree that efforts should be made to reduce unit non-response as much as possible, survey design decisions are never made independent of cost concerns. The salient question, then, is how much is it worth to reduce unit non-response? Here, we need to turn to questions of data quality.

Relatively high rates of non-response are potentially problematic to the representativeness of opinion polls. Those individuals who respond to polls are not perfectly representative of the mass public. In the NES, for example, non-respondents tend to be worse-off financially, are more likely to be black, and are more likely to live in rural areas than those who respond to surveys (Brehm, 1993).[5] Furthermore, surveys routinely over-represent women (Groves & Couper, 1998).

These persistent differences have important implications for survey results. Unit non-responses can cause bias in our point estimates of quantities of interest. For instance, if respondents and non-respondents are different on particular variables of interest, estimates of the mean of those variables will be biased toward their mean value among respondents (Dillman, Eltinge, Groves, & Little, 2002).[6] Conventional wisdom therefore holds that low response rates are problematic. As Weisberg notes, for many researchers, 'A low response rate indicates that the sample size is smaller than desired ... that there may be non-response bias, and that people will be suspicious of the study' (2005, p. 191). Below, I discuss various statistical methods to account for survey non-response. But these methods are not a replacement for the missing data.

Somewhat surprisingly, however, the bulk of research to date has found that the existence of significant differences between respondents and non-respondents does not seem to undermine the representativeness of polls. Brehm (1993) finds that while non-respondents may differ in significant ways from survey respondents, accounting for non-response does not alter estimates of public opinion on political matters very much. Furthermore, while Brehm argued in the early 1990s that worsening response rates could create a situation where estimates of aggregate political opinions are unreliable (1993, chapter 8), recent experiments suggest that these pessimistic predictions might not be met in practice. In 1997, the Pew Research Center for the People & the Press conducted a survey experiment to assess the effects of non-response.[7] Two separate samples were drawn for parallel surveys that included the exact same questions. The first 'standard' survey was conducted over a five-day period and used polling techniques typical of professional survey houses. The second survey was conducted over eight weeks, which allowed the interviewers to contact highly mobile respondents and convince some reluctant respondents to agree to be interviewed. Although, as expected, the response rates differed greatly across the two samples—42% in the standard sample, compared to 71% in the extended sample—the picture of the public's will did not differ significantly across the two surveys.[8] The average difference in the aggregate political attitudes of the two groups was just 2.7 percentage points, less than the margin of errors of the surveys.[9] Only a handful of questions differed by more than three or four percentage points.[10] In 2003, PEW replicated this experiment. Though, as noted above, overall response rates dropped over the six-year period, the researchers again found few attitudinal differences between respondents in the standard survey and those in the rigorous survey. These findings are consistent with broader reviews of existing data collection methods. Krosnick et al. (2005) conclude that even surveys with relatively low response rates are highly representative of the mass public. Furthermore, achieving higher response rates only improves representativeness slightly.

Altogether, the work reviewed here seems to provide a reassuring balm for pollsters. While unit non-response should, in theory, prove damaging to the ability of opinion polls to accurately measure the public's will, in practice it appears that the threat may not be serious. However, this work is not the final word on this matter for two reasons. First, there remains the question of what the existing data can tell us. The Pew study compares parallel surveys with response rates of 30% to those of 60% and finds few differences. It is not clear, though, where the tipping point lies. Is a survey with a 60% response rate equivalent to one with an 80% response rate? What about a survey with a 100% response rate? To draw conclusions from current research requires us to extrapolate well beyond the range of available data, a strategy that could lead to faulty inferences.

Second, it is not clear that representativeness on quantities we happen to measure is sufficient to ensure poll representativeness. Though respondents and non-respondents seem to hold the same views on many political questions, these two groups might differ in other important ways. For instance, the 2003 Pew survey found that respondents in the standard survey were more likely to vote than respondents in the rigorous survey. Perhaps this difference in political engagement extends to other attitudinal indicators we do not measure. Put another way, simply because non-respondents and respondents seem to be similar on quantities we happen to measure does not mean they are the same on quantities we do not measure. If these unmeasured quantities affect answers on particular survey questions, opinion polls might lead us astray. Thus, on the question of whether securing a high response rate is a worthy investment, the jury is still out.

ITEM NON-RESPONSE

On any survey, some respondents will answer some questions, and abstain from others. The phenomenon of item non-response is widespread on surveys. For instance, not a single respondent to the 2004 NES answered every question on the survey. These instances of item non-response—including 'don't know' and 'no opinion' responses—have been of interest to social scientists since the early days of opinion polling, but they have become the subject of increased scholarly study in recent years (see Beatty & Herrmann, 2002; Krosnick, 2002; Berinsky, 2004).

Item non-response has practical implications for the analysis of survey data—how does one analyze data in which, as is typically the case, up to 25% of the sample refuses to disclose their income? If one is conducting political polling for a campaign, how does one treat the 'undecideds'—those respondents who fail to provide a definitive candidate choice? In this section, I review the causes and consequences of item non-response. I focus primarily on attitudinal questions. However, many of the concerns I identify here also apply to understanding item non-response on factual questions, such as measures of income and reports of church attendance (Tourangeau, Rips, & Rasinski, 2000).

Causes of item non-response

The first factor to consider is the source of 'don't know' responses. Just as there are predictable sources of unit non-response that can be found in the characteristics of the interviewer and the interviewed, there are regular determinants of item non-response. These determinants are often divided into three categories: respondent characteristics, questionnaire design issues, and interviewer behavior.

Respondent Characteristics: The most obvious reason that a respondent would choose a 'don't know' response is that they possess personal characteristics that lead them to such a response. Various experimental and non-experimental studies have demonstrated that increasing levels of respondent education, respondent exposure to topic specific information, and interest in the survey topic all reduce 'don't know' responses. In addition

the personality characteristics of a respondent may also affect the likelihood they give a substantive response. For instance, Kam (2003) studied the effect of inter-personal differences in respondents' tendency to engage in and enjoy cognitive activity—measured by the 'Need for Cognition' scale (Cacioppo, Petty, Feinstein, & Jarvis, 1996). Using data from the 2000 NES, she finds that those respondents who score high on the Need for Cognition scale are more likely to answer survey questions.

Question Wording: Factors outside the immediate control of the respondent may also affect the probability of their giving a 'don't know' response. Some topics in the United States, such as reports of income (Hillygus, Nie, Prewitt, & Pals, 2006) and racial attitudes (Berinsky, 2004) engender item non-response because such topics are sensitive and governed by social norms (for a fuller discussion of norms, see Berinsky, 1999, 2002). Presumably, social norms will differ from country to country, and researchers should take appropriate account of such norms.

Beyond the particular topic of the survey, the specific wording of survey questions may affect rates of item non-response. The survey interview can be a difficult and tedious affair. Given these demands, it might be easier for respondents to give a 'don't know' response, and move on to the next question if they have difficulty readily forming a political judgment. To use the words of Krosnick (1991), respondents may engage in 'satisficing' behavior—they may pick the no opinion response rather than engage in effortful cognitive behavior. Thus, some respondents may offer a 'don't know' response because they do not feel they have sufficiently strong views to meet the demands of the question being asked, or because they do not want to pay the mental costs associated with fashioning such views. This behavior may be exacerbated by the structure of the information conveyed from the interviewer to the respondent. The use of a 'full filter'—where respondents are first asked if they have an opinion on a particular issue, and are then asked their opinion—or a 'quasi-filter'—where the 'don't know' option is presented explicitly—may serve as an implicit (if unintentional) signal that the question-answering task ahead of them is especially difficult. As Schwarz notes, full and quasi-filters imply that the forthcoming questions will ask, 'for a careful assessment of the issue, based on considerable knowledge of the facts' (1996, p. 59; see also Krosnick, 2002). The very process of asking the survey question may encourage satisficing behavior.

However, simply because people may satisfice when they answer a survey question with a 'no opinion' filter does not mean they are without thoughts on the question. Hippler and Schwarz (2005), for example, find that those respondents who decline to answer fully filtered questions are willing to provide substantive responses at a more general level of evaluation. In such cases, the decision to give a 'don't know' response may be more a function of the specific survey instrument—such as an opinion filter—than of the particular political predispositions of the respondent.

Opinion filters are not the only question wording decisions that can affect the probability of item non-response. Kinder and Nelson (2005) find that reminding individuals about relevant predispositions through question-wording frames (by including arguments favoring one side or the other in the question) increases the proportion of respondents who offer opinions on survey questions. Kinder and Nelson, moreover, find that these additional opinions are not 'flimsy fabrications created by the momentary presence of persuasive-sounding frames' (2005, p. 110) but are instead the expression of real, potentially relevant political voices. Similarly, Zaller (1990) finds that opinion questions framed using the language of elite discourse yield fewer question abstentions than unframed items. Like Kinder and Nelson, he concludes that these additional answers come without any loss in the quality of response.

Interviewer Behavior: Finally, the characteristics of the interviewer may affect the probability of item non-response. Just as some interviewers are more skilled than others in achieving respondent cooperation, some interviewers are especially capable of obtaining answers to specific questions on a given survey. For instance, Singer, Frankel, and Glassman (1983) find that those interviewers who believed it would be easy to administer a questionnaire were more likely to obtain responses to those items than were interviewers who thought it would be difficult to obtain a response.

The meaning of 'don't know' responses

Given that a variety of factors affect the probability that a respondent will abstain from a given survey question, what meaning should we give to the 'don't know' response? Traditionally, scholars and practitioners of survey research have viewed 'no opinion' responses as useful devices—a way of preventing non-attitudes (Converse, 1964) from contaminating measures of public opinion. However, this view of item non-response proceeds from a particular model of the survey question-answering process as the product of individuals' attempts to reveal their fixed preference on a given policy issue. In this view, people who say 'don't know' simply have no opinion on the matter in question.

Recently, however, a more fluid view of the survey response has emerged, based in part on theories of preference construction developed in cognitive psychology (see, for example, Fischoff, 1991; Slovic, 1995). This view, advanced most forcibly by Zaller and Feldman, argues that 'individuals do not typically possess "true attitudes" on issues, as conventional theorizing assumes, but a series of partially independent and often inconsistent ones' (see also Feldman, 1989; Zaller, 1992, p. 93; Zaller & Feldman, 1992; Tourangeau *et al.*, 2000). According to this line of public opinion research, a survey response is not necessarily a revealed preference. Instead, answers to survey questions can be considered a random draw from an individual's underlying response distribution, which itself is an aggregation across one's potentially diverse feelings and ideas concerning political issues. For instance, Tourangeau *et al.* (2000) argue that respondents answer survey questions by means of a four-step process. Individuals first attempt to comprehend the survey question, and then retrieve information and memories pertinent to the question. Next, they use the retrieved information to make required judgments. Finally they map that judgment onto the survey response options, thereby providing the interviewer with an answer.

Survey answers, then, are a summary judgment of the mass of information that happens to be called to mind when respondents answer a particular question. The types of information encountered about politics in daily life, and even the wording of survey questions, can bring about systematic changes in the base of available information. Because different information may be salient at different times, the response obtained from the same person may change from interview to interview. To use Zaller's (1992) turn of phrase, answers to attitude questions are 'opinion statements'; they do not reveal a single true attitude, but instead they reflect a *sample* of the types of concerns and predispositions people bring to bear when considering issues in the realm of politics.

From this perspective, 'don't know' responses on both attitude questions—such as evaluations of prominent politicians or salient policies—and reports of behavior—such as church attendance and voting behavior—can arise for a variety of reasons. In *Silent Voices* (Berinsky, 2004), I present a model of the survey response focused on the potential costs to the individual of answering specific questions. Such concerns loom especially large in the survey setting, because answering a poll is not only a low cost activity, but also a low benefit activity. Respondents, after all, are no better off materially at the end of the interview than they are at the beginning, regardless of the answers they give. Any psychic benefit they receive from

participating in the survey—such as the fulfillment of the need for self-expression or personal understanding—is achieved in the survey interview by answering the first few questions (Krosnick, 1991). Given the apparent minimal benefits associated with surveys, any costs—even those at the margin—should tip the balance against offering a response. These costs could be the mental effort required to bring together diverse predispositions into a coherent opinion, or they could be the social costs of offending others. Taking as a starting point the model of the survey response advanced by Tourangeau *et al.* (2000), I therefore argue in *Silent Voices* that individuals may come to a 'don't know' answer by two very different routes; either after they first attempt to form an opinion about a particular political controversy or when—if successful in coming to a judgment—they then choose the 'don't know' category when expressing their answer to the survey interviewer. In the first case, the respondent fails to answer the question because of cognitive costs; in the second case, question abstention results from social costs.

What do we lose, then, by taking people at their word when they give a 'don't know' response. At the extremes, certainly, there are some questions that yield meaningless information for certain respondents. For instance, Bishop, Oldendick, Tuchfarber, and Bennet (1980) found that one-third of respondents gave an opinion on a fictitious '1975 Public Affairs Act.' Some respondents, it seems, will answer survey questions even if they have not formed an opinion on a given topic. Surely, then, there must be some issues for some people where 'don't know' is the only legitimate answer. The question, then, is outside of these contrived situations, how often do such situations occur?

My answer is, 'not often.' The decision to abstain from a survey question is certainly a meaningful one. Important information is conveyed by the 'don't know' response—respondents are essentially stating that the costs of providing a substantive answer are too high. However, given that research has shown that 'don't know' responses arise through the interaction of question wording, interviewer behavior, and respondent characteristics, it would be a mistake to attribute 'don't know' responses solely to the absence of meaningful political views on the part of the survey respondent.[11]

Thus, we need to consider the meaning of the 'don't know' response for the expression of public opinion by examining the background correlates of opinion and the answers respondents give to other questions on the same survey. The decision to abstain from a survey question does not necessarily indicates that the respondent is consciously aware of a formed political judgment that she/he reserves from the interviewer. Indeed sometimes a 'don't know' response is just that—the absence of opinion. But the decision to abstain from a survey question does not mean that the respondent is devoid of politically relevant predilections. With the aid of theory and a close examination of the data—using the statistical techniques discussed in the next section—we can learn much about the political predilections of the 'silent voices.'

TREATMENT ON NON-RESPONSE

Given that unit and item non-response are facts of life for survey researchers, how should we analyze our incomplete data? The simplest way is to ignore the problem. In the context of unit non-response, we can simply ignore the fact that some potential respondents were never interviewed and analyze the available data. For item non-response, we can discard those cases with missing data and analyze only those units for which we have complete data. This procedure, known as 'listwise deletion' of missing data, is the norm in social science analysis. In fact, most computer packages automatically delete missing data listwise. This procedure, as Little and Rubin (2002) note, may be satisfactory with small amounts of missing data. However, under certain circumstances, listwise deletion of missing data can lead to serious biases.

Little and Rubin (2002) list three conditions under which missing data may have been generated in the bivariate case. First, if the probability of response is independent of both the dependent and independent variables, the missing data are missing at random (MAR), and the observed data are observed at random (OAR). Alternatively, we may say that the missing data are missing completely at random (MCAR). Under such circumstances, the missing data mechanism may be ignored without any resulting bias in the analysis. Second, if the observation of the value on the dependent variable depends on the independent variable, but not on the value of the dependent variable, the missing data are only MAR. Thus, the observed values of the dependent variable are a random sample of the sampled values conditioning on the independent variables, but are not necessarily a random subsample of the sampled values (Little & Rubin, 2002). If the data is MAR, but not OAR, the missing data mechanism is ignorable for likelihood-based inference, though not for sample-based inference. Finally, if the probability of responses depends on the value of the dependent variable and possibly the independent variable, the data is neither MAR nor OAR. Thus, the missing data mechanism is non-ignorable. In sum, unless the process governing whether data is missing or observed is independent of the dependent variable, the observed data will not be a random subsample of the full data, but rather a *censored* subsample of that data.[12] Thus, unless the data are MCAR, simply deleting the cases with missing data can lead to biased inferences.

To avoid such biases, a number of procedures have been developed to account for missing data. All methods for accounting for either item or unit non-response are by necessity model-based. As Lohr notes, '[i]f we are to make any inference about the non-respondents, we must assume that they are related to the respondents in some way' (1999, p. 254). Sometimes this model is informal. For instance, many pollsters assume that voters who fail to give a

candidate preference in reelection polls—
the undecided voters—will break strongly
against the reelection of incumbent politicians. Blumenthal (2004) terms this theory
the 'incumbent rule.' Elections featuring an
incumbent are seen as a referendum on that
incumbent. Voters first decide whether they
want to fire the politician in office; only
then do they decide whether they wish to
support the challenger. Several pollsters, in
making their election night projections in
2004, followed this rule. Gallup, for instance,
allocated the 3% of respondents who were
undecided by increasing John Kerry's share
by 2% and Ralph Nader's share by 1%,
leading to a projected tie between Kerry
and George W. Bush (Newport & Moore,
2004). Only after election night was it
clear that this implicit model was factually
incorrect.

These informal models only get us so far
and—as the 2004 election example shows—
they can seriously mislead us in some cases.
Statisticians have developed a number of more
formal methods for dealing with missing data.
I first discuss those that account for unit
non-response, then those to account for item
non-response.

Unit non-response

The statistical treatment of unit non-response
depends on the availability of information.
When researchers have a theory of the
patterns of missing data *and* detailed information about the characteristics of non-
respondents, they can employ model-based
approaches, such as selection bias techniques,
to account for the differences between the
sample and the population (Heckman, 1979;
Achen, 1986; Breen, 1996). A prominent
example of this research strategy in political
science is Brehm's (1993) study of 'phantom
respondents.' Brehm takes advantage of information collected in some academic surveys—
such as the NES, the General Social Survey,
and the Detroit Areas Study—about potential
respondents who could or would not be
interviewed (such as the nonrespondent's
age, race, sex, approximate income, and the

accessibility of their housing unit). With this
information, he models jointly the decision
to participate in a survey (the selection
equation) and the decision to engage in
particular politically relevant behaviors, such
as turning out in an election, or voting for a
particular candidate (the outcome equation).
Brehm finds that in some cases, the correlates
of political behavior can change once we
account for non-respondents. He finds, for
example, that the effect of education on
turnout increases once we bring survey non-
respondents into our analysis. In other cases,
Brehm finds that estimates of the determinants of political behavior are unchanged.
For instance, the demographic correlates
of income, such as education, race, and
gender are unaffected once the selection bias
correction is introduced. But these results do
not give researchers license to ignore unit
non-response. As Brehm notes, even though
many models of individual behavior were
changed only slightly with the introduction
of information concerning non-respondents,
there are times when non-response can greatly
affect the estimates of the correlates of
such behaviors. Without accounting for non-
response in our analyses, we will never know
how biased our results might be.

Brehm's cases are rare, however, because
rich information about non-respondents was
available. Most times, though, we only have
information about the population relative
to the sample in the form of auxiliary
information taken from the census. In these
cases, weighting adjustments are typically
applied to reduce the bias in survey estimates
that non-response can cause (Holt & Elliot,
1991; Lohr, 1999; Kalton & Flores-Cervantes,
2003). Though the use of weights to adjust for
non-response is common, there is controversy
about the best way to implement weighting
(see Deville & Sarndal, 1992; Deville,
Sarndal, & Sautory, 1993; Little, 1993; Lohr
1999; Bethlehem, 2002; Gelman & Carlin,
2002; Kalton & Flores-Cervantes, 2003;
Gelman, 2005). One approach commonly
used is raking—also known as iterative
proportional fitting (Deming & Stephan,
1940; Little & Wu, 1991) or rim weighting

(Sharot, 1986). Raking matches cell counts to the marginal distributions of the variables used in the weighting scheme. The raking algorithm works by first matching the rows to the marginal distribution and then the columns. This process is repeated until both the rows and columns match their marginal distributions (see Little & Wu, 1991 for a description of the algorithm). Raking allows for many weighting variables to be included, an important concern for researchers and practitioners, who typically use raking to adjust samples on seven or more variables. However, raking ignores information available in the joint distribution of the weighting variables. Other techniques, such as regression weighting, take advantage of this information. Lohr (1999) provides a useful overview of these different weighting methods.

Item non-response

Statistical techniques can also be used to account for item non-response. If a researcher has a particular theory about the process by which individuals decide whether to answer particular survey questions, she can use an application-specific approach to model the missing data, such as the selection bias model that Brehm used to study unit non-response. In my study of racial attitudes (Berinsky, 1999, 2002, 2004), I used a selection model to estimate the effect of missing data on the correlates and point estimates of such attitudes. My analysis of NES data reveals that public opinion polls overstate support for government efforts to integrate schools and guarantee fair employment. Specifically, selection bias models reveal that some individuals who harbor anti-integrationist sentiments are likely to hide their socially unacceptable opinions behind a 'don't know' response. I find that the same methods that predict that opinion polls understate true opposition to school integration also predict the results of the 1989 New York City mayoral election more accurately than the marginals of pre-election tracking polls.

In the absence of a specific theory about particular patterns of missing data, a common solution to the problem of item non-response is imputation.[13] Essentially imputation procedures involve using various methods to estimate a value for the missing data. With the missing values 'filled in,' researchers can then proceed to analyze the complete data matrix using standard methods of data analysis. Weisberg (2005) provides a detailed overview of various imputation techniques, which have become increasingly sophisticated in recent years. These techniques differ in their particulars of how they fill in missing values. 'Hot Deck' imputation, for instance, imputes missing data with the value obtained on the missing variable for a similar survey participant (with 'similarity' based on the closeness of the 'donor' and 'beggar' cases on other variables of interest (Marker, Judkinds, & Winslee, 2002). Regression imputation, on the other hand, uses a regression equation to model answers to a variable of interest based on other variables in the dataset. This equation is then used to estimate values for non-respondents (Weisberg, 2005). Imputation methods also differ on whether they fill in a single value for a missing case, or provide multiple values, which permits assessment of uncertainty about estimates (see King et al., 2001; Little & Rubin, 2002).

FUTURE RESEARCH

The last 20 years have seen an explosion in the study of survey non-response. Researchers have investigated the causes of unit and item non-response, and have developed new ways to explore the meaning of missing data. Statisticians and applied researchers are developing and employing increasingly sophisticated methods to analyze missing data.

Though we have learned a great deal about survey non-response, there is much work to be done. To date, there has been a large divide in the study of non-response. Scholars study unit non-response and item non-response in isolation, but rarely consider the links between the two processes. Groves and Couper express a common sentiment when they write, 'This is a book about unit non-response, not item non-response. We are interested in what induces people to grant a request for a survey interview from a stranger who appears on their doorstep. We do not study the process by which respondents who begin an interview fail to supply answers to survey questions' (1998, p. 221). But this position flies in the face of the work reviewed in this chapter. Similar factors—such as respondent characteristics and interviewer behavior—affect both unit non-response rates *and* item non-response rates. Furthermore, similar model-based approaches have been applied to fix the problems caused by both types of non-response. For instance, Heckman-style selection bias models have been used to study both unit non-response (Brehm, 1993) and item non-response (Berinsky, 2004). Future work should therefore consider these two forms of non-response together. With a common theoretic perspective in *survey* non-response, we can better understand the meaning and consequences of missing data on surveys.

ACKNOWLEDGMENTS

For helpful comments on earlier drafts of this chapter, I thank Sunshine Hillygus, Chappell Lawson, Lily Tsai, and Ian Yohai. For research assistance, I thank Matthew Gusella.

NOTES

1 Krosnick *et al.* report a variety of response rates based on the different standards codified by AAPOR (2005). To maintain consistency with the NES numbers reported above, I use the RR1 calculation, which is the number of completed interviews (e.g., partially completed interviews are not considered respondents) divided by the sum of the number of eligible households plus the number of households of unknown eligibility.

2 This information is drawn from the NES codebooks of 1996, 1998, 2000, 2002, and 2004 (available at: http://www.umich.edu/~nes/studypages/download/datacenter.htm).

3 At the same time, the Pew center conducted 'rigorous' surveys, designed to mimic academic surveys (see discussion below). The researchers were able to contact nearly all of their potential respondents in 1997 and 2003; both surveys had contact rates of 92%. However, during that period, cooperation rates declined from 74% to 59%, dropping the response rate on the survey 10 points, from 61% to 51%.

4 Krosnick *et al.*'s (2005) study found that while response rates varied greatly from one survey to another, the contact rates for these surveys stayed within a fairly narrow bound of 60% to 70%. Cooperation rates for different surveys determine the variation than can be found across different organizations.

5 An additional problem is that surveys may attract respondents who are not representative of the particular demographic groups to which they belong. Brehm (1993) finds that those who participate in surveys are those who are most interested and most likely to participate in the political world. Thus, individuals who participate in surveys may be unrepresentative of their demographic group.

6 This mean may be expressed, following Kalton (1983) as:

$$\overline{Y} = W_r \overline{Y}_r + W_m \overline{Y}_m$$

where $\overline{Y}$ is the population mean, $\overline{Y}_r$ is the population mean for the respondents, $\overline{Y}_m$ is the population mean for the non-respondents (the subscript r denotes respondents, and the subscript m—for 'missing'—denotes non-respondents), and W_r and W_m are the proportion of the population in these two groups ($W_r + W_m = 1$). Since the survey fails to collect data for the non-respondents, it estimates $\overline{Y}_r$, not the population mean $\overline{Y}$. The difference between $\overline{Y}_r$ and the population parameter $\overline{Y}$ is the bias that results from using the respondent mean in place of the overall mean and is given by:

$$BIAS = W_m \left(\overline{Y}_r - \overline{Y}_m \right)$$

7 This experiment incorporated the PEW poll described above.

8 The gain in response rate in the extended sample reflected increases in both contact and cooperation rates.

9 The samples also were statistically equivalent in their media use and in the background correlates of political opinion. The samples did, however, differ in ways that we would expect from Brehm's work. The standard sample underrepresented whites, the highly affluent, and the well educated. However, these differences underscore the fact that sample differences do not necessarily lead to differences in aggregate opinion.

10 The Pew study did, however, uncover some potential problems. Specifically, it found that reluctant

respondents are more racially conservative than those respondents captured in the standard sample. These differences were not, however, replicated in the 2003 study.

11 Krosnick comes to a similar conclusion, writing, 'Offering a no-opinion response option does not seem to be an effective way to prevent reporting of weak opinions. In fact, because many real attitudes are apparently missed by offering such options, it seems unwise to use them. This is because the vast majority of NO responses are not due to completely lacking an attitude and instead result from a decision not to reveal a potentially embarrassing attitude, ambivalence, or question ambiguity' (2002, p. 99).

12 In other words, if the probability that the *i*th case is not observed depends on the value of the dependent variable, we say that the sample has been censored.

13 Model-based approaches are preferred to imputation methods if researchers have theories of the process that generated the missing data. Even proponents of multiple imputation (King *et al.*, 2001) argue that application-specific approaches are statistically optimal.

REFERENCES

Achen, C. H. (1986). *The statistical analysis of quasi-experiments*. Berkeley: University of California Press.

Beatty, P. & Herrmann, D. (2002). To answer or not to answer: Decision processes related to survey item nonresponse. In R. M. Groves, D. A. Dillman, J. L. Eltinge, & R. J. A. Little (Eds.), *Survey nonresponse* (pp. 71–85). New York: Wiley.

Berinsky, A. J. (1999). The two faces of public opinion. *American Journal of Political Science, 43*, 1209–1230.

Berinsky, A. J. (2002). 'Political context and the survey response: The dynamics of racial policy opinion.' *Journal of Politics, 64*(2), 567–584.

Berinsky, A. J. (2004). *Silent voices: Opinion polls and political representation in America*. Princeton, NJ: Princeton University Press.

Bethlehem, J. G. (2002). Weighting nonresponse adjustments based on auxiliary information. In R. M. Groves, D. A. Dillman, J. L. Eltinge, & R. J. A. Little (Eds.), *Survey nonresponse* (pp. 275–287). New York: Wiley.

Bishop, G. F., Oldendick, R. W., Tuchfarber, A. J., & Bennett, S. E. (1980). Pseudo-opinions on public affairs. *Public Opinion Quarterly, 44*(2), 198–209.

Blumenthal, M. (2004, October 3). The incumbent rule. *Mystery Pollster*. Retrieved January 2, 2006, from http://www.mysterypollster.com/main/2004/10/the_incumbent_r.html.

Breen, R. (1996). *Regression models: Censored, sample selected, or truncated data*. Sage University Paper Series on Quantitative Applications in the Social Sciences, 07–111. Thousand Oaks, CA: Sage.

Brehm, J. (1993). *The phantom respondents: Opinion surveys and political representation*. Ann Arbor: University of Michigan Press.

Cacioppo, J. T., Petty, R. E., Feinstein, J., & Jarvis, W. B. G. (1996). Dispositional differences in cognitive motivation: The life and times of individuals varying in need for cognition. *Psychological Bulletin, 119*, 197–253.

Converse, P. E. (1964). The nature of belief systems in the mass publics. In D. Apter (Ed.), *Ideology and discontent* (pp. 206–261). New York: Free Press.

Curtin, R., Presser, S., & Singer, E. (2005). Changes in telephone survey nonresponse over the past quarter century. *Public Opinion Quarterly, 69*, 87–98.

de Leeuw, E., & de Heer, W. (2002). Trends in household survey nonresponse: A longitudinal and international comparison. In R. M. Groves, D. A. Dillman, J. L. Eltinge, & R. J. A. Little (Eds.), *Survey nonresponse* (pp. 41–54). New York: Wiley.

Deming, W.E., & Stephan, F. F. (1940). On a least squares adjustment of a sample frequency table when the expected marginal totals are known. *Annals of Mathematical Statistics, 11*, 427–444.

Deville, J., & Sarndal, C. (1992). Calibration estimators in survey sampling. *Journal of the American Statistical Association, 87*, 376–382.

Deville, J., Sarndal, C., & Sautory, O. (1993). Generalizing raking procedures in survey sampling. *Journal of the American Statistical Association, 88*, 1013–1020.

Dillman, D. A., Eltinge, J. L., Groves, R. M., & Little, R. J. A. (2002). Survey nonresponse in design, data collection, and analysis. In R. M. Groves, D. A. Dillman, J. L. Eltinge, & R. J. A. Little (Eds.), *Survey nonresponse* (pp. 3–26). New York: Wiley.

Feldman, S. (1989). Measuring issue preferences: The problem of response stability. *Political Analysis, 1*, 25–60.

Fischoff, B. (1991). Value elicitation: Is there anything in there? *American Psychologist, 46*, 835–847.

Gelman, A. (2005). *Struggles with survey-weighting and regression modeling*. New York: Department of Statistics and Department of Political Science, Columbia University.

Gelman, A., & Carlin, J. B. (2002). Poststratification and weighting adjustments. In R. M. Groves, D. A. Dillman, J. L. Eltinge, & R. J. A. Little (Eds.), *Survey nonresponse* (pp. 289–302). New York: Wiley.

Groves, R. M., & Couper, M. (1998). *Nonresponse in household interview surveys*. New York: Wiley.

Heckman, J. J. (1979). Sample selection bias as a specification error. *Econometrica. 47*, 153–161.

Hillygus, D. S., Nie, N. H., Prewitt, K., & Pals, H. (2006). *The hard count: The political and social challenges of census mobilization.* New York: Russell Sage Foundation

Hippler, H J., & Schwarz, N. (1989). 'No opinion'-filters: A cognitive perspective. *International Journal of Public Opinion Research, 1*, 77–87.

Holt, D., & Elliot, D. (1991). Methods of weighting for unit non-response. *The Statistician, 40*(3), 333–342.

Kalton, G. (1983). *Introduction to survey sampling.* Beverly Hills: Sage Publications.

Kalton, G., & Flores-Cervantes, I. (2003). Weighting methods. *Journal of Official Statistics, 19*(2), 81–97.

Kam, C. D. (2003). Thinking more or less: Cognitive effort in the formation of public opinion. Unpublished doctoral dissertation, University of Michigan.

Kinder, D. R., & Nelson, T. M. (2005). 'Democratic debate and real opinions.' In K. Callaghan and F. Schnell (Eds.). *Framing American politics* (pp. 103–122). Pittsburgh: University of Pittsburgh Press.

King, G., Honaker, J., Joseph, A., & Scheve, K. (2001). Analyzing incomplete political science data: An alternative algorithm for multiple imputation. *American Political Science Review, 95*, 49–69.

Krosnick, J. A. (1991). Response strategies for coping with the cognitive demands of attitude measurement in surveys. *Applied Cognitive Psychology, 5*, 213–236.

Krosnick, J. A. (2002). The causes of no-opinion responses to attitude measures in surveys: They are rarely what they appear to be. In R. M. Groves, D. A. Dillman, J. L. Eltinge, & R. J. A. Little (Eds.), *Survey nonresponse* (pp. 87–100). New York: Wiley.

Krosnick, J. A., Holbrook, A., & Pfent, A. (2005). Response rates in surveys by the news media and government contractor survey research firms. Working Paper. Stanford University.

Little, R. J. A. (1993). Post-stratification: A modeler's perspective. *Journal of the American Statistical Association, 88*, 1001–1012.

Little, R. J. A., & Wu, M.-M. (1991). Models for contingency tables with known margins when target and sampled populations differ. *Journal of the American Statistical Association, 86*, 87–95.

Little, R. J. A., & Rubin, D. B. (2002). *Statistical analysis with missing data* (2nd ed.). New York: Wiley.

Lohr, S. (1999). *Sampling: Design and analysis.* Pacific Grove, CA: Duxbury Press.

Luevano, P. (1994, March). *Response rates in the National Election Studies, 1948–1992.* (Technical Report #44). Retrieved August, 6, 2006, from ftp://ftp.electionstudies.org/ftp/nes/bibliography/documents/nes010162.pdf.

Marker, D. A., Judkins, D. R., & Winslee, M. (2002). Large-scale imputation for complex surveys. In R. M. Groves, D. A. Dillman, J. L. Eltinge, & R. J. A. Little (Eds.), *Survey nonresponse* (pp. 329–341). New York: Wiley.

Newport, F., & Moore, D. W. (2004, November 1). *Final poll shows presidential race to be dead heat.* The Gallup Poll. Retrieved July, 28, 2006, from http://poll.gallup.com/content/ default.aspx?CI = 13873.

Schwarz, N. (1996). *Cognition and communication: Judgmental biases, research methods, and the logic of conversation.* Mahwah, NJ: Erlbaum.

Sharot, T. (1986). Weighting survey results. *Journal of the Market Research Society, 28*, 269–284.

Singer E., Frankel, M. R., & Glassman, M. B. (1983). The effect of interviewer characteristics and expectations on response. *Public Opinion Quarterly, 47*, 84–95.

Slovic, P. (1995). The construction of preference. *American Psychologist, 50*, 364–371.

Tourangeau, R., Rips, L., & Rasinski, K. (2000). *The psychology of survey response.* Cambridge: Cambridge University Press.

Weisberg, H. F. (2005). *The total survey error approach: A guide to the new science of survey research.* Chicago: Chicago University Press.

Zaller, J. (1990). Experimental tests of the question-answering model of the mass survey response. *NES Pilot Study Report, No. nes002286.*

Zaller, J. R. (1992). *The nature and origins of mass opinion.* New York: Cambridge University Press.

Zaller, J., & Feldman, S. (1992). A simple theory of the survey response. *American Journal of Political Science, 36*, 579–616.

29

Split Ballots as an Experimental Approach to Public Opinion Research

Thomas Petersen

As a rule, experiments play a relatively minor role in practical survey research, even though they are not, as is often assumed, only an important tool for obtaining insights in the field of psychology. Rather, they enable researchers in the fields of sociology, political science, communication research, market and media research and all other disciplines that use the methods of empirical social research to obtain insights that could not be gained by means of any other methodological approach. The following chapter aims to outline the vital role the experiment has played in the development of the social sciences, while also explaining the basic principle of the split-ballot experiment and discussing the importance of this method in practice. In so doing, the chapter focuses on the use of the split-ballot experiment to analyze questionnaire effects as well as on its varied applications as a tool for uncovering subconscious motives and modes of behavior.

HISTORY OF THE EXPERIMENT

A new approach to scientific evidence

In the history of the sciences, the development of experimental methods has repeatedly proven to be the crucial factor in the evolution of a scientific discipline (see Petersen, 2002, pp. 20ff.). However, the meaning of the term 'experiment' itself has shifted over time, something that occasionally gives rise to misunderstandings even today, since remnants of the word's original meaning still linger, at least in colloquial language (see Schulz, 1970, p. 22).

Roger Bacon (1210–1294), an English Franciscan monk, is regarded as the first person to have advocated the use of experimental methods in scientific endeavors (Bacon, trans. 1964). More than 300 years after Roger Bacon, Francis Bacon (1561–1626) vehemently called for the introduction of the *experimentum* into scientific practice. Like his predecessor, Francis Bacon also did not have the modern controlled scientific experiment in mind, but was instead concerned with the willingness to think empirically and to draw conclusions based on observations rather than relying solely on the authority of the classics (Bacon, 1620/1990). John Stuart Mill (1806–1873) was the first to point out that the experimental method could be used to discover causal relationships (Mill, 1856).

The decisive advantage of the experiment— as the term is understood today—over other scientific procedures is that it produces causal evidence (see Herkner, 1991, p. 18). Researchers need not rely on simply contemplating an empirically observed phenomenon and speculating about the underlying reasons for it; rather, by intervening in a controlled manner, they can attempt to determine the empirical factors on which the phenomenon depends. Hence, the mental leap from empiricism to experimentation is essentially the same as the step from purely theoretical contemplation of an object of study to empirical observation. In both cases, researchers must decide whether to rely solely on their own powers of reason or on their observations. The experiment is thus the logical consequence of empiricism.

The experiment in the social sciences

When the first attempts were made to introduce experimental methods in the newly emerging social sciences in the 19th century, researchers found that the procedures employed in experimental physics or chemistry could not be adopted in unchanged form, since their logic is not suited to the object of investigation in the social sciences. The natural scientist manipulates the key explanatory factor. If the object of the investigation shows any change in response, the change is attributed to the experimental factor. An investigative design of this kind is sufficiently conclusive if the object of investigation cannot undergo any change that is not caused by the experimental

factor (Schulz, 1970, p. 94). In experiments dealing with living organisms—and particularly in experiments in the social sciences—researchers cannot assume that the object of investigation has any fundamentally unchanging 'natural state.' Thus, Campbell and Stanley (1963, pp. 7ff.) logically refer to the use of before-and-after measurements in the social sciences as a 'pre-experimental' method. In 1957, Donald T. Campbell listed various factors that must be considered when conducting an experiment in the social sciences. Among them are external influences aside from the experimental factor, inner change of the subjects during the experiment, or measurement effects.

The solution to this problem in the social sciences has been to examine two (or more) groups of persons simultaneously in parallel investigations. Using this model, at least one experimental group is exposed to the experimental factor—which can be tested in different forms, if need be—whereas the persons in the control group, whose behavior or opinions are also investigated, are not exposed to the experimental factor. This model validly measures the effect of the experimental factor without any interference from the time-dependent disruptive factors mentioned above, as long as the experimental and control groups have exactly the same composition and are treated in exactly the same way—except for the introduction of the experimental stimulus. If these conditions are fulfilled, there is often no need to complete a 'before' measurement.

Other than in the field of psychology, especially in the areas of physiological and social psychology, the experimental method gained only begrudging acceptance. One of the reasons for this was that the method customarily used in psychology, i.e. the laboratory experiment, was not suited to the conditions that are given in other fields of social research. Various aspects of the laboratory experiment like its artificial nature and small samples endanger the validity of the findings in empirical social research. The latter usually focuses on people's opinions and modes of behavior in everyday life and hence on attributes that may fluctuate strongly and that are not, as a rule, homogeneously distributed among the universe being investigated. The solution was the method of the field experiment (the most important variation of which is the split-ballot experiment), which enables researchers to combine the evidentiary logic of the laboratory experiment with the method of the representative survey, thus obtaining findings that are quantitatively generalizable, which is of crucial importance in social research.

The first split-ballot experiments

Not long after the method of the representative survey had become established, the first researchers began employing the split-ballot technique. In 1940, three articles presenting questionnaire experiments were published, one by Elmo Roper, another by Edward G. Benson and a third by Hadley Cantril. The next milestone came in 1944 with the publication of Cantril's book, *Gauging Public Opinion*, which included a detailed description of the split-ballot method and presented the findings of numerous split-ballot experiments.

In the early 1950s, however, interest in the split-ballot method waned. It seemed as if social scientists—or at least the great majority of them—had failed to recognize the possibilities offered by the experiment in social research. In contrast to the field of psychology, where the experiment had long since become a matter of course, there was no long tradition of experimental thinking in the area of social research. Following the publication of Stanley Payne's book, *The Art of Asking Questions*, in 1951, no studies or books dealing with split-ballot experiments to any mentionable degree were published for the next 20 years. It was not until the 1970s, and increasingly since the 1980s, that researchers once again began employing the method of the split-ballot experiment.

The renaissance of the experimental method in survey research was inspired to a great extent by the methods and findings

from the field of cognitive psychology. A major contribution to this development was made by the work of researchers such as Norman Bradburn, George Bishop, Seymour Sudman, Howard Schuman, Stanley Presser and Norbert Schwarz (see, for example Schuman & Presser, 1981; Bishop, Oldendick, & Tuchfarber, 1982; Sudman, Bradburn, & Schwarz, 1996). Since then, split-ballot experiments have gained firm footing as a tool in basic methodological research. Nevertheless, the split-ballot technique still generally tends to be employed in connection with a relatively limited number of research tasks, for example, testing how questions are understood or investigating the rational decision-making strategies people use when giving their responses. Even today, therefore, the manifold possibilities offered by the split-ballot method are still hardly utilized.

The principle of the split-ballot experiment

The basic principle of the split-ballot experiment is quite simple: within the framework of a standardized representative survey, the sample is randomly divided into two (or more) subsamples of equal size. Each of these subsamples is equally representative of the total universe. Respondents in each subsample are interviewed simultaneously and under the same conditions, using a questionnaire that differs with respect only to individual details from group to group, for example, the wording of a certain question, the order in which two questions are presented or the illustrative materials that are presented along with the question. These variations in the questionnaire represent the experimental stimulus to which respondents in the experimental group(s) are exposed.

This approach is so simple and straightforward that the question necessarily arises as to whether the split-ballot technique does in fact meet the conditions of an experiment. Indeed, doubts along these lines were raised for quite some time in the methodological debate in the field of empirical social research. In 1962, for example, Robert Pagès categorically referred to all field experiments—and to split-ballot experiments in particular—as 'quasi-experiments' (Pagès, 1962, p. 439). Yet a glance at four of the conditions that a control-group experiment ought to fulfill shows that split-ballot experiments do in fact meet these theoretical requirements.

1. The experimental group and the control group are identical with respect to all factors: they are both based on equally representative samples, and any differences that may exist are within the margins of error that customarily apply to a random selection of test subjects.
2. The experimental group and the control group are formed simultaneously and before the experimental factor is introduced. The experimental factor is brought into play at the same time for both groups.
3. The control group is completely shielded from the influence of the experimental factor. In each case, the interviews are conducted one-on-one, either via telephone or the Internet or in the respondent's home, and neither the interviewer nor the respondent has any knowledge of the questionnaire employed in the other subgroups.
4. All external and internal conditions of the experiment are exactly the same for both the experimental group and the control group. The only difference between the two groups is the experimental factor. This rule applies not to each individual test subject, but to all groups as a whole. Although the interviews are completed in different locations by different interviewers—and possible interference by third variables cannot be completely excluded—the representativeness of the sample and the large number of interviewers and respondents involved ensure that such interfering variables carry equal weight in all groups, within the margins of statistical error.

Split-ballot experiments thus clearly represent true experiments that are completely suitable as a means of obtaining causal evidence in the social sciences. In fact, split-ballot experiments are actually what is referred to in the natural sciences as 'double-blind experiments,' for ideally, neither respondents nor interviewers are even aware that they are taking part in an experiment, something that can easily be ensured as long as each interviewer receives only one version of the questionnaire.

APPLICATION OF SPLIT-BALLOT EXPERIMENTS

Split-ballot experiments can be used for a number of different purposes. Here, we can distinguish between three main areas: first of all, they can be used in applied research to investigate various technical aspects relating to the questionnaire; second, they can serve as a tool for clarifying concrete investigative tasks; and third, they can be applied in basic methodological research, particularly in connection with questionnaire design (→ *Designing Reliable and Valid Questionnaires*). The following are some of the more specific purposes for which split-ballot experiments can be employed:

Preventing order and context effects

Many response-order effects, albeit not all types of context effects, can be eradicated simply by switching the order of response alternatives and arguments presented in writing, or by rearranging list items in every other interview (Ring, 1974). Although this procedure has become less important over the past decades in telephone surveys, due to improved randomization techniques, it continues to be highly useful in face-to-face surveys.

Testing question wordings

Most of the early publications presenting findings obtained via the split-ballot method focused on split-ballot experiments of this kind. Many of the questionnaire effects observed in the 1940s by Donald Rugg (1941) and others are still viewed as classics even today. The most well known of these is probably Rugg's experiment on respondents' different reactions to the words 'forbid' and 'not allow' (Table 29.1). Nevertheless, these

Table 29.1 Forbidding and not allowing: Donald Rugg's experiment in 1940

Question to subgroup A: 'Do you think the United States should forbid public speeches against democracy?'
Question to subgroup B: 'Do you think the United States should allow public speeches against democracy?'

	United States 1940*	
	Subgroup A (forbid) %	Subgroup B (allow) %
Forbid/not allow	46	62
Not forbid/allow	39	21
Don't know	15	17
	100	100

Note: *Rugg did not indicate the number of respondents
Source: D. Rugg, Experiments in wording questions: II. *Public Opinion Quarterly*, 5, 1941, pp. 91–92, by *permission of Oxford University Press and the American Association for Public Opinion Research*

experiments were problematic, since they often did not allow researchers to draw any conclusions about which of the various question wordings tested had obtained the more valid findings. This was probably the reason why interest in this type of questionnaire experiment waned in the 1950s and was not rekindled until the 1970s, when survey researchers increasingly began turning towards the methods of cognitive psychology. Then and now, this method still represents the only conclusive and reliable way to test the effect of different question wordings (→ *The Psychology of Survey Response*).

Testing the stability of opinions

Even in the early days of empirical social research, the conviction that there are different degrees of firmness in popular opinion had already taken hold among researchers (Tönnies, 1922, pp. 137ff.). Subsequently, Hippler and Schwarz demonstrated that certain questionnaire effects—including effects of the kind revealed by Rugg's classic 'forbid/not allow' experiment—could only be observed among those respondents who had already stated at another point in the questionnaire that they had no clear-cut opinion on the issue in question (Hippler & Schwarz, 1986). This finding can be put to use in practical research. In cases where opinions are firmly held, even extremely suggestive questions give rise to no mentionable effects in split-ballot experiments (Cantril, 1944, p. 45).

During the early stages of the opinion formation process, however, or at times when opinions are shifting radically, even the slightest changes in question wording can have a clear effect. Hence, if strong questionnaire effects are observed at times when opinions would otherwise appear to be stable, this may serve as an early indicator of an upcoming shift in public opinion (Petersen, 2002, pp. 122ff.).

Testing different versions of materials presented to respondents and different lines of reasoning

Particularly in the area of market and media research, simultaneously presenting, for example, four different drafts of an advertisement or advertising text to representative subgroups and then eliciting respondents' reactions to these materials is an elegant and, in many cases, more valid alternative to other measurement procedures that require respondents to compare various drafts, arguments or objects. The advantage of the split-ballot experiment is that respondents do not make a conscious comparison, but instead only assess one particular item. The findings obtained for the various subgroups are not compared until the analysis stage. Thus, respondents make their assessment in a more true-to-life situation than when they are forced into the unaccustomed role of the expert and are asked to make the comparisons themselves, as is the case, for example, with the popular market research technique known as 'conjoint measurement.'

There are a number of different possible variations of this approach: for instance, the 'time-lapse test,' whereby the same poster is repeatedly presented to respondents, thus simulating the effect of habituation to the motif (Noelle-Neumann & Petersen, 2005, pp. 490ff.). Also included here are various benchmarking models, in which the image profiles of competing brand manufacturers are ascertained in different subgroups and then compared, or the 'price-threshold' test, whereby respondents in different subgroups are shown the same product—which is listed at varying prices—and are then asked whether they would be willing to purchase the product (Petersen, 2002, p. 132). A special form of split-ballot experiments is employed in the area of survey research for legal evidence. Here, such experiments are used to obtain conclusive evidence to clarify legal disputes in areas such as fair trading and trade mark law: for example, they can help to determine whether there is a danger that consumers might confuse the packaging of products sold by two different food manufacturers. In such cases, split-ballot experiments often represent the only investigative approach that obtains probative evidence that is accepted by the courts (Zeisel & Kaye, 1997; → *The Use of Surveys as Legal Evidence*).

Split-ballot experiments with indicator questions

Indicator questions represent a way to indirectly measure various issues and circumstances. Gottlieb Schnapper-Arndt (1975) and Emile Durkheim (1961) already described the principle of indicators in the late 19th century: specifically, if a certain situation cannot be measured directly with any reliability, then researchers must resort to questions on aspects that are not of any great interest in themselves, but that allow them to make inferences about the issue or situation actually under investigation. From the early days of survey research to the present, a large variety of questions designed to obtain indirect measurements have been developed. Many of these approaches derive from the field of individual psychology (see Ring, 1992). Indicator questions play a major role in motivation research. In combination with the split-ballot technique, they allow researchers to detect hidden prejudices (see, for instance, one of the earliest examples in Haire, 1950) and even to uncover motives of which respondents themselves are not consciously aware.

Figure 29.1 shows two illustrations presented in a study concerning people's preconceptions about smokers. The question text itself made no mention of the topic of smoking. Instead, respondents were asked to

Figure 29.1 Illustrations for a field experiment on the image of smoking
Source: Allensbach Archives, IfD Survey 4099/I, January 1988. *Reprinted by permission of the Allensbach Institute*

estimate the age of the man depicted and to say whether they found him appealing and whether they believed he was successful at his job. In the subgroup that was shown the picture of the man holding a cigarette in his hand, he was assessed significantly more often as being older, less appealing and less successful professionally than was the case in the control group.

Basic methodological research

This is the most varied and probably the most demanding area in which split-ballot experiments can be employed. No other instrument can reliably demonstrate the diverse effects of questionnaire monotony, the cognitive processes involved in grasping and interpreting question wordings, fluctuating attention levels, heuristic processing of information, suggestive signals imparted by scale categories, or implicit threats that are subjectively perceived by respondents (Petersen, 2002, pp. 151ff.).

ADDITIONAL TYPES OF SURVEY EXPERIMENTS

Although split-ballot experiments represent—in comparative terms—the most widespread variation of survey experiments, they are not the only type of experiment. The same logic that is applied to the questionnaire in split-ballot experiments can also be transferred to just about all other facets of the research process. Thus, experiments have been conducted to test the effects of various sampling procedures (Hochstim & Smith, 1948; Reuband, 1998), different interviewing methods (Petersen, 2000), or various forms of interviewer supervision (Schwarzenauer, 1974).

In addition, other special forms of the field experiment that should be mentioned here are the social experiment—in which some of the test subjects are exposed to the stimulus being investigated under controlled circumstances not only during the interview, but also in a concrete, day-to-day context

(Petersen, 2002, pp. 66ff.)—along with so-called 'quasi-' or 'ex-post-facto' experiments, in which the experimental group and the control group are formed subsequently at the stage of analyzing the data. Strictly speaking, the latter procedure actually represents a variation of the correlation analysis, yet under certain circumstances, this approach can obtain findings that are just about as valid as those of a true experiment (Petersen, 2002, pp. 76ff.).

CONCLUSION

Over the course of history, the development of experimental methods has repeatedly proven to be the decisive factor in the evolution of various scientific disciplines. There is no reason to assume that this does not apply to the social sciences as well. Split-ballot experiments and other types of survey experiments are the logical extension of the shift toward empirical thinking that commenced in the social sciences in the 19th century. It seems highly probable that such experiments will play a key role in shaping the development of empirical social research in the future.

REFERENCES

Bacon, F. (1990). Neues Organon [New Organon]. In W. Krohn (Ed. & Trans.), *Philosophische Bibliothek*. Hamburg: Meiner (Original work published in 1620).

Bacon, R. (1964). *Opus Majus*. (J. H. Bridges, Ed. & Trans.). Frankfurt am Main: Minerva (Reprint).

Benson, E. G. (1940). Three words. *Public Opinion Quarterly, 4*, 130–134.

Bishop, G. F., Oldendick, R. W., & Tuchfarber, A. J. (1982). Effects of presenting one versus two sides of an issue in survey questions. *Public Opinion Quarterly, 46*, 69–85.

Campbell, D. T. (1957). Factors relevant to the validity of experiments in social settings. *Psychological Bulletin, 54*, 297–312.

Campbell, D. T. & Stanley, J. C. (1963). *Experimental and quasi-experimental designs for research*. Boston: Houghton Mifflin.

Cantril, H. (1940). Experiments in the wording of questions. *Public Opinion Quarterly, 4*, 330–332.

Cantril, H. (1944). *Gauging public opinion*. Princeton: Princeton University Press.

Durkheim, E. (1961). *Die Regeln der soziologischen Methode. Les règles de la methode sociologique* [The rules of the sociological method]. Neuwied: Luchterhand.

Haire, M. (1950). Projective techniques in marketing research. *Journal of Marketing, 14,* 649–656.

Herkner, W. (1991). *Lehrbuch Sozialpsychologie* [Manual of social psychology]. Bern: Hans Huber.

Hippler, H.-J. & Schwarz, N. (1986). Not forbidding isn't allowing: The cognitive basis of the forbid-allow-asymmetry. *Public Opinion Quarterly, 50,* 87–96.

Hochstim, J. R. & Smith, D. M. L. (1948). Area sampling or quota control?—Three sampling experiments. *Public Opinion Quarterly, 12,* 71–80.

Mill, J. S. (1856). *A sytem of logic ratiocinative and inductive being a connected view of the principles of evidence and the methods of scientific investigation.* London: John W. Parker and Son.

Noelle-Neumann, E. & Petersen, T. (2005). *Alle, nicht jeder. Einführung in die Methoden der Demoskopie* [All, but not each. Introduction to the methods of survey research] (4th ed.). Berlin: Springer.

Pagès, R. (1962). Das Experiment in der Soziologie [The experiment in sociology]. In R. König (Ed.), *Handbuch der empirischen Sozialforschung* (Vol. 1, pp. 415–450). Stuttgart: Enke.

Payne, S. L. (1951). *The art of asking questions.* Princeton: Princeton University Press.

Petersen, T. (2000). Keine Alternative: Telefon- und Face-to-Face Umfragen [No alternative: Telephone and face-to-face surveys]. In Statistisches Bundesamt (Eds.), *Neue Erhebungsinstrumente und Methodeneffekte.* Stuttgart: Metzler-Poeschel.

Petersen, T. (2002). *Das Experiment in der Umfrageforschung* [The experiment in survey research]. Frankfurt am Main: Campus.

Reuband, K.-H. (1998). Quoten- oder Randomstichproben in der Praxis der Sozialforschung. Gemeinsamkeiten und Unterschiede in der sozialen Zusammensetzung und den Antwortmustern der Befragten [Quota or random samples in practical social research. Commonalities and differences in social composition and response patterns among respondents]. *ZA-Informationen, 43,* 48–80.

Ring, E. (1974). Wie man bei Listenfragen Einflüsse der Reihenfolge ausschalten kann [How to avoid order effects when using list questions]. *Psychologie und Praxis, 17,* 105–113.

Ring, E. (1992). *Signale der Gesellschaft. Psychologische Diagnostik in der Umfrageforschung* [Societal signals. Psychological diagnostics in survey research]. Göttingen: Verlag für angewandte Psychologie.

Roper, E. (1940). Wording questions for the polls. *Public Opinion Quarterly, 4,* 129–130.

Rugg, D. (1941). Experiments in wording questions: II. *Public Opinion Quarterly, 5,* 91–92.

Schnapper-Arndt, G. (1975). Zur Methodologie sozialer Enqueten [On methodology in social inquiries]. In G. Schnapper-Arndt (Ed.), *Hoher Taunus. Eine sozialstatistische Untersuchung in fünf Dorfgemeinden* (pp. 195–223). Allensbach: Verlag für Demoskopie.

Schulz, W. (1970). *Kausalität und Experiment in den Sozialwissenschaften. Methodologie und Forschungstechnik* [Causality and the experiment in the social sciences. Methodology and research techniques]. Mainz: Hase und Koehler.

Schuman, H. & Presser, S. (1981). *Questions and answers in attitude surveys. Experiments on question form, wording, and context.* New York: Academic Press.

Schwarzenauer, W. (1974). An experiment on the effect internal circular letters have on interviewers. *European Research, 2,* 243–247.

Sudman, S., Bradburn, N. M., & Schwarz, N. (1996). *Thinking about answers. The application of cognitive processes to survey methodology.* San Francisco: Jossey-Bass.

Tönnies, F. (1922). *Kritik der öffentlichen Meinung* [A critique of public opinion]. Berlin: Springer.

Zeisel, H. & Kaye, D. (1997). *Prove it with figures. Empirical methods in law and litigation.* New York: Springer.

30

Panel Surveys

Jochen Hansen

Panel surveys measure the *same* variables with *identical* individuals at *several points in time*. They thus obtain *longitudinal data* that could also be collected via normal trend studies—based on similarly composed samples that are *freshly recruited* for each survey. Of course, both panel studies and trend studies are equally adept at measuring *net change* over time. Yet panel studies further enable the researcher to investigate the full extent and direction of the changes— along with the various processes that have contributed to the overall change. Thus, panels reveal how many people changed their position or opinion at all, whether their position changed moderately or substantially, and which new position replaced the old one. In addition, panels allow us to establish which factors either encourage or inhibit loyalty to one position, on the one hand, and reorientation on the other.

Is there really a need for the relatively expensive and time-consuming method of reinterviewing? Would it not suffice to simply ask people about their present, prior or future behavior and sentiments within the framework of a one-time survey? Although respondents usually reply to retrospective questions, research suggests that these questions often provide an incorrect or highly distorted reflection of reality, since people who have in fact changed positions often recall their former position as being in line with their current, new position. For example, by means of panel studies conducted in Germany, we can show that of those voters whose party preference changed in the final months prior to a federal election, about 50% correctly recalled which party they had voted for four years ago when they were asked shortly before changing their preference. After switching to a different party, however, only about one third correctly recalled the party they had last voted for, while a majority of about 50% now claimed to have voted then for the party they currently preferred (Noelle-Neumann, Donsbach, & Kepplinger, 2005, p. 256). Obviously, once changes have occurred respondents tend to align or harmonize their recollection of their former position with their current way of thinking or behavior (see Hansen, 1982, for further examples).

The following gives an overview over the different types of panel surveys, how and where they can be applied, how panel data can be analyzed, and which problems the researcher can face when using this method.

TYPES OF PANELS

The most widely known applications of panel surveys are long-standing panels conducted among consumers or in various commercial channels with the aim of obtaining highly detailed data on both market shares and the characteristics of various goods and services. These surveys are based on samples that are broad enough to provide data that is safeguarded on a regional level. Among the classic providers of such panels—which carry a great weight in the business world—are major institutes like GfK, IRI and Nielsen. In Germany, for instance, the GfK household panel is based on a sample of 20,000 participants. Normally, all important suppliers in a particular market segment subscribe to these regular panel findings, which enable them to track their own market position while also keeping an eye on the competition. Panel data of this kind is collected at regular intervals—i.e. on a daily, weekly or monthly basis—either in written or electronic form. In German television audience research, for instance, audience shares are electronically measured around the clock, with the data being transferred to the research institute daily via an automatic telephone hook-up. The main objective of such studies is to measure continuously such characteristics as: who in the household watches which TV programs, and for how long. Consumer studies focus on aspects such as purchasing frequency and intervals, brands, prices, and sales channels. Another example of a panel study with a very long-term design is the 'Longitudinal Study of Generations,' started in 1971 to investigate intergenerational relations among 300 three-generation families in California (see www.usc.edu/gero/research).

Panels conducted within a limited time frame and with a narrow thematic scope can also obtain highly illuminating findings. The probably most famous study of this kind was conducted by the renowned team of researchers Paul Lazarsfeld, Bernard Berelson and Hazel Gaudet in Erie County, Ohio, USA in 1940, obtaining numerous insights on the effects of election campaigns, the mass media and personal communication that remain valid to this day (Lazarsfeld, Berelson, & Gaudet, 1944/1968). The researchers surveyed an identical sample of 600 persons in seven so-called panel waves over a period of more than six months. In addition, three equally large control groups were interviewed twice, in order to investigate the effects of reinterviewing (the 'panel effect,' see below). The 'Erie County study' has been the model for several election studies although none of these, for reasons of resources, attained the same methodological sophistication.

SPECIFIC RULES AND PROBLEMS OF PANEL SURVEYS

Design and sampling

Panel studies can be designed on a long or relatively short-term basis, depending on the investigative task at hand. They are equally helpful in exploring social and political issues as in studies involving durable and nondurable consumer goods, the media and media effects. Moreover, panels can be conducted at relatively short or long intervals and may comprise many or, in some cases, no more than two waves. The interviews may be highly detailed—or fairly brief—and can be completed either face-to-face, in writing or via telephone. Conducting panels online via the Internet is also feasible, provided that the samples are sufficiently representative of the universe under investigation.

As the Internet becomes ever more prevalent, the idea of interviewing panels online seems to be an increasingly appealing and simple approach: After all, the Internet allows the researcher to locate a large number of respondents relatively quickly and cheaply. However, the findings are at best only representative of the universe of

Internet users, a problem that is defused somewhat as the group of Internet users expands and increasingly comes to resemble a cross-section of the population (→ *Internet Surveys*). Another problem is the sharp decline in respondents' willingness to participate in online-surveys. In representative face-to-face studies conducted among adult Internet users in Germany, respondents were asked if they could imagine being interviewed via the Internet. While in the 1990s almost 50% said they were ready to participate in an online survey, this figure decreased to 35% in 2001, 29% in 2003, and to 27% in 2005 (Institut für Demoskopie Allensbach, 1999–2005).

Continuity of questions

For panel studies conducted over a limited time period or focusing on a single investigative task, the battery of questions is normally rather firmly established right from the start. After only a few survey waves, however, the researcher can easily recognize which variables are especially important and thus absolutely must be asked in each new survey wave—and which ones need only be asked infrequently or even just once. To reduce the unchanging battery of questions to core variables (without any substantial loss of information), statistical-mathematical procedures such as factor, cluster or segmentation analyses should be employed, along with more complex predictive models that pinpoint those variables that play a clearly causal role (while excluding other variables that have little or no explanatory power). In most panel studies by the Allensbach Institute, for instance, no more than 15 to 20 minutes of the total interview are devoted to ascertaining core variables (after they have been tested in the initial survey waves). This time limit leaves enough room for including new topics or more in-depth questions in each wave— without extending the average length of the interview. In this case, panel studies can also replace special studies that would otherwise be necessary and thus save on costs.

Structuring an interview to include a relatively small section of unchanging questions and a larger section of new questions is also conducive to the interview climate: obviously, the larger the section of new questions is, the less likely respondents are to perceive the repeated core questions as onerous, tiring and boring. Moreover, this approach reduces the danger that respondents will be 'conditioned' by repeated interviewing, i.e. that they will succumb to the 'panel effect' (see below) and thus not respond normally. Another benefit of structuring interviews in this way is that respondents are generally more willing to be reinterviewed.

The question of how often panel waves should be conducted depends on what purpose the data is intended to serve. If, for example, the aim is to track every purchase in a particular market, the survey intervals should correspond to the normal purchasing interval in that market. The more the researcher knows about the normal rates of change and various contributing factors, the more he or she is able to prolong the survey interval, as long as the main goal is to depict *strategically important* target groups over time, determining which factors promote party or brand loyalty, for example, or what makes these parties or brands seem either attractive to respondents who were previously indifferent or off-putting to others.

Panel effect

Many panel studies were designed along the lines of the classic panel surveys conducted by Lazarsfeld *et al.* (1944/1968). They thus provided numerous insights regarding not only the effects of election campaigns, the mass media and personal communication, but also the methodological issue known as the 'panel effect,' i.e. the expectation that frequent reinterviewing causes respondents to react abnormally. Lazarsfeld and his colleagues surveyed, within about a half a year, an identical sample of 600 persons seven times, whereas three equally large control groups were interviewed only twice (specifically, in the first and third waves or, respectively, the first and fourth or the first and sixth panel waves). The findings demonstrated that reinterviewing had little or no effect (Glock, 1952)—a fact also largely confirmed by subsequent panel research.

However, there are some indications that response behavior is somewhat more decisive among panel participants: In an election study, for example, about 90% of panel participants stated their voting intention, as compared to about 80% of respondents in independent samples. This complies with evidence from other studies suggesting that the act of being interviewed increases the likelihood of voting (Granberg & Holmberg, 1992). In this context, the fact that panels often focus on one central issue also plays a role, since people who are interested in a particular issue, such as politics, are also more likely to agree to be reinterviewed on that issue than people who are not interested. As a rule, however, the responses—although more decisive—are still distributed proportionally among the different response categories, meaning that this method does correctly measure the relations between the various categories in practice (Hansen, 1982).

Panel mortality

Another reservation associated with panel studies concerns what is known as 'panel mortality,' i.e. the gradual dissolution of the sample over time, for example, when some respondents decline to be reinterviewed, move, or cannot be reached for some other reason. In addition, when panel samples are to be interviewed over a lengthier period of time, they must be designed dynamically. Suppose, for example, that a panel is conducted among eligible voters age 18 and over at the start of a four-year parliamentary term. By the end of the term, the initial sample will no longer contain anyone under the age of 22. Therefore, the panel sample must be expanded in each new wave to include new respondents who have either grown into the universe or, alternatively, who are known, based on prior experience, to be especially likely to drop out of panel samples.

Of course, newly incorporated respondents cannot provide any longitudinal data when they are first interviewed, but such data can be obtained the second time around. By the same token, panel samples must be adjusted when the universe is restricted by a certain attribute, such as a maximum age of 69, or focuses on a specific population, such as jobholders or car drivers. Respondents who no longer fulfill such core criteria when a new wave is conducted do not belong in the universe and must be excluded from the sample.

Provided that the initial survey is prepared by the best methodological standards, one can expect a response rate of 80–90% for the first repeat wave, 70–80% for the second and 60–70% for the third repeat wave (see, for instance, Gruner & Jahr, 2001, 2004). Consequently, if one is aiming to analyze the behavior and attitudes of about 1,000 panel participants in three consecutive waves, one must start with an initial sample of approximately 1,500 respondents. On the other side, the changes measured in panel surveys are more likely to be significant than those ascertained among independently recruited samples of comparable size—since panel surveys measure changes for identical respondents and, therefore, the confidence interval applies only once.

ANALYZING CHANGE

In analyzing the changes measured in panel surveys, we can distinguish (according to Lazarsfeld, 1972) between:

- 'turnover, fluctuation,' which involves investigating whether responses to a repeatedly posed question (for example, on party preferences) either change or stay the same;
- 'qualified change,' whereby respondents are broken down according to assumed independent variables (or attributes), allowing researchers to determine how these 'qualifying factors' influence other variables (for instance, how or whether voting intentions changed among persons who were exposed to campaign advertising by a particular party); and lastly,

- 'concurrent change,' which involves simultaneously tracking several variables and their reciprocal effects over time. Here, the greater the pull exerted by one variable on another, the more clearly it can be interpreted as the causal variable responsible for the change detected.

Fluctuation

Viewed as aggregates, voting intentions and purchasing preferences often appear to remain quite similar over time. As a rule, however, the gross change is substantially greater than the net change. For instance, when analyzing the development of voting intentions in Germany from 1994 to the spring of 1998, we find that the left-leaning Social Democrats (SPD) and the Greens, who ultimately won the 1998 election, increased their share of the vote from 34 to 41%, while the government coalition at the time, consisting of the conservative Christian Democratic Union (CDU/CSU) and the Free Democrats or Liberals (FDP), dropped from 39 to 32%. This development is indicated in Table 30.1 in the vertical total column (for 1994) and the horizontal total line (for 1998). In addition, the table reveals the entire extent of the political shifts, with voting intentions changing among almost half of all German voters (47%) in the time from 1994 to 1998 (all values aside from the boldface diagonal)

and remaining stable among 53% (values in the diagonal).[1]

In addition, the table also shows the exact percentage of voters who migrated to or from the various parties, along with the parties' loyal supporters. In the time from 1994 to 1998, 3% of all voters migrated from the Christian Democrats to the Social Democrats, being joined by 1% from the Liberals, 2% from the Greens, 1% from the Socialists[2] and 6% who had previously favored other parties. In sum, 13% migrated to the Social Democrats (see the values in the second column). At the same time, of those voters who abandoned the Social Democrats, 2% switched to the Christian Democrats, 3% to the Greens, 1% to the Socialists and 3% to other parties, making a total of 9% (see the values in the second line). On balance, therefore, the Social Democrats increased their pool of supporters by four points (from 28 to 32%). With respect to the Christian Democrats, we find that 9% of voters migrated to the Christian Democrats between 1994 and 1998 (see the values in the first column), whereas 14% abandoned the party (see the values in the first line), which thus dropped in the voters' favor from 33 to 28%.

The parties' strengths and weaknesses were also reflected by the degree of stability in voting intentions for the two major parties: Of those voters who favored the Social

Table 30.1 Fluctuation of voting intentions (Party Vote) in Germany, 1994–1998

	PANEL ANALYSIS						
	Voting intentions in Spring 1998 (in percent)						
Voting intention in 1994	Christian Democrats	Social Democrats	Liberals (FDP)	Greens	Socialists	Other	Total
Christian Democrats	19	3	1	2	x	8	33
Social Democrats	2	19	x	3	1	3	28
The Liberals (FDP)	2	1	2	x	0	1	6
The Greens	x	2	x	2	x	2	6
Socialists (PDS)	1	1	x	x	2	x	4
Other	4	6	1	2	1	9	23
Total	28	32	4	9	4	23	100
n =	252	361	46	89	110	271	1129

x = less than 0.5%
Source: Allensbach Archives, IfD Surveys 5113, 5139
Reprinted from: Noelle-Neumann et al., 1999, p. 251—translated by the author. Reprinted with permission from Verlag Karl Alber, Freiburg/München

Democrats in 1994, 68% still intended to vote for this party four years later, as calculated based on the 19% of supporters remaining from the 28% who preferred the party in 1994. In contrast, the share of voters who had favored the Christian Democrats in 1994 and remained loyal to them four years later was considerably lower, at 58% (19% remaining from 33%).

Qualified and concurrent change

To investigate the importance of qualifiers within the framework of a panel study, the 'covarying' variables, which change simultaneously and may mutually influence each other, should ideally be ascertained in each survey wave. Such variables include respondents' political party preference and affinity for the parties' top candidates. By consistently assessing both variables each time, we can determine whether preferences for the parties and the various candidates harmonize over the course of an election campaign. This approach also reveals persons subjected to 'cross pressure,' that is, people who, for instance, like their own party's top candidate less than the candidate running for the opposing party. Panel analyses show how people resolve this conflict during the course of the campaign, i.e. whether they resign themselves to voting for the candidate they dislike—or switch to the party whose candidate they prefer.

'Intermittent' variables are qualifiers that emerge *between* two survey waves. Qualifiers of this kind—for instance, exposure to one of the parties' new TV campaign ads broadcast *after* the first wave—obviously can only be ascertained in the second survey wave. 'Constant' qualifiers are variables like sex, age, or education. Since these variables (usually) do not change, they need only be measured once.

STRATEGIC TARGET GROUPS, IMAGE AND MOTIVATION ANALYSES

Aside from the group of convinced and loyal voters, swing voters represent one of the strategically crucial target groups, which political parties attempt to win over prior to Election Day. Panel studies are an excellent tool for determining how such voters can be attracted, as illustrated by the shift in favor of the Social Democrats in Germany between 1994 and the spring of 1998 shown in Table 30.1. If we take a closer look at the Social Democrats' new supporters in 1998, we find that only 28% believed in 1994 that the Social Democrats would be more likely (than the governing parties at the time) to ensure that there were no new increases in taxes and social welfare contributions. In 1998, however, after switching to the Social Democrats, almost twice as many (51%) were convinced of this. In contrast, among all other voters, confidence in the Social Democrats' ability to prevent such increases actually declined (from 39 to 30%). At the same time, the Social Democrats' new supporters were especially confident that the party would be better at fighting unemployment and shoring up the pension system (Noelle-Neumann *et al.*, 1999, p. 231). Thus, at an early point in time—even months before Election Day—analyses of this kind can detect the decisive motivational patterns that lead to voter fluctuation—while also pinpointing those campaign promises that are not appealing or that voters perhaps even find off-putting.

Focusing on strategic target groups is also important when investigating consumption areas. It is important to define consumers in a way that obtains valid measurements—for example, by including not only regular purchasers, but sporadic customers as well. Here, one very valid technique is to ask about the last purchase made, which is also the best way to ascertain which people just happened to purchase an item by chance. On comparing the latest purchasing data ascertained in two successive waves, we can define the following consumer groups for every brand included in the study: loyal customers (++), new customers (−+), former customers (+−), and two-time non-customers (−−). The percentages of floating and constant consumers should be tracked over time: if, for example, a brand normally obtains a 15% share of new customers from one survey wave to the next, but then obtains only 10% over the next survey interval, one can safely conclude that it is losing its appeal.[3] At the same time, if the share of loyal customers is also declining, then we have all the more reason to believe that the brand is in a crisis situation—especially if there are no signs of a corresponding trend among the competition.

Also, in the economic area, panel analyses allow one to detect the reasons for such fluctuations. For instance, the following response patterns often emerge over time. Among loyal customers of a brand (++), associations with the brand and purchasing motives rarely change, while among brand switchers brand images show much stronger variation, where specifically customers who abandon a brand (+−) associate fewer positive traits with their former brand—and more positive traits with the brand they currently prefer. When a certain trait is associated more strongly with the new brand than it was with the former brand, this gives a good indication of the consumer's motive for changing brands. Conversely, items that are associated to relatively the same extent with both the previous and current brands are clearly not causally related to the consumer's switch (for additional examples, see Hansen, 1981, 1982, 1987).

This indirect analytical approach clearly identifies those conscious and subconscious motives and aspects of a brand's image that play a crucial role when it comes to switching brands, along with showing which aspects are especially helpful in promoting brand loyalty, as well as which ones are not, i.e. those image and motivational elements that are similarly pronounced among competing suppliers.

INTERPRETATION OF UNSTABLE RESPONSES

Of course, doubts as to the scientific legitimacy of such panel findings are sometimes raised, with some researchers contending that shifting attitudes from one wave to the next are to be taken less seriously than responses that remain stable over time. Such qualms may reflect suspicion toward one-time measurements that are not confirmed by retests among the same persons, along with some researchers' exaggerated theoretical expectations regarding certain variables,[4] or simply doubting that instability is plausible in the first place.[5]

When the questions for Inglehart's post-materialism index (→ Assessing Long-Term Value Changes in Societies) were included in a German panel study comprising three waves conducted at monthly intervals, it was found that only 55% of participants gave the same responses in all three consecutive survey waves. Although researchers may have been disappointed by this result, it is hardly an unusual finding in the area of attitudinal measurements. It is equally important to note that practically no respondent mutated during the study from 'materialist' to 'post-materialist' or from 'post-materialist' to 'materialist.' In other words, instability and change often occur only gradually, within a certain attitudinal corridor—and without overstepping its bounds (Porst & Zeifang, 1987; Smith, 1994). Attitudes towards brands also fluctuate considerably, albeit not radically—in the sense of 'delighted today, disdainful tomorrow'—but gradually (Hansen, 1988).

In situations where there is strong attitudinal fluctuation, we may want to consider only respondents with relatively consistent response patterns. In this case, a condition can be created for including respondents in the analysis—for example, only use respondents who choose an item in at least two of three survey waves. This criterion serves to safeguard the findings on a broader statistical base—and experience shows, for example, that we can expect to obtain fairly similar profiles and rankings in image studies as well.

The same applies to habits: an advertising effects panel conducted in three waves over a six-month period found that of almost

100 brands ascertained in six product areas, the brands had twice as many sporadic customers as loyal customers, on average (Gruner & Jahr, 2001; author's own calculation). Similarly, panel studies reveal that readers of most magazines generally do not read regularly the magazine but on an occasional or very infrequent basis. In addition, there is considerable fluctuation between individual titles, with respect to both general interest and special interest titles (Hansen, 1984, 2001; Hansen & Schneller, 2003). Strict analytical models based on the condition of frequent reading would thus primarily ascertain the group of loyal, hard-core readers with high affinity for a particular title—and hence only a minority of the publication's actual readership. Unstable responses obtained over time thus often reflect the most commonplace orientations or modes of behavior—and it would be wrong to dismiss them as being 'imperfectly measured' or resulting from a 'measurement error.'

COMPLEXITY OF PANEL ANALYSES

Even for researchers fairly experienced in dealing with surveys, panel findings are more difficult to understand than the findings of one-time surveys, since it is necessary to comprehend and evaluate both data referring to specific points in time and over time. The findings cited above were depicted in a simple manner, i.e. in the form of percentages or correlations. The more prior knowledge one has in an investigative field and the more accepted the measurement tools are, the simpler it may be to analyze the data in light of the study objective. Without prior knowledge, for example, the researcher would first have to employ a statistical-mathematical model to process the purchasing data obtained for magazine titles in three consecutive panel waves, thus determining the most important structures for each title over time, i.e. the percentage of regular purchasers, sporadic purchasers, and non-purchasers. Equipped with this prior

knowledge—and knowing that the purchasers per wave are validly defined—one can then directly define the analogous target groups (and also project their quantitative significance) by combining all persons who claimed to have bought a particular title in each of the three survey waves into the group of regular purchasers, while including all respondents who bought the title once or twice in the group of sporadic purchasers, and finally, counting all persons who did not cite the title in any survey wave as non-purchasers.

Markus (1979), Kessler and Greenberg (1981), Finkel (1995) and Engel and Reinecke (1996) provide a number of illustrative examples of the complex statistical-mathematical models that can be employed to exclude effects that are attributable to demographic characteristics or factors, such as aging between survey waves, changes in income, and other important factors. Here, readers will find, for instance, descriptions of 'models of reciprocal causation,' which are used to measure cross-lagged effects, synchronous effects and both cross-lagged and synchronous effects in combination—along with 'measurement error models' (Finkel, 1995), techniques such as 'causal log-linear modeling with latent variables and missing data,' as well as 'continuous-time dynamic models for panel data' and 'non-stationary longitudinal LISREL model estimation from incomplete panel data' (Engel & Reinecke, 1996). Although these model-oriented approaches are highly valuable for methodology experts and scholars engaged in basic research on longitudinal data, they do have one disadvantage: their results are not easy to convey to many of the actual recipients (users, financial backers) of the research findings, who often have difficulties understanding the data obtained via such analytical models.

NOTES

1 Reprinted from: Noelle-Neumann, Kepplinger, & Donsbach, 1999, p. 251—translated by the author.

2 The Socialists, officially known as the Party of Democratic Socialism (PDS), are the successor party to the former East German communist party (SED).

3 Given the fact that the differences are beyond the margin of error.

4 'They were presumed to be manifest indicators for some abstract, general, latent orientations' (Jagodzinski, Kühnel, & Schmidt, 1987, p. 7).

5 E.g. Converse (1970): '… somehow it seemed implausible that large proportions of the American population … had shifted their beliefs' (p. 171).

REFERENCES

Converse, P. E. (1970). Attitudes and non-attitudes: Continuation of a dialogue. In E. R. Tufte (Ed.), *The quantitative analysis of social problems* (pp. 168–188). London: Addison-Wesley.

Engel, U., & Reinecke, J. (Eds.). (1996). *Analysis of change: Advanced techniques in panel data analysis.* Berlin, New York: de Gruyter.

Finkel, S. E. (1995). Causal analysis with panel data. *Sage University paper series on quantitative applications in the social sciences, 07–105.* Thousand Oaks, CA: Sage.

Glock, C. (1952). *Participation bias and re-interview effect in panel studies.* Unpublished doctoral dissertation, Columbia University.

Granberg, D., & Holmberg, S. (1992). The Hawthorne effect in election studies: The impact of survey participation on voting. *British Journal of Political Science, 22,* 240–247.

Gruner & Jahr (Eds.). (2001). *Das Gruner+Jahr Werbewirkungspanel* [The Gruner+Jahr advertising effects panel]. Hamburg: Gruner+Jahr.

Gruner & Jahr (Eds.). (2004). *Das PKW Werbewirkungspanel* [The automobile advertising effects panel]. Hamburg: Gruner+Jahr.

Hansen, J. (1981). Persönlich befragte Panels zur validen Erfassung von Wandel, Ursachen und Wirkungen. Ein Modell zur kontinuierlichen und ad-hoc-Forschung. *Interview und Analyse, 8,* 282–291. English version: (1981). Personally interviewed panels for the valid ascertainment of change, causes and effects. A model for continuous and ad hoc research. *Interview und Analyse, 8,* 292–300.

Hansen, J. (1982). *Das Panel: Zur Analyse von Verhaltens- und Einstellungswandel* [The panel: Analyzing behavioral and attitudinal change]. Opladen: Westdeutscher Verlag.

Hansen, J. (1984). Dynamic variables in media research: Findings from a personally interviewed panel. In H. Henry (Ed.), *Readership research: Montreal 1983,* *Proceedings of the 2nd international symposium* (pp. 184–197). North-Holland, Amsterdam: Elsevier Science Publications.

Hansen, J. (1987, June). Qualitative research models in representative longitudinal studies. Paper presented at the ESOMAR Seminar on 'Improving the use of consumer panels for marketing decisions,' Düsseldorf, and in: *ESOMAR, Improving the use of consumer panels for marketing decisions* (pp. 167–188). Amsterdam: ESOMAR.

Hansen, J. (1988). How problematic are random responses in panel studies? *European Research, 16*(1), 34–41.

Hansen, J. (2001). Print media Internet portals: A boon or bust for print media consumption? In IPSOS-RSL (Ed.), *Worldwide Readership Research Symposium, Venice. Session Papers* (pp. 377–391). Harrow.

Hansen, J., & Schneller, J. (2003). Media brands: How much stronger thanks to their Internet presence? In IPSOS-RSL (Ed.), *Worldwide Readership Research Symposium. Cambridge, Massachusetts 2003. Session Papers* (pp. 397–411). Harrow.

Institut für Demoskopie Allensbach (1999–2005). *Allensbacher Computer- und Technik-Analyse (ACTA)* [Allensbach computer and technology analysis].

Jagodzinski, W., Kühnel, S. M., & Schmidt, P. (1987). Is there a 'Socratic effect' in nonexperimental panel studies? Consistency of an attitude toward guestworkers. *Sociological Methods & Research, 15,* 259–302.

Kessler, R. C., & Greenberg, D. F. (1981). *Linear panel analysis: Models of quantitative change.* New York: Academic Press.

Lazarsfeld, P. F. (1972). The problem of measuring turnover. In P. F. Lazarsfeld, A. K. Pasanella, & M. Rosenberg (Eds.), *Continuities in the language of social research* (pp. 358–362). New York: The Free Press.

Lazarsfeld, P. F., Berelson, B. & Gaudet, H. (1968). *The people's choice: How the voter makes up his mind in a presidential campaign* (3rd ed.). New York, London: Columbia University Press. (Original work published in 1944)

Markus, G. B. (1979). *Analyzing panel data.* London, Beverly Hills, CA: Sage.

Noelle-Neumann, E., Donsbach, W., & Kepplinger, H. M. (2005). *Wählerstimmungen in der Mediendemokratie* [Moods among voters in the media democracy]. Freiburg and Munich: Alber.

Noelle-Neumann, E., Kepplinger, H. M., & Donsbach, W. (1999) *Kampa: Meinungsklima und Medienwirkung im Bundestagswahlkampf 1998.* [Kampa: The climate of opinion and media effects during the 1998 federal election campaign]. Freiburg and Munich: Alber.

Porst, R., & Zeifang, K. (1987). Wie stabil sind Umfragedaten? Beschreibung und erste Ergebnisse der Test-Retest-Studie zum ALLBUS 1984 [How stable

is survey data? Description and initial results of a test-retest study in conjunction with the ALLBUS 1984]. *ZUMA-Nachrichten, 20*, 8–31.

Smith, T. (1994): Is there real opinion change? *International Journal of Public Opinion Research, 6*, 187–203.

31

Focus Groups and Public Opinion

David L. Morgan and Collin E. Fellows

INTRODUCTION

This chapter examines two different ways that focus groups have played a role in public opinion. First, it looks at focus groups as a preliminary step in the development of survey questionnaires. In this case, focus groups are especially useful for generating survey content that studies new opinion topics or targets specific subgroups within the broader public. Second, it will consider focus groups as a self-sufficient or 'stand-alone' source of data on public opinion. In this case, focus groups provide an opportunity to hear members of the public discuss their opinions in more complex ways going beyond what people think, to an understanding of why they think the way they do. Academic researchers and those who wish to influence public opinion have each found uses for focus groups as a stand-alone method, and the second section will provide examples of both types of applications.

USES AND PROCEDURES FOR FOCUS GROUPS IN CREATING SURVEYS

This section summarizes the different uses that survey researchers in general and public opinion researchers in particular pursue when they employ focus groups as a preliminary step in creating the content for surveys. The key point here is that focus groups can serve multiple different purposes within the broader goal of creating survey content. Further, the kinds of research designs and concrete procedures that researchers use in their focus groups will vary, depending on the purposes that those groups are supposed to serve. Hence, this section will give an overview of not only the different purposes that focus groups serve when they act as preliminary inputs to survey content, but also the research design implications of those different goals. For simplicity's sake, the discussion on focus group research design assumes that the reader has at least a basic understanding of this topic (e.g., Morgan, 1997; Krueger & Casey, 2000).

There are three broad categories of uses for focus groups (or qualitative methods in general) in creating public opinion surveys, depending on how well the research team already understands the content for the topic in question. At the broadest level, focus groups can serve the purpose of *discovery*, which reveals the fundamental content that needs to be covered in order to measure a topic. At an intermediate level, when the essential content of the topic is already known, then focus groups can help *develop* the kinds of questions that will capture that content. Finally, when the general content for the questions is already established, focus groups can help with the actual *definition* of the item wording. Each of these three uses of focus groups correspond to different strengths of this qualitative method: Discovery highlights the inductive, exploratory nature of hearing from the respondents about their opinions. Development relies on the subjective and interpretative aspects of qualitative research to understand how these opinions summarize the respondents' perspectives on the world. And definition encourages a contextual understanding of how respondents actually speak and react to these topics. (For a more detailed discussion of discovery, development, and definition as preliminary inputs from qualitative research to surveys, see Morgan, 2007.)

Discovery-oriented groups

At the level of discovery, focus groups help explore the range of thinking participants use as they consider a particular domain of public opinion. This is a good example of a case where 'horse race' issues are *not* a good use of focus groups to create survey content, since the basic content is already so cut and dried. In contrast, they can be used to consider topics that address poorly understood issues, such as a ballot measure on a relatively unfamiliar topic or the entry of a new third party into a campaign. While a horse-race question might give a simple summary about *what* potential

voters think, it would give little insight into *why* they think the way they do. In particular, if researchers want to know more about the factors that might shift voters' thinking and their future decisions, then they need to learn more about how the voters think about these issues. Yet, it is hard to know anything about the kinds of questions that should be asked when working with a poorly understood topic. Put simply, discovery-oriented focus groups help a researcher learn which content areas (s)he needs to ask about in order to understand how people think about the issue in question.

At the procedural or design level, discovery-oriented groups tend to be loosely structured, with less moderator control and more freedom for the participants to pursue their own lines of thought. For example, a 90-minute focus group for this purpose might use only three or four questions, with each devoted to a broad topic area. In this case, the role of the moderator would be to facilitate rather than to direct the discussion, encouraging the participants to 'share and compare' their various viewpoints (Morgan, 1997). Instead of pre-written probes to cover specific topics, the moderator would rely on general probes such as 'tell me more about that ...' or 'can you give me an example?' to gain better insight into the source of participants' thinking. The end product of a series of such groups should be an understanding of the basic dimensions or domains that are relevant to the participants' thinking on a given issue.

Development-oriented groups

Focus groups that concentrate on development-oriented goals usually begin with a clear sense of the dimensions and domains that should be included, and thus move on to the goal of locating the best types of questions to ask about those issues. In essence, focus groups at this level should be designed to operationalize an existing set of concepts or interests. Development-oriented focus groups thus seek the concrete elements of a given topic that will do the best job of summarizing or capturing the ways that respondents think about an issue. This may just be a matter of locating two or three questions that 'cover' the key topics—so long as the range of elements involved in the larger issue is relatively small and clear-cut. Alternatively, when the larger issue is more complex, then the focus groups can assist in locating separate questions that will cleanly tap into each of the key elements that are involved in respondents' thinking. The most common example of this kind of complexity is a multi-item scale that needs to cover two or more areas that form subscales. Regardless of the level of complexity involved, the typical goal of development-oriented groups is to locate the kind of specific content areas that can serve as the basis for drafting actual survey questions.

Procedurally, development-oriented focus groups often rely on an intermediate level of structure that makes it possible to hear the participants' own perspectives while also pursuing the research team's specific interests. The most common way to accomplish these dual goals is through what is known as a 'funnel-shaped' series of interview questions. In the beginning, at the broad end of the funnel, the questions follow the same, participant-oriented approach as in a discovery-oriented emphasis, with the moderator serving as a facilitator to bring out the participants' various points of view. One of the major reasons for starting by letting participants express their interests is to hear how much priority they give to the issues that are on the researchers' topic list. This part of the interview typically involves one or two questions that may last from 15 to 30 minutes before a shift toward a more researcher-directed series of questions.

In the narrower section of the funnel format, the moderator concentrates on hearing as much as possible about a set of well-defined topics (often three to five questions), typically using a series of predefined probes to make sure to cover different content areas in each question. More often than not, these topics will already have surfaced in the participants' general discussion, so the moderator can make

transitions into these later questions with phrases such as, 'One thing that has already come up and that we'd like to hear as much as we can about is. ...' Alternatively, if a topic hasn't been raised, that too can generate a useful transition, such as, 'One thing that hasn't come up yet and that we're curious to hear about is the whole issue of . . . .' Both of these alternatives illustrate the end product of development-oriented focus groups: learning as much as possible about a given set of topics, both from the participants' own point of view and from a research-directed point of view.

Definition-oriented groups

Definition-oriented goals are probably the most easily understood purpose for using focus groups, since they focus largely on question wording issues. By this point, it should be clear which topic areas need to be covered in a survey and which kinds of questions are likely to capture the necessary content. What remains is to ensure that the way the questions are asked is in tune with the way that respondents think about and speak about the issues involved. Since its inception, public opinion polling has had to struggle with the problem that seemingly small changes in wording can produce notable shifts in the percentage distribution of responses. Definition-oriented focus groups are largely an attempt to prevent this kind of problem by learning how the participants respond to shifts in the language used to express an issue. This can be an especially sensitive issue in projects where the researcher wants to compare multiple subsamples, particularly where there are cultural differences involved. In that case, the goal is to select one wording that will convey the same basic meaning to each segment of the sample. For example, Krause (2002) used focus groups and a variety of other qualitative methods to ensure that the questions he asked about religion could be meaningfully compared across a sample that was stratified to represent both African-Americans and Europeans-Americans. Regardless of whether the project includes comparisons across specific subsamples, the goal in definition-oriented focus groups is to improve the classic measurement standards in survey research, by making sure that the questions mean the same thing to the respondents that they do to the researchers (validity), and that all respondents interpret the questions consistently and with a minimum of confusion (reliability).

Definition-oriented focus groups typically use a more structured style of moderating. By this point in the process, the researcher should be reasonably familiar with the subject he/she wants to ask about, so he/she mostly needs to investigate alternative ways of phrasing those questions. In this kind of group, the moderator typically walks the participants through a carefully ordered set of questions such as, 'When you think about this issue, what are some of things that come to mind?' Or, 'What difference does it make if, instead, someone says things this way?' Although these types of groups can present candidate wordings for items and ask for participants' responses, the more common approach is to get them to demonstrate how they express their thoughts and feelings about the content area the question is about, while also discussing their reactions to different ways of expressing those thoughts and feelings. The reason for relying less on direct reactions to drafts of questions is because these issues should be dealt with through pretesting and cognitive interviewing (Willis, 2005), which are designed to locate and address question-wording problems. Discussing item wording in focus groups cannot be a substitute for pretesting, because the only truly effective way to determine how a survey question functions is to assess it within the actual context of survey. Hence, one should think of the end product of a set of definition-oriented focus groups as the *tentative* wording for a set of items that will still need to be pretested to determine their final format.

In concluding this section on how focus groups can serve as preliminary inputs to public opinion surveys, it is important to note that the distinctions between discovery-, development-, and definition-oriented uses of focus groups provide a descriptive summary of how focus groups *can* be used for this purpose, rather than a prescriptive requirement for how they *should* be used. In reality, most projects are not likely to operate at one and only one level. For example, a project that was primarily development-oriented might extend the funnel format to do both more discovery-oriented work in the early stages of the discussion and some definition-oriented work at the narrowest end of the funnel. Overall, the principal value of this three-part distinction is to help a researcher to clarify goals, because making decisions about how to design and conduct the groups depends to a great degree on what the researcher wants to get from those groups. Consequently, the next section will also follow a similar organization around the discovery, development, and definition-oriented uses for focus groups.

STAND-ALONE USES FOR FOCUS GROUPS

Discovery-oriented groups

Discovery-oriented focus groups are most useful for understanding the response to new issues or hearing from segments of the public that have not been covered in previous research. In this kind of early stage of exploratory research, a researcher may not even be sure what the questions are. Instead, the researcher needs to ask the participants for help in understanding the range of issues, experiences, and feelings that go into their opinions in this area. It is easy to detect the difficulty of doing surveys in this situation, since there is uncertainty about what questions to ask, and the same problem can cause difficulty for one-on-one qualitative interviews. In contrast, focus groups allow the moderator to ask the group to 'Tell me about . . .' or 'Help me understand . . . .' This goal naturally corresponds to a relatively unstructured format for the focus group, where the moderator's role is primarily to learn from the participants. In addition, however, the moderator's explicit desire to gain a deeper understanding also creates a context where it is legitimate to interrupt the conversation with tactful probes and follow-up questions. Overall, discovery-oriented goals are an area where focus groups provide notable strengths by giving the researcher an ability to 'listen and learn' about things that would be difficult to understand otherwise.

One target for academic research using discovery-oriented focus groups concerns the ways that the public forms opinions on an issue. For example, Mickiewicz (2005) studied how Russian citizens interpreted television news stories, to explore how individuals made sense of the strictly controlled media messages that they received. When the focus groups were shown three government-produced accounts of the opening of a new oil pipeline, they spontaneously supplied the 'trade-offs' between competing goals and interests that were not mentioned, such as environmental damage and diversion of profits. Yet, when the groups watched a final segment where an independent broadcaster gave an almost entirely negative view of the same events, they once again complained about the trade-offs that were ignored in this account (i.e., the positive factors that were the sole content in the earlier coverage). Thus, regardless of the source, the viewers themselves had a well-developed ability to detect and articulate intentionally suppressed tradeoffs and to create their own informed definitions of the missing public opinion options in one-sided accounts. As this example demonstrates, discovery-oriented focus groups are often useful for uncovering not just new elements of public opinion, but also for studying poorly understood aspects of the process by which opinions are generated and used.

Influence attempts generally make less use of discovery-oriented focus groups, simply because this kind of work is largely dedicated to understanding changing opinions about existing issues. One notable exception is the work of Republican political consultant Frank Luntz (2006), whose work has empha-sized the use of focus groups to uncover the basic 'motivational factors' that give a

deeper understanding of the sources of public opinion. For example, Luntz (1994) notes that open-ended survey questions such as 'What is the most important problem facing America today?' seldom find more than 2 to 3% of the respondents answering in terms such as the 'disintegration of morality in American society,' 'break-up of the family,' or 'declining quality of life.' Yet he claims that these three factors account for more than 80% of the broad motivational factors in his surveys, and thus provide the underlying explanations behind more specific concerns about the economy, crime, education, and so on. Interestingly, Luntz's (2006) approach emphasizes a form of 'psychodynamicism' that probes more deeply into why participants feel the way they do, to get at 'the largely subconscious forces which underlie values' (ibid.). The approach obviously runs counter to Lazarsfeld's historic advice about being careful about 'asking why' in survey research, but it also demonstrates the wider range of issues that can be explored in discovery-oriented focus groups.

Development-oriented groups

The core purpose for stand-alone focus groups that emphasize developmental goals is to gain a greater understanding of existing issues. At this stage, the researcher usually has a clear idea what the research questions are, but wants to hear how participants interpret and discuss these topics. Focus groups work well for these purposes because they help the researcher understand the range of consensus and diversity among the opinions within some well-chosen set of participants. A classic example in this regard is Gamson's (1992) book, *Talking Politics*, where he used political cartoons and other 'stimulus material' to hear how groups from different ethnic and socioeco-nomic backgrounds expressed their thoughts about issues of the day. One common format for such groups uses an intermediate degree of structure or moderator control, which encourages a process of 'sharing and comparing' among the participants on topics that are defined by the research team.

Overall, development-oriented focus groups make it possible to learn about participants' perspectives in depth while also providing the opportunity to observe the kinds of interactions involved in expressing 'truly public' opinions.

McGregor (2004) provides a useful example of development-oriented focus groups as a method to investigate how members of the public construct and sustain their opinions through social interaction. The design for the study used group discussions as a microcosm for the reality of every-day conversations, in order to examine the norms and processes that operate in public discourse. McGregor thus created homogeneous groups of environmental activists in each locale; he also chose to minimize the moderator's involvement so that each group's social dynamics and dominant themes could emerge from their discussion. Further, the participants attended multiple focus group sessions, both to track the progression of ideas over time and to allow people to get to know each other. By the second session, the participants were talking much more with each other than with the moderator, providing access to a more active exchange of views. By giving the groups the freedom to construct their own 'storylines,' McGregor could observe not only the development of a core consensus among the participants, but also the ways that marginal perspectives were minimized and ultimately silenced in the process of the ongoing conversations.

Focus groups are uniquely suited to this type of development-oriented use for influencing public opinion because they provide insights into the thinking of the people who are the targets of those influence attempts. By far the best-known example of such focus groups are the 'Willie Horton' ads that Roger Ailes and Lee Atwater created during the 1988 Bush–Dukakis campaign (Runkel, 1989; Jamieson, 1992). The goal was to locate issues that would resonate with registered Democrats who had previously voted for Ronald Reagan. At a focus group session near Paramus N.J., the first question was a request to hear participants' thoughts about whether the country was 'headed in the right direction or the wrong direction.' After steering the discussion toward hearing as much as possible about why the country was headed in the wrong direction—and thus maximizing the participants' sense of frustration—the moderator asked for their reactions to a series of news items. All of the items were actually based on things Dukakis had done, with the specific goal of developing content for 'negative ads' that would help keep these swing voters in the Bush camp. After working through several items related to topics such as failing to control pollution in Boston Harbor, 'lightning struck' when the participants heard the story of a convicted murder and rapist who had committed another murder while on a 'weekend furlough' from a prison in Massachusetts. Although the value of development-oriented focus groups in attempts to influence public opinion is certainly not limited to producing attack ads, the details of this example show how the method can be tailored to meet such a purpose—and hopefully other, more noble ones as well.

Definition-oriented groups

The most useful applications of definition-oriented focus groups typically occur either within relatively well-defined research areas or in the later stages of a multi-part project. The goal in these groups is usually to pursue specific issues in as much depth and detail as possible, including issues of language and nuance that have an impact on how participants interpret topics. The interaction in focus groups can be especially useful for this purpose, because it shows how a range of people think and talk about the subject in a forum that also provides data on their reactions to each other's ways of expressing those thoughts. These groups are typically more structured, because the moderator wants to keep the participants 'on topic' in order to hear as much as possible about what they have to say and how they exchange their different points of view.

This kind of dynamic applies both within single groups and across sets of groups. Within one group, the most useful definition-oriented interaction often involves a process of *differentiation*, where one participant shares an experience or opinion and another person responds with a comparison that begins something like, 'Yes, I really agree with what you're saying, but you also have to consider . . . .' Issues involving differentiation are also important for between-group comparisons, which often involve observing whether groups composed of different categories of participants respond to a topic in distinctive ways. All of these procedures make focus groups an effective tool for defining the more specific aspects of public opinion.

Definition-oriented focus groups tend to be less common among academic researchers, for the simple reason that surveys are the preferred method for accessing opinions at this level of specificity. Studies on framing and media are, however, one place where focus groups have been used for definition-oriented purposes. For example, Gamson (1992) speaks in terms of 'packages' that the media in particular use to portray issues in ways that resonate with desired elements of cultural discourse (such as 'progress through technology' versus 'harmony with nature'). Similarly, McGregor (2004) used the sustained interaction in his repeated focus groups to create 'storylines' that compactly summarized the participants' consensual beliefs, such as preserving 'old growth forests' because of their unique qualities while harvesting 'plantation forests' because they were meant to be sustainable. Kitzinger (2000) provides a somewhat different example within this same general area by demonstrating how beliefs acquired through the media can serve as 'templates' with iconic qualities that shape perceptions of similar issues. In this instance, a seven-year old scandal involving cases of childhood sexual abuse led to an almost 'uncontestable' negative image of social workers in such situations, even though the original news accounts of those events had been strongly challenged in subsequent reporting. What all of these

examples share is a use of focus groups that goes beyond defining how individuals express their opinions, by also considering how exchanges in interactions, messages from the media, and the use of broader cultural assumptions all influence the definition of both personal and public opinion.

In contrast to academic research, which tends to downplay definition-oriented goals as a use for stand-alone focus groups, this is precisely why many of those who seek to influence public opinion rely so heavily on focus groups. In particular, once a potential set of 'messages' has been created, they are often refined in focus groups prior to appearing in their final forms in ads and media campaigns. This is an undeniable element of the complaint that candidates are sold 'like soap.' The work of Frank Luntz once again provides a telling example, showing how his discovery-oriented work on values and other broad motivational factors ultimately gets translated into specific issues. Although a number of politicians and political operatives have claimed credit for reframing inheritance and estate taxes as 'death taxes,' there is little doubt that it was Luntz who did the detailed research on this powerful phrase. More than just the mere wording was involved, however, since Luntz also developed a series of talking points that helped Congressional Republicans define the larger issue in terms of 'fairness,' 'double taxation,' and 'earnings' rather than wealth. Luntz also tested the effectiveness of these ideas with extensive polling, but he began with focus groups to define the message itself. Ultimately, any message is made up of not just its literal content but also a certain amount of packaging that also influences how people will respond. For better or for worse, focus groups are a powerful tool to define both content and packaging in efforts to influence public opinion.

CONCLUSIONS

Focus groups are obviously a research tool that can be used in a great many ways for a variety of different purposes. The first section of this chapter summarized three uses for focus groups within the specific context of developing content for public option surveys. The second section went beyond that particularly well-known combination of focus groups and surveys to illustrate a parallel set of uses for stand-alone focus groups. In the final analysis, however, it is not the focus groups themselves that matter, but how they are used—either to advance our understanding of public opinion or to influence us as members of that public.

REFERENCES

Gamson, W. (1992). *Talking politics.* New York: Cambridge University Press.

Kitzinger, J. (2000). Media templates: patterns of association and the (re)construction of meaning over time. *Media Culture & Society, 22,* 61–84.

Krause, N. (2002). A comprehensive strategy for developing closed-ended survey items for use in studies of older adults. *Journals of Gerontology Series B-Psychological Sciences and Social Sciences, 57,* S263–S274.

Krueger, R., & Casey, M. (2000). *Focus groups: A guide for applied research* (3rd ed.). Thousand Oaks, CA: Sage.

Jamieson, K. (1992). *Dirty politics: Deception, distraction, and democracy.* New York: Oxford University Press.

Luntz, F. (1994, May 16). Focus group research in American politics. *The Polling Report.* Retrieved January 30, 2006, from http://www.pollingreport.com/focus.htm.

Luntz, F. (2006). *Focus groups.* Retrieved January 30, 2006, from http://www.luntz.com/FocusGroups.htm.

McGregor, A. (2004). Doing groups: situating knowledge and creating stories. *Australian Geographer, 35,* 141–149.

Mickiewicz, E. (2005). Excavating concealed tradeoffs: How Russians watch the news. *Political Communication, 22,* 355–380.

Morgan, D. (1997). *Focus groups as qualitative research* (2nd ed.). Thousand Oaks, CA: Sage.

Morgan, D. (2007). *Integrating qualitative and quantitative methods.* Thousand Oaks, CA: Sage.

Runkel, J. (Ed.). (1989). *Campaign for president: The managers look at 1988.* Dover, MA: Auburn House.

Willis, G. (2005). *Cognitive interviewing: A tool for improving questionnaire design.* Thousand Oaks, CA: Sage.

32

Content Analyses and Public Opinion Research

Winfried Schulz

A lasting question of public opinion research concerns the relationship between public opinion and media messages: Do news media mould or mirror public opinion? Generations of scholars speculated about the direction of a hypothetical link and called for valid empirical evidence. As a matter of fact, the methodology is available for answering this question. Numerous studies have demonstrated how the relationship between public opinion and communications can be examined and specified.

This chapter begins with some examples of research settings and theoretical approaches combining public opinion research with analyses of communication content. Thereafter, the basics of content analysis methodology are briefly described. In this context, the instrumental use of the content analysis method for analyzing open-ended survey questions will also be addressed. The next section gives an outline of different methodologies for measuring message exposure as one of the necessary links between communication content and public opinion. The final section

of the chapter discusses linkage analysis designs that can establish evidence of the relationship between news media and public opinion. This is illustrated by examples from empirical research representing different procedures of integrating public opinion data with content analysis results.

TRACING PUBLIC OPINION TO COMMUNICATIONS: RESEARCH APPROACHES

Relating public opinion to media content on both the individual and the macro or system levels is a core element of a number of research approaches. Inquiries into the impact of *election campaign communications* on the voters' opinion formation are a typical example. Already the pioneer study in this field, the legendary Erie County Study conducted by Paul Lazarsfeld and his colleagues, comprised an extensive content analysis of the campaign messages of newspapers, magazines, radio speeches, and newscasts.

On this basis, the authors devoted two chapters of their report to analyzing 'what the voters were told' and to specifying the influences of the radio and the print media (Lazarsfeld, Berelson, & Gaudet, 1944, chaps. XIII and XIV). Since then, it has become almost routine to supplement studies of opinion formation during election campaigns with analyses of campaign communications such as advertising, debates, and news coverage (see, e.g., Kaid, 2004, chaps. 7, 8, and 9).

Agenda-setting, as one of the most intensively researched concepts of media influence in election campaigns and beyond, relates issue coverage in the media to issue salience in the public. A typical agenda-setting study combines survey questions asking people to name the most important problems facing the country with a media analysis focusing on the frequency of issues reported in the news (McCombs & Shaw, 1972; → *Agenda-Setting, Framing and Priming*). *Cultivation theory* is another widely recognized approach in modern communication research that may be mentioned as an example. The basic hypothesis in this context posits a relationship between specific content features of television programs (e.g., an emphasis on violence) and beliefs of the public (e.g., the belief that most people cannot be trusted). A typical cultivation study establishes such a relationship by comparing results of population surveys with content analyses of television programs (Gerbner & Gross, 1976).

Outside academic research, a number of commercial research institutions are continuously monitoring the media coverage of a broad range of topics, organizations, and elite persons, quite often in comparison with public opinion data focusing—for example, on agenda-setting processes and on media influences in election campaigns. In addition to serving their clients, who range from companies to interest groups to government agencies, political parties and politicians, the institutes publish some of their results in newsletters and on their websites.[1]

There are different logical and operational strategies for linking communication content data to public opinion results. The most common—yet weakest—strategy is a conjectural interpretation of aggregated data. The conjectures can go in two directions, either tracing public opinion back to communication content as a stimulus, or inferring from messages in the news media (or other sources) to their impact on public opinion. If either part of the relationship remains unobserved or based on only impressionistic observations instead of systematic research, this strategy is good for generating hypotheses, but not for causal proof.

More valid results will be obtained by measuring and *operationally* integrating both communication content and public opinion. This chapter concentrates on operational strategies including, in addition to public opinion data, three elements: (1) an analysis of communication content, (2) measures of message exposure, and (3) a rationale for connecting public opinion to communication content and establishing the evidence through operational and statistical procedures. Since these methods as well as the relevant studies primarily relate to the news media, the focus here will be on relationships between media messages and public opinion.

CHARACTERIZING COMMUNICATIONS BY CONTENT ANALYSIS

Content analysis is a research technique for systematically identifying characteristics of communications. Most frequently, content analysis is used as a method for making replicable and valid inferences to unobserved elements of the communication process, such as the communicator or the audience. Berelson (1952), in his classical content analysis text book emphasized this purpose, and several other authors agreed (e.g., Holsti, 1969; Krippendorff, 2004). However, in addition to such a 'stand-alone' function, it became increasingly common to implement content analysis as one element of a multi-method design observing—and not just inferring—relationships between different elements of the communication process (Shoemaker & Reese, 1996, chap. 10).

Content analysis procedures aim to transform selected features of messages into data that can be processed by statistical analysis and related to data from other sources like public opinion surveys. This requires, at first, deciding which are the relevant media, messages, or message elements to be included in the analysis. Sampling strategies may be applied for selecting the relevant material on systematic grounds. Second, based on these decisions, the units of analysis have to be defined with reference to semantic or syntactic message features. Typical units of analysis are stories from newspapers or broadcast bulletins, actors or speakers and their utterances ('sound bites'), sentences, and pictures. Third, the researcher has to decide which characteristics of messages—that is, which variables—should be studied. Examples of message variables are *topics* of news stories, *institutional affiliations* of speakers in the news, *evaluations* in utterances, *emotional appeals* of pictures, *space* given to news stories, and *length* of 'sound bites' or of sentences. As a fourth step, the values of each variable are defined. This includes defining the level of measurement of each variable. Content variables are mostly measured on a nominal level (a typical example is a list of topics) or on an ordinal level (e.g., three levels of evaluative direction: positive—neutral—negative). Some formal variables, such as length of the item (in column inches or seconds), can be measured by an interval scale.

The researcher creates a codebook containing the operational definitions of units, variables and values. The codebook provides the instructions for coding the material to be analyzed. The set of variables and values are often called categories (or the coding scheme). For the process of coding—that is, for applying the coding scheme to the media material and thus transforming message features into data—quite often a group of research assistants is employed and trained. In this case, the inter-coder agreement has to be checked by special tests (reliability tests). If verbal messages are analyzed and the

text material is available in computer-readable form, it is possible to employ special software in a computer-assisted coding process.

Full-text archives accessible online, such as the Lexis-Nexis database, are convenient sources particularly for computer-assisted text analysis (see, e.g., Fan, 1988). Likewise, material on the World Wide Web can be exploited for content analysis purposes, also by employing search engines and filtering devices. Useful resources for conventional content analyses are audiovisual media archives holding a great amount of film, television and radio material.

In addition to analyzing already available messages of mass media and other sources such as political documents, speeches, letters and the like, it is also possible to generate messages especially for research purposes and to submit these messages to a content analysis. In public opinion research, responses to open-ended questions serve this function. Mostly, these questions elicit simple and brief answers that can be noted by the interviewer on the spot. Agenda-setting studies, for example, pose an open-ended question asking respondents to name 'the two or three main things which you think the government should concentrate on doing something about,' as in the classical study by McCombs and Shaw (1972). In this case, the answers were coded into 15 categories representing issues and other aspects of the election campaign. Another example is a study by Shah and colleagues examining the cognitive complexity of individuals' responses to radio broadcasts framing the issue of urban growth differently. The authors asked respondents to 'explain the issue of urban growth' and analyzed the answers by using a highly elaborate coding scheme including topics, causes, solutions, actors, as well as relationships between these categories (Shah, Kwak, Schmierbach, & Zubric, 2004). Especially if open-ended questions evoke a bulk of verbal material by a large number of respondents, it will be useful to generate a text file and submit the verbal material to a computer-assisted analysis (see, e.g., Mohler & Zuell, 2001;

West, 2001). In addition to handling vast amounts of material, computer content analysis has the advantage of being highly reliable.

By all means, the definitions and the coding procedures have to meet the basic requirements of empirical research; that is, they have to be valid, precise and reliable (reproducible). There are a number of textbooks providing detailed information about the content analysis methodology and its various applications, including computer-assisted coding (e.g., Neuendorf, 2002; Krippendorff, 2004; see also http://academic.csuohio.edu/kneuendorf/content/).

MEASURING MESSAGE EXPOSURE

When public opinion data are related to mass media content, it will increase the validity of the study if, in addition to content analysis results, information is available about the public's exposure to media and/or messages. There are different ways to access such information.

Audience ratings research is one convenient source providing comprehensive and up-to-date information about the reach and usage of print and electronic media, including the Internet. Routine measures of audiences for television and other media provide specific information, for example, about exposure to content categories such as news or advertising, exposure to specific media outlets (channels, print products or the like), to programs aired at a certain day and time slots, or to specific websites, to single issues of a newspaper or magazine, and even to particular sections or items within an issue. Audience research based on standardized instruments (such as surveys, people meters, and diaries) is mostly commissioned by the media industry and continuously produced by commercial institutes. The data are easily available and quite often exploited for scholarly studies. However, when relating these data to media content, the researcher is usually constrained to comparisons on the aggregate level, which limits the evidence of the study, as will be explained below. If researchers want to examine relationships on the individual level, they inevitably have to measure the respondents' media use in the very survey sample generating the public opinion data for the comparison with the media content.

Recurring measures of media use are included in the General Social Surveys (GSS) of the National Opinion Research Center (NORC) at the University of Chicago and in the American National Election Surveys (ANES), now co-directed by the Institute for Social Research (ISR) at the University of Michigan and the Institute for Research in the Social Sciences (IRiSS) at Stanford University.[2] The GSS has posed identical media questions since the early 1970s, so it is possible to trace long-term trends. In Europe, the Standard Eurobarometer surveys, commissioned by the European Commission and fielded in the member states of the European Community (EC) since the 1980s, regularly include questions about people's use of the media for news on television, in daily papers, on the radio, and about their exposure to media coverage of the EC.[3] In addition, commercial survey organizations, like Gallup, Roper, and others, frequently produce data about media use that may be instrumental in relating public opinion to mass media content.

Since the commercial surveys and also the GSS and ANES studies cover a broad range of topics, there is only room for a few simple questions about the respondent's media exposure. Sample standard versions are: *How often do you read the newspaper— every day, a few times a week, once a week, less than once a week, or never?* or *On an average day, about how many hours do you personally watch television?* (NORC). In addition to inquiries about the frequency of exposure, a number of instruments have been designed for probing various dimensions of media use, for example, asking for reliance on, attention to, and assessment of different media sources. Sample standard versions are: *Where would you say you get most of your news—from newspapers, television, radio, magazines, or somewhere else?* (Roper) or *In general, how much attention did you pay to news about the campaign for President—a great deal, quite a bit, some, very little, or none?* (ANES). Unlike standard surveys, special studies focusing on communication behavior employ more elaborate measures of exposure to and reception of particular messages such as election campaign advertising, televised debates, specific issues, or particular news stories.

One problem with most measures of communication behavior is that they have to rely on the respondent's self-reports. Thus, the validity of the methodology may be questioned (see, e.g., Bartels, 1993). As a study by Shoemaker, Breen, and Wrigley (1998) demonstrates, the results of measuring newspaper exposure may differ considerably depending on how exposure is operationalized. The authors compared two ways of measuring the amount of time spent with reading.[4] Several authors advocate combining questions of exposure with indicators of motivation (like, e.g., message attention, information seeking, media involvement) in order to improve the validity of media use measures (Chaffee & Schleuder, 1986; Shoemaker, Schooler, & Danielson, 1989; Drew & Weaver, 1990; Gantz, Fitzmaurice, & Fink, 1991).

Obviously, the more specifically and the more precisely people's encounters with messages are measured, the more conclusive is the evidence derived from connecting public opinion to communication content. However, elaborate exposure measures require much interview time, so that it is often a question of finding a reasonable compromise between what would be desirable and what is affordable.

ESTABLISHING EVIDENCE: LINKAGE ANALYSIS

Measuring people's message exposure and analyzing the messages people are exposed to are only first steps in drawing relationships between communications and public opinion. Following up on the suggestions of Shoemaker and Reese (1996, chap. 10) for integrating diverse domains of communications research, Neuendorf (2002, pp. 61ff.) distinguishes different levels of interlinking message and audience data. The strongest linkage is established if there is a one-to-one correspondence of the units of analysis of content and audience data. Neuendorf calls this a *first-order linkage*. In this case, the study design comprises all elements of the linkage model illustrated by Figure 32.1.

Relationships between public opinion and communications can be studied on both the micro- and the macro-levels, that is, based on individual-level data or on aggregated data. A typical *micro-level* approach assumes that a person's exposure to a specific message, or a series of messages, may impact on his or her opinions or attitudes. Most studies of election campaign effects on opinion formation take such an approach as it was pioneered by Lazarsfeld *et al.* (1944). *Macro-level* explanations usually attribute the formation or change of public opinion to the societal dissemination of media messages. The 'classical' agenda-setting approach (→ *Agenda-Setting, Framing and Priming*) may be mentioned as one example (McCombs & Shaw, 1972). Another good illustration is a study on 'what moves public opinion' by Page, Shapiro, and Dempsey (1987), which regresses US citizens' policy preferences upon aggregated media content. In all cases the hypothesized

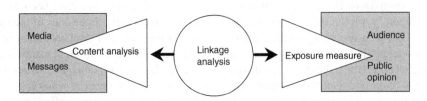

Figure 32.1   The full-model linkage design

relationships are implicitly or explicitly causal in nature.

But the perspective may also be turned around, pursuing, on the micro-level, selection or reception processes by individual audience members when, for example, the research question is how people make sense of media messages (e.g., Neuman, Just, & Crigler, 1992). Macro-level approaches of this type hypothesize that media messages reflect the prevailing mood or the mainstream opinion of the population or of specific population segments (→ *The News as a Reflection of Public Opinion*).[5]

Full model designs with individual level data

Linking message content to public opinion on the individual level may be based on different units of analysis, as there are: (1) the survey respondent as unit, (2) a message unit, or (3) a hybrid unit. Donsbach (1991a) subsumes the two former strategies under the heading 'index model,' since both are characterized by adding the aggregated data of one data set as a new variable to the units of the second data set. In contrast to this, the latter strategy, which Donsbach labels 'the individual data model,' merges individual-level data from both data sets into a new unit of analysis (ibid.). The following examples will illustrate the difference in these procedures.

(1) The respondent as unit of analysis
A groundbreaking agenda-setting study by Erbring, Goldenberg, and Miller (1980) is an example of a full-model design using the survey respondent as the linkage unit. The authors measured the public agenda of the US population with the familiar open-ended question about the most important problems facing the country posed in the 1974 National Election Study. In addition, they asked the respondents which local newspapers they read. The front-page news of the newspapers the respondents actually read was content analyzed in order to specify the relevant media agenda to which they had been exposed.

Finally, the authors matched each respondent with the particular paper he or she had read and merged the (individual-level) survey data with the respective (aggregated) content analysis results (ibid.; Miller, Goldenberg, & Erbring, 1979).[6]

A similar, more recent example is a study by Beck, Dalton, Greene, and Huckfeldt (2002) on the influence of news media and other intermediaries on voting choices. The authors merged four different data sources with a representative survey of the American electorate using the individual respondent as the central unit of analysis. The data sources included content analyses of the respondents' main newspapers and the television networks the respondents watched for news. The content analysis focused on the *actual* bias in both news reporting and editorials, while the interviews investigated the media bias as *perceived* by the respondents.

Other studies make even greater efforts to specify the messages supposed to impact public opinion. For example, a study of public opinion formation on three controversial issues by Kepplinger, Brosius and Staab (1991) included analyses of a broad range of news media outlets such as dailies and weeklies, as well as radio and television programs. These results were merged with the data from a survey of citizens of the German Rhine-Main-Area by assigning to each respondent his/her individual dose of information received on the issues under study.

(2) A message element as unit of analysis
A study by McCombs and Mauro (1977) illustrates the full-model design using a message element for the linkage. The authors examined which characteristics of news stories most strongly influence the level of newspaper readership. The study comprised two parts, a content analysis of a local newspaper and a survey among the readers of that newspaper. The authors measured the readership of each of the 199 items in one day's paper by asking respondents which stories they had noticed, whether they had read some portion of the text, and how much they had read of it.

In addition, the newspaper copy was content analyzed by classifying each story on different content and format characteristics. Finally, the authors assessed each story characteristic as a predictor of the three indicators of readership. In this linkage analysis, the unit of analysis was the single news item with its characteristics as independent variables and the aggregated readership figures per item as dependent variables.

Another example is a study by Naccarato and Neuendorf (1998) who content analyzed magazine advertisements and attributed to each message unit (i.e., advertisement) data about audience responses (e.g., readership and recall measures) from a survey among readers of the magazine. The purpose of this study was to predict readership from the particular form and content attributes of print ads.

(3) A hybrid unit of analysis

Donsbach (1991a, 1991b) constructed a hybrid unit for studying, with a highly elaborate design, how consonance and dissonance between media content and the readers' political predispositions guide audience selectivity. He surveyed readers of two national and two regional German dailies and specified their exposure to political articles in three consecutive issues of the newspapers. The survey included also questions on readers' opinions toward leading politicians covered in the news. In addition, he content analyzed all newspaper articles to which readers had been exposed for a number of format and content characteristics. A crucial content characteristic was the role played by certain political leaders in the news story classified as favorable, unfavorable, or neutral. Donsbach (1991a) created a new unit of analysis defined as 'each potential contact between one reader and one article' (p. 162) in order to merge the information from the news stories with the information from the readership survey. The newly created data set served to investigate how readership behavior was influenced by consonant and dissonant relationships between media content and the readers' political predispositions (ibid.).

Alternatives to the full-model design

Studies operationally relating public opinion to communication content with a full-model design are quite rare, whereas studies missing either or both the content analysis and the exposure measure can be found quite frequently. If the linkage analysis model is incomplete we may speak, in Neuendorf's (2002) terminology, of a *second-order* or a *third-order linkage*.[7] The linkage analysis may be restrained not only due to missing elements but also because it is based on aggregated data. In such cases, the lack of strong empirical evidence at the individual level has to be compensated (or substituted) for with logical reasoning and interpretation.

Very often researchers are content with measuring only people's media exposure in addition to their opinions but not the media content; thus they are leaving the characteristics of the messages people are exposed to unspecified. Moreover, media usage is normally measured only by rough indicators unable to determine exactly which messages people have received (see above section on measuring message exposure). As these studies apply an incomplete model, their evidence of a message-opinion-linkage is limited. Usually, the weakness of the design is compensated for by implying a certain correspondence between media and message content and by taking for granted that people's (self-reported) media contacts result in a specific impact (Maurer, 2003, p. 171).

A more sophisticated reasoning characterizes studies committed to the media dependency hypothesis as defined by Ball-Rokeach and DeFleur (1976). For example, the 'classical' cultivation study relates media content characteristics to audience's beliefs about the 'facts of life,' presupposing that the messages assumed to exert a cultivation effect have been received by the audience. Even if the messages are content analyzed and the study includes measures of media usage (e.g., for identifying heavy television viewers) the design does not conform to the full model as long as the content analysis results are not operationally linked to individual audience members and their respective media exposure.[8] Hence, the evidence has to be supported by ancillary assumptions, for example, that television is a 'common symbolic environment' people cannot elude (Gerbner & Gross, 1976) or—as other authors put it—that 'nearly everyone is exposed either directly or indirectly to what the media broadcast' (Page *et al.*, 1987).

Agenda-setting research is another case in point. If an agenda-setting study relating survey results to the issue agenda of the media is missing a measure of media exposure, the relevant messages that are hypothesized to influence public opinion cannot be specified adequately. In this case the study does not conform to a full-model design.[9] Yet, similar to the 'classical' cultivation approach, it is often presupposed that all media in the respondents' environment present roughly the same issue agenda. Such a situation of *consonant coverage* prevents selective media exposure so that uniform media effects may be expected (Noelle-Neumann, 1973; Peter, 2004).

In principle, studies relying on aggregate-level data for either or both communication content and public opinion are unable to establish a one-to-one correspondence of linkage analysis units. In this case the precise nature of the relationship between individual opinions and aggregate message structures (or of single messages and aggregate public opinion) remains obscure. Unless there is strong evidence for a unique situation such as consonant media coverage, inferences about sub-units within an aggregate population are vulnerable to the *ecological fallacy*.

Linking communication content and public opinion by a time-series design is an operational strategy increasingly used to compensate for the weaknesses of aggregate level data. Statistical methods permitting causal inferences serve to trace changes in media content to changes in public opinion, or vice versa (see, e.g., Fan, 1988; Brosius & Kepplinger, 1990). As Neuendorf (2002, p. 61) argues, a time series study may be considered a 'Type B' *first-order linkage* design since the time unit (such as a week or a month) serves as the operational linkage.[10]

However, only if the time series is set up as a *panel study*—that is, if *identical* persons are interviewed at different time points—does it qualify as a true (or 'Type A') first-order linkage, provided it satisfies all other elements of the full-model design. The specific advantage of a panel study is that it enables tracing changes over time on the individual level and thus examining linkages of individual respondents' opinions and their message exposure. A study by Maurer (2003) is a rare example of a panel study meeting all these conditions.

CONCLUSION

Since the early 1970s Noelle-Neumann has stressed over and again that progress in communication research will be reached by combining and systematically interlinking public opinion data and content analysis results (see, e.g., Noelle-Neumann, 1973; Noelle-Neumann, 1979; see also Shoemaker & Reese, 1990). In the meantime, it has become increasingly common to extend research designs to multi-level and multi-method approaches. The development has been spurred by advancements in statistical methods and data processing techniques. It is especially the complex theoretical models explaining media influences on the individual or on society that call for elaborate research designs integrating different methods of data collection. Due to the theoretical and methodological progress that has been achieved over decades of communication research, the seemingly crucial question of whether the media mold or rather mirror public opinion has turned out to be an ill-defined problem. Depending on the situation, influences going into one direction or the other may prevail, and quite often they go into both directions at the same time, making it more appropriate to speak of an interaction—or even a dynamic transaction—rather than a causal relation (see Part II of this Handbook).

As has been shown, different methodological strategies based on different rationales are instrumental in relating public opinion to communications. Most valid evidence, however, can be compiled only if the study analyzes the message content as well as the message exposure and if there is a one-to-one correspondence of the units of analysis. Yet, studies meeting these conditions are still quite rare.

NOTES

1 This field of applied research was pioneered by Robert and Linda Lichter who founded the Center for Media and Public Affairs (CMPA) in Washington D.C. in 1985 (see http://www.cmpa.com/). In the meantime, institutes with a similar mission are operating in several countries worldwide, for example the Media Tenor institute in Bonn (see http://www.mediatenor.com/).

2 See http://www.umich.edu/~nes/.

3 See http://europa.eu.int/comm/public_opinion/index_en.htm and http://www.gesis.org/en/data_service/eurobarometer/.

4 See also Price (1993) who examined the consequences of varying reference periods in survey question wordings.

5 Macro-level explanations may incorporate micro-level processes (Price, 1988). The spiral of silence theory is a prominent example (Noelle-Neumann, 1984, → Spiral of Silence Theory).

6 As an additional feature of the study 'real world' data, such as unemployment and crime rates, relating to the local contexts of the respondents were collected and merged with the survey and newspaper content data.

7 According to Neuendorf (2002, p. 62) a study should be classified as second-order linkage if it fails to match units with a one-to-one correspondence so that the links may be anecdotal or occasional. From this she distinguishes a third-order linkage characterized by merely assuming a logical relationship between data from different studies.

8 This is, of course, a simplified picture of cultivation research which has, in the meantime, developed quite many facets, including much more elaborate study designs (see Shanahan & Morgan, 1999).

9 There are, of course, variants of agenda-setting research based on individual-level data and a full-model design, like, for example, the study by Erbring et al. (1980) referred to above; see also, for example, Rössler (1999).

10 A study by Schulz (1982) using *events* as linkage unit may be considered as another example of this type. The author identified 555 different events covered by at least two of four selected mass media (TV programs and newspapers) over a three-month period. A content analysis of the media coverage served to characterize these events by their news factors as well as their newsworthiness (indicated by prominence of coverage). These event variables were statistically related to different measures of event awareness investigated by a population survey.

REFERENCES

Ball-Rokeach, S. J., & L. DeFleur, M. (1976). A dependency model of mass-media effects. *Communication Research, 3*, 3–21.

Bartels, L. M. (1993). Messages received: The political impact of media exposure. *American Political Science Review, 87*, 267–285.

Beck, P. A., Dalton, R. J., Greene, S., & Huckfeldt, R. (2002). The social calculus of voting: Interpersonal, media, and organizational influences on presidential choices. *American Political Science Review, 96*, 57–73.

Berelson, B. (1952). *Content analysis in communication research*. Glencoe, Ill. The Free Press.

Brosius, H.-B., & Kepplinger, H. M. (1990). The agenda-setting function of television news. Static and dynamic views. *Communication Research, 17*, 183–211.

Chaffee, S. H., & Schleuder, J. (1986). Measurement and effects of attention to mass media. *Human Communication Research, 13*, 76–107.

Donsbach, W. (1991a). Exposure to political content in newspapers: The impact of cognitive dissonance on readership selectivity. *European Journal of Communication, 6*, 155–186.

Donsbach, W. (1991b). *Medienwirkung trotz Selektion. Einflussfaktoren auf die Zuwendung zu Zeitungsinhalten* [Media effect despite selection. Factors influencing the exposure to newspaper content]. Köln: Böhlau.

Drew, D., & Weaver, D. (1990). Media attention, media exposure, and media effects. *Journalism Quarterly, 67*, 740–748.

Erbring, L., Goldenberg, E., & Miller, A. H. (1980). Front-page news and real-world cues. A new look at agenda-setting by the media. *American Journal of Political Science, 24*, 16–49.

Fan, D. P. (1988). *Predicions of public opinion from the mass media. Computer content analysis and mathematical modeling*. Westport, CT: Greenwood Press.

Gantz, W., Fitzmaurice, M., & Fink, E. (1991). Assessing the active component of information-seeking. *Journalism Quarterly, 68*, 630–637.

Gerbner, G., & Gross, L. (1976). Living with television. The violence profile. *Journal of Communication, 26*, 173–199.

Holsti, O. R. (1969). *Content analysis for the Social Sciences and Humanities*. Reading, Mass.: Addison-Wesley.

Kaid, L. L. (Ed.). (2004). *Handbook of political communication research*. Mahwah, NJ: Lawrence Erlbaum.

Kepplinger, H. M., Brosius, H.-B., & Staab, J. F. (1991). Opinion formation in mediated conflicts and crises: A theory of cognitive-affective media effects. *International Journal of Public Opinion Research, 3*, 132–156.

Krippendorff, K. (2004). *Content analysis. An introduction to its methodology* (2nd ed.). Beverly Hills: Sage.

Lazarsfeld, P. F., Berelson, B. R., & Gaudet, H. (1944). *The people's choice. How the voter makes up his mind in a presidential campaign*. New York: Duell, Sloane & Pearce.

Maurer, M. (2003). *Politikverdrossenheit durch Medienberichte. Eine Paneluntersuchung* [Political malaise through media coverage. A panel study]. Konstanz: UVK.

McCombs, M. E., & Mauro, J. B. (1977). Predicting newspaper readership from content characteristics. *Journalism Quarterly, 54*, 3–7, 49.

McCombs, M. E., & Shaw, D. L. (1972). The agenda-setting function of mass media. *Public Opinion Quarterly, 36*, 176–187.

Miller, A. H., Goldenberg, E. N., & Erbring, L. (1979). Type-set politics: Impact of newspapers on public confidence. *American Political Science Review, 73*, 67–84.

Mohler, P. P., & Zuell, C. (2001). Applied text theory: Quantitative analysis of answers to open-ended questions. In M. D. West (Ed.), *Applications of computer content analysis* (pp. 1–16). Westport, CT: Ablex.

Naccarato, J. L., & Neuendorf, K. A. (1998). Content analysis as a predictive methodology: Recall, readership, and evaluations of business-to-business print advertising. *Journal of Advertising Research, 38*(3), 19–33.

Neuendorf, K. A. (2002). *The content analysis guidebook*. Thousand Oaks: Sage.

Neuman, W. R., Just, M. R., & Crigler, A. N. (1992). *Common knowledge. News and the construction of political meaning*. Chicago: University of Chicago Press.

Noelle-Neumann, E. (1973). Return to the concept of powerful mass media. *Studies of Broadcasting, 9*, 67–112.

Noelle-Neumann, E. (1979). Massenmedien und sozialer Wandel. Methodenkombination in der Wirkungsforschung [Mass media and social change. Combining methods of media effects research]. *Zeitschrift für Soziologie, 8*, 164–182.

Noelle-Neumann, E. (1984). *The spiral of silence. Public opinion—Our social skin*. Chicago: University of Chicago Press.

Page, B. I., Shapiro, R. Y., & Dempsey, G. R. (1987). What moves public opinion? *American Political Science Review, 81*, 23–43.

Peter, J. (2004). Our long 'return to the concept of powerful mass media'. A cross-national comparative investigation of the effects of consonant media coverage. *International Journal of Public Opinion Research, 16*, 144–168.

Price, V. (1988). On the public aspects of opinion. Linking levels of analysis in public opinion research. *Communication Research, 15*, 659–679.

Price, V. (1993). The impact of varying reference periods in survey questions about media use. *Journalism Quarterly, 70*, 615–627.

Rössler, P. (1999). The individual agenda-designing process. How interpersonal communication, egocentric networks, and mass media shape the perception of political issues by individuals. *Communication Research, 26*, 666–700.

Schulz, W. (1982). News structure and people's awareness of political events. *Gazette, 30*, 139–153.

Shah, D. V., Kwak, N., Schmierbach, M., & Zubric, J. (2004). The interplay of news frames on cognitive complexity. *Human Communication Research, 30*, 102–120.

Shanahan, J., & Morgan, M. (1999). *Television and its viewers. Cultivation theory and research*. Cambridge: Cambridge University Press.

Shoemaker, P. J., & Reese, S. D. (1990). Exposure to what? Integrating media content and effect studies. *Journalism Quarterly, 67*, 649–652.

Shoemaker, P. J., & Reese, S. D. (1996). *Mediating the message. Theories of influences on mass media content* (2nd ed.). New York: Longman.

Shoemaker, P. J., Schooler, C., & Danielson, W. A. (1989). Involvement with the media. Recall versus recognition of election information. *Communication Research, 16*, 78–103.

Shoemaker, P. J., Breen, M. J., & Wrigley, B. J. (1998, July). *Measure for measure: Comparing methodologies for determining newspaper exposure*. Paper presented at annual conference of the International Communication Association, Jerusalem.

West, M. D. (Ed.). (2001). *Theory, method, and practice in computer content analysis*. Westport CT: Ablex Publishing.

Measurement of Public Opinion

33

Designing Reliable and Valid Questionnaires

Kenneth A. Rasinski

Obtaining accurate, reliable and valid assessments of public opinion is critical for any survey project, but it is not a simple task. Beyond the necessary substantive expertise needed, the assessment of public opinion requires considerable knowledge, skill, and experience in question wording and questionnaire structure. It requires attention to subtle relationships between questions, and to how those relationships might affect the meaning of the question for the respondent. It also requires an understanding of basic concepts associated with reliability and validity and with techniques employed to produce questions with these qualities and methods to measure the degree of reliability and validity present.

This chapter discusses considerations, concepts and methods related to designing reliable and valid public opinion questionnaires. The discussion attempts to bring together elements from psychometrics—the discipline formally concerned with reliability and validity in measurement; survey methodology, especially focusing on techniques developed to write clear, unambiguous survey questions—and the psychology of survey responding, a discipline aimed at understanding the tasks respondents face as they encounter a survey question.

RELIABILITY AS CONSISTENCY IN RESPONDING OVER TIME

Concepts, techniques and methods for establishing reliability and validity in measurement have been most developed in the area of educational and psychological testing (→ Validation Studies). The psychometrics literature discusses two types of reliability, each relying on the presences of a different type of consistency in responses. The first, test-retest reliability, is consistency in responding across time; it is assessed by observing the magnitude of a measure of association between responses at two time points. If respondents are asked the following question twice: 'Are we spending too much, too little, or about the right amount on improving and protecting the environment?'—one of a set of core questions on the General Social Survey (GSS)—at a two-week interval, and the correlation between responses is, say, 0.8, this would be evidence for temporal stability and would indicate good test-retest reliability, in psychometric terms. Subsequent work has shown that this temporal stability can be increased if measurement error is taken into account (Judd & Milburn, 1980).

While test-retest reliability is an important standard of measurement, Converse (1964) questioned whether it should even be expected in responses to public opinion questions. He based his skepticism on research conducted using the American National Election Survey (ANES). He found generally low correlations between public opinion questions administered to the same respondents at two points in time. Thus, he concluded that most of what we measure in public opinion surveys are 'non-attitudes.'

Two different perspectives on the psychology of survey responding have helped to explain the instability that Converse found. One approach, called the belief-sampling model (Tourangeau, Rips, & Rasinski, 2000), asserts that opinions are reliable to the extent that the survey context causes respondents to access the same belief structures at both measurement points. When a respondent endeavors to answer a question on a public opinion survey, he or she must retrieve relevant information from memory. It is unlikely that all relevant information that a respondent possesses will be retrieved during a survey interview. In a survey, time given for a response is short and the motivation to be thorough is not great (Krosnick, 1991). In addition, cues from prior questions may consciously or unconsciously influence the considerations respondents bring to mind.

The belief sampling mode suggests that it is useful to consider the process of retrieving information related to a survey question as similar to sampling a set of mentally-stored pieces of information from all the information a respondent possessed that he or she could apply to a given question. With regard to public opinion questions, that information may consist of general evaluations, values, knowledge, beliefs, behaviors, or feelings. The belief-sampling model predicts that

public opinion will be stable across time to the extent that there is overlap between the information sampled when answering the question at time 1 and the information sampled when answering the question at time 2.

Tourangeau *et al.* (2000) report on two studies designed to test the belief-sampling model of response stability. In one, a random sample of respondents was interviewed twice by telephone about social issues. After being asked questions about abortion and welfare, respondents were asked to list the considerations they had taken into account when they produced their answers. A second study experimentally varied arguments for or against a fictitious highway project. Respondents were also interviewed twice by telephone. In both studies, correlations between attitudes were higher for respondents who indicated that they employed the same considerations each time. For example, in the first study, those respondents who did not list one overlapping consideration showed an across-time correlation of 0.35 between responses to a question on abortion. Compare this to across-time correlations of 0.79 and 0.84 for those who listed one or two overlapping considerations in their open-ended responses, respectively. In the second study, across-time stability in evaluations of the highway project went from a correlation of 0.71 for those in the condition in which none of the arguments appeared in both interviews to 0.91 and 0.96 in which one or two of the arguments appeared in both interviews.

The results give hope that people do have opinions that are in themselves stable, to a degree, over time. But they show that response stability depends on the question being asked in similar contexts at both points in time. If the question about spending on the environment is asked after a question about spending on programs to assist the poor at one point in time, and after a question about spending on space exploration at another, very different responses might be expected. This is because the information brought to mind by the prior questions would differ in the two contexts. If the different information was related to mental information the respondent might use to make a judgment about spending on the environment, then responses to the environment question might be affected. The effect of context might involve something as subtle as how important spending on the environment might be viewed as after thinking either about spending on programs to assist the poor or spending on space exploration programs.

RELIABILITY AS CONSISTENCY IN RESPONDING TO SIMILAR QUESTIONS

The second type of reliability-related consistency is consistency in responding across similar items. This is called internal consistency and is measured by a statistic called alpha (α), which is defined as the percentage of variance in an unmeasured, or latent, variable that is measured by shared variation among the component items (Crocker & Algina, 1986). Results of a study designed to assess public attitudes toward people with substance abuse disorders are used to illustrate this type of reliability (Rasinski, 2003). Seven public opinion questions were written. Each was derived from a theoretical position about how drug addiction can be stigmatizing. The questions are listed in Table 33.1.

Psychometric analyses were conducted on responses to the questions. The reliability coefficient (α) for these seven questions was

Table 33.1 Questions designed to measure stigma associated with drug addiction

1. AFRAID	I would be afraid to make friends with a person who has completed treatment for drug addiction.
2. EVIL	Drug addicts are evil.
3. LOOK	You can usually tell that a person is a drug addict just by the way they look.
4. SHAME	A drug addict is a shame to his or her family.
5. BLAME	Drug addicts have only themselves to blame for their problems.
6. RELIGION	If people took their religion more seriously they would not become addicted to drugs.
7. DANGER	Drug addicts are dangerous people.

Table 33.2 Item-total correlations and factor loading for the six questions of the drug addiction stigma scale

Variable	Correlation with scale*	Factor loading
DANGER	0.39	0.58
RELIGION	0.36	0.51
BLAME	0.36	0.49
SHAME	0.44	0.66
LOOK	0.38	0.53
EVIL	0.53	0.75
AFRAID	0.45	0.68

Note: *Item-total correlations were computed with the item removed

0.70, indicating that 70% of variance in a latent variable measuring stigma is explained by the correlations among the questions. In addition, an exploratory factor analysis indicated that the questions loaded on only one factor. The item-total correlations are shown in Table 33.2 along with the factor loadings. The reliability coefficient, the factor loadings, and the item-total correlations show that many respondents were answering consistently across questions, thus demonstrating internal consistency.

VALIDITY FROM A PSYCHOMETRICS PERSPECTIVE

For survey questionnaires, a key feature of validity is that it explicitly links a particular survey question to the researcher's purpose for conducting the research. While this may seem obvious and simplistic, it is not. First, researchers may not have a clear sense of purpose in conducting their survey. Second, even if they do, researchers are good at thinking about their purpose in abstract conceptual terms. However, respondents can only properly answer specific, concrete questions. The art of questionnaire development is to map clear, specific, concrete questions to the abstract concepts of the researcher in such a way that the data obtained meet the researcher's goal.

In survey research, Sudman and Bradburn (1982) refer to the purpose of the research as the research objective and, speaking generally, validity is the link between the survey question and the research objective. Specifically, questions may be valid 'on face,' by virtue of their content, by the extent to which they measure the construct intended to be measured, and by their relationship to external criteria (Carmines & Zeller, 1979). There are two indisputable conditions for designing valid survey questions: (1) the investigator must be absolutely clear about the research objective, and (2) the questions must be worded such that their meanings are clear and unambiguous. In short, designing valid questionnaires requires clarity of purpose and of expression.

A basic form of validity is called *face validity* (Mosier, 1947), which indicates that a question should *appear* to measure the desired construct. Thus, a public opinion question such as 'How confident are you that the American economy is moving in the right direction?' might be considered a 'face valid' indicator of confidence in the economy. A question such as 'Do you think that now is a good time to purchase a major appliance?' may be an indicator of consumer confidence, but is not a face-valid one (though it may satisfy some other validity criterion). Face validity is the starting point for most questions about public opinion. A question that appears to measure opinion about a topic, based on the obviousness of its wording, probably does measure opinion on it, provided that the question is written clearly and unambiguously.

Content validity is more elaborate than face validity. Originally, the concept was developed to refer to the process of adequately sampling test questions from a content domain. Public opinion researchers are usually not interested in designing surveys to measure knowledge within content domains. However they often are interested in developing scales representing attitudes within a domain. For example, Rasinski (1987) was interested in developing scales relating to societal fairness for use in a public opinion survey on evaluations of political authorities. To establish content validity, he followed a standard three-step procedure. First, he defined domains

of interest. In this case, they were related to different theoretical definitions of societal fairness. Next, he reviewed published scales and borrowed, adapted and generated 69 items ostensibly related to the definitions. After that, he devised a rating scale based on the definitions of the domains of interest to obtain ratings of the questions. Those questions selected for further testing were the ones that the raters judged as strongly belonging to the fairness domains.

Construct validity pushes well beyond both face and content validity to investigate whether question responses permit arraying respondents along a latent dimension of interest to the researcher. After first selecting questions from a domain, demonstrating the consistency of responses to the items is the second step to establishing construct validity. The third step is to show that the consistency of responding to questions is invariant across methods. Finally, the researcher has to show that the questions in the construct being proposed are related to questions from similar constructs and distinct from questions in dissimilar ones.

Conducting a full construct validity study, which consists of establishing *convergent* and *discriminant* validity through use of multiple tests and multiple measurement techniques (Campbell & Fiske, 1959), is a time consuming process and is rarely done when constructing public opinion questionnaires. At a minimum, many researchers skip the multiple measurement steps, but use statistical techniques to demonstrate convergence and discrimination. For example, Rasinski (1987) used factor analysis to complete the construction of scales related to societal fairness. From the 69 questions that were rated for their relationship to the four fairness domains, 12 met the 'belongingness' criteria. These 12 questions were administered to a group of respondents, and the resulting correlation matrix was factor analyzed. Confirmatory factor analysis was used to see whether the four fairness domains originally proposed held up in the pattern of responses. Results indicated that, in fact, the response pattern was best explained by two domains.

Convergent validity was demonstrated by the relatively good fit of the two-dimensional model to the data.

Discriminant validity was determined by the observation that the two dimensions were negatively correlated to a moderate degree and by the observation that the two fairness scales correlated differently with independent measures of values. The correlations made theoretical sense. One fairness dimension, proportionality, correlated positively with independence and materialism; the other dimension, egalitarianism, correlated positively with valuing helpfulness and forgiveness and was negatively related to materialism. Proportionality was slightly more likely to be endorsed by men than by women and was related to political conservatism, while egalitarianism was related to political liberalism. Thus, observing a pattern of relationships of the newly defined constructs to each other and to other relevant and irrelevant measures was used to complete the process of construct validation.

VALIDITY FROM A SURVEY RESEARCH METHODS PERSPECTIVE

Survey methodologists have been concerned with the quality of survey questions, but consider validity from a slightly different perspective. The focus has traditionally been on paying close attention to the topics that are to be addressed in the surveys and on writing questions that are as clear and unambiguous as possible. Three basic and general principles guide the construction of survey questions. The first principle is that the researcher must have an absolutely ironclad sense of what he or she is after, and ensure that the research ideas are developed in a systematic and logical way before writing a survey question or developing a questionnaire. The second principle is that questions are written in as clear a form as possible, with special attention to whether they accurately reflect the research idea, are fair and balanced in their presentation, and are attentive to the respondents' level of understanding. A third principle involves

question pretesting. Pretesting will help assure that clearly written, unambiguous questions are focused on the topics of interest to the researcher. The purpose of pretesting is to refine questions so that they capture the researcher's intentions in language that is understandable to the vast majority of potential respondents, is fair and balanced, and leaves no room for misinterpretation.

A SURVEY METHODS APPROACH TO RELIABILITY AND VALIDITY

A survey methodological approach to creating reliable and valid public opinion questionnaires considers four key elements. The first concerns how best to develop ideas that can be turned into public opinion questions. The task here is to go from the abstract to the concrete, or, to put it in terms more familiar to researchers, from the construct to its operationalization. Researchers are very good at thinking in terms of abstractions, but survey questions will not yield consistent and meaningful (i.e., valid) responses unless they are rooted in a certain amount of concreteness. The second concerns the important role of question wording and sentence structure. Words, and the sentences in which they are embedded, are tricky beasts. In our general conversations, we use language to ascertain information, much as we would do in a survey question; but we also use words to signal social norms, to persuade, warn, inform, reassure, frighten, clarify, and to confuse. One might say that the words in a survey question come with a lot of potential baggage. In addition, sentences can be written more or less clearly. When we construct questions to ascertain public opinion, we must take care that neither the baggage attached to words nor a convoluted sentence structure circumvent the goals of achieving reliable and valid data that bear on the research objective.

Third, in constructing reliable and valid survey questionnaires, we must go beyond the words themselves and consider the task of the respondent. Recently, much attention has been given to the interaction between the question and the respondent's ability and/or desire to answer the question. Questions that do not take into consideration the respondent's ability to understand, the level of information, the process of making a judgment, and the motivation to respond may suffer in their ability to acquire reliable and valid data. Finally, there is a consideration of the context within which each individual question appears. Taken together, the set of questions constitutes a questionnaire but, to paraphrase a famous maxim, the questionnaire is more than just the sum of its questions. The juxtaposition of questions may result in subtle shifts in meaning such that a prior question might affect responses to a subsequent one (→ *The Psychology of Survey Response*).

Turning ideas into questions

In public opinion research, as in any survey research endeavor, the goal is to make sure that the data are an accurate reflection of the research topics of interest. Fowler (1992) states two conditions for this to be accomplished: (1) survey questions should be understood by all respondents in a consistent way; and (2) survey respondents must interpret the questions in the same way that the survey researcher has intended the question to be interpreted. Fowler recommends beginning each question as an objective. A question objective is simply a statement of the type of information that is needed. From the objective flows the question. Sometimes this is very straightforward. For example, if the objective is to obtain information about age, a question as simple as 'What was your age at your last birthday?' may suffice. However, if the objective is to ask about the relationship between one's religious beliefs and political behavior choices, careful thought must be put to the task of writing a question. A straightforward question asking 'Do your religious beliefs affect your political behaviors?' is so broad that it invites multiple, idiosyncratic, interpretations.

Sudman and Bradburn (1982) state that *research* objectives should be used as a guide for questionnaire construction. A research objective is a desire for knowledge in a particular area; thus, it is an umbrella under which to organize question objectives. Here are some examples of research objectives that might be generated from the recently devastating hurricane Katrina that wiped out good portions of New Orleans and surrounding areas. The hurricane, which hit in September 2005, displaced over a million people. Rebuilding costs may total over $100 billion. A researcher may be interested in a research objective of measuring attitudes about how the reconstruction bill will be paid.

Once a research objective is identified, the difficult task of going to questions that are clear, interpretable, unambiguous and that cover the domain of relevant issues must be confronted. It might be tempting to start with a question that directly paraphrases a research objective. To give an example, let us refocus the research objective in the preceding paragraph to ask who will bear the burden of reconstruction costs. With this in mind, a typical question on a public opinion poll might appear as follows: 'As you may know, the damage from hurricane Katrina may cost as much as $100 billion dollars to repair. Who do you think has most of the responsibility to pay for the costs of the rebuilding – the federal government, state and local government, private industry, or individuals?' This appears to be a question with reasonable face validity that will measure opinion at a very general level. However, it is only one aspect of public opinion on this complex topic. Because it lacks specificity, individual level responses to this question may not be highly stable. Responses may vary depending which of the many facets of the event respondents happened to be thinking about at the moment that they are asked the question. More specific questions, which may elicit responses that are more stable because of their specific references, can be developed by expanding the topic and focusing the scope.

One way to accomplish such expansion is to use a procedure suggested by Booth, Colomb and Williams (2003). These authors suggest a method for honing in on a research thesis, but the procedure is a logical way to develop questions for a thematic and highly specific public opinion questionnaire. First, the authors say, pose a general question. The question area can be easily expanded into sub areas by adding action words or stating a relationship. Typically, applying the technique of asking 'who,' 'what,' 'where,' 'when,' 'why,' and 'how' will suffice. We have already included a 'who' component in our general question (who should bear the costs), but the topic can be further subdivided by applying the other action words. For example, we could ask 'how' questions to ascertain opinion about the best ways for public funds to be utilized in rebuilding. Should local agencies be set up so that those who have incurred uninsured losses can apply for aid, or should this be a centralized process? Should the aid be in the form of loans or grants? Should reconstruction of public works be done through competitive bidding to private contractors or should government departments be responsible for the work? Should a public works program be created that would train local residents to participate directly in the rebuilding? With a little thought, it is not difficult to use this technique to unearth many specific issues related to the research objective of how the reconstruction bill should be paid. At that point, the challenge becomes picking those that are most interesting.

The action/relationship word method also works well with a broad question objective, such as the earlier one asking about the relationship between one's religious beliefs and their political behavior. For example, the proposed question, 'Do your religious beliefs affect your political behaviors?' can be focused by asking specifically about certain religious beliefs and their impact on certain political behaviors. The general question can be translated into something narrow but easily interpretable, such as 'Have you ever donated money to a faith-based political organization?,' or into a slightly broader but still easily interpretable question such as 'Have you ever voted for a political candidate

because his position on the abortion issue was the same as the position held by your religious organization (asked only of people who belong to a religious organization)?'

What can be measured in public opinion surveys?

When considering how questions should be constructed for obtaining reliable and valid public opinion, it is also important to consider what it is that can be measured in public opinion questionnaires. This knowledge gives the public opinion researcher an important toolkit for understanding facets of public responses to topical issues. The more facets that are understood, the greater is the validity of the results. A distinction should be made between obtaining a person's 'opinion' and measuring 'public opinion.' As a formal exercise, public opinion research goes well beyond what we might consider in obtaining a person's opinion about a topic. Public opinion surveys measure attitudes, behaviors, behavioral intentions, beliefs, circumstances, knowledge, values and opinions with respect to a political topic, entity, or event.

For example, consider the common interest of public opinion researchers in public perceptions of whoever occupies the White House. A survey question that asks whether the president should veto a proposed tax increase is an assessment of opinion. Whether the respondent could identify accurately details of the tax increase proposal is an assessment of knowledge. Behavioral intention would be assessed if a question asked whether the president's veto would affect a respondent's vote choice. Asking whether the administration should focus on strengthening the country's defense compared to solving domestic problems is an example of a value choice, because both options refer to a broad agenda rather than to a specific issue. Asking a respondent whether he or she approves of the job the president is doing is probably closer to obtaining an attitude toward the president (i.e., a generalized evaluation) than to a performance assessment. It is impossible to imagine that most citizens have the detailed knowledge necessary to judge the performance of such a multi-faceted, incredibly complex, job. The variety of things one might measure under the rubric of 'public opinion' presents researchers with a wide array of choices with which to understand the political arena.

Question wording and structure

The choice of words is a major consideration for public opinion questions. Studies have shown, for example, that when asking questions about social programs, both the way the program is construed or the implication of positive action in the question stem can affect responses. Using data from several national surveys, Smith (1987) showed that questions asking about programs to assist the poor elicited far more public support than questions asking about social welfare programs. Rasinski (1989) analyzed a set of question wording experiments in the General Social Survey and found that when policy questions were phrased in a more dynamic or active fashion, the public showed more support. In 1986, for example, 48.2% of the public said too little is spent on 'solving the problems of big cities,' compared to 17.7% who said too little is spent on 'assistance to big cities.' Similarly, 36.5% of the public said too little is spent on 'improving the conditions of Blacks,' compared to 27.8% who said too little is spent on 'assistance to Blacks.' Differences of similar magnitude and direction were found when the experiments were conducted in 1984 and 1985.

Questions with words indicating extreme positions may elicit extreme responses. In a classic example from the 1940s, fewer respondents agreed that the US should 'forbid' reporters from a communist country to come into this country to report the news back home than agreed that the US should 'not allow' the foreign reporters (Rugg, 1941). As part of a class exercise, I conducted a question wording experiment as a conceptual replication of this phenomenon. The exercise also demonstrates other principles instructive to questionnaire design. The experiment was

designed to determine whether respondents would be less likely to endorse 'lying' than 'not telling the truth.' As an added feature, each phrase was set in either an absolute context (one should always lie/not tell the truth) or a relative context (one should usually lie/not tell the truth). Students were asked to select a convenience sample of adult respondents who were randomly assigned to one of the four question wordings dealing with telling the truth to a stranger, as listed in Table 33.3. Respondents were instructed to indicate whether they agreed strongly, agreed, disagreed, or disagreed strongly to each question.

Results are shown in Figure 33.1. Three things should be noted. First, more people are willing to agree to 'not tell the truth' than to 'lie,' suggesting the strong wording/extreme response relationship referred to earlier. Second, fewer people agreed with the stronger mandate to 'never' tell the truth than with the weaker injunction that one should 'usually not' tell the truth, again suggesting the strong wording/extreme response relationship. Third, and in contrast, changing the stronger modifier 'always' to the weaker 'usually' did not seem to affect the tendency to reject the strong but unpopular injunction to lie.

Public opinion researchers should be careful to avoid the use of double negatives in writing survey questions. While one might get away with a statement such as 'Increasing property taxes to give teachers a salary rise will not unfairly burden homeowners who have no children in public schools'

Table 33.3   Question wording version

Version	Question
A	You should never tell a person you just met the truth about yourself if he or she asks a personal question.
B	You should usually not tell a person you just met the truth about yourself if he or she asks a personal question.
C	You should always lie to a person you just met if he or she asks a personal question.
D	You should usually lie to a person you just met if he or she asks a personal question.

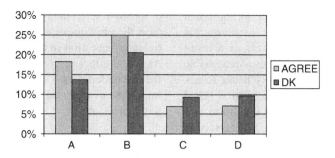

Figure 33.1 Percentage agreeing to question about lying/not telling truth by experimental version

as a piece of prose, this sentence is much too difficult to process as a public opinion question. Under the time pressures of a public opinion survey, the phrase 'not unfairly burden' is likely to be heard as 'unfairly burden,' leading to an interpretation opposite that of the intended one. A clearer statement would be to simply eliminate the word 'not' and allow the respondent to react to the affirmative form.

Sheatsley (1983) points out that an implied double negative may cause problems. In this case, the respondent is asked to approve or disapprove of prohibiting something. He cites a question from a national survey that asked, 'all in all, would you favor or oppose Congress passing a law not allowing any employer to force an employee to retire at any age?' This is clearly a difficult sentence to parse, especially when it is presented verbally, as is the case with most public opinion surveys. This same problematical structure can be seen in versions A and B of the question in Table 33.3. The results presented in Figure 33.1 show that these two versions elicit a higher percentage of 'don't know' responses than versions C and D. This may be less an indication that respondents are more ambivalent about 'not telling the truth' than they are about 'lying' and more an indication that some respondents are confused by having to approve or disapprove a statement of prohibition.

Questions that are double-barreled—those that have two references—often show up in public opinion surveys. For example, a poll conducted nine months after the

September 11 terrorist attacks contained the following question: 'Since the September 11 terrorist attacks, do you personally feel a lot less safe where you live and work, somewhat less safe, only a little less safe, or not at all less safe than you did before?' The difficulty here is that the question asks respondents to judge their feelings of safety at two places, where they live and where they work. For most of us, these are two very different environments—terrorist attacks might be less likely in residential areas than in business areas. So, for many people, this question would be impossible to answer. It would have been better to separate the question into one asking about safety where the respondent lives and one asking about safety where the respondent works (for those that are working). It should also be noted that the double-negative phrasing 'not at all less safe' is awkward. It would have been better to use a bipolar rather than unipolar response format and ask: 'Since the September 11 terrorist attacks do you personally feel very unsafe, somewhat unsafe, somewhat safe, or very safe where you (live or work) compared to before?'

Survey questions should not make presumptions about respondents' beliefs or states of mind. This is illustrated in an item from a news poll also taken nine months after the terrorist attacks. The question reads as follows: 'It has been months since the terrorist attacks. Does that make you feel more afraid because that means another attack may happen soon, or less afraid because that means preventative measures are stopping additional attacks?' First, the question assumes that the respondent experienced fear as a result of the attacks. This may be a reasonable assumption, but it is generally better to ask than assume. Second, the question is based on the premise that the first condition will cause an increase in fear and that the second condition will cause a decrease. However, it should be noted that the faulty construction does not undermine the legitimacy of the research objective. It is usually possible to pull apart some of the ideas embedded within or implied by the faulty question and to express them as separate questions that are more straightforward. One possible breakdown of the question above is as follows: 'How fearful are you that another terrorist attack may happen soon?' (very fearful to not at all fearful), and 'How confident are you that preventative measures are stopping additional terrorist attacks?' (very confident to not at all confident). Taken together, these two questions get at the same ideas, but are less likely to be confusing to respondents and more likely to give information that is readily interpretable.

Question order

The placement of questions in the questionnaire is important to consider. For attitude or opinion questions, related prior questions can affect responses to questions about little known topics, or to questions about which the respondent has mixed feelings. For example, responses to a question about whether the US should have invaded Iraq may be swayed in a positive direction if it is preceded by questions about terrorist attacks in the US and abroad, but in a negative direction if it is preceded by questions about American casualties in Iraq. Tourangeau and his colleagues (Tourangeau, Rasinski, Bradburn, & D'Andrade, 1989) used question-wording experiments in a telephone public opinion survey to examine responses to six target questions about a variety of topics (military policy, civil liberties, social welfare, and abortion) when they were placed after questions that were

designed to set an interpretive context. In each case, the prior questions affected responses to the target question in the expected direction. Also, the effect of context was much larger for respondents who said that the issue was important to them but that they had mixed feelings about it.

RELIABILITY, VALIDITY AND THE PSYCHOLOGICAL TASKS CONFRONTING THE RESPONDENT

Psychologists have paid a considerable amount of attention to the cognitive tasks the survey respondent faces when confronted with a survey question. Developments in this area can help to put some of the technical aspects of writing questions that we have stressed in the preceding sections into context. A simple breakdown of the respondent's experience into the tasks of: (a) question comprehension or interpretation, (b) retrieval or relevant information from memory, (c) forming a judgment, and (d) editing a response has changed the way survey researchers think about question writing and, as we shall see later, has changed the way questions are tested and evaluated (Sudman, Bradburn, & Schwarz, 1996; Tourangeau et al., 2000). Survey researchers evaluate how respondents deal with their questions by pretesting them in a number of ways.

Traditional pretesting

Pretesting can serve several useful purposes, and it should be used whenever possible to establish the reliability and validity of survey questions. First, at a very basic level, pretesting can show whether questions possess enough variability to be useful in further analysis. Sometimes variability is not a requirement for the purposes of the research. If a research question can be answered by responses to a single question, then variability is not necessarily crucial. For example, if a researcher is interested in knowing what the public thinks about whether the US should pull out of the war in Iraq, a result indicating that 90% agree or that 10% agree provides useful information, even though there is little variance in the responses. However, if 90% of the public agree with the statement 'there are too many people getting something for nothing in this society' and the intent is to use the question as a predictor of other responses in order to model public opinion, then the lack of variability is limiting. Second, pretesting is useful in calculating the statistics that are indicators of reliability and validity. In a large and diverse pretest sample, one can calculate measures of internal consistency and conduct the factor analyses necessary to assess psychometric measures of reliability and validity as discussed in our examples.

Cognitive pretesting

Cognitive pretesting (Willis, 2005) is another method of pretesting that emerged directly from the psychological analysis of cognitive tasks involved in survey responding. Cognitive pretesting involves the following steps. First, a set of survey questions is generated, either through borrowing or adapting questions from other researchers or by constructing new ones specific to the topic of interest. Second, a judgment is made about each question as to whether it is likely to pose a problem to respondents in any one of four cognitive areas: interpretation, retrieval of information from memory, forming a judgment, and eliciting a response. Those questions that are judged likely to pose problems are selected for testing with individual respondents in a one-on-one setting.

One or more probe questions are selected for each potentially problematical survey question. The probe questions are open-ended and focus on one of the four cognitive tasks that respondent must confront when answering the question. Probes may query the respondent's understanding of the question— e.g., what sorts of ideas came to mind when the respondent was formulating an answer, how that information was filtered or combined in order to give a response based on the set of response categories presented in the

question, and whether the question was in any way sensitive—such that it would result in the respondent withholding or distorting information.

Typically, a small number of respondents are interviewed, ideally face-to-face. The original survey questions are administered and responses are obtained. Afterwards, the interviewer returns to each question deemed problematical and administers the probes. Open-ended responses to the probes are captured verbatim (usually on a tape recorder) so that the question analyst can study them to pinpoint problems in the question. A set of cognitive interviews may be conducted on, say, eight to ten respondents and the resulting open-ended responses analyzed. Problems with interpretation, retrieval, judgment and responding are assessed, and the questions are improved. The improved questions may be subjected to another round of cognitive interviews using a different set of respondents.

As an example, consider a question that appeared in a recent public opinion poll:

> There have been allegations that President Bush may have benefited from insider information when he sold stock in the Harken Energy Corporation in the early 1990s. Based on what you have read or heard, would you describe President Bush's sale of stock as proper, improper but not illegal, or as illegal?

As survey questions go, this is rather long. If it were administered over the telephone it would certainly pose a challenge to comprehension. One cognitive probe useful for assessing whether comprehension is a problem is to ask the respondent to paraphrase the question, that is, simply to repeat the question in his or her own words. It is likely that this would be a difficult task for many respondents without the text in front of them. Another cognitive probe for assessing comprehension is to ask the respondent to give the meaning of a word or phrase. It is possible that many respondents would not know what 'insider trading' meant even if the question text were visible, such as on a web-administered survey. Including a probe that asks respondents to define the meaning of this potentially obscure term would give information about whether the term should be defined in the question, or whether some other wording should be used.

Sometimes respondents are asked to make very complicated judgments. Consider the following question that appeared on a recent public opinion survey, 'At the present time, do you think environmental protection laws and regulations have gone too far, or not far enough, or have struck about the right balance?' One cognitive probe that might be used to understand the respondent's level of cognitive burden, giving insight into the reliability and validity of the response, could be directed at obtaining the information that was brought to mind by the question. During the cognitive interview, the respondent might be asked, 'What thoughts came to mind as you answered this question?' The respondent might mention some specific laws and regulations or might not be able to mention specific laws and regulations. A follow-up probe might ask how the respondent used the thoughts to come up with their final answer. Again, some respondents might be able to articulate clear decision rules, while others may base their answers on a vague feeling or a wild guess. All of this information is useful to help the researcher understand whether the respondent is interpreting the question as intended, which is, as mentioned, a key component in assessing the question's validity.

CONCLUSION

In this chapter, we discussed concepts and methods related to designing reliable and valid public opinion questionnaires from the psychometrics literature and from the literature on survey methodology. We focused on the importance of selecting questions that elicit consistent responses, that relate empirically to constructs important to the research, and that communicate the research objectives to the respondent in as simple, clear, and unambiguous a way as possible. We explored the meaning of reliability and validity as they appear in the psychometrics literature and addressed validity from a question construction perspective. We focused on rules of question writing and, in particular, on how an understanding of the psychological processes that come into play when a respondent confronts a survey question may affect whether the question is interpreted as the researcher intended, a key component of validity.

Public opinion researchers who are contemplating constructing their own survey instruments need to pay attention to all of these elements of question design. As they search for questions related to their topics, they should select those that have demonstrated empirical reliability and validity by examining any past research using those questions. If they do not have, or cannot find, empirical evidence on question reliability and validity, then they should scrutinize questions as to their construction, using the suggestions contained in this chapter. Pretesting of questions should always be strongly considered. Two methods of pretesting were mentioned, doing a dry-run survey on a small sample and conducting cognitive pretesting. The methods are not mutually exclusive, and they have been used together to assure that the questions on the survey are interpretable, answerable, bear upon the research objectives, and are likely to yield stable, meaningful responses.

REFERENCES

Booth, W. C., Colomb, G. G., & Williams, J. M. (2003). *The Craft of research* (2nd ed.). Chicago: University of Chicago Press.

Campbell, D. T., & Fiske, D. W. (1959). Convergent and discriminant validation by the multitrait-multimethod matrix. *Psychological Bulletin, 56*, 81–105.

Carmines, E. G., & Zeller, R. A. (1979). *Reliability and validity assessment.* Beverly Hills: Sage Publications.

Converse, P. (1964). The nature of belief systems in mass publics. In D. Apter (Ed.), *Ideology and discontent* (pp. 206–261). New York: Free Press.

Crocker, L., & Algina, J. (1986). *Introduction to classical and modern test theory.* New York: Harcourt, Brace Jovanovich.

Fowler, F. J. (1992). How unclear terms affect survey data. *Public Opinion Quarterly, 56*, 218–231.

Judd, C. M., & Milburn, M. A. (1980). The structure of attitude systems in the general public: Comparisons of a structure equation model. *American Sociological Review, 45*, 627–643.

Krosnick, J. A. (1991). Response strategies for coping with the cognitive demands of attitude measures in surveys. *Applied Cognitive Psychology, 5*(3), 213–236.

Mosier, C. I. (1947). A critical examination of the concepts of face validity. *Education and Psychological Measurement, 7*, 191–206.

Rasinski, K. A. (1987). What's fair is fair … or is it? Value difference underlying public views about social justice. *Journal of Personality and Social Psychology, 53*, 201–211.

Rasinski, K. A. (1989). The effect of question wording on support for government spending. *Public Opinion Quarterly, 53*, 388–394.

Rasinski, K. A. (2003). *Stigma associated with drug addiction: Report of a language audit based on the results of a national survey of drug policy.* Washington, DC: Center for Substance Abuse Treatment.

Rugg, D. (1941). Experiments in wording questions: II. *Public Opinion Quarterly, 5*, 91–92.

Sheatsley, P. (1983). Questionnaire construction and item writing. In P. Rossi, J. Wright, & A. Anderson (Eds.), *Handbook of survey research* (pp. 195–230). New York: Academic Press.

Smith, T. W. (1987). That which we call welfare by any other name would smell sweeter: An analysis of the impact of question wording on response patterns. *Public Opinion Quarterly, 51*, 75–83.

Sudman S., & Bradburn, N. (1982). *Asking questions: A practical guide to questionnaire design.* San Francisco: Jossey-Bass Publishers.

Sudman, S., Bradburn, N. M., & Schwarz, N. (1996). *Thinking about answers: The application of cognitive processes to survey methodology.* San Francisco: Jossey-Bass Publishers.

Tourangeau, R., Rasinski, K., Bradburn, N., & D'Andrade, R. (1989). Carryover effects in attitude surveys. *Public Opinion Quarterly, 53*, 495–524.

Tourangeau, R., Rips, L. J., & Rasinski, K. (2000). *The psychology of survey response.* New York: Cambridge University Press.

Willis, G. B. (2005). *Cognitive interviewing: A tool for improving questionnaire design.* Thousand Oaks, CA: Sage Publications.

34

The Psychology of Survey Response

Norbert Schwarz

Since the beginning of public opinion surveys, researchers have been aware that minor changes in question wording, format, or order can profoundly affect respondents' answers (Cantril, 1944; Payne, 1951). Nevertheless, the field has long been characterized by two largely separate streams: rigorous theories of sampling on the one hand, and an experience based 'art of asking questions' on the other hand. This changed since the early 1980s, thanks to a collaboration of survey methodologists and cognitive psychologists, who brought theories of language comprehension, memory, and judgment to bear on the response process (for reviews see Sudman, Bradburn, & Schwarz, 1996; Schwarz, 1999; Tourangeau, Rips, & Rasinski, 2000; and the contributions in Sirken *et al.*, 1999). This chapter highlights key lessons learned, with particular attention to the cognitive and communicative processes underlying answers to attitude questions. For a complementary review of the processes underlying behavioral reports, see Schwarz and Oyserman (2001).

Answering a survey question entails several distinct tasks (Cannell, Marquis, & Laurent, 1977; Tourangeau, 1984; Strack & Martin, 1987). Respondents' first need is to understand the question posed to determine what information they are asked to provide. If the question is an attitude question, they may either retrieve a previously formed judgment from memory or form a judgment on the spot. Because a previously formed judgment that fits the specifics of the question asked is rarely accessible, judgment formation during the interview setting is the most common case. To form a judgment, respondents need to retrieve relevant information from memory. Usually, they will also need to retrieve or construct some standard against which the attitude object is evaluated. Once a 'private' judgment is formed in respondents' minds, they have to communicate it to the researcher. Unless the question is asked in an open response format, they need to format their judgment to fit the response alternatives. Finally, respondents may wish to edit their response before they communicate it, due to self-presentation and social desirability concerns.

The following sections review these tasks in more detail. Throughout, the emphasis is on the theoretical conceptualization of the underlying processes, with illustrations from selected experimental results.

QUESTION COMPREHENSION

Survey textbooks rightly emphasize that researchers should avoid unfamiliar terms and complex syntax in writing survey questions (see Bradburn, Sudman, & Wansink, 2004, for advice; and Belson, 1981, for common problems). This focus on the *literal* or *semantic* meaning of the question, however, misses an important point: Language comprehension is not about words *per se*, but about speaker meaning (Clark & Schober, 1992). When asked, 'What have you done today?' respondents surely understand the words. But to provide an answer, they need to determine what kind of activities the researcher is interested in—should they report that they had a cup of coffee or took a shower, or is that not what the researcher had in mind? Providing an informative answer requires extensive inferences about the questioner's likely intention to determine the *pragmatic meaning* of the question.

To draw these inferences, respondents rely on the tacit assumptions of conversational conduct described by Paul Grice (1975), a philosopher of language. According to Grice's analysis, conversations proceed according to a co-operativeness principle, which can be expressed in the form of four maxims. First, a *maxim of relation* enjoins speakers to make their contribution relevant to the aims of the ongoing conversation. This maxim licenses the use of contextual information in question interpretation and invites respondents to relate the question to the context of the ongoing exchange. Second, a *maxim of quantity* requests speakers to make their contribution as informative as is required, but not more informative than is required. It invites respondents to provide information the questioner seems interested in, rather than other information that may come to mind. Moreover, it discourages the reiteration of information provided earlier, or that 'goes

without saying' (such as, 'taking a shower' in the above example). Third, a *maxim of manner* holds that the contribution should be clear rather than obscure, ambiguous or wordy. This maxim entails an interpretability presumption: research participants can assume that the researcher 'chose his wording so they can understand what he meant—and can do so quickly' (Clark & Schober, 1992, p. 27). Hence, the most obvious meaning seems likely to be the correct one; if an obvious meaning is not apparent, respondents may consult the immediate context to determine one. The researcher's contributions to the conversation include formal aspects of questionnaire design, like the response alternatives, and respondents draw on these features in interpreting the question. Finally, a *maxim of quality* enjoins speakers not to say anything they believe to be false or lack adequate evidence for. These rules of cooperative conversational conduct are essential for understanding how respondents make sense of the questions asked of them (for reviews see Clark & Schober, 1992; Schwarz, 1996).

Question context

In natural conversations, we draw on the content of the ongoing conversation to interpret the next utterance, as licensed by the maxim of relation. The same holds for survey interviews, where respondents draw on the content of *preceding questions*. Hence, a question about 'drugs' acquires a different meaning in the context of health questions rather than crime questions. As a particularly informative example, consider research in which respondents are asked to report their opinion about a highly obscure, or even completely fictitious, issue, such as the 'Agricultural Trade Act of 1978' (e.g., Schuman & Presser, 1981; Bishop, Oldendick, & Tuchfarber, 1986). Apparently confirming public opinion researchers' nightmares, about 30% of respondents report an opinion on such topics, presumably in the absence of any knowledge. Yet, their answers may be more meaningful than assumed.

From a conversational point of view, the sheer fact that a question about some issue is asked presupposes that it exists—or else asking the question would violate every norm of conversational conduct. Respondents have no reason to believe that the researcher would ask a meaningless question and hence draw on contextual information to make sense of it. Once they have assigned a particular meaning to the issue, they have no difficulty reporting a subjectively meaningful opinion. Supporting this assumption, Strack, Schwarz, and Wänke (1991) observed that German university students reported different attitudes toward the introduction of a fictitious 'educational contribution,' depending on the content of a preceding question. Some students were asked to estimate the average tuition fees that students have to pay at US universities (in contrast to Germany, where university education is free), whereas others had to estimate the amount of money that the Swedish government pays every student as financial support. As expected, respondents inferred that the fictitious 'educational contribution' pertained to students having to pay money when it followed the tuition question, but to students receiving money when it followed the financial support question. Accordingly, they reported a more favorable attitude toward the introduction of an 'educational contribution' in the former than in the latter case—hardly a meaningless response.

While the maxim of relation licenses the use of preceding questions in interpreting subsequent ones, the maxim of quantity encourages respondents not to reiterate information they have already provided earlier. This results in unique meaning shifts when closely *related questions* with overlapping meaning are presented. In daily life, one may give the exact same answer when a friend asks how happy one is with life and another asks how satisfied one is— after all, these are closely related concepts and one's friends may just use different words. But if the same friend asks first how happy one is and then follows up with how satisfied one is, he/she may have

different concepts in mind, requiring different and non-redundant answers. Again, the same holds for survey interviews. Strack *et al.* (1991) asked respondents to report on their general happiness and satisfaction with life. When these questions were presented as the last and first questions of two separate questionnaires, presented by different researchers, the two questions correlated, with $r = 0.96$. But when both questions were presented as the last two questions of the first questionnaire, respondents differentiated between happiness and satisfaction, resulting in different mean reports and a significantly lower correlation of $r = 0.75$. Hence, closely related questions can elicit a differential interpretation when presented in close proximity, reflecting that we don't assume that people ask the same thing twice. This can attenuate the internal consistency of multi-item scales.

In natural conversations, we further draw on our knowledge about the speaker to infer the intended meaning of a question. Again, the same applies to research situations, where the *researcher's affiliation* may provide important clues. Norenzayan and Schwarz (1999) presented respondents with newspaper accounts of mass murders and asked them to explain why the mass murder occurred. Depending on conditions, the questionnaire was printed on the letterhead of an alleged 'Institute for Personality Research' or 'Institute for Social Research.' As expected, respondents' explanations showed more attention to personality variables or to social-contextual variables, depending on whether they thought the researcher was a personality psychologist or a social scientist. As requested by norms of conversational conduct, respondents took the researcher's affiliation into account to determine which information would be most relevant to the questioner's likely epistemic interest.

In sum, respondents make systematic use of contextual information. In face-to-face and telephone interviews, this information is limited to what has been provided earlier in the interview. In self-administered surveys, however, respondents can read ahead and can peruse subsequent questions in an effort to make sense of preceding ones, giving rise to systematic influences of later questions on earlier ones (e.g., Schwarz & Hippler, 1995).

Response alternatives

Particularly relevant sources of contextual information are the response alternatives that accompany a question. This has been most extensively addressed in comparisons of *open* and *closed response formats*. Suppose respondents are asked in an open format, 'What have you done today?' To give a meaningful answer, they have to determine which activities may be of interest to the researcher. Observing the maxim of quantity, they are likely to omit activities that the researcher is obviously aware of (e.g., 'I gave a survey interview') or may take for granted anyway (e.g., 'I took a shower'). If respondents were given a list of activities that included giving an interview and taking a shower, most respondents would endorse them. At the same time, such a list would reduce the likelihood that respondents report activities that are not represented on the list (see Schuman & Presser, 1981; Schwarz & Hippler, 1991, for reviews). Both of these questions form effects reflect that response alternatives can clarify the intended meaning of a question and may remind respondents of material that they may otherwise not consider.

These processes can result in pronounced and systematic differences between open and closed question formats. For example, Schuman and Presser (1981, pp. 105ff.) asked respondents what they consider 'the most important thing for children to prepare them for life.' Whereas 62% picked 'To think for themselves' when this alternative was offered as part of a list, only 5% provided an answer that could be assigned to this category in an open response format.

Response alternatives can even affect question interpretation when they are purely 'formal' in nature and apparently devoid of any substantive information. As an example, suppose respondents are asked, 'How successful would you say you have been in life?' accompanied by a rating scale that ranges from 'not at all successful' to 'extremely successful.' To answer this question, they have to determine what the researcher means by 'not at all successful'—does this term refer to the absence of outstanding achievements or to the presence of explicit failures? To do so, they may draw on a feature that the researcher is unlikely to consider informative, namely the *numeric values* of the rating scale. Schwarz, Knäuper, Hippler, Noelle-Neumann, and Clark (1991) presented the above success-in-life question with an 11-point rating scale that ranged either from 0 ('not at all successful') to 10 ('extremely successful'), or from −5 ('not at all successful') to +5 ('extremely successful'). Whereas 34% of the respondents endorsed a value between 0 and 5 on the 0 to 10 scale, only 13% endorsed one of the formally equivalent values between −5 and 0 on the −5 to +5 scale. Figure 34.1 shows the response shift underlying these differences.

Subsequent experiments indicated that this shift is due to differential interpretations of 'not at all successful.' When combined with the numeric value '0,' respondents inferred that the term refers to the absence of outstanding achievements. However, when the same term was combined with the numeric value '−5,' and the scale offered '0' as the mid-point, they inferred that it refers to the presence of explicit failures. In general, a format that ranges from negative to positive numbers conveys that the researcher has a bipolar dimension in mind, where the two poles refer to the presence of opposite attributes. In contrast, a format that uses only positive numbers conveys that the researcher has a unipolar dimension in mind, referring to different degrees of the same attribute.

Other 'formal' characteristics of response scales, like the graphical layout of rating scales or the numeric values of frequency scales, can have a similarly profound impact on respondents' question interpretation (for a review see Schwarz, 1996, chap. 5). While the

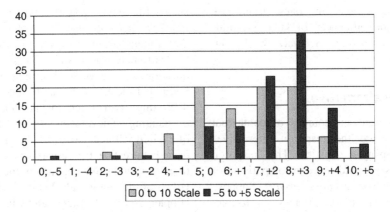

Figure 34.1 Response distribution as a function of the numerical values of the rating scale
Note: Shown is the percentage of respondents who chose the respective scale value when asked, 'How successful would you say you have been in life?' 0 or −5 = 'not at all successful'; 10 or +5 = 'extremely successful.' Adapted from Schwarz, Knäuper, Hippler, Noelle-Neumann, & Clark (1991)

researcher's selection of these formats is often based on convenience or in-house traditions, respondents assume that every contribution of the researcher is relevant to their task, consistent with the maxim of relation. They therefore draw on formal characteristics of the research instrument in making sense of the question asked.

Moreover, respondents work within the *constraints* imposed by the question format (Schuman & Presser, 1981). This is particularly apparent with regard to '*don't know*' (DK) or 'no opinion' responses. Standard survey questions usually omit 'no opinion' as an explicit option, but interviewers accept this response when volunteered. Experimental studies (e.g., Schuman & Presser, 1981) have consistently found that respondents are more likely to report not having an opinion when a DK option is explicitly offered (see Schwarz & Hippler, 1991, for a review). Similarly, many respondents prefer a *middle alternative* between two extreme positions when offered, but endorse another option when the middle alternative is omitted (e.g., Schuman & Presser, 1981). Thus, most respondents assume that the rules of the game call for working within the categories offered, even though a desire to answer otherwise is evident when more choice is provided.

Cognitive pretests

As these findings indicate, question comprehension is not about words—it is about speaker meaning. To determine the speaker's intended meaning, respondents pay close attention to contextual information, bringing the tacit assumptions that govern conversations in daily life (Grice, 1975) to the research situation (Schwarz, 1996). That their responses are systematically affected by minor features of the research instrument highlights how closely they attend to the specifics at hand in their quest to provide informative answers. Unfortunately, their efforts are rarely appreciated by the researcher, who considers these features substantively irrelevant and treats their influence as an undesirable artifact. Nor are researchers likely to note these influences in regular surveys, where control conditions with different question formats are missing, or in regular field pretests, where problems can only be identified when respondents give obviously meaningless answers or complain about the questions asked. What is needed are pretest procedures that deliberately probe respondents' understanding of a question in the context and format in which it will be presented in the actual interview.

Several such *cognitive interviewing* procedures have been developed (see Sudman *et al.*, 1996, chap. 2, and the contributions in Schwarz & Sudman, 1996). Most widely used are *verbal protocols*, in the form of concurrent or retrospective think-aloud procedures. In addition, respondents are often asked to paraphrase the question, thus providing insight into their interpretation of question meaning (see DeMaio & Rothgeb, 1996, for common methods). An alternative, but less sensitive, approach involves detailed analyses of field pretests, known as *behavior coding* (see Fowler & Cannell, 1996). Based on insights from cognitive interviews, Lessler and Forsyth (1996) developed a detailed coding scheme that allows researchers to identify likely question problems in advance. Cognitive pretests that illuminate respondents' understanding of a question within its intended context can be conducted with a relatively small number of respondents, and provide the best available safeguard against later surprises.

RECALLING INFORMATION AND FORMING A JUDGMENT

Once respondents have determined what the researcher is interested in, they need to recall relevant information from memory. In some cases, respondents may have direct access to a recently formed relevant judgment that they can offer as an answer. In most cases, however, they will not find an appropriate answer readily stored in memory, and will need to form a judgment on the spot, drawing on whatever information comes to mind at that time. What renders this process problematic for public opinion research is its high context dependency: what information comes to mind, and how it is used, is strongly influenced by the specifics of the research instrument.

As a general rule, people never retrieve all information that may potentially be relevant to a judgment. Instead, they truncate the search process as soon as enough information has come to mind to form the judgment with sufficient subjective certainty. Accordingly, the judgment is disproportionately influenced by the information that is most accessible at that point in time, e.g., because it has just been used in answering a previous question (Bodenhausen & Wyer, 1987).

Contextual influences on information accessibility are the major contributor to the emergence of question order effects in survey research, along with contextual influences on question interpretation. The underlying processes have been conceptualized in several related models that are consistent with current theorizing in social cognition (e.g., Feldman & Lynch, 1988; Tourangeau, 1992). The next section summarizes the most comprehensive model (Schwarz & Bless, 1992a, 2007), which identifies the conditions under which question order effects emerge and predicts their direction, size, and generalization across related items.

Information accessibility and use: The emergence, direction, and size of question order effects

Attitude questions ask respondents to provide an evaluative judgment. To do so, respondents need to form a mental representation of the target (i.e., the object of judgment), as well as a mental representation of some standard against which the target is evaluated. Both representations are context dependent and include information that is chronically accessible as well as information that is only temporarily accessible—for example, because it was brought to mind by preceding questions. How accessible information influences the judgment depends on how it is used. Information that is *included* in the temporary representation formed of the target results in *assimilation effects*; that is, the inclusion of positive (negative) information results in a more positive (negative) judgment. The size of assimilation effects increases with the amount and extremity of temporarily accessible information and decreases with the amount and extremity of chronically accessible information included in the representation of the target (Bless, Schwarz, & Wänke, 2003).

For example, Schwarz, Strack, and Mai (1991) asked respondents to report their marital satisfaction and their general life-satisfaction in different question orders. When the general life-satisfaction question was asked first, it correlated with marital satisfaction $r = 0.32$. Reversing the question order, however, increased this correlation to $r = 0.67$. This reflects that the marital satisfaction question brought marriage related information to mind that respondents included in the representation formed of their lives in general. This increase in correlation was attenuated, $r = 0.43$, when questions about three different life-domains (job, leisure time, and marriage) preceded the general question, thus bringing more diverse material to mind. Parallel influences were observed in the mean reports. Happily married respondents reported higher, and unhappily married respondents reported lower, general life-satisfaction when their attention was drawn to their marriage by the preceding question.

However, the same piece of accessible information may also elicit a *contrast effect*; that is, a more negative (positive) judgment, the more positive (negative) information is brought to mind. This is the case when the information is *excluded* from, rather than included in, the cognitive representation formed of the target. For example, the above study included a condition in which the marital satisfaction and life-satisfaction questions were introduced with a joint lead-in that read, 'We now have two questions about your life. The first pertains to your marriage and the second to your life in general.' This lead-in was designed to evoke the conversational maxim of quantity, which enjoins speakers to avoid redundancy when answering related questions. Accordingly, respondents who had just reported on their marriage should now disregard this aspect of their lives when answering the general life-satisfaction question. Confirming this prediction, happily

married respondents now reported lower general life-satisfaction, whereas unhappily married respondents reported higher life-satisfaction, indicating that they excluded the positive (negative) marital information from the representation formed of their lives in general. These diverging effects reduced the correlation to $r = 0.18$, from $r = 0.67$ when the same questions were asked in the same order without a joint lead-in. A control condition in which the general life-satisfaction question was reworded to, 'Aside from your marriage, which you already told us about, how satisfied are you with your life in general?' resulted in a highly similar correlation of $r = 0.20$ (Schwarz *et al.*, 1991).

In addition, respondents may use excluded information in constructing a standard of comparison or scale anchor. If the implications of the temporarily accessible information are more extreme than the implications of the chronically accessible information used in constructing a standard, they result in a more extreme standard, eliciting contrast effects for that reason. The size of *comparison based* contrast effects increases with the extremity and amount of temporarily accessible information used in constructing the standard, and decreases with the amount and extremity of chronically accessible information used in making this construction (Bless *et al.*, 2003). Comparison based contrast effects generalize to all targets to which the standard is applicable.

As an example, consider the impact of political scandals on assessments of the trustworthiness of politicians. Not surprisingly, thinking about a politician who was involved in a scandal, say Richard Nixon, decreases trust in politicians in general. This reflects that the exemplar is included in the representation formed of the target 'politicians in general.' If the trustworthiness question pertains to a specific politician, however—say Bill Clinton—the primed exemplar cannot be included in the representation formed of the target—after all, Bill Clinton is not Richard Nixon. In this case, Richard Nixon may serve as a standard of comparison, relative to which Bill Clinton seems very trustworthy. An experiment with German exemplars confirmed these predictions (Schwarz & Bless, 1992b): Thinking about a politician who was involved in a scandal decreased the trustworthiness of politicians in general, but increased the trustworthiness of all specific exemplars assessed, as shown in Figure 34.2.

In general, the same information is likely to result in assimilation effects in the evaluation of superordinate target categories (which allow for the inclusion of all information pertaining to subordinate categories), but in contrast effects in the evaluation of lateral target categories (which are mutually exclusive). These judgmental processes are reflected in a wide range of discrepancies between general and specific judgments in public opinion research. For example, Americans distrust Congress in general, but trust their own representatives (e.g., Erikson, Luttbeg, & Tedin, 1988). Similarly, members of minority groups consistently report high levels of discrimination against their group; yet they also report that their own personal experience was more benign. In each case,

these patterns are to be expected when we take into account that recalling extreme and vivid media examples drives the general and the specific judgments in opposite directions, as predicted on theoretical grounds.

Given the crucial role of inclusion/exclusion operations in the construction of mental representations, it is important to understand their determinants. When thinking about a topic, people generally assume that whatever comes to mind bears on what they are thinking about—or why else would it come to mind now? Hence, the default is to include information that comes to mind in the representation of the target. This renders assimilation effects more likely than contrast effects. In fact, assimilation effects (sometimes referred to as carry-over effects) dominate the survey literature, and many models intended to account for question order effects don't even offer a mechanism for the conceptualization of contrast effects (e.g., Zaller, 1992), which severely limits their usefulness as general theoretical frameworks.

Whereas inclusion is the more common default, the exclusion of information needs

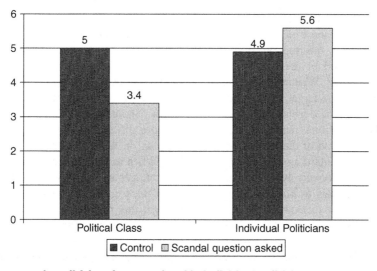

Figure 34.2   Trust in politicians in general and in individual politicians as a function of a preceding scandal question
Note: Respondents rated the trustworthiness of German politicians in general ('political class') or of three individual politicians (averaged); 9 = 'very trustworthy.' Adapted from Schwarz & Bless (1992b)

to be triggered by salient features of the question answering process. Any variable that influences the categorization of information can also determine the emergence of assimilation and contrast effects. These variables can be conceptualized as bearing on three implicit decisions that respondents have to make with regard to topic related information.

The first decision bears on why this information comes to mind. Information that seems to come to mind for the 'wrong reason,' e.g., because respondents are aware of the potential influence of a preceding question, is likely to be excluded. This is more common in experiments that present allegedly separate and independent tasks than in survey interviews, where the questions are seen as part of the same ongoing conversation. The second decision pertains to whether the information that comes to mind bears on the target of judgment or not. The content of the context question, the superordinate or lateral nature of the target category, the extremity of the information or its representativeness for the target category are relevant at this stage (see Schwarz & Bless, 1992a, 2007, for examples). Finally, conversational norms of nonredundancy may elicit the exclusion of previously provided information, as seen above (Schwarz et al., 1991).

Whenever any of these decisions results in the exclusion of information from the representation formed of the target, it will elicit a contrast effect. Whether this contrast effect is limited to the target, or generalizes across related targets, depends on whether the excluded information is merely subtracted from the representation of the target or used in constructing a standard against which the target is evaluated. Conversely, whenever the information that comes to mind is included in the representation formed of the target, it results in an assimilation effect. Hence, the inclusion/exclusion model provides a coherent conceptualization of the emergence, direction, size, and generalization of context effects in attitude measurement. These effects can be reliably produced when the questions are written to clearly operationalize the relevant variables. Of course, this is not

always the case and some questions are too mushy with regard to the conceptual variables to allow strong predictions. Sudman et al. (1996, chap. 5) provide a more extensive discussion of these issues, with detailed examples.

Question order effects are attenuated when related questions are separated by a sufficient number of buffer items, which renders the information brought to mind by the earlier question less accessible (for a review, see Wänke & Schwarz, 1997). Similarly, preceding questions are less likely to influence the judgments of older respondents, due to age-related decline in memory. This age-sensitivity of question order effects can undermine cohort comparisons (for examples see Schwarz & Knäuper, 2000).

Response order effects

Another major source of context effects in attitude measurement is the order in which response alternatives are presented. Response order effects are most reliably obtained when a question presents several plausible response options (see Sudman et al., 1996, chap. 6, for detailed discussions). To understand the underlying processes, suppose a person is asked to provide a few good reasons why 'divorce should be easier to obtain.' The person can easily do so, but he or she could just as easily provide some reasons why 'divorce should be more difficult to obtain.' When such alternatives are juxtaposed within a question (as in 'Should divorce be easier to obtain or more difficult to obtain?'), the outcome depends on which alternative is considered first. When respondents consider 'easier' and generate some supportive thoughts, they are likely to truncate the search process and endorse this response option; but had they considered 'more difficult' the same process would have resulted in an endorsement of that option. Again, respondents' judgment is based on the temporary representation formed of the attitude object, which is, in part, a function of the response option they consider first.

Which option respondents consider first depends on the order and mode in which the response alternatives are presented (Krosnick & Alwin, 1987). When presented in writing, respondents elaborate on the implications of the response options in the order presented. In this mode, an alternative that elicits supporting thoughts is more likely to be endorsed when presented early rather than late on the list, giving rise to *primacy effects*. In contrast, when the alternatives are read to respondents, their opportunity to think about the early ones is limited by the need to listen to later ones. In this case, they are more likely to work backwards, thinking first about the last alternative read to them. When this alternative elicits supporting thoughts, it is likely to be endorsed, giving rise to *recency effects*. Hence, a given alternative is more likely to be endorsed when presented early rather than late in a visual format (primacy effect), but when presented late rather than early in an auditory format (recency effect). Sudman *et al.* (1996, chap. 6) review these processes in more depth.

Response order effects are more pronounced for older and less educated respondents (see Knäuper, 1999, for a meta-analysis), whose limited cognitive resources further enhance the focus on a single response alternative. This age-sensitivity of response order effects can invite misleading conclusions about cohort differences in the reported attitude, suggesting, for example, that older respondents are more liberal than younger respondents under one order condition, but more conservative under the other (Schwarz & Knäuper, 2000).

Attitude strength

Survey researchers have long assumed that attitudes vary in their degree of 'strength,' 'centrality,' or 'crystallization,' and that context effects are limited to attitudes that are weak and not (yet) crystallized (e.g., Cantril, 1944; Converse, 1964; see Krosnick & Abelson, 1992, for a review). Despite its popularity, this hypothesis 'has clearly been disconfirmed' as Krosnick and Abelson (1992, p. 193) concluded after an extensive review. In the most comprehensive test, based on

more than a dozen experiments and different self-report measures of attitude strength, Krosnick and Schuman (1988) found no evidence that context effects are stronger for weak attitudes, except for the not surprising finding that respondents with a weak attitude are more likely to choose a middle alternative. This observation contrasts with findings in other domains, where strongly held attitudes have been found to be more stable over time and less likely to change in response to persuasive messages (see Krosnick & Abelson, 1992, for a review). From a social cognition perspective, this apparent discrepancy is not surprising. First, many context effects reflect differences in respondents' inferences about the pragmatic meaning of the question, resulting in answers to somewhat different questions. These effects are unlikely to be influenced by attitude strength. Second, people process persuasive messages and survey interviews with different background assumptions. They understand that persuaders want to influence them and are prepared to scrutinize their arguments (Friestad & Wright, 1994). In contrast, they assume that survey interviews are intended to assess rather than change their opinions. Moreover, the thoughts brought to mind by preceding questions are their own thoughts, and drawing on these thoughts seems less problematic than accepting the arguments presented by others, who may be following their own agenda. As a result, the question–answer sequence of survey interviews can elicit attitude and behavior change that goes far beyond what skilled persuaders can hope to accomplish (e.g., Morwitz, Johnson, & Schmittlein, 1993).

Finally, it is worth noting that mental construal models of attitude judgment, like the inclusion/exclusion model (Schwarz & Bless, 1992a) presented above, can account for stability as well as change in attitude judgments. Empirically, an attitude is considered 'stable' when respondents provide highly similar judgments at two points in time. From a construal perspective, this is to be expected when the question is presented in the same or a highly similar context or when the amount and extremity of chronically accessible information exceeds the amount and extremity of contextual information. Construal models can therefore conceptualize the context dependency as well as independency of attitude judgments and specify the conditions under which each may be observed (see Schwarz & Bohner, 2001).

FORMATTING THE RESPONSE

Having formed a judgment, respondents usually need to format it to fit the response alternatives provided by the researcher. An issue that needs particular attention at this stage emerges when respondents are asked to rate several items along the same rating scale. As numerous experiments have demonstrated, respondents use the most extreme items of a set to anchor the endpoints of the scale (see Parducci, 1965; Ostrom & Upshaw, 1968). As a result, a given item will be rated as less extreme if presented in the context of a more extreme one than if presented in the context of a less extreme one. This undermines the comparability of ratings across studies when the same item is presented in the context of other, differentially extreme items.

EDITING THE RESPONSE

Finally, respondents may want to edit their response before they communicate it, reflecting considerations of social desirability and self-presentation. This is particularly likely when the question is threatening (see DeMaio, 1984, for a review). Editing is more pronounced in face-to-face interviews than in self-administered questionnaires, which provide a higher degree of confidentiality (e.g., Smith, 1979; Krysan, Schuman, Scott, & Beatty, 1994). All methods designed to reduce socially desirable responding address one of these two factors (see Bradburn et al., 2004, chap. 3, for a review and advice).

Although socially desirable responding is undoubtedly a threat to the validity of survey results, many of the more robust findings

may reflect the impact of several distinct processes. For example, white respondents have frequently been found to mute negative sentiments about African-Americans when the interviewer is black rather than white (e.g., Williams, 1964; Hatchett & Schuman, 1976). From a social desirability perspective, the answers they provide to the interviewer are assumed not to reflect their 'true' attitudes. However, the friendly conversation with a middle class African-American interviewer may itself serve as input into the attitude judgment, resulting in (temporary) 'real' attitude change, much as incidental exposure to the names or pictures of liked African-Americans has been found to affect attitudes toward the group in laboratory experiments (e.g., Bodenhausen, Schwarz, Bless, & Wänke, 1995). Hence, the impact of social desirability *per se* is often difficult to isolate in survey data. Moreover, social desirability certainly affects everyday behavior, including interracial interactions. Its influence should therefore not be regarded as a simple artifact of survey interviewing; nor may we want to eliminate it when our goal is to predict everyday behavior.

CONCLUDING REMARKS

As this selective review illustrates, research into the cognitive and communicative processes underlying survey responses has moved far beyond the 'art of asking questions' (Payne, 1951) and increasingly provides a scientific grounding for questionnaire design. The accumulating insights provide a useful framework for the wording and ordering of questions and the choice of response alternatives (Sudman et al., 1996; Tourangeau et al., 2000). Moreover, the new techniques of cognitive interviewing allow us to identify problems before a survey goes into the field (Schwarz & Sudman, 1996).

At the same time, there is no hope for a silver bullet that eliminates the context dependency of respondents' answers. Instead, the emerging picture is consistent with current research in social and cognitive psychology that emphasizes the situated and constructive nature of human judgment (for reviews see Schwarz, 2000; Smith & Semin, 2004). From this perspective, judgment stands in the service of action, and merely retrieving opinions formed in the past may not serve us well. To guide action, a useful system of judgment should be informed by past experience, but be highly sensitive to the specifics of the present; it should overweight recent experience and experience from similar situations, and take current goals and concerns into account—in short, it should be highly *context sensitive*. Unfortunately, respondents bring this context sensitivity to the interview, where it creates a serious challenge for public opinion research; to the extent that respondents' judgments reflect the immediate context created in the survey interview, generalizations to the population are fraught with uncertainty. There is no reliable solution to this challenge. The best we can do is to increase the odds that we become aware of contextual influences by embedding experiments in regular surveys.

REFERENCES

Belson, W. A. (1981). *The design and understanding of survey questions*. Aldershot: Gower.

Bishop, G. F., Oldendick, R. W., & Tuchfarber, A. J. (1986). Opinions on fictitious issues: the pressure to answer survey questions. *Public Opinion Quarterly, 50*, 240–250.

Bless, H., Schwarz, N., & Wänke, M. (2003). The size of context effects in social judgment. In J. P. Forgas, K. D. Williams & W. von Hippel (Eds.), *Social judgments: Implicit and explicit processes* (pp. 180–197). Cambridge, UK: Cambridge University Press.

Bodenhausen, G. V., & Wyer, R. S. (1987). Social cognition and social reality: Information acquisition and use in the laboratory and the real world. In H. J. Hippler, N. Schwarz & S. Sudman (Eds.), *Social information processing and survey methodology* (pp. 6–41). New York: Springer Verlag.

Bodenhausen, G. V., Schwarz, N., Bless, H., & Wänke, M. (1995). Effects of atypical exemplars on racial beliefs: Enlightened racism or generalized appraisals? *Journal of Experimental Social Psychology, 31*, 48–63.

Bradburn, N., Sudman, S., & Wansink, B. (2004). *Asking questions* (2nd ed.). San Francisco: Jossey Bass.

Cannell, C. F., Marquis, K. H., & Laurent, A. (1977). A summary of studies of interviewing methodology. *Vital and Health Statistics*, Series 2, No. 69 (DHEW Publication No. HRA 77-1343). Washington, DC: Government Printing Office.

Cantril, H. (1944) *Gauging public opinion*. Princeton, NJ: Princeton University Press.

Clark, H. H., & Schober, M. F. (1992). Asking questions and influencing answers. In J. M. Tanur (Ed.), *Questions about questions* (pp. 15–48). New York: Russell-Sage.

Converse, P. E. (1964). The nature of belief systems in the mass public. In D. E. Apter (Ed.), *Ideology and discontent* (pp. 206–261). New York: Free Press.

DeMaio, T. J. (1984). Social desirability and survey measurement: A review. In C. F. Turner & E. Martin (Eds.), *Surveying subjective phenomena* (Vol. 2, pp. 257–281). New York: Russell Sage.

DeMaio, T. J., & Rothgeb, J. M. (1996). Cognitive interviewing techniques: In the lab and in the field. In N. Schwarz & S. Sudman (Eds.), *Answering questions: Methodology for determining cognitive and communicative processes in survey research* (pp. 177–196). San Francisco: Jossey Bass.

Erikson, R. S., Luttbeg, N. R., & Tedin, K.T. (1988). *American public opinion* (3rd ed.). New York: Macmillan.

Feldman, J. M., & Lynch, J. G. (1988). Self-generated validity and other effects of measurement on belief, attitude, intention, and behavior. *Journal of Applied Psychology, 73*, 421–435.

Fowler, F. J., & Cannell, C. F. (1996). Using behavioral coding to identify cognitive problems with survey questions. In N. Schwarz & S. Sudman (Eds.), *Answering questions: Methodology for determining cognitive and communicative processes in survey research* (pp. 15–36). San Francisco: Jossey Bass.

Friestad, M., & Wright, P. (1994). The persuasion knowledge model: How people cope with persuasion attempts. *Journal of Consumer Research, 21*, 1–31.

Grice, H. P. (1975). Logic and conversation. In P. Cole, & J. L. Morgan (Eds.), *Syntax and semantics, Vol. 3: Speech acts* (pp. 41–58). New York: Academic Press.

Hatchett, S., & Schuman, H. (1976). White respondents and race of interviewer effects. *Public Opinion Quarterly, 39*, 523–528.

Knäuper, B. (1999). The impact of age and education on response order effects in attitude measurement. *Public Opinion Quarterly, 63*, 347–370.

Krosnick, J. A., & Abelson, R. P. (1992). The case for measuring attitude strength. In J. M. Tanur (Ed.), *Questions about questions* (pp. 177–203). New York: Russell-Sage.

Krosnick, J. A., & Alwin, D. F. (1987). An evaluation of a cognitive theory of response order effects in survey measurement. *Public Opinion Quarterly, 51,* 201–219.

Krosnick, J. A., & Schuman, H. (1988). Attitude intensity, importance, and certainty and susceptibility to response effects. *Journal of Personality and Social Psychology, 54,* 940–952.

Krysan, M., Schuman, H., Scott, L. J., & Beatty, P. (1994). Response rates and response content in mail versus face-to-face surveys. *Public Opinion Quarterly, 58,* 381–399.

Lessler, J. T., & Forsyth, B. H. (1996). A coding system for appraising questionnaires. In N. Schwarz & S. Sudman (Eds.), *Answering questions: Methodology for determining cognitive and communicative processes in survey research* (pp. 259–292). San Francisco: Jossey Bass.

Morwitz, V., Johnson, E., & Schmittlein, D. (1993). Does measuring intent change behavior? *Journal of Consumer Research, 20,* 46–61.

Norenzayan, A., & Schwarz, N. (1999). Telling what they want to know: Participants tailor causal attributions to researchers' interests. *European Journal of Social Psychology, 29,* 1011–1020.

Ostrom, T. M., & Upshaw, H. S. (1968). Psychological perspective and attitude change. In A. C. Greenwald, T. C. Brock, & T. M. Ostrom (Eds.), *Psychological foundations of attitudes* (pp. 217–242). New York: Academic Press.

Parducci, A. (1965). Category judgments: A range-frequency model. *Psychological Review, 72,* 407–418.

Payne, S. L. (1951). *The art of asking questions.* Princeton: Princeton University Press.

Schuman, H., & Presser, S. (1981). *Questions and answers in attitude surveys.* New York: Academic Press.

Schwarz, N. (1996). *Cognition and communication: Judgmental biases, research methods, and the logic of conversation.* Hillsdale, NJ: Erlbaum.

Schwarz, N. (1999). Self-reports: How the questions shape the answers. *American Psychologist, 54,* 93–105.

Schwarz, N. (2000). Agenda 2000: Attitudes and social judgment—Warmer, more social, and less conscious. *European Journal of Social Psychology, 30,* 149–176.

Schwarz, N., & Bless, H. (1992a). Constructing reality and its alternatives: Assimilation and contrast effects in social judgment. In L. L. Martin & A. Tesser (Eds.), *The construction of social judgments* (pp. 217–245). Hillsdale, NJ: Erlbaum.

Schwarz, N., & Bless, H. (1992b). Scandals and the public's trust in politicians: Assimilation and contrast

effects. *Personality and Social Psychology Bulletin, 18,* 574–579.

Schwarz, N., & Bless, H. (2007). Mental construal processes: The inclusion/exclusion model. In D. A. Stapel & J. Suls (Eds.), *Assimilation and contrast in social psychology* (pp. 119–141) Philadelphia, PA: Psychology Press.

Schwarz, N., & Bohner, G. (2001). The construction of attitudes. In A. Tesser & N. Schwarz (Eds.), *Blackwell handbook of social psychology: Intraindividual processes* (Vol.1, pp. 436–457). Oxford, UK: Blackwell.

Schwarz, N., & Hippler, H. J. (1991). Response alternatives: The impact of their choice and ordering. In P. Biemer, R. Groves, N. Mathiowetz, & S. Sudman (Eds.), *Measurement error in surveys* (pp. 41–56). Chichester: Wiley.

Schwarz, N., & Hippler, H. J. (1995). Subsequent questions may influence answers to preceding questions in mail surveys. *Public Opinion Quarterly, 59,* 93–97.

Schwarz, N., & Knäuper, B. (2000). Cognition, aging, and self-reports. In D. Park & N. Schwarz (Eds.), *Cognitive aging. A primer* (pp. 233–252). Philadelphia, PA: Psychology Press.

Schwarz, N., Knäuper, B., Hippler, H. J., Noelle-Neumann, E., & Clark, F. (1991). Rating scales: Numeric values may change the meaning of scale labels. *Public Opinion Quarterly, 55,* 570–582.

Schwarz, N., & Oyserman, D. (2001). Asking questions about behavior: Cognition, communication and questionnaire construction. *American Journal of Evaluation, 22,* 127–160.

Schwarz, N., Strack, F., & Mai, H.P. (1991). Assimilation and contrast effects in part-whole question sequences: A conversational logic analysis. *Public Opinion Quarterly, 55,* 3–23.

Schwarz, N., & Sudman, S. (1996). *Answering questions: Methodology for determining cognitive and communicative processes in survey research.* San Francisco: Jossey-Bass.

Sirken, M., Hermann, D., Schechter, S., Schwarz, N., Tanur, J., & Tourangeau, R. (Eds.) (1999). *Cognition and survey research.* New York: Wiley.

Smith, E. R., & Semin, G. R. (2004). Socially situated cognition: Cognition in its social context. *Advances in Experimental Social Psychology, 36,* 53–117.

Smith, T. W. (1979). Happiness. *Social Psychology Quarterly, 42,* 18–30.

Strack, F., & Martin, L. (1987). Thinking, judging, and communicating: A process account of context effects in attitude surveys. In H. J. Hippler, N. Schwarz, & S. Sudman (Eds.), *Social information processing and survey methodology* (pp. 123–148). New York: Springer Verlag.

Strack, F., Schwarz, N., & Wänke, M. (1991). Semantic and pragmatic aspects of context effects in social and psychological research. *Social Cognition, 9*, 111–125.

Sudman, S., Bradburn, N. M., & Schwarz, N. (1996). *Thinking about answers: The application of cognitive processes to survey methodology.* San Francisco, CA: Jossey-Bass.

Tourangeau, R. (1984). Cognitive science and survey methods: A cognitive perspective. In T. Jabine, M. Straf, J. Tanur, & R. Tourangeau (Eds.), *Cognitive aspects of survey methodology: Building a bridge between disciplines* (pp. 73–100). Washington, DC: National Academy Press.

Tourangeau, R. (1992). Attitudes as memory structures: belief sampling and context effects. In N. Schwarz & S. Sudman (Eds.), *Context effects in social and psychological research* (pp. 35–47). New York: Springer Verlag.

Tourangeau, R., Rips, L. J., & Rasinski, K. (2000). *The psychology of survey response.* Cambridge: Cambridge University Press.

Wänke, M., & Schwarz, N. (1997). Reducing question order effects: The operation of buffer items. In L. Lyberg, P. Biemer, M. Collins, E. DeLeeuw, C. Dippo, & N. Schwarz (Eds.), *Survey measurement and process quality* (pp. 115–140). Chichester, UK: Wiley.

Williams, J. A. (1964). Interviewer-respondent interaction: A study of bias in the information interview. *Sociometry, 27*, 338–352.

Zaller, J. R. (1992). *The nature and origins of mass opinion.* Cambridge: Cambridge University Press.

35

The Use of Scales in Surveys

Michael Häder

As in the natural sciences, research is conducted in the social sciences in order both to test empirical presumptions and to provide answers to problems. Whereas the natural scientist uses balances, rulers and meters, the social scientist mainly uses scales to obtain information about attitudes, values and intentions. Empirical social science uses methods of scale construction to develop scales. This chapter introduces the most common and established techniques of scale construction. Moreover, it examines the vast variety of measurement instruments employed by the social sciences. Finally two approaches that graphically illustrate the objects under investigation will be discussed. For further details on scaling techniques and related methods see, for example, Borg and Staufenbiel (1997) and Miller (1991).

As a result of both fields relying on measurement, research in both the natural sciences and the social sciences show some similarities. The object to be measured and its characteristics, e.g. the distance from the moon to the earth or the magnitude of a cell, determine the range of measurement instruments to be used. Social scientists also use certain scales to measure

political orientations, norms or past behaviors, among other concepts. These include Likert, Guttman, and Thurstone scaling, and other unfolding techniques that assume a unidimensional attitude structure, as well as Multidimensional Scaling (MDS) that does not. Moreover, Chernoff faces can be used to represent such findings. The purpose of this article is to provide an overview of scaling techniques.

Generally speaking, the objects to be measured are compared with a known equivalent. In the physical sciences, the scale of a ruler depicts the length of a certain object. The mercury's elongation shows a certain temperature. In this sense, numbers are descriptions of objects under investigation (cf. Stevens, 1951). The result of a reading represents data that characterize the measured object. The same applies to social science research. To measure the interest of a certain group of people in policy, for example, a set of questions can be used—for instance: 'Do you read political comments in newspapers?,' 'Do you attend political events?' or 'Do you go to vote?' Every answer depicts a certain value, and the 'total' of all answers reflects one person's interest in a particular policy.

In this regard, the question of whether a measurement instrument is properly working or not—its validity and reliability—are of high importance in both the natural and the social science.

All measurement instruments in the natural sciences as well as in the social sciences are very sensitive. The way a scale is constructed has an influence on respondent's reaction to it. Even little changes in question wording or in the number of statements lead to changes in respondents' behavior. For instance, it is not the same if one asks 'Should that kind of behavior be not allowed?' or 'Should that kind of behavior be forbidden?' Furthermore, one will get different results when using four- or six-point scales. A last example is the following question: 'How much time do you spend watching television?' In the first version, the answer scale is as follows: (a) less than 1/2 hour, (b) 1/2 to 1 hour, (c) more than 1 hour, up to 1½ hours, and (d) more than 1½ hours. The second version is: (a) less than 2 hours, (b) more than 2 hours, up to 2½ hours, (c) more than 2½ hours up to 3 hours, and (d) more than 3 hours. Each version will bring different results for the mean time watching TV question. For more information on the theoretical background to all of this, see the chapter written by Norbert Schwarz in this book (→ *The Psychology of Survey Response*).

The chapter is organized so that the general steps of constructing a scale are examined. They include:

1 Operationalization of the problem under consideration: complex issues should be split, theoretically, into precise dimensions. For example, an attitude towards an object to be measured comprises a cognitive, evaluative and behavioral dimension.
2 The next step is to collect (sometimes up to 100) statements that describe the dimensions used. Such statements are usually called 'items' and are collected from different sources such as the literature, by the researcher's own deliberation, empirical pilot studies, or by analyzing diaries or the like. During the item construction process, unsuitable statements will be discarded. It is important to note that on an average, a researcher starts with about four times as many statements as end up in the final scales. Here is an example: 'The public integration of immigrants is much discussed as a problem. Please list three possible opinions on this topic.' Think aloud answers could be the following: (1) 'Foreigners do enrich our society.' (2) 'Foreigners do threaten our jobs.' (3) 'I am not interested in foreigners.'
3 A third step involves the elimination of duplicate or equivalent statements and a revision of the items collected. In this connection, the researcher takes into consideration that these statements shall later serve as questions in a questionnaire.
4 A further step consists of the standardization of the scales under development. The Likert-scaling technique, Guttman-scaling and the approach of Thurston and Chave are supposed to produce reliable instruments.
5 The statements that remain are employed to construct the final scale used for measurement.

LIKERT SCALES

Likert Scaling is also called the technique of summed ratings (Likert, 1932). Because of its simplicity, it is supposed to be one of the most favored techniques. Only a limited number of statements is needed, and a particular population is asked to assess them. Usually a five-point scale response format is used:

How much you agree with the following statement […]? Do you …

1 Strongly agree
2 Agree
3 Undecided/ Neither agree nor disagree
4 Disagree
5 Strongly disagree

Based on the reaction of the respondent in terms of degrees of agreement or disagreement, response alternatives are weighted, e.g. the answer 'undecided' gets three points. The overall score is obtained by summing the points of all items.

However, some items possibly measure anything but the desired dimension. Those that do not describe the specified issue well need to be determined, because they will be eliminated. The next step is to compare all responses with a reference level. Only items that best fit the reference level are selected for inclusion into a final scale. However, a specific standard value does not exist. Hence the sum of the weights of all items for each respondent is used. It is assumed that the sum of all given responses is a good approximation of the attitude of a respondent under study. Therefore item scores are correlated with total scores (item total correlations). A high correlation suggests the item represents the attitude well. In this manner, the researcher can determine whether all listed items fit the same dimension or not; items with low average item-total correlations can be discarded.

This analysis also shows how well single items discriminate. The attitudes of respondents under consideration can be of different intensity. The researcher can expect the measurement instrument to be sensitive enough to show differences between respondents, that is, to have a discriminating quality. For that purpose, respondents with high scores (the highest quartile) are compared with respondents who obtained only low scores (the lowest quartile). It is obvious that statements answered similarly by both groups have only low discriminating quality. Those items should also be eliminated. In this way, suitable and unsuitable items are gradually identified.

To compensate for the tendency of many respondents to answer 'agree' (cf. Carr, 1971), about half of the items should be negatively formulated to reduce response acquiescence. During analysis, these items need to be recoded in a way that the extent of the respondent's agreement can be considered as an indicator of the intensity of the attitude under study. The total score of each respondent is also called its 'discriminatory power' (cf. Wittenberg, 1998, pp. 95ff.; Wittenberg & Cramer, 2000, pp. 139ff.; Brosius, 2002, pp. 768ff.). Computer software such as SPSS uses reliability analysis to calculate discriminatory power. The result is called the 'Corrected Item-Total Correlation.' Discriminatory power measures the contributory power and adequacy of an item in respect

to the final scale. High discriminatory power indicates close correlation between certain items and the total scores. The output of SPSS indicating 'α if item deleted' depicts another important indication of the final scale's quality. Certain items correlate comparatively weakly with total scores. An increase in the quality of the final scale can be expected from exclusion of this item and is represented by 'Cronbach's α,' which is an indicator of a scale's reliability. Cronbach's α should amount to at least 0.8.

However it is important to say that Cronbach's α does not represent a sufficient measure of the scale's dimensionality (cf. Brosius, 2002, p. 767). The value is much higher if the correlation of the single item with the final score is higher. It is obvious to assume that this is a one-dimensional scale. However it is also easily conceivable that two or more dimensions that highly correlate with each other are measured. To identify such relationships, a factor analysis of the remaining items needs to be performed. The aim is to obtain a single factor that describes all items included in the scale.

SCALOGRAM ANALYSIS

The following is considered to be the underlying assumption for Scalogram Analysis: all of the items in a scale can be ordered with regard to their complexity. This method can be easily illustrated for the items that constitute a test or examination. An examination usually includes questions of different levels of difficulty. The tester assumes that examinees holding comprehensive knowledge are able to answer all questions. Persons holding median levels of knowledge will probably answer only the easy or moderately difficult questions. Finally, examinees with only limited knowledge will probably answer only the easy questions, and people with hardly any knowledge will answer none of the questions asked. Based on this assumption, the exam questions can be sorted in anodic order. Consequently all questions will be answered correctly by a person until a reversal point, after which all the following questions are answered wrong. The position of this point on a scale would represent the obtained mark. In terms of Scalogram-Analysis, the assumption of such a reversal point is also called deterministic step function (cf. Guttman, 1944, 1947). In relation to the number of items n, only $n+1$ combinations of answers should be considered, even though 2^n combinations are possible. In the case of five items only six logically correct combinations do exist, but 2^5 ($2 \times 2 \times 2 \times 2 \times 2 = 32$) are empirically possible. That is 26 combinations are theoretically excluded. They are deemed to be defaults.

One can get a better understanding of Scalogram Analysis by thinking about the extent or the existence of a certain attitude instead of exam knowledge. One variable would achieve the lowest agreement, because it contains the simplest answer that most respondents agree with. Accordingly, respondents will not agree with the contrary variable. Respondents sharing that point of view now highly agree with the issue under study. The remaining items are situated between these two poles, and they can be ordered as above. The quality of such a scale can be determined by the computation of its coefficient of reproducibility (CR). This statistic provides information about the extent to which the assumption of a one-dimensional scale is actually realized. The commonly accepted value of CR should not be less than 0.9, based upon the following calculation:

$$CR = 1 - \text{number of defects}/(\text{number of items} \times \text{number of respondents})$$

By Scalogram Analysis, the resulting scale is ordinal. Accordingly, it is only based on a ranking. Similar to reliability analysis, SPSS software can be used to compute Scalogram Analysis.

THURSTON TECHNIQUE

As mentioned above, the researcher must first assemble a large set of candidate items.

In doing so, the researcher creates a pool of statements with regard to the issue under consideration. Then a group of calibration respondents, heterogeneously assembled, is asked to sort the items into given categories (Thurstone & Chave, 1929). This procedure results in an intensity scale that consists of 11 piles of items representing an evenly graduated series of attitudes from 'extremely positive' (pile 11) through 'extremely negative' (pile 1). Subjects are asked not to answer regarding their own attitudes to the issue under consideration (as is the case with the Likert scale), but rather to rate the given statements. An eleven-point scale printed on a slip of paper and a set of cards, each listing a single item is given to calibration respondents to ease their task. In this manner they can be considered as 'experts.'

At the end, a researcher can first determine whether or not there are statements within the item pool for each of the 11 piles of the scale, and whether the extreme poles of the attitude continuum are sufficiently covered by items. Second, it becomes clear which points of the scale are covered by multiple statements. As a result, the number of given items can possibly be reduced. Third, the dispersion range indicates the quality of each single statement—for example, statements that were equally assigned to all eleven piles by the calibration respondents do very little to measure the attitudes. Compared to this, the unanimous allocation of a given statement to one single pile of the scale by calibration respondents can be interpreted as an indicator of a distinctive phrasing of that statement. At the end of this process, the final scale contains only the items that were not eliminated. Later, in a second step, respondents are asked to show which statements they agree or disagree with. Finally the scores of all items with which a subject agreed are summed. Each item of the derived scale has another scale value, different than the one used to measure each item in it. This scale value is computed on the basis of the variance of the expert's calibration. It is equal to the median (the 50th percentile of the calibration by all the respondents).

UNFOLDING—COOMBS SCALE

The unfolding technique goes back to Coombs (cf. 1950, 1964). Its basic assumption is that all elements of a scale can be arranged in a row and that there is a consensus on this arrangement. This method is explained in detail by both Borg and Staufenbiel (1997, pp. 161ff.) and Bortz and Döring (2002, pp. 227ff.). This technique is illustrated with the following example of political party preference.

- At first, all political parties are arranged on a left-right dimension, and an assumption is made that the spacing between political parties is equal. Coombs called this scale 'I-Scale.' For Germany, this dimension could be (from right to left): REP – FDP – CDU/CSU – SPD – Green Party – PDS.
- This arrangement is considered by all respondents to be mandatory.
- Every person A, B, and C has his or her own ideal point on the scale. This scale is called 'J-Scale.' The hierarchy of Person A is: 1. PDS, 2. Green Party, 3. SPD, 4. CDU/CSU, 5. FDP, 6. REP. Person B preferred: 1. REP, 2. FDP, 3. CDU/CSU, 4. SPD, 5. Green Party, 6. PDS. The sequence of Person C is: 1. CDU/CSU, 2. SPD, 3. FDP, 4. Green Party, 5. PDS, 6. REP.
- Accordingly, each person prefers the political party that is closest to this ideal point. The rating of all other parties is conducted on the basis of the distances from this ideal point.

However, in practice political party preferences are surveyed simultaneously among a number of persons. Based on their empirically determined preferences, an order is compiled for the sample or population. This procedure will only work based on the assumption that the spacings between individual parties are different. Moreover, it is not self-evident that all empirically possible hierarchies can be depicted on a scale.

Subject A can be characterized as politically left orientated. If asked, this person would prefer the Party of Democratic Socialism (PDS) most. Subject C is situated quite centrally on the scale. That person is closed to the Christian Democratic Union (CDU/CSU), followed by the Social Democratic Party (SPD), and so on. Eventually the political party preference of subject B would be reciprocal to that of subject A. Although all three subjects prefer different political parties, it seems highly probable that they perceive the spectrum of political parties in Germany in the same manner. Therefore, the unidimensionality of the Coombs Scale is confirmed.

Taking all six parties, there are $6! = 6 \times 5 \times 4 \times 3 \times 2 \times 1 = 720$ different rank orders that can be compiled. However, in practice there are far fewer rank orders actually used by the respondents. The empirical solution to that scaling problem can be found by searching for inverse rank orders, as was done for subjects A and B. In a narrow sense—with unidimensionality assumed—only the following two rank orders can be determined:

REP → FDP → CDU/CSU → SPD →Green Party → PDS

PDS → Green Party → SPD → CDU/CSU →FDP → REP

In the case of these rankings, the spaces between political parties are similar. However certain empirically observable rank orders cannot be arranged within this model. Only if one takes into account that the FDP is closer to the CDU/CSU than to the REP, does the determined rank ordering for subject C seem plausible.

All in all, Coombs Scales feature the following characteristics:

- They are empirically highly falsifiable: Only $0.5 \times n \times (n-1) + 1 (= 16)$ scales of $n!$ possible scales are admissible.
- They are complex to develop.
- Coombs Scales are metric scales because spaces between political parties can be determined.

CONJOINT ANALYSIS

Originally, Conjoint Analysis was used in market research. It was developed by Luce and Tukey (1964) and is also called Conjoint Measurement (CM). Within empirical social research, this technique has clearly gained in importance over the last several years. For further details see also Backhaus, Erickson, Plinke, and Weiber (2000, pp. 564ff.) and Borg and Staufenbiel (1997, pp. 194ff.).

In the following example illustrating this method, the automobile industry will be used as an example. To simplify matters, it is assumed that the subjective value of a car contains only two relevant factors (A and B). A is the length of the warranty offered (3, 2 or 1 years) and B represents the manufacturing country (Japan or Germany). Subsequently a combination of these two linking elements can be applied to every car. The respondent's task is to rank all possible combinations on each of six cars (3 × 2). Accordingly cars from Japan with a 3-year warranty are best liked, followed by German cars with 3 years warranty. The next is a car from Japan with a 2-year warranty, and so on. Least liked are cars manufactured in Germany with an offered warranty of only one year.

The main aim of CM is to find scale values that can be used to replace the features of the cars. In doing so, the following principles apply: the lower the rank, the higher the preference for a car. The overall preference is determined by summing up the partial-worth utilities of a car. See the following calculation for illustration:

$$y = \mu + \beta A + \beta B$$

where

β represents partial-worth utility for a single feature of a car (A or B);

μ is a constant item;

y is the estimated total utility.

For the example mentioned above, μ (average rank or base utility) is computed as follows:

$$\mu = (1 + 2 + 3 + 4 + 5 + 6)/6 = 3.5$$

β (average of all rank values) is calculated by averaging the measured ranks. In the case of feature A with the one-year warranty, the computation results in rank one and two.

Table 35.1 (Notional) Part-worth utility of the cars under consideration

| | | Characteristic B | | | |
		1	2	pA	pA − p
	1	2	1	1.5	−2.0
Characteristic A	2	3	4	3.5	0
	3	6	5	5.5	2.0
pB		3.6667	3.3333		
pB − p		0.1667	−0.1667		

That is:

$$\beta A = (2 + 1)/2 = 1.5$$

This means that the partial-worth utility of A (1.5) falls below the average of 3.5 by 2.0. Now the partial-worth utilities of both 2- and 3-year warranties and feature B can be determined (see Table 35.1):

$$\beta B = (3 + 4)/2 = 3.5$$

Finally, the total utility of every stimulus can be computed. Here the same calculations can be used and the corresponding values applied. See, for example, the calculation for stimulus 1 (car with an offer of a 1-year warranty):

$$yI = 3.5 + (−2.0) + 0.1667 = 1.667$$

Now all the calculated values can be applied to a table (see Table 35.2).

MULTIDIMENSIONAL SCALING

Multidimensional Scaling (MDS) is a statistical technique that graphically visualizes multidimensional issues in a two-dimensional

Table 35.2 (Notional) Set of use utilities from the example above

Stimulus	p	Y
I	2	1,6667
II	1	1,3333
III	3	3,6667
IV	4	3,3333
V	6	5,6667
VI	5	5,3333

Table 35.3   Items for the evaluation of their own working conditions, European Social Survey 2004 (ESS)

Variable name	Shortened text of the questions asked	Assigning to values
Vrtywrk	A lot of variety in my work	G
Jbrqlrn	Job requires that I keep learning	G
Jbscr	Job is secure	E
Wgdpeft	Wage depends on amount of effort I put into my work	E
Hlpcowk	Get support from co-workers	R
Dcsfwrk	Decide the time I start / finish work	G
Hlthrwk	Health is at risk because of my work	E
Wrkhrd	Job requires very hard work	E
Nevdnjb	Never enough time to get everything done	E
Oprtad	Good opportunities for advancement	G

Source: Second round questionnaire of the ESS, for exact wording see
http://www.europeansocialsurvey.org/

or greater space (cf. Kruskal, 1964; Borg & Groenen, 1997; Borg, 2000). The multidimensional scaling procedure is described below by again employing an example, which is based upon one question from the European social survey 2004 (ESS): 'Please tell me how true each of the following statements is about your current job.' The 10 items displayed in Table 35.3 illustrate these items.

Corresponding questions were presented to respondents holding a job. Subjects were asked to use a five point Likert Scale ranging from 'agree strongly' to 'disagree strongly' to answer the questions. The MDS results can be visualized in a two-dimensional space. For this purpose, all 10 responses were correlated. Items are mapped by points in a two-dimensional space in such a way that the proximity of points to each other indicate either how similar (close to each other) or dissimilar (far off from each other) they are. The results from the SPSS procedure ALSCAL (cf. Young & Lewicky, 1980) are presented in Figure 35.1.

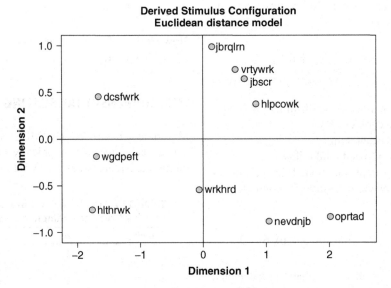

Figure 35.1   Two-dimensional visualization of values via MDS
Population: Europeans in paid work from 26 countries; Sample size: 18.855; Field time: September to December 2004. Source: For data download visit: http://ess.nsd.uib.no

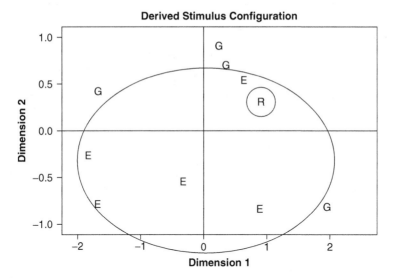

Figure 35.2   Two-dimensional visualization of values via modular partitioning

In the following, the value structure developed by Alderfelder (1972) was tested for whether it is found in the evaluations that respondents' make of their own working conditions. Therefore, Table 35.3 additionally indicates whether items are correlated with Alderfelder's existential-material values (E), growth needs (G) or social-emotional values (R). Moreover, the analysis also tests Alderfelder's assumed value structure (cf. Borg, 2000). For this purpose, a modular partitioning is required that is relatively easy to realize by using a polar pattern. To achieve a better overview, in Figure 35.2 labels for the value dimension are applied to MDS. And in fact, the findings suggest that similarities between Alderfelder's value structure and respondents' judgments on their working conditions can be assumed.

CHERNOFF-FACES

Another possibility for visualizing multivariate characteristics are IconPlots, for example Chernoff Faces, a more trivial form of scaling. Analysis can be computed by software programs such as Statistica. 'IconPlots are multidimensional symbols that represent cases and observational entities' (Statistica Manual, 2005, p. 1). Chernoff Faces display data in the shape of a human face.

Besides Chernoff Faces represented as circles, other symbols such as stars, rays, polygons, columns, lines and profiles can be deployed. The idea behind this is that particular arithmetic charts representing human faces are appropriate for identifying distinctive features in data more quickly. The individual parts of a human face, such as the length of a nose or the height of eyebrows, represent values of the variables by their shape, size, placement and orientation. Simultaneous valuations of 18 situations in which people violently defended themselves against attacks, as well as the sex and age of the respondents, are shown as an example below. One question was, for example: 'A boxer is attacked by four young men in front of a discotheque. He puts the aggressors to flight and slightly hurts them. Was that right or not?' (The wording of the other questions is shown in Table 35.4.) Finally the descriptions of the answers from 12 randomly selected subjects follows the above determined characteristics (see Figure 35.3).

Table 35.4   Assignment of categories of different indicators to characteristics of human faces

Element of face	
Face width	In defence of her parking space a woman suffers from abrasion.
Ear height	A man slightly hurts a bike thief.
Height half of the face	A boxer puts 4 aggressors to flight and slightly hurts them.
Eccentricity upper half	A farmer shoots a fire raiser and heavily hurts him.
Eccentricity lower half	A man shoots four people throwing stones and causes one paraplegia.
Nose length	A housebreaker is killed by stab with a knife.
Position mouth center	A man was knocked down by a stronger one but he fought and stabbed the attacker.
Mouth shape	A driver bothers another driver that subsequently threatens the former. Thereupon the former driver shows a gun and forces the other one to withdraw.
Mouth size	Someone is attacked in a park but is able to defend himself and seriously hurts the attacker.
Height eye center	A house owner sets up a primer containing radio. The radio explodes and harms a housebreaker. He looses one hand.
Eye base	A bar owner heavily hurts two attackers when they intruded.
Eye slant	A man insults another one. During a fight the former gets seriousely injured.
Eye eccentricity	A man slightly hurts a physically superior bike thief.
Eye half length	A boxer puts an attacker to flight and slightly hurts him.
Pupil position	An armed house breaker is killed by a stab with a knife.
Eyebrow height	A man was knocked down by a physically inferior one but he fought and stabbed the attacker.
Eyebrow slope	Someone is attacked in a park. He's able to defend himself and seriously hurts the physically superior attacker.
Eyebrow length	A man bothers another one. The physically inferior former gets seriously hurt during a fight.
Ear radius	Sex of the subject.
Nose size	Age of the subject.

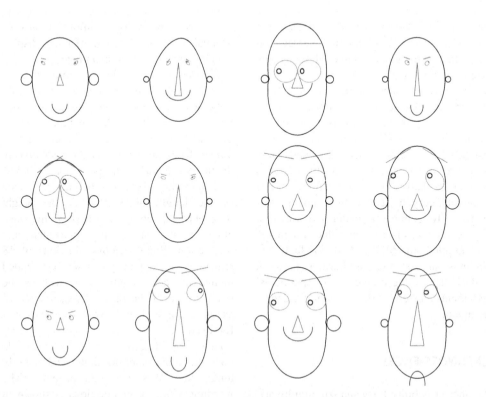

Figure 35.3   Chernoff-Faces to describe the characteristics of 12 subjects
Population: Germans living in housholds from 18 years and older; *Sample size:* The first 12 persons from the data file; *Field time:* October to December 2001. *Source:* Study on Self-defence, Data are available at Central Archive of Empirical Social Research, University of Cologne (ZA), No.ZA4253

SUMMARY AND CONCLUSIONS

At the beginning of this chapter, we focused on the natural sciences and the social sciences. Both have measurement instruments to test empirical presumptions and to provide solutions to problems. The previous discussion shows that the higher the level of measurement in its scientific instruments, the higher the level of the science as a whole. In this chapter, we introduced the most common and established techniques for scale construction in the social sciences. It should be clear now that the development of instrumentation is an important task, and researchers have to pay their full attention to the construction of scales.

REFERENCES

Alderfelder, C.P. (1972). *Existence, relatedness, and growth: Human needs in organizational settings.* New York: Free Press.

Backhaus, K., Erickson, B., Plinke, W., & Weiber, R. (2000): *Multivariate Analysemethoden* [Methods for multivariate analyses]. Heidelberg: Springer.

Borg, I. (2000). Explorative multidimensionale Skalierung [Explorative multidimensional scaling]. *ZUMA How-to-Reihe, 1.* Retrieved January 5, 2007, from http://www.gesis.org/Publikationen/Berichte/ZUMA_How_to/Dokumente/pdf/how-to1ib.pdf.

Borg, I., & Groenen, P. (1997). *Modern multidimensional scaling: Theory and applications.* New York: Springer.

Borg, I., & Staufenbiel, T. (1997). *Theorie und Methoden der Skalierung. Eine Einführung* [Theory and methods for scaling]. Bern: Hans Huber.

Bortz, J., & Döring, N. (2002). *Forschungsmethoden und Evaluation für Human- und Sozialwissenschaftler* [Research methods and evaluation for human- and social researchers] (3rd ed.). Berlin: Springer.

Brosius, F. (2002). *SPSS 11.* Bonn: mitp.

Carr, L. G. (1971). The srole items and acquiescence. *American Sociological Review, 36,* 287–293.

Coombs, C. H. (1950). Psychological scaling without a unit of measurement. *Psychological Review, 57,* 145–158.

Coombs, C. H. (1964). *A theory of data.* New York: Wiley.

Guttman, L. (1944). A basic for scaling qualitative data. *American Sociological Review, 9,* 139–150.

Guttman, L. (1947). The Cornell technique for scale and intensity analysis. *Educational and Psychological Measurement, 7,* 247–279.

Kruskal, J. B. (1964). Multidimensional scaling by optimizing goodness of fit to a nonmetric hypothesis. *Psychometrica, 29,* 115–129.

Likert, R. (1932). A technique for the measurement of attitudes. *Archives of Psychology, 140,* 1–55.

Luce, R. D., & Tukey, J. W. (1964). Simultaneous conjoint measurement: A new type of fundamental measurement. *Journal of Mathematical Psychology, 1,* 1–27.

Statistica Manual (2005). Retrieved February 5, 2007, from http://www.statsoft.com/textbook/stathome.html.

Stevens, S. S. (1951). Mathematics, measurement, and psychophysics. In S. S. Stevens (Ed.), *Handbook of experimental psychology* (pp. 1–49). New York: Wiley.

Miller, D. (1991). *Handbook of Research Design and Social Measurement.* Newbury Park, CA: Sage.

Thurstone, L. L., & Chave, E. J. (1929). *The measurement of attitude.* Chicago: University of Chicago Press.

Young, F. W., & Lewicky, R. (1980). *ALSCAL user guide.* Chapel Hill, NC: Institute for Research in the Social Sciences, University of North Carolina.

Wittenberg, R. (1998). *Grundlagen computerunterstützter Datenanalyse* [Basics for computer aided data analyses]. Stuttgart: Lucius & Lucius.

Wittenberg, R., & Cramer, H. (2000). *Datenanalyse mit SPSS für Windows* [Data analyses with SPSS for Windows] (2nd ed.). Stuttgart: Lucius & Lucius.

36

The Use of Visual Materials in Surveys

Thomas Petersen

Although the use of visual materials plays a major role in applied survey research, this topic is seldom discussed in the methodological literature in the field. There are a variety of reasons for this. To begin with, visual materials are especially important in market and media research—two areas that generally receive little attention in empirical social research. Furthermore, the fact that telephone interviews have, to a great extent, eclipsed traditional face-to-face interviews over recent decades has caused interest in visual materials to wane even further, since visual materials obviously cannot be used in telephone surveys. This trend is problematic for a number of reasons. Aside from narrowing the range of possible questionnaire techniques (see Noelle-Neumann & Petersen, 2000), it also means that key areas of the social sciences can no longer be investigated via the representative survey method. Thus, for example, in many countries today, communication researchers investigating the effect of press photographs or market researchers

conducting surveys on consumer goods are largely forced to rely on surveys that are either not representative or that are geographically limited, because the infrastructure necessary to conduct face-to-face interviews no longer exists.

Couper, Tourangeau, and Kenyon (2004, pp. 257ff.) distinguish between three fundamentally different ways of applying visual materials in surveys: first, visual materials that are intrinsically linked to specific questions, as they are themselves the object of investigation; second, visual materials that serve as supplementary question aids, for example to make the questions easier for respondents to understand; and, third, optical stimuli that are connected to a question or questionnaire but have no independent function in relation to any specific questions. The latter category comprises all of a questionnaire's optical components, such as the color of the paper on which it is printed or the display design and the 'progress bar' used in Internet surveys. Optical elements of this kind are most important in self-administered surveys that are completed in writing or on the Internet, and they also come into play to a certain extent in face-to-face interviews. Although researchers have repeatedly focused on the effects of such optical stimuli (Ring, 1969; Couper, Traugott, & Lamias, 2001; Couper *et al.*, 2004), these elements are not of key concern in the present chapter, which instead aims to outline the various ways of employing those optical stimuli that function as important components of the questions themselves.

VISUAL MATERIALS AS QUESTION AIDS

From the very beginning, the spectrum of investigative materials employed in representative surveys has included not only the questionnaire, but also other materials presented to respondents, such as written lists of response alternatives and lengthier written opinions for respondents to read, along with various visual stimuli. One of the early works in this tradition was George Gallup's dissertation on the 'copytest' method (1928), whereby interviewers present a copy of a newspaper to respondents and then look through it with them page by page. Even more important for the development of visual stimuli employed in representative surveys, however, were influences from the field of psychology.

The simplest and probably most widespread way of employing visual materials in survey research is in the form of question aids such as graphic rating scales that enable respondents to rank thoughts that would otherwise be difficult to express in numerical terms—for example, how strongly they agree with a certain political standpoint—within a structured, numerical framework, which in turn enables researchers to analyze the intensity of respondents' opinions based on quantitative data.

Over the decades, a number of rating scales of various designs were developed to assist respondents in answering questions.

One early example presented in Hadley Cantril's *Gauging Public Opinion* (1944, p. 54) is Daniel Katz's 'voting thermometer,' which allowed respondents to indicate how likely they were to vote in the 1940 US presidential elections. In the 1950s, the Dutch researcher Jan Stapel designed a rating scale that was later named after him that consists of five black boxes and five white boxes stacked on top of one another, enabling respondents to rate issues or individuals positively or negatively (Figure 36.1). This scale has proved to be both extremely useful and valid in many studies, for example, when measuring the popularity of politicians or other public figures (Auer, 1981).

In subsequent decades, a variety of scales were developed utilizing this same basic

Figure 36.1   The Stapel scale

principle, whereby each scale combines a breakdown into numerical intervals with a readily comprehensible optical design illustrating the object of the investigation at hand. Such scales range from simple ladders and measuring tapes to ladders drawn in perspective to symbolize the proximity to or distance from a certain standpoint or issue, up to unconventional models such as that shown in Figure 36.2, meant to measure the subjective feeling of how quickly time passes by at work. In the meantime, numerous experimental investigations have thoroughly documented the effect of such scalar material on response behavior (Smith, 1995; Schwarz, 1996, pp. 46ff.; Petersen, 2002, pp. 203ff., → *The Use of Scales in Surveys*).

Along with rating scales, a great variety of other visual materials are used as question aids—for example, illustrations on which respondents can distribute cards or, when testing geographical knowledge, maps they can mark their responses on.

Dialog questions, which are used in projective tests, represent the borderline to the next category of visual materials that will be dealt with here. Using such dialog illustrations, respondents are shown a sketch of two (or occasionally more) persons drawn in silhouette. As in comic strips, each person has his or her own balloon containing an opinion on a particular issue. Respondents are asked to say which of the two points of view they tend to agree with. This is one of the oldest, most proven question models in survey research. Questions of this kind were first employed in surveys in the United States in the 1940s and were soon adopted in other countries, even though, it is interesting to note, comic strips were not yet an established part of contemporary culture in most of those countries at the time. Illustrations of this kind allow researchers to present somewhat longer and more complex opinions to respondents in a refreshing way, helping to enliven the interview. Questions using this technique are, however, susceptible to order effects.

VISUAL AIDS FOR PSYCHOLOGICAL DIAGNOSTICS IN SURVEY RESEARCH

Projective methods

Projective methods are among the most versatile and scientifically valuable ways in which visual materials can be applied in representative surveys. Like many other question models, such methods were first developed in the field of psychology and then adapted by survey researchers to meet the requirements of structured representative surveys. Using questions of this type, respondents are asked to imagine that they are in a certain situation

Question: 'How quickly does time pass when you are at work? Of course, this is difficult to say, so I've brought along an illustration. The number 1 on the sheet would mean that time almost stands still, and 7 that time passes extremely quickly. Which number from 1 to 7 best applies to the time when you are at work?'

Figure 36.2 Scale: 'How quickly does time pass?'
Source: Allensbach Archives. *Reprinted by permission of the Allensbach Institute*

and to respond from this perspective. In many cases, respondents are given visual materials to help them envision the situation. Projective tests were originally devised in order to learn something about the individual test subjects.

In contrast, projective tests tailored to the requirements of survey research generally aim to ascertain the associative context of a particular object of investigation. Projective tests used in survey research are thus similar to association tests, but they are much more versatile in terms of the forms they can take and the variety of situations in which they can be used. Two of the most well known types of projective tests are sentence completion questions, which are used in conjunction with visual aids, and the thematic apperception test (TAT) devised by Henry and Murray (1943). The method has also been applied in market research. For instance, in a projective test used in a market research survey on the topic of laundry detergents—modeled on the thematic apperception test—respondents are shown an illustration of a woman sitting in a chair and listening to the radio and are then asked the following question: 'Please take a look at this picture. A woman is sitting there and hears the following announcement on the radio: "For your laundry: tried and tested for generations." In your opinion, what does the woman think when she hears that on the radio, what thoughts might come to her mind?'

Other methods derived from psychological diagnostics

Along with projective techniques, there are a number of other question models employing visual aids that derive from single-case diagnostic methods originally developed in the field of psychology, but which can be adapted to the methodological requirements of representative surveys. Examples of such question models include intelligence tests or emotion tests (see Rosenzweig, 1945). Even classic methods from the field of clinical psychology, such as the Rorschach test, can

be employed in representative surveys (Ring, 1992, pp. 177ff.).

When using such methods, one basic logical step has to be taken. As these methods were originally designed to determine the psychological characteristics or psychological state of single individuals, they are generally highly complex and comprise a number of complicated components. As these original investigative approaches would be far too onerous and complex for interviews in representative surveys, they must be radically shortened and simplified. Nevertheless, they still obtain valid findings, since representative surveys do not aim to arrive at a correct diagnosis with respect to specific individuals. Rather, as is true of all analytical questions, such questions aim to distinguish between different segments of the population. This principle is illustrated by the indicator of technical intelligence shown in Figure 36.3. Not every person who correctly responds to a question such as this, which derives from a psychological intelligence test, is necessarily intelligent, but the group of respondents who answered correctly—the box will move downwards because the wheel unwinds more cable than it winds up each time it revolves—will include more intelligent people than the group of those who answered incorrectly.

VISUAL MATERIALS AS THE OBJECT OF INVESTIGATION

Applications in media and market research

Among the different ways that visual materials can be used in structured surveys, the greatest variety can be found in conjunction with those research designs where the visual materials are themselves the objects of investigation and do not just serve as supplementary question aids, although there is no clear-cut boundary between these two categories. The following are but a few of the many ways that question models of this kind can be employed.

Question: 'Which direction will the box move in: upwards, downwards or not at all?'

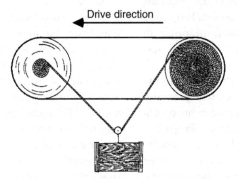

Figure 36.3   An indicator of technical intelligence
Source: Institut für Demoskopie Allensbach (1982). Die Auswirkungen wachsender Technikskepsis auf das Interesse an technisch-naturwissenschaftlichen Studiengängen [The effects of growing skepticism towards technology on interest in studying technical subjects and the natural sciences]. Allensbach Archives, IfD Report No. 2807. *Reprinted by permission of the Allensbach Institute*

Presenting cards and illustrations showing logos, magazine titles, trademarks or other stylized marks is one of the methodologically most uncomplicated ways of employing visual materials in applied survey research. Such materials are commonly used in market and media research, for example, to ascertain newspaper and magazine readership (see Tennstädt, 1984) or brand awareness. The 'copy test' method described above can be viewed as a variation on this same principle. Another example is the dummy test, in which respondents are shown a sample copy of a magazine created especially for the survey and thus not available on the market—for example, a dummy copy of a new title publishers are planning to launch or an edition of a daily newspaper in a proposed new format.

One particularly fruitful technique is combining the presentation of optical stimuli with the principle of the split-ballot experiment, whereby the total survey sample is divided into several randomly selected subgroups (→ *Split Ballots as an Experimental Approach to Public Opinion Research*). If a different illustration is presented to each subgroup and reactions to these illustrations diverge significantly among the various subgroups, this discrepancy can be causally attributed to the varying stimuli—in this case the differences between the illustrations presented (see Petersen, 2002). In contrast to other investigative approaches such as the conjoint measurement method, the split-ballot technique allows researchers, for example, to test the effect of different versions of an advertising billboard without requiring respondents to make the comparison themselves. Instead, respondents make their assessment in a situation that is similar to what they experience in everyday life— that is, each respondent is exposed to only one advertising campaign rather than being required to compare various versions.

In applied research, there are a number of different variations on this simple investigative model that have proven very useful and produced highly valid findings. Along with tests of advertisements and billboards or tests comparing different packaging designs, such tests also include the price threshold test, whereby the different subgroups are shown the same illustration of a particular product, with only one difference: the price. Another special variation of the billboard test is the so-called time-lapse test. Here, the same illustration is presented several times within the course of a lengthier interview, with respondents being asked to evaluate it each time. Tests of this kind simulate what happens when people become accustomed to a particular poster design, which is intended to be part of a major, long-term advertising campaign. Illustrations that are at first assessed positively may ultimately prove unsuitable when presented repeatedly, since respondents quickly grow tired of the design (Noelle-Neumann & Petersen, 2005, pp. 490ff.).

In studies where a large number of different illustrations are to be compared experimentally and for which producing a different version of the questionnaire for each one would be impractical, one possible solution is the card-drawing technique: Here, the illustrations are printed on cards, which the interviewer shuffles, fans out and presents face down to the respondent, who is asked to pick an illustration which then serves as the basis for the subsequent questions. Using this simple procedure, researchers can obtain up to about 10 representative, smaller subgroups because respondents select the cards at random and thus, provided the cards are shuffled thoroughly, the small subgroups formed via this technique are also randomly selected.

One particularly illuminating type of investigation takes advantage of experimental logic to obtain reactions to visual signals without respondents being consciously aware of what they are reacting to. Even subconscious motivations can be ascertained in this manner. An investigative approach of this kind is shown in Figure 36.4, which derives from a study on the image of mouthwash. In the case at hand, there were no previous studies offering any insight into which way the findings might go or what factors could play a role in the image of mouthwash. This problem was solved using the illustration in Figure 36.4, showing several toiletries, in one subsample with and in the other without a bottle of mouthwash on the shelf. Respondents in two randomly selected subgroups were asked to imagine the person to whom the sink belonged and, above all, to say whether they thought he was well groomed. The word 'mouthwash' was not mentioned in any question. And then the following question was asked: 'Suppose this man received a telegram that said, "Run for it! They're on to us!" What could this man have done, what crime might he have committed?' The respondents played along and, in so doing, expressed their subconscious opinion of men who use mouthwash. In the case of the illustration with the mouthwash, respondents generally cited petty crimes. In the other subgroup, respondents predominantly imagined that the sink's owner had perpetrated a violent crime (Ring, 1992, p. 152).

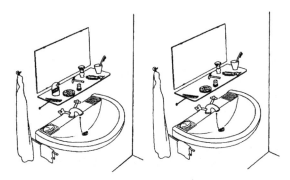

Figure 36.4   Illustrations presented in an experiment on the image of mouthwash
Source: Allensbach Archives, IfD Survey 689/II, 1956/57. *Reprinted by permission of the Allensbach Institute*

Applications in communication research

The same investigative approaches that are employed to measure respondents' reactions to illustrations in market and media research are also used in empirical social research to investigate phenomena such as the effects of visual signals in media reporting. Based on theoretical approaches from the fields of individual psychology, behavioral science and other related disciplines, visual elements can be defined and then systematically manipulated within the framework of a field experiment, thus enabling researchers to test their effect on observers quantitatively. In contrast to laboratory experiments, which are often used when addressing such investigative tasks, presenting visual elements within the framework of a split-ballot experiment has one main advantage. Specifically, not only do the findings reveal any possible effects, but at the same time, they also give us a realistic idea as to the strength of these effects in comparison with other environmental factors that may also have an impact on respondents' reactions (→ *Split Ballots as an Experimental Approach to Public Opinion Research*).

Figure 36.5 shows three variations of an illustration that were presented to respondents in different subgroups to measure the effects of depicting people with a 'plus face' or a 'minus face.' The terms 'plus face' and 'minus face' originate from the field of behavioral research. Biologist Irenäus Eibl-Eibesfeldt remarked: 'If you look at the facial expressions of quarrelling children, you can predict the winner with fairly great certainty. If one child throws his head back a bit, so that his chin is jutting out, and if he looks at the other child and raises his eyebrows in the middle ("plus face") he will most likely be the winner of the conflict .... Losers, on the other hand, tucked in their chins, wrinkled their eyebrows downwards and avoided eye contact' (Eibl-Eibesfeldt, 1986, p. 558, translation by author).

On presentation of one of three illustrations of people, respondents were asked to assess each person using a list of semantically opposite concepts: e.g. strong vs. weak, clever vs. stupid, appealing vs. unappealing, and the like. As observations from behavioral research would lead us to expect, the person depicted with a 'minus face' was perceived by respondents as less appealing and weaker than the person shown with a 'normal face,' that is, where the man is depicted looking straight ahead. In the case of the 'plus face,' the man was also assessed as less appealing but not as considerably weaker than the person depicted with a 'normal face' (Petersen, 2005). Moreover, by taking the research a step further and analyzing the survey findings in conjunction with the results of media content analyses, it was shown that when a prominent public figure is increasingly depicted by the mass media with a 'minus face,'

Figure 36.5   Illustrations presented to test reactions to a person depicted with a 'neutral,' 'plus' or 'minus' face
Source: Allensbach Archives, IfD Surveys 7010 and 7013. *Reprinted by permission of the Allensbach Institute*

the population's assessment of the person also becomes clearly more negative (Petersen & Jandura, 2004).

Other applications

Another special type of illustration used in representative surveys are so-called 'neutralized' illustrations, which are primarily employed in the area of survey research conducted for legal evidence but can also be applied for certain investigative tasks in market research. Using illustrations of this kind, the images of products or product packaging are altered so that the optical elements of the particular product or product packaging are clearly recognizable, whereas other factors that may influence the effect of these elements on respondents and thus diminish the validity of findings are obscured.

In one application in a German survey, the figure showed a neutralized depiction of the packaging of a body care product. The package design and its characteristic optical features were recognizable, but the product name was indecipherable. Illustrations of this kind are employed to determine whether respondents recognize brands purely on the basis of the package shape and color (cf. Noelle-Neumann & Schramm, 1961, pp. 65ff.).

In market research focusing on products, media research, and media effects research, it is often necessary to test respondents' reactions to moving pictures, such as film clips, television news broadcasts, and commercials. Although it is theoretically possible to conduct such tests within the framework of a representative survey, the processes involved are invariably complicated and thus too costly. The most appropriate method in such investigations is the home test, whereby interviewers and respondents watch certain television programs together at a prearranged time or, alternatively, interviewers can be provided with video cassettes or DVDs that they are instructed to play at home. Of course, the latter method has one drawback that is not unproblematic: the representativeness of the sample is limited, since people living in households that do not have a VCR or a DVD player naturally cannot be included. Despite this drawback, the home test continues to be the most reliable, albeit not very widely employed method for testing reactions to moving pictures. Thus, even today, market research designed to test advertising commercials is generally completed within the framework of non-representative studio tests. Analogously, laboratory experiments continue to be the method of choice in academic research.

FUTURE PROSPECTS

In the debate on the future development of survey research, researchers often point somewhat enthusiastically to the many new opportunities offered by online research (→ Internet Surveys). Unlike telephone surveys, which are predominant in many countries today, online surveys would seem to offer practically limitless opportunities to present illustrations, film clips and animated sequences to respondents during the interview. In practice, however, these methods are currently quite limited for a number of reasons. To be sure, practical aspects such as problems respondents may have with compatibility and lack of disk capacity—as well as the fact that, even in leading industrial nations, about half of the population still does not use the Internet—can be viewed as transitional difficulties. Nevertheless, we cannot ignore the fundamental issue of the validity of online surveys, which is at best on a par with written surveys, due to the particularly pronounced tendency toward self-selection, meaning that the online method is not suitable for representative surveys of the population. Still, this method is quite suitable for surveys of certain population groups, such as university professors and students, employees of a company, or members of an organized group or association.

In comparison to surveys conducted purely online, combined approaches may be more promising from a methodological point of view. Here, for example, respondents could be recruited and interviewed by telephone, but then asked to call up the illustrations or film clips used in the interview via the Internet. However, such combined approaches are also only suitable in special cases, since they are relatively complex for respondents. In theory, illustrations and film clips can easily be presented in CAPI surveys. Although this approach plays a role in some areas of market research, the many possibilities theoretically offered by this technology have, for the most part, yet to be fully put into practice.

As this last point shows, the question of whether researchers choose to employ illustrative materials and to refine the array of possible applications is ultimately not a question of the technical options available—after all, they could already resort to the traditional face-to-face survey, which is perfectly suited for such purposes. Rather, this is actually a question of research culture. Due to the predominance of telephone surveys in public opinion research in the 1990s, both practical survey researchers and methodology experts have tended to overlook the possibilities offered by employing visual materials in survey research. The spread of computer-aided face-to-face surveys and online surveys offers—despite the methodological problems that these methods otherwise entail—the best chance to renew the flagging interest in using visual materials and, in so doing, to stop the deterioration in questionnaire methodology that has resulted from researchers' increasing reliance on telephone surveys, and perhaps to even rebuild the spectrum of questionnaire methods available. Such a development would give survey research a major boost in terms of creativity and originality, thus potentially enhancing the scientific contribution that survey findings can make.

REFERENCES

Auer, M. (1981, August). *The Stapel scale: A versatile instrument of survey research.* Paper presented at the annual conference of the World Association of Public Opinion Research (WAPOR), Amsterdam.

Cantril, H. (1944). *Gauging public opinion.* Princeton: Princeton University Press.

Couper, M. P., Traugott, M. W., & Lamias, M. J. (2001). Web survey design and administration. *Public Opinion Quarterly, 65,* 230–253.

Couper, M. P., Tourangeau, R., & Kenyon, K. (2004). Picture this! Exploring visual effects in web surveys. *Public Opinion Quarterly, 68,* 255–266.

Eibl-Eibesfeldt, I. (1986). *Die Biologie des menschlichen Verhaltens. Grundriß der Humanethologie* [The biology of human behavior. An outline of human ethology]. Munich: Piper.

Gallup, G. H. (1928). *An objective method for determining reader interest in the content of a newspaper.* Unpublished doctoral thesis. University of Iowa, Iowa City.

Henry, A., & Murray, M. D. (1943). *Thematic apperception test.* Cambridge, Mass: Harvard University Press.

Noelle-Neumann, E., & Schramm, C. (1961). *Umfrageforschung in der Rechtspraxis* [Survey research as legal evidence]. Weinheim: Verlag Chemie.

Noelle-Neumann, E., & Petersen, T. (2000). Das halbe Instrument, die halbe Reaktion: Zum Vergleich von Telefon- und Face-to-Face-Umfragen [Half an instrument, half a reaction: Comparing telephone and face-to-face interviews]. In V. Hüfken (Ed.), *Methoden in Telefonumfragen* (pp. 183–200). Wiesbaden: Westdeutscher Verlag.

Noelle-Neumann, E., & Petersen, T. (2005). *Alle, nicht jeder. Einführung in die Methoden der Demoskopie* [All, but not each. Introduction to the methods of survey research] (4th ed.). Berlin: Springer.

Petersen, T. (2002). *Das Feldexperiment in der Umfrageforschung* [The field experiment in survey research]. Frankfurt/Main: Campus.

Petersen, T., & Jandura, O. (2004). Der Test von Bildsignalen in Repräsentativumfragen und seine Verknüpfung mit Medieninhaltsanalysen im Bundestagswahlkampf 2002 [Testing visual signals in representative surveys in combination with media content analyses of the 2002 German Federal election campaign]. In T. Knieper & M. G. Müller (Eds.), *Visuelle Wahlkampf-Kommunikation* (pp. 148–167). Cologne: Halem.

Petersen, T. (2005). Testing visual signals in representative surveys. *International Journal of Public Opinion Research, 17,* 456–472.

Ring, E. (1969). Haben Hintergrundfarben des Testmaterials Einfluß auf die Ergebnisse? [Are findings effected by the background colors of test materials?]. *Psychologie und Praxis, 13,* 82–87.

Ring, E. (1992). *Signale der Gesellschaft. Psychologische Diagnostik in der Umfrageforschung* [Societal signals. Psychological diagnostics in survey research]. Göttingen: Verlag für angewandte Psychologie.

Rosenzweig, S. (1945). The picture-association method and its implication in a study of reactions to frustration. *Journal of Personality 14,* 3–23.

Schwarz, N. (1996). *Cognition and communication. Judgmental biases, research methods and the logic of conversation.* Mawah, NJ: Erlbaum.

Smith, T. (1995, May). *Little things matter: A sampler of how differences in questionnaire format can affect survey responses.* Paper presented at the annual conference of the American Association of Public Opinion Research (AAPOR), Fort Lauderdale.

Tennstädt, F. (1984). Effects of differing methods on the level of magazine readership figures. In H. Henry (Ed.), *Readership research: Montreal 1983. Proceedings of the second international symposium* (pp. 229–241). North-Holland, Amsterdam: Elsevier Science.

37

Validation Studies

Michael W. Traugott[1]

The most common form of measurement of contemporary public opinion is with a research design incorporating a survey or poll and specific operationalizations in the form of a variety of questions. These questions, individually or in combination, measure a range of things that are often arrayed along a continuum from attitudes to behaviors, and they are assumed to be reliable and valid (→ *Designing Reliable and Valid Question-naires*). This chapter deals with the ways that a measure becomes validated. The richest literature exists on voting behavior, because it is a relatively common measure in public opinion surveys, and voting records used for validation are easily accessible. However, validation is very important in a number of other research areas where self-reported behavior is a central concept, including health studies of medication or drug use, physician visits, and sexual behavior; consumer research on buying patterns and preferences; and media studies of audience behavior and preferences for specific media and shows.

THE CONCEPT OF VALIDATION

Validity has been an important concern right from the start of survey research (Parry &

Crossley, 1950). Because of some confusion and disagreement about the definition of the concept, there inevitably were differences of opinion about what a validation study is, including what the full process and the significant steps along the way are. The general principle is that a survey question solicits information that can in theory be verified with an external source. One implication of this first principle is that validation is appropriately limited to a behavior where an independent record of it is available. Typically, that source is a set of administrative records that is frequently referred to in the literature as the 'gold standard' to which the self-reported information can be compared through some kind of matching process. Based upon the results of that match, the self-reports are classified as 'accurate' or 'misreports' (sometimes as 'concordant' or not) and are often reported as a rate. In other studies of the accuracy of survey reports, researchers have interviewed the members of pairs or larger groups of individuals who in theory have shared the same experience, comparing their responses for congruency.

Researchers have come to realize that some things that were thought of as behaviors actually have very strong social psychological components associated with them. Secondly, the quality of the records against which the self-reports are checked is often highly variable, making it more or less easy to match them with survey responses from the 'correct' person in the records. It also turns out that there is variation in the abilities of the people who do the record checking, and the resulting matching that determines misreports can change over time and with the conditions under which the checking was done. Finally, the vast number of validation studies is done by comparing information from a survey respondent to that person's administrative record, using name and address as the basis for matching. The process has to account for the potential comparability of Thomas Jones, Thomas A. Jones, Tom Jones, or T. Jones, just to offer a limited number of similar but inexact equivalents that could be found in either source. Women are often more difficult to match than men, for example, because they are the ones who choose to keep their maiden name (or not), or who change their name (or don't) when their marital status changes.

Most of the literature on the sources of misreports focuses on the attributes of the individual respondent, primarily on demographic characteristics, but it is quickly expanding to include other relevant attitudinal and cognitive characteristics. The circumstances of the interview, including the mode of administration ($\rightarrow$ *Face-to-Face Surveys;* $\rightarrow$ *Surveys by Telephone;* $\rightarrow$ *Self-Administered Paper Questionnaires;* $\rightarrow$ *Internet Surveys*) as well as such factors as the presence of others may also affect the propensity to report accurately or misreport. Of course the rates of misreporting may also vary with the attributes of the things being measured, as a function of certain of its properties like social desirability. And the issue of serial or repeated misreporting requires a particular kind of panel design to understand it. When misreporting at the individual level is aggregated to rates, one question is what the appropriate denominator should be for calculating them. In these ways, validation studies represent a microcosm of many of the issues that face the survey research and measurement fields more generally.

STUDIES OF THE VALIDATION OF SELF-REPORTED VOTING BEHAVIOR

The research on this topic has focused on a number of specific questions. What variables are best suited to validation, and what is a 'misreport'? What are the individual level explanations for misreporting? Do the conditions of the interview affect misreporting? And is it possible to minimize misreporting through improved question wording?

Historically, the most frequent focus of validation studies has been self-reported voting behavior, which may be rooted in the early development of public opinion research in conjunction with media organizations that were interested in using polls to supplement their election coverage ($\rightarrow$ *The Historical Roots of Public Opinion Research*). The election of 1936 is linked to the history and rise of polling in the United States, when the *Literary Digest* employed large unrepresentative samples incorrectly to call the race for Landon, while the Gallup Poll used more modern scientific methods to call the race for Roosevelt. The 1948 election in which the public polls said Thomas Dewey would defeat Harry Truman precipitated the initial validation studies.

Validation of individuals' survey responses against administrative records is an expensive enterprise because of the amount of labor required to track down and check the records. When the validation takes place across a wide geographic area, travel can add significantly to the cost as well. For this reason, most validation efforts have been carried out in a limited geographical area. Parry and Crossley (1950) reported on a 1949 study in Denver to validate eight different survey self-reports, including registration and voting, charitable contributions, owning a library card, owning a driver's license, owning a car, age, owning or renting a home, and the presence of a telephone. The researchers constructed eight different self-reported measures of registration and voting alone, and the validation rates, measured as the percentage of all respondents whose answers could be confirmed in various records, ranged from 33% (voted in a set of six elections) to 86% (voted in the 1948 presidential election). These data have been reanalyzed by other researchers, who looked at the characteristics of the misreporters such as age, gender, and socioeconomic status (Cahalan, 1968), and whether the reporting errors were correlated and associated with specific individuals (Presser, 1984). Errors on related items like voting were correlated, but on unrelated items they were not.

The first extensive national validation study was reported by Clausen (1968) following the 1964 election study conducted by the University of Michigan. It compared the lower self-reported turnout estimates from the Current Population Survey, and showed how differences in the two sample designs could explain differences in their self-reported turnout rates, including how having only a post-election interview eliminated the potential stimulus to voting of a pre-election interview. Clausen reported the results of the record check on the basis of all the respondents in the survey, breaking them down by self-reported voters and nonvoters. The validation effort suggested that the misreports are more numerous in the direction of overreporting voting, the socially desirable behavior. He also reports a bias in the self-reported division of the vote that favored the candidate who was advantaged by the short-term forces of the campaign, that is, the one who did better than expected according to a 'normal vote' model.

This work was replicated through self-reports of voting obtained in the 1972–1974–1976 panel of the National Election Study (NES) validated after the 1976 election (Traugott & Katosh, 1979). In that study, the validation of 1976 self-reports were relatively immediate, but that single period of field work was increasingly remote relative to the 1974 and 1972 interviews. The misreporting rates were higher for younger people, those with lower incomes, nonwhites, those having lower levels of citizen duty, and for panel members who had been interviewed fewer

times. These results have been consistently reproduced in other democracies, including Britain (Marsh, 1985; Swaddle & Heath, 1989) and Norway (Granberg & Holmberg, 1991, 1992; Waldahl & Aardal, 2000), as well as in a study comparing those countries with New Zealand and Sweden (Karp & Brockington, 2005).

The use of rates of misreporting based upon the total sample size and the proportion of all misreporters who said they voted was challenged by Anderson and Silver (1986). They suggested a superior aggregated measure is the proportion of nonvoters who claim they voted, because it takes better account of the fact that virtually all misreporters are nonvoters who said they did. Analyzing data from the 1980 NES vote validation study, they report diminished racial disparities in misreporting by using their measure, as well as for such personal characteristics as age, education, and income. In subsequent research, the magnitude of the gap between self-reported turnout and turnout rates in presidential and midterm congressional elections has been rethought as well.

Why respondents misreport?

A variety of explanations for misreporting have been offered, ranging from 'social desirability,' which can explain the direction of misreporting, to memory problems, which can explain errors in the amount as well as the direction of reporting, to source monitoring, an inability to distinguish a specific event from others that are similar. DeMaio (1984) focused research on the concept of 'social desirability,' the tendency for respondents to answer questions in a manner that they think the interviewer wants or that puts them in the best light. The conditions of a validation can affect the result. Presser, Traugott, and Traugott (1990) constructed an index of record quality and mode of access, and found that validation rates improved with record quality. Furthermore, a frequently observed racial difference in overreporting was reduced by half in areas with good quality records, explained in large part by the fact that African-American respondents in the 1988 NES survey disproportionately came from jurisdictions with poor quality records. Traugott and Presser (1992) report on one of the few re-validation studies in which interviewers returned to the places where the 1988 respondents had been validated and tried again, often using a different person to do the work. They reproduced 87% of the 1989 validation results; while the proportion of voters was the same in the two efforts, an equal proportion of respondents (3% and 4%) moved from 'found' to 'not found' and vice versa. Similarly, between 2% and 3% of the respondents moved between 'voter' and 'nonvoter' and vice versa.

Other factors affecting misreporting rates include an individual's personal voting history, which can be constructed by recording during validation how many times a person participated in a specific series of elections in which they had an opportunity to vote. Belli, Traugott, and Beckmann (2001) found that misreporting was in fact higher among those with at least intermittent voting histories rather than habitual nonvoters, suggesting that misremembering might be a less important explanation than some version of self-concept. Some people may think of themselves as habitual voters and in fact do vote fairly regularly; when asked about voting in an election they missed, they answer the survey question in relation to how they generally see themselves rather than in terms of the specific instance.

One important result from validation studies is that misreporters look more like voters than nonvoters. Presser and Traugott (1992) found that in the NES, panel misreporters did not look like habitual voters; that is, 94% of people who misreported in 1976 did not vote in 1974 and 1972. They indirectly test and reject an alternative explanation for misreporting voting, that these people misreport other personal attributes. When they constructed a model to predict the number of votes cast across a series of elections, education was a significant predictor of the self-reported measure but not of the validated measure, perhaps because more

highly educated respondents have a better sense of what is expected of a 'good' citizen than those with lower levels of education.

Belli *et al.* (2001) employed a different approach by assembling a dataset consisting of the information from the seven cross-sectional validation studies conducted by the NES, thereby eliminating some issues associated with panel mortality and the stimulation of a prior interview. When comparing overreporters to validated voters and admitted/validated nonvoters in regressions predicting voting or not voting, they find that demographic characteristics, political attitudes and contextual variables like the date of interview contribute to overreporting. They used two different analytical approaches to show that while each group is unique, overreporters look much more like validated voters than nonvoters.

Research on the likely or probable electorate is one practical area where validated voting information has proved especially useful and important. Public pollsters are interested in estimating who will vote on Election Day as the first step in estimating candidate preference among the voters. But there is no standard measure of who is likely to vote or how a 'likely electorate' should be constructed. Published results from validation studies are critical to evaluating alternative measures and the best way to apply them (Perry, 1960; Traugott & Tucker, 1984; Petrocik, 1991; Freeman & Goldstein, 1996).

Conditions of the interview

In the voting studies, overreporting increases with the amount of elapsed time from Election Day to date of interview (Belli, Traugott, Young, & McGonagle. 1999), suggesting a role for episodic memory. However, research based upon the vote validation studies shows that the presence of others does not affect misreporting (Silver, Abramson, & Anderson, 1986). Going back to the Erie County study in the 1940s, where the authors report that 98% of their respondents in a seven-wave panel study who said they voted actually did, researchers have observed the effects of being interviewed on voting rates as well as the effects of being in a panel on political participation. This panel effect persists in the NES today, and it has been replicated in other countries (Granberg & Holmberg, 1992). And an indication of an intention to vote in a pre-election survey does produce higher rates of misreporting in post-election surveys (Silver et al., 1986).

The research on mode effects suggests that survey techniques that afford greater privacy produce higher levels of reported behaviors that are considered sensitive or less desirable (Acquilino, 1994). This means that self-administered questionnaires, those that employ technologies such as audio computer-assisted telephone interviewing, or web surveys produce higher self-reported levels of such behaviors as smoking than a regular telephone or a face-to-face interview with an interviewer (Moskowitz, 2004). Presser and Stinson (1998) found that reported levels of church attendance were lower when derived from time use diaries and self-administered questionnaires than with standard interviewing techniques involving an interviewer. These results also affected interpretations of whether church attendance had declined rather than remained constant across 30 years. Computerized survey modes will generally produce higher levels of self-reports than their non-computerized equivalents. These differences also appear in a contrast between smoking rates derived from telephone or in-person household surveys of young people and surveys conducted while they are at school.

Attempts to correct for overreporting through modified questions

Given the persistence of the overreporting, it was inevitable that attempts would be made to correct for it at the individual level through improved question wordings. Eckart, Ramstedt, Hibell, Larsson, and Zetterberg (2000) explored different question wordings to reduce the overreport of alcohol consumption in Sweden, for example.

A number of researchers have attempted to revise the wording of the survey questions used to obtain self-reports of voting, and most of them have been unsuccessful. (This is well summarized in Duff, Hanmer, Park, & White, 2004.) However, some wording changes embedded in experiments have produced lower levels of self-reported voting, and some of these reductions have been checked against validated data.

Belli et al. (1999) used a source monitoring perspective in an experimental design to alter the standard NES question, evaluating the results in a national survey as well as a study of Oregon voters. A different introduction to the main question stem as well as different response categories were used. In both studies, the revised question form produced lower self-reported levels of voting, and the effects were proportionately greater the more distant the interview was from Election Day. As a result, the question wording of the NES item was changed, as well as the response categories; but no new introduction was added. This work was partially replicated by Duff et al. (2004) in an NES pilot study in which they experimentally administered the new question with and without the introduction. They found that the introduction and the new response categories reduced overreporting in this midterm election by eight percentage points compared to the revised standard question alone, a significant difference. Because of the experimental design, they were also able to conclude that it was those least likely to vote whose overreporting was reduced the most.

What difference do self-reports or validated measures make?

Given the observed levels of overreporting and the personal characteristics of the misreporters, as well as the fact that misreporters often tend to look like voters, does it make any difference in the development of models of voter turnout or candidate preference whether self-reports or validated measures are used? Accumulating evidence suggests that it does, under some circumstances. Katosh and Traugott (1981) analyzed typical models developed to explain voting using a validated and unvalidated dependent variable, and found that there were no differences in the magnitude of the usual relationships for personal demographic characteristics and social psychological predictors of voting. They also found that misreporters tend to overreport voting for the winner of the general election as well as in the primaries (Wright, 1992; Atkeson, 1999).

The conclusion that misreporting has little effect on models that explain candidate choice may be due to the fact that party identification and candidate evaluations are central explanatory factors in such models, and misreporting does not seem to be correlated with that (Cassel & Sigelman, 2001). At the same time, misreporters have an impact on models of turnout, because similar socioeconomic characteristics are related to both misreporting and participation (Silver et al., 1986; Traugott & Presser, 1992). One especially important predictor affected by misreporting is the role of race (Bernstein, Chadha, & Montjoy, 2001; Cassel, 2003, 2004).

OTHER METHODS OF VALIDATING SURVEY RESPONSES

Several different techniques have been used to validate or triangulate on survey responses. One method is the use of diaries to record events and behaviors as they occur. Typically, aggregated information from samples of diary users are employed to evaluate survey-based measures of the same phenomenon. For example, diary entries about media exposure in studies of time-use have been checked by having small samples of study subjects followed with a video camera. This work showed overreports of the amount of time spent watching television (Robinson, 1985). The rates of bias derived from diaries tend to be low in the aggregate, but higher at the individual level. These results were reproduced in Germany (Scheuch, 1972). A study of parental reports of their young children's viewing habits found a higher correlation between video observation and diary entries than with parental estimates from surveys (Anderson, Field, Collins, Lorch, & Nathan, 1985).

In some studies of health behaviors, validation has been conducted by biological markers assessed by taking samples of bodily fluids (blood and urine) and hair. In a sample of 249 respondents, for example, the correlation between self-reports of the use of 17 dietary and nutritional supplements and the results of the biological assays ranged from 0.65 to 0.78 (Satia-Abouta et al., 2003). A similar approach was used to validate survey self-reports of cocaine and marijuana use among arrestees through a urine test. Some studies found differential misreporting rates for heroin (9%), marijuana (21%), and cocaine (34%), a finding that was replicated in a subsequent study in a different geographical location (Sloan, Bodapati, & Tucker, 2004).

The area of crime statistics has also been a fruitful one for validation studies, employing a number of different techniques, including 'reverse record checks,' to develop survey questions. Starting with samples drawn from lists of known criminals, researchers worked to develop appropriate question forms to maximize accurate reporting. Reverse record checks have also been employed in studies of mental health services parents seek for their children (Fendrich, Johnson, Wislar, & Nageotte, 1999). Some reverse record checks have also used lie detector tests as a means of verifying survey responses (Wentland & Smith, 1993).

OTHER AREAS OF VALIDATION STUDIES

Another form of validation involves asking pairs of individuals or members of larger groups about activities in which they engaged and comparing the level of correspondence in their answers. Such studies have been conducted about the use of contraceptives among partners in 23 different countries, for example, which found that men reported much higher rates of use than women (Becker & Costenbader, 2001). Furthermore, there were differences in the reported use rates depending upon the type of contraceptive device (IUD or oral contraceptive). This is also an area of research in which the interaction between the gender of the interviewer and the respondent affects the quality of the collected data in terms of relative reported use of contraception.

Health care is a research area where the validity of responses is important, because surveys are used to estimate the prevalence of conditions and to develop treatment protocols for them, including diagnoses, medication regimens, and observation patterns. Information from doctor and hospital visits is a typical kind of administrative record available for validity tests. Mathiowetz and Dipko (2000) compared the responses of parents and adolescents about the children's care in an HMO and found that adolescents were more likely to misreport and to overreport, compared to administrative records, the number of their visits to a doctor, date of last visit, and whether they had asthma. Lee *et al.* (1999) showed that parents systematically overreported their children's vaccination status. Udry, Gaughan, Schwingl, and van den Berg (1996) found that only one in five women who had multiple abortions could report the exact date for *each* one in a survey conducted between 10 and 20 years afterward, although nine in ten could report that information for *at least* one of them.

WHAT DO VALIDATION STUDIES TEACH US?

Validation studies remind us about the fragility of the data that we collect in polls and surveys, in the sense that measures of public opinion and behaviors are subject to a number of errors. Based primarily on reports of behavior, we know that levels and types of misreports vary with personal characteristics of the respondents, as well as a variety of psychological forces at work that invoke both social and cognitive aspects of the interview process and the interaction between the respondent and the interviewer. Self-reports are also affected by characteristics of the interview, including the mode of data collection, wording and order of questions, and factors like the presence of others during the interview. Public opinion researchers are interested in these effects because they influence estimates of prevalence as well as the development of models that specify relationships between them and other independent and dependent variables.

Another interesting question is what studies of the validity of measures of behavior tell us about the measurement of attitudes. In these latter studies, the researcher does not know what the 'true' value of an attitude like racism, support for affirmative action, or a woman's right to choose is. But research on the effects of interview context show that the proportion of respondents who express socially desirable views is greatest in the presence of an interviewer in a face-to-face interview and lowest in a self-administered mail survey— suggestive of similar relationships observed in behavioral self-reports that were validated. Therefore the study of validated behaviors can inform our understanding of what we think we know about attitudes as well.

NOTES

1 This work has benefited substantially from the research assistance of Peter Yeung with the support of the Undergraduate Research Opportunity Program at the University of Michigan, which I gratefully acknowledge.

REFERENCES

Acquilino, W. S. (1994). Interview mode effects on surveys of drug and alcohol use. *Public Opinion Quarterly, 58*, 210–240.

Anderson, B., & Silver, B. (1986). Measurement and mismeasurement of the validity of the self-reported vote. *American Journal of Political Science, 30*, 771–785.

Anderson, D. R., Field, D. E., Collins, P. A., Lorch, E. P., & Nathan, J. G. (1985). Estimates of young children's time with television: A methodological comparison of parents reports with time-lapse video home observations. *Child Development, 56*, 1345–1357.

Atkeson, L. R. (1999). Sure, I voted for the winner! Overreport of the primary vote for the party nominee in the national election studies. *Political Behavior, 21*, 197–215.

Becker, S., & Costenbader, E. (2001). Husbands' and wives' reports of contraceptive use. *Studies in Family Planning, 32*, 111–129.

Belli, R., Traugott, M. W., Young, M., & McGonagle, K. (1999). Reducing vote overreporting in surveys: Social desirability, memory failure, and source monitoring. *Public Opinion Quarterly, 31*, 90–108.

Belli, R. F., Traugott, M. W., & Beckmann, M. N. (2001). What leads to voter overreports? Contrasts of overreporters to validated voters and admitted nonvoters in the American national election studies. *Journal of Official Statistics, 17*, 479–498.

Bernstein, R., Chadha, A., & Montjoy, R. (2001). Over-reporting voting: Why it happens and why it matters. *Public Opinion Quarterly, 65*, 22–44.

Cahalan, D. (1968). Correlates of respondent accuracy in the Denver validity survey. *Public Opinion Quarterly, 32*, 607–621.

Cassel, C. A. (2003). Overreporting and electoral participation research. *American Politic Research, 31*, 81–92.

Cassel, C. A. (2004). Voting records and validated voting studies. *Public Opinion Quarterly, 68*, 102–108.

Cassel, C. A., & Sigelman, L. (2001). Misreporters in candidate choice models. *Political Research Quarterly, 54*, 643–655.

Clausen, A. (1968). Response validity: Vote report. *Public Opinion Quarterly, 32*, 588–606.

DeMaio, T. (1984). Social desirability in survey measurement: A review. In C. F. Turner & E. Martin (Eds.), *Surveying subjective phenomenon* (pp. 257–282). New York: Russell Sage.

Duff, B., Hanmer, M. J., Park, W., & White, I. (2004). How good is this excuse? Correcting the over-reporting of voter turnout in the 2002 National Election Study. (ANES Technical Report Series No. nes010872). Retrieved January 5, 2007, from ftp://ftp.electionstudies.org/ftp/nes/bibliography/documents/nes010872.pdf.

Eckart, K., Ramstedt, M., Hibell, B. H., Larsson, S., & Zetterberg, H. L. (2000, May). Can the great errors of surveys measuring alcohol consumption be corrected? Paper presented at the WAPOR annual meeting, Portland, OR. Retrieved January 5, 2007, from http://www.zetterberg.org/Papers/ppr2000a.pdf.

Fendrich, M., Johnson, T., Wislar, J., & Nageotte, C. (1999). The accuracy of parental mental health service reporting: Results from a reverse-record check study.

Journal of the American Academy of Child and Adolescent Psychiatry, 38, 147–155.

Freeman, P., & Goldstein, K. (1996). Building a probable electorate from pre-election polls: A two-stage approach. *Public Opinion Quarterly, 60*, 574–587.

Granberg, D., & Holmberg, S. (1991). Self-reported turnout and voter validation. *American Journal of Political Science, 35*, 448–459.

Granberg, D., & Holmberg, S. (1992). The Hawthorne effect in election studies: The impact of survey participation on voting. *British Journal of Political Science, 22*, 240–248.

Karp, J. A., & Brockington, D. (2005). Social desirability and response validity: A comparative analysis of overreporting voter turnout in five countries. *Journal of Politics, 67*, 825–840.

Katosh, J. P., & Traugott, M. W. (1981). The consequences of validated and self-reported voting measures. *Public Opinion Quarterly, 45*, 519–535.

Lee, L., Brittingham, A., Tourangeau, R., Willis, G., Ching, P., Jobe, J. *et al.* (1999). Are reporting errors due to encoding limitations or retrieval failure? Surveys of child vaccination as a case study. *Applied Cognitive Psychology, 13*, 43–63.

Marsh, C. (1985). Prediction of voting behaviour from a pre-election survey. *Political Studies, 33*, 642–648.

Mathiowetz, N., & Dipko, S. (2000). A comparison of response error by adolescents and adults: Findings from a health care study. *Medical Care, 38*, 374–382.

Moskowitz, J. M. (2004). Assessment of cigarette smoking and smoking susceptibility among youth. *Public Opinion Quarterly, 68*, 565–587.

Parry, H. J., & Crossley, H. M. (1950). Validity of responses to survey questions. *Public Opinion Quarterly, 14*, 61–80.

Perry, P. (1960). Election survey procedures of the Gallup poll. *Public Opinion Quarterly, 24*, 531–542.

Petrocik, J. R. (1991). An algorithm for estimating turnout as a guide to predicting elections. *Public Opinion Quarterly, 55*, 643–647.

Presser, S. (1984). Is inaccuracy on factual survey items item-specific or respondent-specific? *Public Opinion Quarterly, 48*, 344–355.

Presser, S., & Stinson, L. (1998). Data collection mode and social desirability bias in self-reported religious attendance. *American Sociological Review, 63*, 137–145.

Presser, S., & Traugott, M. W. (1992). Little white lies and social science models: Correlated response errors in a panel study of voting. *Public Opinion Quarterly, 56*, 77–86.

Presser, S., Traugott, M. W., & Traugott, S. (1990, November). *Vote 'over' reporting in surveys: The records or the respondents?* Paper presented at the International Conference on Measurement Errors, Tucson, Arizona.

Robinson, J. P. (1985). The validity and reliability of diaries versus alternative time use measures. In F. T. Juster & F. P. Stafford (Eds.), *Time, goods, and well-being* (pp. 33–62). Ann Arbor, MI: Institute for Social Research.

Satia-Abouta, J., Patterson, R. E., King, I. B., Stratton, K. L., Kristal, A. R., Potter, J. D. *et al.* (2003). Reliability and validity of self-report of vitamin and mineral supplement use in the Vitamins and Lifestyle Study. *American Journal of Epidemiology, 157,* 944–954.

Scheuch, E. K. (1972). The time-budget interview. In A. Szalai (Ed.), *The use of time* (pp. 67–87). The Hague: Mouton.

Silver, B. D., Abramson, P. R., & Anderson, B. A. (1986). The presence of others and overreporting of voting in American national elections. *Public Opinion Quarterly, 50,* 228–239.

Sloan, J. J., Bodapati, M. R., & Tucker, T. A. (2004). Respondent misreporting of drug use in self-reports: Social desirability and other correlates. *Journal of Drug Issues, 34,* 269–292.

Swaddle, K., & Heath, A. (1989). Official and reported turnout in the British general election of 1987. *British Journal of Political Science, 19,* 537–551.

Traugott, M. W., & Katosh, J. (1979). Response validity in surveys of voting behavior. *American Journal of Political Science, 43,* 359–377.

Traugott, M. W., & Tucker, C. (1984). Strategies for predicting whether a citizen will vote and estimation of election outcomes. *Public Opinion Quarterly, 48,* 330–343.

Traugott, M. W., & Presser, S. (1992, May). *Re-validation of self-reported vote.* Paper presented at the annual conference of the American Association for Public Opinion Research, St. Petersburg Beach, Florida.

Udry, J. R., Gaughan, M, Schwingl, P. J., & van den Berg, B. J. (1996). A medical record linkage analysis of abortion underreporting. *Family Planning Perspectives, 28,* 228–231.

Waldahl, R., & Aardal, B. (2000). The accuracy of recalled previous voting: Evidence from Norwegian election study panels. *Scandinavian Political Studies, 23,* 373–389.

Wentland, E. J., & Smith, K. W. (1993). *Survey responses: An evaluation of their validity.* San Diego, CA: Academic Press.

Wright, G. C. (1992). Reported versus actual vote: There is a difference and it matters. *Legislative Studies Quarterly, 17,* 131–142.

38

Identifying Value Clusters in Societies

Hans L. Zetterberg

Values are generalized, relatively enduring and consistent priorities for how we want to live. Values belong in the 'vocabulary of motives' (Mills, 1940), not in the realm of instincts and biological needs. Values reveal mankind's aspirations. Needs reveal any creature's wants. Both values and needs answer the question of *why* we act as we do. Lifestyles are bundles of practices centered on some need and/or value. Lifestyles answer the question of *what* we persistently enjoy doing. One and the same value can be expressed by different lifestyles and in different opinions.

Social scientists are primarily interested in values that are shared by many, that is, collective values. There is reason, however, to study also idiosyncratic values, as when social research is focused on the emergence of new values. Value clusters and lifestyles can be used in the presentations of opinion research. This chapter will first focus on values as backgrounds to opinions. We will note how some cardinal values have seeped into the demographic section of the pollsters' questionnaires along with age, sex, and ethnicity. We will then follow how a few pollsters in the United States and Europe introduced values as dominant parts of their questionnaires. Second, we will treat values research not as an auxiliary to opinion research but as a research field in its own right, albeit using much of the same methodology as opinion research. Finally we will touch upon the classical conflict raised by Hegel and Marx about the role of values in the history of humanity, and ask whether survey research can contribute to a resolution.

VALUEGRAPHICS

To account for variations in public opinion researchers have invoked a series of factors that are summarized as characteristics with the ending '-graphics.' *Sociographics*— pioneered by Jahoda, Lazarsfeld, and Zeisel (1933/1960)—invoke the development of opinions in social movements and other groups with much human interaction. Census categories are called *demographics*.

They became known as 'background questions' in the writing of questionnaires. In the analysis of public opinion they became standard table heads. *Psychographics*—explored by Adorno, Frenkel-Brunswik, Levinson, and Sanford (1950)—are invoked when opinions are seen as expressions of personality traits or temperament.

Finally, *valuegraphics* are invoked in the study of opinion when a particular opinion is seen as an expression of 'the spirit of the times and the place.' Studies of the changing value climates have been given labels such as 'mentality history' and 'geography of mentality.' Research into such mentalities can also be supported by opinion polls. Lipset's (1990) study of the continental divide in mentality and social structure between the United States and Canada is historical in the sense that it shows that two nations, not one, emerged from the American Revolution, one 'Whig' and one 'Tory.' His documentation, however, relies in part on present-day opinion polls. An equally comprehensive study by Allardt (1975) deals with mentalities in four Nordic countries and relies almost entirely on survey data.

LIFE ORDERS AND VALUE SPHERES

Some valuegraphics have seeped into the demographics of opinion research. Max Weber spoke of *Wertsphären* (value-spheres) that followed *Lebensordnungen* (life-orders) in a society, each with *Eigengesetzlichkeit* (internal, limited autonomy/freedom). He delineated separate economic, political, intellectual (scientific), religious, familial, and erotic orders and values, although readers may argue about the exact number of spheres and their delineation (Weber, 1920, pp. 542–567/2004, pp. 220–241). If we leave out the microsociological familial and erotic value spheres from Weber's list and add a realm of morality to the remaining, we obtain the six macro-spheres of values about which it might be possible to reach consensus. They are wealth, order, truth, the sacred, virtue, and beauty. Pareto called such values 'utilities'; others have called them 'institutional values'; I prefer to call them 'cardinal values.' Cardinal values are embedded in the major life areas, i.e., in science, economy, polity, art, religion, and morality. Science seeks and produces objective knowledge. The economy seeks and produces riches; the polity seeks and produces order. Art seeks and produces what in the old days was called beauty, and what we today recognize as any emotionally engaging subjective stimulus. Religion seeks and produces sacred meanings. Morality seeks and produces virtue. Each life sphere develops ways to enhance its cardinal value and offer lifestyles for those who want to pursue them (see Table 38.1).

We can learn about the cardinal values by studying economic, political, and juridical history, the history of ideas and learning, the history of religion, of customs, and of art. Much value research is thus embodied in the humanities, not in anthropology or sociology or public opinion research. Our values may be more or less articulated. When we use survey research to measure values, we assume that they are reasonably well articulated among rank-and-files. When we

Table 38.1   Cardinal values, their embedding in life areas and elaboration in life styles assisted by forms of freedom

Life areas	Cardinal values	Life styles	Type of freedom
Science	Knowledge	Learning-buffs	Academic freedom
Economy	Riches	Business-minded	Freedom of trade
Polity	Order	Civic-minded	Civic freedoms
Art	Beauty	Aesthetes	Artistic license
Religion	Sacredness	Believers	Freedom of religion
Morality	Virtue	Do-gooders	Freedom of conscience

use literary or cultural criticism to ascertain values, we may also discover less articulated values.

Public opinion researchers have included in their questionnaires three or four of the six cardinal values among their 'background questions.' Knowledge is routinely measured by questions on levels of education. Riches are measured by questions on income and house ownership. Power is measured when questions on occupation include codes for managers, business owners, and public officials and officeholders. In view of the increasing importance of religion in American politics, background questions on worship have become more common. However, pollsters and their interpreters in the media and the classroom usually assume that the answers belong in the life area of politics.

This error was identified by the French sociologist Pierre Bourdieu (1984) in a provocative lecture entitled 'Public opinion does not exist.' Bourdieu argues (among other things) that by putting the same question to everyone, pollsters wrongly assume that everyone agrees on what the issue is. He takes as an illustration the topic whether or not teachers may use corporal punishment to maintain discipline in schools. Here it is not certain that all respondents see the same issue: 'Questions having to do with moral issues, for example, the punishment of children, relations between teachers and pupils, and so on, are problems which are increasingly perceived as ethical problems as one moves down the social hierarchy, but which can be political problems for the upper classes. One of the distorting effects of surveys is the transformation of ethical responses into political responses by the simple imposition of a particular problematic' (p. 151).

The demographic category of age—a standard in all opinion research—has an indirect relation to values. Historians have showed how big events such as The Great Depression or the two World Wars of the twentieth century affected the opinions of most everyone living through them. With the First World War in mind, Mannheim (1928) identified the transition period between youth and adulthood as a particularly impressionable age. At that age men and women are unusually open to embracing extreme opinions, to recruitment into odd groups, and are quick to go through conversions, be it in the realm of fashion, politics, or religion. He suggested that what happens in this transition period may color much of the outlooks in later life of each generation.

OBSERVING VALUE SHIFTS WITH INTERVIEW SURVEYS

Valuegraphics based on survey data rather than data from literary and historical sources obtained a great boost from the value shifts among young people in the Western publics in the 1960s and 1970s. A youth cult emerged. A mood of exhilaration began to prevail among young people; many boasted that they did not trust anyone over 30.

The backgrounds for these developments were some record years of economic prosperity and the war in Vietnam. Young people protested not only against superpower violence in a developing country, but also against the violence they felt that schools and employers, police, and social-welfare authorities exercised against those who dressed differently (in jeans), smoked differently (marijuana), or went to street demonstrations rather than to class. They stressed informality, not order and hierarchy. They reacted against big cities, big companies and big organizations, and there emerged a belief that small is beautiful. Their dominant values were anti-authoritarian: bureaucracies should give way to networks, and social relations should be egalitarian. Young students, often from a middle-class background, joined an anti-capitalist wave and a massive generation gap arose.

Many pollsters picked up bits and pieces of this turmoil, but only two rose to the occasion and provided comprehensive accounts, one American and one Frenchman. The American was Daniel Yankelovich, a social psychologist (actually trained at the Sorbonne in Paris), and the other was Alain de Vulpian.

Yankelovich conducted an interview study of students on American campuses totally focused on what we later came to call the '1968' values (Yankelovich, 1972). In 1971, his first 'monitor' surveying samples of the entire population was fielded. It included new values (such as elevated 'distrust of advertising') and the old ones (such as the priority of 'beauty in the home'). To cluster answers to value items in questionnaires, Yankelovich used a computer program developed by the US Navy. Values could then be given mathematical representations just like opinions from polls. People with similar values could be identified and presented with different names as value groups. Value trends could be plotted and extrapolated into the future. Every year since the start of this study in 1971, the Yankelovich firm (later called Yankelovich and Partners) has reported on the most telling trends of shifting values—those that have the biggest impact on politics and markets.

In France, Alain de Vulpian (2005) has devoted a lifetime to processes, systems, and dynamics. In the wake of the Paris student revolt of 1968, he developed a system (later called 3SC) for measuring values. He used the then new statistical technique of correspondence analysis to map values. In 1978, he invited pollsters from other European countries who had published on values or lifestyles, or had served clients with such explorations, to participate in a research firm called RISC (Research in Sociocultural Change) incorporated in Switzerland. They included, among others, Elisabeth Nelson, holder of the first UK license to the Yankelovich Monitor, Giampaolo Fabris of Italy, Werner Wyss of Switzerland, and the present author. A focus of this group was to keep up with changes in the value climate by adding revealing items to their value questionnaire. This required sophistication and a sense for the *avant garde,* and made RISC research non-dogmatic, often readable in wide circles and sometimes flamboyant as the use of the title 'Sex in the Snow' for a study of Canadian social values at the end of the millennium (Adams, 1997). Yankelovich and de Vulpian

have relinquished control over their research companies, but the 'Yankelovich Monitor' and 'RISC' have remained brands of value research in marketing circles. Other widely used systems of value measurements that cross borders between valuegraphics and psychographics have been provided by Rokeach (1972), Mitchell (1983), Schwartz and Bilsky (1987, 1990), McCrae and Costa (1990), Schwartz (1992).

In the late 1970s, professor Jan Kerkhofs of the Catholic University of Leuven in Belgium began planning for a study of European values to be carried out in the 10 states that at that time were members of the European Union (EEC). He was less interested in *avant garde* values and more interested in how much of the European heritage of values from Jerusalem, Athens, and Rome remained relevant, and whether any alternative meanings had replaced those of Christianity. He literally set out to read to European respondents each one of the Ten Commandments and ask whether it was applicable today. He received funding from a wealthy Catholic business family, and was able to set up a separate European Value Systems Study Group Foundation with his Dutch colleague Ruud de Moor. They engaged a group of researchers to develop a questionnaire and arrange for the fieldwork: Elisabeth Noelle-Neumann and Renate Köcher from the Institut für Demoskopie in Allensbach in Germany, Jean Stoetzel and Hélène Riffault from Faits et Opinions in Paris, Juan Linz from Data SA in Madrid, Gordon Heald and Meril James from Social Surveys (Gallup Poll) in London, and Stephan Harding who eventually wrote the comprehensive report (Harding, Phillips, & Fogarty, 1986). The survey was a success and was developed and repeated with additional countries, also including non-European ones, in four waves before the turn of the century. By that time an umbrella organization headed by Ronald Inglehart, The World Values Surveys, was in place at the University of Michigan. It covered 65 societies containing over 75% of the world's population. By 2005, World Values Survey data have been utilized in more than 400 publications in more than 20 languages (→ *International Comparative Surveys: Their Purpose, Content and Methodological Challenges*).

Most survey research that we have reviewed so far did not start from a specific theory. Their questionnaires were long. Data reduction and analysis were performed by statistical techniques such as correspondence, cluster, or factor analyses. Efforts to reduce and condense raw empirical data led in due course to a situation in which more theoretical questions could be asked and answered.

THEORY-BASED MEASUREMENTS OF VALUES

Valuegraphic theory can take its lead either from Hegel, and argue that values set the tone for the entire society, or from Marx, and argue that the material base and technology of a society set the tone.

An often retold effort to find regularities in the development of the values of humanity started with Friedrich Hegel (1770–1831). He developed his philosophy around the dialectical method that came to bear his name. Human reasoning develops through its own inner dynamics. It moves, Hegel asserted, through the three stages: thesis, antithesis, and synthesis. They operate through the family, the civil society, and the state; the state was its most complete expression. The spirit of the times (*Zeitgeist*) writes the cultural history. It had moved from Mediterranean antiquity, was located in Western Europe and on its way to North America, which Hegel called 'the land of tomorrow.'

Generally speaking, philosophers and scholars have not been convinced by Hegel but sometimes inspired by him. The Russian-American sociologist Pitirim A. Sorokin was the first to succeed in measuring and quantifying changes in values as they have occurred in history (Sorokin, 1937–1941). He classified the history of the mental on a scale that ranged from 'sensate' concerns to 'ideational' concerns. In sensate mentality, most symbols are clearly and closely associated with the evidence of the senses, especially evidence about the practical artifacts and tools used and the pleasure of the senses. In ideational mentality, they are more divorced from sensual data; symbols refer to other symbols, often highly charged pristine ideals. By recording the relative prevalence of such symbols, one can describe the prevailing mentality. Sorokin did his work prior to opinion polls and his quantifications came from coding paintings, books on the philosophy of life, innovations, war records, and other archived material. They showed that the Zeitgeist of the Western world has fluctuated between sensate and ideational mentalities. Beginning with an ideational environment of ideas in 600 B.C. it oscillated to a sensate mentality when the Roman Empire was at its peak, from there to a new ideational symbolic environment in the late Middle Ages, then to a new sensate mentality in our time. In the late 1930s, Sorokin launched the prediction that the pattern would repeat itself with time, and that the civilization of the West would next move toward a new ideational mentality, a 'New Age.' A Hegelian aspect of Sorokin's theory is that the swings between ideational and sensate mentalities have 'immanent causes,' that is, values swing without external influences— because of factors that are built into the very expressions for the values (Sorokin, 1941, pp. 663ff.). In swift steps toward, say, a consistent ideational mentality, the system of values becomes too remote from material and biological conditions to be effective; too many contacts with everyday realities are lost. We then need to formulate more mundane priorities, and give them a more sensate orientation. Swift steps back to an increasingly coherent materialism lead, in turn, to a loss of contact with human and spiritual realities. The curve swings back to ideational mentality, and so on.

The time-series of value measurements by survey methods have so far been too short (in terms of points in the series) to fully confirm immanent changes. The studies, however, do show the strongest emotive engagement at the two extremes of a value dimension and the weakest in the middle. They share this with many scalable attributes in opinion research. Louis Guttman (1954) discovered this as a mathematical regularity.

The typical pattern of value shifts is to 'lurch first and learn later,' according to Daniel Yankelovich's (2000) summary of his findings. It is as if all of mankind were adolescents, taking exaggerated positions with abrupt switches between them! Yankelovich disagrees with Hegel on one important score: there is no stage of synthesis. Dialectics may develop with a thesis, for example, of tradition, or faithfulness, or materialism, and then an antithesis, for example, of modernity, or pragmatism, or postmaterialism, but they rarely merge into a synthesis; usually the first thesis returns and the process starts all over. The repeated swings between extremes do not mean that dialectic priorities usually revert to any position we can call 'normal.' Normality is a movable feast. With several priorities swinging independently of one another, a balancing point between the extremes rarely occurs, and if one does appear it may be short-lived. An individual's personal priorities may mature and attain balance with age, as Mitchell (1983) argued, but the value environment in society as a whole does not ever seem to attain mature tranquillity.

Marx fitted the dialectical method to the analysis of shifts in technology, production and class relations. The class struggles between the advance of the bourgeoisie (thesis) and its demise by the victorious working class (antithesis) would culminate in a proletarian revolution and communist society (synthesis). Morals, culture, religion—indeed the entire world of ideas in Hegel's 'spirit' and all public opinion—are in Marx's view not causes of but rather reflections of this materialistic dialectic.

By putting Hegel on his feet after having stood on his head, as the common metaphor goes, and using the dialectics on material conditions rather than on symbols and spiritual conditions, Marx achieves a testable theory that can be accepted or rejected by ordinary scholarship. The moving force of history was not any Hegelian spirit, but the technology of production. The latter, owned by the bourgeoisie, the capitalist class, would spread all over the world: 'The need of a constantly expanding market for its products chases the bourgeoisie over the whole surface of the globe. It must nestle everywhere, settle everywhere, establish connections everywhere,' wrote Marx and Engels in their Communist Manifesto.

This anticipation of the globalization of the market economy has proved correct in outline, but the crucial dialectical part of the theory can be rejected on the grounds that its predictions have not turned out to be true. Contrary to Marx's prediction, the proletarian revolution did not come first to the United States, the most advanced capitalist country; it never arrived there, not even as a noticeable public opinion (Lipset & Marks, 2000). Neither have most highly developed industrial nations in Europe, nor in Australia and Japan, seen industrial workers carry out a successful revolution of the Marxist type.

TECHNOLOGY, ECONOMIC CONDITIONS, AND VALUES

The fact that Marx's grand dialectic of production technology has failed does not mean that production and material conditions have no consequences for values. There may even be external forces of communication technology behind the swings described by Sorokin (Zetterberg, 1998, p. 1000). Marshall McLuhan's (1962) criterion for cultural change is the vehicle by means of which the important symbols travel: oral prior to Plato, written until the end of the Middle Ages, printed until the mid-twentieth century, and pictorial in our days. The medium, he argues, affects the message: the values of oral culture are those of wisdom, the values of written culture, on the other hand, are those of knowledge and information. The use of the medium of printed text is harsh and 'manly,' and drives forward instrumental tasks, while the values of pictorial culture are soft and 'womanly,' using the intimate medium of television to express internal states, evoke emotions, maintain harmony and well-being, or its opposite. It is more than a coincidence that Sorokin's main cycle and McLuhan's turning points in the cultural development are located to the third or fourth century before Christ, the mid-fifteenth century, and at the time of the late twentieth century respectively. In recent years, several researchers have stressed the autonomy of media technology more than McLuhan did. They have added the burning of messages into silicon chips as an additional stage to his oral-written-pictorial sequence of communication technologies (e.g., Kittler, 1997). A research race is on to delineate the values that will be promoted by the new silicon networks.

The young Ronald Inglehart (1971) posited the hypothesis that people's values change when they no longer had to concentrate on economic survival. When their societies reached this stage, the values become 'post-materialist.' Inglehart documented a

widespread shift in Western European mentality from a concern with security to a concern with freedom. He did it with a single survey question with four response alternatives, of which the respondents had to choose two: maintaining order in the nation, giving the people more say in important government decisions, fighting rising prices, and protecting freedom of speech.

The respondents who said they would give priority to keeping order and fighting price rises consistently stressed stability and security, that which Inglehart called *materialistic values*. Those who prioritized giving people more say in important decisions and safeguarding freedom of speech consistently stressed political and personal freedom, that which Inglehart called *post-materialist* values. Those who chose one alternative from each group had mixed values. In all, a total of 10,392 persons in France, Germany, Italy, the UK, Belgium and The Netherlands were

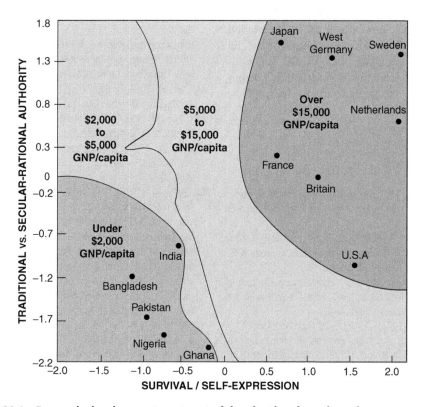

Figure 38.1   Economic development, post-material and rational-secular values
Source: Inglehart & Baker, 2000. *Reprinted by permission of the American Sociological Association*

interviewed in 1970. Many respondents had mixed values, but a consistent finding was that the older generation saw security as more important than the younger generation, while the younger respondents placed a higher priority on freedom compared with the older generation. Inglehart's measurement has been used repeatedly and has generated a vast secondary literature, some of which is critical of, for example, Inglehart's impressionistic view of the satisfaction of material wants. Inglehart himself has refined and developed his thinking beyond the early version (Inglehart, 1990). With data from the World Values Surveys—see Figure 38.1—Inglehart and Baker (2000) show the relation between the economic development and a combination of the values of post-materialism and rational-secular values.

Opinion researchers in the twenty-first century do not design studies to resolve the grand controversy between Hegelian and Marxist orientations. However, it is within their present reach to design studies showing how much of the variation in an opinion can be accounted for by the communication and media technologies used, and by sociographics, demographics, psychographics, and valuegraphics, respectively.

REFERENCES

Adams, M. (1997). *Sex in the snow: Canadian social values at the end of the millennium*. Toronto: Viking.

Adorno, T. W., Frenkel-Brunswik, E., Levinson, D. J., & Sanford, R. N. (1950). *The authoritarian personality*. New York: Harper & Brothers.

Allardt, E. (1975). *Att ha, att älska, att vara. Om välfärd i Norden* [To have, to love, to be. On welfare in the Nordic countries]. Lund: Argos.

Bourdieu, P. (1984). *Questions de sociologie* [Sociology in question]. Paris: Les Éditions de Minuit. English translation by R. Nice (1993). Sociology in question. London: Sage.

Guttman, L. A. (1954). The principle components of scalable attitudes. In P. F. Lazarsfeld (Ed.), *Mathematical thinking in the social sciences* (pp. 216–257). Glencoe, IL: Free Press.

Harding, S., Phillips, D., & Fogarty, M. (1986). *Contrasting values in Western Europe. Unity, diversity and change*. London: Macmillan.

Inglehart, R. (1971). The silent revolution in Europe: Intergenerational change in post-industrial societies. *American Political Science Review, 65*, 991–1017.

Inglehart, R. (1990). *Culture shift in advanced industrial society*. Princeton: Princeton University Press.

Inglehart, R., & Baker, W. E. (2000). Modernization, cultural change and the persistence of traditional values. *American Sociological Review, 65*, 19–55.

Jahoda, M., Lazarsfeld, P. F., & Zeisel, H. (1960). *Die Arbeitslosen von Marienthal. Ein soziographischer Versuch* [The unemployed of Marienthal. A sociographic approach]. Verlag für Demoskopie, Allensbach (Original work published 1933).

Kittler, F. A. (1997). *Literature, media, information systems: Essays by Friedrich A. Kittler* (J. Johnston, Ed.). Amsterdam: Overseas Publishers Association.

Lipset, S. M. (1990). *Continental divide. The values and institutions of the United States and Canada*. New York: Routledge.

Lipset, S. M., & Marks, G. (2000). *It didn't happen here*. New York: Norton.

Mannheim, K. (1928). *Das Problem der Generationen* [The problem of generations]. *Kölner Vierteljahrshefte für Soziologie, 7*, 157–185, 309–330. English translation available in P. Kecskeméti (Ed. & Trans.). (1952). Essays on the sociology of knowledge. New York: Oxford University Press.

McCrae, R. R., & Costa, P. T. (1990). *Personality in adulthood*. New York: Guilford Press.

McLuhan, M. (1962). *The Gutenberg galaxy*. Toronto: University of Toronto Press.

Mills, C. W. (1940). Situated action and the vocabulary of motives. *American Sociological Review, 5*, 904–913.

Mitchell, A. (1983). *The nine American lifestyles*. New York: Macmillan.

Rokeach, M. (1972). *Beliefs, attitudes, and values*. San Francisco: Jossey-Bass.

Schwartz, S. H. (1992). Universals in the content and structure of values. Theoretical advances and empirical tests in 20 countries. In M. Zanna (Ed.), *Advances in experimental social psychology* (pp. 1–65). San Diego: Academic Press.

Schwartz, S. H., & Bilsky, W. (1987). Toward a universal psychological structure of values. *Journal of Personality and Social Psychology, 53*, 550–562.

Schwartz, S. H., & Bilsky, W. (1990). Toward a theory of the universal content and structure of values. *Journal of Personality and Social Psychology, 58*, 878–891.

Sorokin, P. A. (1937–1941). *Social and cultural dynamics* (Vol. 1 (1937), Fluctuations in the forms of art. Vol. 2 (1937), Fluctuations in the systems of truth, ethics, and law. Vol. 3 (1937), Fluctuations of social relationships, war, and revolution. Vol. 4 (1941), Basic problems, principles, and methods). New York: American Book Company.

de Vulpian, A. (2005). *À l'écoute des gens ordinaires: Comment ils transforment le monde* [Listening to ordinary people: How they change the world]. Paris: Dunod.

Yankelovich, D. (1972). *The changing values on campus. Political and personal attitudes of today's college students.* New York: Washington Square Press.

Yankelovich, D. (2000). *How societies learn: Adapting the welfare state to the global economy.* New Brunswick NJ: Transaction Publishers.

Weber, M. (1920). Zwischenbetrachtung [Intermediate reflection]. In M. Weber (Ed.), *Gesammelte Aufsätze zur Religionssoziologie Vol. 1* (pp. 536–573). Tübingen: J.C.B. Mohr (Paul Siebeck). English translation in Whimster, S. (2004). *The essential Weber* (pp. 215–244). London: Routledge.

Zetterberg, H. L. (1998). Cultural values in market and opinion research. In C. McDonald & P. Vangelder (Eds.), *ESOMAR Handbook of marketing and opinion research* (4th ed.). Amsterdam: ESOMAR.

PART IV

The Social and Political Environment of Public Opinion Research

The Status of Public Opinion Research

39

The Legal Status of Public Opinion Research in the World

Wolfgang Donsbach and Uwe Hartung

The freedom to conduct opinion surveys among the people and to publish the results is derived from international or national legal provisions granting rights to people. Restrictions of this freedom, if grounded in law at all, can be found in national laws, such as those on due electoral processes. The liberties from which this freedom is derived include the freedom of speech and expression, the freedom to hold and voice opinions and inform oneself, the freedom of scientific endeavor, and the freedom to conduct businesses. Internationally, these liberties are guaranteed in such bills as the United Nation's Universal Declaration of Human Rights, the Declaration of Principles of the UN's World Summit on the Information Society, the European Convention for the Protection of Human Rights. The national bills of rights are, of course, too diverse to list here, as are the national laws that restrict the freedom to conduct and publish opinion surveys (Donsbach, 2001; Spangenberg, 2003).

In democratic political systems, legal restrictions on the freedom to conduct opinion polls and to publish their results are usually justified by the claim that polls may hurt other legally protected rights such as the inviolability of the election process or peaceful relations between the different groups within a society. By far the most attention has been devoted to the potential infringement of polling upon the electoral process, both by lawmakers setting up restrictions and by the research community defending its freedom. Such impact is usually assumed to be harmful, but the restrictions may be as well. In dealing with this issue, one can distinguish five types of polls (or comparable information) that may have an influence, five entities on which an influence is presumed, and three dimensions in which this is discussed.

This chapter describes the different theoretical and juridical discourses in which limitations and prohibitions of polls are discussed. In the first part, we describe discourses as they occur in democratic countries.

In non-democratic countries, where most of the restrictions exist, there are no discourses (at least no public ones), and the sole motivation to prevent the conduct or the publication of opinion polls is to maintain the power of the ruling authorities. The second part gives some evidence on the actual freedom to conduct and publish polls in countries around the world.

MOTIVATIONS FOR LEGAL RESTRICTIONS ON (PRE-)ELECTION POLLS

Before describing the different discourses on legal restrictions, it makes sense to distinguish between the polling phenomena that some see as problematic and the consequences that they might cause. In the context of restrictions on pre-election polls, we can distinguish between: (1) opinion polls that represent snapshots of opinion at various points in time prior to election day, (2) explicit or implicitly suggested forecasts based on opinion polls prior to election day, (3) predictions based on polls conducted on election day itself (usually in the form of *exit polls*; → *Exit Polls and Pre-Election Polls*), (4) the publication of early returns before voting is over, and (5) projections based on initial results taken from selected voting districts which were chosen according to statistical principles.

The last two forms are rather a matter of electoral law than a matter of the right to conduct opinion research. According to common democratic expectations, the same information should be available to all voters on election day. This also means that nobody should have more or less information than others just because of the place where they live. This occurs, however, in countries where the polling places close at different times. A prominent case is the United States, where as a result of geographical circumstances there are four different time zones, and state law regulates the closing times of polling stations ('western voting phenomenon'). In most countries, early returns are either not possible because of a nation-wide closing

time, or their publication is forbidden (though the Internet now makes it more difficult to enforce the ban). When official results are not available until after the polling stations close, they can no longer have an influence on voting.

Politically, this problem can easily be dealt with in most countries by means of appropriate measures in election legislation, such as similar opening hours for all polling stations and sanctions on election helpers who publish early returns. For this reason, the matter will not be discussed further here. However, the results of studies on the western voting phenomenon (Adams, 2005) in the US describe and explain voters' behavior when they know how other people voted, and this may well be applicable to cases when the knowledge about other voters originates from opinion polls rather than election results.

Opinion snapshots, forecasts and exit polls differ in terms of their validity and their power of persuasion, but not fundamentally as regards their empirical base. They are, in each case, opinion polls based on the survey of a sample by telephone, in face-to-face interviews or—less often—interviews by mail or via Internet and/or e-mail. The difference between these forms is that, as a rule, the closer they get to election day, the greater their accuracy. Consequently, the exit polls on election day are the most reliable—because with greater temporal proximity, there is a greater chance that they will be perceived as an exact representation of the opinions of the population and as such taken seriously. However, in most cases, the results of exit polls will only be available after the real polls have closed, which makes them irrelevant as a factor influencing voting decisions, except in the case where they are leaked online on the Internet before the polls close, as in the US in 2000 and 2004 (Traugott, Highton, & Brady, 2005). This now appears to be under control as a result of new procedures put into place for the 2006 election.

With the other two opinion poll forms, their persuasiveness depends among other things upon whether the institute or media present them as 'forecasts' or as a 'snapshot' of current opinion. Technically, they only differ that in forecasts, the undecideds and no replies are added to one of the parties or to the non-voters, using past experience, specific house procedures and weighting factors specific to election forecasts. Opinion snapshot polls (mixed forms notwithstanding) as a rule are publications of the raw data, routine weighting notwithstanding.

The phenomena upon which election polls can have an effect can basically be divided into three dimensions: the type of effect, the length of the effect, and the system or 'unit' being affected (→ *The Effects of Published Polls on Citizens*).

Type: Distinguishing between direct and indirect effects applies to the question of whether election polls directly influence voter attitudes and behavior or whether they tend to influence other attitudes and behavior that in turn have an indirect influence on voter attitudes and behavior.

Length: Short-term effects (voting intentions) arise more or less directly upon contact with a message. Medium-term effects occur during the course of an election campaign, and long-term effects gradually change the political system or other subsystems of society such as the media.

As regards the *systems affected*, five units can be distinguished: the candidate, the citizen as voter, the political institutions, the political system, and the media. The first case refers to changes in a candidate's strategy and issue positions as a reaction to election polls (→ *The Use of Voter Research in Campaigns*). The second aims at the effect of election polls on the cognition or the behavior of the individual, that is to say, the individual's vote. The third case refers to the effect on public support of a political party. In the fourth case, the point of reference is changes in the rationality of political behavior, and in the last case changes in media contents.

DISCOURSE DIMENSIONS

Roughly speaking, the connections between the cause and effect factors are discussed on three different levels: the legal aspects, aspects related to the theory of democracy, and the social science aspects. The first is of prime interest here, and by nature the first two are more closely interwoven as they deal with predominantly normative issues, that is, questions regarding the area of 'should,' whereas social science aspects aim at an empirical dimension.

The legal discourse

With regard to the legal dimension, the question is whether it is legal, wise, and indeed legally possible to regulate election polls. Restrictions of this type range from a ban on publishing the results of election polls from a certain date onward to generally prohibiting opinion polls or forbidding the use of specific questions.

Several countries introduced such 'embargoes' or 'moratoriums.' According to a survey by the World Association for Public Opinion Research (WAPOR) and the European Society of Opinion and Market Research (ESOMAR) (see below), 30 of the 66 countries surveyed in 2002 currently have restrictions of one kind or another. The most common are publication bans during a specified period prior to the election, for example 15 days in Italy and Greece (Spangenberg, 2003; Smith, 2004).

In constitutional democracies, independent of their specific legal systems, limitations of this kind generally produce concerns about the following areas:

Freedom of the press. In those countries that have enacted a moratorium, it is the rights of the media that first and foremost are restricted. Election polls can be conducted and also made known—to a small group of persons such as those who commission them—but they may not be published in the mass media. This is a serious interference with the freedom of the press and would be unthinkable in many liberally oriented democracies such as the US or the United Kingdom.

Freedom of information for the public. Freedom of the press is granted and protected, among other reasons because it is intended to serve the freedom of information for the public and thus democratic opinion formation. Moratoriums on election polls, from a constitutional point of view, affect the citizens themselves most of all. They divide society into two classes based upon the information they each have: those who are familiar with election poll results because—as political parties, media or large companies—they are able to commission them, and the rest of society, who is not familiar with them because they are denied their only way to access the results of polls—via the media.

The freedom of scientific endeavor of the polling institute and its scholars, that is, the right to select topics and subjects for scholarly investigation and to research them freely according to the appropriate methods. This right, which in German legislation[1] is closely connected with freedom of communication, is so far-reaching that no democracy is known to have forbidden the conduct of election polls completely. An exception is opinion polls on election day itself, which, however, fall under the jurisdiction of election regulations and therefore can be weighted against an equally important right, namely the right to a properly conducted election. Otherwise the constitution only allows restriction of scientific research if it is connected with the investigation of areas that involve fundamental values of society. This is the case, for example, with human genetics.

The economic freedom of the polling organization. In a society with a market economy, this means the vested right of a business enterprise to actively pursue its trade. Since most survey research institutes are private enterprises, they depend upon commissioned work, including commissioned election polls.

In spite of this phalanx of legal rights, there have been, and continue to be, initiatives to introduce bans or tighten restrictions even in democracies and at the initiative of democratic-minded politicians. In Germany, for instance, as in most democratic countries, restricting opinion polls is considered very questionable and would only be legitimate if a serious negative influence were empirically

proven. A law to this effect would not be unconstitutional in principle—it could be justified through Article 38 of the constitution as a precautionary measure to guarantee an 'orderly election.' It would, however, have to be weighed against the rights listed above, and the rights derived from Article 5 (freedom of the press and broadcasting freedom, freedom of information and freedom of scientific endeavor) would provide the greatest obstacles.

After the counting problems in the 2000 presidential election, there was some discussion in the United States about prohibiting opinion polls on election day (exit polls) and possibly the publication of the first projections as long as polling stations are still open in the western part of the country. The discussions have not resulted in changes of the law. A moratorium on opinion polls *prior* to election day would be unthinkable in the US due to the legal-normative strength of the *First Amendment* and the concept of 'prior restraint' that it encompasses.[2] In discussions of this topic among American social scientists or lawyers, restrictions are usually seen as the sign of an underdeveloped democratic system.

The Philippines are a good example of how wisely constitutional judges have defended the freedom of polling (Mangahas, 2004; Social Weather Stations, Incorporated and Kamahalan Publishing Corporation, doing business as Manila Standard vs. Commission on Elections). In 2001, they declared as unconstitutional a freshly-legislated ban on the publication of election surveys. The Manila Supreme Court ruled that the legislation was invalid because 'it imposes prior restraint on the freedom of expression; it is a direct and total suppression of a category of expression even for a limited period.' The Court continued by saying: 'Because of the preferred status of the constitutional rights of speech, expression, and press, such a measure is vitiated by a weighty presumption of invalidity' (*Manila Standard*, 2001; for some background of the case see Mangahas, Guerrero, & Sandoval, 2001).

Another example is a 1998 ruling by the Supreme Court of Canada, which held section 322.1 of the Canada Elections Act unconstitutional. The section had prohibited the publication of poll results in the last three days before the election. The court was not unanimous, but it ruled:

> The doubtful benefits of the ban are outweighed by its deleterious effects. The impact of s. 322.1 on freedom of expression is profound. ... The ban interferes with the rights of voters who want access to the most timely polling information available, and with the rights of the media and pollsters who want to provide it .... Given the state of the evidence adducted on this issue, the postulated harm [of publishing polls shortly before the election, W.D./U.H.] of will seldom occur. The benefits of the ban are, therefore, marginal. The deleterious effects, however, are substantial. The ban ... interferes with the media's reporting function with respect to the election. Further, by denying access to electoral information which some voters may consider useful, the ban interferes not only with their freedom of expression, but also with their perception of the freeness and validity of their vote. In sum, the very serious invasion of the freedom of expression of all Canadians is not outweighed by the speculative and marginal benefits postulated by the government.
> (Thomson Newspapers Co. v. Canada, 1998)[3]

In addition to the legal justification, there is also the question of the feasibility and enforceability of such bans. Even before the introduction of new global communication technologies such as the Internet, there always was the theoretical possibility of gaining access to opinion poll results via the media in neighboring countries. This was particularly the case in densely populated and geographically compact Europe.

Since it is constitutionally more difficult to prohibit the conducting of opinion polls than their publication, some form of results will always be in circulation somewhere. Politicians will always have access to these results because they need them to guide their election campaigns. The media will have them either because the politicians have slipped the results to them or because they commission polls themselves in order to provide suitable background reporting, or even in order to later stand as wise predictors of the outcome. Other members of the 'elites' will also have the results passed to them either from politicians or journalists, most likely with the motive of mobilizing support.

In Belgium—at the time of the incident a country with a moratorium on opinion polls prior to the election—there was a case where stock market speculation took place over election day, and speculators who knew from (unpublished) poll results the probable winner of the election made immense profits. In the 2004 US presidential election, the stock market took a brief plunge when erroneous exit poll results suggesting Democratic candidate John Kerry was leading over President George W. Bush were leaked on the Internet in the afternoon of election day (Fuerbringer, 2004).

The Internet further increases the danger of a two-class society with respect to advance knowledge about likely election results. Sources in a country where an election is about to be held can either anonymously place the data on the web or—if they want to be absolutely sure to avoid legal consequences—provide the results to another source abroad. Someone could circumvent legal restriction in this way and—what is even more serious—again create two classes of voters. The 'digital divide,' the drifting apart of members of society who can use the new information technologies and those who cannot or do not want to use them, will divide the electorate too. The former click onto the corresponding web pages and cast their votes in the awareness of the presumed distribution of votes, and the rest of the population votes without having this information.

The democratic theory discourse

Adherents to restrictions on election polls assume that citizens need to be protected from information that could lead them to actions against their will or their interests. This position denies the citizens' ability to deal with information about opinion distributions wisely and in line with their own objectives. Defenders of the freedom of opinion research hold that such a paternalistic view is inappropriate in a mature democracy. Only in extreme cases of danger from manipulation can it be justified to deny the people access to certain information and opinions. Withholding scientifically ascertained information about the strengths of the various political parties and possible election results certainly does not fall into this category.

Defenders of the freedom of opinion research further hold that, without survey results being freely communicated, the assessment of public opinion in election campaigns would be dominated by statements from politicians and journalists. Indeed, content analyses of German news media have shown that only half of the assessments made in the press on the current standing of parties and candidates or on the expected election outcome are made on the basis of opinion polls. Politicians (about one third) and journalists contribute the other half (Donsbach & Weisbach, 2005). The former are clearly biased and usually made from self-interest, and the latter either reflect personal bias or the influence of the opinion of professional colleagues or profession-specific patterns of perception (Herbst, 1990; Donsbach, 2004; → *The News as a Reflection of Public Opinion*). This position thus does not see a threat to the political culture in the growing visibility of survey results in communication before elections, which in a sense represents an objectification of public opinion assessments.

In spite of the margins of error resulting from the methods and occasional handling errors—or much less often—conscious manipulation, the results of public opinion polls are still a comparatively rational form of information in a sea of partisan and biased statements from other sources about the possible outcome of the election (Lang & Lang, 1984; Donsbach & Antoine, 1990). Again, the Supreme Court in the Philippines made the point as clear as possible: 'To sustain the ban on survey results would sanction the censorship of all speaking by candidates in an election on the ground that the usual bombasts and hyperbolic claims made during the campaign can confuse the voters and thus debase the electoral process.' Noting that a ban on political ads had already been lifted, the Court said the assailed law, in effect, would show a bias by preferring personal opinion to statistical results (*Manila Standard*, 2001).

Adherents of restricting the dissemination of poll results prior to the election also argue that publishing polls might increase *tactical voting*—that is, a voter's decision to adjust his or her vote according to the expected outcome of the election. This is deplored, because a person's vote will not go to the voter's first choice, but to a political party that only ranks second or third in his or her actual preference. This can be a decision to vote for the party that is expected to win the election, thus putting oneself on the winner's side. Or it can also be a decision in favor of a party that the voter would like to see achieve a quorum and make it into parliament. Or it can also be the decision to vote for a party that the voter would like to see strengthened—in order to limit the power of another political party.

In opposition, defenders of the freedom of opinion research hold that tactical voting is not necessarily detrimental to democracy. On the contrary, tactical considerations can help to bring about functioning majorities through coalition formation or prevent one party from assuming a dominating position of power. This, in effect, gives freedom to publish an important democratic function, that of a stabilizing influence on the political party system. This position also holds that, in the end, it is solely the affair of the voters how they make up their minds about whom to vote for. It would be incompatible with the idea of free elections to consciously and intentionally withhold information that is available *and* desired by the voters *and* considered to be relevant.

The social science discourse

Within the social science sphere, the question of whether to restrict the conduct of survey research and/or the publication of its results is discussed in terms of the attention paid to polls, their accuracy and their effects. Studies from different countries have shown that both the voters and the media have increased their attention to surveys in recent decades (Donsbach, 1984; Brettschneider, 1996), that the media have increasingly commissioned polls in this time (Ladd & Benson, 1992; Hardmeier, 2000), and that opinion research is generally approved by the people (Gallup & Moore, 1996; O'Neill, 1996; → *The News Media's Use of Opinion Polls*). In spite of the media's increased attention to polls, much criticism can be formulated against the quality of their reporting of poll results. Research from the US indicates that the responsiveness of the political institution to public opinion increased as the significance of polling grew (Page & Shapiro, 1983).

With regard to accuracy, unavoidable errors (such as those deriving from the time lag between data collection and publication of results or the problem of allocating undecideds) as well as avoidable errors are discussed. Among the latter, aspects such as a lack of professionalism in the field (Lang & Lang, 1991) and the lax application of quality criteria are dealt with. As to intentional or manipulative errors, they are sometimes speculated about, but there is hardly any proof that manipulation occurs in reputable institutes.

As to the effects of opinion polls on opinion formation, empirical results can be summarized as follows:

1 The results are inconclusive and depend to a great degree upon the method used and the particular political circumstances at the time.
2 In general we can say that the more natural the test situation, the weaker the influence that is measured, or there is a lack of a demonstrated influence altogether. Experiments and self-reports give the strongest indications, and natural experiments provide the least indication of an effect of poll results.
3 If there is an influence on voting intention at all, it is more likely to be in the form of a bandwagon effect.
4 Under the prerequisites of certain electoral systems (e.g. the five-percent quorum in Germany) supporters of the smaller party, or the party that requires the smaller party for a coalition, can be convinced by opinion polls to vote for their second choice party (Donsbach, 2001).

As a whole, the effects remain first of all minimal, and second they can be seen as completely harmless. There are various reasons for effects being limited. First, based on probability theory, there are usually several, slightly different election forecasts. Second, election forecasts are quite obviously perceived selectively in favor of one's own opinion. Third, poll results (at least prior to the election) tend to get drowned out amidst the many other statements on the outcome of the election. Fourth, statements, man-in-the-street interviews and the like are apparently much more effective than poll data in influencing expectations of the climate of opinion and also (although the likelihood of this is questioned) voting intentions. Fifth, the significance of election polls for the average citizen is overestimated by both politicians and social scientists. This is because members of both groups have an above-average education and are used to working with information that is presented with quantitative symbols (percentage figures). For lesser educated persons, such comparative percentages remain relatively abstract, and as a result do not create very much of an impression. Furthermore, election polls have an essential significance for politicians and researchers. For the former, they are information about their political fate, and for the latter (at least some of them), they are the way they make their living.

LEGAL SITUATION FOR OPINION RESEARCH IN THE WORLD

The first worldwide survey among opinion researchers dealing with the freedom to conduct opinion polls and publish their results was conducted by the World Association for Public Opinion Research (WAPOR) in 1984. Updates of this study were co-sponsored by WAPOR and ESOMAR (World Association of Research Professionals) and conducted under the auspices of the Foundation for

Information (fi) in 1992, 1996, and 2002. For the 2002 study, a self-completion questionnaire was posted on the fi website, and WAPOR and ESOMAR members conducting polls were invited to participate. In this way, data from 66 countries were gathered.

The study covers almost all of Europe (35 countries) and all of North America, considerable parts of Latin America (12 countries) and the Asian and Pacific region (13 countries), but only two countries each in the Middle East and Africa. The sample of countries is certainly not representative of all countries in the world, as those parts where there are no opinion polls independent of the state are not covered at all, either for financial or political reasons (or both). But given the large number of countries in the study and their distribution over several world regions, the data should give a fair picture of the democratic parts of the world.

Thirty of the 66 countries reported embargoes on the publication of findings before elections, ranging from one to 30 days. The longest embargo was in Luxembourg (30 days), followed by the Republic of Korea (23 days), Greece and Italy (15 days), Slovakia (14 days) and Switzerland (10 days). All other countries with restrictions ruled out the publication of election polls either during the last seven days before the ballots opened or for just one or two days before that. Fifty-six countries were also previously surveyed in 1996. In 15 of them, restrictions were liberalized between 1996 and 2002, and in nine, heavier restrictions (including longer bans) were introduced. The most severe change in a direction towards heavier restrictions occurred in Korea and Greece, countries that newly introduced the bans after 1996. The clearest examples of liberalization were South Africa and Indonesia, who completely lifted their earlier bans of 42 and 21 days respectively, and Turkey, which reduced a 30-day embargo to just 7 days. Italy and Venezuela each reduced their ban by 13 days, down to 15 from 28 in Italy and down to two from 15 in Venezuela. Poland reduced its moratorium from 12 days to just one day (Sulek, forthcoming). All other

changes were smaller. The balance between 1996 and 2002 is therefore tilted somewhat toward liberalization, but restrictions were maintained in many countries. Some countries also witnessed efforts to tighten restrictions, which eventually failed as in Canada, India, or the Philippines (Spangenberg, 2003; Smith, 2004).

Legal regulation goes beyond banning the publication of results before elections. In a few countries, regulations specify which questions cannot be asked or reported, or reported only with a delay, in election surveys. Methodological information such as geographical coverage, sample characteristics, mode and date of interviewing, and the like, are prescribed almost everywhere, but by far in most countries, this is required by self-regulation of the industry rather than by law. Exit polls (usually interviews conducted outside the polling station) are permitted almost everywhere in the countries surveyed; but in a majority of them, the dissemination of the results is restricted until after the ballots have closed. Earlier studies (Rohme, 1992) also revealed some idiosyncratic general regulations such as a ban on questions about the United Nations or the risk of civil war (banned in Greece, publication banned in Argentina, pertaining to the situation in 1992). In some countries, questions on defense issues were not asked (e.g. Chile and Venezuela in 1992).

CONCLUSION

The legal status of public opinion research in the democratic parts of the world is defined between the competing forces of rights enshrined in national and international declarations of liberty, such as the freedom of speech and information, the freedom of scientific endeavor and the freedom to conduct businesses on the one hand, and government regulations focusing mostly on election polling on the other. In undemocratic countries, opinion research is, of course, not conducted at all, or only under supervision of the rulers. The general justification for restricting (pre-)election polls is derived from assumptions about potentially detrimental effects. In the discussion of restrictions, opinion polls proper and the publication of early results have to be distinguished, as they have different kinds of effects. The freedom to conduct and publish opinion research can be justified in *legal discourse* by the rights granted to human beings. In *democratic theory discourse*, it can be defended by arguing that any moratorium on publishing pre-election polls necessarily creates a cleavage between people who know the results and those who do not. In *social science discourse*, the inconclusiveness of the knowledge of the effects of pre-election polls and their harmlessness can be put forth. The most recent empirical study on restrictions to election polling dates from 2002, and shows that slightly less than half of the countries surveyed restricted the publication of opinion research results before elections for periods from one to 30 days, with moratoriums for periods of more than seven days being relatively rare. Recent changes have shown a slight balance to more liberalization, but restrictions remain in effect in many countries.

NOTES

1 Both are in Article 5 of the Grundgesetz (German constitution), paragraphs 1 and 3.

2 'Congress shall make no law respecting an establishment of religion, or prohibiting the free exercise thereof; or abridging the freedom of speech, or of the press; or the right of the people peaceably to assemble, and to petition the Government for a redress of grievances.'

3 Thanks to Robert Chung for providing this ruling, and other information.

REFERENCES

Adams, W. C. (2005). *Election night news and voter turnout: Solving the projection puzzle.* Boulder, CO: Lynne Rienner.

Brettschneider, F. (1996). Wahlumfragen und Medien [Election surveys and the media]. *Politische Vierteljahresschrift, 37,* 475–493.

Donsbach, W. (1984). Die Rolle der Demoskopie in der Wahlkampf-Kommunikation [The role of survey

research in election campaign coverage]. *Zeitschrift für Politik, 31,* 388–407.

Donsbach, W. (2001). *Who's afraid of election polls? Normative and empirical arguments for freedom of pre-election surveys.* Amsterdam: ESOMAR.

Donsbach, W. (2004). Psychology of news decisions. Factors behind journalists' professional behavior. *Journalism, 5,* 131–157.

Donsbach, W., & Antoine, J. (1990). Journalists and the polls: A parallel survey among journalists in France and Germany. *Marketing and Research Today, 18,* 167–174.

Donsbach, W., & Weisbach, K. (2005). Kampf um das Meinungsklima (Battle for the climate of opinion). In E. Noelle-Neumann, W. Donsbach & H. M. Kepplinger (Eds.), *Wählerstimmungen in der Mediendemokratie* (pp. 105–127). Freiburg, München: Alber.

Fuerbringer, J. (2004, November 4). Shares rally as investors welcome election's end. *New York Times.*

Gallup, A., & Moore, D. W. (1996). Younger people today are more positive about polls than their elders. *The Public Perspective, August/September,* 50–53.

Hardmeier, S. (2000). Meinungsumfragen im Journalismus. Nachrichtenwert, Präzision und Publikum [Opinion surveys in journalism: News value, precision, and the public]. *Medien & Kommunikationswissenschaft, 48,* 371–395.

Herbst, S. (1990). Assessing public opinion in the 1930s–1940s: Retrospective views of journalists. *Journalism Quarterly, 67,* 943–949.

Ladd, E. C., & Benson, J. (1992). The growth of news polls in American politics. In T. E. Mann & G. R. Orren (Eds.), *Media polls in American politics* (pp. 19–31). Washington, DC: Brookings Institution.

Lang, K., & Lang, G. E. (1984). The impact of polls on public opinion. In J. L. Martin (Ed.), *Polling and the democratic consensus. The annals of the American Academy of Political and Social Science* (Vol. 472, pp. 129–142). Beverly Hills: Sage.

Lang, K., & Lang, G. E. (1991). The changing professional ethos: A poll of pollsters. *International Journal of Public Opinion Research, 3,* 323–339.

Mangahas, M. (2004). Election survey freedom in the Philippines. *International Journal of Market Research, 46,* 103–107.

Mangahas, M., Guerrero, L. L., & Sandoval, G. (2001, September). *Opinion polling and national elections in the Philippines, 1992–2001.* Paper presented at the Annual Conference of the World Association for Public Opinion Research, Rome, Italy.

Manila Standard (2001, May 6), pp. 1–2.

O'Neill, H. W. (1996). Our greatest interest and most frustrating challenge is how to increase the rate of public participation in polls. *The Public Perspective,* *August/September,* 54–56.

Page, B. I., & Shapiro, R. Y. (1983). Effects of public opinion on policy. *American Political Science Review,* *77,* 175–190.

Rohme, N. (1992, May). The state of the art of public opinion polling worldwide. Paper presented at the WAPOR Annual Conference, St. Petersburg, FL.

Smith, T. W. (2004). Freedom to conduct public opinion polls around the world. *International Journal of Public Opinion Research, 16,* 215–233.

Social Weather Stations, Incorporated and Kamahalan Publishing Corporation, doing business as Manila Standard, petitioners, vs. Commission on Elections, respondent. Supreme Court of the Philippines, G.R. 147571, (2001, May 5). Retrieved January 31, 2007, from http://www. supremecourt.gov.ph/jurisprudence/2001/may2001/ 147571.htm.

Spangenberg, F. (2003). *The freedom to publish* *opinion poll results. Report on a worldwide update.* Amsterdam: Foundation for Information.

Sulek, A. (forthcoming). The struggle for the freedom to publish opinion poll results: The case of Poland. *International Journal of Public Opinion Research.*

Thomson Newspapers Co. v. Canada. (1998). *Supreme* *Court Reports,* pp. 877ff. Retrieved February 23, 2007, from http://www.lexum.umontreal.ca/csc-sec/en/pub/1998/vol1/html/1998scr1_0877.html.

Traugott, M., Highton, B., & Brady, H. E. (2005, March 10). *A review of recent controversies concern-* *ing the 2004 presidential election exit poll.* Report, National Research Commission on Elections and Voting, Social Science Research Council, New York.

40

Attitudes of the Public Toward Public Opinion Research and Polling

Anne Hildreth

The public's sentiment and general understanding of survey research and polling is a topic that joins fundamental principles of democracy with a rapidly changing communication and research environment. With these changes have come significant challenges to those who use surveys as a public research tool. Several cautions surround our interpretation of public opinions on polls, as favorability and selection bias commingle with more standard problems of low response rates and non-response error.

This chapter reviews the public's evaluation of public opinion, primarily represented as polls. It presents the current state of our knowledge in layers. First, it accounts for the best data resources to date and provides a baseline summary of public opinion on polls. Next, it considers polling in the context of policy as a higher quality of data and treats elections as a special instance of a poll in context. The final layer highlights some examples of research that disentangle

attitudes on polls and predispositions from the political and social contexts. The chapter ends with suggestions for future research.

The importance of gauging public sentiment about polls is rooted in their role in democratic processes. A lion's share of our political communication today is conducted through polls, both vertically between the public and elected leaders, and horizontally across the community. Discourse, deliberation, accountability, responsiveness: all of these features of democracy are facilitated by accurate polls and attention to polls, on the part of political leadership and the public. Powerful pointed critiques of polls serve to remind researchers of the costs associated with construing public opinion so narrowly. For a crash course on a range of ways scholars have conceptualized the promise and problems of public opinion polls for democracies, see Gallup and Rae (1940), Blumer (1948), Tilly (1983), Ginsberg (1986), and Herbst (1993, 1998).

DATA RESOURCES (AND PROFESSIONAL RUMINATIONS)

Given the necessity of public confidence to the vitality of the polling enterprise, the public's understanding of the venture is under-researched. In 1944, Goldman found that only 48% of the public in the US had even heard of polling. Since that initial battery of questions gauging familiarity with polls, there have been only a handful of detailed analyses of public attitudes toward polls. More common are short batteries of questions by a polling organization to get a passing reaction.

Several exceptions form the basis of much of what we know about the public's opinion of polls. In the 1980s, Walker Research did a careful analysis of how survey research was perceived by Americans in light of challenges posed by telemarketers. Also in the 1980s, fresh from the poor performance of polls in the 1984 election, Roper asked a lengthy series of questions (Roper, 1986). In 1998, the Council of American Survey Research Organizations (CASRO) conducted a phone and Internet poll on polls. A Gallup survey in 2000 included more than a dozen questions on the topic. In 2001, the Henry J. Kaiser Family Foundation joined with *Public Perspective* magazine in a thorough investigation that compared public attitudes on polls and their role in the political process with the opinions of media and political leaders. This research work by survey organizations has been complemented by regular efforts in the academy to examine the character of public attitudes about surveys and polls, their correlates, and their relationship to sociological and psychological processes.

Even if it has not been the subject of sustained attention from survey organizations, professional concern with the character of public regard has been steady. The 1985 Plenary Session at the jointly held annual meeting of the World Association of Public Opinion Research (WAPOR)/American Association of Public Opinion Researchers (AAPOR) was devoted to addressing the question: Is there a crisis of confidence? Again in 2004 the WAPOR/AAPOR conference theme was 'The public image of survey research.' Zukin's (2006) speech is the most recent in a litany of AAPOR and WAPOR Presidential addresses and presentations by recipients of the Din-erman award that include in their reflections a call for a better understanding of popular attitudes and confidence in survey research. The radical evolution in the communication environment in the last few decades, from answering machines to the Internet, has issued a barrage of challenges to the measurement capacity of polls and the public image of survey research.

DISTINCTIONS AND DIMENSIONS

Before reviewing the evidence on public attitudes about opinion polls, there are fundamental analytical distinctions that help organize the subject and have practical relevance for how one evaluates the quality of opinion on polls. Poll subjects vary; surveying opinions in the policy arena on social issues is distinct from polling on candidate preferences during or on the eve of an election. Marketing research and consumer and product polling are distinct from election and policy research ($\rightarrow$ *Marketing Research;* $\rightarrow$ *The Use of Voter Research in Campaigns*).

Vertical use of polls describes how they are used by political leaders in representational exchange. Horizontal use describes how the public uses polls to understand the larger community context on any given issue. Reports of public opinion on policy are less likely to drive media reports, and they appear to be regarded differently from election polls by the public.

One final distinction operates as a caveat: the extent to which people can distinguish their attitudes about public opinion from their attitudes about media reports of public opinion is difficult to disentangle but important to appreciate. This confluence may be especially significant in gauging popular assessments of election polls. Attention to some of these same distinctions can sharpen the call for future research. These distinctions will structure the following review.

Polling on polls presents an inherent methodological conundrum. A 2000 Fox News/Opinion Dynamics Poll question confronts the issue head on while illustrating the tension of a poll on polls: 'You won't hurt my feelings no matter how you answer this, but how often do you think you can trust the results of public opinion polls?' What Dran (1993) identified as the 'survey equivalent of the Heisenberg principle,' Goyder (1986) referred to as 'the epistemological limitation' of polling on polls: 'employing an instrument to measure its own performance is immediately contradictory.' This Catch-22 muddies the measurement process. It is exacerbated by the failure of many of these general questions on polls to have clear salience for the respondent. The semantics of 'polls' as a referent may be an abstraction, and one that may vary by degree. A question about election polls asked before, during, or after an election may have a clear political referent, especially for respondents attentive to politics; a question about polls in general, coming out of the blue, may be less clear or may bring to mind the respondent's immediate survey experience.

The evidence establishes that the public has generally positive, stable attitudes toward polls in the abstract. Additionally, research that explores attitudes about polls in a specific issue context, and controls for the effects of individual and contextual factors, contributes to our understanding of the factors that shape how polls are consumed and used in negotiating politics.

GENERAL EVALUATIONS

General attitudes about polls in the United States are positive and remarkably stable. As the top panel on Table 40.1 reports, one of the most enduring questions asked, that of 'whether polls are a good thing or a bad thing for the country,' has returned consistently positive evaluations that grow more positive across time, especially when the category for 'or don't they make a difference' was removed as a possible response alternative. This response alternative matters. Academic

research that has repeated the item and retained the middle alternative has returned a less glowing evaluation, at 39% in Kang, Lavrakas, Presser, Price, and Traugott (1998) and 30% in Price and Stroud (2005). In each of these studies, the middle alternative received the plurality response. A similarly positive evaluation of polls is evident when people are asked about the volume of polling, or whether poll results can be trusted.

People also appear to readily assign credibility to polls even while they admit some skepticism. In the 2001 Kaiser survey, 33% replied that polls accurately reflect public thinking 'just about always' and 'most of the time.' A majority responded 'only some of the time.' Both the Roper 1985 survey and the Kaiser 2001 survey found large majorities trust the answers their fellow respondents give: 81% of the Roper sample said nearly all or most of the people interviewed in surveys 'tell the truth,' and 81% of the Kaiser respondents agreed strongly or somewhat that people answer honestly. Moreover, 69% of the Kaiser respondents agreed that professional poll takers try to be careful to ask questions that don't favor one side of an issue. The proportion who report having participated in polls has held steady, at or around 75%, across the last decade.

In comparisons to polls as products, pollsters may fare less well and their evaluation may be heading in the negative direction. This creeping negativism may be one area in which popular evaluations are reacting to the growing partisan polarization of the national political environment and the increase in the political uses of polls. Both the CASRO data and the Kaiser data suggest the public does discriminate between survey research done in support of policy or consumer research versus polling conducted on behalf of political actors or interests. When the title of 'pollsters' was invoked generally, a few recent surveys returned majorities saying they would not trust them. Earlier industry assessments, done by Walker Research and CASRO, suggest that people do discern differences among types of pollsters. Experiments with hypothetical poll reports by Lavrakas, Presser, Traugott, and

Table 40.1   Trends in public attitudes on polls

1. General evaluation of public opinion polls

Evaluation	1956	1963	1990	1996a	1996b
Good	61	65	72	89	81.4
Bad	3	3	24	8	12.4
No difference	28	32		5	
Neither good nor bad	8				

General evaluations:
1956: NORC (n = 1287) In general, do you think public opinion polls are a good thing for the country, or a bad thing, or don't they make any difference one way or the other?
1963: NORC (n = 1515) The next question has to do with public opinion polls. In general do you think public opinion polls are a good thing for the country, or a bad thing, or don't they make any difference one way or the other?
1990: Yankelovich Clancy Shulman (n = 1000) officials sometimes use polls to find out what people think of the issues. In general, do you think this is good practice or a bad practice?
1996a: Gallup (n = 1001) (I'd like to ask you some questions about polls in general, based on what you know or have read or heard about them, not just your experience in this interview.) ... In general, would you say that polls of the opinion of the public are a good thing or a bad thing in our country
1996b: Northern Illinois University (n = 800) In general, would you say polls of the opinion of the public are a good thing or a bad thing in our country?

2. Influence of polls in Washington

Amount	1994	1999	2000	2001	2002
Too Much	37	36	35	38	33
Too Little	52	49	44	41	49
About Right	3	8	8	10	8

Influence in Washington:
1994: Harris Poll (n = 1246) And now a question about the power of different groups in influencing government policy, politicians, and policy makers in Washington. Do you think opinion polls have too much or too little influence on Washington?
1999: Harris Poll (n = 1007) Do you think opinion polls have too much or too little power and influence on Washington?
2000: Harris Poll (n = 1014) And now a question about the power of different groups in influencing government policy, politicians, and policy makers in Washington. Do you think opinion polls have too much or too little power and influence in 2001: Harris Poll (n = 1004) Do you think opinion polls have/ has too much or too little power and influence in Washington?
2002: Harris Poll (n = 1021) How does the power of different groups influence government policy, politicians, and policy makers in Washington? Do you think opinion polls have too much or too little power and influence in Washington?

3. Polls in context

Attitude	1974	1990A	1990B	1998	2003
Positive	44	56	83	63	81
Negative	42	41	14	25	15
DK	14	4	3	12	4

Polls in context:
1974: Gallup (n = 1509). 'Do you think public opinion polls concerning the issue of impeachment [of President Nixon] should be discontinued during the period of the proceedings, or not' (Note: Coding changed so 'positive' = keep polls)
1990A: Gallup (n = 1013). 'Do you think President Bush should stick closely to American public opinion when deciding what steps to take next—including the results of polls like this one—or should President Bush do what he thinks is best regardless of what the American public thinks?'
1990B: Gallup (n = 1013). 'More generally, do you think the results of public opinion polls on the Persian Gulf crisis like this one should be widely published and discussed, or not?'
1998: Chicago Tribute/Market Shares Corporation (n = 700). 'As you know, polls still show that a great majority of Americans approve of the job Clinton is doing as president. Do you think the polls are mostly accurate about how Americans feel about Clinton or do you think the polls are mostly wrong?'
2003: CBS News (n = 681). 'When deciding what to do about Iraq, how much do you think the Bush administration should take into account the views of the American public as expressed in polls like this one—a lot, some, not much, or not at all?'

Table 40.1—(Cont'd)

4. Party differences in perceptions of polls in context

	1998 Evaluation of Clinton in polls	2003 Bush administration and Iraq
Total – positive	63	81
Democrats – positive	82	87
Republicans – positive	42	72
Independents – positive	62	82

Party differences:

1998: Chicago Tribute/Market Shares Corporation ($n = 700$). 'As you know, polls still show that a great majority of Americans approve of the job Clinton is doing as president. Do you think the polls are mostly accurate about how Americans feel about Clinton or do you think the polls are mostly wrong?'

2003: CBS News ($n = 681$). 'When deciding what to do about Iraq, how much do you think the Bush administration should take into account the views of the American public as expressed in polls like this one—a lot, some, not much, or not at all?'

5. Grading pollsters' conduct in the campaign

Grade	1988	1992	1996	1998	2004	2006
A	13	15	11	12	16	20
B	29	31	23	28	26	29
C	29	27	29	30	33	25
D	12	9	11	11	9	7
F	11	6	10	6	8	4
DK/Refused	6	12	16	13	8	15

Grading the pollsters:

2006: Pew Research Center ($n = 1479$) Students are often given the grades A, B, C, D, or Fail to describe the quality of their work. Looking back over the campaign, what grade would you give to each of the following groups for the way they conducted themselves in the campaign? The pollsters.

2004: Pew Research Center ($n = 1209$) 1998: Pew Research Center ($n = 1005$) 1996: Pew Research Center ($n = 1012$) 1992: Times Mirror ($n = 1012$) Students are often given the grades A, B, C, D, or Fail to describe the quality of their work. Looking back over the campaign, what grade would you give to the following group for the way they conducted themselves in the campaign: the pollsters?

Price (1998) suggest that people take into account the identity of a polling organization, and the interest a poll's sponsor might have in a survey's outcome when they evaluate poll reports.

High proportions of respondents do not understand how polling works and may not have the knowledge or interest to differentiate a good poll from a bad one. In his analysis of the Kaiser data, Evans Witt (2001, p. 15) reports that 'Americans recognize their own limitations in dealing intelligently with polls—half of those in the survey had little or no confidence in their ability to judge whether a particular survey was carried out in a fair and scientific manner.' Roper's 1985 poll on polls reports that a clear majority—56%—are skeptical about sampling, a proportion similar to what Kaiser finds in 2001. Roper cites sampling issues as the most frequent reservations

mentioned in the 1985 survey. The Kaiser data returns a similar proportion on a similar question. In that survey, the sample of policy leaders and members of the media are more likely than the public to agree that polling is based on 'sound scientific practices': 50% of the public agreed with that assertion, compared to 75% of the policy leaders and 83% of the media.

Panel 2 on Table 40.1 addresses polls explicitly as a means of vertical political communication: How much influence should they have in reflecting public views? Once again, the trend in the last decade is fairly stable and positive. In 1990, 72% said it was a 'good practice' for 'government officials to use polls to find out what people think.' A similar question in 1996 taps this vertical pathway of political communication in a more proscriptive manner: 74% report that the nation would be 'better off if leaders followed the views of public opinion polls more closely.' By 2005, the proportion responding 'we'd be better off' had declined to 61%. Kang *et al.* (1998) include an extensive battery of questions about surveys and use factor analysis to demonstrate a distinct vertical and horizontal dimension of poll attitudes. They find polls were more positively regarded when the questions were in the horizontal 'interest in others' opinions' dimension relative to their 'government attention to polls' dimension.

A major focus of the 2001 Kaiser Family Foundation research was to evaluate how the public regarded polls compared to other ways to represent public opinion. In that data, a higher proportion of respondents favored a trustee approach to representation over consideration of public opinion polls. The Kaiser respondents were skeptical about how attentive political leaders actually were to the public and to polls. A substantial majority of 76% responded that polls are very and somewhat useful for 'elected and government officials in Washington to understand how the public feels about important issues.' Given an opportunity to choose among different ways in which elected leaders could learn the majority's preferences, equal proportions chose town meetings and constituent contacts as chose conducting a poll.

The Kaiser data reinforces the fact that a fair proportion of the public fail to distinguish an 'equalizing' feature of polls relative to the 'intense' representation associated with constituent mail or town meetings. The Kaiser survey also reflects an American public confidence in polls. After plenty of priming on various dimensions of public opinion, political decision making, and polls, the survey asks participants: 'Do you agree or disagree that public opinion polling is far from perfect, but it is one of the best means we have for communicating what the public is thinking?' A comfortable majority of 84% strongly or somewhat agreed with that statement.

Much of the published analyses of attitudes about polls in countries other than America focus on the election context. However, the jPOLL databank at the Roper Center

for Public Opinion Research, University of Connecticut, includes a question repeated in Japan about whether or not the results of public opinion polls are very useful for society. Asked in slightly different ways in 1992, 1993, and 1998 of a national sample of either voters or adults, between 63% and 80% of the Japanese respondents said polls were very useful or somewhat useful.

Queen's University Canadian Opinion Research Archive contains a question asked five times between 1983 and 1995 to evaluate the level of confidence Canadians have in public opinion polls. There is remarkable stability across this time series with a consistent majority responding they have a lot or some confidence in public opinion polls across the 12-year period. A Gallup Canada question reflects a similar level of stability, but perhaps less confidence when the subject is the honesty of pollsters. When asked how they would rate the honesty and ethical standards of public opinion pollsters, respondents saying 'very high' or 'high' ranged between 28 to 35% across the five survey years from 1995 to 1999.

POLLS IN CONTEXT

Conclusions based on these general positive assessments about surveys are inherently limited. The questions lack a specific issue context or political referent, and therefore don't inform our understanding of how the public actually consumes polls when they encounter them in the media. More recent research has begun to fill the gap by examining how the issue or political context of polling mixes with individual predispositions to influence peoples' assessments of polls.

Panels 3 and 4 on Table 40.1 illustrate evaluations of polls in the context of specific political events. The first panel compares several reports of public assessments of polls on a range of topics, from Nixon's impeachment to the 2003 Iraq invasion. These polls confirm the positive evaluations from panels 1 and 2, but they tell us something more specific about what the public thinks about polls. And they stimulate one to question what is behind some of these differing levels of support for public opinion polls. Panel 4 suggests that partisanship may have a bearing on the evaluation of polls in a particular issue context. In addition to confirming a role for partisanship, studies that examine demographic and political connections have linked age (Dran & Hildreth, 1995), education (Lavrakas, Holley, & Miller, 1991) and socio-economic status (Traugott, 2003) to shaping evaluations of polls.

Academic research has also probed the critical social–psychological dimension of attitudes on polls systematically. Early research by Marsh (1986) investigates the bandwagon and underdog effects of poll reports in an issue context. Dran and Hildreth (1995) establish the sensible correlation between the intensity of opinion on a particular topic and support for the influence of polls. Lavrakas, Presser, Traugott, and Price (1998) find evidence of looking glass perception, whereby people believe polls when they affirm their position and discount them when they do not. Pan, Abisaid, Paek, Sun, and Houden (2005) find evidence of third person effects (→ *Public Opinion and the Third-Person Effect*) in how people regard media reports of polls on issues. De Vreese and Semetko (2002) and Price and Stroud (2005) provide research on whether a third-person effect operates on people's perceptions of polls in elections. Both studies find evidence to support the notion that people are likely to regard others as more susceptible to influence by poll results than themselves.

ELECTIONS AS A SPECIAL CONTEXT

Efforts to gauge public reaction to election polling dominate the polls on polls. While some research has reported a high proportion of negative assessments of horse race polls (Traugott, 1991; Price & Stroud, 2005), polling organizations have reported high marks from the public on their election work in recent years. Even given the media frenzy and the hyperbole about election polls, the final panel on Table 40.1 indicates that a comfortable majority award a passing grade to pollsters for their conduct in campaigns. In 2006 pre-election surveys, more than one media pollster returned a high proportion of respondents saying they would be willing to participate in an exit poll. A stable plurality and usually a majority trust the accuracy of polls in predicting elections.

The timing of a poll in the election cycle affects how it might be used by citizens (Bartels, 1988). A presidential primary occurs in a different information environment than a tracking poll. The timing also affects how likely the public is to see polls reported. These dynamics make elections important opportunities to clarify the conditions under which the public makes use of polls. However, research directed at this puzzle confronts a double whammy of sorts, as it joins measurement issues that surround media effects with the methodological conundrum of polling on polls.

Backing the losing candidate, or the losing side in a referendum, is related to negative assessments of election polls and sometimes for higher levels of support for imposing limitations on poll reports. This finding is consistent with work on policy polls discussed in the prior section. Price and Stroud (2005) use a panel of citizens from the Electronic Dialogue project, a random sample given a web-based survey, to examine how media exposure, political engagement and candidate support in the 2000 election influence attitudes on polls. Their multivariate analysis finds solid evidence of third person bias and a complex set of relationships between attention to media, candidate support, and attitudes toward polls and their reporting. The battery of specific questions on polls in elections is impressive and the respondents are quite negative about polls. Most importantly, Price and Stroud discuss the relationship they find between individual predispositions and attitudes toward polls as a function of the match between disposition and poll message.

De Vreese and Semetko (2002) combine content analysis, focus groups, and panel data to investigate both how polls are reported and public reactions to polls in Denmark's

EU referendum. They posit a typology of poll effects at the individual and institutional levels. The EU election was a highly salient and closely contested decision. Polls were a central part of the newspaper coverage and, in their qualitative and quantitative data, these researchers were regarded as dominating the coverage. Exit polls reported on Election Day were not regarded as negatively as the pre-election polls. De Vreese and Semetko also find third person bias; and, like Price and Stroud, they find high levels of support for restrictions among those who were dissatisfied with the coverage and outcome of the campaign.

The general poll readings reported in Panel 1 of Table 40.1 suggest the public is relatively satisfied with election polls, while these two academic studies paint a less positive picture. These more sober assessments may be a function of the concentrated attention to polls and polling these studies engender, providing respondents an opportunity to reflect what they can think rather than what they do think. More importantly, in both studies, even given this heightened attention, the willingness to support limitations on surveys is limited. Smith (2004) underscores the significance of independent polling in his review of efforts to ban or restrict election polls. He reports polls that show stable majorities in Canada, Denmark, Great Britain, and the United States being against a ban on pre-election polls. His review states that in countries where an attempt has been made to ban or censor polls, support for these prohibitions are more likely to come from parties and elites than the people (→ *Exit Polls and Pre-Election Polls*).

FUTURE CHALLENGES AND FUTURE RESEARCH

The layers of research on polls and the analytical distinctions that have organized this entry frame the research challenges that lie ahead. The Kaiser poll discussed earlier demonstrates how polling and research organizations can contribute to our understanding

of poll consumption and public evaluation. More surveys that give sustained attention to the topic of polling and public opinion are necessary. Probing work like Kaiser's should include attitudes about public opinion on policy questions. However, not all surveys need to give the resources and attention of a Kaiser or a Pew to contribute to our knowledge base. Our understanding of attitudes on public opinion research has been developed through short, replicated series of items, questions asked about the role of the public and polls in an issue context, and wording experiments.

Lamenting the presence of 'polls by the hundreds,' Patterson (2005) names pre-election polls as one of the factors contributing to the poor quality of campaigns and elections in the United States. The silver lining of the American election poll frenzy is the range of information contexts it provides for research. As Price and Stroud point out in their study of the 2000 presidential election, research in one election is still just one election. A rich variety of structures and contexts are offered in local, state, national and international elections, and referendum campaigns.

These more and better polls should be in a feedback loop to assess the progress of the public understanding of polls. There have been continuous calls for better public education toward smarter poll consumption. Volumes like *Polling and the Public* (Asher, 2004) and *The Voter's Guide to Election Polls* (Traugott & Lavrakas, 2004) contribute to popular understanding of the technical details of polls and their essential role in the political system. Both precision journalism and public journalism have provided a communication platform for community level discourse using polls and other mechanisms which represent public views.

Our knowledge of public attitudes about election polls needs to be supplemented with more attention to polls in the context of policy debates. The Lavrakas and Traugott (2000) edited volume and the earlier collection on the 1992 campaign noted above bring together current research that engages a single election context with an appreciation of the importance of polls in the election exchange between the media, candidates, and voters. For example, *Taken by Storm* (Bennett & Paletz, 1994) assembled research on different facets of the relationship between public opinion, the media and the Gulf War, thus allowing scholars to consider the conditions under which there is attentiveness to polls and citizen opinion by the public, political leadership, and the media on a highly salient issue. Better still is work that engages a variety of researchers together from the start on a concerted research agenda and a complex study design. The work of Just *et al.* (1996) in *Crosstalk* is an exemplar of this type of work. Their design exploited macro and micro features of presidential campaigns and employed focus groups, surveys, and interviews to advance our understanding of communication in campaigns.

Surveys that posit general questions about polls may share a quality with early research that sought to evaluate support for democratic values and understand political tolerance. The 'slippage' between the high levels of popular support for free speech (90%) among the American population and the significantly lower level of support for allowing the Klu Klux Klan to march is important to understand (Prothro & Grigg, 1960). Both the abstract support and the applied principle are considered important features of a democracy. So it is also with the distinction between findings of general polls on polls and research that explores public attitudes in a more controlled manner.

ACKNOWLEDGMENT

The author wishes to thank Jeanne Proctor and Shannon Scotece for assistance with this review.

REFERENCES

Asher, H. (2004). *Polling and the public: What every citizen should know*. Washington, DC: CQ Press.

Bartels, L. M. (1988). *Presidential primaries and the dynamics of public choice*. Princeton, NJ: Princeton University Press.

Bennett, L. W., & Paletz, D. (Eds.). (1994). *Taken by storm*. Chicago: University of Chicago Press.

Blumer, H. (1948). Public opinion and public opinion polling. *American Sociological Review, 13*, 542–554.

De Vreese, C. H., & Semetko, H. A. (2002). Public perception of polls and support for restriction on the publication of polls: Denmark's 2000 Euro referendum. *International Journal of Public Opinion Research, 14*, 367–390.

Dran, E. M. (1993, May). *Polls on polling: history and issues*. Paper presented at the annual meeting of the American Association of Public Opinion Researchers, St. Charles, Illinois.

Dran, E. M., & Hildreth, A. (1995). What the public thinks about how we know what it is thinking. *International Journal of Public Opinion Research, 7*, 128–144.

Gallup, G., & Rae, S. F. (1940). *The pulse of democracy*. New York: Simon and Schuster.

Ginsberg, B. (1986). *The captive public*. New York: Basic Books, Inc.

Goldman, E. F. (1944). Poll on the polls. *Public Opinion Quarterly, 8*, 461–467.

Goyder, J. (1986). Surveys on surveys: Limitations and potentialities. *Public Opinion Quarterly, 50*, 27–41.

Herbst, S. (1993). *Numbered voices*. Chicago: University of Chicago Press.

Herbst, S. (1998). *Reading public opinion*. Chicago: University of Chicago Press.

Just, M., Crigler, A., Alger, D. E., Cook, T. E., Kern, M., & West, D. N. (1996). *Crosstalk*. Chicago: University of Chicago Press.

Kang, M., Lavrakas, P., Presser, S., Price, V., & Traugott, M. J. (1998). *Public interest in polling*. Paper presented at the annual conference of the American Association for Public Opinion Research, St. Louis.

Lavarakas, P. J., Holley, J. K., & Miller P. V. (1991). Public reactions to polling news during 1988 presidential campaign. In P. J. Lavrakas, & J. K. Holley (Eds.), *Polling and presidential election coverage* (pp. 135–150). Newbury Park, CA: Sage.

Lavrakas, P. J., Presser, S., Traugott, M. W., & Price, V. (1998, May). *Public opinion about polls: How people decide whether to believe survey results*. Paper presented to the annual meeting of the American Association for Public Opinion Research, St. Louis, MO.

Lavrakas, P. J., & Traugott, M. W. (2000). *Election polls, the news media, and democracy*. Chatham, NJ: Chatham House.

Marsh, C. (1986). Back on the bandwagon: The effect of public opinion polls on public opinion. *British Journal of Political Science, 15*, 51–74.

Pan, Z., Abisaid, J. L., Paek, H., Sun, Y., & Houden, D. (2005). Exploring the perceptual gap in perceived effects of media reports of opinion polls. *International Journal of Public Opinion Research, 18,* 340–348.

Patterson, T. (2005). Of polls, mountains. *Public Opinion Quarterly, 69,* 716–724.

Price, V., & Stroud, J. N. (2005). Public attitudes toward polls: Evidence from the 2000 US presidential election. *International Journal of Public Opinion Research, 18,* 393–421.

Prothro, J. W., & Grigg, C. M. (1960). Fundamental principles of democracy: Bases of agreement and disagreement. *Journal of Politics, 22,* 276–294.

Roper, B. W. (1986). Evaluating the polls with poll data. *Public Opinion Quarterly, 50,* 10–16.

Smith, T. (2004). Freedom to conduct public opinion polls around the world. *International Journal of Public Opinion Research, 8,* 321–327.

Tilly, C. (1983). Speaking your mind without elections, surveys or social movements. *Public Opinion Quarterly, 47,* 461–478.

Traugott, M. W. (1991). Public attitudes about news organizations, campaign coverage, and polls. In P. J. Lavrakas & J. K. Holley (Eds.), *Polling and presidential election coverage* (pp. 135–150). Newbury Park, CA: Sage.

Traugott, M. J. (2003). The nature of belief in a mass public. In MacKuen, M., & Rabinowitz, G. (Eds.), *Electoral democracy* (chap. 8). Ann Arbor, MI: University of Michigan Press.

Traugott, M. W., & Lavrakas, P. J. (2004). *The voter's guide to election polls* (3rd ed.). Maryland: Rowman and Littlefield.

Witt, E. (2001). People who count. *Public Perspectives, 12*(4), 25–28.

Zukin, C. (2006). The future is here! *Public Opinion Quarterly, 70,* 426–442.

41

Attitudes of Journalists Toward Public Opinion Research[1]

David H. Weaver

Journalists are often thought in the US to have a significant influence on public opinion, especially since the advent of the media effects studies of cultivation, agenda-setting, and information processing in the 1960s and 1970s. However, not much has been reported about how journalists generally think about public opinion or the polls regularly used to measure this opinion. Whereas there have been numerous content analyses of news media coverage of polls and public opinion (→ *The News Media's Use of Opinion Polls*), there has been very little systematic research on journalists' opinions about public opinion or the polls used to measure it.

There is some anecdotal evidence on this subject that goes back many years, mainly from prominent journalists such as Walter Lippmann (1922) and onetime muckraker Ray Stannard Baker, who saw the press as representatives of the public at the Paris Peace Conference of 1919 (see Schudson, 1978, p. 164). But there are very few systematic, representative studies of journalists' opinions about public opinion or public opinion

research. One exception is Susan Herbst's survey of 44 US journalists whose careers spanned much of the 1930s and 1940s (Herbst, 1990), which found that journalists developed some innovative and at times misleading strategies for understanding public opinion. These were both systematic and unsystematic in those earlier days when random sample polls were not widely available, including discussions with their colleagues, overhearing conversations in bars and coffee shops, reading letters to the editor and editorials in other newspapers, and receiving telephone calls from readers and listeners.

CONDUCTING AND USING POLLS—AMBIVALENCE OR ANTAGONISM?

Donsbach (1997) argues that there has sometimes been a rivalry between journalists and polls since survey research became more widely used in the 1930s and 1940s. Even though many more news media organizations in the US conducted their own polls between 1976 and 1988 (Ladd & Benson, 1992), and similar trends were found in other countries (Weimann, 1990; Brettschneider, 1991; Yamada & Synodinos, 1994), there is still the potential for polls to conflict with media reports of public opinion and for journalistic values of conflict, oddity, etc. to take precedence over the values of credible survey research (Yankelovitch, 1996; → *The News as a Reflection of Public Opinion*). Lang and Lang (1984) have argued that surveys can be a correction against a 'pluralistic ignorance' produced by the media, and that survey data can limit the effects of the news media on political decision making by providing politicians with alternative sources of information about public thinking.

This potential rivalry was found in a study of French and German journalists' views about polls conducted in 1988 and 1989 by Donsbach and Antoine (1990). They surveyed 118 German and 97 French journalists by mail and found that a third in each country agreed that polls cannot adequately measure public opinion. A third of the German journalists said they thought that polling institutes manipulate the results from time to time to give an advantage to their customers, but only 18% of the French journalists agreed with this. About two-thirds of the journalists in both countries thought that the publication of poll data in the mass media could influence an election outcome, and of those, 58% of the Germans and 48% of the French thought this influence was negative. Slightly more than half (56%) of the German journalists and nearly three-fourths (74%) of the French journalists approved of prohibiting the publication of poll data one week before an election, and only one-third of the German journalists thought that opinion surveys help journalists in fulfilling their tasks as compared with two-thirds of the French.

In spite of these opinions, more than 60% of the journalists from both countries said they believed the media should continue their coverage of political surveys as it was then, and a sizable majority thought that the

publics in their countries had a moderate or large interest in survey results. From these findings, the authors conclude that for German journalists, 'poll data seem to be rather a threat than a helpful information source for assessing public opinion.' They speculate that the negative or ambivalent attitudes of the German journalists toward public opinion research 'might be an expression of their fear to lose political influence which is a major element of their professional motives and role perceptions' (Donsbach & Antoine, 1990, p. 172).

Brettschneider (2002, 2005) conducted surveys of about 700 German journalists who attended the German government's press conferences in July and August of these years, and found that more than 80% in each survey thought that the general public was somewhat or definitely interested in polls and surveys. He also found that two-thirds of these journalists in each year said they sometimes or often used polls and surveys as the main basis for their articles, three-fourths said they used surveys and polls as add-on information when writing about political topics, and about half said that polls and surveys help journalists to fulfill their role in society. Nevertheless, one-fourth in 2002 and nearly one-third in 2005 said that there should be less coverage of the results of polls and surveys, and from 58% in 2002 to 66% in 2005 were in favor of a law to forbid the publishing of polls and survey results one week prior to elections, about the same as Donsbach and Antoine (1990) found in 1988–1989 in their surveys of French and German journalists.

In spite of these reservations about the amount of coverage of polls, two-thirds of the German journalists surveyed in 2002 and 56% in 2005 thought that their colleagues were positive about the use of polls in the media, and only 13–14% thought that they were negative. Two-thirds or more of these German journalists said they believed that polls could really measure public opinion regarding political topics, parties, and politicians. And one-fifth or less said that polling organizations repeatedly manipulated their findings to strengthen the position of the organization that sponsored a survey.

Donsbach and Patterson, in a six-country study of news journalists, found that US journalists were more likely to consider poll results as excellent or good indicators of public opinion than news reports, whereas German journalists were slightly more likely to consider news reports as good measures of public opinion (→ *The News as a Reflection of Public Opinion*). Journalists from all countries were much more likely to consider election results as excellent or good measures of public opinion than news reports, poll results, judgments of well-informed people, letters to the editor, protest demonstrations, editorials, congressional debates, or interest group activities.

This ambivalence about polls and surveys is similar to a finding from a major national telephone survey of 1,149 US journalists in 2002 by Weaver, Beam, Brownlee, Voakes, and Wilhoit (2003, 2007). They found nearly one-fifth of all journalists saying it was not really important for their news organizations to conduct polls to learn citizens' views about issues, although 39% considered it extremely important to give ordinary people a chance to express their views on public affairs and 31% said it was extremely important to include citizens in public affairs stories.

In all, slightly less than one-tenth of all US journalists considered it extremely important for their news organization to conduct polls to learn citizens' priorities on issues. Only 27% said it was quite important to do so, 45% thought it somewhat important, and 18% said it was not really important. These figures suggest that US journalists in general do not consider it very important for their news organizations to conduct polls. In fact, only a little more than one-third said it was extremely or quite important. Daily newspaper and television journalists were most likely to think so (nearly one-half), and radio and news magazine journalists were least likely to say this (about one-sixth).

Donsbach and Antoine (1990) and Brettschneider (2002, 2005) also asked journalists about the kinds of information they would include if they made use of poll data in an article or journalistic piece. They found that the name of the polling organization was most likely to be mentioned (by nearly all journalists surveyed), followed by the organization that funded or released the poll (mentioned by two-thirds to three-fourths), the timing of the interviewing and the size of the sample (mentioned by one-half to two-thirds), the wording of the questions, the definition of the population sampled, the margin of sampling error, and the type of the survey. Actual studies of the reporting of polls summarized in this volume show some differences between what information journalists say they would include about polls and what information actually ends up being presented in these articles (→ *The News Media's Use of Opinion Polls*).

From these findings, Donsbach and Antoine (1990, p. 172) conclude that the German and French journalists they surveyed make use of poll findings primarily as background information in their reporting, and that when reporting about polls 'they are quite negligent in supplying their audience with technical information about the methodological details of the poll.'

JOURNALISTS' ATTITUDES TOWARD SPECIFIC ASPECTS OF OPINION POLLS

Influence of polls on news reporting and values

As mentioned earlier, the surveys of French and German journalists also asked whether polls and surveys help or hinder journalists in fulfilling their roles and tasks. The German journalists surveyed in 1988 were far less likely to say that surveys helped journalists (only one-third thought so) than the French journalists surveyed in 1989 (two-thirds thought so, Donsbach & Antoine, 1990, p. 171), but half the German journalists surveyed in 2002 and 2005 by Brettschneider thought that polls and surveys help journalists.

In the United States, the question was somewhat different. In both the 1992 and 2002 national telephone surveys of journalists, they were asked about the perceived influence of public opinion polls 'on your concept of what is newsworthy' using a five-point scale where '1' meant 'not at all influential' and '5' meant 'very influential.' In 1992, the average rating was 2.5. Ten years later, in 2002, this number had dropped slightly, to 2.3 (Weaver & Wilhoit, 1996; Weaver *et al.*, 2003, 2007).

In 1992, television journalists were most likely to think that polls influenced their news judgment (2.9 on the five-point scale) and news magazine journalists were least likely (2.0), followed closely by those working for the wire services. In 2002, TV journalists were again most likely to rate the influence of polls as high, and news magazine and wire service journalists perceived the least influence. All types of journalists perceived polls as slightly less influential in 2002 than in 1992, except those working for daily newspapers, whose average increased slightly from 2.4 to 2.5.

Thus there are again indications that journalists from France, Germany and the US have ambivalent feelings about polls and surveys. One-third to two-thirds rate polls as helpful in their work, and some (especially those working for television in the US) think that poll findings influence their news judgment. It's clear, though, that these perceptions depend not only on which countries journalists come from, but also on which kinds of news media they work for.

Influence of polls and media on public opinion

French and German journalists were asked in 1988, 1989, 2002, and 2005 about their beliefs concerning the influence of polls published in the media on voters' decisions in elections. About two-thirds in 1988 and 1989 said they thought that poll results could influence voting decisions (Donsbach & Antoine, 1990), and this proportion increased to 83% in 2002 and 2005 (Brettschneider, 2002, 2005). Among those who thought that

polls could have an influence, 58% of the German journalists in 1988 and 48% of the French journalists in 1989 thought it was a negative influence. In 2002, 47% of the German journalists thought the influence was negative, and in 2005, it was 42%. In all cases, then, from two-fifths to three-fifths of the French and German journalists who perceived an influence of published polls on voting decisions thought it was a negative force, compared to 11% or less who thought it was positive.

US journalists in the 1982, 1992, and 2002 studies were asked to estimate the impact of the media on public opinion on a scale where zero indicated no influence and 10 indicated very great influence (Weaver & Wilhoit, 1986, 1996; Weaver *et al.*, 2003). In 1982, the journalists thought that media influence was considerable (a mean of 7.4), as was also true in 1992 (a mean of 7.5) and in 2002 (a mean of 7.4). In all three time periods, then, there was striking agreement among US journalists in their belief that the media have a substantial influence on public opinion. Journalists in the US and Britain estimated more media influence on public opinion than did those in Germany in the early 1980s (Donsbach, 1983), those in France in the late 1980s (McMane, 1998), or those in Mexico in the early 1990s (Wilke, 1998), as Table 41.1 shows.

US, British, Australian (Henningham, 1998), French, Brazilian (Herscovitz & Cardoso, 1998) and Chilean (Wilke, 1998) journalists thought that the media should have somewhat *less* influence on public opinion than they were perceived to have, but journalists in Germany and Algeria (Kirat, 1998) thought that the actual and ideal influence was about the same. Mexican journalists thought that the ideal influence should be a bit greater than the perceived actual influence, perhaps because of government controls on the Mexican press in the early 1990s from the one-party regime there.

In general, however, journalists in most of the countries thought that they should have *less* influence on public opinion than they actually had, a pattern that was also found in South Korea in 1993 using a

Table 41.1   **Journalists' estimates of the actual and ideal influence of the media on public opinion**

	Algeria (1986) (n = 75)	Australia (1992) (n = 1068)	Brazil (1994) (n = 355)	Britain (1981) (n = 405)	Chile (1992) (n = 116)	France (1988) (n = 484)
Actual	7.2	8 (Md)	8 (Mo)	7.3	7.5	5.9
Ideal	7.5	6 (Md)	5 (Mo)	5.9	6.5	4.7

	Germany (1981) (n = 450)	Mexico (1991) (n = 100)	US (1982) (n = 1001)	US (1992) (n = 1156)	US (2002) (n = 1149)
Actual	5.9	6.5	7.4	7.5	7.4
Ideal	6.0	7.4	6.0	5.7	5.8

Note: Except for Australia (medians) and Brazil (modes) all other figures are means on a 10-point scale where '0' indicates 'no influence' and '10' indicates 'very great influence.' The scores for Algerian journalists come from Kirat (1988), for Australian from Henningham (1988), for Brazilian from Herscovitz and Cardoso (1998), for British and German from Donsbach (1983), for Chilean and Mexican from Wilke (1998), for French from McMane (1998), for US journalists in 1982 from Weaver & Wilhoit (1986), for US in 1992 from Weaver & Wilhoit (1996), and for US journalists in 2002 from Weaver *et al.* (2003)

different measuring scale from the one in Table 41.1 (Auh, Lee, & Kang, 1998). This could be because many journalists subscribe to a neutral disseminator role or an ideology of objectivity that runs counter to undue influence over the public. It could also be because these journalists feel somewhat manipulated by powerful news sources that they think are using the media to influence the public, in sometimes undesirable ways. This explanation receives some support from the studies of journalists in France and Germany by Donsbach and Antoine (1990) and Brettschneider (2002, 2005) that found many more journalists saying that media publication of polls shortly before elections was a negative rather than positive influence.

Without including an open-ended question to ask journalists why they think the ideal influence should be lower than the actual, it's only possible to speculate on their reasons for doing so. But it is interesting that in a few countries such as Germany, Algeria and Mexico, journalists did not think that the media had more influence on public opinion than they should have had, and these journalists tended to rate their actual influence on public opinion lower than did US and other journalists.

Turning to the US in 2002, journalists' opinions about the amount of media influence on public opinion did not vary significantly

by type of news medium (daily and weekly newspaper, radio and television, news magazine, or wire service), although the newspaper journalists perceived slightly less media influence on public opinion than did journalists working for other kinds of news media.

However, when asked about how much influence media *should* have on public opinion, the averages were notably lower (5.8 overall on the 10-point scale), and the broadcast journalists working for radio and television estimated this 'ideal' influence the lowest. Thus the difference between the perceived actual influence of media on public opinion and the ideal influence (the influence gap) was greatest for radio and TV journalists and least for daily newspaper journalists in the US in 2002.

Giving ordinary people a voice

The perceived importance of giving ordinary people a chance to express their views on public affairs was asked in the 1992 and 2002 American journalist studies, but not in 1982 or the 1971 national surveys by Johnstone, Slawski, and Bowman (1976). Table 41.2 shows that there was a notable drop of 9.1 percentage points during the past decade in the proportion considering this role 'extremely' important and an increase in those considering it 'somewhat' important. Overall, however,

Table 41.2 US journalists' perceptions of the importance of giving ordinary people a chance to express their views on Public Affairs

	Percentage of US journalists answering		
	1992 (n = 1156)	2002 (n = 1149)	Difference
Extremely important	48.0%	38.9%	−9.1% points
Quite important	30.8	32.9	+2.1
Somewhat important	18.7	25.5	+6.8
Not really important	2.4	2.7	+0.3

Note: The 1992 figures are from Weaver and Wilhoit (1996) and the 2002 figures are from Weaver et al. (2003)

there were very few US journalists who rated this role of the news media as 'not really' important (only 2.4% in 1992 and 2.7% in 2002), but more in 2002 who considered it only somewhat important, suggesting that it was not as high a priority for US journalists in 2002 as it was in the early 1990s.

Among US journalists, those working for weekly or daily newspapers were most likely to consider this function very important (nearly 80% said extremely or quite important), and those working for news magazines were least likely to say this (45%). A similar question was asked in surveys of journalists working in China, Hong Kong, Britain, France and Germany. The percentages of journalists who considered this role very or extremely important were similar, in most cases, to those in the United States (40 to 50%), with the exception of China, where the figure was only 24%. The highest percentages came from Britain (56%) and Finland (53%; Weaver, 1998, pp. 466ff.), where more journalists appear to be committed to giving a voice to ordinary people than in the US or other countries.

CONCLUSIONS

This review of the few published studies of journalists' attitudes about polls and public

opinion suggests that there sometimes has been a tension between journalists and polls since survey research became more widely used in the 1930s and 1940s. Even though many more media organizations now conduct their own polls than in the past, there is still the potential for poll findings to conflict with media reports and analyses of public opinion, and the possibility of journalistic values of conflict, oddity, and immediacy to clash with the values of credible survey research.

The studies of French, German and US journalists in the past 20 years have found ambivalent attitudes about polls and surveys. Substantial majorities of journalists believe that the publication or dissemination of poll results shortly before elections can influence voting decisions, and about half of these journalists think that this influence is negative. Slightly more than half of the German journalists and nearly three-fourths of the French ones approve of prohibiting the publication of poll data one week before an election.

Nevertheless, nearly two-thirds of French and German journalists believe that the media in their countries should continue to report the findings of polls and political surveys at the same rate that they have in the past, and an overwhelming majority of these journalists think that the publics in their countries are quite interested in poll findings. Two-thirds of the journalists say they sometimes or often use polls and surveys as the main basis for their articles, and half say that polls help journalists to fulfill their role in society. More than half of the German journalists think that their colleagues are positive about the use of polls in the media, compared to less than one-sixth who think they are negative. In recent years, two-thirds think that polls really can measure public opinion, and one-fifth or less think that polling organizations manipulate findings to favor a sponsor. Thus it is clear from these findings that French and German journalists are concerned about possible negative effects of polls on voting decisions, but at the same time these journalists find polls useful in their work and valid indicators of public opinion.

This ambivalence about polls and surveys is also evident among US journalists. Only one-tenth of them consider it extremely important for their own news organizations to conduct polls, but two-fifths said it was extremely important to give ordinary people a chance to express their views on public affairs, and one-third thought it extremely important to include citizens in public affairs stories. The perceived importance of conducting polls does vary by type of news medium, with daily newspaper and television journalists most likely to consider polls important. In addition, there is evidence that US journalists think that polls are an important influence on their own news judgment, but this again varies by type of news medium, with TV journalists most likely to think so, and news magazine and wire service journalists least likely.

Another indicator of the ambivalent feelings of journalists regarding public opinion is the difference between how much influence they think they *actually* have on public opinion and how much they *should* have. In most of the dozen or so countries where these questions were asked in the past 25 years, journalists thought that they should have *less* influence on public opinion than they actually had, possibly because they subscribe to a neutral disseminator role or an ideology of objectivity that runs counter to telling people what to think rather than giving them information for forming their own opinions. This feeling is probably correlated with the belief of many journalists that media publication of polls before elections has more negative than positive influences. Further research asking journalists to state in their own words why they feel this way would be illuminating.

But again, these attitudes vary by country and also by type of news medium, making it questionable to generalize about all journalists in all countries. The difference between the perceived *actual* and *ideal* influence of the media on public opinion is smallest for newspaper journalists and greatest for broadcast journalists in the United States, for example. One possible reason for this pattern may be that broadcast journalists think less of the quality of their medium's influence on public opinion than do those working for newspapers, but it's worth noting that television journalists in the US are also most likely to think that polls influence their own news judgment, so this belief may be connected to their tendency to think that their influence on public opinion should be less than they think it is.

Among US journalists in general, there is strong support for giving ordinary people a chance to express their views on public affairs, but much less support for conducting polls to learn those views. Apparently US journalists endorse the expression of public opinion at an individual level, but not at an aggregate level, or at least many of them think that it is not the news media's job to conduct polls.

This chapter confirms that what journalists think about public opinion and polls depends substantially on where they work. There is no monolithic journalistic opinion about public opinion and polls—it depends on what kind of news medium the journalist works for and also in which country he or she works. There are substantial differences in journalists' opinions about public opinion across countries, as Donsbach and Antoine's (1990) study of French and German journalists and Brettschneider's 2002 and 2005 studies of German journalists found, suggesting that journalists' opinions are a function not only of type of news medium, but also of geography and culture. Open-ended questions in future surveys asking why journalists hold these views would likely yield more insights into journalists' attitudes toward polls and public opinion research.

At present, it appears that some of these attitudes of journalists toward public opinion research, polls, and public opinion in general are ambivalent and even contradictory: a grudging respect for the usefulness and validity of polls as measures of public opinion is coupled with a feeling that the effects of polls on journalists and the public are often negative rather than positive. Further research is needed to explore these attitudes in more depth to try to explain their origins and these seeming contradictions.

NOTES

1 David Weaver thanks the John S. and James L. Knight Foundation for its support of the 2002 survey of US journalists reported here, as well as graduate students Eunseong Kim, Leigh Moscowitz and Peter Mwesige for their help with the data analysis and charts. He also thanks his Indiana faculty colleagues Randal Beam (now at the Department of Communication, University of Washington), Bonnie Brownlee, Paul Voakes (now dean of the School of Journalism and Mass Communication at the University of Colorado) and longtime collaborator G. Cleveland Wilhoit for their work on the 2002 survey of US journalists.

REFERENCES

Auh, T. S., Lee, C. K., & Kang, M. K. (1998). Korean journalists in the 1990s. In D. H. Weaver (Ed.), *The global journalist* (pp. 55–69). Cresskill, NJ: Hampton Press.

Brettschneider, F. (1991). *Wahlumfragen. Empirische Befunde zur Darstellung in den Medien und zum Einfluss auf das Wahlverhalten in der Bundesrepublik Deutschland und den USA* [Election polls. Empirical findings regarding the presentation in the media and the influence on voting behavior in Germany and the USA]. Munich: Minerva.

Brettschneider, F. (2002). *Results of a survey of journalists at the German administration's press conferences regarding reporting of polls and surveys.* Paper. University of Augsburg, Communications Research Department.

Brettschneider, F. (2005). *Results of the second survey of journalists at the German administration's press conferences regarding reporting of polls and surveys.* Paper. University of Augsburg, Communications Research Department.

Donsbach, W. (1983). Journalists' concepts of their audience. *Gazette, 32,* 19–36.

Donsbach, W. (1997). Survey research at the end of the twentieth century: Theses and antitheses. *International Journal of Public Opinion Research, 9,* 17–28.

Donsbach, W., & Antoine, J. (1990). Journalists and the polls: A parallel survey among journalists in France and Germany. *Marketing and Research Today, August,* 167–174.

Henningham, J. (1998). Australian journalists. In D. H. Weaver (Ed.), *The global journalist* (pp. 91–107). Cresskill, NJ: Hampton Press.

Herbst, S. (1990). Assessing public opinion in the 1930s–1940s: Retrospective views of journalists. *Journalism Quarterly, 67(4),* 943–949.

Herscovitz, H. G., & Cardoso, A. M. (1998). The Brazilian journalist. In D. H. Weaver (Ed.), *The global journalist* (pp. 417–432). Cresskill, NJ: Hampton Press.

Johnstone, J. W. C., Slawski, E. J., & Bowman, W. W. (1976). *The news people.* Urbana & Chicago: University of Illinois Press.

Kirat, M. (1998). Algerian journalists and their world. In D. H. Weaver (Ed.), *The global journalist* (pp. 323–348). Cresskill, NJ: Hampton Press.

Ladd, E. C., & Benson, J. (1992). The growth of news polls in American politics. In T. E. Mann & G. R. Orren (Eds.), *Media polls in American politics* (pp. 19–31). Washington, DC: Brookings Institution.

Lang, K., & Lang, G. E. (1984). The impact of polls on public opinion. In J. L. Martin (Ed.), *Polling and the democratic consensus* (pp. 129–142). Beverly Hills, CA: Sage.

Lippmann, W. (1922). *Public opinion.* New York: The Free Press.

McMane, A. A. (1998). The French journalists. In D. H. Weaver (Ed.), *The global journalist* (pp. 191–212). Cresskill, NJ: Hampton Press.

Schudson, M. (1978). *Discovering the news.* New York: Basic Books.

Weaver, D. H. (Ed.). (1998). *The global journalist.* Cresskill, NJ: Hampton Press.

Weaver, D. H., & Wilhoit, G. C. (1986). *The American journalist.* Bloomington: Indiana University Press.

Weaver, D. H., & Wilhoit, G. C. (1996). *The American journalist in the 1990s.* Mahwah, NJ: Erlbaum.

Weaver, D., Beam, R., Brownlee, B., Voakes, P., & Wilhoit, G. C. (2003). *The American journalist in the 21st century: Key findings.* Miami, FL: The John S. and James L. Knight Foundation. Also available at http://www.poynter.org/content/content_view.asp?id=28235.

Weaver, D., Beam, R., Brownlee, B., Voakes, P., & Wilhoit, G. C. (2007). *The American journalist in the 21st century: US news people at the dawn of a new millennium.* Mahwah, NJ: Erlbaum.

Weimann, G. (1990). The obsession to forecast: Pre-election polls in the Israeli press. *Public Opinion Quarterly, 54,* 396–408.

Wilke, J. (1998). Journalists in Chile, Ecuador and Mexico. In D. H. Weaver (Ed.), *The global journalist* (pp. 433–452). Cresskill, NJ: Hampton Press.

Yamada, S., & Synodinos, N. E. (1994). Public opinion surveys in Japan. *International Journal of Public Opinion Research, 6,* 118–138.

Yankelovitch, D. (1996). A new direction for survey research. *International Journal of Public Opinion Research, 8,* 1–9.

42

Codes of Ethics and Standards in Survey Research

Tom W. Smith

Standards come in many forms and are created, disseminated, and enforced through various mechanisms. They range from the informal to the legally obligatory and are formed and applied in many different ways. This chapter addresses a number of issues related to standards. First it examines the major types of standards, including common or customary practices, those of professional and trade associations, those of standards organizations, and those of legal authorities. Second, it examines the types of provisions included in the codes established by professional and trade associations, including those that are ethical, disclosure, technical and definitional, and procedural. Third, it looks at the major existing professional and trade associations, focusing on examples of existing professional and trade associations codes regarding disclosure, response rates, and non-response bias. Finally, it looks at the new efforts of the International Organization on Standardization as well as issues of code

enforcement and the role of professionalization.

TYPES OF STANDARDS

First, there are what might be called *common or customary practices*. For example, in the field of survey research (as well as in many other disciplines), it is the general norm to accept only probabilities of 0.05 or smaller as 'statistically significant' and thus scientifically creditable (i.e. the statistical likelihood that the value observed differs from the true value had one interviewed each and every respondent in the population is 5%). Apparently this rule is not codified in any formal standards, but it is widely taught in college courses and applied by peer reviewers, editors, and others at journals, publishers, and funding agencies. Other examples would be the use of null hypotheses, including literature reviews in articles, and acknowledging the funders of research (Smith, 2005).

Second, there are *standards adopted by professional and trade associations.*[1] These may apply only to members (typically with agreement to follow the organizational code being a condition of membership), or may be deemed applicable to all those in a profession or industry regardless of membership. Enforcement, of course, is greatest on members who could be censored or expelled for violating standards, but it has broader impacts proportional to the prestige the association holds (Wilensky, 1964; Freidson, 1984, 1994; Abbott, 1988).

Third, there are *standards adopted by standards organizations.* These differ from professional and trade associations in that they do not represent a particular group and they are not designed to promote and represent professions or industries in general, but to establish standards across many fields. The main international example is the International Organization for Standardization (ISO) and the many national standards organizations affiliated with the ISO (e.g. in the United States the American National Standards Institute or in Togo the Superior Council of Normalization). Standards organizations typically both promulgate rules and certify that organizations are compliant with those rules (Smith, 2005).

Finally, there are *standards established by legislation and regulations* that are legally compulsory. These can be local, national, or international. They may be set directly by legislation or established by regulatory agencies following broad statutory provisions. An example is the restrictions that many countries impose on pre-election polls (Smith, 2004). Enforcement can be through civil suits or criminal prosecutions. Sometimes government agencies will work together with private organizations (usually trade, professional, or standards groups) to formulate and even enforce rules. In addition, governments also set standards by establishing rules for data collected by their own agencies (e.g. the US Bureau of the Census) or by those working for the government (OMB, 1999; Subcommittee on Measuring and Reporting the Quality of Survey Data, 2001; Smith, 2002a).

GENERAL TYPES OF CODES OF PROFESSIONAL AND TRADE ASSOCIATIONS

One hallmark of a profession is the adoption of a code of standards to which members promise to abide and which the association in turn enforces (Wilensky, 1964; Freidson, 1984, 1994; Abbott, 1988).

These codes come in many different varieties. First, there are codes of ethics that stipulate certain general and specific ethical rules. These would include such matters as honesty, avoiding conflicts of interest, and maintaining confidentiality (Crespi, 1998; American Statistical Association, 1999).

Second, there are codes of disclosure that stipulate certain information that must be shared with others about one's professional work (Guide of standards for marketing and social research, n.d.; Hollander, 1992; Kasprzyk & Kalton, 1998; Smith, 2002a). These play a major role in survey research standards, and are discussed below.

Third, there are technical and definitional standards. Essentially these are detailed elaborations on what is meant by other standards. For example, the American Association for Public Opinion Research (AAPOR) and the World Association for Public Opinion Research (WAPOR) both require that the response rate of surveys be reported and both endorse *Standard Definitions* (http://www.aapor.org/pdfs/standarddefs_3.1.pdf) as the way in which those and other outcome rates should be calculated and reported (see also Kasse, 1999; Lynn, Beerten, Laiho, & Martin, 2001).

Fourth, there are procedural standards. These stipulate certain steps or actions that need to be carried out when a professional activity is conducted. For example, checking cases through monitoring centralized telephone calls or recontacts might be stipulated procedures for interview validation (e.g. see recommended procedural standards for legal evidence in Diamond, 1994).

Finally, there are performance or outcome standards. These are acceptable levels that are expected to be reached before work could be deemed as satisfactory. This includes such things as having dual-entry coding show a disagreement rate below a certain level (e.g. less than 2 in 1000) or obtaining a response rate above some minimum (e.g. 60%).

Codes may include all or only some of these types of standards. Typically, ethical standards are the most common, followed by disclosure standards, then technical/definitional standards, and finally the least common procedural and performance/outcome standards. Of course, these types of standards do not work in isolation. Technical/definitional standards often elaborate on what is to be reported in disclosure standards, on how procedural standards are carried out, and whether performance/outcome standards are achieved. Similarly, procedural standards are often stipulated because their use is deemed to be needed to reach various performance standards. Likewise, the procedural and performance standards would be developed to be consistent with basic ethical standards. For example, the ethical requirement for honesty would require that information being disclosed be truthfully reported.

EXISTING PROFESSIONAL AND TRADE ASSOCIATIONS

On one level, public opinion research is well covered by codes of ethics and standards. First, there are the professional and trade associations covering the profession and industry of survey research itself. These include two, major, international professional associations: the European Society for Opinion and Marketing Research (ESOMAR) and WAPOR and many national professional associations such as the AAPOR, the Social Research Associations in Britain, Scotland, and Ireland (SRA), and the British Market Research Association (BMRA). They also include national trade associations such as the Asociacion Mexicana

de Agencias de Investigacion de Mercado y Opinion Publica (AMAI), the Association of the Marketing and Social Research Industry (Canada) (AMSRI), the Council of American Survey Research Organizations (CASRO), the Council of Canadian Survey Research Organizations (CCSRO), the Council for Marketing and Opinion Research (USA) (CMOR), and the National Council of Public Polls (USA) (NCPP).

Second, there are professional and trade associations in closely allied fields: market research, the social sciences, and statistics. In market research, associations include ESOMAR, which bridges the fields of survey and market research, and such other groups as the Advertising Research Foundation (ARF), the Alliance of International Market Research Institutes (AIMRI), the American Marketing Association (AMA), the Marketing Research Association (MRA), the Association of Consumer Research (ACR), the Association of European Market Research Institutes (AEMRI), the European Federation of Associations of Market Research Organizations (EFAMRO), the Market Research Quality Standards Association (MRQSA), the Research Industry Coalition (RIC), the Japanese Market Research Association (JMRA), and such more specialized groups within market research as the Audit Bureau of Circulation (ABC) and the Media Ratings Council (MRC).

The social science disciplines most closely tied to survey research are sociology, political science, psychology, and communications, and they are represented by such cross-national groups as the International Sociological Association (ISA), the International Political Science Association (IPSA), International Association of Applied Psychology and the International Communication Association; and national organizations such as the American Sociological Association (ASA), the American Political Science Association (APSA), the American Psychological Association (APA) and the American Psychological Society (APS). The main international statistical groups are the International Association of Survey Statisticians (IASS) and the International Statistical Institute (ISI). National associations include such examples as the American Statistical Association (AmStat) and the Royal Statistical Society (RSS).

Finally, since public opinion research is often public, the standards of media and journalism associations also come to bear.

EXAMPLES OF EXISTING PROFESSIONAL AND TRADE CODES

Virtually all of these associations have codes of standards, and most have at least some rules that address survey research. The many different associations involved mean that they certainly do not croon with one voice, but to a large degree their tunes are in harmony. Take for example codes of disclosure. A comparison was made of nine documents (codes and supporting documents) by five organizations (AAPOR, CASRO, ESOMAR, NCCP, and WAPOR) (see www.unl.edu/wapor/journalists.doc). All organizations agreed on the reporting of the following elements of a survey: who conducted, who sponsored, sample design, sample size, sampling error, mode of data collection, when collected/dates, question wording, question order, sample population, and response rate. Also, mentioned in most of these codes and related documents were weighting/imputing and the purpose of the survey.

Another example concerns response rates. The codes and official statements of 19 professional, trade, and academic organizations were examined (Smith, 2002a).[2] Three have no codes or any relevant official statements (CMOR, ACR, and IASS). Another three organizations have only brief general statements about doing good, honest research (AMA, ARF, MRA). Yet another three have general pronouncements about being open about methods and sharing technical information with others, but no details on what should be documented (AmStat, ISI, RIC). Then, there are 10 that have some requirement regarding nonresponse (AAPOR, CASRO,

ESOMAR, AEMRI, ERAMRO, MRQSA, NCPP, WAPOR, ABC, and MRC).[3]

Of the eight organizations that have an official journal (AAPOR, WAPOR, ESOMAR, AMA, ARF, ISI, IASS, AmStat), two (AAPOR—*Public Opinion Quarterly* (*POQ*) and WAPOR—*International Journal for Public Opinion Research*) have definite standards about reporting and calculating response rates, two have some general pronouncements that mention nonresponse bias or the response rate (AMA—*Journal of Marketing Research* and ARF—*Journal of Advertising Research*), and one has a marginally relevant standard on data sharing (AmStat—*Journal of the American Statistical Association*).

Of the 10 referring to nonresponse in their codes and statements, all require that response rates (or some related outcome rate) be reported. Only a subset of the 10 that mention nonresponse require anything beyond reporting requirements. Six organizations provide at least some definition of response and/or related outcome rates, and these appear in non-binding documents and statements and not as part of their codes (AAPOR, CASRO, NCPP, ABC, MRC, WAPOR); four provide no definitions (ESOMAR, EFAMRO, AEMRI, MRQSA). Only the AAPOR/WAPOR, CASRO, and ABC definitions are detailed.

Three organizations deal with the issues of nonresponse bias in their codes. The WAPOR code, right after requiring the reporting of the nonresponse rate, calls for information on the 'comparison of the size and characteristics of the actual and anticipated samples' and the ESOMAR and MRSQA codes require in client reports 'discussion of any possible bias due to non-response.'

Three organizations mention nonresponse bias in official documents. AAPOR in its 'Best Practices,' but not its code, urges that nonresponse bias be reported. AmStat addresses the matter in its 'What is a Survey?' series. The AMA in its publication, the *Journal of Market Research*, requires authors to 'not ignore the nonrespondents. They might have different characteristics than the respondents.'

Three organizations deal with procedural and/or performance standards. AAPOR, as part of 'Best Practices,' but not its code, indicates that survey researchers should try to maximize response rates and discuss the means to do. ABC and ARF are more precise in specifying minimum number of calls and details on other efforts that should be employed by media evaluation surveys. Finally, only ABC specifies a minimally acceptable response rate, although even it provides exceptions to its standard.

In addition, professional, trade, and academic organizations have advanced the cause of standards by their general promotion and dissemination of research methods. For example, as Hollander (1992, p. 83) has observed, 'the annual AAPOR conference was recognized early on, together with *POQ*, which is older still, as a means of advancing standards.'

In brief, only the professional, trade, and academic organizations at the core of survey research and in the sub-area of media ratings research take up nonresponse in their codes, official statements, and organizational journals. General market research and statistical organizations do not explicitly deal with nonresponse issues in their codes and standards, and only marginally address these in the guidelines of their official journals. Even among the organizations that do address the matter of nonresponse, the proclaimed standards are mostly minimal. Some, but not automatic, reporting is required by all of the core organizations. However, definitions are provided by only six of the 10 and none include them as part of their codes. Other aspects such as nonresponse bias and performance standards are barely touched upon. Thus, even among those organizations that consider nonresponse, reporting standards are incomplete, technical standards are often lacking and/or regulated to less official status, and performance standards are nearly non-existent.

A final example is the recent, major initiative regarding standards for public opinion research coming from the ISO. In 2003, Technical Committee 225 was established to develop standards for 'market, opinion, and social research.' ISO and its national members are bodies specializing in the development of standards *per se*, and lack detailed knowledge of most specific fields and industries. As such, TC225 relies on advice from technical advisory groups made up of survey researchers in each participating country and international, survey-research associations (ESOMAR and WAPOR) to develop the relevant definitions and rules. In early 2005, a draft international standard was circulated. TC225 considered comments to that draft and formulated a final version in the summer of 2005.

The ISO draft standards (ISO, 2005) are largely consistent with the existing codes of professional and trade associations. Its list of information that must be included in research reports closely confirms to the existing minimum disclosure requirements. The ISO standards go beyond most existing codes in two main regards. First, they spell out the mutual obligations that exist between clients and research service providers (i.e. data collectors or survey firms). This includes stipulating elements that need to be in agreements between them, including such matters as confidentiality of research, documentation requirements, fieldworker training, sub-contracting/outsourcing, effectiveness of quality management system, project schedule, cooperation with client, developing questionnaires and discussion guides, managing sampling, data collection, and analysis, monitoring data collection, handling research documents and materials, reporting research results, and maintaining research records.

Second, it has a number of procedural and performance standards. These include the following: (1) methods for doing translations and level of language competency for the translators, (2) type and hours of training for fieldworkers, (3) validation levels for verifying data collected by fieldworkers, (4) use of ID's by fieldworkers, (5) the notification that potential respondents must receive, (6) documenting the use of respondent incentives, (7) guarantees of respondent confidentiality, and (8) what records should be kept and for how long they should be maintained.

LIVING UP TO AND ENFORCING CODES

Codes are one thing; practice may be another. Codes matter only if they are followed and here the experience of survey and public opinion research is mixed. Three examples will illustrate the present situation and its limitations.

First, a major section of most codes concerns what information about survey methodology must be reported. Repeated studies in different venues indicate that much less information is routinely made available, and even less is typically reported. Presser (1984) examined what methodological information was reported in articles in the top journals in economics, political science, social psychology, sociology, and survey research. He found that in articles using surveys, reporting ranged as follows: (1) sampling method from 4% in economics to 63% in survey research, (2) question wording from 3% in economics to 55% in survey research, (3) mode of data collection from 18% in economics to 78% in social psychology, (4) response rate from 4% in economics to 63% in survey research, (5) year of survey from 20% in social psychology to 82% in political science, and (6) interviewer characteristics from 0% in economics to 60% in social psychology.

Looking at the reporting of response rates, Smith (2002a) found that none of 11 major American organizations conducting public opinion research routinely reported response rates, and even among academic, survey-research organizations reporting was sporadic. He also found that response rates were not usually available from either survey archives or in US government reports. As Presser had found, levels were even low in top academic journals—34% in survey research articles, 29% in sociology, and 20% in political science. In follow-up work, Smith (2002c) found in the 1998–2001 period

that response-rate reporting remained low in political science and sociology, but was improving in survey research. However, even in survey research, in 2001 only 53% of articles reported a response rate and just 33% provided any definition (see also Turner & Martin, 1984; Hardmeier, 1999).

Second, the professional associations are not well suited to handling specific instances of alleged code violations or what are commonly called standards cases. For example, the experience of AAPOR is that formal standards cases involve considerable effort, take a long time to decide, and, under some outcomes (e.g. exoneration or private censure), do not result in educating the profession. The AAPOR procedures are by necessity complex and legalistic in order to protect the rights of the accused. Also, since the handling of standards cases is done by volunteers who must find time to participate, this creates a burden and takes considerable time to adjudicate. AAPOR believes that standards in the field can be better enhanced by methods other than formal standards cases.

Finally, many professions in part enforce their codes through the certification of members. In general, this practice is rare in the field of survey research. For example, in the United States no professional association has established certification. However, that is now changing, and the MRA is currently starting up a Professional Researcher Certification Program (see www.mra-net.org/certification/overview.cfm). Its relationship to MRA's code has not been made clear, but certification will include an 'ethical review process' and the application of 'standards for duties.' Since membership in MRA means acceptance of its code, there will probably be a linkage between the code and certification, and possibly the certification program will increase adherence to and enforcement of the code.

PROFESSIONALIZATION AND CODES

One of the 'necessary elements' of professionalization is the adoption of 'formal codes of ethics ... rules to eliminate the unqualified and unscrupulous, rules to reduce internal competition, and rules to protect clients, and emphasize the service ideal' (Wilensky, 1964, p. 145) and 'codes of ethics may be created both to display concern for the issue [good character] and to provide members with guides to proper performance at work' (Freidson, 1994, p. 174). Survey research has begun to follow the path of professionalization, but has not completed the journey.[4] In the estimation of Wolfgang Donsbach (1997), survey research falls into the category of 'semi-professional.' Among other things, it has been the failure of survey researchers 'to define, maintain, and reinforce standards in their area' (Donsbach, 1997, p. 23) that has deterred full professionalization. As Irving Crespi (1998, p. 77) has noted, 'In accordance with precedents set by law and medicine, developing a code of standards has long been central to the professionalization of any occupation.' He also adds that 'One hallmark of professionals is that they can, and do, meet performance standards.' In Donsbach's analysis (1997, p. 26), the problem is that standards have neither been sufficiently internalized nor adequately enforced:

> We have developed *codes of standards*, but we still miss a high degree of *internalization* in the process of work socialization. We also lack clear and powerful systems of sanctions against those who do not adhere to these standards. It is the professional organizations' task to implement these systems and to enforce the rules.

There are various reasons for the limited adoption and enforcement of standards and the incomplete professionalization of the survey field. First, the survey research profession is divided between commercial and non-commercial sectors. Coordinating the quite different goals and needs of these sectors has been difficult. There has frequently been a split between these sectors on standards and other matters (Smith, 2002a, 2002c). Moreover, trade associations typically only include for-profit firms. In addition, for quite different reasons, both sectors have had particular reasons for failing to pursue professionalization

vigorously. The academics have been the most open to professionalization in general and standards in particular, since most are already members of two types of well-organized professions (university teachers) and their particular disciplines (e.g. statistician, psychologist, sociologist, or the like). But while this socialization has made them open to professionalization and standards, it has also hampered the professionalization of survey research, since the academics already are (usually) professionals twice over, and may have only a secondary interest in survey research as a field/profession. The commercial practitioners have seen themselves more as businesspersons and less as professionals, and many have seen standards as externally imposed constraints (akin to government regulations) that would interfere with their businesses. Of course it is not inevitable that businesses oppose standards and people in business fields would necessarily resist professionalization. For example, the Society of Automobile Engineers was successful from early on in establishing industry-wide standards and recommended practices (Thompson, 1954). However, this has not transpired within the survey-research industry. Suggested reasons for the limited development of cooperation within the survey field include a high level of competition (Bradburn, 1992), and the idea that fewer benefits from collaboration and coordination may exist.[5]

Second, survey research is an information field with strong formative roots in both journalism and politics (Converse, 1987). Some have seen any attempt to regulate the industry (especially by government, but even via self-regulation), as an infringement on their freedom of speech and as undemocratic. They lean more towards an unregulated, marketplace-of-ideas approach.

Third, there are fuzzy boundaries between survey research and other fields such as political consulting and public relations, and those conducting surveys are often more oriented towards and experienced in these other fields than they are in survey research itself (Lang & Lang, 1991). Moreover, at least in the US, this infiltration of survey research by outsiders has been growing over time (ibid.).

In brief, the incomplete professionalization of survey research has retarded the development of professional standards and their enforcement. Incomplete professionalization in turn has resulted from the fractious inter-sectoral and inter-disciplinary nature of survey research, and from the high value placed by practitioners on the ideal of independence and idea that the marketplace itself would exercise sufficient discipline. Attitudes of both economic and intellectual laissez-faire have undermined the adoption and enforcement of standards (Smith, 2002c).

CONCLUSION

Codes of ethics and standards exist for the key professional and trade associations in the field of survey research, and there is a great deal of agreement on their provisions. Standards are most extensive in the area of ethics and disclosure, but technical and procedural standards have been expanding. Since professionalization has only been partially implemented, actual practice has often lagged behind the standards, and enforcement has been limited. However, this situation has begun to change in recent years. For example, AAPOR and WAPOR have adopted *Standard Definitions* for the calculation and reporting of response and other outcome rates, and the ISO is working with professional and trade associations in the field of survey research to formulate international standards. Along with advances in the art and science of conducting survey research, this should lead to a general improvement in data quality and documentation and a strengthening of the survey-research field.

NOTES

1 Trade or industry associations are those in which organizations rather than individuals are the members. Professional and academic associations have individuals as members.

2 The 19 are: AAPOR, ABC, ACR, AEMRI, AMA, AmStat, ARF, CASRO, CMOR, ERAMRO, ESOMAR, IASS, ISI, MRA, MRC, MRQSA, NCPP, RIC, and WAPOR.

3 ARF could be added to this list if its guidelines for newspaper-audience surveys were included, as opposed to its less detailed, general pronouncements.

4 Wilensky (1964) proposes five sequential steps that occupations go through to professionalization: (1) the emergence of the profession, (2) establishing training schools and ultimately university programs, (3) local and then national associations, (4) governmental licensing, and (5) formal codes of ethics. Survey research has only partly achieved the second, for although there are some excellent training programs and university programs, most practitioners are formally trained in other fields (statistics, marketing, psychology, sociology, etc.). Survey research has resisted certification and governmental licensing, although recent support for the proscription of fraudulent practices disguised as surveys (e.g. push polls and sugging—selling under the guise of a survey) have moved the field more in that direction. Only in its early formation of professional associations did survey research fully embrace professionalization. On the development of the survey-research field, see Converse (1987).

5 The setting of a standard gauge for railroads is an example in which several industries benefited. Builders of railroad equipment needed to produce only one size of wheels and axles, shippers gained as transfer costs were reduced, and railroads won increased traffic as unnecessary costs were eliminated.

REFERENCES

Abbott, A. (1988). *The system of professions: An essay on the division of expert labor*. Chicago: University of Chicago Press.

American Statistical Association (1999, November). ASA issues ethical guidelines. *Amstat News, 269*, 10–15.

Bradburn, N. M. (1992). A response to the nonresponse problem. *Public Opinion Quarterly, 56*, 391–397.

Converse, J. M. (1987). *Survey research in the United States: Roots and emergence, 1980–1960*. Berkeley: University of California Press.

Crespi, I. (1998). Ethical considerations when establishing survey standards. *International Journal of Public Opinion Research, 10*, 75–82.

Diamond, S. (1994). Reference guide for survey research. In Federal Judicial Center (Ed.), *Reference manual for scientific evidence* (pp. 221–271). Washington, DC: Federal Judicial Center.

Donsbach, W. (1997). Survey research at the end of the twentieth century: Theses and antitheses.

International Journal for Public Opinion Research, 9, 17–28.

Freidson, E. (1984). The changing nature of professional control. *Annual Review of Sociology, 10,* 1–20.

Freidson, E. (1994). *Professionalism reborn: Theory, prophecy, and policy.* Chicago: University of Chicago Press.

Guide of standards for marketing and social research (n.d.). L'Association de l'industrie de la recherche marketing et sociale, Canada.

Hardmeier, S. (1999). Political poll reporting in Swiss print media: Analysis and suggestions for quality improvement. *International Journal of Public Opinion Research, 11,* 257–274.

Hollander, S. (1992). Survey Standards. In P. B. Sheatsley & W. J. Mitofsky (Eds.), *Meeting place: The history of the American Association for Public Opinion Research* (pp. 65–103). American Association for Public Opinion Research.

ISO (International Organization for Standardization/Technical Committee 225). (2005). *Market, opinion and social research draft international standard.* Madrid: AENOR.

Kasprzyk, D., & Kalton, G. (1998). Measuring and reporting the quality of survey data. In *Proceedings of Statistics Canada Symposium 97: New directions in surveys and censuses* (pp. 179–184). Ottawa: Statistics Canada.

Kasse, M. (1999). *Quality criteria for survey research.* Berlin: Akademie Verlag.

Lang, K., & Lang, G. E. (1991). The changing professional ethos: A poll of pollsters. *International Journal of Public Opinion Research, 3,* 323–339.

Lynn, P. J., Beerten, R., Laiho, J., & Martin, J. (2001). *Recommended standard final outcome categories and standard definitions of response rate for social surveys* (ISER Working paper 2001–23). Essex University, Institute for Social and Economic Research.

OMB (Office of Management and Budget) (1999, June 2). *Implementing guidance for OMB review of agency information collection.* Draft.

Presser, S. (1984). The use of survey data in basic research in the social sciences. In C. F. Turner & E. Martin (Eds.), *Surveying subjective phenomena* (Vol. 2, pp. 93–114). New York: Russell Sage Foundation.

Smith, T. W. (2002a). Developing nonresponse standards. In R. M. Groves, D. A. Dillman, J. L. Eltinge, & R. J. A. Little (Eds.), *Survey nonresponse* (pp. 27–40). New York: John Wiley & Sons.

Smith, T. W. (2002b). Professionalization and Survey-Research Standards, *WAPOR Newsletter,* 3rd quarter: 3–4.

Smith, T. W. (2002c). Reporting survey nonresponse in academic journals. *International Journal of Public Opinion Research, 14,* 469–474.

Smith, T. W. (2004). Freedom to conduct public opinion polls around the world. *International Journal of Public Opinion Research, 16,* 215–223.

Smith, T. W. (2005). *The ISO standards for market, opinion, and social research: A preview.* Paper presented to the annual conference of the American Association for Public Opinion Research, Miami Beach.

Subcommittee on Measuring and Reporting the Quality of Survey Data (2001). *Measuring and reporting sources of error in survey* (Statistical Working Paper No. 31). Washington, DC: OMB.

Thompson, G. V. (1954). Intercompany technical standardization in the early American automobile industry. *Journal of Economic History, 14,* 1–20.

Turner, C. F., & Martin, E. (1984). *Surveying subjective phenomena.* New York: Russell Sage Foundation.

Wilensky, H. L. (1964). The professionalization of everyone? *American Journal of Sociology, 70,* 137–158.

43

Archiving Poll Data

Wolfgang Jagodzinski and
Meinhard Moschner

In contrast to other disciplines, the social sciences have only gradually become fully aware of the importance of a functioning infrastructure that offers support for the whole research process, beginning with the development of a research design, pretesting and sampling, and ending with the archiving of data for extended or secondary data analysis. With the availability of data sets on the Internet in combination with several advanced data retrieval and on-line analysis systems like NESSTAR, Survey Documentation and Analysis (SDA), the Virtual Data Center (VDC), or developments like the CESSDA data portal, the infrastructural services have markedly improved. Data are nowadays accessible not only to the national scientific community, but also on a global level.

The new era has not only facilitated the use of data, however, but also led to new problems: the more easily the data are accessible, the more demanding are the necessary measures of anonymization and data protection that have to be taken. It also has become a question of how journalists and lay people without training in methods

and statistics can be advised to interpret the data appropriately. This chapter focuses on the role of data archives in the social science infrastructure. We will describe why archiving polling data is important, how the concept of archives has developed over time, and which are the most important poll archives from an international perspective.

MOTIVATIONS FOR ARCHIVING RESEARCH DATA

Free and equal access bestows on each data set the status of a collective good. According to the logic of collective action, the primary investigator or the producer of data has little incentive to contribute to the collective good by delivering the data set. Even worse, as long as the publication of books and articles is much more essential to the career of a social scientist than the delivery of a well-documented data set to a data archive, researchers will allocate more time to the former than to the latter activity. Other factors operate in the same direction: if a scientist has spent months and years in building up a data base, he or she will hesitate to make the data accessible to the scientific community before having completely finished their own research with the data. And there may sometimes also be the fear that other scientists may misuse the data by not analyzing them appropriately or disregard rules of data protection. The latter problem is particularly virulent in studies on special subpopulations, especially elite studies.

Fortunately, scientists do not always follow the rationality of the *homo economicus* model. Researchers like Stein Rokkan (1964), Warren Miller (1976) or Erwin K. Scheuch (2003) were convinced that a solid database is a necessary requirement for scientific progress, and they invested time and energy on the collection and documentation of data, not least on the background of their research interests in comparing societies across space and time (Rokkan, 1966). Furthermore, some conditions have changed in favor of the social science infrastructure during the last decades. It is now a widely accepted ethical rule that data have to be stored for replication. Even better, some funding agencies have explicitly stated as a condition that the data of a funded research project have to be delivered to a data archive. The rule that at least publicly funded data collections should be accessible to all scientists has further strengthened this tendency (OECD, 2003).

In those societies where data archives function for a longer time period, a culture of data sharing will emerge. Its prerequisites are competence and mutual trust. The primary investigators have to rely on the professionalism of the data archives and the methodological competence of those who use the data for secondary analyses. The latter have to rely on the competence of the former. If these conditions are met, archived data become an important source of information. Primary investigators who have deposited a well-documented and widely used data set or collection of data to an archive may enhance their reputation significantly. This is a positive, selective incentive for depositing the data.

BENEFITS FROM ARCHIVED DATA FOR THE SCIENTIFIC COMMUNITY

Archived data are a valuable good for the scientific community. First of all, they offer rich material for hypothesis testing. Primary investigators usually focus on a specific set of research questions within a specific research program, so there is ample space for further investigations. Quite often an archive can provide similar data, where a researcher can subsequently evaluate hypotheses that they first developed through analysis of their own single dataset.

Archived questionnaires are also helpful for drafting a new survey. One can examine previous surveys on similar topics. Even if the items in these surveys are not suited for the present investigation, they may at least stimulate the development of more suitable questions.

Archived data can also be used for testing and improving measurement instruments. Existing data allow the examination of the reliability and validity of operationalizations. If the results of these analyses are not satisfying, they may at least be a good starting point for developing refined measurement instruments.

Archived data also permit the study of longitudinal change. They are almost indispensable for the study of opinion and value change. It is true, different researchers rarely have used exactly the same operationalizations and question wordings used in previous studies, and the potential for comparisons over time is therefore much smaller than it might appear at first glance. Fortunately, during the last decades a number of survey programs have been set up which are explicitly also dedicated to the study of social change. The 'General Social Surveys' in the United States (1972ff.), Germany (1980ff.), Poland (1992–2002) and Japan (2000ff.) are to be mentioned here. The European Values Survey (1981ff.) (EVS), the International Social Survey Program (1982ff.) (ISSP) or the European Social Survey (2002ff.) (ESS) in addition permit comparisons between countries

(→ *International Comparative Surveys: Their Purpose, Content and Methodological Challenges*).

It has become quite common to use archived data in courses on method, statistics, or empirical research. These courses are much closer to the practice of empirical research than courses that are based only on textbook examples.

ARCHIVING CONCEPTS AND STANDARDS

Separated in time from the primary research context and its knowledge background, data can only be correctly used if they are supplemented by a *detailed documentation*. The original documentation has to be conserved. Hard copy materials nowadays have to be digitalized including questionnaires in all languages and split versions with their corresponding show cards, fieldwork and methodological reports, interviewer guidelines and so on. International standards are developed for best practice documentation of survey data (ISO 20252: 2006) and their electronic description from survey design and methodology issues down to the variable level (DDI meta-data standards, Blank & Rasmussen, 2004).

Historically, the library tradition of the survey data archive movement that developed with the establishment of the Roper Center after World War II was replaced by the data service concept in the sixties. It emerged in the course of the appearance of the first European data archives (Central Archive, Steinmetz, the predecessors of NSD and UK Data Archive), and the Inter-university Consortium for Political and Social Research in the United States. The data have to be checked for completeness, for agreement with the coding scheme, for consistency of responses with the question routing, as well as for non-meaningful attribute combinations. The cleaning and reformatting of data sets and their documentation down to the variable level became a central part of the archive function. As a result, best practices in social science data

preparation were developed (ICPSR, 2005). Data are archived in such a way that they can be analyzed without difficulties even after a long period of storage. While research projects subject to organizational changes, personal discontinuities, or disintegration are often causes for the loss of valuable data, archives are continuously taking care that data remain readable independent of the life time of storage media, changing software versions, operating systems, and computer platforms (The Royal Statistical Society & the UK Data Archive, 2002). Study descriptions, retrieval systems that operate also for questions and variables, (subject) thesauri and controlled vocabularies nowadays facilitate the finding of relevant data within a rapidly expanding stock of studies and variables. The identification of functionally equivalent measurements across space and time that originally were not designed as comparable measures can be seen as the major challenge in this field.

While data archives formerly were primarily concerned with the processing and documentation of national, predominantly cross-sectional studies, they nowadays invest considerable resources in the processing of large comparative data collections with their increasing needs regarding scope and quality of data documentation. These collections consist of partially or completely harmonized and standardized surveys carried out at different points in time and/or in different populations. The former are relatively rare panel data because they are expensive to produce; many more studies involve repeated cross-sections that are a useful data source for longitudinal analyses and are also useful for comparative studies.

Advanced comparative designs require a documentation of the theoretical models, the context, the translation process, and the methods of data collections in all countries. They often results in complex multi-level data sets with a large set of accompanying documents. The emerging DDI standard will support the efficient capture, maintenance and exchange of all this information at each step of the research process ('data life cycle'). Intense co-operation between archives and (groups of) researchers will help to cope with the growing documentation burden. In large survey programs like the GSS, ESS, EVS or ISSP, this has already been institutionalized. The concept of 'thematic development programs' which has been introduced in the recent data archive re-organization process in the Netherlands (DANS) aims at the same objective.

The number of *comparative studies* is rapidly growing (→ *International Comparative Surveys: Their Purpose, Content and Methodological Challenges*). This may partly be a side effect of globalization, but it has also to do with the insight that we must not generalize results from cross-sectional studies. Social research has become increasingly sensitive to selective and contextual fallacies. What is true for one society need not to be true for a second, even if both societies are more or less at the same level of economic and technological development. Secularization, for instance, may take place in Western Europe, but it need not occur elsewhere in the world. In the following section, we will give a brief overview of some international survey projects and their characteristics. A more comprehensive tabular overview of international data collections and their availability for re-use, including references to related project websites and responsible data archives, has been prepared by Meinhard Moschner and can be found on the web page of GESIS (http://www.gesis.org/ComparativeSurveyOverview/). Table 43.1 gives an overview of the main Social Science data archive web resources.

INTERNATIONAL DATA COLLECTIONS

Development

Even if one is convinced of the usefulness of comparative research, one is not always able to practice it. Comparative survey research is a demanding enterprise. First of all, an efficient infrastructure for conducting survey research is needed in the participating countries. In Germany and many other European countries,

such an infrastructure did not exist before the war. This is the reason why the first surveys that allow for at least some comparisons were carried out by the United States Information Agency (USIA) in the 1950s. These surveys were not conceptualized as a comparative study but tried to collect data on foreign policy orientations like the attitudes towards American and Soviet foreign policy, international relations, arms control, and the like in several European countries, in particular in Germany, Italy, Great Britain and France.[1] It is difficult enough to harmonize data from a single survey program that is not strictly comparative. It is even more complicated to integrate different national cross-sectional studies into a data collection, as projects like *Beliefs in Government* (Kaase & Jennings, 1995) have shown. Even if these studies address the same topics, they rarely use the same measurement instruments. Question wording and response categories frequently differ so that strictly standardized data collections can rarely be built up.

Between 1957 and 1963, the pattern of *Human Concerns Studies* (Cantril, 1965) were carried out in an attempt to investigate the fears and hopes of human beings on several continents. Overall 14 nations participated in the study, among them also Germany and Japan. Unfortunately, the data files for Japan and three other countries are not available. The 'Civic Culture' study of Almond and Verba (1963) presumably is the best known research of this period. The authors introduced a typology of political cultures that they applied to the five countries under investigation— Germany, Great Britain, Italy, Mexico and the United States. Even though the study of Almond and Verba was much criticized, it belongs to the seminal empirical studies of that period.

Several surveys were carried out during the sixties. The magazine *Reader's Digest* sponsored a survey on the life-styles, well-being, and values of the citizens of 12 West European countries. The most famous study of this decade is the 'International Time Budget Study of 1965/66' (Szalai, 1972; Harvey, Szalai, Elliott, Stone, & Clark, 1984), which

Table 43.1   Main data archive web resources

Table 43.1(a)

Data archive networks, initiatives and projects	Website URL
International Federation of Data Organisations for the Social Sciences (IFDO)	http://www.ifdo.org
Council of European Social Science Data Archives (CESSDA)	http://www.cessda.org
East European Data Archive Network (EDAN)	http://www.gesis.org/en/cooperation/data_service/eastern_europe/
Network of Economic and Social Science Infrastructures in Europe (NESSIE)	http://www.nessie-essex.co.uk/
Data Documentation Initiative (DDI)	http://www.icpsr.umich.edu/DDI/
Networked Social Science Tools & Resources (NESSTAR)	http://www.nesstar.org/
Survey Documentation & Analysis (SDA)	http://sda.berkeley.edu/
Unified Access to European Social Science Data Archives (MADIERA)	http://www.madiera.net/
Virtual Data Center (VDC)	http://thedata.org/

Table 43.1(b)

	National data archives[a] by year of (first) establishment		Website URL
US	Roper Center for Public Opinion Research	1946	http://www.ropercenter.uconn.edu/
DE	Central Archive for Empirical Social Research (GESIS-ZA)	1960	http://www.gesis.org/en/za/
US	Inter-university Consortium for Political and Social Research (ICPSR)	1962	http://www.icpsr.umich.edu
NL	Data Archiving & Networked Services (DANS) (Steinmetz Archief)	1964	http://www.dans.knaw.nl
GB	UK Data Archive (UKDA) Economic and Social Data Service (ESDS)	1967	http://www.data-archive.ac.uk/ http://www.esds.ac.uk
IT	ADPSS Sociodata	1970	http://www.sociologiadip.unimib.it/sociodata/
NO	Norwegian Social Science Data Services (NSD)	1971	http://www.nsd.uib.no/english/
DK	Danish Data Archives (DDA)	1973	http://www.dda.dk/
ES	Centro de Investigaciones Sociológicas—Archivo de Estudios Sociales (CIS-ARCES)	1977	http://www.cis.es
SE	Swedish Social Science Data Service (SSD)	1980	http://www.ssd.gu.se/
AU	Australian Social Science Data Archives (ASSDA)	1981	http://assda.anu.edu.au/
FR	Centre de données socio-politiques France (CDSP)	1981	http://cdsp.sciences-po.fr/
IL	Israel Social Sciences Data Center (ISDC)	1985	http://isdc.huji.ac.il/
HU	TARKI—Social Research Informatics Centre	1985	http://www.tarki.hu/
AT	Wiener Institut für Sozialwissenschaftliche Dokumentation und Methodik (WISDOM)	1985	http://www.wisdom.at/
BR	Centro de Estudos de Opinião Pública (CESOP)—Brazilian Survey Data Bank	1992	www.cesop.unicamp.br
CH	Swiss Information and Data Archive Service for the Social Sciences (SIDOS)	1992	http://www.sidos.ch/
ZA	South African Data Archive	1993	http://www.nrf.ac.za/sada/
SI	Social Science Data Archive Slovenia (ADP)	1997	http://www.adp.fdv.uni-lj.si/index_an.html
JP	SSJ Data Archive (Center for Social Science Research on Japan)	1998	http://ssjda.iss.u-tokyo.ac.jp/en/index.html
FI	Finish Social Science Data Archives (FSD)	1999	http://www.fsd.uta.fi/

Note: [a] After 60 years since the founding of the Roper Center, the United States and Western Europe are still hosting more data archives than the rest of the world, and with the exception of Australia, also those with largest collections. Nevertheless data archives have flourished on all continents, and especially in the new Eastern European democracies. Please accept apologies that this short tabular overview is not comprehensive. The selection tries to reflect the historical and/or international importance, including size of holdings, and is intended to include at least one representative from each continent. Herewith in no way a depreciation of the valuable activity of other data archives is intended. Further archives can be located through the respective archive networks IFDO, CESSDA (data archive map) and EDAN. A broad overview is given by E. Mochmann (International Social Science Data Service: Scope and Accessibility. Report for the International Social Science Council (ISSC), Cologne 2002) was conducted in 10 European countries, the United States and Peru. The study allows among other things a comparison of the time use in Western democracies and in the communist East, in particular in Russia.

'Political Action' (Barnes & Kaase, 1979; Jennings & van Deth, 1990) is one of the most important comparative data sets of the 1970s. The study investigates political orientations and political attitudes in seven West European countries and the United States. The database is unique in so far as it also includes a second wave panel for three countries—West Germany, the Netherlands, and the United States. These panels were conducted between 1979 and 1981 and were complemented by a second cross section. The first wave also includes interviews of parents and children and offers a unique opportunity for the investigation of socialization processes (Allerbeck, Jennings, & Rosenmeyer, 1979).

The infrastructure for survey research gradually developed in the decades after the war, but not everywhere with the same speed and success. In Germany, we had a long controversy about quota and random sampling, even though quota sampling can hardly be defended from a statistical point of view (Deville, 1991; Häder & Gabler, 2003). In France, for example, quota sampling nevertheless was predominant until the end of the millennium, and was only recently replaced by random sampling (→ *Sampling*). As a consequence, the national samples of most comparative surveys that were carried out in the last millennium, including in many European countries, were drawn by different methods. Thus, the social research infrastructure even in the affluent West European societies for a long time was far from optimal.

These sampling problems also affected the *Eurobarometer Surveys* (Saris & Kaase, 1997), which started in 1970 under the name of European Communities Studies. In the beginning, from the six founding members, only Belgium, the Netherlands, France, Italy and West Germany participated in the survey, supplemented in advance by Great Britain but excluding Luxembourg. In 1973, the survey was extended to all EC members. Due to the influence of Rabier and Inglehart (Reif & Inglehart, 1991), the Eurobarometer surveys soon became also an instrument for the analysis of change (→ *International Comparative Surveys: Their Purpose, Content and Methodological Challenges*). They are often described and criticized as surveys from and for the European politicians (O'Shea, Bryson, & Jowell, n.d.). It is true that the social sciences had only limited influence on the conceptualization of the surveys. The latter are used by the politicians for testing their popularity or the support of the European citizens for a particular political measure. Nevertheless, the Eurobarometer surveys contain some very interesting information about the European Union. They have included, for instance, an instrument for measuring value change towards postmaterialism for several decades. In this way, a sequence of measurement points has been built up which allows the calculation of the percentages of materialists and postmaterialists in prewar and postwar generations at more than 40 time points from 1970 onwards (→ *Identifying Value Clusters in Societies*).

Potential of data archives: The case of the Eurobarometer

Theories of value change often assume generational change. By means of a data set like the Eurobarometer, we can investigate whether value differences between younger and older generations really persist over longer periods. We can examine, for instance, whether the older generations are permanently more materialistic than the younger ones or whether the differences disappear over time. No other comparative data set permits the analysis of generational stability over a period of more than 30 years with so many measurement points as the Eurobarometer (Jagodzinski, 1996). To be sure, a rigorous test of value change requires observing the same persons repeatedly over time, which is not possible with the Eurobarometer. As long as these panel data do not exist, however, hypotheses about generational change can at least partially be tested with sequences of cross-sections.

While the change and trends in some beliefs and opinions can be empirically investigated in this way, the Eurobarometer surveys have not been conceptualized on the basis of explanatory models, so that the causes and consequences of these changes can only be superficially examined. On balance, the Eurobarometer leaves ambivalent feelings. On the one hand, a huge amount of information has been collected over the years. The Eurobarometers are not only conducted twice a year, they have also been supplemented by additional topical surveys and modules, by the Flash Eurobarometer, the Central and Eastern, and later the Candidate Countries' Eurobarometers. Although Switzerland is not a member of the EU, it nevertheless conducted parallel surveys once a year between 1999 and 2003; in 2005, this was replaced by the biennial MOSAICH project (Measurement and Observation of Social Aspects in Switzerland). The Eurobarometer surveys have become a rich data source, and they have been a source of interesting empirical findings (Bréchon & Cautrès, 1998). Regional barometers are no longer restricted to Western Europe but are now carried out in other parts of the world as well—in Asia, in Africa, and in Latin America. Not all of them are yet available for secondary analyses. A comprehensive data access protocol, as well as a better coordination among the programs, remains a task for the future.

Other comparative studies and international research programs

It is impossible to mention all important studies of the last 30 years. Election research has made great efforts in building up a comparative data base by different strategies. The national election studies can be used for comparative secondary analyses. This often requires an 'ex post harmonization' of the national data, as we call it, which is sometimes possible but often fails. The recently published 'European voter' (Thomassen, 2005) is example of this research strategy. In addition,

comparative data sets have been created, such as the European Election Studies and—as a worldwide enterprise—the Comparative Study of Electoral Systems (Franklin & Wlezien, 2002; Dalton, 2004). The latter is particularly interesting, because it combines macro data about electoral systems with survey data.

Three or four—depending on how one counts—other comparative data sets are highly relevant for the further development of comparative research: the European Values Study (EVS) in combination with the World Value Study, the International Social Survey Program (ISSP) and the European Social Survey (ESS). To a larger extent than the Eurobarometers, these empirical studies are not just surveys but *survey programs*. They do not aim at a single survey but rather a whole series of comparative surveys. The *European Values Study (EVS)* started in 1981 with the intention of investigating the values of the European population: are value differences an obstacle to European integration, or is there a common value basis that facilitates the process of European unification? The first survey included European countries only and was also 'Eurocentric,' in the sense that it focused on European values and beliefs. This perspective changed when Ron Inglehart joined the project in the late 1980s. He transformed the European project into a worldwide enterprise. The second wave of the EVS, which was carried out in 1990, was therefore called *World Values Survey*. In order to transform the formerly European survey, which was based on a Christian worldview, into a global survey, a large number of items have gradually been removed or changed.

This is a high price to pay. Specific cultures can no longer be investigated as comprehensively as in a single study that is tailored to a particular culture. For this and other reasons, the European Values Group decided to conceptualize the third wave of the values survey again as a European study. They also retained the interval of nine years between two adjacent waves. Thus the third EVS took place in 1999 and the fourth will take place in 2008. It was agreed, however, to collapse the data of the EVS 1999 and the WVS 2000 into a single integrated file.[2]

The EVS is at the border of a survey program, because the time interval between two surveys is fairly long. Therefore, the pressure for creating a permanent organization is less strong. This is different with regard to the two other research programs, the *International Social Survey Program (ISSP)* and the *European Social Survey (ESS)*. The ISSP was founded in 1985 as an American-European enterprise. It has gradually changed into a worldwide program with about 40 participating countries. The group has decided to carry out a comparative survey every year on varying topics like the role of government, social inequality, national identity, religion etc. The yearly comparative survey is called a module. By replicating modules in later years, the ISSP also permits the analysis of change. The 'Role of Government' module has already been carried out four times. 'Religion' is another example of a topic that has been surveyed in 1992 and 1998. The module will also be replicated in 2008.

RESOURCES FOR INTERNATIONAL SURVEYS

In order to utilize the full potential for improvements, however, more than loosely organized workgroups are needed. Scientists have to process, analyze, archive and distribute the data continuously, and they have to revisit the sampling procedures, advise the participating countries, and make other proposals for change. This requires resources. It is not sufficient to raise funds for the survey, which in most comparative programs is the duty of the participating countries; it is also necessary to fund a secretariat, organize and fund meetings, pay for data processing and archiving, and create incentives for those who do the difficult and cumbersome work. In ISSP, these overhead costs are shared by a few countries that take the money from their own budget or from some external sources. Therefore, the funding of the overhead in ISSP always remains precarious.

To our knowledge at least, the *European Social Survey (ESS)* (Jowell, Roberts, Fitzgerald, & Gillian, 2006) is the first international survey program that receives such a funding from a supranational organization, namely the EU. It enables the ESS to build up an efficient infrastructure for the whole survey process, beginning with the drafting of the questionnaire, moving to translation, pretesting and sampling, and ending with data distribution and archiving. And the investment pays off. The ESS has become a model for international surveys (Norris, 2004). It has recently been awarded the Descartes Prize—a highly valued European award that so far has only been presented to European hard-core scientists.

The international databases, the documentation standards and the technology for a 'virtual global data archive' are advancing hand in hand. The opportunities for cumulative comparative research are therefore better than ever. The data re-use circle is closed when the results from secondary analysis are linked back to the studies. This will not only inspire new research, but also, in combination with statistical training programs, reduce the risk of inadequate or inappropriate uses of data.

NOTES

1 Due to the initiative of Hans Rattinger, a larger number of the old data sets have been rescued. In cooperation with the Zentralarchiv für Empirische Sozialforschung (ZA) in Cologne, Germany, a total of 65 comparative surveys were transformed into machine-readable documents. In addition, the ZA built up a database of the 47 German surveys that cover a period of about 20 years, from 1952 to 1972. Another 44 surveys are currently being processed and will expand the time horizon up to 1992.

2 The European Value Survey 1999 is archived at the ZA in Cologne. The integrated file of European and World Value Surveys can presently be downloaded at http://www.jdsurvey.net/web/evs1.htm.

REFERENCES

Allerbeck, K. R., Jennings, M. K., & Rosenmeyer, L. (1979). Generations and politics: Political action.

In S. H. Barnes, & M. Kaase (Eds.), *Political action. Mass participation in five Western democracies* (pp. 487–522). Beverly Hills: Sage.

Almond, G. A., & Verba, S. (1963). *The civic culture: Political attitudes and democracy in 5 nations.* Princeton, NJ: Princeton University Press.

Barnes, S. H., & Kaase, M. (1979). *Political action. Mass participation in 5 Western democracies.* Beverly Hills: Sage.

Blank, G., & Rasmussen, K. B. (2004). The data documentation initiative: The value and significance of a worldwide standard. *Social Science Computer Review, 22,* 307–318.

Bréchon, P., & Cautrès, B. (1998). Les enquetes Euro-baromètres: *Analyse comparée des données socio-politiques. Actes du colloque CIDSP-AFSP, Centre d'Informatisation des Données Socio-Politiques, Association Francaise de Science Politique. Grenoble - novembre 1997.* Paris, Montreal: Harmattan.

Cantril, H. (1965). *The patterns of human concern.* New Brunswick, NJ: Rutgers University Press.

Dalton, R. J. (2004). *Democratic challenges, democratic choices: The erosion of political support in advanced industrial democracies.* Oxford: Oxford University Press.

Deville, J.-C. (1991). A theory of quota surveys. *Survey Methodology, 17,* 163–181.

Franklin, M. N., & Wlezien, C. (Eds.). (2002). *The future of election studies.* Amsterdam: Pergamon.

Häder, S., & Gabler, S. (2003). Sampling and estimation. In J. A. Harkness, F. J. R. van de Vijver, & P. Mohler (Eds.), *Cross-cultural survey methods* (pp. 117–134). New Jersey: Wiley Interscience.

Harvey, A. S., Szalai, A., Elliott, D. H., Stone, P. J., & Clark, S. M. (1984). *Time budget research: An ISSC workbook in comparative analysis.* Frankfurt/New York: Campus.

Inter-university Consortium for Political and Social Research (2005). *Guide to social science data preparation and archiving* (3rd ed.). Ann Arbor, Michigan. Retrieved February 5, 2007 from http://www.icpsr.umich.edu/ACCESS/dpm.html.

Jagodzinski, W. (1996). The metamorphosis of life cycle change in longitudinal studies on postmaterialism. In C. Hayashi & E. K. Scheuch (Eds.), *Quantitative social research in Germany and Japan* (pp. 25–52). Opladen: Leske + Budrich.

Jennings, M. K., & van Deth, J. W. (1990). *Continuities in political action: A longitudinal study of political orientations in three Western democracies.* Berlin: Walter de Gruyter.

Jowell, R., Roberts, C., Fitzgerald, R., & Gillian, E. (Eds.). (2006). *Measuring attitudes cross-nationally. Lessons from the European Social Survey.* London: Sage.

Kaase, M., & Jennings, K. (1995). *Beliefs in government* (Volume V). Oxford: Oxford University Press.

Miller, W. E. (1976). The less obvious functions of archiving survey research data. *American Behavioral Scientist, 19,* 409–418.

Norris, P. (2004). From the civic culture to the Afro-Barometer: The expansion in cross-national public opinon surveys. *APSA-Comparative Politics Newsletter.* Retrieved February 5, 2007, from http://ksghome.harvard.edu/~pnorris/Acrobat/APSA-CP.pdf.

OECD Follow Up Group on Issues of Access to Publicly Funded Research Data (2003, March). Promoting access to public research data for scientific, economic, and social development. Final Report. Retrieved February 5, 2007, from http://dataaccess.ucsd.edu/Final_Report_2003.pdf.

O'Shea, R., Bryson, C., & Jowell, R. (n.d.). *Comparative attitudinal research in Europe.* European Social Survey Directorate, National Centre for Social Research, London, on behalf of the central co-ordinating team of the ESS. Retrieved February 5, 2007, from http://naticent02.uuhost.uk.uu.net/ess_docs/comparative_attitudinal_research.doc.

Reif, K., & Inglehart, R. (Eds.). (1991). *Eurobarometer: The dynamics of European public opinion. Essays in honour of Jacques-Rene Rabier.* London: Macmillan.

Rokkan, S. (1964). Archives for secondary analysis of sample survey data: An early inquiry into the prospects of Western Europe. *International Social Science Journal, 16,* 49–62.

Rokkan, S. (1966). *Data archives for the social sciences. Tools and methods of comparative research* (Publications of the International Social Science Council, Vol. 3). Paris/La Hague: Mouton.

The Royal Statistical Society & the UK Data Archive (2002). *Preserving & sharing statistical material.* Essex, Colchester. Retrieved February 5, 2007, from http://www.data-archive.ac.uk/news/publications/PreservingSharing.pdf.

Saris, W. E., & Kaase, M. (Eds.). (1997). *Eurobarometer—Measurement instruments for opinions in Europe* (ZUMA Nachrichten Spezial. Vol. 2). Mannheim: ZUMA.

Scheuch, E. K. (2003). History and visions in the development of data services for the social sciences. *International Social Science Journal, 177,* 385–399.

Szalai, A. (Ed.). (1972). *The use of time. Daily activities of urban and suburban populations in twelve countries.* The Hague, Paris: Mouton.

Thomassen, J. (Ed.). (2005). *The European voter. A comparative study of modern democracies.* Oxford: Oxford University Press.

Uses and Effects of Public Opinion Research

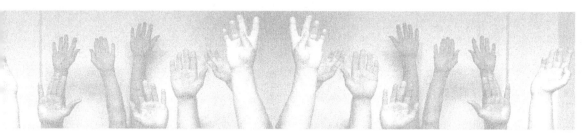

44

The News Media's Use of Opinion Polls

Frank Brettschneider

'The polls have changed journalism, just as the organization of press associations did, just as the advent of half-tone photo engravings did, just as the rise of the columnists and commentators did.' Thus euphorically wrote Eugene Meyer, publisher of the *Washington Post* in 1940 (p. 240). The *Post* was the first subscriber of the *Gallup Poll*, marking the beginning of a new era for the relationship between journalists and pollsters. Today, public opinion polls are an integral component of news coverage. 'Polls are newsworthy: they are topical, relate directly to issues in the news, are up-to-the-moment' (Paletz *et al.*, 1980). They serve many functions: as information sources, as attention-getters, and as a source of journalistic power (Frankovic, 1998, p. 162). Because of their high news value, public opinion polls have increasingly become a standard feature in news reporting over the last decades. According to a worldwide study in 78 countries by Røhme (1997, p. 5), opinion polls were published 'practically every day' or 'regularly' in the major news media—most frequently in newspapers.

One reason for the increase in the media's use of opinion polls lies in the changing relationship between pollsters on the one side and journalists as well as news organizations on the other: from competition and conflict at the beginning to a 'symbiotic' relationship nowadays. The concept of 'precision journalism,' introduced by Philip Meyer during the 1970s, played an important role in those changes. Today, the news media are one of the main clients of polling firms—or they conduct polls on their own.

Especially during election campaigns, polls are under attack from various sides: they are criticized by politicians as well as by some journalists for being misleading and manipulative. Because of their expected influence on the voters' decisions (→ *The Effects of Published Polls on Citizens*), the publication of poll results is banned in many countries of the world during the last days of an election campaign (→ *The Legal Status of Public Opinion Research in the World*). The way journalists report on opinion polls is also criticized: pollsters rate the poll reporting of journalists as 'moderate' (Røhme, 1997, p. 5); problems include the publication of unprofessional poll findings (such as TV studio audience polls or call-in polls), the over-interpretation or misleading interpretations of poll findings by journalists, and poor documentation of polls. Another problem is so-called 'horse-race journalism'—the use of polls in an election campaign to stress entertainment instead of concentrating on political issues. Therefore, this chapter will summarize the findings on the following questions: How did the relationship between journalists and pollsters develop over the last century? How often do news media report about poll results? In what way do they report? Do they disclose methodological information, such as the time of fieldwork or the question wording?

THE RELATIONSHIP BETWEEN POLLS AND THE NEWS MEDIA

Historical roots

In the United States, the relationship between news organizations and polls developed over three stages (Frankovic, 1998). The *first stage (1824–1935)* was dominated by 'straw polls.' According to Frankovic (1998, p. 151), newspapers took a first quantitative account of public opinion in 1824, when the *Niles' Weekly Register* (a Maryland paper) reported a meeting in Delaware, where about 200 people voted on the presidential candidates half a year before Election Day. The *Register* wrote: 'This is something new; but an excellent plan of obtaining the sense of the people' (quoted after Frankovic, 1998, p. 151). Next, the so-called 'straw polls' came to dominate at the end of the nineteenth century. Newspapers sent out questionnaires—mostly to their own readers. These 'polls' were usually not representative of all voters. Already in 1896, the *Chicago Record* conducted a challenging survey. The newspaper sent 833,277 postcard ballots to all registered voters in Chicago. About 240,000 were sent back and adjusted by mathematicians. For a long time, the quality of this survey was unrivaled. After

1900, various newspapers—among others the *Chicago Tribune* and the *New York Tribune*—conducted 'straw polls' with non-representative samples. The non-scientific sampling methods were the main problem of those surveys. Therefore, their prediction of the election often failed miserably, despite high numbers of respondents. The most widely known error was produced by the *Literary Digest* in 1936. The weekly newspaper mailed ballot cards to about 10,000,000 registered voters and failed to predict Franklin D. Roosevelt's victory. At the same time, both George Gallup and Elmo Roper predicted the outcome of the election based on a representative sample of only a few thousand adults (→ *The Start of Modern Public Opinion Research*).

The *second stage (from 1936 until the 1970s)* was dominated by 'syndicated polls' and by 'media sponsored polls.' It started with the success of Gallup's and Roper's accurate predictions of the outcome of the 1936 presidential election. From then on, professional institutes conducted polls based on small but representative samples, and produced a standard news story that they provided to subscriber newspapers or magazines. News media bought these 'syndicated polls' and assured a steady income for the poll institutes. Further, the journalists had information for reports about the public opinion. 'Many newspapers jumped on the polling bandwagon. In May 1940, 118 newspapers subscribed to the Gallup Poll' (Frankovic, 1998, p. 155). In the 1950s, already around 200 newspapers regularly printed columns with the newest Gallup poll results. Also at that time, the first partnerships between individual media and institutes existed—so-called 'media sponsored polls': For example, Roper's polls were conducted for *Fortune* magazine. And Archibald Crossley began polling for the Hearst newspapers. At the end of the 1940s, polls entered radio and television. *CBS* broadcasted the fifteen-minute 'America Speaks: George Gallup Show' on nine Sundays (Frankovic, 1998, p. 155). The news media established these 'media sponsored polls' on an exclusive report basis. Further, they could determine which subject the public would be questioned on. Today, the news media are one of the biggest contractors of political opinion polls.

The *third stage (since the 1970s)* is dominated by 'in-house polls.' The media themselves established polling units inside of their news organization. These units design and carry out polls on their own. New technological and methodological changes stimulated this development as they made it quicker and cheaper to conduct surveys. The news media also used surveys for their market research. In general, partnerships between print and broadcast news organizations were established: *Washington Post/ABC, New York Times/CBS, Wall Street Journal/NBC,* and *CNN/USA Today.* At the end of the 1980s, 82% of all the daily newspapers with a circulation of over 100,000 as well as 56% of all TV-stations conducted their own opinion polls (Ladd & Benson, 1992). 'Thus, the press—the vital "organ" (shaper and mirror) of public opinion in standard treatments of the topic—became inevitably a leading actor in the evolving polling enterprise' (Gollin, 1987, p. 87). The need for instant information and for an ongoing flow of news led to methodological innovations such as exit polls, tracking polls, and instant polls to measure the public's reaction to political debates or breaking news events (→ *Exit Polls and Pre-Election Polls*).

Today, the relationship between news organizations and pollsters can best be described as 'joint venture of ascertaining and reporting public opinion' (Ladd, 1980, p. 576, → *Attitudes of Journalists Toward Public Opinion Research*). Similar developments can be found in other Western democracies—such as Australia (Smith III & Verrall, 1985), Canada (Andersen, 2000), Finland (Suhonen, 2001), Germany (Brettschneider, 1997), Great Britain (Worcester, 1991), Israel (Weimann, 1990), and Switzerland (Hardmeier, 1999).

The establishment of these relationships has not been without criticism. Many critics refer to the misuse of polls. Often they are used as entertainment or 'headline polls' instead of as a tool for in-depth analysis. Another fear is that journalists' lack of knowledge about the conduct and analysis of polls results in low quality 'in-house polls.' Ladd (1980) observed a 'clash of institutional imperatives.' Media have to work fast; they need quick news. In contrast, pollsters have to work precisely. A high-quality poll needs time for the development of a questionnaire, the pre-testing, the fieldwork, and the analysis. In addition, when the news media annex public opinion research, this can lead to a loss of their independence (ibid.; Noelle-Neumann, 1980).

The 'precision journalism' concept

With his books *Precision Journalism* (1973) and *The New Precision Journalism* (1991), Philip Meyer probably has had a great influence on the positive development of the relationship between the news media and public opinion research. The main focus of the concept is 'the application of social and behavioral science research methods to the practice of journalism' (Meyer, 1991, p. 2). Meyer (1991) asks journalists not to fight against polls but to apply them as a useful tool 'to find the facts, to understand them, and to explain them without wasting time' (p. 3). According to his view, one of the traditional functions of journalism, i.e. to recognize and describe social and political phenomena, is now in the responsibility of the social sciences.

Consequently, it would be appropriate to use some social scientific methods and to improve with their help the quality and accuracy of journalism. 'We journalists would be wrong less often if we adapted to our own use some of the research tools of the social scientists' (Meyer, 1973, p. 3). Therefore, journalists could make an educated interpretation of these phenomena through the application of social science methods, including opinion polls. 'The ground rules are no different from those on which we've always operated: find the facts, tell what they mean and do it without wasting time. If there are new tools to enable us to perform this task with greater power, accuracy and insight, then we should make the most of them' (p. 15). Hence he argues that journalists should routinely cite the results of public opinion research and use them for their coverage. Furthermore, journalists should have the knowledge of experts in the field of polls. 'A journalist has to be a database manager, a data processor, and a data analyst' (Meyer, 1991, p. 1). And finally, the news media should conduct polls on their own.

These recommendations are still controversial. For instance, Noelle-Neumann (1980, p. 589) argues against the news media conducting their own surveys: 'I am convinced that he [Meyer] seriously underestimates the difficulties of bringing social research and journalists together.' Social research 'methods and modes of thinking are in many respects utterly alien to journalists' (Noelle-Neumann, 1980, p. 589). Therefore, she prefers a continuous direct encounter between journalists and pollsters by the composition of poll reports. In addition, pollsters should also write their own articles about the poll results—as a 'public opinion research correspondent' (Noelle-Neumann, 1980; similar: Mitofsky, 1995, p. 73). This could guarantee high-quality poll reporting.

However, other critics feel that journalists would compromise their basic professional role of reporting the news when they created news in the form of self-conducted polls (Von Hoffman, 1979). Nevertheless, 'it is clear that precision journalism has become a legitimate genre of reporting, joining interpretive and investigative reporting as a stylistically distinct and professionally accepted approach to news gathering and presentation' (Ismach, 1984, p. 107).

POLLING DATA AS MEDIA CONTENT

In 1980, Roper (1980, p. 48) spoke of a 'pendulum swing from media *resistance* to polls to a media *embrace* of polls.' Ever since, there has been a major increase in the coverage of opinion polls, especially before national elections. In Germany, until the Federal election of 1976, pre-election polls were of little importance to the media (Brettschneider, 1997). Since then, the number of poll reports in the last three months before Election Day in the four national prestige newspapers (*Frankfurter Allgemeine Zeitung, Frankfurter Rundschau, Süddeutsche Zeitung* and *Die Welt*) has grown steadily (Figure 44.1).

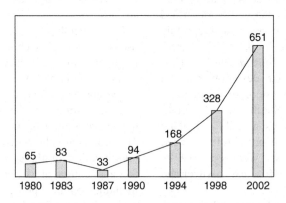

Figure 44.1   Frequency of poll reports within 12 weeks before federal elections in Germany, 1980–2002

Source: Frequency of poll reports published by the four German national newspapers *Frankfurter Allgemeine Zeitung, Frankfurter Rundschau, Süddeutsche Zeitung* and *Die Welt*

Between the election years of 1980 and 2002, it increased ten-fold: from 65 stories in 1980 up to 651 stories in 2002. The increase in poll reports is similar to trends in other countries. In Israel, the number of pre-election poll stories in 15 dailies increased from 16 in 1969 up to 409 in 1988 (Weimann, 1990). In the USA, the number of page one pre-election poll stories in 11 major daily newspapers increased from 102 in 1980 up to 452 in 1992; their share of all election stories rose from 7.1% in 1980 to 22.2% in 1992 (Lavrakas & Bauman, 1995, p. 40). Similar developments were found in Finland (Suhonen, 2001).

This increase is due to changing attitudes of journalists towards polls and to a rise in poll availability. But the general increase in poll reports also shows specific fluctuations. They are defined by the various circumstances of each election: the tighter an election outcome is expected to be and the more personalized an election campaign is, the more poll reports seem to be published. The closer to Election Day, the more poll reports are written and aired. This increase throughout the campaign is caused by a growing public interest in questions concerning the development of the campaign. Linked with this, the news value of poll data also rises. Furthermore, during the last weeks of an election campaign, the number of polls carried out is above average.

QUALITY OF REPORTING OF POLLING DATA IN THE NEWS MEDIA

Criticism

But the overall increase in poll reporting does not mean *per se* an increase in relevant information given to the voters. The following summarizes some of the criticisms of how the news media report polling data.

Diffuse references of journalists to polls: 'Individual poll results do make news, but journalists often refer to findings of "the polls", which are usually unspecified and unsourced [...] Citations of "polls", rather than of a specific poll finding, have

become common' (Frankovic, 1998, p. 162). References to undifferentiated 'polls' appear in an increasing number of stories in American print media (ibid.) as well as in Canadian TV and print media (Andersen, 2000) and in German newspapers (Brettschneider, 1997). Often, diffuse references to 'the polls' are used by journalists to strengthen and to underpin their own interpretations of the campaign. A content analysis of German news media has shown that journalists even tend to synchronize the publication of poll results with their editorial standpoint on parties and candidates (Donsbach & Weisbach, 2005).

Horse-race coverage: This term is an application of a metaphor derived from sports. 'Who's ahead?' 'Who's running behind?' 'Who made gains? Who suffered losses?' In the supporters' opinions, the usage of the 'horse-race metaphor' helps to build public interest for a topic which, otherwise, seems to be incomprehensible, distant, and boring: 'If citizens are more attracted to sports than to politics, why not use sports to teach them about politics?' (Broh, 1980, p. 527). Critics accuse such journalism of not using poll results for the analysis of issues and background information that are relevant for the voting-decision. Instead, entertainment becomes more important than factual information: 'Instead of covering the candidates' qualifications, philosophies, or issue positions, polls have encouraged journalists to treat campaigns as horse races, with a focus on the candidates' popularity, momentum, and size of lead' (Atkin & Gaudino, 1984, p. 124).

Inaccuracies in reporting poll data: Often, journalists interpret the polls incorrectly. 'Opinion change' that lies within the margin of error, is interpreted as a substantial shift in public opinion (Patterson, 2005). Also, poll data are not used as what they are: a momentary snapshot; rather they support an 'obsession to forecast' (Weimann, 1990). Poll data are used to speculate about the election outcome. Journalists frequently try to predict election results by comparing current results with past poll results. As a rule, they leave out the methical characteristics of the studies and do therefore not consider the problems of comparison (e.g. different question wordings or characteristics of the sample).

Disclosure of methodological information

In order to evaluate poll results, the reader needs methodological information, such as question wording, time of fieldwork, the definition of the population for which the survey is representative, and the response rate. This demand led the American Association for Public Opinion Research (AAPOR) in 1969 to develop a list of 'Standards for Minimal Disclosure.' This catalogue was originally intended to specify what the pollster is required to disclose to whomever asks. The AAPOR standards are also used as a guide for the evaluation of poll reports (Paletz *et al.*, 1980; Miller & Hurd, 1982). The presentation of poll results should include information about: the number of respondents, the institution that commissioned the poll, the poll institute that conducted the survey, margin of error of the results, the question wording, the definition of the population, the mode of data collection (written, personal,

on the phone, Internet-based), the time of field work, and the response rate. The World Association for Public Opinion Research (WAPOR) and the European Society for Market and Opinion Research (ESOMAR) have developed similar guidelines as part of their 'Guide to Opinion Polls'.

'Numerous studies in various countries have shown that most media neglect to provide their readers or viewers with the necessary parameters with which it is possible to assess the quality or validity of the results' (Donsbach, 2001, p. 19). However, there are noticeable differences in the frequency with which journalists mention the AAPOR/WAPOR-criteria: The most frequently mentioned are the polling institute, the institution that commissioned the poll, and the time of fieldwork. Information can rarely be found about the mode of data collection and the question wording (Figure 44.2). The sampling error receives almost no attention at all. For Canada, Andersen (2000, p. 292) noticed 'an alarming absence of basic technical information.' Similar findings exist for Israel (Weimann, 1990), Switzerland (Hardmeier, 1999), Finland (Suhonen, 2001) and Germany (Brettschneider, 1997).

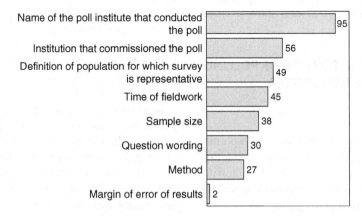

Figure 44.2 Methodological information in poll reports within 12 weeks before federal elections in Germany, 1980–2002 (percentage of reports mentioning certain methodological information)

Source: Reports about recent poll results in which the subject 'poll' is dominating (*n* = 383 poll reports published by the four German national newspapers *Frankfurter Allgemeine Zeitung, Frankfurter Rundschau, Süddeutsche Zeitung* and *Die Welt*)

Moreover, numerous studies show that the frequency of disclosure of methods varies. In the prestige press, the frequency is higher than in the regional or local newspapers. It is higher when pollsters write an article, compared to articles written by journalists. Furthermore, reports about in-house polls have methodical information more often than reports about wire-service and syndicated polls.

There are different viewpoints concerning the usage of methodical information. Some request a 'technical appendix' that embodies all the relevant methodical information. Thus, the voters could make sound judgments about the quality of poll results. Others doubt the value of such an 'appendix.' For example, they believe that mentioning the margin of error would only confuse readers. Even the poll institutes cannot agree upon this matter. The *Harris* organization does not consistently mention the sampling error: 'reporting sampling error serves no function because the public understands that poll results are estimates' (Miller & Hurd, 1982, p. 249). Mitofsky (1995, p. 69) shares this opinion: 'Disclosure of methods is not improving reporting.' Only the knowledgeable pollsters would profit from disclosure, not the journalists or normal readers. Much more important than mentioning methodical information is something else: 'The researcher should discuss the level of the generalizations that can and cannot be made from the data' (Mitofsky, 1995, p. 75).

WHICH WAY TO GO?

The news reports of opinion polls have been increasing during the last century and form a solid element within the public communication—especially within the electoral campaign communication. Yet to be an integral part of the formation of public opinion, the coverage should not only be frequent, but also of high quality. Poll reports should inform, they should not mislead the voters.

The formal aspects of poll reports leave much room for improvement. Methodological information is important in order to judge the reliability, the validity, and the relevance of poll results. But journalists' lack of knowledge about how to work with empirical research methods is one reason for the lack of quality in poll reports. This quality will improve when more journalists learn how to work and apply such methods and, as a result, learn to deal with methodological questions in a more sensitive and competent way. A prerequisite for this will be the efforts of pollsters to make their work more transparent and comprehensible. Apart from this, universities—as has been the case in the United States for a long time—should offer courses for journalists where they get the chance to improve their knowledge of empirical research. Even more important than the methodological part of the story would be an improvement in the adequate interpretation of poll findings. A better education for the journalist could help to avoid false causal explanations of poll data. Once more, the pollsters are in charge: they need to state the limits of the poll data clearly. And they should help journalists to interpret the poll data correctly.

Meyer and Potter (2000, p. 138) conclude: 'Keep the horse-race polls. But do not make them the center of coverage. Do them frequently enough so that too much attention is not focused on any one poll. Resist the temptation to make headline news out of polls whose results are statistically insignificant. Keep poll results in the background like a scoreboard. Use tracking polls only for what they are, a limited measure of the campaign's shifting dynamics. And track trends among subgroups whose support is being contested, such as minorities, women, and old people.' Poll coverage could be a central contribution to citizens' understanding of public opinion, if journalists and news organizations took into account the above listed recommendations. Poll reports could provide the voters with important information concerning their voting decision. Hence, they could strengthen the voice of public opinion against politicians and interest groups.

REFERENCES

Andersen, R. (2000). Reporting public opinion polls: The media and the 1997 Canadian election. *International Journal of Public Opinion Research, 12,* 285–298.

Atkin, C. K., & Gaudino, J. (1984). The impact of polling on the mass media. *ANNALS, 472,* 119–128.

Brettschneider, F. (1997). The press and the polls in Germany, 1980–1994. Poll coverage as an essential part of election campaign reporting. *International Journal of Public Opinion Research, 9,* 248–265.

Broh, C. A. (1980). Horse-race journalism: Reporting the polls in the 1976 presidential election. *Public Opinion Quarterly, 44,* 514–529.

Donsbach, W. (2001). *Who's afraid of election polls? Normative and empirical arguments for the freedom of pre-election surveys.* Amsterdam, Lincoln: ESOMAR/WAPOR.

Donsbach, W., & Weisbach, K. (2005). Kampf um das Meinungsklima. Quellen und Inhalte der Aussagen über den möglichen Wahlausgang [Struggle of the climate of opinion. Sources and content of statements about the possible election outcome]. In E. Noelle-Neumann, W. Donsbach, & H. M. Kepplinger (Eds.), *Wählerstimmungen in der Mediendemokratie* (pp. 104–127). Freiburg, München: Alber.

Frankovic, K. A. (1998). Public opinion and polling. In D. Graber, D. McQuail, & P. Norris (Eds.), *The politics of news. The news of politics* (pp. 150–170). Washington, D.C.: Congressional Quarterly Press.

Gollin, A. E. (1987). Polling and the news media. *Public Opinion Quarterly, 51,* 86–94.

Hardmeier, S. (1999). Political poll reporting in Swiss print media: Analysis and suggestions for quality improvement. *International Journal of Public Opinion Research, 11,* 257–274.

Ismach, A. H. (1984). Polling as news-gathering tool. *ANNALS, 472,* 106–118.

Ladd, E. C. (1980). Polling and the press: The clash of institutional imperatives. *Public Opinion Quarterly, 44,* 574–584.

Ladd, E. C., & Benson, J. (1992). The growth of news polls in American politics. In T. E. Mann & G. R. Orren (Eds.), *Media polls in American politics* (pp. 9–31). Washington, DC: The Brookings Institution.

Lavrakas, P. J., & Bauman, S. L. (1995). Page one use of presidential pre-election polls: 1980–1992. In P. J. Lavrakas, M. W. Traugott, & P. V. Miller (Eds.), *Presidential polls and the news media* (pp. 35–49). Boulder, San Francisco, Oxford: Westview Press.

Meyer, E. (1940). A newspaper publisher looks at the polls. *Public Opinion Quarterly, 4,* 238–240.

Meyer, P. (1973). *Precision journalism. A reporter's introduction to social science methods.* Bloomington, London: Indiana University Press.

Meyer, P. (1991). *The new precision journalism.* Bloomington, Indianapolis: Indiana University Press.

Meyer, P., & Potter, D. (2000). Hidden values: Polls and public journalism. In P. J. Lavrakas & M. W. Traugott (Eds.), *Election polls, the news media, and democracy* (pp. 113–141). New York, London: Chatham House Publishers.

Miller, M. M., & Hurd, R. (1982). Conformity to AAPOR standards in newspaper reporting of public opinion polls. *Public Opinion Quarterly, 46,* 243–249.

Mitofsky, W. J. (1995). How pollsters and reporters can do a better job informing the public: A challenge for campaign '96. In P. J. Lavrakas, M. W. Traugott, & P. V. Miller (Eds.), *Presidential Polls and the News Media* (pp. 69–79). Boulder, San Francisco, Oxford: Westview Press.

Noelle-Neumann, E. (1980). The public opinion research correspondent. *Public Opinion Quarterly, 44,* 585–597.

Paletz, David L., Short, J. Y., Baker, H., Cookman Campbell, B., Cooper, R. J., & and Oeslander, R. M. (1980). Polls in the media: Content, credibility, and consequences. *Public Opinion Quarterly, 44,* 495–513.

Patterson, T. E. (2005). Of polls, mountains: U.S. journalists and their use of election surveys. *Public Opinion Quarterly, 69,* 716–724.

Røhme, N. (1997). *The freedom to publish opinion polls. Report on a worldwide study.* Amsterdam, Chapel Hill: ESOMAR/WAPOR.

Roper, B. W. (1980). The media and the polls: A boxscore. *Public Opinion, 3,* 46.

Smith, T. J., III, & Verrall, D. O. (1985). A critical analysis of Australian television coverage of election opinion polls. *Public Opinion Quarterly, 49,* 58–79.

Suhonen, P. (2001). Opinion polls and journalism: The case of Finland. In S. Splichal (Ed.), *Public opinion and democracy. Vox populi– vox dei?* (pp. 311–335). Cresskill: Hampton Press.

Von Hoffman, N. (1979). Public opinion polls: Newspapers making their own news? *Public Opinion Quarterly, 44,* 572–573.

Weimann, G. (1990). The obsession to forecast: Pre-election polls in the Israeli press. *Public Opinion Quarterly, 54,* 396–408.

Worcester, R. M. (1991). *British public opinion. A guide to the history and methodology of political opinion polling.* Cambridge: Cambridge University Press.

45

The Use of Surveys by Governments and Politicians

Robert M. Eisinger

The history of governments' use of polls is a story about the push and pull between the desire by political elites to gauge public opinion accurately, and the concurrent resistance by political elites to the use of surveys. Simply put, the birth and growth of polling by politicians and government officials have not been met with uniform acceptance or approval. To the contrary, politicians' use of surveys has been a struggle for legitimacy, with recent public officials decrying the use of polls even as they use them. President George W. Bush repeatedly noted when campaigning in 2000 that he governs 'based upon principle and not polls and focus groups' (Green, 2002, p. 11). President Bush's phrasing is peculiar because it leaves room for his polling, but suggests that there is a pejorative connotation in 'governing by polls,' even as his administration uses polls. Polling among politicians, in the United States and elsewhere, continues to grow at a pace that cannot be easily measured, partly because so many agencies and bureaucracies employ surveys of one form or another.

But such growth and reliance on surveys has not yielded comfort on the part of the public or even among the government officials themselves. Polls are used to gauge the will, attitudes and opinions of various publics, but the current trajectory of government's survey use continues to generate alarms, calls for oversight and cautionary statements, much like President Bush's comment above.

This chapter will provide an overview of how surveys are used by governments in democratic regimes, paying closer emphasis to how polls have been used in the United States. The chapter's focus on the US is predicated on the relative abundance of data from that country, and paucity of scholarly studies from elsewhere. In reality, most democracies (and many non-democracies) employ polls when governing. The chapter will describe how US government's use of polls has emerged, noting that the line between campaigning and governing is a blurry one. Simultaneously, this chapter also will highlight the relevant critical theories surrounding survey usage by governments.

Specific attention will be paid to theories about politicians' responsiveness to citizens, and how surveys are used as instruments to facilitate that responsiveness.

SUSPICION OF GOVERNMENT POLLING

Why is it that the phrase 'government polling' is met with dubious derision if not enmity? Why have pollsters developed a reputation as 'Machiavellian plotters whose job it is to think up ways to exploit the public' (Kohut, cited in Green, 2002, p. 11)? The answer lies in the evolution of government's use of polls, especially in its nascent and adolescent stages. Polling was often considered suspicious, avant-garde and deleterious to representative governments. Polling by governmental officials was considered especially dangerous and uncharted. As a result, the history of survey use by and within governments can be best characterized as constantly criticized, even as it increases in volume.

This history of government's use of polls is, at least in the United States, more thematic than linear in nature, in large part because the history of polling by US governments is not easily or logically explained by presidential tenure, Congress, party in power or even by political era. Rather, governmental polling evolves, partly because of technological developments (most obviously the creation of the modern public opinion poll itself), and by the successful employment of surveys over time. That written, criticisms of government's polling recur throughout this evolution, so much so that these criticisms deserve serious analysis when describing how polling by governments has evolved. In short, the scholarly criticisms that governmental surveys employ poor samples, digress from the roots of republicanism, improperly identify the power of group pressure, substitute for or abdicate political leadership, and have created government decision making that replicates a quasi-permanent campaign, all are rooted in a genuine concern that public opinion and its measurement is a powerful political force that

can be used or abused by politicians. Some of these evaluations overstate their cases; others are purely polemical in nature. However, when these critical appraisals are supplemented with a review of how governmental polling commences and ultimately evolves, what emerges is a complex interplay between and among theory and practice, critics and practitioners, and elites and masses.

HISTORY OF GOVERNMENT'S USE OF OPINION POLLS

George Gallup as early proponent

The birth of the modern public opinion poll, and its concomitant use by governments, commences with George Gallup. Gallup arguably served as the most vocal proponent of surveys, delivering speeches as he actively promoted polls as a positive influence on representative government—a quasi-antidote to democratic woes. Gallup forged positive relations with public officials, including President Franklin Delano Roosevelt, and willingly advertised his polling methods as being superior to alternatives. More importantly, Gallup wrote (with Saul Forbes Rae) *The Pulse of Democracy: The Public Opinion Poll and How it Works* a seminal work arguing that polls, while still in their incipient developmental stages, provided more accurate assessments of public opinion than newspapers and interest groups (Gallup & Rae, 1940; see also Eisinger, 2003, p. 142). For Gallup, polls allowed politicians to monitor public opinion, thereby making them more responsive to their constituents and to the mass public. Simultaneously, Gallup also realized that public opinion was a political weapon that could be used by public officials, candidates for office, and political parties. Rather than relying on inaccurate gauges of public attitudes, Gallup believed surveys were the most objective, non-partisan, precise instrument for identifying public opinion. In his view, this accurate vehicle of measurement would improve representative democracy precisely because the alternatives were less accurate, and therefore, were generating and propagating false claims about the public's mood.

The pioneer: Franklin D. Roosevelt

Gallup's clarion call for more polling was taken seriously by the FDR administration. President Roosevelt's advisers and the national Democratic Party already had been employing polls to build the national Democratic Party. One party operative, Emil Hurja, amassed a plethora of public opinion data (straw votes and country fairs, regional maps detailing voting trends, newspaper editorials) in an attempt to identify public opinion, and to use it to the Roosevelt Administration and Democratic Party's advantage. As Gallup's polls were being invented and circulated, Hurja soon employed them into his analyses, establishing himself as political soothsayer and 'prophet extraordinary of the Democratic party,' who 'with questionnaires and frequent samplings of public opinion … checks up reaction to administration policies, to presidential speeches and conferences, to the attitudes of congressional blocs on both sides of the aisle, to Republican lines of attack' (Tucker, 1935, pp. 28ff.; also cited in Eisinger, 2003, p. 84).

Soon thereafter, FDR's advisers were evaluating Gallup data provided by Hadley Cantril, Director of the Office of Public Opinion Research at Princeton University. By 1942, Cantril was interpreting the most accurate public opinion data that existed to White House advisers, doing so discretely and confidentially 'in order to minimize curiosity and preserve the informality of our relationships' (Cantril, 1947, p. 52, also cited in Eisinger, 2003, p. 43). Cantril's outstanding reputation as a preeminent scholar notwithstanding, the government use of surveys had not yet been established as politically acceptable. Polls, and the public opinion that they gauged, were seen as political weapons to be used against members of Congress, interest groups and rival political factions. The *Literary Digest*'s inaccurate 1936 poll that predicted Senator Alf Landon would

defeat FDR served as a reminder that this new polling arsenal was politically volatile, and could backfire with disastrous results. When misused, they would prove politically deadly: the *Digest* poll lost its standing, died an expeditious death, and Gallup stood victorious. When used strategically, surveys would prove immensely important to political leaders in understanding mass opinion, and how the public reacted to political ideas and actions. Cantril's desire for secrecy therefore was understandable when placed in the context that government's use of surveys was entering uncharted territory, about which few people were knowledgeable.

Roll-back under Truman

FDR's use of polls abruptly ceased after his death. His successor, Harry Truman, openly disdained polls, trumpeting in his memoirs how he 'never paid any attention to the polls myself because in my judgment they did not represent a true cross section of American opinion' (Truman, 1956, p. 177, also cited in Eisinger, 2003, p. 45). For Truman, polls inaccurately sampled the public, and worse, made public officials beholden to public opinion at the expense of making unpopular decisions. 'A man who is influenced by the polls or is afraid to make decisions which may make him unpopular is not a man to represent the welfare of the country' (ibid.).

While the US State Department had hired the National Opinion Research Center to conduct public opinion surveys in the early 1940s, Truman's views about polls stalled their growth within and arguably beyond the White House, into other realms of government. Truman's views about polling were shared both by other elected officials and citizens after media polls inaccurately predicted in 1948 that Governor Thomas Dewey would be victorious over President Truman. The infamous 'Dewey defeats Truman' newspaper headline reminded government officials and the public alike that media polls specifically, and all polls more generally, were to be considered circumspect. Polling methodology and poll interpretation were, after all, still in their adolescence. Survey researchers convened to re-examine and discuss the future of polling. Members of the recently formed American Association of Public Opinion Research (founded in 1946–1947) assembled to re-assess how polls could be improved, and more specifically, what went wrong in 1948.

In the late 1950s, Democratic presidential candidate Senator John F. Kennedy hired Lou Harris to conduct polls on his behalf. Harris' polls identified key constituencies that Kennedy needed to woo, most notably citizens who were weary of Kennedy's Catholicism. Kennedy defeated Richard Nixon in 1960 for the presidency, Harris became Kennedy's unofficial White House pollster, and an unofficial tradition was born—the emergence of the victorious campaign pollster becoming the White House (presidential) pollster. This 'tradition' remains became true for virtually every president since JFK. Again, while the literature about other countries is limited, it appears that the party who wins power in parliamentary democracies also retains the pollster who assisted in the electoral victory.

Survey use by governments grows yet again as telephone technology and random digit dialing replace the person-to-person interview. The costs of computing poll data become cheaper than the labor to hire a bevy of nationwide interviewers. Similarly, public opinion, and public opinion polls increasingly become part of what constitutes news (Cantril, 1991, p. 35). US governmental agencies therefore increasingly employed surveys as their techniques had advanced, and because the surveys had now become institutionalized within the political culture.

The pattern to use public opinion polls spread to other countries, although research on the motivations and consequences of its use in these countries is not as extensive a s in the United States. In Germany, for instance, the 1949 new post-world war government under Chancellor Konrad Adenauer commissioned the Institut für Demoskopie Allensbach to supply public opinion data regularly on the performance of the government and on

various political issues. Since 1950, and uninterruptedly since then, the same research institution supplies data for the German federal press agency (Bundespresseamt).

Although in France the nation's president is directly elected by the people (which makes it more likely to use opinion polls for strategic purposes), it took until the 1970s before regular poll usage was established. France's first president after World War II, Charles de Gaulle, opposed opinion polling as well as professional consulting in general. When in 1945 his secretary of information suggested commissioning the French opinion polling institute IFOP for regular opinion polls, de Gaulle refused it. Only after the most important figure in political marketing in France, Michel Bongrand, had successfully counseled for de Gaulle's rival candidate Lecanuet, did the president accept his cooperation. However, it was under the presidency of Valéry Giscard d'Estaing (1974–1981) that polls were used on a more regular basis. Giscard received summaries of representative survey results three times a year. Later, the frequency was increased to monthly reports. It seems that in the French system the use of polls depends heavily on the personality of the president in office. While its use increased with Giscard's successor Francois Mitterand, the current president Jacques Chirac appears to take little notice of polls (Seggelke, 2005, pp. 258ff.).

POLL DATA AS A TOOL FOR POLITICAL RESPONSIVENESS

As government polling became increasingly conducted, so too was it being discredited as exerting a dangerous influence over presidents, legislators, the media and the citizenry. One leader in this battle was Lindsay Rogers, who charged that pollsters 'deliberately [were] misconceiving the nature and our form of government and [were] assuming that we should want to govern ourselves in a national town hall meeting' (Rogers, 1949, p. 65). Not only did Rogers believe that government's use of surveys were inaccurately conceived, he found their use inherently corrupting of the political process. To Rogers, (a) the nature of public opinion could not be measured by a poll, and (b) democratic regimes demanded leadership that resisted the temptation to be overly responsive to public demands.

Rogers' polemical words were shared within the academic community. Herbert Blumer's (1948) *American Sociological Review* article titled 'Public opinion and public opinion polling' was arguably the most intellectually rigorous criticism of polls and polling of the era. Blumer noted the differences in how individuals and groups formed public opinion, simultaneously recognizing that public opinion, however measured, plays a critical role in government: 'Since in every society to some degree, and in our American society to a large degree, there are individuals, committees, boards, legislators, administrators, and executives who have to make the decisions affecting the outcome of the actions of functional groups, such key people become the object of direct and indirect influence or pressure' (p. 544). For Blumer, the problem was not that government polling (or polling more generally) exerted pressure *per se* on public officials, or even that politicians were pressured by citizens' opinion, enlightened or otherwise. Rather, Blumer argued that the modern public opinion poll artificially defined public opinion as the aggregate of individual opinions, thereby misidentifying and inaccurately measuring the group forces that ultimately pressure governmental officials (ibid.). These criticisms received attention in the journalistic, political and academic communities, but government's use of surveys grew in the 1960s and 1970s, in large part because of the decreased costs of polling, and the emergence of the professional pollster.

The use of polls by governments relates to the more general question of responsiveness in a political system. According to Dicey (1914/1963, p. 3), 'the opinion of the governed is the real foundation of all government ... And the assertion that public opinion governs legislation in a particular country, means that laws are there maintained or repealed in accordance with the opinion or wishes of its inhabitants.' Lijphart (1984) advances this argument by contending that 'an ideal democratic government would be one whose actions were always in perfect correspondence with the preferences of all its citizens' (p. 2). In this view, the political system would perform better the more its decisions were in line with current public opinion. No question then, that public opinion polls would be the tool by which governments received valid information about public opinion, just as proposed by George Gallup. However, in representative democracies—which most modern democracies are—power is based on the exercise of popular sovereignty by the people's representatives. The representatives are supposed to act in the people's interest, but not as their proxy representative—i.e., not necessarily always according to their wishes, but with enough authority to deviate from these short-term wishes for the sake of a long-term prosperity of a society. The use of polls by politicians, therefore, is part of a larger debate about representative democracy. In order to locate the people's wishes, those views must be measured. However, when public officials ultimately measure public opinion (by polls, or even by a cruder instrument), it must not be assumed that those same officials are therefore following or responding to the voices of the people.

Roland J. Pennock (1952) has coined the term 'responsiveness' for the degree to which governments or parliaments react to the opinion of the citizens. With the increasing use of poll data by governments and even legislative bodies, the question arose of whether the availability of topical and accurate data on what the people think at a specific point in time might lead the political actors to make political decisions more in line with public opinion in order to gain or preserve power. Miller and Stokes (1963) were the first to test this assumption on an empirical basis by comparing political attitudes in 116 voting districts in the US with the behavior of the representatives in Congress. They found only a moderate relationship between congressmen's roll call votes and their constituency's survey-measured policy preferences.

A methodologically more sophisticated study by Page and Shapiro (1983) compare opinion changes in the population on 357 instances with political decisions on the local, state and federal levels two years before and four years after, for the period between 1935 and 1979. In 43% of the cases political decisions were in line with the changes in public opinion, in 22% they were not, and in 33% there was no change (in most cases because decisions already had been in congruence with public opinion). The authors conclude that opinion clearly moved first and that the congruence was particularly strong when public opinion had changed considerably. For the authors 'democratic responsiveness pervades American politics' (p. 189) and has become stronger over time. Brettschneider (1995) conducted a similar study for political actions of the German parliament and German public opinion. He also found a close relationship between shifts in public opinion and political decisions, but no change over time. Jacobs and Shapiro's (2000) work 'Politicians don't pander' is subtitled 'Political motivation and the loss of democratic responsiveness.' Their work shows that the Clinton administration paid close attention to public opinion, but not in a way that was 'responsive' to citizens' desires about policy preferences. '[P]oliticians ... use research on public opinion to pinpoint the most alluring words, symbols, and arguments in an attempt to move public opinion to support their desired politics' (p. xv).

Studies of this kind have located relationships between public opinion and political decisions, but not the reasons for those relationships. It remains unclear whether the increasing availability of opinion poll data are the reason for this responsiveness and therefore, have led politicians to become more 'populist' and less 'principled.' Most political theorists hold that only weak politicians will sail with the wind of public opinion, and

note that many important decisions were taken against the majority of the people at the time. For instance, decisions of German politicians such as introducing a market system, joining NATO in the 1950s, deploying cruise missiles on German ground in the 1980s (which arguably contributed to the fall of the iron curtain), or the introduction of the European currency, had no opinion majority at their time. It is clearly the political norm that, as Stonecash (2003, p. 3) writes, '[P]oliticians rarely use polling to decide what to support. They use polling to tell them what to stress of the views they already have.' However, poll data create a challenge to this maxim and might, in the long run, make politics more populist.

APPLICATIONS OF POLL DATA IN POLITICAL PRACTICE

Studies mentioned above have measured the relationship between public opinion and political decisions in the aggregate. But how exactly are political polls used by politicians and what are their effects? Several studies have attempted to answer these questions. Brandice Canes-Wrone's (2006) extensive analyses of US presidents and their monitoring of public opinion suggest that their use of polls assists both the public and the presidents:

> [P]residents' involvement with the mass public does shift policy toward majority opinion ... under most conditions a president will not endorse a popular policy he believe is contrary to the interest of society .... Thus presidents' arousing and monitoring of public opinion increase the influence of the populace but not in a way that entails pervasive demagoguery (p. 5).

She notes that presidents occasionally and rarely pander to the public's desires. But overall, attention to mass opinion, often with a sophisticated public opinion apparatus, is done mostly to promote what presidents believe are actions that improve society, and not performed merely to cater to citizens' whims and desires, regardless of their efficacy and value (ibid.).

More recent analyses by Jacobs and Shapiro (2000) confirm this notion of political polling as a means to craft ideas, not to generate or fabricate policies based on the mass opinion poll responses: 'Presidents and legislators carefully track public opinion in order to identify the words, arguments, and symbols that are most likely to be effective in attracting favorable press coverage and ultimately "winning" public support for their desired policies' (p. 7). Jacobs and Shapiro's analysis of the debates surrounding the health care reform debate in 1993 reveals that 'the White House and party leaders in Congress tracked public opinion in order to carefully craft their preferred policy opinion in order to win (rather than follow) public opinion' (p. xviii).

This concept of crafting messages and using surveys to market policies is a recurring theme in the 'government use of polls' literature. Christopher Page's (2006) extensive and unparalleled study on the role of public opinion research by the Canadian government echoes these sentiments. Page delineates that 'while opinion research sometimes promotes responsiveness, it actually has greater influence on other aspects of policy-making such as agenda-setting, and its foremost use is to help governments communicate with citizens to promote support, understanding, compliance and legitimacy' (p. 4).

This practice of using surveys to market ideas, to communicate with the public and to advance policy agendas counters the more cynically expressed perspective that politicians are driven by or beholden to polls. The pollster as a policy marketing and communications adviser makes sense when recognizing how campaigning and governing inevitably and invariably intersect. This blurry line between campaigning and governing exists precisely because public policy advancement demands that a politician successfully market his or her agenda to the public.

In the US, government polling is frequently studied through the eyes of the presidency, not because Congress or other branches of government eschew polling, but rather because the institutionalization of polling has resulted in a permanent campaign that is most pronounced at the presidential level. According to Diane Heith (2004), polls initially provide presidents with guidance about how to strategize about marketing policies. Eventually, she argues, public opinion campaign strategists become White House leaders (p. 11). Heith writes that, the executive branch of the US government employs polls in order to monitor public opinion, and interprets public opinion in ways that resemble a political campaign. 'These former campaign workers continued to rely heavily on polling, and assisted the top echelon of decision makers' reliance on polling. Moreover, the polling apparatus figured prominently in the design of persuasive campaigns selling the president's agenda … the White House used the poll apparatus to design behavior and track responses from a poll-identified constituency: an artificially created campaign-style adversary' (ibid.).

ARE POLLS AN AID OR THREAT TO DEMOCRACY?

As government's use of polling has developed, so too have the criticisms of such government polling. Pierre Bourdieu has suggested that polls serve the interests of political elites, and function to 'impose the illusion that a public opinion exists' (Bourdieu, 1979, p. 125). Benjamin Ginsberg similarly avows that government polling domesticates a potentially rebellious public, as polling allows the state to amass power at the expense of a placated public (Ginsberg, 1986). In a 1992 *Harper's* article titled 'Voting in the passive voice,' Christopher Hitchens re-introduces, endorses and modernizes the criticisms made by Rogers 40 years prior. Hitchens (1992, p. 46) writes, 'Opinion polling was born out of a struggle not to discover the public mind but to master it.'

For Klein (2006), the abundance of polling and monitoring of opinion has replaced political candor and genuine, emotional political discourse that ties government officials and the citizenry. Too many US politicians would be unable to think and act extemporaneously without the guidance of political consultants and pollsters, whose constant assistance in monitoring and gauging their bosses' rhetoric has blanched American politics of flavor. Polling is not the sole cause of the problem, he argues, but an overused instrument that serves as a crutch and substitute for contemporaneous thinking (ibid.).

Alternatively, Frank Newport (2004) suggests that government's use of polls should be increased, and that the dire perspective that polling debilitates democracy is misguided: 'Our elected officials need to move to the point where they give as much or more credence to the accurately measured views of the people as they do to their own attitudes, the view of experts, or the views of special interests ... [p]oliticians might rather defensively admit that they *are* willing to use polling to help figure out the best way to *communicate* their positions to constituents, but not to determine the basic positions in the first place' (p. 283, italics in original). For Newport, problems emerge when leaders opt to avoid measuring public opinion accurately. 'There is no reason why the views of the people, as measured through polls, shouldn't be used directly as a primary basis for establishing or modifying laws or policies' (ibid.).

Is government's use of polls aiding or abetting democratic government? Debates about the role of government's use of surveys will endure, if for no other reason than governments can and will continue to use surveys. Why? Because they remain the most accurate instrument to monitor, gauge, predict, and assess the voice of the people. But even proponents of polls and polling suggest that prudence and discretion are needed. Lawrence Jacobs and Melinda Jackson ask, 'Are the [polling] strategies of political elites endangering the health of a vibrant representative government?' (Jacobs & Jackson in Genovese & Streb, 2004, p. 161)? The authors worry that polls have created a constant public relations campaign that detracts politicians from exercising leadership. Diane Heith (cited in Genovese & Streb, 2004, p. 161) concurs,

stating that 'Polling stands at the heart of the modern candidate-centered presidential campaign' and that the problem of constant campaign and election polling by politicians is a public relations blur that smells of demagoguery.

John Geer (1996, p. xiii) argues that the advent of polls 'has greatly increased the quality of information politicians have about public opinion.' For Geer, polls have effectively killed the era of poor information. Politicians have at their disposal the tools to gauge public opinion, and therefore are better informed now than ever before. This increase in information means that 'well-informed politicians are less likely to take polarized positions on the critical issues that confront the polity' (p. 14).

Polarization has ebbed and flowed, but if history repeats itself, polls will most likely continue to evolve—quantitatively and qualitatively, as will politicians' ability to interpret them. The question is not how the government's use of surveys has grown over the last 70 years, but rather in what form and shape governmental survey usage will evolve in the decades to follow.

REFERENCES

Blumer, H. (1948). Public opinion and public opinion polling. *American Sociological Review, 13,* 542–549.

Bourdieu, P. (1979). Public opinion does not exist. In A. Mattelart & S. Siegelaub (Eds.), *Communication and class struggle: Vol. 1. Capitalism, imperialism* (pp. 124–130). New York: International General.

Brettschneider, F. (1995). Öffentliche Meinung und Politik. Eine empirische Studie zur Responsivität des Deutschen Bundestages [Public opinion and politics. An empirical study on the responsiveness of the German Bundestag]. Opladen: Westdeutscher Verlag.

Canes-Wrone, B. (2006). *Who leads whom? Presidents, policy and the public.* Chicago: University of Chicago Press.

Cantril, H. (1947). *Gauging public opinion.* Princeton, NJ: Princeton University Press.

Cantril, A. H. (1991). *The opinion connection: Polling, politics and the press.* Washington, DC: CQ Press.

Dicey, A. V. (1963). *Lectures on the relationship between law and public and opinion in England during 19th century.* London: Macmillan (Reprinted from 2nd ed., 1914).

Eisinger, R. M. (2003). *The evolution of presidential polling.* New York: Cambridge University Press.

Gallup, G., & Rae, S. F. (1940). *The pulse of democracy: The public-opinion poll and how it works.* New York: Simon and Schuster.

Geer, J. G. (1996). *From tea leaves to opinion polls: A theory of democratic leadership.* New York: Columbia University Press.

Genovese, M. A., & Streb, M. J. (2004). Polling in a robust democracy. In M. A. Genovese & M. J. Streb (Eds.), *Polls and politics: The dilemmas of democracy* (pp. 157–164). Albany: State University of Albany Press.

Genovese, M. A., & Streb, M. J. (Eds.) (2004). *Polls and politics: The dilemmas of democracy.* Albany: State University of Albany Press.

Ginsberg, B. (1986). *The captive public: How mass opinion promotes state power.* New York: Basic Books.

Green, J. (2002, April). The other war room. *Washington Monthly.* Retrieved January 5, 2007, from http://www.washingtonmonthly.com/features/2001/0204.green.html.

Heith, D. J. (2004). *Polling to govern: Public opinion and presidential leadership.* Stanford: Stanford University Press.

Hitchens, C. (1992, April). Voting in the passive voice: What polling has done to American democracy. *Harper's,* 45–52.

Jacobs, L. R., & Shapiro, R. Y. (2000). *Politicians don't pander: Political manipulation and the loss of democratic responsiveness.* Chicago: University of Chicago Press.

Klein, J. (2006). *Politics lost: How American democracy was trivialized by people who think you're stupid.* New York: Random House.

Lijphart, A. (1984). *Democracies. Patterns of majoritarian and consensus government in twenty-one countries.* New Haven, London.

Miller, W., & Stokes, D. E. (1963). Constituency influence in Congress. *American Political Science Review, 57,* 45–56.

Newport, F. (2004). *Polling matters: Why leaders must listen to the wisdom of the people.* New York: Warner Books.

Page, C. (2006). *The roles of public opinion research in Canadian government.* Toronto: University of Toronto Press.

Page, B. I., & Shapiro, R. Y. (1983). Effects of public opinion on policy. *American Political Science Review, 77,* 175–190.

Pennock, J. R. (1952). Responsiveness, responsibility, and majority rule. *American Political Science Review, 46,* 790–807.

Rogers, L. (1949). *The pollsters: Public opinion, politics and democratic leadership.* New York: Knopf.

Seggelke, S. (2005). *Die Kommunikationsstrategien der französischen Staatspräsidenten. Eine vergleichende Studie zur politischen Öffentlichkeitsarbeit in der V. Republik* [Translation]. Doctoral dissertation, University of Paris, France; University of Dresden, Germany.

Stonecash, J. M. (2003). *Political polling: Strategic information in campaigns.* Lanham, MD: Rowman and Littlefield Publishers.

Truman, H. (1956). *Memoirs by Harry S. Truman: Vol. 2, Years of trial and hope* (pp.177–196). New York, Macmillan.

Tucker, R. (1935, January 12). Chart and graph man. *Collier's,* 28–29.

46

The Use of Public Opinion Research in Propaganda

Michael Kunczik and
Eva Johanna Schweitzer

INTRODUCTION

Since the 1920s, propaganda has become a major concern in communication research. Especially the propaganda activities during World War I, the ideological battle in World War II, and the diffusion of the mass media as channels for persuasive messages led communication scientists to concentrate on the content and possible effects of propaganda in a variety of historical and geopolitical contexts. However, the underlying prerequisites of effective propaganda, that is, the application of social science methods to evaluate and prepare propaganda activities, have seldom been questioned. The present chapter therefore attempts to deal with this topic by focusing on case studies, as a complete overview of the use of public opinion research in propaganda is too extensive a task.

Propaganda and propaganda research

Propaganda can be defined as 'the systematic attempt to shape perceptions, manipulate cognitions, and direct behavior to achieve a response that furthers the desired intent of the propagandist' (Jowett & O'Donnell, 1999, p. 6). At that, propaganda activities can be differentiated into the three types of white, gray, and black propaganda, indicating successively lessened degrees of source transparency and identification in persuasive communication. Originally, the term derived from the Latin word *propagare*, which means 'to propagate' or 'to sow.' In communication contexts, it had first been applied by Pope Gregor XV, who founded the *Sacra Congregatio de Propaganda Fide* in 1622. This organization was built to promote the Christian faith in the New World and to oppose the rise of Protestantism. In the fields of politics, military affairs, or the economy, the term propaganda became widely known after the French Revolution and especially after World War I (cf. Bussemer, 2005, pp. 25ff.).

Propaganda often shares a negative or rather pejorative connotation encompassing associations of lies, deception, or manipulation. This is due mainly to its inherent components of intentional and biased communication serving exclusively the fulfillment of personal or organizational interests (cf. Doob, 1989, pp. 374ff.). Since the 1950s, these connotations led to several proposals to eschew the word (cf. Doob, 1989, p. 307) or to replace it by other more technical or euphemistic phrases such as international communications or public diplomacy (cf. Perloff, 1998, p. 198). In addition, attempts were made to separate the concept of propaganda theoretically from advertising or public relations, so as to promote these new professions in persuasion. Edward L. Bernays (1923, p. 212), one of the founding fathers of modern public relations, however, already used propaganda and public relations as synonyms to express calculated persuasive acts of communication.

While propaganda activities can be traced back long into history, systematic research on its content and effects started only in 1927 in Harold D. Lasswell's renowned study *Propaganda Technique in the World War*. He was the first to initiate a scientific analysis of propagandistic means, and also published the first comprehensive bibliography on that topic (cf. Lasswell, Casey, & Smith, 1935). In 1937—the year *Public Opinion Quarterly* appeared for the first time—propaganda research became finally established by the *Institute for Propaganda Analysis* (cf. Doob, 1949, p. 285). This organization examined contemporary propaganda campaigns and published analyses in monthly bulletins and manuals (Doob, 1949, p. 285; Irion, 1952, p. 734). The rise of the mass media as channels of persuasive messages especially in World War II, the subsequent concentration on possible media effects on individuals and society, and the sophistication of empirical measures in the study of attitudes and attitude

change fostered the scientific interest in the analysis of propaganda activities (cf. Mander, 1998, p. x). In fact, propaganda became the major focus of communication research in the following decades (cf. Bussemer, 2005, p. 12) in studies that applied content analyses or experimental designs to understand the attributes, goals, and instruments of the propagandist, the actual content of propagandistic messages, the perception of propaganda, and the initial responses and possible changes of recipients after exposure to propaganda (cf. Doob, 1949, p. 258).

The professionalization of propaganda

Before social science methods entered the field of attitude research in the late 1930s (cf. Nielsen, 1946, p. 3), propaganda was seen by practitioners as 'an art requiring special talent' (Bogart, 1976, p. 195). Instead of systematic baseline surveys and continuous effectiveness studies, which were made possible through accompanying opinion polls, propagandists employed 'little more than skillful guesses' (Fitzgerald, 1957, p. 141) to plan and implement their campaigns (cf. also Carlson, 1957, p. 343). In that way, Leo Bogart (1976, pp. 195ff.) for example postulated: 'It is not mechanical, scientific work. Influencing attitudes requires experience, area knowledge, and instinctive judgment of what is the best argument for the audience. No manual can guide the propagandist. He must have a good mind, genius, sensitivity and knowledge of how the audience thinks and reacts.' This argument was also made by Edward L. Bernays in his work *Propaganda* (1928, p. 49): 'Propaganda ... can never be an exact science for the reason that its subject-matter ... deals with human beings.' Even in modern times, this intuitive understanding of propaganda can sometimes be found, since it suits the self-consciousness and self-promotion of respective practitioners: Manheim (1994, p. 141), for example, analyzed the management of Kuwait's image during the Gulf conflict and found that Hill & Knowlton, the PR firm serving Kuwait's war interests, conducted 'daily tracking polls on Kuwait's image and related variables.' Yet Manheim (1994, pp. 143ff.) argues: 'There is no direct evidence from our interviews that the staff of Hill and Knowlton were operating from an explicit awareness of social scientific knowledge in this area when serving the Kuwait account. To the contrary, they describe their actions as grounded in their many years of experience.'

The reason why propagandists and public relations counsellors at first refrained from employing social science methods in their daily practice lies in the ambivalent and competitive relationship between propaganda professionals and public opinion pollsters. As Fitzgerald (1957, pp. 142ff.) notes, public relation counsellors were, from the very beginning, fighting to establish their profession and to gain recognition in the field of attitude research and persuasion. In that way, opinion pollsters were seen as direct competitors who tried to win clients and to mould the public climate by enigmatic statistics. In fact, the apprehension about quantification might also be a reason for the skepticism prevailing among propagandists with regard to applying social science methods in their daily work (cf. also Noelle-Neumann & Petersen, 2005, pp. 43ff.). According to Rensis Likert (1948), the failure of Gallup to predict the outcome of the 1948 election even reinforced these skeptics of public opinion polling (Gallup forecasted 44.5% for President Truman, who actually received a 50% vote and won the election). Besides this insecurity and inexperience in the use of social statistics, propagandists also complained initially about the additional costs associated with the application of public opinion polls in the preparation of campaigns (cf. Fitzgerald, 1957, p. 143). These were seen as unnecessary as long as the quality and trustworthiness of survey research was questionable.

The functions of public opinion research in propaganda

In practice, propaganda is often associated with the management of public opinion

(cf. Jowett & O'Donnell, 1999, p. 44). Accordingly, the use of public opinion research in propaganda, and also in public relations, might be described in general as a supportive measure to secure the efficiency and goal attainment of public management processes. In that way, survey research fulfills three main functions: On the one hand, public opinion polls enable propagandists to *prepare and plan* their campaigns and persuasive activities in a systematic and precise fashion (cf. Campbell, 1946, p. 16; Carlson, 1957, pp. 343ff.). In detail, opinion polls help to determine attitudes, goals, and needs of relevant publics. This provides the basis for the conceptualization and targeting of effective propagandistic messages in order to suit the purposes of opinion change and image building. Especially in wartime, those measures support the construction and framing of conflict issues, stereotypes, and enemy attributes, and thus contribute to the mobilization of the population.

Besides these functions of propaganda planning and evaluation, the publication of (manipulated) survey research might also serve as a 'legitimating source' (cf. O'Donnell & Jowett, 1989) to *justify and rationalize* political decisions (cf. Herbst, 1992; Jacobs & Shapiro, 1995, p. 188ff.). In political communication, survey research therefore supports the *stabilization of existing power hierarchies* (cf. Fuchs & Pfetsch, 1996, p. 116) when national elites refer to survey results to legitimize their actions and to preserve national upheavals or crises by anticipating means of propaganda. In this context, Jacobs and Shapiro (1995, pp. 188ff.) describe the responsiveness of politicians to survey research as a symbolic or instrumental function of public opinion polling.

CASE STUDIES IN THE PROPAGANDISTIC USE OF PUBLIC OPINION RESEARCH

Case studies from Europe and the United States illustrate the rise of public opinion research in the field of propaganda. This progress was partly the result of activities related to World War II and its coincidence with the diffusion of survey research and systematic studies of public opinion. Moreover, there were also opportunities for the application of persuasion techniques that were very similar to propaganda in the maturing of post-war governments.

Historical developments in Europe

Attempts to identify public opinion in order to plan campaigns have a long history. According to Madame de Stael (cf. Kircheisen, 1912), Napoleon believed that government needed the support of public opinion, and he instigated whispering campaigns. He spread rumors about his political plans to gauge public opinion. Exaggerated reports were circulated so that when his political plans were realized, they appeared more tolerable. In Prussia too, there was a great interest in (published) public opinion. Already in 1816, a 'Literarisches Büro' ('Literary Bureau') systematically collected information about what was said in the news so as to influence the press. Even earlier in 1806, Karl August von Hardenberg had published the famous *Rigaer Denkschrift* (memorandum) in which he emphasized the importance of studying and influencing public opinion. Prussia in those days was reforming its political system in the so-called 'Revolution von oben' ('top-down revolution') (cf. Kunczik, 1997, pp. 71ff.).

In Germany during World War II, the Nazi propagandist Joseph Goebbels kept an eye on public opinion. In an interview, Bernays pointed out (cf. Cutlip, 1994, p. 186): 'Goebbels kept a copy of "Crystallizing public opinion" in his desk and there wasn't a damned thing I could do about it.' In his memoirs (Bernays, 1965, p. 652), he also reports that in the summer 1933 he learned that Goebbels used his book 'as a basis for his destructive campaign against the Jews of Germany. This shocked me, but I knew any human activity can be used for social purposes or misused for antisocial ones. Obviously the attack on Jews in Germany was no emotional outburst of the Nazis, but a deliberate, planned campaign.' Doob (1950, p. 422) states that Goebbels planned and executed propaganda by constantly referring to existing intelligence. Information about public opinion in Germany was mainly obtained from the reports of the *Sicherheitsdienst* (security service). But, as Doob underlines, 'little or none of the intelligence was ever gathered or analyzed systematically.' According to Doob, Goebbels stated that the *Sicherheitsdienst* had conducted 'a statistical investigation ... in the manner of the Gallup Institute'; yet Doob also quotes Goebbels criticizing polls, because he trusted common sense more than polling (cf. Unger, 1965; Boberach, 1984).

In the 1930s, Elisabeth Noelle-Neumann came into contact with this new technique of social science in the United States. In 1940, she completed her dissertation on polling ('Amerikanische Massenumfragen über Politik und Presse,' Frankfurt 1940). According to Schmidtchen (1965, p. 23), the then German chancellor Konrad Adenauer (governing from 1949–1963) signed a contract with her *Institut für Demoskopie Allensbach* in 1950 that employed the organization to analyze German public opinion continually and to give advice to the government on the basis of the respective poll findings. The *U.S. High Commission* (especially its Reaction Analysis Branch) supported the development of German survey research (cf. Schmidtchen, 1965, pp. 31ff.).

After the defeat in World War II, Germans were eager to adopt American social science research techniques. Among the first topics the institute dealt with were surveys concerning the question of who should become Secretary of Foreign Affairs (December 1950), and the reintroduction of a German army. In 1951, the institute polled attitudes towards the chancellor and the so-called 'Saarfrage,' a French protectorate that was reintegrated into Germany in 1957–1959 as the Saarland. Later surveys were conducted concerning European Defense, German reunification, and how to create security against the Russians (cf. Mixa, 2004, p. 25).

Noelle-Neumann (1976) characterized Adenauer as the first German chancellor to accept survey researchers as advisors. Surveys by the Allensbach Institute at the beginning of the 1950s found that Germans had a negative attitude towards entrepreneurs (69% of the employees believed entrepreneurs to be anti-social), and they did not know the meaning of the social market economy. Furthermore, Allensbach found that people seemed to refuse democracy. The institute concluded that the government and entrepreneurs needed a public relations campaign. As a consequence, 'DIE WAAGE/Gemeinschaft zur Förderung des sozialen Ausgleichs' ('The Balance/Society for the Improvement of Social Justice') was founded by German industrials in September 1952. About 100 firms contributed money. While its membership and financing remain unclear, we know that the then German Secretary of Economy, Ludwig Erhard, initiated advertisements for the Soziale Marktwirtschaft between 1955 and 1959. In this context, the first polls concerning the effects of introducing the new German currency (Deutsche Mark)—which was a symbol that the German economic miracle was successful (cf. Schmidtchen, 1965, pp. 237ff.)—were carried out in 1948. According to statute, DIE WAAGE had the task to influence public opinion in favor of entrepreneurship and to support the idea of Soziale Marktwirtschaft whose emphasis was on social responsibility among both employers and the working class.

Greiß (1972, p. 109) acknowledges that statistical analyses cannot prove whether DIE WAAGE finally achieved its aim. Whenever assessing a present state of affairs with regard to some variable (e.g. attitudes towards the market economy) for a large group of subjects, sample surveys are the only adequate method to get an answer. Yet, there are only correlations, for example, between reading advertisements of DIE WAAGE and a positive attitude towards market economy; however they cannot indicate the temporal order necessary for a causal relationship. It may be that people already having a positive attitude about the economy read the advertisements. But it is a fact that in 1950, 56% of the German population did not know what Soziale Marktwirtschaft meant. In 1961, 64% of the population said they were in favor of Soziale Marktwirtschaft. This seems to be a strong indicator for the effectiveness of this long-term campaign.

Developments in the United States

Jacobs and Shapiro (1995, p. 164) emphasize that the White House's interest in tracking public sentiment began in the 1800s, when informal techniques including analysis of newspapers, straw polls, and canvassing to gauge the country's mood were used. Franklin D. Roosevelt was the first president to take an interest in scientific survey research, as he had private polls conducted by his own staff. Those private polls are characterized by Eisinger and Brown (1998, pp. 238ff.) as a 'historic turning point in American politics' because they allowed Roosevelt 'to gauge public opinion without the consent of parties, the media, or Congress.' They argue, 'that some poll reports were intended solely to assess how the president's communication skills could best be improved ...' (p. 248).

In 1939, when war in Europe seemed almost inevitable, Roosevelt, because of isolationist resistance, 'found it a delicate task to change the attitudes of people without unduly alarming them' (Freidel, 1990, pp. 305ff.). Freidel (1990, p. 422) points out: 'Throughout the war Roosevelt closely watched public opinion polls.' Casey (2001) explores how Roosevelt perceived domestic public opinion during the war, especially the extent to which he felt the American people fully shared his conception of Nazism. Casey (2001, p. 33) emphasizes that Roosevelt used the results of polls in his famous *Fireside Chats*: 'Before each speech, Roosevelt and his aides would collect a wealth of information, from polls to press clippings and letters, on the various subjects to be tackled.' But the president did not blindly accept the poll findings: After Pearl Harbor, public opinion in the United States wanted to concentrate war efforts against Japan. The president considered a major offensive in the Pacific unwise because he feared that Germany could defeat the Soviet Union and be stronger than Japan would ever be (Casey, 2001, pp. 84ff.). Therefore, the president campaigned for his 'Germany-first' strategy.

The use of polling by an American president reached new heights during Ronald Reagan's terms. Hedrick Smith (1988, p. 404) emphasizes the influence of the pollster Richard Wirthlin on the Reagan presidency: 'Although Wirthlin never joined the White House staff, as Reagan's $1-million-a-year pollster-strategist (paid by the Republican party) he sat in weekly strategy meetings, his findings often guided the others.' According to Smith (1988, p. 417): 'In Reagan's presidency ... Wirthlin's firm, Decision Making Information, Inc., would "pretest" attitudes before Reagan went barnstorming on issues.' Murray and Howard (2002, p. 541) report that the 'Daily Diary of the President' verifies regular meetings between Ronald Reagan and Richard Wirthlin: an average of one meeting a month. Major public opinion efforts are associated with the breakdown of the 1986 Reykjavik summit, reactions to the Soviet shoot-down of the Korean Airliner 007, the invasion of Grenada, the bombing of Libya in 1986, and the Iran-contra scandal.

The Reagan administration also applied survey research to promote controversial topics in the public. Murray and Howard (2002, p. 540) quote David Gergen, Reagan's Director of Communications, emphasizing that 'Wirthlin's polls were enormously valuable in knowing how to frame issues ... and even more valuable in knowing how to word arguments.' Lou Cannon (1991, p. 342) reports how during the 1980 election campaign Reagan also made use of the discussion about U.S. proprietary rights to the Panama Canal. 'Wirthlin's polls told him that this issue was the then-pending "giveaway" of the canal to Panama.' Reagan won the primary in North Carolina by focusing on this aspect.' But according to Cannon, Reagan's interest in this problem declined after the topic had served its political purpose.

PUBLIC OPINION RESEARCH, PROPAGANDA, AND ETHICS

Paul F. Lazarsfeld, one of the founding fathers of public opinion research, was—like so many of his contemporaries—convinced that the application of social science could help policy and improve the quality of life. The techniques of public opinion research should be used to proliferate the ideals of democracy and freedom. But—as Hanno Hardt (1990, p. 255) emphasizes—'under Lazarsfeld's leadership mass communication research in the United States had become a formidable enterprise which was deeply committed to the commercial interests of the culture industry and the political concern of government.' According to Hardt (1990, p. 253), Lazarsfeld 'was unable to forge his critical research perspective into a major, theoretical statement.' In fact, this use of survey research for private or organizational interests—apart from academic science—has always been a matter of criticism (cf. Lasswell, 1957, pp. 35ff.). Already in 1941, Allard (p. 213) had warned that 'such surveys *in unscrupulous hands* might become effective propaganda weapons' (our emphasis).

The problem lies especially in the misuse of social science methods for purposes of indoctrination and brutal force that builds the groundwork for totalitarian regimes. On that, Murray and Howard (2002, p. 546) emphasize—referring to Reagan—that there is a clear difference between periodically monitoring public reactions on the one hand, and actively using poll data to make strategic decisions on a day-to-day or week-to-week basis on the other. The latter suggests the danger that public opinion research, which started as an attempt to guide public policy in the interest of the people, indeed can be used as an instrument to manipulate public opinion and to cloud the factual circumstances of political decisions. In this way, public opinion research can lose its status of objectivity and neutrality (cf. Altschuler, 1986, p. 298) for the sake of—at best—spin doctoring. As a consequence, opinion pollsters—and the social sciences in general—are in danger of becoming discredited among the public due to their potential to use their knowledge and expertise for dubious interests and goals.

REFERENCES

Allard, W. (1941). A test of propaganda values in public opinion surveys. *Social Forces, 20,* 206–213.

Altschuler, B. E. (1986). Lyndon Johnson and the public polls. *Public Opinion Quarterly, 50,* 285–299.

Bernays, E. L. (1923). *Crystallizing public opinion.* New York: Liveright Publishing Corporation.

Bernays, E. L. (1928). *Propaganda.* New York: Liveright Publishing Corporation.

Bernays, E. L. (1965). *Biography of an idea: Memoirs of public relations counsel Edward L. Bernays.* New York: Simon & Schuster.

Boberach, H. (Ed.) (1984). *Meldungen aus dem Reich: Die geheimen Lageberichte des Sicherheitsdienstes der SS, 1938–1945, Bd. 1* [Reports of the Reich: The secret situation reports of the SS security service, 1938–1945, Vol. 1]. Herrsching: Manfred Pawlak Verlag.

Bogart, L. (1976). *Premises for propaganda: The United States Information Agency's operating assumptions in the Cold War.* New York: Free Press.

Bussemer, T. (2005). *Propaganda: Konzepte und Theorien* [Propaganda: Concepts and theories]. Wiesbaden: VS Verlag für Sozialwissenschaften.

Campbell, A. (1946). The uses of interview surveys in federal administration. *Journal of Social Issues, 2*(2), 14–22.

Cannon, L. (1991). *Ronald Reagan: The role of a lifetime.* New York: Simon & Schuster.

Carlson, R. O. (1957). The use of public relations research by large corporations. *Public Opinion Quarterly, 21,* 341–349.

Casey, S. (2001). *Cautious crusade: Franklin D. Roosevelt, American public opinion, and the war against Nazi Germany.* Oxford: Oxford University Press.

Cutlip, S. M. (1994). *The unseen power: Public relations: A history.* Hillsdale, NJ: Lawrence Erlbaum.

Doob, L. W. (1949). *Public opinion and propaganda.* New York: Henry Holt.

Doob, L. W. (1950). Goebbel's principles of propaganda. *Public Opinion Quarterly, 14,* 419–442.

Doob, L. W. (1989). Propaganda. In E. Barnouw, G. Gerbner, W. Schramm, T. Worth, & L. Gross (Eds.), *International encyclopedia of communications* (Vol. 3, pp. 374–378). New York: Oxford University Press.

Eisinger, R. M., & Brown, J. (1998). Polling as a means toward presidential autonomy: Emil Hurja, Hadley Cantril and the Roosevelt administration. *International Journal of Public Opinion Research, 10,* 237–256.

Fitzgerald, S. E. (1957). Public relations learns to use research. *Public Opinion Quarterly, 21,* 141–146.

Freidel, F. (1990). *Franklin D. Roosevelt: A rendezvous with destiny.* Boston: Little Brown.

Fuchs, D., & Pfetsch, B. (1996). Die Beobachtung der öffentlichen Meinung durch das Regierungssystem [The observation of public opinion by the government system]. In W. van den Daele & F. Neidhardt (Eds.), *Kommunikation und Entscheidung: Politische Funktionen öffentlicher Meinungsbildung und diskursiver Verfahren* (pp. 103–135). Berlin: Ed. Sigma.

Greiß, F. (1972). *Erhards soziale Marktwirtschaft und DIE WAAGE* [Erhard's social market economy and DIE WAAGE]. In G. Schröder (Ed.), *Ludwig Erhard: Beiträge zu seiner politischen Biographie.* Frankfurt am Main: Propyläen.

Hardt, H. (1990). Paul F. Lazarsfeld: Communication research as critical research? In W. R. Langenbucher (Ed.), *Paul F. Lazarsfeld. Die Wiener Tradition der empirischen Sozial- und Kommunikationsforschung* (pp. 243–257). München: Ölschläger.

Herbst, S. (1992). *Numbered voices: How public opinion polling has shaped American politics.* Chicago: University of Chicago Press.

Irion, F. C. (1952). *Public opinion and propaganda.* New York: Thomas Y. Crowell.

Jacobs, L. R., & Shapiro, R. Y. (1995). The rise of presidential polling: The Nixon White House in historical perspective. *Public Opinion Quarterly, 59,* 163–195.

Jowett, G. S., & O'Donnell, V. (1999). *Propaganda and persuasion* (3rd ed.). Thousand Oaks, CA: Sage.

Kircheisen, G. (Ed.) (1912). *Memoiren der Frau von Stael* [Memoirs of Madame de Stael]. Berlin: Morawe & Scheffelt.

Kunczik, M. (1997). *Geschichte der Öffentlichkeitsarbeit in Deutschland* [The history of public relations in Germany]. Köln: Böhlau.

Lasswell, H. D. (1927). *Propaganda technique in the World War.* New York: Knopf.

Lasswell, H. D. (1957). The impact of public opinion research on our society. *Public Opinion Quarterly, 21,* 33–38.

Lasswell, H. D., Casey, R. D., & Smith, B. L. (Eds.) (1935). *Propaganda and promotional activities: An annotated bibliography.* Minneapolis, MN: University of Minnesota Press.

Likert, R. (1948). Public opinion polls. *Scientific American, 179*(6), 7–11.

Mander, M. S. (1998). Preface. In J. Wilke (Ed.), *Propaganda in the 20th century: Contributions to its history* (pp. ix–xii). Cresskill, NJ: Hampton Press.

Manheim, J. B. (1994). Strategic public diplomacy: Managing Kuwait's image during the Gulf conflict. In W. L. Bennett & D. L. Paletz (Eds.), *Taken by storm: The media, public opinion, and U.S. foreign policy in the Gulf War* (pp. 131–148). Chicago: Chicago University Press.

Mixa, S. (2004). *Otto Lenz als PR-Berater von Konrad Adenauer von 1951 bis 1953* [Otto Lenz as pr consultant of Konrad Adenauer from 1951 to 1953]. Unpublished master thesis. University of Mainz, Germany.

Murray, S. K., & Howard, P. (2002). Variation in White House polling operations. Carter to Clinton. *Public Opinion Quarterly, 66*, 527–559.

Nielsen, W. A. (1946). Attitude research and government. *Journal of Social Issues, 2*(2), 2–13.

Noelle-Neumann, E. (1940). *Amerikanische Massenumfragen über Politik und Presse* [American mass surveys about politics and the print media]. Frankfurt am Main: Diesterweg.

Noelle-Neumann, E. (1976). *Konrad Adenauer: Die öffentliche Meinung und Wahlen* [Konrad Adenauer: Public opinion and elections]. In H. Kohl (Ed.), Konrad Adenauer 1876/1976 (pp. 129–139). Stuttgart: Belser.

Noelle-Neumann, E., & Petersen, T. (2005). *Alle, nicht jeder: Einführung in die Methoden der Demoskopie* [All, not everybody: An introduction to the methods of public opinion research] (4th ed.). Berlin: Springer.

O'Donnell, V., & Jowett, G. S. (1989). Propaganda as a form of communication. In T. J. Smith III (Ed.), *Propaganda: A pluralistic perspective* (pp. 49–63). New York: Praeger.

Perloff, R. M. (1998). *Political communication: Politics, press, and public in America.* Mahwah, NJ: Lawrence Erlbaum.

Schmidtchen, G. (1965). *Die befragte Nation. Über den Einfluß der Meinungsforschung auf die Politik* [The interrogated nation: About the influence of public opinion research on politics] (rev. ed.). Frankfurt am Main: Fischer-Bücherei.

Smith, H. (1988). *The power game: How Washington works.* New York: Random House.

Unger, A. L. (1965). The public opinion reports of the Nazi party. *Public Opinion Quarterly, 29*, 565–582.

47

The Effects of Published Polls on Citizens

Sibylle Hardmeier

Modern political opinion polls are accompanied by two constants: the debate about their quality on the one hand (→ *The Methodological Strengths and Weaknesses of Survey Research*), and the debate about their alleged effects in the run-up to elections and voting behavior on the other. The latter includes numerous political efforts (some of which have been implemented) to prohibit publications of opinion polls prior to voting (Foundation for Information, 2003; → *The Legal Status of Public Opinion Research in the World*). Furthermore, this alleged effect goes hand in hand with the strong assumptions of journalists concerning the impact of publishing poll results (Donsbach & Antoine, 1990; Hardmeier, 2000; → *Attitudes of Journalists Toward Public Opinion Research*) and soon gave rise to analyses about the press-polling connection (Crespi, 1980; Ladd, 1980) or the news media's use of polls (→ *The News Media's Use of Opinion Polls*). The effects of published polls on voters are the focus of the present chapter.

The remainder of this chapter is organized along three answers to the question of why there have been so many assumptions about a strong impact of published polls. The first answer implies a differentiation between the dependent variables (effect on what?) and summarizes the corresponding meta-analytical findings. The second answer summarizes the current media impact research that provides important theoretical tools for evaluating possible effects: the role of predispositions as well as issue and campaign characteristics that may intervene in processes of influence. The meta-analytical finding that the literature on polling impact merges very heterogeneous effects gives rise to the third answer: The discussion about effects of opinion polls needs to differentiate to a much greater extent between different effects and possible processes, which at times even cancel each other out. This may again highlight the complexity of these possible effects; however, these statements may also serve as a basis for politicians and researchers to draw some final conclusions.

RESEARCH EVIDENCE

When looking at the history of the debate on the impact of published polls, the persistence of assumptions about a strong impact stands out. This can be explained by two ideal-typical circumstances: either research supports the strong impact assumption or respective research evidence is so modest or contradictory that making such assumptions is particularly easy. In the present case, however, the matter is somewhat more complicated. The body of research is by no means modest. For their meta-analytical overview compiled in 2000, Hardmeier and Roth (2001) identified 34 studies that could be evaluated quantitatively. Moreover, there are more than 30 studies that could be reviewed qualitatively, as well as a comprehensive list of references including numerous recapitulating monographs and various theoretical analyses, most of which follow the traditional line of the Rational Choice Theory.

Thus, research evidence is not at all sparse—but rather confusing as the findings are very disparate. Furthermore, the studies have applied various theoretical approaches and were executed in different disciplines, all of which has led to a lack of mutual reception of the results. All in all, the state of research is characterized by results that do not accumulate very well, so it stands to reason that politicians and regulatory bodies complain about confusing and inconsistent results (Dach, 1997). The present chapter therefore aims to contribute to the accumulation of the state of research, to include literature from non-English speaking areas and to alleviate the prevailing empirical and theoretical confusion. One the one hand, this effort is based on the method of meta-analysis, which allows a quantitative summary of the impact strength measured in published studies. On the other hand, we present an analytical framework to distinguish between possible effects both theoretically as well as in terms of causality.[1]

DISTINGUISHING THE DEPENDENT VARIABLES: EFFECTS ON WHAT?

When discussing effects in the context of opinion polls, it is not mainly the elites (→ *Studying Elite vs Mass Opinion*) that we are concerned with, but the general voters. So we distinguish between two dependent variables or factors that potentially can be influenced: participation in elections on the one hand ('turnout') and the voting behavior or the intention to vote for a specific party or candidate on the other ('preference'). In the first case, we can identify mobilizing and demobilizing effects and the special case of potential effects of exit polls published on Election Day.[2] In the latter case, the effect of changing one's voting intention or actual vote towards the party or candidate (in cases of referenda: issue positions) that are leading in the polls is usually referred to under the generic terms of a 'bandwagon effect'[3]; the effect of changing in the direction of the party, candidate or issue position that is trailing behind in the polls is termed an 'underdog effect.' There are a few other hypotheses, some of which refer to the effects of published polls on so-called 'tactical voting.' For instance, in a multi-party system voters might vote for the party of their second choice in order to facilitate a certain coalition, or to avoid an absolute majority (for an overview of the different effects hypotheses see Donsbach, 2001, p. 22).

Table 47.1 gives an overview of the main characteristics of the studies included in the meta-analysis. The majority of the studies have investigated opinions towards parties or candidates as the dependent variable.

The results of the meta-analysis confirm that this focus on preferences in the context of elections and referenda is well founded: all in all, the influence of polls or exit polls on voter participation is marginal (Hardmeier & Roth, 2001). Statistically, the zero hypothesis cannot be refuted: with the exception of the two findings in the Jackson (1983) study, whose method was heavily criticized,[4] the effect coefficient r_{tet}

Table 47.1   Overview of the findings included in the meta-analysis[a]

Characteristics	n	%
Number of studies	34	100.0
Year of publication		
– Before 1980	12	35.2
– After 1980	22	64.7
Countries		
– USA	53	71.6
– United Kingdom	10	13.5
– Canada	7	9.4
– Germany	3	4.1
– Mixed	1	1.4
	74	100.0
Findings (Unit of analysis)		
Design		
– *Experimental design (field and laboratory)*	51	68.9
– *Survey design (panel and cross-sectional)*	16	21.6
– *Aggregate data*	7	9.5
Dependent variable		
– 1. Turnout	12	16.2
– 2a. Election: election, preferences for and feelings toward a person or party	43	58.1
– 2b. Issues: preferences for and feelings toward an issue	19	25.6
Effects for 2a and 2b		
Bandwagon (*n* = 45); without aggregate data studies	42	–
Underdog (*n* = 17); without aggregate data studies	14	–

Note: [a] The results of this meta-analysis were first presented by Hardmeier and Roth (2001); since then, some adjustments were done. For further detail please consult www.sibylle-hardmeier.com

equals -0.0176.[5] In addition, the Fail-Safe-N-Test[6] suggests the results could easily be refuted. Merely another eight findings without the effect would be required to be able to plead for maintaining the zero hypothesis. Furthermore, the minus sign suggests that opinion polls have a demobilizing effect, if any at all.

There is also no strong effect of published polls on voting intention or voting for a party, candidate or issue position. The impact variables, calculated in terms of a tetrachoric correlation coefficient, are weak: if findings relying on aggregate data are excluded because of their rather weak causal evidence, and if conventional meta-analytical corrections for sample size of the studies (Hunter, Schmidt, & Jackson, 1982, p. 41; Fricke & Treinies, 1985, pp. 124 ff.) are applied,[7] the r_{tet} is 0.1102 (for bandwagon effects) and -0.0336 (for underdog effects), which sums up to a net effect of 0.0536.

If the statistical dependence of some findings originating from the same studies is taken into account, the effect coefficients amount to 0.1205 (for bandwagon effects) and -0.0361 (for underdog effects), which sums up to a net effect of 0.0431 and an absolute effect coefficient value of 0.0787. By conventional standards these are very weak effects, but by no means insignificant when considering the 'real world importance of treatment effects' (Rosenthal & Rubin, 1982, p. 157). If, for instance, published poll results would increase the support for party A by 5 points from 48% to 53%, this would correspond to an r_{tet} value of 0.0875, but it would also change the outcome of the election.

Furthermore, when applying an estimate for significance (z-value) and the Fail-Safe-N-Test along with the meta-analytical methods correction for sample size and test for independence and homogeneity, the weak bandwagon effect will actually turn out to be quite robust. The integrated z-value (15.74) indicates a significant result for the 42 bandwagon findings. Furthermore, more than 55 significant findings implying the opposite effect would be required to fall short of the usual criteria (Fail-Safe-N-Test).

The obvious heterogeneity of the findings suggests that there are important intervening variables such as the methods applied in the study, the year of publication[8] or the way of conveying opinion results to the public. The bandwagon effect is somewhat stronger in (field) experiments (however, there were no replications after 1990), and in studies using trend data rather than snapshot results.

PREDISPOSED VOTERS AND ISSUES

The rather weak effects are not surprising considering the lines of theoretical development in the field of media effects research. While the first theorists of mass media communication proceeded on the assumption that the impact of the media was considerable and influenced the masses psychologically, the first empirical studies demonstrated almost the opposite or a very weak impact, and since the early 1970s, research has been drawing attention to the selective effect of the media. Today, media effects are seen in the context of personal prerequisites and the respective prevailing conditions.

In this, the concept of predisposition is important. It was initially understood as a possible determining factor in (political) behavior, but was then increasingly regarded as the actual perception hurdle or filter (Schmitt-Beck, 2000). Moreover, along with the actual behavioral part in the persuasion processes, information processing became the focus of attention and the object of detailed empirical investigations. As a result, the effect of the media was gradually understood as being based on attitudinal selectivity. This concept highlights two main intervening factors: the interruption of an effect at one of the so-called six levels of information processing (McGuire, 1968), and the influence of cognitive structures or heuristics on information processing (Tversky & Kahneman, 1974).

Predispositions can be defined with regard to social psychology as well as sociology. In the first case, party identification typically acts as a filter; in the second case, this role is assigned to lines of conflict within society. This means that both individuals and issues can be predisposed. Concerning individual predisposition, Ceci and Kain (1982) made an important initiating contribution when they demonstrated that poll-induced effects occur most frequently among the undecided voters. Joslyn (1997) has supported this finding while looking at the intersection of predisposition and public opinion context and differentiating not only between assimilation (for the undecided voters) but also reinforcement and contrast. Furthermore, the concept of predispositions has been shown to be applicable to issues as well. The studies by Hardmeier and Roth (2003), Mutz (1992), and Kaplowitz, Fink, D'Alessio and Armstrong (1983) show that published poll results have a stronger impact when people have weak or no predispositions towards the issue at hand.

On the other side, empirical findings concerning reactions to poll data when people or issues are highly predisposed are less clearcut, and studies found effects in all directions. Along with zero or reinforcing effects, tendencies away from the poll stimulus have been noticed by Joslyn (1997) or Ceci and Kain (1982) at the individual level, and by West (1991) or Hardmeier and Roth 2003 (see Figure 47.1) at the level of issues. Ceci and Kain interpret this as oppositional reactivity, West ascertains an anti-government reflex, and the data reported by Joslyn or Hardmeier and Roth point to a ceiling effect.

This allows establishing another superordinate finding: especially when predisposed subjects are confronted with survey results, their reactions are anything but mechanical. A stimulus does not produce a typical response. The effects thus defy manipulative and deliberate intervention (which is

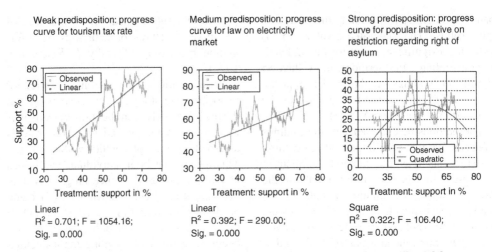

Figure 47.1   Stimulus effect of poll and support (according to degree of predisposition; Hardmeier & Roth 2003)

Notes: Experiment and Treatment: In early May of 2002 a brief survey was conducted with natural science and medicine students in Zurich, Switzerland. Each questionnaire contained one (imaginary) polling result each (between 25% and 75%) on three different issues (initiative on asylum, law on electricity market and tourism tax rate.) A total of 317 persons participated in the quasi-continuous experiment

Analysis: In order to get 'support %' we calculated twice a rolling mean of the cumulative Yes or No, that is, for each treatment x we took into consideration all cases between $x-2.5\%$ and $x+2.5\%$. If for example the range $x-2.5\%$ and $x+2.5\%$ includes 11 Yes and 9 No, then the Support (Yes) would be 55.0%. The replication of this procedure implies that cases closer to the treatment got more weight

a positive aspect), but also currently resist theorizing. While the theoretical arguments for reactions in the direction of the proposed stimulus, that is, a bandwagon effect, seem rather sophisticated (as above), arguments for the counter-reaction, or even an underdog effect, are more frequently developed ad hoc, and with a less well understood theoretical basis. Thus, the simple impact assumption has received yet another differentiated answer.

However, the idea that even issues are predisposed has more scope for development. The fact that some issues can trigger resistance or counter-reactions suggests that this is linked to the nature of the messages conveyed to the public (Zaller, 1992). Evidently there are issues where people lack the cueing messages necessary to identify the direction of impact and the political implications. This was obviously the case with the issue of a revision of the tourism tax rate as shown in Figure 47.1. At the time of the study, the

reform of this law had not even been discussed in parliament.

EXPLANATIONS FOR BANDWAGON EFFECTS

The fact that, even in the context of a meta-analysis, it is difficult to define the quantitative aggregation of the effect of published poll data on voters is also due to the complexity of the underlying processes and the multitude of different approaches used to assess these. A closer look at the body of literature and the theoretical underpinnings used by the respective authors reveal that the term *bandwagon* can at most serve as a generic term. Originally, the term referred to a concept used in crowd psychology which today is no longer very common and represents merely one of many possible models. At least five causal explanations for bandwagon effects can be distinguished.

Contagion

Derived from circus processions through streets with everybody following the bandwagon, that is, the wagon with the music (Collat, Stanley, & Rogowski, 1981), the term was originally used in its literal sense. The theoretical background of this effect can therefore be found in the classics of crowd and advertising psychology. As Kenney and Rice (1994) state, the crucial element driving the herd instinct mechanism is the emotional excitement, the enthusiasm of the crowds.

Gratification

The bandwagon effect, referred to by Kenney and Rice (1994) as 'supporting the winner,' describes an affective reaction as well. However, as in the 'uses and gratifications' approach, this concept describes a media audience who uses content actively and selectively and is stimulated by its own specific motives, even if these are only affective and serve the satisfaction of being on the side of the alleged winner (Bartels, 1988, p. 112). Thus, this theorizing goes beyond the mere contagion hypothesis and there are good reasons to prefer the 'gratification' to the 'supporting the winner' terminology. First, it embeds the effect into an existing media exposure and effects theory; and second the term gratification allows subsuming voter behavior as one specific form of reactions that are all motivated by seeking gratifications for one's own behavior. In this view, it is also the case that motivations to defect from the potential loser in order to avoid disappointment ('throwing the towel,' Kenney & Rice, 1994, p. 925) can be regarded as making an effort to achieve gratification and ensure feeling good emotionally with the seemingly unavoidable outcome of the election or referendum.

Cue taking

The understanding of the bandwagon effect as cue taking represents a newer tradition of media impact and attitude research. It emphasizes that voters, instead of taking the central route of elaboration, may follow cues that are easier to process. In the normative version of this line of theory, some authors claim that cues from poll data can convey group norms and trigger conformity. Voters would modify their preference so that it conforms to the survey-induced stimulus if they perceive an imbalance within the triadic relationship of the person (own preference), others (electorate or poll results), and the attitude object, that is, their voting behavior (see Morwitz & Pluzinski, 1996). Scholars who have more of a sociological understanding of the normative pressure of the 'significant other' apply the reference group theory (Mehrabian, 1998). The response to survey results is similar with both theoretical approaches, no matter whether they tend more towards sociology or social psychology. For reference group theorists, this response occurs even more so if the cues supplied by the poll data convey the attitude of a significant reference group, for example, a peer group.

In the informational version of the cue taking explanation, the poll data activate the so-called 'consensus heuristics' (Lau & Redlawsk, 2001). It suggests that perceiving a social consensus, for example, with regard to a candidate or a referendum, is taken as a cue indicating that one's own standpoint is 'correct,' and the response follows a pattern like 'oh well all those people can't be wrong' (see Ansolabehere & Iyengar, 1994, p. 414; Schmitt-Beck, 1996).

According to the cueing concept, the origins of the bandwagon thesis and most of the arguments in the literature can be understood as an effect of the way that the individual processes information. The underlying assumption of bandwagon effects is a 'peripheral' or 'heuristic' information processing, where the individual does not process the information at hand consciously and systematically. However, the dual-process models of information processing have shown that there are also information and persuasion processes that involve greater cognitive effort.

Cognitive-response

Explicitly following the 'Cognitive Response Theory,' Mutz (1997) demonstrates that poll results can also trigger a process of self-persuasion. At the moment when voters learn that, for instance, one candidate is running well ahead of another, they can contemplate the arguments and motivations for his or her popularity. After sufficient reflection, they may come to the conclusion that there are good reasons to support this candidate. This cognitive model of understanding the effects of published poll results questions the basic assumption of the affective model, which states that low involvement leads to greater effects. In the cognitive response model voters are inspired to perform an act of cognitive information processing, either by a feature of the source (e.g. a survey report providing a lot of arguments for or against a referendum) or an individual feature or a particular motivation such as the 'need for cognition' (Areni, Ferrell, & Wilcox, 2000). This influence should be all the more effective, since attitude change is particularly persistent if it occurs as a result of a cognitive process.

Strategic behavior

Rational models of decision-making behavior necessitate a minimum degree of cognition

as well, at least according to the classic proposition of the theory and if clear preference structures are assumed. In the context of primaries in the USA, Bartels (1988, pp. 108ff.) points out that strategic voters try to maximize the weight of their vote by assessing the viability of candidates at nominations or by avoiding 'wasting' their vote on a candidate without a real chance in elections with more than two candidates. Survey results can thus serve as a basis for decision making, especially in situations that demand a decision between more than two alternatives or candidates or in electoral systems with a quorum. Findings by Forsythe, Rietz and Myerson (1996) and Salisbury (1983) support this hypothesis. Table 47.2 summarizes the theoretical assumptions underlying bandwagon effects.

CONCLUSIONS

The findings of the meta-analysis and the theoretical embedding of the effects suggest that the fears of many politicians and some researchers about the impact of published opinion polls are exaggerated. Often these assumptions not only reflect an outdated idea of media impact, but also overestimate the scope and intensity of the effect. Furthermore, this view neglects the

Table 47.2   Theoretical assumptions about poll effects

Underlying theories	Reaction type	Affective/ cognitive	Information processing	Reactions triggered by poll results
Crowd psychology	contagion	affective	low	I join the masses
Uses and gratifications	gratification	affective	low	It feels good to be on the side of the winners
Cue taking by conformity to reference groups	normative	affective	low	Cue on position of reference group → Don't want to be the only one in my group thinking this way
Cue taking by consensus heuristics	informative	affective	low	Cue on consensus in society → these many people cannot be wrong
Cognitive response theory	self-persuasion	cognitive	high	Why are so many people pro-Bush? They are perhaps right → so I will vote for Bush as well
Rational choice theory	strategic behavior	cognitive	high	Which decision will be as close as possible to my interests, to prevent the worst from happening

possibility that individuals actually want to be influenced by information about the opinions and voting intention of others' reports (cognitive response, strategic voting) or influence corresponding to a 'normal' short-cut decision-making process as in cue taking, which can result as well from any form of political advertising and information dissemination. For instance, in an experiment, Daschmann (2000) has shown that so-called 'exemplars,' that is, man-in-the-street interviews or quotes from concrete people are more influential on people's perceptions of the climate of opinion than poll data. All in all, the stance of strong assumption underestimates the filtering function of predispositions, and advocates of strong impact pay too little attention to the fact that a survey's date of publication or the progress of a campaign are important intervening variables. To put it differently: after all, in a democratic and open society, it is also up to the political actors to employ the respective means of communication or assign resources for public communication and deliberation in order to ensure diversity of opinion and to deliver those cueing messages that voters use to develop resistance and counter-reactions to published poll results. However, pollsters can make a contribution to this as well. With respect to the experiment conducted by Cotter and Stovall (1994), which showed that strong effects of survey results disappear as soon as more background information is provided on candidates, we may draw the following conclusion: pure horse-race journalism limited to a reporting style of 'who's ahead' is also problematic because it does not provide the cueing messages that may prevent a certain effect.

The ban on publications of opinion polls could therefore be shelved in democratic societies. Yet the agenda of scientific research tasks is by no means exhausted. We need to tackle terminological questions, for instance regarding the comprehensive definition of movements away from the bandwagon and movements towards it in a multi-party or multi-candidate context. Furthermore, we still lack the theoretical framework that would allow us to make analytical predictions on possible reactions contrary to the bandwagon effect, for instance the underdog effect. Instead of merely treating them as counter-factual findings that occur by sheer coincidence (Hardmeier & Castiglioni, 2004), we need theoretical assumptions about their occurrence, possibly based on the personality type of the voter. It is possible that different types of people are more prone to one or the other effect but—due to the small effects sizes—we usually lack this differentiation in the data. Most of all, however, we require a systematic body of research on types which would help us to explain different reactions theoretically and ultimately assess them in terms of persistence. Table 47.2 may be a valid input for this research program, but there will be no real progress without methodological innovation. Two aspects deserve special attention in the current debate.

First, the field of research on opinion survey effects quite generally lacks comparative character, as does public opinion research. We know very little about how voters react in what situational contexts, e.g. the type of vote (election or referendum), the electoral system (candidates versus parties, majority versus proportional vote), the campaign phase, the current opinion trend, the kind of issues, or the characteristics of the media system. Second, our analytical perspective should predominately go into greater diachronic detail. If it is true that especially experiments or field experiments without replication of measurement produce stronger effects, this also raises the question of artifact. Maybe such methods or designs just measure the respondents' efforts to deal pragmatically with the interview situation in the short run, but do not reflect a persistent effect of the survey outside the research situation.

NOTES

1 Due to space restrictions, not all the studies can be listed in the bibliography. Please refer to www.sibylle-hardmeier.com for more information.

2 E.g. 'Western Voting' denotes the effect of exit poll results published while the polling stations are still open, as is the case in countries with several time zones like the USA.

3 The so-called 'Big Mo' is discussed predominately in the context of the American primaries. In contrast to the bandwagon concept, the momentum implies a dynamic perspective; see Bartels (1988).

4 Tannenbaum and Kostrich (1983) referred in particular to the large time gap between election and polling, as well as to the 'suspiciously' strong effect. Yet Sudman (1986) and Epstein and Strom (1981) also expressed criticism.

5 In order to get an effect coefficient we calculated a tetrachoric r_{tet}, which is applicable to most data presented in the studies (Fricke & Treinies, 1985, p. 118; Greer, Dunlap, & Beatty, 2003):

$$r_{tet} = \cos \frac{180°}{1 + \sqrt{(bc/ad)}}$$

6 Meta-analysis is vulnerable to the 'file drawer' problem in that studies with non-significant findings are unlikely to be published. Failure to include such studies calls into question meta-analysis findings that are based primarily on published studies. The fail-safe n determines the number of studies with non-significant findings that, if added to the sample, would reduce the combined effect size to a selected level (Orwin, 1983).

7

$$\bar{r} = \frac{\sum n_i * r_i}{N}$$

Thus, a further reason to exclude aggregate data for meta-analytical procedures is provided with this formula: they would get too much weight because of large sample sizes.

8 This could include effects of specific elections that were studied.

REFERENCES

Ansolabehere, S., & Iyengar, S. (1994). Of horseshoes and horse races: Experimental studies of the impact of poll results on electoral behavior. *Political Communication, 11*, 413–430.

Areni, Ch., Ferrell, E. & Wilcox, J. (2000). The persuasive impact of reported opinions on individuals low versus high in need for cognition. *Psychology and Marketing, 17*, 855–875.

Bartels, L. M. (1988). *Presidential primaries and the dynamics of public choice.* Princeton, NJ: Princeton University Press.

Ceci, S. J., & Kain, E. L. (1982). Jumping on the bandwagon with the underdog: The impact of

attitude polls on polling behavior. *Public Opinion Quarterly, 46*, 228–242.

Collat, D. S., Stanley, K., & Rogowski, R. (1981). The end game in presidential nominations. *American Political Science Review, 75*, 426–435.

Cotter, P, & Stovall, J.G. (1994). Is one as good as another? The relative influence of pre-election surveys on voter behavior. *Newspaper Research Journal, 15*(4), 13–19.

Crespi, I. (1980). Polls as journalism. *Public Opinion Quarterly, 44*, 462–476.

Dach, P. (1997). Veröffentlichung von Wahlprognosen: keine verfassungsrechtlichen Bedenken [Publication of election forcast polls—constitutional law doesn't raise objections]. *Zeitschrift für Parlamentsfragen, 28*, 229–235.

Daschmann, G. (2000). Vox pop and the polls: The impact of poll results and voter statements in the media on the perception of a climate of opinion. *International Journal of Public Opinion Research, 12*, 160–181.

Donsbach, W. (2001). *Who's afraid of election polls? Normative and empirical arguments for the freedom of pre-election surveys.* Amsterdam: ESOMAR.

Donsbach, W., & Antoine, J. (1990). Journalists and the polls: A parallel survey among journalists in France and Germany. *Marketing and Research Today, 18*, 167–174.

Epstein, L. K., & Strom, G. (1981). Election night projections and West coast turnout. *American Politics Quarterly, 9*, 479–491.

Forsythe, R., Rietz, T., & Myerson, R. B. (1996). An experimental study of voting rules and polls in three-candidate elections. *International Journal of Game Theory, 25*, 355–383.

Foundation for Information (2003). *The freedom to publish opinion polls. Report on a worldwide update.* Amsterdam/Chapel Hill: ESOMAR / WAPOR.

Fricke, R., & Treinies, G. (1985). *Einführung in die Meta-Analyse* [Introduction to meta-analysis]. Bern: Huber.

Greer, T., Dunlap, W. P., & Beatty, G. O. (2003). A Monte Carlo evaluation of the tetrachoric correlation coefficient. *Educational and Psychological Measurement, 63*, 931–950.

Hardmeier, S. (2000). Meinungsumfragen im Journalismus: Nachrichtenwert, Präzision und Publikum [Journalism's polling: news value, precision and audience]. *Medien & Kommunikationswissenschaft, 48*, 371–395.

Hardmeier, S., & Roth, H. (2001, September). *Towards a systematic assessment of impact of polls on voters: A meta-analytical overview.* Paper presented at the 54th annual conference of the World Association for Public Opinion Research, Rome.

Hardmeier, S., & Roth, H. (2003). Die Erforschung der Wirkung politischer Meinungsumfragen: Lehren vom 'Sonderfall' Schweiz [Researching the influence of public opinion polls: Drawing lessons from the Swiss 'case']. *Politische Vierteljahresschrift, 44,* 174–195.

Hardmeier, S., & Castiglioni, L. (2004, April). *The underdog effect of pre-election poll reporting: Theoretically and empirically underexposed.* Paper presented at the annual conference of the Midwest Political Science Association, Chicago.

Hunter, J. E., Schmidt, F. L., & Jackson, G. B. (1982). *Meta-analysis. Cumulating research findings across studies.* Beverly Hills, CA: Sage.

Jackson, J. E. (1983). Election night reporting and voter turnout. *American Journal of Political Science, 27,* 615–635.

Joslyn, M. R. (1997). The public nature of personal opinion. The impact of collective sentiment on individual appraisal. *Political Behavior, 19,* 337–363.

Kaplowitz, S. A., Fink, E. L., D'Alessio, D., & Armstrong, G. B. (1983). Anonymity, strength of attitude, and the influence of public opinion polls. *Human Communication Research, 10,* 10–25.

Kenney, P. J., & Rice, T. W. (1994). The psychology of political momentum. *Political Research Quarterly, 47,* 923–938.

Ladd, E. C. (1980). Polling and the press: The clash of institutional imperatives. *Public Opinion Quarterly, 44,* 574–584.

Lau, R. R., & Redlawsk, D. P. (2001). Advantages and disadvantages of cognitive heuristics in political decision making. *American Journal of Political Science, 45,* 951–971.

McGuire, W. J. (1968). Personality and attitude change: An information-processing theory. In A. G. Greenwald, T. C. Brock, & T. M. Ostrom (Eds.), *Psychological Foundations of Attitudes* (pp. 171–196). New York: Academic Press.

Mehrabian, A. (1998). Effects of poll reports on voter preferences. *Journal of Applied Social Psychology, 28,* 2119–2130.

Morwitz, V. G., & Pluzinski, C. (1996). Do polls reflect opinions or do opinions reflect polls? The impact of political polling in voter's expectation, preferences, and behavior. *Journal of Consumer Research, 23,* 53–67.

Mutz, D. C. (1992). Impersonal influence: Effects of representations of public opinion on political attitude. *Political Behavior, 14,* 89–122.

Mutz, D. C. (1997). Mechanism of momentum: Does thinking make it so? *Journal of Politics, 59,* 104–125.

Orwin, R. G. (1983). A Fail-Safe N for effect size in meta-analysis. *Journal of Educational Statistics, 8,* 157–159.

Rosenthal, R., & Rubin, D. (1982). A simple general purpose display of magnitude of experimental effect. *Journal of Educational Psychology, 74,* 166–169.

Salisbury, B. R. (1983). Evaluative voting behavior: An experimental examination. *The Western Political Quarterly, 36,* 88–97.

Schmitt-Beck, R. (1996). Mass media, the electorate, and the bandwagon. A study of communication effects on vote choice in Germany. *International Journal of Public Opinion Research, 8,* 266–291.

Schmitt-Beck, R. (2000). *Politische Kommunikation und Wählerverhalten. Ein internationaler Vergleich* [Political communication and voter behavior: an international comparison]. Wiesbaden: Westdeutscher Verlag.

Sudman, S. (1986). Do exit polls influence voting behavior? *Public Opinion Quarterly, 50,* 331–339.

Tannenbaum, P. H., & Kostrich, L. J. (1983). *Turned-on TV / turned-off voters. Policy options for election projections.* Beverly Hills, CA: Sage.

Tversky, A., & Kahneman, D. (1974). Judgment under uncertainty: Heuristics and biases. *Science, 185,* 1124–1131.

West, D. M. (1991). Polling effects in election campaigns. *Political Behavior, 13,* 151–163.

Zaller, J. (1992). *The nature and origins of mass opinion.* Cambridge: Cambridge University Press.

PART V

Special Fields of Application

Special Fields of Application

48

The Use of Surveys as Legal Evidence

Anne Niedermann

Courts, trademark authorities and legal representatives of companies employ survey research findings when precise information about perceptions of consumers or other groups is needed. There is hardly any other area where survey research findings have such immediate impact as when they are presented as evidence to courts, and they result in legally binding rulings and court decisions. Legal decisions, however, can only be legitimately based on survey research if data collection uses proper scientific methods and the studies are neutral, valid and understandable. This chapter gives an overview of areas where survey evidence is used, and its required methodological standards. It does this with an international perspective and illustrations of the cooperation between survey researchers and legal experts.

AREAS OF APPLICATION

Providing survey evidence has gained acceptance in various judicial cultures, particularly in trademark litigation or in cases involving fair trade practices, as well as in antitrust law. The most common application is to determine to what extent members of the general public (consumers) or professionals interpret product names, logos, colors, three-dimensional forms of products or packaging and the like as trademarks in the legal sense (Figure 48.1 gives an example of a 3-D trademark). Other tasks are ascertaining whether a new product exploits the reputation of a well-known brand, or whether two products can be mistaken (Figure 48.2 gives an example of a possible confusion of packaging). In disputes involving fair trade practices and consumer protection, surveys can verify whether an advertising statement, slogan, or product name is actually misleading consumers and producing 'false or unfair advertising.' In antitrust law, surveys can be employed to define relevant product markets from the perspective of consumers or to measure market efficiency.

Survey evidence is not concerned with the population's political views or moral judgments, and is not meant to provide a populist foundation for rulings on such issues. Rather, such surveys provide information on

Figure 48.1   An example of a 3-D trademark
Source: IfD Allensbach 2003. *Reprinted by permission of the Allensbach Institute*

Figure 48.2   An example of a possible confusion of packaging
Source: IfD Allensbach 2003. *Reprinted by permission of the Allensbach Institute*

people's knowledge of, experiences with, or spontaneous reactions to a particular trademark or advertising, or prove the existence or non-existence of certain effects, such as an advertising claim. It is applied in cases where the law or legal precedents refer explicitly to actual circumstances (for example, the attitudes of a target group). Survey evidence also does not solely determine rulings made by courts or government authorities. It is one of several pieces of evidence—though most of the times quite a significant one.

INTERNATIONAL OVERVIEW

Globally, many nations allow survey evidence—most strongly and diversely the

United States and Germany. Knaak identified four factors in law, markets and survey research that explain differences in intensity of the use across countries (1990, pp. 329ff.):

- level of competence attributed to survey research,
- extent to which trademarks are subject to high competitive pressure,
- whether trademark and antitrust law regard the perceptions of the consumers as relevant and
- whether the procedural rules of a country have formally accepted surveys as evidence.

The admissibility of survey evidence has long since been affirmed, not only by judges in continental and northern Europe, but also throughout the formerly reluctant Anglo-American legal circle. The admissibility of surveys as evidence is no longer the issue; the current debate centers on the probative value of a particular survey, on how reliable it is, and to what extent the information is significant, relevant and valid (USA: Federal Rules of Evidence, Rule 703—Bases of Opinion, Testimony by Experts: 299; Sorensen & Sorensen, 1953, p. 1213; Great Britain: Fienberg & Straf, 1982, p. 411; Pattinson, 1990, p. 103; Australia: Skinnon & McDermott, 1998, p. 437). Catalogs of criteria—developed by lawyers—already exist or are being created in different legal cultures laying down the methodological requirements a survey must fulfill in order to be attributed any probative value. These guidelines need to be developed further with increased input from survey researchers and associations.

United States

Survey evidence dates back to the systematic laboratory experiments on the confusion of trademarks conducted by industrial psychologist Hugo Münsterberg at Harvard University around 1910 (Münsterberg, 1913). When polling became established in the US in the 1930s, lab experiments were superseded, first by surveys with extremely broad samples, and later by truly representative population samples.

A major barrier to the acceptance of this type of evidence in the US was that surveys were held to be 'hearsay,' that is inadmissible testimony. The judiciary was troubled by the fact that findings are not ascertained in courtroom cross-examinations, but instead reach the judge 'secondhand,' via interviewers and an expert witness. Some articles by Zeisel corrected this misperception (Zeisel, 1959, 1960). As judges became familiar with representative surveys, they recognized that survey evidence is by no means another form of, or substitute for, cross-examination. They now share the view that surveys are not about proving the truthfulness of an individual testimony, but determine the knowledge, opinions or reactions of the total population (or any relevant section of it). The 'Robin Hood decision' of 1956 was the breakthrough in the US (International Milling Company v. Robin Hood Popcorn Co. Inc., 110 U.S.P.Q. 368 (Comr's. Pat. 1956); cf. Bowen, 1959). In the landmark 'Zippo decision' of 1963, the opinion was upheld that representative surveys fulfilling certain quality requirements are admissible as evidence (Zippo Manufacturing Co. v. Rogers Imports, Inc., 216 F. Supp. 670 (S.D.N.Y. 1963)).

The major area of application in the US is trademark law, specifically issues concerning consumers' perceptions of a brand (distinctiveness, secondary meaning, genericness) and testing whether consumers are mistaking one brand for another (confusion). Also, surveys on deceptive advertising play a major role. Useful overviews are provided by Diamond (2000), Knaak (1990), Evans and Gunn (1989), and Vida (1989, 1992). The US is also the source of important methodological contributions (e.g. Richards, 1990; Zeisel & Kaye, 1997).

Today, survey evidence can be employed throughout the entire Anglo-American legal circle, especially in the United States, Canada (Corbin, Jolliffe, & Gill, 2000), South Africa, Australia and New Zealand (Skinnon & McDermott, 1988), and more recently also in India, Taiwan (Liu, 1997) and in the Philippines. In Japan, surveys have been used as legal evidence for many years in cases concerning trademarks (Aoki, 2004; Iwase, 2004).

Europe

In Europe, Germany and Austria (Prettenhofer, 1954; Hodik, 1983) were the first to apply survey evidence. The German Federal High Court of Justice (BGH) basically accepted this new type of evidence in 1956 (BGH GRUR 1957, 426—Getränkeindustrie, GRUR 1957, 88—Ihr Funkberater; GRUR 1963, 270—Bärenfang). Publications by Noelle-Neumann and Schramm (1960) were especially influential. Now the German Patent Office (DPMA) requires survey evidence on the secondary meaning of a trademark to overcome various legal objections to registration (DPMA, 2004). Appropriate methods are discussed regularly among German survey researchers and legal experts (e.g. Schulz, 1984; Boës & Deutsch, 1996; Eichmann, 1999; Pflüger, 2004; Niedermann, 2006a).

Today, many other European countries use survey evidence, especially the Netherlands (van Nieuwenhoven Helbach, 1983, p. 287) and Sweden (Synnerstad, 1992). Great Britain has joined in after overcoming doubts about admissibility during the 1980s (Morcom, 1984; Pattinson, 1990; Lea, 1999; UK Patent Office/The Trade Marks Registry, 2004). In Italy there is a trend towards more surveys of this type. France, Spain, Portugal and Greece have not yet joined in on this development (Knaak, 1990, pp. 329ff.).

In Switzerland, survey evidence has recently become not only admissible but in fact a prerequisite before registering trademarks of a non-traditional type like colors or 3D-forms of packaging or products (Niedermann & Schneider, 2002; IGE, 2006). The Russian trademark authority accepted survey evidence in 2000 (Rospatent, Order No. 38, March 17, 2000: Rules for the recognition of a trademark as well-known in the Russian Federation).

The European Court of Justice (ECJ) has ruled on survey evidence several times (ECJ GRUR Int. 1998, 795, No. 36—Gut Springenheide; GRUR Int. 1999, 734, No. 24—Lloyd; GRUR Int. 1999, 727, No. 52—Chiemsee; GRUR Int. 2000, 73, No. 25—Chevy; GRUR Int. 2000, 354, No. 31—Lifting Creme; GRUR 2002, 804, No. 62—Philips). As a result, courts of member countries are free to employ surveys for legal evidence.

Since 1996, companies have been able to register 'Community trademarks' with the Office for Harmonization in the Internal Market, Trade Marks and Designs (OHIM), in Alicante, Spain. If objections to registration arise, surveys do in fact affect OHIM's decisions (OHIM, 2004). A content analysis revealed that through 2005, OHIM made reference to surveys in more than 400 of its decisions; and the probability that parties submitting survey evidence will meet with success has been rising (Niedermann, 2006b).

QUALITY IS ESSENTIAL

The survey expert is personally responsible for ensuring the correctness and impartiality of the complete set of survey evidence and signs the report by name. Surveys for legal evidence should be as brief and concise as possible, referring solely to the legal issue at hand. Each question must be carefully considered and clearly warranted, as the risk of objections increases with each additional question. Consideration should also be given to communication. A written report is not only essential documentation; it should explain the procedures employed and highlight the key findings—without, however, anticipating any legal result. Evaluating the findings and their significance in synopsis with other aspects of the case remains the task of the judiciary.

Checklist

Although judicial cultures vary, it is possible to find common quality criteria for survey evidence from the research perspective. The following is a checklist of internationally applicable criteria (Niedermann & Schneider, 2002), with the focus on the validity of the findings, that is, on investigative design and question wording.

Neutrality

1 Does the report refrain from passing its own legal judgments? Are the findings presented in a comprehensive and neutral form? Does it lack any important findings needed to evaluate the results?

Representativeness

2 Was the sample interviewed relevant to the legal issue? Is the survey based on a representative sample of the legally relevant population?

Questionnaire

3 Are the questions neutrally worded? Are all important response alternatives represented equally?
4 Have any visual aids been properly neutralized?
5 Have the legal questions to be addressed been adequately translated into test questions that are both easily understandable and interesting to respondents? Is the questionnaire in tune with the respondents' abilities?
6 Was the questionnaire pretested?

Investigative design and strength of the evidence

7 Are the findings primarily based on responses to direct questions (with low probative value) or do they derive from indirectly ascertained results with high probative value (including indicators, findings of field experiments, split-ballot surveys, along with data analysis)?
8 Is any comparative data provided to help to evaluate results?

Report and documentation

9 Are the findings presented in a written report that also serves to explain the methodological techniques and question wordings used? Are the findings organized and presented in an easily comprehensible way?

10 Does the report contain documentation of the sample (proof of representativeness), the methods employed, and the full questionnaire including original copies of all visual aids?

Methodology is scrutinized far more closely than usual. There is a need for complete transparency. Great care needs to be taken when documenting and archiving the survey. All countries require the complete questionnaire and information on the sample and sampling method in order to check representativeness.

The most important requirement for the survey expert is impartiality. Only a neutral investigative design and an unbiased report are in the interests of the client. On accepting a commission, researchers should make sure the client understands the nature of survey as a scientific investigation with no preordained result. If the data confirms the client's hypotheses, the lawyers have a powerful argument at hand. If not, the report will not be submitted and can be kept as internal information.

PROS AND CONS OF SURVEY EVIDENCE

Reservations against using surveys in a legal context most commonly concern costs and time. Court proceedings may take longer in order to allow time for the survey to be conducted (e.g. Gloy (Spliethoff, 1992, pp. 157ff.; Kreft), 1997: §17 No. 22ff.; Ekey & Klippel, 2003, §8, No. 60). There has to be a balance between costs and the significance of the legal issue. In many cases, the costs associated with conducting a survey are insignificant in comparison to the trademark owner's advertising budget.

One reservation that is occasionally raised is that reliance on surveys makes it more difficult to predict rulings, and there might be less consistency in rulings (e.g. v. Stein, 1970, p. 332; Westermann, 2002, p. 404). Public opinion may appear erratic when it comes to controversial political or moral issues, but measuring awareness of trademarks or consumer behavior tends to produce more stable results because it usually concerns knowledge, long-term attitudes, or reactions. However, the stability of these matters does not imply we need not measure them in every new case to really know them.

Some legal authorities have reservations about the 'imprecision' of survey findings (v. Stein, 1970, p. 332; Westermann, 2002, p. 403). They underestimate how precise surveys are. Survey 'imprecision' is calculable and can be taken into account in the form of margins of error. Even if a finding only provides an approximate measurement or involves broad margins of error, it still allows a more accurate assessment of the situation than if no survey had been conducted.

Current reservations in Europe center around cases concerning the more complex issues of confusion or misleading advertising. The debate is whether the empirical reality ascertained by surveys is at all relevant, or whether judges should define the 'consumer perception' themselves and in a normative way, as attitudes or behaviors that can be expected from a 'sensible' and 'reasonable' consumer (Schweizer, 2000).

Additionally, there are certain psychological difficulties with accepting survey findings. Courts and registration offices may find the use of surveys more arduous than the use of personal assessments to decide on a case. Empirically derived data are sometimes thought of as limiting the level of freedom enjoyed, and as reducing the decision-makers' confidence in their own expertise (Chiotellis & Fikentscher, 1985, p. 3; Pattinson, 1990, p. 102f.).

EFFECTS ON THE LEGAL SYSTEM

The admission of survey evidence has implications for both the legal system and for survey research itself. Researchers must ensure that their methods are transparent, replicable and that they themselves remain impartial. Basing legal decisions on objective data derived from representative surveys is clearly superior to the 'introspection' of a judge or any

other form of subjective assessment of public opinion (Zentes, 1982, p. 435). The superiority is not solely attributable to accuracy—such rulings must also be transparent. Thus, survey evidence exerts pressure on competition, trademark and antitrust law to explain and justify the evaluation of facts. As Tilmann (1984, p. 716) stated: 'If consumers' attitude is ascertained scientifically, the judges' deliberations have to be carried out in broad daylight.'

Presenting survey evidence can often curtail or even avoid legal disputes. Many proceedings are over when impeccably conducted, clear-cut survey findings are introduced, or a settlement is reached on this basis. Interlocutory injunctions are more successful if they are based on empirical evidence—for instance on the awareness of a trademark in a case of confusion.

AN INDEPENDENT DISCIPLINE WITHIN SURVEY RESEARCH

Surveys for legal evidence have evolved into an independent discipline within survey research, one requiring its own investigative tools and methods, just as media research or election research did. Unlike market research, where qualitative methods like focus groups and in-depth interviews play a major role, only surveys representative of an entire country, region or a specific group within the population are suitable. Since it is often necessary to show items to respondents (logos, colors, products, advertisements and the like), face-to-face or CAPI interviewing is most commonly employed. Online interviews may be suitable when the relevant group under study is online regularly, as for example professionals are.

Using models tried and tested in market research like 'brand awareness' is insufficient in most legal contexts, since such data do not clarify the specific legal matter at hand. Approaches and question wordings need to be adapted to the specific legal context, and in most countries there are strict guidelines for conducting surveys and preparing reports (e.g. USA: Federal Rules of Evidence, Rule 703; Diamond, 2000; Germany: DPMA, 2005; Great Britain: UK Patent Office/The Trade Marks Registry, 2004; Switzerland: IGE, 2006; EU: OHIM, 2004).

COOPERATION OF LEGAL EXPERTS AND SURVEY RESEARCHERS

Impeccable sampling and fieldwork are a matter of course in any legal study. But the quality and success of survey evidence depend most on the investigative approach used, and especially on whether the expert is able to translate abstract, complex legal issues into simple, straightforward questions. Standardized methods and tools, which are widely applied in other areas of survey research, are the exception in legal surveys.

Distinguishing between the legal issue at hand (evidentiary issue) and test questions (questions posed to respondents during the interview) allows for a proper division of responsibility between legal and survey experts. Legal experts are responsible for defining the legal problem, that is, for determining the ultimate evidentiary goal as well as the individual building blocks that comprise the evidence. This includes suggestions about the legal definition of the relevant public.

The survey expert is responsible for designing and conducting the survey and analyzing the findings. The expert's most important task is to select appropriate analytical tools, especially with regard to question wording. When it comes to assessing questionnaires, judges, examiners in trademark authorities and lawyers tend to apply personal experiences or principles developed for oral witness examination (Trommsdorf, 1979, pp. 91ff.; Tilmann & Ohde, 1989, p. 236; Spliethoff, 1992, p. 175). However, such principles are not applicable when assessing investigative approaches in survey research. The ultimate decision as to the appropriate investigative approach and question wording must therefore be with the survey expert (Boës & Deutsch, 1996, p. 170). The survey

expert delegates the task of conducting the fieldwork to interviewers. Finally, the survey expert submits a written report detailing the methodology and key findings of the survey—without, however, anticipating the final legal evaluation. The expert may be called upon to explain the methodology, investigative approach and question wording employed (CASRO, Forensic Guidelines). Expert witnesses are also normally present when the case is heard in court and may be called. The expert does far more than simply organize the survey: he or she must bear responsibility for it, be prepared to explain it and, if need be, defend it against any possible objections. Evaluating the findings relative to other aspects of the case remains the task of the judiciary.

Courts, trademark authorities and all other legal experts can assist in the further evolution of survey evidence by quoting the exact wordings of the questions to which they refer in judgments, decisions or papers. Question wordings are by no means 'trade secrets' belonging to individual research companies but, instead, have to be disclosed to fulfill the basic prerequisites that apply to all scientific work, i.e. that findings have to be replicable and verifiable. Overall, the best way to ensure the successful development of survey evidence is not to prescribe question wordings but to agree on procedures and rules for assessing the probative value of surveys (Pagenberg, 1996, p. 324). International comparison shows the soundest studies originate from countries where legal and survey experts work together. This is most likely if surveys are not only commissioned by plaintiffs and defendants, but also by courts or decision-making authorities themselves, like in Germany, for instance.

CONCLUSIONS

Surveys for legal evidence have gained acceptance in many jurisdictions and legal authorities, and have established themselves in many legal cultures as an area of applied survey research. The majority of studies center on trademark, unfair advertising and antitrust law. The neutrality of the research design and questionnaire as well as transparency and documentation of the whole research process is essential in order to secure the probative value of the results. Thus far, little has been published in scientific journals outside the legal sphere about best practices in this field. Also, there is a lack of basic research, e.g. on the extent to which the existing legal concept of a 'rational consumer' actually applies to reality. The process of legal harmonization in the EU is producing an increased demand for international comparative studies. Survey research associations on an international level will have to define common quality criteria for surveys that are suited for submission as legal evidence.

REFERENCES

Aoki, H. (2004). Surveys as evidence in trademark and unfair competition cases. *Intellectual Property Management, 54*, 991–1011.

Boës, U., & Deutsch, V. (1996). Die 'Bekanntheit' nach dem neuen deutschen Markenrecht und ihre Ermittlung durch Meinungsumfragen [Brand awareness in the new German trademark law and its measurement using surveys]. *GRUR, 98*, 168–173.

Bowen, D. C. (1959). Trademarks and psychology. *Journal of the Patent Office Society, 41*, 633–741.

Chiotellis, A., & Fikentscher, W. (Eds.). (1985). *Rechtstatsachenforschung—Methodische Probleme und Beispiele aus dem Schuld- und Wirtschaftsrecht* [Research of legally relevant facts—Methodic problems and examples from law of obligation and commercial law]. Köln: Otto Schmidt.

Council of American Survey Research Organisations (CASRO) Forensic guidelines. Port Jefferson.

Corbin, R. M., Jolliffe, R. S., & Gill, A.K. (2000). *Trial by survey: Survey evidence & the law*. Scarborough. Ontario: Carswell.

Deutsches Patent- und Markenamt (DPMA) (2005). *Richtlinie für die Prüfung von Markenanmeldungen, Abschnitt 5.17: Verkehrsdurchsetzung* [Guideline for the examination of trademark registrations, Section 5.17: Secondary meaning]. Retrieved January 5, 2007, from http://www.dpma. de/formulare/richtlinie.pdf.

Diamond, S. S. (2000). Reference guide on survey research. In Federal Judicial Center (Ed.), *Reference manual on scientific evidence* (2nd ed., pp. 229–276). Washington. Retrieved January 5, 2007, from http: www.air.fjc.gov/public/fjcweb.nsf/pages/16

Eichmann, H. (1999). Gegenwart und Zukunft der Rechtsdemoskopie [Present and future of the use of public opinion for legal evidence]. *GRUR, 101*, 939–955.

Ekey, F. L., & Klippel, D. (2003). Markenrecht [Trademark law]. Heidelberg: C. F. Müller.

Evans, L. E., Jr., & Gunn, D. M. (1989). Trademark surveys. *Trade Mark Reporter, 79*, 1–37.

Fienberg, S. E., & Straf, M.L. (1982). Statistical assessments as evidence. *Journal of the Royal Statistical Society, 44*, 410–421.

Gloy, W. (1997). *Handbuch des Wettbewerbsrechts* [Handbook of competition law] (2nd ed.). München: Beck.

Hodik, K. (1983). Der Grad der Verkehrsgeltung und seine Feststellung [Secondary meaning its degree and measurement]. *ÖBl, 32*, 1–6.

IGE—Institut für Geistiges Eigentum (CH) (2006). *Richtlinien in Markensachen* [Guidelines for trademark issues]. Retrieved January 5, 2007, from http://www.ip4all.ch/D/jurinfo/documents/ 10102d.pdf.

Iwase, Y. (2004, October). *Survey evidence in Japanese trademark litigation*. Paper presented at the AIPLA pre-meeting. Retrieved January 5, 2007, from http://www.jp-ta.jp/committee/005/03_04/ 60122.pdf.

Knaak, R. (1990). The international development of survey practices in trademark and unfair competition law. *IIC, 21*, 327–343.

Lea, G. (1999, February). *Survey evidence: Back to the future*. Paper presented at the seminar of the Intellectual Property Institute, London.

Liu, K. C. (1997). The application of market surveys in trademark law and fair trade law. *National Taiwan University Law Journal, 26*, 173–195.

Morcom, C. (1984). Survey evidence in trade mark proceedings. *EIPR, 7*, 6–10.

Münsterberg, H. (1913). *Psychology and industrial efficiency*. Boston: Houghton Mifflin.

Niedermann, A. (2006a). Empirische Erkenntnisse zur Verkehrsdurchsetzung [Empirical evidence regarding secondary meaning]. *GRUR, 108*, 367–374.

Niedermann, A. (2006b). Surveys as evidence in proceedings before OHIM. *IIC, 37*, 260–276.

Niedermann, A., & Schneider, M. (2002). Der Beitrag der Demoskopie zur Entscheidfindung im schweizerischen Markenrecht: Durchgesetzte Marke—berühmte Marke [The contribution of public opinion research to decision making in Swiss trademark law: prevailing trademark—famous trademark]. *sic!, 6,* 815–840.

van Nieuwenhoven Helbach, E. A. (1983). Het opinie-onderzoek als bewijsmiddel in het mededingingsrecht [Public opinion research as legal evidence in competition law]. In Festschrift für W. L. Haardt-bundel, *Een goede procesorde* (pp. 287–296). Deventer: Kluwer.

Noelle-Neumann, E., & Schramm, C. (1960). *Umfrage-forschung in der Rechtspraxis* [Survey research in legal practice]. Weinheim: Verlag Chemie.

OHIM—Office for Harmonization in the Internal Market (2004). *Guidelines concerning proceedings before the Office for Harmonization in the Internal Market (trade marks and designs), part C, opposition guidelines.* Retrieved January 5, 2007, from http://oami.eu.int/en/mark/marque/pdf/guidelines-oppo-fv.pdf.

Pagenberg, J. (1996). Berühmte und bekannte Marken in Europa [Famous and well-known marks in Europe]. In J. Straus (Ed.), *Aktuelle Herausforderungen des geistigen Eigentums, Festschrift für F.-K. Beier zum 70. Geburtstag,* (pp. 317–332). Köln: Heymanns.

Pattinson, P. G. M. (1990). Market research surveys—Money well spent? The use of survey evidence in passing off proceedings in the U.K. *EIPR, 12,* 99–103.

Pflüger, A. (2004). Der demoskopische Nachweis von Verkehrsgeltung und Verkehrsdurchsetzung [Evidence of secondary meaning by public opinion surveys]. *GRUR, 106,* 652–657.

Prettenhofer, H. (1954). Die Meinungsforschung als Beweis [surveys as evidence]. *ÖJZ, 9,* 556–558.

Richards, J. I. (1990). *Deceptive advertising—Behavioural study of a legal concept.* Hillsdale (N.J.): Lawrence Erlbaum Associates.

Schulz, R. (1984). Die Eintragung eines Warenzeichens kraft Verkehrsdurchsetzung nach §4 Abs.3 WZG aus Sicht der Demoskopie [The registration of a trade mark through secondary meaning according to §4, clause 3 WZG (German trade mark law) from the perspective of public opinion research]. *Markenartikel, 46,* 143–147.

Schweizer, R. (2000). Die Entdeckung der pluralistischen Wirklichkeit [The discovery of the pluralist reality] (3rd ed.). Berlin: Vistas.

Skinnon, J., & McDermott, J. (1988). Market surveys as evidence—Courts still finding faults. *Australian Business Law Review, 26,* 435–449.

Sorensen, R. C., & Sorensen, T.C. (1953). The admissibility and use of opinion research evidence. *New York University Law Review, 28,* 1213–1261.

Spliethoff, H. P. (1992). Verkehrsauffassung und Wettbewerbsrecht. [The perspective of the relevant consumer and competition law.] Baden-Baden: Nomos.

Stein, W. v. (1970). Zur Beurteilung irreführender Werbung ohne demoskopische Gutachten [On the evaluation of deceptive advertising without public opinion surveys]. *WRP, 16,* 332–333.

Synnerstad, K. (1992). *Marknadsundersökningar som bevismedel i varumärkesrättsliga mål och ärenden* [Market research as evidence in trade mark cases]. Stockholm: Juristvölaget.

Tilmann, W. (1984). Die Verkehrsauffassung im Wettbewerbs- und Warenzeichenrecht [The perspective of the relevant consumer in competition and trade mark law]. *GRUR, 86,* 716–723.

Tilmann, W., & Ohde, H. J. (1989). Die Mindestir-reführungsquote [The minimum deception quota]. *GRUR, 91,* 229–239.

Trommsdorff, V. (1979). Das empirische Gutachten als Beweismittel im Wettbewerbsprozeß [Empirical expertise as evidence in competition cases]. *Marketing, 1,* 91–98.

UK Patent Office/The Trade Marks Registry (2004). *Trade Marks Registry work manual,* chap. 6: Examination and practice, sec. 46.5: Survey evidence. Retrieved January 5, 2007, from http://www.patent.gov.uk/tm/reference/workman/chapt6/sec46.

Vida, A. (1989). Die Konsumentenumfrage in der Warenzeichenrechtsprechung der USA [The consumer survey in US trade mark jurisdiction]. *GRUR Int., 38,* 267–280.

Vida, A. (1992). *La preuve par sondage en matiere de signes distinctifs* (étude comparative des droits allemand, américain et français) [Survey evidence on distinctive signs (comparative study of German, American and French law]. Paris: Litec.

Westermann, I. (2002). Bekämpfung irreführender Werbung ohne demoskopische Gutachten [Combat against deceptive advertising without expertise of public opinion research]. *GRUR, 104,* 403–407.

Zeisel, H. (1959). Survey interviewees as witnesses. *Public Opinion Quarterly, 23,* 471–473.

Zeisel, H. (1960). The uniqueness of survey evidence. *Cornell Law Quarterly, 45,* 322–333.

Zeisel, H., & Kaye, D.H. (1997). *Prove it with figures: Empirical methods in law and litigation.* New York: Springer.

Zentes, J. (1982). Forensische Marktforschung [Forensic market research]. *WiSt, 11,* 433–436.

49

Public Opinion and the Economy

Lutz M. Hagen

The economy, in the broadest sense, comprises all actions and institutions driven by the intention to overcome scarcity. In a narrower sense, the concept refers to the production, consumption, and exchange of goods and services that are traded for money on markets. It is in this sense that 'the economy' has established itself as a permanently salient issue of public discourse—particularly concerning its state and growth. The reasons for this can be found in its paramount individual and political relevance in combination with the highly decentralized, complex and hard to control structure and dynamics of modern market economies.

Public opinion, consequently, is frequently driven by economic issues and considerations. Public opinion research has therefore developed the concepts of consumer confidence and business confidence as special indicators of public opinion's economic dimensions.

In the other direction, the performance of single markets and of the national economy as a whole are in many ways heavily dependent on public opinion. It is rational for imperfectly informed market participants to rely on the (perceived) judgment of others. What is more, consumer and business confidence are not only considered to be important factors of the economy, but also definitely have a strong political impact, in that voting behavior and presidential popularity under normal circumstances are well known to depend on the perceived performance of the national economy.

Public opinion has largely been ignored by mainstream economics during recent decades. Recently, behavioral economics is gaining ground again, which, in turn, leads to increased attention to the mass media shaping impressions of markets and the national economy, thus predetermining economic action. Recent economic research is paying more attention to mass media (e.g. studies in behavioral finance) and, at the same time, communication scholars are paying more attention to economic issues.

This shall be discussed in detail in the following five parts. The first and second deal with the way that traditional and modern economic theory respectively incorporate public opinion. The measurement and significance of consumer confidence and business confidence will be discussed in the third part. The fourth part will treat the way that mass media shape economic confidence and otherwise foster interactions between public opinion and the economy, whereas the fifth part deals with the political impact of the state of the economy.

PUBLIC OPINION IN MAINSTREAM ECONOMIC THEORY

Possible influences of public opinion on the performance of single markets or on the economy as a whole have largely been ignored or denied by mainstream economic reasoning. For a long time, mainstream economic reasoning left no room for opinion, let alone public opinion, as a factor in decision making. In particular it is the model of *homo oeconomicus*, starting at the beginning of the 20th century, that formed the core of neoclassical economics by assuming that agents in a given decision situation will act to maximize their own well-being. Also they have at their command all the necessary information on possible choices and means-end relations related to their preferences. It was not until Keynes (1937) that a leading economic scholar would incorporate public opinion into economic theory. Keynes builds on Pigou's (1927) notion that the business cycle is driven by profit expectations of business people, which in turn might not only be set off by substantial economic changes, but also by impulses of a merely 'psychological' nature.

Keynes (1936, pp. 161ff.) in his 'General theory of employment, interest and money' introduced the term 'animal spirits' into the discourse of economics to describe such impulses (cf. Farmer, in press). What is more, he identified the constitutional uncertainty of investment not only as a reason for psychological, but also for social-psychological mechanisms of opinion-formation: 'Knowing that our own individual judgment is worthless, we endeavor to fall back on the judgment of the rest of the world which is perhaps better informed' (Keynes, 1937, p. 214). In another frequently cited passage, he compares investors in stock markets to jurors in a beauty contest who would themselves be rewarded if they chose the picture that the majority rated best (Keynes, 1936, p. 156).

In the economics context, there is another good reason for herd behavior aside from wanting to follow the bandwagon or to avoid isolation. Going along with the majority can produce market gains by anticipating what the majority of participants will do, e.g. selling before everybody else sells makes the price drop, or buying before everybody else does makes the price rise. These and other forms of 'psychological infection' have been elaborated by Jöhr (1978) and identified as causes for the business cycle.

Ideas about co-orientation as a mechanism relevant for economic action have not had much influence on mainstream economics in a long time. Rather, since the last quarter of the 20th century, the economic mainstream has been joined by the new classical economic theory that again took a turn in the direction of the concept of a perfectly informed *homo oeconomicus*. This return is based on the notion of 'rational expectations' that goes back to an influential article by John Muth (1961). Muth did not assume that economic actors can perfectly foresee the future, so his model deviates from *homo oeconomicus*. But he assumes that in their own interest, economic actors will inform themselves using all accessible sources about relevant economic developments. Thus their hindsight will be correct, except for random deviations that cancel out in the aggregate; and their predictions of future events, given a certain constellation of economic data, will essentially be the same as the predictions of the relevant economic theory (Muth, 1961, p. 315).

Recently, researchers are beginning to show that mainstream economics theory might not always be able to make unambiguous predictions about economic developments, even on the basis of complete information about the past. Rather it might be that many different states of equilibrium might be attained, and it depends on some economically irrelevant opinions of the actors which of the possible paths will be realized. If a sufficient number of actors expect a certain possible development, this alone will lead to its realization; as a result, public opinion becomes self-fulfilling. Accordingly, these expectations may be derived from events that originally have no economic significance at all—the so-called sunspots (Benhabib & Farmer, 1999). Sunspot models of the business cycle are seen by many economists as outperforming other types of models. Thus they have evolved to become the foundation of an increasingly strong heterodox strand of economics, contributing to the camel of public opinion again sticking its nose deep into the tent of economic theory.

BEHAVIORAL ECONOMICS

The increasing popularity of sunspot models did foster a new blossoming of behavioral economics, at the core of which lies the conviction that creating a psychological underpinning for economic analysis will improve its explanatory and predictive power. Also, other than the work of mainstream economists with a strong preference for theoretical modeling and simulation, behavioral economics is characterized by a strong empirical focus.

Behavioral economics has a tradition that stems from the time when the social sciences were not yet distinct. Back then, Adam Smith (1759/1892) reasoned about the effects of public opinion on human behavior in 'The theory of moral sentiments'; and Jeremy Bentham, whose utility concept formed the foundation of neoclassical economics, analyzed the psychological substantiation of that concept and at the same time developed theories of public opinion.

Probably the most important theoretical foundation of behavioral economics lies in the concept of bounded rationality. As Simon (1955) demonstrated, it is not only that human decision making under normal circumstances won't be based on an objectively maximizing calculus that processes all the relevant (and true) information. But, what is more, rational decision making in the manner of *homo oeconomicus* mostly is not even rational on a meta level, because the cost of decision making itself can be expected to be higher than its payoff.

Research in behavioral economics thus focuses on the approximate rules of thumb—i.e. heuristics—that guide imperfect judgments and choices. In this respect, the highly influential and mostly experimental work of Tversky and Kahneman (1974) has proven especially useful regarding two heuristics thought to be of high importance. According to the *availability heuristic*, when people make a judgment they will be influenced by information the more likely it is to be retrieved and more easily it can be retrieved instead of by assessing its relevance. According to the *representativeness heuristic*, people judge probabilities by how well data represents a hypothesis or an example represents a class, but they neglect the proper statistical indicators.

As research further shows, public opinion too can serve as a cognitive shortcut in terms of the *consensus heuristic*, the sense that 'the majority is probably right.' Herd behavior is seen by many proponents of behavioral finance as a major force that drives stock markets to overreact to fundamental economic events (Shiller, 2000). Stock analysts are also considered to be prone to herd behavior because they are constantly evaluated against their peers. Thus agents are seen to favor popular and well-known companies because they are less likely to be criticized in case of underperformance (Shleifer, 2000). While theoretically valid reasons for herd behavior in markets can easily be found, it is hard to prove that the unanimous behavior observed in real markets is actually caused by co-orientation and not by economically relevant facts that may simultaneously become known to market participants. Experimental evidence for herding in market situations is scarce and ambiguous so far.

While all kinds of heuristics will, in many cases, lead to reasonably good choices at little decisional cost, as compared to systematic reasoning, they can occasionally lead people far astray. Also, they are the reason for so-called anomalies in rational economic decision making, deviations of judgments and choices from systematic reasoning that can regularly be observed.

When it comes to judgment concerning the state of the national economy, it is also highly likely that heuristics play an important role. After all, a consistent finding of empirical research concerning perceptions of the economy is the fact that most citizens or consumers are able to reproduce or demonstrate only very poor knowledge about the general laws governing the economy. The average ability to verbalize knowledge of the current state of the national economy proves to be just as poor, although respective statistical indicators, most importantly the growth of the Gross Domestic Product (GDP), the unemployment rate or the inflation rate are regularly supplied by official institutions and broadly publicized by the media. Also, the public perception of the economy is marked by a couple of persistent anomalies that are well documented by surveys that assess consumer confidence and business confidence (Hagen, 2005, pp. 200ff.).

CONSUMER CONFIDENCE AND BUSINESS CONFIDENCE

The use of survey research methodologies to track and to forecast economic trends was pioneered by George Katona (1960), another founding father of behavioral economics. The focus of his research lay not explicitly on collective processes of diffusion or opinion formation but rather on their result. Katona developed the consumer sentiment survey so he could empirically support one of his central hypotheses, namely that judgments on the state of the economy would follow a coherent mood that would affect all members of the population, independently of their personal (economic) situation. Katona differed from mainstream economists in so far as he stressed the importance of consumption as

a driving force of business cycles, whereas mainstream macroeconomists focused on investment as an independent factor and saw the consumption of private households as largely predetermined by their respective permanently expected incomes.

Katona introduced an additional factor, viewing consumer expenditures as a function of both capacity (income) and willingness to consume. The latter he considered to be subject to psychological influences whose aggregate he aimed to measure by regular surveys. Thus, George Katona developed the methodology to poll public opinion on the economy. Since 1946, these surveys have been conducted by the Survey Research Center at the University of Michigan, with the Index of Consumer Sentiment being the most prominent outcome.

Nowadays a variety of similar surveys and indexes exist for many developed economies. They consist of a few questions that mainly ask for a rough ordinal rating on a 'better-to-worse' scale of changes in economic circumstances. Usually separate judgments are assessed concerning the household of the respondent on the one hand and the national economy on the other. Furthermore, both aspects will typically be assessed by asking for each about the perceived retrospective and anticipated prospective change in the short run (e.g.: 'Would you say that you and your family living here are better or worse off financially than you were a year ago?'). These questions might be complemented by others concerning, for example, the willingness to buy durable goods. Consumer confidence indexes are calculated by averaging the relative scores on the questions. This procedure is justified by a generally high correlation between the several items.

Although the vast majority of consumers cannot reproduce concrete facts about economic development, many of them have a good feeling for its rough tendency, which is likely to result mainly from evaluative judgments obtained through personal communication or the mass media. Survey answers concerning the development of the personal situation will be even more precise and, if respondents are randomly selected, will on the average mirror the overall trend. Judgments based on random guessing will cancel out in the aggregate.

Thus, consumer confidence indexes do closely follow the statistical indicators of economic development—mainly the growth of the GDP and the change in the unemployment rate (Hagen, 2005, pp. 206ff.). Accordingly, few studies have found that consumer confidence indexes have a significant predictive value on a regular basis if controlled for indicators from official statistics that reflect the objective economic situation at the time of the interviews. But, the indexes do contain some information above and beyond that, and seem to be of predictive use during periods of major economic or social turmoil (Desroches & Gosselin, 2004). Also the polling and reporting of consumer confidence surveys works considerably faster than national accounting, and thus is of value in assessing the current economic situation.

Indexes of business confidence are undisputedly of a much higher predictive value than consumer indexes. Surveys of business confidence are similar to the latter, except that they poll a sample of business organizations. The main questions focus on the respective firm's financial position and the development of its particular markets. Business confidence normally is one of the most important economic leading indicators, preceding the real growth of the GDP by several months. It is hard to find an indicator that will in turn precede business confidence in the course of economic fluctuations. The covariation with real economic development will not be as close as in the case of consumer confidence, controlling for the lag on real development.

The lead of business confidence may either be interpreted as a largely accurate prognosis complying with rational expectations theory or as an indicator of Keynesian animal spirits that shape the economy. According to modern sunspot theories, it could also be a logically inextricable conjugation of both.

The deviation of lay people's judgments about the economy (consumer confidence) from the experts' (business confidence) is in itself an anomaly, especially since business confidence indexes are normally published with a lag of just a few days after the end of the survey period and the media pay a lot of attention to them. But further anomalies can be regularly observed in consumer confidence surveys. Most strikingly, on average, the responses about personal financial situations in consumer surveys are continuously estimated to develop better than the general situation. This is paradox, for the respondents are chosen to form a representative sample of all consumers. This special case of pluralistic ignorance may be attributed to a strong prevalence of negativism in mass media's economic reporting that is well documented by communication research, as noted below.

It is possible that better questioning techniques might lead to better predictive power for consumer surveys. As it is, consumer confidence polling still focuses very much on the perception of manifest economic changes. This might be the wrong strategy, knowing that explicit knowledge about economic developments is scarce among the average consumer. Focusing on mood and emotions instead, even without explicit reference to the economy, seems to be a promising alternative. This goes for the *New Year's mood* as well, which is measured by the percentage of hopes among answers to the question: 'Is it with hopes or with fears that you enter the coming year?' Noelle-Neumann (1989) has pointed to a strong connection between the New Year's mood of the German population, as measured at the end of the old year, and the real growth of the gross national product in the following year. This finding has been sustained by several analyses showing that the New Year's mood outperforms even the German Council of Economic Experts' predictions for the economy that are made at the end of each year on behalf of the government (Hagen, 2005, pp. 277ff.).

ECONOMIC MEDIA EFFECTS

Media effects research shares its theoretical underpinnings in large parts with behavioral economics. Thus at the core of many different effects hypotheses lies the view of humans as basically striving for rational choices according to subjective goals, but being limited by their cognitive capacity. Thus mass media are seen as instruments that are used to overcome cognitive shortcomings. The more useful media are for this purpose, the stronger their effects. Accordingly, the effects of media will be the stronger the more ambiguity exists on an issue, the less experience people have with that issue, and the less alternative information sources exist. These are major tenets of media dependency hypothesis (De Fleur & Ball-Rokeach, 1989) that can be interpreted as underlying different media effects hypotheses, like for example agenda-setting and cultivation.

Now, the economy just like public opinion on a national level is a phenomenon that cannot be overseen by a single person or assessed by interpersonal communication. Therefore, the dependency on and the effects of exposure to the media can be assumed to be strong in this case. While media research has tended to focus on the political sphere and long neglected the economy, this has begun to change.

Meanwhile there is a broad variety of content analyses conducted in many countries showing similar patterns for economic reporting; among these are decontextualized 'numbers reporting,' a high reliance on experts and official sources, frequent tendencies of journalists to instrumentalize economics against governments, and, above all, a striking preference for negative news (Parker, 1997; Hagen, 2005, pp. 71ff.). This last finding above all gives high relevance to investigating how the media affect economic judgments.

Indeed, media effects research has come up with a couple of results unanimously confirming the assumptions of dependency theory. Thus strong empirical evidence exists that when people judge the state of the national economy, they do not generalize from their personal economic situations but rather reproduce mainly what media coverage tells them. On the other hand, little or no evidence can be found that media influence the retrospective assessments of their personal financial or employment situation (Mutz, 1998).

This is very much in line with many results from agenda-setting research showing that the importance of economic issues on aggregate perceptions will regularly depend on their salience in media coverage. This goes particularly for the unemployment issue, which for many decades has been at the top of many nations' public agenda. Hagen (2005, pp. 358ff.) shows strong agenda-setting effects concerning the unemployment issue in Germany that stand in contrast to the fact that personal fear of losing one's job is not affected by media coverage—which is in line with the findings of Mutz and with the dependency hypothesis. As a further result, priming effects on consumer confidence are also revealed: the more that media stress the issue of unemployment, the stronger consumer confidence correlates with changes in the unemployment rate.

The same study shows that in the German case, consumer confidence is clearly influenced by economic judgments from the coverage of leading national newspapers and TV newscasts (controlling for real economic indicators), whereas only weak evidence can be found for effects from those mainstream media on business sentiment. Vice versa, media coverage much stronger seems to be influenced by business confidence than by consumer confidence.

Especially for the US and Great Britain, similar results are documented for consumer confidence, whereas no research seems to have been conducted concerning media effects on business confidence (Blood & Phillips, 1995; Gavin, 1998). The vast majority of studies investigating the influence of the media on consumer confidence do so in the context of an analysis of economic models of voting behavior (see below).

Considering the fact that business sentiment can be seen as an early predictive indicator, if not a driving cause of the economy, a big desideratum of effects research is the need for additional studies of the uses and effects of media coverage by professional actors like CEOs or stock brokers. So far, such research has been almost completely neglected by media studies.

Research grounded in the tradition of behavioral finance, though, has meanwhile yielded quite a number of studies on the impact of media coverage on financial markets. This type of research strongly focuses on the accuracy and price effects of stock recommendations distributed by business media, in particular by the *Wall Street Journal*. Findings normally show that recommendations will lead to the overperformance of recommended stocks. But these effects generally seem to be of very short duration and are very likely to be compensated by countervailing market movements within days, or even minutes (Barber, Lehavy, McNichols, & Trueman, B., 2001; Schuster, 2003).

ECONOMIC MODELS OF VOTING

The research tradition of economic voting as a part of political science rests on the assumption that election outcomes, under normal circumstance, are mainly determined by the state of the economy. It is quite common within this research tradition to build econometric models that regress shares of votes, or respectively the popularity of parties and politicians as measured by public opinion surveys, on other time series. The explanatory variables first and foremost consist of macroeconomic indicators, but might also include specific events in the form of dummy-variables. This class of models is known as the *vote and popularity function* (Nannestad & Paldam, 1994).

Research on the vote and popularity function shows that in different countries, the state of the economy under normal circumstances will always influence election outcomes as long as the government is stable enough to be held responsible and there is no single, unusual issue that dominates the election. In such circumstances, it is usually

the unemployment rate or the inflation rate ('the big two') that exert significant influence. Occasionally the effects of real growth will prevail over unemployment.

Furthermore, most studies show that voters' decisions are guided by their perceptions of the macroeconomic situation rather than their personal economic situation, and by retrospective rather than prospective judgments. Finally voters often prove to be myopic: the effects of economic fluctuations can rarely be detected a year or longer after they occurred. Mostly a lag of three months or less is seen as appropriate for modeling the vote and popularity function.

CONCLUSIONS

Several ongoing developments have been illustrated in the scientific field spanned by public opinion and the economy that indicate new directions. While neoclassical economic theory still dominates, behavioral economics seems to be on the rise and is supported by sunspot models derived from mainstream theory. The project of integrating the behavioral approach with the mainstream of macroeconomics seems promising.

Consumers have greater forecasting powers than the usual surveys of consumer confidence indicate. Their methodology could be refined by incorporating more emotional, less precise questions that might yield better predictions.

Finally, the media, after decades of neglect, have been rediscovered as factors influencing economic judgments and decisions, and media effects research has started to treat economic issues with renewed interest. But still, the impact of media on professional economic decision makers constitutes a blind spot. Furthermore, behavioral economists and even more mainstream economists still widely ignore the mass media's role in the economy. To overcome this deficiency, it would be particularly important to clarify what consequences the media's notorious negativism might really have for economic development.

REFERENCES

Barber, B., Lehavy, R., McNichols, M., & Trueman, B. (2001). Can investors profit from the prophets? Consensus analyst recommendations and stock returns. *The Journal of Finance, 56*, 531–563.

Benhabib, J., & Farmer, R. E. A. (1999). Indeterminacy and sunspots in macroeconomics. In M. Woodford & J. B. Taylor (Eds.), *Handbook of Macroeconomics* (Vol. 1a, pp. 387–448). Amsterdam: Elsevier.

Blood, D. J., & Phillips, P. C. (1995). Recession headlines, consumer sentiment, presidential popularity and the state of the economy: A time series analysis, 1989–1993. *International Journal of Public Opinion Research, 7*, 2–22.

De Fleur, M., & Ball-Rokeach, S. (1989). *Theories of mass communication* (5th ed.). New York: Longman.

Desroches, B., & Gosselin, M.-A. (2004). Evaluating threshold effects in consumer sentiment. *Southern Economic Journal, 70*, 942–952.

Farmer, R. E. A. (in press). Animal spirits. In L. Blume & S. Durlauf (Eds.), *The new Palgrave Dictionary of Economics* (2nd ed.). Palgrave: Macmillan.

Gavin, N. T. (Ed.). (1998). *The economy, media and public knowledge*. London & New York: Leicester University Press.

Hagen, L. (2005). *Konjunkturnachrichten, Konjunkturklima und Konjunktur* [Economic news, economic confidence and the business cycle]. Köln: von Halem.

Jöhr, W. A. (1978). Psychological infection. A cause of business fluctuation. In W. H. Strigel (Ed.), *Problems and instruments of business cycle analysis. A selection of papers presented at the 13th CIRET Conference proceedings, Munich 1977.* Berlin: Springer.

Katona, G. (1960). *The powerful consumer: Psychological studies of the American economy*. New York: McGraw-Hill.

Keynes, J. M. (1936). *The general theory of employment, interest and money*. London: Macmillan / New York: Harcourt.

Keynes, J. M. (1937). The general theory of employment. *The Quarterly Journal of Economics, 51*, 209–223.

Muth, J. F. (1961). Rational expectations and the theory of price movements. *Econometrica, 29,* 315–353.

Mutz, D. C. (1998). *Impersonal influence: How perceptions of mass collectives affect political attitudes*. Cambridge: Cambridge University Press.

Nannestad, P., & Paldam, M. (1994). The VP-function: A survey of the literature on vote and popularity functions after 25 years. *Public Choice, 79*, 213–245.

Noelle-Neumann, E. (1989). The public as prophet: Findings from continuous survey research and their importance for early diagnosis of economic growth. *International Journal of Public Opinion Research, 1*, 136–150.

Pigou. A. C. (1927). *Industrial fluctuations*. London: Macmillan.

Parker, R. (1997). The public, the press and economic news. *Harvard International Journal of Press and Politics, 2*, 127–131.

Schuster, T. (2003). *Fifty-fifty. Stock recommendations and stock prices. Effects and benefits of investment advice in the business media.* (Working paper). University of Leipzig, Institute for Communication and Media Studies.

Shleifer, A. (2000). *Inefficient markets: An introduction to behavioral finance*. Clarendon Lectures: Oxford University Press.

Shiller, R. J. (2000). *Irrational exuberance*. Princeton, NJ: Princeton University Press.

Simon, H. A. (1955). A behavioral model of rational choice. *Quarterly Journal of Economics, 69*, 99–118.

Smith, A. (1759/1892). *The theory of moral sentiments*. New York: Prometheus Books.

Tversky, A., & Kahneman, D. (1974). Judgement under uncertainty: Heuristics and biases. *Science, 185*, 1124–1131.

50

Marketing Research

Humphrey Taylor

What exactly is marketing (or market) research? In what ways is it the same as or different than opinion polling? Chuck Chakrapani (2000, pp. 4ff.) wrote that: 'Traditionally, marketing research has been considered a discipline that primarily uses scientific methods to collect, analyze, and interpret data relevant to marketing of goods and services.' But he went on to say that:

> The acceptance of this definition has prevented marketing researchers from being meaningful partners in the decision-making process. The practice and goal of marketing research should not be just to provide 'input' to decision makers but to gather data and interpret them in light of what is already known and to be a part of the decision-making process. To have continued relevance to management and marketing, we should develop a core body of knowledge. Such knowledge should be supported by extensive empirical evidence. There is no substitute for empirical evidence. Statistical analysis on limited data cannot take the place of empirical evidence.

This is an excellent description of marketing research at its best. However, marketing research certainly includes both quantitative and qualitative research, and qualitative research, by definition, does not provide data for 'extensive empirical evidence.'

Marketing research draws on many different sources for its data, including primary (i.e. 'new') research and secondary research (the analysis of data and other information already available). It does not necessarily involve the use of new data collection, although it usually does. It includes both consumer (actual or potential retail customers) research and business-to-business ('B2B') research where corporate or institutional customers or prospects are interviewed. Like opinion polling, marketing research may be conducted locally, regionally, nationally or internationally.

THE MARKETING RESEARCH INDUSTRY

There is an irony in my writing this chapter on market research in a book about opinion polls. I have written chapters on opinion polls and opinion polling in two large books on marketing research, in which I tried to describe public opinion polling to marketing researchers. Here I am writing primarily for those who are more interested in or more knowledgeable about polling.

Current estimates are that worldwide spending on marketing research in 2006 is $23.3 billion (Inside Research, 2006b), of which $7.7 billion is spent in the United States (Inside Research, 2006a). Spending on public opinion polling, which is usually considered to be part of this industry, is minute by comparison. Of this, approximately 40% (or $9 billion) is spent on custom (or 'ad hoc') research, while 60% is spent on audience measurement (who watches/listens/reads what?) and point of sale reporting (how many packets are sold where?).

Typically, marketing research has grown faster than the economies in most countries, but not at a spectacular rate. Currently, the fastest growing innovation is probably the use of the Internet for data collection, which is estimated to be worth over $1 billion and growing by 30% a year. Worldwide, there are surely tens of thousands of companies, firms and individuals who sell and conduct marketing research, with several thousand in both the United States and Europe. Even in some of the poorest countries, there are a few research firms; for example, I found three in Haiti. Historically, most of the countries which did not allow independent public opinion polling (e.g. the communist countries during the cold war) have allowed some marketing research, even if this was limited to research for government or government-controlled industries. Some countries regulate marketing research; for example, the government of mainland China must approve the questionnaires before any survey research is conducted.

In the overwhelming majority of countries, almost all public opinion polling is conducted by marketing research firms. The United States is unusual in that several of the leading American public opinion polls are conducted not by marketing research firms but by academic institutions, media-owned organizations and a foundation-funding polling organization (The Pew Research Center and its Center for the People and the Press). In the United States and around the world, public opinion polling by marketing research firms only accounts for a minute fraction of their work.

From its earliest days, almost all the methods and techniques used by public opinion polls were first pioneered and developed by marketing research firms. George Gallup was a marketing researcher before he was a pollster. Telephone surveys were conducted by marketing researchers many years before they were used by pollsters. Internet research and many statistical and analytical techniques were only used by pollsters after several years of use in marketing research.

However, the marketing research industry owes a huge debt to public opinion polls. It is always difficult, and often impossible, to validate the accuracy of marketing research. The remarkable accuracy of public opinion polls, notwithstanding their occasional lapses and embarrassments, has provided marketing researchers with the evidence to persuade skeptics of the validity of their other surveys.

One impediment to the better understanding of research issues, methods and applications is the gap between people working in marketing research firms and survey researchers working in academic institutions. The former are more practical and focus on the most cost-effective ways to serve their clients. The latter are much more focused on theory, regardless of cost or timing. After a frustrating day spent working with academic researchers, Donald Stokes, then Dean of Princeton's Woodrow Wilson School said, half in jest: 'You make a living making complicated things simple. Academics make a living making simple things complicated.' This gap is particularly large in the United States, but it exists almost everywhere. The two groups tend to focus on different issues, to read different books and journals, and to go to different conferences. For example, relatively few US marketing researchers go to AAPOR meetings. The polling organizations in the United States that are not also marketing research firms (e.g. the media-owned polls) tend to fall somewhere between academic and commercial researchers.

All too often, these two groups disdain each other. Some academic researchers tend to refer to work by marketing research firms as 'commercial schlock' or by some other pejorative name. Some marketing researchers regard academics as totally impractical theorists, who rarely, if ever, have to meet deadlines, live within a tight budget, or design cost-effective surveys. All of which is a great pity, as both sides have much to learn from each other. We need to bring commercial marketing researchers and academic researchers together much more often. We can both learn from each other. Because many American pollsters are not also marketing researchers, there is a much bigger gap between them than there is in most other countries where the same research firms do both polling and marketing research. This could explain why US pollsters have sometimes been slower to adopt the new methods developed by the marketing research industry (for example, the use of the Internet for data collection, which has been more widely used in Europe than in America).

SIMILARITIES AND DIFFERENCES BETWEEN MARKETING RESEARCH AND PUBLIC OPINION POLLING

The lay public is probably not aware of the relationship between public opinion polling and marketing research, or that most polls are conducted by marketing research firms, or that polling is only a minute tip of the marketing research iceberg. Polling is very visible; marketing research is invisible to all but the small numbers of people who buy, use, or conduct it. Many marketing researchers have decidedly mixed views about opinion polls. Some feel that polling trivializes what they see as the serious business of marketing research; some are probably a little jealous of the publicity generated by the polls; and some have been embarrassed when polls 'get elections wrong.'

The important point here is that many marketing research surveys and polls use basically the same methods, but for different purposes. Public opinion polling measures mostly opinions, although it also measures

voting intentions and past voting, which are behaviors rather than attitudes. Marketing research measures many different things including:

- behavior (e.g. what people have bought or done)
- knowledge, awareness and understanding (e.g. of different products, services, companies and brands)
- attitudes (what consumers like, dislike about different products or services)
- needs (what people would like to have that they do not have)
- beliefs (e.g. their beliefs about companies, products, or services and their attributes)
- motivation (e.g. why they do what they do).

DIFFERENT TYPES AND APPLICATIONS OF MARKETING RESEARCH

Marketing research is used for many different purposes including, but not limited to, the following:

- usage and attitudes studies (what products and services people use and what they think of them)
- brand positioning, brand equity and other brand-related research (what are the strengths and weaknesses of different brands, and how do brands influence buying)
- new product development and new product testing (from the initial concept to, and after, product launch)
- pretesting advertising, and the evaluation (post-testing) of advertising campaigns (with many different theories as to what should be measured and how this should be done)
- customer satisfaction and research on customer loyalty and retention (focusing on repeat purchasing and potential growth)
- media research to measure and describe viewers, listeners and readers (sometimes called 'audience research'), usually conducted for advertising purposes, conducted by many different methods—people meters, TV set meters, diaries and interviews
- communications research, including but not limited to advertising research (for example the development of marketing strategies and public relations campaigns)

- employee attitudes surveys (measuring employee satisfaction and loyalty, reactions to recent events affecting the company, and effectiveness of internal communications)
- business-to-business research, where commercial buyers or intermediaries (wholesalers, doctors, etc.) are surveyed, rather than retail consumers
- site location studies (e.g. where to open a new bank branch or supermarket)
- packaging research (e.g. how to appeal to shoppers scanning many products)
- pricing research
- market segmentation surveys
- corporate image and reputation research
- trade-off research (including but not limited to conjoint analysis).

Those wishing to learn more about marketing research have a thousand different books and several journals and magazines to learn from. Some of the textbooks used in business schools are pretty heavy lifting. I recommend *The ESOMAR Handbook of Marketing and Opinion Research* (edited by Colin McDonald and Phyllis Vangelder, 1998, published by ESOMAR), and *Marketing Research: State of the Art Perspectives* (edited by Chuck Chakrapani, 2000, published by the American Marketing Association or AMA). Both these long books are extremely useful to practitioners. Because they have many chapters on many different topics, it is easy to find what one is looking for. And they are much easier to read than other books which attempt to cover the field. But I should declare my interest: I wrote a chapter in each of them. One, or both, of these books describe the different types and applications of marketing research listed above in considerable detail.

DATA COLLECTION AND SAMPLING METHODS

Many of the data collection and sampling methods used in marketing research surveys are the same as, or similar to, the data collection and sampling methods used in public opinion polling. However the specific methods used vary from survey to survey, from client to client, and from sample to sample. While mail surveys are still used, and Internet-based research is growing very rapidly, the majority of marketing research dollars (as of 2005) are still spent on telephone surveys in the more developed countries, and on in-person surveys in the less developed ones ($\rightarrow$ *Surveys by Telephone;* $\rightarrow$ *Internet Surveys;* $\rightarrow$ *Face-to-Face Surveys;* $\rightarrow$ *Self-Administered Paper Questionaires*). Increasingly, marketing researchers are using 'mixed-mode' research where respondents may be interviewed on the phone, by mail or online.

Of course, marketing research projects vary enormously. Some are in the field for many months, with many attempts made to convert refusals and maximize response rates. Some are conducted over 24 hours with no call-backs made at all. Some involve hundreds of thousands of interviews; some use very small samples, and so on. Marketing researchers use all the tools and methods used by pollsters, plus a lot more. They use random-digit dialing (RDD), CATI, CAPI, diaries, meters and automatic dialers. They also survey many audiences never surveyed by public opinion pollsters:

- Research for the pharmaceutical industry involves collecting huge amounts of data from pharmacists and physicians, nurses, hospital and health insurance managers, as well as patients with specific medical conditions.
- Research for the automotive industry involves the surveying of owners, and purchasers, of specific models of cars and of dealers.
- Research for technology and communications companies involves surveying not just retail consumers but also IT and communications managers, other users of IT and communications systems, purchasing departments and other corporate decision makers and 'influencers.'
- Research for the makers of building materials involves surveying architects and builders.
- Research for airplane manufacturers involves interviewing senior and middle managers of airlines.
- Surveys for consumer products and services and packaged goods firms involve surveying not just consumers but also retailers.

- Surveys for banks, insurance companies and other financial service industries involve interviews with the very rich, as well as with corporate financial officers, risk managers and other bankers. They also involve surveying 'intermediaries' who sell their services such as insurance agents and brokers, consultants and financial planners.
- Research for the travel industry involves surveying frequent flyers, business travelers, travel agents and corporate travel managers.

Obviously, this list could go on and on.

SEGMENTATION

During the 1980s and 1990s, there was an explosion in research involving segmentation. This is based on the assumption that most products and services are sold to very heterogeneous groups of consumers and that it is important to segment the market to understand, and sell to, each of the major segments (→ *The Use of Scales in Surveys*). Initially, most of the segmentation was based on so-called 'psychographics,' in which people were clustered based on their personalities and other psychological factors which might influence their purchasing behavior. However, during the 1990s, a growing number of researchers and their clients realized that broad-brush or generic psychographic variables were not particularly relevant to specific markets for individual products and services. For example, a segmentation which would work well for toothpaste would not work well for banking services. The last few years have therefore seen the rapid growth of segmentation surveys that are based on particular product or service categories.

One reason for the popularity of these segmentation surveys is that they enable advertisers and markets to send out different messages to different segments of potential consumers. In theory this sounds fine, but in practice it is often difficult to find media that are very effective at reaching only one or two segments with the relevant messages. And, where narrowly targeted advertising tactics are used to attract one segment, they may alienate another.

THE USE OF MULTIVARIATE STATISTICAL TECHNIQUES

Like pollsters, most marketing researchers are most comfortable dealing with simple tables and cross-tabulations. However the last 30 years has seen an explosion in the use of a growing number of different statistical techniques. These include:

- analysis of variance
- different types of regression analysis
- discriminate analysis
- factor analysis
- cluster analysis
- multidimensional scaling
- conjoint and other types of trade-off analysis.

For each of these statistical techniques, there are different practices, software packages and methods of analysis. Five different firms may produce very different results when supposedly using the same technique. This is because the design and use of these techniques involves a great deal of judgment, not just cold mathematical science. The problem, however, is that the users of the results of these analyses often have little understanding of the assumptions made. With cross-tabulation, there is only one possible answer if the survey data is tabulated by specific variables. There may be several different answers when different statistical techniques are used, and it is often difficult to know how truly reliable the conclusions are. That is not to downplay the enormous value that many of these techniques provide. But it is a warning to the users to be very careful in choosing the people or companies to do this work.

DIFFERENT APPROACHES TO ORGANIZATION WITHIN MARKETING RESEARCH FIRMS

Most small marketing research firms are either 'jacks of all trades' or specialists in one particular service or industry. For example, they may only do automobile research, or only do advertising research. However, as research firms grow, they can be organized in a number of different ways. All involve teams, whether these work for particular industries, particular clients or provide particular research services.

Although the jargon changes quite often, a common terminology is to talk about 'verticals,' which comprise one or more industries. Computer hardware and software may be considered one vertical. Pharmaceuticals may be another, and so on. 'Horizontals' are teams within a company that focus on particular research methodologies or applications that cut across many different industries. For example, these horizontals may focus on advertising, research, or customer loyalty and retention.

However companies are structured and organized, there is a clear need for both industry expertise and increasingly specialized research expertise. How these two approaches—using verticals and horizontals—are managed is a challenge for many research firms.

MAKING SURE THE RESEARCH IS ADDRESSING THE KEY ISSUES

Most of us in marketing research have delivered surveys that were not very useful, or even useless. A major reason for this is that the people conducting the research did not fully understand why the research was being conducted. All too often, research agencies conduct the research they are asked to conduct without questioning all the ways the research might be used, or what decisions it might influence. It is good practice, therefore, for every research firm to ask the following questions before designing, let alone conducting, research for their clients:

- How will this research be used?
- What decisions might be influenced by the research findings?
- Are there any other ways the research might be useful?

BEWARE OF THE LATEST RESEARCH GIMMICK

Thousands of competing research firms are all trying to differentiate themselves from each other. They are always searching for something new, some new research tool that will give them a competitive advantage. Over the last 40 years (and perhaps longer), marketing researchers have offered their clients hundreds of 'new' research methodologies, including new computerized models, new analytical and statistical techniques, and new questionnaire designs. These have included dozens of 'new' ways to segment markets; measure and predict behavior; differentiate brands, product and services; pre-test new TV commercials; and measure the impact of advertising and marketing campaigns, often using 'branded' research products and services.

Some of these have been very successful and are still widely used many years after they were developed: for example, conjoint analysis and other types of 'trade-off analysis' to understand how different product attributes influence purchasing decisions. However, the overwhelming majority didn't work very well and died after a few years. Buyers of research need to be cautious when research firms pitch their latest new technique, application or methodology, as many of them are mostly sales gimmicks. The hugely increased power of computers have made it possible for 'data-mining' and 'data-integration' to develop and sell very sophisticated new services. How well the buyers understand what they are buying, though, is an open question.

THE APPROPRIATE METHODOLOGY DEPENDS ON HOW THE SURVEY WILL BE USED

How a survey will be used when it is completed should have a big impact on its design, execution and cost. Consider the following different uses or applications of research; virtually all research designs involve such tradeoffs:

1 Surveys intended to generate data for academic papers to be published in peer-reviewed journals:

> Typically these surveys require an 'acceptable' response rate and, therefore, an extended fieldwork period, the use of high quality interviewers, effective refusal conversion, many call-backs and, increasingly, payments to respondents as an incentive to participate in the study. (But, as response rates have declined, so has the meaning of 'acceptable'.) These surveys are therefore much more expensive and require a much longer time in the field than typical polls or marketing research surveys.

2 Surveys intended for use in litigation:

> These surveys also need to be conducted using very high standards. The survey firms must be able to defend their methods and their findings against attacks from hostile expert witnesses and litigators seeking to undermine their validity and credibility.

3 Other surveys that may be publicly released and presented or attacked in litigation:

> Any survey that may be publicly released which compares a client's products services or organization with a competitor's may provoke a legal challenge, and must therefore meet all the same standards as surveys designed specifically for use in litigation.

4 Surveys that will not be publicly released:

> The great majority of research conducted by marketing research firms is never publicly released. It comes in a thousand different shapes and sizes—qualitative and quantitative, large and small, complex and simple, cheap and expensive. The more important the issues addressed and the bigger the decisions the clients will make, the more precision and reliability is usually required.

In choosing the methods used, the research firms should try to ensure that:

1 the level of accuracy and reliability is appropriate to the need;

2 the research is designed to high enough standards to achieve the desired levels of accuracy and reliability;
3 the research is not substantially larger or more expensive than is required to meet the desired levels of accuracy and reliability;
4 the client understands, and accepts, the trade-offs that have been made between quality, timeliness and cost.

It is essential that the research firm and the client discuss and agree on the ways in which the research may be used before the research design is finalized or the contract signed.

FORECASTING RESEARCH

Some of the most important marketing research is intended to answer questions about the future:

- What will be the impact on sales of a new marketing or advertising campaign, a change in prices, or new package?
- Will this new product succeed or fail, and what market share will it achieve?
- How will sales of the service or product be affected by the actions of competitors?
- How will the market change over the next few years?
- Will present trends continue?

Unfortunately, these are incredibly difficult questions to answer, and the answers provided by marketing researchers are probably no better than medium-term economic forecasts or long-range weather forecasts. But, some may argue, polls do a pretty good job of forecasting elections (→ *Exit Polls and Pre-Election Polls*). However, what most pollsters do is to *measure* voting intentions on the eve of an election, making adjustments for differential turnout or abstention and publishing the result as a 'forecast.' And even here, competent pollsters have sometimes produced poor forecasts because of a last-minute swing of opinion, or differential turnout they did not anticipate. In reality this is a good example of the difference between measurement and forecasting.

The problem for marketing researchers is that companies invest billions of dollars in new plant, new products and new campaigns based on assumptions about the future, and therefore need all the help they can get to predict the future. When these assumptions are false, the consequences may be catastrophic. The most notorious case is probably Ford's Edsel car, which failed miserably because Ford's assumptions were wrong. All too often, forecasts are made by projecting current trends into the future. This is risky. As the British economist Alex Cairncross (n.d.) wrote 40 years ago:

> A trend, [to quote the language of Gertrude Stein], is a trend, is a trend. The question is: Will it bend? Will it alter its course, through some unforeseen force and come to a premature end?

Forecasting changes in trends is really difficult. Until now, data-based judgment has probably been more successful than the dozens of very sophisticated computerized models, which have been better at predicting the past than the future!

CONCERNS ABOUT THE ACCURACY AND RELIABILITY OF MARKETING RESEARCH

When marketing researchers measure behavior, knowledge, attitudes, and motivation, or measure the impact of marketing and advertising campaigns, the assumption is that they do this with reasonable accuracy. In practice, we seldom know how accurate or inaccurate most marketing research is, except when it measures something for which we already have other reliable measures (→ *Validation Studies*). In my experience, the quality, and presumably therefore the reliability, of marketing research varies from the exemplary to the truly awful. Unfortunately, many decisions about the design and quality of research are driven by cost and price. As a result, there is a kind of Gresham's law, with 'bad research

often driving out good.' As Ruskin (n.d.) wrote:

> There is scarcely anything in the world that some man cannot make a little worse and sell a little cheaper, and the people who consider price only are this man's lawful prey.

Only rarely, in my experience, do the buyers of marketing research worry much, or at all, about sample design, response rates, weighting procedures, order effects or method effects, or the quality of interviewing—any one of which can seriously damage the accuracy and reliability of the findings. Most clients do not ask for sample dispositions or understand the different definitions of response rates. And, when the clients don't worry about survey methodology, neither do many of those conducting their research. Nobody knows how much unreliable or positively misleading research is conducted and used. My guess is that it is a lot.

DIFFERENT TYPES OF MARKETING RESEARCH FIRMS

There are many different types of marketing research companies, which serve their clients in very different ways. Some companies fall into several of these categories, which include:

1 Very large companies that collect data from panels and slice, dice and sell their data to anyone who will pay for it. Nielsen, IMS and JD Power are probably the best known of these companies.
2 Companies that specialize in data collection mostly using telephone field work or online methodologies. Many of these companies sell their services to other marketing research companies as well as to end-users.
3 Companies that specialize in work for one or more industries. These include some very large companies, such as IMS (pharmaceuticals) and Nielsen (television ratings), as well as medium size and smaller firms such as Greenwich Research (for the banking industry and Wall Street).
4 Companies with 'branded products' such as Millward Brown's advertising research services

or Research International's Micro Test (sales forecasting) and Locator (brand perceptions and images).

5 Global research firms with operations in many different markets (and also many local or single-nation companies).

6 Companies with highly regarded consulting skills who are able to charge premium prices because their judgment and advice are seen to be superior. Often these companies have been led by people with personal relationships with very senior corporate executives. Specialist industry expertise is usually required. Personal charisma rather than corporate competency sometimes distinguishes these companies.

7 Companies (including several of the types listed above) that specialize in advanced statistical techniques and use not only their own survey data but which also 'integrate' (a fashionable word) both proprietary and secondary data from different sources.

THE FUTURE OF MARKETING RESEARCH

Sensible futurists often remind us that we cannot really predict the future, and that 'those who live by the crystal ball often wind up eating ground glass'; Sam Goldwyn told us never to make forecasts, 'especially about the future'; Goose Gossage, the baseball pitcher, allegedly said that 'the future looks a lot like the present, only longer.' We also know that the only certainty is uncertainty and more change. But marketing research is changing, and will continue to do so, so we need to think about the industry's future.

Over the next decade, marketing research will, I believe, change at an ever-increasing pace. However, the changes that will revolutionize our industry will not be increases in knowledge but in the creative use of new technologies, especially the Internet. Jack Honomichl (2000, p. 625), the Boswell (or the Theodore White?) of the marketing research industry has written that all of the following trends will continue:

- More exacting and continuous measurement of human behavior enabled by recent and continuing technological innovations;

- concentration of power, with approximately 25 research companies controlling two-thirds of all research around the world;
- broadening the scope of research, with an emphasis on information that includes MIS/IT, CSM, custom research, business intelligence, and syndicated data services;
- change in leadership, with the prime movers of the industry being technocrats and professional managers rather than researchers themselves; and
- less public cooperation.

I think we can build on Honomichl's predictions, with a fair degree of certainty to include the following:

1 To achieve acceptably high response rates for probability sampling, it will be increasingly necessary to pay substantial incentives to respondents.

2 Pure probability sampling with acceptable response rates will therefore become extremely expensive and, for most research buyers, unaffordable.

3 There will therefore be much research into the biases in (the great majority of) other sampling methods, including 'volunteer' panels and samples, quota sampling, Internet-based samples of willing, self-selected respondents, and quasi-probability sampling with low response rates.

4 This research will show that some non-probability methods work much better than others, that some weighting schemes can reduce many but not all of the biases in our data, and that different weighting schemes will be needed depending on the variables that are being studied.

5 The use of online research will continue to grow rapidly.

6 We will therefore stop debating the biases involved (and the weighting schemes needed) in Internet research as such, and think of the Internet as just another interviewing method, with even more variability in methods, biases, and value, than other data collection methods.

7 The low cost of data collection on the Internet will make it much easier and more affordable for us to test many more experimental designs and to do much more research into different sampling, weighting, question order and question wording issues.

8 Because of the Internet's reach and efficiency, we will often survey much larger samples—10 or

20,000 and more—than we could afford to think of surveying by telephone or in-person.

9 There will be a huge increase in 'narrowcast' research focused on very small sub-segments of the population that are identified by massive screening of very large Internet panels and databases, such as purchasers of specific products or people with particular diseases.

10 It will be common for data collection on the Internet to be conducted in a fraction of the time now needed to conduct large telephone or in-person surveys.

11 The use of video and other visual stimuli in Internet-based research will be commonplace to test new products, packaging, on-line and traditional advertising, in people's homes and offices.

12 Large simultaneous multinational, multilingual surveys will become easier, more affordable and therefore much more common, using the Internet and instant translation systems.

13 Completely new, as yet unthought of, ways to conduct qualitative research will develop, taking advantage of the ability of the Internet to 'bring together' people—consumers, professionals, and corporate decision makers—from all over the world.

14 The growth of highly specialized panels will proliferate not only with important populations such as doctors, IT managers, architects, engineers, purchasing officers, and various types of corporate decision makers, but also with sub-segments of consumers such as owners of expensive cars, very frequent travelers or cancer patients.

15 While the use of the Internet will replace some traditional data collection methods, these will not die. We will still be using some in-person and telephone surveys in 2020. There will always be some things we will be able to do better that way.

16 Privacy will become a much more serious issue, with the need for the industry to protect the public not just from 'sugging' (selling under the guise of conducting research, a kind of commercial 'push polling') and spamming, but also to reassure respondents that they will not be annoyed or embarrassed because they volunteer to participate in surveys. Privacy protection legislation in other countries (later and to a lesser degree in America) will become much more restrictive.

While new research technologies and new, as yet unthought-of, applications will transform the research world, some things—

sadly—will look very much the same. All of the following look like pretty safe forecasts:

- Buyers and sellers of research will still run the gamut from the wonderful to the awful, from the knowledgeable to the ignorant, from the wise to the stupid, and from the sophisticated to the simplistic. And all too many buyers and users of research still won't know the difference.
- Large corporate buyers will continue to go through regular cycles of centralizing their internal marketing research functions, and then decentralizing them again.
- Large corporate buyers will repeat another historical cycle, building up and bringing in their own research talent, then downsizing and outsourcing many research functions, and then investing in their in-house research talent all over again—and so on ad infinitum.
- Marketing researchers will still bemoan their lack of clout and the inability of senior management to understand and make good use of their services.
- Many research buyers will still buy mainly on price and continue to get much poor quality research and unreliable data, on which they will then make bad decisions.
- Too many buyers will still use qualitative research to make judgments and decisions that should be made only with quantitative research.
- Many research buyers will still not make good use—or any use—of their research, because of the difficulties of getting large organizations to change (the 'aircraft carrier' effect).
- Many more research functions will be globalized, with multinational research companies buying in expertise from wherever it can be provided most cost-effectively—for example outsourcing programming to Bangalore or Manila.
- In spite of ever more and better electronic technology, we will still not have achieved the 'paperless office.'
- While modeling and forecasting will become ever more sophisticated—and, I hope, better—forecasting will always be an imprecise and risky business.

Jack Honomichl's forecasts include the concentration of power. This will be fueled by the capital-intensive nature of Internet-based research. But there will always be room for small upstarts with good ideas and minimal capital who will outsource data collection and other services. While the growth of Internet-based research will create a number of capital-intensive battleships—companies that make the investments in Internet panels, online databases of willing respondents ('volunteers') and in the hardware, software, and systems people necessary to be major players—there will also be plenty of opportunities for nimble and creative entrepreneurs to be the speedboats of the industry, pioneering new methods, developing new applications, and selling new services.

For many years, marketing researchers have been forecasting (and hoping) that they will become more consultants than just researchers, that they will interact with senior as opposed to middle managers, and that—as they become more valued for their judgment and their advice—they will be able to charge higher prices. But this may prove to be just wishful thinking.

REFERENCES

Cairncross, A. (n.d.). Quotation available in the *QB Quotations Book*. Retrieved February 13, 2007, from http://www.quotationsbook.com/.

Chakrapani, C. (Ed.). (2000). *Marketing research: State of the art perspectives*. Oxford: Elsevier Books.

Honomichl, J. (2000). Looking to the Future. In C. Chakrapani (Ed.), *Marketing research: State of the art perspectives* (pp. 625ff.). Oxford: Elsevier Books.

Inside Research (2006a). Newsletter, May issue.

Inside Research (2006b). Newsletter, September issue.

McDonald, C., & Vangelder, P. (Eds.). (1998). *The ESOMAR Handbook of marketing and opinion research*. Amsterdam: ESOMAR.

Ruskin, J. (n.d.). Quotation supposedly attributed to J. Ruskin. Quotation available from *Michael Moncur's (Cynical) Quotations*. Retrieved February 13, 2007, from http://quotationspage.com/quote/34145.html.

51

Social Indicators and the Quality of Life

John P. Robinson and Kenneth C. Land

Social indicators are measures of individual attitudes and other personal characteristics that can be used to evaluate individual, aggregated, and national circumstances and how they change over time. Research has been conducted for more than 40 years on the identification and measurement of appropriate social indicators, as well as work devoted to the assembly of time-series data for use in describing and explaining their relationship to human development at the individual and societal levels. This chapter summarizes the historical social indicators movement, including the recent rejuvenation of this area of research.

THE EMERGENCE OF SOCIAL INDICATORS RESEARCH

Ferriss (1988, p. 601) defines social indicators as statistical time series '... used to monitor the social system, helping to identify changes and to guide intervention to alter the course of social change.' The term *social indicators* emerged from the 1960s attempt by the American Academy of Arts and Sciences for the National Aeronautics and Space Administration to anticipate the consequences of the space program. Frustrated by the lack of sufficient data to detect such effects, the Academy project sought to develop a system of statistical and other evidence to anticipate social change. This term gained further momentum from doubts raised in Western industrial societies about economic growth as the major goal of societal progress. There was increasing doubt about whether 'more' should be equated with 'better,' when collective values such as freedom, justice, and the guarantee of natural conditions of life were ignored.

Bauer's (1966) book *Social Indicators* was perhaps the first explicit attempt to establish a 'system of social accounts' that would facilitate a cost–benefit analysis, beyond the market-related aspects of society already indexed by economists. The need for social indicators also was emphasized by public health initiatives conceived of as counterparts to the annual economic reports of governments and addressing major issues in an important area of social concern such as health and illness, social mobility, and alienation. Three decades earlier, Ogburn's (1933) 'Recent social trends' had been a path-breaking contribution to social reporting, although the increased interest in social indicators in the 1960s can also trace its roots to scattered collections of demographic data in Western societies during the seventeenth and eighteenth centuries.

The 1960s' enthusiasm for social indicators became sufficiently strong for Duncan (1969) to describe it as a Social Indicators *Movement*, one that led in the US to the National Science Foundation's support of a Social Science Research Council Center to coordinate indicators as part of a new methodology for the measurement of subjective well-being/quality of life (Campbell & Converse, 1972; Andrews & Withey, 1975, 1976; Campbell, Converse, & Rodgers, 1976). These included periodic sample surveys, like the annual National Opinion Research Center's General Social Survey (GSS), the first volume of the international journal *Social Indicators Research*, and the spread of social reporting to international agencies, such as the United States Nations and the Organization for Economic Cooperation and Development.

After momentum slowed greatly in the 1980s, the *quality-of-life (QOL) concept helped the indicator movement regain* widespread use, through numerous rankings based on well-being indexes of the 'best' places to live, to work, or to do business. The theoretical appeal of the QOL concept is partly due to the perceived importance of measuring individuals' subjective satisfaction with various life domains and with life as a whole. QOL became a concept that bridged marketing research with social indicators. Marketing had far-reaching impacts through its measures of consumer confidence and satisfaction and their impact on satisfaction with life. These attractions led to the mid-1990s' founding of the multi-disciplinary

International Society for Quality-of-Life Studies (see http://www.isqols.org). The great richness of available social data encouraged a return to the task of composite index construction, like (1) the comparisons of nations with respect to the overall quality of life in the *Human Development Index* (United Nations Development Programme, 2004); (2) in the United States, the *Fordham Index of Social Health* (Miringoff & Miringoff, 1999); and (3) the *Child Well-Being Index* developed by Land, Lamb, and Mustillo (2001).

Comprehensive national social reports in the tradition pioneered by Ogburn (1933) and by Olson (1969) clearly have faltered in the United States, but their key ideas of monitoring and forecasting are evident in subject-matter-specific publications, including *Science Indicators* (published by the National Science Foundation), *The Condition of Education* (published by the Department of Education), the *Report to the Nation on Crime and Justice* (published by the Department of Justice), and numerous Census Bureau publications. The Federal Interagency Forum on Child and Family Statistics has begun an annual publication on *America's Children: Key National Indicators of Well-Being*. In addition, numerous private research organizations, policy institutes, and scholars in the US continue to produce reports interpreting social trends.

In contrast, comprehensive social indicators compendia continue to be published in other countries. Examples include the *Datenreport* series published biennially in the Federal Republic of Germany, the *Social and Cultural Report* published biannually by the Social and Cultural Planning Office of The Netherlands, and *Australian Social Trends* published annually by the Australian Bureau of Statistics.[1]

Policy analysts distinguish various ways of affecting public policy, including *problem definition, policy choice and evaluation of alternatives,* and *program monitoring* (MacRae, 1985). However, policy analysts have invariably hoped to shape public policy as articulated by Land and Ferriss (2002). In the language of policy analysis, social indicators are 'target,' 'output' or 'criterion' variables, reflecting changes toward which some public program or project is directed.

TYPES OF SOCIAL INDICATORS

General types

Economist Mancur Olson, the principal author of 'Toward a social report,' characterized a social indicator as a '... statistic of direct normative interest which facilitates concise, comprehensive and balance judgments about the condition of major aspects of a society' (US Department of Health, Education, and Welfare, 1969, p. 97). For Olson, such an indicator is a direct measure of welfare and therefore this type can be called *policy, welfare, or criterion indicators.* If it changes in the 'right' direction, things have gotten better, or people are better off. By this definition, then, statistics on the number of doctors or police officers would not be social indicators, whereas figures on health or crime rates could be.

Life satisfaction and/or happiness indicators as a separate class of social indicators came from Campbell and Converse (1972) and Campbell *et al.* (1976), who monitored key social-psychological states like satisfaction, happiness, and life fulfillment in national in-person surveys. These largely methodological studies explored satisfaction with various aspects ('domains') of one's life, ranging from the highly specific (house, family, and the like) to the global (life-as-a-whole).

There remains the need to link these subjective ratings with objective conditions. Numerous studies have led to a better understanding of these relations (e.g., Cummins, Gullone, & Lau, 2002), even if few of the disputes have been resolved. Subjective QOL indicators may have both trait-like (i.e., a durable psychological condition that differs among individuals and contributes to stability over time and consistency across situations) and state-like (i.e., a condition that is reactive to situational differences) properties

(see, e.g., Stones & Hadjistavropoulos, 1995; Veenhoven, 1998). These debates are important, because if happiness/life satisfaction is only trait-like (that is, everyone has a fixed 'set point' of happiness that changes relatively little despite changes in the external environment), then it is unlikely to respond to economic and social policies designed to improve societies by creating the 'good life.'

With respect to state-like properties, Davis (1984) used accumulated GSS data to document the reaction of personal happiness responses to: (a) 'new money' (recent changes in respondents' financial status as opposed to current income level), (b) 'an old man/lady' (being married or having an intimate living partner), and (c) 'two's company' (a household size of two as compared to living alone or families of three or more). While other studies have identified additional factors, the relevance of intimate living conditions/family status almost always is replicated.

The connection of subjective well-being to income levels has been a particularly intriguing issue, following Easterlin's (1973) conclusion that income differences *between nations* predicted differences in happiness, but that income's association with happiness *within countries* was much weaker. This study has stimulated a large literature on the relationship of income to subjective well-being, as reviewed by Diener and Biswas-Diener (2002) and by Layard (2005). The topic has found its way into popular writings on personal financial philosophies, like Chatzky (2003) and Herper (2004).

Although *descriptive social indicators* may be more or less directly (causally) related to the well-being goals of public policies or programs and thus include policy or criterion indicators, they are not limited to such uses. For instance, in the area of health, descriptive indicators might include preventive indicators (such as the percentage of the population that does not smoke cigarettes), as well as criterion indicators, such as the number of days of activity limitations in the past month or an index of self-reported satisfaction with health. Land (1983) ordered these by their degrees of abstraction—from those requiring only one or two data series and little processing (e.g., an age-specific death rate) to those that involve more complicated processing into a single composite or summary index (e.g., years of life-expectancy at age x). At least in principle, these can be organized into demographic- or time-budget-based systems of social accounts.

Specific types

At least three types of indicators have been collected from national samples: objective, subjective, and time-related indicators. *Objective indicators* can be obtained from surveys, but most are not. Examples include unemployment rates, crime rates, years of life expectancy, health status indices such as the average number of 'healthy' days (or days without activity limitations) in the past month for a specific population, school enrollment rates, average achievement scores on a standardized test, and rates of voting in elections. More survey-derived series include consumer confidence, trust in government and crime victimization. Because they are more developed and familiar, these measures receive limited attention here.

Subjective measures of well-being, such as how happy or satisfied individuals are with their lives, are more tentative or experimental but are now receiving more attention. Pioneering studies in this tradition began in the 1950s, including 'Mental health in the metropolis' (Srole, Langner, Michael, Opler, & Rennie, 1962) and 'Americans view their mental health' (Gurin, Veroff, & Feld, 1960). One influential work during this early period was Bradburn and Caplovitz's (1965) 'Reports on happiness,' in which the authors argued that this ultimately subjective state was open to direct and reliable measurement with clear predictors and consequences. A major output from their study was the 'Affect Balance Scale,' a series of questions about positive and negative mood states over the previous two weeks; surprisingly, the positive and negative measures turned out to be essentially uncorrelated, rather than being at opposite ends of the same dimension (Bradburn, 1969).

A particularly ambitious survey effort was Cantril's (1967) *The Pattern of Human Concerns*, in which the author applied his innovative 'ladder' scale to samples from 14 countries around the world, one of the first international QOL efforts. Among his more striking findings was the very high ladder ratings in Cuba compared to other countries, such as the neighboring Dominican Republic, also at a very low level of economic development (a difference that still holds). Cantril's ladder scale was novel in its ability to collect both open-end qualitative data on respondent criteria for 'the good life,' in addition to quantitative ratings of how close respondents felt they were to reaching these criteria.

The late 1970s saw the first explicit attempts to develop nationally projectable subjective measures centered on life satisfaction, mainly at the Survey Research Center at the University of Michigan. Campbell *et al.* (1976) applied a basic 1 to 7 satisfaction scale to a variety of life aspects, while Andrews and Withey (1976) applied their 1 to 7 'delighted-terrible' scale to many of the same life domains. A major finding in the latter work was that older people were more satisfied with their lives but less happy in relation to younger people. Another 1970s' SRC survey focused on the sub-area of Quality of Employment (Quinn & Staines, 1997).

The second major 1970s' social indicator effort in the US, the General Social Survey, has been far more successful in providing long-term trend data on QOL variables. Moreover, they are readily and publicly available at www//sda.berkeley.edu for interactive secondary analysis. Table 51.1 focuses on 10 direct QOL measures in the GSS—of happiness, satisfaction with marriage, job and community, along with measures of trust in people and feeling rushed. The table shows relatively small but important social trends in the percentage expressing positive QOL responses since the first GSS surveys in the early 1970s. Somewhat larger declines (7 percentage points) are found in marital happiness than overall happiness (down 3 points) over the 30-year period.

Table 51.1   Trends and demographic correlates of 1973–2004 GSS QOL questions (% very happy, satisfied a very great deal 1 = Job; 2 = Family; 3 = City; 4 = Friend; 5 = Health; 6 = Hobby; 7 = Fin, can trust others or always rushed)

Year:	Happy	Happy marriage	Satisfaction (very great deal) with							Trust others	Rushed always
			1	2	3	4	5	6	7		
1972–74	35%	69%	49%	43%	22%	33%	28%	25%	32%	46%	23%*
1975–79	34	66	51	41	19	29	26	24	33	41	18*
1980–84	32	65	47	44	19	30	30	23	27	45	24
1985–89	31	61	46	40	17	29	25	22	30	39	32*
1990–94	31	62	45	41	17	32	24	23	28	36	35*
1995–99	31	63	47	na	na	na	na	na	29	36	30
2000–04	32	62	48	na	na	na	na	na	31	35	31
2004–1972	−3pts	−7	−1	(−2)	(−5)	(−1)	(−4)	(−2)	−1	−11	−8

CORRELATIONS WITH:

Birth factors

Gender (Female)	−01	05	00	−06	−03	−06	05	04	02	04	−04
Age (Older)	03	02	15	−03	22	03	−20	−03	−18	05	27
Race (White)	10	08	08	06	09	13	03	11	12	15	01

Status factors

Income (High)	20	07	15	22	09	14	21	16	26	13	−12
Education (High)	09	06	04	06	00	09	20	18	06	17	−18

Role factors

Married	18	na	13	29	13	06	01	03	11	09	03

Note: *University of Michigan or Maryland national surveys

There are minimal declines in the seven aspects of satisfaction until 1994 (when the time series ended), but notably for city and health satisfaction. Much larger declines are found for trust in people, down 11 points since the early 1970s. The only clear increase is for feeling 'always rushed,' up 8 to 13 points since the late 1970s in two Michigan national surveys. Since this latter finding can also be seen as a negative trend, Table 51.1 contains no evidence of any positive trend in these multiple subjective indicators—one that would mirror the clear economic gains in the US standard of living over that time period.

Correlations of these data with sociodemographics show minor gender differences, although men are slightly happier with their marriages, and women with their family life and friendships. Individuals with higher income, education and occupational status feel happier, are more satisfied with all seven aspects of life, and are more trusting of others. One drawback is they feel more rushed as well. Of the three status factors, income is clearly a more powerful predictor than education or occupation, and this conclusion holds after multivariate controls. In terms of demographic role factors, marriage tends to play a larger role than parenthood or employment. Married people are happier than formerly married or never married people, and they feel more positively about their family situations, jobs and communities as well. That is less true for friendships, hobbies and health. Married people trust others more, although they feel a little more rushed. More comprehensive reviews of QOL correlates can be found in Diener (1984) and Diener and Griffin (1982).

In addition to many QOL items in the GSS (for which Smith, 1992, constructed an interesting overall measure), several subjective indicator measures (mainly in the form of social psychological multi-item scales) are provided in Robinson, Shaver, and Wrights-man (1991), covering such concepts as alien-ation, internal locus of control, self-esteem, authoritarianism and androgeny. Robinson, Shaver, and Wrightsman (1999) expanded the list to include QOL-relevant scales of trust in government, tolerance, political efficacy and political knowledge. The latter volume also includes a review of relevant GSS trends on their items.

Increasing cooperation among social scien-tists in several countries permits international comparisons. Subjective QOL items have been asked regularly in the Eurobarometer surveys since 1973, in the World Value Study since 1980, and more recently, in the European Welfare Survey. The findings from these surveys (along with several comparative surveys of university students) have been conveniently archived in the World Database of Happiness (www1.eur.nl/fsw/happiness), which as of late 2005 contained results from more than 2700 general population surveys in 116 countries (15 of which have more than 20 years of trending) are available in Kalmijn and Veenhoven (2005).

The rank order for 68 nations between 1999 and 2002 shown in Table 51.2 was compiled from this archive and reflects some general country differences found in many such comparisons. It is first clear that high GDP 'Western' countries rate higher on the 0–10 scale (France being a notable exception) than lower GDP, Asian and former Iron Curtain countries. These ratings and the cultural factors behind them are skillfully reviewed in Diener and Tov (in press), who point to 0.58 to 0.84 correlations between GDP and happiness in the literature—noting at the same time that high GDP countries enjoy greater human rights, income equality, educational access and closer friendship and family ties.[2] With regard to money, however, studies show income and wealth having greater impact in poor societies, i.e., those with inadequate food and housing. Similarly, QOL ratings have been found to correlate higher with self-esteem in individualistic countries than in collectivistic countries, where social relationships play a more important role.

Counter to the impression that differences in QOL ratings have become stronger over the years, much as income differences have widened, Veenhoven (1999) finds they have become less variable within and between countries. A second body of impressive international QOL studies has been organized by Cummins (e.g., 1996, 2005), who has developed a 13-item International Well-being Index covering ratings of both personal and national well-being on 11-point scales. Their website identifies researcher connections with more than 40 countries, with translations of the Index into several languages. On a broader reporting level, over a decade ago reports from the multination project, 'Comparative Chart-ing of Social Change' produced similar data. In the case of Germany, Glatzer, Hondrich, Noll, Stier and Wörndl (1992) present data on 17 areas and 78 dimensions of change between 1960 and 1990. Eurostat (2004) published 'Living conditions in Europe' covering a broad range of indicators, much as Noll (2002) summarized trends on several indicators.

Time-based indicators: A newer source of indicator data comes in the form of national surveys, like the Americans' Use of Time project, that employ 'time diaries,' usually complete 24-hour accounts of what survey respondents did on the previous day (Szalai, 1966, 1972; Juster & Stafford, 1985; Robinson & Godbey, 1999). While the welfare or positive benefits of engaging in particular daily activities is not obvious, social observers seem to concur that increases in daily activities like child care, volunteering and other altruistic behaviors, and free time represent improvements in a person's or society's QOL, while increases in time spent on routine housework, repair activities and TV viewing are seen as less desirable.

Interestingly, these diary ratings of activ-ities differ significantly from the responses derived from survey questions. For example, respondents rated their diary work time about one point lower than when asked about their work in general, and the particular TV pro-grams they watched as one point higher than TV viewing in general. Nonetheless, there

Table 51.2 Life satisfaction in various nations (1999–2004)

Nation	Mean[a]	Nation	Mean	Nation	Mean	Nation	Mean
1. Puerto Rico	8.49	9. Finland	7.87	29. Indonesia	6.96	43. Slovakia	6.03	62. Pakistan	4.85
2. Denmark	8.24	10. Netherlands	7.85	30. Nigeria	6.87	44. Estonia	5.93	63. Belarus	4.81
3. Malta	8.21	11. Canada	7.85	31. Croatia	6.68	45. Hungary	5.80	64. Russia	4.56
4. Ireland	8.20	12. Luxembourg	7.81	32. Greece	6.67	46. Bosnia-Herzegovina	5.77	65. Ukraine	4.56
5. Mexico	8.14	13. USA	7.66	33. Philippines	6.65	47. Bangladesh	5.77	66. Moldova	4.56
6. Iceland	8.05	14. Sweden	7.64	34. China	6.53	48. Algeria	5.67	67. Zimbabwe	3.95
7. Austria	8.03	15. Venezuela	7.52	35. Vietnam	6.52	49. Uganda	5.65	68. Tanzania	3.87
8. Northern Ireland	8.00	16. El Salvador	7.50	36. Japan	6.48	50. Montenegro	5.64		
		17. Belgium	7.43	37. Peru	6.44	51. Turkey	5.62		
		18. Germany	7.42	38. Iran	6.38	52. Serbia	5.62		
		19. Great Britain	7.40	39. South Africa	6.31	53. Jordan	5.60		
		20. Argentina	7.30	40. South Korea	6.21	54. Bulgaria	5.50		
		21. Singapore	7.24	41. Poland	6.20	55. Egypt	5.36		
		22. Italy	7.17	42. Morocco	6.06	56. Latvia	5.27		
		23. Chile	7.12			57. Romania	5.23		
		24. Spain	7.09			58. Lithuania	5.20		
		25. Czech Republic	7.06			59. Albania	5.17		
		26. Portugal	7.04			60. India	5.14		
		27. Israel	7.03			61. Macedonia	5.12		
		28. France	7.01						

Note: [a] Standardized measure as described on worlddatabankofhappiness.eur.nl was much more time-frame convergence on other activities, such as ratings of child care and socializing being toward the most enjoyable end of the scale vs. housework and repair activities at the bottom. More recently, Kahneman and his colleagues (2004) have published important new arguments about the need for approaching QOL national measurement using such subjective diary ratings.

Csikszentmihalyi (1990) and his colleagues have devised a technique called the *experience sampling method* (ESM) to collect even more precise time-relevant data on daily activities. This is done at particular moments by collecting a variety of QOL measures when randomly programmed ESM beepers go off at some 15 to 30 points during the day. A limitation of the technique is that it also has only been used with convenience samples with limited generalizability, and it is unlikely to achieve high cooperation rates from respondents in more typical survey settings.

Internationally, time-diary data are now being collected for social accounting purposes in more than 30 other countries, and some of them have collected subjective data on other aspects of daily living, such as for whom each activity was done, the felt time pressure during the activity, and the output from the activity. Since in most of these countries, diary data are collected by central statistical offices that shy away from subjective data (as in the massive new diary collection by the US Census Bureau), few such ratings are available from large enough or generalizable samples to be used for national social accounts.

At the same time, it could be taken as encouraging that the trends in US diary hours do follow a generally hedonistic direction, in that Robinson and Godbey (1999) find people report spending increased time on activities they find more enjoyable in Table 51.3 (like free time activities) and less time on the things they don't like (especially housework). Along the same lines, Bianchi, Robinson and Milkie (2006) report increased time spent on child care, especially interactive or 'fun'

activities with one's child. Moreover, these same long-term *time* trends are found in other countries as well (Bittman, 1998; Gershuny, 2001, 2003). At the same time, there has been no increase in the two highly enjoyable activities of eating and sleeping. Moreover, there may be declines in the major social capital activity of visiting, one of the more popular activities in Table 51.3.

SUMMARY AND CONCLUSIONS

After a notable slowdown in government and scholarly activity related to social indicators in the 1980s, a vibrant and visible international collection of scholars, publications and archives has evolved to share and discuss findings about the public's quality of life in different conditions, countries and historical settings. It is quite clear that these resources and efforts do provide a needed counterbalance to time-series data on 'objective' measures, which have shown considerable improvement in people's economic and political circumstances over the last half-century. It is also clear that more work is needed to explain the gap between external conditions that might lead one to expect closer correspondences between 'objective improvements' (like more money or better health), and what is being detected by subjective QOL measures. While there are some indications that people are spending more time on activities they enjoy more, other ways of measuring QOL in 'real time' face significant challenges in scientific acceptance.

One of the major unresolved issues in this research is the relation between money and happiness. Several pieces of evidence noted above, such as the Table 51.1 correlation with income being about as high as for marital status, the higher Table 51.2 ratings in higher GDP countries, and Davis's (1984) finding of the importance of 'new money,' challenge the conclusion about money not 'buying' happiness. This should ensure that there will be lively debates about what social indicators will be showing in the decades ahead.

Table 51.3   Enjoyment ratings from different diary activities (1985 and 1975 national data, from Robinson & Godbey, 1999, Appendix O)

10-Enjoy a great deal (1985 diary average = 7.0)	1975 General (average = 6.8)
9.3 Sex	
9.2 Play sports	
8.7 Playing/reading with children	8.9 Child care
8.5 Church, religion	
8.5 Sleep	8.6 Play with children
8.2 Meals away	8.0 Socializing, talking
8.2 Socialize, visit others	8.0 Work
8.0 Socialize with family	
8.0 Work breaks	
7.9 Reading	7.5 Sleep
7.8 Meals at home	7.4 Eating
7.8 TV	7.4 Washing, dressing
7.4 Hobbies, crafts	7.3 Church, religion
7.2 Exercise	7.0 Reading
7.2 Baby care	
7.2 Organizations	
7.0 Work	
7.0 Bathing	
6.6 Cooking	6.8 Hobbies
6.6 Other shopping	6.5 Play sports
6.4 Child care	6.5 Cultural events
6.4 Help others	6.2 Cooking
6.3 Work commute	
6.1 Dressing	
5.8 Other housework	5.9 TV
5.5 Grocery shopping	
5.5 Home repairs	5.1 Home repairs
5.2 Pay bills, financial etc.	5.0 Organizations
5.0 Yardwork	
4.9 Clean house	4.6 Grocery shopping
4.9 Laundry	4.3 Other shopping
4.8 Health care, doctor	4.2 Clean house
4.7 Car repair	

0-DISLIKE A GREAT DEAL

NOTES

1 Citations and summary reviews can be found in the newsletter, *SINET: Social Indicators Network News* (http://www.soc.duke.edu/resources/sinet/index.html).

2 Inglehart and Klingeman (2000) found no relation between democracy and QOL after GDP was controlled for.

REFERENCES

Andrews, F., & Withey, S. B. (1975). *Social indicators of well-being in America: the development and measurement of perceptual indicators.* Ann Arbor, Michigan: Institute for Social Research, the University of Michigan.

Andrews, F., & Withey, S. B. (1976). *Social indicators of well being: American's perceptions of life quality.* New York: Plenum.

Bauer, R. A. (Ed.). (1966). *Social indicators.* Cambridge, Mass.: MIT Press.

Bianchi, S., Robinson, J., & Milkie, M. (2006). *Changing rhythms of American family life.* New York: Russell Sage Foundation.

Bittman, M. (1998). The land of the lost long weekend? Trends in free time among working age Australians, 1974–1992. *Society and Leisure, 21,* 352–379.

Bradburn, N. (1969). *The structure of psychological well-being.* Chicago: Aldine.

Bradburn, N., & Caplovitz, D. (1965). *Reports on happiness: a pilot study of behavior related to mental health.* Chicago: Aldine.

Campbell, A., & Converse, P. E. (1972). *The human meaning of social change.* New York: Russell Sage.

Campbell, A., Converse, P. E., & Rodgers, W. L. (1976). *The quality of American life: Perceptions, evaluations, and satisfactions.* New York: Russell Sage Foundation.

Cantril, H. (1967). *The pattern of human concerns.* New Brunswick, NJ: Rutgers University Press.

Chatzky, J. (2003). *You don't have to be rich: Comfort, happiness, and financial security on your own terms.* London: Penguin Books Ltd.

Cummins, R. (1996). The domains of life satisfaction: An attempt to order chaos. *Social Indicators Research, 38,* 303–328.

Cummins, R. (2005). *The Australian Unity Wellbeing Index: 2004 Update.* Paper presented at the 6th Australian Conference on Quality of Life, The Australian Centre on Quality of Life, Deakin University, Australia.

Cummins, R., Gullone, E., & Lau, A. (2002). A model of subjective well-being homeostasis: The role of personality. In E. Gullone & R. Cummins (Eds.), *The universality of subjective wellbeing indicators* (pp. 7–46). Dordrecht, The Netherlands: Kluwer Academic Publishers.

Csikszentmihalyi, M. (1990). *Flow: the psychology of optimal experience.* New York: Harper-Collins.

Davis, J. A. (1984). New money, an old man/lady and 'Two's Company' subjective welfare in the NORC General Social Survey. *Social Indicators Research, 15,* 319–351.

Diener, E. (1984). Subjective well-being. *Psychological Bulletin, 95,* 542–575.

Diener, E., & Griffin, S. (1982). *Subjective well-being: Happiness, life, satisfaction, and morale—Comprehensive bibliography.* Champaign: University of Illinois, Department of Psychology.

Diener, E., & Biswas-Diener, R. (2002). Will money increase subjective well-being? A literature review and guide to needed research. *Social Indicators Research, 57,* 119–169.

Diener, E., & Tov, J. (in press). Culture and subjective well-being. In S. Kitayama & D. Cohen (Eds.), *Handbook of Cultural Psychology.* New York: Guilford.

Duncan, O. D. (1969). *Toward social reporting: Next steps.* New York: Russell Sage Foundation.

Easterlin, R. (1973). Does money buy happiness? *The Public Interest, 30,* 3–10.

Eurostat (2004). *Living conditions in Europe 2003.* Luxembourg: Office of European Communities.

Ferriss, A. L. (1988). The uses of social indicators. *Social Forces, 66,* 601–617.

Gershuny, J. (2001). *Cross-national changes in time-use: some sociological (hi)stories re-examined.* Ben-Gurion University: University of Essex.

Gershuny, J. (2003). *Time use, gender, and public policy regimes.* Oxford University Press.

Glatzer, W., Hondrich, K.-O., Noll, H. H., Stier, K., & Wörndl, B. (1992). *Recent social trends in West Germany, 1960–1990.* Frankfurt am Main: Campus Verlag.

Gurin, G., Veroff, J., & Feld, S. (1960). *Americans view their mental health.* New York: Basic.

Herper, M. (2004, September 21). Money won't buy you happiness. *Forbes,* Retrieved January 5, 2007, from http://www.forbes.com/work/2004/09/21/cx_mh_0921happiness.html.

Inglehart, R., & Klingeman, H. (2000). Genes, culture, democracy and happiness. In E. Diener & E. Suh (Eds.), *Culture and subjective well-being* (pp. 165–183). Cambridge, MA: MIT Press.

Juster, T., & Stafford, F. (1985). *Time, goods, and well-being.* Ann Arbor, Mich.: Survey Research Center, Institute for Social Research, University of Michigan.

Kahneman, D., Krueger, A. B., Schkade, D. A., Schwarz, N., & Stone, A. A. (2004). A survey method for characterizing daily life experience: The day reconstruction method. *Science, 306,* 1776–1780.

Kalmijn, W., & Veenhoven, R. (2005). Measuring inequality of happiness in nations: In search for proper statistics. *Journal of Happiness Studies, 6,* 357–396.

Land, K. C. (1983). Social indicators. *Annual Review of Sociology, 9,* 1–26.

Land, K., Lamb, V. L., & Mustillo, S. K. (2001). Child and youth well-being in the United States, 1975–1998: Some findings from a new index. *Social Indicators Research, 56,* 241–320.

Land, K., & Ferriss, A. L. (2002). Conceptual models for the development and use of social indicators. In W. Glatzer, R. Habich, & K. U. Mayer (Eds.), *Sozialer Wandel und gesellschaftliche Dauerbeobachtung* (pp. 337–352). Opladen: Leske+Budrich.

Layard, P. (2005). *Happiness: lessons from a new science.* New York: Penguin Press.

MacRae, D., Jr. (1985). *Policy indicators: Links between social science and public policy.* Chapel Hill: University of North Carolina Press.

Miringoff, M. L., & Miringoff, M. L. (1999). *The social health of the nation: How America is really doing.* New York: Oxford University Press.

Noll, H.-H. (2002). Towards a European system of social indicators: theoretical framework and system architecture. *Social Indicators Research, 58*, 47–87.

Ogburn, W. (President's Research Committee on Social Trends). (1933). *Recent trends in the United States.* New York: McGraw-Hill.

Olson, M. (1969). *Toward a social report.* Washington, DC: U.S. Government Printing Office.

Quinn, R., & Staines, G. (1997). *The 1977 quality of employment survey: descriptive statistics, with comparison data from the 1969–1970 and the 1972–1973 surveys.* Ann Arbor: Survey Research Center, Institute for Social Research, University of Michigan.

Robinson, J., & Godbey, G. (1999). *Time for life: the surprising ways Americans use their time.* State College, PA: Penn State Press.

Robinson, J., Shaver, P., & Wrightsman, L. (1991). *Measures of personality and social psychological attitudes.* San Diego: Academic Press.

Robinson, J., Shaver, P., & Wrightsman, L. (1999). *Measures of political attitudes.* San Diego: Academic Press.

Smith, T. W. (1992). *Troubles in America: A study of negative life events across time and sub-groups.* (GSS Topical Report No. 40). Chicago.

Srole, L., Langner, I. S., Michael, S. T., Opler, M. K., & Rennie, I. A. C. (1962). *Mental health in the metropolis: The midtown Manhattan study.* New York: McGraw-Hill.

Stones, M. J., & Hadjistavropoulos, T. (1995). Happiness has trait-like and state-like properties: A reply. *Social Indicators Research, 36*, 129–144.

Szalai, A. (1966). Trends in comparative time budget research. *American Behavioral Scientist, 29*, 3–8.

Szalai, A. (1972). *The use of time: Daily activities of urban and suburban populations in twelve countries.* Mouton: The Hague.

United Nations Development Programme (2004). *Human development report 2004.* New York: Oxford University Press.

U.S. Department of Health, Education, and Welfare. (1969). *Toward a social report.* Washington, D.C.: U.S. Government Printing Office.

Veenhoven, R. (1998). Two state-trait discussions on happiness. *Social Indicators Research, 43*, 211–225.

Veenhoven, R. (1999). Quality-of-life in individualistic society. *Social Indicators Research, 48*, 157–186.

52

Assessing Long-Term Value Changes in Societies

Ottar Hellevik

In public opinion research, interest is often focused on the topics of the day. Opinion change is not always a relevant concern, and long-term trends receive even less attention. Single results will, however, become more interesting if they can be seen in relation to a wider framework of changing values and attitudes in society. This chapter deals with how to collect and analyze survey data to assess long-term trends in public opinion.

VALUES IN PUBLIC OPINION RESEARCH

Since the pioneering voter study *The People's Choice* (Lazarsfeld, Berelson, & Gaudet, 1944), social background variables like gender, age, education, and occupation have played a central role in survey analyses of political behavior. Subsequent electoral studies like *The American Voter* (Campbell, Converse, Miller, & Stokes, 1960) used attitudes as important explanatory variables. More recently, Inglehart in *The Silent*

Revolution (1977) explained the growth of new political movements and parties by changes in values. In the causal chain from social characteristics to behavior, values and attitudes have the role of intervening variables, with values as the prior variable and a possible cause of variation in attitudes.

The concept of values is used within several social science disciplines with varying content (Hitlin & Piliavin, 2004). An early definition often cited is the one by Kluckhohn (1951, p. 395): 'A value is a conception, explicit or implicit, distinctive of an individual or characteristic of a group, of the *desirable*, which influences the selection from available modes, means, and ends of action.' Rokeach, pioneering the use of values in survey research (1968), defined values as 'enduring beliefs that a specific mode of conduct is personally or socially preferable to an opposite or converse mode of conduct or end-state of existence' (1973, p. 5). According to Schwartz (1992), values are cognitive representations of three universal human requirements: biologically based organism needs, social interactional requirements for interpersonal coordination, and social institutional demands for group welfare and survival.

Attitudes play a central role in studies of public opinion. The concept refers to favorable or unfavorable evaluations of an object (Eagly & Chaiken, 1993). According to Rokeach (1970), an attitude is an organization of three different kinds of beliefs relating to an object: *descriptive* (regarding the actual properties of the object), *prescriptive* (regarding the ideal properties of such an object), and *evaluative* (positive, neutral or negative emotions, predisposing one for certain modes of action towards the object), resulting from how well the actual properties are experienced to correspond to the ideal ones.

Values are more abstract and general conceptions of ideals affecting prescriptive beliefs for a range of concrete objects. They are also considered more stable, developed during adolescence and remaining relatively unaltered during the rest of a person's life (Mannheim, 1952; Inglehart, 1977, 1990). This implies that aggregate value change will primarily be the result of generational replacement, and accordingly usually gradual and modest in size within short time spans. Attitudes are directly affected by the impact of new experiences and information on their descriptive component, and will therefore be more volatile and susceptible to short-term changes.

Like social background variables, values are general in nature and restricted in number. But while the former constitute a relatively standardized set of explanatory variables included in most opinion surveys, a similar consensus has not yet been reached with regard to values (Hitlin & Piliavin, 2004). In some studies just a single value dimension is used, as exemplified by Inglehart's materialism–postmaterialism index (Inglehart, 1977, 1990). Another case is the left-right self-placement scale used in numerous surveys (Knutsen, 1998; Noelle-Neumann, 1998). More ambitious efforts to capture the entire value set of individuals have been made by Rokeach (1973) and Schwartz, 1992; Schwartz *et al.*, 2001.

Inglehart's work (1977, 1990, 1997; Inglehart & Baker, 2000) prominently illustrates the increasingly central role values play in survey analyses. His index of materialism–postmaterialism has been included in numerous surveys in a lot of countries. A materialist value orientation emphasizes economic and physical security, while a postmaterialist gives higher priority to nonmaterial needs, such as a sense of community and the quality of life. His standard measure is a ranking of four alternatives. A respondent ranking 'Maintain order in the nation' and 'Fight rising prices' as the top two, is classified as a materialist, while ranking 'Protect freedom of speech' and 'Give people more say in the decisions of the government' on top makes one a postmaterialist.

Flanagan has proposed two alternative dimensions, called authoritarian–libertarian and materialism–non-materialism. Two sub-dimensions of the authoritarian–libertarian dimension are strong versus weak social and moral constraints on the self-actualization of the members of a society (1982a).

A comprehensive instrument for measuring values has been developed by Schwartz (1992, 1994). His main dimensions are openness to change versus conservation, and self-enhancement versus self-transcendence. Within the space defined by these two orthogonal dimensions, 10 motivational types of values are located: stimulation and self-direction at the openness to change pole, universalism and benevolence at the self-transcendence pole, conformity, tradition and security at the conservation pole, and finally power, achievement and hedonism near the self-enhancement pole.

A series of extensive value surveys in Norway (Hellevik, 1993, 2002) supports these descriptions of value dimensions and shows how they are related. A factor analysis of 25 value indexes, each made up of two or more agree-disagree propositions, found that the most important value dimension contrasts those who are positive to technological innovations, gender equality, risk taking, spontaneity, and urban life, to those who believe in established traditions, religion, authority, conformity, frugality, respect for law and order. The terms 'modern' versus 'traditional' value orientation or 'change oriented' versus 'stability oriented' have been used to characterize this value dimension.

The second dimension has been termed 'materialistic' versus 'idealistic,' or 'outer' versus 'inner-oriented.' On one side are people valuing economic growth, material possessions and consumption, who put their own desires above concern for other people. On the other side are those who value spirituality, creativity, close interpersonal relations, health, and the environment.

The two value dimensions are independent (orthogonal), defining a two-dimensional cultural space as shown in Figure 52.1. The average on the two axes for those classified as postmaterialists according to Inglehart's standard measure falls in the upper right quadrant of modern idealists, while his materialists are located in the lower left

quadrant of traditional materialists (Hellevik, 1993). The materialist–postmaterialist dimension of Inglehart thus corresponds to the main diagonal in Figure 52.1.

The indicators used by Flanagan (1982a, 1982b) suggest that his dimensions resemble the two axes of Figure 52.1. This is particularly striking when one looks at his two sub-dimensions. The first, degree of social constraints, opposing authority and conformity to autonomy and independence, clearly corresponds to the main diagonal of Figure 52.1 and Inglehart's materialism–postmaterialism dimension. The second corresponds to the bi-diagonal, with, in Flanagan's words, austerity, piety and self-discipline in the lower right corner and self-indulgence, secularism and permissiveness in the upper left.

Finally the dimensions and values discussed by Schwartz (1992, 1994) also clearly resemble the axes of Figure 52.1.

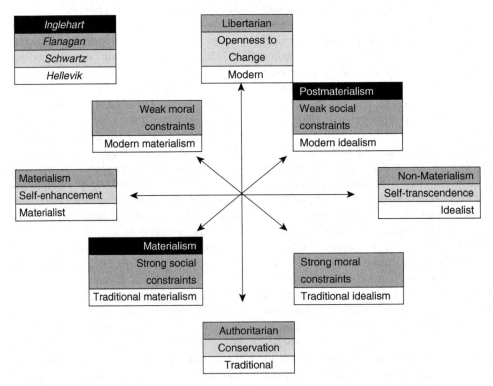

Figure 52.1   Dimensions of value orientation as discussed by Inglehart, Flanagan, Schwartz and Hellevik

This suggests that there is a convergence in the results of value research in post-industrial societies. Allowing for variations in which values are included, how they are measured and how the data are analyzed, the resulting value dimensions seem to constitute axes and diagonals within the same cultural space.

One value dimension often included in analyses of political behavior is the left–right or radical–conservative dimension. In the Norwegian data, it appears as third in importance (Hellevik, 1993). Combined with the first two dimensions of Figure 52.1, we get a three-dimensional cultural space. Including the left–right dimension in the analysis is important when explaining voting or other political phenomena, but it is of less consequence in many other areas.

THEORIES OF VALUE CHANGE

What long-term trends of value change can be expected in societies? According to Inglehart, values reflect the conditions that prevailed during an individual's pre-adult years, more specifically, whether basic needs for physical and economic security were satisfied or not. When they are not met, the individual for the rest of his or her life will be preoccupied with such concerns. Increasing prosperity, giving the new generations a feeling of economic security during their formative years, should produce a shift for the population as a whole along the main diagonal in Figure 52.1, with a growing number of postmaterialists and a declining number of materialists.

Flanagan's discussion suggests a movement along the vertical axis of Figure 52.1, from authoritarian to libertarian values, as the increasing economic surplus of society permits a relaxation of moral and social constraints on activities of its members. He considers the materialism dimension less interesting in the context of cultural change (Flanagan, 1982b).

While Inglehart has presented ample empirical evidence in support of his theory from analyses of longitudinal data for a lot of countries in the 1970s and 1980s, the trend at the end of the century seems to follow the bi- rather than the main diagonal in Figure 52.1, moving towards a new kind of pleasure seeking materialism (Hellevik, 2002). For many families, an improving economy has meant moving from a state of material security during adolescence to one of affluence and immediate gratification of desires. This may have led to increased rather than decreased interest in, and dependence on, possessions and consumption among the young.

BASIC PROCESSES OF CHANGE

There are two basic processes leading to change over time in value distributions for the population as a whole. We have trends originating from the *exchange of individuals* between time one and time two, and trends due to *changing characteristics* for individuals who are present at both points.

With regard to the exchange of individuals, one may further distinguish between generational replacement and migration. These processes will affect the distribution of values and attitudes in a population more strongly the more those entering differ from those leaving, and the larger the share of the population involved in the exchange. For most societies, generational replacement is the dominant source of exchange of individuals. The set of relatively permanent differences in characteristics between pairs of birth cohorts may be called generational or cohort effects.

With regard to individual changes, a distinction can be made between life cycle effects and period effects. The first refers to a regular pattern of changing characteristics common to most individuals during the course of their lifespan, caused by such factors as biological and psychological aging, or changing roles in family and work life. Life cycle effects are differences between individuals at two specific stages of their life cycles. A period effect is a difference between two points in time caused by historical events affecting most members of a population.

The observation of current large differences in values and attitudes between age groups indicates a potential for future change in population distributions. If these differences reflect life cycle effects, however, only minor changes due to the usually modest variations over time in the sizes of age groups will result. The effect of generational replacement is canceled out by individuals changing in the direction of values and attitudes typical of the old. But when the age differences reflect generational effects, cohort replacement will produce increasingly larger changes in population distributions as time passes. This is the levels paradox of change: individual stability may lead to aggregate change, while individual change may result in aggregate stability.

DATA ON CHANGE

The three main approaches to collecting data on change in public opinion research are panel, retrospective and time series studies.

Panel data are collected by interviewing the same sample of respondents at two or more different points in time, showing individual as well as aggregate change (Kasprzyk, Duncan, Kalton, & Singh, 1989, → *Panel Surveys*). Its use in public opinion research is restricted, for a variety of reasons. The method is more expensive than regular surveys due to the extra efforts needed to reach the members of the original sample. It is time consuming if one wishes to study long-term trends, and this design can have problems of sample mortality and panel effects—the influence of repeated interviewing on the respondents.

One possible panel effect is heightened awareness or interest leading to changes in a person's attitudes or behavior, for instance increased participation in elections. Or the effect may be the opposite, a 'freezing' of attitudes caused by having expressed them to the interviewer in a prior wave. 'This freezing may occur when the respondent perceives the interview response to be a sort of public commitment to a position, or when the respondent in a panel survey feels some pressure to be consistent across interviews' (Bridge *et al.*, 1977, p. 57). In relation to

voting, such a panel effect would lead to underestimating the extent of last minute swings in support for a party. Although freezing is often mentioned as a disadvantage of panels, there is little evidence of such an effect according to Waterton and Lievesley (1989). When the time elapsed between the interviews is not years or months but weeks or days, however, the effect may be stronger (Holt, 1989).

Retrospective data are collected by asking a single sample about past as well as present opinions, beliefs, or behaviors in the same interview. The researcher gets instant and inexpensive access to individual level trend data, without problems with regard to comparability of samples or interview methods as in a time series, or the risk of panel effects. It may even be the only approach possible when data is lacking for a prior period of particular interest. The retrospective method has, for instance, been used to study changes in happiness for periods where time series data do not exist, as in analyses of the development in Russia before and after the collapse of the Soviet Union (Saris & Andreenkova, 2001; Veenhoven, 2001). In panels, retrospective questions are used to get information on events in the periods between interviews.

Another reason for using the retrospective approach is economy: the cost compared to a panel will be much lower. Such properties contribute to the appeal of using recall questions in the study of change. But the retrospective approach is faced with a serious methodological problem of its own: the possibility of recall errors.

The problems respondents have in remembering earlier behavior correctly, and even more so attitudes or sentiments, are well known in survey research (Schwarz & Sudman, 1994; Dex 1995). A rich data source for documenting recall error is provided by the question on party vote in prior elections, regularly asked in surveys between elections in order to study change or to use as a weighting variable. In the months immediately after an election, the sample distribution for vote in the prior election usually reflects the outcome quite well. But then the results for some parties start to deviate more and more from the election result, as they gain or lose support among the voters at present. This is the result of a tendency for voters who have changed their party preference to project their present party as their vote in the prior election, thus appearing as stable instead of as party switchers.

Such a tendency towards consistency has been documented by panel studies comparing answers given in a prior interview with answers to a recall question asked at a later point in time. The results demonstrate that political recall is biased in favor of a person's current political views (Markus, 1986).

In a study of trends in feelings of happiness, Hagerty (2003) suggested that retrospective data are preferable to time series data. But when information on even such concrete and highly focused events as a vote in elections is prone to recall errors, even over short time spans, the problem will be all the more serious when respondents are asked to recall an affective state of mind much further back in the past. Instead of using such answers as factual information on past levels of happiness, they should be seen as indicators of how the respondents perceive changes in their life situation (Easterlin, 2002).

Time series data are collected by putting the same questions to different samples at different points in time. This is the approach most commonly used to study trends in public opinion research, and increasingly so as the data archives expand their holdings of surveys and make them more easily accessible. Several cross-national databases providing opportunities for trend analyses of values and attitudes exist. Among the most well known are the Eurobarometer (first survey in 1970, twice a year since 1974), the European Values Study (EVS, waves approximately every tenth year since 1981), the World Values Survey (WVS, first wave in 1981, fourth around 2000), and the International Social Survey Programme (ISSP, started in 1985). Among the earliest national time series surveys are the National Election Studies and the General Social

Survey in the US (the NES and the GSS, from 1952 and 1972 respectively), the ALLBUS in Germany (from 1980) and British Social Attitudes survey (BSA, from in 1983). Similar systematically repeated surveys are available in many countries for shorter or longer periods of time. Information, and in many cases access to the data, is provided on the Internet (see for instance the site of the Eurobarometer, where also links to other archives are given: www.gesis.org/en/data_service/eurobarometer) (→ *International Comparative Surveys: Their Purpose, Content and Methodological Challenges*).

Time series data have their limitations, however. Only change on an aggregate level is captured, and not all the individual shifts adding up to the trend for the population as a whole. Usually, longitudinal data for individuals (panel or retrospective) will show that the proportion of individuals who have changed (gross change) far exceeds the resulting aggregate change (net change). With regard to party preference, for instance, voter movements between pairs of parties usually go in both directions, canceling each other out. The result may be stability on the aggregate level concealing substantial changes on the individual level.

Researchers must therefore take care not to draw unwarranted conclusions from time series data with regard to the behavior of individuals. For many purposes, however, interest is focused on changes for the population as a whole. It is, for instance, the trends in aggregate distributions for party preference or opinions about elected leaders that have political significance.

Finding relevant historical time series in a data archive has the advantage that the analysis of change may start right away, without having to wait for future data collection. One must, however, carefully consider the comparability of the surveys with regard to question wording, sampling, or interview method. Any methodological differences may give rise to artificial trends, which may be hard to distinguish from trends reflecting real changes in society.

It is easy to see that variations in question wording or response format may affect the results. Even identical questions do not always guarantee comparability. The understanding of the words used may change over time, as illustrated by '... an item asked by Gallup (Which American city do you think has the gayest night life?). Today presumably San Francisco would finish well above its 5th place position in 1954' (Smith, 2005, p. 2). Also changes between surveys with regard to the content of the rest of the questionnaire may influence the observed trends due to question order effects. If the definition of the sampling universe, the sampling design or the response rate have changed over time, this may influence trends.

Another possible difference between surveys is a change in interview method. In many countries, a shift from face-to-face to telephone interviewing or to postal self-completion questionnaires is taking place. For answers to questions on sensitive topics, there will be an interviewer effect in face-to-face interviews, which is less pronounced in telephone interviews and absent in mail surveys (→ *Designing Reliable and Valid Questionnaires*).

Ideally the interview method should be the same for all surveys in a time series. If it has been changed, and there is a danger that the respondents feel that certain answers are socially desirable, the time series trend may have a methodological explanation. It has for instance been shown that respondents are more willing to give negative evaluations of persons or organizations in a mail questionnaire than when interviewed face to face (Esaiasson & Granberg, 1993). A shift to self-completion questionnaires accordingly will produce a negative shift in the public's evaluation of politicians and political institutions.

When time series comparability seems satisfactory, the researcher actually avoids some problems of interpretation encountered with single survey results. One example is so-called yea-saying or response acquiescence, the tendency for a respondent to agree to propositions without really having a clear opinion on the matter, brought to attention by the critique by (among others) Couch and Kenniston (1960) of *The authoritarian personality* (Adorno, Frenkel-Brunswick, Levinson, & Sanford, 1950). Yea-saying makes it difficult to estimate the 'true' distribution of attitudes when using this response format. The result may even be a distorted impression of what the majority position on a political issue is. But if it is reasonable to assume that the yea-saying effect is constant over time, the picture of *changes* in public opinion is not affected. The same canceling-out-as-a-constant-factor in a time series analysis may apply to other methodological problems encountered when interpreting results from a single survey.

ANALYSIS OF CHANGE

When longitudinal data are missing, it may be tempting to use *age patterns* as a basis for assessing change. The classical survey analysis *The People's Choice* (Lazarsfeld et al., 1944) reports that Protestants tended to vote for the Republicans, while the majority of Catholics voted for the Democrats. This difference was more pronounced among older than among younger voters. The study interprets the age pattern as a result of growing influence from a person's religious environment on party choice with increasing age—in other words as a life cycle effect.

In another classic, *Political Man*, Lipset (1960) interprets the same empirical results quite differently, as a reflection of generational differences caused by historical events. The younger age groups, growing up in a time of economic depression and social unrest, are less influenced by religious affiliation and more by class background than the older generation, reducing the political distinctiveness of the religious groups among the young.

Both interpretations are compatible with the age pattern, since age in a synchronic data set is an indicator of life cycle stage as well as of cohort membership. To separate the two aspects, one needs longitudinal data. One exception is for variables that do not change for an individual, such as place of birth, education, or first occupation, since any age difference in this case will have to be a generational difference. With values and attitudes, individual changes during the life course cannot be ruled out, and age patterns at any single point in time are ambiguous.

Time series data are often displayed in *trend charts*, making it easier to detect patterns of change by visual inspection. The chart may show results from the population as a whole, or of subgroups within it. Comparative datasets have opened possibilities to contrast trends from different nations, as in Figure 52.2 for self-placement on a left-right scale. There is a tendency for the population mean to move from the 'right' towards the center of the scale, as described in earlier research (Knutsen, 1998; Noelle-Neumann, 1998), with Italy and Denmark as exceptions.

To explain the pattern in a trend chart, historical events may be indicated, or trends for possible causal factors entered in the chart, as when Inglehart included the inflation rate in a chart for trends in postmaterialism in

European countries (1990, p. 94). Time series data are well suited to test the assumption of causal order or sequence of events implied in causal reasoning. To control for spurious covariation in trends, more sophisticated methods than inspecting trend charts are needed, such as multivariate time series regression analysis.

Multivariate time series regression can be used to study the importance of a certain factor for observed trends while controlling for other possible influences (Chatfield, 1989). Time series regression encounters a problem, however, that must be handled carefully in order to avoid serious misinterpretations. When there is a trend of increasing or decreasing values for relevant variables, successive observations for each of them will be correlated (autocorrelation). In such a situation, the results of the regression analysis will be misleading, exaggerating or reducing the importance of an independent variable depending on whether the trend for this variable goes in the same or the opposite direction as that of other relevant variables. One way of dealing with this problem is

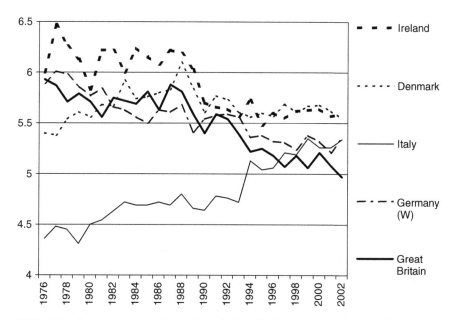

Figure 52.2 Trends in average value on left-right self-placement scale for selected countries 1976–2002 (Left = 1, right = 10)*
*Data from Mannheim Eurobarometer Trend File, provided by www.nsd.uib.no

to include the variables in question in the regression model. An alternative method is filtering of the data (Chatfield, 1989). By removing long-term trends in the data before the analysis, it is possible to see if the short term changes in the assumed causal and effect variables covary. This method has the advantage compared to the control variable method that one does not need data for the confounding variables.

Cohort analysis of time series data makes it possible to establish what kind of basic process of change is at work. The purpose may be to find out whether a pattern of age differences reflects life cycle or generational effects. Or it may be to establish what factor has contributed most to changes in public opinion—generational replacement or historical events (period effects).

A cohort analysis follows persons born within a certain period to see whether the cohort preserves its characteristics over time. With time series data, it is not the same persons but representative samples from the cohorts that are compared, showing aggregate but not individual change. In a standard cohort table, the width of the age classes corresponds to the time span between points of measurement, so that the results for a birth cohort are displayed along a diagonal (Table 52.1). The standard matrix cannot be used if the time span between surveys varies, or if broader age classes than the time interval between surveys permits are necessary to get a sufficient number of respondents in each cell. Two tables/figures are needed, one with birth cohort and time as independent variables, the other with age group and time (Glenn, 1977).

The standard matrix is convenient in that all comparisons of interest can be made within the same table. The vertical columns show differences between age groups at various points in time. In this example involving attitudes towards speeding, the age differences are large. They may reflect a life

Table 52.1 Standard cohort matrix (Percentage saying that it is not acceptable to drive above speed limit. Norwegian Monitor project)

Age	Year					Birth Cohort	Change 2002–1986	
	1986	1990	1994	1998	2002		Cohort	Age
14–17 Young	17	13	13	9	13	1985–88		−4
18–21 Young	17	12	12	7	7	1981–84		−10
22–25	16	14	9	6	5	1977–80		−11
26–29	19	17	10	8	9	1973–76		−10
30–33	25	19	14	8	8	1969–72	−9	−17
34–37	22	25	17	10	10	1965–68	−7	−12
38–41	24	26	21	14	12	1961–64	−4	−12
42–45	26	26	18	14	13	1957–60	−6	−13
46–49	35	27	19	18	13	1953–56	−12	−22
50–53	35	30	22	16	19	1949–52	−3	−16
54–57	40	36	29	18	19	1945–48	−5	−21
58–61	49	43	36	25	22	1941–44	−4	−27
62–65	53	49	41	27	24	1937–40	−11	−29
66–69	69	53	45	35	28	1933–36	−7	−31
70–73 Old	62	66	48	38	37	1929–32	−3	−25
74–77 Old	65	70	56	51	42	1925–28	−7	−23
All	34	31	24	18	17	Mean:	−7	−17
Old–Young	47	56	40	37	30	42		

cycle effect, a cohort effect, or a combination of the two.

The horizontal lines show differences between points in time for each age group. The percentage respecting the speed limits is on the decline for all groups. These changes may be a result of historical events, or reflect generational differences. Finally a diagonal reading, as indicated by the shadowing, shows change within birth cohorts. The respect for speed limits declines within all cohorts, on the average by 7 percentage points. This may be a life cycle and/or a period effect.

With two alternative explanations for the difference between any two cells in the matrix, and sample variation as an additional explanation, definite conclusions cannot be drawn. In many cases the pattern will be clear enough to support a certain interpretation, however, if one following the principle of parsimony (Palmore, 1978), accepting the less complex of the alternative explanations. Since the trend within the cohorts in Table 52.1 is in the opposite direction of what a life cycle effect would produce (away from, rather than closer to, the distribution typical of older people), one may conclude that there is no life cycle effect in this case. The change within the cohorts accordingly is interpreted as a period effect. Since the change for the population as a whole far exceeds the cohort change (17 versus 7 percentage points), we may conclude that generational replacement makes the largest contribution to the overall decline in respect for speed limits in the population.

The cohort analysis provides a better understanding of the processes behind long-term opinion trends. It also may indicate likely future developments in public opinion. Since the large age differences in Table 52.1 represent generational differences, the present trend may be expected to continue, at least in the near future. Period effects are less stable as they depend on historical events and therefore may well change direction in the future.

Since the three variables age, cohort membership and period are perfect combinations of each other, ordinary *multivariate analysis of cohort data* cannot be used to identify their

separate effects on a dependent variable. It has been suggested that the identification problem can be solved by introducing one extra linear restriction, usually one of equality, setting two age, cohort or period effects equal to each other (Mason, Mason, Winsborough, & Poole, 1973). But even if identifiable, the problem remains that the effects found will depend heavily on the equality restriction chosen (Rodgers, 1982), and there is no way of choosing a best fit model (Hagenaars, 1990). Even if the perfect multi-collinearity is broken, it will still be high (Hagenaars, 1990). Finally such analyses are criticized for relying on additive models, assuming that life cycle effects are the same for all cohorts and periods, and likewise for the two other effects (Glenn, 1977).

Due to such problems, some prefer the approach described in the previous section, relying on inspection and simple statistical manipulation of the cohort matrix. Some regard sophisticated multivariate analysis as a mechanical exercise uninformed by theory and outside evidence (Glenn, 1977). Others have more faith in the usefulness of rigorous statistical methods in cohort analysis (Fienberg & Mason, 1985; Hagenaars, 1990).

The amount of information in a cohort table is overwhelming. Limited space will also prevent presentation of results for more than a few variables in an article. This makes a *change diagram*, summarizing the essentials of the pattern of change for a variable as a single point in a two-dimensional space, useful. In Figure 52.3, the results for seven questions of whether violations of specific rules are deemed acceptable or not serve as an empirical illustration of the use of a change diagram (Hellevik, 2002).

Population change between two points in time is indicated along the vertical axis. The horizontal axis shows the difference between the two segments involved in the process of cohort replacement: those who have entered the population and those who have left between the two points in time. The newcomers are those respondents in the 1998 study too young to have been part of the adult population in 1986 (age groups 14–25).

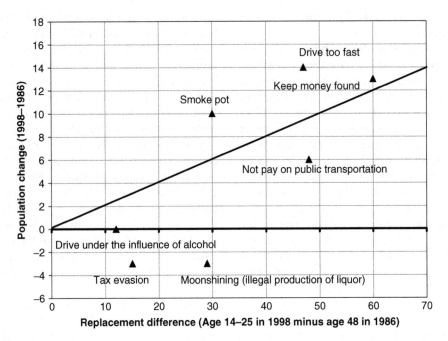

Figure 52.3   Change diagram for indicators of respect for laws and regulations in Norway for the period 1986–1998 (Percentage who feel that the behavior in question is acceptable or under doubt acceptable)

Precisely who among those interviewed in 1986 died in the intervening period, is not known. Their value profile may be represented, however, by that of respondents aged 48 years and above in 1986. Analyses of mortality data for Norway indicate that this group will have the same average age as that of those who departed between 1986 and 1998.

The diagonal in the diagram indicates the replacement effect. This is the difference between newcomers and leavers (replacement difference), weighted by their share of the population. In this empirical example, the replacement involves one-fifth of the population. This means that for each point on the diagonal, the size of the population change equals one fifth of the replacement difference.

The location of a variable in the diagram will indicate whether generation, life cycle or period effects are at work. A position out along the horizontal axis, with no change over time for the population, even though the new cohorts are clearly different from the older

people they replace, indicates that the age difference is the result of life cycle processes (just as for attitudes to drunken driving). The replacement effect is offset by the individual changes undergone by those members of the population present at both points in time. A position on the diagonal means that the effect of replacement exactly equals the population change, suggesting that the age difference is related to cohort membership (attitude to keeping money found).

A position between the diagonal and the horizontal axis indicates a combination of generation and life cycle effects (attitude toward not paying on public transportation). The distance from the axis and up reflects the generation effect, and the distance from the diagonal down the life cycle effect, rendering the population change less than the replacement effect.

A position outside the space between the diagonal and the axis tells us that a period effect has been at work. Positions below the axis show a trend in the opposite direction of what cohort replacement may explain, since the trend for the population as a whole is away from the preferences of the young (attitude to tax evasion and moonshining). The simplest explanation is a life cycle effect accounting for the age differences, and a period effect in the same direction causing the population change.

A position above the diagonal shows a trend in the direction suggested by the age differences, but one that is stronger than what cohort replacement alone may produce (attitude toward speeding and marijuana use). This suggests a combination of generation and period effects working in the same direction, in line with the conclusion from the cohort matrix for speeding (Table 52.1).

FUTURE CHANGE: SCENARIO CONSTRUCTION

An interest in opinion trends in the past may spring from a desire to anticipate what will happen in the future. This is the domain of more or less serious trend analysts, who often seem to base their predictions more on random observations or fanciful speculations than on systematic data analysis. It is possible, however, to use survey data as a basis for creating scenarios, plausible portraits of aspects of possible future situations for a society.

A simple approach is *trend extrapolation*, simply extending the trend of the recent past into the future. If this trend, to a large extent, is the result of period effects, such extrapolation is uncertain. The events and circumstances producing the period effects may change and steer the opinion development in new directions.

More robust prognoses for the future may be derived from the present age–opinion relationship. Such a scenario analysis is made by Abramson and Inglehart (1987), who present a trend chart with two trajectories for the development of postmaterialism in the period from 1985 to 2000. The calculations rest on the assumption that the age pattern in the data reflects stable generational differences. One scenario assumes that new cohorts

entering the adult population will show value orientations similar to those of the youngest age group in the data base, and the other that they will be more postmaterialist. Both scenarios show a modest tendency towards a stronger postmaterialist orientation as a result of generational replacement.

Similar predictions can be made using modified *scenario sample weights*. In public opinion research, weighting respondents to make the sample proportionate with official census statistics for age, sex and region, is a standard procedure. The same procedure can also be used to construct a scenario, but now the 'correct distribution' represents hypothetical future populations. A weighting matrix is defined, by age or cohort and future points in time, separate for men and women. The scenario weights are found by dividing the proportion of the future population in each cell in the matrix by the corresponding proportion for the sample from the present population. The distribution of the future population is defined by the scenario assumptions.

The first set of assumptions concerns such demographic factors as fertility, mortality and migration, and may be based on population prognosis models used by official census authorities. The second set of assumptions concerns the cause of age differences: life cycle versus generation effects. If the age differences are assumed to be caused completely by life cycle effects, the age segments at a future point in time will have the same characteristics as the present segments of identical age. Changes in the overall distribution of characteristics will result from changes in the age distribution of the population, such as the expected increase in the proportion of old people in most industrialized countries.

If a generational effect is assumed to be the sole cause of age differences at present, the characteristics of an age–sex segment at a future point in time will be the same as those of this cohort at present. Instead of an age–sex matrix a birth cohort–sex matrix is used, where the size of older cohorts is reduced over time until it eventually becomes zero, while the size of the new cohorts increases in the scenario populations.

Assuming that both life cycle and generational effects contribute to the age differences, we get mixed scenarios with predicted trends positioned between the pure scenarios according to the degree of the mix. Cohort analysis of time series data provides an empirical basis for choosing realistic scenario assumptions.

Since we do not have data on the new cohorts entering the population at future points in time, a third set of assumptions must be made concerning their characteristics in a generational scenario. One alternative is to assume that they will be identical to the youngest cohort of the present database. Or a sub-segment within this group may be chosen to represent the newcomers, such as those with a high education.

Finally, the consequences of assuming specific historic effects may be tested. This is done by changing the distribution on the variable(s) in question within each age/cohort-sex segment, such as the proportion of unemployed, or of supporters of certain values. The researcher thus ends up with a number of scenario weight variables, one for each set of assumptions for each future point in time. Combined with the original data describing the present, the set of weight variables can be used to analyze different scenario datasets for future situations.

CONCLUSION

Change over time in values and attitudes is a particularly fascinating aspect of the study of public opinion. Data banks providing easy access to steadily expanding time series data bases make it a safe bet that analysis of change will play a more prominent part in public opinion research in the future. Since large age differences in values and attitudes are typical for modern societies, cohort analysis will be a useful instrument to assess the importance of generational, life cycle and period effects. When substantial generational differences in value preferences are found,

important changes in value distributions for a population may be predicted.

REFERENCES

Abramson, P. R., & Inglehart, R. (1987). The future of postmaterialist values: Population replacement effects, 1970–1985 and 1985–2000. *Journal of Politics, 49*, 231–241.

Adorno, T. W., Frenkel-Brunswick, E., Levinson, D. J., & Sanford, R. N. (1950). *The authoritarian personality.* New York: Harper and Row.

Bridge, R. G., Reeder, L. G., Kanouse, D., Kinder, D. R., Nagy, V. T., & Judd, C. M. (1977). Interviewing changes attitudes—sometimes. *Public Opinion Quarterly, 41*, 56–64.

Campbell, A., Converse, P., Miller, W. & Stokes, D. (1960). *The American Voter.* New York: John Wiley & Sons.

Chatfield, C. (1989). *The analysis of time series. An introduction* (4th ed.). London: Chapman and Hall.

Couch, A., & Kenniston, K. (1960). Yeasayers and naysayers: Agreeing response set as a personality variable. *Journal of Abnormal and Social Psychology, 60*, 151–174.

Dex, S. (1995). The reliability of recall data: A literature review. *Bulletin de Methodologie Sociologique, 49* (December), 58–89.

Eagly, A. H., & Chaiken S. (1993). *The psychology of attitudes.* Fort Worth: Harcourt, Brace and Jovanovich.

Easterlin, R. A. (2002). Is reported happiness five years ago comparable to present happiness? A cautionary note. *Journal of Happiness Studies, 2*, 193–198.

Esaiasson, P., & Granberg, D. (1993). Hidden negativism: Evaluation of Swedish parties and their leaders under different survey methods. *International Journal of Public Opinion Research, 5*, 265–277.

Fienberg, S. E., & Mason, W. M. (Eds.). (1985). *Cohort analysis in social research. Beyond the identification problem,* New York: Springer Verlag.

Flanagan, S. C. (1982a). Changing values in advanced industrial society. *Comparative Political Studies, 14*, 403–444.

Flanagan, S. C. (1982b). Measuring value change in advanced industrial society: A rejoinder to Inglehart. *Comparative Political Studies, 15*, 99–128.

Glenn, N. D. (1977). *Cohort Analysis* (Quantitative Applications in the Social Sciences, Vol. 5). Beverly Hills: Sage.

Hagenaars, J. (1990). *Categorical longitudinal data. Loglinear panel, trends and cohort analysis.* Newbury Park: Sage.

Hagerty, M. R. (2003). Was life better in the 'good old days'? Intertemporal judgments of life satisfaction. *Journal of Happiness Studies, 4*, 115–139.

Hellevik, O. (1993). Postmaterialism as a dimension of cultural change. *International Journal of Public Opinion Research, 5*, 211–233.

Hellevik, O. (2002). Age differences in value orientation—life cycle or cohort effect? *International Journal of Public Opinion Research, 14*, 286–302.

Hitlin, S., & Piliavin, J. A. (2004). Values: Reviving a dormant concept. *Annual Review of Sociology, 30*, 359–393.

Holt, D. (1989). Panel conditioning: Discussion. In D. Kasprzyk, G. J. Duncan, G. Kalton & M. P. Singh (Eds.), *Panel Surveys* (pp. 340–347). New York: Wiley.

Inglehart, R. (1977). *The silent revolution—Changing values and political styles among Western publics.* Princeton: Princeton University Press.

Inglehart, R. (1990). *Culture shift in advanced industrial society.* Princeton: Princeton University Press.

Inglehart, R. (1997). *Modernization and Postmodernization. Cultural, Economic and Political Change in 43 Societies.* Princeton: Princeton University Press.

Inglehart, R., & Baker, W. E. (2000). Modernization, cultural change, and the persistence of traditional values. *American Sociological Review, 65*, 19–51.

Kasprzyk, D., Duncan, G. J., Kalton, G., & Singh, M. P. (Eds.). (1989). *Panel Surveys.* New York: Wiley.

Kluckhohn, C. (1951). Values and value-orientations in the theory of action: An exploration in definition and classification. In T. Parsons & E. Shils (Eds.). *Toward a general Theory of Action* (pp. 388–433). New York: Harper and Row.

Knutsen, O. (1998). Europeans move toward the center: A comparative longitudinal study of left-right self-placement in Western Europe. *International Journal of Public Opinion Research, 10*, 292–316.

Lazarsfeld, P., Berelson, B., & Gaudet, H. (1944). *The people's choice.* New York: Columbia University Press.

Lipset, S. M. (1960). *Political Man.* London: Heinemann.

Mannheim, K. (1952). *Essays on the sociology of knowledge.* London: Routledge & Kegan Paul.

Markus, G. B. (1986). Stability and change in political attitudes: Observed, recalled and 'explained'. *Political Behavior, 8*, 21–44.

Mason, K. O., Mason, W. M., Winsborough, H. H., & Poole, W. K. (1973). Some methodological issues in cohort analysis of archival data. *American Sociological Review, 38*, 242–258.

Noelle-Neumann, E. (1998). A shift from the right to the left as an indicator of value change: A battle for the climate of opinion. *International Journal of Public Opinion Research, 10*, 317–334.

Palmore, E. (1978). When can age, period, and cohort be separated? *Social Forces, 57*, 282–295.

Rodgers, W. L. (1982). Estimable functions of age, period, and cohort effects. *American Sociological Review, 47*, 774–787.

Rokeach, M. (1968). The role of values in public opinion research. *Public Opinion Quarterly, 32*, 547–559.

Rokeach, M. (1970). *Beliefs, attitudes and values: A theory of organization and change.* San Francisco: Jossey-Bass.

Rokeach, M. (1973). *The nature of human values.* New York: Free Press.

Saris, W. E., & Andreenkova, A. (2001). What influences subjective well-being in Russia? *Journal of Happiness Studies, 2*, 137–146.

Schwartz, S. H. (1992). Universals in the content and structure of values: theoretical advances and empirical tests in 20 countries. In M.P. Zanna (Ed.), *Advances in experimental social psychology* (pp. 1–65). San Diego: Academic.

Schwartz, S. H. (1994). Are there universal aspects in the structure and content of human values? *Journal of Social Issues, 50*, 19–45.

Schwarz, N. M., & Sudman, S. (Eds.). (1994). *Autobiographical memory and the validity of retrospective reports.* New York: Springer.

Schwartz, S. H., Melech, G., Lehmann, A., Burgess, S., Harris, M., & Owens, V. (2001). Extending the cross-cultural validity of the theory of basic human values with a different method of measurement. *Journal of Cross-Cultural Psychology, 32*, 519–542.

Smith, T. W. (2005). The laws of studying societal change. *Survey Research, 36*, 1–5.

Veenhoven, R. (2001). Are the Russians as unhappy as they say they are? Comparability of self-reports across nations. *Journal of Happiness Studies, 2*, 111–136.

Waterton, J., & Lievesley, D. (1989). Panel conditioning: Discussion. In D. Kasprzyk, G. J. Duncan, G. Kalton & M. P. Singh (Eds.), *Panel surveys* (pp. 319–339). New York: Wiley.

53

Exit Polls and Pre-Election Polls

Kathleen A. Frankovic

Pre-election polls measure vote intention prior to Election Day; exit polls are surveys conducted after voting has occurred. Both types of surveys have become fixtures in democracies, and especially in media reports of elections. They are used both to learn which candidates will win and to explain the intent of voters and the meaning of elections. While one can find examples of the use of polls in earlier elections, scientific pre-election polls began in the mid-twentieth century, and exit polls developed in the 1960s. This chapter reviews the historical and methodological development of both types of polls, their importance to the understanding of elections, and measures that have been used to regulate or limit their use.

Pre-election and exit polls do more than predict an outcome; they provide the basis for understanding what an election means, and put the interpretation of an election in the hands of the voters, not political elites. They have become part of the democratic process: after World War II, polling as well as democracy was brought to Japan by the United States military, and polls were even conducted in Afghanistan and Iraq soon after

the overthrow of the Taliban and Saddam Hussein.

But they are also held to a high standard, and are among the few (if not the only) polls that are tested against an actual outcome—an election result.

THE HISTORY OF PRE-ELECTION POLLS

Pre-election polls have a long history, dating from the 19th century in the United States. In 1824, straw poll counts began appearing in partisan newspapers—suggesting that the public might not agree with the political leaders in their choice of presidential candidates. In some cases, counts of candidate support were taken at public meetings. In others, books were opened for people to register their preference. Some newspapers praised the technique. The *Niles Weekly Register* (1824, May) said of a count taken at a public meeting, 'This is something new; but an excellent plan of obtaining the sense of the people.' Another paper said about a poll book, 'We would recommend to our fellow citizens throughout the Union this mode of ascertaining the sentiments of the people. Let the political managers at Washington and elsewhere know the people's will and, if that is not to decide the question, why let the people know it' (*American Watchman and Delaware Advertiser,* 1824, May 14).

In 1896, the *Chicago Record* sent postcard ballots to every registered Chicago voter, and to a sample of one in ten voters in eight surrounding states. The *Record* mailed a total of 833,277 postcard ballots, at a cost of $60,000; and 240,000 of those sample ballots were returned. The *Record* found that Republican William McKinley was far ahead of the Democrat, William Jennings Bryan. McKinley won, and in Chicago, the *Record*'s pre-election poll results came within four one-hundredths of a percent of the actual election-day tally.

The *Record* justified its polling project in print by its claims of careful representativeness, by the paper's general non-partisanship, and by the claim that knowing the likely results before the election would 'give business the country over the opportunity to secure to new lines without waiting for November 3 to arrive' (*Chicago Record,* 1896). By the 1920s, even papers whose editorial pages were clearly partisan were apparently comfortable reporting straw polls that indicated that their paper's choice for the next election was nonetheless losing the contest for voters.

Between 1900 and 1920, there were close to 20 separate news 'straw polls' in the United States. By 1920, the *Literary Digest* magazine mailed ballot cards to 11,000,000 potential voters, selected predominantly from telephone lists. In later years, car registration lists and some voter registration lists were added to the sampling frame. Although the *Digest* touted its polling as impartial and accurate, and its purpose as assisting in 'the most important piece of news-gathering … in sight at this time … to find out how people are intending to vote' (*The Literary Digest,* 1916), it was also tied to an attempt to increase the magazine's subscriber base. By 1920, many businesses and newspapers

had established market research and advertising research units, so in the 1920s, advertising was full of claims that came from market research.

These news polling operations involved outreach to as many groups as possible, and huge numbers of interviews were carried out (often conducted on street corners). In its 1923 mayoral election poll, the *Chicago Tribune* tabulated more than 85,000 ballots. In the month before the April election, interviews were conducted throughout Chicago, and results were published reporting preferences of each ethnic group (including the 'colored' vote), with special samples of streetcar drivers, moviegoers (noting the differences between first and second show attendees), and white-collar workers in the Loop. The *Tribune* also polled what it described as the 'white native vote,' which was determined by conducting 8,145 *telephone* interviews (perhaps the first ever done) in nine Chicago phone exchanges, covering residences and apartment buildings where 'even the canvassers of the political parties have little or no chance to ascertain the sentiment' (*Chicago Tribune,* 1923, March 25).

But the real emergence of pre-election polls as we now know them came in the United States in the 1930s. Despite the magnitude of the news surveys of the 1920s and early 1930s, and the relative accuracy of many in predicting election outcomes, their success was limited by the unscientific nature of their sampling. However, the polls were carefully thought out; the 1923 telephone poll reached the well-off 'native-born whites,' who would be least likely to be found on the street, where other interviews were conducted.

In 1935, however, both George Gallup and Elmo Roper began conducting a new kind of news poll: Gallup for a consortium of newspapers, and Roper for *Fortune* magazine. The stated goals were democratic and journalistic ones. Gallup co-authored a book called 'The pulse of democracy,' while *Fortune*'s editors in their very first poll report in June 1935, explicitly linked impartial journalism and polls: 'For the journalist and particularly such journalists of fact as the editors of *Fortune* conceive themselves to be, has no preferences as to the facts he hopes to uncover. He prefers, as a journalist, no particular outcome. He is quite as willing to publish the answers that upset his apple cart of preconceptions as to publish the answers that bear him out' (*Fortune*, 1935).

Gallup and Roper, along with Archibald Crossley, who began polling for the Hearst newspapers in 1936, interviewed only a few thousand adults, unlike the tens of thousands in the *Tribune*'s canvass or the millions answering the *Literary Digest* polls. However, samples were selected to ensure that regions, city sizes and economic classes were properly represented.

While not quite true probability samples, they were far more representative than the larger street corner or postcard polls. And in that first test in 1936, the so-called 'scientific' polls successfully predicted a Roosevelt victory. Gallup not only predicted a Roosevelt victory in 1936, but he also predicted the *Literary Digest*'s mistake. The flaws in the *Literary Digest*'s procedures (using lists that in nearly every state were biased in favor of the economically better-off during a Depression) are fairly obvious today. First, by almost always limiting the sampling frame to those owning telephones and automobiles, lower-income voters were excluded, even though by 1936 social class would matter more than state or region in a person's presidential choice. Second, only about two million of the *Digest*'s ten million or so postcard ballots were returned, limiting the polling count to those who both received a questionnaire and bothered to respond—a problem similar to those found in today's call-in polls or Internet surveys.

'Scientific' news polls expanded after 1936. This change in methods meant that news organizations could measure opinion on more subjects and with more questions than straw pollers. In one of the more obvious statements of the pre-war optimism surrounding these polls, Gallup himself praised this ability: 'We can try out any idea,' he crowed, 'we can try out any idea in the world!' By May 1940, 118 newspapers

subscribed to the Gallup Poll. The *Fortune* surveys appeared monthly. Between 1943 and 1948, at least 14 state organizations were conducting their own polls, using methods approximating those of the national pollsters. The *Washington Post* began its own local polling in 1945 in part, it said, to supplement the Gallup poll on national affairs; but also, it claimed, 'to implement the democratic process in the only American community in which residents do not have the right to express their views at the polling booth' (*Washington Post*, 1945).

In the Western democracies, pre-election polling began in the period before World War II and expanded afterwards. The Gallup Organization set up its own branches in some countries, and adopted its techniques to measure parliamentary support, as well as presidential preference. There was a Gallup Institute in Great Britain beginning in 1938, and one in Canada starting in 1935. As democracy spread, so did polling and pre-election polls. This movement towards democracy was occasionally abetted by the US armed forces. After the surrender of Japan, the US occupying forces instituted public opinion polling, and the techniques established in the US were adapted to accommodate at least some Japanese traditions.

Polling spread to Mexico and Latin America after World War II through the work of Joe Belden and others. After the fall of Communism, the development of polling in Russia and Eastern Europe came through sociological institutes and partnerships. There are now polling companies in nearly every country, with pre-election polls conducted wherever there are elections.

There was further growth in the 1970s. In the US, the number of US households with telephones increased to well above 90%; and as a result, surveys could be conducted more cheaply, and data collection could be better controlled. Random-digit-dialing better ensured representativeness, and the speed of data collection was more appropriate for news gathering purposes. In other countries, data collection also moved from in-person to telephone, when possible.

Improving computer technology meant that the time between data collection and analysis continued to shrink, and now polls reacting to campaign events are sometimes conducted and reported within a half hour of an event's occurrence.

METHODS OF PRE-ELECTION POLLS

The earliest scientific pre-election polls, in the 1930s, relied on in-person interviewing. Interviewers were sent to selected locations and required to interview a selected number of men and women, young people and older people, and high status and lower status voters. Completed questionnaires were then returned for tabulation and reporting. The Gallup Organization developed a procedure to speed up the polling for the last few days before an election. Interviewers telegraphed back the responses to specific questions.

This early US polling met with significant successes, until the 1948 election. Their methodology, particularly the reliance on the quota selection process administered by the interviewers themselves, had been questioned by government statisticians like Louis Bean of the Department of Agriculture, Philip M. Hauser and Morris Hansen of the Bureau of the Census, and Rensis Likert, from the Bureau of Agricultural Economics, as well as by some academics. But the assumption of accuracy was basically unchallenged by the media and the public. After the 1948 election, when all the polls predicted a victory by New York State Republican governor Thomas Dewey over incumbent Democratic President Harry Truman, that changed. The Social Science Research Council created a 'blue ribbon' panel to review the process, and recommended the use of probability sampling at all levels of respondent selection, and the elimination of quota selections.

The SSRC report also noted that the pollsters had overestimated the capabilities of the public opinion poll. There was, of course, another source for the problem. What the pollsters had discovered from the 1936,

1940 and 1944 presidential elections was that there were few, if any, changes that could be attributed to the campaign. Consequently, they believed that the lead held by the Republican in the early fall would not be affected by anything either candidate could do. They stopped polling several weeks before the election. After 1948, pollsters would continue to poll until much closer to Election Day. In the 1980s, after in-person interviewing was replaced by telephone interviewing, and following the underestimate of Ronald Reagan's victory margin in the 1980 election, pre-election polling continued through the night before the election.

In other countries, methods have been different, although there too, methodological changes tended to follow problems in election prediction. In Britain, pre-election pollsters mis-predicted the 1992 parliamentary election, wrongly predicting a Labor victory. But the Conservative Party won by eight percentage points. The British Market Research Association conducted its investigation, and found similar problems as in the US in 1948 and 1980. Voters changed their minds at the last minute, but there were also problems with the sampling methods. Most British pollsters opted to remain with in-person quota sampling for the next national election, although they did change their quotas. But others moved to implement greater changes, including the adoption of telephone polls.

The British difficulties in 1992 and the response also underscore a major methodological issue for pre-election polls. Does one weight or adjust the results? The adjustments can range from ensuring that the original sample reflects the population parameters and the probabilities of selection to weighting on past voting behaviors. In addition, there may be adjustments made to make sure that the final published results reflect the opinions of actual voters, not all adults.

Some of those adjustments include the management of voters who refuse to give a preference when asked. Some polling organizations ignore undecided voters and include that percentage in the final pre-election estimate; others remove them and recalculate the percentage for each candidate or party, and others may attempt to allocate them. As Nick Sparrow (1996, p. 16) wrote of the British pre-election polls:

> ICM's adjustment assumes that 60 per cent of them will return to the party they voted for in 1992. This is based on an observation of what the 'don't knows' did in 1992 by reference to ICM's 1992 polls and to the British Election Panel Survey. Another method, favoured by NOP, is to allocate these people to a party they most closely identify with or to the party they think has the best policies on the economy.

He also noted a second possible adjustment, correcting to a degree the past report of voting behavior at the last election. Voters have a tendency, he says, to align their past votes with their present preferences. Using data from the British Election Panel Survey and the British Household Panel Survey, a 'correct' recall of past votes should show a very small Conservative majority for the recall of the 1992 vote. He suggests that by the mid-1990s, quota samples contained too many Labor voters and too few Conservative Party supporters.

In the United States, where turnout in presidential elections totals only about 50% of residents of voting age, the pre-election polls must also make a determination of which respondents will actually vote—the 'likely voters.' This has been done in a variety of ways: with a single question asking the respondent to indicate his or her likelihood of voting, or with several questions asking about prior voting, intent to vote in the coming election, interest and attention to the campaign, and knowledge about the location of the polling place. Paul Perry (1960) of the Gallup Organization described their procedure in *Public Opinion Quarterly*. Selection of likely voters can either be on a respondent basis, or can be on a basis of assigned probability.[1]

As new technologies develop, they have also been applied to pre-election polls. Several companies conduct election polls among a sample of individuals recruited to be part of web panels. Interviews are conducted on line, and the resulting interviews adjusted by demographics and politics to reflect a pre-determined concept of the electorate. Polls have been done using this model in both the United States and Great Britain, with some success.

THE IMPORTANCE OF EXIT POLLS

Exit polls are polls of *voters*, interviewed after they have voted, and no later than Election Day. They may include the interviewing before Election Day of postal, absentee and other early voters. Exit polls are now conducted in many countries, and they may not always be conducted at the polling place, although most are. There are differences in exit polls. Some may be conducted to predict election results and others may be used for later, academic and analytic purposes.

Exit polls can serve three different functions that are not mutually exclusive: predicting election results, describing patterns of voter support for parties, candidates, and issue; and supporting extensive academic research efforts. The main difference between the analysis categories is the speed with which the results are formulated and disseminated.

Exit polls have become part of the ordinary political discourse. Perhaps the first was conducted inadvertently in the United States in 1964 by Ruth Clark. Clark was a well-known newspaper researcher, who began her research career as an interviewer. In 1964, she worked for Lou Harris, and was sent to conduct interviews in Maryland on its primary election day. Tired of door-to-door interviewing looking for voters, she decided to talk with them as they left the polling place. As she put it, 'I told Lou what I had done, and by the [Republican] California primary in June, the exit poll was put to full use,' with Barry Goldwater voters dropping blue beans into a jar, while Nelson Rockefeller voters dropped red beans (Rosenthal, 1998, p. 41).[2] Pollster Lou Harris and statistician David Neft, hired as consultants for CBS News at the start of 1964, used a set of 'key precincts' to project election outcomes.

While Ruth Clark may have invented the exit poll, it became a staple of news election coverage in 1970s and 1980s. CBS News, under the leadership of Warren Mitofsky, began exit polling in 1969, originally to collect voting data in precincts that did not make their vote available at poll closing. It later expanded to a questionnaire that contained questions about voter demographics and issue positions. The process was adopted by other American news organizations and then quickly spread to other countries.

A typical exit poll's methodology is straightforward: first, the selection of polling locations, usually done by probability sampling. To be truly representative, the precincts should be selected to be proportionate to their sizes, with some stratification by geographic location and past vote. Second, it involves the hiring and training of interviewers, to be stationed at the selected poll locations. Third, the voters at the polling locations are sampled, either by interviewing every voter or a probability sample of them (every Nth, with N determined ahead of time depending on the expected size of the precinct). Fourth, a record is kept of non-response—its size and composition. Fifth, the questionnaires must be transmitted to a central location for processing, either physically, by telephone, or electronically.

The first exit poll in Great Britain was conducted in 1974 for ITN by the Harris Organization, followed soon after by exit polling in other Western European countries. Other democracies adopted exit polling soon after—for example, Social Weather Stations conducted its first Election Day poll in the Philippines in 1992, and the first exit polls in Mexico were conducted in 1994. Mitofsky himself did exit polling in the Russian elections starting in 1993, working with the Russian firm CESSI.

There are different types of exit poll questionnaires. Some, as in Britain, simply ask which candidate the respondent voted for. On the other hand, the typical United States exit poll contains 25 questions on both sides of a single sheet of paper about the importance of issues and demographic characteristics. See Figure 53.1 for examples of exit poll questionnaires.

Reporting election results quickly has *always* been important to the news media, not just in order to outshine the competition, but also to minimize electoral uncertainty. In 1896, the *Chicago Record* justified its straw poll of Midwestern states as one that would provide information even before the election.

Election projections can be made in other ways than by interviewing voters as they exit the polling place. While most projections are based on exit polls, interviewing voters after having voted at a polling place, other forecasting models may include:

- CAPI, CATI or other interviews on Election Day with voters after *or before* having cast their votes,
- counts of official votes in a sample of precincts, often known as quick counts,
- a mix of methods.

The most serious methodological issue for exit polls is the level of non-response, as this may result in bias due to those voters most willing to respond. This can affect pre-election polls, too, most notably demonstrated in the experiment conducted by Bischoping and Schuman (1992) in Nicaragua. Interviewer effects can be great in exit polls since they are conducted in person. Paper and pencil questionnaires preserve confidentiality and can reduce the impact (Bishop & Fisher, 1995). But examples of differential non-response have been documented in response rates of voters to interviewers of different races in elections with a racial component (Traugott & Price, 1992), and in other highly intense elections where interviewers may be perceived (correctly or incorrectly) as favoring one or another candidate or party.

These factors must be taken into account when exit polls are used as checks on voting, which has become a standard use for them in new democracies. In recent years, exit poll results in Venezuela and Ukraine have been hailed as better indicators of election outcomes than the vote count. While a well-conducted exit poll can sometimes be one check on voter fraud, sampling error limits any poll's precision. In addition, operational difficulties, including restrictions on carrying out exit polls, and possible bias due to interviewer–respondent interactions must be taken into account before accepting the accuracy of exit polls. In the 2004 US presidential election, exit poll overestimates of the vote for Democrat John Kerry were frequently cited as evidence of fraud by some activists; but all analysis indicated the difference was more likely caused by a differential response rate due to the interviewer–respondent interaction.

CRITICIZING AND RESTRICTING ELECTION POLLS

After the 1948 election, *The New Yorker* wrote:

> The total collapse of the public opinion polls shows that the country is in good health … although you can take a nation's pulse, you can't be sure that the nation hasn't just run up a flight of stairs, and although you can take the nation's blood pressure, you can't be sure that if you came back in 20 minutes you'd get the same reading. This is a damn fine thing. … We are proud of America for clouding up the crystal ball, for telling one thing to a poll-taker, another thing to a voting machine.

NEP National Exit Poll, 2004

National Election Poll

Conducted by Edison/Mitofsky

YOUR ANSWERS ARE CONFIDENTIAL
Please check only ONE response for each question.
VERSION 1

[A] Are you:
1 ☐ Male 2 ☐ Female

[B] Are you:
1 ☐ White
2 ☐ Black
3 ☐ Hispanic/Latino
4 ☐ Asian
5 ☐ Other

[C] In today's election for president, did you just vote for:
1 ☐ John Kerry (Dem)
2 ☐ George W. Bush (Rep)
9 ☐ Other: Who? ___________
0 ☐ Did not vote for president

[D] When did you finally decide for whom to vote in the presidential election?
1 ☐ Just today
2 ☐ In the last three days
3 ☐ Sometime last week
4 ☐ During the last month
5 ☐ Before that

[E] In today's election for U.S. senator, did you just vote for:
1 ☐ Eric Fingerhut (Dem)
2 ☐ George Voinovich (Rep)
9 ☐ Other: Who? ___________
0 ☐ Did not vote for U.S. senator

[F] Which ONE issue mattered most in deciding how you voted for president? *(Check only one)*
1 ☐ Taxes
2 ☐ Education
3 ☐ Iraq
4 ☐ Terrorism
5 ☐ Economy/Jobs
6 ☐ Moral values
7 ☐ Health care

[G] To which age group do you belong?
1 ☐ 18-24
2 ☐ 25-29
3 ☐ 30-39
4 ☐ 40-44
5 ☐ 45-49
6 ☐ 50-59
7 ☐ 60-64
8 ☐ 65-74
9 ☐ 75 or over

[H] How did vote on Issue 1, defining marriage only as a union between a man and a woman?
1 ☐ Yes
2 ☐ No
3 ☐ Did not vote on Issue 1

[I] In today's election for U.S. House of Representatives, did you just vote for:
1 ☐ The Democratic candidate
2 ☐ The Republican candidate
9 ☐ Other: Who? ___________
0 ☐ Did not vote for U.S. House

[J] Do you approve or disapprove of the way George W. Bush is handling his job as president?
1 ☐ Strongly approve
2 ☐ Somewhat approve
3 ☐ Somewhat disapprove
4 ☐ Strongly disapprove

[K] Which ONE candidate quality mattered most in deciding how you voted for president? *(Check only one)*
1 ☐ He cares about people like me
2 ☐ He has strong religious faith
3 ☐ He is honest and trustworthy
4 ☐ He is a strong leader
5 ☐ He is intelligent
6 ☐ He will bring about needed change
7 ☐ He has clear stands on the issues

[L] Are you of Hispanic or Latino descent?
1 ☐ Yes
2 ☐ No

PLEASE TURN THE QUESTIONNAIRE OVER →

OHIO (G-N-V1-2004)

Figure 53.1 NEP National Exit Poll, 2004

[M] Compared to four years ago, is the country:
  1 ☐ Safer from terrorism
  2 ☐ Less safe from terrorism
[N] Do you or does someone in your household belong to a labor union?
  1 ☐ Yes, I do
  2 ☐ Yes, someone else does
  3 ☐ Yes, I do and someone else does
  4 ☐ No one does
[O] How do you feel about the U.S. decision to go to war with Iraq?
  1 ☐ Strongly approve
  2 ☐ Somewhat approve
  3 ☐ Somewhat disapprove
  4 ☐ Strongly disapprove
[P] How do you think things are going for the U.S. in Iraq now?
  1 ☐ Very well
  2 ☐ Somewhat well
  3 ☐ Somewhat badly
  4 ☐ Very badly
[Q] Compared to four years ago, is your family's financial situation:
  1 ☐ Better today
  2 ☐ Worse today
  3 ☐ About the same
[R] If these were the only two presidential candidates on the ballot today, for whom would you have voted?
  1 ☐ John Kerry (Dem)
  2 ☐ George W. Bush (Rep)
  3 ☐ Would not voted for president
[S] Have you ever served in the U.S. military?
  1 ☐ Yes
  2 ☐ No
[T] Are you currently married?
  1 ☐ Yes
  2 ☐ No
[U] Do you have any children under 18 living in your household?
  1 ☐ Yes
  2 ☐ No
	[V] What was the last grade of school you completed?
	  1 ☐ Did not complete high school
	  2 ☐ High school graduate
	  3 ☐ Some college or associate degree
	  4 ☐ College graduate
	  5 ☐ Postgraduate study
	[W] Is this first time you have ever voted?
	  1 ☐ Yes 2 ☐ No
	[X] Are you:
	  1 ☐ Protestant 5 ☐ Jewish
	  2 ☐ Catholic 6 ☐ Muslim
	  3 ☐ Mormon/LDS 7 ☐ Someone else
	  4 ☐ Other Christian 8 ☐ None
	[Y] Would you describe yourself as a born-again or evangelical Christian?
	  1 ☐ Yes 2 ☐ No
	[Z] How often do you attend religious services?
	  1 ☐ More than once a week
	  2 ☐ Once a week
	  3 ☐ A few times a month
	  4 ☐ A few times a year
	  5 ☐ Never
	[AA] No matter how you voted today, do you usually think of yourself as a:
	  1 ☐ Democrat 3 ☐ Independent
	  2 ☐ Republican 4 ☐ Something else
	[AB] On most political matters, do you consider yourself:
	  1 ☐ Liberal
	  2 ☐ Moderate
	  3 ☐ Conservative
	[AC] 2003 total family income:
	  1 ☐ Under $15,000 5 ☐ $75,000-$99,999
	  2 ☐ $15,000-$29,999 6 ☐ $100,000-$149,999
	  3 ☐ $30,000-$49,999 7 ☐ $150,000-$199,999
	  4 ☐ $50,000-$74,999 8 ☐ $200,000 or more
	[AD] What type of telephone service is there in your home that you could use or be reached on? *(Check only one)*
	  1 ☐ Both regular land-line and cell phone service
	  2 ☐ Only regular, land-line phone service
	  3 ☐ Only cell phone service
	  4 ☐ No telephone service at home

Please fold questionnaire and put it in the box. Thank you.

NATIONAL (V1-V2-BACK-2004)

Figure 53.1   Continued

This is an excellent land (*The New Yorker*, 1948).

Before that election, candidate Harry Truman attacked 'poll-happy' Republicans—and meant the pollsters. He said, the 'polls are like sleeping pills, designed to lull the voters into sleeping on Election Day. You might call them sleeping polls … but most of the people are not being fooled. They know that sleeping polls are bad for the system. They affect the mind. An overdose could be fatal' (Truman, 1948).

The politicization of polls is not new. Ever since poll results began making their way to the public directly—mainly through news reports—they have been attacked by people whose interests are served by rejecting the findings. There is a long history of objections from the power elite. In 1896, the Chicago Democratic Party railed against a poll conducted by the independent newspaper, the *Chicago Record*. They called it 'a scheme—one of fraud and debauchery, the first step to do away with popular elections under the law and place the molding of public opinion in the hands of millionaires and corporations.'

In contemporary presidential campaign politics, attacking polls may have become a more important part of campaign strategy. In 1988, Michael Dukakis referred to polls in fewer than 20% of all the speeches he made in the fall campaign. George Bush, who was leading in that election, referred to polls only a third as often as Dukakis. But in 1992, when Bush was trailing, he attacked polls in more than 30 speeches, the equivalent of one in every four times he spoke publicly. And in 1996, Bob Dole talked about the polls even more frequently: in one-third of all his speeches.

In recent elections, campaigns and news stories frequently describe differences in pre-election polls, and raise questions about their methods, including queries about methodologies, how likely voters are defined, question order, weighting, and assumptions about partisanship.

Some governments have attempted to limit the publication of poll results. As late as 2002, at least 30 countries had legal restrictions on the publication of pre-election poll results. There had been little change in the absolute number since 1996, when at least 31 countries were reported to have embargos on the publication of political poll results on or prior to Election Day. Nine of these embargos applied to Election Day only; 46 countries (61%) were reported to have no embargo. Nine countries had increased their time restrictions, while 15 others had decreased theirs, or eliminated them entirely. Countries with limits on the publication of pre-election polls include western European countries like Portugal, Spain and Switzerland, as well as countries in Asia and Latin America (Spangenberg, 2003). In other countries, like Italy, publication is allowed, but with the requirement that the poll report be accompanied by an 'information note' with several specifications related to the poll, which must be published in the media together with the results of the poll as well as recorded on a dedicated website.

As for restricting exit polls, this can be done in ways beyond limits on publication (in the 2002 report, 41 countries restricted publication or broadcast of poll results until after the polling places had closed). In addition, in both the United States and in Hong Kong, there are no government regulations about the release of exit poll information; however, pollsters and news organizations have voluntarily agreed not to report exit poll results until after the polls close.

Just as the bans on reporting pre-election polls can be circumvented by posting results on the Internet, restrictions (whether government-imposed or self-imposed) on reporting exit polls before polls close have also been circumvented, as leaks of exit polling results and their reporting on the Internet have become routine. To help prevent early reports of partial exit poll results in the United States, news organizations agreed after the 2004 election not to receive exit poll information until late in the afternoon of Election Day. Before 5 p.m. on Election Day 2006, two representatives of each organization reviewed the data in a 'quarantine room,' where they had no access to the Internet and had surrendered cell phones and other communication devices before entering. At 5 p.m., the results were transmitted to other members of the member and subscriber organizations.

Governments can institute laws that create operational difficulties for exit pollsters, such as limits on how close to the polling place interviewers can be to conduct their interviews. In the United States, some states have attempted to legislate requirements that exit poll interviewers stand as far as 300 feet (nearly 100 meters) from the polling location, effectively making good sampling of voters impossible. Many of these restrictions (although not all) have been overturned when challenged in court. In some countries, the difficulties of interviewing at the polling place (either through legal restrictions or fear of violence) have forced researchers to use different methodologies, such as in person interviewing at home after people have voted.

The justification for restricting the publication of poll reports both before and on Election Day tends to be phrased as preserving the 'dignity of the democratic process,' according to the 2002 review. Other reasons cited fall under the heading of efforts to prevent poll results from exerting any influence on public opinion. In the majority of countries that have an embargo on publishing poll results before an election, the main enforcers are government agencies or election administration offices.

There is minimal evidence to support the concerns about the impact of pre-election and exit polls. According to one review of studies about the impact of election polling,

> The conclusion is that any effects are difficult to prove and in any case are minimal. Opinion polls do provide a form of 'interpretative assistance' which helps undecided voters make up their mind. But the media are full of such interpretative aids, including interviews and commentaries, and in this perspective, election polls are a relatively neutral and rational 'interpretative aid' (Donsbach, 2001, p. 12).

CONCLUSION

Pre-election polling has a long history. It has set the agenda for political leaders and for news organizations; and good election polls have set the standard for understanding the public's wishes. Polling before elections is now a global phenomenon, and although at the outset it may have had an American identity, the collection of information about voters is now seen as part of the process of global democratization.

Pre-election polling has absorbed the best methods of survey research, especially after the opinion polls have faltered in predicting election outcomes. It has also generated polling innovations, such as the Election Day exit poll, which gives voters the opportunity to express their reasons for casting ballots as they did.

But the value and the perceived accuracy of pre-election polling make it vulnerable to political criticism from those who disagree with the results. And in recent years, there is evidence that the intensity of this criticism has increased.

NOTES

1 See http://www.mysterypollster.com/main/2004/09/how_do_pollster_1.html for a discussion of various likely voter models in the US.

2 Clark had an even more interesting history. A Communist, she and her family immigrated to the Soviet Union after World War II, returning to the US only in 1953. Her daughter Judith was a member of the radical Weather Underground and was sentenced to prison as the result of an armored-car robbery that resulted in the deaths of two policemen and a guard.

REFERENCES

Bishop, G. F., & Fisher, B. S. (1995). 'Secret ballots' and self-reports in an exit-poll experiment. *Public Opinion Quarterly, 59*, 568–588.

Bischoping, K., & Schuman H. (1992). Pens and polls in Nicaragua: An analysis of the 1990 pre-election surveys. *American Journal of Political Science, 36*, 331–350.

Donsbach, W. (2001). *Who's afraid of election polls? Normative and empirical arguments for freedom of pre-election surveys*. Amsterdam: ESOMAR/WAPOR.

Perry, P. (1960). Election survey procedures of the Gallup poll. *Public Opinion Quarterly, 24*, 531–542.

Rosenthal, J. (1998, January 4). Ruth Clark: The right questions. *New York Times Sunday Magazine*, p. 41.

Spangenberg, F. (2003). *Foundation for information report: The freedom to publish opinion poll results: Report on a worldwide update*. Amsterdam: ESOMAR/WAPOR.

Sparrow, N. (1996, February 12). Arena: Polls apart on the voting slips. *The Guardian*, p. 16.

Traugott, M. W., & Price, V. (1992). Review: Exit polls in the 1989 Virginia gubernatorial race: Where did they go wrong? *Public Opinion Quarterly, 56*, 245–253.

Truman, H. (1948, October 26). *Address in the Cleveland Municipal Auditorium*. Truman Presidential Museum and Library. Retrieved February 5, 2007, from http://www.trumanlibrary.org/publicpapers/index.php?pid=2009&st=&st1=

International Comparative Surveys: Their Purpose, Content and Methodological Challenges

Marta Lagos

Sociology is a science based on comparisons, as Durkheim defined it. Comparative surveys are therefore at the core of the development of empirical sociology and political science. International, cross-cultural comparative surveys are the natural extension of that science in a globalized world.

The development of international comparative survey research started in the most developed societies with the highest levels of collaborations, principally in Europe and in the Anglo-Saxon countries. This was a marked difference with the past when social science developed with hardly any interaction; in fact Durkheim and Weber lived no more than 500 kilometers away from each other but never met.

Two types of comparative survey research programs are to be found: on the one hand the ongoing programs that are the main subject of this chapter, and on the other the ad hoc projects. A limited number of ad hoc international comparative research

surveys from past decades can be found in different survey data banks or archives today (→ *Archiving Poll Data*). The first one was the project carried out by Almond and Verba in 1959 in five countries that gave birth to their book *The Civic Culture* (Almond & Verba, 1963). Starting in 1972 and mostly within the European Community, there are a number of surveys (14 altogether) carried out only once, twice or three times in up to 15 countries. Additionally some surveys have been carried out every year or every other year for a number of years (see www.gesis.org).

It is principally after 1990 that ongoing comparative research projects grew in number and had expanded coverage of larger parts of the world, at the time when globalization expanded.

The ongoing international comparative survey research programs can be classified into four main types. The first are the academic studies that try to develop and test theory in the scope of social science: World Value

Survey (WVS); European Value Survey (EVS); Comparative Study of Electoral Systems (CSES); Comparative National Election Program (CNEP); European Social Survey (ESS); and the International Social Survey Program (ISSP). A second type of ongoing comparative surveys are the opinion barometers that have developed as an applied branch of academic surveys, and they are more oriented towards public policy. These surveys monitor the evolution and transformation of societies as a whole. A third type are the commercially oriented surveys on specific subjects like the Corporate Social Responsibility Monitor (CSR) that are being used to study public policy orientations among the international organizations and that are partially available to the general public. Finally a category by itself, the USA-based think tank, the Pew Research Center, has developed a comparative survey program called the Pew Global Attitudes project that monitors USA-related issues in the world and is publicly accessible. This is the only single independent institution that monitors public opinion indicators in a selected sample of countries in the world.

There are other programs based in Universities, like Pipa (Program on International Policy Attitudes) at the University of Maryland USA. Very recent (2006) is also 'The Americas Barometer' based in LAPOP (Latin America Public Opinion Project) at Vanderbilt University, USA. Conducted for USIAD, US Government, in 20 of the 35 countries of The Americas, on Democratic Culture and Audit. This is a category by itself, a barometer of a neighbouring region conducted for a single government.

In spite of the increased amounts of data available, not much has changed since the first international comparative survey in terms of the contribution of these surveys to the development of democratic theory. As Almond and Verba stated, there are still two 'separate tables' (see Almond, 1990; Morlino, 2005). Survey findings have not yet merged into the theory development of social science, with the exception of theories tested and developed by Ronald Inglehart in the World Values Survey.

This poses a twofold challenge, the first one being the task of merging these separate tables and the second to overcome the temptation by many to use 'selected results' to prove particular hypothesis that are not equally proven when considering the overall available data. An increasing amount of literature is being produced with sophisticated selected partial explanatory models, not necessarily developing 'merged tables.' The language barrier necessary to consider the regional and local literature, as well as the necessary specific knowledge of the countries being analyzed, is one of the hindrances. The perverse effect of having so much individual data available is the production of spurious partial interpretation. In other words, the atomization of analysis and geographical spread of scholars, as well as the consideration of partial results, may be delaying rather than accelerating the merging of the two tables.

METHODOLOGY AND APPLICATION

The spread of comparative multicultural surveys has also launched by default the development of a comparative survey methodology discipline, including new research areas and a community of experts. The Comparative Survey Design and Implementation (CSDI) group founded under the leadership of Janet Harkness from ZUMA, a publicly funded research institute in Mannheim, Germany, in 2002 organized research on the methodology for cross-national and cross-cultural surveys. Its key objectives are to provide guidelines and standards for the design and implementation of cross-cultural surveys. The group works on a voluntary self-funding basis that involves a large number of subgroups dedicated to specific subjects in this field (see http://www.gesis.org/Mitarbeiter/zuma/harkness/csdi/Default.htm).

If the object of public opinion surveys is to reflect reality, then comparative surveys aim at reflecting equivalence between different realities. In the case of comparative survey research, the aim should be to recognize and register deviations from reality and their equivalences. Very few countries outside the developed world collect exact statistics. Information is a significant part of the difference between the developed and less developed world; most surveys are conducted on the basis of imperfect information. Registering the level of imperfection of the information upon which samples and designs are made is a necessary challenge to establish equivalence.

In order to attain quality standards, full knowledge of the imperfections and heterogeneity of methods is necessary. Comparative research is comparative when the researchers manage to identify the imperfections and heterogeneity in such a way that it allows them to be considered in the analysis. Roger Jowell offers a list of 10 rules that should be observed in order to 'mitigate' the problems of imperfection and heterogeneity (Jowell, 1998).

One of the main differences between academic projects and projects funded by governments and public money is that academic projects can more easily avoid facing the problems of imperfect information and registering quality standards. In the international comparative research field it is more likely that studies conducted with public and international funds attain higher levels of transparency and result in higher quality conditions than academic studies; the ESS is a good example of this.

The following main aspects have to be addressed when applying multicultural comparative surveys on top of the problem of sampling with imperfect information, considering that the most significant imperfect information lies in the level of knowledge of the involved researchers, who must be capable of understanding the cultures as well as the languages of the countries researched in order to be able to understand the context in which social phenomena take place.

In order to identify the subject matters that can be addressed, one has first to consider the level of knowledge in the sampled population. Second, one must find a question design that is acceptable to diverse cultures. Third, one must phrase the question with such words that it can be translated into different languages without ambiguity.

The cultural differences have to be taken into account. For example barriers or filters to free speech are different in different cultures. Women in some societies are not allowed to talk to strangers (interviewers) other than in the presence of another male member of the family. Castes in India define the communication to the outside world. These differences are not more important than other subtle intangible barriers that cultures pose to the expression of opinions, attitudes and behavior. The difference only lies in the fact that some of them are obvious and others are not.

Another major challenge is the equivalence in the content of words, as well as the expression of a concept with one or more words. The researcher has to be able to define questions using words that mean the same thing in the different cultures to which it is being applied. Universal concepts do not necessarily have universal words. Alone, the word 'democracy' does not exist in every language; in some it must be expressed with a series of words. There are very few, if any, researchers who are capable of evaluating multilingual differences across cultures. This is also an emergent field where not enough capacity is available. No less important is the consideration of the imperfection between the language of survey application and the native language of the respondent that occurs in multilingual countries, turning this into an important restriction for national representative samples.

Scales need careful design, since they can 'force' cultural trends. It is advisable to test scales in the different cultures where they are going to be applied and observe their performance before choosing one. Further attention should be given to modifiers of scales in terms of the response categories. Researchers have to pick modifiers that have the same meaning in different languages. There languages that are softer in their expressions and languages that are harder; a soft modifier in one language can be easily translated into a hard modifier in another language. This difference is responsible for large differences in responses in main comparative questions reported today in the literature (Lagos, 2003). The translation of the questionnaire turns into one of the major sources of imperfection when questions are not carefully designed. This is one of the subjects that receive less attention in international comparative research programs today, and yet may be influencing an important part of the variance found in some results.

The interviewer protocols and sample designs have to be adapted to the differences that these and many other considerations pose. For example, in societies where women have to answer in the presence of men, it must be part of the interviewer protocol differing from that of Western societies. There are also regional differences to account for; in Africa, for example, it is advisable to force a gender quota of 50% to avoid underrepresentation of women due to the many cultural barriers. Interviewer protocols need to include specifics in approaching and obtaining female interviews. A comprehensive list of these kinds of issues can be found at CSDI.

THE SCOPE OF COMPARATIVE RESEARCH

Equivalence is the goal of comparative survey research, but from an international perspective there is a limit to equivalence and comparability. Societies can only be compared in their homogeneities, meaning there are a number of subjects where heterogeneity does not allow comparison. In the extreme, no analysis is possible when all answers are different in such a way that no common coding scheme is feasible. The number of countries that can be included in a given comparison decreases as the number of concepts included increases. The consideration of what public opinion is lies at the heart of comparability, since no issue can be addressed that is not in the domain of public opinion in the societies included.

We find, in fact, no world public opinion *per se* inasmuch as citizens, the general public, do not interact in the world, but mainly in one given society, or a limited group of societies like the European Union. One could speak, therefore, of the existence of a European public opinion in those matters that concern the citizens of the European Union, but one could not speak of a Latin American or an Asian or African public opinion. Hardly any political or social issue of any given society becomes a world issue inasmuch as it does not concern or affect the world population or the population of a given region, even if it is within a shared culture. Interaction between members of those individual societies is not enough for public opinion to exist. The existence of a given public opinion beyond the national borders is a function of the amount of interaction between societies, and the most developed societies with the highest levels of interaction are more likely to develop new dimensions of public opinion that can become the object of comparative research (see Rusciano, 2004).

What researchers do find are issues that are common to many societies and that can be compared as the views that citizens in each society have. These issues are the objective of comparative survey research. Furthermore we also find global issues. A vast majority of the world population, at least that part of the world population that has access to television, is aware of an increasing number of single issues such as wars, terrorism, or natural disasters, that can be called global issues. Some of these issues can be addressed in comparative survey research worldwide. On the other hand, many issues shared by an enlightened international elite produce a world elite opinion that should not be confused with a world *public* opinion.

Comparative survey research can be applied in many aspects that are common to all participating societies in a given research program, in such a way that these aspects are understandable in the exact same way in all languages to which they are translated, with a standardized methodology that targets cultural and functional equivalence and is able to operationalize it. A main quality criterion for comparative survey research is the ability to register and publish individual country design and implementation decisions in order to allow other researchers to assess the level of equivalence. Heterogeneity must be acknowledged as a given and known fact, and it should be the basis upon which comparison is made.

THE ONGOING INTERNATIONAL COMPARATIVE RESEARCH PROGRAMS

The barometers

The word 'Barometer' was first used by the European Commission in 1974 when the Eurobarometer was created, and it has become today a European product expanded to all continents. Five new regional opinion barometers have been launched since the Eurobarometer, starting with New Europe Barometer (NEB) in 1991. The expression 'opinion barometer' is not only used for international comparative surveys but also for national surveys that have tracked the transformation of many societies, especially third wave democracies like the Philippines, Korea, Uruguay, Chile, and Russia, in which 10 to 20 years of data can be found under this name.

The Eurobarometer

The 'Schuijt Report' (Schuijt, 1972) expressed the need to conduct regular surveys of the member countries of the European Commission in order to support the integration process. Jean Jacques Rabier was appointed to devise such an instrument, having conducted the previous comparative surveys from 1970 and 1971. After a pilot study in 1973, he launched in 1974 a biennial survey in all nine member countries called the Eurobarometer. Rabier organized the Eurobarometer with close academic links. At the beginning, the questionnaires were prepared by Rabier, Jean Stoetzel and Ronald Inglehart in French and English, and sent to the institutes that would conduct the surveys. The Eurobarometer has evolved from an academically based survey into a political information instrument for public policy development in the European Union.

The initial objectives were to contribute information about the formation of a 'European conscience,' and so help the economic and political integration process of those societies. The objective of that information policy was to know how, to whom and about what the European Union speaks to Europeans (Rabier, 2003). Today the Eurobarometer is supported by the Institutional Relations and Communications Commissioner of the European Union (see http://europa.eu.int/comm/public_opinion).

The Eurobarometer currently consists of approximately 60 surveys a year; these include a standard biennial face-to-face survey, special, and flash barometers (by telephone) in all member countries. There have been also other series, including the Central and Eastern Eurobarometer (CEEB) carried out annually in up to 20 countries between 1990 and 1997 in European Union non-member countries. Today a central contract for all fieldwork for a fixed number of years is awarded after a competitive process.

The 1970–2002 Mannheim Eurobarometer Trend file, compiled by Hermann Schmitt from Mannheimer Zentrum fur Europäische Sozialforschung (MZES) and Evi Scholz from ZUMA and deposited in the Zentralarchiv für Empirische Sozialforschung (ZA, see http://www.gesis.org/ZA/), is based on the Eurobarometer biannual face-to-face survey data. This is a monumental unique trend file that gathers the longest and largest public opinion comparative research database existing today in the world. With it, one can observe the evolution of European societies over 30 years. Standardized current Eurobarometer data are made available for social science research purposes by cooperation between the Interuniversity Consortium for Political and Social Research (ICPSR), ZA and the Swedish Social Science Data Service (SSDS). The data are also available on their website: http://europa.eu.int/comm/public_opinion/index_en.htm.

An international comparative public opinion barometer can be defined as a comparative survey research program that periodically monitors the evolution of public opinion in a given number of countries representing a region or subregion of the world with identical questions in a defined universe at a given point in time. The Eurobarometer was designed to monitor societies as a whole, while today the expression 'barometer' is used to monitor specific subjects, creating a whole new area of survey research known as opinion barometers. This is the case of the Japan-based Asean Barometer that monitors life styles in Asia. Other differences lie in the application and the periodicity. The Eurobarometer was designed to field identical questionnaires simultaneously in a given number of countries, but only three of the existing barometers apply this principle today. In fact, in Asia and Africa, barometers are not simultaneous in their application. This has to do not only with the heterogeneity of capacities, but also with funding conditions of individual surveys. While the Eurobarometer has central funding, all other barometers depend on ad hoc funding that sometimes necessitates different timings. This creates the additional difference of the time of the study as a factor in interpreting the equivalence of the results.

The regularity with which a barometer is conducted is an important part of the equivalence of its results. The Eurobarometer has been applied biennially without interruption in spring and autumn. The most similar barometer is the 'Latinobarómetro', which has been applied annually across an uninterrupted period of 12 years. All other barometers have no specific periodicity, and waves have taken place dependent on funding or other historical conditions. In other words, the new barometers in Asia and Africa have a long way to go before they can reach the level of equivalence of the Eurobarometer. Central and stable funding lies at the heart of these differences.

The group of scholars involved in the Eurobarometer overlap with those involved in other comparative surveys such as the European Values Survey and the World Values Surveys; after Lazarsfeld and Almond and Verba, they constitute the second generation of pioneers in the field of comparative survey research. Many of the scholars involved in the World Value Surveys are also involved in Barometers or other comparative studies, creating a network of scholars that grew out of these founding fathers of comparative research.

NEB—New Europe Barometer

The Centre for the Study of Public Policy (CSPP), under the direction of Richard Rose, launched the New Europe Barometer NEB in 1991 to monitor responses of public opinion to the transformation of the polity, economy, and society in post-communist countries (see www.abdn.ac.uk/cspp). It completed seven waves that incorporate the New Baltic Barometer and the New Russia Barometer. Altogether this program completed more than 100 surveys involving more than 180,000 respondents in 17 countries. The last wave was conducted in 2004 in 14 countries including the new EU member countries, applicant countries, and post-Soviet countries. The project has had multiple sources of funding over the years. Representative samples of 1,000 or more interviews were conducted in each country. Fieldwork ran over a period of three or four months for each wave, similar to the Eurobarometer. Nevertheless this barometer differs from the Eurobarometer because each wave is applied independently in selected countries, with few countries in all waves. Historically, this barometer comes to an end when the applicant countries become members of the European Union and they start being surveyed by the Eurobarometer. Data are not available through the web.

Latinobarómetro (LB)

The Latinobarómetro was conceived as a replica of the Eurobarometer and was launched in 1995 in eight countries after funding from the European Commission was approved for four countries. The project is carried out by Corporacion Latinobarometro, an NGO based in Santiago de Chile; Marta Lagos is its founding director. Today is it conducted annually in 18 Latin American countries. It has become the most similar barometer to the Eurobarometer; it has a regular annual field period, and a written report is published two months after fieldwork. Today representative samples of 100% of national populations with 1,000 to 1,200 face-to-face interviews are applied in each country. Over 1,000 variables across twelve waves have monitored the transition to democracy in Latin America on attitudes about democracy, the political system, the economy, public policy, values and international relations. The project has had multiple funding sources over the years.

Since 2006, the Latinobarometer has had an online data bank with JD Systems with the first and longest trend of comparative survey research data (1995–2005) available to the general public outside the developed world, in a bilingual format in Spanish and English. This was accomplished after 10 years of negotiating the terms and conditions of contracts with donors to allow their public release, as the data had been only partially available before this. It also is the first public opinion data bank in Spanish (see www.latinobarometro.org).

The Afrobarometer (AB)

In 1999, Robert Mattes from the Institute for Democracy in South Africa (IDASA) and Michael Bratton from Michigan State University gathered a group of scholars in Cape Town, South Africa, including the directors of the existing Latino and New Europe barometers, to launch a comparative survey program that quickly developed into the current Afrobarometer applied in more than a dozen African countries. A third institute joined the project as it grew to cover larger parts of Africa: the Ghana Centre for Democratic Development under the direction of Gyimah Boadi. This is an independent non-partisan research project that measures the social, political and economic atmosphere in Africa. The funding comes from different organizations.

Three waves have been completed, in 1999/2000, 2002/2003; and the third wave in 2005/2006 was conducted in 18 countries. Full results are available for the first wave and second wave. The lag of several years in the release of the data to the general public is another difference from other 'barometers'; because of the academically based funding, the data releases have been linked to the publications of the principal investigator, in accordance with scholarly tradition in the USA. The Afrobarometer is available in the same online system as the Latinobarometer.

The surveys consist of random samples of adult populations with 1,200 face-to-face interviews in 14 countries and interviews with 2,400 cases for Nigeria, South Africa, Kenya and Uganda. These samples represent 85% to 100% of the national populations, based on the number of languages covered in each country (see www.afrobarometer.org).

Asian Barometer (ABS)

In the year 2000, Yunhan Chu from Taipei University and Larry Diamond from Stanford University gathered a group of scholars and professionals from Afro, Latino and other comparative studies in Taipei to launch the Asian Barometer. The first wave was completed in 2002 in 11 countries, and the second was in the field during 2005 and 2006 in 12 countries. The Asian Barometer group now covers 17 countries in Asia, including larger samples for China and India. It is an applied program focusing on political values, attitudes toward democracy, and governance around the region. Face-to-face nationally representative samples of 1,200 or more members of the adult population are interviewed in each country. The project has multiple funding sources. Data from the first wave is available in the same online system as Afro- and Latinobarometer.

In 2003, Yogendra Yadav from the Center for the Study of Developing Societies in New Delhi, India, gathered a group of scholars to launch the South Asian part of the Asian Barometer, adding the last of the larger unsurveyed countries in the world, also known as 'elephant countries' in reference to Brazil, China, India, and other large countries in the world, in terms of population and territory, thus covering the world population. One wave was completed in 2004 in India, Bangladesh, Pakistan, Nepal and Sri Lanka, and its results will be available on the online system after publication by Oxford University Press.

Globalbarometer Surveys (GBS)

Globalbarometer Surveys is a federation of barometers that gathers data from the existing barometers. It is dedicated to the transformation of societies through development of a module of common questions allowing intercultural comparison between regions. The Afro-, Asian and Latinobarometers have a common module and standardized methodology. The first merged dataset contains the first wave of the Asian Barometer and the Afrobarometer and the 2000 wave of the Latinobarometro, altogether comprising 49 countries. The Globalbarometer Surveys network is seeking coordination with the Eurobarometer project in order to expand multicultural comparisons to an additional 24 countries (see www.globalbarometer.net). Also other barometer initiatives are underway in those parts of the world not yet covered, such as the Arabbarometer (www. arabbarometer.org), new member of the Globalbarometer Surveys. This data set will also be uploaded to the online JD system used by the barometers.

A link to the New Europe Barometer was also produced before the expansion of the European Union, and existing historical data was used to publish a chapter on 'Trust in institutions' in the tenth anniversary publication of IDEA International (Bratton, Lagos, Rose, & Chu, 2005).

There are other regional barometers, in addition to those gathered in the Globalbarometers, that refer to specific subjects such as the Asia Barometer (also known as Japan Asean Barometer) or are conducted for a government like 'The Americas Barometer'. Also, the Caribbean, those countries in Europe that are not members of the European Union, and the like, are the next to come, so that we will see new regions with comparative survey results

in the near future, as well as an increasing standardization of access and dissemination of results.

Asia Barometer—Japan Asean Barometer

The first wave of the Asiabarometer, conducted in 2003 in 10 countries under the direction of Takashi Inoguchi from Tokyo University, focused on the daily lives of ordinary people, with their worries, angers, desires and dreams. A source book was published in 2005 by Siglio XXI, and data will be available via the ICPSR. Funding was covered by business donations to the University of Tokyo. The second wave in 2004 was officially called the Japan Asean Barometer and was carried out in 13 countries, focusing on Southeast Asia, but including Japan, Korea and China. It was supported with funding from the Ministry of Foreign Affairs and the University of Tokyo. Surveys consisted of 800 face-to-face interviews (except for Japan) produced through a multi-stage random sample with nationwide coverage, except for China, India, Indonesia and Malaysia (see http://avatoli.ioc.u-tokyo. ac.jp/~asiabarometer/). Data is not available through the web.

International Social Survey Program (ISSP)

The International Social Survey Program (ISSP) is a continuing annual program of cross-national collaboration. It adds a cross-national perspective to existing individual national studies. The ISSP grew out of collaboration between two research institutes in Germany, Allgemeine Bevölkerungsumfragen der Sozialwissenschaften (ALLBUS) and the Zentrum für Umfragen, Methoden and Analysen (ZUMA), and the General Social Survey (GSS) in the United States. In 1982, ALLBUS and GSS included a module on job values, important areas of life, abortion and feminism. Soon a pool of institutes on all continents agreed to develop topical modules of 15 minutes duration to supplement regular national surveys with extensive background variables and make them available to the public. This collaboration has now grown to 39 nations. The surveys are locally funded, and the merging of datasets is performed by the Zentralarchiv für Empirische Sozialforschung (ZA) in Germany. Data from 1985 to 2002 are available at ZA and the ICPSR.

The annual topics for the ISSP are developed by a committee and approved by the annual plenary meeting. The membership is by invitation, and full membership is acquired after having deposited the first data set (see www.issp.org).

The European Values Survey (EVS) and the World Values Survey (WVS)

At the beginning of the 1980s, some of the same scholars involved in the Eurobarometer devised a European survey aimed at researching values. One can find a strong correlation between the development of European integration, the increase in the level of interaction among scholars within and outside Europe, and the formation of a social science community that developed on both sides of the Atlantic. They organized the first pioneer comparative survey research initiatives. Both the European and the World Value surveys are a consequence of this community that initiated comparative survey research, as it is known today. The decades in which these studies were launched correspond to the stable prosperous decades after the Second World War in which the international community was consolidating in all aspects. The launching of these surveys was framed in an expanding world in need of new sources of information, where Europe played a leading role in their development. While the WVS is the largest existing multi-continental comparative survey project, the Eurobarometer is the longest running comparative survey existing today.

The European Values Survey (EVS) was launched under the leadership of Jan Kerkhofs and Ruud de Moor, with Gordon Heald, Juan Linz, Elisabeth Noelle-Neumann, Jacques Rabier and Helene Riffault on the advisory committee. In 1981, the EVS carried out surveys in 10 West European societies, evoking such widespread interest that it expanded to 26 countries. Now it is carried out by the EVS foundation.

Three waves have been conducted, in 1981, 1990 and 1999/2000, covering European countries beyond EU membership. Surveys are based upon face-to-face interviews with representative samples of the adult population of 1,000 cases or more in each country. The surveys focus on basic social, cultural, political, moral and religious values. Cultural and social changes appear dependent upon the stage of socioeconomic development and historical factors specific to a given nation.

The World Values Surveys grew out of the EVS, whose findings suggested that predictable cultural changes were taking place. The second wave of surveys was designed and coordinated by a steering committee consisting of Ruud de Moor, chair; Jan Kerkhofs, co-chair; Karel Dobbelaere, Loek Halman, Stephen Harding, Felix Heunks, Ronald Inglehart, Renate Koecher, Jacques Rabier and Noel Timms. Inglehart organized the surveys in non-European countries and several East European countries, expanding it to all continents; it has become the largest and longest running comparative survey research still in existence today. The WVS has become a Swedish NGO, with a steering committee lead by Ronald Inglehart, after several waves had been run by Inglehart, based at the ISR, University of Michigan.

The World Values Survey is a worldwide investigation of socio-cultural and political change, conducted by a network of social scientists at universities around the world with local funding for each survey, in some cases with supplementary sources. The survey is conducted with nationally representative samples on all six inhabited continents representing 85% of the world population; a total of 79 countries have been surveyed in at least one wave. Both random and quota sampling are used. The populations of China and India are undersampled. The interview length is approximately one hour, and the

Table 54.1   The national composition of the World Values Project

Waves	Countries
1981–1983	19
1990–1993	42
1995–1997	54 plus several regional surveys
1999–2001	60

average sample size is over 1000 cases. Four waves have been carried since 1981 (see Table 54.1); the fifth wave started in 2005 and will continue through 2006/2007 (see www.worldvaluessurvey.org).

Data are available through a newly established online access system designed by JD Systems allowing non-experts to obtain results from individual variables through the web as well as entire data files. The same access system is used by the CSES and Latinobarometers, because it is the most user friendly and best available access system for multinational comparative survey research data, where all barometers of the Globalbarometer network have uploaded their data. The datasets are also archived at the ICPSR and at other major archives.

The World Values Survey project grew through voluntary collaboration and ad hoc financing across successive waves, with a very heterogeneous quality that depended on the level of financial support that a particular survey had, especially in the first waves. Researchers using this data must be aware of the fully documented differences that appear in the full database. The newly established data access and institutional arrangement seeks standardized quality requirements in future waves, starting with the 2005/2006 wave.

The singularity of the World Value Survey is its theoretical framework and development. Unlike any other comparative survey research project, it tests and develops theory. The World Values Surveys were designed to provide a comprehensive measurement of all major areas of human concern, from religion to politics to economic and social life. Two dimensions dominate the picture: (1) traditional/secular-rational, and (2) survival/self-expression values. The traditional/secular-rational values dimension reflects the contrast between societies in which religion is very important and those in which it is not. The second major dimension of cross-cultural variation is linked with the transition from industrial society to post-industrial society—which creates a polarization between survival and self-expression values. Orientations have shifted from traditional toward secular-rational values in almost all industrial societies. This is the only experience in comparative survey research in which 'tables are not separate.'

Comparative Study of Electoral Systems (CSES)

The Comparative Study of Electoral Systems (CSES) is a coordinated comparative project founded in 1995 by Steven Rosenstone, then the director of the American National Election Studies (NES). The CSES grew out of the NES, the National Election Study carried out since 1952 by the Institute for Social Research (ISR) at the University of Michigan. The power of the almost 50 years of longitudinal data on elections was the basis for the establishment of a worldwide program that would produce election surveys on a multicultural longitudinal basis. Many of the scholars involved in the WVS, also based at ISR, took part in the launching of the CSES, contributing to the formation of a worldwide network of scholars in the field of electoral public opinion research. Today CSES has support from the National Science Foundation of the United States and is based in Ann Arbor, Michigan, at the same location as the National Election Study. It is now directed by Ian McAllister. Data are available through JD Systems with online access (see www.cses.org).

This program enables the assembly and systematic analysis of electoral behavior under globally varying institutional conditions. The project design is applied with successive modules; to date, two modules have been applied (see Table 54.2). The project is governed by a steering committee drawn from the members. CSES coordinates the

Table 54.2   The national composition of the CSES Project

Module	Completed	Countries
1	2001	33
2	2005	50
3	beginning 2006 with data collection until elections in 2010	

operation of more than 50 indigenous national election studies across the world. Two sets of information are gathered for each society. One set is composed of information on the institutional arrangements of elections, and the other is a post-election survey about the main election process in each society. This post-election survey consists of a module of questions that is generally included in a wider survey in each participant country designed to last no longer than 10 to 15 minutes. CSES designs, receives, standardizes, cleans, and merges these data, and then makes them freely and immediately available to the world's scholarly community.

Each module has common items and specific objectives. Module 1 addressed the impact of constitutional and electoral systems on democratic performance, social cleavages, and attitudes toward parties, political institutions, and the democratic process. Module 2 refers to accountability and representation. Module 3 considers three aspects of the factors affecting electoral choice: what is the balance between retrospective and prospective choice sets, ideology and performance?

Comparative National Elections Project (CNEP)

The Comparative National Elections Project (CNEP) was launched in the late 1980s as a study of information processes in four established democracies, with Richard Gunther from the Ohio State University as project coordinator. Their website was available as of 2006 and provides access to data produced before the year 2000.

The second wave was applied in new and old democracies with questions on political change and regime consolidation (CNEP II) in nine countries. It is now in its third wave (CNEP III), expanding its coverage to include African and Asian countries with new items on identity and citizen understandings of the meaning and quality of democracy. The CNEP is a project based on aspects of political communication and social structure within the context of election campaigns. It is thus possible to undertake a detailed study of the structuring of partisan politics in new or transformed democracies, and to compare these emerging or evolving institutions and patterns of interaction with those of long-established democracies.

The methodology of the CNEP is mixed. The vast majority of interviews are face-to-face, while some are telephone-based along with one Internet survey. Nationally representative samples of the adult population consisting of 1,000 to 2,500 interviews are applied in each country.

The European Social Survey (ESS)

The European Social Survey was launched in 2002 under the leadership of Max Kaase and the executive direction of Roger Jowell, with the financial support of the European Union. This research program seeks to establish a longitudinal monitoring of public opinion in European societies with the highest quality data standards and stable financial support. This is a project that covers the richest developed democracies with the highest financial support ever given to a comparative research program. It is based on strictly orthodox methodology with exact precision on all aspects of procedures, marking a significant difference from the much looser methodology of comparative research programs in non-developed societies that are underfunded and depend on local or ad hoc financial support for each wave of data. This survey research program is unique and constitutes an exception producing a significant quality difference from all other comparative survey research programs, including the Eurobarometer.

The central aim of the ESS is to develop and conduct a systematic study of changing values, attitudes, attributes and behavior patterns within European polities. Academically driven, but designed to feed into key European policy debates, the ESS measures how people's social values, cultural norms and behavior patterns are distributed, the ways in which they differ within and between nations, and the directions and speeds with which they are changing.

The interviews last an hour and are followed by a short supplement. There is a core module that monitors change and continuity, plus two rotating modules, repeated at intervals, with substantive topics that provide an in-depth focus. Strict fully documented random probability samples at every stage, consisting of 1,500 face-to-face interviews representing the total population of all persons aged 15 and over, are applied in each country every two years. (For the national composition of the ESS project see Table 54.3.)

In fact, programs like CSES or the WVS are applied in countries that have very heterogeneous levels of development where limited or outdated census information makes it impossible to meet ESS methodological standards. In other countries where it would be technically possible to attain ESS standards, such levels of funding are not available. The ESS high quality data only demonstrate again the differences in development between regions of the world (see www.europeansocialsurvey.org). Academically, the question remains open between those who favor the production only

of this level of high quality data, and those who favor the production of minimum standards according to the levels of development of the countries in which surveys are applied. No doubt this requirement for a high level of quality would make barometers outside the developed world impossible to conduct, since funding is always trying to optimize a minimum necessary standard and never a maximum.

Standardization of the differences between different levels of methodology restricted by levels of development in countries is not yet available. CSDI is a program that aims at the development of these issues. The Eurobarometer and GSS are the two standards in Europe and the United States of America that are fully financed by state owned, and as such they constitute the exceptions in comparative social research in a world where most other programs depend on ad hoc funding. The ESS is the first comparative survey research project that is publicly funded to attain the highest quality of comparative survey research ever produced.

Corporate Social Responsibility Monitor (CSR)

The Corporate Social Responsibility Monitor (CSR) is a comparative survey research project carried out by Globescan, Canada, a commercial firm. It focuses on the role of companies in societies. The survey was first conducted in 2000 and has to date completed five waves in over 25 countries from all continents. The survey is conducted with nationally representative samples of 1,000 respondents from the adult population in each country. Globescan has conducted other single comparative surveys in association with Pipa, BBC, and other organizations (see www.globescan.com).

Data have been partially released to the general public. There are other commercial research programs like this on the environment and globalization that also have partially released data for public analysis.

Table 54.3 The national composition of the ESS Project

Wave	Year	Number of countries	Data released
1	2002	21	September 2003
2	2004	24	September 2005
3	2006	24	September 2007

Pew Global Attitudes survey

The Pew Global Attitudes Project released its first survey in 2002, with data from 44 countries on people's assessments of their own lives and their views on the current state of the world. The second survey was released in 2003 with data from 49 countries, focusing on attitudes on globalization and democratization in countries with a significant Muslim population. The series continued into 2006 with different sets of countries interviewed in each year. The program is carried out by the Pew Research Center under the direction of Andrew Kohut. It emphasizes issues, attitudes, and trends most salient for the United States, and is funded by the Pew Charitable Trusts with supplemental grants from the Hewlett Foundation (see www.people-press.org).

CONCLUSIONS

Comparative multicultural survey research is a new field developing in a globalized world with many opportunities for the future. New barometers are on their way to cover new regions. They grow at the speeds of the development of the different regions, sometimes a little ahead of the average of the region, as in the case of Africa and the Afrobarometer, where availability of funding has allowed the application of surveys in countries where neither the capacity nor the tools were available. With such investments, these survey projects contribute to the development of social science in each particular country as well.

A representative sample of countries in the world that covers the known differences in culture and geography is yet to be designed, although first attempts have been made by the Pew Research Program. A new group of scholars is yet to be born, multilingual in Chinese, Hindi, Russian, Arabic, and the European languages, with studies that cover social phenomena common to developing societies. For the moment, what is out there are region and country specialists who

are venturing into comparing their areas with other regions or subregions. We know from available data that Taiwan, Russia and Paraguay have similarities, but no scholar has yet analyzed this comparison. Similarly, Venezuela and Uganda have similarities that have yet to be compared. At the same time, new theory will no doubt develop, with the help of such surveys, to better understand the transformation of these societies. Surely as the discipline expands, the tables will not remain separate. This field is at its starting point, growing at the speed of the levels of interaction among societies. In the meantime, intra-regional comparison is the most common form of analysis, and new regional experts are being trained.

In methodological terms, the spread of comparative surveys to all parts of the world will set new international standards that will no doubt capture the multicultural and diversity elements of development. The resulting data will differ from those of the most developed part of the world. This has been the path other instruments have followed, and survey research, as another example, will follow the same path.

As for results, we have learned with comparative survey research that social phenomena are more homogenous than expected, and at the same time, that culture and history also matter inasmuch as they uniquely shape the evolution of each society. The way that democracy is being consolidated is a concrete example of the value of the combination of these two dimensions, i.e. the homogeneity and specificity of comparative social phenomena. Comparative multicultural interpretations of results are at the beginning of understanding and explaining how these elements combine, and our biggest risk is no doubt to be left with a sea of data and no framework to explain it. Empiricists should therefore not forget to follow the advice of Emile Durkheim to look out of the window. While not diminishing the importance of empirical data, one must nevertheless recognize the simple observation of a living society as a powerful instrument to comprehend its evolution.

REFERENCES

Almond, G. A. (1990). *A discipline divided: Schools and sects in political science.* Newbury Park, Calif.: Sage Publications.

Almond, G. A., & Verba, S. (1963). *The civic culture.* Princeton: Princeton University Press.

Bratton, M., Lagos, M., Rose, R., & Chu, Y. (2005). The people's voice: Trust in political institutions. In International Institute for Democracy and Electoral Assistance IDEA (Eds.), *Ten years of supporting democracy worldwide.* IDEA International. Retrieved February 5, 2007, from http://www.idea.int/publications/anniversary/index.cfm.

Jowell, R. (1998). How comparative is comparative research? *American Behavioural Scientist, 42,* 168–177.

Lagos, M. (2003). Support for and satisfaction with democracy. *International Journal for Public Opinion Research, 15,* 471–487.

Morlino, L. (2005, September). *Still separate tables? Democratic theory and survey research.* Paper presented at the conference on 'Ten years of Latinobarometro,' St Anthony's College, Oxford (UK).

Rabier, J. (2003, October 21). Interview on the occasion of the 30th anniversary of the Eurobarometer posted on the Europa's portal.

Rusciano, F. L. (2004). World opinion. In J. Geer (Ed.), *Public opinion and polling around the world: A historical encyclopedia* (pp. 504–508). Santa Barbara: ABC-CLIO, Inc.

Schuijt, W. (1972). *Rapport sur la politique d'information des Communautés européennes* [Report on the information policy of the European Communities] Document 246/71. European Parliament. Retrieved February 5, 2007, from http://www.euractiv.com/31/images/Schuijt%20Report_tcm31-137655.pdf.

55

The Use of Voter Research in Campaigns

Fred Steeper

Polling and focus groups are used to develop and monitor political campaign strategies. In the United States, presidential campaigns and nearly all campaigns for the US Senate and state governor employ polling, as do many campaigns for the US House of Representatives and for state offices such as Secretary of State and Attorney General. Polling is done in local races as well. It is fair to say that campaign polling is used in most political systems, to a greater or lesser extent depending on available funds. Nevertheless, this chapter will concentrate on its use in the US, because this is where the author has first-hand information and experience. Between the options of giving an in-depth-analysis of the processes in one particular setting, albeit an important political system, and a more general but less concrete international comparison, I have chosen the first alternative.

As important as polling is, it is not the first priority for a political campaign. A campaign's first dollars must go to staffing, fund raising, candidate travel, and various voter contact programs, including direct mail and media advertising. Once the basic essentials are covered in a campaign's budget, a voter research program is added. Typically, a polling program will account for 2% to 5% of a campaign's total budget. While this is a relatively small part of a campaign's budget, it is considered one of the most important areas, which can make a difference between winning and losing.

VOTER RESEARCH DESIGNS AND PROGRAMS

There is a wide variety of survey designs in use today, each one serving a particular purpose. These survey designs include: 'benchmark polls,' 'brushfire polls,' 'strategic polls,' 'monitor polls,' and 'tracking polls' to cite some of their common labels. Campaigns able to afford them put several designs together over the course of a campaign to create a polling or research *program*.

The main distinctions between these polls are the questionnaire length and the sample size. Benchmark or strategic polls have up to 100 separate questions and larger sample sizes. Brushfire or monitor polls have fewer questions and sometimes smaller sample sizes. Tracking polls are in their own category. They use fewer questions and smaller samples on a daily or almost daily basis, with the results usually aggregated over three or more days.

Political polling can begin quite early in the campaign. For example, the first poll often is done almost two years before a statewide election in the US. Several polls plus focus groups are completed well before the final two months of the campaign. A full polling program would use a mix of polling designs over the course of the campaign. The exact *timing* of these polls is almost as important as questionnaire content and sample sizes. A key determinant is when the campaign needs to make certain decisions that depend partly on voter opinion. The most important examples are the decisions needed for the advertising campaign, because it is the single largest share of most campaign budgets. The content of that advertising will be driven partly by voter research. Consequently, the polling program will be coordinated with the needs of the media consultants. The media consultants usually want a strategic poll done just before they need to draft the advertising in order to have the 'freshest' results possible.

For incumbents, a second timing factor is when they learn who their opponents will be. In the US, this often depends on the outcome of primary elections that are spread from March through September of the election year. Strategic polls often are done a week or so after the opponent is known (usually only one because of the strong two-party system in the US) and the 'dust settles' from the opponent's primary victory. Monitor polls and strategic polls are often timed around known events that potentially present the voters with significant new information. A common example is scheduling a poll after a candidate's formal announcement of his or her candidacy. These announcements can generate a flurry of publicity and change or sharpen the shape of the race.

PARLIAMENTARY AND CONGRESSIONAL ELECTIONS

Parliamentary and US Congressional elections present a special case for voter research. These elections must be polled at two levels—the national level and the constituent level. In these elections voters have two sets of considerations—which party they want to control the government and which candidate they prefer to represent their district. The national polls are best to measure the overall advantages and disadvantages a party may have for the election in terms of national issues and the popularity of party leaders. From the national research, a party can develop message strategies to provide the most effective umbrella for all of its district races.

The district research helps a national party determine priorities among all its local races by measuring which are safe, competitive, or not winnable. Determining these priorities can be especially challenging in elections when there is a national 'time for a change' mood. What may look like a 'safe' district in the local polling may actually be a competitive race because of the national forces at play. Similarly, what may appear to be a competitive race in the early local polling may become a one-sided race because of national forces.

The 2006 US congressional elections are a good example of the interplay of local and national forces and the discrepancy that can happen between national and local polling results. For much of 2006, the national surveys were recording extreme 'time for a change' results, with very low approval ratings for President Bush and very high levels of dissatisfaction with the direction of the country. From these results, alone, one would expect a Democratic takeover of Congress. However, the state and district polling for much of 2006 showed Republicans with a reasonable chance of holding both houses of

Congress, albeit by reduced margins. Not until election eve did the local polling indicate an unusually large number of Republican seats were either lost or in jeopardy. Even so, the expectation from the last state and district polls was that Republicans would maintain control of the US Senate by losing no more than four seats, while probably losing control of the US House with a net loss of 16 to 25 districts. Because of the national forces, Republicans ceded control of the Senate with a loss of six seats, and control of the House with a loss of 30 seats.

FOCUS GROUPS, DIAL TESTS, AND ON-LINE TESTS

Campaigns have used traditional focus groups for decades (→ *Focus Groups and Public Opinion*). They are composed of anywhere from six to twelve people (sometimes a few more) with a professional moderator directing a discussion on any number of topics. Alternatively, campaigns use dial groups that mix discussion with quantitative data. A hand held device, 'a dial,' transmits the participants' responses to advertising, the moderator's questions, and other stimuli to an on-site computer (Steeper, 1978). The results are seen by the moderator in the discussion room and by observers from the campaign in a viewing room in real time. Dial groups are often twice the size of conventional focus groups and can be as large as several hundred people, although this option usually is beyond the budget of political campaigns.

Focus groups have two legitimate uses and a third one that is problematic. The two legitimate uses occur when the focus groups are paired with a poll. When focus groups are done *before* the poll, they are used to develop questionnaire content—both the topics to be covered in the poll and the language used in the actual questions—by revealing topics important to voters and the common language people use to describe an issue concern or a candidate perception. When groups are done *after* a poll, they are used to explore and clarify some of the poll's findings.

The problematic use of focus groups occurs when they are *not* paired with a poll. In this instance, strategic conclusions are reached without quantitative verification from a survey. This does happen. While campaigns generally are aware of the unreliability of small groups, there have been a surprising number of important campaign decisions made based on a few focus group discussions without survey verification. This can happen when a campaign is pressured by time or cannot afford poll verification, or both.

Typically, campaigns will recruit 'swing voters,' using varying definitions, to participate in the focus group. However, a wide variety of recruitment criteria come into play. One campaign might recruit only its 'soft' supporters if it is protecting a lead, whereas another might recruit only the 'soft' supporters of the opposition if it is trailing. In both cases, it is recruiting the type of voter who is most relevant to its primary goal— maintaining a lead (searching for messages to reinforce support) or overcoming the opponent's lead (searching for messages to induce switching).

The primary limitations of focus groups are the relatively small number of people in the groups and the group conformity that sometimes happens in small groups. Despite these scientific flaws of focus groups, they are remarkably useful to a campaign. They certainly improve the campaign's survey research in the two ways already described. Moreover, groups do surprisingly well in their problematic use—representing majority opinion or an opinion, at least, shared by a significant minority important to campaign strategy. A common experience with focus groups is to hear very similar discussions repeated in groups at different locations. Indeed, it is quite common that once you have heard discussions from four groups at two locations, or certainly six groups at three locations, 'you have heard it all.'

With the advent of the Internet, campaigns also have begun using on-line advertising tests (→ *Internet Surveys*). On-line tests have the advantage of much larger audience sizes, with several hundred voters viewing the television advertising. They also are significantly less expensive, always a campaign consideration. The major disadvantages of on-line tests are two—fewer ads can be rated at one time, and there is less control over the confidentiality of the ads in the testing stage. A third disadvantage is the constraint on respondent discussion of the ads. On-line tests do allow written comments about the ads. However, campaigns may prefer the more open discussions that occur in both conventional focus groups and dial groups.

IDENTIFYING WINNING MESSAGES

Campaigns have their own research programs to help them develop a winning *message* strategy. At first blush, this might confirm the most contemptuous notion of political campaigns, i.e. candidates say things they think people want to hear, as a result of their polling, rather than presenting what the candidate really believes. The actual experience is much more complex than confirming this cynical view of politics and the role of polling (Jacobs & Shapiro, 2000).

In most campaigns, the largest portion of the campaign budget goes to message delivery to voters through television and radio advertising, direct mail, telephone calls, and Internet web pages and e-mail. All of these communication devices have a limit on the number of messages they can deliver. Besides budget constraints, there is, of course, another major reason for campaigns to limit the number of messages they present the voters—the voters, themselves, have limits on the number of messages they will retain (Goldstein & Ridout, 2004).

While television advertising is the delivery mechanism of choice for all campaigns, it also presents the most severe limitations. From the *hundreds* of topics a campaign could address in its television advertising, *many must choose less than 10*. Even presidential campaigns, with the largest budgets of all, face such a limit, perhaps less than 20 topics that it can adequately cover in their television advertising. This occurs because of the belief that it requires a large amount of money to 'drive home' any single message. There is a difference between a single 'TV spot' and 'a message.' A television spot is a particular ad seen by the public. Several television spots can be communicating essentially the same message, but with different visuals and/or somewhat different language. The media consultants may recommend a television buy anywhere from 600 to 1200 'gross rating points' behind a single message. Even with these limitations, a common mistake of campaigns is that they run *too many* different messages on television rather than not enough messages.

The selection of winning messages is made more difficult by the four broad message categories facing any campaign as shown in Figure 55.1. They include what the campaign says about its candidate; what the campaign says about its opponent; what the campaign says to rebut what the opposition is saying about its candidate; and what the campaign says to rebut what the opposition is saying about the campaign's candidate. One of the most important purposes of polling and focus groups is to identify the most effective messages *within* each of these four categories.

Strategic polls and focus groups can provide information about one or more of these categories. By some point in the campaign, voter research *ideally* will have tested messages in all four categories. (A campaign will measure the other candidate's messages

MESSAGE	By Candidate A	By Candidate B
About Self	Candidate A's statements about Candidate A	Candidate B's statements about Candidate B.
About Opponent	Candidate A's statements about Candidate B	Candidate B's statements about Candidate A.

Figure 55.1   Candidate campaign message categories

to learn which ones are most credible and how to rebut them most effectively). In practice, the research will adequately cover one or two of the message areas and give lesser or no attention to the others. This can be a critical mistake. What to poll is probably the most important research decision a campaign makes.

A second purpose for strategic polling and focus groups is to measure the relative impact *among* the four categories in Figure 55.1. One or two of the categories might be far more important than the others to the final outcome of the election. A campaign needs to know how to allocate its scarce resources to each of these categories. Voter research can tell a campaign that it can win the election by allocating a significant portion of its resources to one or two of the four categories. Conversely, it can tell a campaign it could lose the election if does not allocate significant resources to one or two of the categories.

Frequently, the analysis of the potential effects *among* the four categories directs the campaign to 'negative advertising.' While 'negative advertising' often is criticized in the popular press, its justification comes from objective message testing. The research simply finds that the possible messages the campaign can send about its opponent *moves more voters* than does the information it has about its own candidate.

It is rarely the case, if it happens at all, that the candidate says, 'Find me *any* winning message, and I will use it.' This cynical view of message testing, while popular, is far from the actual experience. For one thing, there are a set of indisputable facts associated with any candidate—a private background, often a public background, and statements made in private and in public. All of these provide a set of parameters for what a campaign can and cannot say. On occasion, candidates have been caught lying about or distorting their backgrounds, and many have made contradictory statements. However, the intention of message testing is to find messages that have solid credibility—messages that will withstand the examination of third parties

(the news media) and will be toughest to rebut by the opposition—in short, messages that will move voters and are true.

To be sure, campaigns do hold their fingers in the air to determine which way the public opinion winds are blowing. They most often do this to decide what things about their candidates to emphasize and what things to downplay. 'Accentuate the positive, eliminate the negative' about its own candidate is a general strategy for all campaigns. A campaign will highlight those issue positions *already held* by the candidate that have *both* substantial majority support and are most relevant to the voters' current issue concerns. It will downplay or obfuscate its candidate's unpopular issue positions. This use of polling, however, is a far cry from the crass view of a candidate deciding his or her positions by which way the wind is blowing.

Of course, there are instances of candidates taking a new issue position based on a compelling poll result. However, in many of these cases, the new issue position is either compatible with candidate's general philosophy or irrelevant to that philosophy. There are also instances of candidates refusing to take a popular position recommended by his or her staff and consultants. And, there are instances of candidates telling the campaign staff and consultants not to even bother testing some position because they will not change what they believe to be right. Many times, the campaign will scrub its questionnaires of any issue strategies that it knows its candidate will not support. In many ways, the candidate forms the message testing rather than the message testing forming the candidate.

What the campaign says is determined by message testing. *When* it delivers these messages can be as important as what it says. A critical part of message strategy is the timing of the four types of messages in Figure 55.1. In important ways, message timing is influenced by who is ahead, 'the horse race.' Measuring the horse race is not just about creating a bandwagon effect with potential donors and the working press. The real purpose is for strategy. Indeed, many campaigns keep their horse race results to themselves.

THE 'HORSE RACE'—AHEAD OR BEHIND AND BY HOW MUCH?

It used to be the case that front-runners were highly unlikely to *initiate* critical messages about their opponents. Front-runners, at one time, also were unlikely to respond to attacks if they thought they had a substantial lead. While not initiating critical messages may still be the norm, it is not as automatic in the strategic thinking of campaign planners as it used to be. Pre-emptive strikes by front-runners are becoming more common. The wisdom of ignoring negative attacks initiated by the underdog has pretty much disappeared in current day strategy assumptions. To make these kinds of strategic decisions, all campaigns want to know if they are ahead or behind, by how much, and among what subgroups.

Types of races

Strategically, the horse race falls into five categories: ahead by a lot, ahead by a little, tied, behind by a little, and behind by a lot. While this scheme is somewhat simplified, campaigns tend to view their strategic situations as falling into one of these categories. The exact quantifications of the categories may vary by campaign and depend more on psychology than science. Being ahead by 10 or more points has a favorable psychological impact on a campaign for no other reason than the weight of having a 'double digit' lead. The strategic evaluation of single digit leads that fall within sampling error can be as much psychological as objective.

The *context* for the horse race result is needed before any strategic planning can begin. To set the context, a campaign reviews the basic popularity of its candidate and the opponent(s) along with the horse race result. Campaign polling has developed a general method of assessing candidate popularity. Campaign polls will ask voters if they are 'aware' of the names of the candidates and, if they are, do they have a 'favorable or unfavorable general impression' of each? To simplify what can be a wide range of results,

candidates fall into one of three situations—popular, relatively unknown, and unpopular. Political pollsters have used these candidate ratings enough times that they have general rules on what can be considered a relatively good or poor rating. A favorable/unfavorable ratio of 3:1 is fairly easy to obtain. Such a ratio is considered 'good,' and the higher the ratio, the stronger the candidate, although the ratio varies for different levels of office. Ratios close to 2:1 are less common and usually indicate something controversial about the candidate. A 1:1 ratio is rare and, when it occurs, it means the candidate is close to unelectable.

Strategic decisions are based on the horse race result *and* the comparison of the popularity of the campaign's candidate with that of the opponent(s). Using the simplified scheme of popular, unknown, and unpopular produces a 3×3 matrix of the possible candidate popularity pairings. When this is overlaid on the five possible horse race outcomes, a campaign can be in any one of 45 situations $(3 \times 3 \times 5)$! For campaign planning, the 'horse race' is really all three of these variables considered together. And, this is not the full basic picture for strategy. The final essential variable is the partisan split of the voters—which candidate has the advantage in terms of the party predispositions of the voters?

An illustration of how all four of these variables affect campaign strategy is as follows. A campaign that is *behind* because its candidate is *unknown* and the opponent (assuming here that there is only one, as is usual) is *popular* knows it has two possible tasks—increase the popularity of its candidate and undercut the popularity of its opponent. If the campaign has the advantage of the *voters' partisan split*, it could reasonably conclude that its main task is to increase the popularity of its candidate. Once this is achieved, the voters' partisan split will produce a victory. If the popular opponent, however, has the advantage of the voters' partisan split, the campaign could reasonably conclude it must undercut the opponent's popularity, i.e. 'go negative'—that it can never win by simply equaling the opponent's popularity.

For all these reasons, a campaign insists on *accuracy* in its private polling. In fact, it could be argued that there is more pressure on accuracy in the applied science of polling than there is for academic surveys or media polls. Based on campaign polling, real and scarce resource allocations are made. The horse race result, analyzed by media markets, is used to make major financial decisions about media buys. The other major scarce resource of any campaign is the candidate's time, and scheduling the candidate is also guided by the horse race result according to media markets and other geographic and demographic subgroups.

Horse race and the public polls

Public polls conducted by mass media outlets are both very useful and a huge annoyance to campaigns (Patterson, 2005). They help fill the time gaps in a campaign's research program. They also can be disruptive to a campaign's planning when the results differ significantly from a campaign's internal polling, or when one public poll is in conflict with the results of another. In addition, a public poll result can itself be a significant *event* in a campaign, either helping or hurting the campaign.

The effects of the public polls notwithstanding, campaigns do incorporate public polls in their own strategic planning. Even presidential campaigns cannot afford to be polling all the time. Public polls are used to fill in the time gaps in a campaign's internal polling program. They can be very useful in telling a campaign that the horse race has not changed since the campaign's last poll, or to alert the campaign that a change possibly has taken place ($\rightarrow$ *Exit Polls and Pre-Election Polls*). Campaigns cannot afford to poll after every event that could possibly change the horse race. When public polls available after such events show no change in the horse race, they save the campaign the expense of doing its own poll to learn this.

In the last part of national campaigns, public polls become more frequent and overlap with the campaign's own polling. They can be disruptive to the campaign when there are inconsistent results among them or with the campaign's polling. Rather than deal with each public poll's horse race result, the campaign will simply track the *average result* of the public polls and leave it to the media outlets to defend their differences.

To weight or not to weight

In US politics, party identifications and race are two of the strongest correlates to voting intentions. The accuracy of the horse race result is dependent on the correct representation of Democrats, Republicans, and African-Americans in a poll. There are two schools of thought about a survey's party identification distribution and whether or not to apply weights to it (Blumenthal, 2004). In one view, the partisan distribution is a legitimate finding like any other finding in the survey. One would no more increase or decrease the number of Republicans or Democrats in the survey than one would weight by the survey's reported voting intentions. Party identification is, after all, an attitude, not a hard demographic like gender, age, or race. The pollster takes whatever party identification distribution there is and reports the horse race, as is.

A second school of thought treats party identification in a more qualified way. Yes, it is an attitude, but it is an attitude with greater stability than many other attitudes and reported intentions. In this view, there can be a correct partisan distribution and an incorrect one. If a particular survey has an incorrect distribution, by chance, weights are applied to change the distribution to one that is considered correct. The correct distribution is based on past polls. Over the course of polling a particular constituency multiple times, one accumulates knowledge of the constituency in terms of its Democratic or Republican advantage. Rather than ignore that knowledge with the next survey, the distribution is compared to prior ones. If it is significantly different from the past surveys, weights are applied.

Late in a campaign, some public polls go to weekly sampling. A sample in one week may have more Republicans than Democrats, and the next week may have more Democrats than Republicans. The purist is stuck defending the position that campaign or other events changed people's party identifications over the one-week period between the two polls. While this is possible, in most cases it is highly unlikely. What is more likely is that sampling and non-sampling error are the reasons for the difference. However, the purist makes no correction for what most likely happened. This is not a trivial matter. A sample that is 3% more Republican will necessarily yield a different ballot result and a possibly different picture of the race than one that is 3% more Democrat. The purist must report the difference in the ballot result as a substantive trend in voting intentions when there may be no trend at all.

Partisan weights often are applied in campaign polling. In doing so, the practitioner is introducing an efficient way to control for partisanship. There are two ways to do this. One is to have an allowable range in the proportions of partisans in the sample. The campaign's pollster may decide a difference of Democrats over Republicans is acceptable if it is within a certain range, e.g. a 3% to 8% Democratic advantage. If a survey is outside that range, it is weighted to the difference it is closest to in that range. The second method is to weight the data to an exact proportion of each partisan group. This method would most likely be used in daily tracking that reports rolling results from the last 2 to 4 days of interviewing.

Likely voters

Measuring the horse race among 'likely voters' has become a common practice in both campaign polling and the public polls. However, there is no generally agreed upon methodology for identifying likely voters (Erikson, Panagopolous, & Wlezien, 2004). Polls report likely voter results as though

the results are as valid as those reported for registered voters or adults. This is not the case. Every poll has its own methodology for identifying likely voters. These reports are frequently based on *a priori* definitions—often reasonable, but without empirical validations. The concept is more complex than may first appear, and the executions can be problematic.

Reporting likely voter results recognizes that what may be true for all eligible voters may not be true for those who will actually vote. The further below a 100% turnout an election has, the more likely the horse race may change. The difference may be a comfortable lead among all eligible voters but only a slight lead among likely voters. For campaigns, the difference can affect their strategies. For the public polls, the difference could mean reporting the race as having a 'clear frontrunner' or one that is 'too close to call'— a distinction that can itself affect the race.

One safe way a campaign can handle the likely voter challenge is to measure its race both among all eligible voters and among its particular way of defining likely voters. Examining the data for both the total sample and the likely voter subsample can help confirm conclusions in a strategic poll. In addition, the campaign can track the election for both populations. Knowing the *change* in the horse race is as important to campaign planning as knowing the margin in the horse race. The trend will almost always be in the same direction for both eligible voters and likely voters. Finally, the total sample and the likely voter subsample often present results within the same general horse race category important for campaign strategy—large lead, small lead, too close to call, small deficit, or large deficit. A campaign needs a reliable likely voter measure because it may show a horse race result in a different strategic category than the one shown in the total sample.

CONCLUSION

Polls and focus groups indisputably help a campaign achieve a winning margin.

Whether or not they further democracy in a positive way is still debated. In this debate, it is curious that polls and focus groups are often cited as though they are separate from public opinion. Editorial writers and even candidates will say public policy should *not* be formed from polls and focus groups, and that candidates should not follow poll and focus group results. But, survey research and focus groups, properly done, do measure public opinion. In a democracy, public opinion is supposed to ultimately rule and campaigns should address the issues the people consider the most important.

A blanket indictment against using polls and focus groups to form public policy and guide the issues the candidate addresses would seem to be an indictment of democracy itself. Certainly, the reliability and validity of a particular poll result should always be open to challenge. With that caveat, polls and focus groups have helped make campaigns and government more responsive to the people, as uncomfortable as that may make some when public opinion goes against their interests.

REFERENCES

Blumenthal, M. (2004, September 28). *Should pollsters weight by party identification?* Pollster.com, Retrieved January 5, 2007 from http://www.pollster.com/faq/should_pollsters_weight_by_par.php.

Erikson, R. S., Panagopolous, C., & Wlezien, C. (2004). Likely (and unlikely) voters and the assessment of campaign dynamics. *Public Opinion Quarterly, 68,* 588–601.

Goldstein, K., & Ridout, T. N. (2004). Measuring the effects of televised political advertising in the United States. *Annual Review of Political Science, 7,* 205–226.

Jacobs, L. R., & Shapiro, R. Y. (2000). *Politicians don't pander.* Chicago: University of Chicago Press.

Patterson, T. (2005). Of polls, mountains: US journalists and their use of election surveys. *Public Opinion Quarterly, 69,* 716–724.

Steeper, F. T. (1978). Public response to Gerald Ford's statement on Eastern Europe in the second debate. In G. F. Bishop, R. G. Meadow, & M. Jackson-Beeck (Eds.), *The presidential debates: Media, electoral, and policy perspectives* (pp. 81–101). New York: Praeger.

Index

CPSIA information can be obtained
at www.ICGtesting.com
Printed in the USA
LVOW04*1419040417

529576LV00019B/403/P